CRICKETERS'
WHO'S WHO
2003

THE CRICKETERS' WHO'S WHO 2003

Introduction by
ROBIN MARTIN-JENKINS

Edited by
CHRIS MARSHALL

Statistics by
RICHARD LOCKWOOD

Photographs by
BILL SMITH
and
GETTY IMAGES

Queen Anne Press

QUEEN ANNE PRESS
a division of Lennard Associates Limited
Mackerye End, Harpenden, Herts AL5 5DR

Published in association with
The Cricketers' Who's Who Limited

First published in Great Britain 2003

British Library Cataloguing in Publication is available

ISBN 1 85291 650 8

Typeset in Times and Univers Condensed
Editor (for Queen Anne Press): Kirsty Ennever
Quiz compiled by Chris Marshall
Cover design by Paul Cooper

Printed and bound by
Butler and Tanner Limited, Frome and London

ACKNOWLEDGEMENTS

Cover photographs by Allsport UK
Some of the long-serving players with Benefits or Testimonials in 2003
Front cover: Ronnie Irani, Alec Stewart, Mark Ealham and Robin Smith
Back: David Leatherdale

The publishers would also like to thank the county clubs, the players
and their families for their assistance in helping to assemble
the information and photographs in this book.

Extra information has also been gathered from the pages of
The Cricketer, The Times, The Sunday Times and CricInfo.com

Thanks also to the following for providing additional photographs:
Birmingham Evening Mail, Bowles Associates, Gordon Child,
John Dawson Cricket Images, Derby Evening Telegraph, East Anglian Daily Times,
Empics, Gloucestershire Echo, John Grainger, Graham Morris, Peter Norton,
Stockport Times, Michael Weeks, Simon Wilkinson, Wolverhampton Express and Star

CONTENTS

INTRODUCTION

'Why are we so bad at cricket then?'

This was the removal man's reaction when told of my profession. It is no longer a reaction I am surprised by. I had, now, been asked this question four times in the past month, the other times being on the street in Hove, at a drinks party in Edinburgh and in a taxi in Mumbai. It would seem, then, that the world perceives there to be something amiss with cricket in Britain.

Who, exactly, is the removal man talking about? Does he refer to the England team itself? The same team who, despite being soundly beaten this winter by Australia (as Australia have soundly beaten all in their path on home grounds in the last decade), have in the last five years had series Test wins against South Africa, West Indies, Zimbabwe, Pakistan and Sri Lanka? Or is he maybe implying it is county cricket that is 'bad', when in fact, during the last few years, the advent of two divisions has sparked new life into an ailing machine. Competition between the counties still gives pleasure to thousands of paying supporters over the length and breadth of the country and to millions more who follow county games in the press or online. CricInfo had 30 million hits for their county scores service in 2001, the year they sponsored the Championship, and last season that rose to 35 million.

I do not blame the removal man for his misplaced gloom. He is merely jumping on the bandwagon of criticism, created by some members of the media, former players, and even some present players. Despite the game's undergoing what, in cricket terms, was a radical change with the recent implementation of two divisions, people are still not satisfied. England players this winter have talked about the need for sweeping changes to the county set-up. Why is it that county cricket comes in for so much stick? Is it really such an inadequate system or is it just being used as a scapegoat for England's failure to win an Ashes series since 1987?

It may be said that when it comes to cricket in this country, we have an obsession for all things Australian. I have no problem with our examining the way the Aussies play the game, extracting their best philosophies and techniques and adapting them to suit the English cricketer. There is no denying the fact that Australian cricketers do a lot right. But so do we, and many an Australian has admitted it, most recently and most prominently none other than Steve Waugh. A system that supports 18 first-class counties, with more than 400 professional cricketers, must contain some benefits.

Probably the biggest criticism of county cricket from the players and media is that there are too many games. It is a fair point. We play, for example, far more one-day domestic cricket than any other country and yet England's results in recent One-Day Internationals have been poor. Does this mean we are not using this extra experience to our advantage? Paradoxically, it may be the reason for England's underachievement in one-day cricket.

Amongst the players, though, opinion is still divided between those that think fewer games would mean more practice, which would lead to a higher standard of play, and those that think that as professional cricketers who are paid good money to play the game we should jolly well be out there every day. The latter school of thought is dwindling in numbers with every 'old' player that retires. The former faction could be split again into those who genuinely believe less cricket increases standards, and those who think fewer games would allow more days with the feet up in front of the TV or more nights on the town. This last category tends to be those who are more worried about their sponsored car and mobile phone than their technique against the turning ball.

I would suggest that, with contracted players getting fewer by the year, these people are now a very small minority and soon this trait will be all but extinct amongst the younger players. Playing staffs are diminishing as budgets are tightened, and there is far less room for complacency than a few years ago. This leaves us with a majority of cricketers in England who think a reduction in the amount of cricket played will lead to an increased standard.

The aim of county cricket should be to replicate Test match cricket as far as it is possible. Players I have spoken to that have made the step up to the highest level believe that the heightened intensity is the most noticeable difference. Sure, the opening bowlers might be a bit quicker and the opposing batsmen might not miss out on any width offered to them, but it is the elements that constitute that magic word 'intensity' which seem to be alien to the fledgling international player. Whether it is the crowd, the TV cameras, the slip fielders muttering within earshot, or the bowler who is at you, always at you, there seems to be an extra kind of pressure. Handling that pressure would appear to be the key to performing at international level.

I would argue that, in its present state, county cricket finds it difficult to reproduce this kind of pressure consistently. It certainly has its moments. There are times during a season when you know you are in a real dogfight. After playing against Surrey at Hove last summer, both Chris Adams and Murray Goodwin stated that batting against a fiery Alex Tudor and a crafty Mushtaq Ahmed on a slow pitch that demanded extreme concentration, with all of the fielders chuntering in their ear between deliveries, was the closest either of them had come to Test match pressure whilst playing at county level. They both used the word intensity.

There would be other such occasions in other games throughout the summer, but for every tense situation I find myself in, if I'm honest, there are times when it's all just a bit too relaxed out on the field. The sun is shining, the wicket is flat, the bowler is tired, down comes the half-volley that gets dispatched for four and he trudges back to his mark. But who can blame him, for in the last week he might have played four days in row, before getting in his car (sponsored, but he doesn't care about that) and driving 250 miles to a hotel in another town where, after a night mixing sleep with reflection on how he bowled in the previous game, he is out on the field again. A new opponent, a new ground, but the same old tired body. No real time to stop and think about what he is doing right or wrong and no time to study and prepare for the next lot of opposition.

I understand that, as professional cricketers, we have a duty to play entertaining cricket regularly throughout the summer months and that if we are to continue to receive the money from television revenue that keeps most of the counties afloat, then we need to earn that money by playing plenty of games. I do think, however, that if we played slightly less than we do at the moment, we would stand a better chance of maintaining the high standards expected of us. With the scrapping of the Benson and Hedges Cup and the freeing up of two weeks in April came the perfect opportunity to reschedule the season. The liberated time could have been spread throughout the summer, giving tired bowlers a vital extra chance to recuperate, or allowing batsmen further practice. Niggles could be treated more completely by the physios and so would have less chance of developing into serious injuries; the very injuries, it could be argued, that effectively ruined any chance we had in the last two Ashes series.

Despite there being three one-day competitions, I propose that too much emphasis is being placed on the Championship. With more international one-day cricket being scheduled each year (sadly it is now the most popular form of the game throughout the world) and with all the revenue it creates, perhaps we should concentrate on getting England to the top of the one-day ladder above all else. As county cricketers, our practice time (what little of it there is) is mainly devoted to the skills required in the longer version of the game. With one less competition, the extra time could have been used to rehearse specific one-day skills, such as bowling yorkers or hitting boundaries at the 'death'. The 16 first-class matches along with the two other one-day competitions would then, in my opinion, have constituted a suitable programme for the season. I fear, therefore, that the decision to replace the Benson and Hedges with another one-day competition may be a flawed one. This year our schedule will be as hectic as ever. It will be intriguing to see if the new 20-over competition will be of any benefit to us as players. The games will be exciting to watch, particularly for children, and I applaud the powers that be for their progressive approach, but I feel their priorities may be wrong. Will the new competition help to produce better cricketers for England? This is the question that should be foremost in anyone's mind when making decisions on the game. County cricket is evolving and many of the recent changes have been clearly for the good. No one could deny, for example, that the implementation of two divisions has made the games more intense and exciting for both players and spectators. There is, however, something that is still missing. There is a certain *je ne sais quoi* that distinguishes the Australian cricketer from the rest of the world; that extra bit of fight and grit that seems to be inherent in his style of play. This kind of tenacity is still absent from the psyche of many English pros.

A reduction in the amount of time spent playing and an increase in practice might be beneficial, but it would not change the innate docility of some English cricketers. There needs to be something else. I am certain that to improve as a cricketer, and to become tougher, you need to be constantly tested by playing against the best opponents possible. To know this is true, you only have to look at how players who languish in county second teams for too long seem to struggle to develop as expected. Does our current set-up allow the best players in England to be persistently tested? Possibly not.

There are clearly some very fine cricketers who are playing second division cricket where they find the going a bit too comfortable. Whilst the two-divisional structure should allow the best players to gravitate to the top division, the inertia present in over a century of Championship cricket means that this will be a slow process. There could be two ways to speed it up: either get rid of a few first-class counties or create a regional competition. I would be wary, however, of reducing the number of counties to an Australian- or South African-style league, with ten or so teams. Part of the charm and uniqueness of county cricket is its accessibility and variety. This year we will play fixtures in Canterbury, Taunton, Birmingham and Edinburgh, to name just a few of the many parts of Britain county cricket will visit. Many loyal supporters would be denied the chance of watching their favourite players if we reduced the number of counties. The answer, in my opinion, would be to keep the County Championship as it stands but create an extra regional competition on top.

Teams from six or seven regions could compete over a six-week period, at the end of which there would be a semi-final and final. In the meantime the County Championship would continue and the players that were picked for their regions could be replaced with younger part-time players from the county's leagues. The 2nd XI Championship would have to go, but that should not be a problem provided county coaches are in close touch with the premier club leagues. In this way, spectators could still watch their teams perform throughout the year, but the best 70 or so cricketers would battle it out against each other in an elite competition that would give the England selectors a chance to see which players really cut the mustard when under pressure. Would it not also help to sharpen the skills of the best players if they were tested in this way?

Opponents of the idea of regional cricket point to the logistical difficulties. Certainly it would make an already crowded fixture list even more confusing, and finding enough decent pitches on which to play all the extra matches could prove problematic. I feel, however, that the benefits of a system that would come as close to Test cricket as is possible in our domestic structure would far outweigh these minor problems. It would be a fairly radical step but one which would complement the many recent changes and improvements to English cricket. Despite the poor overall state of practice facilities at many first-class grounds, the pitches have developed well over the last few years. In the following pages of this book, I'd wager you will find that there are far fewer criticisms of pitches than in previous editions. Although a little on the slow side still (a fact not helped by our climate), they are generally flat and even. Bowlers coming into the game today have to learn to do something with the ball, and young batsmen can develop techniques with the confidence that comes with a true bounce.

Of the other recent developments, the return to the quota of two overseas players per county is long overdue. English players can't fail to learn something when playing with or against an extra international star. Australia aside, England's recent results against the rest of the world have been consistently impressive. Certainly in the last three years, if Test series haven't been won then we have at least been extremely competitive in them. Taking the freakishly talented current Australian Test team out of the equation elevates England to one of the best teams in the world and certainly one of the best to watch. The emergence of attacking cricketers in our ranks, players like Vaughan, Trescothick, Flintoff and Harmison, has arguably been the reason why the game's popularity has not suffered as it might have done, despite our humiliation at the hands of Australia time and again.

People like to see their team win, but above all they want to see exciting cricket. Perhaps the people that condemn cricket in England have become too obsessed with winning. With the collapse of the empire in the 20th century, England long ago relinquished the right to dominance in the sporting world. It should be enough that, in the England team, we have a diverse and improving pool of talent that plays watchable cricket; and that in county cricket we have a system that still gives pleasure to millions, whether they follow it in Hove, Edinburgh or Mumbai.

Robin Martin-Jenkins
February 2003

THE PLAYERS

OVERSEAS PLAYERS IN COUNTY CRICKET

Throughout the book there are 100 quiz questions based on the contribution to
county cricket made by overseas players during the past 50 years.
The answers can be found on page 831.

Editor's Notes

The cricketers listed in this volume include all those who played 1st XI cricket for a first-class county at least once last season, in any form of cricket, and all those registered (at the time of going to press at the end of February) to play for the 18 first-class counties in 2003, even those who have yet to make a first-team appearance. All statistics are complete to the end of the last English season (the Stop press sections for individual players cover subsequent highlights). Figures about 1000 runs, 50 wickets and 50 dismissals in a season refer to matches in England only. All first-class figures include figures for Test matches which are also extracted and listed separately. One-Day 100s and One-Day five wickets in an innings are for the English domestic competitions and all One-Day Internationals, home and abroad. Career records include 'rebel' tours to South Africa. In the interests of space 2002 statistics are not given for those whose appearances in first-class cricket or one-day competitions were only for teams other than the county to which they are now contracted – i.e. universities, Board XIs, minor counties etc (excluding international cricketers on tours to England). These appearances are, however, reflected in their career statistics and reference is made in the Extras section to the team for which they played.

The following abbreviations apply: * means not out; All First – all first-class matches; 1-day Int – One-Day Internationals; 1-day Lge – Norwich Union League (including former Sunday leagues); C&G – C&G Trophy (incl NatWest); B&H – Benson and Hedges Cup (including the Super Cup). The figures for batting and bowling averages refer to the full first-class English list for 2002, followed in brackets by the 2001 figures. Inclusion in the batting averages depends on a minimum of six completed innings; a bowler has to have taken at least ten wickets. Strike rate refers to a bowler's record of balls bowled per wicket taken. This year we have included a new category – Cricket superstitions. Please also note that Worcestershire have ceased awarding caps, presenting 'colours' to each player who appears for the county in the Championship.

Each year in *The Cricketers' Who's Who*, in addition to those cricketers who are playing during the current season, we also include the biographical and career details of those who played in the previous season but retired at the end of it. The purpose of this is to have, on the record, the full and final cricketing achievements of every player when his career has ended.

A book of this complexity and detail has to be prepared several months in advance of the cricket season, and occasionally there are recent changes in a player's circumstances or the structure of the game which cannot be included in time. Many examples of facts, statistics and even opinions which can quickly become outdated in the period between the actual compilation of the book and its publication, months later, will spring to the reader's mind, and I ask him or her to make the necessary commonsense allowance and adjustments.

Chris Marshall, March 2003

ABDUL RAZZAQ
Middlesex

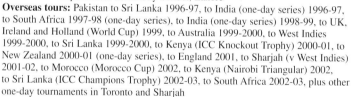

Name: Abdul Razzaq
Role: Right-hand bat, right-arm fast-medium bowler
Born: 2 December 1979, Lahore
Height: 5ft 11in
County debut: 2002
Test debut: 1999-2000
Tests: 21
One-Day Internationals: 112
1st-Class 50s: 13
1st-Class 100s: 6
1st-Class 200s: 1
1st-Class 5 w. in innings: 8
1st-Class 10 w. in match: 2
1st-Class catches: 16
One-Day 5 w. in innings: 3
Place in batting averages: 17th av. 60.66 (2001 174th av. 22.16)
Place in bowling averages: 61st av. 29.11 (2001 94th av. 35.90)
Strike rate: 47.65 (career 50.48)
Education: Furqan Model Secondary School, Lahore
Overseas tours: Pakistan to Sri Lanka 1996-97, to India (one-day series) 1996-97, to South Africa 1997-98 (one-day series), to India (one-day series) 1998-99, to UK, Ireland and Holland (World Cup) 1999, to Australia 1999-2000, to West Indies 1999-2000, to Sri Lanka 1999-2000, to Kenya (ICC Knockout Trophy) 2000-01, to New Zealand 2000-01 (one-day series), to England 2001, to Sharjah (v West Indies) 2001-02, to Morocco (Morocco Cup) 2002, to Kenya (Nairobi Triangular) 2002, to Sri Lanka (ICC Champions Trophy) 2002-03, to South Africa 2002-03, plus other one-day tournaments in Toronto and Sharjah
Overseas teams played for: Khan Research Labs; Lahore Cricket Association
Extras: Took 7-51 on first-class debut, for Lahore City v Karachi Whites 1996-97. Scored 87 v West Indies at Georgetown 1999-2000, in the process sharing with Inzamam-ul-Haq (135) in a record sixth-wicket partnership for Pakistan in Tests v West Indies (206). Took Test hat-trick (Kaluwitharana, Herath, Pushpakumara) v Sri Lanka at Galle in June 2000, becoming the youngest player – and the second Pakistan bowler, after Wasim Akram (twice) – to take a hat-trick in Tests. FICA Young Player of the Year 2001. Man of the Match for his century (134) and match figures of 4-71 in first Test v Bangladesh at Dhaka 2001-02. Returned his best one-day figures of 6-35 v Bangladesh at Dhaka 2001-02. Struck an 84-ball 86 v New Zealand in the second ODI at Rawalpindi 2002, winning Man of the Match award. Joined Middlesex as overseas player in 2002. Scored maiden first-class 200 (203*) v Glamorgan at Cardiff 2002. Scored 43-ball 59 v Australia in the final of the Nairobi Triangular tournament 2002

Best batting: 203* Middlesex v Glamorgan, Cardiff 2002
Best bowling: 7-51 Lahore City v Karachi Whites, Thatta 1996-97
Stop press: Suffered broken left wrist after being struck by a Brett Lee delivery in second Test v Australia in Sharjah 2002-03. Scored maiden ODI century (112) in second ODI v South Africa at Port Elizabeth 2002-03, in the process sharing with Salim Elahi (135) in a second-wicket stand of 267. Selected for Pakistan squad for 2002-03 World Cup

2002 Season

	M	Inns	NO	Runs	HS	Avge	100s	50s	Ct	St	O	M	Runs	Wkts	Avge	Best	5wI	10wM
Test																		
All First	6	9	3	364	203 *	60.66	1	-	1	-	206.3	25	757	26	29.11	7-133	2	-
1-day Int																		
C & G	1	1	0	8	8	8.00	-	-	-	-	10	0	58	1	58.00	1-58	-
B & H																		
1-day Lge	8	6	0	49	24	8.16	-	-	1	-	55.1	5	236	11	21.45	3-19	-

Career Performances

	M	Inns	NO	Runs	HS	Avge	100s	50s	Ct	St	Balls	Runs	Wkts	Avge	Best	5wI	10wM
Test	21	32	3	938	134	32.34	3	4	7	-	3090	1427	44	32.43	4-24	-	-
All First	64	95	15	2730	203 *	34.12	7	13	16	-	10600	6232	210	29.67	7-51	8	2
1-day Int	112	95	22	2032	86	27.83	-	12	13	-	5116	3748	150	24.98	6-35	3
C & G	1	1	0	8	8	8.00	-	-	-	-	60	58	1	58.00	1-58	-
B & H																	
1-day Lge	8	6	0	49	24	8.16	-	-	1	-	331	236	11	21.45	3-19	-

ADAMS, C. J.   Sussex

Name: <u>Christopher</u> John Adams
Role: Right-hand bat, right-arm medium bowler, slip fielder, county captain
Born: 6 May 1970, Whitwell, Derbyshire
Height: 6ft **Weight:** 13st 7lbs
Nickname: Grizzly, Grizwold
County debut: 1988 (Derbyshire), 1998 (Sussex)
County cap: 1992 (Derbyshire), 1998 (Sussex)
Test debut: 1999-2000
Tests: 5
One-Day Internationals: 5
1000 runs in a season: 5
1st-Class 50s: 68
1st-Class 100s: 30
1st-Class 200s: 3

1st-Class catches: 281
One-Day 100s: 16
One-Day 5 w. in innings: 1
Place in batting averages: 54th av. 44.63
(2001 27th av. 51.71)
Place in bowling averages:
(2001 1st av. 11.10)
Strike rate: (career 76.70)
Parents: John and Eluned (Lyn)
Wife and date of marriage: Samantha
Claire, 26 September 1992
Children: Georgia Louise, 4 October 1993;
Sophie Victoria, 13 October 1998
Family links with cricket: Brother David
played 2nd XI cricket for Derbyshire and
Gloucestershire. Father played for Yorkshire
Schools and uncle played for Essex 2nd XI
Education: Tapton House School;
Chesterfield Boys Grammar School; Repton School
Qualifications: 6 O-levels, NCA coaching awards, Executive Development Certificate
in Coaching and Management Skills
Off-season: 'Getting my body back into some semblance'
Overseas tours: Repton School to Barbados 1987; England NCA North to Northern
Ireland 1987; England XI to New Zealand (Cricket Max) 1997; England to South Africa and
Zimbabwe 1999-2000; Sussex to Grenada 2001, 2002; Blade to Barbados 2001
Overseas teams played for: Takapuna, New Zealand 1987-88; Te Puke, New Zealand
1989-90; Primrose, Cape Town, South Africa 1991-92; Canberra Comets, Australia
1998-99; University of NSW, Australia 2000-01
Career highlights to date: 'Has to be Test debut for England'
Cricket moments to forget: 'Our pre-season tour to Grenada [in 2002] and the
resulting death of my colleague Umer Rashid'
Cricketers particularly admired: Mike Atherton, Ian Botham
Young players to look out for: Matt Prior, Tim Ambrose, Rikki Clarke, Kyle Hogg
Other sports played: Football ('mad on it'), golf
Other sports followed: Football (Arsenal FC)
Injuries: Out for five weeks with left knee ligament tear and cartilage tear
Relaxations: 'My kids'
Extras: Represented English Schools U15 and U19, MCC Schools U19 and, in 1989,
England YC. Took two catches as 12th man for England v India at Old Trafford in
1990. Set Derbyshire record for the highest score in the Sunday League (141*) v Kent
at Chesterfield 1992 and record for the fastest century by a Derbyshire batsman (57
minutes, finishing on 140*) v Worcestershire at Worcester 1992. Set record for the
highest score by a Derbyshire No. 3, 239 v Hampshire at Southampton 1996. Released
by Derbyshire at the end of the 1997 season and joined Sussex for 1998 as captain.

Scored 135 and 105 v Essex at Chelmsford 1998, becoming the third player to score centuries in each innings of a match for two counties; he had also done so for Derbyshire. Sussex Player of the Year 1998 and 1999. Set individual one-day record score for Sussex of 163 (off 107 balls) v Middlesex in the National League at Arundel 1999; the innings included nine sixes, a Sussex Sunday/National League record. Top run-scorer in the 1999 National League competition with 798 runs at 79.80. Sussex 1st XI Fielder of the Season 2000. BBC South Cricketer of the Year 2001. B&H Gold Award for his 80* v Hampshire at Hove 2002. Granted a benefit for 2003

Opinions on cricket: 'The game is changing at a rate which is alarming given the fact that the financial increases seem destined to follow a different path.'

Best batting: 239 Derbyshire v Hampshire, Southampton 1996
Best bowling: 4-28 Sussex v Durham, Riverside 2001

2002 Season

	M	Inns	NO	Runs	HS	Avge	100s	50s	Ct	St	O	M	Runs	Wkts	Avge	Best	5wI	10wM
Test																		
All First	10	19	0	848	217	44.63	3	3	2	-	7	1	24	0	-	-	-	-
1-day Int																		
C & G	1	1	0	33	33	33.00	-	-	1	-								
B & H	5	5	2	221	80 *	73.66	-	2	4	-	2	0	12	0	-	-	-	
1-day Lge	10	10	1	303	64 *	33.66	-	2	6	-	2	0	15	0	-	-	-	

Career Performances

	M	Inns	NO	Runs	HS	Avge	100s	50s	Ct	St	Balls	Runs	Wkts	Avge	Best	5wI	10wM
Test	5	8	0	104	31	13.00	-	-	6	-	120	59	1	59.00	1-42	-	-
All First	241	395	29	13784	239	37.66	33	68	281	-	3145	1854	41	45.21	4-28	-	-
1-day Int	5	4	0	71	42	17.75	-	-	3	-							
C & G	26	25	6	1144	129 *	60.21	4	7	10	-	114	91	1	91.00	1-15	-	
B & H	47	44	7	1576	138	42.59	3	11	21	-	198	159	1	159.00	1-41	-	
1-day Lge	185	177	28	5750	163	38.59	9	37	98	-	884	814	27	30.14	5-16	1	

ADAMS, J. H. K.   Hampshire

Name: James Henry Kenneth Adams
Role: Left-hand bat, left-arm medium bowler
Born: 23 September 1980, Winchester
Height: 6ft 1in **Weight:** 13st 7lbs
Nickname: Jimmy, Bison, Baron
County debut: 2002
1st-Class catches: 3
Strike rate: 63.00 (career 63.00)
Parents: Jenny and Mike

Marital status: Single
Family links with cricket: 'Dad played a bit for Kent Schoolboys. Brothers Ben and Tom played/play for Hampshire age groups'
Education: Hursley Keble Memorial; Twyford School; Sherborne School; Loughborough University
Qualifications: 9 GCSEs, 3 A-levels, Level 1 coaching
Career outside cricket: Student
Off-season: 'University'
Overseas tours: England U19 to Sri Lanka (U19 World Cup) 1999-2000; West of England to West Indies 1995; Sherborne School to Pakistan
Overseas teams played for: Woodville, Adelaide 1999-2000; Melville, Perth 2000-01
Career highlights to date: 'England U19 and 2nd XI Championship'

Cricket moments to forget: 'Kidderminster, June 2000'
Cricketers particularly admired: 'Lara, Smith, Thorpe…'
Young players to look out for: J. Francis, J. Tomlinson, C. Denison 'and others from Hants Academy'
Other sports played: Hockey (Dorset age group when 14), football, bass fishing
Other sports followed: Football (Aston Villa); 'fair interest in most sports'
Relaxations: Music, PlayStation, 'kick about with mates'
Extras: Played in U15 World Cup 1996. Hampshire Young Player of the Year 1998. Represented England U19 v Sri Lanka U19 in 'Test' series 2000. Part of Hampshire's 2nd XI Championship winning side 2001. Played for Loughborough University CCE 2002, scoring a century in each innings (103/113) v Kent at Canterbury. Represented British Universities v Sri Lankans at Northampton and v West Indies A (50-over match) at The Parks 2002
Best batting: 48 Hampshire v Sussex, Hove 2002
Best bowling: 2-81 Hampshire v Surrey, West End 2002

2002 Season

	M	Inns	NO	Runs	HS	Avge	100s	50s	Ct	St	O	M	Runs	Wkts	Avge	Best	5wI	10wM
Test																		
All First	3	5	1	88	48	22.00	-	-	3	-	21	4	102	2	51.00	2-81	-	-
1-day Int																		
C & G																			
B & H																			
1-day Lge	3	3	0	28	17	9.33	-	-	2	-	0.1	0	6	0	-		-	-

Career Performances

	M	Inns	NO	Runs	HS	Avge	100s	50s	Ct	St	Balls	Runs	Wkts	Avge	Best	5wI	10wM
Test																	
All First	3	5	1	88	48	22.00	-	-	3	-	126	102	2	51.00	2-81	-	-
1-day Int																	
C & G	·																
B & H																	
1-day Lge	3	3	0	28	17	9.33	-	-	2	-	1	6	0	-		-	-

ADSHEAD, S. J.   Leicestershire

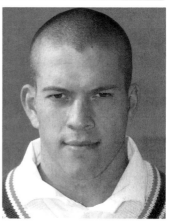

Name: <u>Stephen</u> John Adshead
Role: Right-hand bat, wicket-keeper
Born: 29 January 1980, Worcester
Height: 5ft 8in **Weight:** 12st 7lbs
Nickname: Adzo, Shed, Monkey Boy
County debut: 2000
1st-Class stumpings: 1
Parents: David and Julie
Marital status: Single
Family links with cricket: 'Dad and brother
play local club cricket'
Education: Beoley First; Ridgeway Middle;
Bridley Moor HS, Redditch
Qualifications: 10 GCSEs, 2 A-levels,
ECB Level 2 coaching
Overseas tours: Leicestershire to
Potchefstroom, South Africa 2001
Overseas teams played for: Fish Hoek,
Cape Town 1998-99; Witwatersrand Technical, Johannesburg 1999-2000; Central
Hawke's Bay, New Zealand 2000-01
Career highlights to date: 'Winning AON Trophy 2000; Man of Match in final'
(*Top-scored for Leicestershire 2nd XI with 58*)
Cricketers particularly admired: Alec Stewart, Steve Waugh, Trevor Ward
Young players to look out for: David Brignull
Other sports followed: Football (Nottingham Forest)
Relaxations: Fishing, scuba diving
Extras: Averaged 90 for Worcestershire U19 in county U19 competition in 1998, in
which Worcestershire reached the semi-finals. Played a few games for Worcestershire
2nd XI. Played for Herefordshire in Minor Counties and NatWest 1999. Played for
Leicestershire Board XI in the second round of the C&G 2002, which was played in
September 2001. Did not appear for Leicestershire in a domestic competition in 2002

but played for the county v Indians in a one-day fixture at Leicester. Released by
Leicestershire at the end of the 2002 season
Opinions on cricket: 'Well, I enjoy it!'

2002 Season (did not make any first-class or one-day appearances)

Career Performances

	M	Inns	NO	Runs	HS	Avge	100s	50s	Ct	St	Balls	Runs	Wkts	Avge	Best	5wI	10wM
Test																	
All First	1	1	0	0	0	0.00	-	-	-	1							
1-day Int																	
C & G	3	3	0	70	29	23.33	-	-	3	2							
B & H																	
1-day Lge																	

AFZAAL, U. Nottinghamshire

Name: Usman Afzaal
Role: Left-hand bat, slow left-arm bowler
Born: 9 June 1977, Rawalpindi, Pakistan
Height: 6ft **Weight:** 12st 7lbs
Nickname: Saeed, Gulfraz, Usy Bhai, Trevor
County debut: 1995
County cap: 2000
Test debut: 2001
Tests: 3
1000 runs in a season: 3
1st-Class 50s: 35
1st-Class 100s: 12
1st-Class catches: 60
Place in batting averages: 52nd av. 45.53
(2001 78th av. 37.44)
Place in bowling averages: (2001 145th
av. 57.90)
Strike rate: 95.25 (career 95.10)
Parents: Firdous and Shafi Mahmood
Marital status: Single
Family links with cricket: Older brother Kamran played for NAYC and for
Nottinghamshire U15-U19 ('top player'); younger brother Aqib played for Notts and
England U15; 'Uncle Mac and Uncle Raja great players'
Education: Blue Bell Hill School; Manvers Pierrepont School; South Notts College
Qualifications: Coaching certificates

Career outside cricket: Printing company
Overseas tours: Nottinghamshire to South Africa; England U19 to West Indies 1994-95, to Zimbabwe 1995-96; 'the great ZRK tour to Lahore, Pakistan' 2000; England A to West Indies 2000-01; England to India and New Zealand 2001-02
Overseas teams played for: Victoria Park, Perth
Career highlights to date: 'Playing for England in the Ashes'
Cricket moments to forget: 'Every time I get out'
Cricketers particularly admired: David Gower, Saeed Anwar, Ian Botham, Clive Rice, Uncle Raja and Uncle Mac
Young players to look out for: Bilal Shafayat, Aqib Afzaal, Nadeem Malik
Other sports played: Indoor football
Other sports followed: Football ('a bit of Man U')
Relaxations: 'Praying; spending time with friends and family; listening to Indian music'
Extras: Played for England U15 against South Africa and, in 1994, for England U17 against India. Broke the U16 bowling record in the Texaco Trophy. Won Denis Compton Award 1996. Took wicket (Adam Gilchrist) with third ball in Test cricket v Australia at The Oval 2001. C&G Man of the Match award for his 3-8 (from four overs) and 64* v Ireland at Clontarf 2002
Opinions on cricket: 'Fantastic game. Love it more every day. Give it 100 per cent and enjoy it.'
Best batting: 151* Nottinghamshire v Worcestershire, Trent Bridge 2000
Best bowling: 4-101 Nottinghamshire v Gloucestershire, Trent Bridge 1998

2002 Season

	M	Inns	NO	Runs	HS	Avge	100s	50s	Ct	St	O	M	Runs	Wkts	Avge	Best	5wI	10wM
Test																		
All First	18	32	4	1275	134	45.53	5	6	12	-	63.3	20	180	4	45.00	3-32	-	-
1-day Int																		
C & G	2	2	1	106	64 *	106.00	-	1	1	-	4	0	8	3	2.66	3-8	-	
B & H	5	4	1	44	23	14.66	-	-	1	-	7.1	1	41	2	20.50	1-14	-	
1-day Lge	13	12	0	370	75	30.83	-	3	1	-	24	0	169	6	28.16	3-48	-	

Career Performances

	M	Inns	NO	Runs	HS	Avge	100s	50s	Ct	St	Balls	Runs	Wkts	Avge	Best	5wI	10wM
Test	3	6	1	83	54	16.60	-	1	-	-	54	49	1	49.00	1-49	-	-
All First	121	211	19	6215	151 *	32.36	12	35	60	-	6277	3333	66	50.50	4-101	-	-
1-day Int																	
C & G	8	6	2	225	64 *	56.25	-	1	2	-	90	65	3	21.66	3-8	-	
B & H	18	17	4	425	78	32.69	-	4	3	-	175	155	7	22.14	3-51	-	
1-day Lge	53	46	8	1341	95 *	35.28	-	11	14	-	596	569	21	27.09	3-48	-	

ALDRED, P.

Derbyshire

Name: Paul Aldred
Role: Right-hand bat, right-arm medium bowler
Born: 4 February 1969, Chellaston, Derby
Height: 5ft 10in **Weight:** 12st
Nickname: Jack, Aldo, Mr Ed, Dred
County debut: 1995
County cap: 1999
50 wickets in a season: 1
1st-Class 50s: 1
1st-Class 5 w. in innings: 5
1st-Class 10 w. in match: 1
1st-Class catches: 34
Place in batting averages: (2001 259th av. 10.00)
Place in bowling averages: (2001 143rd av. 57.07)
Strike rate: 88.00 (career 65.44)
Parents: Harry (deceased) and Lynette
Marital status: Single
Family links with cricket: Father played local cricket
Education: Chellaston and Curbar Primary School; Lady Manners, Bakewell
Qualifications: 'None of interest'
Career outside cricket: Builder
Overseas teams played for: Bentley CC, Melbourne 1994-95
Cricketers particularly admired: Ian Botham, Viv Richards
Other sports played: Golf; hockey for Derbyshire U16, U19, U21 and senior squad
Other sports followed: Golf, rugby, horse racing
Relaxations: 'Most sports; golf, fishing, rugby, horse racing'
Extras: Played against New Zealand with NCA in 1994. Played for Derbyshire U21 hockey team at the age of 15. His 1999 season included a spell of 27 wickets in three matches. Released by Derbyshire at the end of the 2002 season
Best batting: 83 Derbyshire v Hampshire, Chesterfield 1997
Best bowling: 7-101 Derbyshire v Lancashire, Derby 1999

2002 Season

	M	Inns	NO	Runs	HS	Avge	100s	50s	Ct	St	O	M	Runs	Wkts	Avge	Best	5wI	10wM
Test																		
All First	2	3	1	40	29	20.00	-	-	2	-	73.2	19	211	5	42.20	2-30	-	-
1-day Int																		
C & G																		
B & H	1	1	0	7	7	7.00	-	-	-	-	9.5	1	52	1	52.00	1-52	-	
1-day Lge																		

Career Performances

	M	Inns	NO	Runs	HS	Avge	100s	50s	Ct	St	Balls	Runs	Wkts	Avge	Best	5wI	10wM
Test																	
All First	60	81	12	806	83	11.68	-	1	34	-	8639	4562	132	34.56	7-101	5	1
1-day Int																	
C & G	5	3	1	21	17	10.50	-	-	1	-	236	151	7	21.57	4-30	-	
B & H	14	6	1	52	24 *	10.40	-	-	2	-	686	523	19	27.52	3-12	-	
1-day Lge	64	35	11	294	39 *	12.25	-	-	11	-	2406	2097	68	30.83	4-41	-	

ALI, K.   Worcestershire

Name: Kabir Ali
Role: Right-hand bat, right-arm medium-fast bowler
Born: 24 November 1980, Birmingham
Height: 6ft **Weight:** 12st 5lbs
Nickname: Kabby, Taxi
County debut: 1999
County colours: 2002
50 wickets in a season: 1
1st-Class 50s: 3
1st-Class 5 w. in innings: 6
1st-Class 10 w. in match: 2
1st-Class catches: 8
One-Day 5 w. in innings: 1
Place in batting averages: 259th av. 15.94
Place in bowling averages: 26th av. 25.08
(2001 4th av. 18.07)
Strike rate: 46.23 (career 48.36)
Parents: Shabir Ali and M. Begum
Marital status: Single
Family links with cricket: Father and uncle played club cricket. Cousin Kadeer Ali also plays for Worcestershire. Cousin Moeen Munir Ali played for England U15 and is now with Warwickshire

Education: Moseley School; Wolverhampton University
Qualifications: GNVQ Leisure and Tourism
Career outside cricket: Student
Off-season: 'Going to Australia with the England Academy'
Overseas tours: Warwickshire U19 to Cape Town 1998; ECB National Academy to Australia and Sri Lanka 2002-03
Overseas teams played for: Midland-Guildford, Perth
Career highlights to date: 'Opening the bowling with Glenn McGrath'
Cricketers particularly admired: Ian Botham, Wasim Akram
Young players to look out for: Kadeer Ali, Moeen Munir, Irfan Shah, Gareth Batty
Other sports played: Football, snooker, badminton
Other sports followed: Football
Relaxations: 'Playing snooker and spending time with family and friends'
Extras: Warwickshire Youth Young Player of the Year award. Won Gold Award on B&H debut for his 4-29 v Glamorgan 2000. Represented England U19 v Sri Lanka U19 in one-day and 'Test' series 2000. NBC Denis Compton Award for the most promising young Worcestershire player 2000. Played for Worcestershire Board XI and Worcestershire in the C&G 2001. Junior Royals Player of the Year 2001. Recorded maiden first-class ten-wicket match return (10-88) v Oxford University CCE at The Parks 2002; his 7-43 in OUCCE's second innings included a burst of six wickets in 21 balls. Recorded maiden Championship ten-wicket match return (10-66) v Gloucestershire at Bristol 2002. Recorded maiden one-day five-wicket return (5-36) v Yorkshire in the NUL at Headingley 2002. Took 3-70 v Glamorgan at Cardiff 2002, in the process reaching 50 Championship wickets in a season for the first time. Professional Cricketers' Association Young Player of the Year 2002. Worcestershire Player of the Year 2002
Opinions on cricket: 'Should play more day/night games.'
Best batting: 51* Worcestershire v Northamptonshire, Northampton 2002
Best bowling: 7-43 Worcestershire v OUCCE, The Parks 2002
Stop press: Called up from the ECB National Academy squad at Adelaide to the England one-day squad in Australia 2002-03 and played for England XI v Australia A at Sydney

2002 Season

	M	Inns	NO	Runs	HS	Avge	100s	50s	Ct	St	O	M	Runs	Wkts	Avge	Best	5wI	10wM
Test																		
All First	17	21	4	271	51*	15.94	-	1	3	-	547.1	129	1781	71	25.08	7-43	5	2
1-day Int																		
C & G	3	2	1	17	9*	17.00	-	-	-	-	21.2	2	112	5	22.40	4-2	-	
B & H	7	2	0	36	27	18.00	-	-	2	-	59	7	201	14	14.35	4-34	-	
1-day Lge	16	9	2	86	24	12.28	-	-	2	-	109	9	557	21	26.52	5-36	1	

Career Performances

	M	Inns	NO	Runs	HS	Avge	100s	50s	Ct	St	Balls	Runs	Wkts	Avge	Best	5wI	10wM
Test																	
All First	32	42	8	633	51 *	18.61	-	3	8	-	5223	2903	108	26.87	7-43	6	2
1-day Int																	
C & G	9	5	1	31	9 *	7.75	-	-	2	-	392	297	15	19.80	4-2	-	
B & H	10	2	0	36	27	18.00	-	-	2	-	448	295	18	16.38	4-29	-	
1-day Lge	34	18	6	110	24	9.16	-	-	6	-	1310	1085	47	23.08	5-36	1	

ALI, K. Worcestershire

Name: Kadeer Ali
Role: Right-hand bat
Born: 7 March 1983, Birmingham
Height: 6ft 2in **Weight:** 10st 7lbs
Nickname: Kaddy
County debut: 2000
1st-Class catches: 3
Place in batting averages: (2001 268th
av. 8.12)
Parents: Munir Ali and Maqsood Begum
Marital status: Single
Family links with cricket: Father a cricket
coach and club cricketer. Brother Moeen
Munir Ali plays for Warwickshire. Cousin
Kabir Ali plays for Worcestershire
Education: Handsworth Grammar; Moseley
Sixth Form College
Qualifications: 5 GCSEs
Career outside cricket: Studying
Overseas tours: England U19 to India 2000-01, to Australia and (U19 World Cup)
New Zealand 2001-02
Cricketers particularly admired: Sachin Tendulkar, Vikram Solanki
Young players to look out for: Kabir Ali
Other sports played: Football
Other sports followed: Football (Liverpool FC)
Relaxations: Listening to music, going out with friends
Extras: Young Player awards at Warwickshire CCC. Played for Worcestershire Board
XI in the NatWest 1999 and in the second round of the C&G 2003, which was played
in September 2002. Represented England U19 v Sri Lanka U19 in 'Test' series 2000
and v West Indies U19 in one-day series (3/3) and 'Test' series (3/3) 2001, scoring
century (155) in the second 'Test' at Trent Bridge. NBC Denis Compton Award for the

most promising young Worcestershire player 2001. Represented England U19 v India U19 in 'Test' series (3/3) and one-day series (3/3) 2002; scored 97 and 111 in the third 'Test' at Northampton, in the process sharing with Bilal Shafayat (118 and 201*) in partnerships of 212 and 256; also scored a 122-ball 125 in the third 'ODI' at Taunton
Best batting: 38 Worcestershire v Middlesex, Worcester 2001

2002 Season

	M	Inns	NO	Runs	HS	Avge	100s	50s	Ct	St	O	M	Runs	Wkts	Avge	Best	5wI	10wM
Test																		
All First																		
1-day Int																		
C & G	1	1	0	66	66	66.00	-	1	-	-	3.3	0	21	0	-		-	-
B & H																		
1-day Lge	1	1	0	57	57	57.00	-	1	-	-								

Career Performances

	M	Inns	NO	Runs	HS	Avge	100s	50s	Ct	St	Balls	Runs	Wkts	Avge	Best	5wI	10wM
Test																	
All First	9	15	0	78	38	5.20	-	-	3	-	102	57	0	-		-	-
1-day Int																	
C & G	2	2	0	90	66	45.00	-	1	-	-	21	21	0	-		-	-
B & H																	
1-day Lge	2	2	0	77	57	38.50	-	1	-	-							

1. Which Australian all-rounder scored 759 Championship runs and took 61 Championship wickets for Surrey in 1996?

ALI, M. M.   Warwickshire

Name: Moeen Munir Ali
Role: Left-hand opening bat, right-arm
off-spin bowler
Born: 18 June 1987, Birmingham
Height: 5ft 9in   **Weight:** 10st
Nickname: Eddy, Elvis, Bart
County debut: No first-team appearance
Parents: Munir Ali and Maqsood Begum
Marital status: Single
Family links with cricket: Brother of Kadeer
Ali; cousin of Kabir Ali. Father is a cricket
coach
Education: Nelson Mandela Community
Primary School; Moseley School
Qualifications: 'Taking GCSEs June 2003'
Career outside cricket: Student
Off-season: 'Further education and to get
into the England U19 set-up'
Overseas tours: Private tour to Pakistan
2002

Career highlights to date: 'Signing two-year contract with Warwickshire. 195* in a
20-over competition'
Cricket moments to forget: 'None'
Cricket superstitions: 'None'
Cricketers particularly admired: Nick Knight, Sanath Jayasuriya, Saeed Anwar,
Wasim Akram, Kabir, Kadeer
Young players to look out for: Omar Munir Ali, Aatil Ali, James Ord
Other sports played: Football
Other sports followed: Football (Liverpool)
Relaxations: 'Enjoy music, eating out, chilling out'
Extras: Represented England U15 2002. Has won five Warwickshire youth awards
since age of 11
Opinions on cricket: 'More youngsters should be given the chance for England and
first-class cricket.'

ALLEN, A. P. W. Warwickshire

Name: Alexander (<u>Sandy</u>) Phillip Wortley Allen
Role: Right-hand bat, wicket-keeper
Born: 13 October 1984, Solihull
Height: 5ft 10in **Weight:** 12st 9lbs
Nickname: Sand
County debut: 2002
Parents: Martyn and Lynne
Marital status: Single
Family links with cricket: 'My grandfather Esmond Lewis kept wicket for Warwickshire'
Education: Knowle Primary School; Arden School, Knowle, Solihull; Solihull Sixth Form College
Qualifications: 8 GCSEs, 'I'm in my last year of a BTEC in Sports Science'
Career outside cricket: College
Off-season: 'Studying for my BTEC Sports Science; training at Warwickshire'

Career highlights to date: 'Keeping wicket for Warwickshire at Edgbaston against West Indies A'
Cricket moments to forget: 'Being hit on the ankle by Tim Bresnan whilst taking off the bowlers during the warm-up before an England U17 game'
Cricket superstitions: 'I always put my left pad on first'
Cricketers particularly admired: Mark Boucher, Darren Gough, Matthew Hayden
Young players to look out for: Moeen Munir, Chris Cheslin
Other sports played: Rugby ('played county; played at Twickenham'), athletics (county), golf
Other sports followed: Football (Birmingham City FC)
Relaxations: 'Snooker, listening to music'
Extras: Played for the Warwickshire Board side that won the last ECB 38-County competition 2002. Played for Warwickshire Board XI in the first round of the C&G 2003, which was played in August 2002
Opinions on cricket: 'National and county academies are improving the standard of English cricket, on technique and fitness.'
Best batting: 18* Warwickshire v West Indies A, Edgbaston 2002

2002 Season

	M	Inns	NO	Runs	HS	Avge	100s	50s	Ct	St	O	M	Runs	Wkts	Avge	Best	5wI	10wM
Test																		
All First	1	1	1	18	18*	-	-	-	-	-								
1-day Int																		
C & G	1	1	0	10	10	10.00	-	-	1	-								
B & H																		
1-day Lge																		

Career Performances

	M	Inns	NO	Runs	HS	Avge	100s	50s	Ct	St	Balls	Runs	Wkts	Avge	Best	5wI	10wM
Test																	
All First	1	1	1	18	18*	-	-	-	-	-							
1-day Int																	
C & G	1	1	0	10	10	10.00	-	-	1	-							
B & H																	
1-day Lge																	

ALLEYNE, D.   Middlesex

Name: David Alleyne
Role: Right-hand bat, wicket-keeper
Born: 17 April 1976, York
Height: 5ft 11in **Weight:** 13st 7lbs
Nickname: Bones, Gears
County debut: 1999 (one-day), 2001
(first-class)
1st-Class catches: 12
Parents: Darcy and Jo
Marital status: Engaged to Dawn
Family links with cricket: Father played for
local club Northampton Exiles
Education: Raglan; Enfield Grammar;
Hertford Regional College, Ware; City and
Islington College
Qualifications: 6 GCSEs, City and Guilds,
BTEC Diploma in Leisure Studies, Level 3
coaching award
Career outside cricket: Coaching; teaching
Off-season: 'Coaching at Middlesex Academy'
Overseas tours: Middlesex to Johannesburg 2000-01
Overseas teams played for: Stratford, New Zealand; Inglewood, New Zealand

1997-98; Sturt, Adelaide 1999-2000; Midland-Guildford, Perth 2000-01; Karori CC, Wellington, New Zealand 2001-02

Career highlights to date: 'Gaining promotion [in Championship] in last game of season!'

Cricketers particularly admired: Viv Richards, Desmond Haynes, Carl Hooper, Jack Russell, Alec Stewart, Keith Piper

Young players to look out for: 'All those who are putting in 110 per cent; they know who they are'

Other sports played: Judo, football

Other sports followed: Football (Liverpool FC)

Injuries: Burst blood vessels in both hands; no time off required

Relaxations: 'Relaxing with Dawn and family'

Extras: Represented Middlesex U11 to U17. London Cricket College (three years). Represented Middlesex Cricket Board. Played football for Middlesex U15 and U16 and for Enfield Borough U16. Middlesex 2nd XI Player of the Year 1999, 2000, 2002

Opinions on cricket: 'Pitches need to be a consistent standard at the start of play. Away teams should get the choice at the toss.'

Best batting: 49* Middlesex v Derbyshire, Derby 2002

2002 Season

	M	Inns	NO	Runs	HS	Avge	100s	50s	Ct	St	O	M	Runs	Wkts	Avge	Best	5wI	10wM
Test																		
All First	3	3	1	93	49*	46.50	-	-	8	-								
1-day Int																		
C & G																		
B & H																		
1-day Lge	7	6	1	26	12	5.20	-	-	3	-								

Career Performances

	M	Inns	NO	Runs	HS	Avge	100s	50s	Ct	St	Balls	Runs	Wkts	Avge	Best	5wI	10wM
Test																	
All First	5	7	1	148	49*	24.66	-	-	12	-							
1-day Int																	
C & G	2	2	0	8	7	4.00	-	-	2	-							
B & H																	
1-day Lge	20	19	1	226	58	12.55	-	1	17	6							

ALLEYNE, M. W.   Gloucestershire

Name: <u>Mark</u> Wayne Alleyne
Role: Right-hand bat, right-arm medium bowler, occasional wicket-keeper, county captain
Born: 23 May 1968, Tottenham, London
Height: 5ft 10in **Weight:** 14st
Nickname: Boo-Boo
County debut: 1986
County cap: 1990
Benefit: 1999
One-Day Internationals: 10
1000 runs in a season: 6
50 wickets in a season: 1
1st-Class 50s: 69
1st-Class 100s: 21
1st-Class 200s: 1
1st-Class 5 w. in innings: 8
1st-Class catches: 253
1st-Class stumpings: 3
One-Day 100s: 4
One-Day 5 w. in innings: 3
Place in batting averages: 177th av. 25.22 (2001 114th av. 31.21)
Place in bowling averages: 149th av. 51.52 (2001 42nd av. 26.31)
Strike rate: 93.88 (career 64.47)
Parents: Euclid (deceased) and Hyacinth
Wife and date of marriage: Louise Maria, 9 October 1998
Family links with cricket: Brother played for Gloucestershire 2nd XI and Middlesex YC. Father played club cricket in Barbados and England
Education: Harrison College, Barbados; Cardinal Pole School, East London
Qualifications: 6 O-levels, NCA Senior Coaching Award, volleyball coaching certificate
Career outside cricket: 'Business and lifestyle management'
Overseas tours: England YC to Sri Lanka 1986-87, to Australia 1987-88; England XI to New Zealand (Cricket Max) 1997; England A to Bangladesh and New Zealand 1999-2000 (captain), to West Indies 2000-01 (captain); England to Australia 1998-99 (CUB Series), to South Africa and Zimbabwe 1999-2000 (one-day series), to Kenya (ICC Knockout Trophy) 2000-01, to Pakistan and Sri Lanka 2000-01 (one-day series)
Career highlights to date: '1) England debut in Brisbane 2) England Man of the Match in East London, South Africa 3) Each one of our five consecutive trophies'
Cricket moments to forget: 'Missing promotion in the Championship and being relegated in the Norwich Union League in the same week [2001]'

Cricketers particularly admired: Gordon Greenidge, Viv Richards, Jack Russell, Steve Waugh

Other sports played: Basketball, football 'and various ball games interpreted by John Bracewell'

Other sports followed: 'Still follow Tottenham religiously but support our local football and rugby teams'

Relaxations: 'Sport crazy but also an avid gardener. Keen historian'

Extras: Graduate of Haringey Cricket College. In 1986 became (at 18 years 54 days) the youngest player to score a century for Gloucestershire, with his 116* v Sussex at Bristol. In 1990 also became the youngest to score a double hundred for the county, with his 256 v Northamptonshire at Northampton. In 1992 struck then highest Sunday League score for Gloucestershire (134*). Cricket Select Sunday League Player of the Year 1992. Scored 112 in the B&H Super Cup final v Yorkshire at Lord's 1999, winning the Man of the Match award. Leading all-rounder in the single-division four-day era of the County Championship with 6409 runs (av. 32.53) and 216 wickets (av. 31.18) 1993-99. Captain of Gloucestershire's one-day double-winning side (NatWest and B&H Super Cup) 1999 and of treble-winning side (NatWest, B&H and Norwich Union National League) 2000. Man of the Match in One-Day International v South Africa at East London February 2000 (53, 3-55 and a catch to dismiss Jonty Rhodes). Played 393 consecutive competitive games, a Gloucestershire record, between 28 July 1990 and 24 June 2000. One of *Wisden*'s Five Cricketers of the Year 2001. Honorary fellowship from University of Gloucestershire, October 2001. Gloucestershire captain since 1997

Best batting: 256 Gloucestershire v Northamptonshire, Northampton 1990

Best bowling: 6-49 Gloucestershire v Middlesex, Lord's 2000

2002 Season

	M	Inns	NO	Runs	HS	Avge	100s	50s	Ct	St	O	M	Runs	Wkts	Avge	Best	5wI	10wM
Test																		
All First	14	25	3	555	142 *	25.22	1	2	12	-	266	59	876	17	51.52	3-76	-	-
1-day Int																		
C & G	3	1	0	28	28	28.00	-	-	-	-	23	3	89	7	12.71	4-27	-	
B & H	6	5	1	119	52	29.75	-	1	2	-	34	1	154	5	30.80	2-32	-	
1-day Lge	14	13	2	423	93	38.45	-	3	5	-	82	2	337	13	25.92	3-30	-	

Career Performances

	M	Inns	NO	Runs	HS	Avge	100s	50s	Ct	St	Balls	Runs	Wkts	Avge	Best	5wI	10wM
Test																	
All First	314	516	48	14512	256	31.00	22	69	259	3	25402	12888	394	32.71	6-49	8	-
1-day Int	10	8	1	151	53	21.57	-	1	3	-	366	280	10	28.00	3-27	-	
C & G	43	34	5	634	73	21.86	-	1	15	-	1791	1131	48	23.56	5-30	1	
B & H	71	61	12	1312	112	26.77	1	4	35	-	2950	2115	67	31.56	5-27	1	
1-day Lge	249	228	47	5243	134 *	28.96	3	23	101	-	8399	6751	220	30.68	5-28	1	

AMBROSE, T. R. Sussex

Name: <u>Timothy</u> Raymond Ambrose
Role: Right-hand bat, wicket-keeper
Born: 1 December 1982, Newcastle,
New South Wales, Australia
Height: 5ft 7in
Nickname: Shambrose
County debut: 2001
1st-Class 50s: 2
1st-Class 100s: 2
1st-Class catches: 9
Place in batting averages: 89th av. 38.00
Parents: Raymond and Sally
Marital status: Single
Family links with cricket: 'Cousin played
Sydney first grade; father is captain of local
grade D4 team'

Education: Tighes Hill, Newcastle;
Merewether Selective High, NSW
Career outside cricket: Greenkeeping
Off-season: 'Training in South Africa'
Overseas tours: Sussex to Grenada 2001, 2002
Overseas teams played for: Wallsend, NSW 2000; Nelson Bay, NSW 2001;
Newcastle, NSW 2002
Career highlights to date: 'Being involved in the [second division] Championship
winning side 2001. Maiden first-class hundred at Headingley'
Cricketers particularly admired: Steve Waugh, Adam Gilchrist, Ian Healy
Young players to look out for: Mike Yardy, Matt Prior, Dominic Clapp,
Carl Hopkinson
Other sports played: Football, squash, golf, rugby league, rugby union, AFL, 'I'll
have a go at anything'
Other sports followed: Rugby league (Newcastle Knights), Australian Rules (Sydney
Swans), football (Tottenham Hotspur)
Relaxations: Guitar, music, surfing
Extras: Captained Newcastle (NSW) U16 1999 Bradman Cup winning side. 'Scored
138 in first ever game.' Played for New South Wales U17. Won NSW Junior Cricketer
of the Year three years running. Played for Eastbourne in the Sussex League in 2000.
Scored 87 and took two catches and a stumping in his second one-day match, in the
Norwich Union League v Lancashire at Hove 2001. Scored 52 on first-class debut v
Warwicks at Edgbaston 2001. C&G Man of the Match award for his 95 v Bucks at
Beaconsfield 2002. Scored maiden first-class century (149) v Yorkshire at Headingley
2002. Holds a British passport and is not considered an overseas player

Opinions on cricket: 'First division should be premier league and more recognised. Great game. Love it.'
Best batting: 149 Sussex v Yorkshire, Headingley 2002

2002 Season

	M	Inns	NO	Runs	HS	Avge	100s	50s	Ct	St	O	M	Runs	Wkts	Avge	Best	5wl	10wM
Test																		
All First	13	22	1	798	149	38.00	2	2	9	-	1	0	1	0	-	-	-	-
1-day Int																		
C & G	3	3	0	111	95	37.00	-	1	1	-								
B & H	6	6	0	230	87	38.33	-	3	9	-								
1-day Lge	12	10	1	113	33 *	12.55	-	-	9	-								

Career Performances

	M	Inns	NO	Runs	HS	Avge	100s	50s	Ct	St	Balls	Runs	Wkts	Avge	Best	5wl	10wM
Test																	
All First	15	25	1	890	149	37.08	2	3	12	-	6	1	0	-	-	-	-
1-day Int																	
C & G	3	3	0	111	95	37.00	-	1	1	-							
B & H	6	6	0	230	87	38.33	-	3	9	-							
1-day Lge	16	14	1	277	87	21.30	-	1	12	3							

AMIN, R. M.   Leicestershire

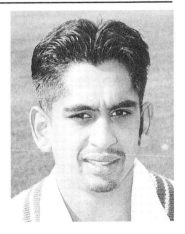

Name: Rupesh Mahesh Amin
Role: Right-hand bat, left-arm orthodox spin bowler
Born: 20 August 1977, Clapham, London
Height: 5ft 11in   **Weight:** 10st 7lbs
Nickname: Idi, Plug, Rups
County debut: 1997 (Surrey)
1st-Class catches: 6
Strike rate: 72.00 (career 98.11)
Parents: Mahesh and Aruna
Marital status: Single
Family links with cricket: Father played club cricket
Education: Stanford Middle School; Riddlesdown High School; John Ruskin Sixth Form
Qualifications: 8 GCSEs, 3 A-levels, ECB Level 1 cricket coaching

Off-season: 'Coaching and training. Playing Sunday league football'
Overseas tours: Bishen Bedi Academy to Sharjah 1999
Overseas teams played for: Manly-Warringah District CC, Sydney 1997-98; University of New South Wales 1999-2000
Career highlights to date: 'Winning County Championship in 1999'
Cricket moments to forget: 'Being hit out of ground by Mal Loye at Whitgift School in NUL'
Cricketers particularly admired: Saqlain Mushtaq, Anil Kumble, Sachin Tendulkar
Young players to look out for: Rikki Clarke, Ravi Bopara
Other sports played: Football (Croydon South FC)
Other sports followed: Football (Liverpool), snooker (Ronnie O'Sullivan), baseball
Relaxations: Going to cinema, eating good food, going out and seeing places
Extras: Played for Croydon District U15 side that won Hobbs Trophy against London Schools. Re-signed by Surrey for 2002 but left at the end of the season and has joined Leicestershire for 2003
Opinions on cricket: 'Not enough rest periods during season to regroup yourself mentally and physically. Too much cricket to be played during a season.'
Best batting: 12 Surrey v Leicestershire, The Oval 1998
Best bowling: 4-87 Surrey v Somerset, The Oval 1999

2002 Season

	M	Inns	NO	Runs	HS	Avge	100s	50s	Ct	St	O	M	Runs	Wkts	Avge	Best	5wI	10wM
Test																		
All First	1	0	0	0	0	-	-	-	-	-	24	8	55	2	27.50	2-40	-	-
1-day Int																		
C & G																		
B & H																		
1-day Lge	1	1	1	0	0 *	-	-	-	-	-	3	0	33	0	-		-	-

Career Performances

	M	Inns	NO	Runs	HS	Avge	100s	50s	Ct	St	Balls	Runs	Wkts	Avge	Best	5wI	10wM
Test																	
All First	15	18	8	35	12	3.50	-	-	6	-	2649	1108	27	41.03	4-87	-	-
1-day Int																	
C & G																	
B & H																	
1-day Lge	4	1	1	0	0 *	-	-	-	1	-	84	97	2	48.50	2-43	-	

ANDERSON, J. M. Lancashire

Name: <u>James</u> Michael Anderson
Role: Left-hand bat, right-arm
medium-fast bowler
Born: 30 July 1982, Burnley
Height: 6ft 2in **Weight:** 12st 7lbs
Nickname: Jimmy
County debut: 2001 (one-day), 2002
(first-class)
50 wickets in a season: 1
1st-Class 5 w. in innings: 3
1st-Class catches: 2
Place in batting averages: 306th av. 7.25
Place in bowling averages: 12th av. 22.28
Strike rate: 39.20 (career 39.20)
Parents: Michael and Catherine
Marital status: Single
Family links with cricket: Father and uncle
played for Burnley

Education: St Mary's RC Primary School; St Theodore's RC High School;
St Theodore's RC Sixth Form Centre – all Burnley
Qualifications: 10 GCSEs, 1 A-level, 1 GNVQ, Level 2 coaching award
Off-season: 'ECB Academy tour to Australia and Sri Lanka'
Overseas tours: Lancashire to Cape Town 2002; ECB National Academy to Australia
2002-03
Career highlights to date: 'Making first-class debut. Taking 50 first-class wickets in
2002 season. Being selected for ECB Academy'
Cricketers particularly admired: Michael Atherton, Darren Gough, Courtney Walsh,
Shaun Pollock
Young players to look out for: David Brown, Jonathan Clare (both Burnley CC)
Other sports played: Golf, football, 'most active sports'
Other sports followed: Football (Burnley FC), golf
Relaxations: 'Television, music, all sports'
Extras: Played for Lancashire Board XI in the NatWest 2000. Represented England
U19 v West Indies U19 in 'Test' series (3/3) 2001, taking 5-45 in the West Indies U19
second innings in the first 'Test' at Leicester. Took hat-trick for Lancashire 2nd XI
2001. Recorded maiden first-class five-wicket return (6-23) v Hampshire at West End
2002. Had match figures of 9-57 (6-41 and 3-16) from 18.5 overs v Somerset at
Blackpool 2002. Took 50 first-class wickets in his first full season 2002
Opinions on cricket: 'Too much cricket is played both at amateur and professional
levels in England. The emphasis seems to be on quantity rather than quality.'
Best batting: 16 Lancashire v Warwickshire, Old Trafford 2002

39

Best bowling: 6-23 Lancashire v Hampshire, West End 2002
Stop press: Called up from the ECB National Academy squad at Adelaide to the England one-day squad for the VB Series in Australia 2002-03 as cover for Andrew Caddick. Made One-Day International debut v Australia at Melbourne in the VB Series 2002-03. Took 1-12 from ten overs (including five successive maidens) v Australia at Adelaide in the VB Series 2002-03. Selected for England squad for 2002-03 World Cup

2002 Season

	M	Inns	NO	Runs	HS	Avge	100s	50s	Ct	St	O	M	Runs	Wkts	Avge	Best	5wI	10wM
Test																		
All First	13	16	8	58	16	7.25	-	-	2	-	326.4	61	1114	50	22.28	6-23	3	-
1-day Int																		
C & G																		
B & H																		
1-day Lge	2	0	0	0	0	-	-	-	1	-	18	3	83	5	16.60	3-42	-	

Career Performances

	M	Inns	NO	Runs	HS	Avge	100s	50s	Ct	St	Balls	Runs	Wkts	Avge	Best	5wI	10wM
Test																	
All First	13	16	8	58	16	7.25	-	-	2	-	1960	1114	50	22.28	6-23	3	-
1-day Int																	
C & G	2	1	1	5	5 *	-	-	-	-	-	120	98	3	32.66	2-64	-	
B & H																	
1-day Lge	3	0	0	0	0	-	-	-	1	-	132	116	6	19.33	3-42	-	

2. In 2000 the members of a hugely successful Test opening pair both captained English first-class counties. Name the batsmen and the counties.

ANDERSON, R. S. G.   Northamptonshire

Name: Ricaldo (<u>Ricky</u>) Sherman
Glenroy Anderson
Role: Right-hand bat, right-arm
medium-fast bowler
Born: 22 September 1976, Hammersmith,
London
Height: 5ft 10in   **Weight:** 11st 11lbs
County debut: 1999 (Essex), 2002
(Northamptonshire)
50 wickets in a season: 1
1st-Class 50s: 2
1st-Class 5 w. in innings: 8
1st-Class 10 w. in match: 1
1st-Class catches: 7
Place in batting averages: 251st av. 16.60
(2001 232nd av. 14.00)
Place in bowling averages: (2001 11th
av. 19.97)
Strike rate: 95.33 (career 50.19)
Parents: Heather and Junior
Marital status: Single
Education: Lyon Park School; Alperton High School; Barnet College; NWL College;
London Cricket College
Qualifications: 6 GCSEs, BTEC National in Engineering
Career outside cricket: 'None yet, but working on it'
Off-season: 'Gym and training at indoor school on cricket skills'
Overseas tours: Middlesex U16 to Jersey; BWIA to Trinidad and Tobago 1998,
1999, 2000
Overseas teams played for: Coronation CC, South Africa 1996-97
Cricketers particularly admired: Malcolm Marshall, Stuart Law, Carl Hooper
Young players to look out for: James Foster
Other sports followed: Football (Liverpool)
Relaxations: Music
Extras: Took 50 first-class wickets in his first season 1999. Left Essex in the 2001-02
off-season and joined Northamptonshire for 2002
Best batting: 67* Essex v Sussex, Chelmsford 2000
Best bowling: 6-34 Essex v Northamptonshire, Ilford 2000

2002 Season

	M	Inns	NO	Runs	HS	Avge	100s	50s	Ct	St	O	M	Runs	Wkts	Avge	Best	5wI	10wM
Test																		
All First	5	10	0	166	51	16.60	-	1	-	-	143	29	550	9	61.11	4-97	-	-
1-day Int																		
C & G	1	1	0	4	4	4.00	-	-	-	-	7	0	53	1	53.00	1-53	-	
B & H	3	1	0	19	19	19.00	-	-	-	-	22	2	85	5	17.00	3-28	-	
1-day Lge	2	2	1	23	22	23.00	-	-	-	-	11	0	71	4	17.75	3-30	-	

Career Performances

	M	Inns	NO	Runs	HS	Avge	100s	50s	Ct	St	Balls	Runs	Wkts	Avge	Best	5wI	10wM
Test																	
All First	37	49	5	637	67 *	14.47	-	2	7	-	5923	3251	118	27.55	6-34	8	1
1-day Int																	
C & G	1	1	0	4	4	4.00	-	-	-	-	42	53	1	53.00	1-53	-	
B & H	7	1	0	19	19	19.00	-	-	1	-	330	257	8	32.12	3-28	-	
1-day Lge	17	14	2	85	22	7.08	-	-	-	-	672	580	11	52.72	3-30	-	

ANGEL, J.   Gloucestershire

Name: Jo Angel
Role: Left-hand bat, right-arm fast bowler
Born: 22 April 1968, Mount Lawley, Perth
Height: 6ft 6in **Weight:** 16st 2lbs
Nickname: Hells, Dust
County debut: 2002 (one-day)
Test debut: 1992-93
Tests: 4
One-Day Internationals: 3
1st-Class 50s: 4
1st-Class 5 w. in innings: 15
1st-Class 10 w. in match: 1
1st-Class catches: 27
Strike rate: (career 51.01)
Education: Eastern Hills Senior High
School, Mount Helena, Western Australia
Off-season: Playing for Western Australia
Overseas tours: Australia to Sri Lanka
(Singer World Series) 1994-95, to Pakistan 1994-95, to New Zealand (NZ Centenary
Tournament) 1994-95; Young Australia (Australia A) to England and Netherlands 1995
Overseas teams played for: Midland-Guildford 1987-88 – ; Western Australia
1991-92 –

Extras: Took 10-140 in Western Australia's innings victory over the New Zealand tourists at Perth 1993-94. Excalibur Award (for upholding the spirit of Western Australian cricket) 2001-02. Western Australia's second highest Sheffield Shield/Pura Cup wicket-taker after Terry Alderman. Played for Leigh in the Liverpool Competition 2002. Was Gloucestershire's overseas player towards the end of the 2002 season, replacing Ian Harvey, absent on international duty

Best batting: 84* Western Australia v New South Wales, Sydney 1993-94
Best bowling: 6-52 Western Australia v Victoria, Perth 2001-02
Stop press: His 6-35 in Queensland's first innings at Perth in the Pura Cup 2002-03 included his 400th first-class wicket

2002 Season

	M	Inns	NO	Runs	HS	Avge	100s	50s	Ct	St	O	M	Runs	Wkts	Avge	Best	5wI	10wM
Test																		
All First																		
1-day Int																		
C & G																		
B & H																		
1-day Lge	3	2	1	12	10 *	12.00	-	-	-	-	25	1	118	4	29.50	2-40	-	

Career Performances

	M	Inns	NO	Runs	HS	Avge	100s	50s	Ct	St	Balls	Runs	Wkts	Avge	Best	5wI	10wM
Test	4	7	1	35	11	5.83	-	-	1	-	748	463	10	46.30	3-54	-	-
All First	108	139	40	1299	84 *	13.12	-	4	27	-	22903	10920	449	24.32	6-52	15	1
1-day Int	3	1	0	0	0	0.00	-	-	-	-	162	113	4	28.25	2-47	-	
C & G																	
B & H																	
1-day Lge	3	2	1	12	10 *	12.00	-	-	-	-	150	118	4	29.50	2-40	-	

3. Hampshire have had two Test players named Marshall. Malcolm was one; who was the other and for which country did he play?

ATRI, V.

Nottinghamshire

Name: Vikram Atri
Role: Right-hand bat, leg-spin bowler
Born: 9 March 1983, Hull
Height: 5ft 7in **Weight:** 9st 6lbs
Nickname: Speedy, Big Dave, Bouffant
County debut: 2002
1st-Class 50s: 1
1st-Class catches: 2
Parents: Gulshan and Kuldip
Marital status: Single
Family links with cricket: Father played
club cricket for a number of years, including
in the Yorkshire and Bradford leagues
Education: Fernwood Junior School;
Fernwood Comprehensive School;
Bilborough College and Loughborough
University
Qualifications: 11 GCSEs, 3½ A-levels,
Level 1 cricket coach
Career outside cricket: 'Currently studying computing and management at
Loughborough University (tax dodger!)'
Off-season: 'Going to Australia to play club cricket'
Career highlights to date: 'Making my first-class debut for Notts against West Indies
A and scoring 98 in debut innings'
Cricket moments to forget: 'Getting out for 98 on first-class debut!'
Cricket superstitions: 'Always put my left pad on first'
Cricketers particularly admired: Sachin Tendulkar, Rahul Dravid, Michael Vaughan,
Shane Warne
Young players to look out for: Bilal Shafayat, John Francis, James Adams
Other sports played: Hockey (Nottinghamshire U13-U18)
Other sports followed: Football ('mad Liverpool supporter'), 'all sports really'
Relaxations: 'Sleeping and generally chilling'
Extras: Played for Nottinghamshire Board XI in the C&G 2001. Played for
Loughborough University CCE 2002, helping them to a clean sweep of all trophies.
Scored 98 on first-class debut v West Indies A at Trent Bridge 2002
Opinions on cricket: 'The game should be more batsman-friendly! Haven't played
long enough to form a valued opinion.'
Best batting: 98 Nottinghamshire v West Indies A, Trent Bridge 2002

2002 Season

	M	Inns	NO	Runs	HS	Avge	100s	50s	Ct	St	O	M	Runs	Wkts	Avge	Best	5wI	10wM
Test																		
All First	1	1	0	98	98	98.00	-	1	2	-								
1-day Int																		
C & G																		
B & H																		
1-day Lge																		

Career Performances

	M	Inns	NO	Runs	HS	Avge	100s	50s	Ct	St	Balls	Runs	Wkts	Avge	Best	5wI	10wM
Test																	
All First	1	1	0	98	98	98.00	-	1	2	-							
1-day Int																	
C & G	1	1	0	0	0	0.00	-	-	-	-							
B & H																	
1-day Lge																	

AVERIS, J. M. M. — Gloucestershire

Name: <u>James</u> Maxwell Michael Averis
Role: Right-hand bat, right-arm fast-medium bowler
Born: 28 May 1974, Bristol
Height: 5ft 11in **Weight:** 13st 7lbs
Nickname: Avo, Fish, Goat
County debut: 1994 (one-day), 1997 (first-class)
County cap: 2001
1st-Class 5 w. in innings: 3
1st-Class catches: 9
One-Day 5 w. in innings: 3
Place in batting averages: 288th av. 10.37 (2001 284th av. 2.18)
Place in bowling averages: 88th av. 33.23 (2001 105th av. 37.69)
Strike rate: 59.07 (career 75.15)
Parents: Mike and Carol
Wife and date of marriage: Anna, 26 October 2002
Family links with cricket: 'Father and grandfather played and have lots of advice'
Education: Bristol Cathedral School; Portsmouth University; St Cross College, Oxford University

Qualifications: 10 GCSEs, 3 A-levels, BSc (Hons) Geographical Science, Diploma in Social Studies (Oxon), FPC I and II

Career outside cricket: Working for advertising agency

Off-season: 'Working and getting hitched. Generally loafing around'

Overseas tours: Bristol Schools to Australia 1990-91; Gloucestershire to Zimbabwe 1997, to South Africa 1999, to Cape Town 2000, to Kimberley 2001, to Stellenbosch 2002; Bristol RFC to South Africa 1996; Oxford University RFC to Japan and Australia 1997

Overseas teams played for: Union CC, Port Elizabeth, South Africa; Kraifontaine, Boland, South Africa 2001

Career highlights to date: 'Winning treble in 2000'

Cricket moments to forget: 'Dropping the biggest dolly in 2000 NatWest final'

Cricket superstitions: 'Must eat on way to ground. Always use same toilet'

Cricketers particularly admired: Viv Richards, Malcolm Marshall, Ian Botham

Young players to look out for: Kabir Ali, Jim Troughton, 'all Glos lads'

Other sports played: Football (Bristol North West), rugby (played for Bristol RFC, captain of South West U21 1995, Oxford Blue 1996)

Other sports followed: Rugby (Bristol RFC), football (Liverpool FC)

Injuries: Out for the 'last couple of weeks' of the season with a torn calf muscle

Relaxations: 'Reading, surfing, eating out'

Extras: Double Oxford Blue in 1996-97. Played in every one-day game in Gloucestershire's treble-winning season 2000. Gloucestershire Player of the Year 2001

Opinions on cricket: 'Each side should include eight England eligible players. Two up/two down. More non-Test grounds used for international games.'

Best batting: 43 Gloucestershire v Nottinghamshire, Bristol 2002

Best bowling: 5-51 Gloucestershire v Nottinghamshire, Bristol 2002

2002 Season

	M	Inns	NO	Runs	HS	Avge	100s	50s	Ct	St	O	M	Runs	Wkts	Avge	Best	5wl	10wM
Test																		
All First	5	8	0	83	43	10.37	-	-	3	-	128	33	432	13	33.23	5-51	1	-
1-day Int																		
C & G	3	1	1	3	3 *	-	-	-	-	-	18	2	85	3	28.33	2-29	-	
B & H	6	2	1	27	20	27.00	-	-	-	-	38	8	187	7	26.71	3-13	-	
1-day Lge	12	7	3	34	20 *	8.50	-	-	3	-	87	3	437	16	27.31	3-44	-	

Career Performances

	M	Inns	NO	Runs	HS	Avge	100s	50s	Ct	St	Balls	Runs	Wkts	Avge	Best	5wl	10wM
Test																	
All First	39	56	11	500	43	11.11	-	-	9	-	6689	4011	89	45.06	5-51	3	-
1-day Int																	
C & G	11	5	4	29	12 *	29.00	-	-	1	-	518	395	18	21.94	4-36	-	
B & H	21	5	1	50	20	12.50	-	-	3	-	934	742	32	23.18	4-8	-	
1-day Lge	56	33	14	158	23 *	8.31	-	-	8	-	2495	1915	85	22.52	5-20	3	

AYMES, A. N.   Hampshire

Name: <u>Adrian</u> Nigel Aymes
Role: Right-hand bat, wicket-keeper
Born: 4 June 1964, Southampton
Height: 6ft **Weight:** 13st
Nickname: Adi
County debut: 1987
County cap: 1991
Benefit: 2000
50 dismissals in a season: 5
1st-Class 50s: 38
1st-Class 100s: 8
1st-Class catches: 516
1st-Class stumpings: 44
Place in batting averages: (2001 67th
av. 40.85)
Strike rate: (career 41.00)
Parents: Michael and Barbara
Wife and date of marriage: Marie,
14 November 1992

Children: Lucie, 9 November 1994
Education: Shirley Middle; Bellemoor Secondary; Hill College
Qualifications: 4 O-levels, 1 A-level, NCA coaching award
Overseas tours: Hampshire CCC to Isle of Wight 1992, to Portugal 1993,
to Guernsey 1994, to Anguilla 1997, to South Africa
Career highlights to date: '1991 NatWest win; 1992 B&H win'
Cricket moments to forget: 'All the semi-final losses'
Cricketers particularly admired: Jack Russell, 'all Hursley Park players'
Young players to look out for: Nicky Peng, 'all Hampshire's youngsters'
Other sports played: Football (Gosport Borough, Lymington, Bristol City trials)
Other sports followed: Non-sport martial arts, football (Arsenal, Southampton)
Relaxations: Spending time with friends and family; 'letting my neighbour "Old Stu"
teach me about wine and food'
Extras: Top-scored with 58 out of 201 on debut v Surrey at The Oval 1987. Equalled
county record of six catches in an innings and ten in a match, v Oxford University at
The Parks 1989. Hampshire Exiles Young Player of the Year 1990. Was quickest
wicket-keeper to 100 dismissals and 1000 runs in the Sunday League. Took 500th first-
class catch (Usman Afzaal off Shaun Udal) v Notts at Trent Bridge 2001. Hampshire
Players' Fielder of the Season Award 2001. Retired at the end of the 2002 season and
took over as manager of Fleet Town FC
Opinions on cricket: 'Still a great game.'
Best batting: 133 Hampshire v Leicestershire, Leicester 1998
Best bowling: 2-101 Hampshire v Nottinghamshire, Trent Bridge 2001

2002 Season

	M	Inns	NO	Runs	HS	Avge	100s	50s	Ct	St	O	M	Runs	Wkts	Avge	Best	5wI	10wM
Test																		
All First	5	7	2	52	22 *	10.40	-	-	16	1								
1-day Int																		
C & G																		
B & H																		
1-day Lge																		

Career Performances

	M	Inns	NO	Runs	HS	Avge	100s	50s	Ct	St	Balls	Runs	Wkts	Avge	Best	5wI	10wM
Test																	
All First	215	314	79	7338	133	31.22	8	38	516	44	246	438	6	73.00	2-101	-	-
1-day Int																	
C & G	25	11	4	277	73 *	39.57	-	2	38	4							
B & H	43	28	8	404	63	20.20	-	1	41	11							
1-day Lge	151	110	43	1511	60 *	22.55	-	3	134	38							

AZHAR MAHMOOD Surrey

Name: Azhar Mahmood Sagar
Role: Right-hand bat, right-arm
fast-medium bowler
Born: 28 February 1975, Rawalpindi
Height: 5ft 11in
County debut: 2002
Test debut: 1997-98
Tests: 21
One-Day Internationals: 121
1st-Class 50s: 15
1st-Class 100s: 4
1st-Class 5 w. in innings: 12
1st-Class 10 w. in match: 3
1st-Class catches: 57
One-Day 5 w. in innings: 3
Place in bowling averages: 1st av. 17.25
Strike rate: 32.80 (career 48.55)
Education: FG No. 1 High School,
Islamabad

Overseas tours: Pakistan Youth to New Zealand 1994-95; Pakistan A to England 1997; Pakistan to India (Pepsi Independence Cup) 1997, to South Africa and Zimbabwe 1997-98, to Bangladesh (Wills International Cup) 1998-99, to India

1998-99, to UK, Ireland and Holland (World Cup) 1999, to Australia 1999-2000, to Sri Lanka 2000, to Kenya (ICC Knockout) 2000-01, to New Zealand 2000-01, to England 2001, to Bangladesh 2001-02, to Australia (Super Challenge II) 2002, to Morocco (Morocco Cup) 2002, to Zimbabwe 2002-03, plus other one-day tournaments in Toronto, Kenya, Sharjah, Bangladesh and Singapore

Overseas teams played for: Islamabad; United Bank; Rawalpindi; Pakistan International Airlines

Extras: Made first-class debut for Islamabad 1993-94. Scored 379 runs (av. 31.58) and topped bowling averages with 40 wickets at 20.72 on Pakistan A tour of England 1997. Scored 128* and 50* on Test debut in the first Test v South Africa at Rawalpindi 1997-98; during first innings shared with Mushtaq Ahmed (59) in a tenth-wicket stand of 151, equalling the world tenth-wicket record in Tests set by Brian Hastings and Richard Collinge for New Zealand v Pakistan at Auckland 1972-73. Took 6-18 v West Indies in the Coca-Cola Champions Trophy in Sharjah 1999-2000 and 5-28 v Sri Lanka in the final of the same competition, winning the Man of the Match award on both occasions. Was Surrey's overseas player at the start of the 2002 season, pending the arrival of Saqlain Mushtaq, absent on international duty; has returned as an overseas player for 2003. Topped English first-class bowling averages 2002 with 20 wickets at 17.25

Best batting: 136 Pakistan v South Africa, Johannesburg 1997-98
Best bowling: 8-61 Surrey v Lancashire, The Oval 2002
Stop press: Selected for Pakistan squad for 2002-03 World Cup

2002 Season

	M	Inns	NO	Runs	HS	Avge	100s	50s	Ct	St	O	M	Runs	Wkts	Avge	Best	5wI	10wM
Test																		
All First	3	4	1	96	64 *	32.00	-	1	3	-	109.2	27	345	20	17.25	8-61	1	-
1-day Int																		
C & G																		
B & H	5	5	0	111	50	22.20	-	1	2	-	43	1	171	7	24.42	4-34	-	
1-day Lge	1	0	0	0	0	-	-	-	-	-	1.4	0	10	1	10.00	1-10	-	

Career Performances

	M	Inns	NO	Runs	HS	Avge	100s	50s	Ct	St	Balls	Runs	Wkts	Avge	Best	5wI	10wM
Test	21	34	4	900	136	30.00	3	1	14	-	3015	1402	39	35.94	4-50	-	-
All First	82	131	17	2887	136	25.32	4	15	57	-	14323	6948	295	23.55	8-61	12	3
1-day Int	121	93	20	1291	67	17.68	-	3	37	-	5439	4111	112	36.70	6-18	3	
C & G																	
B & H	5	5	0	111	50	22.20	-	1	2	-	258	171	7	24.42	4-34	-	
1-day Lge	1	0	0	0	0	-	-	-	-	-	10	10	1	10.00	1-10	-	

BAILEY, T. M. B. Northamptonshire

Name: <u>Tobin</u> Michael Barnaby Bailey
Role: Right-hand bat, wicket-keeper
Born: 28 August 1976, Kettering
Height: 5ft 11in **Weight:** 13st 8lbs
Nickname: Bill, Mad Dog, Scruff
County debut: 1996
1st-Class 50s: 5
1st-Class catches: 65
1st-Class stumpings: 8
Place in batting averages: 217th av. 21.76
(2001 218th av. 16.14)
Parents: Terry and Penny
Marital status: Single
Family links with cricket: 'Step-dad
watches a lot'
Education: Bedford School; Loughborough
University
Qualifications: 3 A-levels, BA (Hons)
Politics, Level II coaching award
Career outside cricket: Coaching

Overseas tours: Bedford to South Africa 1994, to Bermuda; Northamptonshire to
Grenada 2000, 2001
Cricketers particularly admired: Jack Russell, Mike Atherton, Alan Knott
Young players to look out for: Mark Powell
Other sports played: Hockey and tennis (both for Beds at youth level), golf ('badly')
Other sports followed: Rugby (Bedford RFC), football (Leicester City FC)
Relaxations: Watching videos, playing golf and eating out
Extras: Bedfordshire Young Player of the Year and Northants County League Young
Player of the Year in 1995. Holmwoods Schools Cricketer of the Year. Played for
England Schools U19 and was a reserve for the England U19 tour to Zimbabwe
1995-96. Won the BUSA Championship with Loughborough University in 1996 and
captained the university to BUSA Championship shared win with Durham University
in 1998 (final washed out by rain). Represented British Universities 1997 and 1998.
Northamptonshire Young Player of the Year 2000. NBC Denis Compton Award for the
most promising young Northamptonshire player 2000
Best batting: 96* Northamptonshire v Worcestershire, Worcester 2000

2002 Season

	M	Inns	NO	Runs	HS	Avge	100s	50s	Ct	St	O	M	Runs	Wkts	Avge	Best	5wI	10wM
Test																		
All First	17	25	4	457	68	21.76	-	4	43	6								
1-day Int																		
C & G	2	2	0	14	14	7.00	-	-	1	2								
B & H	5	3	2	18	12 *	18.00	-	-	7	2								
1-day Lge	15	11	6	217	44 *	43.40	-	-	19	6								

Career Performances

	M	Inns	NO	Runs	HS	Avge	100s	50s	Ct	St	Balls	Runs	Wkts	Avge	Best	5wI	10wM
Test																	
All First	35	47	7	851	96 *	21.27	-	5	65	8							
1-day Int																	
C & G	3	3	0	18	14	6.00	-	-	1	2							
B & H	15	11	3	115	52	14.37	-	1	12	9							
1-day Lge	28	16	6	276	44 *	27.60	-	-	30	8							

BAKER, T. M. Northamptonshire

Name: <u>Thomas</u> Michael Baker
Role: Right-hand bat, right-arm
medium-fast bowler
Born: 6 July 1981, Dewsbury, West
Yorkshire
Height: 6ft 5in **Weight:** 12st 8lbs
Nickname: Tosh
County debut: 2001 (one-day, Yorkshire)
(*see Extras*)
Parents: Carol and Mike
Marital status: Single
Family links with cricket: 'Grandad played
for Keighley. Brother James plays at Spen
Victoria'
Education: Gomersal First School; Gomersal
Middle School; Whitcliffe Mount School
Qualifications: NCA Level 1 coaching,
BTEC Sports Science, GNVQ Leisure
and Tourism
Career outside cricket: 'Sports scientist'
Off-season: 'Working in accounts at Alltel'
Overseas tours: Yorkshire to Cape Town 2001; Northamptonshire to Grenada 2002

51

Overseas teams played for: Edgemead CC, Cape Town 2000-01
Career highlights to date: 'Making one-day debut on Sky v Derbyshire. Day/night game at Newlands [Cape Town]'
Cricket moments to forget: 'None so far (touch wood)!'
Cricketers particularly admired: Allan Donald, Jacques Kallis
Young players to look out for: Cameron Wake
Other sports played: Golf, football, 'anything'
Other sports followed: Football (Leeds United)
Relaxations: 'Playing golf (poorly); PS2 (godsend)'
Extras: Yorkshire CCC Most Promising Young Cricketer. Took wicket (Steve Stubbings) with first legitimate ball of his career (the first delivery was a wide) v Derbyshire in the B&H at Headingley 2001. Released by Yorkshire at the end of the 2001 season and joined Northamptonshire for 2002. Did not appear for Northants in a domestic competition in 2002 but played for the county v Sri Lankans in a one-day fixture at Northampton. Played for Northamptonshire Board XI in the first round of the C&G 2003, which was played in August 2002
Opinions on cricket: 'Day/night league. Looking forward to 20-over competition.'

2002 Season (did not make any first-class or one-day appearances for his county)

Career Performances

	M	Inns	NO	Runs	HS	Avge	100s	50s	Ct	St	Balls	Runs	Wkts	Avge	Best	5wI	10wM
Test																	
All First																	
1-day Int																	
C & G	1	1	0	63	63	63.00	-	1	-	-	60	49	1	49.00	1-49	-	
B & H	3	1	0	3	3	3.00	-	-	2	-	96	67	3	22.33	2-13	-	
1-day Lge	1	0	0	0	0	-	-	-	1	-	30	22	1	22.00	1-22	-	

BALL, M. C. J. Gloucestershire

Name: <u>Martyn</u> Charles John Ball
Role: Right-hand bat, off-spin bowler, slip fielder
Born: 26 April 1970, Bristol
Height: 5ft 9in **Weight:** 12st 10lbs
Nickname: Benny, Barfo
County debut: 1988
County cap: 1996
Benefit: 2002
1st-Class 50s: 13
1st-Class 5 w. in innings: 11
1st-Class 10 w. in match: 1

1st-Class catches: 193
One-Day 5 w. in innings: 1
Place in batting averages: 247th av. 16.71
(2001 131st av. 29.15)
Place in bowling averages: 117th av. 38.08
(2001 35th av. 25.76)
Strike rate: 74.86 (career 78.65)
Parents: Kenneth Charles and Pamela Wendy
Wife and date of marriage: Mona,
28 September 1991
Children: Kristina, 9 May 1990; Alexandra,
2 August 1993; Harrison, 5 June 1997
Education: Stanshawes Court; King Edmund
Secondary School, Yate; Bath College of
Further Education
Qualifications: 6 O-levels, 2 A-levels,
advanced cricket coach
Career outside cricket: Sports marketing
Overseas tours: Gloucestershire to Namibia 1991, to Kenya 1992, to Sri Lanka 1993,
to Zimbabwe 1996, 1997, to South Africa 1999; MCC to New Zealand 1998-99;
England to India 2001-02
Overseas teams played for: North Melbourne, Australia 1988-89; Old Hararians,
Zimbabwe 1990-91
Cricketers particularly admired: Ian Botham, Vic Marks, John Emburey,
Jack Russell
Young players to look out for: Stephen Pope, Alastair Bressington
Other sports played: Rugby, football (both to county schoolboys level), 'enjoy golf
and skiing'
Other sports followed: 'All sport – massive Man City fan'
Relaxations: 'Spending some quality time at home with family'
Extras: Represented county schools. Played for Young England against Young New
Zealand in 1989. Produced best match bowling figures for the Britannic County
Championship 1993 season – 14-169 against Somerset at Taunton. Called up for
England Test tour of India 2001-02 after withdrawal of Robert Croft. Took 4-15 in 3.5
overs v Sussex at Cheltenham in the NUL 2002. Took over as wicket-keeper while
already acting as substitute fielder for Chris Taylor v Glamorgan at Cardiff 2002,
replacing the injured Jack Russell
Best batting: 71 Gloucestershire v Nottinghamshire, Bristol 1993
Best bowling: 8-46 Gloucestershire v Somerset, Taunton 1993

2002 Season

	M	Inns	NO	Runs	HS	Avge	100s	50s	Ct	St	O	M	Runs	Wkts	Avge	Best	5wI	10wM
Test																		
All First	7	10	3	117	63	16.71	-	1	5	-	287	66	876	23	38.08	6-54	1	-
1-day Int																		
C & G	3	1	1	1	1*	-	-	-	3	-	22.2	0	85	3	28.33	2-16	-	
B & H	3	3	1	45	37*	22.50	-	-	2	-	24	0	95	1	95.00	1-32	-	
1-day Lge	11	7	2	81	45	16.20	-	-	4	-	66.2	1	273	15	18.20	4-15	-	

Career Performances

	M	Inns	NO	Runs	HS	Avge	100s	50s	Ct	St	Balls	Runs	Wkts	Avge	Best	5wI	10wM
Test																	
All First	162	249	46	3949	71	19.45	-	13	193	-	24933	11732	317	37.00	8-46	11	1
1-day Int																	
C & G	28	18	6	162	31	13.50	-	-	19	-	1310	861	29	29.68	3-39	-	
B & H	38	27	6	256	37*	12.19	-	-	19	-	1956	1316	37	35.56	4-23	-	
1-day Lge	146	105	37	908	45	13.35	-	-	55	-	5280	4276	131	32.64	5-42	1	

BANES, M. J. Kent

Name: Matthew (Matt) John Banes
Role: Right-hand bat, right-arm medium bowler
Born: 10 December 1979, Pembury
Height: 5ft 9in **Weight:** 12st 7lbs
Nickname: Bano
County debut: 1999
1st-Class 50s: 3
1st-Class catches: 3
Strike rate: (career 98.00)
Parents: Chris and Jane Ann
Marital status: Single
Education: Holmewood House Prep School; Tonbridge School; Durham University
Qualifications: 10 GCSEs, 4 A-levels
Overseas tours: Tonbridge School to Australia 1996-97; Durham University CC to Cape Town 2000; Yellowhammers to Cape Town 2001-02
Career highlights to date: 'A fifty [53] on debut for Kent v New Zealanders on TV'
Cricketers particularly admired: Mike Atherton, Steve Waugh
Young players to look out for: Rob Ferley, Charlie Van der Gucht

Other sports played: Hockey (Durham University 1st XI)
Other sports followed: Football (Arsenal)
Relaxations: Reading, films, 'Klute'
Extras: Set record for most centuries (11 in three years) for Tonbridge School 1st XI. Played in Old Tonbridgians side that won *The Cricketer* Cup 1999. Scored 53 on first-class debut v New Zealanders at Canterbury 1999. Represented British Universities 2000 and 2001 and v West Indies A (50-over match) at The Parks 2002. Captain of Durham University CCE 2001 and 2002. Played for Kent Board XI in the second round of the C&G 2002, which was played in September 2001, and the second round of the C&G 2003, which was played in September 2002
Best batting: 69 DUCCE v Lancashire, Durham 2002
Best bowling: 3-65 DUCCE v Lancashire, Durham 2001

2002 Season (did not make any first-class or one-day appearances for his county)

Career Performances

	M	Inns	NO	Runs	HS	Avge	100s	50s	Ct	St	Balls	Runs	Wkts	Avge	Best	5wI	10wM
Test																	
All First	10	16	1	349	69	23.26	-	3	3	-	294	175	3	58.33	3-65	-	-
1-day Int																	
C & G	2	2	0	106	82	53.00	-	1	2	-	12	11	1	11.00	1-11	-	
B & H																	
1-day Lge																	

---

4. Which Indian Test player and current commentator played
for Glamorgan from 1987 to 1991?

BARNETT, K. J.   Gloucestershire

Name: <u>Kim</u> John Barnett
Role: Right-hand bat, leg-break bowler
Born: 17 July 1960, Stoke-on-Trent
Height: 6ft **Weight:** 13st
Nickname: The Vicar
County debut: 1979 (Derbyshire),
1999 (Gloucestershire)
County cap: 1982 (Derbyshire),
1999 (Gloucestershire)
Benefit: 1993 (Derbyshire, £37,056)
Test debut: 1988
Tests: 4
One-Day Internationals: 1
1000 runs in a season: 16
1st-Class 50s: 153
1st-Class 100s: 57
1st-Class 200s: 4
1st-Class 5 w. in innings: 3
1st-Class catches: 284
One-Day 100s: 15
One-Day 5 w. in innings: 2
Place in batting averages: 25th av. 53.41 (2001 52nd av. 44.73)
Strike rate: 68.00 (career 75.64)
Parents: Derek and Doreen
Wife and date of marriage: Janet, 8 August 1995
Children: Michael Nicholas, 24 April 1990; Christina Natalie, 11 June 1996;
Gregory John, 26 September 2000
Family links with cricket: 'Father local sportsman, mainly football'
Education: Ipstones C of E; Leek High School, Staffs
Qualifications: 7 O-levels, advanced mathematics
Career outside cricket: Bank clerk
Off-season: Training
Overseas tours: English Schools to India 1977-78; England YC to Australia 1978-79;
England B to Sri Lanka 1985-86 (vice-captain); unofficial English XI to South Africa
1989-90
Overseas teams played for: Boland, South Africa 1980-81, 1982-83
Career highlights to date: 'Captaining Derbyshire to win the 1993 B&H Cup final
without an overseas player against the mighty one-day kings Lancashire'
Cricket moments to forget: 'Relegation from division one of the one-day league in
2001 with poor performances in the last two crucial matches'
Cricketers particularly admired: Gordon Greenidge

Young players to look out for: Chris Taylor, Mark Hardinges
Other sports played: Football (Stafford Rangers, Leek Town)
Other sports followed: Football (Stoke City)
Injuries: Out for two months with a calf injury
Relaxations: Horse racing, golf
Extras: Sir John Hobbs Silver Jubilee Memorial Prize 1975. Played for Staffordshire. Appointed Derbyshire captain 1983, becoming youngest captain of a first-class county; relinquished captaincy at end of 1995 season. One of *Wisden*'s Five Cricketers of the Year 1989. Leading century-maker and run-scorer in all competitions in the history of Derbyshire cricket. Left Derbyshire in 1998-99 off-season and joined Gloucestershire for 1999. Appeared in six successive domestic one-day finals – 1998 NatWest with Derbyshire; 1999 B&H Super Cup and NatWest, 2000 B&H and NatWest and 2001 B&H, all with Gloucestershire; also holds distinction of having played in the first (1981) and last (2000) NatWest finals. Is second highest run-scorer in B&H Cup history behind Graham Gooch (who scored 5176 runs). Scored 101 v Northants in the Norwich Union League at Northampton 2001, passing Graham Gooch's domestic one-day league run record (8573) with his hundredth run; reached 9000 career runs in one-day league v Derbyshire at Derby in the NUL 2002. Carried his bat (for the fourth time in his career) for 182* v Middlesex at Southgate 2002. C&G Man of the Match award (on his 42nd birthday) for his 108 in the quarter-final v Kent at Canterbury 2002
Opinions on cricket: 'Pitches should be as quick as possible, with groundsmen commended for pace and bounce rather than the low, slow pitches often encouraged by management at the expense of development and entertainment!'
Best batting: 239* Derbyshire v Leicestershire, Leicester 1988
Best bowling: 6-28 Derbyshire v Glamorgan, Chesterfield 1991
Stop press: Released by Gloucestershire in the 2002-03 off-season

2002 Season

	M	Inns	NO	Runs	HS	Avge	100s	50s	Ct	St	O	M	Runs	Wkts	Avge	Best	5wI	10wM
Test																		
All First	8	15	3	641	182 *	53.41	3	1	1	-	22.4	6	74	2	37.00	1-7	-	-
1-day Int																		
C & G	3	3	1	171	108	85.50	1	1	-	-	5	0	23	1	23.00	1-23	-	
B & H	6	6	0	182	67	30.33	-	2	1	-	3	0	24	0	-	-	-	
1-day Lge	7	7	0	82	66	11.71	-	1	4	-								

Career Performances

	M	Inns	NO	Runs	HS	Avge	100s	50s	Ct	St	Balls	Runs	Wkts	Avge	Best	5wI	10wM
Test	4	7	0	207	80	29.57	-	2	1	-	36	32	0	-	-	-	-
All First	479	784	76	28593	239 *	40.38	61	153	284	-	14221	7108	188	37.80	6-28	3	-
1-day Int	1	1	0	84	84	84.00	-	1	-	-							
C & G	60	58	4	2203	113 *	40.79	3	15	22	-	820	571	26	21.96	6-24	2	
B & H	109	100	6	3347	115	35.60	4	23	36	-	708	503	16	31.43	3-52	-	
1-day Lge	327	315	43	9002	131 *	33.09	8	48	107	-	1941	1676	62	27.03	4-12	-	

BASSANO, C. W. G.   Derbyshire

Name: Christopher Warwick Godfrey
Bassano
Role: Right-hand bat, leg-spin bowler
Born: 11 September 1975, East London,
South Africa
Height: 6ft 2in **Weight:** 13st 7lbs
Nickname: Bass, Bassy
County debut: 2001
County cap: 2002
1000 runs in a season: 1
1st-Class 50s: 10
1st-Class 100s: 3
1st-Class catches: 18
Place in batting averages: 67th av. 42.52
(2001 57th av. 43.58)
Parents: Brian and Allison
Marital status: Single
Family links with cricket: 'Father played
throughout his life, was a radio commentator, provincial manager, and held
development positions in South Africa; also wrote books on cricket etc.'
Education: Grey School, Port Elizabeth; Launceston Church Grammar School,
Tasmania; University of Tasmania, Hobart
Qualifications: Bachelor of Applied Science (Horticulture)
Career outside cricket: Trout fishing guide
Off-season: 'Fishing and playing cricket in Tasmania as well as spending some time
with the family'
Career highlights to date: 'Being selected to play representative cricket or to play at
a higher level is always a highlight'
Cricket moments to forget: 'Losing'
Cricketers particularly admired: Graeme Pollock, Steve Waugh
Young players to look out for: Tom Lungley, Nathan 'Roach' Dumelow,
Shane Watson (Tasmania)
Other sports played: Hockey
Other sports followed: Rugby union
Relaxations: Fly fishing
Extras: Captained Eastern Province U13 1987-88. Played for Tasmania U16, U17,
U19 (captain), U23 (captain) and 2nd XI. Became the first player to score a century in
each innings of his Championship debut, 186* and 106 v Gloucestershire at Derby
2001; his first innings lasted 8¾ hours and also produced the highest score by a
Derbyshire batsman on Championship debut. Passed 1000 runs in a season for the first
time during his innings of 44 v Middlesex at Derby 2002. Awarded Derbyshire cap

2002. Is diabetic. His ancestry includes a set of brothers from Venice who were musicians at the court of Henry VIII. Is not considered an overseas player

Opinions on cricket: 'As long as each player leaves the game in a better state than when he arrived, we will all be better for it.'

Best batting: 186* Derbyshire v Gloucestershire, Derby 2001

2002 Season

	M	Inns	NO	Runs	HS	Avge	100s	50s	Ct	St	O	M	Runs	Wkts	Avge	Best	5wI	10wM
Test																		
All First	14	26	1	1063	152	42.52	1	8	13	-								
1-day Int																		
C & G																		
B & H	5	4	2	36	22	18.00	-	-	-	-								
1-day Lge	11	11	0	233	61	21.18	-	2	2	-								

Career Performances

	M	Inns	NO	Runs	HS	Avge	100s	50s	Ct	St	Balls	Runs	Wkts	Avge	Best	5wI	10wM
Test																	
All First	22	40	3	1586	186 *	42.86	3	10	18	-	12	11	0	-	-	-	-
1-day Int																	
C & G																	
B & H	6	5	2	45	22	15.00	-	-	1	-							
1-day Lge	19	19	1	413	61	22.94	-	2	4	-							

5. Which Pakistan leg-spinner made his debut for Surrey in 1969?

BATTY, G. J. Worcestershire

Name: <u>Gareth</u> Jon Batty
Role: Right-hand bat, off-spin bowler
Born: 13 October 1977, Yorkshire
Height: 5ft 11in **Weight:** 12st 4lbs
Nickname: Ging, Bats
County debut: 1997 (Yorkshire), 1998 (one-day, Surrey), 1999 (first-class, Surrey), 2002 (Worcestershire)
County colours: 2002 (Worcestershire)
50 wickets in a season: 1
1st-Class 50s: 3
1st-Class 5 w. in innings: 3
1st-Class catches: 11
Place in batting averages: 219th av. 21.34
Place in bowling averages: 71st av. 30.94
Strike rate: 65.69 (career 64.51)
Parents: David and Rosemary
Marital status: Single

Family links with cricket: 'Dad is Yorkshire Academy coach and U17 manager; brother played for Yorkshire and Somerset'
Education: Cullingworth First; Parkside Middle; Bingley Grammar
Qualifications: 9 GCSEs, BTEC Art and Design, coaching certificate
Off-season: ECB National Academy to Australia and Sri Lanka
Overseas tours: England U15 to South Africa 1993; England U19 to Zimbabwe 1995-96, to Pakistan 1996-97; ECB National Academy to Australia and Sri Lanka 2002-03
Overseas teams played for: Marist Newman, Australia
Career highlights to date: 'Every time I'm on the winning team'
Cricket moments to forget: 'Every time I lose'
Cricketers particularly admired: Alec Stewart, Adam Hollioake, Mark Butcher, Saqlain Mushtaq, Ian Salisbury, Graham Thorpe, Ali Brown
Other sports played: Rugby union, golf
Other sports followed: Rugby (Leeds)
Relaxations: Going to the gym
Extras: National U15 bowling award. *Daily Telegraph* Young Player of the Year 1993. Made first-class debut for Yorkshire v Lancashire 1997 in non-Championship match. Joined Surrey for 1998. Scored a 61-ball 54 and took 2-20 v Gloucestershire at Bristol in the Norwich Union League 2001. Surrey Supporters' Club Most Improved Player Award and Young Player of the Year Award 2001. Surrey CCC Young Player of the Year Award 2001. ECB 2nd XI Player of the Year 2001. Released by Surrey at the end of the 2001 season and joined Worcestershire for 2002. Recorded maiden first-class

five-wicket return (6-71) v Essex at Southend 2002. Took 5-60 v Derbyshire at Worcester 2002, in the process reaching 50 Championship wickets in a season for the first time
Opinions on cricket: 'Let's keep the kids interested, whatever it takes.'
Best batting: 74 Worcestershire v Derbyshire, Worcester 2002
Best bowling: 6-71 Worcestershire v Essex, Southend 2002
Stop press: Called up from the ECB National Academy squad in Adelaide to the England one-day squad for the VB Series in Australia 2002-03 as cover for the injured Jeremy Snape. Made One-Day International debut v Australia at Sydney in the VB Series 2002-03

2002 Season

	M	Inns	NO	Runs	HS	Avge	100s	50s	Ct	St	O	M	Runs	Wkts	Avge	Best	5wI	10wM
Test																		
All First	18	27	4	491	74	21.34	-	3	9	-	613.1	162	1733	56	30.94	6-71	3	-
1-day Int																		
C & G	3	2	0	3	2	1.50	-	-	2	-	15	2	69	1	69.00	1-19	-	
B & H	7	5	1	67	22	16.75	-	-	3	-	22	0	119	1	119.00	1-29	-	
1-day Lge	16	13	3	206	54 *	20.60	-	1	5	-	78	0	414	13	31.84	4-36	-	

Career Performances

	M	Inns	NO	Runs	HS	Avge	100s	50s	Ct	St	Balls	Runs	Wkts	Avge	Best	5wI	10wM
Test																	
All First	21	33	5	589	74	21.03	-	3	11	-	3871	1861	60	31.01	6-71	3	-
1-day Int																	
C & G	4	3	0	10	7	3.33	-	-	4	-	146	111	3	37.00	2-42	-	
B & H	7	5	1	67	22	16.75	-	-	3	-	132	119	1	119.00	1-29	-	
1-day Lge	38	34	8	656	83 *	25.23	-	4	11	-	1185	1005	28	35.89	4-36	-	

6. Which former chief executive of Sussex played
for Gloucestershire in 1991?

BATTY, J. N.   Surrey

Name: Jonathan (Jon) Neil Batty
Role: Right-hand bat, wicket-keeper
Born: 18 April 1974, Chesterfield
Height: 5ft 10in **Weight:** 11st 6lbs
Nickname: JB
County debut: 1997
County cap: 2001
50 dismissals in a season: 1
1st-Class 50s: 9
1st-Class 100s: 3
1st-Class catches: 202
1st-Class stumpings: 30
Place in batting averages: 107th av. 35.33
(2001 220th av. 15.93)
Strike rate: (career 78.00)
Parents: Roger and Jill
Marital status: Single
Family links with cricket: Father played to a
high standard of club cricket
Education: Blyth CofE; Oakley Parochial; Wheatley Park; Repton; Durham
University (St Chad's); Keble College, Oxford
Qualifications: 10 GCSEs, 4 A-levels, BSc (Hons) in Natural Sciences, Diploma in
Social Studies (Oxon)
Off-season: 'Working on my game'
Overseas tours: Repton School to Holland 1991; MCC to Bangladesh 1996; Surrey to
South Africa 1997, 2001
Overseas teams played for: Mount Lawley CC, Perth 1997-2002
Career highlights to date: 'Winning three County Championships'
Cricket moments to forget: 'None!'
Cricketers particularly admired: David Gower, Alec Stewart, Jack Russell
Other sports played: Golf, squash
Other sports followed: Football (Nottingham Forest)
Relaxations: Reading, listening to music, movies
Extras: Oxford Blue 1996. Has also played for Oxfordshire and represented Minor
Counties
Opinions on cricket: 'Influx of EU cricketers is complete rubbish and will destroy the
English game if allowed to continue. Where is the need for two overseas players? If
people think they will increase crowds, they are sadly mistaken. Combined with the
EU situation it will be terrible for the game!'
Best batting: 151 Surrey v Somerset, Taunton 2002
Best bowling: 1-21 Surrey v Lancashire, Old Trafford 2000

2002 Season

	M	Inns	NO	Runs	HS	Avge	100s	50s	Ct	St	O	M	Runs	Wkts	Avge	Best	5wl	10wM
Test																		
All First	13	23	2	742	151	35.33	2	3	41	5								
1-day Int																		
C & G	2	1	1	6	6 *	-	-	-	1	-								
B & H																			
1-day Lge	13	8	1	116	30	16.57	-	-	19	2								

Career Performances

	M	Inns	NO	Runs	HS	Avge	100s	50s	Ct	St	Balls	Runs	Wkts	Avge	Best	5wl	10wM
Test																	
All First	82	113	17	2383	151	24.82	3	9	202	30	78	61	1	61.00	1-21	-	-
1-day Int																	
C & G	4	2	1	7	6 *	7.00	-	-	2	-							
B & H	12	9	3	86	26 *	14.33	-	-	9	-							
1-day Lge	63	44	10	471	40	13.85	-	-	65	11							

BELL, I. R. Warwickshire

Name: <u>Ian</u> Ronald Bell
Role: Right-hand bat, right-arm
medium bowler
Born: 11 April 1982, Coventry
Height: 5ft 10in **Weight:** 11st
Nickname: Belly
County debut: 1999
County cap: 2001
1st-Class 50s: 7
1st-Class 100s: 3
1st-Class catches: 19
Place in batting averages: 186th av. 24.37
(2001 9th av. 64.30)
Strike rate: 102.00 (career 102.00)
Parents: Terry and Barbara
Marital status: Single
Family links with cricket: Brother Keith has
played for England U18
Education: Bilton Middle; Princethorpe College, Rugby
Off-season: ECB National Academy to Australia and Sri Lanka
Overseas tours: Warwickshire U19 to Cape Town 1998-99; England U19 to New
Zealand 1998-99, to Malaysia and (U19 World Cup) Sri Lanka 1999-2000, to India

2000-01 (captain); England A to West Indies 2000-01; ECB National Academy to Australia 2001-02, to Sri Lanka 2002-03

Career highlights to date: 'Selection for ECB Academy and as replacement for England A tour to West Indies. Captaining England U19. Receiving my county cap and scoring my first County Championship century'

Cricket moments to forget: 'Being bowled for a duck when making county debut'

Cricketers particularly admired: Michael Atherton, Steve Waugh, Alec Stewart, Nick Knight

Young players to look out for: Keith Bell

Other sports played: Football (was at Coventry City School of Excellence), rugby, golf

Other sports followed: Football (Aston Villa), rugby union (Northampton Saints)

Relaxations: Golf, listening to music

Extras: Played for England U14, U15, U16, U17. Player of the Series for England U19 v New Zealand U19 in 'Test' series 1998-99. Represented England U19 in one-day and 'Test' series v Australia U19 1999. NBC Denis Compton Award for the most promising young Warwickshire player 1999, 2000, 2001. Gray-Nicolls Trophy for Best Young Schools Cricketer 2000. Was England U19 leading run-scorer in 'Test' series in India 2000-01 (332 av. 55.33) and in one-day series (169 av. 56.33). On his return from India, he was drafted into the England A squad in West Indies as injury cover in the batting department and made his England A debut v Leeward Islands at Anguilla. Captained England U19 in one-day and 'Test' series (bar second 'Test') v Sri Lanka U19 2000. Represented England U19 in one-day series (3/3, captain) and 'Test' series (1/3, captain) v West Indies U19 2001. Scored maiden first-class century (130) v Oxford University CCE at The Parks 2001, becoming (at 19 years 56 days) the youngest player to score a first-class century for Warwickshire. Scored maiden Championship century (103) v Nottinghamshire at Edgbaston 2001, becoming (at 19 years 115 days) the youngest Warwickshire batsman to score a Championship 100. Cricket Society's Most Promising Young Cricketer of the Year Award 2001. Scored century (104) in ECB National Academy's innings victory over Commonwealth Bank [Australian] Cricket Academy in Adelaide 2001-02. Called up to the England Test squad in New Zealand 2001-02 as batting cover after Mark Butcher suffered a fractured thumb. B&H Gold Award for his 85* in the quarter-final v Sussex at Hove and for his 65* in the last B&H final, v Essex at Lord's 2002

Best batting: 135 Warwickshire v Derbyshire, Derby 2001

Best bowling: 1-22 Warwickshire v Hampshire, West End 2002

Stop press: Recovered from stress fracture of the back to take part in ECB National Academy tour to Sri Lanka 2002-03

2002 Season

	M	Inns	NO	Runs	HS	Avge	100s	50s	Ct	St		O	M	Runs	Wkts	Avge	Best	5wI	10wM
Test																			
All First	16	28	1	658	77	24.37	-	3	6	-		34	8	89	2	44.50	1-22	-	-
1-day·Int																			
C & G	2	2	0	75	50	37.50	-	1	1	-									
B & H	8	8	2	326	85 *	54.33	-	3	6	-		4	0	24	0	-		-	-
1-day Lge	14	13	1	369	86	30.75	-	3	1	-									

Career Performances

	M	Inns	NO	Runs	HS	Avge	100s	50s	Ct	St		Balls	Runs	Wkts	Avge	Best	5wI	10wM
Test																		
All First	29	47	4	1544	135	35.90	3	7	19	-		306	129	3	43.00	1-22	-	-
1-day Int																		
C & G	3	3	0	85	50	28.33	-	1	1	-		3	2	0	-		-	-
B & H	8	8	2	326	85 *	54.33	-	3	6	-		24	24	0	-		-	-
1-day Lge	15	14	1	417	86	32.07	-	3	1	-								

BENHAM, C. C. Hampshire

Name: Christopher (Chris) Charles Benham
Role: Right-hand bat, right-arm
off-spin bowler
Born: 24 March 1983, Frimley, Surrey
Height: 6ft 1in **Weight:** 13st
Nickname: Benny, Beano
County debut: No first-team appearance
Parents: Frank and Sandie
Marital status: Single
Family links with cricket: 'Both older
brothers, Nick and Andy, played local
club cricket'
Education: Westsfield Junior School; Yateley
Comprehensive School; Yateley Sixth Form
College; Loughborough University
Qualifications: 10 GCSEs, 3 A-levels
Career outside cricket: Studying for Sports
Science and Physical Education degree at
Loughborough University
Overseas tours: West of England U15 to West Indies 1998
Career highlights to date: 'Being part of Hampshire 2nd XI squad that won the 2nd
XI Championship in 2001'

65

Cricketers particularly admired: Ian Botham, Alec Stewart, Steve Waugh, Jacques Kallis
Young players to look out for: James Tomlinson, David Wheeler 'and other young Hampshire Academy players'
Other sports played: Football (school, district and county sides; trials with Swindon and Crystal Palace), tennis, golf
Other sports followed: Football (Arsenal), tennis, 'enjoy watching most sports'
Relaxations: 'Listening to music; having a good night out'
Extras: Played for ESCA U15 v Scotland. Represented England U16 v Denmark. Played for Hampshire Board XI in the C&G 2001. Played for Loughborough University CCE 2002
Opinions on cricket: 'Feel that the technology available in modern sport should be taken advantage of in cricket to prevent controversial decisions.'

2002 Season (did not make any first-class or one-day appearances)

Career Performances

	M	Inns	NO	Runs	HS	Avge	100s	50s	Ct	St	Balls	Runs	Wkts	Avge	Best	5wI	10wM
Test																	
All First																	
1-day Int																	
C & G	1	1	0	0	0	0.00	-	-	-	-							
B & H																	
1-day Lge																	

BENNING, J. G. E.   Surrey

Name: James Graham Edward Benning
Role: Right-hand bat, right-arm medium bowler
Born: 4 May 1983, Mill Hill, London
Height: 6ft **Weight:** 13st
Nickname: Jez, Benno
County debut: 2002 (one-day)
Parents: David and Sandy
Marital status: Single
Family links with cricket: 'Dad played cricket for Middlesex during the early 1970s'
Education: The Beacon School, Chesham Bois; Caterham School
Qualifications: 12 GCSEs, 3 AS-levels
Off-season: 'Going to South Africa on a training camp'
Overseas tours: Surrey YC to Barbados 1999-2000, to Sri Lanka 2002
Overseas teams played for: North Dandenong, Australia 2001-02
Career highlights to date: 'Being part of the High Wycombe side which won the

treble 2002 – league, county cup, *Evening Standard* Trophy (in which I scored 100* at The Oval this year)'

Cricket moments to forget: 'Being bowled by a girl during a junior club game at the age of 11'

Cricketers particularly admired: Alec Stewart, Adam Hollioake, Ali Brown

Young players to look out for: Rikki Clarke, Scott Newman

Other sports followed: Football (Watford)

Relaxations: 'Going to the gym; chilling with friends'

Extras: Played for Buckinghamshire in the C&G 2001. Played for England U15-U19, including representing England U19 v India U19 in 'Test' series (1/3) and one-day series (3/3) 2002

2002 Season

	M	Inns	NO	Runs	HS	Avge	100s	50s	Ct	St	O	M	Runs	Wkts	Avge	Best	5wI	10wM
Test																		
All First																		
1-day Int																		
C & G																		
B & H																		
1-day Lge	1	1	0	10	10	10.00	-	-	-	-	7	0	58	2	29.00	2-58	-	

Career Performances

	M	Inns	NO	Runs	HS	Avge	100s	50s	Ct	St	Balls	Runs	Wkts	Avge	Best	5wI	10wM
Test																	
All First																	
1-day Int																	
C & G	2	2	0	43	23	21.50	-	-	1	-	18	26	1	26.00	1-26	-	
B & H																	
1-day Lge	1	1	0	10	10	10.00	-	-	-	-	42	58	2	29.00	2-58	-	

BETTS, M. M. Warwickshire

Name: Melvyn Morris Betts
Role: Right-hand bat, right-arm
medium-fast bowler
Born: 26 March 1975, Sacriston
Height: 5ft 11in **Weight:** 11st 4lbs
Nickname: Village
County debut: 1993 (Durham),
2001 (Warwickshire)
County cap: 1998 (Durham),
2001 (Warwickshire)
1st-Class 50s: 3
1st-Class 5 w. in innings: 12
1st-Class 10 w. in match: 2
1st-Class catches: 32
Place in batting averages: 199th av. 23.54
(2001 251st av. 11.50)
Place in bowling averages: 148th av. 51.15
(2001 43rd av. 26.45)

Strike rate: 74.60 (career 50.79)
Parents: Melvyn and Shirley
Wife and date of marriage: Angela, 3 October 1998
Children: Chloe
Family links with cricket: Father and uncle played for Sacriston
Education: Fyndoune Comprehensive
Qualifications: 9 GCSEs, plus qualifications in engineering and sports and
recreational studies
Overseas tours: England U19 to Sri Lanka 1993-94; England A to Zimbabwe and
South Africa 1998-99; Durham CCC to South Africa 1996
Career highlights to date: '9-64 v Northamptonshire'
Cricketers particularly admired: David Boon
Young players to look out for: Mark Wagh, Ian Bell, Nicky Peng
Other sports played: Golf
Other sports followed: Football (Newcastle United FC)
Relaxations: 'Local pub with friends outside cricket'
Extras: Played for England U19 in home series against India U19 in 1994. Left
Durham at the end of the 2000 season and joined Warwickshire for 2001. B&H Gold
Award for his 4-22 v Somerset at Taunton 2001. Took 5-22 on his Championship debut
for Warwickshire against his old county, Durham, at Edgbaston 2001
Opinions on cricket: 'Less cricket – more time for training and developing
own game.'
Best batting: 57* Durham v Sussex, Hove 1996
Best bowling: 9-64 Durham v Northamptonshire, Northampton 1997

2002 Season

	M	Inns	NO	Runs	HS	Avge	100s	50s	Ct	St	O	M	Runs	Wkts	Avge	Best	5wI	10wM
Test																		
All First	9	16	5	259	56	23.54	-	1	2	-	248.4	34	1023	20	51.15	3-75	-	-
1-day Int																		
C & G																		
B & H																		
1-day Lge																		

Career Performances

	M	Inns	NO	Runs	HS	Avge	100s	50s	Ct	St	Balls	Runs	Wkts	Avge	Best	5wI	10wM
Test																		
All First	89	132	31	1308	57 *	12.95	-	3	32	-	14325	8250	282	29.25	9-64	12	2
1-day Int																		
C & G	9	7	1	40	14	6.66	-	-	2	-	552	427	15	28.46	4-34	-	
B & H	15	9	4	51	20 *	10.20	-	-	1	-	683	512	19	26.94	4-22	-	
1-day Lge	49	34	16	195	21	10.83	-	-	9	-	2089	1722	53	32.49	4-39	-	

BEVAN, M. G.   Leicestershire

Name: <u>Michael</u> Gwyl Bevan
Role: Left-hand bat, slow left-arm
wrist-spin bowler
Born: 8 May 1970, Canberra, Australia
County debut: 1995 (Yorkshire),
1998 (Sussex), 2002 (Leicestershire)
County cap: 1995 (Yorkshire),
1998 (Sussex)
Test debut: 1994-95
Tests: 18
One-Day Internationals: 183
1000 runs in a season: 3
1st-Class 50s: 71
1st-Class 100s: 52
1st-Class 200s: 3
1st-Class 5 w. in innings: 1
1st-Class 10 w. in match: 1
1st-Class catches: 113
One-Day 100s: 10
One-Day 5 w. in innings: 1
Place in batting averages: 11th av. 63.36
Strike rate: 66.00 (career 73.79)

Wife: Tracy
Education: Australian Cricket Academy (1989)
Off-season: Playing for New South Wales and Australia
Overseas tours: Australia to Sharjah 1994, to Pakistan 1994-95, to India and Pakistan (World Cup) 1995-96, to Sri Lanka 1996-97, to India 1996-97, to South Africa 1996-97, to England 1997, to New Zealand 1997-98, to India and Sharjah 1997-98, to Pakistan and Bangladesh 1998-99 (one-day series), to West Indies 1998-99 (one-day series), to UK, Ireland and Holland (World Cup) 1999, to Sri Lanka 1999-2000 (one-day series), to Zimbabwe 1999-2000 (one-day series), to New Zealand 1999-2000 (one-day series), to South Africa 1999-2000 (one-day series), to Kenya (ICC Knockout Trophy) 2000-01, to India 2000-01 (one-day series), to England 2001 (one-day series), to South Africa 2001-02 (one-day series), to Kenya (Nairobi Triangular) 2002, to Sri Lanka (ICC Champions Trophy) 2002-03
Overseas teams played for: South Australia 1989-90; New South Wales 1990-91 –
Extras: Struck century for South Australia v Western Australia on first-class debut 1989-90. In 1990-91 he became the first player to score a century in five successive Sheffield Shield matches. Made 82 on his Test debut against Pakistan in Karachi, 1994-95. Played for Yorkshire 1995-96 (vice-captain for the 1996 season). Scored 78* to shepherd Australia to victory v West Indies in World Series ODI at Sydney 1995-96; at one point Australia were 38-6 in pursuit of 173. Joined Sussex for 1998 and was appointed vice-captain. Averaged 106.00 in the 1998-99 Australian first-class season. Was in Australia's 1999 World Cup winning side and did not play county cricket that season. Won Man of the Match award for his 185* from 132 balls for a World XI v an Asia XI in Dhaka 2000; chasing 321 for victory, the World XI lost by just one run, Bevan just failing to hit a six from the final ball. Returned to Sussex as overseas player and vice-captain in 2000. Scored 150-plus (166 and 174) in each innings v Nottinghamshire at Hove 2000 as part of a sequence of four scores of 150-plus in five Championship innings. Scored 106 for Australia in the inaugural indoor One-Day International v South Africa at Melbourne 2000. Topped English first-class batting averages in 2000 with 1124 runs at 74.93. Top run-scorer in the 2000 National League competition with 706 runs at 117.66. Sussex Player of the Year 2000. Left Sussex at the end of the 2000 season. Scored 135* in New South Wales's victory over Western Australia in the 2000-01 Mercantile Mutual Cup final at Perth, winning the Man of the Match award. New South Wales Player of the Year 2000-01. Equalled career-best 203* v Western Australia 2001-02, in the process becoming the highest first-class run-scorer in New South Wales cricket history by overtaking Alan Kippax's total of 8005 runs. Man of the Match for his 93-ball century (102*) in Australia's victory over New Zealand in the VB Series One-Day International at Melbourne 2001-02; Australia were at one point 82-6 chasing 246. Joined Leicestershire as overseas player for 2002. Scored a 96-ball century (out for 113) on home debut, in the B&H v Durham at Leicester 2002. B&H Gold Award for his 48 plus two catches and the wicket of Craig White v Yorkshire at Headingley 2002. Left Leicestershire at the end of the 2002 season. ACB central contract 2002-03
Best batting: 203* New South Wales v Western Australia, Sydney 1993-94
                      203* New South Wales v Western Australia, Sydney 2001-02

Best bowling: 6-82 Australia v West Indies, Adelaide 1996-97
Stop press: Selected for Australia squad for 2002-03 World Cup

2002 Season

	M	Inns	NO	Runs	HS	Avge	100s	50s	Ct	St	O	M	Runs	Wkts	Avge	Best	5wI	10wM
Test																		
All First	9	14	3	697	146	63.36	2	4	4	-	33	1	118	3	39.33	3-25	-	-
1-day Int																		
C & G																		
B & H	5	5	1	246	113	61.50	1	1	3	-	5	0	33	1	33.00	1-4	-	
1-day Lge	5	5	2	182	66 *	60.66	-	1	1	-	6	0	38	2	19.00	2-38	-	

Career Performances

	M	Inns	NO	Runs	HS	Avge	100s	50s	Ct	St	Balls	Runs	Wkts	Avge	Best	5wI	10wM
Test	18	30	3	785	91	29.07	-	6	8	-	1285	703	29	24.24	6-82	1	1
All First	206	344	61	15985	203 *	56.48	55	71	113	-	8486	5164	115	44.90	6-82	1	1
1-day Int	183	159	55	5774	108 *	55.51	6	38	59	-	2002	1686	36	46.83	3-36	-	
C & G	11	10	2	456	91 *	57.00	-	5	2	-	223	174	4	43.50	2-47	-	
B & H	21	20	8	1301	157 *	108.41	2	12	4	-	228	218	2	109.00	1-4	-	
1-day Lge	57	55	17	2323	103 *	61.13	2	20	23	-	716	646	38	17.00	5-29	1	

BICHEL, A. J.   Worcestershire

Name: Andrew (<u>Andy</u>) John Bichel
Role: Right-hand bat, right-arm
fast-medium bowler
Born: 27 August 1970, Laidley, Queensland
Height: 5ft 11in **Weight:** 13st 9lbs
Nickname: Bic, Andre
County debut: 2001
County cap: 2001; colours 2002
Test debut: 1996-97
Tests: 6
One-Day Internationals: 32
50 wickets in a season: 1
1st-Class 50s: 10
1st-Class 100s: 1
1st-Class 5 w. in innings: 21
1st-Class 10 w. in match: 4
1st-Class catches: 54
One-Day 100s: 1
One-Day 5 w. in innings: 2

Place in batting averages: 135th av. 30.44 (2001 147th av. 26.12)
Place in bowling averages: 24th av. 25.05 (2001 46th av. 27.33)
Strike rate: 49.50 (career 48.74)
Parents: Trevor and Shirley
Wife: Dionn
Children: Keegan
Family links with cricket: 'Uncle Don played for Queensland. Cricket is a huge part of our family in Southeast Queensland'
Education: Laidley North SS; Laidley High; Ipswich TAFE College
Qualifications: Carpenter and joiner
Career outside cricket: Project management
Off-season: Playing for Queensland
Overseas tours: Queensland Academy to South Africa 1994; Australian Academy to South Africa 1996; Australia A to Scotland and Ireland 1998; Australia to South Africa 1996-97, to England 1997, to New Zealand (one-day series) 1997-98, to Kuala Lumpur (Commonwealth Games) 1998, to West Indies 1998-99, to South Africa 2001-02, to Kenya (Nairobi Triangular) 2002, to Sri Lanka (ICC Champions Trophy) 2002-03
Overseas teams played for: Queensland 1992-93 –
Career highlights to date: 'Queensland winning the Sheffield Shield for the first time in 1994-95. Being selected for Australia in 1997. Playing my first Test for Australia on Australia Day at the Adelaide Oval against West Indies'
Cricket moments to forget: 'Any game that is close that you lose – always makes it hard to forget. But in sport you have to learn from your mistakes'
Cricketers particularly admired: Allan Border, Sachin Tendulkar, Glenn McGrath, Dennis Lillee
Young players to look out for: Simon Katich
Other sports played: Rugby league (first grade TRL); tennis (first grade LTA)
Other sports followed: Rugby league (Brisbane Broncos), AFL (Brisbane Lions)
Relaxations: 'Fishing in my boat on Moreton Bay; going to the beach; golf'
Extras: Sheffield Shield Player of the Year 1996-97. Was due to play for Hampshire as their overseas player in 1998 but was selected for Australia A tour of Scotland and Ireland. Queensland Player of the Year in the 1998-99 Australian season. Took 60 first-class wickets at 20.11 in the 1999-2000 Australian season, including 6-47 for Queensland in Victoria's first innings in the Pura Milk Cup final. Joined Worcestershire as overseas player for 2001. B&H Gold Award for his 100 (his maiden one-day century) v Glamorgan at Cardiff 2001. Won the Dick Lygon Award 2001 as Worcestershire's Player of the Year; was also the Worcestershire Supporters' Association Player of the Year 2001 and the winner of the inaugural Don Kenyon Award for the season's best first-class match-winning performance (113 runs and seven wickets v Glamorgan). His 9-93 v Gloucestershire at Worcester 2002 (just three days after arriving from Australia) was the best innings return by a Worcestershire bowler since Neal Radford took 9-70 v Somerset at Worcester in 1986 and the best innings return in April in Championship history. B&H Gold Awards for his 2-19 from seven

overs v Somerset at Taunton and for his 94* (opening the batting) in the quarter-final v Gloucestershire at Bristol 2002. Has same birthday as the late Sir Donald Bradman. Left Worcestershire at the end of the 2002 season. ACB central contract 2002-03

Opinions on cricket: 'Test and international cricket will always be OK if we keep working and developing the game in schools around the world. Pura Cup and county cricket need to play more day/night cricket because people today like plenty of action, and day/night cricket provides this excitement for everyone that likes cricket.'

Best batting: 110 Queensland v Victoria, Brisbane 1997-98
Best bowling: 9-93 Worcestershire v Gloucestershire, Worcester 2002
Stop press: Selected for Australia squad for 2002-03 World Cup

2002 Season

	M	Inns	NO	Runs	HS	Avge	100s	50s	Ct	St	O	M	Runs	Wkts	Avge	Best	5wI	10wM
Test																		
All First	9	11	2	274	78 *	30.44	-	2	7	-	297	77	902	36	25.05	9-93	1	1
1-day Int																		
C & G	2	2	0	12	11	6.00	-	-	-	-	14	4	43	2	21.50	1-1	-	
B & H	6	5	3	137	94 *	68.50	-	1	1	-	56	8	181	15	12.06	4-24	-	
1-day Lge	5	3	0	13	12	4.33	-	-	2	-	37.4	2	152	7	21.71	3-30	-	

Career Performances

	M	Inns	NO	Runs	HS	Avge	100s	50s	Ct	St	Balls	Runs	Wkts	Avge	Best	5wI	10wM
Test	6	8	0	63	18	7.87	-	-	4	-	972	517	13	39.76	5-60	1	-
All First	98	128	11	2441	110	20.86	1	10	54	-	20181	10093	414	24.37	9-93	21	4
1-day Int	32	20	6	191	27 *	13.64	-	-	7	-	1643	1248	37	33.72	5-19	1	
C & G	5	4	0	42	27	10.50	-	-	-	-	234	145	10	14.50	3-9	-	
B & H	11	10	3	314	100	44.85	1	1	5	-	636	370	24	15.41	4-24	-	
1-day Lge	20	15	1	161	36 *	11.50	-	-	9	-	920	580	34	17.05	5-21	1	

---

7. Name the overseas cricketers who played
for Leicestershire in 2002.

BICKNELL, D. J.   Nottinghamshire

Name: <u>Darren</u> John Bicknell
Role: Left-hand opening bat, occasional slow left-arm bowler
Born: 24 June 1967, Guildford
Height: 6ft 4½in **Weight:** 14st 7lbs
Nickname: Denz, Bickers
County debut: 1987 (Surrey), 2000 (Notts)
County cap: 1990 (Surrey), 2000 (Notts)
Benefit: 1999 (Surrey)
1000 runs in a season: 7
1st-Class 50s: 67
1st-Class 100s: 37
1st-Class 200s: 2
1st-Class catches: 94
One-Day 100s: 10
Place in batting averages: 126th av. 31.91
(2001 83rd av. 36.20)
Strike rate: (career 53.82)
Parents: Vic and Valerie

Wife and date of marriage: Rebecca, 21 September 1992
Children: Lauren Elizabeth, 21 September 1993; Sam, 9 November 1995; Emily, 16 December 1997
Family links with cricket: Brother Martin plays at Surrey
Education: Robert Haining County Secondary; Guildford County College of Technology
Qualifications: 8 O-levels, 2 A-levels, senior coaching award
Career outside cricket: Scottish Courage brewery account manager
Off-season: 'Working for above'
Overseas tours: Surrey to Sharjah 1988, 1989, to Dubai 1990, to Perth 1995; Nottinghamshire to Johannesburg 2000, 2001, 2002; England A to Zimbabwe and Kenya 1989-90, to Pakistan 1990-91, to Bermuda and West Indies 1991-92
Overseas teams played for: Coburg, Melbourne 1986-87
Career highlights to date: 'England A call-up. Debut for Surrey. Being capped by Notts and Surrey. And every time I reach a hundred'
Cricket moments to forget: 'My first-ball dismissal in my debut A 'Test' match v Zimbabwe, and brother Martin getting me out twice'
Cricket superstitions: 'Try and wear same clothes if successful previously'
Cricketers particularly admired: Mark Taylor, David Gower, Angus Fraser, Martin Bicknell
Young players to look out for: Bilal Shafayat, Guy Welton, Rikki Clarke, Kevin Pietersen

Other sports played: Golf (11 handicap)
Other sports followed: Football (West Ham United, Nottingham Forest)
Injuries: Out for eight weeks with a broken left thumb
Relaxations: Family, golf and TV
Extras: Shared Surrey record third-wicket stand of 413 with David Ward v Kent at Canterbury in 1990 – both made career bests. Surrey Batsman of the Year four times. Left Surrey and joined Notts for 2000. Became first English cricketer to take part in more than one partnership of 400-plus when he scored 180* in a first-wicket stand of 406* with Guy Welton (200*) v Warwickshire at Edgbaston 2000; the stand broke several records, including that for the highest Nottinghamshire partnership for any wicket, formerly 398 by Arthur Shrewsbury and William Gunn v Sussex at Trent Bridge 1890, and that for the highest unbeaten first-wicket partnership in Championship history. B&H Gold Awards for his 89 v Lancashire at Trent Bridge and 117* in the quarter-final v Warwickshire at Trent Bridge 2001. Was acting captain of Nottinghamshire in 2001 during the absence through injury of Jason Gallian. Scored 108 v Middlesex at Trent Bridge 2002, in the process sharing with Kevin Pietersen (254*) in a record partnership for any wicket in matches between Nottinghamshire and Middlesex (316)
Opinions on cricket: 'Am enjoying watching England improve – central contracts being a big part of it. English net facilities appalling – general. Teams should socialise more!'
Best batting: 235* Surrey v Nottinghamshire, Trent Bridge 1994
Best bowling: 3-7 Surrey v Sussex, Guildford 1996

2002 Season

	M	Inns	NO	Runs	HS	Avge	100s	50s	Ct	St	O	M	Runs	Wkts	Avge	Best	5wI	10wM
Test																		
All First	13	23	0	734	112	31.91	2	2	5	-								
1-day Int																		
C & G	1	1	0	46	46	46.00	-	-	-	-								
B & H	3	3	0	31	12	10.33	-	-	-	-								
1-day Lge	7	6	0	199	64	33.16	-	2	1	-								

Career Performances

	M	Inns	NO	Runs	HS	Avge	100s	50s	Ct	St	Balls	Runs	Wkts	Avge	Best	5wI	10wM
Test																	
All First	256	449	38	15842	235 *	38.54	39	67	94	-	1238	789	23	34.30	3-7	-	-
1-day Int																	
C & G	24	24	5	906	135 *	47.68	1	5	1	-							
B & H	47	46	5	1708	119	41.65	3	12	16	-							
1-day Lge	142	136	16	4389	125	36.57	6	31	35	-	42	45	2	22.50	1-11	-	

BICKNELL, M. P. Surrey

Name: <u>Martin</u> Paul Bicknell
Role: Right-hand bat, right-arm
fast-medium bowler
Born: 14 January 1969, Guildford
Height: 6ft 4in **Weight:** 15st
Nickname: Bickers
County debut: 1986
County cap: 1989
Benefit: 1997
Test debut: 1993
Tests: 2
One-Day Internationals: 7
50 wickets in a season: 10
1st-Class 50s: 22
1st-Class 100s: 1
1st-Class 5 w. in innings: 37
1st-Class 10 w. in match: 4
1st-Class catches: 89
One-Day 5 w. in innings: 3

Place in batting averages: 151st av. 28.66 (2001 42nd av. 46.75)
Place in bowling averages: 73rd av. 31.38 (2001 17th av. 21.36)
Strike rate: 57.52 (career 51.87)
Parents: Vic and Val
Wife and date of marriage: Loraine, 29 September 1995
Children: Eleanor, 31 March 1995; Charlotte, 22 July 1996
Family links with cricket: 'Brother plays, but with no luck'
Education: Robert Haining County Secondary
Qualifications: 2 O-levels, NCA coach
Career outside cricket: 'Running "Martin Bicknell Golf"'
Overseas tours: England YC to Sri Lanka 1986-87, to Australia 1987-88; England A
to Zimbabwe and Kenya 1989-90, to Bermuda and West Indies 1991-92, to South
Africa 1993-94; England to Australia 1990-91
Career highlights to date: 'A *Wisden* Cricketer of the Year 2001'
Cricket moments to forget: 'It's all been an experience!!'
Cricketers particularly admired: 'All honest county trundlers'
Young players to look out for: Tim Murtagh, Gareth Batty
Other sports played: Golf
Other sports followed: Football (Leeds United), golf
Injuries: Out for several weeks with a broken right wrist
Relaxations: 'Playing golf, reading; spending time with my children'
Extras: His figures of 9 for 45 v Cambridge University at Fenner's in 1988 were the

best for the county for 30 years. Took 7-30 in National League v Glamorgan at The Oval 1999, the best Sunday/National League return by a Surrey bowler. Took 800th first-class wicket (Darren Lehmann) v Yorkshire at The Oval 2000. His 16-119 (including 9-47 in the second innings) v Leicestershire at his home ground of Guildford in 2000 equalled the Surrey record for wickets taken in a match and is the second best match return in Surrey history behind Tony Lock's 16-83 v Kent at Blackheath in 1956. One of *Wisden*'s Five Cricketers of the Year 2001. Scored maiden first-class century (110*) v Kent at Canterbury 2001 out of a total of 193-8, having scored 78 in the first innings and taken 4-47 in Kent's only innings. Scored 748 runs (av. 46.75) and took 72 wickets (av. 21.36) in the County Championship 2001 and won the Wetherell Award for the Cricket Society's leading all-rounder in English first-class cricket for the second successive year. Surrey Supporters' Player of the Year 1993, 1997, 1999, 2000, 2001. Surrey Players' Player of the Year 1997, 1998, 1999, 2000, 2001. Surrey CCC Bowler of the Season Award 2001. Took 6-42 v Kent at The Oval 2002, in the process achieving the feat of having recorded a five-wicket innings return against all 17 counties besides his own

Opinions on cricket: 'Could all the people with a negative effect on the game please find something else to do?'

Best batting: 110* Surrey v Kent, Canterbury 2001

Best bowling: 9-45 Surrey v Cambridge University, The Oval 1988

2002 Season

	M	Inns	NO	Runs	HS	Avge	100s	50s	Ct	St	O	M	Runs	Wkts	Avge	Best	5wI	10wM
Test																		
All First	10	14	5	258	35 *	28.66	-	-	6	-	326	78	1067	34	31.38	6-42	2	-
1-day Int																		
C & G	2	0	0	0	0	-	-	-	1	-	18	1	110	3	36.66	2-84	-	
B & H	3	3	1	16	8 *	8.00	-	-	-	-	24	7	67	4	16.75	3-24	-	
1-day Lge	9	7	1	58	19 *	9.66	-	-	1	-	70.1	10	267	15	17.80	5-26	1	

Career Performances

	M	Inns	NO	Runs	HS	Avge	100s	50s	Ct	St	Balls	Runs	Wkts	Avge	Best	5wI	10wM
Test	2	4	0	26	14	6.50	-	-	-	-	522	263	4	65.75	3-99	-	-
All First	253	307	76	5350	110 *	23.16	1	22	89	-	48343	22748	932	24.40	9-45	37	4
1-day Int	7	6	2	96	31 *	24.00	-	-	2	-	413	347	13	26.69	3-55	-	
C & G	41	19	8	213	66 *	19.36	-	1	17	-	2523	1458	58	25.13	4-35	-	
B & H	66	36	13	380	43	16.52	-	-	13	-	3689	2354	94	25.04	4-38	-	
1-day Lge	187	96	43	742	57 *	14.00	-	1	39	-	8054	5585	230	24.28	7-30	3	

BISHOP, J. E.   Essex

Name: <u>Justin</u> Edward Bishop
Role: Left-hand lower middle order bat,
left-arm fast-medium opening bowler
Born: 4 January 1982, Bury St Edmunds
Height: 6ft **Weight:** 13st 8lbs
Nickname: Bish, Bash, Basher, Tractor Boy
County debut: 1999
1st-Class 5 w. in innings: 1
1st-Class catches: 2
Place in batting averages: 293rd av. 9.85
(2001 271st av. 7.40)
Place in bowling averages: 133rd av. 42.72
(2001 107th av. 38.12)
Strike rate: 65.45 (career 61.10)
Parents: Keith and Anne
Marital status: Girlfriend Lauren
Family links with cricket: 'Dad played
for Bury St Edmunds and Suffolk; Mum
does teas!'

Education: Ickworth Park Primary School; Horringer Court Middle School;
County Upper School, Bury St Edmunds; Durham University
Qualifications: GCSEs, 1 A-level (PE), GNVQ (Advanced) Science, Level 1
coaching awards in cricket and athletics
Career outside cricket: Student
Off-season: 'Working and playing hard at uni'
Overseas tours: England U19 to Malaysia and (U19 World Cup) Sri Lanka
1999-2000, to India 2000-01; British Universities to South Africa 2002
Career highlights to date: 'Taking seven wickets in an U19 "One Day International"
for England v West Indies'
Cricketers particularly admired: Mark Ilott ('ability to swing ball back into
right-handers')
Young players to look out for: Ravinder Bopara, Roger Howlett, Kevin Dobson
Other sports played: Football (Suffolk U15 and 'the mighty "John Snow College
FC"')
Other sports followed: Football (Ipswich Town FC 'on their European tour 2002')
Injuries: Out for eight weeks with a hamstring injury
Relaxations: 'Watching "the Tractor Boyz" win and the Canaries getting stuffed'
Extras: Played for England U15 1997. Represented England U17 at the ECC Colts
Festival in Northern Ireland 1999. Played for Suffolk in the NatWest 2000. Took 7-42
for England U19 in Sri Lanka U19's first innings in third U19 'Test' at Worcester,
August 2000. Took 5-64 in India U19's first innings in the third U19 'Test' at

Hyderabad 2000-01. Represented England U19 v West Indies U19 in one-day series (2/3) and 'Test' series (2/3) 2001, taking 7-41, the best England U19 figures in a 'One-Day International', in second 'ODI' at Chelmsford. Played for Durham University CCE in 2002. Scored 42* in the BUSA Halifax final v Loughborough University CCE at Fenner's 2002 batting at No. 9, sharing in a last-wicket stand of 42 in six overs with James Bruce (22*) that narrowly failed to snatch victory for DUCCE

Best batting: 23* Essex v Worcestershire, Southend 2002
Best bowling: 5-148 Essex v Leicestershire, Chelmsford 2001

2002 Season

	M	Inns	NO	Runs	HS	Avge	100s	50s	Ct	St	O	M	Runs	Wkts	Avge	Best	5wI	10wM
Test																		
All First	6	9	2	69	23 *	9.85	-	-	2	-	120	17	470	11	42.72	3-59	-	-
1-day Int																		
C & G																		
B & H																		
1-day Lge	4	2	2	8	6 *	-	-	-	-	-	22	0	134	5	26.80	3-39	-	

Career Performances

	M	Inns	NO	Runs	HS	Avge	100s	50s	Ct	St	Balls	Runs	Wkts	Avge	Best	5wI	10wM
Test																	
All First	16	22	4	160	23 *	8.88	-	-	2	-	2322	1565	38	41.18	5-148	1	-
1-day Int																	
C & G	3	3	0	3	3	1.00	-	-	-	-	127	78	3	26.00	2-34	-	
B & H																	
1-day Lge	18	12	6	54	16 *	9.00	-	-	3	-	648	598	21	28.47	3-33	-	

8. For which county did Kapil Dev play before moving
to Worcestershire in 1984?

BLACKWELL, I. D.   Somerset

Name: <u>Ian</u> David Blackwell
Role: Left-hand bat, slow left-arm bowler
Born: 10 June 1978, Chesterfield
Height: 6ft 2in **Weight:** 16st 7lbs
Nickname: Blacko, Blackie, Albert, Pip, Yuf
County debut: 1997 (Derbyshire),
2000 (Somerset)
County cap: 2001 (Somerset)
1st-Class 50s: 12
1st-Class 100s: 8
1st-Class 5 w. in innings: 3
1st-Class catches: 27
Place in batting averages: 87th av. 38.21
(2001 31st av. 49.35)
Place in bowling averages: 115th av. 37.72
(2001 128th av. 44.80)

Strike rate: 85.31 (career 95.12)
Parents: John and Marilyn
Children: 'None; just a big, fat, lazy cat – Max'
Family links with cricket: Father played for Derbyshire Over 50s and is also involved at Chesterfield CC
Education: Old Hall Primary School; Manor Community School (GCSEs); Brookfield Community School (A-levels)
Qualifications: 9 GCSEs, 1 A-level, NCA senior coaching award
Career outside cricket: Work in the club office
Off-season: ECB National Academy and touring with England
Overseas tours: Somerset to Cape Town 2000, 2001; England VI to Hong Kong 2001; England to Sri Lanka (ICC Champions Trophy) 2002-03, to Australia 2002-03 (VB Series); ECB National Academy to Australia 2002-03
Overseas teams played for: Delacombe Park CC, Melbourne, Australia 1997, 1999
Career highlights to date: 'By far, the C&G final win v Leicestershire at Lord's 2001. Also getting Steve Waugh out on my debut for Derbyshire 1997; he was my first first-class wicket'
Cricket moments to forget: 'Scoring 0 and 5 against Lancashire in the Championship 1998; in the same game Graham Lloyd hit me for 28 in an over – the Kellogg's factory was in danger!!!'
Cricketers particularly admired: Phillip DeFreitas, Ian Botham, Brian Lara, Glenn McGrath, Jamie Cox, Marcus Trescothick
Players to look out for: Matt Wood, Arul Suppiah, Ian Bell
Other sports played: 'Golf mainly – partner Bully in matchplay – but can turn to most sports'

Other sports followed: Golf, football (Chesterfield FC)

Relaxations: Golf ('but it's not that relaxing!!'); 'use my laptop quite a lot'

Extras: Played for Derbyshire from the age of eight through to the 1st XI. Set record for number of balls lost (seven) in a score of 213* off 156 balls at Bolsover, which included 21 fours and 15 sixes and equalled the Bassetlaw League 1A record. Left Derbyshire at end of 1999 season and joined Somerset for 2000. B&H Gold Award for his 64 v Worcestershire at Worcester 2001. Became first batsman in Championship history to score two centuries (103 and 122) in a match batting at No. 7, v Northants at Northampton 2001; in the process of scoring his 103 he equalled with Keith Dutch the record seventh-wicket partnership for Somerset in matches against Northamptonshire. Scored 102 v Glamorgan at Taunton 2001, in the process sharing with Peter Bowler in a record fifth-wicket stand for Somerset in matches v Glamorgan (163). Scored 100-ball Championship century (out for 114 from 134 balls) v Yorkshire at Taunton 2002; four days later scored 54-ball 79 v Yorkshire in the NUL, also at Taunton. C&G Man of the Match award for his 53-ball 86 in the semi-final v Kent at Taunton 2002. Called up to the England one-day squad for the ICC Champions Trophy in Sri Lanka 2002-03 as a replacement for the injured Andrew Flintoff

Opinions on cricket: 'Having two divisions has increased interest towards the end of the season, but three up/three down is a little excessive. I know there are reasons for it, but two up/two down would be more appropriate.'

Best batting: 122 Somerset v Northamptonshire, Northampton 2001

Best bowling: 5-49 Somerset v Hampshire, West End 2002

Stop press: Made One Day International debut v Zimbabwe at Colombo in the ICC Champions Trophy 2002-03; scored a 68-ball 82 v India at Colombo in his second ODI, also in the ICC Champions Trophy. Selected for England squad for 2002-03 World Cup

2002 Season

	M	Inns	NO	Runs	HS	Avge	100s	50s	Ct	St	O	M	Runs	Wkts	Avge	Best	5wI	10wM
Test																		
All First	14	23	0	879	114	38.21	3	3	4	-	312.5	83	830	22	37.72	5-49	1	-
1-day Int																		
C & G	5	5	1	168	86	42.00	-	1	2	-	42	0	201	2	100.50	1-37	-	
B & H	4	4	0	20	8	5.00	-	-	1	-	17	0	86	4	21.50	3-46	-	
1-day Lge	13	13	0	312	79	24.00	-	3	1	-	69.1	4	384	11	34.90	4-24	-	

Career Performances

	M	Inns	NO	Runs	HS	Avge	100s	50s	Ct	St	Balls	Runs	Wkts	Avge	Best	5wI	10wM
Test																	
All First	68	102	4	2952	122	30.12	8	12	27	-	8847	4082	93	43.89	5-49	3	-
1-day Int																	
C & G	15	14	2	303	86	25.25	-	2	5	-	534	419	8	52.37	2-34	-	
B & H	18	14	1	226	64	17.38	-	1	6	-	288	264	5	52.80	3-46	-	
1-day Lge	65	61	5	1469	97	26.23	-	11	16	-	1970	1569	53	29.60	4-24	-	

BLAIN, J. A. R. Northamptonshire

Name: <u>John</u> Angus Rae Blain
Role: Right-hand bat, right-arm
fast-medium bowler
Born: 4 January 1979, Edinburgh
Height: 6ft 2in **Weight:** 13st 7lbs
Nickname: Blainey, Haggis, Hag
County debut: 1997
One-Day Internationals: 5
1st-Class 5 w. in innings: 1
1st-Class catches: 5
One-Day 5 w. in innings: 2
Place in batting averages: 308th av. 6.71
Place in bowling averages: 154th av. 56.81
(2001 112th av. 39.58)
Strike rate: 72.25 (career 69.94)
Parents: John and Elma
Marital status: Single
Education: Eastfield Primary School;

Penicuik HS; Jewel and Esk Valley College
Qualifications: 8 GCSEs, 1 A-level, HNC Leisure and Recreation, Level 1
coaching award
Overseas tours: Northants CCC to Zimbabwe 1997; Scotland U19 to Holland
(International Youth Tournament) 1994-95, to Bermuda (International Youth
Tournament) 1997, to South Africa (U19 World Cup) 1997-98 (captain);
Scotland to Denmark (European Championships) 1996, to Malaysia (ICC Trophy)
1997, to Malaysia (Commonwealth Games) 1998, to Sharjah 1999, to Canada (ICC
Trophy) 2001
Overseas teams played for: New Plymouth Old Boys, New Zealand 1998-99;
Taranaki Cricket Association, New Zealand 1998-99
Cricketers particularly admired: Devon Malcolm, Steve Waugh
Young players to look out for: Mark Powell
Other sports played: Football (schoolboy forms with Hibernian FC and Falkirk FC,
making youth and reserve team appearances), golf
Other sports followed: Football (Hibernian FC)
Relaxations: 'Listening to music, going out for a drink, going back to Scotland to
spend time with family; watching football, going to the gym and sleeping!'
Extras: Was youngest ever player to play for Scotland national side, at 17 years and
114 days. Played for Scotland in the B&H and NatWest competitions. Made his first-
class debut for Scotland against Ireland in 1996. Took 5-24 on Sunday League debut
for Northamptonshire v Derbyshire at Derby 1997. Represented Scotland in the 1999
World Cup, taking 10 wickets and finishing top of the strike rate chart for the
tournament. B&H Gold Award for his 5-30 v Gloucestershire at Northampton 2002

Best batting: 34 Northamptonshire v Surrey, Northampton 2001
Best bowling: 6-42 Northamptonshire v Kent, Canterbury 2001

2002 Season

	M	Inns	NO	Runs	HS	Avge	100s	50s	Ct	St	O	M	Runs	Wkts	Avge	Best	5wl	10wM
Test																		
All First	7	9	2	47	17 *	6.71	-	-	2	-	192.4	21	909	16	56.81	4-144	-	-
1-day Int																		
C & G	1	1	0	6	6	6.00	-	-	-	-	10	1	47	2	23.50	2-47	-	
B & H	1	0	0	0	0	-	-	-	-	-	8	1	30	5	6.00	5-30	1	
1-day Lge	1	0	0	0	0	-	-	-	-	-	9	0	42	1	42.00	1-42	-	

Career Performances

	M	Inns	NO	Runs	HS	Avge	100s	50s	Ct	St	Balls	Runs	Wkts	Avge	Best	5wl	10wM
Test																	
All First	16	20	7	144	34	11.07	-	-	5	-	2518	1864	36	51.77	6-42	1	-
1-day Int	5	5	1	15	9	3.75	-	-	1	-	223	210	10	21.00	4-37	-	
C & G	2	1	0	6	6	6.00	-	-	1	-	126	103	4	25.75	2-47	-	
B & H	6	3	1	25	11	12.50	-	-	-	-	246	280	10	28.00	5-30	1	
1-day Lge	7	2	2	3	3 *	-	-	-	3	-	306	274	11	24.90	5-24	1	

BLAKEY, R. J. Yorkshire

Name: <u>Richard</u> John Blakey
Role: Right-hand bat, wicket-keeper
Born: 15 January 1967, Huddersfield
Height: 5ft 10in **Weight:** 11st 4lbs
Nickname: Dick
County debut: 1985
County cap: 1987
Benefit: 1998
Test debut: 1992-93
Tests: 2
One-Day Internationals: 3
1000 runs in a season: 5
50 dismissals in a season: 6
1st-Class 50s: 86
1st-Class 100s: 10
1st-Class 200s: 2
1st-Class catches: 746
1st-Class stumpings: 56
One-Day 100s: 3
Place in batting averages: 44th av. 47.31 (2001 142nd av. 27.00)
Strike rate: (career 63.00)

Parents: Brian and Pauline
Wife and date of marriage: Michelle, 28 September 1991
Children: Harrison Brad, 22 September 1993
Family links with cricket: Father played local cricket
Education: Woodhouse Primary; Rastrick Grammar School
Qualifications: 4 O-levels, Senior NCA Coach
Career outside cricket: Started own leisure company
Overseas tours: England YC to West Indies 1984-85; Yorkshire to Barbados 1986-87, to Cape Town 1990-91; England A to Zimbabwe and Kenya 1989-90, to Pakistan 1990-91; England to India and Sri Lanka 1992-93
Overseas teams played for: Waverley, Sydney 1985-87; Mt Waverley, Sydney 1987-88; Bionics, Zimbabwe 1989-90
Cricketers particularly admired: Martyn Moxon, Dermot Reeve, Ian Botham, Alan Knott
Other sports followed: All
Relaxations: All sports, particularly golf and squash, eating out, drawing, photography
Extras: Made record individual score for Yorkshire 2nd XI (273*) v Northamptonshire 2nd XI 1986. Yorkshire's Young Player of the Year 1989. Was awarded a citation by the International Committee for Fair Play in 1995, the only cricketer among the 25 winners worldwide. Scored 60 v Leicestershire at Scarborough in the NUL 2002, in the process sharing with Richard Dawson (41) in a new record eighth-wicket partnership for Yorkshire in the one-day league (89). Scored 103 v Warwickshire at Edgbaston 2002, in the process sharing with Gary Fellows (88) in a new record sixth-wicket partnership for Yorkshire in matches v Warwickshire (175). Vice-captain of Yorkshire 2002. Yorkshire Players' Player of the Year and Club Player of the Year 2002
Best batting: 221 England A v Zimbabwe, Bulawayo 1989-90
Best bowling: 1-68 Yorkshire v Nottinghamshire, Sheffield 1986

2002 Season

	M	Inns	NO	Runs	HS	Avge	100s	50s	Ct	St	O	M	Runs	Wkts	Avge	Best	5wI	10wM
Test																		
All First	16	29	7	1041	103	47.31	1	8	29	1								
1-day Int																		
C & G	5	0	0	0	0	-	-	-	8	-								
B & H	6	6	1	70	34	14.00	-	-	3	2								
1-day Lge	15	12	4	246	60	30.75	-	1	17	5								

Career Performances

	M	Inns	NO	Runs	HS	Avge	100s	50s	Ct	St	Balls	Runs	Wkts	Avge	Best	5wI	10wM
Test	2	4	0	7	6	1.75	-	-	2	-							
All First	335	535	85	14206	221	31.56	12	86	746	56	63	68	1	68.00	1-68	-	-
1-day Int	3	2	0	25	25	12.50	-	-	2	1							
C & G	43	30	11	461	75	24.26	-	2	51	3							
B & H	74	64	18	1308	80 *	28.43	-	6	71	6							
1-day Lge	230	203	50	5292	130 *	34.58	3	27	224	44							

BLOOMFIELD, T. F.   Middlesex

Name: Timothy (<u>Tim</u>) Francis Bloomfield
Role: Right-hand bat, right-arm
fast-medium bowler
Born: 31 May 1973, Ashford, Middlesex
Height: 6ft 2in **Weight:** 14st
Nickname: Bloomers, Boof, Frank
County debut: 1997
County cap: 2001
50 wickets in a season: 1
1st-Class 5 w. in innings: 6
1st-Class catches: 6
Place in batting averages: (2001 272nd
av. 7.08)
Place in bowling averages: (2001 87th
av. 34.18)
Strike rate: 79.85 (career 53.33)
Parents: Richard and Pauline
Marital status: Engaged to Emma

Education: Staines Preparatory School; Halliford Independent School
Qualifications: 8 GCSEs, NCA coaching award
Off-season: Duty manager for OFJ, working on airline flight crew transportation
Overseas tours: Berkshire U25 to Barbados 1996; Middlesex to South Africa 2000;
MCC to Sri Lanka 2001, to Kenya 2002
Career highlights to date: 'Getting capped by Middlesex at Lord's'
Cricket moments to forget: 'All of the 2002 season, having not played due to injury'
Cricket superstitions: 'Nick Compton'
Cricketers particularly admired: Ian Botham, Viv Richards, Angus Fraser
Young players to look out for: Alan Coleman, Nick Compton
Other sports played: Football, golf, tennis, snooker
Other sports followed: Football (Liverpool)
Injuries: Out for most of the 2002 season with hamstring and back injuries
Relaxations: Sport, music, 'nice cold Stella in "the Bells"'
Extras: Has also played for Sussex 2nd XI and Berkshire. Took 4-17 v Somerset at
Southgate in the NatWest 2000, winning the Man of the Match award
Opinions on cricket: 'I think the two division system has been a success. Central
contracts have worked well.'
Best batting: 31* Middlesex v Northamptonshire, Northampton 2002
Best bowling: 5-36 Middlesex v Glamorgan, Cardiff 1999

2002 Season

	M	Inns	NO	Runs	HS	Avge	100s	50s	Ct	St	O	M	Runs	Wkts	Avge	Best	5wI	10wM
Test																		
All First	3	3	2	57	31 *	57.00	-	-	-	-	93.1	20	340	7	48.57	3-45	-	-
1-day Int																		
C & G	1	0	0	0	0	-	-	-	-	-	7.1	1	51	0	-	-	-	-
B & H																		
1-day Lge	5	4	1	16	10	5.33	-	-	3	-	39	2	170	8	21.25	3-28	-	

Career Performances

	M	Inns	NO	Runs	HS	Avge	100s	50s	Ct	St	Balls	Runs	Wkts	Avge	Best	5wI	10wM
Test																	
All First	52	57	24	279	31 *	8.45	-	-	6	-	7894	4808	148	32.48	5-36	6	-
1-day Int																	
C & G	6	2	1	7	7 *	7.00	-	-	-	-	259	191	6	31.83	4-17	-	
B & H	5	2	2	7	7 *	-	-	-	-	-	240	195	2	97.50	1-33	-	
1-day Lge	37	14	5	53	15	5.88	-	-	9	-	1584	1143	34	33.61	3-28	-	

BOJE, N.   Nottinghamshire

Name: Nico (<u>Nicky</u>) Boje
Role: Left-hand bat, slow left-arm bowler
Born: 20 March 1973, Bloemfontein,
South Africa
Nickname: Bodge
Height: 5ft 10in
County debut: 2002
Test debut: 1999-2000
Tests: 19
One-Day Internationals: 79
1st-Class 50s: 27
1st-Class 100s: 5
1st-Class 5 w. in innings: 15
1st-Class 10 w. in match: 1
1st-Class catches: 76
One-Day 100s: 2
One-Day 5 w. in innings: 1
Place in batting averages: 145th av. 29.21
Place in bowling averages: 21st av. 24.85
Strike rate: 52.88 (career 76.50)
Family links with cricket: Elder brother Eduard (E. H. L.) Boje played for Orange
Free State 1989-90

Education: Grey College, Bloemfontein
Off-season: Playing for South Africa
Overseas tours: South Africa A to Zimbabwe 1994-95, to England 1996, to Sri Lanka 1998-99 (vice captain); South Africa U24 to Sri Lanka 1995-96; South Africa to Zimbabwe 1995-96 (one-day series), to India 1996-97, to Bangladesh (Wills International Cup) 1998-99, to New Zealand 1998-99, to UK, Ireland and Holland (World Cup) 1999, to India 1999-2000, to Sharjah (Coca-Cola Cup) 1999-2000, to Sri Lanka 2000, to Australia (Super Challenge) 2000, to Singapore (Singapore Challenge) 2000, to Kenya (ICC Knockout) 2000-01, to West Indies 2000-01, to Australia 2001-02, to Morocco (Morocco Cup) 2002, to Sri Lanka (ICC Champions Trophy) 2002-03
Overseas teams played for: Orange Free State/Free State 1990-91 –
Extras: Represented South Africa Schools 1989-91. Attended South African Academy (Class of 1997). Scored 85 as nightwatchman and had match figures of 7-93 (including 5-83 in the second innings) in second Test v India at Bangalore 1999-2000, winning Man of the Match award. Had scores of 105* (his maiden ODI century), 64 and 129 in the first three One-Day Internationals v New Zealand 2000-01; won Man of the Series award. Man of the Match in the final of the Singapore Challenge, v Pakistan 2000-01 (54 and 1-24). Man of the Match in seventh ODI v Australia at Cape Town 2001-02 (49 and 5-21). Was Nottinghamshire's overseas player in 2002, replacing the injured Chris Cairns. Scored 86 v Leicestershire at Trent Bridge in the NUL 2002, in the process sharing with Jason Gallian (91) in a record fourth-wicket partnership for Nottinghamshire in the one-day league (190). Released by Nottinghamshire at the end of the 2002 season
Best batting: 116 Free State v Western Province, Bloemfontein 1998-99
Best bowling: 6-31 Free State v Boland, Bloemfontein 2001-02
Stop press: Selected for South Africa squad for 2002-03 World Cup

2002 Season

	M	Inns	NO	Runs	HS	Avge	100s	50s	Ct	St	O	M	Runs	Wkts	Avge	Best	5wI	10wM
Test																		
All First	9	16	2	409	84	29.21	-	2	10	-	238	58	671	27	24.85	6-128	2	-
1-day Int																		
C & G	2	1	0	8	8	8.00	-	-	-	-	19	2	65	2	32.50	1-17	-	
B & H																		
1-day Lge	9	8	0	251	86	31.37	-	2	5	-	74	4	328	11	29.81	2-26	-	

Career Performances

	M	Inns	NO	Runs	HS	Avge	100s	50s	Ct	St	Balls	Runs	Wkts	Avge	Best	5wI	10wM
Test	19	28	3	542	85	21.68	-	2	8	-	3471	1452	49	29.63	5-62	2	-
All First	122	180	31	4764	116	31.97	5	27	76	-	25169	10319	329	31.36	6-31	15	1
1-day Int	79	48	9	1077	129	27.61	2	3	24	-	3074	2262	68	33.26	5-21	1	
C & G	2	1	0	8	8	8.00	-	-	-	-	114	65	2	32.50	1-17	-	
B & H																		
1-day Lge	9	8	0	251	86	31.37	-	2	5	-	444	328	11	29.81	2-26	-	

BOND, S. E.   Warwickshire

Name: <u>Shane</u> Edward Bond
Role: Right-hand bat, right-arm fast bowler
Born: 7 June 1975, Christchurch,
New Zealand
County debut: 2002
Test debut: 2001-02
Tests: 6
One-Day Internationals: 13
1st-Class 50s: 1
1st-Class 5 w. in innings: 6
1st-Class catches: 13
One-Day 5 w. in innings: 1
Place in bowling averages: 43rd av. 27.50
Strike rate: 47.83 (career 52.28)
Parents: John and Judith
Wife: Tracy
Education: Papanui High School,
Christchurch
Off-season: Playing for New Zealand
Overseas tours: New Zealand A to India (Buchi Babu Tournament) 2001-02; New Zealand to Australia 2001-02, to West Indies 2001-02, to Sri Lanka (ICC Champions Trophy) 2002-03
Career outside cricket: Police officer
Overseas teams played for: Canterbury 1996-97 –
Extras: Played for Furness in Lancashire League 1999, taking 118 wickets to break the season record for the league. Man of the VB one-day series in Australia 2001-02 with 21 wickets (av. 16.38), including 5-25 v Australia at Adelaide (the third best return by a New Zealand bowler in ODIs). Man of the two-match Test series v West Indies 2002 with 12 wickets (av. 18.00), including 5-78 at Bridgetown and 5-104 at Grenada. Was Warwickshire's overseas player during August 2002, replacing Shaun Pollock, absent on international duty; has returned as an overseas player for 2003. Attended same school in Christchurch as Andrew Caddick
Best batting: 29* Warwickshire v Somerset, Taunton 2002
Best bowling: 5-37 Canterbury v Northern Districts, Gisborne 2001-02
Stop press: Man of the Match (4-21) v Bangladesh at Colombo in the ICC Champions Trophy 2002-03. Took 4-33 from 13.1 overs as New Zealand bowled out India for 121 in their second innings of first Test at Wellington 2002-03. Selected for New Zealand squad for 2002-03 World Cup

2002 Season

	M	Inns	NO	Runs	HS	Avge	100s	50s	Ct	St	O	M	Runs	Wkts	Avge	Best	5wI	10wM
Test																		
All First	3	4	1	64	29 *	21.33	-	-	1	-	95.4	23	330	12	27.50	5-64	1	-
1-day Int																		
C & G																			
B & H																			
1-day Lge	1	0	0	0	0	-	-	-	-	-	9	2	32	0	-		-	-

Career Performances

	M	Inns	NO	Runs	HS	Avge	100s	50s	Ct	St	Balls	Runs	Wkts	Avge	Best	5wI	10wM
Test	6	6	2	40	17	10.00	-	-	4	-	1118	655	26	25.19	5-78	2	-
All First	30	36	13	342	66 *	14.86	-	1	13	-	5280	2693	101	26.66	5-37	6	-
1-day Int	13	6	3	52	19 *	17.33	-	-	4	-	644	486	23	21.13	5-25	1	
C & G																	
B & H																		
1-day Lge	1	0	0	0	0	-	-	-	-	-	54	32	0	-		-	-

BOPARA, R. S. Essex

Name: Ravinder (<u>Ravi</u>) Singh Bopara
Role: Right-hand bat, right-arm fast bowler
Born: 4 May 1985, Newham, London
Height: 5ft 8in **Weight:** 11st 8lbs
Nickname: Puppy
County debut: 2002
1st-Class catches: 6
Place in batting averages: 159th av. 27.50
Strike rate: 96.00 (career 96.00)
Parents: Charanjit Singh Bopara and Baldish Kaur Bopara
Marital status: Single
Education: Central Park School; Brampton Manor School; Barking Abbey Sports College
Qualifications: 7 GCSEs, ECB Level 1 coaching
Career outside cricket: Student
Overseas tours: England U19 to Australia 2002-03
Career highlights to date: '102* against Hertfordshire for Essex 2nd XI on debut 2001. 153* against Yorkshire Academy for England U17 on debut 2001'
Cricket moments to forget: 'I went out to bat once and didn't realise I didn't have a box on until I got hit there'

Cricketers particularly admired: Sachin Tendulkar, Jacques Kallis
Young players to look out for: Tim Bresnan
Other sports played: Football
Other sports followed: Football (Arsenal)
Relaxations: 'I enjoy DJ-ing in my spare time and listening to music (hip-hop, R 'n' B, garage)'
Extras: Played for Development of Excellence XI (South) v West Indies U19 at Arundel 2001. Played for Essex Board XI in the first round of the C&G 2002, which was played in August 2001
Opinions on cricket: 'It is getting more and more competitive and aggressive, which I see as a strong point. Also, to succeed in cricket you not only need talent but you also have to be physically fit, as this can affect one's game and selection.'
Best batting: 48 Essex v Durham, Colchester 2002
Best bowling: 1-43 Essex v Indians, Chelmsford 2002

2002 Season

	M	Inns	NO	Runs	HS	Avge	100s	50s	Ct	St	O	M	Runs	Wkts	Avge	Best	5wI	10wM
Test																		
All First	4	7	1	165	48	27.50	-	-	6	-	16	1	74	1	74.00	1-43	-	-
1-day Int																		
C & G																		
B & H																		
1-day Lge	2	2	0	0	0	0.00	-	-	-	-								

Career Performances

	M	Inns	NO	Runs	HS	Avge	100s	50s	Ct	St	Balls	Runs	Wkts	Avge	Best	5wI	10wM
Test																	
All First	4	7	1	165	48	27.50	-	-	6	-	96	74	1	74.00	1-43	-	-
1-day Int																	
C & G	1	1	0	1	1	1.00	-	-	-	-							
B & H																	
1-day Lge	2	2	0	0	0	0.00	-	-	-	-							

9. Who scored a Somerset season record 11 first-class centuries in 1991?

BOWLER, P. D. Somerset

Name: <u>Peter</u> Duncan Bowler
Role: Right-hand opening bat, occasional off-spin bowler, occasional wicket-keeper
Born: 30 July 1963, Plymouth
Height: 6ft 2in **Weight:** 13st 10lbs
Nickname: Tom
County debut: 1986 (Leicestershire), 1988 (Derbyshire), 1995 (Somerset)
County cap: 1989 (Derbyshire), 1995 (Somerset)
Benefit: 2000 (Somerset)
1000 runs in a season: 9
1st-Class 50s: 93
1st-Class 100s: 39
1st-Class 200s: 3
1st-Class catches: 210
1st-Class stumpings: 1
One-Day 100s: 7
Place in batting averages: 118th av. 33.30 (2001 62nd av. 41.35)
Strike rate: 42.00 (career 96.05)
Parents: Peter and Etta
Wife and date of marriage: Joanne, 10 October 1992
Children: Peter Robert, 21 September 1993; Rebekah, 25 August 1995
Education: Scots College, Sydney, Australia; Daramalan College, Canberra, Australia; Nottingham Trent University
Qualifications: Australian Year 12 certificate, LLB
Cricketers particularly admired: Gus Valence, Rob Jeffery, Bill Carracher, Phil Russell
Other sports followed: Rugby union
Relaxations: Family and reading
Extras: First Leicestershire player to score a first-class century on debut (100* v Hampshire at Leicester 1986). Moved to Derbyshire at the end of the 1987 season and scored a hundred (155*) on debut v Cambridge University at Fenner's 1988, becoming the first player to score hundreds on debut for two counties. His 241* v Hampshire at Portsmouth 1992 is the highest score by a Derbyshire No. 1. First batsman to 2000 runs in 1992, finishing equal leading run-scorer (2044) with Mike Roseberry of Middlesex. Derbyshire Player of the Year 1992. Joined Somerset for 1995. Took over the Somerset captaincy mid-season 1997; relinquished captaincy after 1998 season. Passed 5000 runs in Sunday/National League, v Durham 1999. Top-scoring English batsman in first-class cricket in his benefit season (2000) with 1305 runs (av. 62.14). Scored 164 v Glamorgan at Taunton 2001, in the process sharing with Ian Blackwell in a record fifth-wicket stand for Somerset in matches v Glamorgan (163)

Best batting: 241* Derbyshire v Hampshire, Portsmouth 1992
Best bowling: 3-25 Somerset v Northamptonshire, Taunton 1998

2002 Season

	M	Inns	NO	Runs	HS	Avge	100s	50s	Ct	St	O	M	Runs	Wkts	Avge	Best	5wl	10wM
Test																		
All First	14	25	2	766	94	33.30	-	7	22	-	7	1	23	1	23.00	1-20	-	-
1-day Int																		
C & G	5	5	0	287	104	57.40	1	2	1	-								
B & H	2	2	0	21	21	10.50	-	-	-	-								
1-day Lge	11	11	0	198	53	18.00	-	1	5	-								

Career Performances

	M	Inns	NO	Runs	HS	Avge	100s	50s	Ct	St	Balls	Runs	Wkts	Avge	Best	5wl	10wM
Test																	
All First	293	500	52	18056	241 *	40.30	42	93	210	1	3266	2041	34	60.02	3-25	-	-
1-day Int																	
C & G	36	36	0	1108	111	30.77	2	5	13	-	36	26	0	-		-	-
B & H	57	56	1	1613	109	29.32	2	13	26	1	309	182	5	36.40	1-15	-	
1-day Lge	218	211	19	6325	138 *	32.94	3	51	80	1	308	323	8	40.37	3-31	-	

BRANDY, D. G. Leicestershire

Name: <u>Damian</u> Gareth Brandy
Role: Right-hand bat, right-arm
medium bowler
Born: 14 September 1981, Highgate, London
Height: 6ft 1in **Weight:** 15st 7lbs
Nickname: Damo
County debut: 2002
1st-Class catches: 1
Strike rate: 51.00 (career 51.00)
Parents: Judy May and Aubrey Winston
Marital status: Single
Family links with cricket: 'Dad was an
excellent cricketer who played at various
levels, including representing the Civil
Service at regional level'
Education: Henry Maynard; St John's,
Epping; Harlow College
Qualifications: 10 GCSEs, 3 A-levels, Level
1 ACB coaching award

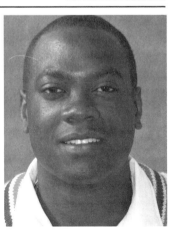

Off-season: 'Travelling to Potch (North-West) South Africa to train with the provincial side under the guidance of Gordon Parsons'
Overseas teams played for: Bankstown, Sydney 2000-01
Career highlights to date: 'Making first-team debut v Somerset under lights at Grace Road. Brilliant night!'
Cricket moments to forget: 'Shouldering arms in two consecutive games against the same team and the same bowler and being bowled first ball each time'
Cricketers particularly admired: Steve Waugh, Curtly Ambrose
Young players to look out for: Luke Wright, Tom New, Damian Brandy
Other sports played: Golf (18 handicap), football (captain of school 1st XI)
Other sports followed: Football (Arsenal)
Relaxations: 'Playing golf, socialising'
Extras: Played for Essex from U11 to 2nd XI. Scored century in first 2nd XI game for Leicestershire, v Durham 2001
Opinions on cricket: 'Standard of pitches should be improved. Cricketers in England settle into comfort zone too easily and need to be pushed.'
Best batting: 23 Leicestershire v Surrey, The Oval 2002
Best bowling: 2-86 Leicestershire v Surrey, The Oval 2002

2002 Season

	M	Inns	NO	Runs	HS	Avge	100s	50s	Ct	St	O	M	Runs	Wkts	Avge	Best	5wI	10wM
Test																		
All First	2	3	0	28	23	9.33	-	-	1	-	17	0	114	2	57.00	2-86	-	-
1-day Int																		
C & G																		
B & H																		
1-day Lge	2	2	0	50	35	25.00	-	-	-	-								

Career Performances

	M	Inns	NO	Runs	HS	Avge	100s	50s	Ct	St	Balls	Runs	Wkts	Avge	Best	5wI	10wM
Test																	
All First	2	3	0	28	23	9.33	-	-	1	-	102	114	2	57.00	2-86	-	-
1-day Int																	
C & G																	
B & H																	
1-day Lge	2	2	0	50	35	25.00	-	-	-	-							

BRANT, S. A. Essex

Name: <u>Scott</u> Andrew Brant
Role: Right-hand bat, left-arm
fast-medium bowler
Born: 26 January 1983, Harare, Zimbabwe
Nickname: Woody
County debut: No first-team appearance
1st-Class catches: 3
Strike rate: (career 48.00)
Education: Nudgee College, Brisbane; Bond
University, Queensland
Qualifications: Studying sports management
Overseas teams played for: Norths (Northern
Suburbs), Brisbane; Queensland
2001-02 –
Other sports played: Hockey, swimming,
triathlon, athletics (all at Zimbabwe Youth level;
pole vault gold medallist at South African junior
championships)
Extras: Born in Zimbabwe and moved to
Australia with his family in 1999. Played for Queensland U19 2000-01. Took 3-34
from ten overs as Norths beat Valley in the final of the 2001-02 Brisbane limited overs
competition at Allan Border Field. Had match figures of 6-54 (3-23 and 3-31) v
Victoria at Brisbane 2001-02 in his second first-class game, winning the Man of the
Match award. Has joined Essex as an overseas player for 2003
Best batting: 19* Queensland v Victoria, Brisbane 2001-02
Best bowling: 3-23 Queensland v Victoria, Brisbane 2001-02

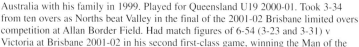

2002 Season (did not make any first-class or one-day appearances)

Career Performances

	M	Inns	NO	Runs	HS	Avge	100s	50s	Ct	St	Balls	Runs	Wkts	Avge	Best	5wI	10wM
Test																	
All First	3	3	2	35	19*	35.00	-	-	3	-	336	126	7	18.00	3-23	-	-
1-day Int																	
C & G																	
B & H																	
1-day Lge																	

BRESNAN, T. T.   Yorkshire

Name: Timothy (<u>Tim</u>) Thomas Bresnan
Role: Right-hand bat, right-arm
fast-medium bowler
Born: 28 February 1985, Pontefract
Height: 6ft **Weight:** 13st
Nickname: Brezy Lad, Brez
County debut: 2001 (one-day)
Parents: Julie and Ray
Marital status: Single
Family links with cricket: 'Dad played local
league cricket'
Education: Three Lane Ends Primary
School; Castleford High School; Pontefract
New College
Qualifications: 8 GCSEs
Off-season: England U19 tour of Australia
Overseas tours: Yorkshire U16 to Cape
Town 2001; England U17 to Australia
2000-01; England U19 to Australia and (U19
World Cup) New Zealand 2001-02,
to Australia 2002-03

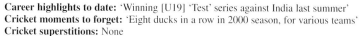

Career highlights to date: 'Winning [U19] 'Test' series against India last summer'
Cricket moments to forget: 'Eight ducks in a row in 2000 season, for various teams'
Cricket superstitions: None
Cricketers particularly admired: Ian Botham
Young players to look out for: Joseph Sayers, Chris Gilbert, David Stiff
Other sports played: Golf, football
Other sports followed: Football (Leeds United)
Relaxations: Golf, PlayStation
Extras: Bunbury Festival Best All-rounder and Most Outstanding Player. Made one-
day debut v Kent at Headingley 2001 aged 16 years 102 days, making him the
youngest player to represent Yorkshire since Paul Jarvis in 1981. Represented England
U19 v India U19 in 'Test' series (2/3) and one-day series (3/3) 2002. Shared new ball
with fellow 17-year-old Nick Thornicroft v Warwicks at Edgbaston in the NUL 2002
Opinions on cricket: 'Local league cricket should be publicised better, drawing better
crowds and should all play 50 overs with circles and fielding restrictions.'

2002 Season

	M	Inns	NO	Runs	HS	Avge	100s	50s	Ct	St	O	M	Runs	Wkts	Avge	Best	5wI	10wM
Test																		
All First																		
1-day Int																		
C & G	1	0	0	0	0	-	-	-	-	-	7	1	18	1	18.00	1-18	-	
B & H	6	4	3	23	16	23.00	-	-	1	-	33	2	119	3	39.66	1-6	-	
1-day Lge	13	7	3	53	22	13.25	-	-	1	-	78.5	4	389	10	38.90	2-27	-	

Career Performances

	M	Inns	NO	Runs	HS	Avge	100s	50s	Ct	St	Balls	Runs	Wkts	Avge	Best	5wI	10wM
Test																	
All First																	
1-day Int																	
C & G	1	0	0	0	0	-	-	-	-	-	42	18	1	18.00	1-18	-
B & H	6	4	3	23	16	23.00	-	-	1	-	198	119	3	39.66	1-6	-
1-day Lge	17	10	5	65	22	13.00	-	-	3	-	611	475	14	33.92	2-27	-

BRESSINGTON, A. N.   Gloucestershire

Name: <u>Alastair</u> Nigel Bressington
Role: Left-hand bat, right-arm fast-medium bowler; all-rounder
Born: 28 November 1979, Bristol
Height: 6ft 1in **Weight:** 14st
Nickname: Magic, Bressy
County debut: 2000
1st-Class catches: 3
Place in bowling averages: (2001 96th av. 36.09)
Strike rate: (career 52.75)
Parents: Adrian and Marjorie
Marital status: Single
Family links with cricket: Brother Nathan plays for Gloucestershire 2nd XI
Education: Croft School, Painswick; Marling Grammar School, Stroud; UWIC
Qualifications: 12 GCSEs, 4 A-levels
Cricketers particularly admired: Jack Russell, Ian Botham
Other sports played: Rugby (Gloucestershire Colts; Gloucester RFC U21; Newbury – National Division 3)
Other sports followed: Rugby (Bristol RFC), football (Liverpool FC)

Relaxations: Music, reading
Extras: Played for Gloucestershire Board XI in the NatWest 1999 and 2000. Took wicket with third ball in first-class cricket v Glamorgan at Bristol 2000 and took five wickets in debut match, including that of Matthew Maynard. Captain of Cardiff University CCE 2001 and 2002
Best batting: 17* Gloucestershire v Hampshire, Cheltenham 2001
Best bowling: 4-36 Gloucestershire v Glamorgan, Bristol 2000

2002 Season

	M	Inns	NO	Runs	HS	Avge	100s	50s	Ct	St	O	M	Runs	Wkts	Avge	Best	5wI	10wM
Test																		
All First																		
1-day Int																		
C & G																		
B & H																		
1-day Lge	1	1	0	22	22	22.00	-	-	-	-	2	0	22	0	-		-	-

Career Performances

	M	Inns	NO	Runs	HS	Avge	100s	50s	Ct	St	Balls	Runs	Wkts	Avge	Best	5wI	10wM
Test																	
All First	6	6	3	42	17 *	14.00	-	-	3	-	844	446	16	27.87	4-36	-	-
1-day Int																	
C & G	3	2	0	98	54	49.00	-	1	2	-	150	86	5	17.20	3-21	-	
B & H																	
1-day Lge	4	3	0	42	22	14.00	-	-	2	-	150	118	1	118.00	1-31	-	

10. Which Australian batsman struck the winning runs
in the 1999 World Cup?

Name: <u>Graeme</u> David Bridge
Role: Right-hand bat, left-arm spin bowler
Born: 4 September 1980, Sunderland
Height: 5ft 8in   **Weight:** 12st 7lbs
Nickname: Bridgadino
County debut: 1999
1st-Class 5 w. in innings: 1
1st-Class catches: 10
Place in batting averages: 269th av. 14.15
(2001 252nd av. 11.36)
Place in bowling averages: 108th av. 35.85
(2001 24th av. 22.94)
Strike rate: 70.80 (career 69.57)
Parents: Anne and John
Marital status: Engaged to Leanne
Family links with cricket: 'Dad played
village cricket <u>badly</u>'
Education: Ryhope Primary School;
Southmoor School

Qualifications: 5 GCSEs
Career outside cricket: 'Admin'
Off-season: 'Training. Socialising with N'Gotty'
Overseas tours: England U19 to New Zealand 1998-99, to Malaysia and
(U19 World Cup) Sri Lanka 1999-2000; Durham to Cape Town 2002
Career highlights to date: 'Getting promoted'
Cricket moments to forget: 'Twisting my ankle on TV. Breaking finger'
Cricketers particularly admired:
David Boon, Martin Love
Young players to look out for: 'Bruno N'Gotty, Moot Peng'
Other sports played: Football
Other sports followed: 'Watching the Mackems [Sunderland] up and down the
country'
Injuries: Out for four weeks with a broken finger
Relaxations: 'Horse racing; the dogs'
Extras: Played in U15 World Cup 1996. Represented England U19 in the one-day
series v Australia U19 1999. Played for Durham Board XI in the NatWest 1999 and in
the second round of the C&G 2003, which was played in September 2002. C&G Man
of the Match award on county one-day debut for his 3-44 v Gloucestershire at Bristol
2001. B&H Gold Award for his 37* and 2-43 v Lancashire at Riverside 2002
Opinions on cricket: 'Tea should be longer.'
Best batting: 49 Durham v Derbyshire, Darlington 2002
Best bowling: 6-84 Durham v Hampshire, Riverside 2001

2002 Season

	M	Inns	NO	Runs	HS	Avge	100s	50s	Ct	St	O	M	Runs	Wkts	Avge	Best	5wI	10wM
Test																		
All First	10	15	2	184	49	14.15	-	-	4	-	247.5	61	753	21	35.85	4-50	-	-
1-day Int																		
C & G	3	2	1	33	19	33.00	-	-	-	-	15.2	0	64	2	32.00	2-36	-	
B & H	5	4	3	98	50 *	98.00	-	1	1	-	42	1	187	6	31.16	2-35	-	
1-day Lge	7	6	1	59	24	11.80	-	-	-	-	53	2	205	9	22.77	3-22	-	

Career Performances

	M	Inns	NO	Runs	HS	Avge	100s	50s	Ct	St	Balls	Runs	Wkts	Avge	Best	5wI	10wM
Test																	
All First	18	30	4	320	49	12.30	-	-	10	-	2783	1276	40	31.90	6-84	1	-
1-day Int																	
C & G	8	6	2	63	19	15.75	-	-	1	-	368	276	7	39.42	3-44	-	
B & H	5	4	3	98	50 *	98.00	-	1	1	-	252	187	6	31.16	2-35	-	
1-day Lge	14	11	4	79	24	11.28	-	-	3	-	624	423	15	28.20	3-22	-	

BRIGNULL, D. S.   Leicestershire

Name: David (<u>Dave</u>) Stephen Brignull
Role: Right-hand bat, right-arm medium-fast bowler
Born: 27 November 1981, Forest Gate, London
Height: 6ft 4in **Weight:** 14st 8lbs
Nickname: Briggers
County debut: 2002 (one-day)
Parents: Sharon Penfold and Stephen Brignull
Marital status: Single
Education: Avenue Junior School; Lancaster Boys School; Wyggeston and Queen Elizabeth I College
Qualifications: 11 GCSEs, 3 A-levels
Career outside cricket: Barman
Overseas tours: Leicestershire U19 to South Africa 2000-01
Overseas teams played for: Lafarge CC, Lichtenburg, South Africa 2000-01
Career highlights to date: 'Debut for England U17 and winning ECC Colts Festival'
Cricket moments to forget: 'First game for Leicestershire 2nd XI – got out first ball against Lancashire'

Cricketers particularly admired: Robin Smith, Darren Gough
Young players to look out for: Tom New
Other sports played: Rugby (Wigston RFC), volleyball (for college team that came fourth in nationals)
Other sports followed: Rugby (Leicester Tigers), football (West Ham)
Relaxations: Listening to music; darts, snooker
Extras: Represented England U17 at the ECC Colts Festival in Northern Ireland 1999. Leicestershire Youth Bowler of the Year and U19 Player of the Season 2001. Hat-trick against Derbyshire U19. Played for Leicestershire Board XI in the NatWest 1999 and the C&G 2001

2002 Season

	M	Inns	NO	Runs	HS	Avge	100s	50s	Ct	St	O	M	Runs	Wkts	Avge	Best	5wI	10wM
Test																		
All First																		
1-day Int																		
C & G																		
B & H																		
1-day Lge	1	1	0	1	1	1.00	-	-	-	-	9	0	52	2	26.00	2-52	-	

Career Performances

	M	Inns	NO	Runs	HS	Avge	100s	50s	Ct	St	Balls	Runs	Wkts	Avge	Best	5wI	10wM
Test																	
All First																	
1-day Int																	
C & G	2	2	1	15	9 *	15.00	-	-	1	-	112	85	4	21.25	2-35	-	
B & H																	
1-day Lge	1	1	0	1	1	1.00	-	-	-	-	54	52	2	26.00	2-52	-	

BROPHY, G. L.   Northamptonshire

Name: <u>Gerard</u> Louis Brophy
Role: Right-hand bat, wicket-keeper
Born: 26 November 1975, Welkom, South Africa
Height: 5ft 11in **Weight:** 12st
Nickname: Scuba
County debut: 2002
1st-Class 50s: 6
1st-Class 100s: 2
1st-Class catches: 78
1st-Class stumpings: 5
Parents: Gerard and Trish
Marital status: Single

Education: Christian Brothers College, Boksburg; Wits Technikon (both South Africa)
Qualifications: Marketing Diploma, Level 2 coach
Off-season: 'Coaching, training'
Overseas tours: South Africa U17 to England 1993; South African Academy to Zimbabwe, Kenya
Overseas teams played for: Gauteng; Free State
Career highlights to date: 'Captaincy of Free State 2000-01. First dismissal [in collaboration] with Allan Donald'
Cricket moments to forget: 'Messing up a live TV interview'
Cricket superstitions: 'Right pad on first and right glove on first'
Cricketers particularly admired: Ray Jennings, Ian Healy, Allan Donald, Hansie Cronje
Young players to look out for: Jacques Rudolph
Other sports played: Golf, rugby
Other sports followed: Golf, rugby
Injuries: Broken rib – no time off required
Relaxations: 'Fishing, travelling, braais, scuba diving'
Extras: Captained South Africa U17. Played for Ireland in the NatWest 2000. Scored maiden Championship century (110) v Glamorgan at Cardiff 2002. Parents live in Brisbane, Australia. Holds a British passport and is not considered an overseas player
Best batting: 185 South African Academy v President's XI, Harare 1999-2000

2002 Season

	M	Inns	NO	Runs	HS	Avge	100s	50s	Ct	St	O	M	Runs	Wkts	Avge	Best	5wI	10wM
Test																		
All First	4	8	3	246	110	49.20	1	1	5	-								
1-day Int																		
C & G																		
B & H																		
1-day Lge	4	4	0	61	54	15.25	-	1	2	-								

Career Performances

	M	Inns	NO	Runs	HS	Avge	100s	50s	Ct	St	Balls	Runs	Wkts	Avge	Best	5wl	10wM
Test																	
All First	27	46	6	1276	185	31.90	2	6	78	5							
1-day Int																	
C & G	1	1	0	15	15	15.00	-	-	-	-							
B & H																	
1-day Lge	4	4	0	61	54	15.25	-	1	2	-							

BROWN, A. D. Surrey

Name: Alistair Duncan Brown
Role: Right-hand bat, off-spin bowler, occasional wicket-keeper
Born: 11 February 1970, Beckenham
Height: 5ft 10in **Weight:** 12st 8lbs
Nickname: Lordy
County debut: 1992
County cap: 1994
Benefit: 2002
One-Day Internationals: 15
1000 runs in a season: 6
1st-Class 50s: 40
1st-Class 100s: 30
1st-Class 200s: 2
1st-Class catches: 180
1st-Class stumpings: 1
One-Day 100s: 14
One-Day 200s: 2
Place in batting averages: 34th av. 50.45 (2001 112th av. 31.50)
Strike rate: (career 816.00)
Parents: Robert and Ann
Wife and date of marriage: Sarah, 10 October 1998
Children: Max Charles, 9 March 2001
Family links with cricket: Father played for Surrey Young Amateurs in the 1950s
Education: Cumnor House School; Caterham School
Qualifications: 5 O-levels, NCA Senior Coach
Overseas tours: England VI to Singapore 1993, 1994, 1995, to Hong Kong 1997; England to Sharjah (Champions Trophy) 1997-98, to Bangladesh (Wills International Cup) 1998-99
Overseas teams played for: North Perth, Western Australia 1989-90
Cricketers particularly admired: Ian Botham, Viv Richards

Other sports played: Golf, football, snooker, 'winner of the Lanzarote Open Pool Championship 1990'

Other sports followed: Football (West Ham United), rugby league (London Broncos)

Extras: Scored three of the eight fastest centuries of the 1992 season (71, 78 & 79 balls). Awarded Man of the Match for his 118 against India in the third One-Day International at Old Trafford 1996. Recorded the highest-ever score in the Sunday League with 203 off 119 balls against Hampshire at Guildford in 1997 and received an individual award at the PCA Dinner for that achievement. Scored 72-ball century v Northamptonshire at The Oval to become joint winner (with Carl Hooper) of the EDS Walter Lawrence Trophy for the fastest first-class 100 of the 1998 season. Scored 31-ball 50 v South Africa in the Texaco Trophy match at Headingley 1998, the fastest 50 in the history of the Texaco Trophy. B&H Gold Award for his 108* in the quarter-final v Sussex at Hove 2001. Surrey CCC Batsman of the Season Award 2001. Scored century (177) v Sussex at The Oval 2002, in the process sharing with Nadeem Shahid (150) in a record fifth-wicket partnership for Surrey v Sussex (262). B&H Gold Award for his 58-ball 73 v Kent at The Oval 2002. C&G Man of the Match award for his 160-ball 268 out of 438-5 v Glamorgan at The Oval 2002; it set a new record for the highest individual score in professional one-day cricket worldwide (overtaking Graeme Pollock's 222 for Eastern Province v Border in 1974) and Brown also became the first batsman to have scored two double centuries in one-day cricket. Scored 107 v Leics at The Oval 2002, in the process sharing with Adam Hollioake (208) in a new record fifth-wicket partnership for Surrey in matches against Leicestershire (282)

Best batting: 295* Surrey v Leicestershire, Oakham School 2000

Best bowling: 1-56 Surrey v Lancashire, Old Trafford 2000

2002 Season

	M	Inns	NO	Runs	HS	Avge	100s	50s	Ct	St	O	M	Runs	Wkts	Avge	Best	5wI	10wM
Test																		
All First	16	26	2	1211	188	50.45	5	3	18	-	3	0	7	0	-	-	-	-
1-day Int																		
C & G	4	4	0	313	268	78.25	1	-	1	-								
B & H	5	5	0	194	97	38.80	-	2	1	-								
1-day Lge	15	15	0	392	94	26.13	-	4	7	-								

Career Performances

	M	Inns	NO	Runs	HS	Avge	100s	50s	Ct	St	Balls	Runs	Wkts	Avge	Best	5wI	10wM
Test																	
All First	170	267	26	10567	295 *	43.84	32	40	180	1	816	432	1	432.00	1-56	-	-
1-day Int	15	15	0	348	118	23.20	1	1	4	-							
C & G	31	27	2	865	268	34.60	1	3	9	-	6	9	0	-	-	-	-
B & H	54	53	7	1695	117 *	36.84	2	8	15	-							
1-day Lge	179	174	5	5318	203	31.46	12	21	59	-	269	252	8	31.50	3-39	-	

BROWN, D. R.   Warwickshire

Name: Douglas (<u>Dougie</u>) Robert Brown
Role: Right-hand bat, right-arm
fast-medium bowler
Born: 29 October 1969, Stirling, Scotland
Height: 6ft 2in **Weight:** 14st 7lbs
Nickname: Hoots
County debut: 1992
County cap: 1995
One-Day Internationals: 9
50 wickets in a season: 3
1st-Class 50s: 31
1st-Class 100s: 2
1st-Class 200s: 1
1st-Class 5 w. in innings: 15
1st-Class 10 w. in match: 4
1st-Class catches: 93
One-Day 5 w. in innings: 1
Place in batting averages: 156th av. 27.95
(2001 73rd av. 39.17)
Place in bowling averages: 86th av. 33.00 (2001 63rd av. 30.57)
Strike rate: 56.96 (career 52.10)
Parents: Alastair and Janette
Wife and date of marriage: Brenda, 2 October 1993
Children: Lauren, 14 September 1998
Family links with cricket: 'Both grandads played a bit'
Education: St John's Primary, Alloa; Alloa Academy; West London Institute of Higher
Education (Borough Road College)
Qualifications: 9 O-Grades, 5 Higher Grades, BEd (Hons) Physical Education,
ECB Level III coach
Career outside cricket: PE teacher
Off-season: Coach to Namibia national team
Overseas tours: Scotland XI to Pakistan 1988-89; England VI to Hong Kong 1997,
2001; England A to Kenya and Sri Lanka 1997-98; England to Sharjah (Champions
Trophy) 1997-98, to West Indies 1997-98 (one-day series), to Bangladesh (Wills
International Cup) 1998
Overseas teams played for: Primrose, Cape Town 1992-93; Vredenburg Saldhana,
Cape Town 1993-94; Eastern Suburbs, Wellington 1995-96; Wellington, New Zealand
1995-96
Career highlights to date: 'Playing in a Lord's final for the first time, in 1995
v Northants'
Cricketers particularly admired: Dermot Reeve, 'and as I play more, the likes of
Devon Malcolm and Phillip DeFreitas, who keep running in each day'

Young players to look out for: Ian Bell 'who looks the genuine article'
Other sports played: Golf
Other sports followed: Football (Alloa Athletic), 'most sports'
Relaxations: Sport, music
Extras: Played football at Hampden Park for Scotland U18. Has played first-class and B&H cricket for Scotland. Scored 1118 runs and took 109 wickets in all first-team county cricket 1997. His maiden first-class century (142) v Northamptonshire at Edgbaston on 15 April 1999 is the earliest Championship 100 in an English season. Scored maiden first-class double century v Sussex at Hove 2000 (203; the highest score recorded by a Warwickshire No. 7), during which he shared in a record Warwickshire partnership for the seventh wicket (289 with Ashley Giles). Took 400th first-class wicket (Mark Davis) v Sussex at Hove 2002. Vice-captain of Warwickshire in 2002. Warwickshire All-rounder of the Year 2002
Best batting: 203 Warwickshire v Sussex, Hove 2000
Best bowling: 8-89 First-Class Counties XI v Pakistan A, Chelmsford 1997

2002 Season

	M	Inns	NO	Runs	HS	Avge	100s	50s	Ct	St	O	M	Runs	Wkts	Avge	Best	5wI	10wM
Test																		
All First	16	28	4	671	79 *	27.95	-	3	9	-	493.4	75	1716	52	33.00	7-110	2	-
1-day Int																		
C & G	2	2	0	8	4	4.00	-	-	2	-	17.4	1	107	3	35.66	2-31	-	
B & H	8	7	1	127	42	21.16	-	-	2	-	74	4	295	16	18.43	3-15	-	
1-day Lge	15	11	1	263	82 *	26.30	-	2	1	-	111.2	7	551	19	29.00	3-43	-	

Career Performances

	M	Inns	NO	Runs	HS	Avge	100s	50s	Ct	St	Balls	Runs	Wkts	Avge	Best	5wI	10wM
Test																	
All First	146	222	29	5482	203	28.40	3	31	93	-	20893	11052	401	27.56	8-89	15	4
1-day Int	9	8	4	99	21	24.75	-	-	1	-	324	305	7	43.57	2-28	-	
C & G	24	23	3	437	70	21.85	-	4	4	-	1154	805	23	35.00	2-18	-	
B & H	42	33	4	736	62	25.37	-	4	11	-	2081	1438	53	27.13	5-31	1	
1-day Lge	133	109	15	2019	82 *	21.47	-	11	35	-	4806	3640	152	23.94	4-42	-	

11. Which South African Test fast bowler played for Kent in 1990?

BROWN, J. F.   Northamptonshire

Name: <u>Jason</u> Fred Brown
Role: Right-hand bat, off-spin bowler
Born: 10 October 1974,
Newcastle-under-Lyme
Height: 6ft   **Weight:** 13st
Nickname: Cheese, Fish, Brownie
County debut: 1996
County cap: 2000
50 wickets in a season: 1
1st-Class 5 w. in innings: 9
1st-Class 10 w. in match: 3
1st-Class catches: 11
Place in batting averages: 285th av. 10.66
(2001 270th av. 8.00)
Place in bowling averages: 126th av. 40.64
(2001 134th av. 50.25)
Strike rate: 75.60 (career 65.91)
Parents: Peter and Cynthia
Wife and date of marriage: Sam, 26
September 1998
Education: St Joseph's RC School, Stoke-on-Trent; St Margaret Ward RC School,
Stoke-on-Trent
Qualifications: 9 GCSEs, Level 1 coaching qualification
Overseas tours: Kidsgrove League U18 to Australia 1990; Northants CCC to
Zimbabwe 1998, to Grenada 2000; England A to West Indies 2000-01; England
to Sri Lanka 2000-01
Overseas teams played for: North East Valley, Dunedin, New Zealand 1996-97
Cricketers particularly admired: John Emburey, Carl Hooper
Young players to look out for: Mark Powell
Other sports played: Golf
Other sports followed: Football (Port Vale)
Relaxations: 'Reading, listening to music, walking my dog Spike'
Extras: Represented Staffordshire at all junior levels and in Minor Counties. Once took
10-16 in a Kidsgrove League game against Haslington U18 playing for Sandyford U18.
Played for Staffordshire in the NatWest 1995. Took 100th first-class wicket in 23rd
match, v Sussex at Northampton 2000, going on to take his 50th wicket of the season in
the same game, only his seventh of the summer
Best batting: 35* Northamptonshire v Leicestershire, Northampton 2001
Best bowling: 7-78 Northamptonshire v Sussex, Northampton 2000

2002 Season

	M	Inns	NO	Runs	HS	Avge	100s	50s	Ct	St	O	M	Runs	Wkts	Avge	Best	5wl	10wM
Test																		
All First	8	11	5	64	19	10.66	-	-	2	-	352.5	76	1138	28	40.64	4-88	-	-
1-day Int																		
C & G	2	2	1	3	3	3.00	-	-	-	-	20	5	77	2	38.50	2-20	-	
B & H																		
1-day Lge	13	4	3	17	16	17.00	-	-	1	-	95.4	7	406	13	31.23	3-30	-	

Career Performances

	M	Inns	NO	Runs	HS	Avge	100s	50s	Ct	St	Balls	Runs	Wkts	Avge	Best	5wl	10wM
Test																	
All First	48	61	27	203	35 *	5.97	-	-	11	-	11996	5571	182	30.60	7-78	9	3
1-day Int																	
C & G	8	5	4	6	3	6.00	-	-	-	-	492	365	9	40.55	3-35	-	
B & H	3	2	2	10	5 *	-	-	-	-	-	156	125	0	-	-	-	
1-day Lge	41	16	8	39 , 16		4.87	-	-	8	-	1835	1271	43	29.55	4-26	-	

BROWN, M. J. Middlesex

Name: <u>Michael</u> James Brown
Role: Right-hand bat, wicket-keeper
Born: 9 February 1980, Burnley
Height: 6ft **Weight:** 11st 9lbs
Nickname: Weasel, Crime, Browny
County debut: 1999
1st-Class 50s: 3
1st-Class catches: 10
Place in batting averages: 191st av. 24.16
(2001 157th av. 24.62)
Parents: Peter and Valerie
Marital status: Single
Family links with cricket: Father played for
Burnley CC (Lancashire League) and some
games for Lancashire 2nd XI in 1970s. Also
played for Southgate CC 1976-78, winning
National Club Knockout in 1977. Brother
David plays for Lancashire U17 and U19
Education: Rosehill Junior School, Burnley; Queen Elizabeth's Grammar School,
Blackburn; Durham University
Qualifications: 10 GCSEs, 4 A-levels, 2.1 Economics/Politics
Off-season: 'Perth – Claremont-Nedlands CC'

Overseas teams played for: Western Province CC, Cape Town 1998-99; Claremont-Nedlands CC, Perth 2002-03

Career highlights to date: 'Watching James Foster slogsweep Mushtaq Ahmed to point, British Universities v Pakistan, May 2001; team bowled out for 74 by Wasim and Waqar – fantastic experience'

Cricket moments to forget: 'Any time I bag them'

Cricketers particularly admired: Dale Benkenstein, Mike Atherton, Glenn McGrath, James Foster

Young players to look out for: Ravi Bopara, David Brown

Other sports played: Football ('town team')

Other sports followed: Football (Burnley FC)

Extras: Lancashire League Under-25 Batsman of the Season 1997, 1998. Represented Lancashire Schools at U11, U13, U15 and U17 level 1989-97. Represented Lancashire U19 Federation 1997-98. Played for Lancashire 2nd XI 1997-98. Represented ECB U19 A v Pakistan U19 in two one-day games 1998. Played for Durham University CCE 2001 and 2002, scoring two fifties (55 and 60*) for DUCCE v Worcestershire at Worcester 2001. Represented British Universities 2001 and v Sri Lankans at Northampton and v West Indies A (50-over match) at The Parks 2002. 'Was at non-striker's end as five wickets fell in one over, Middlesex 2nd XI v Glamorgan 2nd XI, July 2001'

Opinions on cricket: 'Too many passport grabbers. Any chance of some good grass nets?'

Best batting: 60* Durham UCCE v Worcestershire, Worcester 2001

2002 Season

	M	Inns	NO	Runs	HS	Avge	100s	50s	Ct	St	O	M	Runs	Wkts	Avge	Best	5wI	10wM
Test																		
All First	4	6	0	145	57	24.16	-	1	6	-								
1-day Int																		
C & G																		
B & H																		
1-day Lge	1	1	0	18	18	18.00	-	-	-	-								

Career Performances

	M	Inns	NO	Runs	HS	Avge	100s	50s	Ct	St	Balls	Runs	Wkts	Avge	Best	5wI	10wM
Test																	
All First	11	18	3	390	60 *	26.00	-	3	10	-							
1-day Int																	
C & G																	
B & H																	
1-day Lge	1	1	0	18	18	18.00	-	-	-	-							

BROWN, S. J. E.   Durham

Name: <u>Simon</u> John Emmerson Brown
Role: Right-hand bat, left-arm medium-fast bowler, gully fielder
Born: 29 June 1969, Cleadon Village, Sunderland
Height: 6ft 3in **Weight:** 13st
Nickname: Chubby
County debut: 1987 (Northamptonshire), 1992 (Durham)
County cap: 1998 (Durham)
Benefit: 2001 (Durham)
Test debut: 1996
Tests: 1
50 wickets in a season: 7
1st-Class 50s: 2
1st-Class 5 w. in innings: 36
1st-Class 10 w. in match: 2
1st-Class catches: 42
One-Day 5 w. in innings: 2
Place in bowling averages: (2001 29th av. 23.78)
Strike rate: 56.00 (career 52.24)
Parents: Ernest and Doreen
Marital status: Single

Education: Cleadon Village Junior School; Boldon Comprehensive, Tyne & Wear; South Tyneside Marine and Technical College
Qualifications: 6 O-levels, qualified electrician
Career outside cricket: Electrician
Overseas tours: England YC to Sri Lanka 1986-87, to Australia (U19 World Cup) 1987-88; MCC to Bahrain 1994-95
Overseas teams played for: Marist, Christchurch, New Zealand
Cricketers particularly admired: John Lever, Ian Botham, Dennis Lillee
Other sports played: Golf
Relaxations: Playing golf
Extras: Offered basketball scholarship in America. Durham Supporters' Player of the Year 1992. Durham Player of the Year 1994. Took his 500th first-class wicket (Steve Stubbings caught by Martin Speight) v Derbyshire at Darlington 2000. Retired at the end of the 2002 season
Best batting: 69 Durham v Leicestershire, Durham University 1994
Best bowling: 7-51 Durham v Lancashire, Riverside 2000

2002 Season

	M	Inns	NO	Runs	HS	Avge	100s	50s	Ct	St	O	M	Runs	Wkts	Avge	Best	5wI	10wM
Test																		
All First	1	0	0	0	0	-	-	-	-	-	18.4	3	65	2	32.50	2-65	-	-
1-day Int																		
C & G																		
B & H																		
1-day Lge																		

Career Performances

	M	Inns	NO	Runs	HS	Avge	100s	50s	Ct	St	Balls	Runs	Wkts	Avge	Best	5wI	10wM
Test	1	2	1	11	10 *	11.00	-	-	1	-	198	138	2	69.00	1-60	-	-
All First	159	221	72	1796	69	12.05	-	2	42	-	28735	15800	550	28.72	7-51	36	2
1-day Int																	
C & G	12	7	3	20	8	5.00	-	-	1	-	748	503	19	26.47	5-22	1	
B & H	22	9	5	41	12	10.25	-	-	5	-	1199	726	30	24.20	6-30	1	
1-day Lge	77	36	12	156	18	6.50	-	-	17	-	3297	2746	81	33.90	4-20	-	

BRUNNSCHWEILER, I.   Hampshire

Name: Iain Brunnschweiler
Role: Right-hand bat, wicket-keeper
Born: 10 December 1979, Southampton
Height: 6ft **Weight:** 12st 7lbs
Nickname: Bruno, Brown, Brunchy
County debut: 2000
1st-Class catches: 9
Parents: Arthur and Joan
Marital status: Single
Family links with cricket: 'They mostly dislike it!'
Education: Highfield C of E; King Edward VI School, Southampton
Qualifications: 9 GCSEs, 3 A-levels, ECB Level 1 cricket coaching award, UEFA Part B football coaching award
Career outside cricket: Journalism for local paper (*Southern Daily Echo*)
Off-season: 'Writing for the sportsdesk of the *Daily Echo*, then training in Sydney for three months after Christmas'
Overseas tours: England U17 to Bermuda 1997; King Edward VI School to South Africa 1998; Hampshire CCC to Cape Town 2001

Overseas teams played for: Belmont DCC, Newcastle, NSW 1998-99; Nullamara, Perth 2000-01; Perth CC 2001-02
Career highlights to date: 'Hitting the winning runs for Hampshire against Australia in 2001'
Cricket moments to forget: 'Losing the U17 Texaco Trophy final against Northants in 1997 (and getting a golden duck)'
Cricketers particularly admired: Robin Smith, Adi Aymes, Jack Russell, Ian Healy
Young players to look out for: James Tomlinson, Ben Adams, Chris Marlow, Fergus Haycock
Other sports played: Football (Southampton Youth), hockey, rugby
Other sports followed: Football (Southampton FC)
Relaxations: 'Music; going out with my friends and enjoying good food and liquid'
Extras: Played for Hampshire Board XI in the second round of the C&G 2003, which was played in September 2002. 'Longest surname in English county cricket?'
Opinions on cricket: 'People are too opinionated.'
Best batting: 19 Hampshire v New Zealand A, Portsmouth 2000

2002 Season

	M	Inns	NO	Runs	HS	Avge	100s	50s	Ct	St	O	M	Runs	Wkts	Avge	Best	5wl	10wM
Test																		
All First																		
1-day Int																		
C & G	1	1	0	37	37	37.00	-	-	2	-								
B & H																		
1-day Lge	2	1	0	0	0	0.00	-	-	3	-								

Career Performances

	M	Inns	NO	Runs	HS	Avge	100s	50s	Ct	St	Balls	Runs	Wkts	Avge	Best	5wl	10wM
Test																	
All First	2	4	1	33	19	11.00	-	-	9	-							
1-day Int																	
C & G	1	1	0	37	37	37.00	-	-	2	-							
B & H																	
1-day Lge	2	1	0	0	0	0.00	-	-	3	-							

12. Which two Pakistan Test players guested for Somerset against the Australians at Taunton in 2001?

BRYANT, J. D. C. Somerset

Name: James Douglas Campbell Bryant
Role: Right-hand bat, right-arm
medium bowler
Born: 4 February 1976, Durban, South Africa
Height: 6ft **Weight:** 11st 10lbs
Nickname: Ginga
County debut: No first-team appearance
1st-Class 50s: 13
1st-Class 100s: 5
1st-Class catches: 36
Strike rate: (career 32.00)
Parents: Nick and Helen
Marital status: Single
Education: Maritzburg College; University
of Port Elizabeth
Qualifications: BComm (Hons) Business
Management, Level 2 coach
Career outside cricket: Entrepreneur
Overseas tours: South African Academy to
Ireland and Scotland 1999; South Africa A to West Indies 2000-01
Overseas teams played for: Eastern Province 1996-97 – 2002-03
Career highlights to date: '234* v North West and achieving South African highest
first-class batting partnership – 441'
Other sports played: Golf, tennis, squash
Other sports followed: Rugby (Natal Sharks)
Relaxations: 'Reading, watersports, golf'
Extras: Is a British passport holder and is not considered an overseas player
Best batting: 149 Eastern Province v Northerns, Port Elizabeth 1999-2000
Best bowling: 1-22 Eastern Province B v North West, Fochville 1998-99
Stop press: Scored career-best 234* v North West at Potchefstroom in the SuperSport
Series 2002-03, in the process sharing with Carl Bradfield (196) in a new record
partnership for any wicket in South African domestic first-class cricket (441)

---

13. For which county did Sherwin Campbell play in 1996?

Career Performances

	M	Inns	NO	Runs	HS	Avge	100s	50s	Ct	St	Balls	Runs	Wkts	Avge	Best	5wI	10wM
Test																	
All First	44	81	11	2535	149	36.21	5	13	36	-	32	29	1	29.00	1-22	-	-
1-day Int																	
C & G																	
B & H																	
1-day Lge																	

BULBECK, M. P. L. Somerset

Name: <u>Matthew</u> Paul Leonard Bulbeck
Role: Left-hand bat, left-arm medium-fast bowler
Born: 8 November 1979, Taunton
Height: 6ft 4in **Weight:** 15st
Nickname: Bully
County debut: 1998
County cap: 2002
50 wickets in a season: 2
1st-Class 50s: 2
1st-Class 5 w. in innings: 4
1st-Class 10 w. in match: 1
1st-Class catches: 9
One-Day 5 w. in innings: 1
Place in batting averages: 242nd av. 17.95
Place in bowling averages: 90th av. 33.44
Strike rate: 55.24 (career 49.78)
Parents: Paul and Carolyn
Marital status: Girlfriend Helen
Family links with cricket: 'Dad plays for local club'
Education: Bishops Hull Primary School; Castle School; Taunton School; Richard Huish College
Qualifications: 8 GCSEs, Level 1 coaching
Off-season: 'Training with "the Sarge"'
Overseas tours: West of England U15 to West Indies; Somerset U16 to South Africa; England U19 to New Zealand 1998-99; Somerset to Cape Town 1999-2000
Overseas teams played for: Applecross CC, Perth 2002
Career highlights to date: 'Playing in the C&G semi-final v Kent 2002'
Cricket moments to forget: 'Whole of 2001'

Cricket superstitions: 'When walking back to my mark I always turn to my right'
Cricketers particularly admired: Wasim Akram, Graham Rose
Young players to look out for: Adam Champion, James Champion, James Webber
Other sports played: Football, golf (6 handicap)
Other sports followed: Football (Manchester United), golf
Relaxations: 'Spending time with girlfriend; playing golf with Blackie'
Extras: Represented England U19 in one-day and 'Test' series v Australia U19 1999.
NBC Denis Compton Award 1999. Took 58 first-class wickets in 2002 in first full
season after recovery from serious back injury. Awarded Somerset cap 2002
Opinions on cricket: 'Great game!'
Best batting: 76* Somerset v Durham, Riverside 1999
Best bowling: 6-93 Somerset v Lancashire, Taunton 2002

2002 Season

	M	Inns	NO	Runs	HS	Avge	100s	50s	Ct	St	O	M	Runs	Wkts	Avge	Best	5wI	10wM
Test																		
All First	16	27	7	359	53 *	17.95	-	1	3	-	534	93	1940	58	33.44	6-93	1	-
1-day Int																		
C & G	4	2	2	4	4 *	-	-	-	2	-	29	1	160	3	53.33	2-16	-	
B & H	4	3	0	22	14	7.33	-	-	1	-	32	0	168	2	84.00	1-38	-	
1-day Lge	11	6	2	71	24 *	17.75	-	-	-	-	74	5	378	16	23.62	4-39	-	

Career Performances

	M	Inns	NO	Runs	HS	Avge	100s	50s	Ct	St	Balls	Runs	Wkts	Avge	Best	5wI	10wM
Test																	
All First	47	62	24	821	76 *	21.60	-	2	9	-	7568	4615	152	30.36	6-93	4	1
1-day Int																	
C & G	5	2	2	4	4 *	-	-	-	2	-	229	178	8	22.25	5-18	1	
B & H	5	4	1	23	14	7.66	-	-	1	-	234	195	2	97.50	1-38	-	
1-day Lge	20	9	2	78	24 *	11.14	-	-	2	-	720	618	21	29.42	4-39	-	

BURNS, M.   Somerset

Name: Michael Burns
Role: Right-hand bat, right-arm medium bowler, county captain
Born: 6 February 1969, Barrow-in-Furness
Height: 6ft **Weight:** 14st
Nickname: George, Ashley, Butch, Onslow
County debut: 1991 (Warwickshire), 1997 (Somerset)
County cap: 1999 (Somerset)
1000 runs in a season: 1
1st-Class 50s: 37
1st-Class 100s: 4

1st-Class 200s: 1
1st-Class 5 w. in innings: 1
1st-Class catches: 106
1st-Class stumpings: 7
One-Day 100s: 2
Place in batting averages: 95th av. 37.39
(2001 85th av. 35.59)
Place in bowling averages: 125th av. 40.36
(2001 130th av. 44.91)
Strike rate: 55.45 (career 67.69)
Parents: Robert and Linda, stepfather Stan
Wife and date of marriage: Carolyn,
9 October 1994
Children: Elizabeth, 12 January 1997;
Adam, 3 August 2000
Family links with cricket: 'Grandfather was
a great back-garden bowler'
Education: Walney Comprehensive; Barrow
College of Further Education
Qualifications: 'Few CSEs, couple of GCEs', qualified fitter at VSEL in Barrow,
coaching award
Career outside cricket: 'Open to offers'
Off-season: 'Level III coaching course; some academy coaching. Hopefully some
work with Andy Brassington at Finders Keepers Marketing'
Overseas teams played for: Gill College, South Africa 1991-92; Motueka, Nelson,
New Zealand 1992-93; Alex Sports Club, Harare 1993-94; Lindisfarne, Tasmania
1999-2000
Career highlights to date: '2001 Cheltenham & Gloucester final'
Cricket moments to forget: 'Losing the 1999 NatWest final to Gloucestershire'
Cricket superstitions: 'None'
Cricketers particularly admired: Marcus Trescothick
Young players to look out for: Adam Burns ('if he's no good at golf'), Arul Suppiah
Other sports played: Rugby league ('had trials for Barrow RLFC and Carlisle
RLFC'), golf
Other sports followed: Football (Liverpool FC), rugby league (Walney Central
ARLFC)
Injuries: Out for three one-day matches with bruised cartilage and bone in left knee
Relaxations: TV, family, cinema, Indian food
Extras: Played for Cumberland 1989-90. Player of the Tournament at Benson and
Hedges Thailand International Cricket Sixes in 1989. Left Warwickshire and joined
Somerset for the 1997 season. Scored club record of 217 for Lindisfarne in 1999-2000
season. Scored 160 v Oxford Universities at Taunton on 7 April 2000, setting new
record for the earliest ever 100 in a first-class cricket season in this country. His 221 v
Yorkshire at Bath in 2001 set a new record for the highest score by a Somerset pl~
at the ground (overtaking Mark Lathwell's 206 v Surrey in 1994) and for the '

score by a Somerset player against Yorkshire (overtaking Viv Richards' 217 at Harrogate in 1975). C&G Man of the Match award for his 83-ball 71 in the quarter-final v Kent at Canterbury 2001. Had four scores of between 95 and 100 in Championship in 2002; passed 1000 runs in a season for the first time during his innings of 32 v Lancashire at Taunton 2002. Appointed captain of Somerset for 2003

Opinions on cricket: 'Two up/two down in both forms of the game. Prize money needs to be reviewed. Nothing for third in first division and prize money for second in the second is hardly fair.'

Best batting: 221 Somerset v Yorkshire, Bath 2001
Best bowling: 6-54 Somerset v Leicestershire, Taunton 2001

2002 Season

	M	Inns	NO	Runs	HS	Avge	100s	50s	Ct	St	O	M	Runs	Wkts	Avge	Best	5wl	10wM
Test																		
All First	16	30	2	1047	99	37.39	-	9	14	-	101.4	15	444	11	40.36	3-54	-	-
1-day Int																		
C & G	5	5	0	152	72	30.40	-	1	1	-	19	0	123	3	41.00	2-53	-	
B & H	4	4	0	91	61	22.75	-	1	2	-	4	0	27	2	13.50	2-27	-	
1-day Lge	12	12	1	330	54 *	30.00	-	4	8	-	25	0	150	6	25.00	3-22	-	

Career Performances

	M	Inns	NO	Runs	HS	Avge	100s	50s	Ct	St	Balls	Runs	Wkts	Avge	Best	5wl	10wM
Test																	
All First	111	177	8	5298	221	31.34	5	37	106	7	3317	2074	49	42.32	6-54	1	-
1-day Int																	
C & G	23	23	3	592	84 *	29.60	-	4	8	-	300	273	7	39.00	2-30	-	
B & H	30	27	2	698	95	27.92	-	6	9	2	230	216	10	21.60	3-18	-	
1-day Lge	120	112	12	2374	115 *	23.74	2	14	57	9	1035	963	34	28.32	4-39	-	

BURNS, N. D. Leicestershire

Name: <u>Neil</u> David Burns
Role: Left-hand bat, wicket-keeper
Born: 19 September 1965, Chelmsford
Height: 5ft 10in **Weight:** 12st
Nickname: Burnsie, Ern, George
County debut: 1986 (Essex), 1987 (Somerset), 2000 (Leicestershire)
County cap: 1987 (Somerset), 2001 (Leicestershire)
50 dismissals in a season: 5
1st-Class 50s: 40
1st-Class 100s: 7
1st-Class catches: 478
1st-Class stumpings: 38

Place in batting averages: 122nd av. 32.72 (2001 64th av. 41.04)

Parents: Roy and Marie

Family links with cricket: Father played club cricket for Finchley CC; brother Ian captained Essex U19

Education: Mildmay Junior; Moulsham High School

Qualifications: 6 O-levels, advanced cricket coach

Career outside cricket: Neil Burns Company Ltd (NBC), specialising in sports marketing and PR

Overseas tours: England YC to West Indies 1984-85; Essex to Barbados 1985-86; Christians in Sport to India 1989-90

Overseas teams played for: Northerns/Goodwood, Cape Town 1984-87, 1992; Western Province B 1985-86

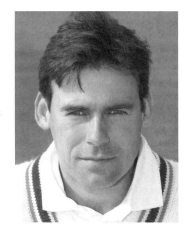

Cricketers particularly admired: Alan Knott, Bob Taylor, Rod Marsh, Graham Gooch, Allan Border, Graeme Pollock, David Gower

Other sports followed: Most sports but particularly soccer (West Ham)

Relaxations: Watching/playing sport, reading newspapers, relaxing at home

Extras: Former schoolboy footballer with Tottenham Hotspur and Orient. Once took a hat-trick of stumpings off Nasser Hussain's leg-breaks for Essex U11 v Berkshire U11. Made eight stumpings in match v Kent 2nd XI at Dartford in 1984. Joined Somerset in 1987 after spending four years at Essex. Scored maiden first-class century (100*) v former county at Chelmsford 1987. Equalled Steve Rhodes's one-day record of four stumpings in an innings, v Kent in Sunday League at Taunton 1991. Retired in 1994. Has also played for Bucks and been their director of cricket. Joined Leicestershire for 2000. Took five catches against his former club Somerset in their first innings at Leicester 2000. Took a Leicestershire record seven catches in an innings against his former club Somerset at Leicester 2001. Scored a 96-ball 90* v Northamptonshire at Leicester in the Norwich Union League 2001, in the process sharing in a Leicestershire competition-record eighth-wicket partnership (116) with Phillip DeFreitas. Scored century (111) then took six first innings catches v Glamorgan at Leicester 2001. Scored 834 runs (av. 41.70) and made 67 dismissals in the Championship 2001, and was the leading first-class wicket-keeper overall in 2001 with 68 dismissals. Leicestershire Player of the Year 2001. Leading wicket-keeper in first division of the Championship 2002 (second overall) with 63 dismissals; also scored 720 Championship runs (av. 32.72). Released by Leicestershire at the end of the 2002 season

Best batting: 166 Somerset v Gloucestershire, Taunton 1990

2002 Season

	M	Inns	NO	Runs	HS	Avge	100s	50s	Ct	St	O	M	Runs	Wkts	Avge	Best	5wI	10wM
Test																		
All First	16	24	2	720	101	32.72	1	5	61	2								
1-day Int																		
C & G	2	2	0	24	18	12.00	-	-	-	3								
B & H	6	5	2	79	44 *	26.33	-	-	4	1								
1-day Lge	16	15	2	308	40	23.69	-	-	15	5								

Career Performances

	M	Inns	NO	Runs	HS	Avge	100s	50s	Ct	St	Balls	Runs	Wkts	Avge	Best	5wI	10wM
Test																	
All First	205	307	65	7376	166	30.47	7	40	478	38	3	8	0	-	-	-	-
1-day Int																	
C & G	29	22	3	277	51	14.57	-	1	34	10							
B & H	47	39	13	630	51	24.23	-	1	41	10							
1-day Lge	151	119	28	1845	90 *	20.27	-	6	160	28							

BUTCHER, G. P. Surrey

Name: <u>Gary</u> Paul Butcher
Role: Right-hand middle-order bat,
right-arm medium bowler
Born: 11 March 1975, Clapham,
London
Height: 5ft 9in **Weight:** 12st
Nickname: Butch, Uncle Bib, Robert,
'the Iron and Steel Business'
County debut: 1994 (Glamorgan),
1999 (Surrey)
1st-Class 50s: 12
1st-Class 100s: 1
1st-Class 5 w. in innings: 2
1st-Class catches: 19
Place in batting averages: (2001 153rd
av. 25.00)
Strike rate: (career 58.11)
Parents: Alan and Elaine
Family links with cricket: Brother Mark plays for Surrey and England. Father Alan
played for Surrey, England, and captained Glamorgan. Uncle Ian played for
Gloucestershire and Leicestershire. Uncle Martin played for Surrey
Education: Cumnor House Prep School, South Croydon; Riddlesdown
Comprehensive; Heath Clark College

Qualifications: 5 GCSEs, BTEC 1st Diploma in Leisure Studies, badminton coaching award, cricket coaching award
Overseas tours: England U18 to Denmark 1993; England U19 to Sri Lanka 1993-94; Glamorgan to Zimbabwe 1995, to Pretoria 1996, to Jersey 1998
Overseas teams played for: Northern Natal, South Africa 1995-96; Hawkesbury Hawks, Sydney 1996-97
Cricketers particularly admired: Brian Lara, Malcolm Marshall, Viv Richards, Curtly Ambrose, Michael Holding, Steve Waugh, David Gower
Young players to look out for: Carl Greenidge
Other sports played: Football
Other sports followed: Football (Liverpool FC)
Relaxations: Music, playing bass guitar, spending time with friends
Extras: Took wicket (N. A. Folland) with first ball on Sunday League debut, for Glamorgan v Somerset at Swansea 1994. Won Glamorgan's Most Improved Player Award 1996. Nominated for Young Player of the Year award 1996. Released by Glamorgan at end of 1998 season and joined Surrey for 1999. Played in three Championship-winning sides in four years (Glamorgan 1997; Surrey 1999, 2000). Took four wickets (Aldred, Munton, Dean, Wharton) in four balls v Derbyshire at The Oval 2000, the first Championship four-in-four since Pat Pocock achieved the feat for Surrey v Sussex at Eastbourne 1972. Man of the Match for his 115-ball 131 in Surrey 2nd XI's victory over Somerset 2nd XI in the 2nd XI Trophy final at Taunton 2001. Released by Surrey at the end of the 2001 season; recalled for one NUL match in 2002
Best batting: 101* Glamorgan v Oxford University, The Parks 1997
Best bowling: 7-77 Glamorgan v Gloucestershire, Bristol 1996

2002 Season

	M	Inns	NO	Runs	HS	Avge	100s	50s	Ct	St	O	M	Runs	Wkts	Avge	Best	5wl	10wM
Test																		
All First																		
1-day Int																		
C & G																		
B & H																		
1-day Lge	1	1	0	9	9	9.00	-	-	-	-	7	0	49	2	24.50	2-49	-	

Career Performances

	M	Inns	NO	Runs	HS	Avge	100s	50s	Ct	St	Balls	Runs	Wkts	Avge	Best	5wl	10wM
Test																	
All First	53	78	12	1841	101 *	27.89	1	12	19	-	3661	2390	63	37.93	7-77	2	-
1-day Int																	
C & G	4	3	1	77	48	38.50	-	-	-	-	120	122	4	30.50	2-33	-	
B & H	14	11	4	59	17	8.42	-	-	1	-	241	214	4	53.50	2-21	-	
1-day Lge	50	41	8	557	47	16.87	-	-	5	-	857	985	20	49.25	4-32	-	

BUTCHER, M. A. Surrey

Name: <u>Mark</u> Alan Butcher
Role: Left-hand bat, right-arm medium bowler
Born: 23 August 1972, Croydon
Height: 5ft 11in **Weight:** 13st
Nickname: Butch, Baz
County debut: 1991
County cap: 1996
Test debut: 1997
Tests: 45
1000 runs in a season: 6
1st-Class 50s: 66
1st-Class 100s: 20
1st-Class 200s: 2
1st-Class 5 w. in innings: 1
1st-Class catches: 179
Place in batting averages: 46th av. 46.80
(2001 19th av. 56.52)
Strike rate: (career 61.73)
Parents: Alan and Elaine
Wife and date of marriage: Judy, 4 October 1997
Children: Alita, 1999
Family links with cricket: Father Alan played for Glamorgan, Surrey and England and is now coach with Surrey; brother Gary played for Glamorgan and Surrey; uncle Ian played for Gloucestershire and Leicestershire; uncle Martin played for Surrey
Education: Cumnor House School; Trinity School; Archbishop Tenison's, Croydon
Qualifications: 5 O-levels, senior coaching award
Career outside cricket: Singer, guitar player
Off-season: Touring Australia with England
Overseas tours: England YC to New Zealand 1990-91; Surrey to Dubai 1990, 1993, to Perth 1995; England A to Australia 1996-97; England to West Indies 1997-98, to Australia 1998-99, to South Africa 1999-2000, to India and New Zealand 2001-02, to Australia 2002-03
Overseas teams played for: South Melbourne, Australia 1993-94; North Perth 1994-95
Cricketers particularly admired: Ian Botham, David Gower, Viv Richards, Larry Gomes, Graham Thorpe, Alec Stewart, Michael Holding
Other sports followed: Football (Crystal Palace)
Relaxations: Music, playing the guitar, novels, wine
Extras: Played his first game for Surrey in 1991 against his father's Glamorgan in the Refuge Assurance League at The Oval, the first-ever match of any sort between first-class counties in which a father and son have been in opposition. Made his maiden Test century (116) v South Africa at Headingley in 1998, winning the Man of the

Match award. His 259 v Leicestershire 1999 was the highest score by a left-hander at Grace Road and the fourth highest individual score recorded there overall. Captained England in third Test v New Zealand at Old Trafford 1999, deputising for Nasser Hussain who missed the match through injury. B&H Gold Award for his 84 in the semi-final v Nottinghamshire at The Oval 2001. His 4-42 in the first Test v Australia at Edgbaston 2001 included four wickets in 14 balls. Scored 145* v Glamorgan 2001, becoming the first Surrey batsman to carry his bat at The Oval since Grahame Clinton did so in 1984. Man of the Match in the fourth Test v Australia at Headingley 2001 for his match-winning 173*, having also scored 47 in the first innings; England's Man of the Series v Australia 2001 with 456 runs (more than any other batsman on either side) at an average of 50.66. Slazenger Sheer Instinct Award 2001 for the cricketer who has impressed the most in the recent season. Captained Surrey in Adam Hollioake's absence during the first part of the 2002 season. B&H Gold Award for his 51 v Middlesex at Lord's 2002. Scored 339 runs (av. 84.75), including two centuries and a 94, in Test series v Sri Lanka 2002 and was named England's Man of the Series. ECB 12-month contract 2002-03

Best batting: 259 Surrey v Leicestershire, Leicester 1999
Best bowling: 5-86 Surrey v Lancashire, Old Trafford 2000
Stop press: Scored century (124) in first innings of England victory in fifth Test at Sydney 2002-03

2002 Season

	M	Inns	NO	Runs	HS	Avge	100s	50s	Ct	St	O	M	Runs	Wkts	Avge	Best	5wI	10wM
Test	7	10	0	551	123	55.10	2	3	5	-	4	1	17	0	-	-	-	-
All First	13	21	1	936	123	46.80	3	5	8	-	12	3	60	0	-	-	-	-
1-day Int																		
C & G																		
B & H	3	3	0	114	62	38.00	-	2	1	-	2	0	12	0	-		-	-
1-day Lge																		

Career Performances

	M	Inns	NO	Runs	HS	Avge	100s	50s	Ct	St	Balls	Runs	Wkts	Avge	Best	5wI	10wM
Test	45	83	3	2651	173 *	33.13	5	11	39	-	566	308	10	30.80	4-42	-	-
All First	190	328	25	11772	259	38.85	22	66	179	-	7161	3874	116	33.39	5-86	1	-
1-day Int																	
C & G	19	19	5	659	91	47.07	-	6	9	-	306	216	5	43.20	2-57	-	
B & H	34	30	6	678	84	28.25	-	4	9	-	492	408	7	58.28	3-37	-	
1-day Lge	91	78	14	1406	85 *	21.96	-	5	27	-	1717	1571	37	42.45	3-23	-	

BYAS, D. Lancashire

Name: David Byas
Role: Left-hand bat
Born: 26 August 1963, Kilham
Height: 6ft 4in **Weight:** 14st 7lbs
Nickname: Bingo, Gadgett
County debut: 1986 (Yorkshire),
2002 (Lancashire)
County cap: 1991 (Yorkshire),
2002 (Lancashire)
Benefit: 2000 (Yorkshire)
1000 runs in a season: 5
1st-Class 50s: 83
1st-Class 100s: 28
1st-Class 200s: 1
1st-Class catches: 366
One-Day 100s: 5
Place in batting averages: 142nd av. 29.73
(2001 49th av. 44.89)

Strike rate: (career 93.16)
Parents: Richard and Anne
Wife and date of marriage: Rachael, 26 October 1990
Children: Olivia, 16 December 1991; Georgia, 30 December 1993; Benjamin, 1997
Family links with cricket: Father played local leagues
Education: Kilham Primary School; Lisvane School, Scarborough;
Scarborough College
Qualifications: 1 O-level (Engineering)
Career outside cricket: Partner in family farming business
Off-season: 'At home with the family and on the farm'
Overseas teams played for: Papatoetoe, Auckland 1990-91
Career highlights to date: 'Leading Yorkshire to County Championship in 2001.
Receiving both my Yorkshire and Lancashire caps!'
Cricket moments to forget: 'Losing B&H final in 1999'
Cricket superstitions: 'Left boot and pad on first'
Cricketers particularly admired: David Gower, Viv Richards, Ian Botham
Young players to look out for: Kyle Hogg, Richard Dawson, Steve Kirby
Other sports played: Hockey (international and county player)
Other sports followed: 'Most other sports'
Injuries: Out for one month with a broken finger
Relaxations: 'Time with the family, and gardening'
Extras: Set Yorkshire League record for runs in a season (1350); became youngest
captain (aged 21) of Scarborough CC in 1985. Runner-up in the Sunday League

averages 1994, breaking John Hampshire's 1976 Sunday League Yorkshire record with 702 runs. Passed Geoffrey Boycott's Yorkshire one-day league run record (5051) v Somerset at Headingley in the Norwich Union League 2001. Captain of Yorkshire 1996-2001. Scored a century (104) and took the final catch in the victory over Glamorgan at his home ground of Scarborough that brought the 2001 County Championship to Yorkshire. Retired at the end of the 2001 season but later accepted an invitation to play for Lancashire in 2002. B&H Gold Award for his 91 in the quarter-final v Leicestershire at Leicester 2002. Scored 101 v Warwickshire at Old Trafford 2002, in the process becoming the first player to have scored a Championship century for both Yorkshire and Lancashire. Awarded Lancashire cap 2002, becoming the first player to be capped by both Yorkshire and Lancashire. Passed 15,000 runs in first-class cricket v Kent at Canterbury 2002. Retired at the end of the 2002 season

Opinions on cricket: 'Two divisions in four-day cricket has done wonders for the competitiveness of the game.'

Best batting: 213 Yorkshire v Worcestershire, Scarborough 1995

Best bowling: 3-55 Yorkshire v Derbyshire, Chesterfield 1990

2002 Season

	M	Inns	NO	Runs	HS	Avge	100s	50s	Ct	St	O	M	Runs	Wkts	Avge	Best	5wI	10wM
Test																		
All First	15	25	2	684	101	29.73	1	4	15	-								
1-day Int																		
C & G	1	1	1	5	5 *	-	-	-	-	-								
B & H	6	6	1	136	91	27.20	-	1	1	-								
1-day Lge	12	11	0	193	78	17.54	-	1	7	-								

Career Performances

	M	Inns	NO	Runs	HS	Avge	100s	50s	Ct	St	Balls	Runs	Wkts	Avge	Best	5wI	10wM
Test																		
All First	283	474	44	15082	213	35.07	29	83	366	-	1118	727	12	60.58	3-55	-	-
1-day Int																		
C & G	35	33	4	917	73 *	31.62	-	8	23	-	18	23	1	23.00	1-23	-	
B & H	64	61	6	1563	116 *	28.41	2	8	18	-	283	155	5	31.00	2-38	-	
1-day Lge	229	222	27	5545	111 *	28.43	3	29	95	-	529	463	19	24.36	3-19	-	

14. Which Somerset overseas player scored 4045 runs in all first-class cricket during the 1987 calendar year?

CADDICK, A. R.   Somerset

Name: <u>Andrew</u> Richard Caddick
Role: Right-hand bat, right-arm
fast-medium bowler
Born: 21 November 1968, Christchurch,
New Zealand
Height: 6ft 5in **Weight:** 14st 13lbs
Nickname: Des, Shack
County debut: 1991
County cap: 1992
Benefit: 1999
Test debut: 1993
Tests: 58
One-Day Internationals: 38
50 wickets in a season: 7
100 wickets in a season: 1
1st-Class 50s: 5
1st-Class 5 w. in innings: 60
1st-Class 10 w. in match: 14
1st-Class catches: 64
One-Day 5 w. in innings: 3

Place in batting averages: 305th av. 7.41 (2001 253rd av. 11.09)
Place in bowling averages: 42nd av. 27.35 (2001 58th av. 29.27)
Strike rate: 52.93 (career 49.23)
Parents: Christopher and Audrey
Wife and date of marriage: Sarah, 27 January 1995
Children: Ashton Faye, 24 August 1998; Fraser Michael, 12 October 2001
Education: Papanui High School, Christchurch, New Zealand
Qualifications: Qualified plasterer and tiler
Career outside cricket: Plasterer and tiler
Off-season: Touring with England
Overseas tours: New Zealand YC to Australia (U19 World Cup) 1987-88,
to England 1988; England A to Australia 1992-93; England to West Indies 1993-94,
to Zimbabwe and New Zealand 1996-97, to West Indies 1997-98, to South Africa and
Zimbabwe 1999-2000, to Kenya (ICC Knockout Trophy) 2000-01, to Pakistan and
Sri Lanka 2000-01, to India (one-day series) and New Zealand 2001-02, to Sri Lanka
(ICC Champions Trophy) 2002-03, to Australia 2002-03
Career highlights to date: 'Bowling West Indies out at Lord's [2000] and thus getting
my name up on the board'
Cricketers particularly admired: Dennis Lillee, Richard Hadlee, Robin Smith,
Jimmy Cook
Other sports followed: 'Mostly all'

Relaxations: Golf

Extras: Rapid Cricketline 2nd XI Championship Player of the Year 1991. Whyte and Mackay Bowler of the Year 1997. Took 105 first-class wickets in 1998 season. Leading wicket-taker in the single-division four-day era of the County Championship with 422 wickets (av. 22.48) 1993-99. England's Man of the Series v New Zealand 1999, taking 20 wickets at an average of 20.60. Returned 7-46 in South Africa's first innings of the third Test at Durban, December 1999; shared Man of the Match award with Gary Kirsten. Cornhill England Player of the Year 1999-2000. Took 5-16 from 13 overs as West Indies were bowled out for 54 in their second innings in the second Test at Lord's 2000. Took 5-14 in fourth Test v West Indies at Headingley 2000, becoming in the process the fifth England bowler to take four wickets in an over in a Test match and recording the cheapest five-wicket Test return by an England bowler since Ian Botham's 5-11 v Australia at Edgbaston in 1981. One of *Wisden*'s Five Cricketers of the Year 2001. Man of the Match in first Test v Pakistan at Lord's 2001 for his match figures of 8-106. Scored a 40-ball 49* v Australia at Edgbaston 2001, in the process sharing with Alec Stewart in the first century stand for the last wicket (103) since 1903-04 for England in Tests v Australia. Withdrew from England Test tour to India 2001-02; replaced by Richard Johnson. Had Test best match figures of 9-172 in the first Test v New Zealand 2001-02, which took place in his birthplace, Christchurch, and was Man of the Match in the second Test at Wellington with first innings figures of 6-63. Took 200th Test wicket (Craig McMillan) in the third Test v New Zealand at Auckland 2001-02. Took 34 wickets (av. 22.73) in five Championship appearances for Somerset 2002. ECB 12-month contract 2002-03

Opinions on cricket: 'I do approve of the two divisional system now in place, but I do believe that only two teams should be relegated or promoted each year.'

Best batting: 92 Somerset v Worcestershire, Worcester 1995

Best bowling: 9-32 Somerset v Lancashire, Taunton 1993

Stop press: Recorded maiden Test ten-wicket match return (3-121 and 7-94) in England victory in fifth Test v Australia at Sydney 2002-03, in the process passing Darren Gough's total of 228 wickets to move into seventh place in the list of England Test wicket-takers. Took 4-35 v Sri Lanka at Adelaide in the VB Series 2002-03, winning Man of the Match award. Selected for England squad for 2002-03 World Cup

2002 Season

	M	Inns	NO	Runs	HS	Avge	100s	50s	Ct	St	O	M	Runs	Wkts	Avge	Best	5wl	10wM
Test	5	6	2	36	14 *	9.00	-	-	-	-	176.1	36	540	14	38.57	4-114	-	-
All First	10	14	2	89	16	7.41	-	-	2	-	423.3	89	1313	48	27.35	6-84	4	-
1-day Int																		
C & G	1	1	1	0	0 *	-	-	-	-	-	9	0	53	0	-		-	-
B & H	2	2	1	5	4 *	5.00	-	-	-	-	15	3	78	2	39.00	1-39	-	
1-day Lge	2	2	0	15	11	7.50	-	-	-	-	18	1	86	2	43.00	2-34	-	

Career Performances

	M	Inns	NO	Runs	HS	Avge	100s	50s	Ct	St	Balls	Runs	Wkts	Avge	Best	5wI	10wM
Test	58	87	11	809	49 *	10.64	-	-	18	-	12532	6309	214	29.48	7-46	12	-
All First	196	263	49	3097	92	14.47	-	5	64	-	42495	21327	863	24.71	9-32	60	14
1-day Int	38	24	9	154	36	10.26	-	-	8	-	2097	1367	48	28.47	4-19	-	
C & G	28	14	6	29	8	3.62	-	-	5	-	1694	940	45	20.88	6-30	2	
B & H	29	19	11	135	38	16.87	-	-	4	-	1569	1099	36	30.52	5-51	1	
1-day Lge	95	38	11	292	39	10.81	-	-	14	-	4139	2989	116	25.76	4-18	-	

CAIRNS, C. L. Nottinghamshire

Name: Christopher (Chris) Lance Cairns
Role: Right-hand bat, right-arm
fast-medium bowler, county one-day captain
Born: 13 June 1970, Picton, New Zealand
Height: 6ft 2in **Weight:** 14st
County debut: 1988
County cap: 1993
Test debut: 1989-90
Tests: 55
One-Day Internationals: 151
1000 runs in a season: 1
50 wickets in a season: 3
1st-Class 50s: 61
1st-Class 100s: 11
1st-Class 5 w. in innings: 29
1st-Class 10 w. in match: 6
1st-Class catches: 71
One-day 100s: 6
One-Day 5 w. in innings: 3
Strike rate: (career 52.18)
Parents: Lance and Sue
Family links with cricket: Father played for New Zealand, uncle played first-class
cricket in New Zealand
Education: Christchurch Boys' High School, New Zealand
Qualifications: 5th and 6th form certificates
Off-season: Playing for New Zealand
Overseas tours: New Zealand YC to Australia (U19 World Cup) 1987-88; New
Zealand to Australia 1989-90, 1993-94, 1997-98, 2001-02, to India 1995-96, 1999-
2000, to India and Pakistan (World Cup) 1995-96, to Pakistan 1996-97, to Zimbabwe
1997-98, 2000-01, to Sri Lanka 1997-98, to UK, Ireland and Holland (World Cup)
1999, to England 1999
Overseas teams played for: Northern Districts 1988-89; Canterbury 1990-91 –

Cricketers particularly admired: Mick Newell, Richard Hadlee, Dennis Lillee
Other sports followed: Most sports
Extras: Represented New Zealand in the 1991-92 World Cup. Hit the fastest first-class hundred of the 1995 season (65 balls for Nottinghamshire v Cambridge University at Fenner's). One of the *New Zealand Cricket Almanack* two Players of the Year 1998, 1999, 2000. New Zealand's Man of the Series on tour of England 1999; performances included 5-31 followed by a 94-ball 80 in final Test at The Oval. Took 7-27 v West Indies at Hamilton 1999-2000, returning 10-100 in the match to make himself and his father Lance the only father and son to have taken ten wickets in a Test match; topped New Zealand series bowling averages with 17 wickets at 9.94 and averaged 51.50 with the bat. Topped New Zealand batting averages in Test series v Australia 1999-2000 (341 runs av. 56.83). National Bank Player of the Year 1999-2000 in New Zealand and won the Redpath Cup for batting and the Winsor Cup for bowling (only the second player, after John Reid in 1954-55, to win the batting and bowling trophies in one year). Canterbury of New Zealand Sportsperson of the Year 2000. One of *Wisden*'s Five Cricketers of the Year 2000. Man of the Match award for his 102* in the ICC Knockout Trophy final v India in Kenya 2000-01. Had first innings figures of 5-146 and scored 61 and 43 in the first Test v Australia at Brisbane 2001-02, his first international match after a year out with a knee injury. Had second innings figures of 7-53 (including 5-7 in 38 balls) v Bangladesh in first Test at Hamilton, December 2001. Captained New Zealand to victory over Australia at Sydney in a VB one-day series match 2001-02 in the absence of the injured Stephen Fleming. Scored a 99-ball 102* in New Zealand's win over South Africa at Brisbane in the VB one-day series 2001-02. Took his 150th One-Day International wicket (Nasser Hussain) v England at Auckland 2001-02 in his 150th One-Day International. Took two wickets in the first over of the first Test v England at Christchurch 2001-02, reducing England to 0-2; suffered a torn knee tendon later in the game that prevented him from rejoining Notts as overseas player for 2002 but has returned for 2003. Appointed one-day captain of Notts for 2003 (*see entry on Jason Gallian*)
Opinions on cricket: 'Great game.'
Best batting: 126 New Zealand v India, Hamilton 1998-99
Best bowling: 8-47 Nottinghamshire v Sussex, Arundel 1995
Stop press: Returned to international cricket in fifth ODI v India at Wellington 2002-03. Selected for New Zealand squad for 2002-03 World Cup

2002 Season (did not make any first-class or one-day appearances)

Career Performances

	M	Inns	NO	Runs	HS	Avge	100s	50s	Ct	St	Balls	Runs	Wkts	Avge	Best	5wl	10wM
Test	55	92	5	2852	126	32.78	4	20	15	-	10445	5675	197	28.80	7-27	12	1
All First	190	297	35	9253	126	35.31	11	61	71	-	31153	16415	597	27.49	8-47	29	6
1-day Int	151	138	14	3614	115	29.14	4	19	49	-	6278	4914	154	31.90	5-42	1	
C & G	7	7	1	306	77	51.00	-	3	2	-	482	279	14	19.92	4-18	-	
B & H	12	8	0	112	46	14.00	-	-	3	-	617	454	16	28.37	4-47	-	
1-day Lge	60	50	10	1655	126*	41.37	2	9	17	-	2363	1858	86	21.60	6-52	2	

CARBERRY, M. A.　　　　　　　　　Kent

Name: <u>Michael</u> Alexander Carberry
Role: Left-hand bat, right-arm
off-spin bowler
Born: 29 September 1980, Croydon
Height: 6ft **Weight:** 12st 7lbs
Nickname: Carbs
County debut: 2001 (Surrey)
1st-Class 50s: 1
1st-Class 100s: 1
1st-Class catches: 8
Place in batting averages: (2001 116th
av. 31.10)
Parents: Maria and Neville
Marital status: Single
Family links with cricket: 'My dad played
club cricket'
Education: Winterbourne Junior School;
St John Rigby RC College

Qualifications: 10 GCSEs
Overseas tours: Surrey U17 to South Africa 1997; England U19 to New Zealand
1998-99, to Malaysia and (U19 World Cup) Sri Lanka 1999-2000
Overseas teams played for: Portland CC, Melbourne
Career highlights to date: 'Getting chance to play first-class cricket'
Cricketers particularly admired: Brian Lara, Steve Waugh, Mark Butcher,
Graham Thorpe
Young players to look out for: Tim Murtagh, Carl Greenidge, Scott Newman
Other sports played: Basketball, football
Other sports followed: Football (Tottenham Hotspur)
Relaxations: 'Nightclubbing, weights, DJ-ing'
Extras: Second schoolboy to score a century for Croydon U13 since Ali Brown.
Scored century (126*) for ECB U18 v Pakistan U19 at Abergavenny 1998.
Represented England U19 in one-day and 'Test' series v Australia U19 1999, scoring
50 in the third 'Test' at Chester-le-Street. Played for Surrey Board XI in 1999
NatWest. NBC Denis Compton Award for the most promising young Surrey player
1999, 2000. Represented England U19 v Sri Lanka U19 in one-day series 2000.
Scored maiden first-class century (153*) v Cambridge University CCE at Fenner's
2002. Left Surrey during the 2002-03 off-season and has joined Kent for 2003
Best batting: 153* Surrey v CUCCE, Fenner's 2002

2002 Season

	M	Inns	NO	Runs	HS	Avge	100s	50s	Ct	St	O	M	Runs	Wkts	Avge	Best	5wl	10wM
Test																		
All First	2	4	1	223	153 *	74.33	1	-	2	-								
1-day Int																		
C & G	1	0	0	0	0	-	-	-	-	-								
B & H	1	1	0	7	7	7.00	-	-	2	-								
1-day Lge	3	3	1	28	19	14.00	-	-	2	-								

Career Performances

	M	Inns	NO	Runs	HS	Avge	100s	50s	Ct	St	Balls	Runs	Wkts	Avge	Best	5wl	10wM
Test																	
All First	8	14	1	534	153 *	41.07	1	1	8	-							
1-day Int																	
C & G	3	2	0	23	19	11.50	-	-	-	-							
B & H	1	1	0	7	7	7.00	-	-	2	-							
1-day Lge	8	8	1	61	20	8.71	-	-	3	-							

CARPENTER, J. R.   Sussex

Name: <u>James</u> Robert Carpenter
Role: Left-hand bat, slow left-arm bowler
Born: 20 October 1975, Birkenhead
Height: 6ft 1in **Weight:** 13st
Nickname: Carps
County debut: 1997
1st-Class 50s: 2
1st-Class catches: 5
Strike rate: (career 129.00)
Parents: John and Jo
Marital status: Single
Family links with cricket: Father played
Minor Counties cricket for Cheshire
Education: Gayton Primary School;
Birkenhead School
Qualifications: 9 GCSEs, 4 A-levels
Overseas tours: Sussex to Grenada 2001
Overseas teams played for: Randwick CC,
Sydney, Australia 1996-99
Cricketers particularly admired: Ian Botham, Allan Border, Steve Waugh
Other sports played: Rugby (Cheshire Schools), football (Liverpool and Everton as
schoolboy, Bolton Wanderers as trialist; Runcorn in Vauxhall Conference)

129

Relaxations: Golf
Extras: Captained MCC Young Professionals at Lord's. *Daily Telegraph* Bowling Award. Wetherell award from the Cricket Society for the year's outstanding schoolboy all-rounder 1991. Leading catcher in AXA League for 1998 season. Retired at the end of the 2002 season
Best batting: 65 Sussex v Nottinghamshire, Trent Bridge 1998
Best bowling: 1-50 Sussex v Nottinghamshire, Hove 1997

2002 Season

	M	Inns	NO	Runs	HS	Avge	100s	50s	Ct	St	O	M	Runs	Wkts	Avge	Best	5wI	10wM
Test																		
All First																		
1-day Int																		
C & G																		
B & H																		
1-day Lge	2	2	0	11	8	5.50	-	-	2	-								

Career Performances

	M	Inns	NO	Runs	HS	Avge	100s	50s	Ct	St	Balls	Runs	Wkts	Avge	Best	5wI	10wM
Test																	
All First	13	24	0	383	65	15.95	-	2	5	-	129	81	1	81.00	1-50	-	-
1-day Int																	
C & G	2	2	0	69	55	34.50	-	1	-	-							
B & H	8	7	2	154	53 *	30.80	-	1	3	-							
1-day Lge	43	34	8	507	64 *	19.50	-	3	25	-	6	15	0	-		-	-

CARTER, N. M.   Warwickshire

Name: <u>Neil</u> Miller Carter
Role: Left-hand bat, left-arm
fast bowler
Born: 29 January 1975, Cape Town, South Africa
Height: 6ft 2in **Weight:** 14st 4lbs
Nickname: Carts
County debut: 2001
1st-Class 50s: 1
1st-Class 100s: 1
1st-Class 5 w. in innings: 3
1st-Class catches: 8
One-Day 5 w. in innings: 1
Strike rate: 68.45 (career 56.68)
Place in batting averages: 59th av. 43.57
Place in bowling averages: 144th av. 47.85 (2001 77th av. 32.57)

Parents: John and Heather
Marital status: Single
Education: Somerset House Preparatory School; Hottentots Holland High School; Cape Technikon
Qualifications: Diploma in Financial Information Systems, Certified Novell Engineer, Level 2 coaching
Career outside cricket: Computers, accounting
Off-season: 'Gym-ing and lying on Clifton Beach'
Overseas tours: SA Country Schools U15 to England 1992; Warwickshire to Cape Town 2001, 2002
Overseas teams played for: Boland 1998-99 – 2001-02
Career highlights to date: 'Winning last B&H Cup in 2002. Winning Standard Bank Cup for Boland 1999-2000'
Cricket moments to forget: 'Any performance under par'
Cricketers particularly admired: Jacques Kallis, Shaun Pollock, Allan Donald
Young players to look out for: Justin Ontong, Graeme Smith
Other sports played: Golf, swimming
Other sports followed: Rugby union (Stormers, Springboks), football (Sheffield Wednesday)
Relaxations: Steam train photography ('gricing'); 'trying to find FMC'
Extras: Made his first-class debut for Boland during the 1999-2000 season. Won Man of the Match award in first one-day match for Warwickshire (4-21 and a 43-ball 40), in C&G Trophy v Essex at Edgbaston 2001. Recorded maiden one-day five-wicket return (5-31) v Durham in the NUL at Edgbaston 2002; also struck 24 from nine balls as opener in the same match. Swept his first ball (the last of the game) for a match-winning four in the B&H semi-final v Lancashire at Old Trafford 2002. Scored maiden first-class century (103) v Sussex at Hove 2002; his 67-ball hundred was the second fastest for Warwickshire since centuries began to be recorded in terms of balls received. Is not considered an overseas player
Opinions on cricket: 'Too many games with too many players "enjoying the ride".'
Best batting: 103 Warwickshire v Sussex, Hove 2002
Best bowling: 6-63 Boland v Griqualand West, Kimberley 2000-01

2002 Season

	M	Inns	NO	Runs	HS	Avge	100s	50s	Ct	St	O	M	Runs	Wkts	Avge	Best	5wI	10wM
Test																		
All First	9	12	5	305	103	43.57	1	1	4	-	228.1	35	957	20	47.85	4-46	-	-
1-day Int																		
C & G	1	1	0	6	6	6.00	-	-	1	-	7	0	45	1	45.00	1-45	-	
B & H	4	2	1	4	4*	4.00	-	-	-	-	26	2	124	5	24.80	3-43	-	
1-day Lge	11	11	4	86	24	12.28	-	-	3	-	83.4	4	440	17	25.88	5-31	1	

Career Performances

	M	Inns	NO	Runs	HS	Avge	100s	50s	Ct	St	Balls	Runs	Wkts	Avge	Best	5wI	10wM
Test																	
All First	24	31	8	449	103	19.52	1	1	8	-	3911	2363	69	34.24	6-63	3	-
1-day Int																	
C & G	4	2	0	46	40	23.00	-	-	1	-	201	142	8	17.75	4-21	-	
B & H	4	2	1	4	4*	4.00	-	-	-	-	156	124	5	24.80	3-43	-	
1-day Lge	15	13	4	99	24	11.00	-	-	3	-	676	559	24	23.29	5-31	1	

CASSAR, M. E.   Northamptonshire

Name: <u>Matthew</u> Edward Cassar
Role: Right-hand bat, right-arm medium-fast bowler, occasional wicket-keeper
Born: 16 October 1972, Sydney, Australia
Height: 6ft **Weight:** 14st
Nickname: Cass, Chach
County debut: 1994 (Derbyshire), 2001 (Northants)
1st-Class 50s: 12
1st-Class 100s: 2
1st-Class 5 w. in innings: 3
1st-Class 10 w. in match: 1
1st-Class catches: 20
One-Day 100s: 4
Place in batting averages: 66th av. 42.87
Place in bowling averages: 59th av. 29.00
Strike rate: 42.56 (career 49.70)
Parents: Edward and Joan
Marital status: Separated
Education: Punchbowl Primary School, Sydney; Sir Joseph Banks High School, Sydney; Manchester Metropolitan University
Qualifications: School certificate and senior coaching award

Overseas tours: Northamptonshire to Grenada 2001
Overseas teams played for: Petersham-Marrickville, Sydney 1988-95, 1999-2001
Career highlights to date: 'Getting Steve Waugh out caught behind first ball during a grade game in Sydney 2000'
Cricket moments to forget: 'My first season at Northamptonshire, when I hardly played because of a groin injury'
Cricketers particularly admired: Dennis Lillee, Viv Richards, Steve Waugh, Rod Marsh, Ian Botham
Other sports played: Golf, squash, tennis, football
Other sports followed: Football (Derby County)
Relaxations: Cinema, music, TV, golf
Extras: Played for New South Wales Colts. Took three wickets in final over of National League match at Southampton 2000, preventing Hampshire scoring the nine runs required for victory. Left Derbyshire at the end of the 2000 season and joined Northamptonshire for 2001. Recorded maiden first-class ten-wicket match return (10-134) v Gloucestershire at Bristol 2002. Released by Northamptonshire at the end of the 2002 season
Best batting: 121 Derbyshire v Sussex, Horsham 1998
Best bowling: 6-34 Northamptonshire v Gloucestershire, Bristol 2002

2002 Season

	M	Inns	NO	Runs	HS	Avge	100s	50s	Ct	St	O	M	Runs	Wkts	Avge	Best	5wI	10wM
Test																		
All First	7	9	1	343	101 *	42.87	1	3	4	-	113.3	18	464	16	29.00	6-34	1	1
1-day Int																		
C & G																		
B & H																		
1-day Lge	9	8	1	177	54	25.28	-	1	3	-	19.5	0	116	1	116.00	1-32	-	

Career Performances

	M	Inns	NO	Runs	HS	Avge	100s	50s	Ct	St	Balls	Runs	Wkts	Avge	Best	5wI	10wM
Test																	
All First	63	98	12	2155	121	25.05	2	12	20	-	4523	2751	91	30.23	6-34	3	1
1-day Int																	
C & G	6	6	1	175	90 *	35.00	-	2	-	-	78	63	1	63.00	1-31	-	
B & H	5	4	0	69	43	17.25	-	-	1	-	126	82	2	41.00	2-8	-	
1-day Lge	55	53	5	1441	134	30.02	4	6	18	-	1054	949	31	30.61	4-29	-	

CATTERALL, D. N.　　　Worcestershire

Name: <u>Duncan</u> Neil Catterall
Role: Right-hand bat, right-arm medium-fast bowler
Born: 19 September 1978, Preston
Height: 5ft 11in　**Weight:** 12st 2lbs
Nickname: Cats
County debut: 1998
1st-Class 50s: 2
1st-Class catches: 1
Strike rate: (career 46.00)
Parents: David and Christine
Marital status: Single
Family links with cricket: Brother plays and father played for Leyland DAF in the Northern League
Education: Horncliffe School, Blackburn; Queen Elizabeth's Grammar School, Blackburn; Loughborough University
Qualifications: 11 GCSEs and 4 A-levels
Overseas tours: Queen Elizabeth's Grammar School to Australia, 1996
Overseas teams played for: Manly CC, Sydney 1999-2000
Cricketers particularly admired: Steve Waugh
Young players to look out for: Kabir Ali
Other sports followed: Football (Preston North End)
Relaxations: Music, socialising
Extras: Represented England Schools U19 in 1998. Released by Worcestershire at the end of the 2002 season
Best batting: 60 Worcestershire v Essex, Chelmsford 1999
　　　　　　　60 Worcestershire v Middlesex, Worcester 1999
Best bowling: 4-50 Worcestershire v West Indians, Worcester 2000

2002 Season

	M	Inns	NO	Runs	HS	Avge	100s	50s	Ct	St	O	M	Runs	Wkts	Avge	Best	5wI	10wM
Test																		
All First																		
1-day Int																		
C & G																		
B & H																		
1-day Lge	1	0	0	0	0	0	-	-	-	-	-	-						

Career Performances

	M	Inns	NO	Runs	HS	Avge	100s	50s	Ct	St	Balls	Runs	Wkts	Avge	Best	5wI	10wM
Test																	
All First	4	5	0	157	60	31.40	-	2	1	-	506	308	11	28.00	4-50	-	-
1-day Int																	
C & G	1	1	0	1	1	1.00	-	-	-	-	57	40	1	40.00	1-40	-	
B & H																		
1-day Lge	12	6	2	27	11 *	6.75	-	-	3	-	336	267	3	89.00	2-35	-	

CAWDRON, M. J.   Northamptonshire

Name: Michael (Mike) John Cawdron
Role: Left-hand bat, right-arm
medium-fast bowler
Born: 7 October 1974, Luton
Height: 6ft 3in **Weight:** 13st 7lbs
Nickname: Muscles
County debut: 1995 (one-day,
Gloucestershire), 1999 (first-class,
Gloucestershire), 2002 (Northamptonshire)
1st-Class 5 w. in innings: 5
1st-Class 10 w. in match: 1
1st-Class catches: 3
Place in batting averages: (2001 247th
av. 11.71)
Place in bowling averages: (2001 120th
av. 41.50)
Strike rate: (career 53.16)
Parents: William and Mandy
Marital status: 'Very single'
Family links with cricket: Father and brother played local village cricket
Education: Cheltenham College
Qualifications: 10 GCSEs, 3 A-levels, NCA coaching award
Overseas tours: West of England U14 to Holland; Cheltenham College to Zimbabwe
1992; Gloucestershire YC to Sri Lanka 1993-94; Gloucestershire Gypsies to
Zimbabwe 1994-95, to Cape Town 1997; Christians in Sport to Zimbabwe 1998,
to South Africa 2000; Gloucestershire to Kimberley and Cape Town 2001
Career highlights to date: 'Playing in 1999 NatWest final v Somerset'
Cricketers particularly admired: Jack Russell, Jeremy Snape, Kim Barnett ('they are
all very tough players who make the most of their talents')
Young players to look out for: David Sales
Other sports followed: Rugby, hockey, rackets, clay-pigeon shooting, golf

Relaxations: Cinema, videos, eating and going out with friends
Extras: Winner of the *Daily Telegraph* Regional Bowling Award 1993. Captain of MCC Schools and ESCA U19 1993. 'Made 50 off 32 balls on Sunday League debut against Essex at my old school' (Cheltenham College). Scored 42 and took 5-35 on first-class debut, v Hampshire at Bristol 1999; went on to take two more five-wicket hauls in his next two Championship games. Released by Gloucestershire at the end of the 2001 season and joined Northamptonshire for 2002
Best batting: 42 Gloucestershire v Hampshire, Bristol 1999
Best bowling: 6-25 First-Class Counties XI v New Zealand A, Milton Keynes 2000

2002 Season

	M	Inns	NO	Runs	HS	Avge	100s	50s	Ct	St	O	M	Runs	Wkts	Avge	Best	5wI	10wM
Test																		
All First																			
1-day Int																			
C & G																			
B & H	2	0	0	0	0	-	-	-	1	-	13	0	91	3	30.33	2-24	-	
1-day Lge	3	2	1	0	0 *	0.00	-	-	-	-	22	1	137	2	68.50	1-18	-	

Career Performances

	M	Inns	NO	Runs	HS	Avge	100s	50s	Ct	St	Balls	Runs	Wkts	Avge	Best	5wI	10wM
Test																	
All First	18	26	4	333	42	15.13	-	-	3	-	2818	1298	53	24.49	6-25	5	1
1-day Int																	
C & G	9	6	3	26	17	8.66	-	-	1	-	420	307	12	25.58	4-34	-	
B & H	14	4	3	16	9 *	16.00	-	-	1	-	606	528	20	26.40	4-28	-	
1-day Lge	35	24	8	251	50	15.68	-	1	4	-	1286	1066	27	39.48	4-17	-	

CHAPPLE, G.   Lancashire

Name: Glen Chapple
Role: Right-hand bat, right-arm medium-fast bowler
Born: 23 January 1974, Skipton, Yorkshire
Height: 6ft 2in **Weight:** 12st 7lbs
Nickname: Chappy, Boris, Boomor, Cheeky
County debut: 1992
County cap: 1994
50 wickets in a season: 4
1st-Class 50s: 12
1st-Class 100s: 2
1st-Class 5 w. in innings: 18
1st-Class 10 w. in match: 1
1st-Class catches: 46

One-Day 5 w. in innings: 4
Place in batting averages: 211th av. 22.40
(2001 118th av. 31.06)
Place in bowling averages: 63rd av. 29.51
(2001 21st av. 22.15)
Strike rate: 59.94 (career 55.40)
Parents: Eileen and Michael
Marital status: Single
Family links with cricket: Father played in
Lancashire League for Nelson and was a
professional for Darwen and Earby
Education: West Craven High School;
Nelson and Colne College
Qualifications: 8 GCSEs, 2 A-levels
Overseas tours: England U18 to Canada
(International Youth Tournament) 1991;
England YC to New Zealand 1990-91, to
Pakistan 1991-92, to India 1992-93; England
A to India 1994-95, to Australia 1996-97; England VI to Hong Kong 2002
Cricketers particularly admired: Dennis Lillee, Robin Smith
Other sports followed: Football (Liverpool), golf
Relaxations: 'Watching films, music, socialising'
Extras: Set record for fastest century in first-class cricket (21 minutes; against
declaration bowling) v Glamorgan at Old Trafford 1993. Man of the Match in the 1996
NatWest final against Essex at Lord's for his 6-18. Shared in a record eighth-wicket
partnership for Lancashire in matches against Northamptonshire (136*) with Warren
Hegg at Northampton 2001, scoring 72*; also scored 31 in the first innings and took
nine wickets in the match. Scored 155 v Somerset at Old Trafford 2001, equalling
Wasim Akram's record, set in 1998 v Nottinghamshire, for the highest score by a
Lancashire No. 8. B&H Gold Award for his 26-ball 42 plus 1-14 v Yorkshire at
Headingley 2002. Scored 55 v Kent at Liverpool 2002, in the process sharing with
Peter Martin (80*) in a record ninth-wicket partnership for Lancashire v Kent (109).
Recorded maiden first-class ten-wicket match return (10-127) v Sussex at Hove 2002.
Lancashire Player of the Year 2002
Best batting: 155 Lancashire v Somerset, Old Trafford 2001
Best bowling: 6-30 Lancashire v Somerset, Blackpool 2002

2002 Season

	M	Inns	NO	Runs	HS	Avge	100s	50s	Ct	St	O	M	Runs	Wkts	Avge	Best	5wI	10wM
Test																		
All First	16	23	1	493	65	22.40	-	4	6	-	539.3	128	1594	54	29.51	6-30	3	1
1-day Int																		
C & G	2	2	1	82	81 *	82.00	-	1	-	-	14.2	1	61	0	-	-	-	-
B & H	7	7	0	106	50	15.14	-	1	4	-	48	6	165	7	23.57	2-26	-	
1-day Lge	14	12	2	125	33	12.50	-	-	-	-	94.4	8	417	11	37.90	3-26	-	

137

Career Performances

	M	Inns	NO	Runs	HS	Avge	100s	50s	Ct	St	Balls	Runs	Wkts	Avge	Best	5wl	10wM
Test																	
All First	146	199	48	3278	155	21.70	2	12	46	-	24266	12319	438	28.12	6-30	18	1
1-day Int																	
C & G	23	14	2	144	81 *	12.00	-	1	6	-	1190	868	27	32.14	6-18	2	
B & H	36	21	7	162	50	11.57	-	1	9	-	1750	1280	40	32.00	5-7	1	
1-day Lge	118	58	16	570	56	13.57	-	2	20	-	4691	3623	126	28.75	6-25	1	

CHERRY, D. D. Glamorgan

Name: <u>Daniel</u> David Cherry
Role: Left-hand bat, right-arm
medium bowler
Born: 7 February 1980, Newport, Gwent
Height: 5ft 9in **Weight:** 13st
Nickname: Rhino, Banners, DC
County debut: 1998
1st-Class catches: 4
Place in batting averages: 256th av. 16.12
Parents: David and Elizabeth
Marital status: Single
Family links with cricket: Father is a
qualified coach and played club cricket
Education: Feltonfleet Prep School,
Cobham, Surrey; Tonbridge School, Kent;
University of Wales, Swansea
Qualifications: 10 GCSEs, 3 A-levels,
degree in History, Level 1 coaching award
Off-season: 'Playing club cricket in Melbourne'
Overseas tours: Tonbridge School to Australia 1996-97; Glamorgan to Cape
Town 2002
Overseas teams played for: Doutta Stars, Melbourne 2002-03
Career highlights to date: 'First-class debut'
Cricket moments to forget: 'Bagging a pair on 2nd XI Championship debut'
Cricketers particularly admired: Michael Atherton, Graham Thorpe,
Steve James
Young players to look out for: Mark Wallace, David Harrison, Ian Thomas,
Jonathan Hughes
Other sports played: Rugby, rackets (Public Schools doubles champion)
Other sports followed: Rugby (Neath), football (Everton)
Relaxations: Reading true crime books, listening to music; 'socialising with the

high-quality clientele that frequents Pembrokeshire's premier nightspot – "The Sands Discotheque Deluxe"'

Extras: Played for ECB U19 XI v Pakistan U19 1998. Awarded Glamorgan 2nd XI cap 2002

Opinions on cricket: 'Development of youngsters is the way forward, not bringing in more overseas and EU-qualified players. All 2nd XI cricket should be played on 1st XI-standard grounds – the quality of pitches is not good enough!'

Best batting: 47 Glamorgan v Gloucestershire, Cheltenham 2002

2002 Season

	M	Inns	NO	Runs	HS	Avge	100s	50s	Ct	St	O	M	Runs	Wkts	Avge	Best	5wI	10wM
Test																		
All First	5	8	0	129	47	16.12	-	-	4	-	3	3	0	0	-	-	-	-
1-day Int																		
C & G																		
B & H																		
1-day Lge																		

Career Performances

	M	Inns	NO	Runs	HS	Avge	100s	50s	Ct	St	Balls	Runs	Wkts	Avge	Best	5wI	10wM
Test																	
All First	6	9	0	140	47	15.55	-	-	4	-	18	0	0	-	-	-	-
1-day Int																	
C & G																	
B & H																	
1-day Lge																	

15. Name the overseas cricketers who played
for Nottinghamshire in 2002.

CHILTON, M. J.   Lancashire

Name: <u>Mark</u> James Chilton
Role: Right-hand bat, right-arm medium bowler
Born: 2 October 1976, Sheffield
Height: 6ft 2in **Weight:** 12st 10lbs
Nickname: Dip, Chill
County debut: 1997
County cap: 2002
1st-Class 50s: 12
1st-Class 100s: 4
1st-Class catches: 56
One-Day 100s: 2
One-Day 5 w. in innings: 1
Place in batting averages: 163rd av. 27.17 (2001 124th av. 29.73)
Strike rate: 142.00 (career 148.80)
Parents: Jim and Sue
Marital status: Single
Family links with cricket: Father played local cricket
Education: Brooklands Primary School; Manchester Grammar School; Durham University
Qualifications: 10 GCSEs, 3 A-levels, BA (Hons) Business Economics, senior coaching award
Off-season: 'North Sydney CC in grade competition'
Overseas tours: Manchester Grammar School to Barbados 1993-94, to South Africa 1995-96; Durham University to Zimbabwe 1997-98
Overseas teams played for: East Torrens, Adelaide 2000-01
Career highlights to date: 'Receiving Lancashire first-team cap!'
Cricket moments to forget: 'Losing off the last ball v Warwicks in B&H semi-final 2002'
Cricket superstitions: 'None'
Cricketers particularly admired: Michael Atherton, David Gower
Young players to look out for: Kyle Hogg, James Anderson
Other sports played: Football, golf
Other sports followed: 'Interest in most sports', football (Manchester United)
Relaxations: 'Music, guitar, relaxing with girlfriend and friends'
Extras: Represented England U14, U15, U17. Awarded England U15 Batsman of the Year in 1992. Played for North of England v New Zealand U19 in 1996. Played for British Universities in 1997 Benson and Hedges Cup, winning the Gold Award against Sussex. Awarded 2nd XI cap 1998. B&H Gold Awards for his 102 (his maiden one-day century) v Nottinghamshire at Old Trafford and for his 101 in the semi-final v

Warwickshire also at Old Trafford 2002. C&G Man of the Match award for his 76* v Derbyshire at Old Trafford 2002. Awarded Lancashire cap 2002

Opinions on cricket: 'The increase in overseas and EU players is a worry. The money should be spent on grass-roots cricket and academies. There must be a minimum of six or seven players in each team eligible to play for England.'

Best batting: 107 Lancashire v DUCCE, Durham 2002

Best bowling: 1-1 Lancashire v Sri Lanka A, Old Trafford 1999

2002 Season

	M	Inns	NO	Runs	HS	Avge	100s	50s	Ct	St	O	M	Runs	Wkts	Avge	Best	5wI	10wM
Test																		
All First	17	29	1	761	107	27.17	1	4	15	-	71	17	226	3	75.33	1-10	-	-
1-day Int																		
C & G	2	2	1	118	76 *	118.00	-	1	-	-								
B & H	7	7	2	270	102	54.00	2	-	3	-	4	0	20	0	-		-	-
1-day Lge	15	14	1	453	84 *	34.84	-	4	4	-	25.4	0	121	3	40.33	1-13	-	

Career Performances

	M	Inns	NO	Runs	HS	Avge	100s	50s	Ct	St	Balls	Runs	Wkts	Avge	Best	5wI	10wM
Test																	
All First	63	104	6	2725	107	27.80	4	12	56	-	744	397	5	79.40	1-1	-	-
1-day Int																	
C & G	5	5	1	230	76 *	57.50	-	2	2	-	42	42	2	21.00	1-20	-	
B & H	21	21	4	621	102	36.52	2	2	8	-	394	338	14	24.14	5-26	1	
1-day Lge	44	41	3	824	84 *	21.68	-	4	8	-	334	303	10	30.30	3-41	-	

16. Which New Zealand Test all-rounder made only one Championship appearance for Middlesex in 1996?

CLAPP, D. A.   Sussex

Name: <u>Dominic</u> Adrian Clapp
Role: Right-hand bat, right-arm
medium bowler
Born: 25 May 1980, Southport, Merseyside
Height: 6ft 0½ **Weight:** 13st 7lbs
Nickname: Hans, Poppa, Gruber, Rhino,
Link, Cornelius
County debut: 2002
Parents: Adrian and Sarah
Marital status: Single
Family links with cricket: Brother plays for
his local club side, Broadwater
Education: Sompting Abbotts Prep School;
Lancing College; Worthing Sixth Form
College
Qualifications: 6 GCSEs, 1 A-level, Level 1
and 2 cricket coach
Career outside cricket: Coaching/journalism

Overseas tours: Sussex U14 to Jersey 1994;
Lancing College to Australia 1996; Sussex U19 to Barbados 1997; Sussex Martlets to
Australia 2000; Sussex
to Grenada 2001
Overseas teams played for: St Bernhards CC, Melbourne
Cricketers particularly admired: Murray Goodwin, Steve Waugh, Jacques Kallis,
Damien Martyn, Mike Atherton, Tony Cottey, Ray Beiber, John Kaye
Young players to look out for: Matt Prior, Ian Bell, Nicky Peng, Ian Hunter,
Lawrence Prittipaul, Jimmy Adams
Other sports played: Tennis (Sussex U10, U11, U12), golf, two-touch football
Other sports followed: Football (Tottenham Hotspur), rugby, golf, tennis,
athletics, boxing
Relaxations: 'Reading newspapers, magazines, books; spending time with my friends;
playing cards'
Extras: Sussex U14 Player of the Year 1994. Set record for highest score in Sussex
Youth cricket, 189 v Middlesex 1998. Played two Development of Excellence games
v Australia U19 1999. Sussex Young Cricketer of the Year 1999. Played for Sussex
Board XI in the NatWest 2000. Released by Sussex at the end of the 2002 season
Best batting: 6 Sussex v Leicestershire, Horsham 2002

2002 Season

	M	Inns	NO	Runs	HS	Avge	100s	50s	Ct	St	O	M	Runs	Wkts	Avge	Best	5wI	10wM
Test																		
All First	1	1	0	6	6	6.00	-	-	-	-								
1-day Int																		
C & G																		
B & H																		
1-day Lge																		

Career Performances

	M	Inns	NO	Runs	HS	Avge	100s	50s	Ct	St	Balls	Runs	Wkts	Avge	Best	5wI	10wM
Test																	
All First	1	1	0	6	6	6.00	-	-	-	-							
1-day Int																	
C & G	2	2	0	14	10	7.00	-	-	-	-	36	46	3	15.33	3-46	-	
B & H																	
1-day Lge																	

CLARKE, A. J.   Essex

Name: Andrew (<u>Andy</u>) John Clarke
Role: Left-hand bat, right-arm
fast-medium bowler
Born: 9 November 1975, Harold Wood,
Essex
Height: 6ft 2in **Weight:** 12st 8lbs
Nickname: Vicram, Nobby, Ken
County debut: 2001 (one-day),
2002 (first-class)
1st-Class 5 w. in innings: 1
1st-Class catches: 1
Strike rate: 31.28 (career 31.28)
Parents: Mary and John (both deceased)
Marital status: Single
Family links with cricket: 'Dad played club
cricket'
Education: Hutton All Saints, Hutton,
Brentwood; St Martins School, Hutton;
Brentwood College of Higher Education
Qualifications: 7 GCSEs, 1 AS-level, 2 A-levels, Level 2 coaching
Career outside cricket: 'Property'
Overseas tours: MCC to Amsterdam 1998

Cricketers particularly admired: 'My dad'
Young players to look out for: Simon Thurston, Steve Cotton, Andy Bliss, Richard Lewis, Simon Lambett, Daniel Shepheard
Other sports played: Football, squash
Other sports followed: Football (West Ham)
Relaxations: 'Listening to music; time with family and friends'
Extras: MCC Young Cricketers cap and Player of the Year 1998. Played for Essex Board XI and Essex in the C&G 2001. Recorded maiden first-class five-wicket return on first-class debut v Glamorgan at Swansea 2002; his 5-54 included three wickets in his first six overs
Opinions on cricket: 'Starts should be later.'
Best batting: 31 Essex v Worcestershire, Southend 2002
Best bowling: 5-54 Essex v Glamorgan, Swansea 2002

2002 Season

	M	Inns	NO	Runs	HS	Avge	100s	50s	Ct	St	O	M	Runs	Wkts	Avge	Best	5wI	10wM
Test																		
All First	2	4	1	42	31	14.00	-	-	1	-	36.3	5	113	7	16.14	5-54	1	-
1-day Int																		
C & G	2	0	0	0	0	-	-	-	2	-	13	0	79	1	79.00	1-42	-	
B & H	7	2	2	3	2 *	-	-	-	1	-	38.4	2	191	12	15.91	4-44	-	
1-day Lge	4	2	1	0	0 *	0.00	-	-	2	-	32.3	1	124	10	12.40	4-30	-	

Career Performances

	M	Inns	NO	Runs	HS	Avge	100s	50s	Ct	St	Balls	Runs	Wkts	Avge	Best	5wI	10wM
Test																	
All First	2	4	1	42	31	14.00	-	-	1	-	219	113	7	16.14	5-54	1	-
1-day Int																	
C & G	4	2	0	9	9	4.50	-	-	2	-	174	117	2	58.50	1-19	-	
B & H	7	2	2	3	2 *	-	-	-	1	-	232	191	12	15.91	4-44	-	
1-day Lge	14	7	2	10	5	2.00	-	-	3	-	519	408	17	24.00	4-30	-	

CLARKE, R.   Surrey

Name: Rikki Clarke
Role: Right-hand bat, right-arm medium-fast bowler
Born: 29 September 1981, Orsett, Essex
Height: 6ft 4½in   **Weight:** 13st 7lbs
Nickname: Clarkey, Gimp
County debut: 2001 (one-day), 2002 (first-class)
1st-Class 50s: 4
1st-Class 100s: 2
1st-Class catches: 9

Place in batting averages: 33rd av. 50.78
Place in bowling averages: 128th av. 41.00
Strike rate: 51.54 (career 51.54)
Parents: Janet and Bob
Marital status: Girlfriend Becky
Family links with cricket: 'Dad was a legend of club cricket. (Ha-ha)'
Education: Godalming Middle School; Broadwater; Godalming College
Qualifications: 5 GCSEs, GNVQ Leisure and Tourism
Off-season: 'National Academy in Oz'
Overseas tours: Surrey U19 to Barbados; MCC Young Cricketers to Cape Town; England to Sri Lanka (ICC Champions Trophy) 2002-03; ECB National Academy to Australia and Sri Lanka 2002-03

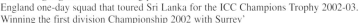

Career highlights to date: 'Being picked for England one-day squad that toured Sri Lanka for the ICC Champions Trophy 2002-03. Winning the first division Championship 2002 with Surrey'
Cricketers particularly admired: Ian Botham, Darren Gough
Young players to look out for: Tim Murtagh, Scott Newman, Jim Troughton, James Anderson
Other sports played: Football, golf, snooker
Other sports followed: Football (Tottenham Hotspur)
Injuries: Out for two weeks with a back injury
Relaxations: 'Golf, snooker, watching films'
Extras: Named after former Tottenham Hotspur and Argentina footballer Ricky Villa. Represented England U17 at the ECC Colts Festival in Northern Ireland 1999. Played for Surrey Board XI in the second round of the C&G 2002, which was played in September 2001. Scored maiden first-class century (107*) on first-class debut v Cambridge University CCE at Fenner's and maiden Championship century (153*) v Somerset at Taunton 2002. Cricket Writers' Young Player of the Year 2002. Surrey Supporters' Young Player of the Year 2002. Surrey Sponsors' Young Player of the Year 2002. Called up to the England one-day squad for the ICC Champions Trophy in Sri Lanka 2002-03 as a replacement for the injured Paul Collingwood
Best batting: 153* Surrey v Somerset, Taunton 2002
Best bowling: 3-41 Surrey v Yorkshire, Guildford 2002

2002 Season

	M	Inns	NO	Runs	HS	Avge	100s	50s	Ct	St	O	M	Runs	Wkts	Avge	Best	5wI	10wM
Test																		
All First	10	16	2	711	153 *	50.78	2	4	9	-	94.3	15	451	11	41.00	3-41	-	-
1-day Int																		
C & G	4	3	0	63	55	21.00	-	1	1	-	16.1	0	115	2	57.50	2-56	-	
B & H																		
1-day Lge	11	11	2	316	98 *	35.11	-	3	5	-	59.2	3	306	7	43.71	2-32	-	

Career Performances

	M	Inns	NO	Runs	HS	Avge	100s	50s	Ct	St	Balls	Runs	Wkts	Avge	Best	5wI	10wM
Test																	
All First	10	16	2	711	153 *	50.78	2	4	9	-	567	451	11	41.00	3-41	-	-
1-day Int																	
C & G	5	4	0	65	55	16.25	-	1	1	-	121	129	3	43.00	2-56	-	
B & H																	
1-day Lge	13	13	2	323	98 *	29.36	-	3	6	-	356	306	7	43.71	2-32	-	

CLIFFORD, I. J. Warwickshire

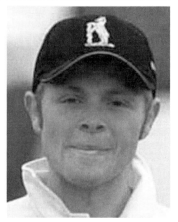

Name: <u>Ian</u> Jeffrey Clifford
Role: Right-hand bat, wicket-keeper
Born: 12 October 1982, Birmingham
Height: 5ft 6in **Weight:** 9st 12lbs
Nickname: Cliffy
County debut: 2002
1st-Class catches: 15
1st-Class stumpings: 1
Place in batting averages: 317th av. 3.33
Parents: Michael and Sheila
Marital status: Single
Education: Castle Bromwich Junior School;
Park Hall Secondary School
Qualifications: Level 1 coaching
Off-season: 'Intend to spend winter in South
Africa after Christmas'
Overseas tours: Warwickshire Development
squad to West Indies 1999-2000
Career highlights to date: 'Taking four catches and a stumping as a substitute fielder'
Cricket moments to forget: 'Coming 317th (bottom) in the County Championship
batting averages 2002'
Cricket superstitions: 'Always walk on the pitch left foot first'

146

Cricketers particularly admired: Keith Piper, Jack Russell, Ian Healy
Young players to look out for: Naqaash Tahir, Moeen Munir, Huw Jones
Other sports played: Cycling
Other sports followed: Football (Aston Villa)
Injuries: Out for one week with a bruised index finger
Extras: Played for Warwickshire Board XI in the C&G 2001 and 2002. Appeared in Championship match v Leicestershire at Edgbaston 2002 as substitute wicket-keeper after Tony Frost suffered a broken finger, later making full debut v Somerset, also at Edgbaston
Opinions on cricket: 'I think that the set-up of the two-divisional system has improved competitiveness right across the county circuit.'
Best batting: 7 Warwickshire v Kent, Edgbaston 2002

2002 Season

	M	Inns	NO	Runs	HS	Avge	100s	50s	Ct	St	O	M	Runs	Wkts	Avge	Best	5wI	10wM
Test																		
All First	4	6	0	20	7	3.33	-	-	15	1								
1-day Int																		
C & G	1	1	1	5	5 *	-	-	-	-	1								
B & H																		
1-day Lge	3	1	0	1	1	1.00	-	-	5	-								

Career Performances

	M	Inns	NO	Runs	HS	Avge	100s	50s	Ct	St	Balls	Runs	Wkts	Avge	Best	5wI	10wM
Test																	
All First	4	6	0	20	7	3.33	-	-	15	1							
1-day Int																	
C & G	2	2	1	8	5 *	8.00	-	-	2	1							
B & H																	
1-day Lge	3	1	0	1	1	1.00	-	-	5	-							

14. In 1999 county cricket boasted two captains who had
or would skipper Tasmania. Name them.

CLINTON, R. S.   Essex

Name: <u>Richard</u> Selvey Clinton
Role: Left-hand opening bat, right-arm medium bowler
Born: 1 September 1981, Sidcup, Kent
Height: 6ft 3in **Weight:** 13st 9lbs
Nickname: Bill, Clint, Norman
County debut: 2001
1st-Class 50s: 2
1st-Class 100s: 1
1st-Class catches: 4
Place in batting averages: 114th av. 34.57 (2001 191st av. 20.21)
Strike rate: (career 27.00)
Parents: Grahame and Catherine
Marital status: Single
Family links with cricket: 'Grandfather and uncles successful club cricketers. Father played professionally for Kent and Surrey'
Education: Harenc Prep School; Colfes School
Qualifications: 9 GCSEs, 3 A-levels
Career outside cricket: Student
Overseas teams played for: Kensington CC, Adelaide; Valleys CC, Brisbane
Career highlights to date: 'Making first-class debut'
Cricket moments to forget: 'Fielding in a Sunday League game against Glamorgan with half-and-half spikes after five days of rain, therefore being unable to stand up or stop running'
Cricketers particularly admired: Graham Thorpe, Mark Butcher, Ricky Ponting
Young players to look out for: Justin Bishop
Other sports played: Football, rugby
Other sports followed: Football (Chelsea FC)
Relaxations: Doing crosswords; playing sport in general; listening to dance music
Extras: Scored 36 and 58* on first-class debut v Surrey at Ilford 2001; scored 56 the following day on Norwich Union League debut v Durham at the same ground. Scored maiden first-class century (107) v Cambridge University CCE at Fenner's 2002. Released by Essex at the end of the 2002 season
Opinions on cricket: 'Should be more use of floodlights to allow Championship games to start and finish later, thereby allowing the supporters to watch the game after work.'
Best batting: 107 Essex v CUCCE, Fenner's 2002
Best bowling: 2-30 Essex v Australians, Chelmsford 2001

2002 Season

	M	Inns	NO	Runs	HS	Avge	100s	50s	Ct	St	O	M	Runs	Wkts	Avge	Best	5wI	10wM
Test																		
All First	5	8	1	242	107	34.57	1	1	2	-								
1-day Int																		
C & G																		
B & H																		
1-day Lge	3	3	1	15	11	7.50	-	-	2	-								

Career Performances

	M	Inns	NO	Runs	HS	Avge	100s	50s	Ct	St	Balls	Runs	Wkts	Avge	Best	5wI	10wM
Test																	
All First	13	23	2	525	107	25.00	1	2	4	-	54	30	2	15.00	2-30	-	-
1-day Int																	
C & G	1	1	0	13	13	13.00	-	-	-	-							
B & H																	
1-day Lge	12	9	3	140	56	23.33	-	1	2	-	18	25	0	-		-	-

CLOUGH, G. D. Nottinghamshire

Name: <u>Gareth</u> David Clough
Role: Right-hand bat, right-arm
medium bowler
Born: 23 May 1978, Leeds
Height: 6ft **Weight:** 12st
Nickname: Banga, Cloughie
County debut: 1998 (Yorkshire),
2001 (Nottinghamshire)
1st-Class catches: 2
Place in batting averages: (2001 282nd
av. 3.66)
Strike rate: 39.00 (career 86.25)
Parents: David and Gillian
Marital status: Single
Family links with cricket: Brother-in-law
plays local league cricket in Leeds
Education: Pudsey Greenside Primary
School; Pudsey Grangefield
Qualifications: 9 GCSEs, 3 A-levels, Level 1 cricket coach
Overseas tours: Yorkshire to Durban and Cape Town 1999; Nottinghamshire to
Johannesburg 2001
Overseas teams played for: Somerset West, Cape Town 1996-97; Deepdene Bears,
Melbourne 1999-2000, 2001-02

Career highlights to date: 'Making my first-class debut – Yorkshire v Glamorgan 1998, Sophia Gardens'
Cricket moments to forget: 'B&H semi-final v Surrey at The Oval 2001' (*Nottinghamshire conceded 361 runs, more than any other first-class county in B&H history, and were then dismissed for 187*)
Cricketers particularly admired: Ian Botham, Steve Waugh
Young players to look out for: Bilal Shafayat, Samit Patel
Other sports played: Golf, football (Royal FC), tennis, snooker, nine-ball pool
Other sports followed: Football (Everton FC), rugby league (Leeds Rhinos)
Relaxations: Socialising with friends, watching films
Extras: Formerly with Yorkshire. Played for Nottinghamshire 2nd XI in 2000, topping the bowling averages with 37 wickets at 19.05 and scoring 400 runs
Opinions on cricket: 'The introduction of a two-divisional structure in the domestic game has made the game more competitive throughout the season, and floodlit games have made cricket more of a spectator sport – which are both big positives.'
Best batting: 33 Yorkshire v Glamorgan, Cardiff 1998
Best bowling: 3-69 Nottinghamshire v Gloucestershire, Trent Bridge 2001

2002 Season

	M	Inns	NO	Runs	HS	Avge	100s	50s	Ct	St	O	M	Runs	Wkts	Avge	Best	5wI	10wM
Test																		
All First	1	1	0	5	5	5.00	-	-	-	-	13	1	61	2	30.50	2-61	-	-
1-day Int																		
C & G	1	0	0	0	0	-	-	-	-	-	6	0	38	0	-		-	-
B & H	5	2	0	3	2	1.50	-	-	4	-	10	0	54	2	27.00	1-6	-	
1-day Lge	1	1	0	22	22	22.00	-	-	-	-	3	0	28	0	-		-	-

Career Performances

	M	Inns	NO	Runs	HS	Avge	100s	50s	Ct	St	Balls	Runs	Wkts	Avge	Best	5wI	10wM
Test																	
All First	6	9	0	61	33	6.77	-	-	2	-	690	425	8	53.12	3-69	-	-
1-day Int																	
C & G	1	0	0	0	0	-	-	-	-	-	36	38	0	-		-	-
B & H	12	3	0	3	2	1.00	-	-	5	-	422	362	9	40.22	2-36	-	
1-day Lge	14	9	2	95	24	13.57	-	-	2	-	535	457	13	35.15	2-33	-	

18. Which South African batsman became the first player to score a century on debut for Derbyshire in the Championship in 1995?

COLEMAN, A. J.
Middlesex

Name: <u>Alan</u> James Coleman
Role: Right-hand bat, right-arm
medium-fast bowler
Born: 13 December 1983, Ashford
Height: 6ft 2in **Weight:** 12st 4lbs
Nickname: Coley
County debut: 2001 (one-day)
Parents: Pamela and Philip
Marital status: Single
Family links with cricket: 'Dad played club
cricket for many years. Brother Chris kept
wicket for Loughborough UCCE and
Derbyshire and Middlesex 2nd XIs'
Education: Bedfont Primary School;
Longford Community School; Loughborough
University ('after gap year')
Qualifications: 11 GCSEs, 3 A-levels, ECB
Level II coach, community sports leader
Off-season: 'Training and coaching (gap year
before university)'
Overseas tours: England U17 to Australia 2000-01
Career highlights to date: 'Making Norwich Union League debut v Sussex in 2001'
Cricketers particularly admired: Owais Shah, 'all the Wycombe House CC boys'
Young players to look out for: Tim Bresnan, Bilal Shafayat, Gary Scott
Other sports played: Football, squash
Other sports followed: Football (Brentford FC)
Injuries: Out for one week with food poisoning; for two weeks with a rib injury
Relaxations: 'Watching Brentford; music; going to the gym'
Opinions on cricket: 'Haven't been playing long enough to say anything. Looking
good so far.'

2002 Season

	M	Inns	NO	Runs	HS	Avge	100s	50s	Ct	St	O	M	Runs	Wkts	Avge	Best	5wl	10wM
Test																		
All First																		
1-day Int																		
C & G																		
B & H																		
1-day Lge	1	1	1	14	14 *	-	-	-	1	-	3	0	31	0	-		-	-

Career Performances

	M	Inns	NO	Runs	HS	Avge	100s	50s	Ct	St	Balls	Runs	Wkts	Avge	Best	5wl	10wM
Test																	
All First																	
1-day Int																	
C & G																	
B & H																	
1-day Lge	4	3	3	29	14 *	-	-	-	2	-	97	92	0	-	-	-	-

COLLINGWOOD, P. D.   Durham

Name: <u>Paul</u> David Collingwood
Role: Right-hand bat, right-arm
medium bowler
Born: 26 May 1976, Shotley Bridge,
Tyneside
Height: 5ft 11in **Weight:** 12st
Nickname: Colly
County debut: 1995 (one-day),
1996 (first-class)
County cap: 1998
One-Day Internationals: 25
1000 runs in a season: 1
1st-Class 50s: 26
1st-Class 100s: 8
1st-Class catches: 92
One-Day 100s: 1
Place in batting averages: 26th av. 53.00
(2001 24th av. 52.76)
Place in bowling averages: 33rd av. 25.80
Strike rate: 58.00 (career 85.63)
Parents: David and Janet
Marital status: Single

Family links with cricket: Father and brother play in the Tyneside Senior League for
Shotley Bridge CC
Education: Benfieldside Junior School; Blackfyne Comprehensive School;
Derwentside College
Qualifications: 9 GCSEs and 2 A-levels
Career outside cricket: 'Hopefully a few years left yet'
Overseas tours: Durham Cricket Academy to Sri Lanka 1996 (captain); England VI
to Hong Kong 2001, 2002; England to Zimbabwe (one-day series) 2001-02, to India
and New Zealand 2001-02 (one-day series), to Australia 2002-03 (VB Series)

Overseas teams played for: Bulleen CC, Melbourne 1995-96, 1996-97 ('won flag on both occasions'); Cornwall CC, Auckland 1997-98; Alberton CC, Johannesburg 1998-99; Richmond CC, Melbourne 2000-01

Career highlights to date: 'Scoring 71* against India in Cuttack'

Cricket moments to forget: 'Being Matthew Walker's (Kent) first first-class wicket'

Cricket superstitions: 'Left pad on first, and wearing them on the wrong legs'

Cricketers particularly admired: Steve Waugh, Jacques Kallis, Glenn McGrath, Shane Warne

Young players to look out for: Gordon Muchall

Other sports played: Golf (9 handicap)

Other sports followed: Football ('The Red and Whites' – Sunderland)

Injuries: Out for five weeks with strained right medial ligament (knee); out for eight weeks-plus with prolapsed disc in neck and loss of right-arm tricep to nerve damage

Extras: Took wicket (David Capel) with first ball on first-class debut against Northants, then scored 91 in Durham's first innings. Durham Player of the Year 2000. Awarded the Ron Brierley Scholarship 2000 through the ECB in conjunction with the Victorian Cricket Association, Australia; joint winner of the Jack Ryder Medal, awarded by the umpires, for his performances in Victorian Premier Cricket 2000-01. B&H Gold Awards for his 89 v Derbyshire at Derby and 95* v Leicestershire at Riverside 2001. Man of the Match (77 and 1-31) in fourth ODI v Zimbabwe at Bulawayo 2001-02; followed up with 56* (50 from 43 balls) in fifth ODI at Bulawayo. Man of the Match in One-Day International v India at Cuttack 2001-02 for his all-round performance, including 71*. Took 4-38 in One-Day International v New Zealand at Napier 2001-02, winning the Man of the Match award. B&H Gold Award for his 51 plus 1-22 v Derbyshire at Riverside 2002. Recorded highest scored by a Durham player at the Riverside ground, 190 v Sri Lankans 2002. Scored maiden one-day century (118*) v Nottinghamshire at Riverside in the NUL 2002. Selected for the England one-day squad for the Champions Trophy in Sri Lanka 2002-03 but was forced to withdraw with a neck injury; replaced by Rikki Clarke

Best batting: 190 Durham v Sri Lanka, Riverside 2002

Best bowling: 4-31 Durham v Derbyshire, Derby 2002

Stop press: Called up to the England Test squad in Australia 2002-03 as batting cover for John Crawley and Michael Vaughan. Scored maiden ODI century (100) v Sri Lanka in the VB Series at Perth 2002-03, winning Man of the Match award; England reached 258-9, having at one point been 122-6. Selected for England squad for 2002-03 World Cup

	M	Inns	NO	Runs	HS	Avge	100s	50s	Ct	St	O	M	Runs	Wkts	Avge	Best	5wl	10wM
Test																		
All First	7	12	0	636	190	53.00	1	4	5	-	96.4	24	258	10	25.80	4-31	-	-
1-day Int	7	6	2	95	38	23.75	-	-	2	-	25	0	196	5	39.20	2-31	-	
C & G																		
B & H	5	5	0	106	51	21.20	-	1	-	-	38	1	199	5	39.80	2-37	-	
1-day Lge	6	6	1	195	118 *	39.00	1	-	5	-	30.4	2	152	8	19.00	2-29	-	

Career Performances

	M	Inns	NO	Runs	HS	Avge	100s	50s	Ct	St	Balls	Runs	Wkts	Avge	Best	5wl	10wM
Test																	
All First	91	157	10	4730	190	32.17	8	26	92	-	5224	2401	61	39.36	4-31	-	-
1-day Int	25	24	6	448	77	24.88	-	3	8	-	589	593	13	45.61	4-38	-	
C & G	11	10	1	262	60	29.11	-	2	1	-	246	196	4	49.00	2-7	-	
B & H	29	28	5	749	95 *	32.56	-	3	11	-	1019	800	23	34.78	4-31	-	
1-day Lge	84	81	7	2106	118 *	28.45	1	14	46	-	1742	1386	48	28.87	3-20	-	

COMPTON, N. R. D.   Middlesex

Name: Nicholas (Nick) Richard
Denis Compton
Role: Right-hand bat, right-arm
off-spin bowler
Born: 26 June 1983, Durban, South Africa
Height: 6ft 1in **Weight:** 12st 8lbs
Nickname: Compo
County debut: 2001 (one-day)
Parents: Richard and Glynis
Marital status: Single
Family links with cricket: Grandfather
Denis Compton played for Middlesex and
England
Education: Clifton, Durban; Hilton
College/DHS, South Africa; Harrow School
Qualifications: 3 A-levels
Overseas tours: England U19 to Australia
and (U19 World Cup) New Zealand 2001-02
Overseas teams played for: University of Western Australia, Perth 2001
Career highlights to date: 'A fifty at age 15 to win a game against a President's XI
which included a number of West Indians'
Cricket moments to forget: 'Dropping three catches against Australia 2002'
Cricketers particularly admired: Jacques Kallis, Damien Martyn

Young players to look out for: Shaun Marsh (Australian), Hasim Amla and Jon Kent (South African), Kyle Hogg, Paul McMahon

Other sports played: Golf (6 handicap), represented Natal at junior level at tennis, hockey, football and rugby

Other sports followed: Football (Arsenal), rugby union (Natal Sharks)

Relaxations: Music, films and friends

Extras: Played for Natal U13 and U15. Represented Harrow v Eton in 1999 (match abandoned), 2000, and 2001 (captain). Natal Academy award 1997. Middlesex U17 Batsman of the Season 1999. Middlesex U19 Player of the Season 2000. NBC Denis Compton Award for the most promising young Middlesex player 2001. Represented England U19 v India U19 in 'Test' series (1/3) 2002

Opinions on cricket: 'Far too individual. Players driven by money and bonuses rather than their so-called passion for the game.'

2002 Season

	M	Inns	NO	Runs	HS	Avge	100s	50s	Ct	St	O	M	Runs	Wkts	Avge	Best	5wI	10wM
Test																		
All First																		
1-day Int																		
C & G																		
B & H																		
1-day Lge	4	4	3	123	86 *	123.00	-	1	-	-	5	0	20	0	-		-	-

Career Performances

	M	Inns	NO	Runs	HS	Avge	100s	50s	Ct	St	Balls	Runs	Wkts	Avge	Best	5wI	10wM
Test																	
All First																	
1-day Int																	
C & G																	
B & H																	
1-day Lge	5	5	3	129	86 *	64.50	-	1	-	-	30	20	0	-		-	-

23. The Waugh twins both played county cricket in 2002. When was the last season in which this occurred and for which counties did they play then?

COOK, J. W.   Northamptonshire

Name: <u>Jeffrey</u> William Cook
Role: Left-hand bat, right-arm
medium bowler
Born: 2 February 1972, Sydney, Australia
Height: 6ft 4in **Weight:** 14st
Nickname: Cookie
County debut: 2000
1st-Class 50s: 9
1st-Class 100s: 2
1st-Class catches: 13
One-Day 100s: 2
Place in batting averages: 105th av. 35.52
(2001 148th av. 26.06)
Strike rate: 88.00 (career 108.00)
Parents: Roma and Les
Wife and date of marriage: Fiona,
10 October 1998
Children: Alexander, 21 April 2000
Family links with cricket: Mother
represented New South Wales
Education: Rockdale Public School, Rockdale, NSW; James Cook High School,
Kogarah, NSW
Qualifications: NCA Level 2 coaching award, ACB Level 1 coaching award
Overseas tours: Northamptonshire to Grenada 2000, 2001
Overseas teams played for: St George DCC, Sydney 1987-93;
Easts CC, Sydney 1999 – 2002
Career highlights to date: 'First [first-class] century (137) v Glos in my second
game. Winning second division of Championship in 2000 with Northants. Fielding for
England v Pakistan at Lord's 2001'
Cricket moments to forget: 'First ever pair – v Yorkshire at Headingley 2001'
Cricketers particularly admired: David Gower, Mark Taylor, Mark Waugh,
Steve Waugh
Young players to look out for: Tobin Bailey
Other sports played: Football, tennis
Other sports followed: Football (Liverpool), rugby league (Parramatta)
Relaxations: 'Time with family'
Extras: Represented NSW at U17, U19 and Colts levels. Represented New South
Wales and Australia at indoor cricket. Played for Northants Board XI in 1999 NatWest,
scoring 130 v Wiltshire at Northampton and winning the Man of the Match award.
Shared in record second-wicket stand for Northants in matches v Surrey (172) with
Mike Hussey at Northampton 2001. B&H Gold Award for his 3-19 v Glamorgan at
Northampton 2002. Is not considered an overseas player

Best batting: 137 Northamptonshire v Gloucestershire, Cheltenham 2000
Best bowling: 2-7 Northamptonshire v OUCCE, The Parks 2002

2002 Season

	M	Inns	NO	Runs	HS	Avge	100s	50s	Ct	St	O	M	Runs	Wkts	Avge	Best	5wI	10wM
Test																		
All First	15	24	3	746	90	35.52	-	4	4	-	132	31	474	9	52.66	2-7	-	-
1-day Int																		
C & G	2	2	0	70	70	35.00	-	1	-	-	8	2	25	1	25.00	1-5	-	
B & H	5	4	2	115	50	57.50	-	1	1	-	19	0	103	4	25.75	3-19	-	
1-day Lge	15	13	1	356	102	29.66	1	1	3	-	78.5	0	385	22	17.50	4-35	-	

Career Performances

	M	Inns	NO	Runs	HS	Avge	100s	50s	Ct	St	Balls	Runs	Wkts	Avge	Best	5wI	10wM
Test																	
All First	35	57	5	1639	137	31.51	2	9	13	-	1080	605	10	60.50	2-7	-	-
1-day Int																	
C & G	6	6	0	305	130	50.83	1	1	-	-	96	75	1	75.00	1-5	-	
B & H	10	9	2	275	86	39.28	-	2	2	-	162	146	4	36.50	3-19	-	
1-day Lge	37	35	1	671	102	19.73	1	2	13	-	581	466	25	18.64	4-35	-	

COOK, S. J. Middlesex

Name: <u>Simon</u> James Cook
Role: Right-hand bat, right-arm
medium-fast bowler
Born: 15 January 1977, Oxford
Height: 6ft 4in **Weight:** 13st
Nickname: Donk, Cookie
County debut: 1997 (one-day),
1999 (first-class)
1st-Class 50s: 2
1st-Class 5 w. in innings: 2
1st-Class catches: 12
Place in batting averages: 249th av. 16.68
(2001 129th av. 29.50)
Place in bowling averages: 40th av. 27.18
(2001 89th av. 34.80)
Strike rate: 45.91 (career 56.55)
Parents: Phil and Sue
Marital status: Single
Education: Botley Primary School; Matthew Arnold School
Qualifications: GCSEs, NVQ Business Administration II

Career outside cricket: Coaching Middlesex youth squads
Off-season: Coaching
Overseas tours: Middlesex to South Africa 2000
Overseas teams played for: Rockingham, Perth 2000-01
Cricketers particularly admired: Angus Fraser, Mark Waugh, Glenn McGrath
Young players to look out for: Jamie Dalrymple, Ed Joyce, Nick Compton,
John Maunders
Other sports followed: Football (Liverpool), 'any other ball sport'
Relaxations: 'Sleeping, playing any sport, watching television and videos'
Extras: Scored career best 93* v Nottinghamshire at Lord's 2001, helping Middlesex
to avoid the follow-on, then took a wicket with the first ball of his opening spell.
Recorded maiden first-class five-wicket return (5-11; 9-62 the match) v Cambridge
University CCE at Fenner's 2002. Recorded maiden Championship five-wicket return
(8-63) v Northamptonshire at Northampton 2002
Best batting: 93* Middlesex v Nottinghamshire, Lord's 2001
Best bowling: 8-63 Middlesex v Northamptonshire, Northampton 2002

2002 Season

	M	Inns	NO	Runs	HS	Avge	100s	50s	Ct	St	O	M	Runs	Wkts	Avge	Best	5wI	10wM
Test																		
All First	15	18	2	267	43 *	16.68	-	-	4	-	367.2	71	1305	48	27.18	8-63	2	-
1-day Int																		
C & G	1	1	1	39	39 *	-	-	-	-	-	10	0	48	2	24.00	2-48	-	
B & H	4	3	0	89	48	29.66	-	-	1	-	29.4	0	143	2	71.50	2-46	-	
1-day Lge	12	9	1	76	21	9.50	-	-	2	-	83	5	367	12	30.58	3-28	-	

Career Performances

	M	Inns	NO	Runs	HS	Avge	100s	50s	Ct	St	Balls	Runs	Wkts	Avge	Best	5wI	10wM
Test																	
All First	42	55	8	885	93 *	18.82	-	2	12	-	5995	3290	106	31.03	8-63	2	-
1-day Int																	
C & G	4	4	2	53	39 *	26.50	-	-	-	-	180	127	4	31.75	2-48	-	
B & H	10	7	0	107	48	15.28	-	-	2	-	478	413	7	59.00	2-46	-	
1-day Lge	52	39	6	394	50	11.93	-	1	9	-	2182	1624	58	28.00	3-16	-	

20. For which county did Rahul Dravid play in 2000?

CORK, D. G.   Derbyshire

Name: <u>Dominic</u> Gerald Cork
Role: Right-hand bat, right-arm fast-medium bowler, county captain
Born: 7 August 1971, Newcastle-under-Lyme, Staffordshire
Height: 6ft 3in **Weight:** 14st 10lbs
Nickname: Corky
County debut: 1990
County cap: 1993
Benefit: 2001
Test debut: 1995
Tests: 37
One-Day Internationals: 30
50 wickets in a season: 6
1st-Class 50s: 39
1st-Class 100s: 4
1st-Class 200s: 1
1st-Class 5 w. in innings: 25
1st-Class 10 w. in match: 3
1st-Class catches: 145
One-Day 5 w. in innings: 4
Place in batting averages: 136th av. 30.43 (2001 161st av. 23.81)
Place in bowling averages: 4th av. 18.90 (2001 137th av. 51.50)
Strike rate: 37.84 (career 53.16)
Parents: Gerald and Mary
Wife and date of marriage: Donna-Marie, 28 August 2000
Children: Ashleigh, 28 April 1990; Gregory Theodore Gerald, 29 September 1994
Family links with cricket: 'Father and brothers played for Betley CC in local North Staffs & South Cheshire League with myself'
Education: The Convent, Newcastle, Staffs; St Joseph's College, Trent Vale, Stoke-on-Trent
Qualifications: 3 O-levels, Level 2 coach
Overseas tours: England YC to Australia 1989-90; England A to Bermuda and West Indies 1991-92, to Australia 1992-93, to South Africa 1993-94, to India 1994-95; England to South Africa 1995-96, to India and Pakistan (World Cup) 1995-96, to New Zealand 1996-97, to Australia 1998-99, to Pakistan and Sri Lanka 2000-01, to Sri Lanka (ICC Champions Trophy) 2002-03
Overseas teams played for: East Shirley, Christchurch, New Zealand 1990-91
Career highlights to date: 'Making my debut for England'
Cricket moments to forget: 'Losing any game'
Cricketers particularly admired: Ian Botham, Malcolm Marshall, Imran Khan
Young players to look out for: Luke Sutton

Other sports played: Football, skiing
Other sports followed: Football (Stoke City)
Extras: Played Minor Counties cricket for Staffordshire in 1989 and 1990. In 1990 he took a wicket in his first over in first-class cricket, v New Zealanders at Derby, and scored a century as nightwatchman for England U19 v Pakistan at Taunton. Took 8-53 before lunch on his 20th birthday, v Essex at Derby 1991. Selected for England A in 1991 – his first full season of first-class cricket. Won the Professional Cricketers' Association (PCA) Young Player of the Year award 1991. Achieved first-class hat-trick against Kent 1994. Took 7-43 on Test debut against West Indies at Lord's 1995, the best innings figures by an England debutant. Achieved hat-trick against the West Indies at Old Trafford in the fourth Test 1995 – the first by an Englishman in Test cricket for 38 years. Voted Player of the Year by the PCA for 1995. Finished at the top of the Whyte and Mackay ratings for bowling in 1995. Cornhill England Player of the Year 1995-96. One of *Wisden*'s Five Cricketers of the Year 1996. Man of the Match in the second Test v West Indies at Lord's 2000; on his recall to the Test side he recorded match figures of 7-52 followed by a match-winning 33* in England's second innings. Scored maiden first-class 200 (200*, the highest score by a Derbyshire No. 8) v Durham at Derby 2000, setting in the process a new record seventh-wicket partnership for Derbyshire (258) with Mathew Dowman. C&G Man of the Match award for his 50 followed by 4-35 v Glamorgan at Cardiff 2001. Was the first bowler to reach 50 first-class wickets in the 2002 season. Derbyshire captain since 1998. Called up to the England one-day squad for the ICC Champions Trophy in Sri Lanka 2002-03, replacing the injured Craig White
Opinions on cricket: 'Too many games. Too little quality. The game should be run by England and counties by owners.'
Best batting: 200* Derbyshire v Durham, Derby 2000
Best bowling: 9-43 Derbyshire v Northamptonshire, Derby 1995

2002 Season

	M	Inns	NO	Runs	HS	Avge	100s	50s	Ct	St	O	M	Runs	Wkts	Avge	Best	5wI	10wM
Test	3	3	0	83	52	27.66	-	1	1	-	80.3	20	259	7	37.00	3-93	-	-
All First	11	16	0	487	80	30.43	-	5	12	-	403.4	101	1210	64	18.90	6-51	5	1
1-day Int																		
C & G	1	1	0	0	0	0.00	-	-	-	-	10	3	36	0	-		-	-
B & H	4	3	0	39	19	13.00	-	-	-	-	18.3	4	66	1	66.00	1-10	-	
1-day Lge	9	9	2	215	51	30.71	-	1	5	-	79.1	14	222	13	17.07	2-20	-	

Career Performances

	M	Inns	NO	Runs	HS	Avge	100s	50s	Ct	St	Balls	Runs	Wkts	Avge	Best	5wI	10wM
Test	37	56	8	864	59	18.00	-	3	18	-	7678	3906	131	29.81	7-43	5	-
All First	206	305	41	6712	200 *	25.42	5	39	145	-	35729	17570	672	26.14	9-43	25	3
1-day Int	30	19	2	174	31 *	10.23	-	-	6	-	1691	1286	41	31.36	3-27	-	
C & G	21	19	4	543	93	36.20	-	6	8	-	1317	797	42	18.97	5-18	2	
B & H	34	26	6	470	92 *	23.50	-	2	15	-	1807	1177	36	32.69	5-49	1	
1-day Lge	107	91	11	1580	83 *	19.75	-	7	49	-	4661	3452	127	27.18	6-21	1	

COSKER, D. A. Glamorgan

Name: <u>Dean</u> Andrew Cosker
Role: Right-hand bat, slow left-arm
spin bowler
Born: 7 January 1978, Weymouth, Dorset
Height: 5ft 10in **Weight:** 12st 5lbs
Nickname: Lurks
County debut: 1996
County cap: 2000
1st-Class 5 w. in innings: 2
1st-Class catches: 63
Place in batting averages: 287th av. 10.45
(2001 221st av. 15.90)
Place in bowling averages: 147th av. 50.60
(2001 121st av. 42.12)
Strike rate: 95.35 (career 78.25)
Parents: Des and Carol
Marital status: Girlfriend Katie
Education: Ravenswood Prep School, Devon;
Millfield School; 'The Cayo Arms, Cathedral Road'
Qualifications: 10 GCSEs, 4 A-levels
Career outside cricket: 'Bodybuilder'
Off-season: 'Reflecting on my season; learning to bat better and turn the ball more!
Working for Lansing Linde Severnside Ltd (materials handling equipment)'
Overseas tours: West of England U15 to West Indies 1993-94; Millfield School to Sri
Lanka 1994-95; England U17 to Holland 1995; England U19 to Pakistan 1996-97;
England A to Kenya and Sri Lanka 1997-98, to Zimbabwe and South Africa 1998-99;
Glamorgan CCC to Cape Town and Jersey
Overseas teams played for: Gordon CC, Sydney 1996-97; Crusaders, Durban
2001-02
Career highlights to date: 'Making my debut for Glamorgan in 1996. My two A
tours. Winning Championship in 1997. Receiving my cap in 2000. Winning the
Norwich Union League in 2002!'
Cricket moments to forget: 'Being told you're not playing. Apart from that a lot of
very happy moments to remember!'
Cricketers particularly admired: Matthew Maynard, Steve Watkin, Steve Barwick,
Hugh Morris
Young players to look out for: Simon Jones, Mark Wallace, Dai Harrison
Other sports played: Football
Other sports followed: Football (Spurs)
Injuries: Out for one game with a dislocated shoulder
Extras: *Daily Telegraph* Regional Bowling Award. England U15 and U17. Played for
U19 TCCB Development of Excellence XI against South Africa U19 in 1995. Played

for England U19 against Zimbabwe U19 in 1997. Leading wicket-taker on England A tour of Zimbabwe and South Africa 1998-99. Third youngest Glamorgan player to receive county cap
Opinions on cricket: 'Enjoy.'
Best batting: 49 Glamorgan v Sussex, Cardiff 1999
Best bowling: 6-140 Glamorgan v Lancashire, Colwyn Bay 1998

2002 Season

	M	Inns	NO	Runs	HS	Avge	100s	50s	Ct	St	O	M	Runs	Wkts	Avge	Best	5wI	10wM
Test																		
All First	10	13	2	115	37	10.45	-	-	8	-	317.5	60	1012	20	50.60	4-135	-	-
1-day Int																		
C & G	1	1	0	0	0	0.00	-	-	-	-	7	0	51	0	-		-	-
B & H	1	1	0	6	6	6.00	-	-	-	-	7.1	0	41	1	41.00	1-41	-	
1-day Lge	13	3	2	8	5	8.00	-	-	7	-	89.5	3	373	13	28.69	4-17	-	

Career Performances

	M	Inns	NO	Runs	HS	Avge	100s	50s	Ct	St	Balls	Runs	Wkts	Avge	Best	5wI	10wM
Test																	
All First	93	109	29	867	49	10.83	-	-	63	-	17451	8203	223	36.78	6-140	2	-
1-day Int																	
C & G	8	5	3	16	5	8.00	-	-	1	-	410	291	8	36.37	3-26	-	
B & H	8	6	2	8	6	2.00	-	-	1	-	331	248	7	35.42	2-26	-	
1-day Lge	66	30	11	180	27 *	9.47	-	-	23	-	2813	2236	72	31.05	4-17	-	

COTTEY, P. A.   Sussex

Name: Phillip Anthony (<u>Tony</u>) Cottey
Role: Right-hand bat
Born: 2 June 1966, Swansea
Height: 5ft 5in **Weight:** 10st 10lbs
Nickname: Cotts, Rudy, Baba
County debut: 1986 (Glamorgan), 1999 (Sussex)
County cap: 1992 (Glamorgan), 1999 (Sussex)
1000 runs in a season: 7
1st-Class 50s: 66
1st-Class 100s: 26
1st-Class 200s: 1
1st-Class catches: 167
Place in batting averages: 128th av. 31.77
Strike rate: (career 91.00)
Parents: Bernard John and Ruth
Wife and date of marriage: Gail, 5 October 1992

Children: Lowri Rhiannon, 16 October 1993; Seren Nia, 6 August 1997
Family links with cricket: Father played club cricket for Swansea CC
Education: Crwys Primary; Bishopston Comprehensive School, Swansea
Qualifications: 9 O-levels, Level 3 coach
Career outside cricket: 'Undecided'
Overseas tours: Glamorgan to La Manga, Barbados, Trinidad, Zimbabwe and Cape Town 1987-96, to Jersey 1998; Sussex to Grenada 2002
Overseas teams played for: Penrith, Sydney 1986-88; Benoni, Johannesburg 1990-93; Eastern Transvaal 1991-92
Career highlights to date: 'Winning Championship with Glamorgan 1997. Winning Sunday League with Glamorgan 1993. Winning second division of one-day league with Sussex 1999'
Cricket moments to forget: 'Any of the four semi-final losses at Glamorgan and the semi-final loss at Gloucestershire 1999 in Super Cup with Sussex'
Cricketers particularly admired: Ian Botham, Matthew Maynard, Sachin Tendulkar, Mark Robinson
Young players to look out for: Tim Ambrose
Other sports played: Golf, road running, soccer
Other sports followed: Rugby (Dunvant RFC), football (Swansea City AFC)
Relaxations: 'Night out with friends; time with family; golf'
Extras: Left school at 16 to play for Swansea City AFC for three years as a professional. Three Welsh Youth caps (one as captain). Glamorgan Player of the Year in 1994. Ran the New York Marathon in 1995 and the Athens Marathon in 1996. Left Glamorgan at the end of the 1998 season and joined Sussex. Sussex Clubman of the Year 1999
Opinions on cricket: 'Two-divisional cricket is great – just worry that an elitist band is going to be created, resulting in some counties going out of business.'
Best batting: 203 Glamorgan v Leicestershire, Swansea 1996
Best bowling: 4-49 Glamorgan v Leicestershire, Swansea 1996

2002 Season

	M	Inns	NO	Runs	HS	Avge	100s	50s	Ct	St	O	M	Runs	Wkts	Avge	Best	5wl	10wM
Test																		
All First	13	22	0	699	137	31.77	3	1	5	-	16.2	5	33	0	-	-	-	-
1-day Int																		
C & G	2	2	0	43	42	21.50	-	-	-	-	6	0	39	0	-	-	-	
B & H	6	5	0	111	61	22.20	-	1	3	-								
1-day Lge	8	7	0	101	43	14.42	-	-	1	-	12	0	50	0	-	-	-	

Career Performances

	M	Inns	NO	Runs	HS	Avge	100s	50s	Ct	St	Balls	Runs	Wkts	Avge	Best	5wI	10wM
Test																	
All First	251	406	51	12908	203	36.36	27	66	167	-	1456	895	16	55.93	4-49	-	-
1-day Int																	
C & G	31	30	7	610	68	26.52	-	4	8	-	186	135	3	45.00	1-9	-	
B & H	45	42	6	749	96	20.80	-	4	18	-	78	53	1	53.00	1-49	-	
1-day Lge	169	144	27	2891	92 *	24.70	-	16	56	-	581	573	15	38.20	4-56	-	

COUSINS, D. M. Northamptonshire

Name: <u>Darren</u> Mark Cousins
Role: Right-hand bat, right-arm
fast-medium bowler
Born: 24 September 1971, Cambridge
Height: 6ft 1in **Weight:** 14st
Nickname: Cuz, Mad Dog, Hooks, T, Gimp
County debut: 1993 (Essex), 1999 (one-day, Surrey), 2000 (Northants)
County cap: 2000 (Northants)
50 wickets in a season: 1
1st-Class 5 w. in innings: 4
1st-Class catches: 12
One-Day 5 w. in innings: 1
Place in batting averages: 282nd av. 11.44
(2001 241st av. 12.42)
Place in bowling averages: 142nd av. 46.54
(2001 78th av. 32.66)
Strike rate: 84.90 (career 58.64)
Parents: Dennis Charles and Deanna Maureen (deceased)
Marital status: 'Living with girlfriend Anna and her two boys Scott and James'
Family links with cricket: Father opened the bowling for and was capped by
Cambridgeshire
Education: Milton Primary School; Impington Village College
Qualifications: 7 GCSEs, basic and senior coaching awards
Career outside cricket: 'Not sure yet but hoping to stay involved in sport in
some way'
Off-season: 'Depends on fitness. Have been picked to go to Fiji and Papua New
Guinea with the MCC in March. Before then, I will find some sort of job!'
Overseas tours: Northamptonshire to Grenada 2000, 2001, 2002
Overseas teams played for: Gold Coast Dolphins, Queensland 1994-95; Maritzburg
Old Boys, Pietermaritzburg, South Africa 1995-96; Shell Harbour, NSW 1996-97;
Bellville, Cape Town 1999-2000; Greenpoint, Cape Town 2000-01

Career highlights to date: 'Winning the second division championship in 2000. Receiving my cap and Player of the Year award. Getting my one and only one-day five-wicket haul at Lord's this year and having Anna and my mates there to see it'

Cricket moments to forget: 'Breaking down live on Sky in my second over two days after getting the five-for at Lord's and not playing again'

Cricket superstitions: 'Try not to get injured!'

People particularly admired: 'Alan Butcher, and everyone who has helped me and my cricket widow Anna'

Young players to look out for: Monty Panesar, Rob White, Mark Powell, Scott and James Gyllenborg

Other sports played: Football (represented Cambridgeshire at all youth levels), swimming (represented Cambridgeshire)

Other sports followed: Rugby and football

Injuries: Out for last third of season ('again!') with foot problems (navicular)

Relaxations: 'All the things professional cricketers shouldn't do'

Extras: Represented Cambridgeshire at every level at cricket. Played for a Bull Development Squad against Australia in 1991, taking four wickets in each innings. Set record both for number of wickets in any single Colts festival (21) and for number of wickets taken in the Hilda Overy Festival overall (74). Spent seven years at Essex, undergoing four back and two knee operations. Awarded 2nd XI cap and Essex Young Player of the Year 1994. Leading Essex wicket-taker in Sunday League and top of the bowling averages in 1994. Essex Cricket Society 2nd XI Player of the Year 1994. Released by Essex at end of 1998 season after only full season on the staff. Played as a pro for Cambridge St Giles and Cambridgeshire 1999. Played three National League matches for Surrey 1999; offered one-year contract at end of 1999 but chose to join Northants for 2000, taking 94 first-class wickets and winning the Player of the Year award. Took all seven wickets to fall (7-120) in Lancashire's second innings at Northampton 2001. Took 100th Championship wicket for Northants (Peter Bowler lbw) v Somerset at Northampton 2001 in only his 23rd Championship match for the county. Recorded maiden one-day five-wicket return (5-22) v Middlesex at Lord's in the NUL 2002

Opinions on cricket: 'Bowling is bloody painful and hard work! Clubs should learn to treat us as human beings and players rather than just pieces of meat!'

Best batting: 29* Northamptonshire v Glamorgan, Northampton 2000

Best bowling: 8-102 Northamptonshire v Yorkshire, Headingley 2001

2002 Season

	M	Inns	NO	Runs	HS	Avge	100s	50s	Ct	St	O	M	Runs	Wkts	Avge	Best	5wI	10wM
Test																		
All First	11	16	7	103	23 *	11.44	-	-	4	-	311.2	67	1024	22	46.54	4-75	-	-
1-day Int																		
C & G	2	2	2	25	17 *	-	-	-	1	-	18	5	64	3	21.33	2-12	-	
B & H	3	1	1	1	1 *	-	-	-	2	-	21.1	3	70	0	-		-	-
1-day Lge	10	2	1	30	21	30.00	-	-	4	-	63.2	6	257	14	18.35	5-22	1	

Career Performances

	M	Inns	NO	Runs	HS	Avge	100s	50s	Ct	St	Balls	Runs	Wkts	Avge	Best	5wI	10wM
Test																	
All First	50	74	22	559	29 *	10.75	-	-	12	-	8914	4656	152	30.63	8-102	4	-
1-day Int																	
C & G	10	6	4	48	17 *	24.00	-	-	3	-	497	376	11	34.18	3-39	-	
B & H	15	6	2	42	12 *	10.50	-	-	6	-	714	485	16	30.31	4-23	-	
1-day Lge	67	27	11	99	21	6.18	-	-	11	-	2849	2131	89	23.94	5-22	1	

COVERDALE, P. S. Northamptonshire

Name: <u>Paul</u> Stephen Coverdale
Role: Right-hand bat, right-arm
medium-fast bowler
Born: 24 July 1983, Harrogate
Height: 5ft 10in **Weight:** 11st 8lbs
Nickname: Covers, Drill Sergeant, Flaps,
'and was known as Toby for most of last
season!'
County debut: No first-team appearance
Parents: Stephen and Jane
Marital status: Single
Family links with cricket: Father played for
Yorkshire CCC and Cambridge University
and is now Chief Executive of
Northamptonshire
Education: Spratton Hall School;
Wellingborough School; Loughborough
University
Qualifications: 9 GCSEs, 3 A-levels, ECB Level I coaching
Career outside cricket: Student
Off-season: 'Studying at Loughborough University'
Overseas tours: Northamptonshire U19 to South Africa 2000
Overseas teams played for: Swanbourne, Perth 2002
Cricket moments to forget: 'Leaving a straight one first ball in a 2nd XI match this
year and then breaking my hand on the changing room wall in anger!'
Cricketers particularly admired: Allan Lamb, Steve Waugh, Michael Atherton,
Jacques Kallis
Young players to look out for: Mark Powell, David Paynter, Monty Panesar,
Andrew Daniels
Other sports played: Rugby, golf, 'the odd bit of boxing'
Other sports followed: Rugby (Northampton Saints), football

Injuries: Out for four weeks with a broken hand; for eight weeks with torn ankle ligaments

Relaxations: 'Socialising and going out with friends; having a few down the Student Union; ruining a great classic on the karaoke; watching and playing sports'

Extras: Progressed through county age groups, captaining at U14, U15, U17 and U19. Played for Northamptonshire Board XI in the C&G 2001, in the first round of the C&G 2002, which was played in August 2001, and in the first round of the C&G 2003, which was played in August 2002. Represented East England Schools U18. Joined the Northants Academy in 2000

Opinions on cricket: 'Beat those Ozzies; win the World Cup; and everything's hunky-dory!'

2002 Season (did not make any first-class or one-day appearances for his county)

Career Performances

	M	Inns	NO	Runs	HS	Avge	100s	50s	Ct	St	Balls	Runs	Wkts	Avge	Best	5wI	10wM
Test																	
All First																	
1-day Int																	
C & G	3	3	0	33	19	11.00	-	-	2	-	96	48	1	48.00	1-21	-	
B & H																	
1-day Lge																	

COWAN, A. P. Essex

Name: <u>Ashley</u> Preston Cowan
Role: Right-hand bat, right-arm fast-medium bowler, 'benefit-only wicket-keeper'
Born: 7 May 1975, Hitchin, Hertfordshire
Height: 6ft 5in **Weight:** 15st
Nickname: Dic Dic, Wallace, Vic
County debut: 1995
County cap: 1997
50 wickets in a season: 1
1st-Class 50s: 9
1st-Class 5 w. in innings: 8
1st-Class catches: 48
One-Day 5 w. in innings: 2
Place in batting averages: 200th av. 23.46 (2001 214th av. 17.14)
Place in bowling averages: 41st av. 27.19 (2001 132nd av. 46.12)

Strike rate: 53.45 (career 59.88)
Parents: Jeff and Pam
Wife and date of marriage: Cath, 14 October 2001
Family links with cricket: 'Father played village cricket. Mother made the teas'
Education: Kingshott Pre-Prep; Framlingham College; 'Essex County Cricket Club'
Qualifications: 8 GCSEs, 3 A-levels
Career outside cricket: Business
Overseas tours: England to West Indies 1997-98
Overseas teams played for: Zingari CC, Durban 1995-97
Career highlights to date: 'Getting England blazer. Winning finals at Lord's'
Cricket moments to forget: 'Any time I get smashed around the park. Losing [NatWest] final at Lord's 1996'
Cricketers particularly admired: Ian Botham, Allan Donald, Curtly Ambrose, Glenn McGrath
Young players to look out for: Mark Pettini, Justin Bishop
Other sports played: Rugby, hockey (Chelmsford), golf (single-figure handicap), squash
Other sports followed: Rugby (Saracens), golf, football ('anybody who plays Man U')
Relaxations: Sports, sleeping, reading
Extras: Played rugby and hockey for East of England U18. Was the youngest person to play for Cambridgeshire. Became first Essex player to take a first-class hat-trick at Castle Park, Colchester, v Gloucestershire in 1996. Took three wickets in four balls in the final over of National League match at Southend 2000 to prevent Glamorgan scoring the six runs needed for victory; the over also contained a run-out
Opinions on cricket: 'More day/night cricket.'
Best batting: 94 Essex v Leicestershire, Leicester 1998
Best bowling: 6-47 Essex v Glamorgan, Cardiff 1999

2002 Season

	M	Inns	NO	Runs	HS	Avge	100s	50s	Ct	St	O	M	Runs	Wkts	Avge	Best	5wI	10wM
Test																		
All First	10	15	2	305	60 *	23.46	-	2	6	-	276.1	70	843	31	27.19	5-68	1	-
1-day Int																		
C & G	3	2	0	8	7	4.00	-	-	-	-	30	5	115	4	28.75	4-27	-	
B & H	7	4	2	71	27 *	35.50	-	-	3	-	60	6	247	9	27.44	3-19	-	
1-day Lge	11	7	2	63	21	12.60	-	-	4	-	84	7	302	19	15.89	4-16	-	

Career Performances

	M	Inns	NO	Runs	HS	Avge	100s	50s	Ct	St	Balls	Runs	Wkts	Avge	Best	5wl	10wM
Test																	
All First	100	149	28	2178	94	18.00	-	9	48	-	16168	8777	270	32.50	6-47	8	-
1-day Int																	
C & G	17	12	4	67	17 *	8.37	-	-	5	-	983	643	23	27.95	4-27	-	
B & H	26	17	10	239	45	34.14	-	-	4	-	1384	992	29	34.20	5-28	1	
1-day Lge	90	69	16	652	40 *	12.30	-	-	36	-	3932	2892	114	25.36	5-14	1	

COX, J. Somerset

Name: Jamie Cox
Role: Right-hand bat, off-spin bowler
Born: 15 October 1969, Burnie, Tasmania
Height: 6ft **Weight:** 12st 7lbs
Nickname: Buzz, Skippy
County debut: 1999
County cap: 1999
1000 runs in a season: 2
1st-Class 50s: 66
1st-Class 100s: 41
1st-Class 200s: 3
1st-Class catches: 90
One-Day 100s: 3
Place in batting averages: 130th av. 31.47
(2001 18th av. 57.45)
Strike rate: (career 129.75)
Parents: David and Kaye
Wife: Helen
Children: Lachlan William Joseph, November 2001
Family links with cricket: Father played State Colts and is life member of local club
Education: Wynyard Primary; Wynyard High; Deakin University
Qualifications: School Certificate, Diploma of Management, Bachelor of Business
degree; currently studying for Diploma of Drafting
Off-season: Playing for Tasmania
Overseas tours: Australia U19 to West Indies 1988; Australia A to Zimbabwe 1989,
to Malaysia (Super 8s) 1997; Australia XI to Zimbabwe 1991-92; Tasmania
to Zimbabwe 1995-96
Overseas teams played for: Tasmania 1987-88 –
Cricketers particularly admired: Ian Botham, Geoff Marsh, David Boon,
Steve Waugh
Other sports played: Golf, soccer ('poorly')

Other sports followed: Australian Rules football (Western Bulldogs)
Relaxations: Music, home design
Extras: First Tasmania player to attend the Australian Cricket Academy, in 1988. Scored 1349 runs in the 1996-97 Australian season, with five 100s, including two in one match v New South Wales. Players' Player of the Year 1996-97. Tasmanian Cricket Player of the Year 1996-97. Scored an unbeaten 115 in the first innings of the 1997-98 Sheffield Shield final v Western Australia, becoming the first player to carry his bat in a Shield final. Joined Somerset as overseas player and captain in 1999 (captain 1999-2002). Became the first Somerset player to score a 200 (216) and a 100 (129*) in a match, v Hampshire at Southampton 1999; scored 153 at the same ground in 2000 to make it three successive scores of 100 or more there. Scored 94 for Australia A v West Indies at Hobart 2000-01. Scored 1070 runs (av. 66.88) in the Pura Cup 2000-01, passing during the season David Boon's record of 9096 career first-class runs for Tasmania to become the state's leading run-scorer. *Wisden Australia* Pura Cup Cricketer of the Year 2000-01; also Pura Cup Player of the Year 2000-01 (voted on by the umpires). Took over captaincy of Tasmania in 1999-2000 in succession to David Boon; handed over to Ricky Ponting for the 2001-02 season. Played in his 140th first-class match for Tasmania against Western Australia at Hobart in January 2002, overtaking David Boon's record of 139 matches to become Tasmania's most-capped first-class player
Opinions on cricket: 'In good shape. Must be careful not to overprotect centrally contracted players. Bonus points to be removed. Points for wins only.'
Best batting: 245 Tasmania v New South Wales, Hobart 1999-2000
Best bowling: 3-46 Somerset v Middlesex, Taunton 1999

2002 Season

	M	Inns	NO	Runs	HS	Avge	100s	50s	Ct	St	O	M	Runs	Wkts	Avge	Best	5wI	10wM
Test																		
All First	13	25	2	724	176	31.47	1	3	6	-								
1-day Int																		
C & G	4	4	0	144	64	36.00	-	1	4	-	7	0	33	1	33.00	1-33	-	
B & H	4	4	0	31	25	7.75	-	-	3	-								
1-day Lge	10	10	0	298	99	29.80	-	3	3	-								

Career Performances

	M	Inns	NO	Runs	HS	Avge	100s	50s	Ct	St	Balls	Runs	Wkts	Avge	Best	5wI	10wM
Test																	
All First	209	369	26	15294	245	44.58	44	66	90	-	519	323	4	80.75	3-46	-	-
1-day Int																	
C & G	15	15	1	574	114	41.00	1	3	6	-	42	33	1	33.00	1-33	-	
B & H	11	11	0	300	72	27.27	-	3	4	-							
1-day Lge	52	52	1	1707	110	33.47	2	11	23	-	96	82	3	27.33	3-28	-	

CRAVEN, V. J. Yorkshire

Name: <u>Victor</u> John Craven
Role: Left-hand middle/top order bat,
right-arm medium bowler
Born: 31 July 1980, Harrogate
Height: 6ft **Weight:** 13st 8lbs
Nickname: Cow, Magoo
County debut: 2000
1st-Class 50s: 5
1st-Class catches: 16
Place in batting averages: 201st av. 23.10
Strike rate: 90.00 (career 216.00)
Parents: Vic and Sue
Marital status: Single
Family links with cricket: 'Father played
local cricket and introduced me to the game'
Education: Beckwithshaw County Primary;
Harrogate Grammar School

Qualifications: 10 GCSEs, GNVQ
(Advanced) Business, Level 2 cricket
coaching
Career outside cricket: Gym instructor
Overseas tours: Yorkshire to South Africa
Overseas teams played for: Tatura CC, Victoria 1998-99; Deepdene Bears,
Melbourne 2000-01
Career highlights to date: 'Playing against West Indies and scoring 53 [for Yorkshire
in 2000]'
Cricket moments to forget: 'All bad drops and misfields'
Cricketers particularly admired: Michael Atherton, Graham Thorpe
Young players to look out for: John Sadler, Michael Lumb
Other sports played: Soccer, golf, snooker
Other sports followed: Football (Leeds United), rugby league (Leeds Rhinos)
Relaxations: 'Cinema, gym, socialising with pals'
Extras: Has Yorkshire 2nd XI cap
Best batting: 72 Yorkshire v Hampshire, West End 2002
Best bowling: 1-25 Yorkshire v Leicestershire, Scarborough 2002

2002 Season

	M	Inns	NO	Runs	HS	Avge	100s	50s	Ct	St	O	M	Runs	Wkts	Avge	Best	5wI	10wM
Test																		
All First	11	21	2	439	72	23.10	-	3	8	-	15	3	56	1	56.00	1-25	-	-
1-day Int																		
C & G																		
B & H																		
1-day Lge	6	6	0	105	59	17.50	-	1	1	-	2	0	21	1	21.00	1-21	-	

Career Performances

	M	Inns	NO	Runs	HS	Avge	100s	50s	Ct	St	Balls	Runs	Wkts	Avge	Best	5wI	10wM
Test																	
All First	21	36	4	723	72	22.59	-	5	16	-	216	140	1	140.00	1-25	-	-
1-day Int																	
C & G	1	1	0	26	26	26.00	-	-	-	-							
B & H	1	1	0	1	1	1.00	-	-	1	-							
1-day Lge	14	14	0	248	59	17.71	-	2	6	-	12	21	1	21.00	1-21	-	

CRAWLEY, J. P. Hampshire

Name: <u>John</u> Paul Crawley
Role: Right-hand bat, occasional wicket-keeper
Born: 21 September 1971, Maldon, Essex
Height: 6ft 2in **Weight:** 13st 2lbs
Nickname: Creeps, Jonty, JC
County debut: 1990 (Lancashire), 2002 (Hampshire)
County cap: 1994 (Lancashire), 2002 (Hampshire)
Test debut: 1994
Tests: 34
One-Day Internationals: 13
1000 runs in a season: 8
1st-Class 50s: 97
1st-Class 100s: 36
1st-Class 200s: 6
1st-Class catches: 170
One-Day 100s: 5
Place in batting averages: 23rd av. 53.80 (2001 69th av. 40.81)
Strike rate: (career 132.00)
Parents: Frank and Jean

Family links with cricket: Father played in Manchester Association; brother Mark played for Lancashire and Nottinghamshire; brother Peter plays for Warrington CC and has played for Scottish Universities and Cambridge University; uncle was excellent fast bowler; godfather umpires in Manchester Association
Education: Manchester Grammar School; Trinity College, Cambridge
Qualifications: 10 O-levels, 2 AO-Levels, 3 A-levels, 2 S-levels, BA in History
Overseas tours: England YC to Australia 1989-90, to New Zealand 1990-91 (captain); England A to South Africa 1993-94, to West Indies 2000-01; England to Australia 1994-95, 1998-99, 2002-03, to South Africa 1995-96, to Zimbabwe and New Zealand 1996-97, to West Indies 1997-98
Overseas teams played for: Midland-Guildford, Perth 1990
Cricketers particularly admired: Michael Atherton, Neil Fairbrother, Graham Gooch, Alec Stewart, David Gower, Allan Donald, Ian Salisbury
Other sports followed: Football (Manchester United), golf
Relaxations: 'Playing or trying to play the guitar'
Extras: Sir John Hobbs Silver Jubilee Memorial Prize 1987. Played for England YC in three home series – v New Zealand 1989, Pakistan 1990 and Australia (as captain) 1991. First to score 1000 runs in U19 'Tests'. Scored 286 for England A against Eastern Province at Port Elizabeth in 1994, the highest score by an Englishman on an England or England A tour for almost 30 years. Finished top of the first-class batting averages on England's tour to South Africa in 1995-96 with 336 runs at 67.20. Lancashire vice-captain for the 1998 season. Scored century in each innings (124 and 136) v Glamorgan at Colwyn Bay 1998. Topped English first-class batting averages for 1998 season (1851 runs; av. 74.04). Lancashire Player of the Year 1998. Lancashire captain 1999-2001. Left Lancashire during the 2001-02 off-season and joined Hampshire for 2002. Scored 272 on debut for Hampshire v Kent at Canterbury 2002, passing Denis Baldry's Hampshire debut record of 151 set in 1959 v Glamorgan and F. E. Lacey's 1884 record for the highest individual score for Hampshire v Kent (211); also became one of only five English batsmen to have made five first-class scores of 250 or above. B&H Gold Award for his 103* v Middlesex at West End 2002. Recalled to Test side in 2002 for first time since 1998-99 and scored 64 and 100* in second Test after recall, v India at Lord's. Awarded Hampshire cap 2002
Best batting: 286 England A v Eastern Province, Port Elizabeth 1993-94
Best bowling: 1-90 Lancashire v Sussex, Hove 1992

2002 Season

	M	Inns	NO	Runs	HS	Avge	100s	50s	Ct	St	O	M	Runs	Wkts	Avge	Best	5wI	10wM
Test	5	8	2	309	100 *	51.50	1	1	-	-								
All First	15	25	4	1130	272	53.80	2	7	8	-								
1-day Int																		
C & G	1	1	1	113	113 *	-		1	-	-								
B & H	5	5	1	155	103 *	38.75	1	-	-	-								
1-day Lge	9	9	0	211	52	23.44	-	1	1	-								

Career Performances

	M	Inns	NO	Runs	HS	Avge	100s	50s	Ct	St	Balls	Runs	Wkts	Avge	Best	5wl	10wM
Test	34	55	7	1638	156 *	34.12	4	8	26	-							
All First	252	412	40	17660	286	47.47	42	97	170	-	132	201	1	201.00	1-90	-	-
1-day Int	13	12	1	235	73	21.36	-	2	1	1							
C & G	27	26	4	927	113 *	42.13	2	5	9	-	6	4	0	-		-	-
B & H	54	52	2	1677	114	33.54	2	9	15	-							
1-day Lge	120	117	9	2977	100	27.56	1	19	33	3							

CROFT, R. D. B. Glamorgan

Name: <u>Robert</u> Damien Bale Croft
Role: Right-hand bat, off-spin bowler,
county vice-captain
Born: 25 May 1970, Morriston, Swansea
Height: 5ft 11in **Weight:** 13st 7lbs
Nickname: Crofty
County debut: 1989
County cap: 1992
Benefit: 2000
Test debut: 1996
Tests: 21
One-Day Internationals: 50
50 wickets in a season: 5
1st-Class 50s: 37
1st-Class 100s: 3
1st-Class 5 w. in innings: 31
1st-Class 10 w. in match: 5
1st-Class catches: 134
One-Day 100s: 2
One-Day 5 w. in innings: 1
Place in batting averages: 104th av. 35.57 (2001 141st av. 27.15)
Place in bowling averages: 132nd av. 42.52 (2001 109th av. 38.62)
Strike rate: 92.85 (career 80.04)
Parents: Malcolm and Susan
Wife: Marie
Children: Callum James Bale Croft
Family links with cricket: Father and grandfather played league cricket
Education: Hendy CP School; St John Lloyd Catholic School, Llanelli; Neath Tertiary
College; West Glamorgan Institute of Higher Education
Qualifications: 6 O-levels, OND Business Studies, HND Business Studies,
NCA senior coaching certificate

Overseas tours: England A to Bermuda and West Indies 1991-92, to South Africa 1993-94; England to Zimbabwe and New Zealand 1996-97, to West Indies 1997-98, to Australia 1998-99, to Sharjah (Coca-Cola Cup) 1998-99, to Sri Lanka 2000-01

Career highlights to date: 'Playing for England and winning the Championship with Glamorgan in 1997'

Cricket moments to forget: 'None. This career is too short to forget any of it'

Cricketers particularly admired: Ian Botham, Viv Richards, Shane Warne

Young players to look out for: 'Everyone at Glamorgan'

Other sports played: 'Give anything a go'

Other sports followed: Football (Liverpool FC), rugby (Llanelli and Wales)

Interests/relaxations: 'Everything'

Extras: Captained England South to victory in International Youth Tournament 1989 and was voted Player of the Tournament. Glamorgan Young Player of the Year 1992. Scored Test-best 37* at Old Trafford 1998, resisting for 190 minutes to deny South Africa victory. Represented England in the 1999 World Cup. Made his 16th England Test appearance v West Indies at Edgbaston 2000, passing Jeff Jones's total of 15 Tests to become the most capped Welshman. Had match figures of 10-191 from 90.3 overs v Northamptonshire at Cardiff 2001. Honorary fellow of West Glamorgan Institute of Higher Education. Selected for England Test party to India and New Zealand 2001-02 but withdrew from tour to India and was replaced by Martyn Ball; subsequently omitted from revised party to New Zealand. Glamorgan vice-captain since 2002. Scored 69-ball 119 v Surrey at The Oval in the C&G 2002, striking each of Martin Bicknell's first five balls for four as Glamorgan made 429 in reply to Surrey's 438-5

Opinions on cricket: 'Too many people sticking their noses in when they haven't got a clue what they are talking about.'

Best batting: 143 Glamorgan v Somerset, Taunton 1995

Best bowling: 8-66 Glamorgan v Warwickshire, Swansea 1992

2002 Season

	M	Inns	NO	Runs	HS	Avge	100s	50s	Ct	St	O	M	Runs	Wkts	Avge	Best	5wI	10wM
Test																		
All First	17	24	3	747	101*	35.57	1	5	8	-	619	138	1701	40	42.52	5-71	1	-
1-day Int																		
C & G	2	2	0	142	119	71.00	1	-	-	-	18	0	102	1	102.00	1-62	-	
B & H	4	4	0	70	33	17.50	-	-	-	-	25	0	124	4	31.00	2-51	-	
1-day Lge	16	16	0	327	59	20.43	-	1	6	-	117.2	2	550	28	19.64	4-40	-	

Career Performances

	M	Inns	NO	Runs	HS	Avge	100s	50s	Ct	St	Balls	Runs	Wkts	Avge	Best	5wI	10wM
Test	21	34	8	421	37*	16.19	-	-	10	-	4619	1825	49	37.24	5-95	1	-
All First	266	386	75	7927	143	25.48	3	37	134	-	57311	26103	716	36.45	8-66	31	5
1-day Int	50	36	12	344	32	14.33	-	-	11	-	2466	1743	45	38.73	3-51	-	
C & G	34	28	6	568	119	25.81	1	3	5	-	2032	1269	40	31.72	4-47	-	
B & H	42	37	8	792	77	27.31	-	5	9	-	2171	1459	45	32.42	4-30	-	
1-day Lge	168	141	28	2613	114*	23.12	1	11	47	-	7044	5142	175	29.38	6-20	1	

CROOK, S. P. Lancashire

Name: <u>Steven</u> Paul Crook
Role: Right-hand bat, right-arm
fast-medium bowler
Born: 28 May 1983, Adelaide, Australia
Height: 5ft 11in **Weight:** 13st
Nickname: Crooky, Hairdo
County debut: No first-team appearance
Parents: Martyn Crook (father), Sue Carey
(mother), Doug Carey (stepfather)
Marital status: Single
Family links with cricket: 'Brother Andrew'
Education: St Augustines Primary; Rostrevor
College; Magill University
Qualifications: Matriculation
Off-season: 'Visiting family in Australia'
Overseas tours: Australia U19 to New
Zealand (U19 World Cup) 2001-02
Overseas teams played for: South Australia
Redbacks
Career highlights to date: 'Signing two-year contract with Lancashire'
Cricket moments to forget: 'Getting the yips!'
Cricket superstitions: 'None'
Cricketers particularly admired: Brett Lee, Shoaib Akhtar
Young players to look out for: Paul Horton (Lancashire)
Other sports played: Football (Australia U17 trials)
Other sports followed: Football (Tottenham Hotspur FC)
Injuries: Out for six weeks with shin splints
Relaxations: Playing golf
Extras: Attended Australian Institute of Sport Cricket Academy. Represented South
Australia U13-U19. Member of Australia U19 World Cup squad 2001-02. Is not
considered an overseas player
Opinions on cricket: 'Cricket has reached an exciting time, with so many
opportunities for young players who show great potential.'

---

21. Which New Zealand Test cricketer, who also played rugby union for
England, made his debut for Warwickshire in 1948?

176

CROWE, C. D. Leicestershire

Name: <u>Carl</u> Daniel Crowe
Role: Right-hand bat, right-arm off-spinner
Born: 25 November 1975, Leicester
Height: 6ft **Weight:** 12st 7lbs
Nickname: 'Crowey!'
County debut: 1995
1st-Class catches: 18
Place in batting averages: 268th av. 14.33
(2001 269th av. 8.11)
Place in bowling averages: 112th av. 37.06
Strike rate: 72.50 (career 68.70)
Parents: Jeannette and Eddie (deceased)
Wife and date of marriage:
Helen, 14 October 2000
Family links with cricket: Brother Craig has
played for Leicestershire 2nd XI
Education: Lutterworth High School;
Lutterworth Grammar School

Qualifications: 11 GCSEs, 2 A-levels, NCA
Senior Coach
Career outside cricket: 'Business world'
Overseas tours: Leicestershire U19 to South Africa 1993-94; Leicestershire to
Holland 1996, 1998, to Barbados 1998, to Sri Lanka 1999, to Anguilla 2000, to South
Africa 2001
Overseas teams played for: Old Mentonians, Melbourne 1997-99
Career highlights to date: 'Championship medal'
Cricket moments to forget: 'Playing and missing in nets to Wardy last June [2001]'
Cricketers particularly admired: The Waughs
Other sports played: 'Try all sports.' 'Had a hole in one'
Other sports followed: 'Support Leicester at everything and follow Spurs'
Relaxations: 'PS2; reading true crime and military operations'
Extras: Played for Leicestershire U12-U19 and Midlands Schools U14-U19. One of
the Cricketers of the Festival at Cambridge U19 Festival 1994. Won Leics 2nd XI
batting award 1998. Played in Leicestershire's victory in the AON Trophy final 2000.
B&H Gold Award for his 1-7 from four overs (in a game shortened to 22 overs per
side) v Nottinghamshire at Leicester 2002. Released by Leicestershire at the end of the
2002 season
Opinions on cricket: 'Day/night games are the way forward.'
Best batting: 44* Leicestershire v Northamptonshire, Northampton 1999
Best bowling: 4-47 Leicestershire v Surrey, The Oval 2001

2002 Season

	M	Inns	NO	Runs	HS	Avge	100s	50s	Ct	St	O	M	Runs	Wkts	Avge	Best	5wI	10wM
Test																		
All First	12	16	4	172	34	14.33	-	-	4	-	193.2	51	593	16	37.06	4-63	-	-
1-day Int																		
C & G	2	2	1	1	1	1.00	-	-	-	-	11	0	56	0	-		-	-
B & H	6	4	3	58	23 *	58.00	-	-	-	-	30	0	107	6	17.83	3-35	-	
1-day Lge	14	6	2	22	8	5.50	-	-	3	-	90.2	0	484	16	30.25	3-40	-	

Career Performances

	M	Inns	NO	Runs	HS	Avge	100s	50s	Ct	St	Balls	Runs	Wkts	Avge	Best	5wI	10wM
Test																	
All First	38	49	10	581	44 *	14.89	-	-	18	-	3916	1925	57	33.77	4-47	-	-
1-day Int																	
C & G	2	2	1	1	1	1.00	-	-	-	-	66	56	0	-		-	-
B & H	6	4	3	58	23 *	58.00	-	-	-	-	180	107	6	17.83	3-35	-	
1-day Lge	19	9	4	36	8	7.20	-	-	5	-	593	524	20	26.20	4-30	-	

CUNLIFFE, R. J. Leicestershire

Name: <u>Robert</u> John Cunliffe
Role: Right-hand bat
Born: 8 November 1973, Oxford
Height: 5ft 10in **Weight:** 13st
County debut: 1993 (one-day, Gloucs),
1994 (first-class, Gloucs), 2002 (Leics)
1st-Class 50s: 10
1st-Class 100s: 3
1st-Class catches: 53
One-Day 100s: 3
Place in batting averages: 271st av. 13.44
(2001 192nd av. 20.14)
Parents: Barry and Janet
Wife and date of marriage: Claire Louise,
25 November 2000
Children: Benjamin Michael, 22 August
2000
Family links with cricket: 'Dad played in
his younger days for his wife's village team and was groundsman for nine years at
Banbury Twenty CC'
Education: Grimsbury Primary; Banbury School; Banbury Technical College
Qualifications: Carpentry course, coaching award

Off-season: 'Bringing up the newborn [daughter born December 2002]; sleeping when possible'
Overseas tours: England U19 to India 1992-93
Overseas teams played for: Richmond City CC, Melbourne 1995-97
Cricketers particularly admired: Robin Smith
Other sports played: Football
Extras: Played in England U19 home series against West Indies U19 in 1993. B&H Gold Award for his 143-ball 137 v Surrey at The Oval 1996; scored 116* in following round v Ireland, sharing in a Gloucestershire record B&H partnership (221) with A. J. Wright (123). Scored 61 in the B&H Super Cup final at Lord's 1999, in the process sharing in a third-wicket partnership of 157 from 156 balls with Mark Alleyne (112). Left Gloucestershire during the 2001-02 off-season and joined Leicestershire for 2002
Best batting: 190* Gloucestershire v Oxford University, Bristol 1995

2002 Season

	M	Inns	NO	Runs	HS	Avge	100s	50s	Ct	St	O	M	Runs	Wkts	Avge	Best	5wl	10wM
Test																		
All First	5	10	1	121	30	13.44	-	-	1	-	1.1	0	3	0	-	-	-	-
1-day Int																		
C & G																		
B & H	2	2	1	11	9 *	11.00	-	-	1	-								
1-day Lge	8	5	0	70	28	14.00	-	-	3	-								

Career Performances

	M	Inns	NO	Runs	HS	Avge	100s	50s	Ct	St	Balls	Runs	Wkts	Avge	Best	5wl	10wM
Test																	
All First	67	113	7	2542	190 *	23.98	3	10	53	-	7	3	0	-	-	-	-
1-day Int																	
C & G	12	10	0	234	69	23.40	-	1	2	-							
B & H	28	27	4	921	137 *	40.04	3	5	12	-							
1-day Lge	47	42	5	779	66	21.05	-	5	12	-							

22. Name the overseas cricketers who played for Yorkshire in 2002.

CURRIE, M. R.   Lancashire

Name: <u>Mark</u> Robert Currie
Role: Right-hand bat, right-arm
off-spin bowler
Born: 22 September 1979, Manchester
Height: 6ft **Weight:** 12st 7lbs
Nickname: Ruby, Cuz
County debut: 2002
Parents: Martin and Jennifer
Marital status: Single
Family links with cricket: Father and
brothers played local club cricket
Education: Vernon Junior School, Poynton;
Poynton County High School; City of
Westminster College
Qualifications: 9 GCSEs, GNVQ Leisure
and Tourism and Sports Leader award, Level
II coaching

Career outside cricket: Coaching
Off-season: 'Training and playing golf'
Overseas tours: Cheshire U17 to Sydney 1997; MCC Young Professionals to South
Africa 2000
Overseas teams played for: Hamersley Carine, Perth 2000-02
Career highlights to date: 'Getting a contract and first-team debut'
Cricket moments to forget: 'Breaking my index finger – twice'
Cricket superstitions: 'None'
Cricketers particularly admired: Mark Waugh, Damien Martyn, Sachin Tendulkar
Young players to look out for: Kyle Hogg, Jimmy Anderson
Other sports played: Football, golf
Other sports followed: Football (Manchester City FC)
Injuries: Out for six weeks with a broken finger
Relaxations: 'Listening to music, going out with friends, golf'
Extras: Four years with MCC Young Professionals. Has played for Cheshire since
1997; represented Cheshire in the C&G 2001, the second round of the C&G 2002,
which was played in September 2001, and the second round of the C&G 2003, which
was played in September 2002. Leading run-scorer in league from which Hammersley
Carine (Perth) were promoted 2001-02
Opinions on cricket: 'More competitive since the introduction of two divisions. This
will be my first season, so not really able to comment.'
Best batting: 48* Lancashire v West Indies A, Liverpool 2002

2002 Season

	M	Inns	NO	Runs	HS	Avge	100s	50s	Ct	St		O	M	Runs	Wkts	Avge	Best	5wI	10wM
Test																			
All First	1	2	1	50	48 *	50.00	-	-	-	-									
1-day Int																			
C & G	1	1	0	94	94	94.00	-	1	1	-									
B & H																			
1-day Lge																			

Career Performances

	M	Inns	NO	Runs	HS	Avge	100s	50s	Ct	St	Balls	Runs	Wkts	Avge	Best	5wI	10wM
Test																	
All First	1	2	1	50	48 *	50.00	-	-	-	-							
1-day Int																	
C & G	3	3	0	118	94	39.33	-	1	1	-							
B & H																	
1-day Lge																	

DAGNALL, C. E. Leicestershire

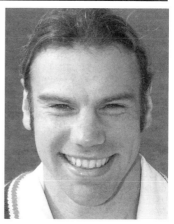

Name: <u>Charles</u> Edward Dagnall
Role: Right-hand 'boundary number 1',
right-arm medium 'dobber'
Born: 10 July 1976, Bury, Lancashire
Height: 6ft 3in **Weight:** '14st on a
bowling day; 17st on a batting day'
Nickname: Daggers
County debut: 1999 (Warwickshire),
2002 (Leicestershire)
1st-Class 5 w. in innings: 1
1st-Class catches: 1
Place in bowling averages: (2001 26th
av. 23.25)
Strike rate: 78.00 (career 51.10)
Parents: Mike and Jackie
Marital status: Single 'still!'
Family links with cricket: 'Dad ran
town team'
Education: Bolton School; Bridgewater School, Worsley; UMIST
Qualifications: 9 GCSEs, 4 A-levels, BSc (Hons) Chemistry
Career outside cricket: Singer (Frisco Crabbe and the Atlantic Frantics); presenter for
BBC Radio Leicester

Off-season: 'Playing in New Zealand; trying to break the 80mph barrier. Intend to do another degree'

Overseas tours: Warwickshire to Bloemfontein 2000, to Cape Town 2001

Overseas teams played for: Newtown and Chilwell, Geelong, Australia 1994-95; St Josephs, Geelong 1998-99

Career highlights to date: 'Winning B&H Gold Award v Worcestershire [at Worcester] in 2001. And also getting my full quota of bouncers in for one over v Worcestershire at Kidderminster'

Cricket moments to forget: 'Alan Richardson getting 91 v Hampshire'

Cricket superstitions: 'Stop bowling filthy half-volleys'

Cricketers particularly admired: 'All the Leicestershire over-35 bowlers. Amazing effort'

Young players to look out for: Alan Richardson, Jamie Spires, Luke Wright, 'Phillip DeFreitas, Devon Malcolm'

Other sports played: Golf, football, tennis, Scrabble

Other sports followed: Football (Burnley FC, 'still hate Stoke'); NFL (Tampa Bay Buccaneers)

Injuries: Out for about three months with a lateral tear in a hip muscle

Relaxations: 'Educating the masses about music; meeting new people; talking; playing the bass guitar with the world famous band Two Tone Deaf'

Extras: Played for Cumberland. Man of the Match in the Board XI final 1999 (Warwickshire v Essex). Topped Warwickshire 2nd XI batting averages 1998 and was third in bowling averages. Awarded Warwickshire 2nd XI cap 1999. Took a wicket with his fourth ball in first-class cricket v Oxford University at The Parks 1999. B&H Gold Award for his 21* batting at No. 11 (following 2-18) v Worcestershire at Worcester 2001. Left Warwickshire at the end of the 2001 season and joined Leicestershire for 2002

Opinions on cricket: 'The loan system, which at the moment is useless, could be a huge success. Ask me for details. Also, is two overseas players the answer? Somehow I doubt it. Let's plunge that money into youth systems.'

Best batting: 16 Leicestershire v Yorkshire, Leicester 2002

Best bowling: 6-50 Warwickshire v Derbyshire, Derby 2001

2002 Season

	M	Inns	NO	Runs	HS	Avge	100s	50s	Ct	St	O	M	Runs	Wkts	Avge	Best	5wI	10wM
Test																		
All First	4	5	1	33	16	8.25	-	-	1	-	91	24	270	7	38.57	3-55	-	-
1-day Int																		
C & G																			
B & H																			
1-day Lge	5	3	0	58	28	19.33	-	-	-	-	41	2	179	6	29.83	3-56	-	

Career Performances

	M	Inns	NO	Runs	HS	Avge	100s	50s	Ct	St	Balls	Runs	Wkts	Avge	Best	5wI	10wM
Test																	
All First	10	9	3	45	16	7.50	-	-	1	-	1533	818	30	27.26	6-50	1	-
1-day Int																	
C & G	1	1	0	4	4	4.00	-	-	-	-	54	37	1	37.00	1-37	-	
B & H	3	1	1	21	21 *	-	-	-	1	-	174	125	4	31.25	2-18	-	
1-day Lge	22	6	1	64	28	12.80	-	-	1	-	1031	622	31	20.06	4-34	-	

DAKIN, J. M. Essex

Name: <u>Jonathan</u> Michael Dakin
Role: Left-hand bat, right-arm
medium-fast bowler
Born: 28 February 1973, Hitchin, Herts
Height: 6ft 6in **Weight:** 16st
Nickname: JD, Babe Ruth, Jack,
Deuce, Rosie
County debut: 1993 (Leicestershire),
2002 (Essex)
County cap: 2000 (Leicestershire)
1st-Class 50s: 11
1st-Class 100s: 5
1st-Class catches: 19
One-Day 100s: 2
One-Day 5 w. in innings: 1
Place in batting averages: 221st av. 21.11
(2001 200th av. 19.18)
Place in bowling averages: 68th av. 30.82
(2001 44th av. 26.68)
Strike rate: 54.05 (career 66.71)
Parents: Fred John and Gloria May
Marital status: Single
Family links with cricket: 'Brother keeps winning trophies with club Ivanhoe'
Education: King Edward VII School, Johannesburg, South Africa
Qualifications: Matriculation
Off-season: 'North Hobart Demons (Tasmania)'
Overseas tours: Rutland Tourists to Jersey 1992; Leicestershire CCC to South Africa
1996, 1997, to Barbados, to Sri Lanka, to Anguilla
Overseas teams played for: Wanderers, South Africa 1986-92; Alberts, South Africa
1993; Kaponga CC, New Zealand 1995-96; North Hobart, Tasmania 2001-03
Career highlights to date: 'Getting promoted in both divisions for Essex'

Cricket moments to forget: 'This year's [2002] B&H final at Lord's. That makes three losses in a row there in finals'

Cricketers particularly admired: Phil Simmons, Devon Malcolm, Pete Evans

Players to look out for: Mark Pettini, Ravi Bopara, Darren Maddy

Other sports played: Golf

Other sports followed: Rugby union (Leicester Tigers)

Injuries: Out for two weeks with 'a dodgy hamstring'

Relaxations: Eating out

Extras: Won three Bain Hogg trophies in four years. Scored 193 against Middlesex in the Bain Hogg in 1996. Won the Gold Award against Durham in the 1996 B&H. C&G Man of the Match award for his 179 v Wales at Swansea 2001; it was the fourth highest individual score in Gillette/NatWest/C&G history and the highest in the 50-over format of the competition. Left Leicestershire at the end of the 2001 season and joined Essex for 2002

Opinions on cricket: 'Sunday League should be 40 overs. The choice should be left to away team captains so no toss is needed. This will stop doctored pitches.'

Best batting: 190 Leicestershire v Northamptonshire, Northampton 1997

Best bowling: 4-17 Essex v Middlesex, Chelmsford 2002

2002 Season

	M	Inns	NO	Runs	HS	Avge	100s	50s	Ct	St	O	M	Runs	Wkts	Avge	Best	5wI	10wM
Test																		
All First	14	20	3	359	57	21.11	-	1	3	-	360.2	77	1233	40	30.82	4-17	-	-
1-day Int																		
C & G	3	2	0	21	17	10.50	-	-	-	-	27.5	3	123	3	41.00	2-51	-	
B & H	7	5	1	42	18	10.50	-	-	1	-	38	3	165	5	33.00	3-47	-	
1-day Lge	14	11	4	250	45 *	35.71	-	-	4	-	76	5	334	11	30.36	2-32	-	

Career Performances

	M	Inns	NO	Runs	HS	Avge	100s	50s	Ct	St	Balls	Runs	Wkts	Avge	Best	5wI	10wM
Test																	
All First	63	91	9	2316	190	28.24	5	11	19	-	7606	3983	114	34.93	4-17	-	-
1-day Int																	
C & G	13	12	0	296	179	24.66	1	-	1	-	491	347	10	34.70	2-23	-	
B & H	28	22	6	444	108 *	27.75	1	-	7	-	892	704	21	33.52	3-47	-	
1-day Lge	116	100	16	1574	68 *	18.73	-	2	23	-	3183	2662	96	27.72	5-30	1	

DALE, A.   Glamorgan

Name: Adrian Dale
Role: Right-hand bat, right-arm medium bowler
Born: 24 October 1968, Johannesburg, South Africa
Height: 5ft 11in **Weight:** 12st
Nickname: Arthur
County debut: 1989
County cap: 1992
Benefit: 2002
1000 runs in a season: 4
1st-Class 50s: 56
1st-Class 100s: 20
1st-Class 200s: 2
1st-Class 5 w. in innings: 4
1st-Class catches: 92
One-Day 100s: 2
One-Day 5 w. in innings: 2

Place in batting averages: 96th av. 37.34 (2001 28th av. 51.30)
Strike rate: 125.00 (career 70.61)
Parents: John and Maureen
Wife and date of marriage: Ruth, 9 January 1999
Children: Jessica, 12 January 2001; Luke, December 2002
Family links with cricket: Father played occasionally for Glamorgan 2nd XI
Education: Chepstow Primary School; Chepstow Comprehensive; Swansea University
Qualifications: 9 O-levels, 3 A-levels, BA (Hons) Economics
Career outside cricket: Estate agency. Glamorgan marketing department
Off-season: 'Busy with the end of my benefit year'
Overseas tours: Welsh Schools U16 to Australia 1986-87; Combined Universities to Barbados 1988-89; Glamorgan to Trinidad 1989-90, 1991-92, to Zimbabwe 1990-91, to Cape Town 1992-93, 1999, 2002; England A to South Africa 1993-94
Overseas teams played for: Bionics, Zimbabwe 1990-91; Cornwall, New Zealand 1991-93, 1995-97
Career highlights to date: '1997 County Championship win'
Cricket moments to forget: 'Losing the 2000 B&H Cup final at Lord's'
Cricket superstitions: 'None'
Cricketers particularly admired: Ian Botham, Michael Holding, Mike Gatting
Young players to look out for: 'There's good young talent at Glamorgan'
Other sports followed: Football (Arsenal), rugby union (Wales)
Injuries: Out for one Championship match with an ankle injury

Relaxations: Travelling, eating out

Extras: Played in successful Combined Universities sides of 1989 and 1990. Only batsman to score two half-centuries against the West Indies tourists in the same match in 1991. Took a wicket with his first delivery at Lord's. Recorded Glamorgan's then best one-day bowling figures, 6-22, against Durham 1993. Shared in Glamorgan's highest ever partnership, 425*, with Viv Richards against Middlesex 1993. Scored two centuries in a match (108/113) v Gloucestershire at Cardiff 1999. Glamorgan CCC Player of the Year 2000, 2001. Vice-captain of Glamorgan in 2001. Glamorgan Supporters' Player of the Year 2001. Scored 109 v Nottinghamshire at Colwyn Bay 2002, in the process sharing with Steve James (184) in a record fourth-wicket partnership for Glamorgan in matches against Nottinghamshire (217)

Opinions on cricket: 'The two divisions system is working well, although there should be less prize money for teams winning the second division and more for those doing well in the first division.'

Best batting: 214* Glamorgan v Middlesex, Cardiff 1993
Best bowling: 6-18 Glamorgan v Warwickshire, Cardiff 1993

2002 Season

	M	Inns	NO	Runs	HS	Avge	100s	50s	Ct	St	O	M	Runs	Wkts	Avge	Best	5wI	10wM
Test																		
All First	16	24	1	859	127 *	37.34	2	3	7	-	125	25	459	6	76.50	1-15	-	-
1-day Int																		
C & G	2	2	1	92	49	92.00	-	-	-	-	10	0	76	0	-		-	-
B & H	4	4	0	84	42	21.00	-	-	1	-	10.1	2	43	2	21.50	1-15	-	
1-day Lge	16	13	2	354	78 *	32.18	-	3	1	-	84	2	377	17	22.17	3-28	-	

Career Performances

	M	Inns	NO	Runs	HS	Avge	100s	50s	Ct	St	Balls	Runs	Wkts	Avge	Best	5wI	10wM
Test																	
All First	229	373	31	11688	214 *	34.17	22	56	92	-	15111	8073	214	37.72	6-18	4	-
1-day Int																	
C & G	36	33	4	897	110	30.93	1	3	6	-	1400	1022	29	35.24	3-15	-	
B & H	48	47	7	1157	100	28.92	1	3	13	-	1787	1290	45	28.66	5-41	1	
1-day Lge	192	165	22	4081	82	28.53	-	24	40	-	5873	4974	161	30.89	6-22	1	

23. Which Pakistan Test cricketer was captain of Kent in 1977?

DALEY, J. A. Durham

Name: <u>James</u> Arthur Daley
Role: Right-hand bat
Born: 24 September 1973, Sunderland
Height: 5ft 11in **Weight:** 12st
Nickname: Bebs, Jonty
County debut: 1992
County cap: 1999
1st-Class 50s: 20
1st-Class 100s: 4
1st-Class catches: 44
One-Day 100s: 1
Place in batting averages: (2001 134th
av. 28.53)
Strike rate: (career 126.00)
Parents: William and Christine
Marital status: Single
Family links with cricket: Brother played
representative cricket for Durham
Education: Hetton Comprehensive
Qualifications: 5 GCSEs
Career outside cricket: Travel agent
Overseas tours: Durham to Zimbabwe 1991-92; England U19 to India 1992-93;
England XI to Holland 1993
Cricketers particularly admired: David Graveney, Wayne Larkins, Jimmy Adams
Other sports followed: Most sports
Relaxations: Socialising, listening to all types of music
Extras: Scored three centuries in 1991 for MCC Young Cricketers at Lord's. Northern
Electric Foundation for Sport award winner 1992. Retired at the end of the 2002
season
Best batting: 159* Durham v Hampshire, Portsmouth 1994
Best bowling: 1-12 Durham v Cambridge University, Fenner's 1998

2002 Season

	M	Inns	NO	Runs	HS	Avge	100s	50s	Ct	St	O	M	Runs	Wkts	Avge	Best	5wI	10wM
Test																		
All First	3	6	1	130	59 *	26.00	-	1	1	-								
1-day Int																		
C & G																		
B & H																		
1-day Lge																		

Career Performances

	M	Inns	NO	Runs	HS	Avge	100s	50s	Ct	St	Balls	Runs	Wkts	Avge	Best	5wl	10wM
Test																	
All First	94	164	13	4272	159 *	28.29	4	20	44	-	126	81	1	81.00	1-12	-	-
1-day Int																	
C & G																	
B & H	16	15	1	298	92	21.28	-	2	-	-	12	19	0	-		-	-
1-day Lge	51	47	9	1260	105	33.15	1	7	11	-	1	4	0	-		-	-

DALRYMPLE, J. W. M.   Middlesex

Name: James (Jamie) William
Murray Dalrymple
Role: Right-hand bat, off-spin bowler
Born: 21 January 1981, Nairobi, Kenya
Height: 6ft **Weight:** 13st 7lbs
Nickname: JD, Pest
County debut: 2000 (one-day),
2001 (first-class)
1st-Class 50s: 2
1st-Class 100s: 2
1st-Class catches: 10
Place in batting averages: 79th av. 41.15
(2001 172nd av. 22.55)
Place in bowling averages: (2001 144th
av. 57.80)
Strike rate: 122.66 (career 122.31)
Parents: Douglas and Patricia
Marital status: Single
Family links with cricket: 'Dad played lots of club cricket.' Brother Simon played for
Oxford University in 2002
Education: Ashfold School, Dorton; Radley College, Abingdon; St Peter's College,
Oxford University
Qualifications: 10 GCSEs, 5 A-levels
Off-season: At university
Overseas tours: Middlesex to South Africa 2000
Career highlights to date: 'Four-day debut. Being part of an [NUL] win with 16
required off the last over. Man of the Match in Norwich Union League v Essex'
Cricket moments to forget: 'Any duck. Dropping any catches'
Cricketers particularly admired: 'Many – Gower, Hooper, the Waughs,
Ian Botham …'
Young players to look out for: Nick Compton, Tom Mees

Other sports played: Rugby (college), hockey (university)
Other sports followed: Football (Tottenham), rugby (Northampton RUFC)
Relaxations: Reading, music
Extras: Represented England U19 v Sri Lanka U19 in one-day and 'Test' series 2000. Played for Oxford University CCE 2001 and 2002 (captain 2002); made first-class debut for OUCCE against his county club, Middlesex, at The Parks 2001. Represented British Universities 2001 and captained British Universities v Sri Lankans at Northampton and v West Indies A (50-over match) at The Parks 2002. Scored maiden first-class century (148) for OUCCE v Gloucestershire at The Parks 2002, following up with 54* in the second innings. Oxford Blue 2001 and 2002; captained Oxford in 2002 Varsity Match at The Parks (taking 4-152 from 52.4 overs in Cambridge's only innings and scoring 48 and 137) and in the 2002 Charles Fry Trophy (50-over) match at Lord's (scoring 78 and taking 4-42)
Opinions on cricket: 'There are too many games played on poor pitches throughout the levels of the game. There seems to be more talk than action at times in cricket.'
Best batting: 148 OUCCE v Gloucestershire, The Parks 2002
Best bowling: 4-86 Oxford University v Cambridge University, Fenner's 2001

2002 Season

	M	Inns	NO	Runs	HS	Avge	100s	50s	Ct	St	O	M	Runs	Wkts	Avge	Best	5wl	10wM
Test																		
All First	8	14	1	535	148	41.15	2	1	2	-	122.4	20	467	6	77.83	4-152	-	-
1-day Int																		
C & G																		
B & H																		
1-day Lge	11	10	1	227	52	25.22	-	1	8	-	59	1	306	10	30.60	2-25	-	

Career Performances

	M	Inns	NO	Runs	HS	Avge	100s	50s	Ct	St	Balls	Runs	Wkts	Avge	Best	5wl	10wM
Test																	
All First	13	24	2	738	148	33.54	2	2	10	-	1957	1045	16	65.31	4-86	-	-
1-day Int																	
C & G																	
B & H																	
1-day Lge	21	18	4	341	52	24.35	-	1	10	-	621	500	18	27.77	4-14	-	

DAVIES, A. P. Glamorgan

Name: <u>Andrew</u> Philip Davies
Role: Left-hand bat, right-arm
medium bowler
Born: 7 November 1976, Neath
Height: 6ft **Weight:** 12st
Nickname: Diver, Snowy, Gazza, T-shirt
County debut: 1995
1st-Class 5 w. in innings: 1
1st-Class catches: 3
One-Day 5 w. in innings: 2
Place in batting averages: 295th av. 9.66
(2001 230th av. 14.16)
Place in bowling averages: 51st av. 28.00
Strike rate: 46.53 (career 58.22)
Parents: Anne and Phil
Wife and date of marriage: Nerys,
1 February 2003
Family links with cricket: Brother plays
local cricket with father
Education: Coedffranc; Dwr-y-Felin Comprehensive School; Christ College, Brecon
Qualifications: 6 GCSEs, A-levels, Level 2 coach
Career outside cricket: Sales rep
Off-season: 'Preparing for wedding; working for Lansing Linde'
Overseas tours: Wales MC to Barbados; Glamorgan to Pretoria, to Cape Town
Overseas teams played for: Marist CC, Whangarei, New Zealand 1995-96
Career highlights to date: 'Winning division two of NUL 2001. Winning division
one of NUL 2002. Beating Surrey at The Oval in Championship 2001. Bowling
Steve Waugh'
Cricket moments to forget: 'Bowling at the end at Canterbury and getting hit for six.
Memory soon went on balcony when Steve James lifted NUL division one trophy!'
Cricket superstitions: 'Praying before every NUL ball bowled in the first 15'
Cricketers particularly admired: 'All those who kept nerve at Canterbury'
Young players to look out for: Dave and Adam Harrison, Mark Wallace, Ian Thomas,
Simon Jones, Jonny Hughes, Leighton Jones
Other sports played: 'Used to play football (trials for Birmingham City)'
Other sports followed: Football (Swansea City)
Relaxations: 'Listening to music; beating Leighton Jones at pool or snooker'
Extras: Wales U19 Player of the Year 1995. Wales Player of the Year 1996. 2nd XI
cap 1998. 2nd XI Player of the Year 1998, 1999. 1st XI Player of the Month August-
September 1998. Recorded maiden one-day five-wicket return (5-39; five of the top
six) v Essex at Cardiff in the Norwich Union League 2001. Glamorgan's leading

wicket-taker (21) in the Norwich Union League 2001. Took 5-19 from nine overs in the C&G v Lincolnshire at Sleaford 2002. Recorded maiden first-class five-wicket return (5-79) v Worcestershire at Cardiff 2002

Opinions on cricket: 'No ball – batters get free hit; if bowler beats bat, batters have candlestick. Let's make it even more of a batter's game. Make bats wider, shorten stumps, pitch longer, every batter gets four lives.'

Best batting: 40 Glamorgan v Essex, Cardiff 2001

Best bowling: 5-79 Glamorgan v Worcestershire, Cardiff 2002

2002 Season

	M	Inns	NO	Runs	HS	Avge	100s	50s	Ct	St	O	M	Runs	Wkts	Avge	Best	5wI	10wM
Test																		
All First	5	6	0	58	30	9.66	-	-	-	-	116.2	14	420	15	28.00	5-79	1	-
1-day Int																		
C & G	2	1	0	1	1	1.00	-	-	-	-	17	3	107	5	21.40	5-19	1	
B & H	2	2	2	15	8 *	-	-	-	-	-	18	0	97	1	97.00	1-44	-	
1-day Lge	15	5	3	15	11 *	7.50	-	-	2	-	110.2	7	518	21	24.66	4-33	-	

Career Performances

	M	Inns	NO	Runs	HS	Avge	100s	50s	Ct	St	Balls	Runs	Wkts	Avge	Best	5wI	10wM
Test																	
All First	18	22	3	222	40	11.68	-	-	3	-	2329	1364	40	34.10	5-79	1	-
1-day Int																	
C & G	2	1	0	1	1	1.00	-	-	-	-	102	107	5	21.40	5-19	1	
B & H	6	3	3	18	8 *	-	-	-	-	-	333	286	3	95.33	1-38	-	
1-day Lge	35	15	8	77	24	11.00	-	-	6	-	1445	1100	54	20.37	5-39	1	

---

24. Which Sri Lankan batsman scored 255 and 116 for Kent
v Derbyshire at Maidstone in 1995?

DAVIES, M. A.　　　　　　　　　　　　Durham

Name: <u>Mark</u> Anthony Davies
Role: Right-hand bat, right-arm
fast-medium bowler
Born: 4 October 1980, Stockton-on-Tees
Height: 6ft 3in **Weight:** 13st
Nickname: Davo
County debut: 1998 (one-day),
2002 (first-class)
1st-Class 5 w. in innings: 1
1st-Class catches: 3
Place in batting averages: 284th av. 10.82
Place in bowling averages: 34th av. 26.16
Strike rate: 59.63 (career 59.63)
Parents: Howard and Mandy
Marital status: Single
Education: Priors Mill C of E School;
Northfield School, Billingham; Stockton
Sixth Form College

Qualifications: 5 GCSEs, NVQ Level 3 Sport and Recreation
Overseas tours: Durham to South Africa 2002
Overseas teams played for: North Kalgoorlie CC, Western Australia
Career highlights to date: 'Gaining promotion in the NUL 2001'
Cricketers particularly admired: Glenn McGrath
Young players to look out for: Kabir Ali
Other sports played: Football, golf, boxing
Other sports followed: Football (Middlesbrough)
Relaxations: Socialising, golf
Extras: Represented England U19 in one-day series v Sri Lanka U19 2000. Played for
Durham Board XI in the NatWest 2000 and for Durham Board XI and Durham in the
C&G 2001. Recorded maiden first-class five-wicket return (5-61) v Glamorgan at
Riverside 2002. Attended Durham Academy
Best batting: 33 Durham v Derbyshire, Darlington 2002
Best bowling: 5-61 Durham v Glamorgan, Riverside 2002

2002 Season

	M	Inns	NO	Runs	HS	Avge	100s	50s	Ct	St	O	M	Runs	Wkts	Avge	Best	5wI	10wM
Test																		
All First	14	24	7	184	33	10.82	-	-	3	-	357.5	106	942	36	26.16	5-61	1	-
1-day Int																		
C & G	2	1	0	2	2	2.00	-	-	-	-	11	2	55	0	-		-	-
B & H	3	1	1	18	18*	-	-	-	-	-	19	2	83	2	41.50	1-12	-	
1-day Lge	16	11	3	77	31*	9.62	-	-	6	-	112	8	464	16	29.00	3-41	-	

Career Performances

	M	Inns	NO	Runs	HS	Avge	100s	50s	Ct	St	Balls	Runs	Wkts	Avge	Best	5wI	10wM
Test																	
All First	14	24	7	184	33	10.82	-	-	3	-	2147	942	36	26.16	5-61	1	-
1-day Int																	
C & G	8	5	1	8	6	2.00	-	-	-	-	342	220	5	44.00	1-11	-	
B & H	3	1	1	18	18 *	-	-	-	-	-	114	83	2	41.50	1-12	-	
1-day Lge	23	15	3	91	31 *	7.58	-	-	7	-	960	657	28	23.46	4-13	-	

DAVIS, M. J. G.   Sussex

Name: <u>Mark</u> Jeffrey Gronow Davis
Role: Right-hand bat, right-arm
off-spin bowler
Born: 10 October 1971, Port Elizabeth,
South Africa
Height: 6ft 2in **Weight:** 12st 8lbs
Nickname: Doxy, Davo, Sparky
County debut: 2001
County cap: 2002
1st-Class 50s: 7
1st-Class 100s: 1
1st-Class 5 w. in innings: 5
1st-Class 10 w. in match: 1
1st-Class catches: 57
Place in batting averages: 170th av. 26.33
(2001 158th av. 24.38)
Place in bowling averages: 118th av. 38.60
(2001 114th av. 39.83)
Strike rate: 74.42 (career 78.72)
Parents: Jeremy and Marilyn
Wife and date of marriage: Candice, 8 April 2000
Family links with cricket: 'Father supports Sussex. My brothers, William and Patrick,
play league cricket in Sussex'
Education: Woodridge Preparatory School; Grey High School; University of Pretoria
Qualifications: BA Psychology and English
Off-season: 'Head coach of UPE International Cricket Academy in Port Elizabeth'
Overseas tours: South Africa U24 to Sri Lanka 1995; Northern Transvaal to
Zimbabwe 1992-93, to Kenya 1994-95, 1995-96
Overseas teams played for: Northern Transvaal/Northerns 1991-92 – 2000-01
Cricket moments to forget: 'Being bowled by our physio Stuart Osborne during a
net session'

Cricketers particularly admired: 'The Sussex team', Malcolm Marshall, Tim May, Roy Pienaar, Shane Warne
Young players to look out for: Tim Ambrose, Matt Prior
Other sports played: Golf, tennis
Other sports followed: Rugby ('support the Springboks'), football (Middlesbrough)
Injuries: Out for two and a half weeks after breaking a hand v Somerset
Relaxations: 'Golf, music, going out with friends, watching good movies'
Extras: Made first-class debut for Northern Transvaal B 1990-91. Captain of Northern Transvaal/Northerns 1997-2000, during which time the province won the first two trophies in its history. Represented South Africa A v Zimbabwe 1995. Member of MCC; played for MCC against Sri Lanka A at Shenley in 1999 and against New Zealand A at The Parks in 2000. B&H Gold Award for his 2-47 and 15 key runs at the 'death' v Surrey at Hove 2002. Scored maiden first-class century (111) v Somerset at Taunton 2002, in the process sharing with Robin Martin-Jenkins (205*) in a record eighth-wicket partnership for Sussex (291); the stand fell one run short of the record eighth-wicket partnership in English first-class cricket, set by Bobby Peel and Lord Hawke for Yorkshire v Warwickshire at Birmingham in 1896. Awarded Sussex cap 2002. Is not considered an overseas player
Opinions on cricket: 'Still the best game in the world.'
Best batting: 111 Sussex v Somerset, Taunton 2002
Best bowling: 8-37 Northerns B v North West, Potchefstroom 1994-95

2002 Season

	M	Inns	NO	Runs	HS	Avge	100s	50s	Ct	St	O	M	Runs	Wkts	Avge	Best	5wI	10wM
Test																		
All First	15	22	4	474	111	26.33	1	2	7	-	347.2	71	1081	28	38.60	6-97	1	-
1-day Int																		
C & G	3	1	1	1	1*	-	-	-	-	-	30	1	127	1	127.00	1-28	-	
B & H	6	2	1	18	15	18.00	-	-	1	-	48	2	190	4	47.50	2-47	-	
1-day Lge	15	10	3	116	28	16.57	-	-	5	-	105.2	4	423	17	24.88	3-40	-	

Career Performances

	M	Inns	NO	Runs	HS	Avge	100s	50s	Ct	St	Balls	Runs	Wkts	Avge	Best	5wI	10wM
Test																	
All First	100	155	25	2427	111	18.66	1	7	57	-	15194	6768	193	35.06	8-37	5	1
1-day Int																	
C & G	5	3	3	42	30*	-	-	-	-	-	300	186	4	46.50	2-37	-	
B & H	10	4	3	20	15	20.00	-	-	2	-	524	335	6	55.83	2-47	-	
1-day Lge	29	18	4	203	28	14.50	-	-	6	-	1263	946	29	32.62	4-24	-	

DAWSON, R. K. J.   Yorkshire

Name: <u>Richard</u> Kevin James Dawson
Role: Right-hand bat, right-arm
off-spin bowler
Born: 4 August 1980, Doncaster
Height: 6ft 4in **Weight:** 11st 4lbs
Nickname: Billy Dog
County debut: 2001
Test debut: 2001-02
Tests: 3
1st-Class 50s: 2
1st-Class 5 w. in innings: 4
1st-Class catches: 9
Place in batting averages: 215th av. 22.21
(2001 264th av. 9.50)
Place in bowling averages: 120th av. 38.77
(2001 84th av. 33.80)
Strike rate: 73.32 (career 73.78)
Parents: Kevin and Pat
Marital status: Single
Family links with cricket: Brother Gareth plays for Doncaster Town CC
Education: Hill House Preparatory School; Batley GS; Exeter University
Qualifications: 10 GCSEs, 4 A-levels, degree in Exercise and Sports Science
Off-season: Touring with England
Overseas tours: England U18 to Bermuda 1997; England U19 to New Zealand
1998-99; England to India and New Zealand 2001-02, to Australia 2002-03; ECB
National Academy to Sri Lanka 2002-03
Cricketers particularly admired: Steve Waugh, Graeme Swann
Young players to look out for: Graeme Bridge, Ian Bell
Other sports played: Football
Other sports followed: Football (Doncaster Rovers FC)
Relaxations: Sleeping, listening to music
Extras: Captained England U15. Sir John Hobbs Silver Jubilee Memorial Prize 1995.
Played for Devon 1999 and 2000. Represented England U19 in one-day and 'Test'
series v Australia U19 in 1999. Has Yorkshire 2nd XI cap. Captained British
Universities 2000. NBC Denis Compton Award for the most promising young
Yorkshire player 2001. Made Test debut in first Test v India at Mohali 2001-02, taking
4-134 in India's first innings. Scored 41 v Leicestershire at Scarborough in the NUL
2002, in the process sharing with Richard Blakey (60) in a new record eighth-wicket
partnership for Yorkshire in the one-day league (89)
Best batting: 87 Yorkshire v Kent, Canterbury 2002
Best bowling: 6-82 Yorkshire v Glamorgan, Scarborough 2001
Stop press: Added to ECB National Academy squad for tour to Sri Lanka 2002-03

2002 Season

	M	Inns	NO	Runs	HS	Avge	100s	50s	Ct	St	O	M	Runs	Wkts	Avge	Best	5wI	10wM
Test																		
All First	15	24	1	511	87	22.21	-	2	2	-	488.5	104	1551	40	38.77	5-42	2	-
1-day Int																		
C & G	4	0	0	0	0	-	-	-	1	-	33.4	0	180	4	45.00	4-34	-	
B & H	3	3	2	16	8	16.00	-	-	1	-	7.3	0	35	5	7.00	4-13	-	
1-day Lge	13	10	0	100	41	10.00	-	-	1	-	66	0	333	13	25.61	4-37	-	

Career Performances

	M	Inns	NO	Runs	HS	Avge	100s	50s	Ct	St	Balls	Runs	Wkts	Avge	Best	5wI	10wM
Test	3	5	1	27	11	6.75	-	-	1	-	540	279	6	46.50	4-134	-	-
All First	31	46	5	737	87	17.97	-	2	9	-	5829	3108	79	39.34	6-82	4	-
1-day Int																	
C & G	9	3	0	14	7	4.66	-	-	2	-	435	339	9	37.66	4-34	-	
B & H	3	3	2	16	8	16.00	-	-	1	-	45	35	5	7.00	4-13	-	
1-day Lge	23	17	1	125	41	7.81	-	-	5	-	738	599	22	27.22	4-37	-	

DEAN, K. J.   Derbyshire

Name: Kevin James Dean
Role: Left-hand bat, left-arm
'slow-medium' bowler ('because I always
bowl into the wind, don't I, Corky?')
Born: 16 October 1975, Derby
Height: 6ft 5in **Weight:** 14st
Nickname: Deany, Red Face,
The Wall, George
County debut: 1996
County cap: 1998
50 wickets in a season: 2
1st-Class 50s: 2
1st-Class 5 w. in innings: 14
1st-Class 10 w. in match: 4
1st-Class catches: 13
One-Day 5 w. in innings: 1
Place in batting averages: 226th av. 20.41
(2001 248th av. 11.70)
Place in bowling averages: 17th av. 23.50 (2001 37th av. 26.11)
Strike rate: 42.65 (career 41.19)
Parents: Ken and Dorothy
Marital status: Single

Education: Waterhouses Primary School; Leek High School; Leek College of Further Education
Qualifications: 8 GCSEs, 3 A-levels, 1 AS-level
Career outside cricket: Working for Ladbrokes
Off-season: 'Working for Ladbrokes at Derby County and Uttoxeter Racecourse. Writing for cricnet.com. And babysitting for A.J. Harris'
Overseas tours: MCC to Australia 2002-03
Overseas teams played for: Sturt CC, Adelaide 1996-97
Career highlights to date: 'Can't split – 1) Hitting the winning runs against Australia for Derbys in 1997; 2) Getting either hat-trick'
Cricket moments to forget: 'Losing in the NatWest final [1998]'
Cricket superstitions: 'Last person out of changing room for first session of fielding'
Cricketers particularly admired: Dominic Cork, Wasim Akram, Michael Holding
Young players to look out for: Tom Lungley, Lian Wharton ('if he ever bowls'), Mark Davies, Jacob Harris
Other sports played: Football ('influential playmaker in the Derby Rejects football team, winners of the Premier League at Derby's JJB Soccerdome; also play for the "White Hart" in Duffield'), golf, tennis, snooker
Other sports followed: Football (Derby County), horse racing
Injuries: 'Windburn due to continual running into the wind; no time out of game, just a red face'
Relaxations: 'Going horse racing. Talking with Sutts and trying to keep it vaguely interesting. Fleecing fruit machines with Tetley, but not casinos, yet!'
Extras: A member of the Staffordshire U16 Texaco winning team. Achieved first-class hat-trick against Kent at Derby 1998. Took second first-class hat-trick (Habib, Kumble, Ormond) v Leicestershire at Leicester 2000. Joint leading wicket-taker in English first-class cricket 2002 (with Martin Saggers) with 83 wickets (av. 23.50). Derbyshire Player of the Year 2002 (jointly with Michael DiVenuto)
Best batting: 54* Derbyshire v Worcestershire, Derby 2002
Best bowling: 8-52 Derbyshire v Kent, Canterbury 2000

2002 Season

	M	Inns	NO	Runs	HS	Avge	100s	50s	Ct	St	O	M	Runs	Wkts	Avge	Best	5wI	10wM
Test																		
All First	17	26	9	347	54 *	20.41	-	2	6	-	590	148	1951	83	23.50	7-42	3	2
1-day Int																		
C & G																		
B & H	3	1	0	1	1	1.00	-	-	-	-	17	1	71	1	71.00	1-6	-	
1-day Lge	12	8	3	46	16 *	9.20	-	-	4	-	92	12	422	18	23.44	4-33	-	

Career Performances

	M	Inns	NO	Runs	HS	Avge	100s	50s	Ct	St	Balls	Runs	Wkts	Avge	Best	5wl	10wM
Test																	
All First	73	96	34	794	54 *	12.80	-	2	13	-	11987	6676	291	22.94	8-52	14	4
1-day Int																	
C & G	11	3	2	8	8	8.00	-	-	4	-	630	421	20	21.05	3-13	-	
B & H	9	3	1	21	14 *	10.50	-	-	-	-	342	282	6	47.00	2-62	-	
1-day Lge	68	32	18	158	16 *	11.28	-	-	13	-	2900	2272	78	29.12	5-32	1	

DEFREITAS, P. A. J. Leicestershire

Name: <u>Phillip</u> Anthony Jason DeFreitas
Role: Right-hand bat, right-arm
fast-medium bowler, county captain
Born: 18 February 1966, Scotts Head,
Dominica
Height: 6ft **Weight:** 13st 7lbs
Nickname: Padge, Daffy, Linchy
County debut: 1985 (Leics),
1989 (Lancs), 1994 (Derbys)
County cap: 1986 (Leics),
1989 (Lancs), 1994 (Derbys)
Test debut: 1986-87
Tests: 44
One-Day Internationals: 103
50 wickets in a season: 13
1st-Class 50s: 51
1st-Class 100s: 9
1st-Class 5 w. in innings: 57
1st-Class 10 w. in match: 5
1st-Class catches: 120
One-Day 5 w. in innings: 6

Place in batting averages: 147th av. 29.00 (2001 194th av. 19.69)
Place in bowling averages: 72nd av. 31.25 (2001 47th av. 27.47)
Strike rate: 66.66 (career 57.72)
Parents: Sybil and Martin
Marital status: Divorced
Children: Alexandra Elizabeth Jane, 5 August 1991
Family links with cricket: Father played in Windward Islands. All six brothers play
Education: Willesden High School
Qualifications: 2 O-levels
Overseas tours: England YC to West Indies 1984-85; England to Australia 1986-87,

to Pakistan, Australia and New Zealand 1987-88, to India (Nehru Cup) and West Indies 1989-90, to Australia 1990-91, to New Zealand 1991-92, to India and Sri Lanka 1992-93, to Australia 1994-95, to South Africa 1995-96, to India and Pakistan (World Cup) 1995-96; England XI to New Zealand (Cricket Max) 1997

Overseas teams played for: Port Adelaide, South Australia 1985; Mosman, Sydney 1988; Boland, South Africa 1993-94, 1995-96

Cricketers particularly admired: Ian Botham, Geoff Boycott, Mike Gatting, Viv Richards, Malcolm Marshall, David Hughes, Neil Fairbrother

Young players to look out for: Charlie Dagnall, Luke Wright

Other sports followed: Football (Manchester City)

Extras: Left Leicestershire and joined Lancashire at end of 1988 season. Man of the Match in 1990 NatWest Trophy final. One of *Wisden*'s Five Cricketers of the Year 1992. Man of the Tournament in the Hong Kong Sixes 1993. Left Lancashire at the end of the 1993 season and joined Derbyshire. Player of the Series against New Zealand 1994. Captained Derbyshire for part of 1997 season after the departure of Dean Jones. Is the only playing English cricketer to have appeared in two World Cup finals. Took 1000th first-class wicket (Usman Afzaal caught by Karl Krikken) v Notts at Trent Bridge 1999. Left Derbyshire at end of 1999 season and rejoined Leicestershire for 2000. Scored 97 and 123* v Lancashire at Leicester 2000 (also bowled 47 overs in Lancashire's only innings). Shared in a Leicestershire record eighth-wicket partnership for the one-day league (116) with Neil Burns v Northamptonshire at Leicester in the Norwich Union League 2001. Took 6-65 v Glamorgan at Cardiff 2001, in the process achieving the feat of having recorded a five-wicket innings return against all 18 counties. Struck a 22-ball Championship 50 (out for 51) v Lancashire at Old Trafford 2002, following up with 6-101 in Lancashire's first innings. Passed 10,000 runs in first-class cricket v Somerset at Leicester 2002 to achieve the career double of 10,000 runs and 1000 wickets. Appointed captain of Leicestershire for 2003

Opinions on cricket: '1. First division players should get paid more than second division players. 2. Prize money should be paid only to first division; the reward for second division teams is to get promoted to play for prize money. 3. Championship games should never follow day/night games.'

Best batting: 123* Leicestershire v Lancashire, Leicester 2000

Best bowling: 7-21 Lancashire v Middlesex, Lord's 1989

2002 Season

	M	Inns	NO	Runs	HS	Avge	100s	50s	Ct	St	O	M	Runs	Wkts	Avge	Best	5wI	10wM
Test																		
All First	16	23	2	609	114	29.00	1	3	10	-	566.4	150	1594	51	31.25	6-101	2	-
1-day Int																		
C & G	2	2	0	35	30	17.50	-	-	1	-	17	3	49	0	-	-	-	-
B & H	4	2	0	27	15	13.50	-	-	1	-	21.1	1	83	3	27.66	2-25	-	
1-day Lge	13	12	4	237	49	29.62	-	-	-	-	95.2	9	342	18	19.00	4-24	-	

Career Performances

	M	Inns	NO	Runs	HS	Avge	100s	50s	Ct	St	Balls	Runs	Wkts	Avge	Best	5wl	10wM
Test	44	68	5	934	88	14.82	-	4	14	-	9838	4700	140	33.57	7-70	4	-
All First	339	481	45	10042	123 *	23.03	9	51	120	-	66092	31896	1145	27.85	7-21	57	5
1-day Int	103	66	23	690	67	16.04	-	1	26	-	5712	3775	115	32.82	4-35	-	
C & G	45	29	4	462	69	18.48	-	1	8	-	2715	1419	57	24.89	5-13	4	
B & H	67	45	9	763	75 *	21.19	-	3	17	-	3554	2043	90	22.70	5-16	1	
1-day Lge	211	162	28	2588	72 *	19.31	-	6	37	-	8693	6258	226	27.69	5-26	1	

DENNING, N. A.   Essex

Name: Nicholas (Nick) Alexander Denning
Role: Right-hand bat, right-arm
fast-medium bowler
Born: 3 October 1978, Ascot
Height: 5ft 11in **Weight:** 11st 7lbs
Nickname: Denzil, Nudger
County debut: No first-team appearance
Parents: John Philip and Jill Patricia
Marital status: Single
Family links with cricket: Father played and
brother played up to Berkshire U19
Education: Hall Grove Prep School, Surrey;
Bradfield College, Berkshire; Cheltenham
and Gloucester College of Higher Education
Qualifications: 9 GCSEs, 3 A-levels, degree
in Sports and Exercise Sciences, Sports
Massage Therapy, ECB Level 2 coaching
Career outside cricket: Fitness training
Off-season: 'Working in the gym at Lord's and getting fit'
Overseas tours: Bradfield College to Barbados 1997; MCC YC to Cape Town 2000
Overseas teams played for: CBC Old Boys 2000-01
Career highlights to date: 'Signing for Essex and being capped by Berkshire'

Cricket moments to forget: 'Bagging a pair while on trial'

Cricket superstitions: 'Always turn the same direction when I reach my bowling mark'

Cricketers particularly admired: Darren Gough, Mike Atherton, Allan Donald

Young players to look out for: James Morris (Berkshire)

Other sports played: 'Most sports but nothing too competitive'

Other sports followed: 'Follow most sports', football (Arsenal)

Relaxations: 'Relaxing with friends and family and going on holiday'

Extras: Played for Berkshire, including appearances in the first round of the C&G 2002, which was played in August 2001, and the first and second rounds of the C&G 2003, which were played in August and September 2002. Took 6-42 from 19.5 overs, including a spell of 6-4, v Cornwall at Wash Common in the Minor Counties Championship 2002

Opinions on cricket: 'Introduction of two-division cricket is good for the game as it encourages competition throughout the whole of the season.'

2002 Season (did not make any first-class or one-day appearances for his county)

Career Performances

	M	Inns	NO	Runs	HS	Avge	100s	50s	Ct	St	Balls	Runs	Wkts	Avge	Best	5wl	10wM
Test																	
All First																	
1-day Int																	
C & G	3	1	1	1	1*	-	-	-	-	-	162	119	4	29.75	3-22	-	
B & H																	
1-day Lge																	

25. Who took four wickets in four balls on his county debut
v Leicestershire in the B&H Cup 1996?

DIVENUTO, M. J.　　　　　Derbyshire

Name: <u>Michael</u> James DiVenuto
Role: Left-hand bat, right-arm medium/leg-break bowler, county vice-captain
Born: 12 December 1973, Hobart, Tasmania
Height: 5ft 11in **Weight:** 12st 12lbs
Nickname: Diva
County debut: 1999 (Sussex), 2000 (Derbyshire)
County cap: 1999 (Sussex), 2000 (Derbyshire)
One-Day Internationals: 9
1000 runs in a season: 3
1st-Class 50s: 66
1st-Class 100s: 20
1st-Class 200s: 1
1st-Class catches: 155
One-Day 100s: 2
Place in batting averages: 15th av. 61.52 (2001 48th av. 45.08)
Strike rate: (career 144.60)
Parents: Enrico and Elizabeth
Marital status: Single
Family links with cricket: 'Dad and older brother Peter both played grade cricket in Tasmania.' Brother Peter also plays for Italy
Education: St Peter's School, Hobart; St Virgil's College, Hobart
Qualifications: HSC (5 x Level III subjects), Level 3 cricket coach
Career outside cricket: Part-time sports journalist with Southern Cross TV, Hobart
Off-season: Playing for Tasmania
Overseas tours: Australian Cricket Academy to India and Sri Lanka 1993, to South Africa 1996; Australia A to Malaysia (Super 8s) 1997 (captain), to Scotland and Ireland 1998 (captain), to Los Angeles 1999; Australia to South Africa 1996-97 (one-day series), to Hong Kong (Super 6s) 1997, to Malaysia (Super 8s) 1998; Tasmania to Zimbabwe 1995-96
Overseas teams played for: North Hobart CC, Tasmania; Kingborough, Tasmania; Tasmania 1991-92 –
Career highlights to date: 'Playing for Australia. Man of the Match award v South Africa at Johannesburg 1997. Dismissing Jamie Cox at Taunton in 1999, my first wicket in first-class cricket'
Cricket moments to forget: 'Being dismissed by Jamie Cox at Taunton in 1999, *his* first wicket in first-class cricket'
Cricketers particularly admired: David Boon, Dean Jones, Kepler Wessels, Mark and Steve Waugh

Young players to look out for: Steve Selwood
Other sports played: Australian Rules (Tasmanian U15, U16 and Sandy Bay FC)
Other sports followed: Australian Rules football (Geelong Cats)
Injuries: Out for two and a half months of the 2001-02 Australian season with an ankle injury
Relaxations: Golf, sleeping and eating
Extras: Scored then career-best 189 v Western Australia in 1997-98 Sheffield Shield final, contributing more than 50 per cent of Tasmania's total in their second innings. Joined Sussex as overseas player for 1999. Joined Derbyshire as overseas player for 2000. Scored 173* v Derbyshire Board XI at Derby in NatWest 2000, a record for Derbyshire in one-day cricket. B&H Gold Award for his 108 v Leicestershire at Leicester 2001. Took five slip catches in an innings v Durham at Riverside 2001, later scoring 111 in victory chase. Scored maiden first-class double hundred (230) v Northamptonshire at Derby 2002, in the process setting a new record for the highest individual innings for Derbyshire v Northamptonshire. Carried his bat for 192* v Middlesex at Lord's 2002; also scored 113 in the second innings. Derbyshire Player of the Year 2002 (jointly with Kevin Dean). Vice-captain of Derbyshire since 2002
Opinions on cricket: 'The game's in good shape. Always on the lookout for ways to improve. The 20-over game should be interesting!'
Best batting: 230 Derbyshire v Northamptonshire, Derby 2002
Best bowling: 1-0 Tasmania v Queensland, Brisbane 1999-2000

2002 Season

	M	Inns	NO	Runs	HS	Avge	100s	50s	Ct	St	O	M	Runs	Wkts	Avge	Best	5wI	10wM
Test																		
All First	15	28	3	1538	230	61.52	4	7	29	-								
1-day Int																		
C & G	1	1	0	10	10	10.00	-	-	-	-								
B & H	5	4	0	60	30	15.00	-	-	-	-								
1-day Lge	13	13	0	325	94	25.00	-	2	2	-								

Career Performances

	M	Inns	NO	Runs	HS	Avge	100s	50s	Ct	St	Balls	Runs	Wkts	Avge	Best	5wI	10wM
Test																	
All First	154	267	15	10566	230	41.92	21	66	155	-	723	406	5	81.20	1-0	-	-
1-day Int	9	9	0	241	89	26.77	-	2	1	-							
C & G	6	6	1	358	173 *	71.60	1	2	4	-							
B & H	17	15	1	492	108	35.14	1	2	4	-							
1-day Lge	55	55	4	1635	94 *	32.05	-	11	15	-	30	30	0	-		-	-

DONALD, A. A. — Worcestershire

Name: <u>Allan</u> Anthony Donald
Role: Right-hand bat, right-arm fast bowler
Born: 20 October 1966, Bloemfontein, South Africa
Height: 6ft 3in **Weight:** 14st
County debut: 1987 (Warwickshire), 2002 (Worcestershire)
County cap: 1989 (Warwickshire), 2002 (Worcestershire colours)
Benefit: 1999 (Warwickshire)
Test debut: 1991-92
Tests: 72
One-Day Internationals: 147
50 wickets in a season: 5
1st-Class 50s: 2
1st-Class 5 w. in innings: 66
1st-Class 10 w. in match: 9
1st-Class catches: 112
One-Day 5 w. in innings: 10
Strike rate: 28.80 (career 48.21)
Parents: Stuart and Francine

Wife and date of marriage: Tina, 21 September 1991
Children: Hannah and Oliver
Family links with cricket: Father and uncle played club cricket
Education: Grey College; Technical High School, Bloemfontein
Qualifications: Matriculation
Off-season: Playing for South Africa
Overseas tours: South Africa to India (one-day series) 1991-92, to Zimbabwe (one-day series) 1991-92, to Australia and New Zealand (World Cup) 1991-92, to West Indies 1991-92, 2000-01, to Sri Lanka 1993-94, to Australia 1993-94, 1997-98, 2001-02, to England 1994, 1998, to New Zealand 1994-95, 1998-99, to Zimbabwe 1995-96, 1999-2000, to India, Pakistan and Sri Lanka (World Cup) 1995-96, to India 1996-97, 1999-2000, to Pakistan 1997-98, to UK, Ireland and Holland (World Cup) 1999, to Kenya (ICC Knockout Trophy) 2000-01, to Morocco (Morocco Cup) 2002, to Sri Lanka (ICC Champions Trophy) 2002-03
Overseas teams played for: Orange Free State/Free State 1985-86 –
Cricketers particularly admired: Richard Hadlee, Malcolm Marshall, Gladstone Small, Andy Lloyd, Eddie Barlow
Other sports followed: Rugby, golf, tennis
Relaxations: 'Listening to music, having a barbecue, playing golf and having a few beers with my friends'

Extras: Played for South African XI v Australian XI in 1986-87 and v English XI in 1989-90. Toured with South Africa on first-ever visit to India and to West Indies in 1991-92. One of *Wisden*'s Five Cricketers of the Year 1992. Voted Man of the Series against England 1995-96, finishing with 19 wickets at an average of 26.15. Was awarded his country's highest sporting honour when he was presented with a Gold Medal by Nelson Mandela at an awards ceremony in Pretoria on 15 August 1997. Was South Africa's Man of the Series v England 1998, finishing with 33 wickets at an average of 19.78. Became the first South African to take 200 Test wickets, v Sri Lanka 1998, then became the first South African to take 300 Test wickets, in the first Test v New Zealand at Bloemfontein (his home city) in November 2000. Played for Warwickshire 1987-2000 (except 1994, 1996, 1998), retiring from county cricket at the end of the 2000 season. Retired from Test cricket in February 2002. Played for Knowle & Dorridge in the Birmingham & District Premier League 2002. Was Worcestershire's overseas player during June 2002, replacing Andy Bichel, absent on international duty. Took 5-77 in his single first-class match for Worcestershire 2002, v Durham at Riverside, including a wicket (Jon Lewis) with his first Championship delivery for the county

Best batting: 55* South Africans v Tasmania, Devonport 1997-98

Best bowling: 8-37 Orange Free State v Transvaal, Johannesburg 1986-87

Stop press: Took his 250th ODI wicket v West Indies at Colombo in the ICC Champions Trophy 2002-03. Selected for South Africa squad for 2002-03 World Cup. Retired from international cricket after the 2002-03 World Cup

2002 Season

	M	Inns	NO	Runs	HS	Avge	100s	50s	Ct	St	O	M	Runs	Wkts	Avge	Best	5wI	10wM
Test																		
All First	1	1	1	5	5 *	-	-	-	-	-	24	3	77	5	15.40	5-77	1	-
1-day Int																		
C & G	1	0	0	0	0	-	-	-	-	-	10	3	24	1	24.00	1-24	-	
B & H	1	1	0	10	10	10.00	-	-	-	-	10	0	54	0	-	-	-	
1-day Lge	3	1	0	0	0	0.00	-	-	-	-	15.4	3	54	2	27.00	2-27	-	

Career Performances

	M	Inns	NO	Runs	HS	Avge	100s	50s	Ct	St	Balls	Runs	Wkts	Avge	Best	5wI	10wM
Test	72	94	34	645	37	10.75	-	-	18	-	15519	7344	330	22.25	8-71	20	3
All First	308	359	137	2681	55 *	12.07	-	2	112	-	57229	26937	1187	22.69	8-37	66	9
1-day Int	147	36	16	88	13	4.40	-	-	24	-	7728	5288	248	21.32	6-23	2	
C & G	36	11	6	39	14 *	7.80	-	-	4	-	2210	1263	88	14.35	5-12	5	
B & H	31	17	8	99	23 *	11.00	-	-	4	-	1655	1140	39	29.23	5-25	1	
1-day Lge	85	30	15	158	18 *	10.53	-	-	18	-	3665	2408	121	19.90	6-15	2	

DOWMAN, M. P.   Derbyshire

Name: <u>Mathew</u> Peter Dowman
Role: Left-hand bat, right-arm
medium bowler
Born: 10 May 1974, Grantham
Height: 5ft 10in **Weight:** 12st
Nickname: Doomer
County debut: 1993 (one-day,
Nottinghamshire), 1994 (first-class,
Nottinghamshire), 2000 (Derbyshire)
County cap: 1998 (Nottinghamshire),
2000 (Derbyshire)
1000 runs in a season: 1
1st-Class 50s: 18
1st-Class 100s: 9
1st-Class catches: 56
Place in batting averages: 220th av. 21.28
(2001 171st av. 22.68)
Place in bowling averages: 13th av. 22.30
Strike rate: 43.20 (career 75.94)
Parents: Clive and Jackie
Wife and date of marriage: Joanne, 6 October 2001
Family links with cricket: 'Dad and three brothers all used to play for Grantham
Town; two brothers represented Lincolnshire Schools and Lincolnshire U19'
Education: Earlsfield County Primary; St Hugh's Comprehensive; Grantham College
Qualifications: 3 GCSEs, national sports award, senior coach
Overseas tours: Lincolnshire U16 to Zimbabwe 1988-89; England U19 to India
1992-93; Nottinghamshire to Cape Town 1992-93, to Johannesburg 1996-97, 1997-98,
1998-99; Derbyshire to Portugal 2000
Overseas teams played for: South Barwon, Geelong, Melbourne 1995-96; East
Shirley, Christchurch, New Zealand 1997-98 ('didn't complete season')
Career highlights to date: 'Probably 145* v Pakistan on my birthday [2001], plus
any first-class hundred scored'
Cricket moments to forget: 'Dropping a catch and breaking my nose for Notts v
Derbys'
Cricketers particularly admired: Robin Smith, Mike Gatting, Malcolm Marshall,
Jimmy Adams
Young players to look out for: Nathan Dumelow
Other sports played: Golf (9 handicap), squash
Other sports followed: Ice hockey (Nottingham Panthers, New York Rangers), 'most
football', golf
Relaxations: 'TV, generally relaxing at home; golf, films, music'

Extras: Played in winning Midlands team at ESCA Festival 1989. Set record for most runs in a season for Lincolnshire Schools and record for most runs in Lincolnshire Schools career. Played for England U19 in home series against West Indies in 1993, scoring 267 in second 'Test'. Winner of the 1997 Uncapped Whyte and Mackay Batting Award. Released by Nottinghamshire at end of 1999 season and joined Derbyshire for 2000. Scored 140 v Durham at Derby 2000, in the process sharing with Dominic Cork in a new record seventh-wicket partnership for Derbyshire (258). B&H Gold Award for his 76* against his old county, Nottinghamshire, at Derby 2001. Captained Derbyshire to victory in four-day match v West Indies A at Derby 2002, in the process taking 4-28 and scoring an 87-ball 71. Scored 45 v Gloucestershire at Bristol in the NUL 2002, in the process sharing with Steve Selwood (93) in a new record sixth-wicket partnership for Derbyshire in the one-day league (123). Released by Derbyshire at the end of the 2002 season

Opinions on cricket: 'One way or another the third umpire issue needs to be resolved. There is too much talk about their role rather than the cricket being played. There is a role for them in the game, but the people at the top don't seem to know what that is or how much power to give them.'

Best batting: 149 Nottinghamshire v Leicestershire, Leicester 1997
Best bowling: 4-28 Derbyshire v West Indies A, Derby 2002

2002 Season

	M	Inns	NO	Runs	HS	Avge	100s	50s	Ct	St	O	M	Runs	Wkts	Avge	Best	5wI	10wM
Test																		
All First	8	14	0	298	71	21.28	-	1	6	-	72	24	223	10	22.30	4-28	-	-
1-day Int																		
C & G	1	1	0	10	10	10.00	-	-	-	-								
B & H																		
1-day Lge	14	13	1	195	45	16.25	-	-	1	-	79	5	312	17	18.35	3-38	-	

Career Performances

	M	Inns	NO	Runs	HS	Avge	100s	50s	Ct	St	Balls	Runs	Wkts	Avge	Best	5wI	10wM
Test																	
All First	101	178	11	4648	149	27.83	9	18	56	-	2658	1394	35	39.82	4-28	-	-
1-day Int																	
C & G	10	9	0	180	47	20.00	-	-	3	-	222	134	4	33.50	2-49	-	
B & H	24	19	4	600	92	40.00	-	4	5	-	398	299	14	21.35	3-21	-	
1-day Lge	104	103	5	1788	74 *	18.24	-	6	22	-	1487	1283	38	33.76	3-38	-	

DRIVER, R. C. Lancashire

Name: <u>Ryan</u> Craig Driver
Role: Left-hand bat, right-arm
medium bowler
Born: 30 April 1979, Truro
Height: 6ft 4in **Weight:** 15st
Nickname: Screw
County debut: 1998 (Worcestershire),
2001 (Lancashire)
1st-Class 50s: 2
1st-Class 5 w. in innings: 1
1st-Class catches: 13
Place in batting averages: 234th av. 18.83
(2001 249th av. 11.62)
Place in bowling averages: 45th av. 27.58
Strike rate: 52.50 (career 51.57)
Parents: Les and Jan
Marital status: Engaged
Family links with cricket: Grandfather and
uncle played club cricket. Father was captain of Truro CC for six years and still plays
in Cornwall League. Mother and fiancée keen supporters
Education: St Gluvias CP and Trewirgie School, Redruth; Redruth Technology
College; Durham University
Qualifications: 9 GCSEs, 3 A-levels, 2.2 degree in Sport in Community, Level 3
coaching award
Overseas tours: ESCA West U14 to West Indies 1993-94; Cornwall Colts to South
Africa 1996, 1997; Lancashire to South Africa 2001
Career highlights to date: 'Man of the Match award, Worcestershire v
Gloucestershire in NatWest Trophy 2000'
Cricket moments to forget: 'Ducking a yorker from Ian Hunter in 2nd XI game at
Old Trafford and having stumps spread everywhere'
Cricketers particularly admired: Steve Waugh
Young players to look out for: Kadeer Ali, Adam Barber
Other sports played: Football ('apparently')
Other sports followed: Football (Derby County)
Relaxations: Music, 'getting beaten at squash by Tim Roberts'
Extras: CSCA Batting Award 1993-96. Played for Cornwall CCC from 1995. West
Region *Daily Telegraph* Batsman of the Year 1995. Played for ESCA U19 and MCC
Schools in 1997. England Schoolboy Cricketer of the Year 1997. 2nd XI Player of the
Month August/September 1998. Durham University 1st XI 1998-2000; played in
Durham University's BUSA Championship winning side 1999. Won NatWest Man of
the Match award for his 61* v Gloucestershire 2000 (the game was later declared void

and replayed but award stood). British Universities 1999-2000. Durham University Sportsman of the Year 2000. Released by Worcestershire at the end of the 2000 season and joined Lancashire for 2001. Recorded maiden first-class five-wicket return (5-70) v West Indies A at Liverpool 2002. Released by Lancs at the end of the 2002 season

Best batting: 64 Worcestershire v Sussex, Worcester 2000
Best bowling: 5-70 Lancashire v West Indies A, Liverpool 2002

2002 Season

	M	Inns	NO	Runs	HS	Avge	100s	50s	Ct	St	O	M	Runs	Wkts	Avge	Best	5wI	10wM
Test																		
All First	5	8	2	113	56	18.83	-	1	5	-	105	28	331	12	27.58	5-70	1	-
1-day Int																		
C & G																		
B & H																		
1-day Lge	5	4	0	30	25	7.50	-	-	-	-	35	2	162	0	-		-	-

Career Performances

	M	Inns	NO	Runs	HS	Avge	100s	50s	Ct	St	Balls	Runs	Wkts	Avge	Best	5wI	10wM
Test																	
All First	25	43	6	686	64	18.54	-	2	13	-	722	408	14	29.14	5-70	1	-
1-day Int																	
C & G	3	3	1	61	61 *	30.50	-	1	-	-							
B & H																	
1-day Lge	16	15	0	170	52	11.33	-	1	1	-	264	227	1	227.00	1-17	-	

26. Which overseas player was second in the 1994 first-class batting averages with 2066 runs at an average of 89.82?

DUMELOW, N. R. C.   Derbyshire

Name: <u>Nathan</u> Robert Charles Dumelow
Role: Right-hand bat, right-arm
off-spin bowler
Born: 30 April 1981, Derby
Height: 5ft 10in **Weight:** 12st 2lbs
Nickname: Pig
County debut: 2001
1st-Class 50s: 3
1st-Class catches: 3
Place in batting averages: (2001 182nd
av. 21.71)
Place in bowling averages: (2001 138th
av. 51.64)
Strike rate: (career 92.50)
Parents: Kate and Robert
Marital status: Single
Family links with cricket: 'Dad plays for
Derbyshire Over 50s'
Education: Foremark Hall; Denstone College
Qualifications: 7 GCSEs
Career outside cricket: Farmer
Off-season: 'Playing in Tasmania again'
Overseas tours: Derbyshire U16 to Barbados; Derbyshire U17 to South Africa
Overseas teams played for: Schoeman Park CC, Bloemfontein 2000-01
Career highlights to date: 'Taking four wickets against Pakistan [2001]'
Cricket moments to forget: 'Day/night game v Worcestershire' (*Took 2-59 from five
overs as Worcs posted 288-6 and beat Derbys by 138 runs at Derby in the NUL 2001*)
Cricketers particularly admired: Viv Richards
Young players to look out for: Lian Wharton, Chris Bassano, Tom Lungley
Other sports played: Golf, snooker
Other sports followed: Football (Derby County FC)
Injuries: Knee injury early in the season
Relaxations: Fishing, shooting
Extras: Won all Derbyshire age-group awards. Played for Derbyshire Board XI in the
NatWest 1999 and 2000. Took 4-81 on first-class debut v Pakistanis at Derby 2001,
including the wickets of Yousuf Youhana, Inzamam-ul-Haq and Abdul Razzaq. Scored
50* on Championship debut v Hampshire at Derby 2001. Derbyshire's Most Improved
Player 2001. Won eight awards while playing club cricket in Tasmania 2001-02,
including those for best batting and bowling averages and for fair play
Opinions on cricket: 'More young players should play.'
Best batting: 61 Derbyshire v Middlesex, Southgate 2001
Best bowling: 4-81 Derbyshire v Pakistanis, Derby 2001

2002 Season

	M	Inns	NO	Runs	HS	Avge	100s	50s	Ct	St	O	M	Runs	Wkts	Avge	Best	5wI	10wM
Test																		
All First	2	3	0	80	56	26.66	-	1	1	-	30	5	145	0	-	-	-	-
1-day Int																		
C & G																		
B & H	1	1	0	11	11	11.00	-	-	-	-	9	1	28	0	-	-	-	-
1-day Lge	5	5	0	125	52	25.00	-	1	-	-	28.4	0	129	5	25.80	3-24	-	

Career Performances

	M	Inns	NO	Runs	HS	Avge	100s	50s	Ct	St	Balls	Runs	Wkts	Avge	Best	5wI	10wM
Test																	
All First	11	18	1	384	61	22.58	-	3	3	-	1295	868	14	62.00	4-81	-	-
1-day Int																	
C & G	3	3	0	56	32	18.66	-	-	-	-	132	90	2	45.00	2-21	-	
B & H	2	2	0	29	18	14.50	-	-	-	-	114	74	1	74.00	1-46	-	
1-day Lge	15	14	2	270	52	22.50	-	1	1	-	562	474	16	29.62	3-24	-	

DURSTON, W. J. Somerset

Name: Wesley (Wes) John Durston
Role: Right-hand bat, right-arm off-spin bowler; all-rounder
Born: 6 October 1980, Taunton
Height: 5ft 10in **Weight:** 12st
Nickname: Fred, Ace
County debut: 2002
1st-Class 50s: 1
1st-Class catches: 1
Strike rate: 84.00 (career 84.00)
Parents: Gillian and Steven
Marital status: Engaged to Christina Henshaw
Family links with cricket: 'Dad and my two brothers, Dan and Greg, all play. On occasions all four played in same local team (Compton Dundon)'
Education: Edgarley Hall; Millfield School; University College Worcester
Qualifications: 10 GCSEs, 2 A-levels, BSc Sports Studies ('results pending'), ECB Level 1 cricket coaching
Career outside cricket: Coaching

Off-season: 'Finding a house to live with Christina, and training and working hard at my game'
Overseas tours: West of England to West Indies 1996
Career highlights to date: 'Three centuries (106, 162*, 126) in three days at Tonbridge Festival for Millfield School 1999. First-class debut v West Indies A 2002, scoring 26 and 55, and the match tied chasing 453 to win'
Cricket moments to forget: 'Scoring 0 v Kent, being lbw and breaking left big toe in NUL 2002'
Cricket superstitions: 'Right foot on and off field first. Placing my right inner glove in my pocket while I bat'
Cricketers particularly admired: Brian Lara, Graham Gooch, Muttiah Muralitharan
Young players to look out for: James Hildreth, Richard Timms, Judd Doughty, Tom Goodey
Other sports played: Hockey (Shrewsbury HC and Shropshire; also West of England U21), golf ('occasionally')
Other sports followed: Football 'passionately' (Man Utd), 'any sport that's on TV'
Injuries: Out for end of 2002 season after breaking left big toe in August
Relaxations: 'Spending time with fiancée; computers (Internet); watching sport'
Extras: Captained winning Lord's Taverners team v Shrewsbury School at Trent Bridge 1996. Wetherell Schools All-rounder Award 1999; scored 956 runs and took 35 wickets. Played for Somerset Board XI in the NatWest 2000 and in the first round of the C&G 2003, which was played in August 2002. Captained Somerset 2nd XI on occasion in 2002. Scored 44-ball 55 on first-class debut at Taunton 2002 as Somerset, chasing 454 to win, tied with West Indies A
Opinions on cricket: 'As there is so much one-day cricket in the county game, more attention should be given to this in the 2nd XI. The AON Trophy does not provide enough practice of this format for cricketers in the 2nd XI. And this should be where new structures are trialled, such as the new 20 over format.'
Best batting: 55 Somerset v West Indies A, Taunton 2002
Best bowling: 1-25 Somerset v West Indies A, Taunton 2002

2002 Season

	M	Inns	NO	Runs	HS	Avge	100s	50s	Ct	St	O	M	Runs	Wkts	Avge	Best	5wI	10wM
Test																		
All First	1	2	0	81	55	40.50	-	1	1	-	14	0	65	1	65.00	1-25	-	-
1-day Int																		
C & G	1	1	0	50	50	50.00	-	1	-	-	10	1	43	1	43.00	1-43	-	
B & H																		
1-day Lge	2	2	0	0	0	0.00	-	-	-	-	2	0	19	0	-		-	-

Career Performances

	M	Inns	NO	Runs	HS	Avge	100s	50s	Ct	St		Balls	Runs	Wkts	Avge	Best	5wl	10wM
Test																		
All First	1	2	0	81	55	40.50	-	1	1	-		84	65	1	65.00	1-25	-	-
1-day Int																		
C & G	2	2	0	75	50	37.50	-	1	-	-		84	75	2	37.50	1-32	-	
B & H																		
1-day Lge	2	2	0	0	0	0.00	-	-	-	-		12	19	0	-		-	-

DUTCH, K. P.   Somerset

Name: <u>Keith</u> Philip Dutch
Role: Right-hand bat, off-spin bowler
Born: 21 March 1973, Harrow, Middlesex
Height: 5ft 9in **Weight:** 11st 4lbs
Nickname: Dutchy, Oik
County debut: 1993 (Middlesex),
2001 (Somerset)
County cap: 2001 (Somerset)
1st-Class 50s: 8
1st-Class 100s: 1
1st-Class 5 w. in innings: 1
1st-Class catches: 61
One-Day 5 w. in innings: 2
Place in batting averages: 240th av. 18.00
(2001 130th av. 29.44)
Place in bowling averages: 153rd av. 56.80
(2001 98th av. 36.22)
Strike rate: 107.40 (career 71.27)
Parents: Alan and Ann
Wife and date of marriage: Emma, 11 November 2000
Children: Lauren Beth Amy, 15 January 1999
Family links with cricket: Father coached
Education: Nower Hill High School, Pinner; Weald College, Harrow
Qualifications: 5 GCSEs, 1 AS-level, staff tutor coach
Off-season: Coaching
Overseas tours: MCC to Central and East Africa 1997, to Canada 2000-01
Overseas teams played for: Worcester United, South Africa 1992-93; Geelong City, Australia, 1994; Rygersdal CC, Cape Town 1997-98
Career highlights to date: 'Man of the Match award in C&G semi-final and winning C&G final 2001'
Cricketers particularly admired: Mark Ramprakash, John Emburey

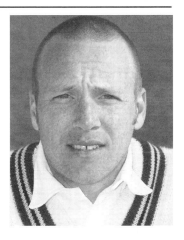

Young players to look out for: Owais Shah, David Nash, Stephen Peters, Ed Joyce
Other sports followed: Football (Arsenal FC)
Relaxations: Music, TV and shopping for clothes
Extras: Middlesex 2nd XI Player of the Year 1995. In 1996 scored over 1,000 2nd XI Championship runs and took 63 wickets, setting in the process a record for the highest-ever batting total (261 v Somerset) and best bowling figures (15 for 157 v Leicestershire) by a Middlesex player in the history of the 2nd XI Championship. 2nd XI Championship Player of the Year in 1993, 1996 and 1999. Took five catches in Cambridge University's first innings at Fenner's 2000. Scored 91 and took 6-62 (both then career bests) in a single day v Essex at Chelmsford 2000. Released by Middlesex at the end of the 2000 season and joined Somerset for 2001. Scored 84 v Northamptonshire at Northampton 2001, in the process equalling, partnered by Ian Blackwell, the Somerset record seventh-wicket stand in matches against Northamptonshire. C&G Man of the Match award for his 54-ball 61 in the semi-final v Warwickshire at Taunton 2001
Opinions on cricket: 'Going in right direction. Could benefit from a few less counties. Two divisions seems to be strengthening the game.'
Best batting: 118 Somerset v Essex, Taunton 2001
Best bowling: 6-62 Middlesex v Essex, Chelmsford 2000

2002 Season

	M	Inns	NO	Runs	HS	Avge	100s	50s	Ct	St	O	M	Runs	Wkts	Avge	Best	5wI	10wM
Test																		
All First	16	27	3	432	74	18.00	-	2	20	-	268.3	59	852	15	56.80	3-104	-	-
1-day Int																		
C & G	5	4	3	40	13 *	40.00	-	-	4	-	28	1	125	3	41.66	3-26	-	
B & H	4	3	0	77	45	25.66	-	-	-	-	26	0	147	5	29.40	2-43	-	
1-day Lge	15	14	3	210	64	19.09	-	1	10	-	99.4	4	457	12	38.08	2-0	-	

Career Performances

	M	Inns	NO	Runs	HS	Avge	100s	50s	Ct	St	Balls	Runs	Wkts	Avge	Best	5wI	10wM
Test																	
All First	59	84	9	1459	118	19.45	1	8	61	-	6272	3311	88	37.62	6-62	1	
1-day Int																	
C & G	19	15	8	268	61 *	38.28	-	1	15	-	816	568	16	35.50	3-26	-	
B & H	16	15	2	221	55	17.00	-	1	2	-	564	433	17	25.47	4-42	-	
1-day Lge	92	80	20	1064	64	17.73	-	3	33	-	3197	2490	96	25.93	6-40	2	

EALHAM, M. A.   Kent

Name: <u>Mark</u> Alan Ealham
Role: Right-hand bat, right-arm medium bowler; all-rounder
Born: 27 August 1969, Ashford, Kent
Height: 5ft 10in **Weight:** 14st
Nickname: Ealy, Border, Skater
County debut: 1989
County cap: 1992
Test debut: 1996
Tests: 8
One-Day Internationals: 64
1000 runs in a season: 1
1st-Class 50s: 45
1st-Class 100s: 6
1st-Class 5 w. in innings: 16
1st-Class 10 w. in match: 1
1st-Class catches: 78
One-Day 100s: 1
One-Day 5 w. in innings: 4

Place in batting averages: 109th av. 34.94 (2001 168th av. 23.00)
Place in bowling averages: 98th av. 34.07 (2001 25th av. 22.96)
Strike rate: 75.21 (career 60.54)
Parents: Alan and Sue
Wife and date of marriage: Kirsty, 24 February 1996
Children: George, 8 March 2002
Family links with cricket: Father played for Kent
Education: Chartham; Stour Valley Secondary School
Qualifications: 9 CSEs
Career outside cricket: Plumber
Overseas tours: England A to Australia 1996-97, to Kenya and Sri Lanka 1997-98; England VI to Hong Kong 1997, 2001; England to Sharjah (Champions Trophy) 1997-98, to Bangladesh (Wills International Cup) 1998, to Australia 1998-99 (CUB Series), to Sharjah (Coca-Cola Cup) 1998-99, to South Africa and Zimbabwe 1999-2000 (one-day series), to Kenya (ICC Knockout Trophy) 2000-01, to Pakistan and Sri Lanka 2000-01 (one-day series)
Overseas teams played for: South Perth, Australia 1992-93; University, Perth 1993-94
Cricketers particularly admired: Ian Botham, Viv Richards, Robin Smith, Steve Waugh, Paul Blackmore and Albert 'for his F and G'
Other sports followed: Football (Manchester United), 'and most other sports'
Injuries: Out for three weeks with a broken finger; for three weeks with a foot injury

Relaxations: Playing golf and snooker, watching films
Extras: Set record for fastest Sunday League century (44 balls), v Derbyshire at Maidstone 1995. Represented England in the 1999 World Cup. Returned a new England best One-Day International bowling analysis with his 5-15 v Zimbabwe at Kimberley in January 2000; all five were lbw. Vice-captain of Kent 2001. Scored 83* v Sussex at Tunbridge Wells 2002, in the process sharing with Ben Trott (26) in a ground record tenth-wicket partnership for Kent (77). Scored 74* and took 4-45 v Indians in a 50-over match at Canterbury 2002. Granted a benefit for 2003
Opinions on cricket: 'Two-divisional cricket is a success, but only two teams from each division to go up and down.'
Best batting: 153* Kent v Northamptonshire, Canterbury 2001
Best bowling: 8-36 Kent v Warwickshire, Edgbaston 1996

2002 Season

	M	Inns	NO	Runs	HS	Avge	100s	50s	Ct	St	O	M	Runs	Wkts	Avge	Best	5wI	10wM
Test																		
All First	14	24	7	594	83 *	34.94	-	3	14	-	351	107	954	28	34.07	3-22	-	-
1-day Int																		
C & G	4	3	0	95	47	31.66	-	-	1	-	33	1	132	3	44.00	1-33	-	
B & H																		
1-day Lge	13	12	1	291	75	26.45	-	2	4	-	95.1	5	397	20	19.85	3-18	-	

Career Performances

	M	Inns	NO	Runs	HS	Avge	100s	50s	Ct	St	Balls	Runs	Wkts	Avge	Best	5wI	10wM
Test	8	13	3	210	53 *	21.00	-	2	4	-	1060	488	17	28.70	4-21	-	-
All First	175	279	47	7230	153 *	31.16	6	45	78	-	23430	11120	387	28.73	8-36	16	1
1-day Int	64	45	4	716	45	17.46	-	-	9	-	3222	2193	67	32.73	5-15	2	
C & G	28	25	7	539	58 *	29.94	-	2	7	-	1505	790	34	23.23	4-10	-	
B & H	46	42	9	908	75	27.51	-	7	17	-	2290	1481	69	21.46	4-17	-	
1-day Lge	164	138	36	2625	112	25.73	1	11	43	-	6570	4845	167	29.01	6-53	2	

27. For which county did Jacques Kallis play in 1997?

EDWARDS, N.   Somerset

Name: Neil Edwards
Role: Left-hand bat, right-arm
leg-spin bowler
Born: 14 October 1983, Truro, Cornwall
Height: 6ft 3in **Weight:** 14st 3lbs
Nickname: Nige, Toastman, Shanesy
County debut: 2002
1st-Class catches: 1
Parents: Lynn and John
Marital status: Single
Family links with cricket: 'Uncle Jeff
played Minor Counties for Cornwall. Cousin
Tim played for Worcestershire'
Education: St Hilary School; Cape Cornwall
School; Richard Huish College
Qualifications: 11 GCSEs, 3 A-levels,
Level 1 coach
Career outside cricket: Student
Off-season: 'England U19 tour to Australia; training'
Overseas tours: Cornwall U13 to South Africa 1997; West of England to West Indies
1999; Somerset Academy to Australia 2002; England U19 to Australia 2002-03
Career highlights to date: 'First-class debut v West Indies A at Taunton. Being
selected for England U19 tour of Australia'
Cricket moments to forget: 'Golden duck on debut for Cornwall at only 16 years old'
Cricket superstitions: 'Never change batting gloves'
Cricketers particularly admired: Michael Blackmore, Marcus Trescothick,
Matt Hayden
Young players to look out for: Tom Edwards, Ryan Edwards, Steve Richards
Other sports played: Football ('local club')
Other sports followed: Football (Stoke City FC)
Relaxations: 'Spending time back in Cornwall with family, girlfriend and friends'
Extras: Scored 213 for Cornwall U19 v Dorset U19 at 16 years old
Opinions on cricket: 'More one-day cricket. Wider use of floodlit cricket.'
Best batting: 31 Somerset v West Indies A, Taunton 2002
Stop press: Scored a second innings 97 in England U19's victory over Australia U19
in the first 'Test' at Adelaide 2002-03

2002 Season

	M	Inns	NO	Runs	HS	Avge	100s	50s	Ct	St	O	M	Runs	Wkts	Avge	Best	5wI	10wM
Test																		
All First	1	2	0	58	31	29.00	-	-	1	-								
1-day Int																		
C & G																		
B & H																		
1-day Lge																		

Career Performances

	M	Inns	NO	Runs	HS	Avge	100s	50s	Ct	St	Balls	Runs	Wkts	Avge	Best	5wI	10wM
Test																		
All First	1	2	0	58	31	29.00	-	-	1	-							
1-day Int																		
C & G																		
B & H																		
1-day Lge																		

ELLIOTT, M. T. G.   Yorkshire

Name: <u>Matthew</u> Thomas Gray Elliott
Role: Left-hand bat, left-arm
orthodox bowler
Born: 28 September 1971, Chelsea,
Victoria, Australia
Height: 6ft 3in **Weight:** 13st 8lbs
Nickname: Hoarse
County debut: 2000 (Glamorgan),
2002 (Yorkshire)
County cap: 2000 (Glamorgan)
Test debut: 1996-97
Tests: 20
One-Day Internationals: 1
1000 runs in a season: 1
1st-Class 50s: 55
1st-Class 100s: 33
1st-Class 200s: 2
1st-Class catches: 161
One-Day 100s: 4
Place in batting averages: 22nd av. 54.11
Strike rate: 96.00 (career 110.10)
Parents: John and Glenda

218

Wife and date of marriage: Megan, 11 December 1994
Children: Zachary, 22 November 1997; Samuel, 18 February 2000
Education: Lancaster Primary School/St Augustines; Kyabram Secondary College
Qualifications: VCE
Off-season: 'Playing for Victoria'
Overseas tours: Young Australia (Australia A) to England and Netherlands 1995;
Australia to South Africa 1996-97, to England 1997, to West Indies 1998-99
Career highlights to date: 'Taking the 2002 C&G Trophy through Scarborough on an
open-top bus with a police escort!'
Cricket moments to forget: 'Being dismissed by Dean Cosker at Sophia Gardens in
'97!'
Cricket superstitions: 'Always put left shoe on first'
Cricketers particularly admired: Shane Warne, Allan Border, Steve Waugh
Young players to look out for: Cameron White (Victoria), James Anderson
Other sports played: Australian Rules football
Other sports followed: Australian Rules football (Collingwood FC)
Relaxations: 'Fishing; reading biographies; drinking Corona'
Extras: Scored 556 runs (av. 55.60) in the 1997 Ashes series, including 199 in the
fourth Test at Headingley. One of *Wisden*'s Five Cricketers of the Year 1998. Sheffield
Shield Player of the Year 1995-96 and 1998-99. Was Glamorgan's overseas player in
2000. Scored century (117) in his first Championship innings for Glamorgan, v
Warwickshire at Edgbaston 2000. Scored 177 in helping to set county record first-
wicket partnership of 374 with Stephen James v Sussex at Colwyn Bay 2000; James
went on to score 309*. Victoria's one-day captain 2001-02, becoming overall skipper
for the remainder of the campaign on the retirement of Paul Reiffel during the season;
also Victoria's One-Day Player of the Season 2001-02 (431 runs; av. 47.88). Was
Yorkshire's overseas player for the latter part of 2002, replacing Darren Lehmann,
absent first through injury and then international duty. C&G Man of the Match award
for his 128* in the final v Somerset at Lord's 2002. Averaged 54.11 from his five
Championship matches and 88.66 (including two centuries) from his five NUL
appearances during his 2002 stay. Has returned as an overseas player for 2003
Opinions on cricket: 'Would like to see umpires be more entertaining with their
signals (*à la* Leslie Nielsen in *Naked Gun*).'
Best batting: 203 Victoria v Tasmania, Melbourne 1995-96
Best bowling: 1-3 Victoria v Tasmania, Melbourne 1998-99

2002 Season

	M	Inns	NO	Runs	HS	Avge	100s	50s	Ct	St	O	M	Runs	Wkts	Avge	Best	5wI	10wM
Test																		
All First	5	10	1	487	127	54.11	1	4	7	-	16	1	77	1	77.00	1-64	-	-
1-day Int																		
C & G	1	1	1	128	128 *	-		1	-	-	-	-						
B & H																		
1-day Lge	5	5	2	266	115 *	88.66	2		-	-	-	-						

Career Performances

	M	Inns	NO	Runs	HS	Avge	100s	50s	Ct	St	Balls	Runs	Wkts	Avge	Best	5wI	10wM
Test	20	34	1	1171	199	35.48	3	4	13	-	12	4	0	-	-	-	-
All First	136	252	20	11503	203	49.58	35	55	161	-	1101	640	10	64.00	1-3	-	-
1-day Int	1	1	0	1	1	1.00	-	-	-	-							
C & G	4	4	1	309	156	103.00	2	-	-	-							
B & H	6	6	0	60	29	10.00	-	-	5	-							
1-day Lge	16	16	4	695	115 *	57.91	2	4	5	-	18	10	0	-	-	-	

ELSTUB, C. J. Yorkshire

Name: <u>Christopher</u> John Elstub
Role: Right-hand bat, right-arm
medium-fast bowler
Born: 3 February 1981, Dewsbury
Height: 5ft 11in **Weight:** 12st
Nickname: Shrub, Elly
County debut: 2000
1st-Class catches: 2
Strike rate: 246.00 (career 69.90)
Parents: Richard and Susan
Marital status: Single
Family links with cricket: Father played
club cricket and for Yorkshire 2nd XI
Education: Gomersal Middle School;
Whitcliffe Mount School; Leeds Metropolitan
University
Qualifications: 9 GCSEs, 1 A-level, GNVQ
(Advanced) Leisure and Tourism, NCA
coaching award Levels 1 and 2

Career outside cricket: Teacher
Cricketers particularly admired: Darren Gough, Darren Lehmann, Courtney Walsh
Young players to look out for: Michael Lumb, Joe Sayers
Other sports played: Hockey (Bradford)
Other sports followed: Football (Emley FC and Manchester United)
Relaxations: Sleeping, listening to music, socialising with friends
Extras: Played for Bradford/Leeds University CCE 2001 and 2002 (captain 2002).
Represented British Universities 2001 and v West Indies A (50-over match) at The
Parks 2002. Released by Yorkshire at the end of the 2002 season
Best batting: 18* Yorkshire v Sussex, Arundel 2002
Best bowling: 3-37 Yorkshire v West Indians, Headingley 2000

2002 Season

	M	Inns	NO	Runs	HS	Avge	100s	50s	Ct	St	O	M	Runs	Wkts	Avge	Best	5wI	10wM
Test																		
All First	2	3	3	22	18 *	-	-	-	1	-	41	7	181	1	181.00	1-16	-	-
1-day Int																		
C & G																		
B & H																		
1-day Lge	1	1	1	4	4 *	-	-	-	-	-	7	2	31	1	31.00	1-31	-	

Career Performances

	M	Inns	NO	Runs	HS	Avge	100s	50s	Ct	St	Balls	Runs	Wkts	Avge	Best	5wI	10wM
Test																	
All First	7	9	7	34	18 *	17.00	-	-	2	-	769	421	11	38.27	3-37	-	-
1-day Int																	
C & G																	
B & H																	
1-day Lge	9	3	3	4	4 *	-	-	-	-	-	362	259	11	23.54	4-25	-	

FAIRBROTHER, N. H. Lancashire

Name: <u>Neil</u> Harvey Fairbrother
Role: Left-hand bat, left-arm medium bowler
Born: 9 September 1963, Warrington
Height: 5ft 8in **Weight:** 11st 4lbs
Nickname: Harvey
County debut: 1982
County cap: 1985
Benefit: 1995
Test debut: 1987
Tests: 10
One-Day Internationals: 75
1000 runs in a season: 10
1st-Class 50s: 104
1st-Class 100s: 43
1st-Class 200s: 3
1st-Class 300s: 1
1st-Class catches: 290
One-Day 100s: 7
Place in batting averages: 206th av. 22.55 (2001 10th av. 62.60)
Strike rate: (career 113.57)
Parents: Les and Barbara
Wife and date of marriage: Audrey, 23 September 1988
Children: Rachael Elizabeth, 4 April 1991; Sam, 3 April 1994

Family links with cricket: Father and two uncles played local league cricket
Education: St Margaret's Church of England School, Oxford; Lymm Grammar School
Qualifications: 5 O-levels
Overseas tours: England A to Pakistan 1990-91; England to Sharjah 1986-87, to India and Pakistan (World Cup) 1987-88, to Australia and New Zealand 1987-88, to New Zealand 1991-92, to India 1992-93, to Australia 1994-95, to South Africa 1995-96, to India and Pakistan (World Cup) 1995-96, to Bangladesh (Wills International Cup) 1998-99, to Australia 1998-99 (CUB Series), to Sharjah (Coca-Cola Cup) 1998-99
Cricketers particularly admired: Clive Lloyd, Allan Border, David Gower
Other sports followed: Football, rugby union, rugby league
Relaxations: Music and playing sport
Extras: 'I was named after the Australian cricketer Neil Harvey, who was my mum's favourite cricketer.' Played for England YC v Australia 1983. His 366 v Surrey in 1990 was the third (now fourth) highest score ever made in the County Championship, the second highest first-class score by a Lancashire batsman and the highest individual score recorded at The Oval; during the innings he shared in a Lancashire record partnership for the third wicket (364) with Michael Atherton. Appointed Lancashire captain for 1992 but resigned in 1993. Has appeared in ten domestic one-day finals, a record he shares with Derek Underwood. Represented England in the 1999 World Cup. Passed 20,000 career first-class runs v Northamptonshire at Old Trafford 2001. Retired at the end of the 2002 season; has become a player's agent, numbering Andrew Flintoff among his clients
Best batting: 366 Lancashire v Surrey, The Oval 1990
Best bowling: 2-91 Lancashire v Nottinghamshire, Old Trafford 1987

2002 Season

	M	Inns	NO	Runs	HS	Avge	100s	50s	Ct	St	O	M	Runs	Wkts	Avge	Best	5wI	10wM
Test																		
All First	12	19	1	406	101	22.55	1	-	10	-	6	0	27	0	-	-	-	-
1-day Int																		
C & G	1	1	0	15	15	15.00	-	-	1	-								
B & H	1	1	0	1	1	1.00	-	-	-	-								
1-day Lge	10	9	0	34	14	3.77	-	-	1	-	2	0	17	0	-	-	-	

Career Performances

	M	Inns	NO	Runs	HS	Avge	100s	50s	Ct	St	Balls	Runs	Wkts	Avge	Best	5wI	10wM
Test	10	15	1	219	83	15.64	-	1	4	-	12	9	0	-	-	-	-
All First	366	580	80	20612	366	41.22	47	104	290	-	795	500	7	71.42	2-91	-	-
1-day Int	75	71	18	2092	113	39.47	1	16	33	-	6	9	0	-	-	-	
C & G	50	47	10	1685	93 *	45.54	-	13	24	-	48	44	1	44.00	1-28	-	
B & H	85	81	23	2850	116 *	49.13	1	23	36	-	54	67	1	67.00	1-17	-	
1-day Lge	259	240	59	6995	116 *	38.64	5	48	75	-	60	65	1	65.00	1-33	-	

FARROW, J. C.   Worcestershire

Name: <u>Jonathan</u> Colin Farrow
Role: Right-hand bat, right-arm fast bowler
Born: 22 February 1984, Stockport
Nickname: Faz, Jonny
County debut: No first-team appearance
Parents: Colin and Susan
Marital status: Single
Family links with cricket: Father plays
club cricket
Education: Etchells Primary School,
Stockport; Kingsway High,
Stockport/Wilmslow High, Cheshire;
University College, Worcester
Qualifications: 9 GCSEs, 3 A-levels
Off-season: 'At university'
Career highlights to date: '7-63 for
Cheshire U19 v Staffordshire U19'
Cricket superstitions: 'None'
Cricketers particularly admired: Glenn McGrath
Other sports played: Football, badminton
Other sports followed: Football (Manchester United)
Extras: Played for Cheshire in the first and second rounds of the C&G 2003, which
were played in August and September 2002

2002 Season (did not make any first-class or one-day appearances for his county)

Career Performances

	M	Inns	NO	Runs	HS	Avge	100s	50s	Ct	St	Balls	Runs	Wkts	Avge	Best	5wI	10wM
Test																	
All First																	
1-day Int																	
C & G	2	0	0	0	0	-	-	-	-	-	90	109	2	54.50	2-81	-	
B & H																	
1-day Lge																	

FELLOWS, G. M. Yorkshire

Name: <u>Gary</u> Matthew Fellows
Role: Right-hand bat, right-arm medium bowler
Born: 30 July 1978, Halifax
Height: 5ft 9in **Weight:** 11st 2lbs
Nickname: Mousey
County debut: 1998
1st-Class 50s: 5
1st-Class 100s: 1
1st-Class catches: 22
Place in batting averages: 160th av. 27.38 (2001 135th av. 28.43)
Place in bowling averages: (2001 81st av. 33.16)
Strike rate: 55.37 (career 75.96)
Parents: Eric and Tina
Marital status: Single
Family links with cricket: 'Dad played; brothers still do'

Education: Whitehill Primary School; North Halifax Grammar School – both Illingworth, Halifax
Qualifications: 10 GCSEs, 1 A-level, Level 1 coaching award
Career outside cricket: Fitness training
Off-season: 'Relax until Christmas; fitness course after'
Overseas teams played for: Bulawayo Athletic Club, Zimbabwe 1996-97
Career highlights to date: 'Winning the Championship and the C&G Trophy'
Cricket moments to forget: 'Relegation!'
Cricket superstitions: 'Left pad on first'
Cricketers particularly admired: Craig White, Mark Waugh
Other sports played: Football (on Bradford City books for one season)
Other sports followed: Football (Halifax Town)
Relaxations: Most sports 'and a laugh with the lads after the game'. Golf
Extras: Awarded Yorkshire 2nd XI cap 1998. C&G Man of the Match award for his 89-ball 80* v Surrey at Headingley 2001. Scored 50 and took 4-19 v Durham at Headingley in the NUL 2002. Scored 109 v Lancashire at Old Trafford 2002, becoming the seventh Yorkshire batsman to record his maiden first-class century in a Roses match. Scored 88 v Warwickshire at Edgbaston 2002, in the process sharing with Richard Blakey (103) in a new record sixth-wicket partnership for Yorkshire in matches v Warwickshire (175)
Best batting: 109 Yorkshire v Lancashire, Old Trafford 2002
Best bowling: 3-23 Yorkshire v Essex, Chelmsford 2001

2002 Season

	M	Inns	NO	Runs	HS	Avge	100s	50s	Ct	St	O	M	Runs	Wkts	Avge	Best	5wI	10wM
Test																		
All First	10	18	0	493	109	27.38	1	1	9	-	73.5	9	315	8	39.37	3-90	-	-
1-day Int																		
C & G	5	2	2	86	68 *	-	-	1	2	-								
B & H	6	6	1	34	13 *	6.80	-	-	2	-	14.4	0	83	6	13.83	3-31	-	
1-day Lge	15	12	4	243	50	30.37	-	1	6	-	33.5	2	220	5	44.00	4-19	-	

Career Performances

	M	Inns	NO	Runs	HS	Avge	100s	50s	Ct	St	Balls	Runs	Wkts	Avge	Best	5wI	10wM
Test																	
All First	42	66	6	1450	109	24.16	1	5	22	-	2279	1180	30	39.33	3-23	-	-
1-day Int																	
C & G	12	8	3	230	80 *	46.00	-	2	3	-	72	55	0	-	-	-	-
B & H	20	18	4	219	38	15.64	-	-	3	-	238	192	9	21.33	3-31	-	
1-day Lge	59	49	7	884	67	21.04	-	4	18	-	566	538	13	41.38	4-19	-	

FERLEY, R. S.   Kent

Name: <u>Robert</u> Steven Ferley
Role: Right-hand bat, left-arm spin bowler
Born: 4 February 1982, Norwich
Height: 5ft 8in **Weight:** 12st 4lbs
Nickname: Mr Shaky Shake, Billy Bob, Bob Turkey
County debut: No first-team appearance
1st-Class catches: 2
Strike rate: 65.25 (career 74.80)
Parents: Pam and Tim (divorced)
Marital status: Single
Education: North Wootton CP; King Edward VII High School; Sutton Valence School (A-levels); Grey College, Durham University
Qualifications: 10 GCSEs, 3 A-levels
Career outside cricket: Student
Off-season: University
Overseas tours: England U19 to India 2000-01; British Universities to South Africa 2002
Career highlights to date: 'Dismissing Charles Clarke for a golden duck. Dismissing Charles Clarke to all parts of the boundary'
Cricketers particularly admired: Steve Waugh, Steve Marsh, Min Patel, Charles Clarke

Young players to look out for: James Tredwell
Other sports played: Rugby, hockey, tennis, football
Other sports followed: Football (Liverpool)
Relaxations: 'Films, interior design, keeping fit'
Extras: Represented England U17 at the ECC Colts Festival in Northern Ireland 1999. Took 4-32 (including 3-2 in nine balls) on his 19th birthday to help England U19 to victory over India U19 in the second 'One-Day International' at Vijayawada 2000-01. Played for Durham University CCE 2001 and 2002. Represented British Universities 2001 and v Sri Lankans at Northampton and v West Indies A (50-over match) at The Parks 2002. Represented England U19 v West Indies U19 in one-day series (3/3) 2001. Played for Kent Board XI in the second round of the C&G 2002, which was played in September 2001, and in the second round of the C&G 2003, which was played in September 2002
Opinions on cricket: 'I love the game. I want to be involved as long as possible.'
Best batting: 37* DUCCE v Lancashire, Durham 2002
Best bowling: 4-83 DUCCE v Nottinghamshire, Trent Bridge 2002

2002 Season (did not make any first-class or one-day appearances for his county)

Career Performances

	M	Inns	NO	Runs	HS	Avge	100s	50s	Ct	St	Balls	Runs	Wkts	Avge	Best	5wI	10wM
Test																	
All First	8	10	3	137	37 *	19.57	-	-	2	-	1122	640	15	42.66	4-83	-	-
1-day Int																	
C & G	2	1	0	6	6	6.00	-	-	-	-	82	43	3	14.33	2-30	-	
B & H																	
1-day Lge																	

FISHER, I. D.   Gloucestershire

Name: Ian Douglas Fisher
Role: Left-hand bat, left-arm spin bowler
Born: 31 March 1976, Bradford
Height: 5ft 11in **Weight:** 13st 6lbs
Nickname: Fish, Flash, Fishy
County debut: 1995-96 (Yorkshire), 2002 (Gloucestershire)
1st-Class 50s: 6
1st-Class 100s: 1
1st-Class 5 w. in innings: 3
1st-Class catches: 9
Place in batting averages: 183rd av. 24.69
Place in bowling averages: 151st av. 53.90
Strike rate: 96.37 (career 80.57)

Parents: Geoff and Linda
Marital status: Single
Family links with cricket: Father played club cricket
Education: Denholme First School; Parkside Middle School; Beckfoot Grammar School
Qualifications: 9 GCSEs, NCA coaching award, sports leader's award, lifesaver (bronze), YMCA gym instructor
Off-season: 'Training, resting'
Overseas tours: Yorkshire to Zimbabwe 1996, to South Africa 1998, 1999, 2001, to Perth 2000; MCC to Sri Lanka 2001
Overseas teams played for: Somerset West, Cape Town 1994-95; Petone Riverside, Wellington, New Zealand 1997-98
Career highlights to date: 'Winning the Championship with Yorkshire [2001]'
Cricket moments to forget: 'My pair'
Cricketers particularly admired: Darren Lehmann, Shane Warne
Young players to look out for: Tim Bresnan
Other sports played: Football (Westbrook)
Other sports followed: Football (Leeds United)
Relaxations: Music, movies, catching up with friends, shopping, eating out
Extras: Played England U17 and Yorkshire Schools U15, U16 and Yorkshire U19. Yorkshire 2nd XI cap. Bowled the last first-class ball delivered at the Northlands Road ground, Southampton, September 2000. Released by Yorkshire at the end of the 2001 season and joined Gloucestershire for 2002. Scored maiden first-class century (103*) v Essex at Gloucester 2002, in the process sharing with Jack Russell (107) in a record seventh-wicket partnership for Gloucestershire in matches v Essex (207)
Best batting: 103* Gloucestershire v Essex, Gloucester 2002
Best bowling: 5-35 Yorkshire v Mashonaland, Harare 1995-96

2002 Season

	M	Inns	NO	Runs	HS	Avge	100s	50s	Ct	St	O	M	Runs	Wkts	Avge	Best	5wI	10wM
Test																		
All First	16	26	3	568	103 *	24.69	1	4	8	-	514	103	1725	32	53.90	5-87	1	-
1-day Int																		
C & G																		
B & H																		
1-day Lge	3	3	1	10	6	5.00	-	-	-	-	21.1	0	111	3	37.00	1-11	-	

Career Performances

	M	Inns	NO	Runs	HS	Avge	100s	50s	Ct	St	Balls	Runs	Wkts	Avge	Best	5wI	10wM
Test																	
All First	40	58	12	1113	103 *	24.19	1	6	9	-	6043	3109	75	41.45	5-35	3	
1-day Int																	
C & G	3	1	0	5	5	5.00	-	-	2	-	150	87	3	29.00	1-21	-	
B & H	1	0	0	0	0	-	-	-	1	-	48	26	1	26.00	1-26	-	
1-day Lge	27	14	4	73	20	7.30	-	-	3	-	970	706	28	25.21	3-20	-	

FLEMING, D. W. Warwickshire

Name: <u>Damien</u> William Fleming
Role: Right-hand bat, right-arm
fast-medium bowler
Born: 24 April 1970, Bentley, Perth,
Australia
Height: 6ft
County debut: 2002 (one-day)
Test debut: 1994-95
Tests: 20
One-Day Internationals: 88
1st-Class 50s: 4
1st-Class 5 w. in innings: 13
1st-Class 10 w. in match: 1
1st-Class catches: 54
One-Day 5 w. in innings: 1
Strike rate: (career 61.10)
Education: Heatherhill HS, Victoria; Deakin
University, Victoria

Off-season: Playing for South Australia
Overseas tours: Australia to South Africa 1993-94, to Sharjah (Pepsi Austral-Asia
Cup) 1993-94, to Sri Lanka (Singer World Series) 1994-95, to Pakistan 1994-95, to
West Indies 1994-95, to India and Pakistan (World Cup) 1995-96, to Sri Lanka (Singer
World Series) 1996-97, to India 1996-97, 1997-98, to Sharjah (Coca-Cola Cup) 1997-
98, to Bangladesh (Wills International Cup) 1998-99, to Pakistan 1998-99, to West
Indies 1998-99 (one-day series), to UK, Ireland and Holland (World Cup) 1999, to Sri
Lanka and Zimbabwe 1999-2000, to New Zealand 1999-2000, to India 2000-01, to
England 2001
Overseas teams played for: Victoria 1989-90 – 2001-02; South Australia 2002-03 –
Extras: Became only the third player to take a hat-trick (Aamer Malik, Inzamam-ul-
Haq, Salim Malik) on Test debut, in the second Test v Pakistan at Rawalpindi 1994-95.
Bowler of the Series in the Coca-Cola Cup, Sharjah 1997-98. Man of the Match (5-46
and 4-45) in the second Test v England at Perth 1998-99. Played in Australia's World

Cup winning team 1999. Was Warwickshire's overseas player towards the end of the 2002 season, replacing Shaun Pollock, absent on international duty

Best batting: 71* Australia v England, Brisbane 1998-99
Best bowling: 7-90 Victoria v South Australia, Adelaide 1992-93

2002 Season

	M	Inns	NO	Runs	HS	Avge	100s	50s	Ct	St	O	M	Runs	Wkts	Avge	Best	5wI	10wM
Test																		
All First																		
1-day Int																		
C & G																		
B & H																		
1-day Lge	1	0	0	0	0	-	-	-	-	-	4	0	25	0	-	-	-	

Career Performances

	M	Inns	NO	Runs	HS	Avge	100s	50s	Ct	St	Balls	Runs	Wkts	Avge	Best	5wI	10wM
Test	20	19	3	305	71 *	19.06	-	2	9	-	4129	1942	75	25.89	5-30	3	-
All First	112	134	38	1437	71 *	14.96	-	4	54	-	22975	10508	376	27.94	7-90	13	1
1-day Int	88	31	18	152	29	11.69	-	-	14	-	4619	3402	134	25.38	5-36	1	
C & G																	
B & H																	
1-day Lge	1	0	0	0	0	-	-	-	-	-	24	25	0	-	-	-	

FLEMING, M. V. Kent

Name: Matthew Valentine Fleming
Role: Right-hand bat, right-arm medium bowler
Born: 12 December 1964, Macclesfield
Height: 5ft 11ins **Weight:** 13st
Nickname: Jazzer
County debut: 1988
County cap: 1990
Benefit: 2001
One-Day Internationals: 11
1st-Class 50s: 42
1st-Class 100s: 11
1st-Class 5 w. in innings: 2
1st-Class catches: 83
One-Day 100s: 4
One-Day 5 w. in innings: 3
Place in batting averages: 137th av. 30.14 (2001 177th av. 21.83)

Place in bowling averages: (2001 118th av. 41.36)
Strike rate: 102.00 (career 76.87)
Parents: Valentine and Elizabeth
Wife and date of marriage: Caroline, 23 September 1989
Children: Hannah, 9 October 1992; Victoria, 16 June 1994;
Mathilda, 13 February 1997
Family links with cricket: Great-grandfather C.F.H. Leslie played four Tests for
England on 1882-83 tour of Australia; once hit an all-run seven at Lord's. Father
played for Eton 2nd XI; mother opened the bowling for Heathfield School
Education: St Aubyns School, Rottingdean; Eton College
Qualifications: 8 O-levels, 3 A-levels, granted short-service commission in Royal
Green Jackets 1985
Overseas tours: England VI to Hong Kong 1997; England to Sharjah (Champions
Trophy) 1997-98, to West Indies 1997-98 (one-day series), to Bangladesh (Wills
International Cup) 1998
Overseas teams played for: Avendale, Cape Town 1983-84
Other sports played: 'Most sports; none with distinction'
Other sports followed: Football (Arsenal), rugby union (London Wasps)
Injuries: Torn hip flexor and hip bone injury
Relaxations: 'Field sports, bonfiring, my family'
Extras: Is great-nephew of James Bond author Ian Fleming. First two scoring shots in
Championship cricket were sixes. Out twice before lunch batting at number three for
Kent against West Indies in 1995. Took 4-13 and scored a 20-ball 63* (reaching 50
from 16 balls) in a reduced (ten-over) AXA League match v Yorkshire at Canterbury in
1996. Player of the Tournament in the 1997 Hong Kong Sixes. Director of *The
Cricketer* magazine. Shared in a new NatWest record sixth-wicket stand of 226 with
Nigel Llong v Cheshire at Bowdon 1999, scoring 117* in the process; the second 50 of
his 100 came off 13 balls. Ran out four opposition batsmen, including three in four
balls, with direct hits on the stumps v Surrey at Canterbury in the Norwich Union
League 2001. Top-scored with 58 and took 5-40 v Gloucestershire at Bristol and
scored 125 and took 3-28 v Northamptonshire at Canterbury in the Norwich Union
League 2001. Kent Player of the Year (Cowdrey Award) 2001. Captain of Kent
1999-2001; club captain and one-day captain of Kent 2002 (*see entry on David
Fulton*). Won the Walter Lawrence Trophy (for the fastest first-class century of the
season in terms of balls received) for his 66-ball century (out for 102) v Sri Lankans at
Canterbury 2002. C&G Man of the Match award for his 56 and 3-4 (from four overs)
v Norfolk at Manor Park 2002. Retired at the end of the 2002 season
Best batting: 138 Kent v Essex, Canterbury 1997
138 Kent v Worcestershire, Worcester 1999
Best bowling: 5-51 Kent v Nottinghamshire, Trent Bridge 1997

2002 Season

	M	Inns	NO	Runs	HS	Avge	100s	50s	Ct	St	O	M	Runs	Wkts	Avge	Best	5wI	10wM
Test																		
All First	5	8	1	211	102	30.14	1	-	-	-	102	19	292	6	48.66	4-68	-	-
1-day Int																		
C & G	3	3	0	172	63	57.33	-	3	3	-	24	2	125	7	17.85	3-4	-	
B & H	5	5	1	85	50	21.25	-	1	-	-	39.2	3	171	6	28.50	3-12	-	
1-day Lge	14	14	0	332	68	23.71	-	2	3	-	97.2	6	419	14	29.92	4-22	-	

Career Performances

	M	Inns	NO	Runs	HS	Avge	100s	50s	Ct	St	Balls	Runs	Wkts	Avge	Best	5wI	10wM
Test																	
All First	219	348	43	9206	138	30.18	11	42	83	-	22293	10415	290	35.91	5-51	2	-
1-day Int	11	10	1	139	33	15.44	-	-	1	-	523	434	17	25.52	4-45	-	
C & G	28	26	2	679	117 *	28.29	1	4	14	-	1155	767	30	25.56	3-4	-	
B & H	59	54	4	1221	105 *	24.42	1	6	17	-	2742	1928	78	24.71	5-27	2	
1-day Lge	212	188	24	4009	125	24.44	2	17	47	-	7713	6450	250	25.80	5-40	1	

FLINTOFF, A. Lancashire

Name: Andrew Flintoff
Role: Right-hand bat, right-arm
fast-medium bowler
Born: 6 December 1977, Preston
Height: 6ft 4in
County debut: 1995
County cap: 1998
Test debut: 1998
Tests: 21
One-Day Internationals: 46
1st-Class 50s: 22
1st-Class 100s: 9
1st-Class 5 w. in innings: 1
1st-Class catches: 113
One-Day 100s: 2
Place in batting averages: 152nd av. 28.40
(2001 115th av. 31.18)
Place in bowling averages: 152nd av. 54.85
(2001 110th av. 38.73)
Strike rate: 107.57 (career 77.40)
Parents: Colin and Susan
Family links with cricket: Brother Chris and father both play local league cricket

Education: Greenlands County Primary; Ribbleton Hall High School
Qualifications: 9 GCSEs
Off-season: Touring with England
Overseas tours: England Schools U15 to South Africa 1993; England U19 to West Indies 1994-95, to Zimbabwe 1995-96, to Pakistan 1996-97 (captain); England A to Kenya and Sri Lanka 1997-98, to Zimbabwe and South Africa 1998-99; England to Sharjah (Coca-Cola Cup) 1998-99, to South Africa and Zimbabwe 1999-2000, to Kenya (ICC Knockout Trophy) 2000-01, to Pakistan and (one-day series) Sri Lanka 2000-01, to Zimbabwe (one-day series) 2001-02, to India and New Zealand 2001-02, to Australia 2002-03; ECB National Academy to Australia 2001-02; England VI to Hong Kong 2001
Cricketers particularly admired: Jason Gallian, John Crawley, Stephen Titchard, Warren Hegg
Other sports followed: Football (Preston North End and Liverpool FC)
Relaxations: Listening to music and sleeping
Extras: Won a *Daily Telegraph* regional award for batting. Represented England U14 to U19. Captained England U19 in the series against Zimbabwe U19 in 1997. Scored 61 off 24 balls in Championship match v Surrey at Old Trafford in June 1998, including 34 from one over by Alex Tudor. Became the 50th recipient of the Cricket Writers' Club Young Player of the Year award in September 1998. Professional Cricketers' Association's Young Player of the Year 1998. Topped England A batting averages for tour to Zimbabwe and South Africa 1998-99 with 542 runs at an average of 77.42. Struck 50 (including four sixes) on One-Day International debut, v Pakistan, Sharjah 1998-99. Scored 143 off 66 balls, including nine sixes, in National League v Essex at Chelmsford 1999. His 160 v Yorkshire at Old Trafford 1999 included 111 runs before lunch, the first century before lunch by a Lancashire batsman in a Roses match. Won the EDS Walter Lawrence Trophy 1999 (for the fastest first-class century of the season) for his hundred off 61 balls (before lunch) for Lancashire v Gloucestershire at Bristol. Represented England in the 1999 World Cup. NatWest Man of the Match award for his 111-ball 135* in the quarter-final v Surrey at The Oval 2000. Lancashire Player of the Year 2000. Struck 84 from 60 balls to win Man of the Match award in England's victory in the first One-Day International v Pakistan at Karachi 2000-01. C&G Man of the Match awards for his 2-19 and 65* v Sussex at Old Trafford and his 2-46 and 72* in the quarter-final v Durham at Blackpool 2001. Vice-captain of Lancashire in 2002. Called up from the ECB National Academy tour in Australia into the England Test squad in India 2001-02, recording Test best bowling figures (4-50) in the third Test at Bangalore to win the Man of the Match award. Scored 36-ball 50 (52) in One-Day International v India at Delhi 2001-02, then scored 40 and took 3-38 in England's series-equalling victory at Mumbai (Bombay). Man of the Match for his 4-17 in One-Day International v New Zealand at Auckland 2001-02. Scored maiden Test century (137) v New Zealand in the first Test at Christchurch 2001-02, in the process sharing with Graham Thorpe in a stand of 281 that set several new records, including that for the highest sixth-wicket partnership for England in Tests; he struck five fours and a six from the first 12 deliveries he received and reached his hundred from 114 balls. Struck a 44-ball 75 in the second Test v New

Zealand at Wellington 2001-02; it included the third fastest England Test 50 in terms of balls faced (33). Scored a 75-ball century (out for 137) v Surrey at The Oval 2002, on a day on which 17 wickets fell. Man of the Match award for his 28-ball 50* (the fastest ODI fifty by an England player) and 3-49 v Sri Lanka at Trent Bridge in the NatWest Series 2002. Selected for the England one-day squad for the ICC Champions Trophy in Sri Lanka 2002-03 but was ruled out after a hernia operation; replaced by Ian Blackwell. ECB 12-month contract 2002-03

Best batting: 160 Lancashire v Yorkshire, Old Trafford 1999
Best bowling: 5-24 Lancashire v Hampshire, Southampton 1999
Stop press: Forced to return home early from England tour of Australia 2002-03 after failing to recover fully from hernia operation; replaced in England one-day squad by Adam Hollioake; returned to Australia ahead of VB Series finals. Selected for England squad for 2002-03 World Cup

2002 Season

	M	Inns	NO	Runs	HS	Avge	100s	50s	Ct	St	O	M	Runs	Wkts	Avge	Best	5wl	10wM
Test	6	8	0	141	59	17.62	-	1	7	-	219	45	669	11	60.81	2-22	-	-
All First	7	10	0	284	137	28.40	1	1	8	-	251	53	768	14	54.85	2-22	-	-
1-day Int	7	6	1	190	51	38.00	-	2	3	-	52.1	0	276	9	30.66	3-49	-	
C & G	2	1	0	45	45	45.00	-	-	1	-	14	2	70	2	35.00	2-46	-	
B & H	4	3	0	87	47	29.00	-	-	3	-	37.2	8	111	6	18.50	4-11	-	
1-day Lge	2	2	0	4	3	2.00	-	-	-	-	10	0	60	1	60.00	1-56	-	

Career Performances

	M	Inns	NO	Runs	HS	Avge	100s	50s	Ct	St	Balls	Runs	Wkts	Avge	Best	5wl	10wM
Test	21	33	0	643	137	19.48	1	2	14	-	3251	1556	33	47.15	4-50	-	-
All First	96	150	10	4551	160	32.50	9	22	113	-	8282	3824	107	35.73	5-24	1	-
1-day Int	46	38	3	847	84	24.20	-	5	15	-	1312	1067	36	29.63	4-17	-	
C & G	19	16	4	612	135 *	51.00	1	3	11	-	569	364	10	36.40	2-19	-	
B & H	24	20	1	432	92	22.73	-	2	12	-	794	416	20	20.80	4-11	-	
1-day Lge	56	55	2	1286	143	24.26	1	6	14	-	1295	960	44	21.81	4-24	-	

28. Which South African pace bowler took 85 first-class wickets
at an average of 14.73 for Middlesex in 1980?

FLOWER, A.   Essex

Name: Andrew (<u>Andy</u>) Flower
Role: Left-hand bat, wicket-keeper,
occasional right-arm medium/off-spin bowler
Born: 28 April 1968, Cape Town,
South Africa
Height: 5ft 10in
Nickname: Petals
County debut: 2002
County cap: 2002
Test debut: 1992-93
Tests: 61
One-Day Internationals: 195
1000 runs in a season: 1
1st-Class 50s: 52
1st-Class 100s: 26
1st-Class 200s: 2
1st-Class catches: 288
1st-Class stumpings: 21
One-Day 100s: 3
Place in batting averages: 36th av. 50.04
Strike rate: (career 124.50)
Family links with cricket: Younger brother Grant also plays for Zimbabwe
Education: North Park School, Harare; Vainona High School
Overseas tours: Zimbabwe to Australia and New Zealand (World Cup) 1991-92,
to India 1992-93, to Pakistan 1993-94, to Australia (one-day series) 1994-95, to New
Zealand 1995-96, to India and Pakistan (World Cup) 1995-96, to Sri Lanka and
Pakistan 1996-97, to Sri Lanka and New Zealand 1997-98, to Bangladesh (Wills
International Cup) 1998-99, to Pakistan 1998-99, to UK, Ireland and Holland (World
Cup) 1999, to Singapore (Singapore Challenge) 1999-2000, to Kenya (LG Cup) 1999-
2000, to South Africa 1999-2000, to West Indies 1999-2000, to England 2000, to
Kenya (ICC Knockout) 2000-01, to India 2000-01, to New Zealand and Australia
2000-01, to Bangladesh, Sri Lanka and India 2001-02, to Sri Lanka (ICC Champions
Trophy) 2002-03
Overseas teams played for: Mashonaland 1993-94 –
Other sports played: Tennis, squash; rugby, hockey (at school)
Extras: Captained Zimbabwe Schools. Made first-class debut for ZCU President's XI
v Young West Indies at Harare 1986. Has represented Zimbabwe since 1988-89.
Scored century (115*) on One-Day International debut v Sri Lanka at New Plymouth
in the 1992 World Cup, batting right through the Zimbabwe innings. Appeared in
Zimbabwe's inaugural Test, v India at Harare 1992-93, scoring 59. Captain of
Zimbabwe 1993-94 – 1995-96 and 1999-2000. Scored 156 v Pakistan at Harare 1994-
95 in Zimbabwe's first Test win, in the process sharing with Grant Flower (201*) in a

fourth-wicket stand of 269, the highest partnership between brothers in Test cricket and at the time the highest partnership for Zimbabwe for any wicket in Tests. Scored 100* v Pakistan at Bulawayo 1997-98, in the process sharing with Murray Goodwin in a new record partnership for Zimbabwe for any wicket in Tests (277*). Scored maiden Test double century (232*) v India at Nagpur 2000-01 to help save the match after Zimbabwe had followed on; was Man of the Series, having scored 183*, 70 and 55 in his other three innings for a series average of 270.00. Scored 73 v Bangladesh at Bulawayo 2000-01, in the process equalling Everton Weekes's world record, set 1947-49, of seven consecutive Test half-centuries. FICA International Player of the Year 2001. Scored 142 and 199* v South Africa in the first Test at Harare 2001, becoming the first wicket-keeper to score a century in each innings of a Test match and the first Zimbabwe player to reach 4000 Test runs; his performance took him to the top of the PricewaterhouseCoopers ratings for Test batsmen, making him the first wicket-keeper/batsman to achieve the feat. Equalled Zimbabwe's highest individual score in One-Day Internationals with his 142* (century from 97 balls) v England in the third One-Day International at Harare 2001-02, in the process sharing with Heath Streak in a new world record seventh-wicket partnership for ODIs (130). Scored century in each innings (114/156*) for Mashonaland in the Logan Cup 2001-02 v Mashonaland A, for whom brother Grant scored 235* in the first innings. One of *Wisden*'s Five Cricketers of the Year 2002. Joined Essex as overseas player for 2002. B&H Gold Awards for his 98 plus three catches v Surrey and for his 79* v Hampshire, both at Chelmsford 2002. Ended the season with an average of more than 50 in each of the four domestic competitions. Awarded Essex cap 2002

Best batting: 232* Zimbabwe v India, Nagpur 2000-01
Best bowling: 1-1 Mashonaland v Mashonaland CD, Harare South 1993-94
Stop press: Scored 145 v India at Colombo in the ICC Champions Trophy 2002-03, in the process improving on his own (shared) record for the highest individual score for Zimbabwe in ODIs. Selected for Zimbabwe squad for 2002-03 World Cup and has announced that he will retire from international cricket after that competition

2002 Season

	M	Inns	NO	Runs	HS	Avge	100s	50s	Ct	St	O	M	Runs	Wkts	Avge	Best	5wI	10wM
Test																		
All First	16	29	6	1151	172 *	50.04	2	6	35	1	6	0	19	0	-	-	-	-
1-day Int																		
C & G	3	2	0	120	75	60.00	-	1	4	-								
B & H	7	7	1	308	98	51.33	-	2	12	-								
1-day Lge	14	14	4	506	80	50.60	-	6	16	4								

Career Performances

	M	Inns	NO	Runs	HS	Avge	100s	50s	Ct	St		Balls	Runs	Wkts	Avge	Best	5wI	10wM
Test	61	108	19	4655	232 *	52.30	12	26	149	9		1	0	0	-	-	-	-
All First	143	239	49	10116	232 *	53.24	28	52	288	21		498	208	4	52.00	1-1	-	-
1-day Int	195	192	14	5988	142 *	33.64	3	48	136	32		30	23	0	-		-	-
C & G	3	2	0	120	75	60.00	-	1	4	-								
B & H	7	7	1	308	98	51.33	-	2	12	-								
1-day Lge	14	14	4	506	80	50.60	-	6	16	4								

FLOWER, G. W. Leicestershire

Name: <u>Grant</u> William Flower
Role: Right-hand bat, slow left-arm bowler
Born: 20 December 1970, Harare, Zimbabwe
Height: 5ft 10in
County debut: 2002
Test debut: 1992-93
Tests: 61
One-Day Internationals: 182
1st-Class 50s: 45
1st-Class 100s: 12
1st-Class 200s: 3
1st-Class 5 w. in innings: 2
1st-Class catches: 113
One-Day 100s: 5
Strike rate: 35.00 (career 84.69)
Family links with cricket: Younger brother
of Andy Flower
Education: North Park School, Harare;
St George's College, Harare
Overseas tours: Zimbabwe to India 1992-93, to Pakistan 1993-94, to Australia (one-day series) 1994-95, to New Zealand 1995-96, to India and Pakistan (World Cup) 1995-96, to Sri Lanka and Pakistan 1996-97, to Sri Lanka and New Zealand 1997-98, to Bangladesh (Wills International Cup) 1998-99, to Pakistan 1998-99, to UK, Ireland and Holland (World Cup) 1999, to Singapore (Singapore Challenge) 1999-2000, to Kenya (LG Cup) 1999-2000, to South Africa 1999-2000, to West Indies 1999-2000, to England 2000, to Kenya (ICC Knockout) 2000-01, to India 2000-01, to New Zealand and Australia 2000-01, to Bangladesh, Sri Lanka and India 2001-02, to Sri Lanka (ICC Champions Trophy) 2002-03
Overseas teams played for: Mashonaland 1996-97 –
Extras: Made first-class debut for Zimbabwe v England A at Bulawayo 1989-90. Appeared in Zimbabwe's inaugural Test, v India at Harare 1992-93, scoring 82. Scored

201* v Pakistan at Harare 1994-95 in Zimbabwe's first Test win, in the process sharing with Andy Flower (156) in a fourth-wicket stand of 269, the highest partnership between brothers in Test cricket and at the time the highest partnership for Zimbabwe for any wicket in Tests. Became the first player to score a hundred in each innings of a Test for Zimbabwe (104/151) in the first Test v New Zealand at Harare 1997-98; Man of the Series (two matches) with 387 runs (av. 96.75). Scored 156* in the first Test v Pakistan at Bulawayo 1997-98, in the process becoming the second Zimbabwe player to carry his bat in a Test and the first to score five Test centuries. Scored 235* for Mashonaland A in the Logan Cup 2001-02 v Mashonaland, for whom brother Andy scored a century in each innings (114/156*). Was Leicestershire's overseas player during June 2002, replacing Michael Bevan, absent on international duty
Best batting: 242* Mashonaland v Matabeleland, Harare 1996-97
Best bowling: 7-31 Zimbabweans v Lahore City, Lahore 1998-99
Stop press: Scored century (105*) in fourth ODI v Pakistan at Harare 2002-03 to help post a total of 210; at one point Zimbabwe had been 41-6. Selected for Zimbabwe squad for 2002-03 World Cup

2002 Season

	M	Inns	NO	Runs	HS	Avge	100s	50s	Ct	St	O	M	Runs	Wkts	Avge	Best	5wI	10wM
Test																		
All First	1	2	0	82	75	41.00	-	1	1	-	35	12	98	6	16.33	4-66	-	-
1-day Int																		
C & G	1	1	0	3	3	3.00	-	-	1	-	10	0	33	2	16.50	2-33	-	
B & H																		
1-day Lge	3	2	0	22	19	11.00	-	-	-	-	14.2	0	62	1	62.00	1-43	-	

Career Performances

	M	Inns	NO	Runs	HS	Avge	100s	50s	Ct	St	Balls	Runs	Wkts	Avge	Best	5wI	10wM
Test	61	112	5	3162	201 *	29.55	6	13	37	-	3294	1503	25	60.12	4-41	-	-
All First	130	229	18	7890	242 *	37.39	15	45	113	-	9401	4187	111	37.72	7-31	2	-
1-day Int	182	180	14	5566	142 *	33.53	5	33	67	-	4209	3252	86	37.81	4-32	-	
C & G	2	2	0	11	8	5.50	-	-	1	-	66	33	2	16.50	2-33	-	
B & H																		
1-day Lge	3	2	0	22	19	11.00	-	-	-	-	86	62	1	62.00	1-43	-	

29. Which batsman holds the Hampshire records for the highest individual scores in all three domestic one-day competitions?

FOSTER, J. S.　　　　　　　　　　　　Essex

Name: <u>James</u> Savin Foster
Role: Right-hand bat, wicket-keeper
Born: 15 April 1980, Whipps Cross, London
Height: 6ft **Weight:** 12st
Nickname: Fozzy, Chief
County debut: 2000
County cap: 2001
Test debut: 2001-02
Tests: 6
1st-Class 50s: 6
1st-Class 100s: 1
1st-Class catches: 78
1st-Class stumpings: 11
Place in batting averages: (2001 143rd
av. 26.56)
Parents: Martin and Diana
Marital status: Single
Family links with cricket: 'Dad played for
Essex Amateurs'

Education: Forest School; Durham University
Qualifications: 10 GCSEs, 3 A-levels, hockey and cricket Level 1 coaching awards
Off-season: 'Touring Australia with England'
Overseas tours: BUSA to South Africa 1999; Durham University to South Africa
1999, to Vienna (European Indoor Championships) 1999; England A to West Indies
2000-01; England to Zimbabwe (one-day series) 2001-02, to India and New Zealand
2001-02, to Australia 2002-03
Career highlights to date: 'Playing for my country'
Cricket moments to forget: 'None yet'
Cricketers particularly admired: Nasser Hussain, Stuart Law, Robert Rollins,
Ian Healy, Jack Russell, Alec Stewart, Adam Gilchrist
Young players to look out for: John Chambers, Adnan Akram, Arfan Akram,
Tony Palladino, Ravi Bopara, Michael Brown, Steven Miel
Other sports played: Hockey (Essex U21), tennis (played for GB U14 v Sweden
U14; national training squad)
Other sports followed: Football (Wimbledon FC)
Injuries: Out for two months with a broken ulna (left arm); for one and a half months
with a broken left thumb
Relaxations: Socialising, 'Klute and Rixy's'
Extras: Essex U17 Player of the Year 1997. Represented ECB U19 v Pakistan U19
1998. Represented England U19 v Australia U19 in 'Test' series 1999. Represented
BUSA v South Africa Universities 1999, v New Zealand A and Zimbabweans 2000
and v Pakistan 2001. Scored 52 on Championship debut v Glamorgan at Southend

2000. Awarded 2nd XI cap at end of 2000 season. Voted Essex Cricket Society 2nd XI Player of the Year 2000. Scored 53 on England A debut v Guyana in Grenada 2000-01. Played for Durham University CCE in 2001. NBC Denis Compton Award for the most promising young Essex player 2001. Scored 40 in second Test v India at Ahmedabad 2001-02, in the process sharing with Craig White in a record seventh-wicket partnership for England in Tests in India (105)

Opinions on cricket: 'Less first-class cricket should be played, and county cricket regulations should comply with those of Test/international cricket. Lunch and tea should be longer.'

Best batting: 103 DUCCE v Worcestershire, Worcester 2001

2002 Season

	M	Inns	NO	Runs	HS	Avge	100s	50s	Ct	St	O	M	Runs	Wkts	Avge	Best	5wl	10wM
Test																		
All First	4	4	0	80	36	20.00	-	-	9	1								
1-day Int																		
C & G																		
B & H																		
1-day Lge	3	3	0	20	14	6.66	-	-	5	1								

Career Performances

	M	Inns	NO	Runs	HS	Avge	100s	50s	Ct	St	Balls	Runs	Wkts	Avge	Best	5wl	10wM
Test	6	10	3	201	48	28.71	-	-	14	1							
All First	36	53	7	1236	103	26.86	1	6	78	11	12	6	0	-	-	-	-
1-day Int																	
C & G	1	1	0	33	33	33.00	-	-	2	-							
B & H																	
1-day Lge	23	22	8	308	56 *	22.00	-	1	28	3							

30. Who was Durham's overseas player in their inaugural first-class season of 1992?

FRANCIS, J. D.   Hampshire

Name: <u>John</u> Daniel Francis
Role: Left-hand bat, slow left-arm bowler
Born: 13 November 1980, Bromley, Kent
Height: 5ft 11in   **Weight:** 13st
Nickname: Long John, Franky, Junior
County debut: 2001
1st-Class 50s: 4
1st-Class catches: 7
One-Day 100s: 1
Place in batting averages: 204th av. 23.00
Strike rate: 12.00 (career 24.00)
Parents: Linda and Daniel
Marital status: Single
Family links with cricket: Brother Simon
played for Hampshire 1997-2001; now plays
for Somerset. Father played club cricket.
Grandfather played for the services
Education: Yardley Court, Tonbridge; King
Edward VI, Southampton; Durham and Loughborough Universities
Qualifications: 10 GCSEs, 3 A-levels, ECB Level 1 coaching award
Off-season: Studying at Loughborough University
Overseas tours: Twyford School to Barbados 1993; West of England U15 to West
Indies 1995; King Edward VI, Southampton to South Africa 1998; Durham University
to South Africa 2000; British Universities to South Africa 2002
Career highlights to date: 'Scoring maiden century for Hampshire in NUL match v
Northamptonshire at the Rose Bowl 2002 in 83 balls'
Cricket moments to forget: 'Getting first ever pair, in a match v Yorkshire'
Cricket superstitions: 'Too many to say'
Cricketers particularly admired: Matthew Hayden, Garry Sobers, Robin Smith,
Simon Francis
Young players to look out for: Mark Powell, Monty Panesar, Andrew Dunn,
Simon Francis
Other sports played: Hockey (England U18), golf, squash
Relaxations: Drawing and painting, socialising
Extras: Hampshire Young Sportsman of the Year 1995. Sir John Hobbs Silver Jubilee
Memorial Prize for outstanding U16 player of the year 1996. Leading run-scorer in
U15 World Cup 1996. Played for Loughborough University CCE in 2001 and 2002;
scored a century (107) v Leicestershire at Leicester 2001. Scored 189* for British
Universities v South Africa Universities in South Africa 2002. Represented British
Universities v Sri Lankans at Northampton and v West Indies A (50-over match) at
The Parks 2002. Scored maiden one-day century (103*) v Northamptonshire at West
End in the NUL 2002

Best batting: 82 Hampshire v Leicestershire, Leicester 2002
Best bowling: 1-1 Hampshire v Leicestershire, Leicester 2002

2002 Season

	M	Inns	NO	Runs	HS	Avge	100s	50s	Ct	St	O	M	Runs	Wkts	Avge	Best	5wl	10wM
Test																		
All First	10	17	0	391	82	23.00	-	3	6	-	2	1	1	1	1.00	1-1	-	-
1-day Int																		
C & G																		
B & H																		
1-day Lge	10	10	2	339	103 *	42.37	1	2	2	-								

Career Performances

	M	Inns	NO	Runs	HS	Avge	100s	50s	Ct	St	Balls	Runs	Wkts	Avge	Best	5wl	10wM
Test																	
All First	12	21	2	522	82	27.47	-	4	7	-	48	35	2	17.50	1-1	-	-
1-day Int																	
C & G																	
B & H																	
1-day Lge	16	16	5	528	103 *	48.00	1	4	3	-							

FRANCIS, S. R. G.   Somerset

Name: <u>Simon</u> Richard George Francis
Role: Right-hand bat, right-arm
fast-medium bowler
Born: 15 August 1978, Bromley, Kent
Height: 6ft 2in **Weight:** 15st
Nickname: Franco, Sorg
County debut: 1997 (Hampshire),
2002 (Somerset)
1st-Class 5 w. in innings: 1
1st-Class catches: 1
Place in batting averages: 300th av. 8.37
Place in bowling averages: 94th av. 33.82
Strike rate: 47.67 (career 64.84)
Parents: Daniel and Linda
Marital status: Single
Family links with cricket: Brother John
plays for Hampshire. Father played club
cricket. Grandfather played for the Navy
Education: Yardley Court, Tonbridge/Twyford, Winchester; King Edward VI,
Southampton; Durham University

Qualifications: 9 GCSEs, 1 AS-Level, 3 A-levels, BA (Hons) Sport in the Community, Level 1 coaching in hockey, Level III coaching in cricket
Career outside cricket: Cricket and hockey coaching
Off-season: 'Training in this country with several holidays'
Overseas tours: England U17 to Holland (International Youth Tournament) 1995; England U19 to Pakistan 1996-97; Durham University to Zimbabwe 1997-98; Hampshire to Boland 2001
Overseas teams played for: Maties (Stellenbosch University), South Africa 2000; Melville CC, Perth 2001
Career highlights to date: 'Run out in semi-final of C&G v Kent and five wickets v Warwickshire' (*His run out of Kent's James Golding with a direct hit from the prone position was described as the 'turning point of the match' by his coach Kevin Shine*)
Cricket moments to forget: 'Whole of the B&H competition 2002'
Cricket superstitions: 'Not applicable'
Cricketers particularly admired: Malcolm Marshall, Richard Hadlee, Allan Donald, Graham Dilley
Young players to look out for: John Francis
Other sports played: Golf, hockey (England U18 1995)
Injuries: Out for four weeks with a broken finger
Relaxations: 'Films, sleeping, reading, listening to music'
Extras: *Daily Telegraph* West Region Bowling Award U15. Played in Durham University's BUSA Championship-winning side 1999. Put on 90 for the tenth wicket with Dimitri Mascarenhas v Surrey at The Oval 2000, the pair falling just two runs short of pulling off a remarkable Championship victory. Released by Hampshire at the end of the 2001 season and joined Somerset for 2002. Recorded maiden first-class five-wicket return (5-73) v Warwickshire at Taunton 2002
Opinions on cricket: 'More day/night games – more entertaining; bigger crowds.'
Best batting: 30* Hampshire v Surrey, The Oval 2000
Best bowling: 5-73 Somerset v Warwickshire, Taunton 2002

2002 Season

	M	Inns	NO	Runs	HS	Avge	100s	50s	Ct	St	O	M	Runs	Wkts	Avge	Best	5wI	10wM
Test																		
All First	10	16	8	67	17	8.37	-	-	-	-	222.3	26	947	28	33.82	5-73	1	-
1-day Int																		
C & G																		
B & H	3	2	1	22	21	22.00	-	-	1	-	23	0	179	2	89.50	1-49	-	
1-day Lge	10	6	3	64	27	21.33	-	-	3	-	70	5	384	13	29.53	4-60	-	

Career Performances

	M	Inns	NO	Runs	HS	Avge	100s	50s	Ct	St	Balls	Runs	Wkts	Avge	Best	5wl	10wM
Test																	
All First	26	38	18	158	30 *	7.90	-	-	1	-	3437	2179	53	41.11	5-73	1	-
1-day Int																	
C & G	1	0	0	0	0	-	-	-	-	-	36	10	0	-	-	-	-
B & H	3	2	1	22	21	22.00	-	-	1	-	138	179	2	89.50	1-49	-	
1-day Lge	20	11	6	82	27	16.40	-	-	5	-	768	626	19	32.94	4-60	-	

FRANKS, P. J. Nottinghamshire

Name: Paul John Franks
Role: Left-hand bat, right-arm fast-medium bowler, county vice-captain
Born: 3 February 1979, Sutton-in-Ashfield
Height: 6ft 1½in **Weight:** 13st 10lbs
Nickname: Pike, Franno, The General
County debut: 1996
County cap: 1999
One-Day Internationals: 1
50 wickets in a season: 2
1st-Class 50s: 11
1st-Class 5 w. in innings: 9
1st-Class catches: 32
One-Day 5 w. in innings: 2
Place in batting averages: 179th av. 25.08
Place in bowling averages: 28th av. 25.40 (2001 80th av. 33.00)
Strike rate: 44.03 (career 53.49)
Parents: Pat and John
Marital status: Single
Family links with cricket: 'Dad was a local league legend'
Education: Walter D'Ayncourt Primary School; Minster School, Southwell; West Notts College
Qualifications: 7 GCSEs, GNVQ (Advanced) Leisure Management, coaching Level 1
Off-season: Playing club cricket in New Zealand
Overseas tours: England U19 to Pakistan 1996-97, to South Africa (including U19 World Cup) 1997-98; England A to Zimbabwe and South Africa 1998-99, to Bangladesh and New Zealand 1999-2000, to West Indies 2000-01; Notts CCC to South Africa 1998, 1999
Career highlights to date: 'England [one-day] debut v West Indies on home ground in 2000'

Cricket moments to forget: 'Any time I get my poles removed or go the distance'
Cricketers particularly admired: Glenn McGrath, Mike Atherton, Allan Donald, Phil 'bowls like me' DeFreitas
Young players to look out for: Kyle Hogg, Nadeem Malik, Bilal Shafayat, Matt Prior, Richard Hodgkinson
Other sports played: Golf
Other sports followed: Football (Mansfield Town)
Relaxations: 'Taking it generally steady'
Extras: Became youngest ever Notts player (and third-youngest player ever in English first-class cricket, aged 18 years 163 days) to take a hat-trick, v Warwickshire at Trent Bridge in July 1997. Won U19 World Cup winner's medal in Johannesburg 1998. Attended Dennis Lillee coaching school, Chennai (Madras), March 1997, February 1998 and March 1999. NBC Denis Compton Award 1999. Cricket Writers' Young Player of the Year 2000. Scored 85 v Middlesex at Lord's 2001, in the process sharing in a record seventh-wicket stand for Notts in matches against Middlesex (199) with Kevin Pietersen. Appointed vice-captain of Nottinghamshire for 2003
Best batting: 85 Nottinghamshire v Middlesex, Lord's 2001
Best bowling: 7-56 Nottinghamshire v Middlesex, Lord's 2000

2002 Season

	M	Inns	NO	Runs	HS	Avge	100s	50s	Ct	St	O	M	Runs	Wkts	Avge	Best	5wl	10wM
Test																		
All First	10	14	2	301	67	25.08	-	3	2	-	234.5	53	813	32	25.40	5-51	1	-
1-day Int																		
C & G	2	0	0	0	0	-	-	-	-	-	14	0	107	1	107.00	1-39	-	
B & H																		
1-day Lge	9	7	2	131	60	26.20	-	1	1	-	60.2	1	350	10	35.00	3-31	-	

Career Performances

	M	Inns	NO	Runs	HS	Avge	100s	50s	Ct	St	Balls	Runs	Wkts	Avge	Best	5wl	10wM
Test																	
All First	81	119	21	2163	85	22.07	-	11	32	-	14176	7247	265	27.34	7-56	9	-
1-day Int	1	1	0	4	4	4.00	-	-	1	-	54	48	0	-	-	-	
C & G	11	7	3	110	26 *	27.50	-	-	3	-	564	436	16	27.25	3-7	-	
B & H	10	4	2	32	14	16.00	-	-	-	-	492	362	8	45.25	2-14	-	
1-day Lge	59	45	18	504	60	18.66	-	1	7	-	2600	2063	80	25.78	6-27	2	

FRASER, A. R. C. Middlesex

Name: <u>Angus</u> Robert Charles Fraser
Role: Right-hand lower-order bat,
right-arm medium-fast bowler
Born: 8 August 1965, Billinge, Wigan
Height: 6ft 6in **Weight:** 16st
Nickname: Gus, Lard, Wiggy, Recall
County debut: 1984
County cap: 1988
Benefit: 1997
Test debut: 1989
Tests: 46
One-Day Internationals: 42
50 wickets in a season: 7
1st-Class 50s: 2
1st-Class 5 w. in innings: 36
1st-Class 10 w. in match: 5
1st-Class catches: 54
One-Day 5 w. in innings: 1

Place in batting averages: (2001 242nd av. 12.41)
Place in bowling averages: (2001 104th av. 37.62)
Strike rate: 61.71 (career 63.51)
Parents: Don and Irene
Wife and date of marriage: Denise, March 1996
Children: Alexander Charles Mitchell, May 1993; Bethan Louise, July 1995
Family links with cricket: 'Mum and Dad keen followers. Brother Alastair played for Middlesex, Essex, then Middlesex again'
Education: Weald Junior and Middle School; Gayton High School, Harrow; Orange Hill Senior High School, Edgware
Qualifications: 7 O-levels, qualified cricket coach
Career outside cricket: Cricket writer
Overseas tours: Thames Valley Gentlemen to Barbados 1985; Middlesex to La Manga 1985, 1986, to Portugal 1991-93, to Malta 2001; England to India (Nehru Cup) 1989-90, to West Indies 1989-90, 1993-94, 1997-98, to Australia 1990-91, 1994-95, 1998-99, to South Africa 1995-96, to Sharjah (Coca-Cola Cup) 1998-99
Overseas teams played for: Plimmerton, Wellington 1985-86, 1987-88; Western Suburbs, Sydney 1988-89, 1994-95
Career highlights: 'Difficult to pull out one. Fortunately there have been a few highlights. Obviously playing and winning games/series for England and winning trophies for Middlesex stand out'
Cricket moments to forget: 'Remember the bad days as they make the good ones feel that much better. I have no regrets'

Cricketers particularly admired: Graham Gooch, Curtly Ambrose, Courtney Walsh, Allan Border, Mike Atherton
Young players to look out for: Chris Tremlett, Ian Bell, 'the Middlesex top six'
Other sports played: 'Golf with a sombrero on'
Other sports followed: 'Follow Liverpool FC keenly. Enjoy watching rugby internationals at my local rugby club, Harrow'
Relaxations: Spending time with family, golf, Liverpool FC, drinking good red wine
Extras: Middlesex Player of the Year 1988 and 1989. Took a hat-trick v Sussex at Lord's in the Benson and Hedges Cup 1988. Took his 100th Test wicket (Brian Lara) in second Test v West Indies at Lord's 1995. Finished 2nd in the Whyte and Mackay bowling ratings for 1995. One of *Wisden*'s Five Cricketers of the Year 1996. His 8-53 (11-110 the match) at Trinidad 1997-98 is the best innings return by an English bowler against the West Indies, home or away. Peter Smith Award 1998. Winner of the Kumala Cape Wines 'Century of Bottles' award for the best individual performance against the 1998 South Africans. Awarded MBE in New Year honours list 1999. Represented England in 1999 World Cup. Captain of Middlesex 2001 and at the beginning of the 2002 season, until his retirement to join the media. Took 5-61 on his final first-class appearance, at Lord's v Nottinghamshire 2002
Opinions on cricket: 'The greed of players will lead to their premature exclusion from the game. Higher salaries don't make you a better player. Reward success, not potential. You have to work hard for success.'
Best batting: 92 Middlesex v Surrey, The Oval 1990
Best bowling: 8-53 England v West Indies, Port of Spain 1997-98

2002 Season

	M	Inns	NO	Runs	HS	Avge	100s	50s	Ct	St	O	M	Runs	Wkts	Avge	Best	5wI	10wM
Test																		
All First	2	2	0	36	20	18.00	-	-	-	-	72	26	190	7	27.14	5-61	1	-
1-day Int																		
C & G																		
B & H	4	2	2	1	1 *	-	-	-	-	-	34	4	115	3	38.33	2-34	-	
1-day Lge																		

Career Performances

	M	Inns	NO	Runs	HS	Avge	100s	50s	Ct	St	Balls	Runs	Wkts	Avge	Best	5wl	10wM
Test	46	67	15	388	32	7.46	-	-	9	-	10876	4836	177	27.32	8-53	13	2
All First	290	344	82	2934	92	11.19	-	2	54	-	56275	24277	886	27.40	8-53	36	5
1-day Int	42	20	9	141	38 *	12.81	-	-	5	-	2392	1412	47	30.04	4-22	-	
C & G	36	13	10	80	19	26.66	-	-	6	-	2301	1180	50	23.60	4-34	-	
B & H	54	29	16	129	30 *	9.92	-	-	10	-	3129	1831	66	27.74	4-49	-	
1-day Lge	188	77	35	489	33	11.64	-	-	30	-	8418	5397	213	25.33	5-32	1	

FROST, T.   Warwickshire

Name: Tony Frost
Role: Right-hand bat, wicket-keeper
Born: 17 November 1975, Stoke-on-Trent
Height: 5ft 10in **Weight:** 10st 6lbs
County debut: 1997
County cap: 1999
1st-Class 50s: 4
1st-Class 100s: 2
1st-Class catches: 82
1st-Class stumpings: 7
Place in batting averages: 132nd av. 30.80
Parents: Ivan and Christine
Marital status: Single
Family links with cricket: Father played for
Staffordshire
Education: James Brinkley High School;
Stoke-on-Trent College
Qualifications: 5 GCSEs
Overseas tours: Kidsgrove U18 to Australia 1990-91
Cricketers particularly admired: Ashley Giles 'could be described as a legend',
'Pop' Welch and George Burns 'in the JT bracket'
Other sports followed: Football, golf
Relaxations: Listening to music, watching films, reading aircraft magazines
Extras: Represented Staffordshire at all levels from U11 to U19. Won Texaco U16
competition with Staffordshire in 1992. Played for Development of Excellence XI U17
v South Africa and U18 v West Indies and U19 v India. Scored maiden Championship
century (103) v Yorkshire at Edgbaston 2002
Best batting: 111* Warwickshire v Oxford University, The Parks 1998

2002 Season

	M	Inns	NO	Runs	HS	Avge	100s	50s	Ct	St	O	M	Runs	Wkts	Avge	Best	5wI	10wM
Test																		
All First	7	11	1	308	103	30.80	1	1	6	2	1	0	9	0	-		-	-
1-day Int																		
C & G	1	1	0	9	9	9.00	-	-	1	-								
B & H	2	1	1	4	4 *	-	-	-	2	-								
1-day Lge	6	3	2	29	17	29.00	-	-	7	-								

Career Performances

	M	Inns	NO	Runs	HS	Avge	100s	50s	Ct	St	Balls	Runs	Wkts	Avge	Best	5wl	10wM
Test																	
All First	38	56	7	1220	111 *	24.89	2	4	82	7	12	15	0	-		-	-
1-day Int																	
C & G	3	3	0	14	9	4.66	-	-	5	1							
B & H	5	3	2	15	10 *	15.00	-	-	5	-							
1-day Lge	29	12	5	117	22 *	16.71	-	-	22	3							

FULTON, D. P. Kent

Name: David (<u>Dave</u>) Paul Fulton
Role: Right-hand top-order bat, left-arm spin
bowler, occasional wicket-keeper,
county captain
Born: 15 November 1971, Lewisham
Height: 6ft 2in **Weight:** 12st 7lbs
Nickname: Tav, Rave
County debut: 1992
County cap: 1998
1000 runs in a season: 2
1st-Class 50s: 34
1st-Class 100s: 18
1st-Class 200s: 2
1st-Class catches: 218
Place in batting averages: 57th av. 43.80
(2001 5th av. 75.68)
Strike rate: (career 175.00)
Parents: John and Ann

Marital status: 'Cohabiting with Claudine, my better half'
Family links with cricket: Father played for village
Education: Otford County Primary; The Judd School, Tonbridge; University of Kent
at Canterbury
Qualifications: 10 GCSEs, 3 A-levels, BA (Hons) Politics and International Relations,
advanced cricket coach, rugby coach, gym instructor qualification
Career outside cricket: Journalist
Off-season: 'Column for *Kent on Sunday*; other media activities'
Overseas tours: Kent SCA U17 to Singapore and New Zealand 1987-88; Kent to
France 1998, to Port Elizabeth 2001
Overseas teams played for: Avendale CC, Cape Town 1993-94; Victoria CC,
Cape Town 1994-95; University of WA, Perth 1995-96; Petersham-Marrickville CC,
Sydney 1998-99, 1999-2000

Career highlights to date: 'Will Kendall caught and bowled Fulton (first and only first-class victim). PCA Player of the Year 2001'

Cricket moments to forget: 'Already forgotten'

Cricketers particularly admired: Gordon Greenidge, Graham Gooch, Courtney Walsh, Steve Waugh

Young players to look out for: James Tredwell, Rob Joseph

Other sports played: Chess (England junior), table tennis ('top 10 in UK as a junior'; played for South England juniors); rugby, football, tennis, golf, squash

Other sports followed: Football (Nottingham Forest), rugby (Harlequins)

Relaxations: 'Reading, music, fitness; walking Poppy, our dog'

Extras: Was the last person to catch Viv Richards in a first-class match, in 1993. Set record for the longest innings ever played by a Kent batsman in scoring his 207 against Yorkshire at Maidstone in 1998. Has best catching strike rate in Kent fielding history. Scored double century (208*) and century (104*) v Somerset at Canterbury 2001, also taking seven catches in the match; followed up with 197 v Northamptonshire at Northampton in next Championship innings. Scored 196 v Northamptonshire at Canterbury 2001, in the process equalling Arthur Fagg's 1938 season tally of nine centuries for Kent, one behind Frank Woolley's Kent record of ten, set in 1928 and 1934. First batsman to 1000 first-class runs in 2001 and the season's leading English batsman in terms of runs scored (second overall) and average (fifth overall) with 1892 runs (av. 75.68). Kent Batsman of the Year (Denness Award) 2001. PCA Player of the Year 2001. Captain of Kent in County Championship 2002 (*see entry on Matthew Fleming*); appointed captain of Kent for 2003

Opinions on cricket: 'I'm concerned about EU-qualified players flooding into our game. Counties while trying to run their businesses successfully must not lose sight of the bigger picture.'

Best batting: 208* Kent v Somerset, Canterbury 2001

Best bowling: 1-37 Kent v Oxford University, Canterbury 1996

2002 Season

	M	Inns	NO	Runs	HS	Avge	100s	50s	Ct	St	O	M	Runs	Wkts	Avge	Best	5wI	10wM
Test																		
All First	17	33	2	1358	177	43.80	4	4	33	-								
1-day Int																		
C & G	4	4	1	159	62	53.00	-	1	1	-								
B & H	5	4	0	165	80	41.25	-	1	1	-								
1-day Lge	10	10	1	192	41 *	21.33	-	-	2	-								

Career Performances

	M	Inns	NO	Runs	HS	Avge	100s	50s	Ct	St	Balls	Runs	Wkts	Avge	Best	5wI	10wM
Test																	
All First	142	250	16	8543	208 *	36.50	20	34	218	-	175	112	1	112.00	1-37	-	-
1-day Int																	
C & G	15	15	1	351	63	25.07	-	2	9	-	6	9	0	-		-	-
B & H	7	6	0	207	80	34.50	-	1	4	-							
1-day Lge	43	43	1	730	82	17.38	-	2	20	-							

GAIT, A. I. Derbyshire

Name: <u>Andrew</u> Ian Gait
Role: Right-hand opening bat
Born: 19 December 1978, Bulawayo, Zimbabwe
Height: 6ft 1in **Weight:** 13st 7lbs
Nickname: Bob, Gaitor, The Hammer
County debut: 2002
1st-Class 50s: 13
1st-Class 100s: 3
1st-Class catches: 33
Place in batting averages: 133rd av. 30.71
Parents: Roger and Hazel
Marital status: Single
Education: Warner Beach Primary School, KwaZulu-Natal, South Africa; Kearsney College, KwaZulu-Natal; 'studying through University of South Africa'
Qualifications: Level 2 coaching, studying for Bachelor of Commerce degree
Career outside cricket: 'Busy studying, coaching, and barman'
Off-season: Back in South Africa visiting family; possibly travelling
Overseas tours: South African National Academy to Kenya and Zimbabwe 1998
Overseas teams played for: Free State 1998-2001
Career highlights to date: 'Chasing 400-plus in fourth innings and winning v Natal 1999-2000; scored 101'
Cricket moments to forget: 'Losing to Natal in a Standard Bank game in the 2000-01 season' (*Free State lost by 12 runs under the Duckworth/Lewis method, four wickets falling in a single over bowled by Jonathan Bastow*)
Cricketers particularly admired: Allan Donald, Steve Waugh, Jacques Kallis
Young players to look out for: Kevin Pietersen, Jim Troughton, Graeme Smith
Other sports played: Squash, kick boxing

Other sports followed: Rugby (Natal Sharks)

Relaxations: Gym, running; beach, outdoors; music

Extras: Represented South Africa U19 in U19 World Cup 1997-98. Set Free State record for highest individual score in one-day cricket (138*). Scored 101 in the highest successful fourth-innings run chase by a South African province – 443 by Free State v KwaZulu-Natal at Durban 1999-2000. Scored maiden Championship century (175) v Northamptonshire at Northampton 2002. Holds a British passport and is not considered an overseas player

Opinions on cricket: 'I found the 2002 season to be a great learning experience for me. I think one plays too much cricket in the UK and the pitches need to be better!'

Best batting: 175 Derbyshire v Northamptonshire, Northampton 2002

2002 Season

	M	Inns	NO	Runs	HS	Avge	100s	50s	Ct	St	O	M	Runs	Wkts	Avge	Best	5wI	10wM
Test																		
All First	17	33	1	983	175	30.71	1	8	14	-								
1-day Int																		
C & G	1	1	0	0	0	0.00	-	-	-	-								
B & H																		
1-day Lge	8	8	0	102	30	12.75	-	-	3	-								

Career Performances

	M	Inns	NO	Runs	HS	Avge	100s	50s	Ct	St	Balls	Runs	Wkts	Avge	Best	5wI	10wM
Test																	
All First	36	68	1	1920	175	28.65	3	13	33	-							
1-day Int																	
C & G	1	1	0	0	0	0.00	-	-	-	-							
B & H																	
1-day Lge	8	8	0	102	30	12.75	-	-	3	-							

31. Who was capped by Worcestershire in 1991 and is now the county's director of cricket?

GALE, A. W.   Yorkshire

Name: <u>Andrew</u> William Gale
Role: Left-hand bat
Born: 28 November 1983, Dewsbury
Height: 6ft 2in **Weight:** 13st
Nickname: Galey
County debut: No first-team appearance
Parents: Denise and Alan
Marital status: Single
Education: Gomersal First School;
Heckmondwike Grammar/Whitcliffe Mount
Qualifications: 10 GCSEs, 3 A-levels,
Level 1 cricket coaching
Off-season: Touring with England U19
Overseas tours: England U17 to Australia
2001; England U19 to Australia 2002-03;
Yorkshire to Grenada 2002
Career highlights to date: '164 for
Yorkshire 2nd XI v Leicestershire 2nd XI
2002. 77 for England U19 v India U19 2002'
Cricket superstitions: 'Don't like odd numbers'
Cricketers particularly admired: Marcus Trescothick, Michael Vaughan
Young players to look out for: Tim Bresnan, Bilal Shafayat
Other sports played: Football, golf
Other sports followed: Football (Huddersfield Town)
Relaxations: 'Golf and listening to music'
Extras: Has played for England since U15 level. Played for Yorkshire Board XI in the
C&G 2002 and in the second round of the C&G 2003, which was played in September
2002. Yorkshire League Young Batsman of the Year 2002

2002 Season (did not make any first-class or one-day appearances for his county)

Career Performances

	M	Inns	NO	Runs	HS	Avge	100s	50s	Ct	St	Balls	Runs	Wkts	Avge	Best	5wl	10wM
Test																	
All First																		
1-day Int																		
C & G	3	3	0	35	17	11.66	-	-	1	-							
B & H																		
1-day Lge																		

GALLIAN, J. E. R.   Nottinghamshire

Name: <u>Jason</u> Edward Riche Gallian
Role: Right-hand bat, right-arm
medium bowler, county club captain and
captain in first-class cricket
Born: 25 June 1971, Manly, NSW, Australia
Height: 6ft **Weight:** 14st
Nickname: Gal
County debut: 1990 (Lancashire),
1998 (Nottinghamshire)
County cap: 1994 (Lancashire),
1998 (Nottinghamshire)

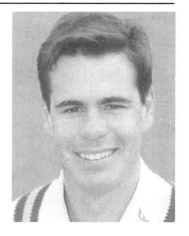

Test debut: 1995
Tests: 3
1000 runs in a season: 3
1st-Class 50s: 42
1st-Class 100s: 21
1st-Class 300s: 1
1st-Class 5 w. in innings: 1
1st-Class catches: 128
One-Day 100s: 7
One-Day 5 w. in innings: 1
Place in batting averages: 74th av. 41.80
Strike rate: (career 71.40)
Parents: Ray and Marilyn
Wife and date of marriage: Charlotte, 2 October 1999
Children: Tom, 12 April 2001
Family links with cricket: Father played for Stockport
Education: The Pittwater House Schools, Australia; Oxford University
Qualifications: Higher School Certificate, Diploma in Social Studies
(Keble College, Oxford)
Off-season: 'Australia over the Christmas period. Best man at mate's wedding.
Looking for employment'
Overseas tours: Australia U20 to West Indies 1989-90; England A to India 1994-95,
to Pakistan 1995-96, to Australia 1996-97; England to South Africa 1995-96;
Nottinghamshire to Johannesburg 2000, to South Africa 2001
Overseas teams played for: NSW U19 1988-89; NSW Colts and NSW 2nd XI 1990-
91; Manly 1993-94
Career highlights to date: 'Playing Test cricket'
Cricket moments to forget: 'Breaking a finger in my first Test match'
Cricket superstitions: 'None'
Cricketers particularly admired: Desmond Haynes, Mike Gatting
Young players to look out for: Bilal Shafayat

Other sports followed: Rugby league and union, football

Relaxations: Listening to music, playing golf

Extras: Represented Australia YC 1988-90; was captain v England YC 1989-90. Represented Australia U20 and U21 1991-92. Took wicket of D. A. Hagan of Oxford University with his first ball in first-class cricket 1990. Played for Oxford University in 1992 and for Combined Universities in the B&H Cup 1992. Captained Oxford University 1993. Recorded highest individual score in history of Old Trafford with his 312 v Derbyshire in 1996. Left Lancashire during the 1997-98 off-season and joined Nottinghamshire for 1998, being appointed captain after resignation of Paul Johnson; appointed Nottinghamshire club captain and captain in first-class cricket for 2003 (*see entry on Chris Cairns*). Scored 91 v Leicestershire at Trent Bridge in the NUL 2002, in the process sharing with Nicky Boje (86) in a record fourth-wicket partnership for Nottinghamshire in the one-day league (190). Scored 111* opening the innings as Nottinghamshire reached 323-9 to beat Derbyshire in the Championship at Derby 2002; at one point Nottinghamshire had been 170-5 and his stand of 46* with Greg Smith was a Nottinghamshire record for the last wicket to win a match

Opinions on cricket: 'Two divisions is very good. Four-day cricket needs to be more intense.'

Best batting: 312 Lancashire v Derbyshire, Old Trafford 1996

Best bowling: 6-115 Lancashire v Surrey, Southport 1996

2002 Season

	M	Inns	NO	Runs	HS	Avge	100s	50s	Ct	St	O	M	Runs	Wkts	Avge	Best	5wI	10wM
Test																		
All First	16	29	3	1087	171	41.80	4	6	16	-								
1-day Int																		
C & G	2	2	0	74	69	37.00	-	1	2	-								
B & H	5	4	0	103	56	25.75	-	1	1	-								
1-day Lge	12	12	1	307	91	27.90	-	2	2	-								

Career Performances

	M	Inns	NO	Runs	HS	Avge	100s	50s	Ct	St	Balls	Runs	Wkts	Avge	Best	5wI	10wM
Test	3	6	0	74	28	12.33	-	-	1	-	84	62	0	-	-	-	-
All First	157	274	26	9211	312	37.14	22	42	128	-	6712	3825	94	40.69	6-115	1	-
1-day Int																	
C & G	16	16	1	516	101 *	34.40	1	4	10	-	162	122	1	122.00	1-11	-	
B & H	39	37	2	1098	134	31.37	2	7	7	-	725	621	17	36.52	5-15	1	
1-day Lge	102	100	10	2963	130	32.92	4	16	34	-	844	825	28	29.46	2-10	-	

GANNON, B. W.   Gloucestershire

Name: Benjamin Ward Gannon
Role: Right-hand bat, right-arm
medium bowler
Born: 5 September 1975, Oxford
Height: 6ft 3in **Weight:** 13st 7lbs
Nickname: Louis, Ganja
County debut: 1999
1st-Class 5 w. in innings: 3
1st-Class catches: 8
Place in bowling averages: 129th av. 41.73
Strike rate: 64.80 (career 50.84)
Parents: Martin and Jane
Marital status: Single
Education: Dragon School, Oxford;
Abingdon School; Cheltenham and
Gloucester College of Higher Education
Qualifications: 3 A-levels, BSc (Hons)
Sports Science and Physical Geography,

coaching awards in football, rugby and cricket, fitness qualifications
Overseas tours: Gloucestershire to Zimbabwe 1997, to South Africa 2000, 2001;
Forest Nomads to Zimbabwe 1998
Overseas teams played for: Waverley, Sydney 1993-94; Union CC, Port Elizabeth
2000; Easterns CC, Cape Town 2001
Career highlights to date: 'Making debut against Glamorgan'
Cricketers particularly admired: Courtney Walsh, Curtly Ambrose, Glenn McGrath,
'Syd' Lawrence
Young players to look out for: Steve Harmison, Simon Jones
Other sports played: 'I'll have a go at most sports'
Other sports followed: Boxing, rugby, tennis, athletics, climbing
Relaxations: Listening to music, keeping fit, travelling, photography
Extras: NBC Denis Compton Award 1999. Released by Gloucestershire at the end of
the 2002 season
Opinions on cricket: 'Opinions often fall on deaf ears anyway, so take the view that the
individual should be given the responsibility and trust to make his/her own destiny.'
Best batting: 28 Gloucestershire v Essex, Colchester 2000
Best bowling: 6-80 Gloucestershire v Glamorgan, Cardiff 1999

2002 Season

	M	Inns	NO	Runs	HS	Avge	100s	50s	Ct	St	O	M	Runs	Wkts	Avge	Best	5wI	10wM
Test																		
All First	7	8	4	31	14	7.75	-	-	1	-	162	36	626	15	41.73	3-41	-	-
1-day Int																		
C & G																			
B & H																			
1-day Lge																			

Career Performances

	M	Inns	NO	Runs	HS	Avge	100s	50s	Ct	St	Balls	Runs	Wkts	Avge	Best	5wI	10wM
Test																	
All First	31	36	16	187	28	9.35	-	-	8	-	4322	2730	85	32.11	6-80	3	-
1-day Int																	
C & G																		
B & H																		
1-day Lge																		

GAZZARD, C. M. Somerset

Name: <u>Carl</u> Matthew Gazzard
Role: Right-hand bat, wicket-keeper
Born: 15 April 1982, Penzance
Height: 6ft **Weight:** 13st
Nickname: Gazza, Sling Boy
County debut: 2002
1st-Class catches: 3
1st-Class stumpings: 1
Parents: Paul and Alison
Marital status: Single
Family links with cricket: Father and
brother both played for Cornwall Schools;
mother's a keen follower
Education: St Mary's Roman Catholic
School, Penzance; Mounts Bay
Comprehensive; Richard Huish College,
Taunton
Qualifications: 10 GCSEs, 2 A-levels, Level
1 and 2 coaching
Off-season: 'Playing grade cricket in Perth'
Overseas tours: Cornwall Schools U13 to Johannesburg; West of England U15 to
West Indies; Somerset Academy to Durban 1999
Overseas teams played for: Subiaco-Floreat, Perth 2000-01

Career highlights to date: 'England U19 v Sri Lanka U19 2000 – 3-0 victory in ODIs and 1st "Test" victory. First-class debut v West Indies A'
Cricket moments to forget: 'Dislocating my shoulder in Perth – kept me out for 2001 season'
Cricket superstitions: 'None'
Cricketers particularly admired: Marcus Trescothick, Graham Rose
Young players to look out for: Arul Suppiah, Peter Trego
Other sports played: Football (played through the age groups for Cornwall)
Other sports followed: Football (West Ham United)
Injuries: Out for the last four weeks of the season with a fractured little finger
Relaxations: 'Any sport, watching TV, socialising'
Extras: Played for England U13, U14, U15, U19. Won the Graham Kersey Award for Best Wicket-keeper at Bunbury Festival. Played for Cornwall in Minor Counties aged 16 and in the NatWest Trophy 1999
Best batting: 24 Somerset v West Indies A, Taunton 2002

2002 Season

	M	Inns	NO	Runs	HS	Avge	100s	50s	Ct	St	O	M	Runs	Wkts	Avge	Best	5wI	10wM
Test																		
All First	1	2	0	31	24	15.50	-	-	3	1								
1-day Int																		
C & G																		
B & H																		
1-day Lge																		

Career Performances

	M	Inns	NO	Runs	HS	Avge	100s	50s	Ct	St	Balls	Runs	Wkts	Avge	Best	5wI	10wM
Test																	
All First	1	2	0	31	24	15.50	-	-	3	1							
1-day Int																	
C & G	1	1	0	16	16	16.00	-	-	2	-							
B & H																	
1-day Lge																	

---

95. Who played Test cricket for India in 1946, made his Warwickshire debut in 1948 and went on to captain Pakistan in their inaugural Test in 1952-53?

GIDDINS, E. S. H. Hampshire

Name: Edward (<u>Ed</u>) Simon Hunter Giddins
Role: Right-hand bat, right-arm
medium-fast swing bowler
Born: 20 July 1971, Eastbourne
Height: 6ft 4in **Weight:** 14st
Nickname: Chief
County debut: 1991 (Sussex),
1998 (Warwickshire), 2001 (Surrey)
County cap: 1994 (Sussex),
1998 (Warwickshire)
Test debut: 1999
Tests: 4
50 wickets in a season: 4
1st-Class 5 w. in innings: 22
1st-Class 10 w. in match: 2
1st-Class catches: 22
One-Day 5 w. in innings: 2
Place in batting averages: (2001 276th
av. 6.00)
Place in bowling averages: 91st av. 33.45 (2001 102nd av. 36.73)
Strike rate: 63.50 (career 53.30)
Parents: Simon and Pauline
Marital status: 'Attached to Claire'
Children: Isabella, 28 May 2002
Education: St Bede's School, Eastbourne; Eastbourne College
Qualifications: 8 O-levels, 2 A-levels, Level 1 coaching certificate
Career outside cricket: 'Property developer and hen-party transporter'
Off-season: 'I own a limousine company with a difference (the vehicles are fire
engines). My co-owner Tom Porter (ex-Chippendale) and I specialise in hen parties'
Overseas tours: England A to Pakistan 1995-96
Overseas teams played for: Mosman, Sydney 1994-95
Career highlights to date: '5-15 and Man of the Match at Lord's 2000. B&H Cup
win with Surrey 2001'
Cricket superstitions: 'Left first'
Cricketers particularly admired: Ian Gould, Eddie Hemmings
Other sports played: Golf
Other sports followed: Football (Fulham FC)
Relaxations: Travel
Extras: Joined Warwickshire for the 1998 season. Recorded maiden Test five-wicket
return (5-15; 7-42 in match) in the first Test v Zimbabwe, Lord's 2000, winning the
Man of the Match award. Left Warwickshire during the 2000-01 off-season and joined
Surrey for 2001. C&G Man of the Match award v Surrey Board XI at Guildford 2001.

Left Surrey at the end of the 2002 season and has joined Hampshire for 2003
Best batting: 34 Sussex v Essex, Hove 1995
Best bowling: 6-47 Sussex v Yorkshire, Eastbourne 1996

2002 Season

	M	Inns	NO	Runs	HS	Avge	100s	50s	Ct	St	O	M	Runs	Wkts	Avge	Best	5wl	10wM
Test																		
All First	7	7	4	23	9	7.66	-	-	1	-	232.5	49	736	22	33.45	4-113	-	-
1-day Int																		
C & G	4	0	0	0	0	-	-	-	1	-	29	2	186	4	46.50	2-9	-	
B & H	4	3	1	5	5*	2.50	-	-	-	-	34	3	150	0	-	-	-	
1-day Lge	14	7	6	26	13*	26.00	-	-	4	-	107	10	435	30	14.50	5-20	1	

Career Performances

	M	Inns	NO	Runs	HS	Avge	100s	50s	Ct	St	Balls	Runs	Wkts	Avge	Best	5wl	10wM
Test	4	7	3	10	7	2.50	-	-	-	-	444	240	12	20.00	5-15	1	-
All First	144	171	73	524	34	5.34	-	-	22	-	24787	13226	465	28.44	6-47	22	2
1-day Int																	
C & G	23	7	4	27	13	9.00	-	-	5	-	1337	878	25	35.12	3-24	-	
B & H	33	13	7	13	5*	2.16	-	-	7	-	1724	1108	38	29.15	5-21	1	
1-day Lge	124	50	22	67	13*	2.39	-	-	22	-	5291	4112	148	27.78	5-20	1	

GIDMAN, A. P. R.   Gloucestershire

Name: Alexander (<u>Alex</u>) Peter
Richard Gidman
Role: Right-hand bat, right-arm fast-medium
bowler; all-rounder
Born: 22 June 1981, High Wycombe
Height: 6ft 2in **Weight:** 13st 8lbs
Nickname: A.P.R., Gidders, Giddo
County debut: 2001 (one-day),
2002 (first-class)
1st-Class 50s: 4
1st-Class 100s: 1
1st-Class catches: 5
Place in batting averages: 110th av. 34.87
Place in bowling averages: 136th av. 44.20
Strike rate: 59.40 (career 59.40)
Parents: Alistair and Jane
Marital status: Single
Family links with cricket: 'All male family
members love it. Younger brother plays GCCC Youth'

Education: Dean Close; Wycliffe College
Qualifications: 7 GCSEs, 1 A-level, GNVQ in Leisure and Tourism
Overseas tours: MCC Young Cricketers to Cape Town 1999
Overseas teams played for: Albion, New Zealand
Career highlights to date: 'Debut for Gloucestershire'
Cricket moments to forget: 'Surrey 2nd XI scoring 400 v MCC Young Cricketers in one-day game'
Cricketers particularly admired: Steve Waugh, Brett Lee
Young players to look out for: Will Gidman, Mark Wright
Other sports played: Rugby (Gloucester U17 trials), football (Stroud district)
Other sports followed: Rugby (Gloucester RFC), football (Wolverhampton Wanderers)
Relaxations: Golf, drinking coffee
Extras: Played for Gloucestershire Board XI in the C&G 2001 and in the first and second rounds of the C&G 2002, which were played in August and September 2001. Scored 67 on first-class debut v Derbyshire at Derby 2002. Scored maiden first-class century (117) v Northamptonshire at Bristol 2002
Opinions on cricket: 'Encourage people to be positive rather than negative towards the game.'
Best batting: 117 Gloucestershire v Northamptonshire, Bristol 2002
Best bowling: 3-33 Gloucestershire v Middlesex, Cheltenham 2002

2002 Season

	M	Inns	NO	Runs	HS	Avge	100s	50s	Ct	St	O	M	Runs	Wkts	Avge	Best	5wI	10wM
Test																		
All First	10	17	1	558	117	34.87	1	4	5	-	99	16	442	10	44.20	3-33	-	-
1-day Int																		
C & G	1	1	0	11	11	11.00	-	-	-	-								
B & H	2	0	0	0	0	-	-	-	-	-	4	0	26	0	-	-	-	
1-day Lge	10	8	1	137	48	19.57	-	-	4	-	7	0	46	3	15.33	3-46	-	

Career Performances

	M	Inns	NO	Runs	HS	Avge	100s	50s	Ct	St	Balls	Runs	Wkts	Avge	Best	5wI	10wM
Test																	
All First	10	17	1	558	117	34.87	1	4	5	-	594	442	10	44.20	3-33	-	-
1-day Int																	
C & G	4	4	0	61	23	15.25	-	-	1	-	129	106	1	106.00	1-43	-	
B & H	2	0	0	0	0	-	-	-	-	-	24	26	0	-	-	-	
1-day Lge	11	9	1	144	48	18.00	-	-	4	-	42	46	3	15.33	3-46	-	

GILES, A. F. Warwickshire

Name: <u>Ashley</u> Fraser Giles
Role: Right-hand bat, slow left-arm bowler
Born: 19 March 1973, Chertsey
Height: 6ft 4in **Weight:** 15st 7lbs
Nickname: Splash, Skinny
County debut: 1993
County cap: 1996
Test debut: 1998
Tests: 18
One-Day Internationals: 21
50 wickets in a season: 2
1st-Class 50s: 14
1st-Class 100s: 3
1st-Class 5 w. in innings: 19
1st-Class 10 w. in match: 3
1st-Class catches: 55
One-Day 100s: 1
One-Day 5 w. in innings: 3
Place in batting averages: 216th av. 22.00
Place in bowling averages: 95th av. 33.94 (2001 93rd av. 35.75)
Strike rate: 69.86 (career 69.16)
Parents: Michael and Paula
Wife and date of marriage: Stine, 9 October 1999
Children: Anders Fraser, 29 May 2000; Matilde, February 2002
Family links with cricket: 'Dad played and brother Andrew still plays club cricket at Ripley, Surrey'
Education: Kingfield Primary School, Old Woking; George Abbott County Secondary, Burpham, Guildford
Qualifications: 9 GCSEs, 2 A-levels, coaching certificate
Off-season: Touring with England to Australia
Overseas tours: Surrey U19 to Barbados 1990-91; Warwickshire to Cape Town 1996, 1997, to Bloemfontein 1998; England A to Australia 1996-97, to Kenya and Sri Lanka 1997-98; England to Sharjah (Champions Trophy) 1997-98, to Bangladesh (Wills International Cup) 1998, to Australia 1998-99 (CUB Series), to South Africa and Zimbabwe 1999-2000 (one-day series), to Kenya (ICC Knockout Trophy) 2000-01, to Pakistan and Sri Lanka 2000-01, to India and New Zealand 2001-02, to Sri Lanka (ICC Champions Trophy) 2002-03, to Australia 2002-03
Overseas teams played for: Vredenburg/Saldanha, Cape Town 1992-95; Avendale CC, Cape Town 1995-96
Cricketers particularly admired: Dermot Reeve, Tim Munton, Dougie Brown, Ian Botham
Young players to look out for: Ian Bell

Other sports played: Golf (14 handicap), football ('Klinsmann')
Other sports followed: Football (QPR)
Relaxations: 'Cinema, music, spending lots of time with my family'
Extras: Surrey Young Cricketer of the Year 1991. Scored 83 v Worcestershire at Worcester 1996, in the process sharing in then record Warwickshire partnership for tenth wicket (141) with Tim Munton. NBC Denis Compton Award for Warwickshire in 1996. Warwickshire Player of the Year in 1996 and 2000. Warwickshire Most Improved Player 1996. Cricket Society's Leading Young All-rounder 1996. Scored hundred (123*) and took five wickets in an innings (5-28) in same match (v Oxford University at The Parks) in 1999, the first time this feat had been performed by a Warwickshire player since Tom Cartwright achieved it v Lancashire at Edgbaston in 1961. Shared in record Warwickshire partnership for seventh wicket (289 with Dougie Brown v Sussex at Hove 2000), in the process scoring 128*, the best by a Warwickshire No. 8. Took 23 wickets (12-135 and 11-196) in two games v Northamptonshire 2000. Took 17 Test wickets in series v Pakistan 2000-01, the highest total by an England bowler in a series in Pakistan. Returned figures of 4-11 from 9.1 overs as Sri Lanka were bowled out for 81 in their second innings of the third Test at Colombo 2000-01. Returned innings figures of 5-67 from 43.3 overs v India at Ahmedabad 2001-02 on his return to Test cricket after an Achilles tendon operation in July 2001. Man of the Match for his 5-57 (including spell of 5-10 in 19 balls) in One-Day International v India at Delhi 2001-02. Took three wickets for no runs in ten balls to finish Sri Lanka's second innings in third Test at Old Trafford 2002, leaving England six overs to make 50 runs for victory. Scored 68 v Kent at Edgbaston 2002, in the process sharing with Jim Troughton (115) in a record sixth-wicket partnership for Warwickshire in matches against Kent (124). ECB 12-month contract 2002-03
Best batting: 128* Warwickshire v Sussex, Hove 2000
Best bowling: 8-90 Warwickshire v Northamptonshire, Northampton 2000
Stop press: Suffered fractured left wrist after being struck by a ball from Steve Harmison during net practice ahead of the second Test v Australia at Adelaide 2002-03. Selected for England squad for 2002-03 World Cup

2002 Season

	M	Inns	NO	Runs	HS	Avge	100s	50s	Ct	St	O	M	Runs	Wkts	Avge	Best	5wI	10wM
Test	5	6	0	130	45	21.66	-	-	2	-	203.3	34	544	11	49.45	4-62	-	-
All First	9	12	0	264	68	22.00	-	1	3	-	419.1	67	1222	36	33.94	7-142	3	1
1-day Int	4	1	1	2	2 *	-	-	-	-	-	30	1	157	5	31.40	3-39	-	
C & G																		
B & H	5	2	1	24	21 *	24.00	-	-	-	-	50	2	193	7	27.57	2-29	-	
1-day Lge	4	2	1	3	2	3.00	-	-	1	-	29.1	1	127	4	31.75	3-27	-	

Career Performances

	M	Inns	NO	Runs	HS	Avge	100s	50s	Ct	St	Balls	Runs	Wkts	Avge	Best	5wI	10wM
Test	18	26	5	307	45	14.61	-	-	11	-	4657	1911	49	39.00	5-67	2	-
All First	124	168	34	3546	128 *	26.46	3	14	55	-	26213	10429	379	27.51	8-90	19	3
1-day Int	21	12	4	93	21 *	11.62	-	-	4	-	984	793	22	36.04	5-57	1	
C & G	20	14	4	373	107	37.30	1	2	3	-	1067	703	31	22.67	5-21	1	
B & H	24	16	4	212	37	17.66	-	-	9	-	1012	747	29	25.75	3-22	-	
1-day Lge	85	55	12	769	57	17.88	-	1	27	-	3168	2298	111	20.70	5-36	1	

GOLDING, J. M. Kent

Name: <u>James</u> Matthew Golding
Role: Right-hand bat, right-arm
fast-medium bowler; all-rounder
Born: 19 July 1977, Canterbury
Height: 6ft 4in **Weight:** 16st 7lbs
Nickname: Goldy, Jingo
County debut: 1999
1st-Class catches: 2
Place in batting averages: (2001 227th
av. 15.00)
Strike rate: 60.16 (career 83.00)
Parents: Marilyn and Adrian
Marital status: Single
Education: St Anne's, Canterbury; Kent
College, Canterbury; University College,
Worcester
Qualifications: 9 GCSEs, 3 A-levels,
BSc (Hons) Geography with Sports Science,
Level II cricket coach, Level I hockey coach

Overseas tours: Kent to Port Elizabeth 2001
Overseas teams played for: Kensington District CC, Adelaide 1995-96; Balcatta CC,
Perth 2000-01
Career highlights to date: 'Kent winning Norwich Union League 2001'
Cricket moments to forget: 'Being struck into the top tier of the Frank Woolley Stand
at Canterbury'
Cricketers particularly admired: Ian Botham, David Gower, Jacques Kallis,
Allan Donald, Graeme Hick
Young players to look out for: Robin Jackson, Ian Gascoigne, Andy Alford,
Rupert Swetman
Other sports played: 'All ball sports, particularly hockey, golf and tennis'
Other sports followed: 'Keep an eye on most, apart from horse racing'

Relaxations: Socialising, other sports, gym
Extras: Played for Kent Board XI in the NatWest 1999, winning the Man of the Match award v Hampshire in the third round. Made first-class debut for Kent v New Zealanders 1999 while still an amateur; his first wicket was New Zealand captain Stephen Fleming. Took 4-42 v Indians in a 50-over match at Canterbury 2002. Released by Kent at the end of the 2002 season
Opinions on cricket: 'More day/nighters – encourages younger audience.'
Best batting: 32 Kent v Warwickshire, Maidstone 2002
Best bowling: 4-76 Kent v Sri Lankans, Canterbury 2002

2002 Season

	M	Inns	NO	Runs	HS	Avge	100s	50s	Ct	St	O	M	Runs	Wkts	Avge	Best	5wI	10wM
Test																		
All First	4	5	3	113	32	56.50	-	-	-	-	60.1	10	195	6	32.50	4-76	-	-
1-day Int																		
C & G	2	2	0	13	13	6.50	-	-	-	-	12.1	1	68	1	68.00	1-38	-	
B & H	4	3	1	52	34 *	26.00	-	-	1	-	30	3	138	4	34.50	2-24	-	
1-day Lge	12	8	4	128	47 *	32.00	-	-	3	-	72	4	324	18	18.00	3-23	-	

Career Performances

	M	Inns	NO	Runs	HS	Avge	100s	50s	Ct	St	Balls	Runs	Wkts	Avge	Best	5wI	10wM
Test																	
All First	11	16	7	224	32	24.88	-	-	2	-	1162	637	14	45.50	4-76	-	-
1-day Int																	
C & G	6	4	0	65	47	16.25	-	-	2	-	241	228	1	228.00	1-38	-	
B & H	11	8	3	135	34 *	27.00	-	-	3	-	415	346	15	23.06	3-20	-	
1-day Lge	20	15	6	170	47 *	18.88	-	-	3	-	714	501	23	21.78	3-23	-	

GOODE, C. M.   Northamptonshire

Name: Christopher (<u>Chris</u>) Martin Goode
Role: Right-hand bat, right-arm fast-medium bowler; all-rounder
Born: 12 October 1984, Kettering
Height: 6ft 2in **Weight:** 12st 2lbs
Nickname: Goodey
County debut: No first-team appearance
Parents: Martin and Carla
Marital status: Single
Family links with cricket: 'Dad played at local level'
Education: Finedon Mulso C of E Junior School; Huxlow Comprehensive, Irthlingborough; Tresham College, Kettering
Qualifications: 9 GCSEs, AS-level Sports Studies, Level 1 coaching
Career outside cricket: Full-time education

Off-season: 'Getting fitter'
Overseas tours: Northamptonshire U19 to South Africa 2000, 2002
Career highlights to date: 'Playing in Costcutter U15 World Cup 2000'
Cricket moments to forget: 'Getting beaten by Pakistan in the semi-final of the U15 World Cup'
Cricketers particularly admired: Allan Donald, Mal Loye, Mike Hussey
Young players to look out for: Tim Bresnan, Samit Patel
Other sports played: Football ('toured Italy with Northampton Town U16 1999')
Other sports followed: Football (Man Utd)
Injuries: Out for a quarter of the season with a back problem
Relaxations: Music
Extras: Represented England U15 in Costcutter U15 World Challenge 2000, taking 4-22 v India in opening game
Opinions on cricket: 'Enjoy it!'

GOODWIN, M. W. Sussex

Name: <u>Murray</u> William Goodwin
Role: Right-hand bat, right-arm medium/leg-spin bowler
Born: 11 December 1972, Harare, Zimbabwe
Height: 5ft 9in **Weight:** 11st 2lbs
Nickname: Muzza, Fuzz, Goodie
County debut: 2001
County cap: 2001
Test debut: 1997-98
Tests: 19
One-Day Internationals: 71
1000 runs in a season: 2
1st-Class 50s: 30
1st-Class 100s: 20
1st-Class 200s: 1
1st-Class catches: 67
One-Day 100s: 4
Place in batting averages: 68th av. 42.10 (2001 12th av. 61.25)

Strike rate: (career 95.00)
Parents: Penny and George
Wife and date of marriage: Tarsha, 13 December 1997
Family links with cricket: 'Dad is a coach. Eldest brother played for Zimbabwe'
Education: St Johns, Harare, Zimbabwe; Newtonmoore Senior High, Bunbury, Western Australia
Qualifications: Level II coach
Career outside cricket: Coaching, commentating; business
Off-season: Playing for Western Australia
Overseas tours: Australian Cricket Academy to South Africa 1992, to Sri Lanka and India 1993; Zimbabwe to Sri Lanka and New Zealand 1997-98, to Bangladesh (Wills International Cup) 1998-99, to Pakistan 1998-99, to UK, Ireland and Holland (World Cup) 1999, to South Africa 1999-2000, to West Indies 1999-2000, to England 2000
Overseas teams played for: Excelsior, Holland 1997; Mashonaland 1997-98 – 1998-99; Western Australia 1994-95 – 1996-97, 2000-01 –
Career highlights to date: 'Playing international cricket'
Cricket moments to forget: 'Test against Sri Lanka – we felt the umpiring to be very dubious' (*In the second Test v Zimbabwe 1997-98 at Colombo, chasing 326 to win, Sri Lanka won by five wickets having been 137 for five*)
Cricketers particularly admired: Allan Border, Steve Waugh, Curtly Ambrose, Sachin Tendulkar
Young players to look out for: Shaun Marsh
Other sports played: Hockey (WA Country), golf, tennis
Other sports followed: 'All'
Relaxations: 'Socialising with friends'
Extras: Emigrated to Australia aged 13. Attended Australian Cricket Academy. Made first-class debut for Western Australia v England, Perth 1994-95, scoring 91 and 77. Scored century (111) in only his second One-Day International, v Sri Lanka at Colombo 1997-98, winning Man of the Match award. Scored 166* v Pakistan at Bulawayo 1997-98, in the process sharing with Andy Flower in the highest partnership for Zimbabwe for any wicket in Tests (277*). Scored 148* for Zimbabwe v England in second Test at Trent Bridge 2000, winning Man of the Match award. Scored 112* v West Indies in NatWest Triangular Series at Riverside 2000, winning Man of the Match award. Retired from international cricket in 2000. Scored 167 for Western Australia v New South Wales at Perth in the Mercantile Mutual Cup 2000-01, setting a new record for the highest individual score in Australian domestic one-day cricket. Joined Sussex as overseas player for 2001. B&H Gold Award for his 108 v Middlesex at Hove 2001. Scored maiden first-class double century (203*) v Nottinghamshire at Trent Bridge 2001, having already scored a century (115) in the first innings; in the process of scoring his 203* he shared with Richard Montgomerie in a record partnership for any wicket for Sussex in matches against Notts (372*). Scored 87 v Essex at Hove in the Norwich Union League 2001, in the process sharing with Richard Montgomerie in a Sussex record opening partnership in the one-day league (176). Joint Sussex Player of the Year (with Richard Montgomerie) 2001. B&H Gold Award for his 62-ball 85* v Kent at Canterbury 2002

Opinions on cricket: 'Play long hours and lots of practice for little financial gain.'
Best batting: 203* Sussex v Nottinghamshire, Trent Bridge 2001
Best bowling: 2-23 Zimbabweans v Lahore City, Lahore 1998-99

2002 Season

	M	Inns	NO	Runs	HS	Avge	100s	50s	Ct	St	O	M	Runs	Wkts	Avge	Best	5wI	10wM
Test																		
All First	16	28	0	1179	162	42.10	5	3	13	-	2	1	1	0	-	-	-	-
1-day Int																		
C & G	3	3	1	158	110 *	79.00	1	-	-	-	2	0	28	0	-	-	-	
B & H	6	6	1	146	85 *	29.20	-	1	4	-								
1-day Lge	16	15	2	350	76 *	26.92	-	2	6	-								

Career Performances

	M	Inns	NO	Runs	HS	Avge	100s	50s	Ct	St	Balls	Runs	Wkts	Avge	Best	5wI	10wM
Test	19	37	4	1414	166 *	42.84	3	8	10	-	118	69	0	-	-	-	-
All First	96	169	13	6935	203 *	44.45	21	30	67	-	665	338	7	48.28	2-23	-	-
1-day Int	71	70	3	1818	112 *	27.13	2	8	20	-	248	210	4	52.50	1-12	-	
C & G	6	6	1	267	110 *	53.40	1	1	-	-	42	56	1	56.00	1-28	-	
B & H	10	10	1	368	108	40.88	1	2	5	-							
1-day Lge	31	30	5	834	87	33.36	-	8	10	-							

GOUGH, D.   *Yorkshire*

Name: Darren Gough
Role: Right-hand bat, right-arm fast bowler
Born: 18 September 1970, Barnsley
Height: 5ft 11in   **Weight:** 13st 9lbs
Nickname: Rhino, Dazzler
County debut: 1989
County cap: 1993
Benefit: 2001
Test debut: 1994
Tests: 56
One-Day Internationals: 111
50 wickets in a season: 4
1st-Class 50s: 12
1st-Class 100s: 1
1st-Class 5 w. in innings: 27
1st-Class 10 w. in match: 3
1st-Class catches: 41
One-Day 5 w. in innings: 6

Place in batting averages: (2001 176th av. 21.90)
Place in bowling averages: (2001 66th av. 31.07)
Strike rate: 57.00 (career 49.88)
Parents: Trevor and Christine
Children: Liam James, 24 November 1994; Brennan Kyle, 9 December 1997
Education: St Helens Junior; Priory Comprehensive; Airedale and Wharfdale College (part-time)
Qualifications: 2 O-levels, 5 CSEs, BTEC Leisure, NCA coaching award
Off-season: Touring Australia with England
Overseas tours: England YC to Australia 1989-90; Yorkshire to Barbados 1989-90, to South Africa 1991-92, 1992-93; England A to South Africa 1993-94; England to Australia 1994-95, 1998-99, 2002-03, to South Africa 1995-96, to India and Pakistan (World Cup) 1995-96, to Zimbabwe and New Zealand 1996-97, to Sharjah (Coca-Cola Cup) 1998-99, to South Africa and Zimbabwe 1999-2000, to Kenya (ICC Knockout Trophy) 2000-01, to Pakistan and Sri Lanka 2000-01, to India and New Zealand 2001-02 (one-day series)
Overseas teams played for: East Shirley, Christchurch, New Zealand 1991-92
Cricketers particularly admired: Shane Warne, Steve Waugh, Ian Botham, Michael Atherton, Malcolm Marshall
Young players to look out for: Michael Lumb
Other sports played: Golf, football
Other sports followed: Football (Barnsley and Tottenham Hotspur)
Relaxations: Golf, cinema
Extras: Scored 65 in his first Test innings, v New Zealand at Old Trafford 1994, batting at No. 9. Yorkshire Sports Personality of the Year 1994. Cornhill England Player of the Year 1994-95. Took a hat-trick against Kent at Headingley in 1995. Whyte and Mackay Bowler of the Year in 1996. England Player of the Series in the Texaco one-day rubber v South Africa 1998. Took 100th Test wicket (Jonty Rhodes) v South Africa at Headingley 1998. Took Test hat-trick (Healy, MacGill, Miller) v Australia at Sydney in January 1999, the first Ashes hat-trick by an England bowler since J. Hearne's at Leeds in 1899. Was third English cricketer to reach 100 One-Day International wickets. *Sheffield Star* Sports Personality of the Year. Cornhill England Player of the Year (for the second time) 1998-99. One of *Wisden*'s Five Cricketers of the Year 1999. Represented England in the 1999 World Cup. Won Freeserve Fast Ball award 2000 (for the fastest recorded ball bowled in a televised match) for a delivery timed at 93.1 mph at Lord's on 20 May during the first Test v Zimbabwe. Took 25 Test wickets v West Indies 2000 and was named England's Man of the Series. Man of the Series v Sri Lanka 2000-01 (14 wickets; av. 19.57). *GQ* Sportsman of the Year 2001. Vodafone England Cricketer of the Year 2000-01. Took 200th Test wicket (Rashid Latif) v Pakistan at Lord's 2001 in his 50th Test, in the same match passing John Snow's total of 202 wickets to move into seventh place in the list of England Test wicket-takers (*see entry on Andrew Caddick*); his 5-61 in Pakistan's first innings was also his first Test five-wicket return at Lord's. Took 146th ODI wicket (Shahid Afridi) v Pakistan at Headingley 2001, passing Ian Botham's England record of 145 ODI wickets. Made himself unavailable for Test tour of India 2001-02. Became first

England bowler to take 150 One-Day International wickets, v India at Cuttack 2001-02. Selected for the England one-day squad for the ICC Champions Trophy in Sri Lanka 2002-03 but was forced to withdraw with a knee injury; replaced by James Kirtley

Best batting: 121 Yorkshire v Warwickshire, Headingley 1996
Best bowling: 7-28 Yorkshire v Lancashire, Headingley 1995
Stop press: Forced to return home early from England tour of Australia 2002-03 after failing to recover from an injury to his right knee

2002 Season

	M	Inns	NO	Runs	HS	Avge	100s	50s	Ct	St	O	M	Runs	Wkts	Avge	Best	5wI	10wM
Test																		
All First	1	0	0	0	0	-	-	-	-	-	19	3	85	2	42.50	2-85	-	-
1-day Int	5	3	2	10	7 *	10.00	-	-	1	-	41	1	230	6	38.33	3-45	-	
C & G	1	0	0	0	0	-	-	-	-	-	10	0	52	2	26.00	2-52	-	
B & H																		
1-day Lge																		

Career Performances

	M	Inns	NO	Runs	HS	Avge	100s	50s	Ct	St	Balls	Runs	Wkts	Avge	Best	5wI	10wM
Test	56	83	18	806	65	12.40	-	2	12	-	11503	6288	228	27.57	6-42	9	-
All First	193	260	50	3379	121	16.09	1	12	41	-	35272	18712	707	26.46	7-28	27	3
1-day Int	111	71	29	455	45	10.83	-	-	17	-	6096	4384	174	25.19	5-44	2	
C & G	27	14	1	234	46	18.00	-	-	3	-	1703	991	56	17.69	7-27	2	
B & H	39	19	6	177	48 *	13.61	-	-	11	-	2042	1245	45	27.66	4-17	-	
1-day Lge	106	70	20	673	72 *	13.46	-	1	19	-	4563	3291	135	24.37	5-13	2	

33. Which South African topped the Leicestershire batting averages in 1995 with 1301 Championship runs at an average of 52.04?

GOUGH, M. A.   Durham

Name: <u>Michael</u> Andrew Gough
Role: Right-hand bat, off-spin bowler, specialist gully fielder
Born: 18 December 1979, Hartlepool
Height: 6ft 5in **Weight:** 14st
Nickname: Besty
County debut: 1998
1st-Class 50s: 11
1st-Class 100s: 2
1st-Class 5 w. in innings: 1
1st-Class catches: 49
One-Day 100s: 1
Place in batting averages: 31st av. 51.33 (2001 196th av. 19.56)
Place in bowling averages: (2001 71st av. 32.07)
Strike rate: 123.00 (career 85.70)
Parents: Michael and Jean
Marital status: Engaged

Family links with cricket: 'Dad played Minor Counties cricket for Durham. Cousin Paul played for Durham U19. Uncle John was a good opening bat'
Education: Sacred Heart RC Primary School, Hartlepool; English Martyrs School and Sixth Form College, Hartlepool
Qualifications: 10 GCSEs, cricket coaching award
Off-season: 'Training; keeping in touch with (team-mate) Thorpy'
Overseas tours: Durham U21 to Sri Lanka November 1996; Durham to Sri Lanka 2001, to South Africa 2002; England U17 to Bermuda (International Youth Tournament) June 1997; England U19 to South Africa (including U19 World Cup) 1997-98, to New Zealand 1998-99 (captain); England A to Bangladesh and New Zealand 1999-2000
Overseas teams played for: Claremont-Nedlands, Perth 2001
Cricket superstitions: 'Left pad first, and left foot on and off pitch first'
Cricketers particularly admired: Brad Hodge, Jacques Kallis, Sachin Tendulkar, Rahul Dravid, Ronnie Irani
Young players to look out for: Gordon Muchall, Liam Plunkett, Gary Scott, Nigel Kent ('football!')
Other sports played: Football (had trials with Arsenal, Sheffield United and Hartlepool, and attended Middlesbrough FC School of Excellence)
Other sports followed: Football (Hartlepool United season-ticket holder)
Relaxations: 'Cinema, TV, socialising, eating out, football, music'
Extras: Captained North of England and England U15. Part of winning England U17 team at the International Youth Tournament in Bermuda 1997. Durham CCC Young

Player of the Year 1997. Scored 62 on first-class debut, against Essex at Riverside 1998. Became youngest player to score a first-class century for Durham, 123 against Cambridge University at Fenner's 1998, aged 18 years and 151 days. Captained England U19 v Australia U19 in one-day and 'Test' series 1999. C&G Man of the Match award for his 132 (his maiden one-day century) v Wales at Cardiff 2002. Scored maiden Championship century (103) v Essex at Colchester 2002. Carried his bat for 75* v Essex at Riverside 2002

Opinions on cricket: 'Far too much cricket played; not enough time for rest and preparation. Reduce amount of overs in a day. Extend tea break by ten minutes. Need to improve pitches and practice facilities.'

Best batting: 123 Durham v Cambridge University, Fenner's 1998

Best bowling: 5-66 Durham v Middlesex, Riverside 2001

2002 Season

	M	Inns	NO	Runs	HS	Avge	100s	50s	Ct	St	O	M	Runs	Wkts	Avge	Best	5wI	10wM
Test																		
All First	8	14	2	616	103	51.33	1	3	6	-	41	9	132	2	66.00	2-22	-	-
1-day Int																		
C & G	1	1	0	132	132	132.00	1	-	-	-	3	0	7	0	-		-	-
B & H	1	1	1	32	32 *	-	-	-	-	-								
1-day Lge	11	11	0	226	57	20.54	-	2	4	-	51.1	1	263	6	43.83	3-26	-	

Career Performances

	M	Inns	NO	Runs	HS	Avge	100s	50s	Ct	St	Balls	Runs	Wkts	Avge	Best	5wI	10wM
Test																	
All First	54	94	3	2368	123	26.02	2	11	49	-	2314	1241	27	45.96	5-66	1	-
1-day Int																	
C & G	5	4	0	195	132	48.75	1	-	2	-	84	71	0	-		-	-
B & H	7	7	1	168	58	28.00	-	1	2	-	199	152	6	25.33	3-36	-	
1-day Lge	27	24	3	449	57	21.38	-	2	7	-	697	585	13	45.00	3-26	-	

34. Name the overseas cricketers who played for Surrey in 2002.

GRANT, J. B. Essex

Name: Joseph (<u>Joe</u>) Benjamin Grant
Role: Right-hand bat, right-arm
fast-medium bowler
Born: 17 December 1967, White House,
St James, Jamaica
County debut: 2001
1st-Class 5 w. in innings: 1
1st-Class catches: 6
Place in batting averages: 302nd av. 8.00
Place in bowling averages: 85th av. 32.90
Strike rate: 48.69 (career 56.17)
Overseas teams played for: Jamaica
1990-91 – 1995-96
Extras: Opened the bowling for Jamaica with
Courtney Walsh. Has played in the Yorkshire
leagues. Played for Cambridgeshire in the
Minor Counties Championship in 2001,
taking 21 wickets (av. 12.38) in three

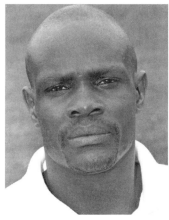

matches. Recorded maiden first-class five-wicket return (5-38) v Cambridge University
CCE at Fenner's 2002. Is not considered an overseas player
Best batting: 36* Jamaica v Guyana, Albion 1994-95
Best bowling: 5-38 Essex v CUCCE, Fenner's 2002

2002 Season

	M	Inns	NO	Runs	HS	Avge	100s	50s	Ct	St	O	M	Runs	Wkts	Avge	Best	5wl	10wM
Test																		
All First	11	12	4	64	30	8.00	-	-	-	-	267.5	50	1086	33	32.90	5-38	1	-
1-day Int																		
C & G																		
B & H																		
1-day Lge	6	2	0	2	2	1.00	-	-	3	-	37	4	127	8	15.87	3-13	-	

Career Performances

	M	Inns	NO	Runs	HS	Avge	100s	50s	Ct	St	Balls	Runs	Wkts	Avge	Best	5wl	10wM
Test																	
All First	26	31	13	154	36*	8.55	-	-	6	-	3146	2066	56	36.89	5-38	1	-
1-day Int																	
C & G																	
B & H																	
1-day Lge	6	2	0	2	2	1.00	-	-	3	-	222	127	8	15.87	3-13	-	

GRAY, A. K. D.

Yorkshire

Name: Andrew (<u>Andy</u>) Kenneth
Donovan Gray
Role: Right-hand bat, right-arm
off-spin bowler
Born: 19 May 1974, Armadale,
Western Australia
Nickname: Graysie
County debut: 2001
1st-Class 50s: 1
1st-Class catches: 2
Place in bowling averages: (2001 53rd
av. 28.10)
Strike rate: 116.40 (career 75.60)
Overseas teams played for: Willetton,
Western Australia
Extras: Played for Wilberfoss in division one
of the York Senior League. Played for
Scarborough CC for part of 2001. Played for

Worcestershire 2nd XI v Yorkshire 2nd XI at Scarborough 2001 before joining
Yorkshire. Is not considered an overseas player
Best batting: 74* Yorkshire v Leicestershire, Scarborough 2002
Best bowling: 4-128 Yorkshire v Surrey, The Oval 2001

2002 Season

	M	Inns	NO	Runs	HS	Avge	100s	50s	Ct	St	O	M	Runs	Wkts	Avge	Best	5wI	10wM
Test																		
All First	4	6	1	193	74 *	38.60	-	1	-	-	97	17	297	5	59.40	3-62	-	-
1-day Int																		
C & G																		
B & H	3	3	1	17	10 *	8.50	-	-	-	-	12	0	50	1	50.00	1-33	-	
1-day Lge	5	2	0	7	6	3.50	-	-	-	-	25	1	131	7	18.71	4-34	-	

Career Performances

	M	Inns	NO	Runs	HS	Avge	100s	50s	Ct	St	Balls	Runs	Wkts	Avge	Best	5wI	10wM
Test																	
All First	7	10	1	197	74 *	21.88	-	1	2	-	1134	578	15	38.53	4-128	-	-
1-day Int																	
C & G																	
B & H	3	3	1	17	10 *	8.50	-	-	-	-	72	50	1	50.00	1-33	-	
1-day Lge	7	4	1	28	19 *	9.33	-	-	1	-	205	180	8	22.50	4-34	-	

GRAYSON, A. P.   Essex

Name: Adrian <u>Paul</u> Grayson
Role: Right-hand opening bat, left-arm spin bowler, county vice-captain
Born: 31 March 1971, Ripon
Height: 6ft 1in **Weight:** 12st
Nickname: Larry
County debut: 1990 (Yorkshire), 1996 (Essex)
County cap: 1996 (Essex)
One-Day Internationals: 2
1000 runs in a season: 4
1st-Class 50s: 38
1st-Class 100s: 15
1st-Class 5 w. in innings: 1
1st-Class catches: 116
Place in batting averages: 115th av. 34.33 (2001 33rd av. 49.03)
Strike rate: 52.50 (career 91.53)
Parents: Adrian and Carol
Wife and date of marriage: Alison, 30 September 1994
Children: Oliver, 30 January 1997; Beth, 3 February 1999
Family links with cricket: 'Father is a staff coach; brother Simon plays when free from football commitments'
Education: Bedale; Bedale Comprehensive School
Qualifications: 8 CSEs, BTEC in Leisure Studies, Level 2 cricket coach
Off-season: 'Working for Ridley's Brewery. Football coach at Felsted School'
Overseas tours: England YC to Australia 1989-90; England to Kenya (ICC Knockout Trophy) 2000-01, to Pakistan 2000-01 (one-day series), to Zimbabwe (one-day series) 2001-02; Yorkshire to Barbados 1989-90, to Cape Town 1991, 1992, 1993, to Leeward Islands 1994
Overseas teams played for: Petone, Wellington 1991-92, 1995-96
Career highlights to date: 'Playing for England. All the trophies won with Essex'
Cricket moments to forget: 'Being bowled out for 57 in NatWest final 1996'
Cricket superstitions: 'Have a lucky vest. Left pad on first'
Cricketers particularly admired: Graham Gooch, Martyn Moxon, Darren Gough
Young players to look out for: Oliver Grayson, Ravi Bopara
Other sports played: Golf (16 handicap), football (Essex CCC charity side; was offered apprentice forms with Middlesbrough FC at 16 but signed for Yorkshire)
Other sports followed: Football (Leeds United)
Injuries: Out for eight weeks after knee surgery
Relaxations: 'Spending time with my wife and children; playing golf; watching football'

Extras: Played for England YC v New Zealand YC 1989 and Pakistan YC 1990. Yorkshire Player of the Year 1994. Released by Yorkshire at end of 1995 and joined Essex for 1996. Essex Player of the Year 1997, 2001. B&H Gold Award v Middlesex at Chelmsford 2001. Scored two centuries (173 and 149) in match v Northamptonshire at Northampton 2001. Vice-captain of Essex since 2002

Opinions on cricket: 'Three sides promoted and relegated is one too many. No heavy roller should be used after the start of the match. Better one-day pitches.'

Best batting: 189 Essex v Glamorgan, Chelmsford 2001

Best bowling: 5-20 Essex v Yorkshire, Scarborough 2001

2002 Season

	M	Inns	NO	Runs	HS	Avge	100s	50s	Ct	St	O	M	Runs	Wkts	Avge	Best	5wI	10wM
Test																		
All First	7	9	0	309	105	34.33	1	1	7	-	70	18	176	8	22.00	3-21	-	-
1-day Int																		
C & G	2	0	0	0	0	-	-	-	1	-	8	1	53	0	-	-	-	
B & H	7	5	3	103	49 *	51.50	-	-	2	-	41	0	158	2	79.00	1-30	-	
1-day Lge	8	5	1	97	29	24.25	-	-	3	-	45.3	2	167	8	20.87	3-27	-	

Career Performances

	M	Inns	NO	Runs	HS	Avge	100s	50s	Ct	St	Balls	Runs	Wkts	Avge	Best	5wI	10wM
Test																	
All First	165	270	23	7902	189	31.99	15	38	116	-	11625	5418	127	42.66	5-20	1	-
1-day Int	2	2	0	6	6	3.00	-	-	1	-	90	60	3	20.00	3-40	-	
C & G	26	20	1	446	82 *	23.47	-	3	8	-	1037	790	25	31.60	3-24	-	
B & H	38	31	9	511	49 *	23.22	-	-	9	-	1431	991	30	33.03	3-30	-	
1-day Lge	150	123	18	2018	69 *	19.21	-	6	42	-	5063	4287	138	31.06	4-25	-	

35. Which of the following is the odd man out: a) Rohan Kanhai; b) Alvin Kallicharran; c) Garfield Sobers; d) Lance Gibbs?

GREEN, J. A. G.   Sussex

Name: <u>Jeremy</u> Arthur Graham Green
Role: Right-hand bat, right-arm
fast-medium bowler
Born: 17 September 1984, Cuckfield
Height: 6ft 2in **Weight:** 12st
Nickname: Jez
County debut: No first-team appearance
(*see Extras*)
Parents: David and Janis
Marital status: Single
Family links with cricket: Father is
chairman of Sussex CCC
Education: Twineham School/Mowden
School; Lancing College
Qualifications: 11 GCSEs
Career outside cricket: Student
Off-season: At school
Overseas tours: Sussex Academy to Sri

Lanka 2001
Career highlights to date: '102 in the Sussex League to save Steyning from
relegation'
Cricket moments to forget: 'None'
Cricket superstitions: 'None'
Cricketers particularly admired: Ian Botham, Jacques Kallis
Other sports played: Golf, football, hockey, skiing
Relaxations: 'Music, friends'
Extras: Is a Sussex Academy player and has not appeared for the county in a domestic
competition but played for Sussex v West Indies A in a limited overs fixture at Hove
2002

GREENIDGE, C. G.   Northamptonshire

Name: <u>Carl</u> Gary Greenidge
Role: Right-hand bat, right-arm
fast bowler
Born: 20 April 1978, Basingstoke
Height: 5ft 10in **Weight:** 12st 7lbs
Nickname: Carlos, Carlito, G
County debut: 1998 (one-day, Surrey), 1999 (first-class, Surrey),
2002 (Northamptonshire)

50 wickets in a season: 1
1st-Class 5 w. in innings: 4
1st-Class catches: 10
Place in batting averages: 298th av. 9.41
Place in bowling averages: 76th av. 31.71
Strike rate: 48.79 (career 50.09)
Parents: Gordon and Anita
Marital status: Single
Family links with cricket: Father Gordon played for Hampshire and West Indies, as did cousin (on mother's side) Andy Roberts
Education: St Paul's, Barbados; St Michael's, Barbados; Heathcote School, Chingford; City of Westminster College
Qualifications: GNVQ Leisure and Tourism, NCA senior coaching award
Cricketers particularly admired: Malcolm Marshall, Dennis Lillee, Carl Hooper, Mark Waugh, Graham Thorpe, Ricaldo Anderson, Muazam Ali, Gareth Batty, Rupesh Amin, 'and many more'
Other sports followed: Football (Arsenal), basketball (LA Lakers)
Relaxations: 'Music, kung fu movies, PlayStation, and my bed'
Extras: Spent a year on Lord's groundstaff. Took 5-60 (8-124 the match) on Championship debut for Surrey, v Yorkshire at The Oval 1999. Released by Surrey at the end of the 2001 season and joined Northamptonshire for 2002
Best batting: 46 Northamptonshire v Derbyshire, Derby 2002
Best bowling: 6-40 Northamptonshire v Durham, Riverside 2002

2002 Season

	M	Inns	NO	Runs	HS	Avge	100s	50s	Ct	St	O	M	Runs	Wkts	Avge	Best	5wI	10wM
Test																		
All First	15	19	2	160	46	9.41	-	-	7	-	431	67	1681	53	31.71	6-40	3	-
1-day Int																		
C & G	1	1	0	12	12	12.00	-	-	1	-	10	0	73	1	73.00	1-73	-	
B & H	4	1	0	3	3	3.00	-	-	-	-	33.4	5	152	4	38.00	2-29	-	
1-day Lge	12	7	0	45	20	6.42	-	-	3	-	90.3	10	448	17	26.35	3-22	-	

Career Performances

	M	Inns	NO	Runs	HS	Avge	100s	50s	Ct	St	Balls	Runs	Wkts	Avge	Best	5wI	10wM
Test																	
All First	20	24	2	189	46	8.59	-	-	10	-	3256	2018	65	31.04	6-40	4	-
1-day Int																	
C & G	3	1	0	12	12	12.00	-	-	1	-	144	160	1	160.00	1-73	-	
B & H	5	1	0	3	3	3.00	-	-	-	-	226	174	4	43.50	2-29	-	
1-day Lge	25	12	3	51	20	5.66	-	-	10	-	977	851	26	32.73	3-22	-	

GROVE, J. O.   Leicestershire

Name: <u>Jamie</u> Oliver Grove
Role: Right-hand bat, right-arm
fast-medium bowler
Born: 3 July 1979, Bury St Edmunds
Height: 6ft 2in **Weight:** 12st 6lbs
Nickname: Groover, Grover
County debut: 1998 (Essex),
2000 (Somerset), 2002 (Leicestershire)
1st-Class 5 w. in innings: 1
1st-Class catches: 2
Strike rate: 210.00 (career 66.33)
Parents: Chris and Pat
Marital status: Single
Family links with cricket: 'Dad played
Minor Counties and brother plays local
cricket. Mum is a keen fan!'
Education: Whepstead Primary School; St
James Middle School, Bury St Edmunds;
County Upper School, Bury St Edmunds; Saxon Training College
Qualifications: 9 GCSEs, Modern Apprenticeship in Precision Engineering
Career outside cricket: Engineer
Overseas tours: England U19 to South Africa (including U19 World Cup) 1997-98
Career highlights to date: 'Taking five wickets on debut for Somerset'
Cricket moments to forget: 'Anything that involved me being hit out of the park'
Cricketers particularly admired: Ian Botham
Young players to look out for: Sam Waterson, Taylor Waterson, Matthew Wood
(Somerset), Pete Trego
Other sports played: 'All sports'
Other sports followed: Football (West Ham United)
Relaxations: 'Listening to music, chillin' with mates'
Extras: Played for England at U15, U17 and U19 level. Was part of the successful
England U19 World Cup winning squad in South Africa in 1997-98. Released by
Essex at the end of the 1999 season and joined Somerset for 2000. Recorded maiden
first-class five-wicket return (5-90) v Leicestershire at Leicester 2000 on debut for
Somerset. Member of Somerset's 2nd XI Trophy runners-up side 2001. Member of
Somerset's C&G Trophy winning squad 2001. Released by Somerset at the end of the
2001 season and joined Leicestershire for 2002
Opinions on cricket: 'Take every day as it comes.'
Best batting: 33 Essex v Surrey, Chelmsford 1998
Best bowling: 5-90 Somerset v Leicestershire, Leicester 2000

2002 Season

	M	Inns	NO	Runs	HS	Avge	100s	50s	Ct	St	O	M	Runs	Wkts	Avge	Best	5wI	10wM
Test																		
All First	2	4	0	13	6	3.25	-	-	-	-	35	6	152	1	152.00	1-75	-	-
1-day Int																		
C & G	1	0	0	0	0	-	-	-	-	-	4	0	14	0	-		-	-
B & H	6	2	2	11	9*	-	-	-	1	-	42	6	176	6	29.33	2-22	-	
1-day Lge	14	6	1	22	13	4.40	-	-	4	-	104	8	481	17	28.29	3-29	-	

Career Performances

	M	Inns	NO	Runs	HS	Avge	100s	50s	Ct	St	Balls	Runs	Wkts	Avge	Best	5wI	10wM
Test																	
All First	24	31	9	204	33	9.27	-	-	2	-	2786	2025	42	48.21	5-90	1	-
1-day Int																	
C & G	2	0	0	0	0	-	-	-	-	-	84	50	4	12.50	4-36	-	
B & H	6	2	2	11	9*	-	-	-	1	-	252	176	6	29.33	2-22	-	
1-day Lge	26	9	2	31	13	4.42	-	-	7	-	1104	919	26	35.34	3-24	-	

GUEST, C. S. Worcestershire

Name: Chris S. Guest
Role: Right-hand bat, right-arm
medium-fast bowler
Born: 5 July 1984, Wolverhampton
Height: 6ft 5in **Weight:** 15st 10lbs
Nickname: Guesty, Jo
County debut: No first-team appearance
Parents: Pam and Shaun
Marital status: Single
Family links with cricket: 'Dad played for
Fordhouses CC for 25 years'
Education: Perton Middle School; Codsall
High School; Leeds Metropolitan University
Qualifications: 11 GCSEs, 4 A-levels, Level
1 cricket coach
Career outside cricket: Student
Off-season: 'Studying'
Overseas tours: Staffordshire to Barbados
2000
Career highlights to date: 'Making 2nd XI debut'
Cricketers particularly admired: Curtly Ambrose, Glenn McGrath, Courtney Walsh
Other sports played: Football, badminton

Other sports followed: Football (Wolverhampton Wanderers)
Relaxations: 'Going to the gym; listening to music; socialising with friends'

GUNTER, N. E. L. Derbyshire

Name: <u>Neil</u> Edward Lloyd Gunter
Role: Left-hand bat, right-arm
medium-fast bowler
Born: 12 May 1981, Basingstoke
Height: 6ft
Nickname: Wolfie, Human Kiwi Fruit,
Missing Link
County debut: 2002
1st-Class catches: 3
Strike rate: 38.37 (career 38.37)
Parents: Tim and Caroline
Marital status: Single
Family links with cricket: 'Dad played club
cricket for The Mote, Maidstone'
Education: Woolton Hill Primary School;
The Clere School; Newbury College
Qualifications: GCSEs and A-levels
Off-season: 'Playing for Port Adelaide'

Overseas teams played for: Port Adelaide, South Australia 2002-03
Career highlights to date: 'Signing for Derbyshire'
Cricket moments to forget: 'NUL debut v Gloucestershire' (*Had figures of 0-80 from nine overs and was out first ball at Bristol 2002*)
Cricketers particularly admired: Kevin Dean, Paul Aldred
Young players to look out for: Nathan Dumelow
Other sports played: Snooker
Other sports followed: 'Passing interest in most sports'
Relaxations: 'Cinema, socialising, music'
Extras: Berkshire Young Player of the Year 2000. Played for Berkshire in the C&G 2001. MCC groundstaff 2001. Took 4-14 from eight overs (plus 2-39 in the first innings) on first-class debut v West Indies A at Derby 2002
Opinions on cricket: 'There are a lot more good players than are credited for. Improvements concerning the game should be done with the paying public more in mind.'
Best batting: 18 Derbyshire v West Indies A, Derby 2002
Best bowling: 4-14 Derbyshire v West Indies A, Derby 2002

2002 Season

	M	Inns	NO	Runs	HS	Avge	100s	50s	Ct	St	O	M	Runs	Wkts	Avge	Best	5wI	10wM
Test																		
All First	2	3	0	18	18	6.00	-	-	3	-	51.1	18	153	8	19.12	4-14	-	-
1-day Int																		
C & G																		
B & H																		
1-day Lge	2	1	0	0	0	0.00	-	-	-	-	12	0	91	0	-		-	-

Career Performances

	M	Inns	NO	Runs	HS	Avge	100s	50s	Ct	St	Balls	Runs	Wkts	Avge	Best	5wI	10wM
Test																	
All First	2	3	0	18	18	6.00	-	-	3	-	307	153	8	19.12	4-14	-	-
1-day Int																	
C & G	1	1	0	5	5	5.00	-	-	-	-	24	25	0	-		-	-
B & H																	
1-day Lge	2	1	0	0	0	0.00	-	-	-	-	72	91	0	-		-	-

GUY, S. M. — Yorkshire

Name: Simon Mark Guy
Role: Right-hand bat, wicket-keeper
Born: 17 November 1978, Rotherham
Height: 5ft 7in **Weight:** 10st 7lbs
Nickname: Rat
County debut: 2000
1st-Class catches: 21
1st-Class stumpings: 2
Parents: Darrell and Denise
Wife and date of marriage: Suzanne, 13 October 2001
Family links with cricket: 'Father played for Notts and Worcs 2nd XI and for Rotherham Town CC. Brothers play local cricket for Treeton CC'
Education: Listerdale Junior School; Wickersley Comprehensive School
Qualifications: GNVQ in Leisure and Recreation, qualified cricket coach, 'two years at the Yorkshire Cricket School under Ralph Middlebrook'
Career outside cricket: Currently consultant for Evolution Sportswear based in Rotherham
Off-season: 'Spending time with my family and preparing for a hard season'

Overseas tours: Yorkshire to South Africa 1999, 2001, to Grenada 2002

Overseas teams played for: Orange Cyrus, NSW 1999-2000

Career highlights to date: 'Playing the last ever County Championship game at Southampton and winning off the last ball with 13 Yorkshire and past Yorkshire men on the pitch at the same time'

Cricket moments to forget: 'On my debut against the Zimbabweans, smashing a door after getting out – but I still say it was an accident'

Cricket superstitions: 'This book is not big enough'

Cricketers particularly admired: Darren Lehmann, Jack Russell

Young players to look out for: Joe Sayers

Other sports played: 'I like to play all sports', rugby (currently Darlington RUFC; also played for South Yorkshire and Yorkshire)

Other sports followed: Rugby (Rotherham RUFC), 'Treeton Welfare CC, where all my family play'

Relaxations: 'Playing all sports, socialising with friends, watching cartoons, and eating a lot'

Extras: Set fifth-wicket partnership record in Yorkshire League (199 unbroken). Topped Yorkshire 2nd XI batting averages 1998 (106.00). Awarded 2nd XI cap 2000. Took five catches in an innings for first time for Yorkshire 1st XI 2000. Did not appear for Yorkshire in a domestic competition in 2002 but played for the county v West Indies A in a one-day fixture at Headingley

Best batting: 42 Yorkshire v Somerset, Taunton 2000

2002 Season (did not make any first-class or one-day appearances)

Career Performances

	M	Inns	NO	Runs	HS	Avge	100s	50s	Ct	St	Balls	Runs	Wkts	Avge	Best	5wl	10wM
Test																	
All First	7	11	3	148	42	18.50	-	-	21	2	24	8	0	-	-	-	-
1-day Int																	
C & G																	
B & H																	
1-day Lge																	

36. Which Australian batsman topped the 2000 first-class averages with 1124 runs at 74.93?

HABIB, A.   Essex

Name: Aftab Habib
Role: Right-hand bat
Born: 7 February 1972, Reading
Height: 5ft 9in **Weight:** 12st
Nickname: Afie, Tabby, Inzy, Habiby
County debut: 1992 (Middlesex),
1995 (Leicestershire), 2002 (Essex)
County cap: 1998 (Leicestershire),
2002 (Essex)
Test debut: 1999
Tests: 2
1000 runs in a season: 2
1st-Class 50s: 34
1st-Class 100s: 16
1st-Class 200s: 1
1st-Class catches: 59
One-Day 100s: 1

Place in batting averages: 56th av. 43.81
(2001 65th av. 41.00)
Parents: Tahira (deceased) and Hussain
Marital status: Single
Family links with cricket: Cousin of Zahid Sadiq (ex-Surrey and Derbyshire)
Education: Alfred Sutton Primary School; Edgarley Hall (Millfield Preparatory
School); Taunton School
Qualifications: 7 GCSEs, Level 2 coaching
Career outside cricket: 'Some sort of teaching'
Off-season: 'At home relaxing; going travelling'
Overseas tours: Berkshire CCC to South Africa 1996; England YC to Australia
1989-90, to New Zealand 1990-91; England A to Bangladesh and New Zealand 1999-
2000, to West Indies 2000-01
Overseas teams played for: Globe Wakatu, Nelson, New Zealand 1992-93,
1996-97; Riccarton CC, Christchurch, New Zealand 1997-98
Career highlights to date: 'Playing for England in 1999'
Cricket moments to forget: 'Losing three one-day finals and a Test match at Lord's'
Cricketers particularly admired: 'Whole Essex team', Sachin Tendulkar, Javed
Miandad, Mark Waugh, Andy Flower
Young players to look out for: Ravi Bopara, Mark Pettini, Will Jefferson, 'cousin
Furaz Amjad'
Other sports played: 'Enjoy most sports', football (Reading Schools)
Other sports followed: Football (Reading FC, Liverpool), rugby (Leicester Tigers,
New Zealand All Blacks)
Injuries: Out for four weeks with a dislocated finger

Relaxations: 'Music, reading, golf, cinema'
Extras: Played for England U15-U19. Middlesex 2nd XI Seaxe Player of the Year 1992.
Released by Middlesex at end of 1994 season. Played for Berkshire. Leicestershire 2nd XI
Player of the Year in 1995. With James Whitaker, set then record partnership for
Leicestershire for fifth wicket (320), v Worcestershire at Leicester in 1996. Championship
medals with Leicestershire in 1996 and 1998. Gold Award winner in the 1997 Benson and
Hedges Cup with 111 against Durham at Chester-le-Street. Scored 101* for England A v
New Zealand A to help save the first 'Test' at Lincoln 1999-2000. Left Leicestershire
during the 2001-02 off-season and joined Essex for 2002. Awarded Essex cap 2002
Opinions on cricket: 'Less matches would improve level of quality of games.'
Best batting: 215 Leicestershire v Worcestershire, Leicester 1996

2002 Season

	M	Inns	NO	Runs	HS	Avge	100s	50s	Ct	St	O	M	Runs	Wkts	Avge	Best	5wl	10wM
Test																		
All First	15	25	3	964	123	43.81	2	8	12	-								
1-day Int																		
C & G	3	2	1	69	40	69.00	-	-	1	-								
B & H	7	6	1	139	46	27.80	-	-	3	-								
1-day Lge	8	6	0	162	53	27.00	-	2	4	-								

Career Performances

	M	Inns	NO	Runs	HS	Avge	100s	50s	Ct	St	Balls	Runs	Wkts	Avge	Best	5wl	10wM
Test	2	3	0	26	19	8.66	-	-	-	-							
All First	118	175	26	6650	215	44.63	17	34	59	-	48	52	0	-	-	-	-
1-day Int																	
C & G	18	14	2	326	67	27.16	-	2	6	-	10	11	2	5.50	2-5	-
B & H	28	23	3	536	111	26.80	1	2	13	-							
1-day Lge	80	70	16	1509	99 *	27.94	-	7	27	-	1	4	0	-	-	-

HALL, A. J. Worcestershire

Name: Andrew James Hall
Role: Right-hand bat, right-arm fast-medium bowler; all-rounder
Born: 31 July 1975, Johannesburg, South Africa
County debut: No first-team appearance
Test debut: 2001-02
Tests: 2
One-Day Internationals: 20
1st-Class 50s: 14
1st-Class 100s: 2
1st-Class 5 w. in innings: 5

1st-Class catches: 25
Strike rate: (career 56.59)
Education: Hoërskool Alberton
Overseas tours: South Africa to Sri Lanka 2000, to Australia (Super Challenge) 2000, to Singapore (Singapore Challenge) 2000-01, to Kenya (ICC Knockout) 2000-01
Overseas teams played for: Transvaal/Gauteng; Easterns
Extras: Played indoor cricket for South Africa. Made first-class debut for Transvaal v Zimbabwe A at Johannesburg 1995-96. Was shot in the hand by a mugger in 1998. Played for Durham Board XI in the NatWest 1999 and for Suffolk in the C&G 2002. Man of the Match in tied indoor ODI v Australia at Melbourne 2000 for his 37 followed by 2-8 from three overs. Made Test debut in second

Test v Australia at Cape Town 2001-02, scoring 70 batting at No. 8. Has joined Worcestershire as an overseas player for 2003
Best batting: 153 Easterns v North West, Benoni 2001-02
Best bowling: 5-20 Gauteng v Eastern Province, Johannesburg 1999-2000
Stop press: Had match figures of 5-20 from 13 overs in first Test v Sri Lanka at Johannesburg 2002-03, including a second innings analysis of 3-1 from two overs. Had match figures of 11-99 (6-77 and 5-22) in the SuperSport Series final 2002-03, winning the Man of the Match award; was also Man of the Series with 265 runs (av. 33.12) and 36 wickets (av. 12.94). Selected for South Africa squad for 2002-03 World Cup

---

2002 Season (did not make any first-class or one-day appearances for his county)

Career Performances

	M	Inns	NO	Runs	HS	Avge	100s	50s	Ct	St	Balls	Runs	Wkts	Avge	Best	5wI	10wM
Test	2	3	1	97	70	48.50	-	1	1	-	163	108	1	108-00	1-35	-	-
All First	44	62	11	1831	153	35.90	2	14	25	-	6961	3212	123	26.11	5-20	5	-
1-day Int	20	19	2	412	81	24.23	-	1	8	-	256	208	5	41.60	2-8	-	
C & G	4	4	0	172	78	43.00	-	2	2	-	204	138	6	23.00	4-33	-	
B & H																	
1-day Lge																	

HAMBLIN, J. R. C. Hampshire

Name: James Rupert Christopher Hamblin
Role: Right-hand bat, right-arm
fast-medium bowler
Born: 16 August 1978, Pembury, Kent
Height: 6ft **Weight:** 14st
Nickname: Hambo
County debut: 2001
1st-Class 50s: 1
1st-Class catches: 4
Place in batting averages: 241st av. 18.00
Strike rate: 81.00 (career 84.85)
Parents: Bryan and Amanda
Marital status: Single
Family links with cricket: 'Father (C.B.
Hamblin) played for Oxford University
1971-73 and scored a first-class hundred'
Education: Vinehall Preparatory School;
Charterhouse School; University of the West
of England, Bristol
Qualifications: 9 GCSEs, 2 A-levels, BA (Hons) Social Science
Off-season: 'Perth, Western Australia, post-Christmas 2002'
Overseas tours: British Universities to South Africa 1999; Hampshire to
Cape Town 2000
Overseas teams played for: Harare Sports Club, Zimbabwe 1996-97; Old
Edwardians, Johannesburg 2000-01; Melville, Perth 2001-02
Career highlights to date: 'Hampshire v Sussex 2001 – 61 and 3-23'
Cricket moments to forget: 'Missing out on the Hampshire v Australians game 2001'
Cricketers particularly admired: Jim Williams, James Kirtley
Young players to look out for: John Francis, James Pyemont, Mark Hardinges
Other sports played: Rackets, golf, 'any sport really'
Other sports followed: 'All sports'
Relaxations: Playing golf and snooker
Extras: 2nd XI Player of the Month for August/September 1999 and for
August/September 2001. Played in Charterhouse Friars' *Cricketer* Cup winning side
2000; scored 174 for Charterhouse Friars v Old Whitgiftians in the first round of the
2002 *Cricketer* Cup. Took 3-23 and scored a 42-ball 61 (50 from 28 balls) v Sussex at
Hove in the Norwich Union League 2001
Opinions on cricket: 'Great to see clubs and countries having the confidence to play
younger cricketers.'
Best batting: 50 Hampshire v Kent, West End 2002
Best bowling: 2-44 Hampshire v Indians, West End 2002

2002 Season

	M	Inns	NO	Runs	HS	Avge	100s	50s	Ct	St	O	M	Runs	Wkts	Avge	Best	5wI	10wM
Test																		
All First	5	9	0	162	50	18.00	-	1	4	-	81	9	373	6	62.16	2-44	-	-
1-day Int																		
C & G																		
B & H	5	5	0	98	39	19.60	-	-	-	-	35.4	0	203	2	101.50	1-38	-	
1-day Lge	6	6	0	34	13	5.66	-	-	2	-	17	0	107	2	53.50	1-13	-	

Career Performances

	M	Inns	NO	Runs	HS	Avge	100s	50s	Ct	St	Balls	Runs	Wkts	Avge	Best	5wI	10wM
Test																	
All First	6	10	0	167	50	16.70	-	1	4	-	594	461	7	65.85	2-44	-	-
1-day Int																	
C & G																	
B & H	5	5	0	98	39	19.60	-	-	-	-	214	203	2	101.50	1-38	-	
1-day Lge	20	14	2	163	61	13.58	-	1	7	-	618	538	19	28.31	4-29	-	

HAMILTON, G. M.   Yorkshire

Name: <u>Gavin</u> Mark Hamilton
Role: Left-hand bat, right-arm medium-fast bowler
Born: 16 September 1974, Broxburn
Height: 6ft 3in **Weight:** 13st
Nickname: Hammy, Jock, Dits, 'anything Scottish'
County debut: 1994
County cap: 1998
Test debut: 1999-2000
Tests: 1
One-Day Internationals: 5
50 wickets in a season: 1
1st-Class 50s: 14
1st-Class 100s: 1
1st-Class 5 w. in innings: 9
1st-Class 10 w. in match: 2
1st-Class catches: 27
One-Day 5 w. in innings: 2
Place in batting averages: (2001 238th av. 12.66)
Place in bowling averages: (2001 36th av. 25.84)
Strike rate: 72.00 (career 49.05)

Parents: Gavin and Wendy
Marital status: Single
Family links with cricket: Father 'long-term fast bowler at club level' (Sidcup, Kent; West Lothian, Scotland). Brother opening bat for Sidcup CC and has opened batting for Scotland
Education: Dulverton Primary School, New Eltham; Hurstmere School, Sidcup
Qualifications: 10 GCSEs and two coaching awards
Overseas tours: England to South Africa and Zimbabwe 1999-2000; Yorkshire pre-season tours to South Africa, Zimbabwe and West Indies
Overseas teams played for: Welling, Municipals, and Stellenbosch University – all South Africa; Spotswood, Melbourne
Cricketers particularly admired: Craig White, Mark Robinson, Chris Adams
Young players to look out for: Matthew Wood, Vikram Solanki, Gary Fellows
Other sports played: Golf ('a lot of it'), football (Arsenal YTS)
Other sports followed: Football (Falkirk FC)
Relaxations: Listening to music and reading the paper
Extras: Took ten wickets and scored 149 runs v Glamorgan at Cardiff in 1998, the second best all-round contribution in Yorkshire history. Wetherell Award for the Cricket Society's leading all-rounder in English first-class cricket 1998; Yorkshire Players' Player of the Year 1998; Yorkshire Supporters' Player of the Year 1998. Scored 76 for Scotland v Pakistan at Chester-le-Street in the 1999 World Cup, the first 50 scored by a Scotland player in World Cup cricket. Scored 217 runs (av. 54.25) in the 1999 World Cup, more than any England batsman. Finished in top 15 of first-class batting and bowling averages 1999. Scored 57* and took 5-34 v Sussex Sharks in the National League at Scarborough 2000
Best batting: 125 Yorkshire v Hampshire, Headingley 2000
Best bowling: 7-50 Yorkshire v Surrey, Headingley 1998

2002 Season

	M	Inns	NO	Runs	HS	Avge	100s	50s	Ct	St	O	M	Runs	Wkts	Avge	Best	5wI	10wM
Test							-	-	-	-							-	-
All First	2	4	0	23	11	5.75	-	-	-	-	12	2	65	1	65.00	1-48	-	-
1-day Int																		
C & G																		
B & H																		
1-day Lge																		

Career Performances

	M	Inns	NO	Runs	HS	Avge	100s	50s	Ct	St	Balls	Runs	Wkts	Avge	Best	5wI	10wM
Test	1	2	0	0	0	0.00	-	-	-	-	90	63	0	-	-	-	-
All First	80	107	20	2253	125	25.89	1	14	27	-	11724	6067	239	25.38	7-50	9	2
1-day Int	5	5	1	217	76	54.25	-	2	1	-	214	149	3	49.66	2-36	-	
C & G	11	9	3	148	39	24.66	-	-	3	-	504	340	19	17.89	3-27	-	
B & H	19	11	4	178	31	25.42	-	-	1	-	772	516	22	23.45	4-33	-	
1-day Lge	71	50	12	712	57 *	18.73	-	2	11	-	2435	2033	81	25.09	5-16	2	

HANCOCK, T. H. C. Gloucestershire

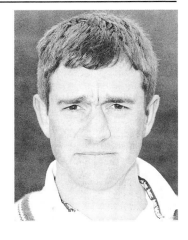

Name: Timothy (<u>Tim</u>) Harold
Coulter Hancock
Role: Right-hand bat, right-arm
medium bowler
Born: 20 April 1972, Reading
Height: 5ft 11in **Weight:** 12st 7lbs
Nickname: Herbie
County debut: 1991
County cap: 1998
1000 runs in a season: 1
1st-Class 50s: 42
1st-Class 100s: 6
1st-Class 200s: 1
1st-Class catches: 96
One-Day 100s: 1
One-Day 5 w. in innings: 1
Place in batting averages: 148th av. 29.00
(2001 187th av. 20.90)
Strike rate: (career 65.38)
Parents: John and Jennifer
Wife and date of marriage: Rachael, 26 September 1998
Children: George, 30 January 2000; Annabel Rachael, 28 August 2001
Family links with cricket: 'Dad and brother very keen players'
Education: St Piran's, Maidenhead; St Edward's, Oxford; Henley College
Qualifications: 8 GCSEs, senior coaching award
Overseas tours: Gloucestershire to Kenya 1991, to Sri Lanka 1992-93, to Zimbabwe
(two visits)
Overseas teams played for: CBC Old Boys, Bloemfontein 1991-92; Wynnum
Manley, Brisbane 1992-93; Harlequins, Durban 1994-95
Career highlights to date: 'Winning at Lord's four times and doing the treble in
one-day competitions in 2000'
Cricket moments to forget: 'Breaking my hand in fielding practice days before the
2001 B&H final'
Cricketers particularly admired: Viv Richards, Gordon Greenidge, Ian Botham
Young players to look out for: 'Nicky Peng of Durham has plenty of talent'
Other sports played: Hockey, golf
Other sports followed: 'I like to play and watch rugby, but don't do either enough'
Relaxations: 'Family life and a round of golf'
Extras: Played hockey for Oxfordshire U19. Vice-captain of Gloucestershire 2000-02.
Scored maiden one-day century (110) to win Man of the Match award in the NatWest
quarter-final v Northamptonshire at Bristol 2000

Opinions on cricket: 'I feel the way the game is marketed needs to change. Certainly the game should be spun a bit more positively.'
Best batting: 220* Gloucestershire v Nottinghamshire, Trent Bridge 1998
Best bowling: 3-5 Gloucestershire v Essex, Colchester 1998

2002 Season

	M	Inns	NO	Runs	HS	Avge	100s	50s	Ct	St	O	M	Runs	Wkts	Avge	Best	5wI	10wM
Test																		
All First	9	17	3	406	112	29.00	1	2	1	-								
1-day Int																		
C & G	1	1	0	0	0	0.00	-	-	-	-								
B & H																		
1-day Lge	7	6	0	86	45	14.33	-	-	3	-								

Career Performances

	M	Inns	NO	Runs	HS	Avge	100s	50s	Ct	St	Balls	Runs	Wkts	Avge	Best	5wI	10wM
Test																	
All First	159	279	19	7143	220 *	27.47	7	42	96	-	2877	1658	44	37.68	3-5	-	-
1-day Int																	
C & G	18	17	0	659	110	38.76	1	5	6	-	233	178	13	13.69	6-58	1	
B & H	40	37	3	843	71 *	24.79	-	3	8	-	337	264	10	26.40	3-13	-	
1-day Lge	130	119	2	2117	73	18.09	-	8	47	-	696	654	22	29.72	3-18	-	

HARBHAJAN SINGH Lancashire

Name: Harbhajan Singh
Role: Right-hand bat, right-arm
off-spin bowler
Born: 3 July 1980, Jalandhar, Punjab
Nickname: Bhajji
County debut: No first-team appearance
Test debut: 1997-98
Tests: 28
One-Day Internationals: 51
1st-Class 50s: 5
1st-Class 5 w. in innings: 19
1st-Class 10 w. in match: 3
1st-Class catches: 29
One-Day 5 w. in innings: 1
Place in batting averages: 162nd av. 27.25
Place in bowling averages: 47th av. 27.60
Strike rate: 52.14 (career 55.28)

Overseas tours: India to Sharjah (Coca-Cola Cup) 1997-98, to Sri Lanka (Singer Akai Nidahas Trophy) 1998, to Zimbabwe 1998-99, to New Zealand 1998-99, to Sri Lanka (Asian Test Championship) 1998-99, to Zimbabwe 2001, to Sri Lanka 2001, to South Africa 2001-02, to West Indies 2001-02, to England 2002, to Sri Lanka (ICC Champions Trophy) 2002-03, to New Zealand 2002-03

Overseas teams played for: Punjab

Extras: Popularly nicknamed the 'Turbanator'. Took 32 wickets (av. 17.03) in three-Test series v Australia 2000-01, breaking Bishen Bedi's 1977-78 Indian series record v Australia of 31 wickets (in five Tests) and winning Man of the Series award; he returned match figures of 4-132, 13-196 (becoming in the process the first Indian to take a Test hat-trick – Ponting, Gilchrist, Warne) and 15-217. Had match figures of 7-110 in India's victory over England in first Test at Mohali 2001-02 and 6-149 in second Test at Ahmedabad. Had match figures of 8-132 (2-70 and 6-62) in second Test v Zimbabwe at Delhi 2001-02, winning Man of the Match award. Had match figures of 8-180 in fifth Test v West Indies at Kingston 2001-02. His 33-ball fifty (out for 54) in the second Test v England at Trent Bridge 2002 was the second fastest for India in Tests behind Kapil Dev's 30-ball fifty v Pakistan at Karachi 1982-83. Took 5-115 in England's first innings of fourth Test at The Oval 2002. Has joined Lancashire as an overseas player for 2003

Best batting: 84 Punjab v Haryana, Amritsar 2000-01

Best bowling: 8-84 India v Australia, Chennai (Madras) 2000-01

Stop press: Took 20 wickets (av. 16.75 and including second innings figures of 7-48 in first Test at Mumbai) in three-match rubber v West Indies 2002-03, winning Man of the Series award. Selected for India squad for 2002-03 World Cup

2002 Season

	M	Inns	NO	Runs	HS	Avge	100s	50s	Ct	St	O	M	Runs	Wkts	Avge	Best	5wI	10wM
Test	3	4	0	90	54	22.50	-	1	-	-	135.4	23	410	12	34.16	5-115	1	-
All First	8	10	2	218	54	27.25	-	1	1	-	243.2	43	773	28	27.60	7-83	2	-
1-day Int	3	2	0	15	15	7.50	-	-	-	-	30	0	149	4	37.25	4-46	-	
C & G																		
B & H																		
1-day Lge																		

Career Performances

	M	Inns	NO	Runs	HS	Avge	100s	50s	Ct	St	Balls	Runs	Wkts	Avge	Best	5wI	10wM
Test	28	41	8	405	66	12.27	-	2	7	-	7493	3401	119	28.57	8-84	9	2
All First	75	100	22	1469	84	18.83	-	5	29	-	17359	8022	314	25.54	8-84	19	3
1-day Int	51	28	8	259	46	12.95	-	-	16	-	2794	1925	71	27.11	5-43	1	
C & G																	
B & H																	
1-day Lge																	

HARDINGES, M. A.　　　　　Gloucestershire

Name: <u>Mark</u> Andrew Hardinges
Role: Right-hand bat, right-arm
medium-fast bowler
Born: 5 February 1978, Gloucester
Height: 6ft 1in　**Weight:** 13st 7lbs
Nickname: Dinges
County debut: 1999
1st-Class 100s: 1
1st-Class catches: 2
Strike rate: (career 98.40)
Parents: David and Jean
Marital status: Single
Family links with cricket: Brother and
father played club cricket
Education: Hillstone School; Malvern
College; Bath University
Qualifications: 10 GCSEs, 3 A-levels,
BSc (Hons) Economics and Politics

Overseas tours: Malvern College to South Africa 1996; Gloucestershire to South
Africa 1999, 2000
Overseas teams played for: Newtown and Chilwell, Geelong, Australia 1997
Career highlights to date: 'Norwich Union debut v Notts 2001 – scored 65 and set
domestic one-day seventh-wicket partnership record (164) with J. Snape. Also Lord's
final v Surrey'
Cricket moments to forget: 'Glos v Somerset [Norwich Union 2001] – bowled three
overs for 30 and was run out for 0 on Sky TV'
Cricketers particularly admired: Kim Barnett, Steve Waugh, Mark Alleyne
Young players to look out for: Stephen Pope, James Pearson, Neil Stovold, David
Nash, Gavin Franklin
Other sports played: Golf, tennis (Gloucester U14), football (university first team)
Other sports followed: Football (Tottenham)
Relaxations: Golf
Extras: Represented British Universities in 2000. Scored 65 v Nottinghamshire at
Trent Bridge on Norwich Union League debut 2001, in the process sharing in a
record seventh-wicket partnership for domestic one-day competitions (164) with
Jeremy Snape. Scored maiden first-class century (172) on his only first-class
appearance of 2002, v Oxford University CCE at The Parks. C&G Man of the Match
award for his 4-19 v Shropshire at Shrewsbury School 2002
Opinions on cricket: 'Pre-match preparation is having too much emphasis on it.
Warm-up should start at 10.00. Practise your skills!'
Best batting: 172 Gloucestershire v OUCCE, The Parks 2002
Best bowling: 2-16 Gloucestershire v Essex, Bristol 2000

2002 Season

	M	Inns	NO	Runs	HS	Avge	100s	50s	Ct	St	O	M	Runs	Wkts	Avge	Best	5wl	10wM
Test																		
All First	1	1	0	172	172	172.00	1	-	-	-	12	2	45	0	-	-	-	-
1-day Int																		
C & G	3	2	0	13	12	6.50	-	-	1	-	12	3	38	5	7.60	4-19	-	
B & H	2	1	0	31	31	31.00	-	-	1	-	10	0	37	0	-	-	-	
1-day Lge	6	6	2	51	29	12.75	-	-	3	-	45	2	202	5	40.40	2-37	-	

Career Performances

	M	Inns	NO	Runs	HS	Avge	100s	50s	Ct	St	Balls	Runs	Wkts	Avge	Best	5wl	10wM
Test																	
All First	8	8	0	232	172	29.00	1	-	2	-	984	499	10	49.90	2-16	-	-
1-day Int																	
C & G	4	3	0	13	12	4.33	-	-	2	-	90	49	6	8.16	4-19	-	
B & H	3	2	0	43	31	21.50	-	-	1	-	102	68	1	68.00	1-31	-	
1-day Lge	14	14	4	165	65	16.50	-	1	4	-	462	371	8	46.37	2-37	-	

HARMISON, S. J.   Durham

Name: <u>Stephen</u> James Harmison
Role: Right-hand bat, right-arm
fast bowler
Born: 23 October 1978, Ashington,
Northumberland
Height: 6ft 4in **Weight:** 14st
Nickname: Harmy
County debut: 1996
County cap: 1999
Test debut: 2002
Tests: 1
50 wickets in a season: 2
1st-Class 5 w. in innings: 5
1st-Class catches: 13
Place in batting averages: 310th av. 5.86
(2001 263rd av. 9.70)
Place in bowling averages: 66th av. 30.33
(2001 95th av. 36.05)
Strike rate: 58.96 (career 60.88)
Parents: Jimmy and Margaret
Wife and date of marriage: Hayley, 8 October 1999
Children: Emily Alice, 1 June 1999; Abbie

Family links with cricket: Brothers Ben and James have both played for Northumberland
Education: Ashington High School
Off-season: Touring Australia with England
Overseas tours: England U19 to Pakistan 1996-97; England A to Zimbabwe and South Africa 1998-99; ECB National Academy to Australia 2001-02; England to Australia 2002-03
Career highlights to date: 'Playing for England v India at Trent Bridge [2002]'
Cricketers particularly admired: David Boon, Courtney Walsh
Young players to look out for: Gordon Muchall, Kyle Hogg, James Anderson
Other sports played: Football (played for Ashington in Northern League), golf, snooker
Other sports followed: Football ('Newcastle United season-ticket holder')
Injuries: Out for ten weeks with an intercostal problem
Relaxations: Spending time with family
Extras: Represented Northumberland U17. Was selected for England A tours of Bangladesh and New Zealand 1999-2000 and West Indies 2000-01 but was forced to withdraw through injury. Returned match figures of 7-120 (4-78 and 3-42) in ECB National Academy's innings victory over Commonwealth Bank [Australian] Cricket Academy in Adelaide 2001-02. Made Test debut in second Test v India at Trent Bridge 2002
Best batting: 36 Durham v Kent, Canterbury 1998
　　　　　　　　36 Durham v Worcestershire, Worcester 1998
Best bowling: 6-111 Durham v Sussex, Riverside 2001
Stop press: Made One-Day International debut v Sri Lanka at Brisbane in the VB Series 2002-03. Selected for England squad for 2002-03 World Cup

2002 Season

	M	Inns	NO	Runs	HS	Avge	100s	50s	Ct	St	O	M	Runs	Wkts	Avge	Best	5wI	10wM
Test	1	1	0	3	3	3.00	-	-	-	-	49	12	120	5	24.00	3-57	-	-
All First	11	18	3	88	19 *	5.86	-	-	4	-	324.2	75	1001	33	30.33	5-65	1	-
1-day Int																		
C & G																		
B & H	2	1	0	0	0	0.00	-	-	1	-	20	1	112	1	112.00	1-63	-	
1-day Lge	3	1	0	3	3	3.00	-	-	-	-	26	0	117	5	23.40	2-39	-	

Career Performances

	M	Inns	NO	Runs	HS	Avge	100s	50s	Ct	St	Balls	Runs	Wkts	Avge	Best	5wI	10wM
Test	1	1	0	3	3	3.00	-	-	-	-	294	120	5	24.00	3-57	-	-
All First	69	99	25	628	36	8.48	-	-	13	-	13152	6754	216	31.26	6-111	5	-
1-day Int																	
C & G	3	3	1	4	2 *	2.00	-	-	1	-	132	122	2	61.00	1-34	-	
B & H	10	5	2	17	8 *	5.66	-	-	1	-	468	393	10	39.30	2-34	-	
1-day Lge	24	10	5	27	11 *	5.40	-	-	3	-	1061	903	24	37.62	4-43	-	

HARRIS, A. J. Nottinghamshire

Name: <u>Andrew</u> James Harris
Role: Right-hand bat, right-arm
fast-medium bowler
Born: 26 June 1973, Ashton-under-Lyne,
Lancashire
Height: 6ft **Weight:** 11st 9lbs
Nickname: AJ, Honest
County debut: 1994 (Derbyshire),
2000 (Nottinghamshire)
County cap: 1996 (Derbyshire),
2000 (Nottinghamshire)
50 wickets in a season: 1
1st-Class 5 w. in innings: 12
1st-Class 10 w. in match: 3
1st-Class catches: 26
One Day 5 w. in innings: 1
Place in batting averages: 281st av. 11.61
(2001 275th av. 6.07)
Place in bowling averages: 10th av. 22.01 (2001 111th av. 39.17)
Strike rate: 37.04 (career 51.82)
Parents: Norman (deceased) and Joyce
Wife and date of marriage: Kate, 7 October 2000
Children: Jacob Alexander, 28 August 2002
Education: Tintwistle Primary School; Hadfield Comprehensive School;
Glossopdale Community College
Qualifications: 6 GCSEs, 1 A-level
Career outside cricket: Studying book-keeping and accountancy
Off-season: As above
Overseas tours: England A to Australia 1996-97
Overseas teams played for: Ginninderra West Belconnen, Australian Capital Territory
1992-93; Victoria University of Wellington CC, New Zealand 1997-98
Career highlights to date: 'Helping Nottinghamshire achieve first-division status in
the Frizzell Championship for 2003'
Cricket moments to forget: 'Having forgotten my shirt I had to walk out to field in
the last Norwich Union game of the 2001 season (which happened to be on TV)
wearing the diminutive Guy Welton's shirt'
Cricket superstitions: 'None'
Cricketers particularly admired: Merv Hughes, Allan Donald
Young players to look out for: Bilal Shafayat
Other sports played: Golf, snooker, 'as well as being player/manager of the Derby
Rejects, winners of the winter '01 season of the JJB Soccerdome Six-a-Side Monday
Night Premier Division'

Other sports followed: Football ('watching Man City win a place in Europe!')
Relaxations: 'Good food, good wine and the odd game of golf'
Extras: Left Derbyshire at end of the 1999 season and joined Notts for 2000. Scored 41* v Northamptonshire at Northampton 2002, in the process sharing with Paul McMahon in a record last-wicket stand for Nottinghamshire in matches v Northamptonshire (68). Took 50 first-class wickets (67) in a season for the first time 2002. Nottinghamshire Player of the Year 2002
Best batting: 41* Nottinghamshire v Northamptonshire, Northampton 2002
Best bowling: 7-54 Nottinghamshire v Northamptonshire, Trent Bridge 2002

2002 Season

	M	Inns	NO	Runs	HS	Avge	100s	50s	Ct	St	O	M	Runs	Wkts	Avge	Best	5wI	10wM
Test																		
All First	14	20	7	151	41 *	11.61	-	-	6	-	413.4	93	1475	67	22.01	7-54	3	2
1-day Int																		
C & G	2	0	0	0	0	-	-	-	-	-	18	3	59	2	29.50	2-17	-	
B & H	5	2	0	3	3	1.50	-	-	-	-	33.2	1	190	11	17.27	4-42	-	
1-day Lge	10	6	3	34	16 *	11.33	-	-	1	-	73.5	3	457	6	76.16	2-47	-	

Career Performances

	M	Inns	NO	Runs	HS	Avge	100s	50s	Ct	St	Balls	Runs	Wkts	Avge	Best	5wI	10wM
Test																	
All First	80	114	31	775	41 *	9.33	-	-	26	-	14303	8465	276	30.67	7-54	12	3
1-day Int																	
C & G	11	5	3	21	11 *	10.50	-	-	1	-	601	402	11	36.54	3-10	-	
B & H	18	7	1	15	5	2.50	-	-	4	-	872	727	29	25.06	4-42	-	
1-day Lge	74	28	13	109	16 *	7.26	-	-	17	-	3179	2816	92	30.60	5-35	1	

HARRISON, D. S.   Glamorgan

Name: <u>David</u> Stuart Harrison
Role: Right-hand bat, right-arm medium-fast bowler, occasional wicket-keeper; all-rounder
Born: 31 July 1981, Newport
Height: 6ft 4in **Weight:** 15st
Nickname: Harry, Hazza, Sunroof, Moorhead, Butter
County debut: 1999
One-Day 5 w. in innings: 1
Strike rate: 78.00 (career 106.50)
Parents: Stuart and Susan
Marital status: 'Single!!'
Family links with cricket: 'Dad played for Glamorgan in early 1970s (bowling his

old school seamers!); brother Adam in England U19 squad to Australia 2002-03'

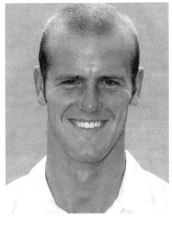

Education: Greenlawn Junior School, Pontypool; West Monmouth Comprehensive, Pontypool; Pontypool College

Qualifications: 8 GCSEs, 2 A-levels, Levels 1 and 2 coaching awards

Career outside cricket: 'Qualified school caretaker!'

Off-season: 'I will be selling Christmas trees until December; going to Cape Town for World Cup'

Overseas tours: Gwent U15 to Cape Town 1996; Wales U16 to Jersey 1996, 1997; England U19 to Malaysia and (U19 World Cup) Sri Lanka 1999-2000; Glamorgan to Cape Town 2002

Overseas teams played for: Claremont, Cape Town 2002 (during Glamorgan tour)

Career highlights to date: 'Winning NUL division one title at Canterbury [2002]. Making my Glamorgan debut April 1999 – fifth youngest ever to play for Glamorgan in County Championship!'

Cricket moments to forget: 'Being abused by Dave Houghton on Sky TV for my poor throwing from the boundary (can't hide on TV!)'

Cricketers particularly admired: Matthew Maynard, Craig White

Young players to look out for: Mark Powell, 'little brother Adam'

Other sports played: Squash (Wales U13-U15), 'handy golfer', five-a-side football (Super Dragon Rovers), curling

Other sports followed: Football (Cardiff City)

Injuries: Out for about a month with knee and side injuries

Relaxations: 'Sleeping, Sky Digital, JD and Coke, walking my dog Jake, socialising'

Extras: Represented Glamorgan U12-U19. Represented England at U17, U18 and U19 levels. Missed U19 tour to New Zealand 1998-99 and home series v Australia U19 1999 through back injury. Represented England U19 v Sri Lanka U19 in 'Test' series 2000. Recorded maiden one-day five-wicket return (5-26), then struck a career-best 37* from 35 balls v Yorkshire at Headingley in the NUL 2002

Opinions on cricket: 'It's a great thing to get paid for something you love doing. Make the most of it because you never know what's around the corner.'

Best batting: 27 Glamorgan v Gloucestershire, Bristol 2000

Best bowling: 2-79 Glamorgan v Northamptonshire, Cardiff 2002

2002 Season

	M	Inns	NO	Runs	HS	Avge	100s	50s	Ct	St	O	M	Runs	Wkts	Avge	Best	5wI	10wM
Test																		
All First	1	1	0	0	0	0.00	-	-	-	-	39	6	132	3	44.00	2-79	-	-
1-day Int																		
C & G																		
B & H																		
1-day Lge	5	4	3	55	37 *	55.00	-	-	1	-	37	2	185	9	20.55	5-26	1	

Career Performances

	M	Inns	NO	Runs	HS	Avge	100s	50s	Ct	St	Balls	Runs	Wkts	Avge	Best	5wI	10wM
Test																	
All First	4	5	0	56	27	11.20	-	-	-	-	426	241	4	60.25	2-79	-	-
1-day Int																	
C & G																	
B & H																	
1-day Lge	8	7	4	66	37 *	22.00	-	-	2	-	306	281	9	31.22	5-26	1	

HARRITY, M. A.   Worcestershire

Name: <u>Mark</u> Andrew Harrity
Role: Right-hand bat, left-arm fast bowler
Born: 9 March 1974, Adelaide, Australia
Height: 6ft 4in **Weight:** 13st 9lbs
Nickname: Hags
County debut: No first-team appearance
1st-Class 5 w. in innings: 2
1st-Class catches: 25
Strike rate: (career 69.65)
Parents: Stuart and Judith
Marital status: Engaged to Laura
Children: Lachlan, 1 August 2000
Education: Taperoo Primary School;
Taperoo High School
Career outside cricket: 'Father to Lachlan'
Off-season: 'Returning to Australia to do coaching work with the South Australian Cricket Association and play grade cricket with West Torrens'
Overseas tours: Young Australia (Australia A) to England and Netherlands 1995
Overseas teams played for: West Torrens; South Australia 1993-94 – 2002-03
Career highlights to date: 'Winning the Sheffield Shield with South Australia in 1995-96'

Cricket moments to forget: 'Bringing up Dean Jones' 100 after kicking the ball into the boundary for four runs in 1994'

Cricket superstitions: 'Always wear sweatband on left wrist and always wear towel'

Cricketers particularly admired: Dean Jones, Jason Gillespie

Young players to look out for: Michael Clarke (NSW), Shaun Tait (South Australia), Trent Kelly (South Australia)

Other sports played: Australian Rules ('past footballer')

Other sports followed: Australian Rules (Port Power)

Relaxations: 'Play piano and guitar'

Extras: Selected for Prime Minister's XI v West Indians at Canberra 1995-96 and for Prime Minister's XI v England tourists at Canberra 1998-99, taking 3-46. Played for Australian XI v West Indians at Brisbane 1995-96. One of South Australia's leading wicket-takers for several seasons (one-day and four-day), topping the state's wicket-taking list in the ING Cup 2001-02 with 17 wickets (av. 19.76). Has name on Adelaide Oval locker for ten years' service (locker was previously that of Sir Donald Bradman and Les Favell)

Opnions on cricket: 'Strong opinion that if a fielder claims a catch the batsman should walk, with no third umpire input. Lots of up-and-coming talent from all countries coming through the ranks.'

Best batting: 19 South Australia v Victoria, Melbourne 2001-02

Best bowling: 5-65 South Australia v Tasmania, Hobart 2001-02

2002 Season (did not make any first-class or one-day appearances)

Career Performances

	M	Inns	NO	Runs	HS	Avge	100s	50s	Ct	St	Balls	Runs	Wkts	Avge	Best	5wl	10wM
Test																	
All First	70	85	43	220	19	5.23	-	-	25	-	13373	7273	192	37.88	5-65	2	-
1-day Int																	
C & G																	
B & H																	
1-day Lge																	

---

37. For which two first-class counties did Franklyn Stephenson play before joining Sussex in 1992?

HARVEY, I. J. Gloucestershire

Name: Ian Joseph Harvey
Role: Right-hand bat, right-arm
fast-medium bowler
Born: 10 April 1972, Wonthaggi,
Victoria, Australia
Height: 5ft 9in **Weight:** 12st 8lbs
Nickname: Freak
County debut: 1999
County cap: 1999
One-Day Internationals: 43
1st-Class 50s: 30
1st-Class 100s: 8
1st-Class 5 w. in innings: 13
1st-Class 10 w. in match: 2
1st-Class catches: 78
One-Day 5 w. in innings: 6
Place in batting averages: 60th av. 43.33
(2001 68th av. 40.84)

Place in bowling averages: 5th av. 19.03 (2001 7th av. 18.85)
Strike rate: 32.64 (career 55.62)
Family links with cricket: Brothers play club cricket in Australia
Education: Wonthaggi Technical College
Overseas tours: Australian Academy to New Zealand 1994-95; Australia to Sharjah
(Coca-Cola Cup) 1997-98, to New Zealand 1999-2000 (one-day series), to Kenya
(ICC Knockout Trophy) 2000-01, to India 2000-01 (one-day series), to England 2001
(one-day series), to South Africa 2001-02 (one-day series); Australia A to South Africa
2002-03
Overseas teams played for: Dandenong, Victoria; Fitzroy-Doncaster, Victoria;
Victoria 1993-94 –
Extras: The nickname 'Freak' is a reference to his brilliant fielding and was
reportedly coined by Shane Warne. Attended Commonwealth Bank [Australian]
Cricket Academy 1994. Took a wicket (Jonty Rhodes) with his second ball in One-Day
International cricket in 1997-98. Top scorer (57) for Victoria in their Mercantile
Mutual Cup final victory over New South Wales 1998-99. Joined Gloucestershire in
1999 as overseas player. Top wicket-taker in the 1999 National League competition
with 30 wickets at 15.80. Had match figures of 10-32 from 25 overs (and scored 60 in
Gloucestershire's only innings) v Sussex at Hove 2000. B&H Gold Awards for his 5-
32 v Warwickshire at Edgbaston and 92 (followed by 2-35) v Worcestershire at Bristol
2001. Won the Walter Lawrence Trophy for the season's fastest first-class hundred
with his 61-ball century (ending up with 104 from 65) v Derbyshire at Bristol 2001;
also took 5-89 in Derbyshire's second innings. B&H Gold Awards for his 4-21 v

Worcestershire at Worcester and for his 5-20 v Somerset at Bristol 2002. Took hat-trick (Knight,
N. Smith, Bell) v Warwickshire at Bristol in the B&H 2002. Took 4-41 then scored a 37-ball 56 v Lancashire at Bristol in the NUL 2002. Struck a 103-ball 123 (100 from 72 balls) in the Championship v Glamorgan at Cardiff 2002. ACB central contract 2002-03

Best batting: 136 Victoria v South Australia, Melbourne 1995-96
Best bowling: 7-44 Victoria v South Australia, Melbourne 1996-97
Stop press: Selected for Australia squad for 2002-03 World Cup

2002 Season

	M	Inns	NO	Runs	HS	Avge	100s	50s	Ct	St	O	M	Runs	Wkts	Avge	Best	5wI	10wM
Test																		
All First	6	10	1	390	123	43.33	1	2	6	-	152.2	29	533	28	19.03	6-68	3	1
1-day Int																		
C & G	2	2	0	27	27	13.50	-	-	-	-	16.3	0	87	3	29.00	3-25	-	
B & H	5	5	1	107	34	26.75	-	-	2	-	42.5	6	118	18	6.55	5-20	1	
1-day Lge	10	9	1	348	68 *	43.50	-	4	7	-	68.4	5	289	17	17.00	4-41	-	

Career Performances

	M	Inns	NO	Runs	HS	Avge	100s	50s	Ct	St	Balls	Runs	Wkts	Avge	Best	5wI	10wM
Test																	
All First	105	175	14	5193	136	32.25	8	30	78	-	16409	7962	295	26.98	7-44	13	2
1-day Int	43	32	8	429	47 *	17.87	-	-	13	-	2074	1626	47	34.59	4-28	-	
C & G	14	13	0	217	47	16.69	-	-	6	-	726	458	28	16.35	4-29	-	
B & H	18	16	1	451	92	30.06	-	2	5	-	954	566	50	11.32	5-20	3	
1-day Lge	47	46	3	1270	68 *	29.53	-	8	13	-	2117	1396	91	15.34	5-19	3	

38. Which Pakistan fast bowler took 113 County Championship wickets in 1991?

HATCH, N. G. Durham

Name: <u>Nicholas</u> Guy Hatch
Role: Right-hand bat, right-arm
medium-fast bowler
Born: 21 April 1979, Darlington
Height: 6ft 7in **Weight:** 14st 10lbs
Nickname: Tony
County debut: 2001
1st-Class catches: 3
Place in batting averages: (2001 219th
av. 16.12)
Place in bowling averages: (2001 83rd
av. 33.34)
Strike rate: 82.55 (career 63.85)
Parents: Mike and Paula
Marital status: Single
Family links with cricket: Father played
club cricket with Darlington CC for over 20
years. Brother plays club cricket in London
Education: Raventhorpe Prep School; Barnard Castle School; Hull University
Qualifications: 11 GCSEs, 5 A-levels, BA History and Politics
Overseas teams played for: Claremont-Nedlands CC, Perth 2000-01, 2001-02
Career highlights to date: 'First-class debut'
Cricketers particularly admired: Courtney Walsh, Steve Waugh, Curtly Ambrose
Young players to look out for: Nicky Peng, Gordon Muchall
Other sports played: Rugby union (played for North of England U19)
Other sports followed: All sports
Relaxations: Reading, socialising with friends
Extras: Represented British Universities v New Zealand A in one-day match 2000
Best batting: 24 Durham v Sussex, Riverside 2001
Best bowling: 4-61 Durham v Worcestershire, Riverside 2002

2002 Season

	M	Inns	NO	Runs	HS	Avge	100s	50s	Ct	St	O	M	Runs	Wkts	Avge	Best	5wI	10wM
Test																		
All First	4	4	2	12	6 *	6.00	-	-	2	-	123.5	26	444	9	49.33	4-61	-	-
1-day Int																		
C & G	1	0	0	0	0	-	-	-	-	-	7	3	14	1	14.00	1-14	-	
B & H	1	0	0	0	0	-	-	-	2	-	10	2	37	2	18.50	2-37	-	
1-day Lge	3	2	1	25	20 *	25.00	-	-	-	-	19	1	134	2	67.00	1-34	-	

Career Performances

	M	Inns	NO	Runs	HS	Avge	100s	50s	Ct	St	Balls	Runs	Wkts	Avge	Best	5wI	10wM
Test																	
All First	13	20	10	141	24	14.10	-	-	3	-	2235	1311	35	37.45	4-61	-	-
1-day Int																	
C & G	2	0	0	0	0	-	-	-	-	-	102	65	3	21.66	2-51	-	
B & H	1	0	0	0	0	-	-	-	2	-	60	37	2	18.50	2-37	-	
1-day Lge	8	4	2	38	20 *	19.00	-	-	-	-	312	278	9	30.88	3-26	-	

HAYNES, J. J. Lancashire

Name: Jamie Jonathan Haynes
Role: Right-hand bat, wicket-keeper
Born: 5 July 1974, Bristol
Height: 5ft 10in **Weight:** 12st 8lbs
Nickname: JJ, Haynes-bomb
County debut: 1996
1st-Class 50s: 3
1st-Class catches: 32
1st-Class stumpings: 2
Place in batting averages: (2001 216th av. 16.62)
Parents: Steve Haynes and Moiya Ford
Marital status: Engaged to Michelle Tyrrell
Family links with cricket: 'Father and uncle both played for Gloucestershire. American uncle Carl number one cricket fan in New York'
Education: Garran Primary, Canberra, Australia; St Edmunds College, Canberra; University of Canberra ('nearly completed BA Sports Media')
Qualifications: Year 12 Certificate, coaching certificate
Career outside cricket: 'Dabbling in journalism; hoping to work with our club sponsor'
Off-season: Training as part of 12-month contract at Lancashire; 'trying to beat Chappy at golf'
Overseas tours: Lancashire CCC to Cape Town 1999
Overseas teams played for: Weston Creek CC, Canberra; Queanbeyan CC, Canberra; Tuggeranong Valley CC, Canberra 1995-96; South Canberra CC 1996-97
Career highlights to date: 'Making first-class debut'
Cricket moments to forget: 'Losing four front teeth while keeping wicket'
Cricket superstitions: 'Too many to mention – never cross on stairs if you are forced to cross fingers'

Cricketers particularly admired: Ian Healy, Jack Russell, Steve Waugh, Stuart Law, Mike Atherton, Carl Butrum

Young players to look out for: Kyle Hogg, James Anderson

Other sports played: Australian Rules football (Queanbeyan Tigers)

Other sports followed: Football (Manchester United, 'a soft spot for Burnley FC as well'), Australian Rules (Carlton)

Relaxations: 'Cooking, drinking, playing golf'

Extras: Top scorer with 80 as nightwatchman in Lancashire's first innings v Sri Lanka A at Old Trafford 1999

Opinions on cricket: 'Two overseas players is a backward step for English cricket. It should be abolished at the end of the year.'

Best batting: 80 Lancashire v Sri Lanka A, Old Trafford 1999

2002 Season

	M	Inns	NO	Runs	HS	Avge	100s	50s	Ct	St	O	M	Runs	Wkts	Avge	Best	5wI	10wM
Test																		
All First	3	4	1	70	53	23.33	-	1	4	-								
1-day Int																		
C & G																		
B & H																		
1-day Lge	3	2	1	9	7 *	9.00	-	-	8	1								

Career Performances

	M	Inns	NO	Runs	HS	Avge	100s	50s	Ct	St	Balls	Runs	Wkts	Avge	Best	5wI	10wM
Test																	
All First	14	21	4	418	80	24.58	-	3	32	2							
1-day Int																	
C & G	1	1	1	59	59 *	-	-	1	1	-							
B & H	1	1	0	29	29	29.00	-	-	2	-							
1-day Lge	10	5	1	32	12	8.00	-	-	13	3							

HAYWARD, M.   Worcestershire

Name: Mornantau (<u>Nantie</u>) Hayward

Role: Right-hand bat, right-arm fast bowler

Born: 6 March 1977, Uitenhage, South Africa

County debut: No first-team appearance

Test debut: 1999-2000

Tests: 10

One-Day Internationals: 21

1st-Class 50s: 1

1st-Class 5 w. in innings: 6

1st-Class 10 w. in match: 2
1st-Class catches: 19
Strike rate: (career 54.37)
Education: Daniel Pienaar Technical High
Overseas tours: South Africa to England 1998, to India 1999-2000, to Sharjah (Coca-Cola Cup) 1999-2000, to Sri Lanka 2000, to Australia (Super Challenge) 2000, to Australia 2001-02
Overseas teams played for: Eastern Province 1995-96 –
Extras: Represented South Africa Schools 1995. Made first-class debut for Eastern Province B v Zimbabwe Board XI at Harare 1995-96. Made Test debut in second Test v England at Port Elizabeth 1999-2000, taking 4-75 in England's first innings. Man of the Match award for his 4-31 in fifth Coca-Cola

Cup match v India at Sharjah 1999-2000. Has joined Worcestershire as an overseas player for 2003
Best batting: 55* Eastern Province v Boland, Port Elizabeth 1997-98
Best bowling: 6-31 Eastern Province v Easterns, Port Elizabeth 1999-2000
Stop press: Recorded maiden Test five-wicket return (5-56) in first Test v Pakistan at Durban 2002-03

2002 Season (did not make any first-class or one-day appearances)

Career Performances

	M	Inns	NO	Runs	HS	Avge	100s	50s	Ct	St	Balls	Runs	Wkts	Avge	Best	5wI	10wM
Test	10	13	6	59	14	8.42	-	-	1	-	1949	1003	32	31.34	4-75	-	-
All First	60	60	23	545	55*	14.72	-	.1	19	-	11418	5997	210	28.55	6-31	6	2
1-day Int	21	5	1	12	4	3.00	-	-	4	-	993	858	21	40.85	4-31	-	
C & G																	
B & H																	
1-day Lge																	

---

39. Which New Zealand Test all-rounder scored 983 Championship runs and took 54 Championship wickets for Nottinghamshire in 1992?

HEGG, W. K.   Lancashire

Name: Warren Kevin Hegg
Role: Right-hand bat, wicket-keeper,
county captain
Born: 23 February 1968, Manchester
Height: 5ft 9in **Weight:** 12st 10lbs
Nickname: Chucky
County debut: 1986
County cap: 1989
Benefit: 1999 (£178,000)
Test debut: 1998-99
Tests: 2
50 dismissals in a season: 6
1st-Class 50s: 50
1st-Class 100s: 7
1st-Class catches: 747
1st-Class stumpings: 81
Place in batting averages: 228th av. 19.80
(2001 34th av. 48.87)

Parents: Kevin (deceased) and Glenda
Wife and date of marriage: Joanne, 29 October 1994
Children: Chloe Louise, 13 November 1998
Family links with cricket: Brother Martin plays in local leagues
Education: Unsworth High School; Stand College, Whitefield
Qualifications: 5 O-levels, 7 CSEs, qualified coach
Career outside cricket: Runs Parkfield Inn at Whitefield, near Manchester
Overseas tours: NCA North U19 to Bermuda 1985; England YC to Sri Lanka 1986-87,
to Australia (U19 World Cup) 1987-88; England A to Pakistan and Sri Lanka 1990-91,
to Australia 1996-97; England to Australia 1998-99, to India and New Zealand 2001-02
Overseas teams played for: Sheffield, Tasmania 1988-90, 1992-93
Cricketers particularly admired: Ian Botham, Alan Knott, Bob Taylor,
Gehan Mendis, Ian Healy
Other sports played: Football (Old Standians)
Other sports followed: Rugby league (Salford City Reds), football (Man United)
Relaxations: 'Golf, golf, golf'
Extras: Became youngest player for 30 years to score a century for Lancashire with
his 130 v Northamptonshire at Northampton in 1987 aged 19 in his fourth first-class
game. Took 11 catches in match v Derbyshire at Chesterfield in 1989, equalling world
first-class record. Wombwell Cricket Lovers' Society joint Wicket-keeper of the Year
1993. Vice-captain of Lancashire in 1999 and 2001. Scored 107* v Northamptonshire
at Northampton 2001, in the process sharing in a record eighth-wicket partnership for
Lancashire in matches against Northants (136*) with Glen Chapple. Lancashire Player

of the Year 2001. Lancashire captain since 2002, the first wicket-keeper to hold the post in an official capacity

Best batting: 134 Lancashire v Leicestershire, Old Trafford 1996

2002 Season

	M	Inns	NO	Runs	HS	Avge	100s	50s	Ct	St	O	M	Runs	Wkts	Avge	Best	5wI	10wM
Test																		
All First	16	23	2	416	62	19.80	-	1	44	2								
1-day Int																		
C & G	1	0	0	0	0	-	-	-	-	1								
B & H	7	5	2	68	26	22.66	-	-	9	1								
1-day Lge	12	10	1	167	54	18.55	-	1	15	1								

Career Performances

	M	Inns	NO	Runs	HS	Avge	100s	50s	Ct	St	Balls	Runs	Wkts	Avge	Best	5wI	10wM
Test	2	4	0	30	15	7.50	-	-	8	-							
All First	305	446	83	9984	134	27.50	7	50	747	81	6	7	0	-	-	-	-
1-day Int																	
C & G	43	22	1	411	60	19.57	-	1	49	7							
B & H	79	43	16	690	81	25.55	-	2	105	7							
1-day Lge	223	138	51	1745	54	20.05	-	2	229	39							

HEMP, D. L. Glamorgan

Name: <u>David</u> Lloyd Hemp
Role: Left-hand bat, right-arm medium bowler
Born: 15 November 1970, Hamilton, Bermuda
Height: 6ft 1in **Weight:** 13st
Nickname: Hempy, Mad Dog, Soc
County debut: 1991 (Glamorgan), 1997 (Warwickshire)
County cap: 1994 (Glamorgan), 1997 (Warwickshire)
1000 runs in a season: 3
1st-Class 50s: 46
1st-Class 100s: 18
1st-Class catches: 113
One-Day 100s: 5
Place in batting averages: 155th av. 28.05 (2001 32nd av. 49.35)

Strike rate: (career 60.70)
Parents: Clive and Elisabeth
Wife and date of marriage: Angie, 16 March 1996
Children: Cameron, January 2002
Family links with cricket: Brother Tim plays for Swansea CC
Education: Parklands Junior; Olchfa Comprehensive School; Millfield School; West Glamorgan Institute of Higher Education; Birmingham University
Qualifications: 5 O-levels, 2 A-levels, Level III coaching award
Off-season: 'Finishing MBA degree at Birmingham University'
Overseas tours: Welsh Cricket Association U18 to Barbados 1986; Welsh Schools U19 to Australia 1987-88; Glamorgan to Trinidad 1990; South Wales Cricket Association to New Zealand and Australia 1991-92; England A to India 1994-95
Overseas teams played for: Crusaders, Durban 1992-98
Career highlights to date: 'Career best 186 not out v Worcestershire 2001'
Cricket superstitions: 'None'
Cricketers particularly admired: David Gower, Viv Richards
Young players to look out for: Ian Bell, Mark Wallace, Jon Hughes
Other sports followed: Football (Swansea City, West Ham United)
Relaxations: 'Golf, listening to music, reading'
Extras: In 1989 scored 104* and 101* for Welsh Schools U19 v Scottish Schools U19 and 120 and 102* v Irish Schools U19. Scored 258* for Wales v MCC 1991. Left Glamorgan at the end of the 1996 season and joined Warwickshire. Scored two 100s (138 and 114*) v Hampshire at Southampton 1997. Vice-captain of Warwickshire in 2001. Left Warwickshire in the 2001-02 off-season and rejoined Glamorgan for 2002. Scored 88-ball 102 v Surrey at The Oval in the C&G 2002 as Glamorgan made 429 in reply to Surrey's 438-5. Scored 108 v Northamptonshire at Cardiff 2002, in the process sharing with Matthew Maynard (151) in a new record second-wicket partnership for Glamorgan in matches against Northamptonshire (252)
Opinions on cricket: 'Reduce amount of cricket played, which would allow for more quality practice in between games. Bowlers would remain fairly fresh all season. Batters should become more disciplined because of less innings, which would hopefully raise standard and competitiveness of cricket played. Away captain should have choice of whether to bat or bowl. Cricketers are only as good as the surface they play on. Improve the wickets, which will improve the standard of players. Pitch inspectors less tolerant; more points deducted for poor surfaces. Keep two divisions with three up/three down as majority of games will remain competitive up till end of season.'
Best batting: 186* Warwickshire v Worcestershire, Edgbaston 2001
Best bowling: 3-23 Glamorgan v South Africa A, Cardiff 1996

2002 Season

	M	Inns	NO	Runs	HS	Avge	100s	50s	Ct	St	O	M	Runs	Wkts	Avge	Best	5wI	10wM
Test																		
All First	12	20	2	505	108	28.05	1	2	6	-								
1-day Int																		
C & G	2	2	0	111	102	55.50	1	-	-	-								
B & H	4	4	0	117	62	29.25	-	1	2	-								
1-day Lge	11	11	1	195	55 *	19.50	-	1	6	-								

Career Performances

	M	Inns	NO	Runs	HS	Avge	100s	50s	Ct	St	Balls	Runs	Wkts	Avge	Best	5wI	10wM
Test																		
All First	173	288	26	8970	186 *	34.23	18	46	113	-	1032	778	17	45.76	3-23	-	-
1-day Int																		
C & G	23	22	2	864	112	43.20	4	3	5	-	48	43	1	43.00	1-40	-	
B & H	26	24	0	663	121	27.62	1	5	4	-	49	32	4	8.00	4-32	-	
1-day Lge	121	105	12	1859	83 *	19.98	-	8	51	-	74	86	3	28.66	2-43	-	

HEWITT, J. P.   Kent

Name: James Peter Hewitt
Role: Left-hand bat, right-arm
medium-fast bowler
Born: 26 February 1976, Southwark, London
Height: 6ft 3in **Weight:** 14st 7lbs
Nickname: Hewie, Shoes, Dog, Carlo,
Duke B ('ask Rob Ferley')
County debut: 1995 (one-day, Middlesex),
1996 (first-class, Middlesex), 2002 (Kent)
County cap: 1998 (Middlesex)
50 wickets in a season: 1
1st-Class 50s: 3
1st-Class 5 w. in innings: 5
1st-Class catches: 23
Place in bowling averages: (2001 108th
av. 38.60)
Strike rate: (career 49.91)
Parents: Gill and Terry
Marital status: Engaged to Joanne
Family links with cricket: 'Father and grandfather both played; Mum watches'
Education: Buckingham Primary School, Hampton; Teddington School, Middlesex;
Richmond College; City of Westminster College

Qualifications: GCSEs; City and Guilds Parts I, II and III in Recreation and Leisure; GNVQ Leisure and Tourism; coaching Levels I, II, III and advanced staff coach
Career outside cricket: Coaching
Off-season: 'Getting fit; coaching; going to Perth after Christmas'
Overseas teams played for: University, Perth 1997-98; Shenton Park 2000-02
Career highlights to date: 'Beating Australians at Lord's for Middlesex [2001]'
Cricket moments to forget: 'Every time not picked (quite a lot over past couple of years!)'
Cricket superstitions: 'Same routine every time go out to bat'
Cricketers particularly admired: Richard Hadlee, Jacques Kallis, Sachin Tendulkar, Damien Martyn, Adam Hollioake ('not just for cricket')
Young players to look out for: Joe Denly, Scott Newman, Simon Cosden, Charlie Hempreys
Other sports played: Athletics ('represented South of England at cross-country'), football ('played for Chelsea Youth'); 'I will play all sports'
Other sports followed: Football (Chelsea – 'the Mighty Blues')
Relaxations: 'Spending time with family and friends'
Extras: First Middlesex bowler since J. H. S. Hunt in 1902 to take a wicket with first ball in first-class cricket (R. I. Dawson of Gloucestershire at Lord's 1996). Released by Middlesex at the end of the 2001 season and joined Kent for 2002
Opinions on cricket: 'Too many back-door cricketers. Second-team pitches outside first-class grounds are poor. Tea should be half an hour.'
Best batting: 75 Middlesex v Essex, Chelmsford 1997
Best bowling: 6-14 Middlesex v Glamorgan, Cardiff 1997

2002 Season

	M	Inns	NO	Runs	HS	Avge	100s	50s	Ct	St	O	M	Runs	Wkts	Avge	Best	5wI	10wM
Test																		
All First	1	1	1	48	48 *	-	-	-	-	-	26	5	92	0	-	-	-	-
1-day Int																		
C & G																			
B & H																			
1-day Lge	1	0	0	0	0	-	-	-	-	-	2	0	20	1	20.00	1-20	-	

Career Performances

	M	Inns	NO	Runs	HS	Avge	100s	50s	Ct	St	Balls	Runs	Wkts	Avge	Best	5wI	10wM
Test																	
All First	61	82	13	1264	75	18.31	-	3	23	-	8485	4948	170	29.10	6-14	5	-
1-day Int																	
C & G	6	3	2	23	14 *	23.00	-	-	2	-	288	249	4	62.25	1-26	-	
B & H	9	5	0	30	14	6.00	-	-	2	-	444	384	6	64.00	2-49	-	
1-day Lge	59	34	13	268	32 *	12.76	-	-	19	-	2067	1546	56	27.60	4-24	-	

HEWSON, D. R. Derbyshire

Name: Dominic (<u>Dom</u>) Robert Hewson
Role: Right-hand bat, right-arm
medium bowler
Born: 3 October 1974, Cheltenham
Height: 5ft 9in **Weight:** 13st
Nickname: Chopper
County debut: 1996 (Gloucestershire),
2002 (Derbyshire)
1st-Class 50s: 14
1st-Class 100s: 3
1st-Class catches: 30
Place in batting averages: 224th av. 20.68
(2001 87th av. 35.47)
Strike rate: (career 150.00)
Parents: Robert and Julie
Wife and date of marriage:
Amy, 14 October 2000
Education: Cheltenham College; University
of West of England

Qualifications: 10 GCSEs, 3 A-levels, City and Guilds in Tree Surgery
Career outside cricket: Tree surgeon
Overseas teams played for: Constantia, Cape Town 1995-96; Central, Hawke's Bay,
New Zealand 1998-99
Career highlights to date: 'Playing at Gloucestershire CCC during their successes of
1999 and 2000'
Cricketers particularly admired: Courtney Walsh
Other sports followed: Rugby (Gloucester RFC)
Relaxations: Seeing friends, fishing, and watching sport
Extras: Made debut for Gloucestershire 2nd XI in July 1993. Left Gloucestershire in
the 2001-02 off-season and joined Derbyshire for 2002. Scored century (102*) on
debut for Derbyshire v Glamorgan at Cardiff 2002
Best batting: 168 Gloucestershire v Derbyshire, Bristol 2001
Best bowling: 1-7 Gloucestershire v Kent, Bristol 1998

2002 Season

	M	Inns	NO	Runs	HS	Avge	100s	50s	Ct	St	O	M	Runs	Wkts	Avge	Best	5wI	10wM
Test																		
All First	11	20	1	393	102*	20.68	1	1	7	-	13	4	33	0	-	-	-	-
1-day Int																		
C & G	1	1	0	63	63	63.00	-	1	-	-								
B & H	5	4	1	81	46	27.00	-	-	1	-	3	0	9	0	-	-	-	-
1-day Lge	5	5	0	56	32	11.20	-	-	-	-								

Career Performances

	M	Inns	NO	Runs	HS	Avge	100s	50s	Ct	St	Balls	Runs	Wkts	Avge	Best	5wl	10wM
Test																	
All First	62	114	8	2565	168	24.19	3	14	30	-	150	77	1	77.00	1-7	-	-
1-day Int																	
C & G	6	6	0	204	63	34.00	-	1	1	-							
B & H	10	8	2	143	46	23.83	-	-	2	-	18	9	0	-		-	-
1-day Lge	25	21	0	290	52	13.80	-	1	5	-							

HICK, G. A.   Worcestershire

Name: <u>Graeme</u> Ashley Hick
Role: Right-hand bat, off-spin bowler
Born: 23 May 1966, Harare, Zimbabwe
Height: 6ft 3in **Weight:** 14st 4lbs
Nickname: Hicky, Ash
County debut: 1984
County cap: 1986; colours 2002
Benefit: 1999
Test debut: 1991
Tests: 65
One-Day Internationals: 120
1000 runs in a season: 17
1st-Class 50s: 133
1st-Class 100s: 107
1st-Class 200s: 11
1st-Class 300s: 2
1st-Class 400s: 1
1st-Class 5 w. in innings: 5
1st-Class 10 w. in match: 1
1st-Class catches: 553
One-Day 100s: 31
One-Day 5 w. in innings: 1

Place in batting averages: 19th av. 55.88 (2001 20th av. 56.36)
Strike rate: (career 89.64)
Parents: John and Eve
Wife and date of marriage: Jackie, 5 October 1991
Children: Lauren Amy, 12 September 1992; Jordan Ashley, 5 September 1995
Family links with cricket: Father has served on Zimbabwe Cricket Union Board of
Control since 1984 and played representative cricket in Zimbabwe
Education: Banket Primary; Prince Edward Boys' High School, Zimbabwe
Qualifications: 4 O-levels, NCA coaching award

Overseas tours: Zimbabwe to England (World Cup) 1983, to Sri Lanka 1983-84, to England 1985; England to New Zealand and Australia (World Cup) 1991-92, to India and Sri Lanka 1992-93, to West Indies 1993-94, to Australia 1994-95, to South Africa 1995-96, to India and Pakistan (World Cup) 1995-96, to Sharjah 1997-98, to West Indies 1997-98 (one-day series), to Bangladesh (Wills International Cup) 1998-99, to Australia 1998-99, to Sharjah (Coca-Cola Cup) 1998-99, to South Africa and Zimbabwe 1999-2000 (one-day series), to Kenya (ICC Knockout Trophy) 2000-01, to Pakistan and Sri Lanka 2000-01

Overseas teams played for: Old Hararians, Zimbabwe 1982-90; Northern Districts, New Zealand 1987-89; Queensland 1990-91; Auckland 1997-98

Cricketers particularly admired: Steve Waugh, Glenn McGrath

Other sports played: Golf ('relaxation'), hockey (played for Zimbabwe)

Other sports followed: Football (Liverpool FC), golf, tennis, squash, hockey

Injuries: Broke thumb in last Championship match of 2002 season

Relaxations: 'Leaning against Steve Rhodes at first slip'

Extras: Youngest player participating in 1983 Prudential World Cup (aged 17); youngest player to represent Zimbabwe. In 1986, at age 20, he became the youngest player to score 2000 runs in an English season. One of *Wisden*'s Five Cricketers of the Year 1987. In 1988 he made 405* v Somerset at Taunton, the highest individual first-class score in England since A. C. MacLaren's 424 for Lancashire v Somerset at Taunton in 1895, and scored 1000 first-class runs by end of May, hitting a record 410 runs in April. In 1990 became youngest batsman ever to make 50 first-class centuries and scored 645 runs without being dismissed – a record for English cricket. Also in 1990 became the fastest to 10,000 runs in county cricket (179 innings). Qualified as an English player in 1991. Finished third in the Whyte and Mackay batting ratings in 1995 and top of the first-class batting averages in 1997. Scored hundredth first-class 100 (132) v Sussex at Worcester in 1998 with his second 100 of the match; at the age of 32, he became the second youngest player after Wally Hammond to score one hundred 100s; received an Individual Performance Award from the PCA in recognition of his achievement. Represented England in the 1999 World Cup. Scored two centuries in a match (101 and 150) for the fourth time, v Essex at Chelmsford 1999. Won One-Day International Man of the Match awards v Zimbabwe, the country of his birth, for his match-winning 87* at Bulawayo and his 80 and 5-33 at Harare, February 2000. Scored 101 in England's only innings in his first Test v Zimbabwe at Lord's 2000; it was his first Test century at Lord's. Scored 40 in match-winning 91-run partnership with Graham Thorpe in third Test v Pakistan at Karachi 2000-01. Scored 200* v Durham at Riverside 2001, in the process equalling Sir Donald Bradman's career figure of 117 hundreds and achieving the feat of having recorded centuries against each of the other 17 counties, both home and away. Passed Allan Lamb's career total of 32,502 runs during the 2001 season, becoming the highest scoring African-born cricketer. Scored 315* v Durham at Worcester 2002 to become only the fifth batsman to have scored three triple hundreds; it was also the highest individual score by a Worcestershire batsman at the ground, overtaking Glenn Turner's 311 in 1982. Scored 69 in Worcestershire's second innings v Middlesex at Worcester 2002, in the process passing 35,000 runs in first-class cricket. Scored 77* v Kent at Worcester in the NUL

2002, in the process becoming only the third player to record 8000 runs in the one-day league. Captain of Worcestershire 2000-02
Opinions on cricket: 'Wickets still need to improve!'
Best batting: 405* Worcestershire v Somerset, Taunton 1988
Best bowling: 5-18 Worcestershire v Leicestershire, Worcester 1995

2002 Season

	M	Inns	NO	Runs	HS	Avge	100s	50s	Ct	St	O	M	Runs	Wkts	Avge	Best	5wI	10wM
Test																		
All First	18	30	4	1453	315 *	55.88	4	6	30	-	24	7	79	0	-		-	-
1-day Int																		
C & G	3	3	1	192	117 *	96.00	1	-	2	-								
B & H	7	7	0	140	66	20.00	-	1	6	-								
1-day Lge	15	14	2	482	141 *	40.16	1	2	6	-	6	0	37	1	37.00	1-24	-	

Career Performances

	M	Inns	NO	Runs	HS	Avge	100s	50s	Ct	St	Balls	Runs	Wkts	Avge	Best	5wI	10wM
Test	65	114	6	3383	178	31.32	6	18	90	-	3057	1306	23	56.78	4-126	-	-
All First	440	725	69	35246	405 *	53.72	121	133	553	-	20709	10205	231	44.17	5-18	5	1
1-day Int	120	118	15	3846	126 *	37.33	5	27	64	-	1236	1026	30	34.20	5-33	1	
C & G	46	46	8	2142	172 *	56.36	7	9	25	-	1247	791	23	34.39	4-54	-	
B & H	77	75	13	2962	127 *	47.77	7	20	51	-	852	628	18	34.88	3-23	-	
1-day Lge	230	219	36	8071	141 *	44.10	12	57	78	-	2852	2477	88	28.14	4-21	-	

HOCKLEY, J. B.   Kent

Name: James Bernard Hockley
Role: Right-hand bat, right-arm off-spin bowler
Born: 16 April 1979, Beckenham
Height: 6ft 2in **Weight:** 12st 7lbs
Nickname: Hockers, Ice
County debut: 1998
1st-Class 50s: 1
1st-Class catches: 9
One-Day 100s: 1
Place in batting averages: 289th av. 10.25 (2001 233rd av. 13.83)
Strike rate: (career 122.00)
Parents: Bernard and Joan
Wife and date of marriage: Wendy, 28 September 2001
Education: Churchfields Primary School, Beckenham; Kelsey Park Secondary School, Beckenham
Qualifications: 7 GCSEs, NCA coaching award Level 1
Career outside cricket: Coaching

Overseas tours: Kent to Jamaica 1999, to South Africa 2001
Overseas teams played for: North City, Wellington 1999-2000
Career highlights to date: 'Winning the Norwich Union League trophy with Kent in 2001'
Cricket moments to forget: 'Playing at Lord's for the first time – out for a duck and dropped a catch!'
Cricketers particularly admired: Ian Botham, Aravinda De Silva, Carl Hooper
Young players to look out for: Ben Trott, Rob Key, Geraint Jones
Other sports played: Football, golf, snooker
Other sports followed: Football (Arsenal)
Relaxations: 'Spending time with my wife; listening to music; beating Martin Saggers at golf'

Extras: AKCL Player of the Year Award in 1995. Equalled Trevor Ward's Kent U15 batting record with a total of 1,000 runs in the season. Kent Schools Player of the Year in 1996. Scored a 102-ball 90 in title-clinching Norwich Union League victory v Warwickshire at Edgbaston 2001. B&H Gold Award for his 32-ball 33* v Middlesex at Canterbury 2002. C&G Man of the Match award for his 107-ball 121 (his maiden one-day century) v Warwickshire at Canterbury 2002. Released by Kent at the end of the 2002 season
Opinions on cricket: 'Two divisional system seems to be a success; lots of competitive cricket to make better, tougher players. In my opinion we should make better use of the technology available so that umpires can correctly make decisions that could either make or break a game.'
Best batting: 74 Kent v Zimbabweans, Canterbury 2000
Best bowling: 1-21 Kent v Glamorgan, Maidstone 2001

2002 Season

	M	Inns	NO	Runs	HS	Avge	100s	50s	Ct	St	O	M	Runs	Wkts	Avge	Best	5wI	10wM
Test																		
All First	5	9	1	82	46	10.25	-	-	1	-								
1-day Int																		
C & G	4	4	0	176	121	44.00	1	-	-	-	4	0	35	1	35.00	1-35	-	
B & H	5	5	1	71	33 *	17.75	-	-	2	-								
1-day Lge	11	11	0	213	58	19.36	-	1	6	-								

Career Performances

	M	Inns	NO	Runs	HS	Avge	100s	50s	Ct	St	Balls	Runs	Wkts	Avge	Best	5wI	10wM
Test																	
All First	19	30	2	423	74	15.10	-	1	9	-	366	233	3	77.66	1-21	-	-
1-day Int																	
C & G	8	8	1	251	121	35.85	1	-	-	-	24	35	1	35.00	1-35	-	
B & H	11	10	1	177	55	19.66	-	1	2	-							
1-day Lge	36	35	3	879	90	27.46	-	5	17	-							

HODD, A. J. Sussex

Name: <u>Andrew</u> John Hodd
Role: Right-hand bat, wicket-keeper
Born: 12 January 1984, Chichester
Height: 5ft 8in **Weight:** 10st 5lbs
Nickname: Hoddy
County debut: No first-team appearance
(*see* **Extras**)
Parents: Karen and Adrian
Marital status: Single
Family links with cricket: 'Long line of
enthusiastic club cricketers'
Education: Little Common CP School;
Bexhill High School/Bexhill Sixth Form
College; 'I may take up a place at
Loughborough University in 2003'
Qualifications: 9 GCSEs, 4 A-levels, ECB
Level 1 coaching certificate
Off-season: England U19 tour to Australia
Overseas tours: South of England U14 to West Indies 1998; Sussex Academy to
South Africa 1999, to Sri Lanka 2001; England U17 to Australia 2001; England U19
to Australia 2002-03
Career highlights to date: 'Winning the first four-day U19 'Test' against Australia in
Adelaide, January 2003'
Cricket moments to forget: 'Scoring a duck on my first appearance at the Melbourne
Cricket Ground'
Cricket superstitions: 'Always follow a set routine in the changing room and always
have a cup of coffee before the start of a game'
Cricketers particularly admired: Alec Stewart
Young players to look out for: Ollie Rayner (Sussex), David Stiff (Yorkshire)
Other sports played: 'Football for fun'
Other sports followed: Football (Liverpool)

316

Relaxations: 'Cinema, cooking, music'
Extras: Played for England U14, U15, U17 and U19. Graham Kersey Trophy, Bunbury 1999. Several junior Player of the Year awards at Sussex. Played for Sussex Board XI in the second round of the C&G 2003, which was played in September 2002. Sussex County League Young Player of the Year 2002. Is a Sussex Academy player and has not appeared for the county in a domestic competition but played for Sussex v West Indies A in a limited overs fixture at Hove 2002
Opinions on cricket: 'The usual gripes – too much cricket played, poor wickets. I do think the academy system, given time, will produce the top players needed by England.'

2002 Season (did not make any first-class or one-day appearances for his county)

Career Performances

	M	Inns	NO	Runs	HS	Avge	100s	50s	Ct	St	Balls	Runs	Wkts	Avge	Best	5wI	10wM
Test																	
All First																	
1-day Int																	
C & G	1	1	0	1	1	1.00	-	-	1	-							
B & H																	
1-day Lge																	

HODGE, B. J. Leicestershire

Name: Bradley (<u>Brad</u>) John Hodge
Role: Right-hand bat, right-arm
off-spin bowler
Born: 29 December 1974, Sandringham,
Victoria, Australia
Height: 5ft 9in **Weight:** 12st 6lbs
Nickname: Bunk
County debut: 2002 (Durham)
1st-Class 50s: 28
1st-Class 100s: 16
1st-Class catches: 48
Place in batting averages: 106th av. 35.50
Strike rate: 136.00 (career 74.91)
Off-season: Playing for Victoria
Overseas tours: Commonwealth Bank
Cricket Academy to Zimbabwe 1998-99
Overseas teams played for:
Victoria 1993-94 –

Career highlights to date: First game for Victoria. Century in each innings v South Australia, Adelaide 2001-02
Cricketers particularly admired: Allan Border, Dennis Lillee, Dean Jones, Sachin Tendulkar
Other sports played/followed: Australian Rules football (Melbourne), golf, tennis, soccer, skiing
Extras: Attended Commonwealth Bank [Australian] Cricket Academy 1993. Leading run-scorer for Victoria in the Sheffield Shield in his first season (1993-94) with 903 runs (av. 50.16), including one century and seven 50s. Represented Australia A v Sri Lanka 1998-99, v India A 1999, v Pakistan 1999-2000, v West Indies and Zimbabwe 2000-01. Victoria's Pura Cup Player of the Year 2000-01 (973 runs; av. 54.06); also Victoria's leading run-scorer in the Mercantile Mutual Cup 2000-01 (374 runs; av. 46.75). Scored two centuries in match (140/110*), v South Australia at Adelaide 2001-02. Victoria's Pura Cup Player of the Year for the second successive season 2001-02 (858 runs; av. 57.20) and winner of the national Pura Cup Player of the Season Award 2001-02 (jointly with Jimmy Maher of Queensland). Was Durham's overseas player from late July 2002, replacing the injured Martin Love; has joined Leicestershire as an overseas player for 2003
Best batting: 140 Victoria v South Australia, Adelaide 2001-02
Best bowling: 4-17 Australia A v West Indians, Hobart 2000-01

2002 Season

	M	Inns	NO	Runs	HS	Avge	100s	50s	Ct	St	O	M	Runs	Wkts	Avge	Best	5wI	10wM
Test																		
All First	4	8	0	284	73	35.50	-	2	3	-	22.4	4	102	1	102.00	1-28	-	-
1-day Int																		
C & G																			
B & H																			
1-day Lge	3	3	1	195	91 *	97.50	-	2	3	-	7	0	29	1	29.00	1-15	-	

Career Performances

	M	Inns	NO	Runs	HS	Avge	100s	50s	Ct	St	Balls	Runs	Wkts	Avge	Best	5wI	10wM
Test																	
All First	90	167	17	5930	140	39.53	16	28	48	-	2772	1497	37	40.45	4-17	-	-
1-day Int																	
C & G																		
B & H																		
1-day Lge	3	3	1	195	91 *	97.50	-	2	3	-	42	29	1	29.00	1-15	-	

HOGG, K. W. Lancashire

Name: <u>Kyle</u> William Hogg
Role: Left-hand bat, right-arm fast-medium bowler
Born: 2 July 1983, Birmingham
Height: 6ft 4in **Weight:** 13st
Nickname: Hoggy, Boss
County debut: 2001
1st-Class 50s: 1
1st-Class 5 w. in innings: 1
1st-Class catches: 5
Place in batting averages: 278th av. 12.11
Place in bowling averages: 83rd av. 32.68
Strike rate: 55.26 (career 50.18)
Parents: Sharon Ramadhin and William Hogg
Marital status: Single
Family links with cricket: 'Dad played for Lancs and Warwickshire; grandad Sonny Ramadhin played for Lancs and West Indies'

Education: St Anne's, Oldham; Saddleworth High School
Qualifications: GCSEs
Off-season: 'ECB Academy'
Overseas tours: England U19 to India 2000-01, to Australia and (U19 World Cup) New Zealand 2001-02; Lancashire to South Africa; ECB National Academy to Australia and Sri Lanka 2002-03
Career highlights to date: 'Debut; first first-class 50 and five-wicket haul'
Cricket moments to forget: '[B&H 2002] semi-final v Warwickshire'
Cricket superstitions: 'None'
Cricketers particularly admired: Andrew Flintoff
Young players to look out for: Gordon Muchall, Tim Bresnan, Graham Wagg
Other sports played: Football
Other sports followed: Football (Man Utd)
Injuries: Out for three weeks with an injury to the left knee
Relaxations: 'Going out with mates'
Extras: Represented England U19 v West Indies U19 in one-day series (2/3) and 'Test' series (2/3) 2001, taking 5-88 (including three wickets in four balls) in the first innings of the second 'Test' at Trent Bridge. NBC Denis Compton Award for the most promising young Lancashire player 2001. Recorded maiden first-class five-wicket return (5-48) on Championship debut v Leicestershire at Old Trafford 2002. Represented England U19 v India U19 in 'Test' series (2/3) and one-day series (3/3) 2002, scoring century (103) in second 'ODI' at Taunton

Opinions on cricket: 'Seems to be a lot of cricket and travelling and not enough days to recover.'
Best batting: 50 Lancashire v Somerset, Taunton 2002
Best bowling: 5-48 Lancashire v Leicestershire, Old Trafford 2002
Stop press: Included in provisional England squad of 30 for the 2002-03 World Cup

2002 Season

	M	Inns	NO	Runs	HS	Avge	100s	50s	Ct	St	O	M	Runs	Wkts	Avge	Best	5wI	10wM
Test																		
All First	7	9	0	109	50	12.11	-	1	5	-	175	41	621	19	32.68	5-48	1	-
1-day Int																		
C & G	2	1	0	0	0	0.00	-	-	-	-	9	2	44	2	22.00	2-27	-	
B & H	6	2	1	6	6*	6.00	-	-	2	-	38	7	112	9	12.44	2-17	-	
1-day Lge	12	8	3	103	24	20.60	-	-	3	-	79.5	6	343	15	22.86	4-20	-	

Career Performances

	M	Inns	NO	Runs	HS	Avge	100s	50s	Ct	St	Balls	Runs	Wkts	Avge	Best	5wI	10wM
Test																	
All First	8	10	0	128	50	12.80	-	1	5	-	1104	638	22	29.00	5-48	1	-
1-day Int																	
C & G	2	1	0	0	0	0.00	-	-	-	-	54	44	2	22.00	2-27	-	
B & H	6	2	1	6	6*	6.00	-	-	2	-	228	112	9	12.44	2-17	-	
1-day Lge	14	8	3	103	24	20.60	-	-	4	-	533	379	16	23.68	4-20	-	

HOGGARD, M. J. Yorkshire

Name: <u>Matthew</u> James Hoggard
Role: Right-hand bat, right-arm fast-medium bowler
Born: 31 December 1976, Leeds
Height: 6ft 2in **Weight:** 14st
Nickname: Oggie
County debut: 1996
County cap: 2000
Test debut: 2000
Tests: 15
One-Day Internationals: 16
50 wickets in a season: 1
1st-Class 5 w. in innings: 10
1st-Class catches: 14
One-Day 5 w. in innings: 4
Place in batting averages: 261st av. 15.83 (2001 285th av. 1.83)
Place in bowling averages: 104th av. 34.72 (2001 23rd av. 22.90)
Strike rate: 60.66 (career 50.92)

Parents: Margaret and John
Marital status: Living with girlfriend Sarah
Family links with cricket: 'Dad is a cricket badger'
Education: Lowtown Junior and Infants; Pudsey Grangefield
Qualifications: GCSEs and A-levels
Off-season: Touring with England
Overseas tours: Yorkshire CCC to South Africa; England U19 to Zimbabwe 1995-96; England to Kenya (ICC Knockout Trophy) 2000-01, to Pakistan and Sri Lanka 2000-01, to Zimbabwe (one-day series) 2001-02, to India and New Zealand 2001-02, to Sri Lanka (ICC Champions Trophy) 2002-03, to Australia 2002-03
Overseas teams played for: Pirates, Johannesburg 1995-97; Free State 1998-2000
Career highlights to date: 'Taking my first Test wicket (Younis Khan)'
Cricketers particularly admired: Allan Donald, Courtney Walsh
Young players to look out for: Joe Sayers, Michael Lumb, Tim Bresnan
Other sports played: Rugby
Other sports followed: Rugby league (Leeds Rhinos)
Relaxations: Dog walking
Extras: Was top wicket-taker in the 2000 National League competition with 37 wickets at 12.37, in the process superseding Howard Cooper's Yorkshire one-day league season record of 29 wickets set in 1975. PCA Young Player of the Year 2000. Returned match figures of 8-30 (4-13 and 4-17) from 22.3 overs v Pakistan Board XI at Lahore 2000-01 and took 17 wickets in total in his two matches in Pakistan. Was called up to England one-day squad for NatWest Series halfway through Yorkshire v Kent Championship match at Headingley 2001 and replaced by Steve Kirby. Man of the Match (3-37) in the second ODI v Zimbabwe at Harare 2001-02. Recorded maiden ODI five-wicket return (5-49) in third ODI v Zimbabwe at Harare 2001-02. Took 7-63 in New Zealand's first innings in the first Test at Christchurch 2001-02, the best innings return by an England opening bowler in Tests v New Zealand. Had match figures of 7-147 (2-55 and 5-92) to win the Man of the Match award in the second Test v Sri Lanka at Edgbaston 2002; also scored 17* in England's innings, sharing in a record tenth-wicket stand for England in Tests v Sri Lanka (91) with Graham Thorpe, during which the latter moved from 61 to 123. ECB 12-month contract 2002-03
Opinions on cricket: 'The two league system has worked well with vital games being played at the end of the season, but I think we need zonal teams to make the sides stronger – e.g. Yorkshire, Lancashire, Durham could play Surrey, Essex, Middlesex.'
Best batting: 32 England v India, Trent Bridge 2002
Best bowling: 7-63 England v New Zealand, Christchurch 2001-02
Stop press: Selected for England squad for 2002-03 World Cup

2002 Season

	M	Inns	NO	Runs	HS	Avge	100s	50s	Ct	St	O	M	Runs	Wkts	Avge	Best	5wI	10wM
Test	7	8	4	67	32	16.75	-	-	3	-	293	57	982	28	35.07	5-92	1	-
All First	9	11	5	95	32	15.83	-	-	3	-	364	71	1250	36	34.72	5-92	1	-
1-day Int	4	0	0	0	0	-	-	-	1	-	27.5	0	189	3	63.00	1-25	-	
C & G	4	0	0	0	0	-	-	-	1	-	37.2	2	168	10	16.80	5-65	1	
B & H	3	2	2	8	7 *	-	-	-	1	-	22.5	3	120	3	40.00	1-22	-	
1-day Lge	3	1	0	0	0	0.00	-	-	1	-	27	5	100	7	14.28	3-44	-	

Career Performances

	M	Inns	NO	Runs	HS	Avge	100s	50s	Ct	St	Balls	Runs	Wkts	Avge	Best	5wI	10wM
Test	15	20	9	94	32	8.54	-	-	4	-	3451	1886	60	31.43	7-63	2	-
All First	70	85	29	384	32	6.85	-	-	14	-	13342	6540	262	24.96	7-63	10	-
1-day Int	16	3	2	5	4 *	5.00	-	-	3	-	791	667	24	27.79	5-49	1	
C & G	5	0	0	0	0	-	-	-	1	-	254	174	10	17.40	5-65	1	
B & H	11	3	3	10	7 *	-	-	-	1	-	498	350	13	26.92	4-39	-	
1-day Lge	34	14	7	15	5 *	2.14	-	-	4	-	1530	1037	59	17.57	5-28	2	

HOLLIOAKE, A. J.　　　　　　　　Surrey

Name: <u>Adam</u> John Hollioake
Role: Right-hand bat, right-arm
medium bowler, county captain
Born: 5 September 1971,
Melbourne, Australia
Height: 5ft 11in **Weight:** 14st
Nickname: Smokey
County debut: 1992 (one-day),
1993 (first-class)
County cap: 1995
Test debut: 1997
Tests: 4
One-Day Internationals: 35
1000 runs in a season: 2
1st-Class 50s: 50
1st-Class 100s: 14
1st-Class 200s: 1
1st-Class 5 w. in innings: 1
1st-Class catches: 140
One-Day 100s: 2
One-Day 5 w. in innings: 6
Place in batting averages: 9th av. 67.09 (2001 70th av. 39.89)

Strike rate: 45.60 (career 72.78)
Parents: John and Daria
Wife: Sherryn
Children: Bennaya, 25 May 2002
Education: St Joseph's College, Sydney; St Patrick's College, Ballarat, Australia; St George's College, Weybridge; Surrey Tutorial College, Guildford
Qualifications: GCSEs, A-levels
Career outside cricket: Property developer
Off-season: 'In Australia'
Overseas tours: School trip to Zimbabwe; Surrey YC to Australia; England YC to New Zealand 1990-91; England A to Australia 1996-97 (captain); England VI to Hong Kong 1997 (captain), 2002; England to Sharjah (Champions Trophy) 1997-98 (captain), to West Indies 1997-98 (captain in one-day series), to Bangladesh (Wills International Cup) 1998-99 (captain), to Australia 1998-99 (CUB Series), to Sharjah (Coca-Cola Cup) 1998-99
Overseas teams played for: Fremantle, Western Australia 1990-91; North Shore, Sydney 1992-93; Geelong, Victoria; North Perth, Western Australia 1995-97
Career highlights to date: 'Getting my first wicket bowling leg spin'
Cricket moments to forget: 'Getting hit on my helmet by Glen Chapple'
Cricket superstitions: 'None'
Cricketers particularly admired: 'Every cricketer who gives their best and takes up the challenge to compete'
Young players to look out for: Rikki Clarke, Tim Murtagh, Scott Newman
Other sports played: Rugby (played for London Counties, Middlesex and South of England; England U18 trialist)
Extras: Scored a century (123) on first-class debut against Derbyshire at Ilkeston 1993. Surrey Young Player of the Year 1993. Scored fastest ever one-day 50 – in 15 balls v Yorkshire in the Sunday League at Scarborough 1994. Scored two centuries in match (128/117*) v Somerset at Taunton 1996. His 39 wickets in the Sunday League in 1996 is a season record for the domestic one-day league. Surrey Supporters' Player of the Year and Surrey Players' Player of the Year 1996. Man of the Match in the first One-Day International against Australia at Headingley in 1997. Captained England in the Texaco Trophy one-day series v South Africa 1998. Represented England in the 1999 World Cup. Coached Hong Kong in the Asian Cricket Council Trophy in Sharjah 2000. Took 5-77 and made two run-outs v Glamorgan at The Oval in the C&G 2002 as Surrey bowled Glamorgan out for 429 in reply to their own 438-5. C&G Man of the Match award for his 59-ball 117* (century from 52 balls) in the quarter-final v Sussex at Hove 2002. Scored a 103-ball 122* (out of 225) as Surrey avoided the follow-on v Kent at Canterbury 2002; the innings contained 98 in boundaries, one six striking an elderly woman spectator, to whom Hollioake later presented the ball, signed. Scored maiden first-class double century (208) v Leicestershire at The Oval 2002, in the process sharing with Alistair Brown (107) in a new record fifth-wicket partnership for Surrey in matches against Leicestershire (282). Surrey captain since 1997
Opinions on cricket: 'We are lucky to have such a good game to play, and it is an honour for me to have the opportunity to compete every day.'

Best batting: 208 Surrey v Leicestershire, The Oval 2002
Best bowling: 5-62 Surrey v Glamorgan, Swansea 1998
Stop press: Called up to England one-day squad for the VB Series in Australia 2002-03 as a replacement for the injured Andrew Flintoff

2002 Season

	M	Inns	NO	Runs	HS	Avge	100s	50s	Ct	St	O	M	Runs	Wkts	Avge	Best	5wI	10wM
Test																		
All First	9	13	2	738	208	67.09	2	5	10	-	38	1	182	5	36.40	2-39	-	-
1-day Int																		
C & G	3	3	1	137	117 *	68.50	1	-	-	-	15.5	0	127	7	18.14	5-77	1	
B & H																		
1-day Lge	12	10	2	214	42 *	26.75	-	-	9	-	64.2	2	319	23	13.86	5-43	1	

Career Performances

	M	Inns	NO	Runs	HS	Avge	100s	50s	Ct	St	Balls	Runs	Wkts	Avge	Best	5wI	10wM
Test	4	6	0	65	45	10.83	-	-	4	-	144	67	2	33.50	2-31	-	-
All First	148	225	19	8276	208	40.17	15	50	140	-	7861	4341	108	40.19	5-62	1	-
1-day Int	35	30	6	606	83 *	25.25	-	3	13	-	1208	1019	32	31.84	4-23	-	
C & G	27	21	4	617	117 *	36.29	1	3	10	-	873	745	30	24.83	5-77	1	
B & H	40	31	3	720	85	25.71	-	4	12	-	1346	1171	42	27.88	4-34	-	
1-day Lge	139	126	18	2915	111	26.99	1	12	41	-	4418	4067	200	20.33	5-29	5	

HOLLOWAY, P. C. L.   Somerset

Name: <u>Piran</u> Christopher Laity Holloway
Role: Left-hand bat, off-spin bowler, wicket-keeper
Born: 1 October 1970, Helston, Cornwall
Height: 5ft 8in   **Weight:** 11st 5lbs
Nickname: Oggy, Leg, Piras
County debut: 1988 (Warwickshire), 1994 (Somerset)
County cap: 1997 (Somerset)
1st-Class 50s: 31
1st-Class 100s: 9
1st-Class catches: 86
1st-Class stumpings: 1
One-Day 100s: 3
Place in batting averages: 120th av. 32.92 (2001 137th av. 28.35)
Parents: Chris and Mary

Family links with cricket: 'Mum and Dad are keen'
Education: Nansloe CP School, Helston; Millfield School; Taunton School; Loughborough University
Qualifications: 7 O-levels, 2 A-levels, BSc (Hons) Sports Science
Career outside cricket: Coaching
Overseas tours: Millfield School to Barbados 1986; England YC to Australia 1989-90; Warwickshire CCC to Cape Town 1992, 1993; Somerset CCC to Holland 1994
Overseas teams played for: North Perth, 1993-94; Nedlands, Perth 1994-96; Claremont-Nedlands, Perth 1996-98
Cricketers particularly admired: Ian Botham, David Gower
Young players to look out for: Matt Bulbeck, Steve Harmison
Other sports followed: Squash, football, rugby, tennis, surfing
Relaxations: Music, surfing, travel
Extras: Sir John Hobbs Silver Jubilee Memorial Prize 1986. Played Young England for three years. Was fourth in the county averages in 1991 (av. 65.75). Somerset Young Player of the Year 1995. Scored the most runs in A-grade cricket in Perth in 1997-98 season, in which Claremont-Nedlands won the Bank West Cup. Scored 78 v Glamorgan at Cardiff 2001, in the process sharing with Marcus Trescothick (147) in a record opening partnership for Somerset in matches against Glamorgan (240)
Best batting: 168 Somerset v Middlesex, Uxbridge 1996

2002 Season

	M	Inns	NO	Runs	HS	Avge	100s	50s	Ct	St	O	M	Runs	Wkts	Avge	Best	5wI	10wM
Test																		
All First	7	13	0	428	88	32.92	-	3	4	-								
1-day Int																		
C & G																		
B & H																		
1-day Lge	8	8	1	163	112 *	23.28	1	-	-	-								

Career Performances

	M	Inns	NO	Runs	HS	Avge	100s	50s	Ct	St	Balls	Runs	Wkts	Avge	Best	5wI	10wM
Test																	
All First	126	213	28	5786	168	31.27	9	31	86	1	76	69	0	-	-	-	-
1-day Int																	
C & G	16	15	3	549	90	45.75	-	4	8	1							
B & H	11	11	1	233	78	23.30	-	2	8	-							
1-day Lge	102	92	17	1905	117	25.40	3	10	36	7							

HOPKINSON, C. D.   Sussex

Name: <u>Carl</u> Daniel Hopkinson
Role: Right-hand bat, right-arm medium-fast
bowler; 'batter that bowls'
Born: 14 September 1981, Brighton
Height: 5ft 11in
Nickname: Hoppo
County debut: 2001 (one-day), 2002
(first-class)
1st-Class catches: 2
Strike rate: 42.00 (career 42.00)
Parents: Jane and Jerry
Marital status: Single
Family links with cricket: 'Dad played in
the local team, which got me interested, and
coached me from a young age'
Education: Barcombe; Chailey;
Brighton College
Qualifications: 7 GCSEs, 3 A-levels,
Level 1 coaching
Overseas tours: Tours to India 1997-98, to South Africa 1999
Overseas teams played for: Rockingham-Mandurah, Western Australia 2000-01
Career highlights to date: 'Playing in my first day/night game on TV; also my debut'
Cricket moments to forget: 'Playing on my debut and taking guard before the
incoming batsman was announced; in other words, they didn't know who I was!'
Cricketers particularly admired: Dennis Lillee, Ian Botham, Viv Richards,
Graham Thorpe
Young players to look out for: Krishna Singh
Other sports played: Rugby ('won Rosslyn Park National Sevens'), squash, football
Other sports followed: Football (Leeds United and Brighton & Hove Albion)
Relaxations: 'Going out in Brighton with my mates, cinema etc.'
Extras: South of England and England squads until U17. Sussex Young Player of the
Year 2000. 2nd XI Fielder of the Year 2001. Played for Sussex Board XI in the C&G
2001 and in the second round of the C&G 2002, which was played in September 2001.
Took wicket (John Wood) with his third ball on county debut, in the Norwich Union
League v Lancashire at Hove 2001. Took four catches and achieved a run out v
Glamorgan at Hove in the Norwich Union League 2001
Opinions on cricket: 'I like the idea of the new academies that are being set up.
Having come through an academy, they seem like a superb opportunity for the players
involved. Apart from that, I think I need to play a little more cricket to further my
opinions.'
Best batting: 33 Sussex v Warwickshire, Hove 2002
Best bowling: 1-35 Sussex v Warwickshire, Hove 2002

2002 Season

	M	Inns	NO	Runs	HS	Avge	100s	50s	Ct	St	O	M	Runs	Wkts	Avge	Best	5wI	10wM
Test																		
All First	1	2	0	42	33	21.00	-	-	2	-	7	0	35	1	35.00	1-35	-	-
1-day Int																		
C & G																		
B & H																		
1-day Lge	2	2	0	14	12	7.00	-	-	1	-	2	0	16	1	16.00	1-16	-	

Career Performances

	M	Inns	NO	Runs	HS	Avge	100s	50s	Ct	St	Balls	Runs	Wkts	Avge	Best	5wI	10wM
Test																	
All First	1	2	0	42	33	21.00	-	-	2	-	42	35	1	35.00	1-35	-	-
1-day Int																	
C & G	2	2	0	58	43	29.00	-	-	1	-	90	88	0	-	-	-	-
B & H																	
1-day Lge	4	3	1	24	12	12.00	-	-	6	-	24	18	2	9.00	1-2	-	

HOUSE, W. J. — Sussex

Name: William (<u>Will</u>) John House
Role: Left-hand top-order bat, right-arm medium bowler
Born: 16 March 1976, Sheffield
Height: 5ft 10in **Weight:** 13st
Nickname: Housey, Curry, Etna
County debut: 1997 (Kent), 2000 (Sussex)
1st-Class 50s: 8
1st-Class 100s: 2
1st-Class catches: 21
One-Day 5 w. in innings: 1
Strike rate: (career 365.75)
Parents: Bill and Anna
Marital status: Girlfriend Felicity
Family links with cricket: 'Dad played in the Yorkshire League and now plays with both my brothers for "the Chart"'
Education: British School in the Netherlands, The Hague; Sevenoaks School; University of Cambridge (Gonville and Caius College)
Qualifications: 11 GCSEs, International Baccalaureate, BA (Hons) History, NCA coaching award

Career outside cricket: 'Working for Long Reach International (www.longreachint.com) – company providing expertise to the managers of the commercial and risk management activities of sport'
Overseas tours: MCC to Australia 1999, to Bangladesh 2000; Sussex to Grenada 2001
Overseas teams played for: Royal Hague CC 1985-89; University CC, Adelaide 1994-95
Career highlights to date: 'First first-class hundred'
Cricket moments to forget: 'Getting out for two on my Championship debut for Kent in 1997 and it then starting to rain just as I was walking off – terrible feeling'
Cricketers particularly admired: David Gower, Ian Botham
Young players to look out for: Tim Ambrose, Matt Prior
Other sports played: Rugby (Cambridge University U21 XV 1996-97), football (Cambridge Blue 1998)
Other sports followed: Rugby, football (Sheffield Wednesday), golf
Injuries: No bowling for six weeks because of a side strain
Relaxations: Music, history
Extras: Cricket Society's leading all-rounder in schools cricket in 1993. Scored maiden first-class century (136 from 123 balls) for Cambridge University v Derbyshire at Fenner's 1996 in only his second first-class match. Kent CCC's Most Improved Player 1996. Cambridge University's Player of the Year 1996 and 1998. Benson and Hedges Gold Awards for British Universities v Surrey 1997 (93 runs) and v Gloucestershire 1998 (5-34). Left Kent at end of 1999 season and joined Sussex for 2000. Retired at the end of the 2002 season, striking a six from his last ball in professional cricket, v Hampshire at Hove in the NUL
Opinions on cricket: 'Two divisions has helped ensure intense cricket right through to the end of the season. There seems little doubt now that a gulf in standard will open up sooner rather than later between the two divisions and will inevitably result in division one attracting greater interest and revenue. Twenty-over cricket has come a year too late!'
Best batting: 136 Cambridge University v Derbyshire, Fenner's 1996
Best bowling: 1-34 Cambridge University v Oxford University, Lord's 1998
1-34 Sussex v Glamorgan, Colwyn Bay 2000

2002 Season

	M	Inns	NO	Runs	HS	Avge	100s	50s	Ct	St	O	M	Runs	Wkts	Avge	Best	5wl	10wM
Test																		
All First																		
1-day Int																		
C & G	2	2	0	19	18	9.50	-	-	3	-	7	0	28	0	-	-	-	-
B & H	6	5	1	42	20	10.50	-	-	-	-	16	0	110	2	55.00	1-30	-	
1-day Lge	13	12	2	138	31	13.80	-	-	4	-	10.5	0	40	2	20.00	1-8	-	

Career Performances

	M	Inns	NO	Runs	HS	Avge	100s	50s	Ct	St	Balls	Runs	Wkts	Avge	Best	5wI	10wM
Test																	
All First	37	57	8	1443	136	29.44	2	8	21	-	1463	964	4	241.00	1-34	-	-
1-day Int																	
C & G	6	5	0	57	18	11.40	-	-	6	-	90	75	0	-	-	-	-
B & H	25	24	1	447	93	19.43	-	2	4	-	281	300	12	25.00	5-58	1	
1-day Lge	63	55	10	958	80 *	21.28	-	1	12	-	589	465	15	31.00	3-34	-	

HUGHES, J. Glamorgan

Name: Jonathan Hughes
Role: Right-hand bat, right-arm
medium bowler
Born: 30 June 1981, Pontypridd
Height: 5ft 11in
Nickname: Jonny, Tuck Box, Hughesy
County debut: 2001
1st-Class 50s: 1
1st-Class catches: 2
Place in batting averages: 182nd av. 25.00
Parents: Steve and Anne
Marital status: Single
Family links with cricket: 'Dad and brothers
Matthew (17) and Gareth (23) play for
Hopkinstown'
Education: Trehoplyn; Coed y Lan
Comprehensive, Pontypridd
Qualifications: MCC coaching badges
Overseas tours: Hopkinstown to Barbados 1998
Overseas teams played for: Easts-Redlands, Brisbane 2000, 2001
Career highlights to date: 'Debut v Surrey for Glamorgan in County Championship'
Cricketers particularly admired: Matthew Maynard, Ian Botham
Young players to look out for: Mark Wallace
Other sports played: Football (Hopkinstown)
Other sports followed: Rugby (Pontypridd), football (Everton)
Relaxations: Going to the pub
Extras: Captained Welsh Schools. Was on Lord's groundstaff 1998-99. Glamorgan
2nd XI Player of the Year 2001. Glamorgan Young Player of the Year 2001. Scored 74,
including 14 fours, v Worcestershire at Worcester 2002 in his second first-class match
Opinions on cricket: 'Just get on with it.'
Best batting: 74 Glamorgan v Worcestershire, Worcester 2002

2002 Season

	M	Inns	NO	Runs	HS	Avge	100s	50s	Ct	St	O	M	Runs	Wkts	Avge	Best	5wl	10wM
Test																		
All First	7	10	1	225	74	25.00	-	1	2	-								
1-day Int																		
C & G																		
B & H																		
1-day Lge	1	1	0	9	9	9.00	-	-	-	-								

Career Performances

	M	Inns	NO	Runs	HS	Avge	100s	50s	Ct	St	Balls	Runs	Wkts	Avge	Best	5wl	10wM
Test																	
All First	8	12	1	312	74	28.36	-	1	2	-							
1-day Int																	
C & G																	
B & H																	
1-day Lge	1	1	0	9	9	9.00	-	-	-	-							

HUNT, T. A. Middlesex

Name: <u>Thomas</u> Aaron Hunt
Role: Left-hand bat, right-arm
medium-fast bowler
Born: 19 January 1982, Melbourne, Australia
Height: 6ft 3in **Weight:** 13st 4lbs
Nickname: Hopalong, Peg-leg
County debut: 2002 (*see* **Extras**)
Strike rate: 56.50 (career 56.50)
Parents: Jennifer Hunt and Tim Woodbridge
Marital status: Single
Education: Brackenbury, Hammersmith;
Acton High; St Clement Danes
Qualifications: 9 GCSEs, 1 A-level, Level 1
coaching award
Cricket moments to forget: '1st XI debut at
Lord's [v Australians 2001]'
Cricketers particularly admired:
Curtly Ambrose, Waqar Younis
Young players to look out for: Ian Bell
Other sports played: 'Keen skier, also played school and Sunday league football'
Other sports followed: Football (Man Utd)
Relaxations: 'Music; spending time with girlfriend'

Extras: Made 1st XI debut for Middlesex v Australians in a one-day fixture at Lord's 2001 but did not appear for the county in first-class cricket or domestic competition until 2002
Best batting: 3 Middlesex v Sri Lankans, Shenley 2002
Best bowling: 3-43 Middlesex v CUCCE, Fenner's 2002

2002 Season

	M	Inns	NO	Runs	HS	Avge	100s	50s	Ct	St	O	M	Runs	Wkts	Avge	Best	5wI	10wM
Test																		
All First	2	1	0	3	3	3.00	-	-	-	-	37.4	3	189	4	47.25	3-43	-	-
1-day Int																		
C & G																		
B & H																		
1-day Lge	3	1	0	0	0	0.00	-	-	1	-	15	0	80	1	80.00	1-24	-	

Career Performances

	M	Inns	NO	Runs	HS	Avge	100s	50s	Ct	St	Balls	Runs	Wkts	Avge	Best	5wI	10wM
Test																	
All First	2	1	0	3	3	3.00	-	-	-	-	226	189	4	47.25	3-43	-	-
1-day Int																	
C & G																	
B & H																	
1-day Lge	3	1	0	0	0	0.00	-	-	1	-	90	80	1	80.00	1-24	-	

40. In 2001 who became the first overseas player
to be capped by three counties?

HUNTER, I. D.   Durham

Name: Ian David Hunter
Role: Right-hand bat, right-arm
fast-medium bowler
Born: 11 September 1979, Durham City
Height: 6ft 2in **Weight:** 12st 7lbs
Nickname: Sticks, Hunts
County debut: 1999 (one-day),
2000 (first-class)
1st-Class 50s: 2
1st-Class catches: 6
Place in batting averages: 237th av. 18.54
(2001 210th av. 18.09)
Place in bowling averages: 119th av. 38.75
(2001 123rd av. 43.75)
Strike rate: 61.80 (career 65.28)
Parents: Ken and Linda
Marital status: Single
Family links with cricket: Brother plays for

local village side
Education: Sacriston Junior School; Fyndoune Community College, Sacriston; New
College, Durham
Qualifications: 9 GCSEs, 1 A-level (PE), BTEC National Diploma in Sports Science,
Level I and II cricket coaching awards
Off-season: 'Being an interior designer'
Overseas tours: Durham U21 to Sri Lanka 1996; Durham to Cape Town 2002
Career highlights to date: 'Scoring 63 on first-class debut' (*v Leicestershire at
Riverside 2000 as nightwatchman*)
Cricket superstitions: 'Always put my left pad on first'
Cricketers particularly admired: Allan Donald, Steve Waugh
Other sports played: Football, golf
Other sports followed: Football (Durham City AFC)
Relaxations: Socialising with friends; keeping fit, golf, football
Extras: Set a new Durham best analysis for the 2nd XI Championship with his 11-155
v Lancashire 2nd XI 1999. Represented England U19 in 'Test' series v Australia U19
1999. Played for Durham Board XI in the C&G 2001 and in the second round of the
C&G 2002, which was played in September 2001
Opinions on cricket: 'Pitches are becoming increasingly flat! More day/night cricket
– "it's a right laugh".'
Best batting: 65 Durham v Northamptonshire, Northampton 2002
Best bowling: 4-55 Durham v Warwickshire, Edgbaston 2001

2002 Season

	M	Inns	NO	Runs	HS	Avge	100s	50s	Ct	St	O	M	Runs	Wkts	Avge	Best	5wI	10wM
Test																		
All First	8	12	1	204	65	18.54	-	1	2	-	206	42	775	20	38.75	3-44	-	-
1-day Int																		
C & G																		
B & H	5	5	1	70	39	17.50	-	-	1	-	45	3	220	7	31.42	2-22	-	
1-day Lge	10	6	0	43	16	7.16	-	-	4	-	71	5	387	7	55.28	2-42	-	

Career Performances

	M	Inns	NO	Runs	HS	Avge	100s	50s	Ct	St	Balls	Runs	Wkts	Avge	Best	5wI	10wM
Test																	
All First	19	30	4	486	65	18.69	-	2	6	-	2742	1703	42	40.54	4-55	-	-
1-day Int																	
C & G	2	2	0	14	13	7.00	-	-	-	-	78	47	1	47.00	1-29	-	
B & H	9	7	2	71	39	14.20	-	-	3	-	486	384	12	32.00	4-48	-	
1-day Lge	34	19	4	127	21	8.46	-	-	7	-	1410	1135	36	31.52	4-29	-	

HUSSAIN, N.　　　　　Essex

Name: Nasser Hussain
Role: Right-hand bat, leg-break bowler, county club captain
Born: 28 March 1968, Madras, India
Height: 6ft　**Weight:** 12st 7lbs
Nickname: Nashwan
County debut: 1987
County cap: 1989
Benefit: 1999 (£271,500)
Test debut: 1989-90
Tests: 76
One-Day Internationals: 72
1000 runs in a season: 5
1st-Class 50s: 94
1st-Class 100s: 46
1st-Class 200s: 1
1st-Class catches: 330
One-Day 100s: 7
Place in batting averages: 81st av. 40.25 (2001 93rd av. 34.00)
Strike rate: (career 156.00)
Parents: Joe and Shireen
Wife and date of marriage: Karen, 24 September 1993

Children: Jacob, 8 June 2001; Joel, 18 November 2002

Family links with cricket: Father played zonal cricket in India. Played for Madras in Ranji Trophy 1966-67. Brother Mel played for Hampshire. Brother Abbas played for Essex 2nd XI

Education: Forest School, Snaresbrook; Durham University

Qualifications: 10 O-levels, 3 A-levels, BSc (Hons) in Natural Sciences, NCA cricket coaching award

Off-season: Touring with England

Overseas tours: England YC to Sri Lanka 1986-87, to Australia (U19 World Cup) 1987-88; England A to Pakistan and Sri Lanka 1990-91, to Bermuda and West Indies 1991-92, to Pakistan 1995-96 (captain); England to India (Nehru Cup) 1989-90, to West Indies 1989-90, 1993-94, 1997-98, to Zimbabwe and New Zealand 1996-97, to Australia 1998-99, 2002-03 (captain), to South Africa and Zimbabwe 1999-2000 (captain), to Kenya (ICC Knockout Trophy) 2000-01 (captain), to Pakistan and Sri Lanka 2000-01 (captain), to Zimbabwe (one-day series) 2001-02 (captain), to India and New Zealand 2001-02 (captain), to Sri Lanka (ICC Champions Trophy) 2002-03 (captain)

Overseas teams played for: Madras 1986-87; Adelaide University 1990; Petersham, Sydney 1992-93; Stellenbosch University, South Africa 1994-95; Primrose, Cape Town

Cricketers particularly admired: Mark Waugh, Graham Gooch, Sachin Tendulkar

Other sports played: Golf (10 handicap), football

Other sports followed: Football (Leeds United)

Relaxations: Listening to music. Watching television

Extras: Played for England Schools U15 for two years (one as captain). Became youngest player to play for Essex Schools U11 at the age of eight and U15 at the age of 12. Took hat-trick for Essex U11 v Berkshire U11 – all stumped by Neil Burns. Cricket Writers' Club Young Cricketer of the Year 1989. Set records for third (347* v Lancashire at Ilford 1992), fourth (314 v Surrey at The Oval 1991) and fifth (316 v Leicestershire at Leicester 1991) wicket partnerships for Essex (with Mark Waugh, Salim Malik and Mike Garnham respectively). Essex Player of the Year 1993. Appointed Essex vice-captain 1996. Finished 2nd in the Whyte and Mackay batting ratings in 1995. Appointed England vice-captain in 1996-97. Scored 207 in the first Test v Australia at Edgbaston 1997, in the process sharing with Graham Thorpe (138) in record fourth-wicket partnership for England in Tests v Australia (288). Appointed Essex captain for 1999. Represented England in the 1999 World Cup. Appointed England captain after 1999 World Cup. Topped England batting averages in the 1999-2000 Test series v South Africa with 370 runs at 61.66; during the series he became the first player to bat for 1000 minutes in Test cricket without being out. Handed over Essex 1st XI captaincy to Ronnie Irani at the start of the 2000 season but remains Essex club captain. In 2000 led England to victory in the NatWest triangular one-day series, to a Test series win over Zimbabwe, and to a first Test series win over West Indies for 31 years; followed up with series wins in Pakistan and Sri Lanka in the winter of 2000-01, which made England only the second touring side to win two Test rubbers on the sub-continent in the same season. npower Contribution to Cricket

Award 2001. Awarded OBE in New Year honours list 2001-02. Scored 106 in first innings of first Test v New Zealand at Christchurch 2001-02, coming to the wicket with England at 0-2 and being last out with the score on 228; was England's top run-scorer in the three-match series with 280 (av. 56.00). Vodafone England Cricketer of the Year 2001-02. B&H Gold Award for his 144-ball 136* in the quarter-final v Yorkshire at Chelmsford 2002; two days later struck a 99-ball 96 in the C&G v Middlesex, also at Chelmsford. C&G Man of the Match award for his 83* v Lancashire at Chelmsford 2002. Scored maiden ODI century (115) v India in the final of the NatWest Series at Lord's 2002. Man of the Match for his first innings 155 and his captaincy in the first Test v India at Lord's 2002. Scored 110 in England's second innings of the third Test v India at Headingley 2002, in the process passing 2000 Test runs as England captain. ECB 12-month contract 2002-03
Best batting: 207 England v Australia, Edgbaston 1997
Best bowling: 1-38 Essex v Worcestershire, Kidderminster 1992
Stop press: Scored 75 and 72 in England victory v Australia in fifth Test at Sydney 2002-03. Appointed captain of England squad for 2002-03 World Cup. Resigned as England one-day captain at the end of the 2002-03 World Cup

2002 Season

	M	Inns	NO	Runs	HS	Avge	100s	50s	Ct	St	O	M	Runs	Wkts	Avge	Best	5wI	10wM
Test	7	10	0	478	155	47.80	2	2	6	-								
All First	8	12	0	483	155	40.25	2	2	8	-								
1-day Int	7	7	1	244	115	40.66	1	1	3									
C & G	3	3	1	186	96	93.00	-	2	3									
B & H	5	5	1	260	136 *	65.00	1	-	-	-								
1-day Lge																		

Career Performances

	M	Inns	NO	Runs	HS	Avge	100s	50s	Ct	St	Balls	Runs	Wkts	Avge	Best	5wI	10wM
Test	76	134	13	4484	207	37.05	12	23	53	-	30	15	0	-	-	-	-
All First	303	491	48	18555	207	41.88	47	94	330	-	312	323	2	161.50	1-38	-	-
1-day Int	72	72	10	1954	115	31.51	1	13	36	-							
C & G	31	29	4	1099	108	43.96	2	6	22	-							
B & H	58	53	9	2148	136 *	48.81	3	17	23	-							
1-day Lge	145	134	18	3692	114	31.82	1	25	63	-							

41. Who scored 2395 runs in his first full season for Hampshire in 1968?

HUSSEY, M. E. K.   Northamptonshire

Name: Michael (<u>Mike</u>) Edward
Killeen Hussey
Role: Left-hand bat, right-arm medium
bowler, county captain
Born: 27 May 1975, Perth, Western Australia
Height: 6ft **Weight:** 12st 7lbs
Nickname: Huss
County debut: 2001
County cap: 2001
1000 runs in a season: 2
1st-Class 50s: 40
1st-Class 100s: 20
1st-Class 200s: 2
1st-Class 300s: 2
1st-Class catches: 107
One-Day 100s: 2
Place in batting averages: 8th av. 68.66
(2001 4th av. 79.03)
Strike rate: (career 95.60)
Parents: Helen and Ted
Wife: Amy

Family links with cricket: Brother Dave was in the Western Australia state squad and
now plays for Victoria
Education: Whitfords Catholic; Prendiville; Curtin
Career outside cricket: Teacher
Overseas tours: Australia U19 to India 1993-94; Australian Cricket Academy to
Pakistan 1995; Australia A to Scotland and Ireland 1998, to South Africa 2002-03
Overseas teams played for: Wanneroo, Western Australia; Western Australia
1994-95 –
Cricketers particularly admired: Steve Waugh, Mark Taylor, Sachin Tendulkar,
Dennis Lillee
Young players to look out for: Shaun Marsh
Other sports played: Golf, squash, tennis
Other sports followed: Australian Rules (West Coast Eagles), football (Man Utd)
Relaxations: Movies, beach
Extras: Attended Commonwealth Bank [Australian] Cricket Academy 1995. Finished
third in the Sheffield Shield Player of the Year award in his first full season 1995-96.
Sir Donald Bradman Young Cricketer of the Year 1998. Excalibur Award (Western
Australia) 1998-2000. Scored maiden Mercantile Cup century (100*) v Victoria at
Melbourne 1999-2000, sharing in a competition record sixth-wicket partnership of 173
with Brad Hogg. Carried his bat for 172* v South Australia in the Pura Milk Cup

1999-2000. Joined Northamptonshire as overseas player for 2001. B&H Gold Awards for his 93 v Warwickshire at Northampton and 114* v Glamorgan at Cardiff (his maiden century for Northants) 2001. Shared in record second-wicket stand for Northants in matches v Surrey (172) with Jeff Cook at Northampton 2001. Scored maiden first-class triple century (329*) v Essex at Northampton 2001, in the process overtaking Mal Loye's record for the highest individual score by a Northants player (322*); followed up with a 33-ball 70* in the second innings and was on the field for the entire match. Scored 208 v Somerset at Taunton 2001, in the process sharing with Russell Warren (144) in a record third-wicket partnership for Northants in matches against Somerset (287). Leading run-scorer in English first-class cricket 2001 with 2055 runs (all in the Championship) at 79.03, at the same time becoming the first Northants batsman to score 2000 Championship runs in a season since Allan Lamb did so in 1981; Northamptonshire Player of the Year 2001 and 2002, the first player to win the award twice in succession. Leading run-scorer in Australia's one-day ING Cup 2001-02 with 440 runs (av. 55.00); in the match v New South Wales at Perth, struck sponsor's sign at square leg with a sweep shot, winning a $200,000 prize. Northamptonshire captain since 2002. B&H Gold Award for his 87 v Somerset at Taunton 2002. Was first batsman to reach 1000 first-class runs in the 2002 season. Scored 310* v Gloucestershire at Bristol 2002, in the process sharing with Graeme Swann (183) in a stand of 318; was on the field for the entire match. ACB central contract 2002-03

Best batting: 329* Northamptonshire v Essex, Northampton 2001
Best bowling: 2-21 Western Australia v Queensland, Perth 1998-99

2002 Season

	M	Inns	NO	Runs	HS	Avge	100s	50s	Ct	St	O	M	Runs	Wkts	Avge	Best	5wI	10wM
Test																		
All First	13	23	2	1442	310 *	68.66	5	4	21	-								
1-day Int																		
C & G	2	2	0	27	15	13.50	-	-	-	-								
B & H	5	5	0	266	87	53.20	-	3	1	-								
1-day Lge	10	10	2	394	110	49.25	1	3	6	-								

Career Performances

	M	Inns	NO	Runs	HS	Avge	100s	50s	Ct	St	Balls	Runs	Wkts	Avge	Best	5wI	10wM
Test																	
All First	112	203	15	9500	329 *	50.53	24	40	107	-	478	269	5	53.80	2-21	-	-
1-day Int																	
C & G	4	4	0	94	59	23.50	-	1	1	-	30	30	1	30.00	1-20	-	
B & H	10	10	1	519	114 *	57.66	1	4	4	-	18	15	1	15.00	1-15	-	
1-day Lge	25	25	3	904	110	41.09	1	7	10	-							

HUTCHISON, P. M.   Sussex

Name: <u>Paul</u> Michael Hutchison
Role: Left-hand bat, left-arm swing bowler
Born: 9 June 1977, Leeds
Height: 6ft 4in **Weight:** 13st
Nickname: Hutch
County debut: 1995-96 (Yorkshire),
2002 (Sussex)
County cap: 1998 (Yorkshire)
50 wickets in a season: 1
1st-Class 5 w. in innings: 7
1st-Class 10 w. in match: 1
1st-Class catches: 9
Strike rate: 79.00 (career 43.93)
Parents: David Hutchison and Rita Laycock
(deceased)
Marital status: Engaged to Emma
Family links with cricket: Brother Richard
plays for Pudsey St Lawrence CC in the
Bradford League
Education: Pudsey Greenside; Pudsey Crawshaw; 'just listening to Richard
Montgomerie and Robin Martin-Jenkins!'
Qualifications: 8 GCSEs, GNVQ Leisure and Tourism, qualified cricket coach,
basic IT ('thanks to PCA')
Off-season: 'Training like mad in Brighton getting ready for the summer'
Overseas tours: England U19 to Zimbabwe 1995-96; England A to Kenya and Sri
Lanka 1997-98, to Zimbabwe and South Africa 1998-99; Yorkshire to Zimbabwe and
Botswana 1996, to South Africa 1998, 1999, 2001; Sussex to Grenada 2002
Career highlights to date: 'My Championship debut at Portsmouth – 7-50. My
Yorkshire cap. My two England A tours'
Cricket moments to forget: 'Last season!'
Cricket superstitions: 'Always turn right at end of run-up'
Cricketers particularly admired: Matt Maynard, Neil Fairbrother, Courtney Walsh,
Craig White, Darren Gough, Graham Dilley, Malcolm Marshall
Young players to look out for: Michael Lumb, Tim Ambrose, Matt Prior, John Sadler
Other sports played: Golf, football
Other sports followed: 'Most sports; anything on Sky Sports; any team from my area
(Leeds/Bradford)'
Injuries: Out for about three months with shin splints
Relaxations: Golf, cinema, socialising with friends
Extras: Represented England at U17, U18 and U19 levels. Played for Pudsey St
Lawrence in the Bradford League. Had a place at the Yorkshire Academy. Took 7-38
on first first-class appearance of 1997, against Pakistan A. Took 7-50 against

Hampshire at Portsmouth 1997, the best Championship debut figures for Yorkshire since Wilfred Rhodes took 7-24 v Somerset in 1898. Voted Wombwell Cricket Lovers' Young Player of the Year for 1997. Released by Yorkshire at the end of the 2001 season and joined Sussex for 2002

Opinions on cricket: 'Great game to be involved with. Two divisions is a success. Would probably change it to two up/two down as gaining promotion to the top flight from third place is too easy. Floodlit matches are also a success as they get the crowds in. TV coverage is also improving, which then lends itself to better marketing for the players. Every county should have an academy. In favour of two overseas players as the standard should rise.'

Best batting: 30 Yorkshire v Essex, Scarborough 1998
Best bowling: 7-31 Yorkshire v Sussex, Hove 1998

2002 Season

	M	Inns	NO	Runs	HS	Avge	100s	50s	Ct	St	O	M	Runs	Wkts	Avge	Best	5wl	10wM
Test																		
All First	3	5	2	29	20 *	9.66	-	-	-	-	79	6	389	6	64.83	3-146	-	-
1-day Int																		
C & G																		
B & H																		
1-day Lge	2	2	0	13	12	6.50	-	-	2	-	15	1	76	3	25.33	3-38	-	

Career Performances

	M	Inns	NO	Runs	HS	Avge	100s	50s	Ct	St	Balls	Runs	Wkts	Avge	Best	5wl	10wM
Test																	
All First	47	50	27	229	30	9.95	-	-	9	-	7074	3951	161	24.54	7-31	7	1
1-day Int																	
C & G	3	1	1	4	4 *	-	-	-	-	-	132	62	5	12.40	3-18	-	
B & H	6	2	2	6	4 *	-	-	-	-	-	191	112	10	11.20	3-14	-	
1-day Lge	25	10	5	21	12	4.20	-	-	5	-	1010	746	31	24.06	4-34	-	

42. Which South African future coach of Bangladesh made his debut for Derbyshire in 1976?

HUTTON, B. L.   Middlesex

Name: Benjamin (<u>Ben</u>) Leonard Hutton
Role: Left-hand bat, right-arm
medium bowler
Born: 29 January 1977, Johannesburg,
South Africa
Height: 6ft 2in **Weight:** 12st
Nickname: Gibbo, The Gibbonian
County debut: 1999
1st-Class 50s: 9
1st-Class 100s: 4
1st-Class catches: 53
One-Day 5 w. in innings: 1
Place in batting averages: 150th av. 28.77
(2001 72nd av. 39.30)
Strike rate: 55.33 (career 79.11)
Parents: Charmaine and Richard
Marital status: Single
Family links with cricket: Sir Leonard
Hutton (grandfather) Yorkshire and England; Richard Hutton (father) Yorkshire and
England; Ben Brocklehurst (grandfather) Somerset
Education: Holmewood House Prep School; Radley College; Durham University
Qualifications: 10 GCSEs, 3 A-levels, BA (Hons) Social Sciences, NCA
coaching award
Career outside cricket: 'Apprentice insurance broker!'
Off-season: 'Broadening my horizons beyond the game, that will allow me to develop
a trade alongside cricket'
Overseas tours: Durham University to Zimbabwe 1997-98; Middlesex to Portugal
1996, 1997, 1998, to South Africa 1999, to Malta 2001, to Bombay 2003; MCC to
Italy
Overseas teams played for: Pirates CC, Johannesburg 1996; Wanderers CC,
Johannesburg 1997; Gosnells, Perth 2000-01, 2001-02
Career highlights to date: 'First first-class 100 (2001). Scoring 73 against the world
champions (Australians) 2001. Securing promotion to [County Championship] first
division 2002'
Cricket moments to forget: 'Breaking my hand v Gloucestershire 2001. Recording
the first pair of my career 2002'
Cricket superstitions: 'Not sitting within ten yards of David Nash in any dressing
room!'
Cricketers particularly admired: 'My grandfathers – Len Hutton and Ben
Brocklehurst; my father – Richard Hutton; Angus Fraser'
Young players to look out for: Nick Compton, Darren Moon
Other sports played: Golf (12 handicap), rackets

Other sports followed: 'All sports, except motor racing'
Injuries: Side strain ('prevented from bowling very fast for three months')
Relaxations: 'Reading (insurance textbooks!), music'
Extras: BUSA Halifax medal 1997. Opened for Middlesex v Essex at Southend 1999 with Andrew Strauss, his former opening partner at Radley. Played in Durham University's BUSA Championship winning side 1999. His maiden first-class century, 133 v Oxford University CCE at The Parks, was the first first-class century of the 2001 season
Opinions on cricket: 'It doesn't look like the game in this country is developing as quickly as our Australian counterparts' game. Is the answer to play a 20-over "slogathon"? I think not. Are the Aussies laughing at us? I think so!'
Best batting: 139 Middlesex v Derbyshire, Southgate 2001
Best bowling: 4-37 Middlesex v Sri Lankans, Shenley 2002

2002 Season

	M	Inns	NO	Runs	HS	Avge	100s	50s	Ct	St	O	M	Runs	Wkts	Avge	Best	5wI	10wM
Test																		
All First	11	19	1	518	116	28.77	1	4	20	-	83	20	262	9	29.11	4-37	-	-
1-day Int																		
C & G	1	0	0	0	0	-	-	-	-	-	2	0	16	0	-		-	-
B & H	4	4	1	57	27 *	19.00	-	-	1	-	6	0	36	0	-		-	-
1-day Lge	9	8	1	177	71 *	25.28	-	2	3	-	38	0	226	6	37.66	2-34	-	

Career Performances

	M	Inns	NO	Runs	HS	Avge	100s	50s	Ct	St	Balls	Runs	Wkts	Avge	Best	5wI	10wM
Test																	
All First	44	72	5	1833	139	27.35	4	9	53	-	1424	838	18	46.55	4-37	-	-
1-day Int																	
C & G	2	1	0	14	14	14.00	-	-	1	-	48	58	2	29.00	2-42	-	
B & H	13	10	1	127	52	14.11	-	1	5	-	205	188	5	37.60	2-43	-	
1-day Lge	32	26	3	536	77	23.30	-	3	14	-	678	610	20	30.50	5-45	1	

43. For which English counties did the brothers Mushtaq and Sadiq Mohammad play Championship cricket?

HYAM, B. J.   Essex

Name: <u>Barry</u> James Hyam
Role: Right-hand bat, wicket-keeper
Born: 9 September 1975, Romford
Height: 5ft 11in **Weight:** 12st
Nickname: Bazza
County debut: 1993
County cap: 1999
50 dismissals in a season: 1
1st-Class 50s: 3
1st-Class catches: 168
1st-Class stumpings: 13
Place in batting averages: (2001 185th
av. 21.42)
Parents: Peter and Gloria
Wife and date of marriage: Villene,
30 September 2000
Family links with cricket: 'Mum and Dad
are keen fans; brother Matthew is captain of
Harold Wood CC; brother Richard plays for Harold Wood'

Education: Marshalls Park; Havering Sixth Form College; Westminster College;
Capel Manor College
Qualifications: 9 GCSEs, 1 A-level, NCA coaching award
Career outside cricket: Artist, garden designer and landscaper
Off-season: 'Developing my garden design and landscaping business; also producing
some limited edition drawings and prints'
Overseas tours: MCC to Bangladesh 1999-2000
Career highlights to date: 'Receiving my county cap'
Cricket moments to forget: 'I can't remember!'
Cricket superstitions: 'None'
Cricketers particularly admired: Jack Russell, Nasser Hussain
Young players to look out for: Ravinder Bopara
Other sports played: Golf, football
Other sports followed: Football (West Ham United)
Relaxations: 'Drawing, gardening'
Extras: Made first-class debut on his 18th birthday. Joint leading wicket-keeper (along
with Steve Rhodes) in first-class cricket in the 2000 season with 55 dismissals
Best batting: 63 Essex v Glamorgan, Chelmsford 2001

2002 Season

	M	Inns	NO	Runs	HS	Avge	100s	50s	Ct	St	O	M	Runs	Wkts	Avge	Best	5wI	10wM
Test																		
All First	1	2	1	28	16 *	28.00	-	-	-	2								
1-day Int																		
C & G																		
B & H																		
1-day Lge																		

Career Performances

	M	Inns	NO	Runs	HS	Avge	100s	50s	Ct	St	Balls	Runs	Wkts	Avge	Best	5wI	10wM
Test																	
All First	61	97	12	1409	63	16.57	-	3	168	13	12	8	0	-		-	-
1-day Int																	
C & G	4	3	1	41	36 *	20.50	-	-	2	1							
B & H	6	5	0	49	24	9.80	-	-	2	1							
1-day Lge	33	23	5	217	37	12.05	-	-	27	4							

ILOTT, M. C.　　　　　　Essex

Name: <u>Mark</u> Christopher Ilott
Role: Left-hand bat, left-arm medium-fast swing bowler
Born: 27 August 1970, Watford
Height: 6ft 1in **Weight:** 13st 8lbs
Nickname: Ramble, Chook
County debut: 1988
County cap: 1993
Benefit: 2002
Test debut: 1993
Tests: 5
50 wickets in a season: 5
1st-Class 50s: 4
1st-Class 5 w. in innings: 27
1st-Class 10 w. in match: 3
1st-Class catches: 54
One-Day 5 w. in innings: 1
Place in batting averages: (2001 215th av. 16.90)
Place in bowling averages: 123rd av. 39.93 (2001 85th av. 34.11)
Strike rate: 72.68 (career 55.85)
Parents: John and Glenys

Wife and date of marriage: Sandra, 14 October 1994
Children: James Christopher Mark, 6 October 1996; Madeleine-Rose, 3 March 1999
Family links with cricket: 'Father now umpires at Minor Counties level. Brother skippers Langleybury in the Hertfordshire League Premier Division'
Education: Kingsway Junior; Francis Combe Secondary Modern
Qualifications: 8 O-levels, 2 A-levels, first two coaching awards, diploma in Fitness and Nutrition
Career outside cricket: 'Hospitality business and website publisher'
Overseas tours: England A to Sri Lanka 1990-91, to Australia 1992-93, to South Africa 1993-94, to India 1994-95; England to South Africa 1995-96
Overseas teams played for: East Torrens District, Adelaide 1989-91
Career highlights: 'England games – all five of them. B&H victory 1998; NatWest victory 1997; Essex cap 1993'
Cricket moments to forget: 'The various times I have limped off with injury, or when Keith Newell dispatched [the ball] all over Chelmsford for 40 in two overs [2001]'
Cricketers particularly admired: Malcolm Marshall, Graham Gooch, John Lever, Nasser Hussain
Young players to look out for: James Foster, Justin Bishop
Other sports played: Snooker, badminton
Other sports followed: Football (Liverpool and Watford)
Relaxations: Guitar playing and cutting grass ('no one's in particular')
Extras: Took his 450th wicket for Essex (Nick Knight) v Warwickshire at Chelmsford 1999. Retired at the end of the 2002 season
Best batting: 60 England A v Warwickshire, Edgbaston 1995
Best bowling: 9-19 Essex v Northamptonshire, Luton 1995

2002 Season

	M	Inns	NO	Runs	HS	Avge	100s	50s	Ct	St	O	M	Runs	Wkts	Avge	Best	5wI	10wM
Test																		
All First	6	5	3	45	28	22.50	-	-	4	-	193.5	45	639	16	39.93	4-67	-	-
1-day Int																		
C & G																		
B & H																		
1-day Lge																		

Career Performances

	M	Inns	NO	Runs	HS	Avge	100s	50s	Ct	St	Balls	Runs	Wkts	Avge	Best	5wI	10wM
Test	5	6	2	28	15	7.00	-	-	-	-	1042	542	12	45.16	3-48	-	-
All First	192	245	52	2830	60	14.66	-	4	54	-	35359	17537	633	27.70	9-19	27	3
1-day Int																	
C & G	23	13	6	125	54 *	17.85	-	1	6	-	1440	876	25	35.04	3-20	-	
B & H	36	14	4	107	26 *	10.70	-	-	4	-	1944	1205	56	21.51	5-21	1	
1-day Lge	122	75	27	522	56 *	10.87	-	1	20	-	5126	3892	147	26.47	4-15	-	

INNES, K. J. Sussex

Name: <u>Kevin</u> John Innes
Role: Right-hand bat, right-arm
medium bowler
Born: 24 September 1975, Wellingborough
Height: 5ft 10in **Weight:** 11st 5lbs
Nickname: KJ, Squirrel, Ernie
County debut: 1994 (Northamptonshire),
2002 (Sussex)
1st-Class 50s: 3
1st-Class catches: 13
Place in batting averages: 127th av. 31.86
(2001 229th av. 14.33)
Place in bowling averages: 57th av. 28.75
Strike rate: 55.55 (career 53.77)
Parents: Peter and Jane
Wife and date of marriage: Caroline, 2001
Education: Boothville Middle School;

Weston Favell Upper School, Northampton
Qualifications: 6 GCSEs, 4 O-levels, Level 3 Staff 1 coach
Off-season: 'Coaching in Northampton; relaxing; playing golf, snooker, squash'
Overseas tours: England U18 to South Africa 1992-93, to Denmark 1993; England
U19 to Sri Lanka 1993-94
Overseas teams played for: Karori, New Zealand 1995-97
Cricketers particularly admired: Glenn McGrath, Steve Waugh
Young players to look out for: Mark Powell
Other sports played: Golf, snooker, fishing
Relaxations: 'Spending time with my wife; sleeping and eating out; music, reading
books/magazines'
Extras: Won the MCC Lord's Taverners Award U13 and U15. Became youngest
player to play for Northants 2nd XI, aged 14 years 9 months. Played for England U19
in home series against India U19 in 1994. 2nd XI Championship Player of the Year
1998. Left Northamptonshire during the 2001-02 off-season and joined Sussex for
2002
Best batting: 63 Northamptonshire v Lancashire, Northampton 1996
Best bowling: 4-41 Sussex v Surrey, Hove 2002

2002 Season

	M	Inns	NO	Runs	HS	Avge	100s	50s	Ct	St	O	M	Runs	Wkts	Avge	Best	5wI	10wM
Test																		
All First	13	22	7	478	60 *	31.86	-	2	3	-	268.3	65	834	29	28.75	4-41	-	-
1-day Int																		
C & G	2	1	0	1	1	1.00	-	-	1	-	13	0	83	0	-		-	-
B & H																		
1-day Lge	12	8	3	193	50 *	38.60	-	1	3	-	62.1	5	284	10	28.40	4-26	-	

Career Performances

	M	Inns	NO	Runs	HS	Avge	100s	50s	Ct	St	Balls	Runs	Wkts	Avge	Best	5wI	10wM
Test																	
All First	34	54	13	1000	63	24.39	-	3	13	-	3603	1951	67	29.11	4-41	-	-
1-day Int																	
C & G	7	4	2	34	25	17.00	-	-	3	-	201	197	5	39.40	3-26	-	
B & H	9	5	1	76	37	19.00	-	-	-	-	427	372	6	62.00	1-25	-	
1-day Lge	54	36	13	573	55	24.91	-	2	15	-	1701	1500	52	28.84	4-26	-	

INNESS, M. W. H. Northamptonshire

Name: <u>Mathew</u> William Hunter Inness
Role: Left-hand bat, left-arm
fast-medium bowler
Born: 13 January 1978, East Melbourne,
Victoria, Australia
Height: 6ft **Weight:** 13st 8lbs
Nickname: Minnie
County debut: 2002
1st-Class 5 w. in innings: 6
1st-Class 10 w. in match: 2
1st-Class catches: 17
Place in bowling averages: 56th av. 28.60
Strike rate: 46.66 (career 52.82)
Off-season: Playing for Victoria
Overseas teams played for:
Victoria 1997-98 –
Career highlights to date: Taking a hat-trick
against New South Wales
Cricketers particularly admired: Shane Warne
Other sports played: Australian Rules football (Victorian Schoolboys)
Other sports followed: Australian Rules football (Hawthorn)
Extras: Has attended Commonwealth Bank [Australian] Cricket Academy as a player

(1997) and on a coaching scholarship. Had match figures of 11-108 v New South Wales at Richmond 1999-2000, including his first Pura Cup five-wicket returns and a hat-trick. Represented Australia A v West Indians at Hobart 2000-01. Topped Pura Cup bowling averages 2001-02 with 31 wickets at 19.26. Was Northamptonshire's overseas player for the latter part of the 2002 season, replacing Mike Hussey, absent on international duty

Best batting: 27 Victoria v New South Wales, Melbourne 1997-98
Best bowling: 7-19 Victoria v New South Wales, Sydney 2001-02

2002 Season

	M	Inns	NO	Runs	HS	Avge	100s	50s	Ct	St	O	M	Runs	Wkts	Avge	Best	5wI	10wM
Test																		
All First	4	4	1	66	25	22.00	-	-	5	-	116.4	25	429	15	28.60	7-90	1	-
1-day Int																		
C & G																		
B & H																		
1-day Lge	5	3	1	4	2 *	2.00	-	-	-	-	43	3	197	5	39.40	2-28	-	

Career Performances

	M	Inns	NO	Runs	HS	Avge	100s	50s	Ct	St	Balls	Runs	Wkts	Avge	Best	5wI	10wM
Test																	
All First	45	47	17	143	27	4.76	-	-	17	-	8610	4064	163	24.93	7-19	6	2
1-day Int																	
C & G																	
B & H																	
1-day Lge	5	3	1	4	2 *	2.00	-	-	-	-	258	197	5	39.40	2-28	-	

44. Victoria's all-time leading wicket-taker joined
Nottinghamshire as overseas player for 2000 as a replacement for the injured
Shoaib Akhtar. Name him.

IRANI, R. C. Essex

Name: Ronald (<u>Ronnie</u>) Charles Irani
Role: Right-hand bat, right-arm
medium bowler, county 1st XI captain
Born: 26 October 1971, Leigh, Lancashire
Height: 6ft 4in **Weight:** 14st 4lbs
Nickname: Reggie
County debut: 1990 (Lancashire),
1994 (Essex)
County cap: 1994 (Essex)
Test debut: 1996
Tests: 3
One-Day Internationals: 17
1000 runs in a season: 5
50 wickets in a season: 1
1st-Class 50s: 50
1st-Class 100s: 17
1st-Class 200s: 1
1st-Class 5 w. in innings: 9
1st-Class catches: 64
One-Day 100s: 3
One-Day 5 w. in innings: 4
Place in batting averages: 16th av. 61.06 (2001 132nd av. 28.85)
Place in bowling averages: 6th av. 20.37 (2001 72nd av. 32.50)
Strike rate: 47.13 (career 59.97)
Parents: Jimmy and Anne
Wife's name: Lorraine
Children: Simone
Family links with cricket: 'Father played league cricket for over 30 years. Mum did teas for years as well'
Education: Church Road Primary School; Smithills Comprehensive School
Qualifications: 9 GCSEs
Off-season: Touring with England
Overseas tours: England YC to Australia 1989-90; England A to Pakistan 1995-96, to Bangladesh and New Zealand 1999-2000; England to Zimbabwe and New Zealand 1996-97, to Sri Lanka (ICC Champions Trophy) 2002-03, to Australia 2002-03 (VB Series); England VI to Hong Kong 2002
Overseas teams played for: Technicol Natal, Durban 1992-93; Eden-Roskill, Auckland 1993-94
Career highlights to date: 'Playing for England. Winning one-day trophies with Essex'
Cricketers particularly admired: Graham Gooch, Javed Miandad, Viv Richards, Wasim Akram

Young players to look out for: Will Jefferson, Justin Bishop
Other sports played: Golf, pool
Other sports followed: Football (Manchester United), Muay Thai boxing
Relaxations: Fly fishing
Extras: Played for England YC in home series v Australian YC 1991, scoring a century and three 50s in six innings and being named Bull Man of the Series. Appointed vice-captain of Essex in 1999. Achieved double of 1000 first-class runs and 50 first-class wickets in 1999. Took over 1st XI captaincy of Essex at the start of the 2000 season, Nasser Hussain remaining as club captain. His then career best innings of 168* v Glamorgan at Cardiff 2000 lasted nine hours and 20 minutes, during which time he received 479 balls. Scored a 55-ball century (ending up 108*) v Glamorgan at Chelmsford in the Norwich Union League 2001. Recorded a five-wicket innings return (5-58) and scored a century (119) for Essex v Surrey at Ilford 2001, following up with a wicket with the first ball of his opening spell in Surrey's second innings. B&H Gold Awards for his 47 and 5-36 (his maiden five-wicket return in the B&H) v Sussex at Chelmsford, for his 32-ball 50* v Kent at Canterbury and for his 57 and 3-30 in the semi-final v Worcestershire at Chelmsford 2002. C&G Man of the Match award for his 86* plus 2-47 v Middlesex at Chelmsford 2002. Struck a 70-ball century (101) to set up a Championship victory v Derbyshire at Chelmsford 2002. Scored maiden first-class double century (207*) v Northamptonshire at Ilford 2002. Took a season record 20 wickets in the 2002 B&H. Man of the Match award v India at The Oval in the NatWest Series 2002 for his 53 (his maiden ODI fifty) and 5-26 (his maiden ODI five-wicket return and the best ODI analysis recorded at The Oval); also named 'Fans' Player of the Series'. Granted a benefit for 2003
Opinions on cricket: 'Would like to see more money in the game all round; not just wages but facilities, stadiums etc.'
Best batting: 207* Essex v Northamptonshire, Ilford 2002
Best bowling: 6-71 Essex v Nottinghamshire, Trent Bridge 2002
Stop press: Took 4-37 v Zimbabwe at Colombo in the ICC Champions Trophy 2002-03. Captained England XI v Sir Donald Bradman XI at Bowral 2002-03. Selected for England squad for 2002-03 World Cup

2002 Season

	M	Inns	NO	Runs	HS	Avge	100s	50s	Ct	St	O	M	Runs	Wkts	Avge	Best	5wI	10wM
Test																		
All First	12	19	3	977	207 *	61.06	3	1	-		227.5	72	591	29	20.37	6-71	1	-
1-day Int	7	6	1	169	53	33.80	-	1	2	-	60	2	252	8	31.50	5-26	1	
C & G	3	2	1	118	86 *	118.00	-	1	-	-	28	2	129	4	32.25	2-47	-	
B & H	7	7	2	214	57	42.80	-	2	4	-	64.3	10	262	20	13.10	5-28	2	
1-day Lge	10	10	3	235	51 *	33.57	-	2	2	-	75.2	9	324	16	20.25	3-29	-	

Career Performances

	M	Inns	NO	Runs	HS	Avge	100s	50s	Ct	St	Balls	Runs	Wkts	Avge	Best	5wI	10wM
Test	3	5	0	86	41	17.20	-	-	2	-	192	112	3	37.33	1-22	-	-
All First	173	285	35	9438	207 *	37.75	18	50	64	-	19789	9762	330	29.58	6-71	9	-
1-day Int	17	16	3	247	53	19.00	-	1	4	-	689	498	12	41.50	5-26	1	
C & G	24	21	3	830	124	46.11	1	7	7	-	1412	949	34	27.91	4-41	-	
B & H	36	30	4	991	82 *	38.11	-	6	10	-	1755	1291	58	22.25	5-28	2	
1-day Lge	139	132	21	3023	108 *	27.23	2	16	32	-	5078	3831	160	23.94	5-33	1	

JAMES, S. P. Glamorgan

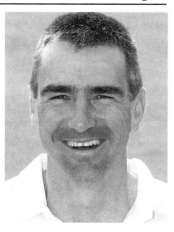

Name: Stephen Peter James
Role: Right-hand opening bat, county captain
Born: 7 September 1967, Lydney
Height: 6ft **Weight:** 13st
Nickname: Sid, Jamo
County debut: 1985
County cap: 1992
Benefit: 2001
Test debut: 1998
Tests: 2
1000 runs in a season: 9
1st-Class 50s: 58
1st-Class 100s: 41
1st-Class 200s: 5
1st-Class 300s: 1
1st-Class catches: 172
One-Day 100s: 7
Place in batting averages: 27th av. 52.90
(2001 39th av. 47.33)
Parents: Peter and Margaret
Wife and date of marriage: Jane Louise, 26 September 1997
Children: Bethan Amy, 28 August 1998 ('during Test match!')
Family links with cricket: Father played for Gloucestershire 2nd XI. Distant relative of Dominic Ostler
Education: Monmouth School; University College, Swansea; Cambridge University
Qualifications: BA (Hons) Wales – Classics; BA (Hons) Cantab – Land Economy
Off-season: 'Rugby writing for *Sunday Telegraph*, as well as columns for *South Wales Argus* and *Western Mail*'
Overseas tours: Welsh Schools to Barbados 1984; Monmouth Schools to Sri Lanka 1985; Combined Universities to Barbados 1989; Glamorgan to Trinidad 1989-90, to Zimbabwe 1990-91, to Cape Town 1993-94, to Pretoria 1995-96; England A to Kenya and Sri Lanka 1997-98 (vice-captain)

Overseas teams played for: Bionics, Zimbabwe 1990-92; Universals Sports Club, Zimbabwe 1992-96

Career highlights to date: 'Hitting winning runs to win the Championship in 1997'

Cricket moments to forget: 'Pair in a day, Luton 1992'

Cricketers particularly admired: Michael Atherton, Graham Burgess

Young players to look out for: 'All our youngsters at Glamorgan', Rob White

Other sports played/followed: Rugby union (Cardiff RFC and Lydney RFC; 'played for Lydney, Gloucestershire and Cambridge University and was on bench for Varsity Match'), football (West Ham United)

Injuries: Out for the last two weeks of the 2002 season with a broken finger that required surgery; also needed operation on a recurring knee problem

Relaxations: Reading, *Telegraph* crosswords, videos, weight-training

Extras: Scored maiden century (106) in only second first-class innings, v Oxford University at The Parks 1987. In 1995 broke Matthew Maynard's club record for number of one-day runs in a season with 1263; in same season, also broke Hugh Morris's club record for number of Sunday League runs in a season with 815. First player to reach 1000 runs in 1997 and was voted the Cricketer of the Year by both the Wombwell Cricket Lovers' Society and the PCA. Appointed vice-captain of Glamorgan in 1999. Set record for highest post-war score by a Glamorgan batsman, with 259* v Notts at Colwyn Bay 1999 (his fifth successive century v Notts and still the highest score by a Glamorgan No. 1), beating Matthew Maynard's 243 in 1991. Set record (batting at No. 2) for highest individual score ever by a Glamorgan batsman, with 309* v Sussex at Colwyn Bay in 2000, setting in the process a new record first-wicket partnership for Glamorgan of 374 with Matthew Elliott (177); during his innings he also became the first Glamorgan batsman to record five scores of 200-plus. Captained Wales to victory over an England XI in a one-day warm-up match at Cardiff 2002, top-scoring with 83*. Scored 184 v Nottinghamshire at Colwyn Bay 2002, in the process sharing with Adrian Dale (109) in a record fourth-wicket partnership for Glamorgan in matches against Nottinghamshire (217) and bringing his Championship total at the ground in his three innings since 1999 (did not play there in 2001) to 752 for once out. Captain of Glamorgan since 2001

Opinions on cricket: 'EU cricketers – what a joke!'

Best batting: 309* Glamorgan v Sussex, Colwyn Bay 2000

2002 Season

	M	Inns	NO	Runs	HS	Avge	100s	50s	Ct	St	O	M	Runs	Wkts	Avge	Best	5wI	10wM
Test																		
All First	14	22	1	1111	249	52.90	4	3	7	-								
1-day Int																		
C & G	1	1	0	47	47	47.00	-	-	-	-								
B & H	4	4	0	16	14	4.00	-	-	-	-								
1-day Lge	12	11	3	305	86	38.12	-	3	2	-								

Career Performances

	M	Inns	NO	Runs	HS	Avge	100s	50s	Ct	St	Balls	Runs	Wkts	Avge	Best	5wI	10wM
Test	2	4	0	71	36	17.75	-	-	-	-							
All First	244	422	33	15876	309 *	40.81	47	58	172	-	2	3	0	-	-	-	-
1-day Int																	
C & G	30	29	3	1144	123	44.00	3	6	9	-							
B & H	47	47	4	1340	135	31.16	2	9	12	-							
1-day Lge	152	146	20	4292	107	34.06	2	32	35	-							

JARVIS, P. W. Somerset

Name: <u>Paul</u> William Jarvis
Role: Right-hand bat, right-arm
fast-medium bowler
Born: 29 June 1965, Redcar
Height: 5ft 11in **Weight:** 12st 7lbs
Nickname: Gnash, Jarv, Krusty
County debut: 1981 (Yorkshire),
1994 (Sussex), 1999 (Somerset)
County cap: 1986 (Yorkshire), 1994
(Sussex)
Test debut: 1987-88
Tests: 9
One-Day Internationals: 16
50 wickets in a season: 4
1st-Class 50s: 10
1st-Class 5 w. in innings: 22
1st-Class 10 w. in match: 3
1st-Class catches: 66
One-Day 5 w. in innings: 6
Strike rate: (career 54.31)
Parents: Malcolm and Marjorie
Children: Alexander Michael, 13 June 1989; Isabella Grace, 21 March 1993
Education: Bydales Comprehensive School, Marske, Cleveland
Qualifications: 4 O-levels, advanced cricket coach
Overseas tours: Yorkshire to St Lucia and Barbados 1987, to South Africa 1991;
England to India and Pakistan (World Cup) 1987-88, to Pakistan 1987-88, to Australia
and New Zealand 1987-88, to India and Sri Lanka 1992-93; unofficial England XI to
South Africa 1989-90
Overseas teams played for: Mosman Middle Harbour, Sydney 1984-85; Avendale,
Cape Town 1985-86; Manly-Warringah, Sydney 1987; Onslow, Wellington 1994-95
Cricketers particularly admired: Ian Botham, Malcolm Marshall

Young players to look out for: Matt Bulbeck
Other sports followed: Football
Relaxations: 'Eating out, drinking real ale and good wine'
Extras: In 1981 became youngest player ever to play for Yorkshire in County Championship (16 years, 2 months, 13 days). Became youngest player to take hat-trick in Sunday League, v Derbyshire at Derby 1982, and youngest to take first-class hat-trick for Yorkshire (20 years, 25 days), v Derbyshire at Chesterfield 1985. Played for England YC v West Indies 1982 and Australia 1983. Retired at the end of the 2000 season; re-signed as emergency cover during 2002 and released at the end of the season
Best batting: 80 Yorkshire v Northamptonshire, Scarborough 1992
Best bowling: 7-55 Yorkshire v Surrey, Headingley 1986

2002 Season

	M	Inns	NO	Runs	HS	Avge	100s	50s	Ct	St	O	M	Runs	Wkts	Avge	Best	5wl	10wM
Test																		
All First																		
1-day Int																		
C & G	1	0	0	0	0	-	-	-	-	-	2	0	25	0	-		-	-
B & H																		
1-day Lge	1	1	0	0	0	0.00	-	-	-	-	8	0	54	2	27.00	2-54	-	

Career Performances

	M	Inns	NO	Runs	HS	Avge	100s	50s	Ct	St	Balls	Runs	Wkts	Avge	Best	5wl	10wM
Test	9	15	2	132	29 *	10.15	-	-	2	-	1912	965	21	45.95	4-107	-	-
All First	215	268	67	3373	80	16.78	-	10	66	-	35525	18914	654	28.92	7-55	22	3
1-day Int	16	8	2	31	16 *	5.16	-	-	1	-	879	672	24	28.00	5-35	1	
C & G	29	16	5	177	34 *	16.09	-	-	7	-	1718	1231	36	34.19	5-55	1	
B & H	50	27	9	353	63	19.61	-	1	4	-	2750	1709	78	21.91	4-34	-	
1-day Lge	164	97	32	693	43	10.66	-	-	35	-	6982	5403	233	23.18	6-27	4	

45. Who was Leicestershire's overseas player in 1999?

JEFFERSON, W. I.   Essex

Name: William (<u>Will</u>) Ingleby Jefferson
Role: Right-hand bat, right-arm
medium bowler
Born: 25 October 1979, Derby ('but native
of Norfolk')
Height: 6ft 10½in **Weight:** 15st 2lbs
Nickname: Jeffo
County debut: 2000
County cap: 2002
1st-Class 50s: 3
1st-Class 100s: 2
1st-Class catches: 20
One-Day 100s: 2
Place in batting averages: 124th av. 32.60
Parents: Richard and Pauline
Marital status: Single
Family links with cricket: Grandfather
Jefferson played for the Army and Combined
Services in the 1920s. Father, R. I. Jefferson, played for Cambridge University 1961
and Surrey 1961-66
Education: Beeston Hall School, Norfolk; Oundle School, Northants;
Durham University
Qualifications: 9 GCSEs, 3 A-levels, BA (Hons) Sport in the Community, Levels 1
and 2 cricket coaching awards
Off-season: 'Spending four months in Perth at Paul Terry Academy'
Overseas tours: Oundle School to South Africa 1995
Overseas teams played for: Young People's Club, Paarl, South Africa 1998-99
Career highlights to date: 'Being awarded county cap on final day of the 2002
season. Scoring 165* to help beat Notts and secure 2002 second division
Championship'
Cricket moments to forget: 'Losing to Loughborough in the final of the BUSA
Championships in 2000 off the last ball of the match'
Cricketers particularly admired: Mark Waugh, Shaun Pollock, Jacques Kallis,
Steve Waugh, Nasser Hussain
Young players to look out for: Jamie Dalrymple, Justin Ontong (South African)
Other sports played: Golf (12 handicap), tennis, swimming
Other sports followed: 'Follow most sports'
Relaxations: 'Spending time with my girlfriend; listening to music; catching up with
family and friends'
Extras: Aged 15, received a letter handwritten by Sir Colin Cowdrey congratulating
him on scoring 83 and 106* in his two games in the Sun Life of Canada U15 Club
Championships. Holmwoods School Cricketer of the Year 1998. Represented British

Universities 2000, 2001 and v Sri Lankans at Northampton 2002. Played for Durham University CCE 2001 and 2002. Scored maiden first-class century (109) v Glamorgan at Chelmsford 2002. Scored maiden one-day century 111* v Middlesex at Lord's in the NUL 2002. Awarded Essex cap 2002

Opinions on cricket: 'How can you expect fitness and performance levels to be maintained and players to remain physically and mentally fresh with such a congested fixture list?'

Best batting: 165* Essex v Nottinghamshire, Chelmsford 2002

2002 Season

	M	Inns	NO	Runs	HS	Avge	100s	50s	Ct	St	O	M	Runs	Wkts	Avge	Best	5wI	10wM
Test																		
All First	15	29	4	815	165 *	32.60	2	2	17	-								
1-day Int																		
C & G																		
B & H																		
1-day Lge	13	13	1	421	111 *	35.08	2	-	8	-								

Career Performances

	M	Inns	NO	Runs	HS	Avge	100s	50s	Ct	St	Balls	Runs	Wkts	Avge	Best	5wI	10wM
Test																	
All First	20	37	4	1021	165 *	30.93	2	3	20	-							
1-day Int																	
C & G																	
B & H																	
1-day Lge	17	17	1	540	111 *	33.75	2	2	9	-							

46. For which county did Allan Border play in 1986 and 1988?

JOHNSON, N. C.   Hampshire

Name: <u>Neil</u> Clarkson Johnson
Role: Left-hand bat, right-arm
fast-medium bowler
Born: 24 January 1970, Harare, Zimbabwe
Nickname: Johnno
County debut: 1997 (Leicestershire),
2001 (Hampshire)
County cap: 1997 (Leicestershire),
2001 (Hampshire)
Test debut: 1998-99
Tests: 13
One-Day Internationals: 48
1000 runs in a season: 1
1st-Class 50s: 50
1st-Class 100s: 9
1st-Class 5 w. in innings: 2
1st-Class catches: 196
One-Day 100s: 6

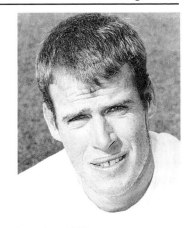

Place in batting averages: 129th av. 31.74 (2001 53rd av. 44.70)
Place in bowling averages: 111th av. 37.00 (2001 113th av. 39.60)
Strike rate: 66.09 (career 62.70)
Education: Kingswood College, Grahamstown, South Africa; University of
Port Elizabeth
Overseas tours: South Africa A to Zimbabwe 1994-95; Zimbabwe to Pakistan
1998-99, to South Africa 1999-2000, to West Indies 1999-2000, to England 2000
Overseas teams played for: Eastern Province B 1989-90 – 1991-92; Natal 1992-93 –
1997-98; Matabeleland 1998-99; Western Province 2000-01 –
Extras: Moved from Zimbabwe to South Africa at the age of ten. Represented Eastern
Province Schools, opening the bowling with Brett Schultz. Represented South African
Schools 1988. Leicestershire's overseas player in 1997. Became Zimbabwean citizen
once again in 1998. Scored maiden Test century (107, after going in on hat-trick ball)
in his second Test, for Zimbabwe v Pakistan at Peshawar 1998-99. Scored 59 and took
4-42 v Kenya, scored 76 and took 3-27 v South Africa and scored 132* v Australia in
the 1999 World Cup, winning Man of the Match award on each occasion. Scored 95*
in the NatWest Triangular Series international v West Indies at Bristol 2000, winning
the Man of the Match award. Retired from international cricket after the NatWest
Triangular Series v England and West Indies in 2000. Joined Hampshire as overseas
player for 2001. Man of the Match for his 88 and 29-ball 37 in Hampshire's victory
over the Australians in the Vodafone Challenge match at West End 2001. Awarded
Hampshire cap 2001. Released by Hampshire at the end of the 2002 season
Best batting: 150 Leicestershire v Lancashire, Leicester 1997
Best bowling: 5-79 Natal v Boland, Stellenbosch 1993-94

2002 Season

	M	Inns	NO	Runs	HS	Avge	100s	50s	Ct	St	O	M	Runs	Wkts	Avge	Best	5wI	10wM
Test																		
All First	17	29	2	857	117	31.74	1	6	27	-	242.2	52	814	22	37.00	3-22	-	-
1-day Int																		
C & G	2	2	1	118	66 *	118.00	-	2	4	-	10	0	55	1	55.00	1-27	-	
B & H	5	5	0	98	46	19.60	-	-	1	-	21	0	113	1	113.00	1-46	-	
1-day Lge	15	15	0	408	92	27.20	-	3	13	-	77	3	396	12	33.00	3-42	-	

Career Performances

	M	Inns	NO	Runs	HS	Avge	100s	50s	Ct	St	Balls	Runs	Wkts	Avge	Best	5wI	10wM
Test	13	23	1	532	107	24.18	-	4	12	-	1186	594	15	39.60	4-77	-	-
All First	147	229	27	6928	150	34.29	9	50	196	-	13921	7190	222	32.38	5-79	2	-
1-day Int	48	48	2	1679	132 *	36.50	4	6	19	-	1503	1220	35	34.85	4-42	-	
C & G	5	5	2	250	113 *	83.33	1	2	5	-	96	101	1	101.00	1-27	-	
B & H	17	17	2	305	58	20.33	-	2	3	-	588	540	12	45.00	3-41	-	
1-day Lge	41	41	2	1189	105 *	30.48	1	7	34	-	1142	1083	36	30.08	3-37	-	

JOHNSON, P.   Nottinghamshire

Name: Paul Johnson
Role: Right-hand bat, right-arm
'occasional' bowler
Born: 24 April 1965, Newark
Height: 'Below average' **Weight:** 'Above average'
Nickname: Johno, Midge
County debut: 1982
County cap: 1986
Benefit: 1995
1000 runs in a season: 8
1st-Class 50s: 119
1st-Class 100s: 40
1st-Class catches: 236
1st-Class stumpings: 1
One-Day 100s: 13
Place in batting averages: 138th av. 30.09
(2001 117th av. 31.09)
Strike rate: (career 109.00)
Parents: Donald Edward and Joyce
Wife and date of marriage: Jackie, 24 December 1993
Children: Ruth, 28 September 1994; Eve, 9 September 1996

Family links with cricket: Father played local cricket and is a qualified coach
Education: Grove Comprehensive School, Newark
Qualifications: 9 CSEs, Level 3 coach
Career outside cricket: Coaching
Overseas tours: England A to Bermuda and West Indies 1991-92; Christians in Sport to Zimbabwe 1997, 1998
Overseas teams played for: RAU Johannesburg 1985-86; Hutt District, Wellington, New Zealand 1988-89
Career highlights: 'Winning all four domestic honours'
Cricket moments to forget: 'Losing never gets easier!'
Cricketers particularly admired: Clive Rice, Mike Gatting, Michael Atherton
Young players to look out for: Gary Pratt, Samit Patel
Other sports played: '"Royal Oak" pool team, golf, squash, indoor powerboat racing'
Other sports followed: Ice hockey (Nottingham Panthers), football (Nottingham Forest)
Relaxations: Listening to music, crosswords and reading autobiographies
Extras: Played for English Schools in 1980-81 and England YC 1982 and 1983. Youngest player to join the Nottinghamshire staff. Made 235 for Nottinghamshire 2nd XI, July 1982, aged 17. Scored 125 v Gloucestershire at Bristol 1983, in the process becoming (at 18 years 128 days) the then youngest player to score a first-class century for Nottinghamshire (now Bilal Shafayat). Won Man of the Match award in his first NatWest game (101* v Staffordshire) in 1985, but missed the final owing to appendicitis. Sunday morning soccer referee in Nottingham. Took over the Nottinghamshire captaincy from Tim Robinson at the start of the 1996 season; relinquished captaincy during 1998 season. Against Surrey at Trent Bridge 2001, passed Derek Randall's record of 7062 runs to become Notts highest run-scorer in the domestic one-day league. Scored 96 v Derbyshire at Trent Bridge 2002, in the process passing 20,000 runs in first-class cricket (later became the eleventh batsman to score 20,000 first-class runs for Nottinghamshire, v Worcestershire at Kidderminster 2002); also passed 10,000 runs in one-day cricket during the 2002 season, becoming the only uncapped current player to have achieved this 'double'. Retired at the end of the 2002 season to become Nottinghamshire club coach
Opinions on cricket: 'Too many people have too many opinions who have not played too many matches.'
Best batting: 187 Nottinghamshire v Lancashire, Old Trafford 1993
Best bowling: 1-9 Nottinghamshire v Cambridge University, Trent Bridge 1984

2002 Season

	M	Inns	NO	Runs	HS	Avge	100s	50s	Ct	St	O	M	Runs	Wkts	Avge	Best	5wI	10wM
Test																		
All First	14	25	3	662	96	30.09	-	5	7	-	1.2	0	12	0	-	-	-	-
1-day Int																		
C & G	1	1	1	25	25*	-	-	-	-	-								
B & H	2	2	0	34	21	17.00	-	-	1	-								
1-day Lge	12	10	0	151	36	15.10	-	-	-	-								

Career Performances

	M	Inns	NO	Runs	HS	Avge	100s	50s	Ct	St	Balls	Runs	Wkts	Avge	Best	5wI	10wM
Test																	
All First	371	624	60	20534	187	36.40	40	119	236	1	654	617	6	102.83	1-9	-	-
1-day Int																	
C & G	39	38	3	1083	146	30.94	3	3	12	-	18	20	0	-		-	-
B & H	71	66	13	1711	104 *	32.28	2	11	16	-							
1-day Lge	269	253	29	7225	167 *	32.25	8	42	80	-	5	3	1	3.00	1-2	-	

JOHNSON, R. L. Somerset

Name: <u>Richard</u> Leonard Johnson
Role: Right-hand bat, right-arm
fast-medium bowler
Born: 29 December 1974, Chertsey
Height: 6ft 2in **Weight:** 14st 3lbs
Nickname: Jono, Lenny, The Greek
County debut: 1992 (Middlesex),
2001 (Somerset)
County cap: 1995 (Middlesex),
2001 (Somerset)
50 wickets in a season: 4
1st-Class 50s: 6
1st-Class 5 w. in innings: 14
1st-Class 10 w. in match: 3
1st-Class catches: 47
One-Day 5 w. in innings: 1
Place in batting averages: 212th av. 22.30

(2001 111th av. 31.58)
Place in bowling averages: 8th av. 21.25 (2001 28th av. 23.77)
Strike rate: 42.86 (career 49.85)
Parents: Roger and Mary Anne
Marital status: Engaged
Family links with cricket: Father and grandfather played club cricket
Education: Chennestone; Sunbury Manor School; Spelthorne College
Qualifications: 9 GCSEs, A-level in Physical Education, NCA senior coaching award
Off-season: 'Mainly relaxing and getting my body ready for next season'
Overseas tours: England U18 to South Africa 1992-93; England U19 to Sri Lanka
1993-94; England A to India 1994-95; MCC to Bangladesh 1999-2000, to Canada
2000-01; England to India 2001-02
Career highlights to date: 'Taking all ten wickets v Derby. Getting called up for
England. Winning C&G Trophy [2001]'

Cricket moments to forget: 'Losing C&G final [2002]'
Cricketers particularly admired: Ian Botham, Richard Hadlee and Angus Fraser 'for his quality bowling and his dedication to moaning'
Young players to look out for: Matthew Wood, Ed Joyce
Other sports followed: Football (Tottenham), rugby (London Irish)
Injuries: Out for two periods of four weeks with a pulled hamstring
Relaxations: 'Eating out with fiancée and friends; having a few beers with Nashy and listening to him gloating about Middlesex's promotion'
Extras: Represented Middlesex at all levels from U11. Took 10 for 45 v Derbyshire in July 1994, becoming the first person to take ten wickets in an English first-class innings since Ian Thomson (Sussex) in 1964; also most economical ten-wicket haul since Hedley Verity's 10 for 10 in 1932. Left Middlesex at the end of the 2000 season and joined Somerset for 2001. Took five wickets in an innings in his first two Championship matches for Somerset – 5-107 v Lancashire and 5-106 v Glamorgan. Included in England squad for third, fourth and fifth Tests v Australia 2001. Called up for England Test tour of India 2001-02 after withdrawal of Andrew Caddick
Opinions on cricket: 'Overseas players are vital to keep the standard of domestic cricket high, but the situation with EU-qualified players has to be looked at.'
Best batting: 69 Middlesex v Essex, Chelmsford 2000
Best bowling: 10-45 Middlesex v Derbyshire, Derby 1994

2002 Season

	M	Inns	NO	Runs	HS	Avge	100s	50s	Ct	St	O	M	Runs	Wkts	Avge	Best	5wI	10wM
Test																		
All First	9	17	4	290	61	22.30	-	1	2	-	307.1	66	914	43	21.25	7-43	2	1
1-day Int																		
C & G	3	1	0	2	2	2.00	-	-	1	-	28	4	140	5	28.00	3-51	-	
B & H	2	1	1	1	1 *	-	-	-	1	-	14	1	80	1	80.00	1-43	-	
1-day Lge	2	1	0	25	25	25.00	-	-	-	-	16	1	60	5	12.00	3-41	-	

Career Performances

	M	Inns	NO	Runs	HS	Avge	100s	50s	Ct	St	Balls	Runs	Wkts	Avge	Best	5wI	10wM
Test																	
All First	115	164	22	2422	69	17.05	-	6	47	-	19143	10181	384	26.51	10-45	14	3
1-day Int																	
C & G	24	14	3	178	45 *	16.18	-	-	4	-	1260	927	36	25.75	5-50	1	
B & H	21	15	1	155	26	11.07	-	-	3	-	1110	844	23	36.69	3-33	-	
1-day Lge	90	61	16	529	29	11.75	-	-	9	-	3704	3137	97	32.34	4-45	-	

JONES, G. O. Kent

Name: <u>Geraint</u> Owen Jones
Role: Right-hand bat, wicket-keeper
Born: 14 July 1976, Kundiawa,
Papua New Guinea
Height: 5ft 10in **Weight:** 11st
Nickname: Jonesy, Oink
County debut: 2001
1st-Class 50s: 1
1st-Class catches: 6
Parents: Emrys
Marital status: Single
Family links with cricket: 'Father was
the star off-spinner for Blaenau Ffestiniog
School side'
Education: Wilsonton Primary School,
Toowoomba, Queensland, Australia;
Harristown State High School, Toowoomba;
MacGregor State HS, Brisbane
Qualifications: NVQ Level 3 Pharmacy Technician
Overseas tours: Beenleigh-Logan U19 to New Zealand 1995
Overseas teams played for: Beenleigh-Logan, Brisbane 1995-98
Career highlights to date: 'NUL debut v Surrey at The Oval. Didn't know much
about Saqlain's first ball, but did all right from then on'
Cricket moments to forget: 'Kent 2nd XI v Nottinghamshire 2nd XI 2001 – out lbw
in first innings leaving one down legside which swung back and hit my right pad dead
in front of all three stumps'
Cricketers particularly admired: Ian Healy, Steve Waugh, Jack Russell
Young players to look out for: Robert Key, James Hockley, Ben Phillips, Rob Ferley
Other sports played: Rugby
Other sports followed: Rugby (Crickhowell RFC)
Relaxations: 'Golf, video sessions with Rob Ferley'
Extras: Scored a 39-ball 39 on Norwich Union League debut v Surrey at The Oval
2001, having arrived at the crease with his side on 59 for 5. Scored maiden first-class
50 (76*) v Sri Lankans at Canterbury 2002 in only his second first-class match. Is not
considered an overseas player
Opinions on cricket: 'Second XI competition needs to mirror first-class, not in terms
of games played but promotion and relegation, otherwise season just drifts along if you
don't play any first-team cricket. More floodlit cricket required – gets the crowds in
and enjoying the sport.'
Best batting: 76* Kent v Sri Lankans, Canterbury 2002

2002 Season

	M	Inns	NO	Runs	HS	Avge	100s	50s	Ct	St	O	M	Runs	Wkts	Avge	Best	5wI	10wM
Test																		
All First	4	4	1	162	76 *	54.00	-	1	5	-								
1-day Int																		
C & G																		
B & H																		
1-day Lge	7	7	2	96	28	19.20	-	-	1	-								

Career Performances

	M	Inns	NO	Runs	HS	Avge	100s	50s	Ct	St	Balls	Runs	Wkts	Avge	Best	5wI	10wM
Test																	
All First	5	5	1	167	76 *	41.75	-	1	6	-	6	4	0	-	-	-	-
1-day Int																	
C & G	1	0	0	0	0	-	-	-	1	-							
B & H																	
1-day Lge	11	11	2	155	39	17.22	-	-	1	-							

JONES, H. R. Warwickshire

Name: Huw Rhys Jones
Role: Right-hand bat, leg-spin bowler
Born: 23 November 1980, Oxford
Height: 6ft **Weight:** 13st 3lbs
Nickname: Jonah, Bones
County debut: 2002 (one-day)
1st-Class 50s: 2
1st-Class catches: 5
Place in batting averages: 218th av. 21.66
Parents: John and Elizabeth
Marital status: Single
Family links with cricket: 'Dad played club cricket for Leamington'
Education: Telford School; Trinity School; Warwick Sixth Form; Oxford Brookes University
Qualifications: 8 GCSEs, 3 A-levels
Career outside cricket: Oxford Brookes University
Off-season: 'Studying, finishing degree; then I would like to play in Australia to learn some cricket there'
Overseas tours: Warwickshire U19 to Cape Town 1998

Overseas teams played for: Karori CC, Wellington, New Zealand; Hams Tech CC, Border, South Africa

Career highlights to date: 'Scoring 97 against Worcestershire in first-class game for OUCCE. Making my debut for Warwickshire 1st XI against Glamorgan'

Cricket moments to forget: 'Being lbw on 97 against Worcestershire and missing chance to get maiden first-class hundred'

Cricketers particularly admired: Michael Vaughan, Matthew Hayden, Sachin Tendulkar

Young players to look out for: Graham Charlesworth, Stewart Reeve, Patrick Wolf

Other sports played: Basketball, football, golf, snooker

Other sports followed: Football (Arsenal FC)

Relaxations: 'Going out with mates; spending time with girlfriend'

Extras: Played in U15 World Cup 1996. Played for Oxford University CCE 2001 and 2002, scoring 97 v Worcestershire at The Parks 2002 and 114 v Loughborough in the UCCE final at Lord's 2002. Represented British Universities v West Indies A (50-over match) at The Parks 2002. Played for Warwickshire Board XI in the C&G 2002 – including the second round, which was played in September 2001; C&G Man of the Match award for his 72 v Leicestershire at Coventry 2002. Played for the Warwickshire Board XI side that won the final ECB 38-County competition 2002

Opinions on cricket: 'Twenty-over game a good idea. More floodlit cricket – it attracts crowds. Tighten up qualifications on British-qualified players.'

Best batting: 97 OUCCE v Worcestershire, The Parks 2002

2002 Season

	M	Inns	NO	Runs	HS	Avge	100s	50s	Ct	St	O	M	Runs	Wkts	Avge	Best	5wI	10wM
Test																		
All First	3	6	0	130	97	21.66	-	1	3	-								
1-day Int																		
C & G	1	1	0	72	72	72.00	-	1	-	-								
B & H																		
1-day Lge	1	1	0	6	6	6.00	-	-	-	-								

Career Performances

	M	Inns	NO	Runs	HS	Avge	100s	50s	Ct	St	Balls	Runs	Wkts	Avge	Best	5wI	10wM
Test																	
All First	5	10	1	220	97	24.44	-	2	5	-							
1-day Int																	
C & G	2	2	0	82	72	41.00	-	1	-	-							
B & H																	
1-day Lge	1	1	0	6	6	6.00	-	-	-	-							

JONES, I. Middlesex

Name: Ian Jones
Role: Right-hand bat, right-arm
fast bowler
Born: 11 March 1977, London
Height: 6ft 4in **Weight:** 17st
Nickname: Bubba, Jonah
County debut: 1999 (Somerset),
2002 (Middlesex)
Strike rate: 33.75 (career 61.10)
Parents: Dianne and Ronnie
Marital status: Single
Family links with cricket: Brother plays in
Durham League for Kimblesworth CC
Education: Fyndoune Community College,
Sacriston, Durham
Qualifications: 9 GCSEs, City and Guilds
Diploma in Engineering, Level 1 coaching
award
Overseas tours: Durham Academy to Sri Lanka 1996
Cricketers particularly admired: Glenn McGrath, Andrew Caddick, Allan Donald
Young players to look out for: Matt Bulbeck, Ian Blackwell, Ian Hunter
Other sports played: Football, shooting
Other sports followed: Football (Sunderland AFC)
Relaxations: 'Shooting, walking, listening to music'
Extras: First player to sign on at Durham Cricket Academy. Played for Somerset
Board XI in the C&G 2001. Took 3-14 v Surrey at The Oval in the Norwich Union
League 2001 after being called up from the stands to replace Richard Johnson, who
was unwell. Released by Somerset at the end of the 2001 season. Was with Middlesex
on a trial basis 2002; released at the end of the season
Best batting: 35 Somerset v Durham, Riverside 1999
Best bowling: 3-72 Middlesex v Gloucestershire, Southgate 2002

2002 Season

	M	Inns	NO	Runs	HS	Avge	100s	50s	Ct	St	O	M	Runs	Wkts	Avge	Best	5wI	10wM
Test																		
All First	1	1	0	29	29	29.00	-	-	-	-	22.3	3	100	4	25.00	3-72	-	-
1-day Int																		
C & G																		
B & H																		
1-day Lge	7	1	0	6	6	6.00	-	-	3	-	41.1	1	211	6	35.16	2-32	-	

Career Performances

	M	Inns	NO	Runs	HS	Avge	100s	50s	Ct	St	Balls	Runs	Wkts	Avge	Best	5wI	10wM
Test																	
All First	4	5	1	107	35	26.75	-	-	-	-	611	441	10	44.10	3-72	-	-
1-day Int																	
C & G	1	1	0	6	6	6.00	-	-	1	-	60	33	2	16.50	2-33	-	
B & H																	
1-day Lge	9	2	1	11	6	11.00	-	-	3	-	302	278	10	27.80	3-14	-	

JONES, P. S. Somerset

Name: Philip Steffan Jones
Role: Right-hand bat, right-arm fast bowler
Born: 9 February 1974, Llanelli
Height: 6ft 1in **Weight:** 14st ('fighting weight')
Nickname: Jona, Cracker, Myfanwy
County debut: 1997
50 wickets in a season: 1
1st-Class 50s: 1
1st-Class 100s: 1
1st-Class 5 w. in innings: 4
1st-Class 10 w. in match: 1
1st-Class catches: 14
One-Day 5 w. in innings: 1
Place in batting averages: (2001 217th av. 16.36)
Place in bowling averages: 137th av. 44.47 (2001 86th av. 34.15)
Strike rate: 75.57 (career 62.92)
Parents: Lyndon and Ann
Wife and date of marriage: Alexandra Louise, 12 October 2002

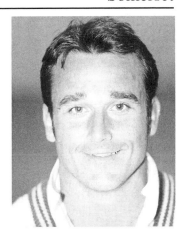

Family links with cricket: Father played for Glamorgan 2nd XI and Wales Schools; also played first-class rugby for Swansea and Llanelli
Education: Llangennech Primary School; Ysgol Gyfun y Strade, Llanelli; Loughborough University; Homerton College, Cambridge University
Qualifications: BSc Sports Science, PGCE in Physical Education
Career outside cricket: Teaching and fitness training; coaching
Off-season: 'Training even harder but smarter than all the other pre-seasons'
Overseas tours: Wales Minor Counties to Barbados 1996; Somerset CCC to South Africa 1999, 2000
Overseas teams played for: 'Llangennech and Wales! (We did give them a game, sir!)'

Career highlights to date: '2001 Lord's final (C&G) v Leicestershire. Wales beating England 2002 (catching Banger!)'
Cricket moments to forget: 'Being left out of the NatWest final at Lord's 1999'
Cricket superstitions: 'Training like mad in the winter; being better prepared than everyone else'
Cricketers particularly admired: 'Banger' (Marcus Trescothick), Brett Lee, Shoaib Akhtar
Young players to look out for: Rikki Clarke, Matt Prior, James Anderson
Other sports played: Rugby union (Wales Schools, U18, Youth; Swansea, Bristol, Exeter and Moseley)
Other sports followed: Baseball, rugby union, athletics
Injuries: Ankle ligament injury ('ruined my 2002 season')
Relaxations: 'Fitness training; spending time with my new wife, Alex'
Extras: Schoolboy international from U13 to U19. Represented Wales Minor Counties. Took nine wickets (6-67 and 3-81) in the Varsity Match at Lord's 1997. Took 59 first-class wickets in 2001. Recorded maiden first-class ten-wicket match return (10-156) v Warwickshire at Edgbaston 2002. Played first-class cricket and first-class rugby for two years ('last dual professional sportsman')
Opinions on cricket: 'The best inspiration is not to outdo others but to outdo ourselves.'
Best batting: 105 Somerset v New Zealanders, Taunton 1999
Best bowling: 6-67 Cambridge University v Oxford University, Lord's 1997

2002 Season

	M	Inns	NO	Runs	HS	Avge	100s	50s	Ct	St	O	M	Runs	Wkts	Avge	Best	5wI	10wM
Test																		
All First	7	8	3	76	37 *	15.20	-	-	-	-	239.2	45	845	19	44.47	6-110	1	1
1-day Int																		
C & G	5	0	0	0	0	-	-	-	-	-	43.1	1	219	8	27.37	3-47	-	
B & H																		
1-day Lge	12	9	5	36	10	9.00	-	-	2	-	87.4	3	532	22	24.18	4-72	-	

Career Performances

	M	Inns	NO	Runs	HS	Avge	100s	50s	Ct	St	Balls	Runs	Wkts	Avge	Best	5wI	10wM
Test																	
All First	61	72	21	832	105	16.31	1	1	14	-	10446	5983	166	36.04	6-67	4	1
1-day Int																	
C & G	18	4	3	47	26 *	47.00	-	-	2	-	902	766	24	31.91	4-25	-	
B & H	13	7	4	35	12	11.66	-	-	2	-	589	403	13	31.00	3-38	-	
1-day Lge	71	39	21	166	27	9.22	-	-	13	-	3124	2739	116	23.61	5-23	1	

JONES, S. P.   Glamorgan

Name: <u>Simon</u> Philip Jones
Role: Left-hand bat, right-arm fast bowler
Born: 25 December 1978, Morriston
Height: 6ft 3in   **Weight:** 15st
Nickname: Horse, Racehorse, Raymond, Ray
County debut: 1998
County cap: 2002
Test debut: 2002
Tests: 1
1st-Class 5 w. in innings: 3
1st-Class catches: 8
Place in batting averages: 239th av. 18.16
(2001 266th av. 8.30)
Place in bowling averages: 44th av. 27.52
(2001 139th av. 52.17)
Strike rate: 48.57 (career 59.36)
Parents: Irene and Jeff
Marital status: Single
Family links with cricket: 'Dad played for Glamorgan and England'
Education: Halfway CP School; Coedcae Comprehensive School; Millfield School
Qualifications: 12 GCSEs, 1 A-level, basic and senior coaching awards
Off-season: 'England Ashes tour'
Overseas tours: Dyfed Schools to Zimbabwe 1994; Glamorgan to South Africa 1998;
ECB National Academy to Australia 2001-02; England to Australia 2002-03
Career highlights to date: 'Debut for England v India at Lord's'
Cricket superstitions: 'Put right bowling boot on first'
Cricketers particularly admired: Allan Donald, 'my dad'
Young players to look out for: Ian Bell, Nicky Peng, Steve Harmison, Rob Key,
Bilal Shafayat
Other sports played: Football (Leeds Utd trialist)
Injuries: Out for six weeks with a rib cartilage injury
Relaxations: 'Feeding the ducks. Having a few pots'
Extras: Struck a 14-ball 46 (including six sixes and two fours) v Yorkshire at
Scarborough 2001. NBC Denis Compton Award for the most promising young
Glamorgan player 2001. Made Test debut in the first Test v India at Lord's 2002,
striking a 43-ball 44 (more runs than his father scored in his Test career); the Joneses
are the eleventh father and son to have played in Tests for England. Awarded
Glamorgan cap 2002
Opinions on cricket: 'More rest needed.'
Best batting: 46 Glamorgan v Yorkshire, Scarborough 2001
Best bowling: 6-45 Glamorgan v Derbyshire, Cardiff 2002
Stop press: Took 5-78 for England XI v Western Australia at Perth 2002-03. Forced to

return home early from England tour of Australia 2002-03 after rupturing the anterior cruciate ligament of his right knee while fielding during the first Test at Brisbane

2002 Season

	M	Inns	NO	Runs	HS	Avge	100s	50s	Ct	St	O	M	Runs	Wkts	Avge	Best	5wI	10wM
Test	1	1	0	44	44	44.00	-	-	-	-	38	3	129	4	32.25	2-61	-	-
All First	13	18	6	218	44	18.16	-	-	5	-	323.5	53	1101	40	27.52	6-45	2	-
1-day Int																		
C & G																			
B & H	2	2	1	5	4	5.00	-	-	-	-	9	0	59	0	-		-	-
1-day Lge																			

Career Performances

	M	Inns	NO	Runs	HS	Avge	100s	50s	Ct	St	Balls	Runs	Wkts	Avge	Best	5wI	10wM
Test	1	1	0	44	44	44.00	-	-	-	-	228	129	4	32.25	2-61	-	-
All First	39	48	13	393	46	11.22	-	-	8	-	5521	3483	93	37.45	6-45	3	-
1-day Int																	
C & G	1	0	0	0	0	-	-	-	-	-	30	30	0	-		-	-
B & H	3	2	1	5	4	5.00	-	-	-	-	84	106	0	-		-	-
1-day Lge	1	1	1	12	12 *	-	-	-	-	-	42	39	1	39.00	1-39	-	

JOYCE, E. C.   Middlesex

Name: Edmund (<u>Ed</u>) Christopher Joyce
Role: Left-hand bat, right-arm medium bowler, occasional wicket-keeper
Born: 22 September 1978, Dublin
Height: 5ft 10in **Weight:** 12st 3lbs
Nickname: Joycie, Spud
County debut: 1999
County cap: 2002
1000 runs in a season: 1
1st-Class 50s: 7
1st-Class 100s: 6
1st-Class catches: 30
Place in batting averages: 29th av. 52.79
Strike rate: 108.00 (career 222.00)
Parents: Maureen and Jim
Marital status: Single
Family links with cricket: 'Two of my four brothers have played for Ireland and two of my four sisters (twins) have played for Ireland's ladies'

Education: St Patrick's, Bray; Presentation College, Bray, County Wicklow; Trinity College, Dublin

Qualifications: Irish Leaving Certificate, BA (Hons) Economics and Geography

Career outside cricket: 'Would like to run my own business sometime in the future'

Off-season: 'Going back to Ireland until Christmas to see my family, and then travelling somewhere hot to train'

Overseas tours: Ireland U19 to Bermuda (International Youth Tournament) 1997, to South Africa (U19 World Cup) 1997-98; Ireland to Canada (ICC Trophy) 2001

Overseas teams played for: Coburg CC, Melbourne 1996-97; University CC, Perth 2001-02

Career highlights to date: 'Making hundred at Lord's in 2001'

Cricket moments to forget: 'Trying to play Mohammad Ali [Derbyshire] with my handle and gloves exclusively'

Cricket superstitions: 'None'

Cricketers particularly admired: Larry Gomes, Brian Lara

Young players to look out for: Eoin Morgan, Nick Compton

Other sports played: Golf, rugby, soccer, snooker

Other sports followed: Rugby (Leinster), football (Manchester United)

Injuries: Out for one one-day match with an injured shoulder; also sprained left ankle badly in pre-season

Relaxations: Cinema, eating out, listening to music

Extras: Leinster U19 to Oxford Festival. Was only player to score a century (105 v Denmark Colts) at the International Youth Tournament, Bermuda 1997. Has represented Ireland senior side since 1997, including appearances in the Triple Crown tournament and the NatWest. NBC Denis Compton Award for the most promising young Middlesex player 2000. Scored maiden first-class century (104) v Warwickshire at Lord's 2001, becoming the first born and bred Irishman to record a 100 in the County Championship. Scored 125 v Worcestershire at Worcester 2002, in the process reaching 1000 runs in a season for the first time. Awarded Middlesex cap 2002. Is not considered an overseas player

Opinions on cricket: 'Two-division cricket is good, but it should only be two up/two down. There are too many games in the Norwich Union League. I think the 20-over cricket will be a success and hope all the counties put out full teams for it.'

Best batting: 129 Middlesex v Derbyshire, Lord's 2002

Best bowling: 1-20 Middlesex v CUCCE, Fenner's 2002

2002 Season

	M	Inns	NO	Runs	HS	Avge	100s	50s	Ct	St	O	M	Runs	Wkts	Avge	Best	5wI	10wM
Test																		
All First	18	27	3	1267	129	52.79	4	6	16	-	18	2	74	1	74.00	1-20	-	-
1-day Int																		
C & G	1	1	0	10	10	10.00	-	-	-	-								
B & H	4	3	0	81	53	27.00	-	1	1	-								
1-day Lge	14	13	0	224	58	17.23	-	1	5	-								

Career Performances

	M	Inns	NO	Runs	HS	Avge	100s	50s	Ct	St	Balls	Runs	Wkts	Avge	Best	5wl	10wM
Test																	
All First	30	46	5	1787	129	43.58	6	7	30	-		222	176	1	176.00	1-20	-	-
1-day Int																	
C & G	6	6	2	206	73	51.50	-	1	1	-							
B & H	7	6	0	157	53	26.16	-	1	2	-							
1-day Lge	26	24	3	417	58	19.85	-	1	9	-							

KAIF, M. Leicestershire

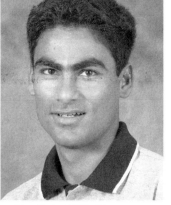

Name: Mohammad Kaif
Role: Right-hand bat, right-arm
off-spin bowler
Born: 1 December 1980, Allahabad, India
County debut: 2002
Test debut: 1999-2000
Tests: 4
One-Day Internationals: 18
1st-Class 50s: 16
1st-Class 100s: 5
1st-Class catches: 25
Strike rate: (career 70.62)
Overseas tours: India U15 to England (U15
World Cup) 1996; India U19 to South Africa
(U19 World Cup) 1997-98, to Sri Lanka (U19
World Cup) 1999-2000 (captain); India A to
West Indies 1999-2000; India to West Indies
2001-02 (one-day series), to England 2002,
to Sri Lanka (ICC Champions Trophy) 2002-03, to New Zealand 2002-03
Overseas teams played for: Uttar Pradesh 1997-98 –
Extras: A member of the India U15 side that won the U15 World Cup (Lombard
Challenge) 1996. Represented India U19 v Sri Lanka U19 1998-99. Captained India
U19 to victory in the U19 World Cup in Sri Lanka 1999-2000. Player of the
Tournament in the 1999-2000 Challenger Trophy (India v India A v India B). Attended
Indian National Cricket Academy. Scored 75-ball 87* in India's victory in the NatWest
Series final v England at Lord's 2002, sharing in a stand of 121 from 106 balls with
Yuvraj Singh and winning the Man of the Match award. Was Leicestershire's overseas
player during August 2002, replacing Michael Bevan, absent on international duty
Best batting: 136 India A v South Africa A, Kimberley 2001-02
Best bowling: 3-4 Uttar Pradesh v Vidharba, Kanpur 2001-02
Stop press: Scored 111* v Zimbabwe at Colombo in the ICC Champions Trophy

2002-03, setting a new world record for the highest score by a No. 7 in ODIs. Selected for India squad for 2002-03 World Cup

2002 Season

	M	Inns	NO	Runs	HS	Avge	100s	50s	Ct	St		O	M	Runs	Wkts	Avge		Best	5wI	10wM
Test																				
All First	2	4	1	140	77	46.66	-	1	-	-		7	0	43	0	-		-	-	-
1-day Int	7	5	3	174	87 *	87.00	-	1	4	-										
C & G																				
B & H																				
1-day Lge	1	1	1	60	60 *	-	-	-	1	1	-									

Career Performances

	M	Inns	NO	Runs	HS	Avge	100s	50s	Ct	St		Balls	Runs	Wkts	Avge		Best	5wI	10wM
Test	4	8	1	141	37	20.14	-	-	1	-		18	4	0	-		-	-	-
All First	44	69	9	2559	136	42.65	5	16	25	-		1130	498	16	31.12		3-4	-	-
1-day Int	18	14	4	452	87 *	45.20	-	3	7	-									
C & G																			
B & H																			
1-day Lge	1	1	1	60	60 *	-	-	-	1	1	-								

KASPROWICZ, M. S. Glamorgan

Name: <u>Michael</u> Scott Kasprowicz
Role: Right-hand bat, right-arm fast bowler
Born: 10 February 1972, Brisbane, Australia
Height: 6ft 4in **Weight:** 15st 5lbs
Nickname: Kasper
County debut: 1994 (Essex),
1999 (Leicestershire), 2002 (Glamorgan)
County cap: 1994 (Essex), 1999
(Leicestershire), 2002 (Glamorgan)
Test debut: 1996-97
Tests: 17
One-Day Internationals: 16
50 wickets in a season: 3
1st-Class 50s: 9
1st-Class 5 w. in innings: 37
1st-Class 10 w. in match: 4
1st-Class catches: 63
One-Day 5 w. in innings: 1
Place in batting averages: 144th av. 29.33
Place in bowling averages: 37th av. 26.66

Strike rate: 47.39 (career 51.31)
Parents: Wally and Joan
Wife and date of marriage: Lindsay, 5 December 2002
Family links with cricket/rugby: 'Brother Adam represented Queensland U17 and U19. Brother Simon plays for NSW Waratahs in Super 12 rugby competition'
Education: Marshall Road; Brisbane State High School
Qualifications: Level 2 cricket coaching
Off-season: 'Playing for Queensland Bulls'
Overseas tours: Australia YC to England 1991; Young Australia (Australia A) to England and Netherlands 1995; Australia to England 1997, to India 1997-98, 2000-01, to Sharjah (Coca-Cola Cup) 1997-98, to Bangladesh (Wills International Cup) 1998-99
Overseas teams played for: Queensland 1989-90 –
Career highlights to date: 'Representing Australia and receiving baggy green cap. Glamorgan 2002 NUL title win'
Cricketers particularly admired: Dennis Lillee, Steve Waugh
Young players to look out for: Mark Wallace, David Harrison, 'Matthew Maynard'
Other sports played: Rugby (Australian Schoolboys 1989, including tour of New Zealand)
Other sports followed: Rugby league (Brisbane Broncos), Australian Rules football (Brisbane Lions)
Injuries: Out for three weeks with a strained left hamstring
Relaxations: 'Fishing, beach, music'
Extras: Played for Queensland U17 and U19 and made his Queensland debut aged 17. Played for Australia U17. Took nine wickets in first 'Test' at Grace Road, Leicester, on Australia YC tour to England 1991. Attended Australian Cricket Academy 1991. Was second leading wicket-taker in the Sheffield Shield 1992-93 with 51 wickets (av. 24.13). Was Essex's overseas player in 1994. Took 7-36 in second innings of sixth Test v England at The Oval 1997. Took 5-28 from 18 overs in the second innings of the third Test v India at Bangalore 1997-98. Was Leicestershire's overseas player in 1999. Joined Glamorgan as overseas player for 2002 and has returned for 2003. Took wickets (Robinson, Middlebrook) with the first two balls of Essex's second innings at Swansea 2002. Awarded Glamorgan cap 2002
Opinions on cricket: 'By giving the "benefit of the doubt" to the bowler we will have a fun, quick game. Instead of the ball just missing leg stump, it will just hit it.'
Best batting: 92 Australians v India A, Nagpur 2000-01
Best bowling: 7-36 Australia v England, The Oval 1997

2002 Season

	M	Inns	NO	Runs	HS	Avge	100s	50s	Ct	St	O	M	Runs	Wkts	Avge	Best	5wl	10wM
Test																		
All First	12	19	7	352	72 *	29.33	-	1	7	-	418.4	78	1413	53	26.66	6-47	4	1
1-day Int																		
C & G	2	1	0	25	25	25.00	-	-	-	-	18.5	2	81	4	20.25	3-28	-	
B & H	4	4	2	61	33 *	30.50	-	-	-	-	31	7	124	2	62.00	1-16	-	
1-day Lge	11	7	3	58	13	14.50	-	-	4	-	89.2	6	359	16	22.43	4-28	-	

Career Performances

	M	Inns	NO	Runs	HS	Avge	100s	50s	Ct	St	Balls	Runs	Wkts	Avge	Best	5wI	10wM
Test	17	23	5	234	25	13.00	-	-	6	-	3338	1739	47	37.00	7-36	2	-
All First	166	218	48	3052	92	17.95	-	9	63	-	33557	17442	654	26.66	7-36	37	4
1-day Int	16	8	6	62	28 *	31.00	-	-	3	-	817	709	22	32.22	3-50	-	
C & G	4	3	0	53	25	17.66	-	-	-	-	245	168	10	16.80	5-60	1	
B & H	7	5	2	101	40	33.66	-	-	1	-	336	236	6	39.33	2-36	-	
1-day Lge	39	28	5	252	38	10.95	-	-	6	-	1705	1252	45	27.82	4-28	-	

KATICH, S. M. Hampshire

Name: <u>Simon</u> Mathew Katich
Role: Left-hand bat, left-arm
wrist-spin bowler
Born: 21 August 1975, Midland,
Western Australia
Height: 6ft **Weight:** 12st 8lbs
Nickname: Kat
County debut: 2000 (Durham),
2002 (Yorkshire)
County cap: 2000 (Durham)
Test debut: 2001
Tests: 1
One-Day Internationals: 1
1000 runs in a season: 1
1st-Class 50s: 24
1st-Class 100s: 15
1st-Class 200s: 1
1st-Class catches: 76
Strike rate: (career 88.65)
Parents: Vince and Kerry
Marital status: Single
Education: Trinity College, Perth; University of Western Australia
Qualifications: Bachelor of Commerce degree
Off-season: Playing in Australia
Overseas tours: Australian Cricket Academy to South Africa 1996; Australia to Sri
Lanka and Zimbabwe 1999-2000, to England 2001; Australia A to South Africa
2002-03 (vice-captain)
Overseas teams played for: Western Australia 1996-97 – 2001-02; New South Wales
2002-03
Career highlights to date: 'Test debut at Leeds'
Cricket moments to forget: 'None'

Cricket superstitions: 'Like to wear old gear'
Cricketers particularly admired: Viv Richards, David Gower
Young players to look out for: Michael Clarke (NSW)
Other sports played: Australian Rules, hockey, golf
Other sports followed: Australian Rules (Richmond), football (Newcastle United)
Relaxations: 'Movies, beach'
Extras: Attended Commonwealth Bank [Australian] Cricket Academy 1996. Scored century (106) for Western Australia v England at Perth 1998-99. Captained ACB Chairman's XI v England 1998-99. Scored 115 in Western Australia's first innings in their 1998-99 Sheffield Shield final victory. *Wisden Australia*'s Sheffield Shield Cricketer of the Year 1998-99. Was Durham's overseas player in 2000. Took over as captain of Western Australia during 2000-01 season after retirement of Tom Moody. Finished the 2000-01 season with a Western Australian record 1145 Pura Cup runs (av. 71.56), having become the first WA batsman to score a century against each of the other states (two v Queensland, home and away) in a single season. Was Yorkshire's overseas player during June 2002, replacing Darren Lehmann, absent on international duty; has joined Hampshire as an overseas player for 2003. Vice-captain of New South Wales 2002-03
Opinions on cricket: 'The game needs less of the third umpire!'
Best batting: 228* Western Australia v South Australia, Perth 2000-01
Best bowling: 3-21 Australians v Somerset, Taunton 2001

2002 Season

	M	Inns	NO	Runs	HS	Avge	100s	50s	Ct	St	O	M	Runs	Wkts	Avge	Best	5wI	10wM
Test																		
All First	1	2	0	37	21	18.50	-	-	1	-	2	0	25	0	-	-	-	-
1-day Int																		
C & G	1	1	1	40	40 *	-	-	-	-	-								
B & H																		
1-day Lge	2	2	1	39	39 *	39.00	-	-	2	-								

Career Performances

	M	Inns	NO	Runs	HS	Avge	100s	50s	Ct	St	Balls	Runs	Wkts	Avge	Best	5wI	10wM
Test	1	2	1	15	15	15.00	-	-	1	-							
All First	74	131	21	5383	228 *	48.93	16	24	76	-	1773	1085	20	54.25	3-21	-	-
1-day Int	1	0	0	0	0	-	-	-	-	-							
C & G	3	3	1	84	40 *	42.00	-	-	1	-							
B & H	6	6	0	116	62	19.33	-	2	5	-	6	8	0	-	-	-	-
1-day Lge	18	18	4	637	70 *	45.50	-	6	10	-	102	94	2	47.00	1-25	-	

KEEDY, G.   Lancashire

Name: Gary Keedy
Role: Left-hand bat, slow left-arm bowler
Born: 27 November 1974, Wakefield
Height: 5ft 11in **Weight:** 12st 4lbs
Nickname: Keeds
County debut: 1994 (Yorkshire),
1995 (Lancashire)
County cap: 2000 (Lancashire)
1st-Class 50s: 1
1st-Class 5 w. in innings: 7
1st-Class 10 w. in match: 2
1st-Class catches: 25
One-Day 5 w. in innings: 1
Place in batting averages: 262nd av. 15.64
(2001 250th av. 11.57)
Place in bowling averages: 122nd av. 39.78
(2001 117th av. 41.07)
Strike rate: 79.57 (career 79.26)
Parents: Roy and Pat
Marital status: Engaged
Family links with cricket: Twin brother plays for Castleford in the Yorkshire League
Education: Green Lane; Garforth Comprehensive
Qualifications: 8 GCSEs, Level 2 coaching award
Off-season: 12-month contract
Overseas tours: England U18 to South Africa 1992-93, to Denmark 1994;
England U19 to Sri Lanka 1993-94; Lancashire to Portugal 1995, to Jamaica 1996,
to South Africa 1997
Overseas teams played for: Frankston, Melbourne 1995-96
Career highlights to date: 'Probably bowling Yorkshire out at Headingley. My
involvement with Lancashire in general; receiving my county cap was a proud
moment'
Cricketers particularly admired: Shane Warne, Graham Gooch
Young players to look out for: Kyle Hogg, James Anderson
Other sports played: Football, snooker
Other sports followed: Football (Leeds United), rugby league (Leeds Rhinos)
Relaxations: PlayStation
Extras: Player of the Series for England U19 v West Indies U19 in 1993. Graduate of
the Yorkshire Cricket Academy. Played for England U19 in the home series against
India U19 in 1994. His match return of 10-155 v Durham at Old Trafford 2000
included second innings figures of 6-56 from 50 overs. Scored 25* v Sussex at Old
Trafford 2002, in the process sharing with Stuart Law (218) in a tenth-wicket stand of
145 that avoided the follow-on

Opinions on cricket: 'Do we need overseas players? Let's find out who's the best team without them!'

Best batting: 57 Lancashire v Yorkshire, Headingley 2002
Best bowling: 6-56 Lancashire v Durham, Old Trafford 2000

2002 Season

	M	Inns	NO	Runs	HS	Avge	100s	50s	Ct	St	O	M	Runs	Wkts	Avge	Best	5wI	10wM
Test																		
All First	16	22	8	219	57	15.64	-	1	4	-	437.4	102	1313	33	39.78	5-122	1	-
1-day Int																		
C & G																			
B & H																			
1-day Lge	2	1	1	10	10 *	-	-	-	-	-	14	0	78	3	26.00	2-28	-	

Career Performances

	M	Inns	NO	Runs	HS	Avge	100s	50s	Ct	St	Balls	Runs	Wkts	Avge	Best	5wI	10wM
Test																	
All First	94	111	57	663	57	12.27	-	1	25	-	18311	8445	231	36.55	6-56	7	2
1-day Int																	
C & G	1	0	0	0	0	-	-	-	-	-	60	40	1	40.00	1-40	-	
B & H																	
1-day Lge	14	4	2	13	10 *	6.50	-	-	1	-	484	439	14	31.35	5-30	1	

KEEGAN, C. B. Middlesex

Name: <u>Chad</u> Blake Keegan
Role: Right-hand bat, right-arm fast-medium bowler
Born: 30 July 1979, Sandton, South Africa
Height: 6ft 1in **Weight:** 12st
Nickname: Wick
County debut: 2001
1st-Class catches: 4
One-Day 5 w. in innings: 1
Place in batting averages: 313th av. 5.80 (2001 278th av. 5.62)
Place in bowling averages: 138th av. 45.00 (2001 79th av. 32.66)
Strike rate: 66.89 (career 61.91)
Parents: Sharon and Blake
Marital status: Single
Education: Northlands Senior Primary,

Durban, South Africa; Durban High School
Qualifications: YMCA fitness instructor
Overseas tours: MCC to Argentina and Chile 2001
Overseas teams played for: Durban High School Old Boys 1994-97; Crusaders, Durban 1998-99
Career highlights to date: 'Beating Australia at Lord's and getting Steve Waugh's wicket [2001]'
Cricket moments to forget: 'Getting hit for eight off the first ball of an innings by Atherton'
Cricketers particularly admired: Malcolm Marshall, Neil Johnson
Young players to look out for: Thos ('Mare Man') Hunt
Other sports played: 'Any extreme sports, golf'
Other sports followed: Football (Liverpool)
Relaxations: 'Making and listening to music (guitar); sketching'
Extras: Represented KwaZulu-Natal U13, KwaZulu-Natal Schools, KwaZulu-Natal U19, KwaZulu-Natal Academy. MCC Young Cricketer. Is not considered an overseas player
Opinions on cricket: 'More floodlit games.'
Best batting: 30* Middlesex v Warwickshire, Edgbaston 2001
Best bowling: 4-47 Middlesex v Worcestershire, Worcester 2002

2002 Season

	M	Inns	NO	Runs	HS	Avge	100s	50s	Ct	St	O	M	Runs	Wkts	Avge	Best	5wI	10wM
Test																		
All First	9	10	0	58	24	5.80	-	-	3	-	211.5	32	855	19	45.00	4-47	-	-
1-day Int																		
C & G																		
B & H	4	3	2	34	24	34.00	-	-	-	-	31	3	155	6	25.83	3-24	-	
1-day Lge	11	5	4	20	12 *	20.00	-	-	3	-	87.2	7	416	13	32.00	2-22	-	

Career Performances

	M	Inns	NO	Runs	HS	Avge	100s	50s	Ct	St	Balls	Runs	Wkts	Avge	Best	5wI	10wM
Test																	
All First	16	20	2	103	30 *	5.72	-	-	4	-	2291	1443	37	39.00	4-47	-	-
1-day Int																	
C & G																	
B & H	9	6	3	38	24	12.66	-	-	1	-	438	356	12	29.66	3-24	-	
1-day Lge	25	16	7	92	16	10.22	-	-	5	-	1165	877	39	22.48	5-17	1	

KENDALL, W. S.   Hampshire

Name: William (<u>Will</u>) Salwey Kendall
Role: Right-hand bat, right-arm medium
bowler, occasional wicket-keeper, county
vice-captain
Born: 18 December 1973, Wimbledon,
London
Height: 5ft 10in **Weight:** 12st 7lbs
Nickname: Villy, Lemon, Baldy, Wiggy,
Wilbur, Fish
County debut: 1996
County cap: 1999
1000 runs in a season: 3
1st-Class 50s: 31
1st-Class 100s: 8
1st-Class 200s: 1
1st-Class catches: 105
One-Day 100s: 1
Place in batting averages: 187th av. 24.31
(2001 165th av. 23.62)
Strike rate: 127.33 (career 89.76)

Parents: Tom and Sue
Wife and date of marriage: Emily, 27 September 2002
Family links with cricket: Father played club cricket with East Horsley, Hampshire
Hogs and MCC. Older brother James played for Durham University. Younger brother,
Ed, took new ball for Nottingham University
Education: Bradfield College, Berkshire; Keble College, Oxford University
Qualifications: 10 GCSEs, 3 A-levels, 1 AS-level, BA (Hons) Modern History
Career outside cricket: 'Dabbling in a little journalism'
Off-season: 'From New Year onwards, playing club cricket in Cape Town and on tour
in West Africa with MCC'
Overseas tours: Bradfield College to Barbados 1991; Troubadours to Argentina 1997;
Hampshire CCC to Anguilla 1997, to Cape Town 2001; MCC to Kenya 2001-02, to
West Africa 2003
Overseas teams played for: Frankston Peninsula CC, Melbourne 1997-98
Career highlights to date: 'Being part of the Hampshire side that beat the Aussies in
2001 – an unforgettable three days. Receiving my county cap on the same day I made
my career best score v Sussex 1999'
Cricket moments to forget: 'Plenty of my batting efforts over the past two years'
Cricketers particularly admired: Robin Smith, Graham Thorpe, Mark Ramprakash,
Shane Warne, 'and anyone playing over 36'
Young players to look out for: James Adams, James Tomlinson, John Francis,
Tom Burroughs

Other sports played: Hockey (Oxford Blue), football (Independent Schools 1992, Old Bradfieldians, Corinthian Casuals; offered terms by Reading), squash, golf

Other sports followed: 'All sports; an interest in Tottenham Hotspur FC'

Injuries: Out for one one-day game with a shoulder strain

Relaxations: Playing or watching sport, socialising with friends, relaxing at home; 'hacking up golf courses, travelling and quiet days with wife, Emily'

Extras: Surrey Young Cricketer of the Year 1992. Awarded Gray-Nicolls Trophy for Schoolboy Cricketer of the Year in memory of Len Newbery 1992. Made first-class debut for Oxford University in 1994. Hampshire Exiles Player of the Year for 1996. Hampshire Cricket Society Player of the Year 2000. Vice-captain of Hampshire since 2001. Carried his bat for 53* v Leicestershire at West End 2002. Scored maiden one-day century (110*) v Middlesex at West End in the NUL 2002

Opinions on cricket: 'We clearly need to up the standard, but regional cricket is not the answer. Why not restrict full-time county staffs to 17-18, abandon registration and allow all players outside of this core to be free agents? Counties could receive less central funding and be allowed to sink or swim – the cream will soon rise. And bring back an "A" side for summer and winter matches. They should truly be England's 2nd XI.'

Best batting: 201 Hampshire v Sussex, Southampton 1999

Best bowling: 3-37 Oxford University v Derbyshire, The Parks 1995

2002 Season

	M	Inns	NO	Runs	HS	Avge	100s	50s	Ct	St	O	M	Runs	Wkts	Avge	Best	5wI	10wM
Test																		
All First	17	31	2	705	88	24.31	-	4	12	-	63.4	14	186	3	62.00	1-8	-	-
1-day Int																		
C & G	2	0	0	0	0	-	-	-	2	-	7	0	26	1	26.00	1-8	-	
B & H	4	3	1	36	34 *	18.00	-	-	3	-	19	2	90	2	45.00	2-48	-	
1-day Lge	15	14	2	367	110 *	30.58	1	1	5	-	9	0	57	1	57.00	1-32	-	

Career Performances

	M	Inns	NO	Runs	HS	Avge	100s	50s	Ct	St	Balls	Runs	Wkts	Avge	Best	5wI	10wM
Test																	
All First	123	203	24	6193	201	34.59	9	31	105	-	1167	639	13	49.15	3-37	-	-
1-day Int																	
C & G	11	8	2	127	39	21.16	-	-	5	-	42	26	1	26.00	1-8	-	
B & H	20	18	2	260	34 *	16.25	-	-	5	-	114	90	2	45.00	2-48	-	
1-day Lge	79	71	10	1437	110 *	23.55	1	5	38	-	66	79	1	79.00	1-32	-	

KENWAY, D. A. Hampshire

Name: <u>Derek</u> Anthony Kenway
Role: Right-hand bat, wicket-keeper
Born: 12 June 1978, Fareham
Height: 6ft **Weight:** 14st 7lbs
Nickname: Kenners, Big Dog
County debut: 1997
County cap: 2001
1000 runs in a season: 1
1st-Class 50s: 16
1st-Class 100s: 4
1st-Class catches: 59
1st-Class stumpings: 1
Place in batting averages: 238th av. 18.30
(2001 92nd av. 34.51)
Strike rate: (career 42.00)
Parents: Keith and Geraldine
Marital status: Single
Family links with cricket: Brother plays
local club cricket

Education: Botley Primary School; St George's, Southampton; Barton Peveril College
Qualifications: 6 GCSEs, NCA coaching award
Overseas tours: West of England U15 to West Indies 1993; ECB National Academy
to Australia 2001-02
Overseas teams played for: Beaumaris CC, Melbourne 1997-98
Career highlights to date: 'Being picked for the Academy'
Cricket moments to forget: 'Leaving a straight one on my debut'
Cricketers particularly admired: Steve Waugh
Young players to look out for: Chris Tremlett
Other sports played: Football, 'all pub games (local teams)'
Other sports followed: Football (Southampton FC)
Relaxations: 'Music, TV, sleeping'
Extras: *Daily Telegraph* Batting Award (West) 1994. Southern League Young Player
of the Year 1996. NBC Denis Compton Award 1999. Hampshire Cricket Society Player
of the Year 2001. Scored half-century (60) in ECB National Academy's innings victory
over Commonwealth Bank [Australian] Cricket Academy in Adelaide 2001-02. C&G
Man of the Match award for his 76 v Kent Board XI at Folkestone 2002
Best batting: 166 Hampshire v Nottinghamshire, West End 2001
Best bowling: 1-5 Hampshire v Warwickshire, Southampton 1997

2002 Season

	M	Inns	NO	Runs	HS	Avge	100s	50s	Ct	St		O	M	Runs	Wkts	Avge	Best	5wl	10wM
Test																			
All First	8	15	2	238	54	18.30	-	1	15	-		1	0	8	0	-		-	-
1-day Int																			
C & G	2	2	0	106	76	53.00	-	1	-	-									
B & H	5	5	0	117	40	23.40	-	-	2	-									
1-day Lge	8	8	0	164	50	20.50	-	1	2	-									

Career Performances

	M	Inns	NO	Runs	HS	Avge	100s	50s	Ct	St		Balls	Runs	Wkts	Avge	Best	5wl	10wM
Test																		
All First	62	110	13	3050	166	31.44	4	16	59	1		126	150	3	50.00	1-5	-	-
1-day Int																		
C & G	5	5	0	232	76	46.40	-	2	1	1								
B & H	14	13	0	269	47	20.69	-	-	7	1								
1-day Lge	53	49	2	1244	93 *	26.46	-	9	28	4								

KERR, J. I. D.   Derbyshire

Name: <u>Jason</u> Ian Douglas Kerr
Role: Right-hand bat, right-arm fast-medium bowler, (wicket-keeper 'if required')
Born: 7 April 1974, Bolton
Height: 6ft 3in **Weight:** 12st 6lbs
Nickname: Dogage, Keardog
County debut: 1993 (Somerset), 2002 (Derbyshire)
1st-Class 50s: 8
1st-Class 5 w. in innings: 2
1st-Class catches: 18
Place in batting averages: 141st av. 29.90 (2001 160th av. 23.85)
Place in bowling averages: 127th av. 40.75
Strike rate: 55.25 (career 62.58)
Parents: Len and Janet
Marital status: Single
Education: Withins High School; Bolton Met College
Qualifications: 5 GCSEs, BTEC National Diploma in Business Studies, cricket coach
Off-season: 'The gym will become my second home! Studying (if I get around to it). Recovering from six months' baby-sitting Luke Sutton and monitoring his eating disorder!'

Overseas tours: England U19 to India 1992-93; Lancashire U19 to Isle of Man; MCC to Kenya 2002
Overseas teams played for: Gordon CC, Sydney, Australia 1994-95; Taita CC, Wellington, New Zealand 1996-97; Subiaco-Floreat, Perth
Cricketers particularly admired: Kevin Dean, Graeme Welch
Young players to look out for: Steve Selwood
Other sports followed: Football (Bolton 'The Great' Wanderers)
Extras: His 7-23 v Leics at Taunton 1999 included a spell of 5-6 from 3.1 overs. Completed hat-trick (Lara, McLean, Collymore) v West Indians at Taunton 2000 in his first game of the 2000 season; Collymore was also his 100th first-class wicket. Left Somerset in the 2001-02 off-season and joined Derbyshire for 2002. Scored 65* batting at No. 9 to help Derbyshire to victory v Northamptonshire in the NUL at Derby 2002
Best batting: 80 Somerset v West Indians, Taunton 1995
Best bowling: 7-23 Somerset v Leicestershire, Taunton 1999

2002 Season

	M	Inns	NO	Runs	HS	Avge	100s	50s	Ct	St	O	M	Runs	Wkts	Avge	Best	5wI	10wM
Test																		
All First	7	12	2	299	68	29.90	-	3	2	-	147.2	29	652	16	40.75	4-32	-	-
1-day Int																		
C & G	1	1	0	0	0	0.00	-	-	-	-	6.1	0	46	0	-		-	-
B & H	1	1	0	0	0	0.00	-	-	-	-	1	0	4	0	-		-	-
1-day Lge	15	13	2	227	65 *	20.63	-	1	5	-	106.4	4	441	15	29.40	3-27	-	

Career Performances

	M	Inns	NO	Runs	HS	Avge	100s	50s	Ct	St	Balls	Runs	Wkts	Avge	Best	5wI	10wM
Test																	
All First	65	95	18	1693	80	21.98	-	8	18	-	8074	5210	129	40.38	7-23	2	-
1-day Int																	
C & G	11	9	2	43	21	6.14	-	-	2	-	427	392	9	43.55	3-32	-	
B & H	13	8	1	60	17	8.57	-	-	-	-	539	374	18	20.77	3-14	-	
1-day Lge	88	60	16	666	65 *	15.13	-	2	16	-	3365	2942	97	30.32	4-28	-	

47. Which West Indies fast bowler topped the 1994 first-class bowling averages with 77 wickets at an average of 14.45?

KEY, R. W. T.   Kent

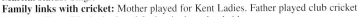

Name: <u>Robert</u> William Trevor Key
Role: Right-hand bat, off-spin bowler
Born: 12 May 1979, Dulwich, London
Height: 6ft 1in **Weight:** 12st 7lbs
Nickname: Keysy
County debut: 1998
County cap: 2001
Test debut: 2002
Tests: 2
1000 runs in a season: 2
1st-Class 50s: 24
1st-Class 100s: 10
1st-Class catches: 56
One-Day 100s: 1
Place in batting averages: 71st av. 41.83
(2001 46th av. 45.75)
Parents: Trevor and Lynn
Marital status: Single
Family links with cricket: Mother played for Kent Ladies. Father played club cricket in Derby. Sister Elizabeth played for her junior school side
Education: Worsley Bridge Primary School; Langley Park Boys' School
Qualifications: 10 GCSEs, NCA coaching award, GNVQ Business Studies
Career outside cricket: 'Work in the futures market'
Off-season: Touring with England
Overseas tours: Kent U13 to Holland; England U17 to Bermuda (International Youth Tournament) 1997; England U19 to South Africa (including U19 World Cup) 1997-98; England A to Zimbabwe and South Africa 1998-99; ECB National Academy to Australia 2001-02, to Sri Lanka 2002-03; England to Australia 2002-03
Overseas teams played for: Greenpoint CC, Cape Town 1996-97
Cricket moments to forget: 'Any time I have lost to Min at cards'
Cricketers particularly admired: Min Patel, Neil Taylor, Alan Wells, Mark Ealham 'for his enthusiasm'
Other sports played: Hockey, football, snooker
Other sports followed: Football (Chelsea), basketball (Chicago Bulls)
Extras: Played for England U17 and England U19 Development XI. Also played for South England U14 and U19. County tennis player. Played for England U19 against Zimbabwe U19 in 1997 and captained the England U17 side to victory in the International Youth Tournament in Bermuda in July. Played for the victorious England side in the U19 World Cup in South Africa 1997-98. Shared England U19 Man of the Series award with Graeme Swann v Pakistan U19 1998. Scored century (119) v Pakistanis at Canterbury 2001 on his 22nd birthday. Scored a 33-ball 50 in title-clinching Norwich Union League victory v Warwickshire at Edgbaston 2001. NBC

Denis Compton Award for the most promising young Kent player 2001. Scored century (177) in ECB National Academy's innings victory over Commonwealth Bank [Australian] Cricket Academy in Adelaide 2001-02. Scored maiden one-day century (114 from 98 balls) v Nottinghamshire in the NUL at Trent Bridge 2002. Made Test debut in second Test v India at Trent Bridge 2002. Selected for the England tour of Australia 2002-03 as a replacement for Graham Thorpe

Best batting: 160 Kent v Hampshire, Canterbury 2002

Stop press: Scored 174* for England XI v Australia A at Hobart 2002-03. Added to ECB National Academy squad for tour to Sri Lanka 2002-03

2002 Season

	M	Inns	NO	Runs	HS	Avge	100s	50s	Ct	St	O	M	Runs	Wkts	Avge	Best	5wI	10wM
Test	2	3	0	81	34	27.00	-	-	2	-								
All First	17	31	1	1255	160	41.83	3	6	12	-								
1-day Int																		
C & G	4	4	0	201	77	50.25	-	2	1	-								
B & H	5	5	0	86	59	17.20	-	1	1	-								
1-day Lge	13	13	1	483	114	40.25	1	3	2	-								

Career Performances

	M	Inns	NO	Runs	HS	Avge	100s	50s	Ct	St	Balls	Runs	Wkts	Avge	Best	5wI	10wM
Test	2	3	0	81	34	27.00	-	-	2	-							
All First	87	149	4	4620	160	31.86	10	24	56	-	70	40	0	-	-	-	-
1-day Int																	
C & G	11	11	1	446	77	44.60	-	5	2	-							
B & H	11	10	0	187	59	18.70	-	1	2	-							
1-day Lge	49	45	5	1280	114	32.00	1	10	5	-							

KHAN, A.   Kent

Name: Amjad Khan
Role: Right-hand bat, right-arm fast bowler
Born: 14 October 1980, Copenhagen, Denmark
Height: 6ft **Weight:** 11st 7lbs
County debut: 2001
50 wickets in a season: 1
1st-Class 50s: 1
1st-Class 5 w. in innings: 4
1st-Class catches: 5
Place in batting averages: 263rd av. 15.21
Place in bowling averages: 77th av. 31.80
Strike rate: 46.19 (career 46.25)
Parents: Aslam and Raisa

Marital status: Single
Education: Skolen på Duevej, Denmark; Falkonërgårdens Gymnasium
Overseas tours: Denmark U19 to Canada 1996, to Bermuda 1997, to South Africa and Wales 1998, to Ireland 1999; Denmark to Holland 1998, to Zimbabwe 1999, to Canada (ICC Trophy) 2001
Overseas teams played for: Kjøbenhavns Boldklub, Denmark
Cricketers particularly admired: Wasim Akram, Sachin Tendulkar, Allan Donald
Other sports followed: Football (Denmark)
Relaxations: Working out, listening to music, sleeping
Extras: The youngest Danish international ever, at age of 17. Played for Denmark in the NatWest Trophy 1999 and 2000. Recorded

maiden first-class five-wicket return (6-52) v Yorkshire at Canterbury 2002 in his third Championship match. Took 6-56 and then scored maiden first-class fifty (58) v Sussex at Hove 2002. Took 50 first-class wickets (63) in his first full season 2002. Is not considered an overseas player
Best batting: 58 Kent v Sussex, Hove 2002
Best bowling: 6-52 Kent v Yorkshire, Canterbury 2002

2002 Season

	M	Inns	NO	Runs	HS	Avge	100s	50s	Ct	St	O	M	Runs	Wkts	Avge	Best	5wI	10wM
Test																		
All First	16	19	5	213	58	15.21	-	1	5	-	485	75	2004	63	31.80	6-52	4	-
1-day Int																		
C & G	3	1	0	13	13	13.00	-	-	2	-	20	0	105	2	52.50	2-50	-	
B & H	1	1	0	0	0	0.00	-	-	-	-	10	0	62	1	62.00	1-62	-	
1-day Lge	3	2	0	27	21	13.50	-	-	-	-	20	1	100	3	33.33	2-47	-	

Career Performances

	M	Inns	NO	Runs	HS	Avge	100s	50s	Ct	St	Balls	Runs	Wkts	Avge	Best	5wI	10wM
Test																	
All First	17	19	5	213	58	15.21	-	1	5	-	2960	2050	64	32.03	6-52	4	-
1-day Int																	
C & G	5	3	0	15	13	5.00	-	-	2	-	225	198	5	39.60	2-38	-	
B & H	3	2	1	0	0 *	0.00	-	-	-	-	96	97	2	48.50	1-23	-	
1-day Lge	3	2	0	27	21	13.50	-	-	-	-	120	100	3	33.33	2-47	-	

Name: <u>Rawait</u> Mahmood Khan
Role: Right-hand bat
Born: 5 March 1982, Birmingham
Height: 5ft 9in **Weight:** 9st 7lbs
Nickname: Ray
County debut: 2001
1st-Class 50s: 1
Parents: Hashim Khan and Barish Begum
Marital status: Single
Family links with cricket: Father played for
Warwickshire 2nd XI. Brother Zubair was
also with Derbyshire
Education: Parkhill School; Moseley School;
Solihull College
Cricketers particularly admired:
Steve Waugh
Other sports played: Football, badminton
Relaxations: 'Socialising with friends'
Extras: Played for Derbyshire Board XI in the NatWest 2000. Scored 91 v Indians at
Derby 2002 in his second first-class match
Best batting: 91 Derbyshire v Indians, Derby 2002

2002 Season

	M	Inns	NO	Runs	HS	Avge	100s	50s	Ct	St	O	M	Runs	Wkts	Avge	Best	5wI	10wM
Test																		
All First	1	1	0	91	91	91.00	-	1	-	-	3	0	15	0	-	-	-	-
1-day Int																		
C & G																		
B & H																		
1-day Lge																		

Career Performances

	M	Inns	NO	Runs	HS	Avge	100s	50s	Ct	St	Balls	Runs	Wkts	Avge	Best	5wI	10wM
Test																	
All First	2	3	0	109	91	36.33	-	1	-	-	18	15	0	-	-	-	-
1-day Int																	
C & G	1	1	0	29	29	29.00	-	-	-	-							
B & H																	
1-day Lge																	

KILLEEN, N. Durham

Name: Neil Killeen
Role: Right-hand bat, right-arm
medium-fast bowler
Born: 17 October 1975, Shotley Bridge
Height: 6ft 1in **Weight:** 15st
Nickname: Killer, Bully, Quinny,
Squeaky, Bull
County debut: 1995
County cap: 1999
50 wickets in a season: 1
1st-Class 5 w. in innings: 6
1st-Class catches: 17
One-Day 5 w. in innings: 2
Place in batting averages: 286th av. 10.47
Place in bowling averages: 75th av. 31.48
(2001 13th av. 20.18)
Strike rate: 63.43 (career 57.23)
Parents: Glen and Thora
Wife and date of marriage: Clare Louise, 5 February 2000
Children: Jonathan David
Family links with cricket: 'Dad best armchair player in the game'
Education: Anfield Plain; Greencroft Comprehensive School; Derwentside College,
University of Teesside
Qualifications: 8 GCSEs, 2 A-levels, first year Sports Science, Level III coaching
award, Level I staff coach
Career outside cricket: Cricket coaching
Overseas tours: Durham CCC to Zimbabwe 1992; England U19 to West Indies
1994-95; MCC to Bangladesh 1999-2000
Career highlights to date: 'My county cap and first-class debut'
Cricket moments to forget: 'Injury causing me to miss most of 2001 season'
Cricketers particularly admired: Ian Botham, Curtly Ambrose, Courtney Walsh,
David Boon
Young players to look out for: Nicky Peng
Other sports played: Athletics (English Schools javelin)
Sports followed: Football (Sunderland AFC), cricket (Anfield Plain CC)
Relaxations: 'Good food, good wine; golf; spending time with wife and family'
Extras: Was first Durham bowler to take five wickets in a Sunday League game
(5-26 v Northamptonshire at Northampton 1995). Took three wickets in final over of
National League game at Derby 2000, preventing Derbyshire scoring the six runs
required for victory. B&H Gold Award for his 4-18 v Lancashire at Liverpool 2001
Best batting: 48 Durham v Somerset, Riverside 1995
Best bowling: 7-85 Durham v Leicestershire, Leicester 1999

2002 Season

	M	Inns	NO	Runs	HS	Avge	100s	50s	Ct	St	O	M	Runs	Wkts	Avge	Best	5wI	10wM
Test																		
All First	15	22	5	178	27 *	10.47	-	-	5	-	391.1	108	1165	37	31.48	4-26	-	-
1-day Int																		
C & G	2	1	0	1	1	1.00	-	-	-	-	12	2	51	2	25.50	1-12	-	
B & H	5	3	1	22	15	11.00	-	-	-	-	47.2	8	131	11	11.90	3-12	-	
1-day Lge	16	10	6	56	22 *	14.00	-	-	3	-	131.4	15	562	30	18.73	4-12	-	

Career Performances

	M	Inns	NO	Runs	HS	Avge	100s	50s	Ct	St	Balls	Runs	Wkts	Avge	Best	5wI	10wM
Test																	
All First	60	86	17	807	48	11.69	-	-	17	-	10073	5003	176	28.42	7-85	6	-
1-day Int																	
C & G	8	5	1	5	2	1.25	-	-	1	-	420	268	10	26.80	2-15	-	
B & H	32	17	5	82	24 *	6.83	-	-	7	-	1706	1088	42	25.90	4-18	-	
1-day Lge	86	52	20	335	32	10.46	-	-	15	-	3851	2957	123	24.04	6-31	2	

KING, R. E.   Northamptonshire

Name: <u>Richard</u> Eric King
Role: Right-hand bat, left-arm
fast-medium bowler
Born: 3 January 1984, Hitchin
Height: 6ft **Weight:** 12st 6lbs
Nickname: Dingy, Ding Dong, Kingy
County debut: No first-team appearance
Parents: Roger and Rosemary
Marital status: Single
Education: Fernwood School; Bedford
Modern School; Loughborough University
Qualifications: 10 GCSEs, 3 A-levels,
Level 1 ECB coach
Career outside cricket: Loughborough
University
Off-season: 'At university. Developing my
game'
Overseas tours: Bedford Modern to
Barbados 1999; Northamptonshire YC to South Africa 2002
Career highlights to date: 'Second XI debut – scored 66*. Captaining England
Schools against India U19'
Cricket moments to forget: 'Nothing – no mistakes are made; all learning
experiences'

Cricketers particularly admired: Shane Warne, Ian Botham, Viv Richards, Damien Martyn
Young players to look out for: David Paynter, Monty Panesar
Other sports played: Rugby (Midlands XV)
Other sports followed: Rugby
Relaxations: 'Listening to music; seeing friends'
Extras: MCC Lord's Taverners Player of the Year U13. MCC Young Player of the Year 1997. Broke school record with 200* (from 140 balls) in 2001, then scored 185* a week later. Played for Northamptonshire Board XI in the first round of the C&G 2002, which was played in August 2001, and in the first round of the C&G 2003, which was played in August 2002. Northamptonshire Academy 2002
Opinions on cricket: 'Best sport in the world!'

2002 Season (did not make any first-class or one-day appearances for his county)

Career Performances

	M	Inns	NO	Runs	HS	Avge	100s	50s	Ct	St	Balls	Runs	Wkts	Avge	Best	5wl	10wM
Test																	
All First																	
1-day Int																	
C & G	2	2	0	2	2	1.00	-	-	1	-	90	66	2	33.00	2-39	-	
B & H																	
1-day Lge																	

48. Which Australian Test all-rounder made his debut for Northamptonshire in 1951?

KIRBY, S. P. Yorkshire

Name: <u>Steven</u> Paul Kirby
Role: Right-hand bat, right-arm fast bowler
Born: 4 October 1977, Bury
Height: 6ft 3in **Weight:** 12st 10lbs
Nickname: Tango
County debut: 2001
1st-Class 50s: 1
1st-Class 5 w. in innings: 4
1st-Class 10 w. in match: 1
1st-Class catches: 4
Place in batting averages: 291st av. 10.07
(2001 274th av. 6.12)
Place in bowling averages: 100th av. 34.10
(2001 16th av. 20.85)
Strike rate: 53.70 (career 43.69)
Parents: Paul and Allison
Marital status: Engaged
Education: St Joseph's Primary, Heywood,
Lancs; Elton High School, Walshaw, Bury, Lancs; Bury College
Qualifications: 10 GCSEs, BTEC/GNVQ Advanced Leisure and Tourism,
Level 1 coaching award
Career outside cricket: Sports management
Overseas tours: Yorkshire to Grenada 2001; ECB National Academy to Australia
2001-02
Overseas teams played for: Egmont Plains, New Zealand 1997-98
Career highlights to date: 'Being selected to go to Australia with the Academy'
Cricketers particularly admired: Michael Atherton, Curtly Ambrose, Malcolm
Marshall, Glenn McGrath, Darren Gough
Young players to look out for: Tim Bresnan, John Sadler, Ian Bell
Other sports played: Basketball, table tennis, tennis, squash, golf
Other sports followed: Football (Manchester United), rugby (Leicester Tigers),
golf (Tiger Woods)
Relaxations: 'Spending time with my girlfriend and family and friends; socialising;
golf and playing any other sports; big *Star Trek* fan'
Extras: Formerly with Leicestershire. Took 14 wickets (41-18-47-14) in one day for
Egmont Plains v Hawera in a New Zealand club match 1997-98. Took 7-50 in Kent's
second innings at Headingley 2001, the best bowling figures by a Yorkshire player on
first-class debut (Paul Hutchison's similar figures were on his Championship debut
only); Kirby had replaced Matthew Hoggard (called up for England) halfway through
the match. Took 12-72 against Leicestershire, his former club, at Headingley 2001.
Awarded Yorkshire 2nd XI cap 2001. Returned first innings figures of 4-100 in ECB

National Academy's victory over Commonwealth Bank [Australian] Cricket Academy in Adelaide 2001-02

Opinions on cricket: '1. We play too much cricket, which reduces a) intensity; b) recovery; c) preparation. 2. Pitches are too inconsistent – a) bad techniques; b) lack of fast bowlers. 3. Need to have better practice facilities.'

Best batting: 57 Yorkshire v Hampshire, Headingley 2002
Best bowling: 7-50 Yorkshire v Kent, Headingley 2001

2002 Season

	M	Inns	NO	Runs	HS	Avge	100s	50s	Ct	St	O	M	Runs	Wkts	Avge	Best	5wI	10wM
Test																		
All First	10	17	3	141	57	10.07	-	1	-	-	331.1	68	1262	37	34.10	5-129	1	-
1-day Int																		
C & G																			
B & H	1	1	0	0	0	0.00	-	-	-	-	5	1	43	0	-		-	-
1-day Lge	4	2	0	2	1	1.00	-	-	-	-	33.4	1	197	3	65.66	2-40	-	

Career Performances

	M	Inns	NO	Runs	HS	Avge	100s	50s	Ct	St	Balls	Runs	Wkts	Avge	Best	5wI	10wM
Test																	
All First	20	27	5	190	57	8.63	-	1	4	-	3670	2242	84	26.69	7-50	4	1
1-day Int																	
C & G	1	1	0	0	0	0.00	-	-	-	-	60	53	1	53.00	1-53	-	
B & H	1	1	0	0	0	0.00	-	-	-	-	30	43	0	-		-	-
1-day Lge	8	3	1	6	4 *	3.00	-	-	1	-	364	355	9	39.44	3-35	-	

49. Which Zimbabwe cricketer was Hampshire's overseas player in 1995?

KIRTLEY, R. J. Sussex

Name: Robert <u>James</u> Kirtley
Role: Right-hand bat, right-arm
fast-medium bowler, county vice-captain
Born: 10 January 1975, Eastbourne
Height: 6ft **Weight:** 12st
Nickname: Ambi, Hurtler, Springer
County debut: 1995
County cap: 1998
One-Day Internationals: 7
50 wickets in a season: 5
1st-Class 50s: 2
1st-Class 5 w. in innings: 24
1st-Class 10 w. in match: 4
1st-Class catches: 33
One-Day 5 w. in innings: 2
Place in batting averages: 277th av. 12.16
(2001 254th av. 10.88)
Place in bowling averages: 15th av. 22.62
(2001 27th av. 23.32)
Strike rate: 42.90 (career 47.51)
Parents: Bob and Pip
Wife and date of marriage: Jenny, 26 October 2002
Family links with cricket: Brother plays league cricket
Education: St Andrews School, Eastbourne; Clifton College, Bristol
Qualifications: 9 GCSEs, 2 A-levels, NCA coaching first level
Career outside cricket: 'Teaching?'
Off-season: Touring Sri Lanka with England one-day team
Overseas tours: Sussex YC to Barbados 1993, to Sri Lanka 1995; Sussex to Grenada
2001; England A to Bangladesh and New Zealand 1999-2000; England to Zimbabwe
(one-day series) 2001-02, to Sri Lanka (ICC Champions Trophy) 2002-03
Overseas teams played for: Mashonaland, Zimbabwe 1996-97; Namibian Cricket
Board/Wanderers, Windhoek, Namibia 1998-99
Career highlights to date: 'Winning the second division Championship with Sussex
[2001]. Being selected for the England one-day squad. Hopefully more to come'
Cricket moments to forget: 'The three times I've bagged a pair'
Cricketers particularly admired: Curtly Ambrose, Jim Andrew, Darren Gough
Other sports followed: Hockey, golf, football (Brighton & Hove Albion)
Injuries: Out for four weeks with a broken hand
Relaxations: 'Inviting friends round for a braai (barbeque) and enjoying a cold beer
with them'
Extras: Played in the Mashonaland side which defeated England on their 1996-97 tour
of Zimbabwe, taking seven wickets in the match. Winner of an NBC Denis Compton

Award for promising cricketers 1997. Vice-captain of Sussex since 2001. Took hat-trick (A. Morris, Z. Morris, Aymes) in the B&H v Hampshire at West End 2001. Leading wicket-taker in English first-class cricket 2001 with 75 wickets (av. 23.32); took 102 wickets in all county cricket 2001. Made One-Day International debut in first ODI v Zimbabwe at Harare 2001-02. Has taken 50 wickets in a season for five consecutive years. Called up to the England one-day squad for the ICC Champions Trophy in Sri Lanka 2002-03 as a replacement for the injured Darren Gough. Sussex Player of the Year 2002

Opinions on cricket: 'Pitches, particularly one-day pitches, need to be of the highest quality. It would provide entertainment and develop skills that are required for playing at international level, where pitches on the whole are superb.'

Best batting: 59 Sussex v Durham, Eastbourne 1998
Best bowling: 7-21 Sussex v Hampshire, Southampton 1999
Stop press: Called up to the England one-day squad for the VB Series in Australia 2002-03 as a replacement for the injured Darren Gough

2002 Season

	M	Inns	NO	Runs	HS	Avge	100s	50s	Ct	St	O	M	Runs	Wkts	Avge	Best	5wI	10wM
Test																		
All First	11	15	3	146	36 *	12.16	-	-	4	-	379	94	1199	53	22.62	6-107	4	1
1-day Int	4	0	0	0	0	-	-	-	3	-	36	1	211	3	70.33	2-40	-	
C & G	2	0	0	0	0	-	-	-	-	-	17.1	3	58	5	11.60	3-46	-	
B & H	6	1	0	1	1	1.00	-	-	6	-	57	5	206	14	14.71	5-33	1	
1-day Lge	9	4	2	26	19 *	13.00	-	-	1	-	57.2	8	229	12	19.08	3-49	-	

Career Performances

	M	Inns	NO	Runs	HS	Avge	100s	50s	Ct	St	Balls	Runs	Wkts	Avge	Best	5wI	10wM
Test																	
All First	104	146	41	1116	59	10.62	-	2	33	-	19150	10036	403	24.90	7-21	24	4
1-day Int	7	1	0	1	1	1.00	-	-	5	-	362	305	6	50.83	2-33	-	
C & G	10	3	1	13	7 *	6.50	-	-	1	-	565	402	20	20.10	5-39	1	
B & H	17	6	2	26	10 *	6.50	-	-	9	-	953	632	34	18.58	5-33	1	
1-day Lge	84	38	21	201	19 *	11.82	-	-	22	-	3437	2648	119	22.25	4-21	-	

KLUSENER, L.   Nottinghamshire

Name: Lance Klusener
Role: Left-hand bat, right-arm
medium-fast bowler
Born: 4 September 1971, Durban,
South Africa
Height: 6ft **Weight:** 12st 10lbs
Nickname: Zulu
County debut: 2002
Test debut: 1996-97
Tests: 48
One-Day Internationals: 137
1st-Class 50s: 20
1st-Class 100s: 6
1st-Class 5 w. in innings: 11
1st-Class 10 w. in match: 3
1st-Class catches: 64
One-Day 100s: 2
One-Day 5 w. in innings: 6
Strike rate: 120.00 (career 56.00)

Parents: Peter and Dawn
Wife and date of marriage: Isabelle, 13 May 2000
Children: Matthew, 17 February 2002
Education: Durban High School; Durban Technikon
Off-season: 'Fishing, hunting and family'; playing for South Africa
Overseas tours: South Africa to India 1996-97, to Pakistan 1997-98, to Australia
1997-98, to England 1998, to New Zealand 1998-99, to UK, Ireland and Holland
(World Cup) 1999, to Kenya (LG Cup) 1999-2000, to India 1999-2000, to Sharjah
(Coca-Cola Cup) 1999-2000, to Sri Lanka 2000, to Australia (Super Challenge) 2000,
to Singapore (Singapore Challenge) 2000, to Kenya (ICC Knockout) 2000-01, to West
Indies 2000-01, to Zimbabwe 2001, to Australia 2001-02, to Morocco (Morocco Cup)
2002, to Sri Lanka (ICC Champions Trophy) 2002-03
Overseas teams played for: Natal/KwaZulu-Natal 1993-94 –
Career highlights to date: 'World Cup Man of the Tournament [1999]'
Cricketers particularly admired: Malcolm Marshall
Young players to look out for: Kevin Pietersen, Hashim Amla
Other sports played: Golf
Other sports followed: Rugby (Sharks)
Extras: Returned the best analysis by a South African on Test debut – 8-64 in India's
second innings of the second Test at Kolkata (Calcutta) 1996-97. Struck his maiden
Test century off an even 100 balls (102*) in the second Test v India at Cape Town
1996-97, setting a record for the quickest Test hundred by a South African in terms of
balls faced and sharing with Brian McMillan in a record eighth-wicket partnership for

South Africa in Tests v India (147*). Has won numerous ODI awards, including Player of the Tournament in World Cup 1999. Scored 174 in the second Test v England at Port Elizabeth 1999-2000, setting a record for the highest individual Test score at the ground and sharing with Mark Boucher in a record eighth-wicket stand for South Africa in Tests v England (119). One of *Wisden*'s Five Cricketers of the Year 2000. Topped South Africa's Test batting averages on tour of Sri Lanka 2000 (275 runs; av. 68.75) and was Man of the Series. Scored a 77-ball 83 v Australia in the first ODI at Johannesburg 2001-02, having arrived at the crease with South Africa on 66-6. Was Nottinghamshire's overseas player at the start of the 2002 season, pending the arrival of Nicky Boje. B&H Gold Award for his 68 and 2-31 v Durham at Trent Bridge 2002
Best batting: 174 South Africa v England, Port Elizabeth 1999-2000
Best bowling: 8-34 Natal v Western Province, Durban 1995-96
Stop press: Selected for South Africa squad for 2002-03 World Cup

2002 Season

	M	Inns	NO	Runs	HS	Avge	100s	50s	Ct	St	O	M	Runs	Wkts	Avge	Best	5wI	10wM
Test																		
All First	1	2	0	42	42	21.00	-	-	1	-	20	4	88	1	88.00	1-88	-	-
1-day Int																		
C & G																		
B & H	5	5	2	144	68	48.00	-	1	1	-	33	0	162	4	40.50	2-31	-	
1-day Lge																		

Career Performances

	M	Inns	NO	Runs	HS	Avge	100s	50s	Ct	St	Balls	Runs	Wkts	Avge	Best	5wI	10wM
Test	48	68	11	1904	174	33.40	4	8	33	-	6683	2924	78	37.48	8-64	2	-
All First	109	150	31	4047	174	34.00	6	20	64	-	16971	8071	303	26.63	8-34	11	3
1-day Int	137	113	40	3129	103 *	42.86	2	17	29	-	5966	4662	165	28.25	6-49	6	
C & G																	
B & H	5	5	2	144	68	48.00	-	1	1	-	198	162	4	40.50	2-31	-	
1-day Lge																	

KNIGHT, N. V.   Warwickshire

Name: <u>Nicholas</u> Verity Knight
Role: Left-hand bat, right-arm medium-fast
bowler, close fielder
Born: 28 November 1969, Watford
Height: 6ft 1in **Weight:** 13st
Nickname: Stitch, Fungus
County debut: 1991 (Essex),
1995 (Warwickshire)
County cap: 1994 (Essex),
1995 (Warwickshire)
Test debut: 1995
Tests: 17
One-Day Internationals: 83
1000 runs in a season: 3
1st-Class 50s: 53
1st-Class 100s: 26
1st-Class 200s: 3
1st-Class catches: 242
One-Day 100s: 17

Place in batting averages: 2nd av. 95.00 (2001 54th av. 44.64)
Strike rate: (career 159.00)
Parents: John and Rosemary
Wife and date of marriage: Trudie, 3 October 1998
Family links with cricket: Father played for Cambridgeshire. Brother Andy plays
club cricket in local Cambridge leagues
Education: St John's School, Cambridge; Felsted Prep; Felsted School;
Loughborough University
Qualifications: 9 O-levels, 3 A-levels, BSc (Hons) Sociology, coaching qualification
Off-season: Touring with England
Overseas tours: Felsted School to Australia 1986-87; England A to India 1994-95, to
Pakistan 1995-96, to Kenya and Sri Lanka 1997-98; England to Zimbabwe and New
Zealand 1996-97, to Sharjah (Champions Trophy) 1997-98, to West Indies 1997-98
(one-day series), to Bangladesh (Wills International Cup) 1998, to Australia 1998-99
(CUB Series), to Sharjah (Coca-Cola Cup) 1998-99, to South Africa and Zimbabwe
1999-2000 (one-day series), to Sri Lanka 2000-01 (one-day series), to Zimbabwe
(one-day series) 2001-02, to India and New Zealand 2001-02 (one-day series), to Sri
Lanka (ICC Champions Trophy) 2002-03, to Australia 2002-03 (VB Series)
Overseas teams played for: Northern Districts, Sydney 1991-92; East Torrens,
Adelaide 1992-94
Cricketers particularly admired: David Gower, Graham Gooch
Other sports played: Rugby, hockey
Relaxations: Eating good food, painting

Extras: Captained English Schools 1987 and 1988, England YC v New Zealand 1989 and Combined Universities 1991. Played hockey for Essex and Young England. Played rugby for Eastern Counties. Won *Daily Telegraph* award 1988; voted Gray-Nicolls Cricketer of the Year 1988, Cricket Society Most Promising Young Cricketer of the Year 1989, Essex Young Player of the Year 1991 and Essex U19 Player of the Year. Left Essex at the end of the 1994 season to join Warwickshire. Scored successive centuries (113 and 125*) in the Texaco Trophy against Pakistan in 1996. Man of the Match after striking 96 off 117 balls in first Test v Zimbabwe at Bulawayo 1996-97 as England chased 205 for victory; he was run out off the last ball of the match while attempting the winning run and the match was drawn with the scores level (the first such Test result). Won successive one-day Man of the Match awards v West Indies 1997-98. Warwickshire vice-captain 1999. Member of England's 1999 World Cup squad. With Anurag Singh, shared in record NatWest first-wicket stand for Warwickshire (185), v Hampshire at Edgbaston 2000. B&H Gold Award for his 107* v Glamorgan at Edgbaston 2001 (his second century in two days). Man of the Match (80*) in fifth ODI v Zimbabwe at Bulawayo 2001-02 and Man of the Series (302 runs; av. 100.67). Scored 105 in England's One-Day International victory over India at Delhi 2001-02. B&H Gold Award for his 126* v Somerset at Edgbaston 2002; his 100 took him past Alvin Kallicharran's record of 12 one-day centuries for Warwickshire. Carried his bat for 255* v Hampshire at Edgbaston 2002, in the process sharing with Alan Richardson (91) in a tenth-wicket stand of 214, which was a county best for the last wicket and the fifth highest tenth-wicket partnership in Championship history overall. Carried his bat (for the second time in the season) for 245* v Sussex at Edgbaston 2002, becoming the first batsman to score two double centuries in a season for Warwickshire since Alvin Kallicharran did so in 1982; also scored 97 in second innings. Scored 79 v Yorkshire at Headingley 2002, in the process passing 1000 Championship runs for the season from only ten completed innings; also scored 109 in the second innings. Leading English player (second overall) in the 2002 first-class batting averages with 1520 runs at 95.00. Warwickshire Batsman of the Year 2002
Best batting: 255* Warwickshire v Hampshire, Edgbaston 2002
Best bowling: 1-61 Essex v Middlesex, Uxbridge 1994
Stop press: Scored unbeaten century (111*) v Australia at Sydney in the VB Series 2002-03, following up with 70 in the next match, also v Australia, at Melbourne; leading run-scorer in the VB Series 2002-03 with 461 runs (av. 51.22). Selected for England squad for 2002-03 World Cup

2002 Season

	M	Inns	NO	Runs	HS	Avge	100s	50s	Ct	St	O	M	Runs	Wkts	Avge	Best	5wI	10wM
Test																		
All First	10	19	3	1520	255 *	95.00	5	5	10	-								
1-day Int	7	7	1	142	31	23.66	-	-	2	-								
C & G	2	2	0	79	54	39.50	-	1	3	-								
B & H	8	8	1	157	126 *	22.42	1	-	5	-								
1-day Lge	10	10	0	255	86	25.50	-	1	3	-								

Career Performances

	M	Inns	NO	Runs	HS	Avge	100s	50s	Ct	St	Balls	Runs	Wkts	Avge	Best	5wI	10wM
Test	17	30	0	719	113	23.96	1	4	26	-							
All First	176	293	30	11544	255 *	43.89	29	53	242	-	159	191	1	191.00	1-61	-	-
1-day Int	83	83	9	3015	125 *	40.74	4	20	34	-							
C & G	27	27	2	1054	151	42.16	4	4	12	-							
B & H	49	45	5	1383	126 *	34.57	5	4	15	-	6	4	0	-	-	-	-
1-day Lge	134	122	16	3391	134	31.99	4	15	55	-	84	85	2	42.50	1-14	-	

KOENIG, S. G.   Middlesex

Name: <u>Sven</u> Gaëtan Koenig
Role: Left-hand bat
Born: 9 December 1973, Durban, South Africa
Height: 5ft 9in **Weight:** 12st 2lbs
Nickname: Blackie, Kuala
County debut: 2002
County cap: 2002
1000 runs in a season: 1
1st-Class 50s: 32
1st-Class 100s: 11
1st-Class catches: 52
One-Day 100s: 1
Place in batting averages: 48th av. 46.33
Strike rate: (career 122.00)
Parents: Gaëtan and Barbara
Wife and date of marriage:
Catherine, 27 December 2002
Education: Highbury; Hilton College; University of Cape Town
Qualifications: Law degree, Economics degree, Level 2 coach
Career outside cricket: Business
Off-season: 'Mexico/USA October-December 2002. Wedding 27 December 2002; honeymoon in Mauritius January 2003'
Overseas tours: Western Province to Australia 1995; South Africa A to England 1996; Transvaal to Australia 1997
Overseas teams played for: Western Province 1993-96; Transvaal/Gauteng 1997-2000
Career highlights to date: 'Playing at Lord's – debut at Lord's v Notts'
Cricket moments to forget: 'First-ball duck – lbw Malcolm Marshall – on Currie Cup debut, Western Province v Natal'
Cricket superstitions: 'None'

Cricketers particularly admired: Desmond Haynes, Steve Waugh, Gary Kirsten
Young players to look out for: Nick Compton, Ed Cowan (Sydney University), Kabir Ali
Other sports played: Golf, surfing
Other sports followed: Rugby (Springboks), football (Newcastle United)
Injuries: Injury to right knee, but no time off required
Interests/relaxations: Surfing, fishing, business
Extras: South African Young Player of the Year 1994. Leading run-scorer in South African domestic first-class cricket 2000-01 with 789 runs (av. 60.69). Gauteng Player of the Year 2000-01. Scored century (141*) on first-class debut for Middlesex v Cambridge University CCE at Fenner's and another (100) on Championship debut for the county v Durham at Riverside 2002. Scored maiden one-day century for Middlesex (116) v Essex at Chelmsford in the C&G 2002. Scored 1000 Championship runs in his debut season for Middlesex. Awarded Middlesex cap 2002. Holds an Italian passport and is not considered an overseas player
Opinions on cricket: 'Championship matches should end on Friday, giving an extra day for pitch and player preparation for Sunday League matches.'
Best batting: 155 Gauteng v Griqualand West, Kimberley 2000-01
Best bowling: 1-0 Gauteng/Northerns v Sri Lanka A, Johannesburg 1999-2000

2002 Season

	M	Inns	NO	Runs	HS	Avge	100s	50s	Ct	St	O	M	Runs	Wkts	Avge	Best	5wI	10wM
Test																		
All First	18	29	2	1251	141 *	46.33	4	7	6	-								
1-day Int																		
C & G	1	1	0	116	116	116.00	1	-	-	-								
B & H	4	4	0	71	30	17.75	-	-	1	-								
1-day Lge	12	11	1	104	43 *	10.40	-	-	3	-								

Career Performances

	M	Inns	NO	Runs	HS	Avge	100s	50s	Ct	St	Balls	Runs	Wkts	Avge	Best	5wI	10wM
Test																	
All First	93	160	7	5893	155	38.51	11	32	52	-	122	67	1	67.00	1-0	-	-
1-day Int																	
C & G	1	1	0	116	116	116.00	1	-	-	-							
B & H	4	4	0	71	30	17.75	-	-	1	-							
1-day Lge	12	11	1	104	43 *	10.40	-	-	3	-							

KRIKKEN, K. M.   Derbyshire

Name: <u>Karl</u> Matthew Krikken
Role: Right-hand bat, wicket-keeper
Born: 9 April 1969, Bolton
Height: 5ft 10in **Weight:** 13st 3lbs
Nickname: Krikk, Krude
County debut: 1987 (one-day),
1989 (first-class)
County cap: 1992
Benefit: 2002
50 dismissals in a season: 5
1st-Class 50s: 25
1st-Class 100s: 1
1st-Class catches: 526
1st-Class stumpings: 31
Place in batting averages: 283rd av. 11.26
(2001 179th av. 21.75)
Strike rate: (career 134.00)
Parents: Brian and Irene

Wife and date of marriage: Leesha, 3 October 1998
Children: Harry Evan, 20 December 1996; Chester, 19 December 1998
Family links with cricket: Father played for Lancashire and Worcestershire
Education: Horwich Parish Church School; Rivington and Blackrod High School and
Sixth Form College
Qualifications: 6 O-levels, 3 A-levels, Level 3 coaching award
Overseas tours: Derbyshire to Bermuda 1993, to Spain 1997, to Portugal 2000
Overseas teams played for: CBC Old Boys, Kimberley, South Africa 1988-89;
Green Island, Dunedin, New Zealand 1990-91; United CC, Cape Town 1992-93;
Rivertonians, Cape Town 1993-94; Longford CC, Victoria, Australia
Career highlights to date: 'Winning B&H in 1993. Winning Sunday League in 1990.
Runners-up in Nat West 1998 and Championship 1996'
Cricket moments to forget: 'Enjoyed all of it'
Cricketers particularly admired: Kim Barnett, Bob Taylor, Derek Randall,
Jack Russell, Alan Hill
Young players to look out for: 'Derbyshire will come of age in a few years'
Other sports played: 'Keg ball', volleyball, football
Other sports followed: Football (Wigan Athletic FC, Bolton Wanderers FC)
Relaxations: Family
Extras: Derbyshire Supporters' Player of the Year 1991 and 1996; Derbyshire
Clubman of the Year 1993. Derbyshire vice-captain 1998-2000. Made 500th first-class
dismissal when he caught Will Kendall off Nathan Dumelow v Hampshire at Derby
2001. Appointed 2nd XI coach for 2003

Best batting: 104 Derbyshire v Lancashire, Old Trafford 1996
Best bowling: 1-54 Derbyshire v Hampshire, Derby 1999

2002 Season

	M	Inns	NO	Runs	HS	Avge	100s	50s	Ct	St	O	M	Runs	Wkts	Avge	Best	5wI	10wM
Test																		
All First	9	16	1	169	48	11.26	-	-	26	-								
1-day Int																		
C & G																		
B & H	5	2	1	19	15 *	19.00	-	-	2	-								
1-day Lge	1	0	0	0	0	-	-	-	2	1								

Career Performances

	M	Inns	NO	Runs	HS	Avge	100s	50s	Ct	St	Balls	Runs	Wkts	Avge	Best	5wI	10wM
Test																	
All First	213	321	60	5710	104	21.87	1	25	526	31	134	121	1	121.00	1-54	-	-
1-day Int																	
C & G	20	12	5	201	55	28.71	-	1	15	1							
B & H	42	26	10	333	42 *	20.81	-	-	35	8							
1-day Lge	137	99	33	1137	44 *	17.22	-	-	145	34							

LAMPITT, S. R. Worcestershire

Name: <u>Stuart</u> Richard Lampitt
Role: Right-hand bat, right-arm
fast-medium bowler
Born: 29 July 1966, Wolverhampton
Height: 5ft 11in **Weight:** 14st
Nickname: Jed
County debut: 1985
County cap: 1989
Benefit: 2000
50 wickets in a season: 7
1st-Class 50s: 20
1st-Class 100s: 1
1st-Class 5 w. in innings: 20
1st-Class catches: 148
One-Day 5 w. in innings: 3
Place in batting averages: (2001 150th
av. 25.62)
Place in bowling averages: (2001 51st
av. 27.87)
Strike rate: (career 53.32)

Parents: Joseph Charles and Muriel-Ann
Wife and date of marriage: Clare Jeanette, 31 March 2001
Children: Joseph Stuart, 4 September 2001
Education: Maidensbridge Primary School, Wall Heath; The Kingswinford School;
Dudley College of Technology
Qualifications: 7 O-levels, BTEC Diploma in Business Studies, Level III cricket
coach
Career outside cricket: Cricket Development Officer, Worcestershire Cricket Board
Off-season: 'Beginning my new role as CDO of the Worcestershire Cricket Board on
1 October 2002'
Overseas tours: NCA U19 South to Bermuda 1985; Worcestershire to Bahamas 1990,
to Zimbabwe 1991, 1994, to South Africa 1993, to Barbados 1996, to Portugal 2000
Overseas teams played for: Mangere, Auckland 1986-88; University of Western
Australia, Perth 1991-93
Career highlights to date: 'Lucky enough to have been a part of Worcestershire CCC
teams winning every domestic honour'
Cricket moments to forget: 'Every time I'm dismissed or hit for a boundary'
Cricket superstitions: 'None'
Cricketers particularly admired: Ian Botham, Wasim Akram, Malcolm Marshall,
Richard Hadlee
Young players to look out for: 'The clever ones'
Other sports played: Football, golf (5 handicap; club champion Stourbridge GC
1999)
Other sports followed: Football (Wolverhampton Wanderers FC)
Relaxations: 'Enjoying my family; socialising!'
Extras: Took five wickets and made 42 for Stourbridge in the final of the William
Younger Cup at Lord's 1986. One of the Whittingdale Young Players of the Year 1989.
Retired at the end of the 2002 season and is now development officer with
Worcestershire Cricket Board
Opinions on cricket: 'Great game!'
Best batting: 122 Worcestershire v Middlesex, Lord's 1994
Best bowling: 7-45 Worcestershire v Warwickshire, Worcester 2000

2002 Season

	M	Inns	NO	Runs	HS	Avge	100s	50s	Ct	St	O	M	Runs	Wkts	Avge	Best	5wI	10wM
Test																		
All First																		
1-day Int																		
C & G	3	1	0	5	5	5.00	-	-	-	-	21	0	112	3	37.33	1-10	-	
B & H	7	3	1	31	20 *	15.50	-	-	4	-	55	6	178	4	44.50	3-28	-	
1-day Lge	14	6	5	20	10 *	20.00	-	-	1	-	97.1	9	419	15	27.93	3-33	-	

Career Performances

	M	Inns	NO	Runs	HS	Avge	100s	50s	Ct	St	Balls	Runs	Wkts	Avge	Best	5wI	10wM
Test																	
All First	236	311	74	5649	122	23.83	1	20	148	-	32049	17224	601	28.65	7-45	20	-
1-day Int																	
C & G	33	23	5	247	54	13.72	-	1	8	-	1696	1228	49	25.06	5-22	1	
B & H	54	29	12	361	41	21.23	-	-	18	-	2734	1764	77	22.90	6-26	1	
1-day Lge	209	124	47	1414	41 *	18.36	-	-	60	-	7708	5851	236	24.79	5-67	1	

LANEY, J. S. Hampshire

Name: Jason Scott Laney
Role: Right-hand bat, occasional
off-spin bowler
Born: 27 April 1973, Winchester
Height: 5ft 10in **Weight:** 13st 7lbs
Nickname: Chucky, Hurler, Crickethead,
Cricket Badger
County debut: 1993 (one-day),
1995 (first-class)
County cap: 1996
1000 runs in a season: 1
1st-Class 50s: 26
1st-Class 100s: 5
1st-Class catches: 72
One-Day 100s: 2
Place in batting averages: 213th av. 22.23
Strike rate: (career 192.00)
Parents: Geoff and Pam
Marital status: Single
Family links with cricket: Grandfather played good club cricket
Education: Pewsey Vale Comprehensive; St John's, Marlborough;
Leeds Metropolitan University
Qualifications: 8 GCSEs, 2 A-levels, BA (Hons) in Human Movement Studies
Overseas tours: England U18 to Canada (International Youth Tournament) 1991
Overseas teams played for: Waikato, New Zealand 1994-95; Matabeleland and Old
Miltonians, Zimbabwe 1995-96; DHS Old Boys, South Africa 1996-97
Cricketers particularly admired: Rupert Cox, Ian Botham, Robin Smith,
Malcolm Marshall
Young players to look out for: Lawrence Prittipaul, Chris Tremlett, Jimmy Adams
Other sports played: Golf, cards
Other sports followed: Football (Swindon Town FC)

Extras: Hampshire Young Cricketer of the Year 1995. Scored 153 v Norfolk at Southampton 1996 to become the first Hampshire cricketer to score a century before lunch on debut in the NatWest Trophy; in the process shared with John Stephenson (107) in a then competition record stand for the first wicket (269). Released by Hampshire at the end of the 2002 season
Best batting: 112 Hampshire v Oxford University, The Parks 1996
Best bowling: 1-24 Hampshire v Northamptonshire, Northampton 1999

2002 Season

	M	Inns	NO	Runs	HS	Avge	100s	50s	Ct	St	O	M	Runs	Wkts	Avge	Best	5wl	10wM
Test																		
All First	7	13	0	289	89	22.23	-	1	7	-								
1-day Int																		
C & G	1	1	0	0	0	0.00	-	-	-	-								
B & H																		
1-day Lge	7	7	0	197	71	28.14	-	1	1	-								

Career Performances

	M	Inns	NO	Runs	HS	Avge	100s	50s	Ct	St	Balls	Runs	Wkts	Avge	Best	5wl	10wM
Test																	
All First	87	153	5	4414	112	29.82	5	26	72	-	384	224	2	112.00	1-24	-	-
1-day Int																	
C & G	16	15	1	658	153	47.00	1	3	6	-							
B & H	21	20	0	303	41	15.15	-	-	3								
1-day Lge	84	84	2	1916	106 *	23.36	1	8	21	-	3	9	0	-	-	-	-

LARAMAN, A. W.   Somerset

Name: Aaron William Laraman
Role: Right-hand bat, right-arm medium-fast bowler
Born: 10 January 1979, London
Height: 6ft 5in **Weight:** 14st 7lbs
Nickname: Az, Lazza, Shanky, Long
County debut: 1998 (Middlesex)
1st-Class 50s: 1
1st-Class catches: 5
One-Day 5 w. in innings: 2
Place in batting averages: 119th av. 33.00
Place in bowling averages: 99th av. 34.07
Strike rate: 58.37 (career 52.45)
Parents: William and Lynda
Marital status: Single
Education: St Paul's C of E School; Enfield Grammar School

Qualifications: 8 GCSEs
Career outside cricket: Cricket coaching in winter
Overseas tours: England U17 to Holland 1995; England U19 to South Africa 1997-98
Overseas teams played for: Burnside CC, Christchurch, New Zealand 1999-2000; Willetton CC, Perth 2000-01
Career highlights to date: 'Making my debut at Lord's in 1998'
Cricketers particularly admired: Steve Waugh, Glenn McGrath, Michael Atherton
Young players to look out for: Lee Wooldridge
Other sports followed: Football (Arsenal)
Relaxations: Working out at the gym, football, golf
Extras: Enfield Grammar School cap at the age of 13. Middlesex Colts cap. Seaxe 2nd XI Player of the Year 1997. Took 4-39 on NatWest debut v Nottinghamshire at Lord's 2000. Scored 95-ball 82* as Middlesex successfully chased 240 to win County Championship match v Gloucestershire at Southgate 2002. Left Middlesex at the end of the 2002 season and has joined Somerset for 2003

Best batting: 82* Middlesex v Gloucestershire, Southgate 2002
Best bowling: 4-33 Middlesex v Cambridge University, Fenner's 2000

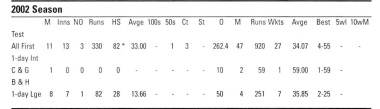

2002 Season

	M	Inns	NO	Runs	HS	Avge	100s	50s	Ct	St	O	M	Runs	Wkts	Avge	Best	5wI	10wM
Test																		
All First	11	13	3	330	82*	33.00	-	1	3	-	262.4	47	920	27	34.07	4-55	-	-
1-day Int																		
C & G	1	0	0	0	0	-	-	-	-	-	10	2	59	1	59.00	1-59	-	
B & H																		
1-day Lge	8	7	1	82	28	13.66	-	-	-	-	50	4	251	7	35.85	2-25	-	

Career Performances

	M	Inns	NO	Runs	HS	Avge	100s	50s	Ct	St	Balls	Runs	Wkts	Avge	Best	5wI	10wM
Test																	
All First	14	14	3	359	82*	32.63	-	1	5	-	1731	995	33	30.15	4-33	-	-
1-day Int																	
C & G	5	2	1	18	16*	18.00	-	-	2	-	201	125	9	13.88	4-39	-	
B & H																	
1-day Lge	18	15	5	115	28	11.50	-	-	4	-	700	550	24	22.91	6-42	2	

LAW, D. R. Durham

Name: <u>Danny</u> Richard Law
Role: Right-hand bat, right-arm medium-fast bowler
Born: 13 July 1975, London
Height: 6ft 5in **Weight:** 16st
Nickname: Desperate
County debut: 1993 (Sussex), 1997 (Essex), 2001 (Durham)
County cap: 1996 (Sussex), 2001 (Durham)
1st-Class 50s: 14
1st-Class 100s: 2
1st-Class 5 w. in innings: 8
1st-Class catches: 55
Place in batting averages: 153rd av. 28.11 (2001 166th av. 23.44)
Place in bowling averages: (2001 39th av. 26.26)
Strike rate: 72.85 (career 53.87)
Parents: Richard (deceased) and Claudette
Marital status: Separated
Children: Sade
Family links with cricket: Cousins play club cricket in Northampton
Education: St Andrews; Wolverstone Hall/Steyning Grammar School
Qualifications: Coach
Overseas tours: Sussex Schools U16 to Jersey 1991; England U18 to South Africa 1992-93, to Denmark 1993; England U19 to Sri Lanka 1993-94; Dulwich CC to Kenya and Uganda 2000-01
Overseas teams played for: Ashburton CC, Melbourne 1992-94; Essendon, Melbourne 1995-96
Career highlights to date: 'Winning two trophies with Essex. Being capped at Sussex and also at Durham'
Cricketers particularly admired: Viv Richards, Ian Botham, Michael Holding, Simon Brown, Martin Love, Stuart Law
Young players to look out for: Nicky Peng, Andy Pratt, Paul Collingwood, Steve Harmison
Other sports played: Golf ('badly')
Other sports followed: Football (Man Utd)
Relaxations: Cinema, music, PlayStation
Extras: Winner of Denis Compton Award 1996. Left Sussex during the 1996-97 off-season and joined Essex for 1997. Took Championship hat-trick v Durham at Riverside 1998. Left Essex at the end of the 2000 season and joined Durham for 2001. Scored maiden Championship century (103) v Hampshire at Riverside 2001, in the

process sharing with James Brinkley in a record seventh-wicket partnership for Durham (127). Awarded Durham cap 2001

Opinions on cricket: 'Keep it interesting.'

Best batting: 115 Sussex v Young Australia, Hove 1995

Best bowling: 6-53 Durham v Hampshire, West End 2001

2002 Season

	M	Inns	NO	Runs	HS	Avge	100s	50s	Ct	St	O	M	Runs	Wkts	Avge	Best	5wI	10wM
Test																		
All First	6	10	1	253	72 *	28.11	-	2	2	-	85	17	330	7	47.14	3-41	-	-
1-day Int																		
C & G	1	1	0	24	24	24.00	-	-	-	-	4	0	14	1	14.00	1-14	-	
B & H																		
1-day Lge	11	9	0	84	28	9.33	-	-	1	-	44.1	0	321	4	80.25	2-67	-	

Career Performances

	M	Inns	NO	Runs	HS	Avge	100s	50s	Ct	St	Balls	Runs	Wkts	Avge	Best	5wI	10wM
Test																	
All First	102	160	7	3171	115	20.72	2	14	55	-	10829	6647	201	33.06	6-53	8	-
1-day Int																	
C & G	18	14	1	251	47	19.30	-	-	4	-	355	322	10	32.20	3-51	-	
B & H	16	15	3	248	57 *	20.66	-	1	3	-	288	241	4	60.25	2-22	-	
1-day Lge	110	95	14	1732	82	21.38	-	5	21	-	2290	2082	65	32.03	3-26	-	

50. Which West Indies and Kent all-rounder scored 1157 runs and took 96 wickets in 1968?

LAW, S. G. — Lancashire

Name: <u>Stuart</u> Grant Law
Role: Right-hand bat, right-arm
leg-spin bowler
Born: 18 October 1968, Brisbane, Australia
Height: 6ft 1in **Weight:** 13st
Nickname: Lawry, Judge, LA
County debut: 1996 (Essex),
2002 (Lancashire)
County cap: 1996 (Essex),
2002 (Lancashire)
Test debut: 1995-96
Tests: 1
One-Day Internationals: 54
1000 runs in a season: 7
1st-Class 50s: 92
1st-Class 100s: 53
1st-Class 200s: 3
1st-Class 5 w. in innings: 1
1st-Class catches: 292
One-Day 100s: 13

Place in batting averages: 28th av. 52.86 (2001 7th av. 65.55)
Strike rate: 148.00 (career 99.19)
Parents: Grant and Pam
Wife and date of marriage: Debbie-Lee, 31 December 1998
Children: Max, 9 January 2002
Family links with cricket: 'Cricket has always been in the family'
Education: Stafford State School; Craigslea State High School; Brisbane State
High School
Qualifications: Level 2 cricket coach
Off-season: 'Playing for Queensland in Pura Cup'
Overseas tours: Young Australia (Australia A) to England and Netherlands 1995
(captain); Australia to India and Pakistan (World Cup) 1995-96, to Sri Lanka (Singer
World Series), India and South Africa 1996-97, to New Zealand (one-day series)
1997-98
Overseas teams played for: Queensland Bulls 1988-89 –
Career highlights to date: 'Playing for Australia. Captaining Queensland to their first
Sheffield Shield [title] win'
Cricket superstitions: 'None'
Cricketers particularly admired: Viv Richards, Greg Chappell
Young players to look out for: Jim Anderson
Other sports played: Golf, tennis
Other sports followed: Rugby league (Brisbane Broncos)

Injuries: Broke hand in February 2002
Relaxations: 'Spending time with family, friends; going to the beach'
Extras: Made his first-class debut for Queensland as a 19-year-old, scoring 179 on only his second appearance. Sheffield Shield Player of the Year 1990-91. Shared with Martin Love in record third-wicket partnership for Queensland (326), v Tasmania at Brisbane 1994-95. Is the most successful captain in Australian domestic cricket history, having captained Queensland to their first Sheffield Shield title in 1994-95, to their second in 1996-97, to the title in the first three Pura Cup competitions in 1999-2000, 2000-01 and 2001-02 (to equal Richie Benaud's feat of captaining his state to five titles) and to three one-day titles. Made his Test debut for Australia against Sri Lanka at Perth in 1995-96 and scored an unbeaten 54. Man of the Match for his 71-ball 80* in the 1997 NatWest final v Warwickshire at Lord's. One of *Wisden*'s Five Cricketers of the Year 1998. Set record for the fastest century in Australian domestic one-day cricket – 74 balls for Queensland v Tasmania at Brisbane 1998-99 (ended up 103*). Scored centuries (159 and 113*) in each innings v Yorkshire at Chelmsford 1999. Topped the English first-class batting averages for 1999 (1833 runs at 73.32). Professional Cricketers' Association Player of the Year 1999. Man of the Match in inaugural Pura Milk Cup Final 1999-2000. Scored 116* and 123* v Lancashire at Old Trafford 2001, becoming the first player since Glamorgan's Hugh Morris in 1995 to score unbeaten centuries in each innings of a match; followed up with a 90-ball century (ending up with 108) v Lancashire in the ensuing Norwich Union League match at the same ground. Left Essex at the end of the 2001 season and joined Lancashire as overseas player for 2002. Became Queensland's most-capped player when he passed Sam Trimble's record of 133 first-class appearances for the state, v Tasmania at the Gabba 2001-02. Stood down as captain of Queensland at the end of the 2001-02 Australian season. Scored 218 (his maiden century for Lancashire) v Sussex at Old Trafford 2002, in the process sharing with Gary Keedy (25*) in a tenth-wicket stand of 145 that avoided the follow-on. Awarded Lancashire cap 2002
Opinions on cricket: 'No consistency in policing the laws of the game.'
Best batting: 263 Essex v Somerset, Chelmsford 1999
Best bowling: 5-39 Queensland v Tasmania, Brisbane 1995-96

2002 Season

	M	Inns	NO	Runs	HS	Avge	100s	50s	Ct	St	O	M	Runs	Wkts	Avge	Best	5wI	10wM
Test																		
All First	15	26	3	1216	218	52.86	2	6	21	-	24.4	5	72	1	72.00	1-24	-	-
1-day Int																		
C & G	2	1	0	4	4	4.00	-	-	3	-								
B & H	7	5	0	90	47	18.00	-	-	4	-								
1-day Lge	12	12	1	561	133	51.00	1	4	2	-	8.2	0	41	3	13.66	3-41	-	

Career Performances

	M	Inns	NO	Runs	HS	Avge	100s	50s	Ct	St	Balls	Runs	Wkts	Avge	Best	5wI	10wM
Test	1	1	1	54	54 *	-	-	1	1	-	18	9	0	-	-	-	-
All First	259	432	47	19122	263	49.66	56	92	292	-	8134	4029	82	49.13	5-39	1	-
1-day Int	54	51	5	1237	110	26.89	1	7	12	-	807	635	12	52.91	2-22	-	
C & G	18	16	1	710	107	47.33	3	3	15	-	439	366	8	45.75	2-36	-	
B & H	29	26	0	760	116	29.23	1	3	16	-	384	351	9	39.00	2-13	-	
1-day Lge	94	92	5	3232	133	37.14	8	13	36	-	954	832	25	33.28	4-37	-	

LEATHERDALE, D. A. Worcestershire

Name: <u>David</u> Anthony Leatherdale
Role: Right-hand bat, right-arm medium bowler, cover fielder
Born: 26 November 1967, Bradford
Height: 5ft 10in **Weight:** 11st
Nickname: Lugsy, Spock
County debut: 1988
County cap: 1994; colours 2002
1000 runs in a season: 1
1st-Class 50s: 52
1st-Class 100s: 14
1st-Class 5 w. in innings: 2
1st-Class catches: 149
One-Day 5 w. in innings: 1
Place in batting averages: 61st av. 43.31
(2001 164th av. 23.75)
Place in bowling averages: 89th av. 33.43
(2001 99th av. 36.25)
Strike rate: 52.68 (career 53.36)
Parents: Paul and Rosalyn
Wife: Vanessa
Children: Callum Edward, 6 July 1990; Christian Ellis, 6 March 1995
Family links with cricket: Father played local cricket; brother-in-law played for England YC in 1979
Education: Bolton Royd Primary School; Pudsey Grangefield Secondary School
Qualifications: 8 O-levels, 3 A-levels, NCA coaching award (stage 1)
Overseas tours: England Indoor to Australia and New Zealand 1994-95
Overseas teams played for: Pretoria Police, South Africa 1987-88
Career highlights to date: '5-10 v Australia 1997'
Cricketers particularly admired: Mark Scott, George Batty, Peter Kippax
Other sports followed: Football, American football

Relaxations: Golf

Extras: Scored century (147*) v Northamptonshire at Northampton 2002, in the process sharing with Stephen Peters (146) in a record fourth-wicket partnership for Worcestershire in matches against Northamptonshire (239). B&H Gold Award for his 43* plus 2-18 and a run-out v Warwickshire at Edgbaston 2002. Recorded maiden one-day five-wicket return (5-9) in the NUL v Durham at Riverside 2002. Scored 120 v Nottinghamshire at Trent Bridge 2002, in the process sharing with Steve Rhodes (124) in a new record seventh-wicket partnership for Worcestershire (256). Granted a benefit for 2003

Best batting: 157 Worcestershire v Somerset, Worcester 1991

Best bowling: 5-20 Worcestershire v Gloucestershire, Worcester 1998

2002 Season

	M	Inns	NO	Runs	HS	Avge	100s	50s	Ct	St	O	M	Runs	Wkts	Avge	Best	5wI	10wM
Test																		
All First	14	23	4	823	154	43.31	2	4	4	-	140.3	22	535	16	33.43	4-23	-	-
1-day Int																		
C & G	3	2	0	45	40	22.50	-	-	2	-	16	0	81	3	27.00	2-35	-	
B & H	7	6	2	118	43 *	29.50	-	-	2	-	37	1	154	4	38.50	2-18	-	
1-day Lge	16	13	1	347	66	28.91	-	3	1	-	63.3	4	283	15	18.86	5-9	1	

Career Performances

	M	Inns	NO	Runs	HS	Avge	100s	50s	Ct	St	Balls	Runs	Wkts	Avge	Best	5wI	10wM
Test																	
All First	210	339	41	9839	157	33.01	14	52	149	-	6777	3969	127	31.25	5-20	2	-
1-day Int																	
C & G	30	26	2	480	53	20.00	-	1	13	-	412	353	10	35.30	3-14	-	
B & H	43	35	9	658	66	25.30	-	4	11	-	891	618	23	26.86	4-13	-	
1-day Lge	188	158	24	2811	70 *	20.97	-	12	84	-	2322	1898	91	20.85	5-9	1	

51. Which Australian cricketer scored the fastest first-class century of 2001 from 61 deliveries?

LEE, S.   Worcestershire

Name: Shane Lee
Role: Right-hand bat, right-arm
medium bowler
Born: 8 August 1973, Wollongong,
New South Wales, Australia
Height: 6ft 2in
County debut: 1996 (Somerset),
2002 (Worcestershire)
County cap: 1996 (Somerset),
2002 (Worcestershire colours)
One-Day Internationals: 45
1000 runs in a season: 1
1st-Class 50s: 24
1st-Class 100s: 12
1st-Class catches: 74
One-Day 100s: 1
One-Day 5 w. in innings: 1
Strike rate: (career 67.96)
Parents: Robert and Helen
Family links with cricket: Elder brother of Brett Lee (NSW and Australia)
Education: Balarang Primary School; Oak Flats Senior High School;
Wollongong University
Qualifications: High School Certificate
Off-season: Playing for New South Wales
Overseas tours: Australian Cricket Academy to India and Sri Lanka 1993; Australia
U19 to New Zealand; Australia to India, Pakistan and Sri Lanka (World Cup) 1995-96,
to West Indies 1998-99 (one-day series), to UK, Ireland and Holland (World Cup)
1999, to New Zealand 1999-2000 (one-day series), to South Africa (one-day series)
1999-2000, to Kenya (ICC Knockout) 2000-01, to India 2000-01 (one-day series)
Overseas teams played for: New South Wales 1992-93 –
Extras: Attended Australian Cricket Academy 1993. Was Somerset's overseas player
in 1996, scoring 1300 first-class runs (av. 61.90) and taking 40 wickets. Vice-captain
of New South Wales 2000-01, 2001-02, captaining in the absence of Steve Waugh on
international duty. Was Worcestershire's overseas player for the latter part of the 2002
season, replacing Andy Bichel, absent on international duty
Best batting: 183* New South Wales v South Australia, Adelaide 1997-98
Best bowling: 4-20 New South Wales v Tasmania, Sydney 1995-96

2002 Season

	M	Inns	NO	Runs	HS	Avge	100s	50s	Ct	St	O	M	Runs	Wkts	Avge	Best	5wI	10wM
Test																		
All First	2	2	0	80	48	40.00	-	-	-	-	0.2	0	8	0	-	-	-	-
1-day Int																		
C & G																			
B & H																			
1-day Lge	3	2	0	77	41	38.50	-	-	1	-	3	0	39	0	-	-	-	

Career Performances

	M	Inns	NO	Runs	HS	Avge	100s	50s	Ct	St	Balls	Runs	Wkts	Avge	Best	5wI	10wM
Test																	
All First	93	151	22	5071	183 *	39.31	12	24	74	-	10195	6078	150	40.52	4-20	-	-
1-day Int	45	35	8	477	47	17.66	-	-	23	-	1706	1245	48	25.93	5-33	1	
C & G	3	3	0	122	104	40.66	1	-	1	-	101	83	0	-	-	-	
B & H	5	5	1	63	23	15.75	-	-	2	-	242	245	6	40.83	3-60	-	
1-day Lge	19	17	4	519	71 *	39.92	-	5	8	-	713	657	25	26.28	4-40	-	

LEHMANN, D. S. Yorkshire

Name: <u>Darren</u> Scott Lehmann
Role: Left-hand bat, slow left-arm bowler
Born: 5 February 1970, Gawler, Australia
Nickname: Boof
Height: 5ft 11in **Weight:** 14st 2lbs
County debut: 1997
County cap: 1997
Test debut: 1997-98
Tests: 5
One-Day Internationals: 78
1000 runs in a season: 4
1st-Class 50s: 85
1st-Class 100s: 53
1st-Class 200s: 8
1st-Class catches: 112
One-Day 100s: 9
Place in batting averages: 10th av. 66.82
(2001 2nd av. 83.29)
Place in bowling averages: (2001 64th av. 30.66)
Strike rate: 88.88 (career 83.42)
Marital status: Married
Off-season: Playing for South Australia and Australia

Overseas tours: Australia to Sri Lanka (Singer World Series) 1996-97, to New Zealand (one-day series) 1997-98, to Sharjah (Coca-Cola Cup) 1997-98, to India 1997-98, to Pakistan 1998-99, to Bangladesh (Wills International Cup) 1998-99, to West Indies 1998-99 (one-day series), to UK, Ireland and Holland (World Cup) 1999, to Sri Lanka 1999-2000 (one-day series), to Zimbabwe 1999-2000 (one-day series), to India 2000-01 (one-day series), to South Africa 2001-02, to Sri Lanka (ICC Champions Trophy) 2002-03

Overseas teams played for: Salisbury District CC (now Northern Districts), Adelaide; South Australia 1987-88 – 1989-90; Victoria 1990-91 – 1992-93; South Australia 1993-94 –

Other sports followed: Australian Football League (Adelaide Crows)

Relaxations: Golf, watching sport

Extras: Represented South Australia at all age groups. Scored 1128 runs (av. 57.50) in his first full Sheffield Shield season. Man of the Match in CUB second final v England at Melbourne 1998-99. Played in Australia's 1999 World Cup winning side, striking the winning runs in the final v Pakistan at Lord's. Scored 1142 runs at 63.44 (including seven centuries) in the 1999-2000 Australian season and was Pura Milk Cup Player of the Year; was also voted Interstate Cricketer of the Year 1999-2000 at the inaugural Allan Border Medal awards January 2000. Won the EDS Walter Lawrence Trophy for the fastest first-class century of the 2000 season – 89 balls for Yorkshire v Kent at Canterbury. Top run-scorer in English first-class cricket 2000 with 1477 runs at an average of 67.13. Scored a 44-ball 63 for South Australia v Western Australia at Adelaide 2000-01, in the process overtaking Dean Jones's total of 2122 runs to become the highest scoring batsman in Australian domestic one-day cricket. Voted State Player of the Year (for the second successive year) 2000-01. One of *Wisden*'s Five Cricketers of the Year 2001. B&H Gold Awards for his 114-ball 103 v Derbyshire at Headingley, 1-13 and 35 v Lancashire at Liverpool and 76-ball 88 v Durham at Headingley 2001 (three Gold Awards in eight days). Became only the fourth player to score a Roses match double century with his 288-ball 252 v Lancashire at Headingley 2001. Scored 106* v Surrey at Headingley 2001, in the process sharing with Matthew Wood in a record third-wicket partnership for Yorkshire in matches against Surrey. His 103-ball 191, including 11 sixes, v Nottinghamshire at Scarborough in the Norwich Union League 2001 is the second highest score in the domestic one-day league, behind Alistair Brown's 203 for Surrey v Hampshire in 1997. Captain of South Australia since 1998-99. Vice-captain of Yorkshire in 2001. Yorkshire Player of the Year 2001. Became the highest scoring batsman in Sheffield Shield/Pura Cup history when he passed Jamie Siddons's career competition total of 10,643 runs v Victoria 2001-02. Named State Player of the Year (for the third successive year) 2001-02. Captain of Yorkshire 2002, the first overseas player to be appointed to the office. Scored 187 v Lancashire at Headingley 2002, in the process sharing with Anthony McGrath (165) in a record third-wicket partnership for Yorkshire at Headingley (317). ACB central contract 2002-03

Best batting: 255 South Australia v Queensland, Adelaide 1996-97

Best bowling: 4-42 Yorkshire v Kent, Maidstone 1998

Stop press: Scored first ODI century in Australia (119) v Sri Lanka at Perth in the VB

Series 2002-03, winning Man of the Match award. Selected for Australia squad for 2002-03 World Cup

2002 Season

	M	Inns	NO	Runs	HS	Avge	100s	50s	Ct	St	O	M	Runs	Wkts	Avge	Best	5wI	10wM
Test																		
All First	10	18	1	1136	216	66.82	3	7	5	-	133.2	32	346	9	38.44	3-40	-	-
1-day Int																		
C & G	3	2	1	72	54 *	72.00	-	1	-	-	20	0	72	7	10.28	4-26	-	
B & H	6	6	0	267	89	44.50	-	3	3	-	29	0	109	4	27.25	3-29	-	
1-day Lge	7	7	1	354	104	59.00	1	3	4	-	42	0	206	7	29.42	2-23	-	

Career Performances

	M	Inns	NO	Runs	HS	Avge	100s	50s	Ct	St	Balls	Runs	Wkts	Avge	Best	5wI	10wM
Test	5	8	0	228	98	28.50	-	2	3	-	102	45	2	22.50	1-6	-	-
All First	208	355	23	18849	255	56.77	61	85	112	-	5339	2565	64	40.07	4-42	-	-
1-day Int	78	71	14	2048	110 *	35.92	2	11	16	-	829	719	22	32.68	2-4	-	
C & G	13	11	2	350	105	38.88	1	2	2	-	300	184	14	13.14	4-26	-	
B & H	30	30	4	1285	119	49.42	3	8	13	-	468	306	12	25.50	3-29	-	
1-day Lge	65	65	8	2769	191	48.57	3	21	23	-	1267	930	36	25.83	3-31	-	

LEWIS, J.   Gloucestershire

Name: Jonathan (Jon) Lewis
Role: Right-hand bat,
right-arm fast-medium bowler
Born: 26 August 1975, Aylesbury
Height: 6ft 2in **Weight:** 13st
Nickname: Lewy, JJ, Nugget
County debut: 1995
County cap: 1998
50 wickets in a season: 3
1st-Class 50s: 3
1st-Class 5 w. in innings: 15
1st-Class 10 w. in match: 2
1st-Class catches: 25
Place in batting averages: 267th av. 14.36
Place in bowling averages: 116th av. 37.77
(2001 19th av. 21.61)
Strike rate: 73.11 (career 54.91)
Parents: John and Jane
Marital status: Single

Education: Lawn Primary, Swindon; Churchfields Secondary, Swindon; Swindon College

Qualifications: 9 GCSEs, BTEC in Leisure and Hospitality

Overseas tours: Bath Schools to New South Wales 1993; England A to West Indies 2000-01

Overseas teams played for: Marist, Christchurch, New Zealand 1994-95; Richmond City, Melbourne 1995-96; Wanderers, Johannesburg; Techs CC, Cape Town

Cricketers particularly admired: Courtney Walsh, Jack Russell

Young players to look out for: Chris Taylor

Other sports played: Golf, football (Bristol North West FC)

Other sports followed: Football (Swindon Town FC)

Relaxations: 'Chilling out'

Extras: Was on Northamptonshire staff in 1994 but made no first-team appearance. His 62 v Worcestershire at Cheltenham 1999 is the highest score by a Gloucestershire No. 11. Took Championship hat-trick (Gallian, Afzaal and Morris) v Nottinghamshire at Trent Bridge 2000. Leading first-class wicket-taker among English bowlers in 2000 with 72 wickets (av. 20.91). Gloucestershire Player of the Year 2000. B&H Gold Award for his 4-23 in the quarter-final v Durham at Bristol 2001

Best batting: 62 Gloucestershire v Worcestershire, Cheltenham 1999

Best bowling: 8-95 Gloucestershire v Zimbabweans, Gloucester 2000

2002 Season

	M	Inns	NO	Runs	HS	Avge	100s	50s	Ct	St	O	M	Runs	Wkts	Avge	Best	5wI	10wM
Test																		
All First	16	25	6	273	57	14.36	-	1	6	-	536.1	137	1662	44	37.77	6-54	2	1
1-day Int																		
C & G	1	0	0	0	0	-	-	-	1	-	8.2	1	39	0	-		-	-
B & H	6	2	1	1	1 *	1.00	-	-	1	-	51.4	4	194	8	24.25	4-41	-	
1-day Lge	6	4	2	51	27 *	25.50	-	-	-	-	49	6	231	9	25.66	4-22	-	

Career Performances

	M	Inns	NO	Runs	HS	Avge	100s	50s	Ct	St	Balls	Runs	Wkts	Avge	Best	5wI	10wM
Test																	
All First	102	152	31	1479	62	12.22	-	3	25	-	18560	9287	338	27.47	8-95	15	2
1-day Int																	
C & G	8	5	3	14	6 *	7.00	-	-	6	-	430	261	9	29.00	3-27	-	
B & H	26	11	6	71	33 *	14.20	-	-	4	-	1372	970	37	26.21	4-23	-	
1-day Lge	62	40	16	272	27 *	11.33	-	-	9	-	2560	2057	67	30.70	4-22	-	

LEWIS, J. J. B.   Durham

Name: Jonathan (<u>Jon</u>) James Benjamin Lewis
Role: Right-hand bat, county captain
Born: 21 May 1970, Isleworth, Middlesex
Height: 5ft 9in **Weight:** 12st
Nickname: Judge, JJ
County debut: 1990 (Essex), 1997 (Durham)
County cap: 1994 (Essex), 1998 (Durham)
1000 runs in a season: 3
1st-Class 50s: 46
1st-Class 100s: 13
1st-Class 200s: 1
1st-Class catches: 92
One-Day 100s: 1
Place in batting averages: 198th av. 23.64
(2001 105th av. 32.25)
Strike rate: (career 120.00)
Parents: Ted and Nina
Wife and date of marriage: Fiona,
6 July 1999
Family links with cricket: Father played county schools. Uncle is a lifelong Somerset supporter. Sister is right-arm medium-fast bowler for Cisco
Education: King Edward VI School, Chelmsford; Roehampton Institute of Higher Education
Qualifications: 5 O-levels, 3 A-levels, BSc (Hons) Sports Science, NCA Senior Coach
Off-season: 'In South Africa'
Overseas tours: Durham to Cape Town 2002
Overseas teams played for: Old Hararians, Zimbabwe 1991-92; Taita District, New Zealand 1992-93; Eshowe and Zululand, South Africa 1994-95; Richards Bay, South Africa 1996-97; Empangeni, Natal 1997-98; Eshowe 1998-2002
Cricketers particularly admired: John Childs, Greg Matthews, Alan Walker, Shane Warne
Young players to look out for: 'Plenty of talent about. We'll see who wants it most'
Other sports followed: Soccer (West Ham United), rugby (Newcastle Falcons), 'most sports really'
Injuries: Out for last month of the season after operation on left groin
Relaxations: Sleep
Extras: Hit century (116*) on first-class debut in Essex's final Championship match of the 1990 season, v Surrey at The Oval. Joined Durham for the 1997 season. Scored a double century on his debut for Durham (210* v Oxford University), placing him in a small club, alongside Peter Bowler and Neil Taylor, of players who have scored centuries on debut for two different counties. Captain of Durham since the latter stages of the 2000 season. Scored 112 v Nottinghamshire at Riverside 2001, in the process

sharing in Durham's highest Championship partnership for any wicket (258) with Martin Love
Opinions on cricket: 'Central contracts appear to be working well, but I thought the emphasis was going to be on young fast bowlers.'
Best batting: 210* Durham v Oxford University, The Parks 1997
Best bowling: 1-73 Durham v Surrey, Riverside 1998

2002 Season

	M	Inns	NO	Runs	HS	Avge	100s	50s	Ct	St	O	M	Runs	Wkts	Avge	Best	5wI	10wM
Test																		
All First	11	18	1	402	102	23.64	1	2	2	-								
1-day Int																		
C & G	2	2	1	61	31	61.00	-	-	-	-								
B & H	5	5	0	120	31	24.00	-	-	2	-								
1-day Lge	13	12	3	282	52	31.33	-	1	3	-								

Career Performances

	M	Inns	NO	Runs	HS	Avge	100s	50s	Ct	St	Balls	Runs	Wkts	Avge	Best	5wI	10wM
Test																	
All First	151	267	22	8026	210 *	32.75	14	46	92	-	120	121	1	121.00	1-73	-	-
1-day Int																	
C & G	17	17	4	297	65 *	22.84	-	1	1	-							
B & H	31	30	6	748	67	31.16	-	3	7	-							
1-day Lge	129	114	26	2594	102	29.47	1	15	21	-	8	35	0	-		-	-

LEWRY, J. D.   Sussex

Name: <u>Jason</u> David Lewry
Role: Left-hand bat, left-arm fast-medium bowler
Born: 2 April 1971, Worthing
Height: 6ft 3in **Weight:** 14st 7lbs ('depending on time of year!')
Nickname: Lewie, Urco
County debut: 1994
County cap: 1996
Benefit: 2002
50 wickets in a season: 4
1st-Class 5 w. in innings: 21
1st-Class 10 w. in match: 3
1st-Class catches: 22
Place in batting averages: 299th av. 9.10 (2001 228th av. 14.42)
Place in bowling averages: 113th av. 37.18 (2001 38th av. 26.23)
Strike rate: 55.36 (career 49.25)
Parents: David and Veronica

Wife and date of marriage: Naomi Madeleine, 18 August 1997

Children: William, 14 February 1998; Louis, 20 November 2000

Family links with cricket: Father coaches

Education: Thomas à Becket, Worthing; Durrington High School, Worthing; Worthing Sixth Form College

Qualifications: 6 O-levels, 3 GCSEs, City and Guilds, NCA Award

Career outside cricket: 'Still looking, but with more urgency with each passing year!'

Overseas tours: Goring CC to Isle of Wight 1992, 1993; England A to Zimbabwe and South Africa 1998-99

Career highlights to date: 'Seven wickets in 14 balls v Hampshire at Hove 2001. The second most (most by a seamer) outstanding spell of wicket-taking in first-class cricket' (*After Pat Pocock's seven in 11 for Surrey v Sussex at Eastbourne in 1972*)

Cricket moments to forget: 'King pair, Eastbourne 1995'

Cricketers particularly admired: David Gower, Martin Andrews

Other sports played: Golf, squash; darts, pool ('anything you can do in a pub')

Other sports followed: Football (West Ham United)

Relaxations: Golf, pub games, films

Opinions on cricket: 'A return to "English county cricket" would be good.'

Best batting: 47 Sussex v Gloucestershire, Hove 2001

Best bowling: 7-38 Sussex v Derbyshire, Derby 1999

2002 Season

	M	Inns	NO	Runs	HS	Avge	100s	50s	Ct	St	O	M	Runs	Wkts	Avge	Best	5wI	10wM
Test																		
All First	10	15	5	91	21 *	9.10	-	-	5	-	304.3	45	1227	33	37.18	5-88	1	-
1-day Int																		
C & G																			
B & H																			
1-day Lge	2	2	1	1	1	1.00	-	-	2	-	13.2	1	66	1	66.00	1-29	-	

Career Performances

	M	Inns	NO	Runs	HS	Avge	100s	50s	Ct	St	Balls	Runs	Wkts	Avge	Best	5wI	10wM
Test																	
All First	101	141	32	1056	47	9.68	-	-	22	-	17878	9716	363	26.76	7-38	21	3
1-day Int																	
C & G	8	5	3	35	16	17.50	-	-	-	-	504	330	15	22.00	4-42	-	
B & H	12	8	2	69	14 *	11.50	-	-	-	-	624	498	10	49.80	2-32	-	
1-day Lge	34	19	7	44	10 *	3.66	-	-	7	-	1410	1138	45	25.28	4-29	-	

LIPTROT, C. G.   Worcestershire

Name: <u>Christopher</u> George Liptrot
Role: Left-hand bat, right-arm
fast-medium bowler
Born: 13 February 1980, Wigan
Height: 6ft 3in **Weight:** 13st 9lbs
Nickname: Lippy
County debut: 1999
County colours: 2002
1st-Class 50s: 1
1st-Class 5 w. in innings: 2
1st-Class catches: 9
Place in batting averages: (2001 237th
av. 12.80)
Place in bowling averages: (2001 48th
av. 27.60)
Strike rate: 73.50 (career 57.25)
Parents: Brian and Susan
Marital status: Single

Family links with cricket: 'My father and brother played local league cricket in
Wigan'
Education: Highfield Primary School; The Deanery High School, Wigan
Qualifications: 9 GCSEs
Overseas tours: Northwest Select XI to South Africa 1998; Forest Nomads to
Thailand 2000
Overseas teams played for: Sunshine Coast, Brisbane 1999-2000
Career highlights to date: 'Taking five wickets [5-51] on home debut against
Surrey 1999'
Cricketers particularly admired: Glenn McGrath, Graeme Hick
Young players to look out for: Kabir Ali
Other sports played: Football, rugby
Other sports followed: Football (Everton FC), rugby league (Wigan Warriors)

Relaxations: Music, spending time with friends
Extras: Represented England U19 in one-day and 'Test' series v Australia U19 1999.
NBC Denis Compton Award 1999. Worcestershire scholarship to Perth 2001.
Worcestershire Supporters' Association Uncapped Player of the Year 2001
Best batting: 61 Worcestershire v Warwickshire, Edgbaston 1999
Best bowling: 6-44 Worcestershire v Warwickshire, Worcester 2000

2002 Season

	M	Inns	NO	Runs	HS	Avge	100s	50s	Ct	St	O	M	Runs	Wkts	Avge	Best	5wI	10wM
Test																		
All First	2	3	0	32	16	10.66	-	-	-	-	49	5	210	4	52.50	2-51	-	-
1-day Int																		
C & G																		
B & H																		
1-day Lge																		

Career Performances

	M	Inns	NO	Runs	HS	Avge	100s	50s	Ct	St	Balls	Runs	Wkts	Avge	Best	5wI	10wM
Test																	
All First	29	36	11	303	61	12.12	-	1	9	-	3779	2165	66	32.80	6-44	2	-
1-day Int																	
C & G	1	1	1	2	2 *	-	-	-	-	-	30	12	2	6.00	2-12	-	
B & H	1	1	0	3	3	3.00	-	-	1	-	24	11	0	-	-	-	
1-day Lge	6	3	3	18	15 *	-	-	-	1	-	163	176	6	29.33	3-44	-	

52. Which West Indies all-rounder scored 1186 Championship
runs and took 56 Championship wickets for Leicestershire in 1996?

LLOYD, G. D.   Lancashire

Name: <u>Graham</u> David Lloyd
Role: Right-hand bat, right-arm
medium bowler
Born: 1 July 1969, Accrington
Height: 5ft 9in **Weight:** 12st 10lbs
Nickname: Bumble
County debut: 1988
County cap: 1992
Benefit: 2001
One-Day Internationals: 5
1000 runs in a season: 5
1st-Class 50s: 64
1st-Class 100s: 21
1st-Class 200s: 3
1st-Class catches: 140
One-Day 100s: 3
Place in batting averages: 94th av. 37.41
Strike rate: (career 169.50)

Parents: David and Susan
Wife and date of marriage: Sharon, 11 October 1997
Children: Joseph, 20 December 1998
Family links with cricket: Father played for Lancashire and England
Education: Peel Park Primary; Hollins County High School, Accrington
Qualifications: 3 O-levels, Level 2 coaching certificate
Career outside cricket: Bookmaker
Overseas tours: England A to Australia 1992-93; Lancashire CCC to Guernsey 1995;
England VI to Hong Kong 1997; England to Bangladesh (Wills International Cup)
1998
Overseas teams played for: Maroochydore CC, Queensland 1988-89 and 1991-95
Cricketers particularly admired: Steve Waugh
Young players to look out for: James Anderson, Kyle Hogg
Other sports played: Football, tennis
Other sports followed: Football (Manchester United)
Relaxations: Horse racing
Extras: Won the EDS Walter Lawrence Trophy (for the fastest century of the season)
two years running: 1996 (70 balls v Essex) and 1997 (73 balls v Leicestershire).
Lancashire Player of the Year 1996. Scored 109 before lunch (having been 17*
overnight; eventually out for 126) v Somerset at Old Trafford 2000. Retired at the end
of the 2002 season
Opinions on cricket: 'People are too quick to blame county cricket if England do
badly. No mention of anything when England do well.'

Best batting: 241 Lancashire v Essex, Chelmsford 1996
Best bowling: 1-4 Lancashire v Warwickshire, Edgbaston 1996

2002 Season

	M	Inns	NO	Runs	HS	Avge	100s	50s	Ct	St	O	M	Runs	Wkts	Avge	Best	5wI	10wM
Test																		
All First	7	13	1	449	80	37.41	-	5	4	-								
1-day Int																		
C & G	2	1	0	27	27	27.00	-	-	1	-								
B & H	7	5	1	80	49 *	20.00	-	-	-	-								
1-day Lge	12	11	2	160	41	17.77	-	-	6	-								

Career Performances

	M	Inns	NO	Runs	HS	Avge	100s	50s	Ct	St	Balls	Runs	Wkts	Avge	Best	5wI	10wM
Test																	
All First	203	323	28	11279	241	38.23	24	64	140	-	339	440	2	220.00	1-4	-	-
1-day Int	5	4	1	39	22	13.00	-	-	2	-							
C & G	33	25	4	629	96	29.95	-	3	8	-	30	35	1	35.00	1-23	-	
B & H	61	50	13	956	81 *	25.83	-	3	9	-	30	50	0	-	-	-	
1-day Lge	191	174	30	4263	134	29.60	3	22	46	-	12	18	0	-	-	-	

LOGAN, R. J.   Nottinghamshire

Name: <u>Richard</u> James Logan
Role: Right-hand bat, right-arm fast bowler
Born: 28 January 1980, Stone, Staffs
Height: 6ft 1in **Weight:** 13st 9lbs
Nickname: Gus, Logie
County debut: 1999 (Northants),
2001 (Notts)
1st-Class 5 w. in innings: 4
1st-Class catches: 11
One-Day 5 w. in innings: 1
Place in batting averages: 297th av. 9.53
(2001 239th av. 12.46)
Place in bowling averages: 96th av. 34.02
(2001 69th av. 31.97)
Strike rate: 54.77 (career 51.94)
Marital status: Single
Family links with cricket: Father played for
local club Cannock as batsman/wicket-keeper
Education: Walhouse C of E School, Cannock; Wolverhampton Grammar School
Qualifications: 11 GCSEs, 1 A-level, coaching awards (hockey and cricket)

Overseas tours: England U17 to Bermuda (International Youth Tournament) 1997; England U19 to South Africa (including U19 World Cup) 1997-98, to New Zealand 1998-99

Overseas teams played for: St George, Sydney 1999-2000

Cricketers particularly admired: Sir Richard Hadlee, Malcolm Marshall

Young players to look out for: Mark Powell

Other sports played: Hockey (Cannock – 'also played for Staffordshire from age 9 and for Midlands U14')

Other sports followed: Football (Wolverhampton Wanderers)

Relaxations: 'Spending time with my mates. Training'

Extras: Played for Staffordshire at every level from U11 to U19, and as captain from U13 to U17. Played for Midlands U14 and U15 (both as captain) and HMC Schools U15. 1995 *Daily Telegraph*/Lombard U15 Midlands Bowler and Batsman of the Year. Played for Northamptonshire U17 and U19 national champions in 1997. Has played for England U15, U17 and U19, including one-day and 'Test' series v Australia U19 1999. Left Northamptonshire in the 2000-01 off-season and joined Nottinghamshire for 2001. C&G Man of the Match award for his 5-24 v Suffolk at Mildenhall 2001; it was his maiden one-day five-wicket return

Best batting: 37* Nottinghamshire v Hampshire, Trent Bridge 2001

Best bowling: 6-93 Nottinghamshire v Derbyshire, Trent Bridge 2001

2002 Season

	M	Inns	NO	Runs	HS	Avge	100s	50s	Ct	St	O	M	Runs	Wkts	Avge	Best	5wI	10wM
Test																		
All First	13	19	4	143	32	9.53	-	-	5	-	319.3	71	1191	35	34.02	4-64	-	-
1-day Int																		
C & G																		
B & H																		
1-day Lge	8	4	1	24	15	8.00	-	-	3	-	54	3	359	6	59.83	2-31	-	

Career Performances

	M	Inns	NO	Runs	HS	Avge	100s	50s	Ct	St	Balls	Runs	Wkts	Avge	Best	5wI	10wM
Test																	
All First	31	44	7	357	37 *	9.64	-	-	11	-	5039	3197	97	32.95	6-93	4	-
1-day Int																	
C & G	2	1	0	0	0	0.00	-	-	1	-	120	53	6	8.83	5-24	1	
B & H	4	1	0	1	1	1.00	-	-	-	-	216	160	7	22.85	3-52	-	
1-day Lge	23	14	4	107	24	10.70	-	-	8	-	877	962	19	50.63	2-31	-	

LOUDON, A. G. R. Kent

Name: <u>Alexander</u> Guy Rushworth Loudon
Role: Right-hand bat, right-arm
off-spin bowler
Born: 6 September 1980, London
Height: 6ft 3in **Weight:** 14st 8lbs
Nickname: Noisy, Minor, A-Lo, Minotaur
County debut: 2002 (one-day)
1st-Class catches: 6
Strike rate: 78.25 (career 61.85)
Parents: Jane and James
Marital status: Single
Family links with cricket: Brother and
father played for Hampshire 2nd XI
Education: Wellesley House; Eton College;
Durham University
Qualifications: 9 GCSEs, 1 AO-level,
3 A-levels, ECB Level 1 coaching
Career outside cricket: Student
Off-season: 'Studying'
Overseas tours: Kent U11 to Holland 1990; Eton College to South Africa 1995;
England U19 to Malaysia and (U19 World Cup) Sri Lanka 1999-2000; Kent to
South Africa 2002
Career highlights to date: 'Hitting the ball over the tree at Canterbury'
Cricket moments to forget: 'Running out my brother at school'
Cricketers particularly admired: Steve Waugh, Michael Atherton
Young players to look out for: 'George Ealham'
Other sports played: Rugby (Durham University 1st XV), golf, squash, rackets
Other sports followed: Football (Man Utd), rugby (British Lions), WWE ('especially
"the Animal" and "the Dentist"')
Injuries: Torn intercostal
Relaxations: 'Eating, sleeping and Sky Sports'
Extras: Captained England in U15 World Cup 1996. Len Newbery Award for Best
Schools Cricketer 1999. NBC Denis Compton Award for the most promising young
Kent player 1999. Silk Trophy batting award 1999. Played for Durham University
CCE 2001 and 2002. Played for Kent Board XI in the second round of the C&G 2002,
which was played in September 2001. Played for the Eton Ramblers *Cricketer* Cup
winning side 2001, scoring 64 in the final
Opinions on cricket: '1. There should be fewer matches to enable players to practise
and rest more. 2. The game needs to sell itself more to the public and media to
maintain and enhance supporter bases.'
Best batting: 39 DUCCE v Lancashire, Durham 2001
Best bowling: 3-86 DUCCE v Worcestershire, Worcester 2001

2002 Season

	M	Inns	NO	Runs	HS	Avge	100s	50s	Ct	St	O	M	Runs	Wkts	Avge	Best	5wI	10wM
Test																		
All First	3	5	0	54	35	10.80	-	-	5	-	52.1	10	190	4	47.50	2-60	-	-
1-day Int																		
C & G																		
B & H																		
1-day Lge	2	2	0	32	21	16.00	-	-	-	-								

Career Performances

	M	Inns	NO	Runs	HS	Avge	100s	50s	Ct	St	Balls	Runs	Wkts	Avge	Best	5wI	10wM
Test																	
All First	5	7	0	96	39	13.71	-	-	6	-	433	276	7	39.42	3-86	-	-
1-day Int																	
C & G	1	1	0	53	53	53.00	-	1	-	-	6	4	0	-		-	-
B & H																	
1-day Lge	2	2	0	32	21	16.00	-	-	-	-							

LOVE, M. L.   Durham

Name: <u>Martin</u> Lloyd Love
Role: Right-hand bat
Born: 30 March 1974, Mundubbera, Queensland, Australia
Height: 6ft **Weight:** 13st
Nickname: Handles
County debut: 2001
County cap: 2001
1000 runs in a season: 1
1st-Class 50s: 46
1st-Class 100s: 18
1st-Class 200s: 4
1st-Class catches: 142
Place in batting averages: 4th av. 82.28 (2001 29th av. 50.51)
Strike rate: (career 6.00)
Parents: Ormond and Evelyn
Marital status: Engaged to Deborah
Education: Mundubbera State School; Toowoomba Grammar School; University of Queensland
Qualifications: Bachelor of Physiotherapy, Level 2 coach
Career outside cricket: Physiotherapist

Off-season: 'Playing for Queensland Bulls'
Overseas tours: Australia U19 to New Zealand 1992-93; Young Australia (Australia A) to England and Netherlands 1995
Overseas teams played for: Queensland Bulls 1992-93 –
Career highlights to date: 'Member of Queensland's first ever Sheffield Shield winning team 1994-95'
Cricket moments to forget: 'Any duck'
Cricket superstitions: 'Left pad on first'
Cricketers particularly admired: Allan Border
Young players to look out for: Gordon Muchall
Other sports played: Golf
Other sports followed: AFL (Brisbane Lions), rugby union (Queensland Reds)
Injuries: Out for most of the 2002 season with a broken right little finger
Relaxations: 'Home renovation'
Extras: Represented Queensland U17 (1990-91) and U19 (1991-93). Made debut for Queensland in 1992-93 Sheffield Shield final v New South Wales. Shared with Stuart Law in record third-wicket partnership for Queensland (326), v Tasmania at Brisbane 1994-95. Scored century (146) in 1994-95 Sheffield Shield final v South Australia at Brisbane. Shared with Matthew Hayden in record second-wicket partnership for Queensland (368*), v Tasmania at Hobart 1995-96. Scored century (100) in 1999-2000 Pura Milk Cup final v Victoria at Albion. Scored 76 for Australia A v West Indies at Hobart 2000-01. Won the Ian Healy Trophy for Queensland Player of the Year 2000-01. Joined Durham as overseas player in 2001. Scored his first century for Durham (149*) v Nottinghamshire at Riverside 2001, in the process sharing in Durham's highest Championship partnership for any wicket (258) with Jon Lewis. Leading run-scorer in the Pura Cup 2001-02 with 1108 (av. 65.18). Made the highest ever individual score by a Durham batsman (251) v Middlesex at Lord's 2002. ACB central contract 2002-03
Opinions on cricket: 'Young players need to be given more responsibility earlier in their careers to fully develop their potential.'
Best batting: 251 Durham v Middlesex, Lord's 2002
Best bowling: 1-5 Queensland v Western Australia, Brisbane 1997-98
Stop press: Scored two double centuries against the England touring side 2002-03 – 250 for Queensland at Brisbane and 201* for Australia A at Hobart. Made Test debut in fourth Test v England at Melbourne 2002-03, scoring 62* in Australia's first innings. Named State Player of the Year at the 2003 Allan Border Medal awards

2002 Season

	M	Inns	NO	Runs	HS	Avge	100s	50s	Ct	St	O	M	Runs	Wkts	Avge	Best	5wI	10wM
Test																		
All First	6	8	1	576	251	82.28	2	2	3	-								
1-day Int																		
C & G	1	1	0	23	23	23.00	-	-	-	-								
B & H	5	5	0	77	34	15.40	-	-	3	-								
1-day Lge	3	3	0	50	36	16.66	-	-	2	-								

Career Performances

	M	Inns	NO	Runs	HS	Avge	100s	50s	Ct	St	Balls	Runs	Wkts	Avge	Best	5wl	10wM
Test																	
All First	123	212	17	9412	251	48.26	22	46	142	-	6	5	1	5.00	1-5	-	-
1-day Int																	
C & G	4	4	0	132	51	33.00	-	1	1	-							
B & H	9	9	0	182	59	20.22	-	1	7	-							
1-day Lge	16	16	1	481	89	32.06	-	2	10	-	12	7	0	-	-	-	-

LOYE, M. B. Lancashire

Name: <u>Malachy</u> Bernard Loye
Role: Right-hand bat, off-spin bowler,
occasional wicket-keeper
Born: 27 September 1972, Northampton
Height: 6ft 3in **Weight:** 14st
Nickname: Mal, Chairman, Jacko,
Shermenator
County debut: 1991 (Northamptonshire)
County cap: 1994 (Northamptonshire)
1000 runs in a season: 2
1st-Class 50s: 35
1st-Class 100s: 19
1st-Class 200s: 1
1st-Class 300s: 1
1st-Class catches: 75
One-Day 100s: 4
Place in batting averages: 102nd av. 36.57
(2001 21st av. 55.72)

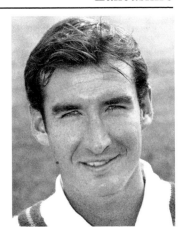

Parents: Patrick and Anne
Marital status: Single
Family links with cricket: Father and brother played for Cogenhoe CC
in Northampton
Education: Brixworth Primary School; Moulton Comprehensive School
Qualifications: GCSEs, 'numerous coaching certificates'
Career outside cricket: 'Impersonator, singer, actor'
Off-season: 'At home mostly training, strumming etc.'
Overseas tours: England U18 to Canada (International Youth Tournament) 1991;
England U19 to Pakistan 1991-92; England A to South Africa 1993-94, to Zimbabwe
and South Africa 1998-99; Northamptonshire to Cape Town 1993, to Zimbabwe 1995,
1998, to Johannesburg 1996, to Grenada 2001, 2002
Overseas teams played for: Riccarton, Christchurch, New Zealand 1992-95; Onslow,

Wellington, New Zealand 1995-96; North Perth, Australia 1997-98; Claremont, Perth 2001

Career highlights to date: 'PCA Player of the Year 1998'

Cricket moments to forget: 'Not being picked for 1995 and 1996 cup finals'

Cricket superstitions: 'None'

Cricketers particularly admired: Wayne Larkins, Gordon Greenidge, Curtly Ambrose, Devon Malcolm, Peter Carlstein, David Capel

Young players to look out for: Monty Panesar

Other sports followed: Football (Liverpool, Northampton Town), rugby union (Ireland), boxing

Relaxations: 'Playing the guitar, swimming, singing, reading. Having the odd large night out!'

Extras: Played for England YC in the home series against Australia YC in 1991 and for England U19 against Sri Lanka U19 in 1992. PCA Young Player of the Year and Whittingdale Young Player of the Year 1993. Shared in a county record opening stand of 372 with Richard Montgomerie as Northamptonshire followed on v Yorkshire at Northampton 1996. His 322* v Glamorgan at Northampton in 1998 was the highest individual first-class score for the county until surpassed in 2001 by Mike Hussey's 329*; during his innings, Loye put on 401 with David Ripley, setting a new fifth-wicket record for first-class cricket in England. PCA Player of the Year 1998. Scored century (123) v Sri Lankans in a 50-over match at Northampton 2002. Scored century in each innings (105/104*) v Nottinghamshire at Northampton 2002. Left Northamptonshire at the end of the 2002 season and has joined Lancashire for 2003

Opinions on cricket: 'Divisional system should be two up/two down, otherwise teams can have an ordinary season yet still get promoted.'

Best batting: 322* Northamptonshire v Glamorgan, Northampton 1998

2002 Season

	M	Inns	NO	Runs	HS	Avge	100s	50s	Ct	St	O	M	Runs	Wkts	Avge	Best	5wI	10wM
Test																		
All First	13	22	1	768	139	36.57	4	1	7	-	2	1	1	0	-	-	-	-
1-day Int																		
C & G	2	2	0	45	34	22.50	-	-	1	-								
B & H	5	5	1	169	57	42.25	-	3	1	-								
1-day Lge	12	12	2	410	101 *	41.00	1	2	2	-								

Career Performances

	M	Inns	NO	Runs	HS	Avge	100s	50s	Ct	St	Balls	Runs	Wkts	Avge	Best	5wI	10wM
Test																	
All First	151	243	23	8349	322 *	37.95	21	35	75	-	25	44	0	-	-	-	-
1-day Int																	
C & G	21	20	4	527	124 *	32.93	1	1	5	-							
B & H	33	33	6	857	77	31.74	-	7	10	-							
1-day Lge	120	116	11	3379	122	32.18	3	22	23	-							

LUCAS, D. S.   Nottinghamshire

Name: <u>David</u> Scott Lucas
Role: Right-hand bat, left-arm medium-fast bowler
Born: 19 August 1978, Nottingham
Height: 6ft 3in   **Weight:** 13st 3lbs
Nickname: Muke, Lukey
County debut: 1999
1st-Class 5 w. in innings: 1
1st-Class catches: 3
Place in batting averages: (2001 209th av. 18.12)
Strike rate: 87.00 (career 60.30)
Parents: Mary and Terry
Marital status: With partner
Education: Horsendale Primary School; Djanogly City Technology College, Nottingham
Qualifications: 6 GCSEs, pass in Computer-Aided Design
Off-season: 'Coaching; hopefully going back to Australia'
Overseas tours: England (Indoor) to Australia (Indoor Cricket World Cup) 1998
Overseas teams played for: Bankstown-Canterbury Bulldogs, Sydney 1996-97; Wanneroo, Perth 2001-02
Career highlights to date: 'Getting Man of the Match against Derbyshire in a close fixture'
Cricket moments to forget: 'The whole of 2001 and most of 2002!'
Cricket superstitions: 'Always walk back to the left of my mark when bowling. Always put left pad on first'
Cricketers particularly admired: Wasim Akram, Glenn McGrath, Steve Waugh, Damien Martyn
Young players to look out for: Kevin Pietersen, Bilal Shafayat
Other sports played: Indoor cricket, football
Other sports followed: Football (Arsenal FC)
Injuries: Torn thigh muscle
Relaxations: 'Food, cars, PS2, movies'
Extras: Won Yorkshire League with Rotherham in 1996. NBC Denis Compton Award for the most promising young Nottinghamshire player 2000
Best batting: 49 Nottinghamshire v DUCCE, Trent Bridge 2002
Best bowling: 5-104 Nottinghamshire v Essex, Trent Bridge 1999

2002 Season

	M	Inns	NO	Runs	HS	Avge	100s	50s	Ct	St	O	M	Runs	Wkts	Avge	Best	5wI	10wM
Test																		
All First	1	1	0	49	49	49.00	-	-	-	-	29	11	56	2	28.00	1-21	-	-
1-day Int																		
C & G																			
B & H																			
1-day Lge	7	3	1	8	8	4.00	-	-	1	-	49	3	289	12	24.08	3-13	-	

Career Performances

	M	Inns	NO	Runs	HS	Avge	100s	50s	Ct	St	Balls	Runs	Wkts	Avge	Best	5wI	10wM
Test																	
All First	22	28	8	436	49	21.80	-	-	3	-	3136	1909	52	36.71	5-104	1	-
1-day Int																	
C & G	1	1	1	14	14 *	-	-	-	-	-	36	40	0	-		-	-
B & H	2	0	0	0	0	-	-	-	-	-	54	61	1	61.00	1-33	-	
1-day Lge	23	8	2	36	19 *	6.00	-	-	3	-	951	881	31	28.41	4-27	-	

LUMB, M. J.   *Yorkshire*

Name: <u>Michael</u> John Lumb
Role: Left-hand bat, right-arm medium bowler
Born: 12 February 1980, Johannesburg, South Africa
Height: 6ft **Weight:** 13st
Nickname: China, Joe
County debut: 2000
1st-Class 50s: 6
1st-Class 100s: 2
1st-Class catches: 8
Place in batting averages: 167th av. 26.79 (2001 81st av. 36.33)
Strike rate: (career 21.00)
Parents: Richard and Sue
Marital status: Single

Family links with cricket: Father played for Yorkshire. Uncle played for Natal
Education: Montrose Primary School; St Stithians College
Qualifications: Matriculation
Off-season: 'South Africa playing cricket'
Overseas tours: Transvaal U19 to Barbados; Yorkshire to Cape Town 2001, to Grenada 2002

Overseas teams played for: Pirates CC, Johannesburg; Wanderers CC, Johannesburg
Career highlights to date: 'Championship winners 2001'
Cricket moments to forget: 'Injuring knee 2001'
Cricket superstitions: 'None'
Cricketers particularly admired: 'Dad', Graham Thorpe, Darren Lehmann, Craig White, Jacques Kallis
Young players to look out for: Grant Elliott, Matthew Prior
Other sports played: Golf
Other sports followed: Rugby union (Sharks in Super 12, Leeds Tykes)
Relaxations: 'Golf, socialising with friends'
Extras: Has Yorkshire 2nd XI cap. Scored 66* on first-class debut v Zimbabweans at Headingley 2000. Scored maiden first-class century (122) v Leicestershire at Headingley 2001; the Lumbs thus became only the fourth father and son to have scored centuries for Yorkshire
Opinions on cricket: 'Splitting the Championship has proved to be exciting and I think it's a good idea. Changes must be made to make the game more appealing to spectators, to get bigger crowds in.'
Best batting: 124 Yorkshire v Surrey, Guildford, 2002
Best bowling: 2-10 Yorkshire v Kent, Canterbury 2001

2002 Season

	M	Inns	NO	Runs	HS	Avge	100s	50s	Ct	St	O	M	Runs	Wkts	Avge	Best	5wI	10wM
Test																		
All First	16	30	1	777	124	26.79	1	4	8	-	3	0	16	0	-	-	-	-
1-day Int																		
C & G	2	1	0	23	23	23.00	-	-	1	-								
B & H	4	4	0	74	43	18.50	-	-	-	-								
1-day Lge	11	11	1	275	73	27.50	-	1	5									

Career Performances

	M	Inns	NO	Runs	HS	Avge	100s	50s	Ct	St	Balls	Runs	Wkts	Avge	Best	5wI	10wM
Test																	
All First	21	39	3	1063	124	29.52	2	6	8	-	42	26	2	13.00	2-10	-	-
1-day Int																	
C & G	4	3	0	64	30	21.33	-	-	1	-							
B & H	11	9	1	126	43	15.75	-	-	3	-							
1-day Lge	18	17	2	399	73	26.60	-	2	7	-							

LUNGLEY, T.   Derbyshire

Name: Tom Lungley
Role: Left-hand bat, right-arm
medium bowler
Born: 25 July 1979, Derby
Height: 6ft 2in **Weight:** 13st
Nickname: Lungfish, Monkfish, Sweaty,
Full Moon, Half Moon, Lungo
County debut: 2000
1st-Class catches: 4
Place in batting averages: 275th av. 12.92
(2001 224th av. 15.42)
Place in bowling averages: 19th av. 24.47
(2001 125th av. 43.91)
Strike rate: 41.52 (career 44.00)
Parents: Richard and Christina
Marital status: 'Taken'
Family links with cricket: 'Dad was captain
of Derby Road CC. Grandad was bat maker
in younger days'

Education: Risley Lower Grammar School; Saint John Houghton School; South East
Derbyshire College
Qualifications: 9 GCSEs, Sport and Recreation Levels 1 and 2, pool lifeguard
qualification, coaching qualifications in cricket, tennis, basketball, football and
volleyball
Career outside cricket: Painter and decorator
Off-season: 'Working and spending time with my lovely girlfriend Kate. Spending
time on sleep education programme'
Overseas teams played for: Delacombe Park, Melbourne 1999-2000
Cricket moments to forget: 'Unable to speak when interviewed by Sybil Ruscoe on
Channel 4 Cricket Roadshow (live)'
Cricket superstitions: 'Always eat Jaffa Cake before play'
Cricketers particularly admired: Ian Botham, Dennis Lillee, Courtney Walsh, Curtly
Ambrose, Brian Lara, Richard Hadlee, Glenn McGrath
Other sports played: 'Enjoy playing most sports, mainly football and basketball'
Other sports followed: Football (Derby County), basketball (Derby Storm)
Injuries: Broken thumb; 'had trouble with insomnia mid-season'
Relaxations: 'Spending all my time with girlfriend; walking my dogs'
Extras: First homegrown cricketer to become professional from Ockbrook and
Borrowash CC. Scored 109 in Derbyshire Cup final 2000, winning Man of the Match
award
Best batting: 47 Derbyshire v Warwickshire, Derby 2001
Best bowling: 3-10 Derbyshire v Cambridge University, Fenner's 2000

	M	Inns	NO	Runs	HS	Avge	100s	50s	Ct	St	O	M	Runs	Wkts	Avge	Best	5wI	10wM
Test																		
All First	7	13	0	168	44	12.92	-	-	4	-	117.4	32	416	17	24.47	3-43	-	-
1-day Int																		
C & G	1	1	0	3	3	3.00	-	-	-	-	3.1	0	28	0	-		-	-
B & H	5	2	0	29	17	14.50	-	-	1	-	30	2	129	7	18.42	3-29	-	
1-day Lge	7	5	3	42	12 *	21.00	-	-	1	-	48.4	1	225	8	28.12	2-29	-	

Career Performances

	M	Inns	NO	Runs	HS	Avge	100s	50s	Ct	St	Balls	Runs	Wkts	Avge	Best	5wI	10wM
Test																	
All First	14	24	4	276	47	13.80	-	-	4	-	1540	984	35	28.11	3-10	-	-
1-day Int																	
C & G	2	2	0	6	3	3.00	-	-	-	-	43	52	0	-	-	-	-
B & H	6	3	0	29	17	9.66	-	-	1	-	240	184	10	18.40	3-29	-	
1-day Lge	18	11	4	142	45	20.28	-	-	2	-	808	594	29	20.48	4-28	-	

MacGILL, S. C. G. Nottinghamshire

Name: <u>Stuart</u> Charles Glyndwr MacGill
Role: Right-hand bat, right-arm
leg-spin bowler
Born: 25 February 1971, Mount Lawley,
Perth, Australia
Height: 6ft
County debut: 1997 (Somerset),
2002 (Nottinghamshire)
County cap: 2002 (Nottinghamshire)
Test debut: 1997-98
Tests: 17
One-Day Internationals: 3
1st-Class 50s: 1
1st-Class 5 w. in innings: 18
1st-Class 10 w. in match: 3
1st-Class catches: 45
Place in batting averages: 301st av. 8.00
Place in bowling averages: 16th av. 23.25
Strike rate: 34.15 (career 51.99)
Family links with cricket: Father (T. M. D. MacGill) played for Western Australia
1968-69 – 1972-73); grandfather (C. W. T. MacGill) played for Western Australia
1938-39 – 1950-51

Education: Christ Church GS, Perth
Off-season: Playing for Australia/New South Wales
Overseas tours: Australia to India 1997-98, to Pakistan 1998-99, to West Indies 1998-99, to Sri Lanka and Zimbabwe 1999-2000, to South Africa 2001-02
Overseas teams played for: Western Australia 1993-94; New South Wales 1996-97 –
Extras: Attended Commonwealth Bank [Australian] Cricket Academy 1991. Played for Devon in the NatWest 1997, 1998. Played one first-class match for Somerset 1997, v Pakistan A at Taunton. Was leading wicket-taker in Test series v England 1998-99 with 27 wickets (av. 17.70), including match figures of 12-107 in the fifth Test at Sydney. Took 4-19 on ODI debut v Pakistan at Sydney in the Carlton and United Series 1999-2000, winning Man of the Match award. Took 7-104 in the West Indies first innings in the fifth Test at Sydney 2000-01. Was leading wicket-taker in Australia's one-day ING Cup 2001-02 with 21 at 18.14. Was Nottinghamshire's overseas player for two periods during the 2002 season, replacing Nicky Boje, absent on international duty. Took 5-63 v Worcestershire at Kidderminster 2002, becoming the first bowler since Garfield Sobers in 1968 to record a five-wicket return on Championship debut for Nottinghamshire; followed up with figures of 14-165 in next match, v Middlesex at Trent Bridge; took 40 wickets (av. 23.25) overall in his six Championship matches for Nottinghamshire 2002. Awarded Nottinghamshire cap 2002; has returned to Nottinghamshire as an overseas player for 2003. ACB central contract 2002-03
Best batting: 53 New South Wales v South Australia, Sydney 2001-02
Best bowling: 8-111 Nottinghamshire v Middlesex, Trent Bridge 2002
Stop press: Bowled 84 overs for his match figures of 7-260 (2-108 and 5-152) in the fourth Test v England at Melbourne 2002-03

2002 Season

	M	Inns	NO	Runs	HS	Avge	100s	50s	Ct	St	O	M	Runs	Wkts	Avge	Best	5wI	10wM
Test																		
All First	6	7	1	48	22	8.00	-	-	5	-	227.4	37	930	40	23.25	8-111	4	1
1-day Int																		
C & G																		
B & H																		
1-day Lge	4	3	1	12	6	6.00	-	-	3	-	29	1	125	3	41.66	2-38	-	

Career Performances

	M	Inns	NO	Runs	HS	Avge	100s	50s	Ct	St	Balls	Runs	Wkts	Avge	Best	5wI	10wM
Test	17	23	2	228	43	10.85	-	-	12	-	4139	2051	82	25.01	7-50	4	1
All First	75	102	21	778	53	9.60	-	1	45	-	16949	9291	326	28.50	8-111	18	3
1-day Int	3	2	1	1	1	1.00	-	-	2	-	180	105	6	17.50	4-19	-	
C & G	2	2	0	4	4	2.00	-	-	-	-	120	59	2	29.50	1-29	-	
B & H																	
1-day Lge	4	3	1	12	6	6.00	-	-	3	-	174	125	3	41.66	2-38	-	

MADDY, D. L. Leicestershire

Name: <u>Darren</u> Lee Maddy
Role: Right-hand opening bat, right-arm medium bowler
Born: 23 May 1974, Leicester
Height: 5ft 9in **Weight:** 11st
Nickname: Roaster, Dazza, Fire Starter
County debut: 1993 (one-day), 1994 (first-class)
County cap: 1996
Test debut: 1999
Tests: 3
One-Day Internationals: 8
1000 runs in a season: 3
1st-Class 50s: 35
1st-Class 100s: 15
1st-Class 200s: 1
1st-Class 5 w. in innings: 3
1st-Class catches: 156
One-Day 100s: 5
Place in batting averages: 42nd av. 47.48 (2001 204th av. 18.60)
Place in bowling averages: 18th av. 23.83 (2001 56th av. 28.71)
Strike rate: 46.67 (career 56.32)
Parents: William Arthur and Hilary Jean
Wife and date of marriage: Justine Marie, 7 October 2000
Family links with cricket: Father and younger brother, Greg, play club cricket
Education: Herrick Junior School, Leicester; Roundhill, Thurmaston; Wreake Valley, Syston
Qualifications: 8 GCSEs
Career outside cricket: 'Undecided'
Off-season: 'Playing grade cricket in Perth'
Overseas tours: Leicestershire to Bloemfontein 1995, to Western Transvaal 1996, to Durban 1997, to Barbados 1998, to Anguilla 2000, to Potchefstroom 2001; England A to Kenya and Sri Lanka 1997-98, to Zimbabwe and South Africa 1998-99; England to South Africa and Zimbabwe 1999-2000
Overseas teams played for: Wanderers, Johannesburg 1992-93; Northern Free State, South Africa 1993-95; Rhodes University, South Africa 1995-97; Sunshine CC, Grenada 2002; Perth CC, 2002-03
Career highlights to date: 'Winning two Championship medals. Playing for England'
Cricket moments to forget: 'Too many to mention. I hate losing a cricket match and I hate getting out – losing two Lord's finals and finishing second in the Norwich Union League'

Cricketers particularly admired: Graham Gooch, Michael Atherton, Ian Botham, Viv Richards, Richard Hadlee

Young players to look out for: Damian Brandy, Luke and Ashley Wright

Other sports played: Touch rugby, golf, squash, 5-a-side football

Other sports followed: Rugby (Leicester Tigers), football (Leicester City), baseball, golf, boxing – 'most sports really except for horse racing and motor racing'

Injuries: Elevated first rib; mild osteoarthritis in left hip; stress fracture in right shin – no time off required

Relaxations: 'Going to the gym, playing sport, spending time with my wife, Justine; listening to music, watching TV, going on holiday, scuba diving, bungee jumping, playing the drums'

Extras: In 1994, set a new 2nd XI Championship run aggregate record (1498), the previous best having stood since 1961, and won the Rapid Cricketline 2nd XI Championship Player of the Year award. Was leading run-scorer on England A's 1997-98 tour with 687 runs at 68.7. In 1998, broke the record for the number of runs scored in the B&H competition in one season (629), previously held by Graham Gooch (591), also setting a record for the most B&H Gold Awards won in one season (five). Scored 110 for First Class Counties Select XI in one-day match v Sri Lanka A at Riverside 1999. Scored 133 for England XI in one-day match v Combined Border/Eastern Province Invitation XI at Alice 1999-2000. B&H Gold Award for his 4-34 v Lancashire at Old Trafford 2002. Had first innings figures of 5-104 and then scored 81 and 94 v Surrey at Leicester 2002

Opinions on cricket: 'Why is it that we play 25 days out of 28 at the start of the season and then have three whole weeks off mid-season? I don't believe we play too much cricket, but I would like to see the fixtures spread evenly throughout the year, instead of playing too much cricket in a short period of time and then nothing for two weeks or so. Also I think day/night cricket is fantastic, but why do we have to start a Championship game the very next day? After a late finish, players, umpires and spectators need a day to recover. Too many EU-qualified players being allowed to play. Counties should make a mutual decision on how many we should allow to play. I think two per county along with two overseas players should be more than enough. Twenty-over cricket is a refreshing idea to attract new sponsors and a bigger audience, but to have to travel two hours or more to play a 20-over "slogathon" seems a long way to go.'

Best batting: 202 England A v Kenya, Nairobi 1997-98

Best bowling: 5-37 Leicestershire v Hampshire, West End 2002

2002 Season

	M	Inns	NO	Runs	HS	Avge	100s	50s	Ct	St	O	M	Runs	Wkts	Avge	Best	5wI	10wM
Test																		
All First	16	29	4	1187	156	47.48	2	8	22	-	334.3	78	1025	43	23.83	5-37	2	-
1-day Int																		
C & G	2	2	0	6	6	3.00	-	-	1	-	18.3	1	97	3	32.33	2-46	-	
B & H	6	4	0	42	19	10.50	-	-	4	-	42.4	3	179	12	14.91	4-34	-	
1-day Lge	15	14	5	225	50 *	25.00	-	1	5	-	88.2	3	461	9	51.22	4-36	-	

Career Performances

	M	Inns	NO	Runs	HS	Avge	100s	50s	Ct	St	Balls	Runs	Wkts	Avge	Best	5wl	10wM
Test	3	4	0	46	24	11.50	-	-	4	-	84	40	0	-	-	-	-
All First	154	247	15	7465	202	32.17	16	35	156	-	5520	2914	98	29.73	5-37	3	-
1-day Int	8	6	0	113	53	18.83	-	1	1	-							
C & G	20	18	2	402	89	25.12	-	2	8	-	407	345	10	34.50	2-38	-	
B & H	38	36	4	1396	151	43.62	4	7	14	-	657	521	22	23.68	4-34	-	
1-day Lge	134	121	18	2793	106 *	27.11	1	17	44	-	2326	2062	74	27.86	4-16	-	

MAHMOOD, S. I. Lancashire

Name: <u>Sajid</u> Iqbal Mahmood
Role: Right-hand bat, right-arm medium-fast bowler
Born: 21 December 1981, Bolton
County debut: 2002
Extras: Played for Lancashire Board XI in the first round of the C&G 2002, which was played in August 2001. His second over in first-class cricket v Hampshire at Old Trafford 2002 lasted in excess of 67 hours, having been interrupted by bad light and rain
Best batting: 18 Lancashire v Hampshire, Old Trafford 2002

2002 Season

	M	Inns	NO	Runs	HS	Avge	100s	50s	Ct	St	O	M	Runs	Wkts	Avge	Best	5wl	10wM
Test																		
All First	1	1	0	18	18	18.00	-	-	-	-	2	1	6	0	-	-	-	-
1-day Int																		
C & G																		
B & H																		
1-day Lge	1	0	0	0	0	-	-	-	-	-	8	0	31	0	-	-	-	

Career Performances

	M	Inns	NO	Runs	HS	Avge	100s	50s	Ct	St	Balls	Runs	Wkts	Avge	Best	5wI	10wM
Test																	
All First	1	1	0	18	18	18.00	-	-	-	-	12	6	0	-	-	-	-
1-day Int																	
C & G	1	1	0	11	11	11.00	-	-	-	-	24	37	0	-	-	-	
B & H																	
1-day Lge	1	0	0	0	0	-	-	-	-	-	48	31	0	-	-	-	

MALCOLM, D. E.   Leicestershire

Name: <u>Devon</u> Eugene Malcolm
Role: Right-hand bat, right-arm fast bowler
Born: 22 February 1963, Kingston, Jamaica
Height: 6ft 2½in **Weight:** 16st 2lbs
Nickname: Dude
County debut: 1984 (Derbyshire),
1998 (Northamptonshire), 2001
(Leicestershire)
County cap: 1989 (Derbyshire),
1999 (Northamptonshire), 2001
(Leicestershire)
Benefit: 1997 (Derbyshire)
Test debut: 1989
Tests: 40
One-Day Internationals: 10
50 wickets in a season: 9
1st-Class 50s: 2
1st-Class 5 w. in innings: 45
1st-Class 10 w. in match: 9
1st-Class catches: 45
One-Day 5 w. in innings: 2
Place in batting averages: 292nd av. 9.85 (2001 265th av. 9.00)
Place in bowling averages: 67th av. 30.43 (2001 54th av. 28.64)
Strike rate: 47.78 (career 50.69)
Parents: Albert and Brendalee (deceased)
Wife and date of marriage: Jennifer, 15 October 1989
Children: Erica, 11 June 1991; Natalie, 25 June 1993; Stephany, 11 July 1995
Education: St Elizabeth Technical High School, Jamaica; Richmond College,
Sheffield; Derby College of Higher Education
Qualifications: O-levels, HND Business Studies, Level II coaching certificate
Off-season: 'Australia (fast-bowling competition); South Africa'

Overseas tours: England to West Indies 1989-90, to Australia 1990-91, to India and Sri Lanka 1992-93, to West Indies 1993-94, to Australia 1994-95, to South Africa 1995-96; England A to Bermuda and West Indies 1991-92; Christians in Sport to South Africa 2000

Overseas teams played for: Ellerslie, Auckland 1985-87

Career highlights to date: '9-57, England v South Africa, The Oval 1994'

Cricket moments to forget: 'South Africa tour 1996'

Cricket superstitions: 'Left boot on first'

Cricketers particularly admired: Sir Richard Hadlee, Michael Holding, Viv Richards, Steve Waugh

Young players to look out for: Darren Stevens

Other sports played: Table tennis

Other sports followed: Football (Man United), boxing

Relaxations: 'Cooking, listening to music'

Extras: Played league cricket for Sheffield Works and Sheffield United; he once took six wickets for no runs off 15 deliveries. Became eligible to play for England in 1987. Had match figures of 10 for 137 v West Indies in Port-of-Spain Test 1989-90. Took 9-57 v South Africa at The Oval in 1994; received the 'Century of Bottles' Award for this best performance against the touring South Africans. Was one of *Wisden*'s Five Cricketers of the Year 1995. Joined Northamptonshire for 1998. Left Northants at the end of the 2000 season and joined Leicestershire for 2001, taking 5-78 v Lancashire at Leicester in his second Championship match for the county. First bowler to reach 50 first-class wickets in the 2001 season. His 6-72 v Yorkshire at Leicester 2002 included his 1000th first-class wicket (Victor Craven)

Opinions on cricket: 'Not happy with third umpire being involved in lbw decision – this takes away the human element from cricket. Totally against two overseas players. Top overseas players are already centrally contracted, therefore not available.'

Best batting: 51 Derbyshire v Surrey, Derby 1989

Best bowling: 9-57 England v South Africa, The Oval 1994

2002 Season

	M	Inns	NO	Runs	HS	Avge	100s	50s	Ct	St	O	M	Runs	Wkts	Avge	Best	5wl	10wM
Test																		
All First	16	22	8	138	44	9.85	-	-	4	-	477.5	79	1826	60	30.43	7-76	4	1
1-day Int																		
C & G	2	1	0	0	0	0.00	-	-	2	-	19	3	65	4	16.25	3-24	-	
B & H																		
1-day Lge	2	0	0	0	0	-	-	-	-	-	18	2	96	3	32.00	2-36	-	

Career Performances

	M	Inns	NO	Runs	HS	Avge	100s	50s	Ct	St	Balls	Runs	Wkts	Avge	Best	5wI	10wM
Test	40	58	19	236	29	6.05	-	-	7	-	8480	4748	128	37.09	9-57	5	2
All First	300	362	113	1958	51	7.86	-	2	45	-	52725	31619	1040	30.40	9-57	45	9
1-day Int	10	5	2	9	4	3.00	-	-	1	-	526	404	16	25.25	3-40	-	
C & G	30	14	1	31	10 *	2.38	-	-	4	-	1757	1117	43	25.97	7-35	1	
B & H	43	23	6	114	16	6.70	-	-	6	-	2354	1715	62	27.66	5-27	1	
1-day Lge	94	38	13	155	42	6.20	-	-	10	-	4003	3369	119	28.31	4-21	-	

MALIK, M. N. Nottinghamshire

Name: Muhammad Nadeem Malik
Role: Right-hand bat, right-arm
fast-medium bowler
Born: 6 October 1982, Nottingham
Height: 6ft 5in **Weight:** 14st
Nickname: Nigel, Nige, Gerz
County debut: 2001
1st-Class 5 w. in innings: 2
1st-Class catches: 1
Place in batting averages: 315th av. 5.50
Place in bowling averages: 30th av. 25.54
(2001 119th av. 41.40)
Strike rate: 40.00 (career 47.00)
Parents: Abdul and Arshad
Marital status: Single
Education: Meadows Primary School;
Wilford Meadows Secondary School;
Bilborough College
Qualifications: 9 GCSEs
Overseas tours: ZRK to Pakistan 2000; Nottinghamshire to South Africa 2001;
England U19 to India 2000-01, to Australia and (U19 World Cup) New Zealand
2001-02
Career highlights to date: '5-57 against Derbyshire 2001'
Cricket moments to forget: 'Norwich Union match v Yorkshire at Scarborough 2001
– Lehmann 191'
Cricketers particularly admired: Glenn McGrath, Wasim Akram, Curtly Ambrose
Young players to look out for: Bilal Shafayat, Gordon Muchall
Other sports played: Football
Other sports followed: Football
Relaxations: Music, games consoles
Extras: Took 15 wickets at an average of 19.40 for Nottinghamshire 2nd XI 2000.

Played for Nottinghamshire Board XI in the NatWest 2000. Represented England U19 v West Indies U19 in one-day series (1/3) 2001. Represented England U19 v India U19 in 'Test' series (3/3) 2002
Best batting: 19 Nottinghamshire v Middlesex, Lord's 2002
Best bowling: 5-57 Nottinghamshire v Derbyshire, Trent Bridge 2001

2002 Season

	M	Inns	NO	Runs	HS	Avge	100s	50s	Ct	St	O	M	Runs	Wkts	Avge	Best	5wI	10wM
Test																		
All First	7	7	1	33	19	5.50	-	-	1	-	146.4	29	562	22	25.54	5-67	1	-
1-day Int																		
C & G	1	0	0	0	0	-	-	-	-	-	2	0	12	0	-	-	-	-
B & H	5	2	1	8	8 *	8.00	-	-	1	-	29	1	132	3	44.00	1-8	-	
1-day Lge	6	4	3	17	11	17.00	-	-	3	-	37	1	229	1	229.00	1-48	-	

Career Performances

	M	Inns	NO	Runs	HS	Avge	100s	50s	Ct	St	Balls	Runs	Wkts	Avge	Best	5wI	10wM
Test																	
All First	12	13	6	45	19	6.42	-	-	1	-	1504	976	32	30.50	5-57	2	-
1-day Int																	
C & G	2	1	1	1	1 *	-	-	-	-	-	48	32	0	-	-	-	-
B & H	7	2	1	8	8 *	8.00	-	-	1	-	252	194	4	48.50	1-8	-	
1-day Lge	11	6	4	21	11	10.50	-	-	3	-	462	434	6	72.33	2-34	-	

MANN, C.   Durham

Name: Christopher (Chris) Mann
Role: Right-hand bat, right-arm medium bowler
Born: 14 April 1981, South Shields
Height: 6ft 1in **Weight:** 10st 10lbs
Nickname: Norman
County debut: No first-team appearance
Parents: Pat and Harry
Marital status: Single
Family links with cricket: Father has played for Marsden CC for 35 years
Education: Biddick Hall Primary School; Boldon Comprehensive; South Tyneside College
Qualifications: 6 GCSEs, Level 2 cricket coach
Overseas teams played for: Bulleen CC, Melbourne 2001-02
Career highlights to date: 'Being told by Geoff Cook at the end of the 2001 season that I was going to be given a two-year professional contract with Durham'
Cricket moments to forget: 'Injuring my back in the 2000 season and being told by the specialist not to bowl again'

Cricketers particularly admired:
Mike Atherton, Steve Waugh
Young players to look out for:
Graham Onions, Liam Plunkett
Other sports played: Football (South
Tyneside; goalkeeper 1988-96)
Other sports followed: Football
(Manchester United)
Relaxations: Listening to music, going to the
cinema, relaxing with family and friends
Extras: Captain of Durham Cricket Academy
2001. Played for Durham Board XI in the
second round of the C&G 2002, which was
played in September 2001

2002 Season (did not make any first-class or one-day appearances)

Career Performances

	M	Inns	NO	Runs	HS	Avge	100s	50s	Ct	St	Balls	Runs	Wkts	Avge	Best	5wI	10wM
Test																	
All First																	
1-day Int																	
C & G	1	1	0	7	7	7.00	-	-	1	-							
B & H																	
1-day Lge																	

53. Which Australian scored 237 for Gloucestershire
v Derbyshire at Cheltenham in 1997?

MARTIN, P. J.　　　　　　　　Lancashire

Name: <u>Peter</u> James Martin
Role: Right-hand bat, right-arm
fast-medium bowler
Born: 15 November 1968, Accrington
Height: 6ft 4in　**Weight:** 15st 7lbs
Nickname: Digger
County debut: 1989
County cap: 1994
Benefit: 2002
Test debut: 1995
Tests: 8
One-Day Internationals: 20
50 wickets in a season: 3
1st-Class 50s: 7
1st-Class 100s: 2
1st-Class 5 w. in innings: 16
1st-Class 10 w. in match: 1
1st-Class catches: 46
One-Day 5 w. in innings: 6

Place in batting averages: 86th av. 38.36 (2001 203rd av. 18.77)
Place in bowling averages: 7th av. 21.24 (2001 59th av. 29.36)
Strike rate: 51.16 (career 60.20)
Parents: Keith and Catherine
Wife and date of marriage: Bethan, 3 October 1998
Children: Oliver, 14 August 2001
Education: Danum School, Doncaster; University of Central Lancashire, Preston
Qualifications: 6 O-levels, 2 A-levels, PGCM (UCLAN), Levels 1 and 2 coaching
certificates
Career outside cricket: 'Painting'
Off-season: 'Benefit year end; painting'
Overseas tours: England YC to Australia (U19 World Cup) 1987-88, 'and various
other tours with English Schools and NAYC'; England to South Africa 1995-96, to
India and Pakistan (World Cup) 1995-96, to Sharjah (Champions Trophy) 1997-98,
to Bangladesh (Wills International Cup) 1998-99
Overseas teams played for: Southern Districts, Beerwah, Queensland 1988-89; South
Launceston, Tasmania 1989-90; South Canberra, ACT 1990-92
Career highlights to date: 'Playing for England and Lord's finals with Lancashire.
Managing to play for this long!'
Cricket moments to forget: 'Not many, thankfully'
Cricket superstitions: 'None'
Cricketers particularly admired: 'Loads'
Young players to look out for: Kyle Hogg, James Anderson

Other sports played: Golf, soccer
Injuries: Fractured rib
Relaxations: 'Painting, cooking, wine, family, outdoor stuff'
Extras: Played for England A v Sri Lankans 1991. His 78* v Durham at Old Trafford 1997 is the equal highest score by a Lancashire No. 11 (although Paul Allott was dismissed v Gloucestershire at Bristol in 1985). Scored 80* v Kent at Liverpool 2002, in the process sharing with Glen Chapple (55) in a record ninth-wicket partnership for Lancashire v Kent (109). Scored 117* v Warwickshire at Old Trafford 2002, setting a new record for the highest score by a Lancashire No. 10
Best batting: 133 Lancashire v Durham, Gateshead Fell 1992
Best bowling: 8-32 Lancashire v Middlesex, Uxbridge 1997

2002 Season

	M	Inns	NO	Runs	HS	Avge	100s	50s	Ct	St	O	M	Runs	Wkts	Avge	Best	5wl	10wM
Test																		
All First	12	16	5	422	117 *	38.36	1	1	4	-	452	143	1126	53	21.24	5-54	1	-
1-day Int																		
C & G	2	1	1	1	1 *	-	-	-	-	-	15	1	39	2	19.50	2-21	-	
B & H	5	2	1	10	5 *	10.00	-	-	1	-	42	6	166	8	20.75	2-23	-	
1-day Lge	12	7	3	47	23 *	11.75	-	-	3	-	90	11	310	18	17.22	3-18	-	

Career Performances

	M	Inns	NO	Runs	HS	Avge	100s	50s	Ct	St	Balls	Runs	Wkts	Avge	Best	5wl	10wM
Test	8	13	0	115	29	8.84	-	-	6	-	1452	580	17	34.11	4-60	-	-
All First	192	227	59	3415	133	20.32	2	7	46	-	33412	15063	555	27.14	8-32	16	1
1-day Int	20	13	7	38	6	6.33	-	-	1	-	1048	806	27	29.85	4-44	-	
C & G	29	11	8	106	31 *	35.33	-	-	1	-	1670	947	55	17.21	5-16	2	
B & H	42	14	10	56	11 *	14.00	-	-	13	-	2252	1546	59	26.20	3-31	-	
1-day Lge	131	42	21	238	35 *	11.33	-	-	25	-	5305	3717	168	22.12	5-21	4	

54. Which cricketer made his debut for Sussex in 1976 and went on to play in Tests for Australia and South Africa?

MARTIN-JENKINS, R. S. C.   Sussex

Name: <u>Robin</u> Simon Christopher
Martin-Jenkins
Role: Right-hand bat, right-arm
fast-medium bowler
Born: 28 October 1975, Guildford
Height: 6ft 5in **Weight:** 14st
Nickname: Tucker
County debut: 1995
County cap: 2000
1000 runs in a season: 1
1st-Class 50s: 15
1st-Class 100s: 1
1st-Class 200s: 1
1st-Class 5 w. in innings: 4
1st-Class catches: 16
Place in batting averages: 69th av. 42.00
(2001 38th av. 47.63)

Place in bowling averages: 109th av. 36.02
(2001 68th av. 31.83)
Strike rate: 68.82 (career 61.02)
Parents: Christopher and Judy
Wife and date of marriage: Flora, 19 February 2000
Family links with cricket: Father is *The Times* chief cricket correspondent and *TMS* commentator. Brother captains the Radley Rangers
Education: Cranleigh Prep School, Surrey; Radley College, Oxon; Durham University
Qualifications: 10 GCSEs, 3 A-levels, 1 AS-level, Grade 3 bassoon (with merit), BA (Hons) Social Sciences, Don Mackenzie School of Professional Photography Certificate
Career outside cricket: 'Weekly columnist for *Brighton Argus*. Photographer for "Goodnightie Company"'
Off-season: 'Gym. MCC tour. Few weeks in India (Madras or Bombay)'
Overseas tours: Radley College to Barbados 1992; Sussex U19 to Sri Lanka 1995; Durham University to Vienna 1995; MCC to Kenya 1999; Sussex to Grenada 2001, 2002
Overseas teams played for: Lima CC, Peru 1994; Bellville CC, Cape Town 2000-01
Career highlights to date: 'Winning National League Division Two in 1999. Scoring maiden first-class century in same match that Sussex won to take second division Championship 2001. Scoring maiden first-class 200 v Somerset at Taunton 2002'
Cricket moments to forget: 'I can't remember'
Cricket superstitions: 'Never bowl first at Colwyn Bay'
Cricketers particularly admired: Angus Fraser, Robin Smith, Umer Rashid, Ben Hollioake, Adam Hollioake

Young players to look out for: Krishna Singh
Other sports played: Golf, tennis, Rugby fives
Other sports followed: Rugby, football (Liverpool)
Relaxations: Photography, guitar, reading, TV, films
Extras: Played for ESCA from U15 to U19. *Daily Telegraph* Bowling Award 1994. European Player of the Year, Vienna 1995. Best Performance Award for Sussex 1998. NBC Denis Compton Award for the most promising young Sussex player 1998, 1999, 2000. Scored maiden first-class century (113) v Gloucestershire at Hove 2001, including 109 between lunch and tea on the first day. Scored 80* out of 246 and followed up with 5-37 v Hampshire in Championship match at West End 2002. Scored maiden first-class double century (205*) v Somerset at Taunton 2002, in the process sharing with Mark Davis (111) in a record eighth-wicket partnership for Sussex (291); the stand fell one run short of the record eighth-wicket partnership in English first-class cricket, set by Bobby Peel and Lord Hawke for Yorkshire v Warwickshire at Birmingham in 1896. Passed 1000 runs in a season for the first time (v Warwickshire at Hove) 2002
Opinions on cricket: '1. Counties should play each other once in each division – then play-off matches with a semi-final and final to decide champions. 2. Practice facilities at all county grounds need to get better.'
Best batting: 205* Sussex v Somerset, Taunton 2002
Best bowling: 7-51 Sussex v Leicestershire, Horsham 2002

2002 Season

	M	Inns	NO	Runs	HS	Avge	100s	50s	Ct	St	O	M	Runs	Wkts	Avge	Best	5wI	10wM
Test																		
All First	16	28	4	1008	205 *	42.00	1	5	1	-	470.2	100	1477	41	36.02	7-51	2	-
1-day Int																		
C & G	3	3	2	29	15	29.00	-	-	1	-	28	4	111	3	37.00	2-65	-	
B & H	6	5	1	46	26 *	11.50	-	-	-	-	59	8	220	12	18.33	4-22	-	
1-day Lge	16	12	1	206	50	18.72	-	1	2	-	107.5	19	384	11	34.90	2-21	-	

Career Performances

	M	Inns	NO	Runs	HS	Avge	100s	50s	Ct	St	Balls	Runs	Wkts	Avge	Best	5wI	10wM
Test																	
All First	69	112	14	2944	205 *	30.04	2	15	16	-	10252	5307	168	31.58	7-51	4	-
1-day Int																	
C & G	5	4	2	45	16	22.50	-	-	1	-	288	163	7	23.28	2-24	-	
B & H	26	22	2	227	45	11.35	-	-	2	-	1385	971	41	23.68	4-22	-	
1-day Lge	70	48	4	538	50	12.22	-	1	20	-	2885	1918	58	33.06	3-20	-	

MASCARENHAS, A. D.   Hampshire

Name: Adrian <u>Dimitri</u> Mascarenhas
Role: Right-hand bat, right-arm
medium bowler
Born: 30 October 1977, Chiswick, London
Height: 6ft 2in **Weight:** 11st 7lbs
Nickname: Dimi, D-Train
County debut: 1996
County cap: 1998
1st-Class 50s: 13
1st-Class 100s: 2
1st-Class 5 w. in innings: 5
1st-Class catches: 34
One-Day 5 w. in innings: 1
Place in batting averages: 194th av. 23.91
(2001 156th av. 24.83)
Place in bowling averages: 69th av. 30.83
(2001 33rd av. 25.37)
Strike rate: 68.24 (career 66.19)
Parents: Malik and Pauline
Marital status: Single

Family links with cricket: Uncle played in Sri Lanka and brothers both play for
Melville CC in Perth, Western Australia
Education: Our Lady's Primary, Melbourne; Trinity College, Perth
Qualifications: Level 2 coaching
Career outside cricket: Personal trainer
Off-season: 'Relaxing in Perth, Western Australia'
Overseas teams played for: Melville CC, Perth 1991-2000
Career highlights to date: 'Debut for Hampshire 1996 – 6-88 v Glamorgan'
Cricketers particularly admired: Viv Richards, Malcolm Marshall, the Waugh twins
Young players to look out for: John Francis, Jimmy Adams
Other sports followed: Australian Rules (Collingwood)
Relaxations: Tennis, golf, Australian Rules
Extras: Played for Western Australia at U17 and U19 level as captain. Took 6-88 on
first-class debut, for Hampshire v Glamorgan at Southampton 1996, the best analysis
by a Hampshire bowler on first-class debut since 1899. Won NatWest Man of the
Match awards in semi-final v Lancashire 1998 (3-28 and 73) and in quarter-final v
Middlesex 2000 (4-25). Put on 90 for the tenth wicket with Simon Francis v Surrey at
The Oval 2000, the pair falling just two runs short of pulling off a remarkable
Championship victory. Scorer of the first Championship century recorded at the Rose
Bowl (104) v Worcestershire 2001. Recorded maiden one-day five-wicket return
(5-27), and contributed 39*, v Gloucestershire at West End in the NUL 2002

Best batting: 104 Hampshire v Worcestershire, West End 2001
Best bowling: 6-26 Hampshire v Middlesex, West End 2001

2002 Season

	M	Inns	NO	Runs	HS	Avge	100s	50s	Ct	St	O	M	Runs	Wkts	Avge	Best	5wI	10wM
Test																		
All First	16	26	2	574	94	23.91	-	2	8	-	420.5	144	1141	37	30.83	5-87	1	-
1-day Int																		
C & G	2	1	0	20	20	20.00	-	-	-	-	18	1	82	2	41.00	1-34	-	
B & H	3	3	1	7	5	3.50	-	-	3	-	30	5	84	8	10.50	3-19	-	
1-day Lge	15	14	3	171	39 *	15.54	-	-	3	-	126.2	13	506	24	21.08	5-27	1	

Career Performances

	M	Inns	NO	Runs	HS	Avge	100s	50s	Ct	St	Balls	Runs	Wkts	Avge	Best	5wI	10wM
Test																	
All First	86	128	13	2678	104	23.28	2	13	34	-	11650	5534	176	31.44	6-26	5	-
1-day Int																	
C & G	13	11	4	307	73	43.85	-	2	2	-	654	385	20	19.25	4-25	-	
B & H	19	18	3	244	53	16.26	-	2	3	-	840	556	19	29.26	4-28	-	
1-day Lge	83	72	9	1092	79	17.33	-	6	24	-	3337	2407	102	23.59	5-27	1	

MASON, M. S. Worcestershire

Name: Matthew (<u>Matt</u>) Sean Mason
Role: Right-hand bat, right-arm
fast-medium bowler
Born: 20 March 1974, Claremont,
Perth, Western Australia
Height: 6ft 5in **Weight:** 16st
Nickname: Mase, Alvin, Chipmunk
County debut: 2002
County colours: 2002
1st-Class 50s: 1
1st-Class 5 w. in innings: 1
1st-Class catches: 2
Place in batting averages: 243rd av. 17.83
Place in bowling averages: 50th av. 27.86
Strike rate: 61.27 (career 72.38)
Parents: Bill and Sue
Marital status: Single
Family links with cricket: Brother Simon
plays for Wanneroo District CC
Education: St Bridgets Primary, Perth; Mazenod College, Perth

Qualifications: Level 1 ACB coach
Career outside cricket: Sales consultant with Nissan Motor Company
Off-season: 'Playing cricket in Western Australia'
Overseas teams played for: Western Australia 1996-1998
Career highlights to date: 'First-class debut [for Western Australia] v Queensland at WACA. First five-wicket haul in first-class cricket, v Notts'
Cricket moments to forget: 'Any time I lose!'
Cricketers particularly admired: Justin Langer, Damien Martyn
Young players to look out for: James Pipe, Kabir Ali
Other sports played: Golf, tennis, Australian Rules football
Other sports followed: Rugby league (Bradford Bulls), rugby union (Wallabies)
Injuries: Out for five weeks with a shoulder injury
Relaxations: 'Listening to music; going to the movies; the beach'
Extras: Recorded maiden first-class five-wicket return (5-50) v Nottinghamshire at Kidderminster 2002. Scored maiden first-class fifty (50) from 27 balls v Derbyshire at Worcester 2002. Holds an Irish passport and is not considered an overseas player
Opinions on cricket: 'Fully support the two overseas player rule. Anything that makes the game more competitive and challenges us more as players should be welcomed.'
Best batting: 50 Worcestershire v Derbyshire, Worcester 2002
Best bowling: 5-50 Worcestershire v Nottinghamshire, Kidderminster 2002

2002 Season

	M	Inns	NO	Runs	HS	Avge	100s	50s	Ct	St	O	M	Runs	Wkts	Avge	Best	5wI	10wM
Test																		
All First	7	8	2	107	50	17.83	-	1	1	-	224.4	55	613	22	27.86	5-50	1	-
1-day Int																		
C & G	2	1	0	1	1	1.00	-	-	-	-	18.3	1	119	3	39.66	2-58	-	
B & H	3	0	0	0	0	-	-	-	-	-	24	2	109	7	15.57	3-33	-	
1-day Lge	9	3	1	11	6	5.50	-	-	1	-	58.5	5	250	11	22.72	3-37	-	

Career Performances

	M	Inns	NO	Runs	HS	Avge	100s	50s	Ct	St	Balls	Runs	Wkts	Avge	Best	5wI	10wM
Test																	
All First	10	13	3	117	50	11.70	-	1	2	-	1882	862	26	33.15	5-50	1	-
1-day Int																	
C & G	2	1	0	1	1	1.00	-	-	-	-	111	119	3	39.66	2-58	-	
B & H	3	0	0	0	0	-	-	-	-	-	144	109	7	15.57	3-33	-	
1-day Lge	9	3	1	11	6	5.50	-	-	1	-	353	250	11	22.72	3-37	-	

MASTERS, D. D. Leicestershire

Name: <u>David</u> Daniel Masters
Role: Right-hand bat, right-arm
medium-fast bowler
Born: 22 April 1978, Chatham
Height: 6ft 4ins **Weight:** 12st 5lbs
Nickname: Hod, Race Horse, Hoddy
County debut: 2000 (Kent)
1st-Class 50s: 1
1st-Class 5 w. in innings: 3
1st-Class catches: 9
One-Day 5 w. in innings: 1
Place in batting averages: 248th av. 16.71
Place in bowling averages: 114th av. 37.56
Strike rate: 63.43 (career 58.96)
Parents: Kevin and Tracey
Marital status: Single
Family links with cricket:

'Dad was on staff at Kent 1983-86'
Education: Luton Junior School; Fort Luton High School; Mid-Kent College
Qualifications: 8 GCSEs, GNVQ in Leisure and Tourism, qualified coach in cricket,
football and athletics, bricklayer and plasterer
Career outside cricket: Builder
Overseas teams played for: Double View, Perth 1998-99
Cricketers particularly admired: Ian Botham
Young players to look out for: 'My brother Daniel Masters'
Other sports played: Football, boxing 'and most other sports'
Other sports followed: Football (Manchester United)
Relaxations: 'Going out with mates'
Extras: His 6-27 v Durham at Tunbridge Wells 2000 included a final spell of 4-9 from
10.2 overs. Joint Kent Player of the Year 2000 (with Martin Saggers). NBC Denis
Compton Award for the most promising young Kent player 2000. Recorded maiden
one-day five-wicket return (5-20) v Durham at Maidstone in the NUL 2002. Left Kent
at the end of the 2002 season and has joined Leicestershire for 2003
Best batting: 68 Kent v Warwickshire, Edgbaston 2002
Best bowling: 6-27 Kent v Durham, Tunbridge Wells 2000

2002 Season

	M	Inns	NO	Runs	HS	Avge	100s	50s	Ct	St	O	M	Runs	Wkts	Avge	Best	5wI	10wM
Test																		
All First	8	7	0	117	68	16.71	-	1	3	-	243.1	47	864	23	37.56	4-36	-	-
1-day Int																		
C & G	1	1	0	0	0	0.00	-	-	-	-	7	0	58	0	-		-	-
B & H	2	1	0	0	0	0.00	-	-	-	-	20	1	105	3	35.00	2-44	-	-
1-day Lge	8	5	3	30	8 *	15.00	-	-	-	-	51	2	282	6	47.00	5-20	1	

Career Performances

	M	Inns	NO	Runs	HS	Avge	100s	50s	Ct	St	Balls	Runs	Wkts	Avge	Best	5wI	10wM
Test																	
All First	28	30	9	196	68	9.33	-	1	9	-	4599	2304	78	29.53	6-27	3	-
1-day Int																	
C & G	3	2	0	1	1	0.50	-	-	-	-	151	117	1	117.00	1-23	-	-
B & H	8	3	1	18	12 *	9.00	-	-	1	-	322	241	5	48.20	2-44	-	-
1-day Lge	22	14	5	63	10 *	7.00	-	-	2	-	901	715	15	47.66	5-20	1	-

MAUNDERS, J. K.   Leicestershire

Name: <u>John</u> Kenneth Maunders
Role: Left-hand bat, right-arm
medium bowler
Born: 4 April 1981, Ashford, Middlesex
Height: 5ft 10in   **Weight:** 12st 7lbs
Nickname: Racing Johnny, Chop
County debut: 1999 (Middlesex)
1st-Class catches: 1
Parents: Kenny and Lynn
Marital status: Single
Family links with cricket: 'Grandfather and
one uncle played quite well, and other uncle
(Nigel) tried hard but never really got to grips
with the concept!'
Education: Ashford Park Primary School;
Ashford High School; Spelthorne College
Qualifications: 10 GCSEs, coaching award
Career outside cricket: Cricket coach

Off-season: 'Plenty of coaching. Working in the office at Pacemaker (consistently
making amends for Glen Nash's mistakes)'
Overseas tours: England U19 to New Zealand 1998-99, to Malaysia and (U19 World
Cup) Sri Lanka 1999-2000

Overseas teams played for: University, Perth 2001-02
Career highlights to date: 'Representing England U19'
Cricket moments to forget: 'Glen Nash hitting me for 24 in an over and claiming my wicket twice!!'
Cricket superstitions: 'A few little ones!'
Cricketers particularly admired: Justin Langer, Alec Stewart
Young players to look out for: 'I coach quite a few talented youngsters who could become very good'
Other sports played: Squash, football, hockey
Other sports followed: Football, racing
Relaxations: 'Spending time with girlfriend Lauren; eating out; socialising with friends and family; consistently winning cash off Spencer "Bitter" Collins; watching most sports; spending time with little Rosie'
Extras: Awarded junior county cap at the age of 12. Has been Seaxe Player of Year. Represented England U17 and U19. NBC Denis Compton Award 1999. Played for Middlesex Board XI in the C&G 2001. Released by Middlesex at the end of the 2002 season and has joined Leicestershire for 2003
Best batting: 9 Middlesex v Cambridge University, Fenner's 1999

2002 Season (did not make any first-class or one-day appearances)

Career Performances

	M	Inns	NO	Runs	HS	Avge	100s	50s	Ct	St	Balls	Runs	Wkts	Avge	Best	5wI	10wM
Test																	
All First	1	2	0	13	9	6.50	-	-	1	-							
1-day Int																	
C & G	1	1	0	11	11	11.00	-	-	-	-	13	18	0	-		-	-
B & H																	
1-day Lge	2	2	0	55	49	27.50	-	-	1	-							

55. Which Somerset and former New South Wales cricketer (later to become a first-class umpire) scored 3019 first-class runs in 1961?

MAYNARD, M. P.   Glamorgan

Name: <u>Matthew</u> Peter Maynard
Role: Right-hand bat, occasional wicket-keeper
Born: 21 March 1966, Oldham, Lancashire
Height: 5ft 11in **Weight:** 13st
Nickname: Ollie, Wilf
County debut: 1985
County cap: 1987
Benefit: 1996
Test debut: 1988
Tests: 4
One-Day Internationals: 14
1000 runs in a season: 11
1st-Class 50s: 123
1st-Class 100s: 48
1st-Class 200s: 3
1st-Class catches: 346
1st-Class stumpings: 7
One-Day 100s: 13
Place in batting averages: 20th av. 55.68 (2001 119th av. 31.05)
Strike rate: (career 186.16)
Parents: Ken (deceased) and Pat
Wife and date of marriage: Susan, 27 September 1986
Children: Tom, 25 March 1989; Ceri Lloyd, 5 August 1993
Family links with cricket: Father played for many years for Duckinfield. Brother Charles plays for St Fagans. Son Tom plays
Education: Ysgol David Hughes, Menai Bridge, Anglesey
Qualifications: Cricket coach
Career outside cricket: Commercial property specialist with Thomas Carroll Group Ltd
Overseas tours: North Wales XI to Barbados 1982; Glamorgan to Barbados 1982, to South Africa 1993; unofficial England XI to South Africa 1989-90; HKCC (Australia) to Bangkok and Hong Kong 1990; England VI to Hong Kong 1992, 1994, 2001 (captain), 2002 (captain); England to West Indies 1993-94; England XI to New Zealand (Cricket Max) 1997 (captain)
Overseas teams played for: St Joseph's, Whakatane, New Zealand 1986-88; Gosnells, Perth, Western Australia 1988-89; Papakura and Northern Districts, New Zealand 1990-91; Morrinsville College and Northern Districts, New Zealand 1991-92; Otago, New Zealand 1996-97
Career highlights to date: 'Leading Glamorgan to the County Championship in 1997. Playing for England'
Cricket moments to forget: 'Playing unsuccessfully for England'

Cricketers particularly admired: Ian Botham, Viv Richards, David Gower
Young players to look out for: Tom Maynard
Other sports played: Golf, football
Other sports followed: Rugby, football
Relaxations: 'Spending time with my wife and family and relaxing'
Extras: Scored century (102) on first-class debut v Yorkshire at Swansea in 1985, reaching his 100 with three successive straight sixes and becoming the youngest centurion for Glamorgan and the first Glamorgan debutant to score a century since F. B. Pinch did so in 1921; he scored 1000 runs in his first full season. In 1987 set record for fastest 50 for Glamorgan (14 mins) v Yorkshire and became youngest player to be awarded Glamorgan cap. Voted Young Cricketer of the Year 1988 by the Cricket Writers' Club. Scored 987 runs in July 1991, including a century in each innings (129/126) v Gloucestershire at Cheltenham. His 243 v Hampshire at Southampton 1991 is the highest score by a Glamorgan No. 4. Captained Glamorgan for most of 1992 in Alan Butcher's absence; Glamorgan captain 1996-2000. Voted Wombwell Cricket Lovers' Society captain of the year for 1997. Was one of *Wisden*'s Five Cricketers of the Year 1998. Appointed honorary fellow of University of Wales, Bangor. Set new Glamorgan one-day record stand for third wicket (204) with Jacques Kallis in National League match v Surrey at Pontypridd 1999. Passed 20,000 first-class runs during his 186 in Glamorgan's first innings v Yorkshire at Headingley 1999. Won Gold Award in the B&H Cup final 2000 for his 104 from 118 balls, having also won the award in the semi-final v Surrey for his 109 from 115 balls. Scored a century in each innings (140/118*) v Gloucestershire at Cheltenham 2002 (as he also did in 1991), in the process passing 20,000 runs in first-class cricket for Glamorgan. Scored 150-ball 151 v Northamptonshire at Cardiff 2002, in the process sharing with David Hemp (108) in a new record second-wicket partnership for Glamorgan in matches against Northamptonshire (252). Glamorgan Player of the Year 2002
Opinions on cricket: 'Why are people so keen to criticise our national team? I wish they could be a lot more upbeat and get behind the team.'
Best batting: 243 Glamorgan v Hampshire, Southampton 1991
Best bowling: 3-21 Glamorgan v Oxford University, The Parks 1987

2002 Season

	M	Inns	NO	Runs	HS	Avge	100s	50s	Ct	St	O	M	Runs	Wkts	Avge	Best	5wI	10wM
Test																		
All First	13	20	1	1058	151	55.68	3	6	14	-	1	0	5	0	-	-	-	-
1-day Int																		
C & G	1	1	0	21	21	21.00	-	-	-	-								
B & H	2	2	1	33	32	33.00	-	-	1	-								
1-day Lge	14	13	2	482	87	43.81	-	4	14	-								

Career Performances

	M	Inns	NO	Runs	HS	Avge	100s	50s	Ct	St	Balls	Runs	Wkts	Avge	Best	5wI	10wM
Test	4	8	0	87	35	10.87	-	-	3								
All First	363	589	57	22576	243	42.43	51	123	346	7	1117	866	6	144.33	3-21	-	-
1-day Int	14	12	1	156	41	14.18	-	-	3	-							
C & G	45	43	4	1690	151 *	43.33	2	13	23	1	18	8	0	-	-	-	-
B & H	61	61	7	2358	151 *	43.66	6	11	20	-	30	38	0	-	-	-	-
1-day Lge	241	232	24	6950	132	33.41	5	46	109	4	64	64	1	64.00	1-13	-	

McCOUBREY, A. G. A. M.   Essex

Name: <u>Adrian</u> George Agustus
Mathew McCoubrey
Role: Right-hand bat, right-arm
fast-medium bowler
Born: 3 April 1980, Ballymena,
Northern Ireland
Height: 5ft 10in **Weight:** 11st
Nickname: Scoobie, Coubs, Coubsy
County debut: No first-team appearance
Parents: Ronald and Josephine
Marital status: Single
Family links with cricket: Father played
town cricket
Education: Lisnamurrican Primary;
Cambridge House Boys' Grammar School;
Queen's University of Belfast
Qualifications: 9 GCSEs, 3 A-levels, BEng
(Hons) Aeronautical Engineering (2.1)
Career outside cricket: Engineer
Off-season: 'Training with the Irish winter squad for the start of the 2003 season'
Overseas tours: Ireland to Canada (ICC Trophy) 2001
Career highlights to date: 'First Irish senior cap 1999. Playing against Australia at
Ormeau, Belfast 2001. Signing professional contract with Essex'
Cricket moments to forget: 'Not qualifying for 2003 World Cup'
Cricket superstitions: 'Will not play any match without wearing the Star of David
around my neck'
Cricketers particularly admired: Darren Gough, Glenn McGrath
Other sports played: Football, hockey
Other sports followed: Football (Liverpool FC)
Injuries: Out for half of the season with a quad strain
Relaxations: 'Swimming, reading, surfing the Net'

Extras: Has 23 senior Ireland caps; represented Ireland in the C&G 2002 and in the first round of the C&G 2003, which was played in August 2002. Ballymena Adult Sportsperson of the Year 2001

2002 Season (did not make any first-class or one-day appearances for his county)

Career Performances

	M	Inns	NO	Runs	HS	Avge	100s	50s	Ct	St	Balls	Runs	Wkts	Avge	Best	5wI	10wM
Test																	
All First																	
1-day Int																	
C & G	4	3	0	13	11	4.33	-	-	-	-	162	85	3	28.33	2-20	-	
B & H																	
1-day Lge																	

McGARRY, A. C.   Essex

Name: <u>Andrew</u> Charles McGarry
Role: Right-hand bat, right-arm fast-medium bowler
Born: 8 November 1981, Basildon
Height: 6ft 5in **Weight:** 12st 7lbs
Nickname: Rodders
County debut: 1999
1st-Class catches: 3
Place in bowling averages: (2001 146th av. 63.70)
Strike rate: 170.50 (career 82.31)
Parents: Christine and George
Marital status: Single
Family links with cricket: Father played, and eldest brother plays recreational cricket
Education: Widford Lodge Preparatory School, Chelmsford; King Edward VI GS, Chelmsford; South East Essex College of Arts and Technology, Southend
Qualifications: 9 GCSEs, Level 1 and 2 ECB coaching awards
Overseas tours: England U19 to India 2000-01
Cricketers particularly admired: Ian Botham, Allan Donald
Young players to look out for: Justin Bishop, Monty Panesar, Mark Pettini
Other sports played: Basketball, volleyball, football
Other sports followed: Football (Aston Villa)
Relaxations: Going out, listening to music

Extras: First Brian Johnston Scholarship winner 1996. NBC Denis Compton Award for the most promising young Essex player 2000. Represented England U19 v West Indies U19 in one-day series (1/3) and 'Test' series (2/3) 2001

Opinions on cricket: 'Two division cricket has created a much more competitive season.'

Best batting: 11* Essex v CUCCE, Fenner's 2002

Best bowling: 3-29 Essex v Worcestershire, Chelmsford 2000

2002 Season

	M	Inns	NO	Runs	HS	Avge	100s	50s	Ct	St	O	M	Runs	Wkts	Avge	Best	5wI	10wM
Test																		
All First	3	4	2	16	11*	8.00	-	-	1	-	56.5	9	228	2	114.00	2-23	-	-
1-day Int																		
C & G																		
B & H																		
1-day Lge	3	1	0	1	1	1.00	-	-	-	-	17.3	1	125	2	62.50	2-35	-	

Career Performances

	M	Inns	NO	Runs	HS	Avge	100s	50s	Ct	St	Balls	Runs	Wkts	Avge	Best	5wI	10wM
Test																	
All First	13	16	11	22	11*	4.40	-	-	3	-	1811	1241	22	56.40	3-29	-	-
1-day Int																	
C & G																	
B & H	3	1	1	0	0*	-	-	-	-	-	150	98	4	24.50	2-34	-	
1-day Lge	12	3	1	2	1	1.00	-	-	1	-	279	259	6	43.16	2-20	-	

McGRATH, A.   Yorkshire

Name: Anthony McGrath
Role: Right-hand bat, right-arm medium bowler, county captain
Born: 6 October 1975, Bradford
Height: 6ft 2in **Weight:** 14st 7lbs
Nickname: Gripper, Mags, Terry
County debut: 1995
County cap: 1999
1st-Class 50s: 24
1st-Class 100s: 9
1st-Class catches: 70
One-Day 100s: 2
Place in batting averages: 125th av. 32.12 (2001 106th av. 32.07)
Place in bowling averages: 48th av. 27.66
Strike rate: 58.16 (career 60.61)
Parents: Terry and Kath

Marital status: Single
Education: St Winefrides; St Blaize; Yorkshire Martyrs Collegiate School
Qualifications: 9 GCSEs, BTEC National Diploma in Leisure Studies, senior coaching award
Overseas tours: England U19 to West Indies 1994-95; England A to Pakistan 1995-96, to Australia 1996-97; MCC to Bangladesh 1999-2000
Overseas teams played for: Deep Dene, Melbourne 1998-99; Wanneroo, Perth 1999-2001
Career highlights to date: 'Championship win 2001. C&G Trophy 2002'
Cricket moments to forget: 'Losing semi-final to Lancashire 1996. Relegation to Division Two 2002'
Cricketers particularly admired: Darren Lehmann, Robin Smith
Young players to look out for: Michael Lumb, John Sadler
Other sports followed: 'Most sports', football (Manchester United)
Injuries: Out for three weeks with a groin injury
Relaxations: 'Music; spending time with friends; eating out'
Extras: Captained Yorkshire Schools U13, U14, U15 and U16; captained English Schools U17. Bradford League Young Cricketer of the Year 1992 and 1993. Played for England U17, and for England U19 in home series against India U19 1994. Appeared as 12th man for England in the first Test against West Indies at Headingley in 1995. C&G Man of the Match for his 72* in the quarter-final v Essex at Chelmsford 2002. Scored 165 v Lancashire at Headingley 2002, in the process sharing with Darren Lehmann (187) in a record third-wicket partnership for Yorkshire at Headingley (317). Appointed captain of Yorkshire for 2003
Opinions on cricket: 'I still think there is too much cricket crammed into the season. Fewer Championship games in the season would allow for more preparation and planning, enabling more quality cricket to be played.'
Best batting: 165 Yorkshire v Lancashire, Headingley 2002
Best bowling: 4-49 Yorkshire v Hampshire, West End 2002
Stop press: Included in provisional England squad of 30 for the 2002-03 World Cup

56. For which county did Anil Kumble play in a) 1995; b) 2000?

2002 Season

	M	Inns	NO	Runs	HS	Avge	100s	50s	Ct	St	O	M	Runs	Wkts	Avge	Best	5wI	10wM
Test																		
All First	14	26	1	803	165	32.12	1	3	7	-	174.3	38	498	18	27.66	4-49	-	-
1-day Int																		
C & G	5	3	2	142	72 *	142.00	-	1	2	-	18	0	96	2	48.00	1-33	-	
B & H	6	6	0	101	48	16.83	-	-	-									
1-day Lge	14	13	2	376	85 *	34.18	-	3	4	-	56	3	259	7	37.00	3-39	-	

Career Performances

	M	Inns	NO	Runs	HS	Avge	100s	50s	Ct	St	Balls	Runs	Wkts	Avge	Best	5wI	10wM
Test																	
All First	116	199	13	5520	165	29.67	9	24	70	-	2182	1079	36	29.97	4-49	-	-
1-day Int																	
C & G	20	17	3	644	84	46.00	-	6	8	-	150	133	2	66.50	1-33	-	
B & H	33	31	1	740	109 *	24.66	1	1	11	-	12	10	2	5.00	2-10	-	
1-day Lge	93	85	15	2284	102	32.62	1	15	27	-	609	447	15	29.80	3-39	-	

McLEAN, N. A. M.   Somerset

Name: <u>Nixon</u> Alexei McNamara McLean
Role: Left-hand bat, right-arm fast bowler
Born: 20 July 1973, Stubbs, St Vincent
Height: 6ft 5in
Nickname: Nicko
County debut: 1998 (Hampshire)
County cap: 1998 (Hampshire)
Test debut: 1997-98
Tests: 19
One-Day Internationals: 44
50 wickets in a season: 1
1st-Class 50s: 2
1st-Class 5 w. in innings: 11
1st-Class 10 w. in match: 1
1st-Class catches: 29
Strike rate: (career 52.96)
Marital status: Single
Family links with cricket: Brother
(R. McLean) played for Windward Islands
Education: Carapan SS, St Vincent
Overseas tours: West Indies to Australia 1996-97, to Bangladesh (Wills International Cup) 1998-99, to South Africa 1998-99, to Bangladesh (one-day series) 1999-2000,

to Sharjah (Coca-Cola Champions' Trophy) 1999-2000, to England 2000, to Australia 2000-01; West Indies A to South Africa 1997-98

Overseas teams played for: Windward Islands; KwaZulu-Natal 2001-02 –

Extras: Was Hampshire's overseas player 1998-99, taking 62 first-class wickets (av. 25.40) in 1998. Took 44 wickets (av. 16.27) in KwaZulu-Natal's Supersport Series title win 2001-02, including 6-84 in the Northerns first innings in the final at Durban; also took 15 wickets at 15.33 in KwaZulu-Natal's successful Standard Bank Cup campaign 2001-02. Has joined Somerset as an overseas player for 2003

Best batting: 70 Hampshire v Surrey, Guildford 1999

Best bowling: 7-28 West Indies v Free State, Bloemfontein 1998-99

Stop press: Selected for West Indies squad for 2002-03 World Cup

---

2002 Season (did not make any first-class or one-day appearances)

Career Performances

	M	Inns	NO	Runs	HS	Avge	100s	50s	Ct	St	Balls	Runs	Wkts	Avge	Best	5wI	10wM
Test	19	32	2	368	46	12.26	-	-	5	-	3299	1873	44	42.56	3-53	-	
All First	100	158	22	1811	70	13.31	-	2	29	-	17477	9036	330	27.38	7-28	11	1
1-day Int	44	33	8	309	50*	12.36	-	1	8	-	2084	1691	46	36.76	3-21	-	
C & G	6	6	3	112	36	37.33	-	-	-	-	307	177	9	19.66	3-27	-	
B & H	5	4	1	35	28*	11.66	-	-	2	-	271	230	2	115.00	1-32	-	
1-day Lge	31	24	3	280	32	13.33	-	-	3	-	1242	1016	40	25.40	3-27	-	

57. Whose Worcestershire season record of ten first-class centuries did Graeme Hick equal in 1988?

McMAHON, P. J. Nottinghamshire

Name: <u>Paul</u> Joseph McMahon
Role: Right-hand bat, off-spin bowler
Born: 12 March 1983, Wigan
Height: 6ft 1in **Weight:** 11st 7lbs
Nickname: Vince, Macca, Boffin, Kenneth
County debut: 2002
Strike rate: 68.50 (career 68.50)
Parents: Gerry and Teresa
Marital status: Single
Family links with cricket: 'Dad was club professional in Lancashire and Cheshire leagues; now plays for Notts Over 50s and for Wollaton in Notts Premier League. Mum makes teas and is learning how to find scores on Ceefax'

Education: St Teresa's RC Primary, Nottingham; Trinity RC Comprehensive, Nottingham; Wadham College, Oxford University
Qualifications: 11 GCSEs, 4 A-levels
Career outside cricket: Student
Off-season: 'First year of law degree at Oxford University'
Overseas tours: England U19 to Australia and (U19 World Cup) New Zealand 2001-02; Nottinghamshire to South Africa 2002
Career highlights to date: 'Captaining England U19 against India U19, and taking eight wickets [4-47 and 4-58] in the victory at Northampton in the deciding final "Test"'
Cricket moments to forget: 'I've tried to learn from them all!'
Cricketers particularly admired: Mike Atherton, Steve Waugh, Nasser Hussain
Young players to look out for: 'All the many young players at Notts'
Other sports played: Football (represented Nottingham City Schools U15), tennis ('badly'), golf ('even worse')
Other sports followed: Football (Wimbledon)
Injuries: 'Third-degree burns from diving on the hard shoulder at Taunton; various strains and niggles – no games missed'
Relaxations: Music, reading, current affairs, 'doing the Wheelhouse quiz'
Extras: Has played for Notts at every level from U11 to 1st XI. Second graduate of Nottinghamshire CCC Academy ('Bilal Shafayat was the first'). Took 45 wickets at an average of 18.82 in 2nd XI Championship 2002. Man of the Match in England's opening game of the 2001-02 U19 World Cup, taking 5-25 against Nepal. Captain of England U19 in 'Test' (3/3) and one-day (3/3) series aganst India U19 2002; leading wicket-taker in 'Test' series with ten wickets (av. 22.2). Shared with Andrew Harris

(41*) in a record last-wicket stand for Nottinghamshire in matches v Northamptonshire (68), at Northampton 2002

Opinions on cricket: 'I feel very lucky to be part of this great game.'
Best batting: 15 Nottinghamshire v Northamptonshire, Northampton 2002
Best bowling: 2-22 Nottinghamshire v West Indies A, Trent Bridge 2002

2002 Season

	M	Inns	NO	Runs	HS	Avge	100s	50s	Ct	St	O	M	Runs	Wkts	Avge	Best	5wI	10wM
Test																		
All First	2	3	0	15	15	5.00	-	-	-	-	22.5	2	103	2	51.50	2-22	-	-
1-day Int																		
C & G																			
B & H																			
1-day Lge																			

Career Performances

	M	Inns	NO	Runs	HS	Avge	100s	50s	Ct	St	Balls	Runs	Wkts	Avge	Best	5wI	10wM
Test																	
All First	2	3	0	15	15	5.00	-	-	-	-	137	103	2	51.50	2-22	-	-
1-day Int																	
C & G																		
B & H																		
1-day Lge																		

58. Who was Nottinghamshire's overseas player in 1998 and for which county had he played the previous season?

MEES, T.   Warwickshire

Name: Thomas (<u>Tom</u>) Mees
Role: Right-hand bat, right-arm
fast-medium bowler
Born: 8 June 1981, Wolverhampton
Height: 6ft 3in **Weight:** 13st
Nickname: Meesy, Meesdog
County debut: No first-team appearance
1st-Class 5 w. in innings: 1
1st-Class catches: 1
Strike rate: 48.00 (career 52.60)
Parents: Mark and Christina
Marital status: Single
Family links with cricket: 'Cousin Simon
played for Worcestershire Youth. Dad played
for Cosely and umpires'
Education: Worcester Royal Grammar Prep
School; Worcester Royal Grammar School;
King Edward VI College, Stourbridge;
Oxford Brookes University

Qualifications: 9 GCSEs, 3 A-levels, ECB Level 1 coaching award
Overseas tours: British Universities to South Africa 2002
Overseas teams played for: Railways, Albany, Western Australia 1999-2000
Career highlights to date: 'Taking 6-64 v Middlesex on first-class debut for
Oxford UCCE 2001'
Cricket moments to forget: 'Playing in a Birmingham League match for Old Hill v
Walsall, mistaking the umpire for the wicket-keeper and throwing the ball over the
umpire's head for four overthrows off the last ball of the game with the opposition
needing two to win!'
Cricketers particularly admired: Ian Botham, Andrew Flintoff
Young players to look out for: Jamie Dalrymple, Matt Stillwell, Patrick Wolff,
Ian Bell, Graham Wagg
Other sports played: Golf, football, tennis
Other sports followed: Football (Liverpool FC)
Relaxations: Playing golf, spending time with friends, shopping, going out
Extras: Played for Worcestershire Board XI in the NatWest 1999. Has played for
Warwickshire 2nd XI. Played for Oxford University CCE in 2001 and 2002. Played for
Warwickshire Board XI in the C&G 2001 and in the first and second rounds of the
C&G 2002, which were played in August and September 2001. Recorded maiden
first-class five-wicket return (6-64) for OUCCE on first-class debut v Middlesex at
The Parks 2001. Represented British Universities v West Indies A (50-over match) at
The Parks 2002

Opinions on cricket: 'Regional cricket should be introduced at start of season and against tourists as a trial, and then possibly used more frequently. Day/night cricket should be played more frequently. County Championship could be divided into three divisions.'

Best batting: 13 OUCCE v Worcestershire, The Parks 2002

Best bowling: 6-64 OUCCE v Middlesex, The Parks 2001

2002 Season (did not make any first-class or one-day appearances for his county)

Career Performances

	M	Inns	NO	Runs	HS	Avge	100s	50s	Ct	St	Balls	Runs	Wkts	Avge	Best	5wI	10wM
Test																	
All First	4	6	0	28	13	4.66	-	-	1	-	789	492	15	32.80	6-64	1	-
1-day Int																	
C & G	4	2	1	4	4 *	4.00	-	-	-	-	198	144	3	48.00	3-19	-	
B & H																	
1-day Lge																	

MIDDLEBROOK, J. D. Essex

Name: <u>James</u> Daniel Middlebrook
Role: Right-hand bat, off-spin bowler
Born: 13 May 1977, Leeds
Height: 6ft 1in **Weight:** 13st
Nickname: Brooky, Midi, Midders, Midhouse, Dog
County debut: 1998 (Yorkshire), 2002 (Essex)
1st-Class 50s: 2
1st-Class 5 w. in innings: 1
1st-Class 10 w. in match: 1
1st-Class catches: 21
Place in batting averages: 244th av. 17.37
Place in bowling averages: 139th av. 45.68
Strike rate: 87.68 (career 74.66)
Parents: Ralph and Mavis
Marital status: Single
Family links with cricket: 'Dad is a senior staff coach'
Education: Greenside, Pudsey; Crawshaw, Pudsey ('at these schools with Paul Hutchison')
Qualifications: NVQ Level 2 in Coaching Sport and Recreation, ECB senior coach
Off-season: 'India; Cape Town'

Overseas tours: Yorkshire CCC to Guernsey
Overseas teams played for: Stokes Valley CC, New Zealand; Gold Coast Dolphins, Brisbane; Surfers Paradise CC, Brisbane
Cricketers particularly admired: John Emburey, Ian Botham
Young players to look out for: Ravinder Bopara
Other sports played: Golf, tennis, squash, badminton
Other sports followed: Football (Leeds United), athletics
Relaxations: 'Any music – MTV – sleeping, socialising, catching up with old friends'
Extras: Played for Pudsey Congs from age of seven. Played for Yorkshire at all age levels U11 to 1st XI. Awarded Yorkshire 2nd XI cap 1998. His maiden first-class five-wicket return (6-82) v Hampshire at Southampton 2000 included a spell of four wickets in five balls. Released by Yorkshire at the end of the 2001 season and joined Essex for 2002
Best batting: 84 Yorkshire v Essex, Chelmsford 2001
Best bowling: 6-82 Yorkshire v Hampshire, Southampton 2000

2002 Season

	M	Inns	NO	Runs	HS	Avge	100s	50s	Ct	St	O	M	Runs	Wkts	Avge	Best	5wl	10wM
Test																		
All First	18	28	4	417	67	17.37	-	1	7	-	555.2	121	1736	38	45.68	4-38	-	-
1-day Int																		
C & G	2	1	1	6	6 *	-	-	-	-	-	13	0	73	1	73.00	1-46	-	
B & H	5	2	1	24	15 *	24.00	-	-	2	-								
1-day Lge	14	9	2	65	19	9.28	-	-	4	-	81	6	320	19	16.84	4-33	-	

Career Performances

	M	Inns	NO	Runs	HS	Avge	100s	50s	Ct	St	Balls	Runs	Wkts	Avge	Best	5wl	10wM
Test																	
All First	41	59	7	902	84	17.34	-	2	21	-	6496	3194	87	36.71	6-82	1	1
1-day Int																	
C & G	4	2	2	12	6 *	-	-	-	3	-	126	111	1	111.00	1-46	-	
B & H	7	3	1	27	15 *	13.50	-	-	3	-	84	75	0	-	-	-	
1-day Lge	28	18	4	117	19	8.35	-	-	5	-	1050	737	32	23.03	4-33	-	

MILLER, D. J.   Surrey

Name: <u>Daniel</u> James Miller
Role: Left-hand bat, right-arm fast bowler
Born: 12 June 1983, Hammersmith, London
Height: 6ft 4in **Weight:** 14st 4lbs
Nickname: Windy, Funky
County debut: 2002 (one-day)
Parents: Gillian and Keith

Marital status: Single
Family links with cricket: 'My dad's got the name but no ability'
Education: Ewell Castle Junior School; Ewell Castle Senior School; Kingston College
Qualifications: 9 GCSEs, 4 A-levels
Off-season: 'At Loughborough University'
Overseas tours: Surrey Cricket Board to Barbados 1999
Career highlights to date: 'Making first-team debut at Surrey in NUL'
Cricket superstitions: 'Copying the preparation of a good day'
Cricketers particularly admired: David Morgan, Ian Botham, Alec Stewart, Graham Thorpe, Glenn McGrath
Young players to look out for: Neil Saker, Chris Murtagh, Simon Day

Other sports played: Football (Kingstonian Youth)
Other sports followed: Football (Tottenham Hotspur), 'all rugby union'
Injuries: Out for three weeks with a nerve injury in right shoulder
Relaxations: 'Going to Cheam Sports Club (Rome)'
Extras: Appeared in one NUL match in 2002; is a Surrey Academy player
Opinions on cricket: 'It's tough being a bowler; it's certainly a batsman's game!'

2002 Season

	M	Inns	NO	Runs	HS	Avge	100s	50s	Ct	St	O	M	Runs	Wkts	Avge	Best	5wI	10wM
Test																		
All First																		
1-day Int																		
C & G																		
B & H																		
1-day Lge	1	1	0	1	1	1.00	-	-	-	-	7	0	32	0	-		-	-

Career Performances

	M	Inns	NO	Runs	HS	Avge	100s	50s	Ct	St	Balls	Runs	Wkts	Avge	Best	5wI	10wM
Test																	
All First																	
1-day Int																	
C & G																	
B & H																	
1-day Lge	1	1	0	1	1	1.00	-	-	-	-	42	32	0	-		-	-

MOHAMMAD ALI　　　　　Derbyshire

Name: Syed Mohammad Ali Bukhari
Role: Right-hand bat, left-arm
fast-medium bowler
Born: 8 November 1973, Bahawalpur, Punjab
County debut: 2002
1st-Class 50s: 4
1st-Class 5 w. in innings: 11
1st-Class 10 w. in match: 2
1st-Class catches: 24
Place in batting averages: 264th av. 15.13
Place in bowling averages: 110th av. 36.34
Strike rate: 51.70 (career 51.60)
Overseas teams played for: Numerous,
including Bahawalpur, Islamabad Cricket
Association, Lahore Cricket Association,
Railways and United Bank
Extras: Nephew of Taslim Arif who played
for Pakistan 1979-80. Played for Glamorgan
2nd XI 2000 and 2001. Struck a 38-ball 53 on debut for Derbyshire v Durham at
Derby 2002, batting at No. 9. Is not considered an overseas player
Best batting: 92 Bahawalpur v Lahore City, Rahimyarkhan 1997-98
Best bowling: 6-37 Railways v National Bank, Faisalabad 1993-94

2002 Season

	M	Inns	NO	Runs	HS	Avge	100s	50s	Ct	St	O	M	Runs	Wkts	Avge	Best	5wI	10wM
Test																		
All First	15	24	2	333	53	15.13	-	1	5	-	405	63	1708	47	36.34	3-48	-	-
1-day Int																		
C & G	1	1	0	19	19	19.00	-	-	-	-	3	0	22	0	-	-	-	-
B & H	4	2	0	0	0	0.00	-	-	-	-	13	0	86	1	86.00	1-54	-	-
1-day Lge	2	2	1	12	10 *	12.00	-	-	-	-	14	0	66	4	16.50	3-42	-	-

Career Performances

	M	Inns	NO	Runs	HS	Avge	100s	50s	Ct	St	Balls	Runs	Wkts	Avge	Best	5wI	10wM
Test																	
All First	70	89	22	1036	92	15.46	-	4	24	-	11662	7061	226	31.24	6-37	11	2
1-day Int																	
C & G	1	1	0	19	19	19.00	-	-	-	-	18	22	0	-	-	-	-
B & H	4	2	0	0	0	0.00	-	-	-	-	78	86	1	86.00	1-54	-	-
1-day Lge	2	2	1	12	10 *	12.00	-	-	-	-	84	66	4	16.50	3-42	-	-

MONTGOMERIE, R. R. Sussex

Name: <u>Richard</u> Robert Montgomerie
Role: Right-hand opening bat
Born: 3 July 1971, Rugby
Height: 5ft 10in **Weight:** 13st
Nickname: Monty
County debut: 1991 (Northamptonshire), 1999 (Sussex)
County cap: 1995 (Northamptonshire), 1999 (Sussex)
1000 runs in a season: 4
1st-Class 50s: 46
1st-Class 100s: 23
1st-Class catches: 153
One-Day 100s: 3
Place in batting averages: 88th av. 38.00 (2001 14th av. 58.75)
Strike rate: (career 180.00)
Parents: Robert and Gillian
Marital status: Single
Family links with cricket: Father captained Oxfordshire
Education: Bilton Grange; Rugby School; Worcester College, Oxford University
Qualifications: 12 O-levels, 4 A-levels, BA (Hons) Chemistry, Level II coaching
Off-season: 'Trips to China and Australia'
Overseas tours: Oxford University to Namibia 1991; Northamptonshire to Zimbabwe and Johannesburg; Christians in Sport to South Africa 2000; Sussex to Grenada 2001, 2002
Overseas teams played for: Sydney University CC 1995-96
Career highlights to date: 'Two Lord's finals. Winning second division of National League in 1999 and second division of County Championship in 2001. A hundred [157] v Australians [at Hove 2001]'
Cricket moments to forget: 'Running [Northants] captain Allan Lamb out on my Championship debut … as his runner'
Cricketers particularly admired: Steve Waugh, Mark Robinson
Young players to look out for: Matt Prior, Tim Ambrose – 'there seem to be more quality young players coming through in the last couple of years'
Other sports followed: Golf, rackets, real tennis 'and many others'
Relaxations: Any sport, good television, reading and 'occasionally testing my brain'
Extras: Oxford rackets Blue 1990. Scored unbeaten 50 in each innings of 1991 Varsity match. Faced first ball delivered by Durham in first-class cricket, for Oxford University at The Parks 1992. Was Oxford University captain in 1994; also captained Combined Universities 1994. Released by Northants at the end of the 1998 season and joined Sussex for 1999. Scored his first 100 for Sussex (113*) against his former

county at Hove 1999. Scored 160* v Nottinghamshire at Trent Bridge 2001; in the process he shared with Murray Goodwin in a record partnership for any wicket for Sussex in matches against Notts (372*), superseding his own record (292) set with Michael Bevan at Hove in 2000. Scored 108 (his maiden one-day league century) v Essex at Hove in the Norwich Union League 2001, in the process sharing with Murray Goodwin in a Sussex record opening partnership in the one-day league (176). Man of the Match award for his 157 in the Vodafone Challenge match against the Australians at Hove 2001. Joint Sussex Player of the Year (with Murray Goodwin) 2001. Carried his bat for 122* v Leicestershire at Horsham 2002. C&G Man of the Match award for his 126* v Leicestershire at Leicester 2002

Opinions on cricket: '20/20 cricket should be exciting to play in and watch. We must all be willing to give it a go and let it mature. Any success in Australia this (last) winter will be an excellent achievement.'

Best batting: 196 Sussex v Hampshire, Hove 2002

Best bowling: 1-0 Sussex v Middlesex, Lord's 2001

2002 Season

	M	Inns	NO	Runs	HS	Avge	100s	50s	Ct	St	O	M	Runs	Wkts	Avge	Best	5wI	10wM
Test																		
All First	16	28	1	1026	196	38.00	2	4	16	-	6	2	10	0	-		-	-	-
1-day Int																		
C & G	3	3	1	241	126 *	120.50	1	1	2	-								
B & H	6	6	1	329	85	65.80	-	4	2	-								
1-day Lge	14	14	2	178	31	14.83	-	-	4	-								

Career Performances

	M	Inns	NO	Runs	HS	Avge	100s	50s	Ct	St	Balls	Runs	Wkts	Avge	Best	5wI	10wM
Test																	
All First	164	288	27	9534	196	36.52	23	46	153	-	180	99	1	99.00	1-0	-	-
1-day Int																	
C & G	15	15	4	755	126 *	68.63	2	6	5	-							
B & H	31	29	3	972	85	37.38	-	7	5	-	6	0	0	-	-	-	-
1-day Lge	94	93	7	2721	108	31.63	1	20	23	-							

59. For which county did Sachin Tendulkar play in 1992?

MOORE, S. C.   Worcestershire

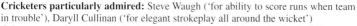

Name: <u>Stephen</u> Colin Moore
Role: Right-hand top-order bat, right-arm
medium bowler
Born: 4 November 1980, Johannesburg,
South Africa
Height: 6ft 1in **Weight:** 13st
Nickname: Circles, Mandy
County debut: No first-team appearance
Parents: Shane and Carrol
Marital status: Single
Education: St Stithians Preparatory School;
St Stithians College, Johannesburg;
Exeter University
Career outside cricket: 'Studying for an
MEng in electronic engineering'
Overseas tours: Wanderers Colts U19 to
England 1996
Overseas teams played for: Wanderers,
Johannesburg 1995-99
Cricketers particularly admired: Steve Waugh ('for ability to score runs when team
in trouble'), Daryll Cullinan ('for elegant strokeplay all around the wicket')
Other sports played: Tennis (university 1st team; ranked in top 15 South African
juniors), hockey (university 1st XI)
Other sports followed: Rugby (Springboks)
Relaxations: 'Wildlife; inflatable boating and other watersports; music (saxophone
and guitar)'
Extras: Is not considered an overseas player

60. Who scored 161* on his Championship debut for Gloucestershire v
Surrey at The Oval in 1995?

MORRIS, A. C.   Hampshire

Name: Alexander (<u>Alex</u>) Corfield Morris
Role: Left-hand bat, right-arm
medium-fast bowler
Born: 4 October 1976, Barnsley
Height: 6ft 4in **Weight:** 14st
Nickname: Almo
County debut: 1995 (Yorkshire),
1998 (Hampshire)
County cap: 2001 (Hampshire)
50 wickets in a season: 2
1st-Class 50s: 7
1st-Class 5 w. in innings: 5
1st-Class 10 w. in match: 1
1st-Class catches: 32
Place in batting averages: (2001 155th
av. 24.88)
Place in bowling averages: (2001 52nd
av. 28.00)
Strike rate: (career 50.42)
Parents: Janet and Chris
Marital status: Girlfriend Helen
Family links with cricket: Brother Zac played for Hampshire and Yorkshire
Education: Wilthorpe Primary School; Holgate School, Barnsley; Barnsley College
Qualifications: 4 GCSEs, BTEC National Diploma in Sports Science, senior cricket
coach
Off-season: 'Living it up in Sydney'
Overseas tours: England U19 to West Indies 1994-95, to Zimbabwe 1995-96;
England VI to Hong Kong 1996; Michael Vaughan XI to Tenerife 1996; Craig Dudley
XI to Cyprus 1997; Anthony McGrath XI to Gran Canaria 1998; Alex Morris XI to
Cyprus 1999; 'Ayia Napa 2002'
Overseas teams played for: South Sydney 2002
Cricket moments to forget: 'Out off the last ball of the last game at Northlands Road,
v Yorkshire 2000'
Other sports played: Football (junior with Barnsley and Rotherham; trials for
Nottingham Forest and Leeds)
Other sports followed: Football (Barnsley FC)
Injuries: Fracture of facet joint in back; played as batsman
Relaxations: 'Bondi Beach'
Extras: Played for Yorkshire U11-U19; made debut for 2nd XI at age 16. Played for
England U15 against Barbados and in 1994 for both England U17 and U19 against
India. Left Yorkshire and signed for Hampshire along with his brother Zac for the 1998
season. Awarded Hampshire cap 2001

Best batting: 65 Hampshire v Sussex, West End 2001
Best bowling: 5-39 Hampshire v Durham, Riverside 2001

2002 Season

	M	Inns	NO	Runs	HS	Avge	100s	50s	Ct	St	O	M	Runs	Wkts	Avge	Best	5wI	10wM
Test																		
All First	2	2	0	36	24	18.00	-	-	-	-	29	5	112	0	-		-	-
1-day Int																		
C & G																			
B & H																			
1-day Lge																			

Career Performances

	M	Inns	NO	Runs	HS	Avge	100s	50s	Ct	St	Balls	Runs	Wkts	Avge	Best	5wI	10wM
Test																	
All First	60	78	12	1325	65	20.07	-	7	32	-	7867	4119	156	26.40	5-39	5	1
1-day Int																	
C & G	3	2	2	4	3 *	-	-	-	1	-	132	125	2	62.50	1-43	-	
B & H	5	3	1	46	25 *	23.00	-	-	2	-	186	135	6	22.50	3-49	-	
1-day Lge	32	19	5	232	48 *	16.57	-	-	6	-	792	708	26	27.23	4-49	-	

MUCHALL, G. J. Durham

Name: <u>Gordon</u> James Muchall
Role: Right-hand bat, right-arm
medium-fast bowler
Born: 2 November 1982,
Newcastle upon Tyne
Height: 6ft **Weight:** 13st 5lbs
Nickname: Manson, West, Cannon,
Melon, Lecter
County debut: 2002
1st-Class 50s: 3
1st-Class 100s: 1
1st-Class catches: 14
Place in batting averages: 185th av. 24.52
Strike rate: 64.50 (career 64.50)
Parents: Mary and Arthur
Marital status: Single
Family links with cricket: Grandfather
played for Northumberland. Younger brother
(Paul) is in England U15 squad
Education: Newlands Prep School, Newcastle; Durham School

Qualifications: 8 GCSEs, 2 A-levels
Career outside cricket: Laying patios
Off-season: 'Going away with the Academy'
Overseas tours: England U19 to India 2000-01, to Australia and (U19 World Cup) New Zealand 2001-02; ECB National Academy to Australia and Sri Lanka 2002-03
Overseas teams played for: Fremantle 2001-02
Career highlights to date: '127 at Lord's for Durham. 253 for England U19 v India U19'
Cricket moments to forget: 'With the opposition needing four off the last ball to win, going into the long barrier position and the ball bouncing over my head for four'
Cricketers particularly admired: Jacques Kallis, Ian Botham, Steve Waugh, Darren Gough
Young players to look out for: Paul Muchall, Kyle Hogg, Kadeer Ali, Nadeem Malik
Other sports played: Rugby (at school)
Other sports followed: Football (Newcastle United), rugby (Newcastle Falcons and England)
Relaxations: Listening to music, socialising with friends
Extras: Represented England U19 v West Indies U19 in one-day series (3/3) and 'Test' series (2/3) 2001. Played for Durham Board XI in the second round of the C&G 2002, which was played in September 2001. Scored maiden first-class century (127) v Middlesex at Lord's 2002. Represented England U19 v India U19 in 'Test' series (3/3) 2002, scoring 254 in the first 'Test' at Cardiff; it was the third highest individual score in the history of U19 international cricket. Cricket Society's Most Promising Young Cricketer of the Year Award 2002
Opinions on cricket: 'More day/night cricket.'
Best batting: 127 Durham v Middlesex, Lord's 2002
Best bowling: 2-52 Durham v Northamptonshire, Riverside 2002

2002 Season

	M	Inns	NO	Runs	HS	Avge	100s	50s	Ct	St	O	M	Runs	Wkts	Avge	Best	5wI	10wM
Test																		
All First	15	25	0	613	127	24.52	1	3	14	-	43	6	194	4	48.50	2-52	-	-
1-day Int																		
C & G	1	1	0	3	3	3.00	-	-	-	-								
B & H																		
1-day Lge	9	9	1	228	81	28.50	-	1	3	-								

Career Performances

	M	Inns	NO	Runs	HS	Avge	100s	50s	Ct	St	Balls	Runs	Wkts	Avge	Best	5wl	10wM
Test																	
All First	15	25	0	613	127	24.52	1	3	14	-		258	194	4	48.50	2-52	-	-
1-day Int																	
C & G	2	2	0	22	19	11.00	-	-	2	-		12	11	0	-		-	-
B & H																	
1-day Lge	9	9	1	228	81	28.50	-	1	3	-							

MULLALLY, A. D. — Hampshire

Name: <u>Alan</u> David Mullally
Role: Right-hand bat, left-arm fast bowler
Born: 12 July 1969, Southend
Height: 6ft 4in **Weight:** 14st
Nickname: Spider
County debut: 1988 (Hampshire),
1990 (Leicestershire)
County cap: 1993 (Leicestershire),
2000 (Hampshire – *see* **Extras**)
Test debut: 1996
Tests: 19
One-Day Internationals: 50
50 wickets in a season: 5
1st-Class 50s: 2
1st-Class 5 w. in innings: 30
1st-Class 10 w. in match: 4
1st-Class catches: 41
One-Day 5 w. in innings: 2
Place in batting averages: 316th av. 4.90 (2001 256th av. 10.25)
Place in bowling averages: 27th av. 25.13 (2001 5th av. 18.50)
Strike rate: 60.43 (career 60.61)
Parents: Mick and Ann
Wife and date of marriage: Chelsey, 1997
Family links with cricket: 'Younger brother is better'
Education: Cannington Primary and High School, Perth, Australia; Wembley and Carlisle Technical College
Overseas tours: Western Australia to India; Leicestershire to Jamaica 1992-93; England to Zimbabwe and New Zealand 1996-97, to Australia 1998-99, to Sharjah (Coca-Cola Cup) 1998-99, to South Africa and Zimbabwe 1999-2000, to Sri Lanka 2000-01 (one-day series)
Overseas teams played for: Western Australia 1987-90; Victoria 1990-91

Career highlights to date: 'Career best 9-93 v Derbyshire. Man of the Match in World Cup [v Zimbabwe 1999] and CUB Series v Australia [1998-99]'
Cricket moments to forget: 'Sunday League v Middlesex' (*At the Rose Bowl in 2001, Middlesex took 35 runs off the last 13 deliveries of the game to win*)
Cricketers particularly admired: Robin Smith
Young players to look out for: Derek Kenway
Other sports followed: Australian Rules football, basketball, most sports
Relaxations: Fishing, music
Extras: English-qualified as he was born in Southend, he made his first-class debut for Western Australia in the 1987-88 Sheffield Shield final, and played for Australian YC 1988-89. Played one match for Hampshire in 1988 before joining Leicestershire. Represented England in the 1999 World Cup. Left Leicestershire at end of 1999 season and rejoined Hampshire for 2000. Took 5-18 as Hampshire bowled out the Australians for 97 at West End 2001
Opinions on cricket: 'Too much cricket. Too many teams.'
Best batting: 75 Leicestershire v Middlesex, Leicester 1996
Best bowling: 9-93 Hampshire v Derbyshire, Derby 2000

2002 Season

	M	Inns	NO	Runs	HS	Avge	100s	50s	Ct	St	O	M	Runs	Wkts	Avge	Best	5wI	10wM
Test																		
All First	13	16	5	54	23	4.90	-	-	1	-	463.2	145	1156	46	25.13	6-56	1	-
1-day Int																		
C & G	2	0	0	0	0	-	-	-	-	-	19	2	69	2	34.50	1-16	-	
B & H	5	4	2	12	7	6.00	-	-	-	-	50	11	173	5	34.60	2-29	-	
1-day Lge	8	5	3	19	9 *	9.50	-	-	1	-	65	7	244	7	34.85	2-17	-	

Career Performances

	M	Inns	NO	Runs	HS	Avge	100s	50s	Ct	St	Balls	Runs	Wkts	Avge	Best	5wI	10wM
Test	19	27	4	127	24	5.52	-	-	6	-	4525	1812	58	31.24	5-105	1	-
All First	212	238	62	1510	75	8.57	-	2	41	-	40796	18578	673	27.60	9-93	30	4
1-day Int	50	25	10	86	20	5.73	-	-	8	-	2698	1728	63	27.42	4-18	-	
C & G	27	10	5	58	19 *	11.60	-	-	3	-	1656	935	44	21.25	5-18	1	
B & H	54	24	9	70	13	4.66	-	-	2	-	2934	1839	51	36.05	3-33	-	
1-day Lge	124	57	26	246	38	7.93	-	-	21	-	5578	3855	137	28.13	5-15	1	

61. Which South African batsman scored four successive County Championship centuries for Essex in 1977?

MURTAGH, T. J. Surrey

Name: Timothy (<u>Tim</u>) James Murtagh
Role: Left-hand bat, right-arm
fast-medium bowler
Born: 2 August 1981, Lambeth, London
Height: 6ft 2in **Weight:** 12st
Nickname: Browser, Murts, Human
Headband
County debut: 2000 (one-day),
2001 (first-class)
1st-Class 5 w. in innings: 2
1st-Class catches: 3
Place in bowling averages: 22nd av. 24.94
Strike rate: 43.11 (career 37.92)
Parents: Dominic and Elizabeth
Marital status: Single
Family links with cricket: 'Chris, younger
brother, plays in Surrey age-group cricket and
is in their Development of Excellence
Programme; Uncle Andy (A. J. Murtagh) played for Hampshire'
Education: Regina Coeli, Purley, Surrey; John Fisher, Purley, Surrey; St Mary's
University, Twickenham
Qualifications: 10 GCSEs, 2 A-levels
Career outside cricket: Student (Sports Science and Media Studies)
Overseas tours: Surrey U17 to South Africa 1997; England U19 to Malaysia and
(U19 World Cup) Sri Lanka 1999-2000; British Universities to South Africa 2002
Cricketers particularly admired: Darren Gough, Glenn McGrath
Young players to look out for: James Benning, Jon Hammond
Other sports played: Rugby (was captain of John Fisher 2nd XV), skiing ('in the past')
Other sports followed: Football (Liverpool FC), rugby
Relaxations: Playing golf, watching sport, films, reading
Extras: Represented British Universities 2000, 2001 and v Sri Lankans at
Northampton and v West Indies A (50-over match) at The Parks 2002. Represented
England U19 in one-day and 'Test' series v Sri Lanka U19 2000; named Player of the
Series. Played for Surrey Board XI and Surrey in the C&G 2001. NBC Denis
Compton Award for the most promising young Surrey player 2001. Recorded maiden
Championship five-wicket return (5-39) v Leicestershire at The Oval 2002
Best batting: 22* British Universities v Pakistanis, Trent Bridge 2001
Best bowling: 6-86 British Universities v Pakistanis, Trent Bridge 2001

2002 Season

	M	Inns	NO	Runs	HS	Avge	100s	50s	Ct	St	O	M	Runs	Wkts	Avge	Best	5wI	10wM
Test																		
All First	5	7	3	50	22	12.50	-	-	3	-	122.1	23	424	17	24.94	5-39	1	-
1-day Int																		
C & G																		
B & H																		
1-day Lge	9	6	2	32	14 *	8.00	-	-	3	-	77.3	3	353	13	27.15	3-38	-	

Career Performances

	M	Inns	NO	Runs	HS	Avge	100s	50s	Ct	St	Balls	Runs	Wkts	Avge	Best	5wI	10wM
Test																	
All First	8	11	5	86	22 *	14.33	-	-	3	-	948	544	25	21.76	6-86	2	-
1-day Int																	
C & G	2	2	0	13	11	6.50	-	-	1	-	108	86	2	43.00	1-40	-	
B & H																	
1-day Lge	18	12	6	44	14 *	7.33	-	-	4	-	884	717	24	29.87	4-31	-	

MUSHTAQ AHMED   Sussex

Name: Mushtaq Ahmed
Role: Right-hand bat, leg-spin bowler
Born: 28 June 1970, Sahiwal, Pakistan
Height: 5ft 4in
Nickname: Mushy
County debut: 1993 (Somerset),
2002 (Surrey)
County cap: 1993 (Somerset)
Test debut: 1991-92
Tests: 50
One-Day Internationals: 143
50 wickets in a season: 3
1st-Class 50s: 11
1st-Class 5w. in innings: 59
1st-Class 10w. in match: 16
1st-Class catches: 94
One-Day 5 w. in innings: 3
Strike rate: 78.75 (career 52.82)
Marital status: Married
Overseas tours: Pakistan to Australia 1989-90, 1995-96, to New Zealand and
Australia (World Cup) 1991-92, to England 1992, 1996, to New Zealand 1992-93,
1993-94, 1995-96, 2000-01, to West Indies 1992-93, 1999-2000, to Sri Lanka 1994-95,

1996-97, 2000, to South Africa 1997-98, to Zimbabwe 1997-98, to India 1998-99, to UK, Ireland and Holland (World Cup) 1999

Overseas teams played for: Multan; United Bank; Lahore; Peshawar; National Bank

Cricketers particularly admired: Viv Richards

Other sports followed: Football (Brazil), hockey

Relaxations: Watching videos, eating, spending time with family

Extras: Made first-class debut for Multan v Hyderabad 1986-87. Had first innings figures of 6-81 for Punjab Chief Minister's XI against England tourists at Sahiwal 1987-88. Took 16 wickets in the 1991-92 World Cup, finishing as second highest wicket-taker for Pakistan after Wasim Akram. Somerset's overseas player 1993-95 and 1997-98; Player of the Year 1993. Took 9-198 and 9-186 in successive Tests on Pakistan's tour of Australia 1995-96, following up with 10-171 (including 7-56) in next Test v New Zealand eight days later. Represented Pakistan in 1995-96 World Cup. Man of the Test series v England 1996 (17 wickets; av. 26.29) and v South Africa 1997-98 (14; 27.57). One of *Wisden*'s Five Cricketers of the Year 1997. Released by Somerset at end of 1998 season. Played for Little Stoke in the North Staffordshire/South Cheshire League 2002. Was Surrey's overseas player during August 2002, replacing Saqlain Mushtaq, absent on international duty. Has joined Sussex as an overseas player for 2003

Best batting: 90 Somerset v Sussex, Taunton 1993

Best bowling: 9-93 Multan v Peshawar, Sahiwal 1986-87

2002 Season

	M	Inns	NO	Runs	HS	Avge	100s	50s	Ct	St	O	M	Runs	Wkts	Avge	Best	5wI	10wM
Test																		
All First	2	3	0	66	47	22.00	-	-	1	-	105	23	305	8	38.12	5-71	1	-
1-day Int																		
C & G																		
B & H																		
1-day Lge	1	1	0	16	16	16.00	-	-	-	-	9	2	19	1	19.00	1-19	-	

Career Performances

	M	Inns	NO	Runs	HS	Avge	100s	50s	Ct	St	Balls	Runs	Wkts	Avge	Best	5wI	10wM
Test	50	70	15	636	59	11.56	-	2	22	-	12226	5902	183	32.25	7-56	10	3
All First	206	261	32	3267	90	14.26	-	11	94	-	46057	22848	872	26.20	9-93	59	16
1-day Int	143	76	34	399	34 *	9.50	-	-	30	-	7487	5296	161	32.89	5-36	1	
C & G	11	7	3	100	35	25.00	-	-	4	-	754	362	22	16.45	5-26	1	
B & H	14	10	1	119	31	13.22	-	-	-	-	738	443	20	22.15	7-24	1	
1-day Lge	57	43	12	361	41	11.64	-	-	5	-	2420	1673	56	29.87	3-17	-	

MUSTARD, P. Durham

Name: Philip Mustard
Role: Left-hand bat, wicket-keeper
Born: 8 October 1982, Sunderland
Nickname: Colonel
County debut: 2002
1st-Class 50s: 1
1st-Class catches: 2
Parents: Maureen
Marital status: Single
Education: Usworth Grange; Usworth Comprehensive
Career outside cricket: Landscaping
Cricket moments to forget: 'The first game I played I went out to bat and got a first-ball duck, then went out to keep wicket and dropped catches'
Cricketers particularly admired: Mike Atherton ('professionalism')
Young players to look out for: Nicky Peng
Other sports followed: Football (Middlesbrough)
Relaxations: 'Socialising with friends down the pub'
Extras: Played for Durham Board XI in the NatWest 2000, in the C&G 2001 and in the second round of the C&G 2002, which was played in September 2001. Scored 77-ball 75 on first-class debut v Sri Lankans at Riverside 2002. Represented England U19 v India U19 in one-day series (3/3) 2002
Best batting: 75 Durham v Sri Lankans, Riverside 2002

2002 Season

	M	Inns	NO	Runs	HS	Avge	100s	50s	Ct	St	O	M	Runs	Wkts	Avge	Best	5wI	10wM
Test																		
All First	1	1	0	75	75	75.00	-	1	2	-								
1-day Int																		
C & G																		
B & H																		
1-day Lge																		

Career Performances

	M	Inns	NO	Runs	HS	Avge	100s	50s	Ct	St	Balls	Runs	Wkts	Avge	Best	5wI	10wM
Test																	
All First	1	1	0	75	75	75.00	-	1	2	-							
1-day Int																	
C & G	5	4	1	14	8	4.66	-	-	7	3							
B & H																	
1-day Lge																	

NAPIER, G. R.   Essex

Name: <u>Graham</u> Richard Napier
Role: Right-hand bat, right-arm
medium bowler
Born: 6 January 1980, Colchester
Height: 5ft 10in **Weight:** 12st 7lbs
Nickname: Plank, Napes
County debut: 1997
1st-Class 50s: 3
1st-Class 100s: 1
1st-Class catches: 16
One-Day 5 w. in innings: 1
Place in batting averages: 222nd av. 20.90
(2001 110th av. 31.62)
Place in bowling averages: 78th av. 31.95
(2001 106th av. 37.75)
Strike rate: 51.60 (career 52.24)
Parents: Roger and Carol
Marital status: Single
Family links with cricket: Father played for Palmers Boys School 1st XI (1965-68),
Essex Police divisional teams, and Harwich Immigration CC. 'Now makes guest
appearances on Walton beach'
Education: Myland School, Colchester; Gilberd School, Colchester
Qualifications: NCA coaching award
Overseas tours: England U17 to Bermuda (International Youth Tournament) 1997;
England U19 to South Africa (including U19 World Cup) 1997-98
Overseas teams played for: Campbelltown CC, Sydney 2000-01; North Perth,
Western Australia 2001-02
Career highlights to date: 'Testing myself against the world's best and scoring
some runs'
Cricket moments to forget: 'Being 12th man at Lord's and after a drinks break
dropping the empties on a tray, towels, jumpers and anything else thrown at me in
front of the MCC members'

Young players to look out for: Will Jefferson, Mark Pettini
Other sports followed: Football ('The Tractor Boys' – Ipswich Town FC)
Extras: Represented England U19 in one-day and 'Test' series v Australia U19 1999. Man of the Match award for Essex Board XI v Lancashire Board XI in the NatWest 2000. Scored 73 (losing three cricket balls in the process) and recorded maiden one-day five-wicket return (6-29) v Worcestershire at Chelmsford in the Norwich Union League 2001
Opinions on cricket: 'The introduction of the cricket academy is the best move the ECB have made to help the progress of young cricketers into the first-class and hopefully the international game. Longer lunch and tea breaks.'
Best batting: 104 Essex v CUCCE, Fenner's 2001
Best bowling: 3-47 Essex v Durham, Colchester 2002

2002 Season

	M	Inns	NO	Runs	HS	Avge	100s	50s	Ct	St	O	M	Runs	Wkts	Avge	Best	5wI	10wM
Test																		
All First	9	13	2	230	54 *	20.90	-	1	6	-	172	33	639	20	31.95	3-47	-	-
1-day Int																		
C & G	2	2	1	16	12 *	16.00	-	-	-	-	17	0	81	4	20.25	2-34	-	
B & H	5	5	0	92	41	18.40	-	-	6	-	5.2	0	31	1	31.00	1-31	-	
1-day Lge	15	12	2	150	50	15.00	-	1	7	-	90	6	446	18	24.77	3-10	-	

Career Performances

	M	Inns	NO	Runs	HS	Avge	100s	50s	Ct	St	Balls	Runs	Wkts	Avge	Best	5wI	10wM
Test																	
All First	25	37	4	843	104	25.54	1	3	16	-	1927	1277	37	34.51	3-47	-	-
1-day Int																	
C & G	5	5	1	112	79	28.00	-	1	-	-	144	118	5	23.60	2-34	-	
B & H	10	8	1	118	41	16.85	-	-	6	-	122	138	1	138.00	1-31	-	
1-day Lge	51	41	2	624	78	16.00	-	4	14	-	944	783	32	24.46	6-29	1	

NASH, C. D. Sussex

Name: Christopher (<u>Chris</u>) David Nash
Role: Right-hand bat, right-arm off-spin bowler
Born: 19 May 1983, Cuckfield
Height: 5ft 11in **Weight:** 12st 8lbs
Nickname: Nashy, Nashdog, Spidey
County debut: 2002
1st-Class catches: 1
Strike rate: 105.00 (career 105.00)
Parents: Nick and Jane
Marital status: Single

Family links with cricket: Brother played Sussex 2nd XI and Sussex age groups
Education: Heron Way Primary School; Collyers Sixth Form College; Loughborough University (Sports Science degree)
Qualifications: 11 GCSEs, 3 A-levels
Career outside cricket: University student
Off-season: 'Studying at Loughborough and training with the [Loughborough] Academy'
Overseas tours: Sussex Academy to Cape Town 1999
Career highlights to date: 'First-class debut v Warwickshire at Edgbaston July 2002, taking first wicket in third over'
Cricket moments to forget: 'Getting out first ball on debut (lbw Carter), then having to stand at the non-striker's end for four balls to see if I had to face on a pair in the second innings'

Cricketers particularly admired: Mark 'Milton' Nash, Ryan Leverton, Mark Upton, Luke Marshall, Howard Leasey, Paul Farbrace
Young players to look out for: Richard Hawkes, Lewis Jenkins, Andrew Hodd
Other sports played: Squash (county level; Loughborough University team), football (Horsham FC)
Other sports followed: Rugby, football (Horsham), cricket (Horsham)
Relaxations: 'Fishing, listening to music, going out with friends, training, squash'
Extras: Represented England U15, U17, U18, U19, captaining at U17 and U18 levels; represented England U17 at the ECC Colts Festival in Northern Ireland 1999. Sussex League Young Player of the Year 2001. Played for Loughborough University CCE treble-winning side 2002, scoring 85 v Oxford in the UCCE final at Lord's. Appeared in one Championship match for Sussex 2002; is a Sussex Academy player
Opinions on cricket: 'Cricketers are here to entertain the crowd, so keep the game positive and fun all the time.'
Best bowling: 1-81 Sussex v Warwickshire, Edgbaston 2002

2002 Season

	M	Inns	NO	Runs	HS	Avge	100s	50s	Ct	St	O	M	Runs	Wkts	Avge	Best	5wI	10wM
Test																		
All First	1	2	1	0	0 *	0.00	-	-	1	-	35	1	171	2	85.50	1-81	-	-
1-day Int																		
C & G																			
B & H																			
1-day Lge																			

Career Performances

	M	Inns	NO	Runs	HS	Avge	100s	50s	Ct	St	Balls	Runs	Wkts	Avge	Best	5wI	10wM
Test																	
All First	1	2	1	0	0 *	0.00	-	-	1	-	210	171	2	85.50	1-81	-	-
1-day Int																	
C & G																	
B & H																	
1-day Lge																	

NASH, D. C. Middlesex

Name: <u>David</u> Charles Nash
Role: Right-hand bat, wicket-keeper
Born: 19 January 1978, Chertsey
Height: 5ft 7in **Weight:** 11st 5lbs
Nickname: Nashy, Knocker
County debut: 1995 (one-day), 1997 (first-class)
County cap: 1999
50 dismissals in a season: 1
1st-Class 50s: 15
1st-Class 100s: 4
1st-Class catches: 171
1st-Class stumpings: 14
Place in batting averages: 49th av. 46.14
(2001 101st av. 32.71)
Strike rate: (career 19.00)
Parents: David and Christine
Marital status: Single
Family links with cricket: 'Father played
club cricket; brother plays now and again for Ashford CC; mother is avid watcher and
tea lady'
Education: Chennestone County Middle; Sunbury Manor; Malvern College, Worcs
Qualifications: 9 O-levels, 1 A-level, Levels 1 and 2 cricket coaching, qualified
football referee
Career outside cricket: Qualified cricket coach
Off-season: 'Playing club cricket in Perth for Fremantle'
Overseas tours: England U15 to South Africa 1993; British Airways Youth Team to
West Indies 1993-94; England U19 to Zimbabwe 1995-96, to Pakistan 1996-97;
England A to Kenya and Sri Lanka 1997-98
Overseas teams played for: Fremantle, Perth 2000-01, 2002-03
Career highlights to date: 'Touring with England A and scoring first hundred for
Middlesex at Lord's v Somerset'

Cricket moments to forget: 'All golden ducks'

Cricket superstitions: 'Too many to mention'

Cricketers particularly admired: Angus Fraser, and Andrew Strauss 'for his amazing ability to keep going in all fitness runs when he's knackered after the first 50 yards'

Young players to look out for: Ed Joyce

Other sports played: Rugby, football ('played for Millwall U15 and my district side'), 'and most other sports'

Other sports followed: Rugby (London Irish), football (Chelsea), cricket ('closely watching Richard Johnson's figures on Teletext')

Injuries: Out for 'a couple of games' with back and hamstrings; 'earache listening to all Andy Strauss's excuses as to why his weight is ballooning'

Relaxations: 'Listening to music, watching sport and socialising with friends'

Extras: Represented Middlesex at all ages. Played for England U14, U15, U17 and U19. Once took six wickets in six balls when aged 11 – 'when I could bowl!' *Daily Telegraph* Southern England Batting Award 1993. Seaxe Young Player of the Year 1993. Scored 67 in the B&H v Sussex at Lord's 2002, in the process sharing with Ashley Noffke (58) in a record eighth-wicket partnership for the competition

Opinions on cricket: 'More floodlit cricket should be played – it's the way forward to get the crowds in; and Lord's having lights would be a bonus. The technological side of the game is good with umpires getting help in run-outs, but we don't need to add to this. One-day teams should consist of at least three players under 23. Second-team cricket should mirror first-class, with pitches in particular needing to improve. The two-league system is good and has added to the competitiveness, especially at the end of the season!'

Best batting: 114 Middlesex v Somerset, Lord's 1998

Best bowling: 1-8 Middlesex v Essex, Chelmsford 1997

2002 Season

	M	Inns	NO	Runs	HS	Avge	100s	50s	Ct	St	O	M	Runs	Wkts	Avge	Best	5wI	10wM
Test																		
All First	15	19	5	646	100	46.14	1	4	36	1								
1-day Int																		
C & G	1	0	0	0	0	-	-	-	1	-								
B & H	4	2	0	82	67	41.00	-	1	5	-								
1-day Lge	9	6	3	111	32 *	37.00	-	-	10	-								

Career Performances

	M	Inns	NO	Runs	HS	Avge	100s	50s	Ct	St	Balls	Runs	Wkts	Avge	Best	5wI	10wM
Test																	
All First	86	119	22	3002	114	30.94	4	15	171	14	19	19	1	19.00	1-8	-	-
1-day Int																	
C & G	4	2	0	61	58	30.50	-	1	2	-							
B & H	14	9	3	148	67	24.66	-	1	15	4							
1-day Lge	61	46	11	724	57 *	20.68	-	1	51	11							

NEL, A.   Northamptonshire

Name: Andre Nel
Role: Right-hand bat, right-arm
fast-medium bowler
Born: 15 July 1977, Germiston, Gauteng,
South Africa
County debut: No first-team appearance
Test debut: 2001-02
Tests: 3
One-Day Internationals: 7
1st-Class 5 w. in innings: 7
1st-Class catches: 11
Strike rate: (career 49.86)
Education: Hoërskool Dr E.G. Jansen,
Boksburg

Overseas tours: South African Academy to
Ireland and Scotland 1999; South Africa to
West Indies 2000-01, to Zimbabwe 2001-02
Overseas teams played for: Easterns
Extras: Made One-Day International debut in sixth ODI v West Indies at Port of Spain
2000-01, taking 3-20. Made Test debut in first Test v Zimbabwe at Harare 2001-02,
taking 4-53 in Zimbabwe's first innings. Took 31 wickets (av. 9.19) in four matches for
Easterns in the 2001-02 SuperSport Series. Played for South Africa A v India A in
one-day match at Lenasia 2001-02, taking 4-34. Has joined Northamptonshire as an
overseas player for 2003
Best batting: 44 Easterns v Free State, Benoni 2000-01
Best bowling: 6-25 Easterns v Gauteng, Johannesburg 2001-02

2002 Season (did not make any first-class or one-day appearances)

Career Performances

	M	Inns	NO	Runs	HS	Avge	100s	50s	Ct	St	Balls	Runs	Wkts	Avge	Best	5wI	10wM
Test	3	2	0	7	7	3.50	-	-	-	-	513	289	8	36.12	4-53	-	-
All First	35	39	16	262	44	11.39	-	-	11	-	6483	2600	130	20.00	6-25	7	-
1-day Int	7	2	2	3	3*	-	-	-	2	-	359	241	10	24.10	3-20	-	
C & G																	
B & H																	
1-day Lge																	

NEW, T. J. — Leicestershire

Name: Thomas (Tom) James New
Role: Left-hand bat, wicket-keeper
Born: 18 January 1985, Sutton-in-Ashfield
Height: 5ft 10in **Weight:** 9st 7lbs
Nickname: Newy
County debut: No first-team appearance
Parents: Martin and Louise
Marital status: Single
Education: Croft School; Quarrydale Comprehensive
Qualifications: GCSEs
Off-season: 'Staying in England – working on fitness, working on weaknesses'
Overseas teams played for: Geelong Cement, Victoria 2001-02
Career highlights to date: 'Captaining England U15 in Costcutter World Challenge 2000'
Cricket moments to forget: 'Losing semi-final of Costcutter World Challenge 2000 to Pakistan'
Cricket superstitions: 'None'
Cricketers particularly admired: Ian Healy, Jack Russell
Young players to look out for: Luke Wright
Other sports played: Rugby (County U14/U15), football
Other sports followed: Football (Mansfield Town FC)
Relaxations: 'Golf, music'
Extras: Played for Notts U12, U13, U15, U16 and Midlands U13, U14, U15. Captained England U15 in Costcutter World Challenge [U15 World Cup] 2000. Sir John Hobbs Silver Jubilee Memorial Prize 2000. England U17-U19 squads 2000-03; reserve for U19 tour to Australia 2002-03. Played for Leicestershire Board XI in the C&G 2001 and in the first round of the C&G 2003, which was played in August 2002

2002 Season (did not make any first-class or one-day appearances for his county)

Career Performances

	M	Inns	NO	Runs	HS	Avge	100s	50s	Ct	St	Balls	Runs	Wkts	Avge	Best	5wI	10wM
Test																	
All First																	
1-day Int																	
C & G	2	2	0	9	6	4.50	-	-	-	-							
B & H																	
1-day Lge																	

NEWELL, K.　　　　　　　　　　Glamorgan

Name: Keith Newell
Role: Right-hand bat, right-arm medium bowler
Born: 25 March 1972, Crawley
Height: 6ft **Weight:** 13st
Nickname: Croc, Nightstalker, Greavsie
County debut: 1993 (one-day, Sussex), 1995 (first-class, Sussex), 1999 (Glamorgan)
1st-Class 50s: 11
1st-Class 100s: 5
1st-Class catches: 25
One-Day 100s: 1
One-Day 5 w. in innings: 1
Place in batting averages: (2001 100th av. 32.88)
Strike rate: (career 85.45)
Parents: Peter Charles and Julie Anne
Marital status: Single
Family links with cricket: Brother Mark played for Sussex and Derbyshire. Brother Jonathan has played for Sussex U17 and U19
Education: Gossops Green Junior School; Ifield Community College
Qualifications: 'A few GCSEs', coaching certificate
Career outside cricket: Cricket coach
Overseas teams played for: Zimbabwe Universals 1989-90; Bulawayo Athletic Club 1991-92, 1995-96; Riverside CC, Wellington 1992-93; Randwick CC, Sydney 1998-99; Balmain Tigers, Sydney 2001-02
Cricketers particularly admired: Ian Botham, Alan Wells
Young players to look out for: Simon Jones, Mark Wallace, 'Kirbs'
Other sports played: Table tennis
Other sports followed: Football (Spurs)
Relaxations: 'Watching films and going out every now and then'
Extras: Released by Sussex at end of 1998 season and joined Glamorgan. Scored a 53-ball 97 to set up victory for Glamorgan against Essex at Chelmsford in the Norwich Union League 2001. Released by Glamorgan at the end of the 2002 season
Best batting: 135 Sussex v West Indians, Hove 1995
Best bowling: 4-61 Sussex v Kent, Horsham 1997

2002 Season

	M	Inns	NO	Runs	HS	Avge	100s	50s	Ct	St	O	M	Runs	Wkts	Avge	Best	5wI	10wM
Test																		
All First																		
1-day Int																		
C & G	1	1	0	12	12	12.00	-	-	-	-								
B & H	4	4	0	34	13	8.50	-	-	-	-	2	0	16	1	16.00	1-16	-	
1-day Lge	1	1	0	4	4	4.00	-	-	-	-								

Career Performances

	M	Inns	NO	Runs	HS	Avge	100s	50s	Ct	St	Balls	Runs	Wkts	Avge	Best	5wI	10wM
Test																	
All First	72	123	14	2930	135	26.88	5	11	25	-	2051	1023	24	42.62	4-61	-	-
1-day Int																	
C & G	12	10	2	429	129	53.62	1	2	1	-	268	213	3	71.00	1-31	-	
B & H	25	23	1	411	62 *	18.68	-	1	3	-	351	306	8	38.25	3-37	-	
1-day Lge	87	78	5	1641	97	22.47	-	7	15	-	1139	947	29	32.65	5-33	1	

NEWMAN, S. A.   Surrey

Name: Scott Alexander Newman
Role: Left-hand bat
Born: 3 November 1979, Epsom
Height: 6ft 1in **Weight:** 13st 7lbs
Nickname: Seve, Scotty
County debut: 2001 (one-day),
2002 (first-class)
1st-Class 50s: 1
1st-Class 100s: 1
1st-Class catches: 3
Parents: Ken and Sandy
Marital status: Engaged
Children: Lemoy, 1985;
Brandon, 8 September 2002
Family links with cricket: 'Dad and brother
both played'
Education: Cumnor House School, Purley;
Trinity School, Croydon; Brighton University
Qualifications: 10 GCSEs, GNVQ (Advanced) Business Studies
Career outside cricket: 'Father'
Off-season: 'Training hard and changing nappies'
Overseas tours: SCB to Barbados

Overseas teams played for: Mount Lawley CC, Perth
Career highlights to date: 'First-class debut 2002 – 99'
Cricket moments to forget: 'Plinking it on TV against Derby'
Cricketers particularly admired: 'All of the Surrey dressing room (especially Tim Murtagh)'
Young players to look out for: 'Anybody who loves the game'
Other sports played: Football, rugby ('most sports really')
Other sports followed: Rugby, football, American sports
Relaxations: 'Music and chilling out with my family'
Extras: Played for Surrey Board XI in the C&G 2001 and in the second round of the C&G 2002, which was played in September 2001. Scored 99 on first-class debut v Hampshire at The Oval 2002. Scored maiden first-class century (183) v Leicestershire at The Oval 2002, in the process sharing with Ian Ward (118) in a new record opening partnership for Surrey in matches v Leicestershire (227)
Opinions on cricket: 'Less EU players; more English youngsters to be picked.'
Best batting: 183 Surrey v Leicestershire, The Oval 2002

2002 Season

	M	Inns	NO	Runs	HS	Avge	100s	50s	Ct	St	O	M	Runs	Wkts	Avge	Best	5wI	10wM
Test																		
All First	3	5	0	322	183	64.40	1	1	3	-								
1-day Int																		
C & G																		
B & H	1	1	0	14	14	14.00	-	-	-	-								
1-day Lge	3	3	0	71	37	23.66	-	-	-	-								

Career Performances

	M	Inns	NO	Runs	HS	Avge	100s	50s	Ct	St	Balls	Runs	Wkts	Avge	Best	5wI	10wM
Test																	
All First	3	5	0	322	183	64.40	1	1	3	-							
1-day Int																	
C & G	3	3	0	100	49	33.33	-	-	1	-							
B & H	1	1	0	14	14	14.00	-	-	-	-							
1-day Lge	5	5	0	81	37	16.20	-	-	-	-							

62. Which Pakistan Test player scored 2074 first-class runs for Glamorgan and Cambridge University in 1972?

NIXON, P. A.   Leicestershire

Name: <u>Paul</u> Andrew Nixon
Role: Left-hand bat, wicket-keeper
Born: 21 October 1970, Carlisle
Height: 6ft **Weight:** 12st 10lbs
Nickname: Badger, Nico, Nobby
County debut: 1989 (Leicestershire),
2000 (Kent)
County cap: 1994 (Leicestershire),
2000 (Kent)
1000 runs in a season: 1
50 dismissals in a season: 6
1st-Class 50s: 36
1st-Class 100s: 13
1st-Class catches: 619
1st-Class stumpings: 50
Place in batting averages: 90th av. 37.60
(2001 77th av. 38.29)
Parents: Brian and Sylvia
Wife and date of marriage: Jen, 9 October 1999
Family links with cricket: 'Grandad and father played local league cricket. Mum made the teas for Edenhall CC, Penrith'
Education: Langwathby Primary; Ullswater High
Qualifications: 2 O-levels, 6 GCSEs, coaching certificates
Career outside cricket: 'Used to be farming. Father sold up'
Off-season: 'Moving up to Leicester; then Australia after Christmas'
Overseas tours: Cumbria Schools U15 to Denmark 1985; Leicestershire to Barbados, to Jamaica, to Holland, to Johannesburg, to Bloemfontein; MCC to Bangladesh 1999-2000; England A to India and Bangladesh 1994-95; England to Pakistan and Sri Lanka 2000-01
Overseas teams played for: Melville, Western Australia; North Fremantle, Western Australia; Mitchells Plain, Cape Town 1993; Primrose CC, Cape Town 1995-96
Career highlights to date: 'Winning the Championship in 1996 with Leicestershire. Receiving phone call from David Graveney advising me of England [tour] selection'
Cricket moments to forget: 'Losing Lord's one-day finals'
Cricketers particularly admired: David Gower, Ian Botham, Ian Healy, Viv Richards
Young players to look out for: Rob Key, James Troughton
Other sports played: Golf, training with Leicester Tigers rugby team
Other sports followed: Football (Leicester City, Carlisle United, Liverpool), rugby (Leicester Tigers)
Relaxations: Team-building; winning books and tapes; health hydros
Extras: County captain of Cumbria at football, cricket and rugby. Youngest person to score a century against Yorkshire (at U15). Played for England U15. Played in Minor

Counties Championship for Cumberland at 16. MCC Young Pro in 1988. Took eight catches in debut match v Warwickshire at Hinckley in 1989. Played for Carlisle United. Leicestershire Young Player of the Year two years running. In 1994 became only second Leicestershire wicket-keeper to score 1000 runs in a season (1046). Voted Cumbria Sports Personality of the Year 1994-95. Was part of Leicestershire's County Championship winning side in 1996 and 1998. Left Leicestershire at end of 1999 season and joined Kent for 2000. Captained First-Class Counties Select XI v New Zealand A at Milton Keynes 2000. B&H Gold Award for his 65* v Surrey at Canterbury 2001 and for his 42 (plus three catches) v Hampshire at West End 2002. Scored 60 v Worcestershire at Canterbury in the NUL 2002, in the process sharing with Matthew Walker (94) in a record sixth-wicket partnership for Kent in the one-day league (116). Played 300 first-class games in succession and has missed only four Championship matches since debut in 1989. Released by Kent at the end of the 2002 season and has rejoined Leicestershire for 2003

Opinions on cricket: '1. "Premier Division" rather than "Division One". 2. Regional cricket against tourists. 3. Start season four weeks later so we go on into October. 4. Bats should have any company's name on them. 5. All kids under 16 should only pay £10 per year membership. 6. Two teams go up, two teams go down in Championship divisions.'

Best batting: 134* Kent v Hampshire, Canterbury 2000

2002 Season

	M	Inns	NO	Runs	HS	Avge	100s	50s	Ct	St	O	M	Runs	Wkts	Avge	Best	5wI	10wM
Test																		
All First	16	30	7	865	103	37.60	1		6	49	4	0.3	0	8	0	-	-	-	-
1-day Int																		
C & G	4	4	2	119	39 *	59.50	-	-	3	3								
B & H	5	4	0	71	42	17.75	-	-	7	1								
1-day Lge	16	16	4	341	60	28.41	-	1	20	6								

Career Performances

	M	Inns	NO	Runs	HS	Avge	100s	50s	Ct	St	Balls	Runs	Wkts	Avge	Best	5wI	10wM
Test																	
All First	236	339	77	8482	134 *	32.37	13	36	619	50	33	22	0	-	-	-	-
1-day Int																	
C & G	31	25	10	465	51	31.00	-	1	38	10							
B & H	39	31	7	558	65 *	23.25	-	2	47	7							
1-day Lge	184	161	29	2917	96 *	22.09	-	12	180	41							

NOFFKE, A. A. — Middlesex

Name: <u>Ashley</u> Allan Noffke
Role: Right-hand bat, right-arm fast bowler; all-rounder
Born: 30 April 1977, Sunshine Coast, Queensland, Australia
Height: 6ft 3in **Weight:** 14st
Nickname: Noffers, Wombat
County debut: 2002
1st-Class 50s: 2
1st-Class 5 w. in innings: 6
1st-Class 10 w. in match: 1
1st-Class catches: 10
Place in batting averages: 207th av. 22.55
Place in bowling averages: 25th av. 25.06
Strike rate: 40.68 (career 50.28)
Parents: Rob & Lesley Simpson and Allan Noffke

Wife and date of marriage: Michelle, 8 April 2000
Family links with cricket: Father played club cricket
Education: Buderim Primary; Immanuel Lutheran College; Sunshine Coast University
Qualifications: Bachelor of Business, ACB Level 2 coaching certificate
Off-season: Playing cricket for Queensland
Overseas tours: Commonwealth Bank Cricket Academy to Zimbabwe 1998-99; Australia to England 2001
Overseas teams played for: Queensland 1998 –
Career highlights to date: 'Man of the Match in a winning Pura Cup final for Queensland. Being selected for Australia for 2001 Ashes tour'
Cricket moments to forget: 'Rolling my ankle playing for Australia v Sussex, forcing me home from the Ashes tour'
Cricket superstitions: 'None'
Cricketers particularly admired: Steve Waugh
Young players to look out for: Ed Joyce, Lee Carseldine, Jerry Cassell
Other sports played: Golf
Other sports followed: Rugby league, rugby union, 'enjoy all sports'
Relaxations: Fishing
Extras: Leading wicket-taker in Brisbane first-grade cricket competition 1997-98 and 1998-99. Made first-class debut for Commonwealth Bank [Australian] Cricket Academy v Zimbabwe Cricket Academy XI 1998-99. Queensland Academy of Sport Player of the Year 1998-99. Man of the Match in the Pura Cup final v Victoria 2000-01 for his 7-120 and 43 runs batting as nightwatchman. Awarded an ACB contract 2001-02 on his 24th birthday, after just six first-class matches. Called up for Australia

tour to England 2001 as a replacement for the injured Nathan Bracken. Sunshine Coast Sportstar of the Year 2001. Was Middlesex's overseas player for two periods during the 2002 season, replacing Abdul Razzaq, absent on international duty; has returned as an overseas player for 2003. Scored 58 in the B&H v Sussex at Lord's 2002, in the process sharing with David Nash (67) in a record eighth-wicket partnership for the competition. Took a career-best 8-24 from 15 overs v Derbyshire at Derby 2002, including a spell of 7-6 from 35 balls; took 4-84 in the second innings for a maiden first-class ten-wicket match return

Best batting: 76 Middlesex v Worcestershire, Worcester 2002
Best bowling: 8-24 Middlesex v Derbyshire, Derby 2002
Stop press: Represented Australia A v England tourists at Hobart 2002-03

2002 Season

	M	Inns	NO	Runs	HS	Avge	100s	50s	Ct	St	O	M	Runs	Wkts	Avge	Best	5wl	10wM
Test																		
All First	8	10	1	203	76	22.55	-	1	3	-	305.1	57	1128	45	25.06	8-24	3	1
1-day Int																		
C & G																		
B & H	4	2	0	58	58	29.00	-	1	1	-	34	4	166	8	20.75	4-34	-	
1-day Lge																		

Career Performances

	M	Inns	NO	Runs	HS	Avge	100s	50s	Ct	St	Balls	Runs	Wkts	Avge	Best	5wl	10wM
Test																	
All First	28	31	6	610	76	24.40	-	2	10	-	5733	3143	114	27.57	8-24	6	1
1-day Int																	
C & G																	
B & H	4	2	0	58	58	29.00	-	1	1	-	204	166	8	20.75	4-34	-	
1-day Lge																	

NOON, W. M.   Nottinghamshire

Name: Wayne Michael Noon
Role: Right-hand bat, wicket-keeper
Born: 5 February 1971, Grimsby
Height: 5ft 9in **Weight:** 11st 7lbs
Nickname: Noonie, Spain Boon
County debut: 1988 (one-day, Northants), 1989 (first-class, Northants), 1994 (Notts)
County cap: 1995 (Notts)
1st-Class 50s: 12
1st-Class catches: 188
1st-Class stumpings: 20
Parents: Trafford and Rosemary

Marital status: Married
Education: Caistor Grammar School
Qualifications: 5 O-levels
Career outside cricket: Manager of
G. Atkins (bookmakers)
Overseas tours: Lincolnshire U15 to
Pakistan 1984; Rutland tourists to South
Africa 1988; England YC to Australia 1989-
90 (captain); Northamptonshire to Durban
1992, to Cape Town 1993
Overseas teams played for: Burnside West,
Christchurch, New Zealand 1989-90,
1995-96; Rivertonians, Cape Town 1993-94;
Canterbury, Christchurch 1994-95
Cricketers particularly admired:
Ian Botham
Other sports followed: Football (Lincoln
City), horse racing (flat)
Relaxations: 'Having a bet. Eating out and having a pint'
Extras: Played for England YC v New Zealand YC 1989; captain v Pakistan YC 1990.
Was the 1000th player to appear in the Sunday League competition. Broke the Northants
record for most 2nd XI hundreds in one season in 1993. Took seven catches for Notts in
Kent's first innings at Trent Bridge 1999, breaking Bruce French's county record of six.
Appointed 2nd XI captain for 2003. Granted a benefit for 2003
Best batting: 83 Nottinghamshire v Northamptonshire, Northampton 1997

2002 Season

	M	Inns	NO	Runs	HS	Avge	100s	50s	Ct	St	O	M	Runs	Wkts	Avge	Best	5wI	10wM
Test																		
All First	1	1	0	15	15	15.00	-	-	1	-								
1-day Int																		
C & G																		
B & H																		
1-day Lge																		

Career Performances

	M	Inns	NO	Runs	HS	Avge	100s	50s	Ct	St	Balls	Runs	Wkts	Avge	Best	5wI	10wM
Test																	
All First	90	141	22	2489	83	20.91	-	12	188	20	30	34	0	-	-	-	-
1-day Int																	
C & G	7	4	1	73	34	24.33	-	-	4	2							
B & H	18	11	3	152	46	19.00	-	-	9	4							
1-day Lge	81	52	14	477	38	12.55	-	-	62	15							

ORMOND, J.   Surrey

Name: James Ormond
Role: Right-hand bat, right-arm fast-'ish'
bowler, can also bowl off spin
Born: 20 August 1977, Walsgrave, Coventry
Height: 6ft 3in **Weight:** 15st
Nickname: Jimmy, Horse
County debut: 1995 (Leicestershire),
2002 (Surrey)
County cap: 1999 (Leicestershire)
Test debut: 2001
Tests: 2
50 wickets in a season: 2
1st-Class 50s: 1
1st-Class 5 w. in innings: 15
1st-Class 10 w. in match: 1
1st-Class catches: 18
Place in batting averages: 257th av. 16.00
(2001 199th av. 19.30)
Place in bowling averages: 105th av. 34.90 (2001 57th av. 28.91)
Strike rate: 57.07 (career 52.43)
Parents: Richard and Margaret
Marital status: Single
Family links with cricket: 'Dad played years of cricket in Warwickshire'
Education: St Anthony's, Bedworth; St Thomas More, Nuneaton; North Warwickshire
College of Further Education
Qualifications: 6 GCSEs
Overseas tours: England U19 to Zimbabwe 1995-96; England A to Kenya and Sri
Lanka 1997-98; England to India and New Zealand 2001-02
Overseas teams played for: Sydney University CC 1996, 1998, 1999
Cricketers particularly admired: Curtly Ambrose, Courtney Walsh, Allan Donald,
Sachin Tendulkar, Brian Lara, Steve Griffin
Young players to look out for: Darren Stevens
Other sports played: Football, mountain biking, 'anything'
Other sports followed: Football (Coventry City)
Relaxations: Spending time with friends and family
Extras: Played for the Development of Excellence side and England U19 against
South Africa U19 in 1995. Played for England U19 against New Zealand U19 in 1996.
Won Leicestershire's 2nd XI bowling award. NBC Denis Compton Award for the most
promising young Leicestershire player 1998, 1999, 2000. B&H Gold Award for his
4-25 v Yorkshire at Leicester 2001. Left Leicestershire in the 2001-02 off-season and
joined Surrey for 2002. Recorded maiden first-class ten-wicket match return (10-178)
v Warwickshire at The Oval 2002

Best batting: 50* Leicestershire v Warwickshire, Leicester 1999
Best bowling: 6-33 Leicestershire v Somerset, Leicester 1998

2002 Season

	M	Inns	NO	Runs	HS	Avge	100s	50s	Ct	St	O	M	Runs	Wkts	Avge	Best	5wI	10wM
Test																		
All First	15	17	4	208	43 *	16.00	-	-	6	-	485.1	87	1780	51	34.90	5-62	2	1
1-day Int																		
C & G	4	1	1	5	5 *	-	-	-	2	-	24.1	0	164	0	-	-	-	
B & H	4	3	1	19	14 *	9.50	-	-	-	-	32.2	2	160	8	20.00	3-52	-	
1-day Lge	2	0	0	0	0	-	-	-	1	-	9	0	25	0	-	-	-	

Career Performances

	M	Inns	NO	Runs	HS	Avge	100s	50s	Ct	St	Balls	Runs	Wkts	Avge	Best	5wI	10wM
Test	2	4	1	38	18	12.66	-	-	-	-	372	185	2	92.50	1-70	-	-
All First	80	94	22	997	50 *	13.84	-	1	18	-	14577	7707	278	27.72	6-33	15	1
1-day Int																	
C & G	12	6	4	34	18 *	17.00	-	-	3	-	607	456	10	45.60	2-16	-	
B & H	15	11	4	59	14 *	8.42	-	-	3	-	720	492	27	18.22	4-25	-	
1-day Lge	53	32	18	173	18	12.35	-	-	11	-	2259	1519	68	22.33	4-12	-	

OSTLER, D. P. Warwickshire

Name: <u>Dominic</u> Piers Ostler
Role: Right-hand bat, right-arm medium bowler
Born: 15 July 1970, Solihull
Height: 6ft 2in **Weight:** 14st
Nickname: Ossie
County debut: 1990
County cap: 1991
Benefit: 2000
1000 runs in a season: 6
1st-Class 50s: 66
1st-Class 100s: 14
1st-Class 200s: 2
1st-Class catches: 256
One-Day 100s: 3
Place in batting averages: 62nd av. 43.29
(2001 40th av. 47.27)
Strike rate: (career 239.00)
Parents: Mike and Ann
Wife and date of marriage: Karen, 14 October 2000

Family links with cricket: Brother used to play for Knowle and Dorridge CC
Education: Our Lady of the Wayside; Princethorpe College; Solihull College of Technology
Qualifications: 4 O-levels, A-levels, City and Guilds Recreation Course
Career outside cricket: 'In business'
Off-season: 'Spending time with the wife; playing snooker for Shirley Social Club; bit of golf; trying to earn some money'
Overseas tours: Gladstone Small's Benefit Tour to Barbados 1991; England A to Pakistan 1995-96; England XI to New Zealand (Cricket Max) 1997; Andy Moles' Benefit Tour to Barbados 1997
Overseas teams played for: Avendale CC, Cape Town 1991-92
Career highlights to date: 'Winning eight trophies'
Cricket moments to forget: 'Dropping a slip catch in final at Lord's'
Cricket superstitions: 'None'
Cricketers particularly admired: Jason Ratcliffe, Simon Millington, Graeme Welch
Young players to look out for: Ian Bell, Nick Warren
Other sports played: Golf, snooker
Other sports followed: Football (Birmingham City FC)
Injuries: Out for three weeks with a broken finger
Relaxations: 'Spending time with wife, Karen; snooker and golf'
Extras: Was a member of the Warwickshire U19 side that won the Esso U19 County Festivals in 1988 and 1989. Has collected winner's medals for the B&H Cup, County Championship, NatWest Trophy and Sunday League. Scored 134* off 114 balls v Gloucestershire at Edgbaston in the Norwich Union League 2001, equalling Nick Knight's Warwickshire record for the highest individual score in the one-day league. Scored 175 v Somerset at Edgbaston 2002, in the process passing 10,000 runs in first-class cricket. Scored 240-ball 225 v Yorkshire at Edgbaston 2002
Opinions on cricket: 'Got to improve wickets. Longer tea interval – 20 minutes is no good to anyone!'
Best batting: 225 Warwickshire v Yorkshire, Edgbaston 2002
Best bowling: 1-46 Warwickshire v Middlesex, Edgbaston 2000

2002 Season

	M	Inns	NO	Runs	HS	Avge	100s	50s	Ct	St	O	M	Runs	Wkts	Avge	Best	5wI	10wM
Test																		
All First	14	25	1	1039	225	43.29	2	5	24	-	1	0	13	0	-	-	-	-
1-day Int																		
C & G	2	2	0	8	8	4.00	-	-	1	-								
B & H	1	1	0	17	17	17.00	-	-	1	-								
1-day Lge	13	13	2	465	103 *	42.27	1	2	5	-								

Career Performances

	M	Inns	NO	Runs	HS	Avge	100s	50s	Ct	St	Balls	Runs	Wkts	Avge	Best	5wI	10wM
Test																	
All First	200	328	25	10737	225	35.43	16	66	256	-	239	262	1	262.00	1-46	-	-
1-day Int																	
C & G	42	41	4	1134	104	30.64	1	8	20	-	15	10	1	10.00	1-4	-	
B & H	41	39	5	1274	87	37.47	-	10	19	-							
1-day Lge	172	162	24	4565	134 *	33.07	2	31	53	-	6	4	0	-		-	-

PANESAR, M. S. Northamptonshire

Name: <u>Mudhsuden</u> Singh Panesar
Role: Left-hand bat, slow left-arm bowler
Born: 25 April 1982, Luton
Height: 6ft 1in **Weight:** 12st 7lbs
Nickname: Monty
County debut: 2001
1st-Class catches: 3
Place in bowling averages: 82nd av. 32.58
(2001 74th av. 32.54)
Strike rate: 67.35 (career 62.64)
Parents: Paramjit and Gursharan
Marital status: Single
Family links with cricket: 'Dad played local
cricket'
Education: St Matthew's Junior School;
Stopsley High School; Bedford Modern
School; Loughborough University
Qualifications: 10 GCSEs, 3 A-levels
Off-season : 'Academy'
Overseas tours: Bedford Modern School to Barbados 1999; England U19 to India
2000-01; Northamptonshire to Grenada 2001-02; British Universities to South Africa
2002; ECB National Academy to Australia and Sri Lanka 2002-03
Cricketers particularly admired: Sachin Tendulkar, Steve Waugh, Matthew Hayden,
Rahul Dravid
Other sports played: Badminton, tennis, snooker
Other sports followed: Football (Arsenal), tennis (Pete Sampras)
Relaxations: Music, cars, wildlife
Extras: Represented England U19 v Sri Lanka U19 in one-day and 'Test' series
2000 and v West Indies U19 in 'Test' series (1/3) 2001. Had match figures of 8-131
on first-class debut v Leicestershire at Northampton 2001, including 4-11 in the
second innings. NBC Denis Compton Award for the most promising young

Northamptonshire player 2001. Played for Loughborough University CCE 2002.
Represented British Universities v Sri Lankans at Northampton and v West Indies A
(50-over match) at The Parks 2002
Best batting: 10 Northamptonshire v Leicestershire, Northampton 2001
Best bowling: 4-11 Northamptonshire v Leicestershire, Northampton 2001

2002 Season

	M	Inns	NO	Runs	HS	Avge	100s	50s	Ct	St	O	M	Runs	Wkts	Avge	Best	5wI	10wM
Test																		
All First	6	6	2	4	2 *	1.00	-	-	3	-	190.5	55	554	17	32.58	4-42	-	-
1-day Int																		
C & G																			
B & H																			
1-day Lge	1	1	1	16	16 *	-	-	-	-	-	9	0	26	0	-		-	-

Career Performances

	M	Inns	NO	Runs	HS	Avge	100s	50s	Ct	St	Balls	Runs	Wkts	Avge	Best	5wI	10wM
Test																	
All First	8	9	4	19	10	3.80	-	-	3	-	1754	912	28	32.57	4-11	-	-
1-day Int																	
C & G																		
B & H																		
1-day Lge	1	1	1	16	16 *	-	-	-	-	-	54	26	0	-		-	-

---

63. Which Leicestershire batsman who played for Ceylon
(Sri Lanka) in the 1950s scored an eight-minute fifty v Nottinghamshire
at Trent Bridge in 1965?

PARK, C. L.   Northamptonshire

Name: Christopher (Chris) Leslie Park
Role: Right-hand bat, wicket-keeper
Born: 22 July 1983, Poole
Height: 5ft 8in **Weight:** 10st 2lbs
Nickname: Parklife, Parkside, Brenda
County debut: No first-team appearance
Parents: Basil and Madge
Marital status: Single (girlfriend Jenny)
Family links with cricket: 'Dad plays for
local teams with two brothers'
Education: Hayeswood First School; St
Michaels Middle/Upper School;
QE Sixth Form
Career outside cricket: Fitness instructor
Off-season: 'Relaxing back down home;
working; seeing girlfriend; enjoying myself;
training'

Career highlights to date: '2nd XI debut.
Colts Player of the Year 2002. Young Player of the Year (league) 2002'
Cricket moments to forget: 'Sharing hotel room with Adam Shantry/Tom Huggins'
Cricket superstitions: 'Never sit next to Adam Shantry in changing room'
Cricketers particularly admired: Adam Gilchrist
Young players to look out for: Adam Shantry, Mark Powell, Chris Goode
Other sports played: Football (YTS contract with AFC Bournemouth)
Other sports followed: Football (Bournemouth, Man Utd)
Injuries: Broken fingers
Relaxations: 'Music, shopping, sleeping, fishing'
Extras: Played for Dorset in the second round of the C&G 2002, which was played in
September 2001, and for Northamptonshire Board XI in the first round of the C&G
2003, which was played in August 2002. Northamptonshire Colts Player of the Year
2002. Northamptonshire Championship Young Player of the Year 2002. Is
Northamptonshire Academy player
Opinions on cricket: 'Intense; too serious – people should be playing with a smile on
their face.'

Career Performances

	M	Inns	NO	Runs	HS	Avge	100s	50s	Ct	St	Balls	Runs	Wkts	Avge	Best	5wI	10wM
Test																	
All First																	
1-day Int																	
C & G	2	2	0	38	35	19.00	-	-	1	-							
B & H																	
1-day Lge																	

PARKIN, O. T. Glamorgan

Name: <u>Owen</u> Thomas Parkin
Role: Right-hand bat, right-arm medium-fast swing bowler
Born: 24 September 1972, Coventry
Height: 6ft 3in **Weight:** 13st
Nickname: Parky, Cala, Long-term, Off-road
County debut: 1994
1st-Class 5 w. in innings: 2
1st-Class catches: 11
One-Day 5 w. in innings: 1
Strike rate: 71.71 (career 56.32)
Parents: Vernon Cyrus and Sarah Patricia
Wife and date of marriage: Diane Margaret, 29 September 2001
Children: Benjamin Lewis, January 2003
Family links with cricket: 'None – but enjoyed by all family'
Education: Summerbee Juniors; Bournemouth School; Bath University
Qualifications: 9 GCSEs, 4 A-levels, 1 S-level, BSc (Hons) Mathematics
Career outside cricket: Marketing department of GCCC
Off-season: 'As above'
Overseas tours: Dorset Youth to Denmark
Overseas teams played for: Kew, Melbourne 1992-93; North Balwyn, Melbourne 1994-95; Balmain, Sydney 1997-99; ATW Clubites, Bundaberg, Queensland 1999-2000
Career highlights to date: 'Lord's final, and hitting winning runs against Derby in 2000' (*The latter batting at No. 11 in NUL after 10 required off 14 balls*)
Cricket moments to forget: 'Dropping Chris Adams at Hove 2000'

Cricket superstitions: 'Never cross on the stairs (Sophia Gardens)'
Cricketers particularly admired: Malcolm Marshall, Richard Hadlee
Young players to look out for: Adam Harrison
Other sports played: 'Most sports socially'
Other sports followed: Rugby, football (Nottingham Forest), golf
Relaxations: '*Telegraph* crossword'
Extras: Played for Dorset in the NatWest Trophy 1992 and 1993. ASW Young Player of the Month July 1994. Took 5 for 28 v Sussex on debut in Sunday League at Hove 1996 – a Glamorgan record
Opinions on cricket: 'Not overly pleased with the advent of two overseas players and the influx of "Euro" players. We keep hearing "invest in academies – bring the young players on" and yet close the door on them to another place in the team. Seems hypocritical to me! I like the idea of the 20-over game – the more self-financing cricket we play the better. Why not change Championship cricket to three six-sided leagues (ten games – perfect both from a player's perspective and commercially)?'
Best batting: 24* Glamorgan v Essex, Chelmsford 1998
Best bowling: 5-24 Glamorgan v Somerset, Cardiff, 1998

2002 Season

	M	Inns	NO	Runs	HS	Avge	100s	50s	Ct	St	O	M	Runs	Wkts	Avge	Best	5wI	10wM
Test																		
All First	3	3	0	23	16	7.66	-	-	1	-	83.4	19	247	7	35.28	2-47	-	-
1-day Int																		
C & G																		
B & H	3	2	0	1	1	0.50	-	-	1	-	19.4	1	94	2	47.00	1-31	-	
1-day Lge	5	1	1	14	14 *	-	-	-	1	-	34.3	3	179	6	29.83	2-44	-	

Career Performances

	M	Inns	NO	Runs	HS	Avge	100s	50s	Ct	St	Balls	Runs	Wkts	Avge	Best	5wI	10wM
Test																	
All First	40	47	20	226	24 *	8.37	-	-	11	-	6027	2992	107	27.96	5-24	2	-
1-day Int																	
C & G	11	5	2	3	2	1.00	-	-	5	-	520	361	10	36.10	3-23	-	
B & H	11	7	3	17	8	4.25	-	-	3	-	502	404	16	25.25	4-60	-	
1-day Lge	73	26	11	57	14 *	3.80	-	-	14	-	3101	2452	97	25.27	5-28	1	

PARSONS, K. A.   Somerset

Name: <u>Keith</u> Alan Parsons
Role: Right-hand bat, right-arm
medium bowler
Born: 2 May 1973, Taunton
Height: 6ft 1in **Weight:** 14st 7lbs
Nickname: Pilot, Pars, Orv
County debut: 1992
County cap: 1999
1st-Class 50s: 23
1st-Class 100s: 5
1st-Class 5 w. in innings: 2
1st-Class catches: 98
One-day 100s: 1
Place in batting averages: 189th av. 24.20
(2001 82nd av. 36.28)
Place in bowling averages: 121st av. 39.52
Strike rate: 61.85 (career 75.33)

Parents: Alan and Lynne
Wife and date of marriage: Sharon, 12 January 2002
Children: Joseph Luke, 17 October 2002
Family links with cricket: Identical twin brother, Kevin, was on the Somerset staff
1992-94 and now captains the Somerset Board XI. Father played six seasons for
Somerset 2nd XI and captained National Civil Service XI
Education: Bishop Henderson Primary School; The Castle School, Taunton; Richard
Huish Sixth Form College, Taunton
Qualifications: 8 GCSEs, 3 A-levels, NCA senior coach
Off-season: 'Working for Set Square Recruitment Agency in Taunton'
Overseas tours: Castle School to Barbados 1989; Somerset CCC to Cape Town 1999,
2000, 2001
Overseas teams played for: Kapiti Old Boys, Horowhenua, New Zealand 1992-93;
Taita District, Wellington, New Zealand 1993-96; Wembley Downs CC, Perth 1998
Career highlights to date: 'C&G final 2001 v Leicestershire – great to win a trophy,
and Man of the Match capped a dream day'
Cricket moments to forget: 'Any bad days at Taunton'
Cricket superstitions: 'None'
Cricketers particularly admired: Andy Caddick, Marcus Trescothick,
Glenn McGrath, Saqlain Mushtaq
Other sports followed: Rugby union (Bath RFC), football (Nottingham Forest FC),
golf, horse racing
Relaxations: Playing golf, watching movies, listening to music 'and the odd social
pint of beer'

504

Extras: Captained two National Cup winning sides – Taunton St Andrews in National U15 Club Championship and Richard Huish College in National U17 School Championship. Represented English Schools at U15 and U19 level. Somerset Young Player of the Year 1993. C&G Man of the Match award for his 52-ball 60* (including sixes from the last two balls of the innings) and 2-40 in the final v Leicestershire at Lord's 2001. C&G Man of the Match award for his 100-ball 121 (his maiden one-day century) in the quarter-final v Worcestershire at Taunton 2002 (also took 2-37, two catches and completed a run-out)

Opinions on cricket: 'With the increasing number of EU-qualified players becoming available, I am worried about opportunities for youngsters to play first-team cricket, especially as we are also having two overseas players.'

Best batting: 193* Somerset v West Indians, Taunton 2000
Best bowling: 5-13 Somerset v Lancashire, Taunton 2000

2002 Season

	M	Inns	NO	Runs	HS	Avge	100s	50s	Ct	St	O	M	Runs	Wkts	Avge	Best	5wI	10wM
Test																		
All First	15	26	2	581	68	24.20	-	4	16	-	216.3	30	830	21	39.52	3-44	-	-
1-day Int																		
C & G	5	5	1	242	121	60.50	1	-	2	-	32	0	166	6	27.66	4-55	-	
B & H	4	4	1	45	25 *	15.00	-	-	1	-	13	1	61	2	30.50	1-17	-	
1-day Lge	13	13	1	383	73	31.91	-	3	7	-	54	2	253	4	63.25	3-29	-	

Career Performances

	M	Inns	NO	Runs	HS	Avge	100s	50s	Ct	St	Balls	Runs	Wkts	Avge	Best	5wI	10wM
Test																	
All First	107	174	17	4285	193 *	27.29	5	23	98	-	6328	3552	84	42.28	5-13	2	-
1-day Int																	
C & G	27	25	8	730	121	42.94	1	2	7	-	1136	858	32	26.81	4-43	-	
B & H	22	19	6	277	72	21.30	-	1	11	-	486	455	6	75.83	2-60	-	
1-day Lge	115	97	16	2099	73	25.91	-	11	46	-	2676	2184	57	38.31	3-21	-	

64. Which Pakistan fast bowler was Northamptonshire's overseas player in 1997?

PARSONS, M.   Somerset

Name: Michael Parsons
Role: Right-hand bat, right-arm
medium-fast bowler
Born: 26 November 1984, Taunton
Height: 5ft 11in **Weight:** 12st 2lbs
Nickname: Pars
County debut: 2002 (one-day)
Parents: Dave and Hilary
Marital status: Single
Education: Staplegrove; Ladymead
Secondary; Richard Huish Sixth Form
Qualifications: 10 GCSEs
Off-season: South West Academy, Somerset
Overseas tours: ESCA West Region U15 to
West Indies 2000; Somerset U19 Cricket
Academy to Australia 2002
Career highlights to date: '1st XI debut –
Somerset Sabres v Leicestershire Foxes in
NUL 2002, aged 17 (live on Sky TV)'
Cricket moments to forget: 'Dropped catch in above match, live on Sky TV'
Cricket superstitions: 'None'
Cricketers particularly admired: Allan Donald, Glenn McGrath
Young players to look out for: Michael Parsons
Other sports followed: Football (Man United)
Injuries: Out for one month with a side injury
Relaxations: 'Music, PlayStation'
Extras: England U15 and U17. Bowler of ESCA West Region U15 tour to West Indies
2000. Played for Somerset Board XI in the first round of the C&G 2003, which was
played in August 2002
Opinions on cricket: 'Still needs a more professional attitude of mind at county level.
Still too much old school and regional politics re national selection.'

2002 Season

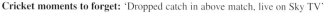

	M	Inns	NO	Runs	HS	Avge	100s	50s	Ct	St	O	M	Runs	Wkts	Avge	Best	5wI	10wM
Test																		
All First																			
1-day Int																			
C & G	1	1	0	0	0	0.00	-	-	-	-	10	0	70	3	23.33	3-70	-	
B & H																			
1-day Lge	1	0	0	0	0	-	-	-	-	-	5	1	26	0	-		-	-

Career Performances

	M	Inns	NO	Runs	HS	Avge	100s	50s	Ct	St	Balls	Runs	Wkts	Avge	Best	5wI	10wM
Test																	
All First																	
1-day Int																	
C & G	1	1	0	0	0	0.00	-	-	-	-	60	70	3	23.33	3-70	-	
B & H																	
1-day Lge	1	0	0	0	0	-	-	-	-	-	30	26	0	-		-	-

PATEL, M. M. Kent

Name: Minal (<u>Min</u>) Mahesh Patel
Role: Right-hand bat, slow left-arm
orthodox bowler
Born: 7 July 1970, Bombay, India
Height: 5ft 7in **Weight:** 9st 10lbs
Nickname: Ho Chi, Diamond, Geez
County debut: 1989
County cap: 1994
Test debut: 1996
Tests: 2
50 wickets in a season: 3
1st-Class 50s: 11
1st-Class 5 w. in innings: 23
1st-Class 10 w. in match: 9
1st-Class catches: 88
Place in batting averages: 82nd av. 40.07
(2001 223rd av. 15.43)
Place in bowling averages: 92nd av. 33.50
(2001 65th av. 30.70)
Strike rate: 87.58 (career 73.66)
Parents: Mahesh and Aruna
Wife and date of marriage: Karuna, 8 October 1995
Family links with cricket: Father played good club cricket in India,
Africa and England
Education: Maypole CP; Dartford Grammar School; Manchester Polytechnic
Qualifications: 6 O-levels, 3 A-levels, BA (Hons) Economics
Career outside cricket: Writes for *Racing Post*
Overseas tours: Dartford GS to Barbados 1988; England A to India and Bangladesh
1994-95; MCC to Malta 1997, 1999, to Fiji, Sydney and Hong Kong 1998, to East and
Central Africa 1999, to Bangladesh 1999-2000 (captain), to Argentina and Chile 2001;
Kent to Port Elizabeth 2001; Club Cricket Conference to Australia 2002

Overseas teams played for: St Augustine's, Cape Town 1993-94; Alberton, Johannesburg 1997-98

Career highlights to date: 'Winning 2001 Norwich Union League at Edgbaston. First Test cap. Any match-winning performance for Kent'

Cricket moments to forget: 'Being left out of the final XI for the Lord's Test v India 1996'

Cricketers particularly admired: Derek Underwood, Aravinda de Silva

Young players to look out for: Rob Key

Other sports played: Golf, snooker

Other sports followed: Football (Tottenham Hotspur), 'most sports that you can name'

Relaxations: Spread betting, DJ-ing, golf

Extras: Played for English Schools 1988, 1989 and NCA England South 1989. Was voted Kent League Young Player of the Year 1987 while playing for Blackheath. First six overs in NatWest Trophy were all maidens. Whittingdale Young Player of the Year 1994

Best batting: 82 Kent v Leicestershire, Canterbury 2002

Best bowling: 8-96 Kent v Lancashire, Canterbury 1994

2002 Season

	M	Inns	NO	Runs	HS	Avge	100s	50s	Ct	St	O	M	Runs	Wkts	Avge	Best	5wI	10wM
Test																		
All First	16	20	6	561	82	40.07	-	5	9	-	525.3	152	1206	36	33.50	5-56	1	-
1-day Int																		
C & G																		
B & H																		
1-day Lge	3	2	1	13	12 *	13.00	-	-	1	-	21.2	4	80	4	20.00	2-6	-	

Career Performances

	M	Inns	NO	Runs	HS	Avge	100s	50s	Ct	St	Balls	Runs	Wkts	Avge	Best	5wI	10wM
Test	2	2	0	45	27	22.50	-	-	2	-	276	180	1	180.00	1-101	-	-
All First	160	214	44	2925	82	17.20	-	11	88	-	34621	14484	470	30.81	8-96	23	9
1-day Int																	
C & G	14	5	2	45	27 *	15.00	-	-	5	-	662	399	11	36.27	2-29	-	
B & H	18	10	6	59	18 *	14.75	-	-	5	-	750	580	11	52.72	2-29	-	
1-day Lge	41	24	7	122	15	7.17	-	-	13	-	1714	1283	50	25.66	3-22	-	

PATEL, S. R. Nottinghamshire

Name: Samit (<u>Sam</u>) Rohit Patel
Role: Right-hand bat, slow left-arm bowler; all-rounder
Born: 30 November 1984, Leicester
Height: 5ft 8in **Weight:** 12st
County debut: 2002
Parents: Rohit and Sejal
Marital status: Single
Family links with cricket: 'Dad plays local cricket in Derbyshire County League. Younger brother plays for Notts U13 and is in the Midland U13 squad'
Education: Worksop College
Qualifications: 'Still studying for A-levels'
Off-season: 'In Australia with England U19'
Overseas tours: England U17 to Australia 2001; England U19 to Australia and (U19 World Cup) New Zealand 2001-02, to Australia 2002-03

Career highlights to date: 'Playing for England U15 in World Cup. Becoming England Cricketer of the Year'
Cricket superstitions: 'None'
Cricketers particularly admired: Sachin Tendulkar, Steve Waugh
Young players to look out for: Bilal Shafayat, Akhil Patel
Other sports played: Rugby, hockey, 'any sport really'
Other sports followed: Football (Nottingham Forest), rugby (Leicester Tigers)
Relaxations: 'Watching Nottingham Forest, music and sport'
Extras: Winner of inaugural BBC *Test Match Special* U15 Young Cricketer of the Year Award 2000. Represented England U19 v India U19 in 'Test' series (1/3) and one-day series (3/3) 2002
Best batting: 35 Nottinghamshire v West Indies A, Trent Bridge 2002

2002 Season

	M	Inns	NO	Runs	HS	Avge	100s	50s	Ct	St	O	M	Runs	Wkts	Avge	Best	5wI	10wM
Test																		
All First	1	1	0	35	35	35.00	-	-	-	-								
1-day Int																		
C & G																		
B & H																		
1-day Lge	3	1	0	18	18	18.00	-	-	-	-	8	1	44	3	14.66	2-14	-	

Career Performances

	M	Inns	NO	Runs	HS	Avge	100s	50s	Ct	St	Balls	Runs	Wkts	Avge	Best	5wl	10wM
Test																	
All First	1	1	0	35	35	35.00	-	-	-	-							
1-day Int																	
C & G																	
B & H																	
1-day Lge	3	1	0	18	18	18.00	-	-	-	-	48	44	3	14.66	2-14	-	

PATTISON, I. Durham

Name: Ian Pattison
Role: Right-hand bat, right-arm
medium bowler
Born: 5 May 1982, Sunderland
Height: 5ft 10in **Weight:** 13st
Nickname: Patta, Patto
County debut: 2002
1st-Class catches: 2
Place in batting averages: 290th av. 10.16
Strike rate: 54.00 (career 54.00)
Parents: Stewart and Janice
Marital status: Single
Family links with cricket: 'Brother plays in
local premier league'
Education: New Seaham Primary School;
Seaham Comprehensive
Qualifications: 6 GCSEs, Level 1 coaching
award

Off-season: 'In Australia'
Overseas tours: England U19 to Malaysia and (U19 World Cup) Sri Lanka 1999-
2000, to India 2000-01
Career highlights to date: 'Making debuts for Durham first team in 2002 – against
Glamorgan at Riverside in Championship and against Somerset in one-day game at
Taunton'
Cricket moments to forget: 'My debuts – the Championship game was over in a day
and a half; in the one-day game we got hammered'
Cricketers particularly admired: Steve Waugh, Craig White, Jacques Kallis,
Darren Gough
Young players to look out for: Gordon Muchall
Other sports followed: 'Most'
Relaxations: 'Horse racing; sleeping; working out; socialising'

Extras: Played for Durham Board XI in the NatWest 2000 and in the second round of the C&G 2002, which was played in September 2001
Opinions on cricket: 'Play more day/night cricket.'
Best batting: 27 Durham v Gloucestershire, Bristol 2002
Best bowling: 3-41 Durham v Essex, Riverside 2002

2002 Season

	M	Inns	NO	Runs	HS	Avge	100s	50s	Ct	St	O	M	Runs	Wkts	Avge	Best	5wI	10wM
Test																		
All First	3	6	0	61	27	10.16	-	-	2	-	36	9	167	4	41.75	3-41	-	-
1-day Int																		
C & G																		
B & H																		
1-day Lge	1	1	0	0	0	0.00	-	-	-	-	4	1	29	0	-	-	-	

Career Performances

	M	Inns	NO	Runs	HS	Avge	100s	50s	Ct	St	Balls	Runs	Wkts	Avge	Best	5wI	10wM
Test																	
All First	3	6	0	61	27	10.16	-	-	2	-	216	167	4	41.75	3-41	-	-
1-day Int																	
C & G	4	4	2	57	48 *	28.50	-	-	2	-	114	88	3	29.33	1-25	-	
B & H																	
1-day Lge	1	1	0	0	0	0.00	-	-	-	-	24	29	0	-	-	-	

65. For which county did West Indies Test batsman Ron Headley
(father of Dean) play from 1958 to 1974?

PAYNTER, D. E.   Northamptonshire

Name: <u>David</u> Edward Paynter
Role: Right-hand bat, right-arm off-spin bowler
Born: 25 January 1981, Truro
Height: 6ft 2½in **Weight:** 12st 7lbs
Nickname: Paints
County debut: 2002
1st-Class catches: 2
One-Day 100s: 1
Parents: Mark and Carole
Marital status: Single
Family links with cricket: Great-grandfather (Eddie Paynter) played for Lancashire (1926-1945) and England and was on the Bodyline tour
Education: Larchmont First School; Clayton Middle School
Qualifications: 9 GCSEs, Level I, II and III coaching awards
Overseas tours: Yorkshire U19 to India 1998-99
Overseas teams played for: Grafton, Auckland 1999-2001
Cricketers particularly admired: Mark Waugh, Ricky Ponting
Young players to look out for: John Sadler, Daren Drake, Craig Mowatt
Other sports played: Table tennis (Yorkshire U14), rugby (Queensbury RFC)
Other sports followed: Football (Bradford City), rugby league (Bradford Bulls)
Relaxations: Gym work, listening to music, socialising with friends
Extras: Bradford League Young Player of the Year 2000. Has attended Yorkshire and Northamptonshire academies. Played for Worcestershire 2nd XI in 2000. Played for Northamptonshire Board XI in the C&G 2001, scoring 104 on competition debut v Northamptonshire at Northampton
Best batting: 20 Northamptonshire v Durham, Northampton 2002

2002 Season

	M	Inns	NO	Runs	HS	Avge	100s	50s	Ct	St	O	M	Runs	Wkts	Avge	Best	5wI	10wM
Test																		
All First	2	4	1	32	20	10.66	-	-	2	-								
1-day Int																		
C & G																		
B & H																		
1-day Lge	2	2	0	29	18	14.50	-	-	-	-	2	0	27	1	27.00	1-27	-	

Career Performances

	M	Inns	NO	Runs	HS	Avge	100s	50s	Ct	St	Balls	Runs	Wkts	Avge	Best	5wI	10wM
Test																	
All First	2	4	1	32	20	10.66	-	-	2	-							
1-day Int																	
C & G	1	1	0	104	104	104.00	1	-	-	-	36	46	0	-		-	-
B & H																	
1-day Lge	2	2	0	29	18	14.50	-	-	-	-	12	27	1	27.00	1-27	-	

PEARSON, J. A.   Gloucestershire

Name: James Alexander Pearson
Role: Left-hand bat
Born: 11 September 1983, Bristol
Height: 5ft 10in **Weight:** 12st 7lbs
Nickname: JP
County debut: 2002
1st-Class 50s: 1
1st-Class catches: 2
Parents: Milverton and Faith
Marital status: Single
Family links with cricket: 'Dad played club cricket'
Education: St Teresa's/Ashley Down; Clifton College
Qualifications: 5 GCSEs, 3 A-levels, GNVQ
Off-season: 'Going to Australia with England U19'
Overseas tours: England U19 to Australia 2002-03
Career highlights to date: 'Making 51 opening the batting on debut v Northamptonshire'
Cricketers particularly admired: Brian Lara, Courtney Walsh, Ricky Ponting
Young players to look out for: Alex Gidman, Liam Plunkett
Other sports played: 'A bit of footy now and then'
Other sports followed: Football (Arsenal)
Relaxations: 'Listening to music and going clubbing'
Extras: Played for Gloucestershire Board XI in the C&G 2001 and in the second round of the C&G 2002, which was played in September 2001. Scored 51 on debut v Northamptonshire at Bristol 2002. Represented England U19 v India U19 in one-day series (1/3) 2002
Best batting: 51 Gloucestershire v Northamptonshire, Bristol 2002

2002 Season

	M	Inns	NO	Runs	HS	Avge	100s	50s	Ct	St	O	M	Runs	Wkts	Avge	Best	5wl	10wM
Test																		
All First	3	6	1	114	51	22.80	-	1	2	-								
1-day Int																		
C & G																		
B & H																		
1-day Lge																		

Career Performances

	M	Inns	NO	Runs	HS	Avge	100s	50s	Ct	St	Balls	Runs	Wkts	Avge	Best	5wl	10wM
Test																	
All First	3	6	1	114	51	22.80	-	1	2	-							
1-day Int																	
C & G	2	2	0	7	7	3.50	-	-	-	-	18	29	1	29.00	1-29	-	
B & H																	
1-day Lge																	

PENBERTHY, A. L.   Northamptonshire

Name: Anthony (<u>Tony</u>) Leonard Penberthy
Role: Left-hand bat, right-arm medium bowler, county vice-captain
Born: 1 September 1969, Troon, Cornwall
Height: 6ft 1in **Weight:** 12st 7lbs
Nickname: Berth, Penbers, Sir Leonard, Denzil
County debut: 1989
County cap: 1994
Benefit: 2002
1st-Class 50s: 40
1st-Class 100s: 10
1st-Class 5 w. in innings: 4
1st-Class catches: 108
One-Day 5 w. in innings: 4
Place in batting averages: 76th av. 41.31 (2001 66th av. 40.95)
Place in bowling averages: 145th av. 49.00 (2001 115th av. 40.76)
Strike rate: 103.05 (career 73.99)
Parents: Gerald (deceased) and Wendy
Wife and date of marriage: Rebecca, 9 November 1996

Children: Georgia Lily, 4 March 1998; Harry Jake, 5 October 2000
Family links with cricket: Father played in local leagues in Cornwall and became a qualified umpire instructor
Education: Troon County Primary; Camborne Comprehensive
Qualifications: 3 O-levels, 3 CSEs, Levels 1 and 2 coaching certificates
Career outside cricket: Coaching
Off-season: 'Finishing off the benefit year and re-introducing myself to the family'
Overseas tours: Druids to Zimbabwe 1988; Northants to Durban 1992, to Cape Town 1993, to Zimbabwe 1995, 1998, to Johannesburg 1996, to Grenada 2000, 2001
Career highlights to date: 'Wicket of Mark Taylor with first ball in first-class cricket' (*Caught behind, June 1989*)
Cricket moments to forget: 'A pair in the same game'
Cricketers particularly admired: Ian Botham, David Gower, Dennis Lillee, Viv Richards, Eldine Baptiste
Young players to look out for: Mark Powell, Monty Panesar
Other sports played: Football (trials for Plymouth Argyle), golf
Other sports followed: Football (West Ham United), rugby (Northampton Saints)
Relaxations: Listening to music, watching films and comedy programmes, 'walking my Irish setter'
Extras: Played for England YC v New Zealand YC 1989. Took only the second Sunday/National League hat-trick in Northants history v Somerset at Northampton in 1999. Vice-captain of Northamptonshire since 2001. Scored 132* v Glamorgan at Northampton 2001, in the process sharing with Russell Warren in a record sixth-wicket partnership for Northants in matches against Glamorgan (250). Took his 158th one-day league wicket (Trevor Ward) v Leicestershire at Northampton 2001 to pass Peter Willey's county record in the competition. Scored 80 v Somerset at Northampton 2001, in the process sharing with David Ripley in a record eighth-wicket partnership for Northants in matches against Somerset (161); also shared with Curtly Ambrose in the previous record stand – 145 at Taunton in 1994. B&H Gold Award for his 53 and 2-18 v Worcestershire at Northampton 2002
Opinions on cricket: 'Two divisional system has led to more competitive cricket. Wickets must improve, and the pitch liaison officers should be more consistent with their findings. Standard of balls has improved. Not too sure I'm looking forward to the 20-over comp next year – surely it's a game for the youngsters!'
Best batting: 132* Northamptonshire v Glamorgan, Northampton 2001
Best bowling: 5-37 Northamptonshire v Glamorgan, Swansea 1993

2002 Season

	M	Inns	NO	Runs	HS	Avge	100s	50s	Ct	St	O	M	Runs	Wkts	Avge	Best	5wI	10wM
Test																		
All First	16	25	3	909	130 *	41.31	2	5	9	-	292	76	833	17	49.00	3-21	-	-
1-day Int																		
C & G	2	2	0	39	39	19.50	-	-	1	-	18	1	60	1	60.00	1-17	-	
B & H	5	4	0	111	53	27.75	-	1	-	-	36.5	7	128	8	16.00	3-6	-	
1-day Lge	15	13	3	329	64	32.90	-	3	5	-	123	9	473	16	29.56	3-31	-	

Career Performances

	M	Inns	NO	Runs	HS	Avge	100s	50s	Ct	St	Balls	Runs	Wkts	Avge	Best	5wI	10wM
Test																	
All First	179	267	29	7119	132 *	29.91	10	40	108	-	17092	8997	231	38.94	5-37	4	-
1-day Int																	
C & G	30	21	2	462	79	24.31	-	4	10	-	1393	1005	25	40.20	5-56	1	
B & H	41	32	6	754	62	29.00	-	4	9	-	1873	1285	37	34.72	3-6	-	
1-day Lge	166	138	28	2672	81 *	24.29	-	15	42	-	6132	4905	174	28.18	5-29	3	

PENG, N.   Durham

Name: Nicky Peng
Role: Right-hand bat
Born: 18 September 1982,
Newcastle upon Tyne
Height: 6ft 3in   **Weight:** 12st
Nickname: Pengy, King
County debut: 2000
County cap: 2001
1st-Class 50s: 6
1st-Class 100s: 2
1st-Class catches: 17
One-Day 100s: 3
Place in batting averages: 190th av. 24.19
(2001 146th av. 26.23)
Parents: Linda and Wilf
Marital status: Single
Education: Royal Grammar School,
Newcastle upon Tyne
Qualifications: 10 GCSEs
Overseas tours: England U19 to India 2000-01, to Australia and (U19 World Cup)
New Zealand 2001-02 (captain); ECB National Academy to Australia 2001-02;
Durham to South Africa 2002

Career highlights to date: 'Scoring 119 for Durham v Hampshire in June [2001] in C&G match'
Cricket moments to forget: 'Every time I get out!'
Cricketers particularly admired: Mike Atherton, Steve Waugh
Young players to look out for: Gordon Muchall, Ian Bell, Mark Wallace
Other sports followed: Football, rugby (Newcastle, and especially England)
Relaxations: Socialising with friends; music and films
Extras: Full name Nicky Peng Gillender. Has represented England at U14, U15, U17 and U19 levels. Represented Minor Counties at age 15. Sir John Hobbs Silver Jubilee Memorial Prize 1998. Scored 98 on his Championship debut v Surrey at Riverside 2000. Represented England U19 v Sri Lanka U19 in one-day and 'Test' series 2000 (scoring 123 in second 'Test' at Northampton) and v West Indies U19 in 'Test' series (2/3) 2001 (captain in first 'Test'). Scored 132 in England's first innings in the second U19 'Test' at Chennai (Madras) 2000-01. NBC Denis Compton Award for the most promising young Durham player 2000, 2001. C&G Man of the Match award for his 119 v Hampshire at Riverside 2001. Durham CCC Young Player of the Year 2001. Awarded Durham cap 2001. PCA Young Player of the Year 2001
Opinions on cricket: 'Setting up of the National Academy is a major step forward for the development of young players.'
Best batting: 108 Durham v Derbyshire, Derby 2002

2002 Season

	M	Inns	NO	Runs	HS	Avge	100s	50s	Ct	St	O	M	Runs	Wkts	Avge	Best	5wI	10wM
Test																		
All First	12	21	0	508	108	24.19	1	2	8	-	1	0	2	0	-	-	-	-
1-day Int																		
C & G	2	2	0	24	23	12.00	-	-	-	-								
B & H	5	5	0	179	72	35.80	-	2	1	-								
1-day Lge	14	14	1	178	38	13.69	-	-	6	-								

Career Performances

	M	Inns	NO	Runs	HS	Avge	100s	50s	Ct	St	Balls	Runs	Wkts	Avge	Best	5wI	10wM
Test																	
All First	33	58	2	1290	108	23.03	2	6	17	-	6	2	0	-	-	-	-
1-day Int																	
C & G	5	5	0	173	119	34.60	1	-	1	-							
B & H	12	11	0	244	72	22.18	-	2	1	-							
1-day Lge	31	31	2	719	121	24.79	2	2	10	-							

PENNEY, T. L. Warwickshire

Name: Trevor Lionel Penney
Role: Right-hand bat, leg-break bowler, occasional wicket-keeper
Born: 12 June 1968, Harare, Zimbabwe
Height: 6ft **Weight:** 11st 2lbs
Nickname: TP, Blondie
County debut: 1992
County cap: 1994
1000 runs in a season: 2
1st-Class 50s: 36
1st-Class 100s: 15
1st-Class catches: 93
1st-Class stumpings: 2
Strike rate: (career 43.16)
Parents: George and Bets
Wife and date of marriage: Deborah-Anne, 19 December 1992
Children: Samantha Anne, 20 August 1995; Kevin, 7 June 1998
Family links with cricket: Father played club cricket. Brother Stephen captained Zimbabwe Schools
Education: Blakiston Junior School; Prince Edward Boys High School, Zimbabwe
Qualifications: 3 O-levels
Overseas tours: Zimbabwe U24 to England 1984; Zimbabwe to Sri Lanka 1987; ICC Associates team to Australia (U19 World Cup) 1987-88 (captain)
Overseas teams played for: Old Hararians, Zimbabwe 1983-89, 1992-98; Scarborough, Perth 1989-90; Avendale, South Africa 1990-91; Boland, South Africa 1991-92; Mashonaland, Zimbabwe 1993-94, 1997-98 –
Cricketers particularly admired: Colin Bland, Ian Botham, Allan Donald, Steve Waugh
Other sports played: Hockey (Zimbabwe and Africa), squash, tennis, golf and white water rafting
Other sports followed: Basketball (Chicago Bulls), American football (San Francisco 49ers), Formula One motor racing
Relaxations: 'Spending time with my family'
Extras: Played for Zimbabwe against Sri Lanka in 1987. Played hockey for Zimbabwe 1984-87 and also made the African team who played Asia in 1987. Scored century (102*) on first-class debut for Warwickshire, v Cambridge University at Fenner's 1992. Qualified to play for England in 1992. Captained Old Hararians to victory in three Zimbabwe domestic trophies 1998-99. Coach of Zimbabwe Board XI 2000-01. C&G Man of the Match award for his 58* in the quarter-final v Yorkshire at Headingley 2001. Warwickshire 2nd XI captain in 2002; took part in a third-wicket

stand of 397 with Jonathan Trott v Somerset 2nd XI at Knowle & Dorridge. Granted a benefit for 2003

Best batting: 151 Warwickshire v Middlesex, Lord's 1992
Best bowling: 3-18 Mashonaland v Mashonaland U24, Harare 1993-94

2002 Season

	M	Inns	NO	Runs	HS	Avge	100s	50s	Ct	St	O	M	Runs	Wkts	Avge	Best	5wI	10wM
Test																		
All First																		
1-day Int																		
C & G	1	1	0	2	2	2.00	-	-	1	-								
B & H	8	8	1	86	24	12.28	-	-	2	-								
1-day Lge	6	5	1	132	50	33.00	-	1	-	-								

Career Performances

	M	Inns	NO	Runs	HS	Avge	100s	50s	Ct	St	Balls	Runs	Wkts	Avge	Best	5wI	10wM
Test																	
All First	157	246	45	7954	151	39.57	15	36	93	2	259	184	6	30.66	3-18	-	-
1-day Int																	
C & G	39	36	10	837	90	32.19	-	3	22	-	13	16	1	16.00	1-8	-	
B & H	47	42	8	845	73 *	24.85	-	4	16	1							
1-day Lge	152	130	42	2467	83 *	28.03	-	10	54	-	6	2	0	-	-	-	

PETERS, S. D.   Worcestershire

Name: <u>Stephen</u> David Peters
Role: Right-hand bat, leg-break bowler
Born: 10 December 1978, Harold Wood, Essex
Height: 5ft 11in **Weight:** 11st
Nickname: Geezer, Pedro
County debut: 1996 (Essex), 2002 (Worcestershire)
County colours: 2002 (Worcestershire)
1st-Class 50s: 13
1st-Class 100s: 4
1st-Class catches: 52
Place in batting averages: 75th av. 41.68 (2001 175th av. 22.08)
Strike rate: (career 23.00)
Parents: Brian and Lesley
Marital status: Single

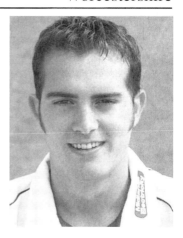

Family links with cricket: 'All family is linked with Upminster CC'
Education: Upminster Junior School; Coopers Company and Coborn School
Qualifications: 9 GCSEs
Off-season: 'Perth, Australia'
Overseas tours: Essex U14 to Barbados; Essex U15 to Hong Kong; England U19 to Pakistan 1996-97, to South Africa (including U19 World Cup) 1997-98
Overseas teams played for: Cornwall CC, Auckland, New Zealand 2001-02
Career highlights to date: 'Winning B&H Cup in 1998 with Essex. Gaining [Championship] promotion in 2000 with Essex'
Cricket superstitions: 'Tried to bin them all in 2002'
Cricketers particularly admired: 'Anyone who plays at the top level'
Young players to look out for: Gareth Batty, Kabir Ali
Other sports played: Football, golf
Other sports followed: Football (West Ham United)
Injuries: Out for seven weeks with a broken thumb
Relaxations: 'My sofa; keeping in touch with my mates'
Extras: Sir John Hobbs Silver Jubilee Memorial Prize 1994; a *Daily Telegraph* Regional Batting Award 1994. Represented England at U14, U15, U17 and U19. Scored century (110) on county debut v Cambridge University at Fenner's 1996, in the process becoming (at 17 years 194 days) the youngest player to score a first-class century for Essex. Essex Young Player of the Year 1996. Scored a century (107) and was Man of the Match in the U19 World Cup final in South Africa 1997-98. Left Essex during the 2001-02 off-season and joined Worcestershire for 2002. Scored maiden Championship century (146) v Northamptonshire at Northampton 2002, in the process sharing with David Leatherdale (147*) in a record fourth-wicket partnership for Worcestershire in matches against Northamptonshire (239)
Opinions on cricket: 'Twenty overs should be fun and attract a different audience.'
Best batting: 146 Worcestershire v Northamptonshire, Northampton 2002
Best bowling: 1-19 Essex v Oxford University, Chelmsford 1999

2002 Season

	M	Inns	NO	Runs	HS	Avge	100s	50s	Ct	St	O	M	Runs	Wkts	Avge	Best	5wI	10wM
Test																		
All First	10	16	0	667	146	41.68	2	3	6	-								
1-day Int																		
C & G	1	1	0	18	18	18.00	-	-	-	-								
B & H	5	5	0	101	52	20.20	-	1	-	-								
1-day Lge	9	8	0	107	29	13.37	-	-	-	-								

Career Performances

	M	Inns	NO	Runs	HS	Avge	100s	50s	Ct	St	Balls	Runs	Wkts	Avge	Best	5wl	10wM
Test																	
All First	72	118	15	2912	146	28.27	4	13	52	-	23	19	1	19.00	1-19	-	-
1-day Int																	
C & G	6	6	0	102	58	17.00	-	1	3	-							
B & H	18	16	1	366	58 *	24.40	-	2	3	-							
1-day Lge	65	57	3	914	73 *	16.92	-	4	15	-							

PETTINI, M. L. Essex

Name: <u>Mark</u> Lewis Pettini
Role: Right-hand bat, right-arm medium bowler, wicket-keeper
Born: 7 August 1983, Brighton
Height: 5ft 11in **Weight:** 10st 12lbs
Nickname: Swampy, Michelle
County debut: 2001
1st-Class 50s: 2
1st-Class catches: 3
Place in batting averages: 172nd av. 26.16
Parents: Pauline and Max
Marital status: Single
Family links with cricket: 'Brother Tom plays. Mum and Dad are very keen supporters while Grandad plays a demon game of beach cricket'
Education: Avalon Primary School, Sydney, Australia; Meridian Primary School;

Comberton Village College and Hills Road Sixth Form College, Cambridge; Cardiff University
Qualifications: 10 GCSEs, 3 A-levels, Level 1 cricket coaching award
Off-season: 'Studying at Cardiff University'
Overseas tours: England U19 to Australia and (U19 World Cup) New Zealand 2001-02
Career highlights to date: 'Playing first-team cricket last summer [2002]'
Cricket moments to forget: 'Losing three U19 One-Day Internationals to India last summer [2002]'
Cricketers particularly admired: Brian Lara, Steve Waugh, Sachin Tendulkar, 'all the Essex 1st team'
Young players to look out for: 'Brother Tom'
Other sports played: Tennis, swimming ('keeping fit'), table tennis

Other sports followed: Tennis, basketball
Relaxations: Fishing, watching sport, sleeping
Extras: Captained Cambridgeshire county sides U11-U16. Took hat-trick against Bedfordshire U12. Highest score of 173* v Hampshire U16 1999. Played for Development of Excellence XI (South) v West Indies U19 at Arundel 2001. Represented England U19 v India U19 in 'Test' series (2/3) and one-day series (3/3) 2002. Essex 2nd XI Player of the Year 2002
Best batting: 64 Essex v Durham, Colchester 2002

2002 Season

	M	Inns	NO	Runs	HS	Avge	100s	50s	Ct	St	O	M	Runs	Wkts	Avge	Best	5wI	10wM
Test																		
All First	3	6	0	157	64	26.16	-	2	2	-								
1-day Int																		
C & G	1	1	0	3	3	3.00	-	-	1	-								
B & H																		
1-day Lge	9	8	0	179	75	22.37	-	2	2	-								

Career Performances

	M	Inns	NO	Runs	HS	Avge	100s	50s	Ct	St	Balls	Runs	Wkts	Avge	Best	5wI	10wM
Test																	
All First	4	8	0	199	64	24.87	-	2	3	-							
1-day Int																	
C & G	1	1	0	3	3	3.00	-	-	1	-							
B & H																	
1-day Lge	11	9	0	193	75	21.44	-	2	3	-							

PHILLIPS, B. J.   Northamptonshire

Name: <u>Ben</u> James Phillips
Role: Right-hand bat, right-arm fast-medium bowler
Born: 30 September 1975, Lewisham, London
Height: 6ft 6in **Weight:** 15st
Nickname: Bennyphil, Bus
County debut: 1996 (Kent), 2002 (Northamptonshire)
1st-Class 50s: 2
1st-Class 100s: 1
1st-Class 5 w. in innings: 2
1st-Class catches: 8
Strike rate: 25.50 (career 55.05)
Parents: Glynis and Trevor
Wife and date of marriage: Sarah Jane, 20 January 2003
Family links with cricket: Father and brother both keen club cricketers for Hayes CC (Kent)

Education: St Joseph's Primary, Bromley; Langley Park School for Boys, Beckenham; Langley Park Sixth Form
Qualifications: 9 GCSEs, 3 A-levels
Career outside cricket: Personal training
Off-season: 'Following the Saints; three weeks in Cape Town for Christmas; bit of this, bit of that'
Overseas tours: Northamptonshire to Grenada 2002
Overseas teams played for: University of Queensland, Australia 1993-94; Cape Technikon Greenpoint, Cape Town 1994-95, 1996-98; University of Western Australia, Perth 1998-99; Valley, Brisbane 2001-02
Career highlights to date: '100* v Lancashire, Old Trafford 1997'
Cricket moments to forget: 'Having to leave the field in a televised game against Worcestershire with a shoulder injury that kept me out for most of last season – that would be up there'

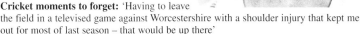

Cricket superstitions: 'Arrive at the ground early – hate rushing!'
Cricketers particularly admired: Glenn McGrath, Jason Gillespie
Young players to look out for: Jake Phillips, Monty Panesar
Other sports played: 'Going to try to get into golf this winter [2002-03]'
Other sports followed: Football (West Ham United), rugby (Northampton Saints)
Injuries: Out for 'too long' with a mystery shoulder injury
Relaxations: 'Enjoy swimming, watching a good movie, and just generally like spending time with family and friends'
Extras: Represented England U19 Schools in 1993-94. Set Langley Park School record for the fastest half-century, off 11 balls. Released by Kent at the end of the 2001 season and joined Northamptonshire for 2002
Best batting: 100* Kent v Lancashire, Old Trafford 1997
Best bowling: 5-47 Kent v Sussex, Horsham 1997

2002 Season

	M	Inns	NO	Runs	HS	Avge	100s	50s	Ct	St	O	M	Runs	Wkts	Avge	Best	5wI	10wM
Test																		
All First	1	1	0	17	17	17.00	-	-	-	-	17	5	41	4	10.25	3-28	-	-
1-day Int																		
C & G																			
B & H	2	1	1	3	3*	-	-	-	-	-	9	2	32	2	16.00	2-28	-	
1-day Lge																			

Career Performances

	M	Inns	NO	Runs	HS	Avge	100s	50s	Ct	St	Balls	Runs	Wkts	Avge	Best	5wI	10wM
Test																	
All First	28	40	4	601	100 *	16.69	1	2	8	-	3799	1955	69	28.33	5-47	2	-
1-day Int																	
C & G	2	1	1	9	9 *	-	-	-	1	-	90	67	3	22.33	3-14	-	
B & H	8	4	2	4	3 *	2.00	-	-	1	-	296	188	12	15.66	3-13	-	
1-day Lge	18	8	2	49	29	8.16	-	-	7	-	562	443	20	22.15	4-25	-	

PHILLIPS, N. C.   Durham

Name: <u>Nicholas</u> Charles Phillips
Role: Right-hand bat, off-spin bowler
Born: 10 May 1974, Pembury, Kent
Height: 6ft **Weight:** 12st 5lbs
Nickname: Captain Chaos
County debut: 1994 (Sussex),
1998 (Durham)
County cap: 2001 (Durham)
1st-Class 50s: 4
1st-Class 5 w. in innings: 4
1st-Class 10 w. in match: 1
1st-Class catches: 35
Place in batting averages: 205th av. 22.60
(2001 240th av. 12.42)
Place in bowling averages: 79th av. 31.95
(2001 116th av. 40.82)
Strike rate: 60.00 (career 85.84)
Parents: Robert and Joan
Marital status: Single

Family links with cricket: Father plays club cricket for Hastings. Represents Sussex Over 50s and has represented Kent 2nd XI, Kent League XI and has scored over 100 club 100s
Education: Hilden Grange School, Tonbridge; St Thomas's School, Winchelsea; William Parker School, Hastings
Qualifications: 8 GCSEs, Level 2 coaching award
Career outside cricket: Physiotherapy assistant
Overseas tours: Sussex U18 to India 1990-91; Durham to Cape Town 2002
Overseas teams played for: Marist CC, Auckland 1996-97; Taita Districts, Wellington, New Zealand 1998-99
Career highlights to date: 'Taking over captaincy for the last six weeks of the [2002] season. Promotion to Division One of NUL 2001'

Cricket superstitions: 'Make sure I put my glasses on before the start of play'
Cricketers particularly admired: Eddie Hemmings, Brad 'the Cannon' Hodge
Young players to look out for: 'Fred' Muchall
Other sports played: Hockey (Sussex U14 and U16)
Other sports followed: Football (West Ham)
Injuries: Out for four weeks with a fractured spinning finger
Relaxations: 'Spending time with friends and girlfriend. Listening to music. Eating out and socialising with fellow players'
Extras: Represented England U19 in home series against West Indies U19 in 1993. Released by Sussex at the end of the 1997 season and joined Durham. Returned the best figures for a Durham spinner since the county attained first-class status with his 12-268 v Glamorgan at Cardiff 1999. Took 3-0 from four overs as Durham bowled out Derbyshire to win Championship match at Darlington 2002. Captained Durham during the latter part of the 2002 season in the absence, injured, of Jon Lewis
Best batting: 58* Durham v Essex, Colchester 2002
Best bowling: 6-97 Durham v Glamorgan, Cardiff 1999

2002 Season

	M	Inns	NO	Runs	HS	Avge	100s	50s	Ct	St	O	M	Runs	Wkts	Avge	Best	5wI	10wM
Test																		
All First	10	16	6	226	58 *	22.60	-	1	4	-	210	47	671	21	31.95	4-103	-	-
1-day Int																		
C & G	1	1	0	10	10	10.00	-	-	-	-	3	0	32	0	-		-	-
B & H																		
1-day Lge	9	5	0	32	17	6.40	-	-	3	-	77	0	384	15	25.60	3-38	-	

Career Performances

	M	Inns	NO	Runs	HS	Avge	100s	50s	Ct	St	Balls	Runs	Wkts	Avge	Best	5wI	10wM
Test																	
All First	64	96	22	1171	58 *	15.82	-	4	35	-	10645	5561	124	44.84	6-97	4	1
1-day Int																	
C & G	7	5	0	52	21	10.40	-	-	-	-	287	172	4	43.00	2-16	-	
B & H	13	8	1	50	16	7.14	-	-	7	-	629	452	16	28.25	3-17	-	
1-day Lge	80	54	12	429	38 *	10.21	-	-	22	-	3269	2642	92	28.71	4-13	-	

---

66. Who became the first cricketer to score a
double century and a century in a match three times, for Gloucestershire
v Sussex at Cheltenham in 1977?

PHILLIPS, T. J. Essex

Name: Timothy (Tim) James Phillips
Role: Left-hand bat, slow left-arm bowler
Born: 13 March 1981, Cambridge
Height: 6ft **Weight:** 12st 4lbs
Nickname: Pips, TP
County debut: 1999
1st-Class 50s: 1
1st-Class catches: 7
Place in batting averages: 154th av. 28.10
(2001 260th av. 10.00)
Place in bowling averages: 143rd av. 46.88
Strike rate: 69.94 (career 80.59)
Parents: Martin (deceased) and Carolyn
Marital status: Single
Family links with cricket: Father played in
Lancashire League, then local cricket for
villages in Essex. Brother, Nick, played for
Essex Schools, and now plays for Saffron
Walden in the Essex League
Education: Felsted Preparatory School; Felsted School; Durham University
Qualifications: 10 GCSEs, 3 A-levels
Overseas tours: Felsted School to Australia 1995-96; England U19 to Malaysia and
(U19 World Cup) Sri Lanka 1999-2000
Career highlights to date: 'Four wickets v Sri Lanka A on debut for Essex'
Cricket moments to forget: 'Essex Schools U11 debut – bowled for 0, first ball'
Cricketers particularly admired: Phil Tufnell
Young players to look out for: Mark Pettini, David Randall
Other sports played: Hockey (Essex Schools U14, U15; East of England U21 trials),
'squash and golf socially'
Other sports followed: 'Like watching rugby union and league, follow football a bit
(Cambridge United!)'
Relaxations: Socialising, cinema, playing golf
Extras: Winner of *Daily Telegraph* U14 National Bowling Award 1995. Holmwoods
School Cricketer of the Year runner-up 1997 and 1998. Broke Nick Knight's and
Elliott Wilson's record for runs in a season for Felsted School, scoring 1200. NBC
Denis Compton Award 1999. Played for Durham University CCE 2001 and 2002,
scoring 75 v Durham at Riverside 2002
Opinions on cricket: 'There should be a more structured close season, keeping up
fitness and working on technical problems. The new academy can only be good for the
future of the game.'
Best batting: 75 DUCCE v Durham, Riverside 2002
Best bowling: 4-42 Essex v Sri Lanka A, Chelmsford 1999

2002 Season

	M	Inns	NO	Runs	HS	Avge	100s	50s	Ct	St	O	M	Runs	Wkts	Avge	Best	5wI	10wM
Test																		
All First	8	13	3	281	75	28.10	-	1	6	-	209.5	32	844	18	46.88	4-102	-	-
1-day Int																		
C & G	1	1	1	4	4 *	-	-	-	-	-	5	0	27	0	-		-	-
B & H																			
1-day Lge	4	4	2	14	6	7.00	-	-	1	-	22	0	114	4	28.50	2-36	-	

Career Performances

	M	Inns	NO	Runs	HS	Avge	100s	50s	Ct	St	Balls	Runs	Wkts	Avge	Best	5wI	10wM
Test																	
All First	17	25	3	388	75	17.63	-	1	7	-	2579	1704	32	53.25	4-42	-	-
1-day Int																	
C & G	1	1	1	4	4 *	-	-	-	-	-	30	27	0	-		-	-
B & H																	
1-day Lge	6	6	2	16	6	4.00	-	-	2	-	210	182	6	30.33	2-36	-

PIETERSEN, K. P.   Nottinghamshire

Name: <u>Kevin</u> Peter Pietersen
Role: Right-hand bat, right-arm
off-spin bowler
Born: 27 June 1980, Pietermaritzburg,
South Africa
Height: 6ft 4in **Weight:** 14st 9lbs
Nickname: KP, Kapes
County debut: 2001
County cap: 2002
1000 runs in a season: 1
1st-Class 50s: 8
1st-Class 100s: 6
1st-Class 200s: 2
1st-Class catches: 36
One-Day 100s: 2
Place in batting averages: 14th av. 62.21
(2001 17th av. 57.95)
Strike rate: 74.40 (career 93.59)
Parents: Jannie and Penny
Marital status: Single
Education: Clarendon, Pietermaritzburg; Merchiston Preparatory School; Maritzburg
College; University of South Africa

Qualifications: 3 A-levels
Off-season: 'Playing in Sydney, Australia, for Sydney University'
Overseas tours: Natal to Zimbabwe 1999-2000, to Australia 2000-01;
Nottinghamshire to South Africa 2001, 2002
Overseas teams played for: Rovers, Durban 1997 – 2001-02; Natal Dolphins 1997-98
– 2000-01; Sydney University 2002-03
Career highlights to date: 'Making four consecutive 100s for Notts in August 2002,
including a personal best of 254 not out'
Cricket moments to forget: 'Breaking my leg against Glamorgan in August 2002 in
an NUL game'
Cricketers particularly admired: Shaun Pollock, Errol Stewart
Young players to look out for: Ed Joyce, Jamie Troughton, Rich Logan
Other sports played: Golf, swimming ('represented my state in 1992-93'), running
Other sports followed: Formula One (Ferrari), rugby (Natal Sharks)
Injuries: Out for five weeks with a broken leg
Relaxations: 'Going to game reserves and chilling with mates'
Extras: Played for South African Schools B 1997. Merit award for cricket from Natal
1997. Scored 61* and had figures of 4-141 from 56 overs for KwaZulu-Natal v
England on their 1999-2000 tour of South Africa. Scored maiden first-class century
(165*) v Middlesex at Lord's 2001, in the process sharing in a record seventh-wicket
stand for Notts in matches against Middlesex (199) with Paul Franks. Youngest Notts
player to score a 200 in a first-class match (218* v Derbyshire at Derby 2001). Scored
1275 runs in first season of county cricket 2001. Scored 254* v Middlesex at Trent
Bridge 2002 (the highest post-war Championship score by a Nottinghamshire
batsman), in the process sharing with Darren Bicknell (108) in a record partnership for
any wicket in matches between Nottinghamshire and Middlesex (316). Three days
later, scored maiden one-day century (122 from 100 balls) v Somerset at Trent Bridge
in the NUL; next day scored another century (147 from 101 balls), also v Somerset, at
Taunton in the NUL; followed up with a further century (116) in next Championship
match, v Gloucestershire at Trent Bridge. NUL Player of the Month August 2002;
PCA Player of the Month August 2002. Awarded Nottinghamshire cap 2002. Holds a
British passport and is not considered an overseas player
Opinions on cricket: 'Coming from South Africa where you play eight first-class
games a season and one one-day competition, I was completely drained come the end
of the season. So much cricket is played, but the only way to learn the game is to play.
Brilliant!!!'
Best batting: 254* Nottinghamshire v Middlesex, Trent Bridge 2002
Best bowling: 4-141 KwaZulu-Natal v England, Durban 1999-2000

2002 Season

	M	Inns	NO	Runs	HS	Avge	100s	50s	Ct	St	O	M	Runs	Wkts	Avge	Best	5wI	10wM
Test																		
All First	12	17	3	871	254 *	62.21	4	-	12	-	62	13	226	5	45.20	2-54	-	-
1-day Int																		
C & G	2	1	0	24	24	24.00	-	-	-	-	13	1	49	0	-		-	-
B & H	5	4	0	57	29	14.25	-	-	2	-	28	0	138	2	69.00	2-36	-	-
1-day Lge	11	10	2	515	147	64.37	2	1	6	-	14.1	0	106	2	53.00	2-29	-	-

Career Performances

	M	Inns	NO	Runs	HS	Avge	100s	50s	Ct	St	Balls	Runs	Wkts	Avge	Best	5wI	10wM
Test																	
All First	37	56	9	2399	254 *	51.04	8	8	36	-	3463	1755	37	47.43	4-141	-	-
1-day Int																	
C & G	4	2	0	39	24	19.50	-	-	2	-	84	62	0	-		-	-
B & H	12	9	5	228	78 *	57.00	-	1	6	-	498	362	5	72.40	2-36	-	-
1-day Lge	27	26	6	901	147	45.05	2	4	13	-	613	586	13	45.07	3-39	-	

PIPE, D. J.   Worcestershire

Name: David James Pipe
Role: Right-hand bat, wicket-keeper
Born: 16 December 1977, Bradford
Height: 5ft 10in **Weight:** 11st 7lbs
Nickname: Pipes, Pipey, Pip
County debut: 1998
County colours: 2002
1st-Class 50s: 1
1st-Class catches: 18
1st-Class stumpings: 3
Parents: David and Dorothy
Marital status: Single
Family links with cricket: 'My dad and
uncle played in the local league'
Education: Stocks Lane Primary School;
Hainsworth Moor Middle School;
Queensbury School; BICC
Qualifications: 8 GCSEs, BTEC National in
Business and Finance, HND Leisure Studies, senior coaching award
Career outside cricket: Coaching and studying
Overseas teams played for: Leeming Spartans CC and South Metropolitan Cricket
Association, Perth 1998-99; Manly CC, Australia 1999-2002

Cricketers particularly admired: Adam Gilchrist
Other sports followed: Rugby league (Bradford Bulls, Northern Eagles), football (Bradford City), boxing ('all British fighters'), AFL (West Coast Eagles)
Relaxations: Watching sport, watching films, playing golf, socialising with friends, listening to music
Extras: MCC School of Merit Wilf Slack Memorial Trophy winner 1995. Awarded 2nd XI cap 1999. Played for Worcestershire Board XI in NatWest 2000. Scored 54 on Championship debut v Warwickshire at Worcester 2000. Played for Worcestershire Board XI and Worcestershire in the C&G 2001; took eight catches for the latter v Hertfordshire at Hertford to set a new NatWest/C&G record for most catches in a match by a wicket-keeper, beating Alec Stewart's seven v Glamorgan in the NatWest 1994
Best batting: 54 Worcestershire v Warwickshire, Worcester 2000

2002 Season

	M	Inns	NO	Runs	HS	Avge	100s	50s	Ct	St	O	M	Runs	Wkts	Avge	Best	5wI	10wM
Test																		
All First	3	4	0	64	26	16.00	-	-	12	1								
1-day Int																		
C & G																		
B & H																		
1-day Lge	4	4	1	36	20	12.00	-	-	3	4								

Career Performances

	M	Inns	NO	Runs	HS	Avge	100s	50s	Ct	St	Balls	Runs	Wkts	Avge	Best	5wI	10wM
Test																	
All First	11	16	0	251	54	15.68	-	1	18	3							
1-day Int																	
C & G	3	2	0	60	56	30.00	-	1	11	-							
B & H																	
1-day Lge	11	10	1	168	45	18.66	-	-	3	5							

PIPER, K. J.   Warwickshire

Name: <u>Keith</u> John Piper
Role: Right-hand bat, wicket-keeper
Born: 18 December 1969, Leicester
Height: 5ft 7in **Weight:** 10st 8lbs
Nickname: Tubbsy, Garden Boy
County debut: 1989
County cap: 1992
Benefit: 2001

50 dismissals in a season: 2
1st-Class 50s: 14
1st-Class 100s: 2
1st-Class catches: 490
1st-Class stumpings: 33
Place in batting averages: 253rd av. 16.30
(2001 86th av. 35.50)
Strike rate: (career 34.00)
Parents: John and Charlotte
Marital status: Single
Family links with cricket: Father plays club
cricket in Leicester
Education: Seven Sisters Junior;
Somerset Senior
Qualifications: Senior coaching award,
basketball coaching award, volleyball
coaching award
Overseas tours: Haringey Cricket College to
Barbados 1986, to Trinidad 1987, to Jamaica 1988; Warwickshire to La Manga 1989,
to St Lucia 1990; England A to India 1994-95, to Pakistan 1995-96
Overseas teams played for: Desmond Haynes's XI, Barbados v Haringey Cricket College
Cricketers particularly admired: Jack Russell, Alec Stewart, Dermot Reeve,
Colin Metson
Other sports followed: Snooker, football, tennis
Relaxations: Music, eating
Extras: London Young Cricketer of the Year 1989 and in the last five 1992. Played for
England YC 1989. Was batting partner (116*) to Brian Lara when he reached his 501*,
v Durham at Edgbaston 1994
Best batting: 116* Warwickshire v Durham, Edgbaston 1994
Best bowling: 1-57 Warwickshire v Nottinghamshire, Edgbaston 1992

2002 Season

	M	Inns	NO	Runs	HS	Avge	100s	50s	Ct	St	O	M	Runs	Wkts	Avge	Best	5wI	10wM
Test																		
All First	8	12	2	163	64 *	16.30	-	1	14	1								
1-day Int																		
C & G	1	1	0	3	3	3.00	-	-	-	-								
B & H	6	4	2	33	13 *	16.50	-	-	5	-								
1-day Lge	7	5	1	46	17	11.50	-	-	8	4								

Career Performances

	M	Inns	NO	Runs	HS	Avge	100s	50s	Ct	St	Balls	Runs	Wkts	Avge	Best	5wI	10wM
Test																	
All First	195	268	44	4481	116 *	20.00	2	14	490	33	34	60	1	60.00	1-57	-	-
1-day Int																	
C & G	39	20	10	181	19	18.10	-	-	47	7							
B & H	40	28	10	190	29	10.55	-	-	47	5							
1-day Lge	129	66	34	521	38 *	16.28	-	-	128	35							

POLLOCK, S. M.   Warwickshire

Name: <u>Shaun</u> Maclean Pollock
Role: Right-hand bat, right-arm fast-medium bowler
Born: 16 July 1973, Port Elizabeth, South Africa
Height: 6ft 3in **Weight:** 13st 5lbs
Nickname: Polly
County debut: 1996
County cap: 1996
Test debut: 1995-96
Tests: 63
One-Day Internationals: 164
1st-Class 50s: 27
1st-Class 100s: 6
1st-Class 5 w. in innings: 20
1st-Class 10 w. in match: 2
1st-Class catches: 94
One-Day 100s: 1
One-Day 5 w. in innings: 6
Place in batting averages: 181st av. 25.00
Place in bowling averages: 35th av. 26.17
Strike rate: 64.60 (career 56.74)
Parents: Peter and Inez
Marital status: Married
Family links with cricket: Father Peter played for Eastern Province and South Africa (1959-71) and was convenor of selectors for national teams. Uncle Graeme played for Eastern Province, Transvaal and South Africa (1960-86) and is a national selector
Education: Northlands Primary School, Durban, Natal; Northwood, Durban, Natal; Natal University
Qualifications: B Comm
Off-season: Playing for South Africa

Overseas tours: South Africa Tertiary Team to Kenya and Zimbabwe 1994-95; South Africa U24 to Sri Lanka 1995-96; South Africa VI to Hong Kong Sixes 1995; South Africa to India and Pakistan (World Cup) 1995-96, to Pakistan 1997-98, to Australia 1997-98, to England 1998, to New Zealand 1998-99, to UK, Ireland and Holland (World Cup) 1999, to Zimbabwe 1999-2000, to India 1999-2000, to Sri Lanka 2000 (captain), to Australia (Super Challenge) 2000-01 (captain), to Kenya (ICC Knockout) 2000-01 (captain), to West Indies 2000-01 (captain), to Zimbabwe 2001-02 (captain), to Australia 2001-02 (captain), to Morocco (Morocco Cup) 2002 (captain), to Sri Lanka 2002-03 (ICC Champions Trophy) (captain)
Overseas teams played for: Natal/KwaZulu-Natal 1991-92 –
Cricketers particularly admired: Brian McMillan, Malcolm Marshall, Clive Rice
Other sports followed: Golf, hockey, tennis, rugby and soccer
Relaxations: Watching sport, spending time with friends and listening to music
Extras: Played for Natal Nuffield team and then selected for South Africa Schools in 1991. Made first-class debut for Natal B v Western Province B at Pietermaritzburg 1991-92. Was voted Player of the Series in the South Africa v England one-day series 1995-96. Won B&H Gold Award on Warwickshire debut v Leicestershire at Edgbaston 1996, during which game he became the first bowler to take four wickets (Macmillan, Whitaker, Robinson, Maddy) in four balls in the competition, ending up with 6-21. One of South Africa's five Players of the Year 1996, 1998 and 2001. Took 7-87 from 41 overs in Australia's first innings of the third Test at Adelaide 1997-98. Appointed captain of South Africa in April 2000. Was Man of the Series v Sri Lanka 2000-01, during which he became the second South African bowler to pass 200 Test wickets (at Durban) and scored a 95-ball maiden Test century (111 at Centurion, batting at No. 9). Topped batting averages (302 runs av. 75.50) and was second in bowling averages (20 wickets av. 23.20) in Test series in West Indies 2000-01, in the process scoring his second Test century batting at No. 9 (106*) in the third Test at Bridgetown and picking up Man of the Series award for Test and one-day matches. Recorded maiden Test ten-wicket match return (10-147) in the first Test v India at Bloemfontein 2001-02, winning Man of the Match award. Scored 113* in the unofficial 'Test' v India at Centurion 2001-02, winning Man of the Match award. Rejoined Warwickshire as overseas player for 2002. B&H Gold Award for his 64 and 4-12 v Glamorgan at Cardiff 2002. C&G Man of the Match award for his 47 plus 0-9 from eight overs v Staffordshire at Stone 2002. Scored maiden one-day century (111*) v Worcestershire at Worcester in the NUL 2002. Left Warwickshire at the end of the 2002 season
Best batting: 150* Warwickshire v Glamorgan, Edgbaston 1996
Best bowling: 7-33 Natal v Border, East London 1995-96
Stop press: Became only the fourth player in Test history to run out of partners on 99* in second Test v Sri Lanka at Centurion 2002-03. Scored 51-ball 57 then took 3-12 from 9.5 overs in first ODI v Pakistan at Durban 2002-03. Appointed captain of South Africa squad for 2002-03 World Cup

2002 Season

	M	Inns	NO	Runs	HS	Avge	100s	50s	Ct	St	O	M	Runs	Wkts	Avge	Best	5wI	10wM
Test																		
All First	10	18	1	425	66	25.00	-	4	13	-	301.3	101	733	28	26.17	4-37	-	-
1-day Int																		
C & G	2	2	0	56	47	28.00	-	-	-	-	16	4	49	1	49.00	1-40	-	
B & H	8	8	0	162	64	20.25	-	1	1	-	71.5	13	207	15	13.80	4-12	-	
1-day Lge	10	8	3	332	111 *	66.40	1	1	4	-	79.2	10	273	21	13.00	4-36	-	

Career Performances

	M	Inns	NO	Runs	HS	Avge	100s	50s	Ct	St	Balls	Runs	Wkts	Avge	Best	5wI	10wM
Test	63	91	20	2242	111	31.57	2	10	41	-	14145	5410	261	20.72	7-87	14	1
All First	133	194	36	5244	150 *	33.18	6	27	94	-	27464	10694	484	22.09	7-33	20	2
1-day Int	164	109	38	1646	75	23.18	-	6	64	-	8628	5504	230	23.93	6-35	4	
C & G	4	4	0	96	47	24.00	-	-	-	-	198	111	5	22.20	4-37	-	
B & H	15	12	2	260	64	26.00	-	2	2	-	815	484	30	16.13	6-21	2	
1-day Lge	24	19	5	605	111 *	43.21	1	3	7	-	1103	660	46	14.34	4-36	-	

POPE, S. P. Gloucestershire

Name: <u>Stephen</u> Patrick Pope
Role: Right-hand bat, wicket-keeper
Born: 25 January 1983, Cheltenham
Height: 5ft 8in **Weight:** 12st
Nickame: Bod
County debut: No first-team appearance
Parents: John and Patricia
Marital status: Single
Education: Leckhampton Primary School;
Cheltenham Bournside Comprehensive
Qualifications: 11 GCSEs, 2 A-levels
Off-season: 'Getting fit in South Africa'
Overseas tours: ESCA South West U15 to
West Indies 1998; England U19 to Australia
and (U19 World Cup) New Zealand 2001-02;
Gloucestershire to South Africa 2002
Overseas teams played for: St Kilda,
Melbourne 2001-02
Career highlights to date: 'Playing for England U19 in the World Cup 2002'
Cricketers particularly admired: Jack Russell, David Partridge
Young players to look out for: Kadeer Ali, Mark Pettini, Nicky Peng
Other sports played: Rugby union (scrum half for England U16 v Portugal and
Wales; England U18 Development Squad)

Other sports followed: Football (Arsenal FC)

Relaxations: 'Going out with my friends'

Extras: Has represented England at U14, U15, U17 and U19 levels. Played for Gloucestershire Board XI in the NatWest 1999 and 2000, in the C&G 2001 and in the second round of the C&G 2002, which was played in September 2001. NBC Denis Compton Award for the most promising young Gloucestershire player 2001. Represented England U19 v West Indies U19 in one-day series (3/3) and 'Test' series (1/3) 2001 and v India U19 in 'Test' series (3/3) 2002

Opinions on cricket: 'Unless wicket-keepers are given regular specialist coaching, it is impossible to develop your full potential at an early age.'

2002 Season (did not make any first-class or one-day appearances)

Career Performances

	M	Inns	NO	Runs	HS	Avge	100s	50s	Ct	St	Balls	Runs	Wkts	Avge	Best	5wI	10wM
Test																	
All First																	
1-day Int																	
C & G	5	4	0	22	15	5.50	-	-	10	1							
B & H																	
1-day Lge																	

67. Which Australian leg-spinning Test all-rounder qualified to play for Somerset in 1956?

POTHAS, N.   Hampshire

Name: Nicolas (<u>Nic</u>) Pothas
Role: Right-hand bat, wicket-keeper
Born: 18 November 1973, Johannesburg, South Africa
Height: 6ft 1in **Weight:** 13st 7lbs
Nickname: Skeg
County debut: 2002
One-Day Internationals: 3
1st-Class 50s: 22
1st-Class 100s: 7
1st-Class catches: 268
1st-Class stumpings: 26
Place in batting averages: 195th av. 23.88
Parents: Emmanuel and Penelope
Marital status: 'Very single'
Family links with cricket: 'Greek by nationality, therefore clearly none'
Education: King Edward VII Preparatory School; King Edward VII High School; Rand Afrikaans University
Career outside cricket: 'Own two clothing businesses – 1) sport and corporate clothing; 2) fashion clothing'
Off-season: 'Coaching the University Premier League team; running my businesses'
Overseas tours: South Africa A to England 1996, to Sri Lanka 1998-99, to West Indies 2000-01; Gauteng to Australia 1997; South Africa to Singapore (Singapore Challenge) 2000-01
Overseas teams played for: Transvaal/Gauteng 1993-94 – 2001-02
Career highlights to date: 'First tour for South Africa A. Playing for South Africa'
Cricket superstitions: 'Too many to mention'
Cricketers particularly admired: Ray Jennings, Jimmy Cook, Robin Smith
Young players to look out for: John Francis, Chris Tremlett
Other sports played: Hockey (South Africa U21, Transvaal)
Other sports followed: Football (Manchester United)
Injuries: Out for two games with a slight knee cartilage tear
Relaxations: 'Shopping; designing clothes; sleeping; gym'
Extras: Scored maiden first-class century (147) for South African Students v England tourists at Pietermaritzburg 1995-96. Benson and Hedges Young Player of the Year 1996. Transvaal Player of the Year 1996, 1998. Was stand-by wicket-keeper for South Africa's tour to West Indies 2000-01. Holds a Greek passport and is not considered an overseas player
Opinions on cricket: 'Need to make the game more spectator-friendly – looks like administrators are listening. Administrators should listen to player input far more.'
Best batting: 165 Gauteng v KwaZulu-Natal, Johannesburg 1998-99

2002 Season

	M	Inns	NO	Runs	HS	Avge	100s	50s	Ct	St	O	M	Runs	Wkts	Avge	Best	5wl	10wM
Test																		
All First	16	26	1	597	99	23.88	-	5	30	4								
1-day Int																		
C & G	2	1	1	10	10 *	-	-	-	2	-								
B & H	5	5	0	48	26	9.60	-	-	7	-								
1-day Lge	13	12	7	280	53 *	56.00	-	2	19	1								

Career Performances

	M	Inns	NO	Runs	HS	Avge	100s	50s	Ct	St	Balls	Runs	Wkts	Avge	Best	5wl	10wM
Test																	
All First	102	159	26	4487	165	33.73	7	22	268	26	6	5	0	-	-	-	-
1-day Int	3	1	0	24	24	24.00	-	-	4	1							
C & G	2	1	1	10	10 *	-	-	-	2	-							
B & H	5	5	0	48	26	9.60	-	-	7	-							
1-day Lge	13	12	7	280	53 *	56.00	-	2	19	1							

POWELL, M. J.   Northamptonshire

Name: <u>Mark</u> John Powell
Role: Right-hand bat, right-arm medium bowler
Born: 4 November 1980, Northampton
Height: 5ft 11in **Weight:** 11st 6lbs
Nickname: Piggy, Perfect, Powelly
County debut: 2000
1st-Class 100s: 2
1st-Class catches: 6
Parents: David and Philippa
Marital status: Single
Education: Flore Primary, Northants; Campion School, Bugbrooke, Northants; Loughborough University
Qualifications: 10 GCSEs, 3 A-levels, BSc (Hons) Information Management and Business Studies, Level 1 coach
Off-season: 'Perth, Australia – club cricket'
Overseas tours: Northamptonshire U19 to South Africa 2000
Career highlights to date: 'Scoring maiden first-class hundred against Gloucestershire and breaking Northants opening partnership record at the same time. Captaining Loughborough to the "clean sweep" of university trophies for the second year running'

Cricket moments to forget: 'Bagging a pair on 2nd XI debut when 16'
Cricketers particularly admired: Adam Gilchrist, Marcus Trescothick, Rahul Dravid
Young players to look out for: Robert White, John Francis, Steve Selwood
Other sports played: Golf
Other sports followed: Football (Tottenham Hotspur), rugby union (Northampton Saints)
Injuries: Out for three weeks with a chipped knuckle
Relaxations: 'Cinema, watching sport'
Extras: Played for England U15 in inaugural U15 World Cup 1996; knocked out in semi-finals by Pakistan at Headingley. Played for Midlands U19 v Australia U19 1999. 2nd XI Player of the Month August/September 2000. Scored 50 in Loughborough University's BUSA Championship final win at Fenner's 2000. Captained Loughborough University to BUSA Championship and UCCE title in 2001 and 2002; scored 96* v Oxford in UCCE final at Lord's 2002 and 44 v Durham in the BUSA final at Fenner's 2002. Scored century (124*) for Loughborough UCCE v Hampshire at West End 2002. Scored maiden first-class century (107) v Gloucestershire at Northampton 2002 in his third Championship match, in the process sharing with Rob White (277; also a maiden first-class century) in a new record opening partnership for Northamptonshire (375); followed up with a second century (108*) in next Championship match v Glamorgan at Cardiff
Opinions on cricket: 'Too many slow, low wickets in Youth/2nd XI games, which don't help produce good first-class/Test match players.'
Best batting: 108* Northamptonshire v Glamorgan, Cardiff 2002

2002 Season

	M	Inns	NO	Runs	HS	Avge	100s	50s	Ct	St	O	M	Runs	Wkts	Avge	Best	5wI	10wM
Test																		
All First	3	5	1	289	108 *	72.25	2	-	6	-								
1-day Int																		
C & G																		
B & H																		
1-day Lge	2	2	0	66	64	33.00	-	1	-	-								

Career Performances

	M	Inns	NO	Runs	HS	Avge	100s	50s	Ct	St	Balls	Runs	Wkts	Avge	Best	5wI	10wM
Test																	
All First	4	7	1	291	108 *	48.50	2	-	6	-							
1-day Int																	
C & G																	
B & H																	
1-day Lge	2	2	0	66	64	33.00	-	1	-	-							

POWELL, M. J. Warwickshire

Name: <u>Michael</u> James Powell
Role: Right-hand opening bat, right-arm
medium bowler, county captain
Born: 5 April 1975, Bolton
Height: 5ft 10in **Weight:** 11st
Nickname: Arthur, Powelly
County debut: 1996
County cap: 1999
1000 runs in a season: 1
1st-Class 50s: 25
1st-Class 100s: 7
1st-Class 200s: 1
1st-Class catches: 72
One-Day 100s: 1
One-Day 5 w. in innings: 1
Place in batting averages: 139th av. 30.06
(2001 113th av. 31.45)
Strike rate: 114.00 (career 102.60)
Parents: Terry and Pat
Wife and date of marriage: Sarah, 26 October 1996
Family links with cricket: 'Father played as a youngster. Brother represented
Warwickshire youth teams'
Education: Horwich Parish C of E School; Rivington and Blackrod High School,
Horwich; Lawrence Sheriff Boys Grammar School, Rugby
Qualifications: 6 GCSEs, 2 A-levels, Levels I-III coaching awards
Career outside cricket: PE teacher
Overseas tours: England U18 to South Africa 1992-93 (captain), to Denmark 1993
(captain); England U19 to Sri Lanka 1993-94; England A to West Indies 2000-01
Overseas teams played for: Avendale CC, Cape Town 1994-95, 1996-97, 2000-01;
Griqualand West, South Africa 2001-02
Cricketers particularly admired: Ian Botham, Dermot Reeve, Roger Twose
Young players to look out for: Graham Wagg, Ian Bell
Other sports played: Rugby (Warwickshire U16-U18), golf
Other sports followed: Football (Manchester United – 'who else?')
Relaxations: Golf, snooker, 'spending time with my wife Sarah'
Extras: Captained Warwickshire age-group sides U14-U19. Captained England U17
and U18. Became first uncapped Warwickshire player for 49 years to carry his bat, for
70* out of 130 v Nottinghamshire at Edgbaston 1998. Scored 106 v Essex at
Chelmsford 2000, in the process sharing with Mark Wagh (137) in a record first-
wicket stand for Warwickshire in matches v Essex (230). Scored 96 v Barbados at
Bridgetown 2000-01, in the process sharing with Ian Ward (135) in a record opening
stand for England A (224). B&H Gold Award for his 101* (his maiden one-day

539

century) v Northamptonshire at Edgbaston 2002. Recorded maiden one-day five-wicket return (5-40) v Kent at Canterbury in the C&G 2002. Captain of Warwickshire since 2001

Best batting: 236 Warwickshire v OUCCE, The Parks 2001
Best bowling: 2-16 Warwickshire v Oxford University, The Parks 1998

2002 Season

	M	Inns	NO	Runs	HS	Avge	100s	50s	Ct	St	O	M	Runs	Wkts	Avge	Best	5wl	10wM
Test																		
All First	17	31	2	872	103	30.06	1	6	13	-	57	7	210	3	70.00	2-29	-	-
1-day Int																		
C & G	2	2	0	22	16	11.00	-	-	1	-	7	0	40	5	8.00	5-40	1	
B & H	8	8	2	263	101 *	43.83	1	1	3	-	11.3	0	60	2	30.00	2-22	-	
1-day Lge	13	11	1	219	39	21.90	-	-	11	-	35	1	203	8	25.37	3-44	-	

Career Performances

	M	Inns	NO	Runs	HS	Avge	100s	50s	Ct	St	Balls	Runs	Wkts	Avge	Best	5wl	10wM
Test																	
All First	90	147	5	4492	236	31.63	8	25	72	-	1026	534	10	53.40	2-16	-	-
1-day Int																	
C & G	11	11	1	171	39	17.10	-	-	8	-	42	40	5	8.00	5-40	1	
B & H	14	14	3	401	101 *	36.45	1	2	6	-	201	165	4	41.25	2-22	-	
1-day Lge	47	38	5	805	78	24.39	-	2	19	-	462	408	14	29.14	3-44	-	

POWELL, M. J. Glamorgan

Name: <u>Michael</u> John Powell
Role: Right-hand bat
Born: 3 February 1977, Abergavenny
Height: 6ft 1in **Weight:** 14st 8lbs
Nickname: Powelly
County debut: 1997
County cap: 2000
1000 runs in a season: 2
1st-Class 50s: 25
1st-Class 100s: 10
1st-Class 200s: 1
1st-Class catches: 46
Place in batting averages: 35th av. 50.08 (2001 126th av. 29.60)
Strike rate: (career 82.00)
Parents: Linda and John
Marital status: Single
Family links with cricket: 'Dad John and Uncle Mike both played for Abergavenny'

Education: Crickhowell Primary School; Crickhowell Secondary School; Pontypool College
Qualifications: 5 GCSEs, BTEC National Diploma in Sports Science, Level 1 coaching award
Off-season: 'Nets and training'
Overseas tours: Glamorgan to Cape Town 1999, 2002
Overseas teams played for: Wests, Brisbane 1996-97; Cornwall CC, Auckland 1998-99, 2000-01
Career highlights to date: 'Glamorgan's 1997 season and Glamorgan's 2002 season'
Cricket moments to forget: 'You wouldn't want to forget any of it'
Cricket superstitions: 'None'
Cricketers particularly admired: Adam Hollioake
Other sports played: Rugby (Crickhowell RFC)
Other sports followed: Rugby (Cardiff)
Relaxations: Eating and sleeping
Extras: Scored 200 not out on his first-class debut v Oxford University at The Parks 1997. Scored 1210 runs at 75.63 in the 1997 2nd XI Championship, the second-highest ever total behind Alan Brazier's 1212 for Surrey 2nd XI in 1948. 2nd XI Championship Player of the Year 1997. NBC Denis Compton Award for the most promising young Glamorgan player 2000. Acted as 12th man in third Test v Sri Lanka at Old Trafford 2002, taking the catch that ended Sri Lanka's second innings and left England with a victory target of 50 runs in six overs
Opinions on cricket: 'Great game.'
Best batting: 200* Glamorgan v Oxford University, The Parks 1997
Best bowling: 2-39 Glamorgan v Oxford University, The Parks 1999

2002 Season

	M	Inns	NO	Runs	HS	Avge	100s	50s	Ct	St	O	M	Runs	Wkts	Avge	Best	5wI	10wM
Test																		
All First	16	26	3	1152	135	50.08	3	7	7	-	6	0	21	0	-	-	-	-
1-day Int																			
C & G	2	2	1	5	5 *	5.00	-	-	1	-								
B & H	4	4	0	86	51	21.50	-	1	1	-								
1-day Lge	15	13	1	393	74	32.75	-	2	7	-								

Career Performances

	M	Inns	NO	Runs	HS	Avge	100s	50s	Ct	St		Balls	Runs	Wkts	Avge	Best	5wI	10wM
Test																		
All First	86	140	15	4862	200 *	38.89	11	25	46	-		164	132	2	66.00	2-39	-	-
1-day Int																		
C & G	9	9	2	116	52	16.57	-	1	3	-								
B & H	15	15	0	380	67	25.33	-	3	5	-								
1-day Lge	78	72	12	1595	86	26.58	-	5	25	-								

PRATT, A.   Durham

Name: Andrew Pratt
Role: Left-hand bat, wicket-keeper
Born: 4 March 1975, Bishop Auckland
Height: 5ft 11in **Weight:** 12st
Nickname: The Claw
County debut: 1997
County cap: 2001
50 dismissals in a season: 1
1st-Class 50s: 6
1st-Class catches: 102
1st-Class stumpings: 10
Place in batting averages: 225th av. 20.59
(2001 193rd av. 19.83)
Parents: Gordon and Brenda
Marital status: Engaged to Laura
Family links with cricket: One brother was
with MCC Young Cricketers for four years.
Younger brother Gary also plays for Durham.
Father played for many years in Durham
Education: Willington Junior School; Willington Parkside Comprehensive School;
Durham New College
Qualifications: 9 GCSEs, Advanced Diploma in Information Technology, qualified
cricket coach
Off-season: 'Recovering; training'
Overseas tours: Durham Academy to Sri Lanka
Overseas teams played for: Hallam, Melbourne 1997-98
Career highlights to date: 'Making debut for Durham'
Cricketers particularly admired: Alan Knott, Jack Russell
Other sports followed: Football (Middlesbrough FC)
Relaxations: 'Music, drinking'
Extras: Played for Durham County Schools at all levels and for the North of England

U15. Played for MCC Young Cricketers for three years. He and brother Gary became the first brothers to play in a Championship match for Durham, against Lancashire at Old Trafford 2000. Durham Player of the Year 2001

Opinions on cricket: 'Less games, more practice.'

Best batting: 93 Durham v Gloucestershire, Riverside 2002

2002 Season

	M	Inns	NO	Runs	HS	Avge	100s	50s	Ct	St	O	M	Runs	Wkts	Avge	Best	5wI	10wM
Test																		
All First	17	30	3	556	93	20.59	-	3	42	3								
1-day Int																		
C & G	2	2	0	19	13	9.50	-	-	2	-								
B & H	5	5	1	81	38	20.25	-	-	3	-								
1-day Lge	16	13	3	192	59	19.20	-	1	19	6								

Career Performances

	M	Inns	NO	Runs	HS	Avge	100s	50s	Ct	St	Balls	Runs	Wkts	Avge	Best	5wI	10wM
Test																	
All First	43	71	8	1263	93	20.04	-	6	102	10							
1-day Int																	
C & G	5	4	1	52	26 *	17.33	-	-	5	1							
B & H	11	8	4	103	38	25.75	-	-	8	3							
1-day Lge	39	33	8	530	86	21.20	-	3	38	15							

68. Which Australian batsman topped the 1999 first-class averages with 1833 runs at 73.32?

PRATT, G. J.   Durham

Name: <u>Gary</u> Joseph Pratt
Role: Left-hand bat, off-spin bowler
Born: 22 December 1981, Bishop Auckland
Height: 5ft 11in **Weight:** 11st
Nickname: Gazza
County debut: 2000
1st-Class 50s: 4
1st-Class catches: 14
Place in batting averages: 158th av. 27.62
Parents: Gordon and Brenda
Marital status: Single
Family links with cricket: Father played for
many years in Durham and one brother was
on Lord's groundstaff (MCC Young
Cricketers). Brother Andrew also plays for
Durham
Education: Crook Junior School;
Willington Parkside
Qualifications: 9 GCSEs
Overseas tours: England U19 to Malaysia and (U19 World Cup) Sri Lanka
1999-2000, to India 2000-01
Overseas teams played for: Melville, Perth 2001-02
Career highlights to date: 'Being the first brothers to play for Durham'
Cricketers particularly admired: Graham Thorpe, David Gower
Other sports played: Football ('ex-Sheffield Wednesday')
Relaxations: Music, cinema
Extras: Represented England U17 at the ECC Colts Festival in Northern Ireland 1999.
NBC Denis Compton Award 1999. On his first-class debut, against Lancashire at Old
Trafford 2000, he and brother Andrew became the first brothers to play in a
Championship match for Durham. Scored century (114) for England U19 v India U19
in third 'Test' at Hyderabad 2000-01. Represented England U19 v Sri Lanka U19 in
one-day and 'Test' series 2000 and v West Indies U19 in one-day series (3/3) and
'Test' series (3/3) 2001, scoring century (100) in second 'One-Day International' at
Chelmsford and another (188) in the second 'Test' at Trent Bridge. Played for Durham
Board XI in the second round of the C&G 2002, which was played in September 2001.
Durham Player of the Year 2002
Best batting: 78 Durham v Northamptonshire, Northampton 2002

2002 Season

	M	Inns	NO	Runs	HS	Avge	100s	50s	Ct	St	O	M	Runs	Wkts	Avge	Best	5wI	10wM
Test																		
All First	16	27	0	746	78	27.62	-	4	12	-	2.3	0	12	0	-	-	-	-
1-day Int																		
C & G	2	2	0	103	89	51.50	-	1	-	-								
B & H	5	5	0	60	23	12.00	-	-	1	-								
1-day Lge	16	16	4	306	84 *	25.50	-	3	6	-								

Career Performances

	M	Inns	NO	Runs	HS	Avge	100s	50s	Ct	St	Balls	Runs	Wkts	Avge	Best	5wI	10wM
Test																	
All First	20	34	0	838	78	24.64	-	4	14	-	15	12	0	-	-	-	-
1-day Int																	
C & G	3	3	0	135	89	45.00	-	1	-	-							
B & H	5	5	0	60	23	12.00	-	-	1	-							
1-day Lge	16	16	4	306	84 *	25.50	-	3	6	-							

PRETORIUS, D.   Durham

Name: Dewald Pretorius
Role: Right-hand bat, right-arm fast bowler
Born: 6 December 1977, Pretoria, South Africa
County debut: No first-team appearance
Test debut: 2001-02
Tests: 1
1st-Class 5 w. in innings: 6
1st-Class catches: 8
Strike rate: (career 46.76)
Overseas tours: South African Academy to Ireland and Scotland 1999
Overseas teams played for: Free State 1998-99 –
Extras: Was leading wicket-taker in South African first-class cricket 2001-02 with 42 wickets (av. 23.35) in nine matches. Represented South Africa A v Australians at Port Elizabeth 2001-02, taking 5-148 in the tourists' only innings. Made Test debut in second Test v Australia at Cape Town 2001-02. Played for South North in ECB North East Premier League 2002. Has joined Durham as an overseas player for 2003
Best batting: 43 Free State v Western Province, Bloemfontein 1998-99
Best bowling: 6-49 South Africa A v India A, Bloemfontein 2001-02

2002 Season (did not make any first-class or one-day appearances)

Career Performances

	M	Inns	NO	Runs	HS	Avge	100s	50s	Ct	St	Balls	Runs	Wkts	Avge	Best	5wI	10wM
Test	1	2	1	5	5*	5.00	-	-	-	-	150	132	1	132.00	1-60	-	-
All First	34	40	9	275	43	8.87	-	-	8	-	6501	3282	139	23.61	6-49	6	-
1-day Int																	
C & G																	
B & H																	
1-day Lge																	

PRIOR, M. J. Sussex

Name: Matthew (<u>Matt</u>) James Prior
Role: Right-hand bat, wicket-keeper
Born: 26 February 1982, Johannesburg, South Africa
Height: 5ft 11½in **Weight:** 12st 12lbs
County debut: 2001
1st-Class 50s: 6
1st-Class 100s: 1
1st-Class catches: 78
1st-Class stumpings: 4
Place in batting averages: 131st av. 30.87 (2001 195th av. 19.68)
Parents: Michael and Terri
Marital status: Single
Education: King Edward VII Prep School, Johannesburg; Brighton College, East Sussex
Qualifications: 9 GCSEs, 3 A-levels, Level 1 coaching certificate
Career outside cricket: 'Occasional coach'
Off-season: 'Training in gym until Christmas; going to Cape Town for eight weeks in January'
Overseas tours: Brighton College to India 1997-98; Sussex Academy to Cape Town 1999; Sussex to Grenada 2001
Career highlights to date: 'Maiden century. First-class debut. Winning second division Championship [2001]'
Cricket moments to forget: 'Falling onto stumps at the Rose Bowl on Sky'
Cricket superstitions: 'Too many to name all of them'
Cricketers particularly admired: Steve Waugh, Murray Goodwin, Mark Boucher
Young players to look out for: Mike Yardy, Tim Ambrose

Other sports played: Golf
Other sports followed: Football (Arsenal), golf
Relaxations: 'Gym, golf'
Extras: Has played for Sussex since U12. Represented England U14-U19, captaining England U17. Attended Sussex Academy. Played for Sussex Board XI in NatWest 2000. Reserve for England U19 tour to India 2000-01. Represented England U19 v West Indies U19 in 'Test' series (2/3) 2001, scoring 57 and 51 in the first 'Test' at Leicester. NBC Denis Compton Award for the most promising young Sussex player 2001. Struck a 55-ball 73 v Essex in the NUL at Horsham 2002. Scored maiden first-class century (102*) v Hampshire at Hove 2002, becoming the first Sussex wicket-keeper for five years to score a century
Opinions on cricket: 'Please refer to Michael Howard Yardy'
Best batting: 102* Sussex v Hampshire, Hove 2002

2002 Season

	M	Inns	NO	Runs	HS	Avge	100s	50s	Ct	St	O	M	Runs	Wkts	Avge	Best	5wl	10wM
Test																		
All First	16	27	3	741	102 *	30.87	1	5	39	2								
1-day Int																		
C & G	2	1	0	34	34	34.00	-	-	2	-								
B & H																		
1-day Lge	10	8	0	141	73	17.62	-	1	4	1								

Career Performances

	M	Inns	NO	Runs	HS	Avge	100s	50s	Ct	St	Balls	Runs	Wkts	Avge	Best	5wl	10wM
Test																		
All First	32	51	5	1174	102 *	25.52	1	6	78	4								
1-day Int																		
C & G	5	4	0	57	34	14.25	-	-	6	-								
B & H	4	3	0	12	6	4.00	-	-	2	2								
1-day Lge	21	16	1	191	73	12.73	-	1	10	2								

---

69. Which two West Indies fast bowlers headed Surrey's first-class bowling averages in 1987?

PRITTIPAUL, L. R.   Hampshire

Name: <u>Lawrence</u> Roland Prittipaul
Role: Right-hand bat, right-arm
medium bowler
Born: 19 October 1979, Portsmouth
Height: 6ft **Weight:** 13st
Nickname: Lozza, Lawrie, Lol, Shep,
Pretty Boy, Throat
County debut: 1999 (one-day),
2000 (first-class)
1st-Class 50s: 2
1st-Class 100s: 1
1st-Class catches: 8
Place in batting averages: 304th av. 7.50
(2001 206th av. 18.33)
Strike rate: 77.00 (career 127.00)
Parents: Roland and Christine
Marital status: Engaged to Kim
Family links with cricket: 'Dad plays for
Southsea. Cousin Shivnarine Chanderpaul plays for the West Indies'
Education: Meon First and Middle School, Portsmouth; St John's College, Southsea;
Portsmouth College
Qualifications: GCSEs, GNVQ, Level 2 coaching, first-aider, lifeguard, 'chippy'
Career outside cricket: 'Radio, journalism, sports massage; working for Fleet UK
and Exbury Developments'
Off-season: 'Going on holiday and relaxing'
Overseas tours: Hampshire to Cape Town 2001; MCC to Nigeria 2003
Overseas teams played for: Milnerton, Cape Town 1999-2001; King Edwards,
Johannesburg 2002
Career highlights to date: 'Home debut 152 (broke county record). Any game my
father comes to watch'
Cricket moments to forget: 'Last season, 2002'
Cricketers particularly admired: 'Dad', Jon Ayling, Tony Middleton, Carl Hooper,
Shane Warne
Young players to look out for: James Tomlinson, 'Deano' Wilson
Other sports played: Tennis, table tennis, pool
Other sports followed: Football ('Pompey FC')
Injuries: Out for one game with a thigh injury
Relaxations: 'Relaxing on a beach!'
Extras: Scored first century at age 13 for St John's College. Played for Hants Colts
from age 11 to 18; took 29 wickets and broke bowling record aged 11. Represented
England U17. Scored 185 for Hants U19 in 1998. Won Player of the Year award in
Southern League 1998. Scored over 1000 runs for Hants 2nd XI in 1999. Played for

Hampshire Board XI in the NatWest 1999. Scored 152 on home debut, v Derbyshire at Southampton 2000, breaking Dennis Baldry's Hampshire home Championship debut record of 151 set in 1959. Hampshire Young Player of the Year 2000

Opinions on cricket: 'Too many games and not enough quality. Need time to prepare to correct mistakes and form!'

Best batting: 152 Hampshire v Derbyshire, Southampton 2000
Best bowling: 2-43 Hampshire v Surrey, The Oval 2002

2002 Season

	M	Inns	NO	Runs	HS	Avge	100s	50s	Ct	St	O	M	Runs	Wkts	Avge	Best	5wI	10wM
Test																		
All First	3	6	0	45	32	7.50	-	-	1	-	38.3	10	108	3	36.00	2-43	-	-
1-day Int																		
C & G																		
B & H	1	0	0	0	0	-	-	-	-	-	5	0	21	1	21.00	1-21	-	
1-day Lge	12	9	1	43	20	5.37	-	-	-	-	68.1	3	356	9	39.55	3-33	-	

Career Performances

	M	Inns	NO	Runs	HS	Avge	100s	50s	Ct	St	Balls	Runs	Wkts	Avge	Best	5wI	10wM
Test																	
All First	14	21	0	508	152	24.19	1	2	8	-	381	194	3	64.66	2-43	-	-
1-day Int																	
C & G	4	4	0	75	30	18.75	-	-	3	-	156	125	4	31.25	2-53	-	
B & H	1	0	0	0	0	-	-	-	-	-	30	21	1	21.00	1-21	-	
1-day Lge	33	25	3	331	61	15.04	-	1	8	-	433	388	9	43.11	3-33	-	

70. Which Sussex batsman scored 203* for India v England at Delhi in 1963-64?

PYEMONT, J. P.   Derbyshire

Name: <u>James</u> Patrick Pyemont
Role: Right-hand top-order bat,
off-spin bowler
Born: 10 April 1978, Eastbourne
Height: 6ft **Weight:** 11st 7lbs
Nickname: Pumper, Pyeko, Pye, Pyemo,
Piggy, Pykethon
County debut: 1997 (Sussex),
1999 (Derbyshire)
1st-Class 50s: 5
1st-Class 100s: 1
1st-Class catches: 22
Place in batting averages: 245th av. 17.28
(2001 190th av. 20.87)
Place in bowling averages: (2001 136th
av. 51.20)
Strike rate: 93.00 (career 108.83)
Parents: Christopher and Christina
Marital status: Single
Family links with cricket: Father played for Cambridge University and Sussex
2nd XI
Education: St Bede's School, Eastbourne; Tonbridge School, Kent; Trinity Hall,
Cambridge University
Qualifications: 9 GCSEs, 3 A-levels, BA (Hons) Classics, PGCE, NCA qualified
coach
Career outside cricket: Teaching, journalism, 'dabbling'
Off-season: 'Pursuing a few ideas and getting stronger'
Overseas tours: Sussex U19 to Barbados 1993; Cambridge University to Pakistan 1999;
British Universities to South Africa 1999
Career highlights to date: 'Scoring maiden first-class 100 at Lord's' (*124 in the
Varsity match 2000*)
Cricket moments to forget: 'First couple of balls in Championship cricket!'
(*Recorded a king pair on Championship debut, Derbyshire v Surrey 1999*)
Cricketers particularly admired: David Gower
Young players to look out for: Stephen Stubbings
Other sports played: 'Anything'
Other sports followed: Football (Brighton & Hove Albion)
Relaxations: Reading, films
Extras: Played in the Old Tonbridgians sides that won the *Cricketer* Cup 1998-99 and
2002. Joined Derbyshire in 1999 from Sussex. Represented British Universities 2000
and 2001 (captain v Pakistanis 2001). Acted as 12th man for England v Australia at
Headingley 2001. Played for Cambridge University CCE in 2001. Cambridge Blue

1998-2001 (captain 2000). Released by Derbyshire at the end of the 2002 season
Opinions on cricket: 'Cricket is a game.'
Best batting: 124 Cambridge University v Oxford University, Lord's 2000
Best bowling: 4-101 Cambridge University v Oxford University, Fenner's 2001

2002 Season

	M	Inns	NO	Runs	HS	Avge	100s	50s	Ct	St	O	M	Runs	Wkts	Avge	Best	5wl	10wM
Test																		
All First	4	7	0	121	43	17.28	-	-	2	-	15.3	2	70	1	70.00	1-37	-	-
1-day Int																		
C & G																		
B & H																		
1-day Lge																		

Career Performances

	M	Inns	NO	Runs	HS	Avge	100s	50s	Ct	St	Balls	Runs	Wkts	Avge	Best	5wl	10wM
Test																	
All First	38	58	4	1126	124	20.85	1	5	22	-	1306	743	12	61.91	4-101	-	-
1-day Int																	
C & G																	
B & H	5	5	0	74	25	14.80	-	-	3	-							
1-day Lge	18	18	1	227	50	13.35	-	1	7	-							

PYRAH, R. M.   Yorkshire

Name: <u>Richard</u> Michael Pyrah
Role: Right-hand bat, right-arm medium bowler
Born: 1 November 1982, Dewsbury
Height: 6ft **Weight:** 12st
Nickname: Fez
County debut: No first-team appearance
Parents: Mick and Lesley
Marital status: Single
Family links with cricket: 'Dad played local cricket'
Education: Holy Trinity; Ossett School
Qualifications: Level 1 coaching
Off-season: 'Training hard'
Overseas teams played for: Taranaki, New Zealand 2001-02
Career highlights to date: 'Five-wicket haul v Somerset in C&G 2002. Signing pro contract'

Cricket superstitions: 'Yellow grips'
Cricketers particularly admired: Michael Vaughan, Jacques Kallis
Young players to look out for: Tim Bresnan, Andrew Gale
Other sports played: Football, golf, rugby
Other sports followed: Football (Leeds United)
Relaxations: XBox
Extras: Played for Yorkshire Board XI in the C&G 2001 and 2002, winning Man of the Match award for his 5-50 (plus 26 runs) v Somerset at Scarborough in the third round 2002; also played for Yorkshire Board XI in the second round of the C&G 2003, which was played in September 2002

2002 Season (did not make any first-class or one-day appearances for his county)

Career Performances

	M	Inns	NO	Runs	HS	Avge	100s	50s	Ct	St	Balls	Runs	Wkts	Avge	Best	5wI	10wM
Test																	
All First																	
1-day Int																	
C & G	4	4	0	106	27	26.50	-	-	2	-	102	98	7	14.00	5-50	1	
B & H																	
1-day Lge																	

RAMPRAKASH, M. R. Surrey

Name: <u>Mark</u> Ravindra Ramprakash
Role: Right-hand bat, right arm off-spin bowler
Born: 5 September 1969, Bushey, Herts
Height: 5ft 10in **Weight:** 12st 4lbs
Nickname: Ramps, Bloodaxe
County debut: 1987 (Middlesex), 2001 (Surrey)
County cap: 1990 (Middlesex), 2002 (Surrey)
Benefit: 2000 (Middlesex)
Test debut: 1991
Tests: 52
One-Day Internationals: 18
1000 runs in a season: 12
1st-Class 50s: 108
1st-Class 100s: 53
1st-Class 200s: 7
1st-Class catches: 187

One-Day 100s: 9
One-Day 5 w. in innings: 1
Place in batting averages: 18th av. 56.85 (2001 30th av. 49.72)
Strike rate: (career 121.90)
Parents: Deonarine and Jennifer
Date of marriage: 24 September 1993
Family links with cricket: Father played club cricket in Guyana
Education: Gayton High School; Harrow Weald Sixth Form College
Qualifications: 6 O-levels, 2 A-levels
Off-season: Studying for Level 2 football coaching certificate
Overseas tours: England YC to Sri Lanka 1986-87, to Australia (U19 World Cup)
1987-88; England A to Pakistan 1990-91, to West Indies 1991-92, to India 1994-95
(vice-captain); Lion Cubs to Barbados 1993; England to New Zealand 1991-92,
to West Indies 1993-94, to Australia 1994-95, to South Africa 1995-96, to West Indies
1997-98, to Australia 1998-99, to South Africa 1999-2000, to Zimbabwe (one-day
series) 2001-02, to India and New Zealand 2001-02
Overseas teams played for: Nairobi Jafferys, Kenya 1988; North Melbourne 1989
Cricketers particularly admired: 'All the great all-rounders'
Other sports followed: Snooker, football (Arsenal)
Relaxations: 'Being at home with the family, going to movies, eating out'
Extras: Played for Middlesex 2nd XI aged 16 and made first-team debut for
Middlesex aged 17. Voted Best U15 Schoolboy of 1985 by Cricket Society (Sir John
Hobbs Silver Jubilee Memorial Prize), Best Young Cricketer of 1986 and Cricket
Society's Most Promising Young Cricketer of the Year in 1988. Man of the Match for
his 56 in Middlesex's NatWest Trophy final win in 1988, on his debut in the
competition. Played for England YC v New Zealand YC in 1989. Scored century in
each innings (100*/125) v Kent at Canterbury 1990, becoming (at 20 years, 325 days)
the youngest batsman to score twin centuries in the Championship. Won Cricket
Writers' Young Cricketer of the Year award 1991. Finished top of the Whyte and
Mackay batting ratings in 1995 and again in 1997. Appointed Middlesex captain
during 1997 season after Mike Gatting stood down. Scored maiden Test 100 (154)
v West Indies at Bridgetown 1997-98, sharing in a record sixth-wicket partnership for
England in Tests v West Indies (205) with Graham Thorpe and receiving Man of the
Match award. Achieved feat of scoring a century against all other first-class counties
with his 128* v Glamorgan at Lord's in 1998. Became the first player to score three
200s v Surrey with his 209* at Lord's 1999. Stood down as Middlesex captain at end
of 1999 season. Leading run-scorer in the single-division four-day era of the County
Championship with 8392 runs (av. 56.32) 1993-99. Scored two centuries (110*/112) in
the match v Sussex at Southgate 2000 to become the first Middlesex player to record
100s in each innings of a game on four occasions; his 112 in the second innings was
his 50th first-class century. Left Middlesex in the 2000-01 off-season and joined
Surrey for 2001. Scored century (146) on Championship debut for Surrey v Kent at
The Oval 2001. B&H Gold Award for his 97* v Essex at The Oval 2001. C&G Man of
the Match award for his 101* v Scotland at Edinburgh 2002. Scored 218 (and 53)
v Somerset at Taunton 2002, following up with 210* v Warwickshire at The Oval to

become the first player to score a double hundred in successive Championship matches since Aravinda de Silva for Kent in 1995. Awarded Surrey cap 2002
Best batting: 235 Middlesex v Yorkshire, Headingley 1995
Best bowling: 3-32 Middlesex v Glamorgan, Lord's 1998

2002 Season

	M	Inns	NO	Runs	HS	Avge	100s	50s	Ct	St	O	M	Runs	Wkts	Avge	Best	5wI	10wM
Test																		
All First	15	25	4	1194	218	56.85	4	6	6	-	8	1	23	0	-		-	-
1-day Int																		
C & G	4	4	2	297	107 *	148.50	2	1	2	-								
B & H	4	4	1	118	70 *	39.33	-	1	-	-	6	0	31	1	31.00	1-31	-	
1-day Lge	15	15	3	537	87 *	44.75	-	5	3	-	5.2	0	32	2	16.00	2-19	-	

Career Performances

	M	Inns	NO	Runs	HS	Avge	100s	50s	Ct	St	Balls	Runs	Wkts	Avge	Best	5wI	10wM
Test	52	92	6	2350	154	27.32	2	12	39	-	895	477	4	119.25	1-2	-	-
All First	325	537	66	21779	235	46.23	60	108	187	-	3901	2064	32	64.50	3-32	-	-
1-day Int	18	18	4	376	51	26.85	-	1	8	-	132	108	4	27.00	3-28	-	
C & G	36	35	3	1217	107 *	38.03	3	5	18	-	360	217	9	24.11	2-15	-	
B & H	51	50	10	1678	119 *	41.95	2	10	19	-	300	220	10	22.00	3-35	-	
1-day Lge	182	174	31	5871	147 *	41.05	4	43	56	-	534	480	17	28.23	5-38	1	

RANDALL, S. J. — Nottinghamshire

Name: <u>Stephen</u> John Randall
Role: Right-hand bat, right-arm off-spin bowler
Born: 9 June 1980, Nottingham
Height: 5ft 10in **Weight:** 11st
Nickname: Rags, Rago
County debut: 1999
1st-Class catches: 5
Place in batting averages: (2001 245th av. 12.16)
Strike rate: (career 198.12)
Parents: Robert and Glenda
Marital status: Single
Family links with cricket: 'Dad played in local bucket bangers league for 15 years'
Education: Heyman; West Bridgford School
Qualifications: 9 GCSEs, Level 2 coach
Overseas tours: England U17 to Bermuda

1997; Nottinghamshire to South Africa 1998, 1999, 2000, 2001
Career highlights to date: 'Bowling Matt Dowman'
Cricket moments to forget: 'Dropping Mr Cork on 9; he went on to make 129'
Cricketers particularly admired: Tim Robinson, Robert Croft, Eddie Hemmings, Paul Franks
Young players to look out for: Kev Pietersen, Richard Logan
Other sports played: Golf, tennis
Other sports followed: Football (Mansfield Town)
Extras: Played for Nottinghamshire Board XI in the NatWest 1999
Opinions on cricket: 'Fantastic.'
Best batting: 28 Nottinghamshire v Gloucestershire, Bristol 2001
Best bowling: 2-64 Nottinghamshire v Derbyshire, Trent Bridge 2001

2002 Season

	M	Inns	NO	Runs	HS	Avge	100s	50s	Ct	St	O	M	Runs	Wkts	Avge	Best	5wl	10wM
Test																		
All First	2	3	0	13	8	4.33	-	-	1	-	33	6	140	0	-	-	-	-
1-day Int																		
C & G																		
B & H																		
1-day Lge	11	7	3	67	25	16.75	-	-	4	-	88	2	399	8	49.87	2-37	-	

Career Performances

	M	Inns	NO	Runs	HS	Avge	100s	50s	Ct	St	Balls	Runs	Wkts	Avge	Best	5wl	10wM
Test																	
All First	10	15	2	116	28	8.92	-	-	5	-	1585	951	8	118.87	2-64	-	-
1-day Int																	
C & G	1	1	0	1	1	1.00	-	-	-	-	60	43	0	-	-	-	
B & H																	
1-day Lge	13	9	5	95	25	23.75	-	-	4	-	606	485	11	44.09	3-44	-	

---

71. Which Leicestershire overseas player of the late 1960s
and 1970s was nicknamed 'Garth'?

RASHID, S.   Sussex

Name: Shaun Rashid
Role: Right-hand bat, right-arm
medium-fast bowler
Born: 1 March 1977, Burnley
Height: 5ft 11in **Weight:** 12st 7lbs
Nickname: Rash
County debut: No first-team appearance
Parents: Shahid and Ann
Marital status: Single
Family links with cricket: 'Dad played
cricket in the local Asian leagues in his
heyday; apparently "legendary" throughout
his career according to some friends'
Education: Stoneyholme Primary,
Burnley/Walter Street Primary, Brierfield;
Mansfield High School, Brierfield; Burnley
College; De Montfort University, Bedford
Qualifications: National Diploma in Sports

Science; various coaching awards; 'was studying for a degree'
Career outside cricket: 'Was a student; temporarily on hold'
Off-season: 'Spending two months at the University of Port Elizabeth International
Cricket Academy 2003 getting fit for the forthcoming season'
Overseas teams played for: UPE Cricket Academy 2003
Career highlights to date: 'Took 9-27, including hat-trick, during a club game for
Bedford Town CC. Man of the Match in C&G game v Holland 2002'
Cricket moments to forget: 'Getting smashed around the park by Andy Roberts,
Bedfordshire captain, during a club game last year [2002]; he eventually went on to
score a hundred and something!'
Cricketers particularly admired: Viv Richards, Allan Donald, Andy Roberts
(Bedfordshire)
Young players to look out for: Shahbaz Rashid ('little brother'), Vishal and Bharat
Tripathi, Tim Ambrose
Other sports played: Badminton, pool, golf, 'generally like to participate in most
sports'
Other sports followed: Football (Burnley FC)
Relaxations: 'Socialising with team-mates; reading and listening to various music;
learning to play the guitar at present'
Extras: Bedfordshire Young Player of the Year 2001. Holds Bedford Town record for
most National Championship wickets in a season. Played for Bedfordshire in the C&G
2001 and 2002; also played for Bedfordshire in the second round of the C&G 2003,
which was played in September 2002, winning Man of the match award for his 4-30
v Holland at Luton

Opinions on cricket: 'Great having two overseas players per club this year. It will hopefully make teams stronger but could restrict talented players playing first-class cricket. Players will, however, learn from their experiences on and off the field.'

2002 Season (did not make any first-class or one-day appearances for his county)

Career Performances

	M	Inns	NO	Runs	HS	Avge	100s	50s	Ct	St	Balls	Runs	Wkts	Avge	Best	5wl	10wM
Test																	
All First																	
1-day Int																	
C & G	6	2	2	11	9 *	-	-	-	1	-	332	254	15	16.93	4-30	-	
B & H																	
1-day Lge																	

RATCLIFFE, J. D. Surrey

Name: <u>Jason</u> David Ratcliffe
Role: Right-hand bat, right-arm medium/off-spin bowler, slip fielder; all-rounder
Born: 19 June 1969, Solihull
Height: 6ft 4in **Weight:** 14st 7lbs
Nickname: Ratters, Fridge
County debut: 1988 (Warwickshire), 1995 (Surrey)
County cap: 1998 (Surrey)
1st-Class 50s: 38
1st-Class 100s: 5
1st-Class 5 w. in innings: 1
1st-Class catches: 68
One-Day 100s: 1
Strike rate: 36.00 (career 60.88)
Parents: David and Sheila
Wife and date of marriage: Andrea, 7 January 1995

Children: Samuel Taylor, 11 September 2001
Family links with cricket: Father (D.P. Ratcliffe) played for Warwickshire 1956-62
Education: Meadow Green Primary School; Sharmans Cross Secondary School; Solihull Sixth Form College
Qualifications: 6 O-levels, 3 A-levels, NCA staff coach
Career outside cricket: Sports PR and marketing
Overseas tours: NCA (South) to Ireland 1988; Warwickshire to South Africa 1991-92
Overseas teams played for: West End, Kimberley, South Africa 1987-88; Belmont,

Newcastle, NSW 1990-91; Penrith, Sydney 1992-94; Parramatta, Sydney 1999-2000
Cricketers particularly admired: Dom Ostler, Gladstone Small
Young players to look out for: Tim Murtagh
Other sports followed: Football (Birmingham City FC)
Relaxations: Music, reading, eating out
Extras: Has won Championship winner's medals with Warwickshire and Surrey, a NatWest winner's medal (Warwicks), a Sunday League winner's medal (Surrey) and a B&H winner's medal (Surrey). Struck a 31-ball 53 and took 4-44 v Essex at Guildford in his final NUL match 2002. Retired at the end of the 2002 season
Best batting: 135 Surrey v Worcestershire, Worcester 1997
Best bowling: 6-48 Surrey v Sri Lanka A, The Oval 1999

2002 Season

	M	Inns	NO	Runs	HS	Avge	100s	50s	Ct	St	O	M	Runs	Wkts	Avge	Best	5wI	10wM
Test																		
All First	1	2	1	16	13	16.00	-	-	-	-	6	4	14	1	14.00	1-0	-	-
1-day Int																		
C & G	1	0	0	0	0	-	-	-	-	-	4	0	33	1	33.00	1-33	-	
B & H																			
1-day Lge	2	1	0	53	53	53.00	-	1	-	-	17	0	85	6	14.16	4-44	-	

Career Performances

	M	Inns	NO	Runs	HS	Avge	100s	50s	Ct	St	Balls	Runs	Wkts	Avge	Best	5wI	10wM
Test																	
All First	136	244	14	6561	135	28.52	5	38	68	-	1644	911	27	33.74	6-48	1	-
1-day Int																	
C & G	19	16	1	492	105	32.80	1	3	1	-	144	135	2	67.50	1-17	-	
B & H	16	13	3	170	41	17.00	-	-	6	-	185	121	8	15.12	3-15	-	
1-day Lge	72	61	8	1084	82	20.45	-	6	21	-	1204	927	28	33.10	4-44	-	

RAWNSLEY, M. J.   Worcestershire

Name: <u>Matthew</u> James Rawnsley
Role: Right-hand bat, slow left-arm bowler
Born: 8 June 1976, Birmingham
Height: 6ft 3in **Weight:** 12st 8lbs
Nickname: Scrawny, Dog
County debut: 1996
County colours: 2002
1st-Class 5 w. in innings: 3
1st-Class 10 w. in match: 1
1st-Class catches: 22
One-Day 5 w. in innings: 1

Place in batting averages: (2001 236th av. 13.12)
Place in bowling averages: (2001 129th av. 44.85)
Strike rate: 279.00 (career 96.32)
Parents: Christopher (deceased) and June
Marital status: Single
Education: Northfield Manor Primary School, Birmingham; Bourneville Secondary School, Birmingham; Brynteg Comprehensive, Bridgend
Qualifications: 9 GCSEs, 4 A-levels, NCA coaching award, qualified canoe instructor
Overseas tours: Worcestershire CCC to Zimbabwe 1997; Forest Nomads to Zimbabwe 1999
Overseas teams played for: Kumeu, Auckland 1995-96; Sunrise Sports Club, Harare, Zimbabwe 1996-97; Old Hararians, 1999-2000; Waitakere, Auckland 2001-02
Career highlights to date: 'Playing against Australia at Worcester [2001]'
Cricket moments to forget: 'Being relegated into second division of Norwich Union League last game of the season 2000'
Cricketers particularly admired: Richard Illingworth
Young players to look out for: Kadeer Ali
Other sports played: Hockey (Wales U18), rugby (Greater Birmingham, North Midlands Colts), badminton (Glamorgan Schools)
Other sports followed: Rugby ('support my bro, who plays for Selly Oak in Birmingham')
Extras: Set record for the most wickets at the Oxford Festival (27). Warwickshire U19 Player of the Year in 1995. Took ten wickets and scored 133 not out against Gloucestershire 2nd XI in 1997. Worcestershire Denis Compton Award recipient 1997. Released by Worcestershire at the end of the 2002 season
Opinions on cricket: 'People don't realise how good things are until they are gone.'
Best batting: 39 Worcestershire v Hampshire, Worcester 2001
Best bowling: 6-44 Worcestershire v Oxford University, The Parks 1998

2002 Season

	M	Inns	NO	Runs	HS	Avge	100s	50s	Ct	St	O	M	Runs	Wkts	Avge	Best	5wl	10wM
Test																		
All First	4	3	1	20	9 *	10.00	-	-	2	-	93	28	274	2	137.00	1-26	-	-
1-day Int																		
C & G																		
B & H																		
1-day Lge	2	1	1	1	1 *	-	-	-	-	-	11.4	0	39	3	13.00	2-19	-	

Career Performances

	M	Inns	NO	Runs	HS	Avge	100s	50s	Ct	St	Balls	Runs	Wkts	Avge	Best	5wI	10wM
Test																	
All First	46	57	10	529	39	11.25	-	-	22	-	7128	3283	74	44.36	6-44	3	1
1-day Int																	
C & G	6	4	1	19	12	6.33	-	-	1	-	324	224	6	37.33	2-36	-	
B & H	5	2	0	1	1	0.50	-	-	2	-	218	179	4	44.75	1-30	-	
1-day Lge	40	17	6	47	7	4.27	-	-	8	-	1409	1085	40	27.12	5-26	1	

READ, C. M. W.   Nottinghamshire

Name: <u>Christopher</u> Mark Wells Read
Role: Right-hand bat, wicket-keeper
Born: 10 August 1978, Paignton
Height: 5ft 8in **Weight:** 10st 6lbs
Nickname: Readie, Muttley
County debut: 1997 (one-day, Glos),
1998 (Notts)
County cap: 1999 (Notts)
Test debut: 1999
Tests: 3
One-Day Internationals: 9
50 dismissals in a season: 2
1st-Class 50s: 15
1st-Class 100s: 2
1st-Class catches: 283
1st-Class stumpings: 9
Place in batting averages: 113th av. 34.65
(2001 122nd av. 30.27)

Parents: Geoffrey and Carolyn
Marital status: Single
Family links with cricket: 'Dad is now "chairman of selectors" at Paignton CC!'
Education: Roselands Primary School; Torquay Boys' Grammar School;
University of Bath; Loughborough University
Qualifications: 9 GCSEs, 4 A-levels, senior coaching award
Off-season: 'ECB National Academy'
Overseas tours: West of England U13 to Holland 1991; West of England U15 to West
Indies 1992-93; England U17 to Holland (ICC Youth tournament) 1995; England U19
to Pakistan 1996-97; England A to Kenya and Sri Lanka 1997-98, to Zimbabwe and
South Africa 1998-99, to West Indies 2000-01; England to South Africa and Zimbabwe
1999-2000; British Universities to South Africa 2002; ECB National Academy to
Australia and Sri Lanka 2002-03

Career highlights to date: 'Test match debut v New Zealand, Edgbaston 1999'
Cricket moments to forget: 'Ducking a slower ball from Chris Cairns in second Test v New Zealand at Lord's 1999'
Cricketers particularly admired: Adam Gilchrist, Bruce French, Alan Knott, Bob Taylor, Jack Russell, Ian Healy
Young players to look out for: Bilal Shafayat, Gary Pratt
Other sports played: Hockey (Devon U18, U21; West of England U17)
Other sports followed: Football (Torquay United)
Relaxations: 'Reading, listening to music, keeping fit and going out with friends'
Extras: Represented Devon in Minor Counties Championship and NatWest in 1995, 1996 and 1997, the county winning the Minor Counties Championship three years running. Played for England U18 against New Zealand U19 in 1996 and for England U19 in the series against Zimbabwe U19 1997. Was selected for the England A tour to Kenya and Sri Lanka aged 18 and without having played a first-class game. Joined Nottinghamshire for 1998 season. Recorded eight dismissals on Test debut in the first Test v New Zealand at Edgbaston 1999. Scored 69 v Warwickshire at Edgbaston in the NUL 2002, in the process passing 1000 runs for Nottinghamshire in the one-day league. Leading wicket-keeper in English first-class cricket 2002 with 68 dismissals (also scored 797 runs at 34.65)
Opinions on cricket: 'In day/night cricket in this country the ECB has recognised that six or eight light towers are required to illuminate the field, yet in domestic day/night games only four are used due to the large financing costs, but the players are subsequently expected to play in sub-standard conditions in often crucial games.'
Best batting: 160 Nottinghamshire v Warwickshire, Trent Bridge 1999
Stop press: Called up from ECB National Academy squad in Adelaide to England one-day squad in Australia 2002-03 and played v Prime Minister's XI in Canberra

2002 Season

	M	Inns	NO	Runs	HS	Avge	100s	50s	Ct	St	O	M	Runs	Wkts	Avge	Best	5wI	10wM
Test																		
All First	18	28	5	797	127	34.65	1	4	66	2								
1-day Int																		
C & G	2	1	1	51	51 *	-	-	-	1	1	2							
B & H	5	4	2	82	36 *	41.00	-	-	7	1								
1-day Lge	15	13	1	297	69	24.75	-	1	12	7								

Career Performances

	M	Inns	NO	Runs	HS	Avge	100s	50s	Ct	St	Balls	Runs	Wkts	Avge	Best	5wI	10wM
Test	3	4	0	38	37	9.50	-	-	10	1							
All First	99	150	24	3330	160	26.42	2	15	283	9	18	25	0	-	-	-	-
1-day Int	9	6	2	70	26 *	17.50	-	-	11	2							
C & G	13	10	3	182	51 *	26.00	-	1	12	5							
B & H	16	11	4	145	36 *	20.71	-	-	15	5							
1-day Lge	72	60	10	1042	69	20.84	-	2	82	15							

REES, T. M.   Lancashire

Name: Timothy (Tim) Martyn Rees
Role: Right-hand top-order bat, occasional
off-spin bowler
Born: 4 September 1984
Height: 6ft 1in **Weight:** 10st 4lbs
Nickname: Reescy
County debut: 2002
1st-Class catches: 1
Parents: Simon and Rosey
Marital status: Girlfriend
Education: High Lawn CP; Canon Slade
Qualifications: 9 GCSEs
Off-season: 'Finishing A-levels and playing
football'
Overseas tours: England U17 to Australia
2001

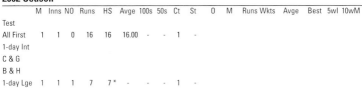

Career highlights to date: 'Lancs 1st XI
debut v Somerset in Championship'
Cricket moments to forget: 'Getting 3 v Glamorgan 2nd XI on my 18th birthday!'
Cricket superstitions: 'Too many to mention'
Cricketers particularly admired: Michael Vaughan, Sachin Tendulkar
Young players to look out for: Bilal Shafayat
Other sports followed: Football (Bolton Wanderers FC)
Relaxations: 'Playing football; going to the cinema with friends; shopping'
Best batting: 16 Lancashire v Somerset, Taunton 2002

2002 Season

	M	Inns	NO	Runs	HS	Avge	100s	50s	Ct	St	O	M	Runs	Wkts	Avge	Best	5wl	10wM
Test																		
All First	1	1	0	16	16	16.00	-	-	1	-								
1-day Int																		
C & G																		
B & H																		
1-day Lge	1	1	1	7	7 *	-	-	-	1	-								

Career Performances

	M	Inns	NO	Runs	HS	Avge	100s	50s	Ct	St	Balls	Runs	Wkts	Avge	Best	5wl	10wM
Test																	
All First	1	1	0	16	16	16.00	-	-	1	-							
1-day Int																	
C & G																	
B & H																	
1-day Lge	1	1	1	7	7 *	-	-	-	1	-							

RHODES, J. N.   Gloucestershire

Name: Jonathan (<u>Jonty</u>) Neil Rhodes
Role: Right-hand bat, right-arm
medium bowler
Born: 27 July 1969, Pietermaritzburg,
South Africa
Height: 5ft 8in
County debut: No first-team appearance
Test debut: 1992-93
Tests: 52
One-day Internationals: 231
1st-Class 50s: 45
1st-Class 100s: 17
1st-Class catches: 121
One-Day 100s: 2
Strike rate: (career 138.00)
Wife: Kate
Children: Daniella
Family links with cricket: Brother (C. B.
Rhodes) played for Eastern Province B and Natal B 1990-93
Education: Maritzburg College; Natal University (Pietermaritzburg)
Overseas tours: South Africa to Australia and New Zealand (World Cup) 1991-92, to
West Indies 1991-92, to Sri Lanka 1993-94, to India (Hero Cup) 1993-94, to Australia
1993-94, to England 1994, to New Zealand 1994-95, to India and Pakistan (World
Cup) 1995-96, to Sharjah (Pepsi Cup) 1995-96, to India 1996-97, to Pakistan 1997-98,
to Australia 1997-98, to England 1998, to Bangladesh (Wills International Cup)
1998-99, to New Zealand 1998-99, to UK, Ireland and Holland (World Cup) 1999, to
Zimbabwe 1999-2000, to Sri Lanka 2000, to Australia (Super Challenge) 2000, to
Kenya (ICC Knockout) 2000-01, to West Indies 2000-01 (one-day series), to
Zimbabwe 2001-02 (one-day series), to Australia (VB Series) 2001-02, to Morocco
(Morocco Cup) 2002, to Sri Lanka (ICC Champions Trophy) 2002-03
Overseas teams played for: Natal/KwaZulu-Natal 1988-89 –

Career highlights to date: 1992 World Cup, including South Africa debut v Australia and running out Inzamam-ul-Haq v Pakistan; taking five catches v West Indies in ODI at Mumbai (Bombay) 1993-94; 117 v England at Lord's 1998
Cricketers particularly admired: Shane Warne (as bowler), Steve Waugh (as batsman), Mark Taylor (as fielder), Hansie Cronje (as captain and batsman to bat with)
Other sports played: Football, hockey
Other sports followed: Basketball (NBA)
Relaxations: Reading
Extras: Represented Natal Nuffield Schools and South Africa Schools 1986-87. Represented South Africa in the 1991-92, 1995-96 and 1999 World Cups. One of South Africa's five Players of the Year 1992, 1999. Scored 40 and took ODI world-record five catches v West Indies at Mumbai (Bombay) in Hero Cup 1993-94, winning Man of the Match award; has won numerous other ODI awards, including Man of the Series in Standard Bank International Series in South Africa 1997-98 and in Texaco Trophy in England 1998. Scored 117 in second Test v England at Lord's 1998, in the process sharing with Hansie Cronje (81) in a then record fifth-wicket partnership for South Africa in Tests (184) and winning Man of the Match award. Scored 95-ball 103* in fifth Test v West Indies at Centurion 1998-99, reaching his century with a six and winning Man of the Match award. One of *Wisden*'s Five Cricketers of the Year 1999. Played for Ireland 1999. Scored 74 and 154 in the SuperSport Series final 2001-02 v Northerns at Durban, winning Man of the Match award. Appointed Patron of the ICC Cricket World Cup 2003 national volunteers programme. Has joined Gloucestershire as an overseas player for 2003
Best batting: 172 KwaZulu-Natal v Griqualand West, Kimberley 2001-02
Best bowling: 1-13 Natal v Northerns, Durban 1990-91
Stop press: Voted best fielder in the world (75 per cent of vote) in a poll of international players held during the ICC Champions Trophy in Sri Lanka 2002-03. His image features on a 50-cent South African coin released in October 2002 to commemorate the 2003 World Cup. Scored a 92-ball 98 in first ODI v Pakistan at Durban and a 95-ball 81 in the fifth at Cape Town 2002-03, winning the Man of the Match award on both occasions. Selected for South Africa squad for 2002-03 World Cup; retired from international cricket (with a South African record 245 ODI caps) after breaking hand in second pool match against Kenya

2002 Season (did not make any first-class or one-day appearances)

Career Performances

	M	Inns	NO	Runs	HS	Avge	100s	50s	Ct	St	Balls	Runs	Wkts	Avge	Best	5wI	10wM
Test	52	80	9	2532	117	35.66	3	17	34	-	12	5	0	-	-	-	-
All First	148	234	26	8167	172	39.26	17	45	121	-	138	65	1	65.00	1-13	-	-
1-day Int	231	209	48	5630	121	34.96	2	30	100	-	14	4	0	-	-	-	-
C & G																	
B & H																		
1-day Lge																		

RHODES, S. J. Worcestershire

Name: Steven (<u>Steve</u>) John Rhodes
Role: Right-hand bat, wicket-keeper,
county vice-captain
Born: 17 June 1964, Bradford
Height: 5ft 8in **Weight:** 12st 8lbs
Nickname: Bumpy
County debut: 1981 (Yorkshire),
1985 (Worcestershire)
County cap: 1986 (Worcestershire;
colours, 2002)
Benefit: 1996
Test debut: 1994
Tests: 11
One-Day Internationals: 9
1000 runs in a season: 2
50 dismissals in a season: 13
1st-Class 50s: 68
1st-Class 100s: 12
1st-Class catches: 1056
1st-Class stumpings: 118

Place in batting averages: 83rd av. 39.75 (2001 94th av. 34.00)
Parents: William Ernest and Norma Kathleen
Wife and date of marriage: Judy Ann, 6 March 1993
Children: Holly Jade, 20 August 1985; George Harry, 26 October 1993;
Lily Amber, 3 March 1995
Family links with cricket: Father played for Nottinghamshire 1959-64
Education: Bradford Moor Junior School; Lapage St Middle; Carlton-Bolling
Comprehensive, Bradford
Qualifications: 4 O-levels, Level III coach, 'attended Bradford Management Centre
for ECB – Coaching and Management Skills course'
Career outside cricket: Marketing department at Worcestershire CCC; cricket
coaching
Off-season: 'Coaching; participating in Level IV coaching course'
Overseas tours: England A to Sri Lanka 1986, to Zimbabwe and Kenya 1989-90, to
Pakistan 1990-91, to West Indies 1991-92, to South Africa 1993-94; England to
Australia 1994-95; MCC to Kenya 1999; Blade Group to Barbados 2000-01
Overseas teams played for: Past Bros, Bundaberg, Queensland; Avis Vogeltown,
New Plymouth, New Zealand; Melville, Perth, Australia
Cricketers particularly admired: Richard Hadlee, Ian Healy, Glenn McGrath
Young players to look out for: Ed Joyce
Other sports followed: Rugby league (Bradford Bulls), horse racing

Injuries: Dislocated finger; out for about three weeks in two spells with a torn quadricep

Relaxations: Horse racing

Extras: Played for England YC v Australia YC in 1983 and set record for most victims in an innings for England YC. Youngest wicket-keeper to play for Yorkshire. Released by Yorkshire to join Worcestershire at end of 1984 season. Set one-day record of four stumpings in an innings v Warwickshire in Sunday League at Edgbaston 1986. One of *Wisden*'s Five Cricketers of the Year 1995. Overtook David Bairstow (257) as the wicket-keeper with the most dismissals in the Sunday League, v Essex 1997. Made 1000th first-class dismissal of his career when he caught Graeme Swann off Alamgir Sheriyar v Northants at Northampton 1999. Equalled his own Worcestershire record for the most catches in a match with nine v Gloucestershire at Worcester 2000. Vice-captain of Worcestershire since 2001. Took 1000th first-class catch during the 2001 season. Coach of Zimbabwe U19 squad to U19 World Cup in New Zealand 2001-02. Scored 124 v Nottinghamshire at Trent Bridge 2002, in the process sharing with David Leatherdale (120) in a new record seventh-wicket partnership for Worcestershire (256)

Opinions on cricket: 'EU players – I understand that nothing can be done due to European law, but what is going to happen to our English-qualified youngsters? If the ECB were to deduct finances to counties for signing EU players they would think twice about signing them and the result would be signing a young English player.'

Best batting: 124 Worcestershire v Nottinghamshire, Trent Bridge 2002

2002 Season

	M	Inns	NO	Runs	HS	Avge	100s	50s	Ct	St	O	M	Runs	Wkts	Avge	Best	5wI	10wM
Test																		
All First	15	22	6	636	124	39.75	1	2	37	4								
1-day Int																		
C & G	3	2	1	19	15	19.00	-	-	4	1								
B & H	7	3	0	56	41	18.66	-	-	6	1								
1-day Lge	12	7	3	94	42	23.50	-	-	10	4								

Career Performances

	M	Inns	NO	Runs	HS	Avge	100s	50s	Ct	St	Balls	Runs	Wkts	Avge	Best	5wI	10wM
Test	11	17	5	294	65 *	24.50	-	1	46	3							
All First	412	583	155	14097	124	32.93	12	68	1056	118	6	30	0	-	-	-	-
1-day Int	9	8	2	107	56	17.83	-	1	9	2							
C & G	49	38	14	537	61	22.37	-	3	61	10	6	1	0	-	-	-	
B & H	81	54	8	638	51 *	13.86	-	1	102	11							
1-day Lge	271	173	55	2334	48 *	19.77	-	-	287	87							

RICHARDS, M. A.   Middlesex

Name: <u>Mali</u> Alexander Richards
Role: Left-hand bat
Born: 2 September 1983, Taunton
County debut: No first-team appearance
Parents: Vivian and Miriam
Family links with cricket: Father is West
Indies legend Viv Richards
Education: Cheltenham College
Overseas teams played for: Antigua and
Barbuda
Extras: Scored 958 runs for Cheltenham
College in 2001. Has played for
Gloucestershire 2nd XI. Played for Antigua
and Barbuda v Guyana in the Red Stripe
Bowl 2002-03. Is not considered an overseas
player

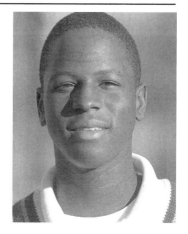

RICHARDSON, A.   Warwickshire

Name: Alan Richardson
Role: Right-hand bat, right-arm
medium bowler
Born: 6 May 1975, Newcastle-under-Lyme,
Staffs
Height: 6ft 3in **Weight:** 13st
Nickname: Richo
County debut: 1995 (Derbyshire),
1999 (Warwickshire)
County cap: 2002 (Warwickshire)
1st-Class 50s: 1
1st-Class 5 w. in innings: 4
1st-Class 10 w. in match: 1
1st-Class catches: 15
One-Day 5 w. in innings: 1
Place in batting averages: 252nd av. 16.50
Place in bowling averages: 23rd av. 25.02
(2001 45th av. 27.30)

Strike rate: 47.42 (career 60.18)
Parents: Roy and Sandra
Marital status: Single
Family links with cricket: 'Dad played for and captained Little Stoke 3rd XI'
Education: Manor Hill First School; Walton Priory Middle School; Alleyne's High School, Stone; Stafford College of Further Education
Qualifications: 8 GCSEs, 2 A-levels, 2 AS-levels, senior cricket coach
Career outside cricket: 'Cutting grass'
Off-season: 'Watching Stoke City and thrashing Mark Wagh at squash'
Overseas tours: Derbyshire to Malaga 1995; Warwickshire to Bloemfontein 2000, to Cape Town 2001
Overseas teams played for: Northern Natal, South Africa 1994-96; Hawkesbury CC, Sydney 1997-99; Northern Districts, Sydney 1999-2000, 2001-02
Career highlights to date: 'Getting capped by my native Staffordshire. Any attempted catch by Charlie Dagnall. Oh, and 8-51'
Cricket moments to forget: 'Grasping a tie from the open jaws of victory for Little Stoke in 1998. A true club pro at his best!'
Cricketers particularly admired: Angus Fraser, Tim Parmenter, Andrew Powers, and Jason Fellows 'for pure determination despite ability'
Young players to look out for: Jamie Spires, Jim Troughton, Nick Warren, Ed Dawes
Other sports played: 'Part of sound defensive unit for the Bears football team. Hoof!!!'
Other sports followed: 'One of the many passionate and knowledgeable Stoke City fans'
Relaxations: 'Music, football and "Station"'
Extras: *Cricket World* award for best bowling performance in Oxford U19 Festival (8-60 v Devon). Topped Minor Counties bowling averages with Staffordshire 1998 and won Minor Counties bowling award. Most Improved 2nd XI Player 1999. Outstanding Performance of the Year 1999 for his 8-51 v Gloucestershire on home debut; besides being the season's best analysis, it was the best return by a Warwickshire player on debut at Edgbaston. Scored 91 v Hampshire at Edgbaston 2002; it was the highest score by a Warwickshire No. 11 and in scoring it he shared with Nick Knight (255*) in a tenth-wicket stand of 214, which was a county best for the last wicket and the fifth highest tenth-wicket partnership in Championship history overall. Recorded maiden one-day five-wicket return (5-35) v Staffordshire (his native county) at Stone in the C&G 2002. His 8-46 in the second innings v Sussex at Edgbaston 2002 was the best return by a Warwickshire bowler since Bob Willis's 8-32 v Gloucestershire at Bristol in 1977. Awarded Warwickshire cap 2002
Opinions on cricket: 'Tea breaks have to be longer. Will someone in authority please listen to me?! No need for two overseas players – most counties already have three or four anyway!'
Best batting: 91 Warwickshire v Hampshire, Edgbaston 2002
Best bowling: 8-46 Warwickshire v Sussex, Edgbaston 2002

2002 Season

	M	Inns	NO	Runs	HS	Avge	100s	50s	Ct	St	O	M	Runs	Wkts	Avge	Best	5wI	10wM
Test																		
All First	10	12	4	132	91	16.50	-	1	5	-	300.2	64	951	38	25.02	8-46	2	-
1-day Int																		
C & G	1	1	1	1	1*	-	-	-	1	-	10	1	35	5	7.00	5-35	1	
B & H	6	2	1	6	5	6.00	-	-	2	-	46	3	188	6	31.33	4-21	-	
1-day Lge	4	2	1	9	8	9.00	-	-	1	-	29	1	178	3	59.33	1-30	-	

Career Performances

	M	Inns	NO	Runs	HS	Avge	100s	50s	Ct	St	Balls	Runs	Wkts	Avge	Best	5wI	10wM
Test																	
All First	43	39	18	208	91	9.90	-	1	15	-	7644	3573	127	28.13	8-46	4	1
1-day Int																	
C & G	4	4	1	4	3	1.33	-	-	1	-	228	151	6	25.16	5-35	1	
B & H	9	4	2	8	5	4.00	-	-	2	-	348	236	7	33.71	4-21	-	
1-day Lge	16	6	4	28	11*	14.00	-	-	2	-	661	539	17	31.70	3-17	-	

RICHARDSON, S. A.   *Yorkshire*

Name: <u>Scott</u> Andrew Richardson
Role: Right-hand bat, right-arm
medium bowler
Born: 5 September 1977, Oldham
Height: 6ft 2in **Weight:** 13st 6lbs
Nickname: Richo, Tickle
County debut: 2000
1st-Class 50s: 2
1st-Class catches: 8
Place in batting averages: (2001 159th
av. 23.88)
Parents: Mike and Anne
Marital status: Single ('girlfriend Denise')
Family links with cricket: 'Dad is an ex-
professional in local leagues. He owns
Romida Sports (specialist cricket shop)'
Education: Hulme Grammar School,
Oldham; Manchester Grammar School
Qualifications: 11 GCSEs, 2 A-levels
Career outside cricket: 'Work for Romida Sports'
Off-season: 'Either playing in Australia or working at Romida Sports'
Overseas tours: Manchester GS to Barbados 1993, to Cape Town 1995; MCC to
Philadelphia 2000; Yorkshire to Grenada 2002

Overseas teams played for: Easts-Redlands, Brisbane 1996-98; Redbank Plains, Queensland 1998-99
Career highlights to date: 'Making Championship debut'
Cricket moments to forget: 'Getting the "yips" when throwing the ball as 12th man in an NUL game 2001'
Cricket superstitions: 'Too many to mention'
Cricketers particularly admired: Michael Atherton, Robin Smith
Young players to look out for: David Stiff
Other sports played: Golf, football
Other sports followed: Football (Manchester United), rugby league (Oldham)
Relaxations: 'Watching Man Utd and Oldham rugby league side; movies; playing golf'
Extras: Lancashire Schools U19 Player of the Year 1995. Scored 69 v Kent at Headingley 2001, sharing in the process in the highest first-wicket partnership (152) for Yorkshire in matches against Kent for 49 years with Matthew Wood
Opinions on cricket: 'Need to keep 2nd XI because the step from board/league cricket to first-class would be too big.'
Best batting: 69 Yorkshire v Kent, Headingley 2001

2002 Season

	M	Inns	NO	Runs	HS	Avge	100s	50s	Ct	St	O	M	Runs	Wkts	Avge	Best	5wI	10wM
Test																		
All First	2	4	0	45	29	11.25	-	-	2	-								
1-day Int																		
C & G																		
B & H																		
1-day Lge																		

Career Performances

	M	Inns	NO	Runs	HS	Avge	100s	50s	Ct	St	Balls	Runs	Wkts	Avge	Best	5wI	10wM
Test																	
All First	10	17	2	274	69	18.26	-	2	8	-							
1-day Int																	
C & G																	
B & H																	
1-day Lge																	

ROBERTS, T. W.   Lancashire

Name: Timothy (Tim) William Roberts
Role: Right-hand bat, right-arm
off-spin bowler
Born: 4 March 1978, Kettering
Height: 5ft 7½in **Weight:** 11st
Nickname: Robbo
County debut: 2001
1st-Class catches: 2
Parents: David and Shirley
Marital status: Single
Family links with cricket: 'Brother Andy
was a leg-spinner at Northants; now captains
Bedfordshire. Dad Dave had trials for
Northants'
Education: Our Lady's Convent, Kettering;
Bishop Stopford School, Kettering;
Durham University
Qualifications: 2.1 degree in Geology,
Level 3 cricket coach

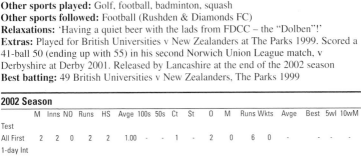

Overseas tours: England U17 to Holland 1995; Lancashire to South Africa
2000, 2001
Overseas teams played for: Eastern Suburbs, Wellington, New Zealand 1999-2000
Cricketers particularly admired: Andy Roberts, Ricky Ponting, Sachin Tendulkar,
Wayne Larkins
Young players to look out for: N. Coles, N. Brown, A. Daniels, S. Brett, M. Henson
Other sports played: Golf, football, badminton, squash
Other sports followed: Football (Rushden & Diamonds FC)
Relaxations: 'Having a quiet beer with the lads from FDCC – the "Dolben"!'
Extras: Played for British Universities v New Zealanders at The Parks 1999. Scored a
41-ball 50 (ending up with 55) in his second Norwich Union League match, v
Derbyshire at Derby 2001. Released by Lancashire at the end of the 2002 season
Best batting: 49 British Universities v New Zealanders, The Parks 1999

2002 Season

	M	Inns	NO	Runs	HS	Avge	100s	50s	Ct	St	O	M	Runs	Wkts	Avge	Best	5wI	10wM
Test																		
All First	2	2	0	2	2	1.00	-	-	1	-	2	0	6	0	-	-	-	-
1-day Int																		
C & G																			
B & H	4	3	0	48	33	16.00	-	-	1	-								
1-day Lge	2	2	0	14	14	7.00	-	-	1	-								

Career Performances

	M	Inns	NO	Runs	HS	Avge	100s	50s	Ct	St	Balls	Runs	Wkts	Avge	Best	5wI	10wM
Test																	
All First	5	7	0	110	49	15.71	-	-	2	-	12	6	0	-	-	-	-
1-day Int																	
C & G																	
B & H	4	3	0	48	33	16.00	-	-	1	-							
1-day Lge	5	5	0	82	55	16.40	-	1	1	-	18	14	0	-	-	-	

ROBINSON, D. D. J. Essex

Name: <u>Darren</u> David John Robinson
Role: Right-hand bat, leg-spin bowler
Born: 2 March 1973, Braintree, Essex
Height: 5ft 11in **Weight:** 14st
Nickname: Pies, Pie Shop, Robbo
County debut: 1993
County cap: 1997
1000 runs in a season: 1
1st-Class 50s: 29
1st-Class 100s: 14
1st-Class 200s: 1
1st-Class catches: 104
One-Day 100s: 3
Place in batting averages: 50th av. 46.06
(2001 99th av. 32.93)
Parents: Dorothy (deceased) and David
Wife and date of marriage: Alyssa,
2 December 2001
Children: Kalli, 20 July 1998; Cameron, 20 May 2000
Family links with cricket: Father plays club cricket for Halstead
Education: Tabor High School, Braintree; Chelmsford College of Further Education
Qualifications: 5 GCSEs, BTEC National Diploma in Building and Construction
Career outside cricket: Site investigation and surveying
Off-season: 'Drinking beer with my mates'
Overseas tours: England U18 to Canada (International Youth Tournament) 1991;
England U19 to Pakistan 1991-92
Overseas teams played for: Waverley, Sydney 1992-94; Eden Roskill CC,
Auckland 1995-96
Career highlights to date: 'Every trophy we have won'
Cricket moments to forget: 'Being bowled out for 57 against Lancashire in the
NatWest final [1996]'

Cricket superstitions: 'None'
Cricketers particularly admired: Steve Hale, David Denny
Young players to look out for: Ravinder Bopara, Mark Pettini
Other sports played: Football, golf, squash
Other sports followed: Golf, football, rugby, swimming
Injuries: Most of winter 2002-03 spent recovering from operation for double stress fracture of the back
Relaxations: 'Reading crime novels, music, eating out, pubs'
Extras: *Daily Telegraph* Batting Award 1988. International Youth Tournament in Canada batting award 1991. Scored two centuries (102 and 118*) in match v Leicestershire at Chelmsford 2001. Scored Championship career-best 175 v Gloucestershire at Gloucester 2002 while captaining Essex in the absence of Ronnie Irani on international duty. Scored 119 v Glamorgan at Chelmsford 2002, in the process passing 1000 first-class runs in a season for the first time. Essex Player of the Year 2002
Opinions on cricket: 'Not sure two overseas players is a good idea. Too many talented young players are going to be released to finance them; also, many clubs cannot afford them. There should only be two up and down from each division. Also, longer for tea break – maybe extend to 30 minutes.'
Best batting: 200 Essex v New Zealanders, Chelmsford 1999

2002 Season

	M	Inns	NO	Runs	HS	Avge	100s	50s	Ct	St	O	M	Runs	Wkts	Avge	Best	5wI	10wM
Test																		
All First	18	34	2	1474	175	46.06	5	6	17	-	9	1	54	0	-	-	-	-
1-day Int																		
C & G	3	3	0	128	59	42.66	-	2	1	-								
B & H	6	6	0	113	46	18.83	-	-	-	-								
1-day Lge	14	14	0	369	76	26.35	-	3	7	-								

Career Performances

	M	Inns	NO	Runs	HS	Avge	100s	50s	Ct	St	Balls	Runs	Wkts	Avge	Best	5wI	10wM
Test																	
All First	125	220	11	6557	200	31.37	15	29	104	-	165	153	0	-	-	-	-
1-day Int																	
C & G	19	17	1	405	62	25.31	-	4	6	-							
B & H	26	24	3	633	137 *	30.14	2	1	3	-							
1-day Lge	102	100	8	2358	129 *	25.63	1	12	31	-	17	26	1	26.00	1-7	-	

ROBINSON, M. A.   Sussex

Name: <u>Mark</u> Andrew Robinson
Role: Right-hand bat, right-arm fast-medium bowler
Born: 23 November 1966, Hull
Height: 6ft 3in **Weight:** 13st
Nickname: Coddy, Smokie, Tiger, Storm, Rodney
County debut: 1987 (Northamptonshire), 1991 (Yorkshire), 1996 (Sussex)
County cap: 1990 (Northamptonshire), 1992 (Yorkshire), 1997 (Sussex)
50 wickets in a season: 1
1st-Class 5 w. in innings: 13
1st-Class 10 w. in match: 2
1st-Class catches: 41
Place in batting averages: (2001 281st av. 4.00)

Place in bowling averages: (2001 8th av. 19.33)
Strike rate: 48.00 (career 64.53)
Parents: Malcolm and Joan
Wife and date of marriage: Julia, 8 October 1994
Children: Samuel Lewis, 11 January 1996; Eleanor Grace, 20 July 2000
Family links with cricket: Grandfather a prominent local cricketer and 'father was hostile bowler in the back garden'
Education: Fifth Avenue Primary; Endike Junior High; Hull Grammar School
Qualifications: 6 O-levels, 2 A-levels, advanced cricket coach, badminton coach, rugby union coach
Career outside cricket: Self-employed cricket coach
Overseas tours: England U19 North to Bermuda; Yorkshire to Cape Town 1991-92, 1992-93, to West Indies 1993-94; Sussex to Grenada 2001
Overseas teams played for: East Shirley, Canterbury, New Zealand 1987-89; Canterbury, New Zealand 1989-98
Career highlights to date: '9-37 v Northants'
Cricket moments to forget: 'Don't want to forget any moment of what is a privileged existence'
Cricketers particularly admired: Peter Moores, Keith Greenfield, Tony Cottey 'and any other player who lives for the game'
Young players to look out for: Steve Patterson, Joe Sayers, Matt Prior, Tim Ambrose, Sam Robinson
Other sports played: Football
Other sports followed: Football (Hull City), 'all sports'

Extras: Took hat-trick with first three balls of innings in Yorkshire League playing for Hull v Doncaster. First player to win Yorkshire U19 Bowler of the Season in two successive years, 1984 and 1985. Northamptonshire Uncapped Player of the Year in 1989. Endured a world record 12 innings without scoring a run in 1990. Sussex Clubman of the Year 1997 and 1998. Scored 500th first-class run on the same day as he took 500th first-class wicket v Surrey at Hove 1999. Was not out in ten successive innings during 1999-2000, equalling the record for county cricket. B&H Gold Award for his 4-29 v Kent at Hastings 2001. His 5-59 v Durham at Hove 2001 included his 200th wicket for Sussex. Appointed Sussex club coach for 2003

Opinions on cricket: 'Never trust a man who likes green sweets.'

Best batting: 27 Sussex v Lancashire, Old Trafford 1997

Best bowling: 9-37 Yorkshire v Northamptonshire, Harrogate 1993

2002 Season

	M	Inns	NO	Runs	HS	Avge	100s	50s	Ct	St	O	M	Runs	Wkts	Avge	Best	5wI	10wM
Test																		
All First	1	2	1	10	6	10.00	-	-	-	-	40	8	138	5	27.60	3-57	-	-
1-day Int																		
C & G																		
B & H																		
1-day Lge	5	4	2	15	7 *	7.50	-	-	-	-	28	3	201	6	33.50	2-38	-	

Career Performances

	M	Inns	NO	Runs	HS	Avge	100s	50s	Ct	St	Balls	Runs	Wkts	Avge	Best	5wI	10wM
Test																	
All First	229	259	112	590	27	4.01	-	-	41	-	37689	17807	584	30.49	9-37	13	2
1-day Int																	
C & G	29	11	7	19	8 *	4.75	-	-	3	-	1908	1042	38	27.42	4-32	-	
B & H	34	15	7	12	5	1.50	-	-	6	-	1906	1131	43	26.30	4-29	-	
1-day Lge	176	69	31	127	15 *	3.34	-	-	16	-	7780	5488	171	32.09	4-23	-	

72. Who took 106 County Championship wickets
in 1998 at the age of 35?

ROLLINS, A. S. Northamptonshire

Name: <u>Adrian</u> Stewart Rollins
Role: Right-hand bat, right-arm 'medium rubbish'
Born: 8 February 1972, Barking
Height: 6ft 5in **Weight:** 'Lighter than last year'
Nickname: Rollie, Blaah
County debut: 1993 (Derbyshire), 2000 (Northants)
County cap: 1995 (Derbyshire)
1000 runs in a season: 3
1st-Class 50s: 40
1st-Class 100s: 11
1st-Class 200s: 2
1st-Class catches: 109
1st-Class stumpings: 1
One-Day 100s: 1
Place in batting averages: 73rd av. 41.81 (2001 163rd av. 23.77)
Strike rate: (career 90.00)
Parents: Marva
Children: Jared Terrell, 1 June 1999; Jordell Deane, 30 September 2001
Family links with cricket: 'Brother [Robert] was at Essex [1991-99]. Other brother plays when he gets permission from his missus'
Education: Avenue Primary, Manor Park, London; Little Ilford Comprehensive, Manor Park, London; Open University
Qualifications: 10 GCSEs, 4 A-levels, BAWLA leader's award, CCPR Community Sports Leader's award, Diploma in Sports Psychology, Certificate in Social Sciences (Open University)
Career outside cricket: 'Psychologist, so I can find out how far up I am on the fruitcake scale'
Off-season: 'Getting my coat, drying my eyes and scooping my chins up'
Overseas tours: London Federation of Boys Clubs to Barbados 1987; Northamptonshire to Grenada 2000, 2001
Overseas teams played for: Kaponga, Taranaki, New Zealand 1993-94; Taranaki, New Zealand 2000-02 (captain)
Career highlights to date: 'Hundred before lunch v Glamorgan at Chesterfield 1997'
Cricket moments to forget: 'Getting injured taking a catch versus Notts [2002]. It cost me dearly – I bust my wrist'
Cricket superstitions: 'Don't get out to rubbish'
Cricketers particularly admired: Phillip DeFreitas, Malcolm Marshall, David Gower, Viv Richards, Gordon Greenidge, Desmond Haynes, Michael Holding

Young players to look out for: Jared and Jordell Rollins ('Gonna run world cricket. Remember where you heard it')
Other sports played: Badminton (Essex at junior level), 'racketball master', chess
Other sports followed: Football (West Ham), basketball (LA Lakers)
Injuries: Out for two and a half months with damaged wrist cartilage
Relaxations: 'I don't know how to relax; I have kids'
Extras: Made Championship debut on same day as brother. Became 500th first-class player for Derbyshire, for whom he was named Young Player of the Year 1993. Scored maiden first-class century (118) v Glamorgan at Derby 1995, becoming the 100th player to score a hundred for Derbyshire. In 1995 set record for the highest score by a Derbyshire opener to carry his bat – his 200 not out v Gloucestershire was also the longest innings by a Derbyshire player, and he became the youngest English-qualified Derbyshire double centurion. Voted Derbyshire Player of the Year for 1995. Took part in record third-wicket partnership for Derbyshire (316*) with Kim Barnett against Leicestershire 1997. Left Derbyshire at the end of the 1999 season and joined Northamptonshire for 2000. Retired during the 2002-03 off-season because of ruptured ligaments of the wrist
Opinions on cricket: 'If you can play cricket for a fair amount of time and maintain your sanity, then you are a champion. Clichés should be banned from dressing rooms.'
Best batting: 210 Derbyshire v Hampshire, Chesterfield 1997
Best bowling: 1-19 Derbyshire v Essex, Chelmsford 1995

2002 Season

	M	Inns	NO	Runs	HS	Avge	100s	50s	Ct	St	O	M	Runs	Wkts	Avge	Best	5wI	10wM
Test																		
All First	6	12	1	460	107	41.81	1	2	6	-								
1-day Int																		
C & G																		
B & H																		
1-day Lge																		

Career Performances

	M	Inns	NO	Runs	HS	Avge	100s	50s	Ct	St	Balls	Runs	Wkts	Avge	Best	5wI	10wM
Test																	
All First	129	233	20	7331	210	34.41	13	40	109	1	90	122	1	122.00	1-19	-	-
1-day Int																	
C & G	14	13	0	323	80	24.84	-	3	9	-							
B & H	12	12	1	263	70 *	23.90	-	2	2	-							
1-day Lge	73	67	6	1139	126 *	18.67	1	1	29	-	12	15	0	-	-	-	-

ROSE, G. D.   Somerset

Name: <u>Graham</u> David Rose
Role: Right-hand bat, right-arm fast-medium bowler, first slip
Born: 12 April 1964, Tottenham, London
Height: 6ft 4in **Weight:** 15st 7lbs
Nickname: Rosie, Hagar
County debut: 1985 (Middlesex), 1987 (Somerset)
County cap: 1988 (Somerset)
Benefit: 1997 (Somerset, £91,500)
1000 runs in a season: 1
50 wickets in a season: 5
1st-Class 50s: 41
1st-Class 100s: 11
1st-Class 5 w. in innings: 15
1st-Class 10 w. in match: 1
1st-Class catches: 117
One-Day 100s: 2
Strike rate: (career 56.85)

Parents: William and Edna
Wife and date of marriage: Teresa Julie, 19 September 1987
Children: Georgina Charlotte, 6 December 1990; Felix William Michael, 11 August 1997
Family links with cricket: Father and brothers have played club cricket
Education: Northumberland Park School, Tottenham
Qualifications: 6 O-levels, 4 A-levels, NCA coaching certificate
Overseas teams played for: Carey Park, Bunbury, Western Australia 1984-85; Fremantle, Perth 1986-87; Paarl, Cape Town 1988-89
Cricketers particularly admired: Andrew Caddick, Jimmy Cook, Richard Hadlee, Malcolm Marshall, Mushtaq Ahmed
Young players to look out for: Matthew Bulbeck, Peter Trego
Other sports followed: Football, rugby, golf
Relaxations: Wine, golf, 'Georgina and Felix'
Extras: Played for England YC v Australia YC 1983. Took 6-41 on Middlesex debut v Worcestershire at Worcester 1985 (the best innings figures by a Middlesex bowler on first-class debut), then scored 95 on debut for Somerset v Lancashire at Taunton 1987. Completed double of 1000 runs and 50 wickets in first-class cricket in 1990 and set records for fastest recorded centuries in NatWest Trophy (36 balls v Devon at Torquay) and Sunday League (46 balls v Glamorgan at Neath; since bettered). Scored 1097 runs and took 100 wickets in all first-team county cricket 1997. Cricket Society's All-rounder of the Year 1997. Retired at the end of the 2002 season
Best batting: 191 Somerset v Sussex, Taunton 1997
Best bowling: 7-47 Somerset v Nottinghamshire, Taunton 1996

2002 Season

	M	Inns	NO	Runs	HS	Avge	100s	50s	Ct	St	O	M	Runs	Wkts	Avge	Best	5wI	10wM
Test																		
All First	3	4	0	84	32	21.00	-	-	1	-	30	10	95	0	-		-	-
1-day Int																		
C & G	1	1	0	0	0	0.00	-	-	-	-	7	1	13	1	13.00	1-13	-	
B & H																		
1-day Lge	3	3	1	43	20 *	21.50	-	-	1	-	23	1	110	2	55.00	1-29	-	

Career Performances

	M	Inns	NO	Runs	HS	Avge	100s	50s	Ct	St	Balls	Runs	Wkts	Avge	Best	5wI	10wM
Test																	
All First	251	347	63	8737	191	30.76	11	41	117	-	34338	17963	604	29.74	7-47	15	1
1-day Int																	
C & G	26	22	3	372	110	19.57	1	1	4	-	1408	902	30	30.06	3-11	-	
B & H	56	49	5	926	79	21.04	-	4	12	-	2968	1968	68	28.94	4-21	-	
1-day Lge	208	180	35	3725	148	25.68	1	19	52	-	8198	6046	200	30.23	4-26	-	

RUSSELL, R. C.   Gloucestershire

Name: Robert Charles (Jack) Russell
Role: Left-hand bat, wicket-keeper
Born: 15 August 1963, Stroud
Height: 5ft 8¼in **Weight:** 9st 9lbs
County debut: 1981
County cap: 1985
Benefit: 1994
Test debut: 1988
Tests: 54
One-Day Internationals: 40
1000 runs in a season: 1
50 dismissals in a season: 15
1st-Class 50s: 86
1st-Class 100s: 11
1st-Class catches: 1159
1st-Class stumpings: 123
One-Day 100s: 2
Place in batting averages: 53rd av. 45.04
(2001 79th av. 37.30)
Strike rate: (career 56.00)
Parents: John (deceased) and Jennifer
Wife and date of marriage: Aileen Ann, 6 March 1985

Children: Stepson, Marcus Anthony, 1980; Elizabeth Ann, March 1988; Victoria, 1989; Charles David, 1991; Katherine Jane, 1996

Family links with cricket: 'Late father and late brother played club cricket (plus other sports)'

Education: Uplands County Primary School; Archway Comprehensive School; Bristol Polytechnic ('walked out after two months of accountancy course. Couldn't understand the sociology and economics – wanted to play cricket instead')

Qualifications: 7 O-levels, 2 A-levels

Career outside cricket: Professional artist

Off-season: 'Painting'

Overseas tours: England A to Australia 1992-93 (vice-captain); England to Pakistan 1987-88, to India and West Indies 1989-90, to Australia 1990-91, to New Zealand 1991-92, to West Indies 1993-94, to Australia 1994-95, to South Africa 1995-96, to Pakistan and India (World Cup) 1995-96, to Zimbabwe and New Zealand 1996-97, to West Indies 1997-98, to Bangladesh (Wills International Cup) 1998-99

Career highlights to date: 'Running down the steps and onto the ground at Lord's to make Test debut'

Cricket moments to forget: 'All ducks and missed chances!'

Cricket superstitions: 'None (if you believe that, you'll believe anything!). Too many to mention'

Cricketers particularly admired: Alan Knott, Bob Taylor, Ian Botham, Sir Don Bradman, Rodney Marsh, 'and other greats'

Others sports played: None – 'no time! Too busy painting'

Other sports followed: Football, rugby, snooker, 'anything competitive'

Relaxations: Playing cricket and painting pictures. 'I love comedians and comedies. Life is too short, you need to laugh as much as you can'

Extras: Became youngest Gloucestershire wicket-keeper (17 years 307 days) and set record for most dismissals in a match on first-class debut: 8 (7 caught, 1 stumped) for Gloucestershire v Sri Lankans at Bristol 1981. Hat-trick of catches v Surrey at The Oval 1986 (one off Courtney Walsh; two off David Lawrence). Was chosen as England's Man of the Test Series, England v Australia 1989 and was one of *Wisden's* Five Cricketers of the Year 1990. Opened Jack Russell Gallery in Chipping Sodbury, South Gloucestershire, in 1995; his paintings are sold and displayed in museums and private collections all around the world. *Jack Russell – Unleashed*, an autobiography, made the top ten bestsellers in 1997. Has website: http://www.jackrussell.co.uk. Captain of Gloucestershire and Player of the Year 1995. Broke Bob Taylor's long-standing world record for the number of dismissals in a Test match with 11 (all caught) in the second Test v South Africa at Johannesburg 1995-96; his 27 Test dismissals in the series is a record for England. Awarded MBE in 1996 for services to cricket. Was the Whyte and Mackay wicket-keeper/batsman of the year 1995, 1996, 1997. Became seventh wicket-keeper to take 1000 first-class catches when he caught Tim Robinson v Notts at Bristol 1999. Set a new NatWest dismissals record by claiming his 67th victim (Adrian Rollins) v Derbyshire at Bristol 1999. Man of the Match in Gloucestershire's NatWest final victory over Somerset 1999. Conceded no byes in Northamptonshire's 746 v Gloucestershire at Bristol 2002, bettering the previous world record for a clean sheet in first-class cricket – 716 by Srinivasan Reuben Paul of Tamil Nadu v Karnataka in 1995-96. Scored 107 v Essex at Gloucester 2002, in the process sharing with Ian Fisher (103*) in a record seventh-wicket partnership for Gloucestershire in matches v Essex (207). Took six catches in an innings for Gloucestershire for the first time, v Durham at Bristol 2002. During 2002 season passed Gloucestershire record for most first-class runs by a wicket-keeper and equalled club record for most first-class dismissals (1016 by Jack Board). Winner of Cricket Writers' Club Peter Smith Award (for presentation of cricket to the public) 2002. Recent painting commissions include 'The Cenotaph' for Royal British Legion; 'Field Marshals of the British Army' for Army Benevolent Fund (hanging National Army Museum, London); Duke of Edinburgh; Duke of Kent

Best batting: 129* England v Boland, Paarl 1995-96
Best bowling: 1-4 Gloucestershire v West Indians, Bristol 1991

2002 Season

	M	Inns	NO	Runs	HS	Avge	100s	50s	Ct	St	O	M	Runs	Wkts	Avge	Best	5wI	10wM
Test																		
All First	17	28	6	991	119 *	45.04	3	5	39	2								
1-day Int																		
C & G	3	1	0	66	66	66.00	-	1	4	2								
B & H	6	3	2	39	25 *	39.00	-	-	8	-								
1-day Lge	15	10	1	138	42	15.33	-	-	21	5								

Career Performances

	M	Inns	NO	Runs	HS	Avge	100s	50s	Ct	St	Balls	Runs	Wkts	Avge	Best	5wI	10wM
Test	54	86	16	1897	128 *	27.10	2	6	153	12							
All First	452	672	140	16395	129 *	30.81	11	86	1159	123	56	68	1	68.00	1-4	-	-
1-day Int	40	31	7	423	50	17.62	-	1	41	6							
C & G	56	42	11	888	84	28.64	-	4	79	15							
B & H	84	61	23	1215	119 *	31.97	1	5	86	15							
1-day Lge	266	209	46	3719	108	22.81	1	15	227	54							

73. Name the overseas cricketers who played for
Warwickshire in 2002.

SADLER, J. L. Leicestershire

Name: <u>John</u> Leonard Sadler
Role: Left-hand bat
Born: 19 November 1981, Dewsbury
Height: 5ft 11in **Weight:** 12st 6lbs
Nickname: Sads
County debut: No first-team appearance
(*see* **Extras**)
Parents: Mike and Sue
Marital status: Single
Family links with cricket: Father played and
now coaches. Brothers Dave and Jamie play
for Ossett in Central Yorkshire League; both
played for Yorkshire youth teams
Education: St Ignatius Primary, Ossett;
St Thomas à Becket Comprehensive, Wakefield
Qualifications: 9 GCSEs, Level 1 coaching
award
Off-season: 'Playing club cricket for Tuart
Hill, Perth'

Overseas tours: England U19 to Malaysia and (U19 World Cup) Sri Lanka
1999-2000, to India 2000-01; Yorkshire to Grenada 2002
Overseas teams played for: Tuart Hill, Perth 2001-03
Career highlights to date: 'Selection for England youth teams. Award of Yorkshire
2nd XI cap. Debut for Yorkshire v West Indies A'
Cricket moments to forget: 'Injury to knee in Sri Lanka January 2000, leading to
early return to England from U19 World Cup squad'
Cricketers particularly admired: Sachin Tendulkar, Graham Thorpe, Robin Smith
Young players to look out for: Ian Bell, Nicky Peng, Tim Bresnan
Other sports played: Football
Other sports followed: Football (Leeds United), rugby league (Leeds Rhinos)
Relaxations: 'Socialising with friends, keeping fit, sleeping'
Extras: Played for Yorkshire Schools at all levels and joined Yorkshire Academy 1998.
Yorkshire Supporters' Club Young Player of the Year 1998. Represented England at
U14, U15, U17, U18 and U19 levels; represented England U17 at the ECC Colts
Festival in Northern Ireland 1999. Represented England U19 v Sri Lanka U19 in one-
day series 2000 and v West Indies in one-day (3/3) and Test (1/3) series 2001. Played
for Yorkshire Board XI in the NatWest 1999. Did not appear for Yorkshire in a
domestic competition in 2002 but played for the county v West Indies A in a one-day
fixture at Headingley. Awarded Yorkshire 2nd XI cap 2002. Released by Yorkshire at
the end of the 2002 season and has joined Leicestershire for 2003
Opinions on cricket: 'The best game and the hardest at times.'

2002 Season (did not make any first-class or one-day appearances)

Career Performances

	M	Inns	NO	Runs	HS	Avge	100s	50s	Ct	St	Balls	Runs	Wkts	Avge	Best	5wI	10wM
Test																	
All First																	
1-day Int																	
C & G	1	1	0	9	9	9.00	-	-	-	-							
B & H																	
1-day Lge																	

SAGGERS, M. J.   Kent

Name: <u>Martin</u> John Saggers
Role: Right-hand bat ('should perhaps try left-handed after last year's efforts'), right-arm fast-medium bowler
Born: 23 May 1972, King's Lynn
Height: 6ft 2in **Weight:** 14st 2lbs
Nickname: Saggs, Saggy Bits, Bits of Aloo, Jurgen Burgen
County debut: 1996 (Durham), 1999 (Kent)
County cap: 2001 (Kent)
50 wickets in a season: 3
1st-Class 50s: 1
1st-Class 5 w. in innings: 13
1st-Class catches: 13
One-Day 5 w. in innings: 1
Place in batting averages: 314th av. 5.61 (2001 243rd av. 12.33)
Place in bowling averages: 9th av. 21.51 (2001 30th av. 24.23)
Strike rate: 41.27 (career 44.24)
Parents: Brian and Edna
Marital status: Single
Family links with cricket: Grandfather played in the Essex League
Education: Roseberry Avenue Primary School; Springwood High School; University of Huddersfield
Qualifications: BA (Hons) Architectural Studies International
Career outside cricket: 'A bit of coaching, and helping run the club website'
Off-season: 'Training in the gym; working very hard on my batting (I need all the help I can get). Disappearing off to South Africa for six weeks (yes, Min, to see the elephants and giraffes)'

Overseas tours: England VI to Hong Kong 2002
Overseas teams played for: Randburg CC, Johannesburg 1996-98, 2000-01; Southern
Suburbs CC, Johannesburg 1998-99
Career highlights to date: 'Winning the Norwich Union League [2001]'
Cricket moments to forget: 'There is not really one particular moment, it is more a
combination of a few – i.e. all the ducks that I have amassed over the past season'
Cricket superstitions: 'Getting a corner spot in the changing room'
Cricketers particularly admired: Neil Foster, Graham Dilley, Allan Donald,
Richard Ellison, Willie Garbers
Young players to look out for: Amjad Khan, Duncan Bousted, John Payne
Other sports played: Golf (14 handicap), 'and any other sport where you can run
around like a headless chicken'
Other sports followed: Football (Spurs), 'anything that is shown on Sky Sports
channels'
Injuries: 'Just the odd pulled muscle at the beginning of the season'
Relaxations: 'Going on safari in the Kruger National Park in South Africa. Also
spending many an hour in the jacuzzi'
Extras: Released by Durham at end of the 1998 season and joined Kent. Took career
best 7-79 against his old county, Durham, at Riverside 2000. Won Most Promising
Uncapped Player Award 2000. Joint Kent Player of the Year 2000 (with David
Masters). Took two hat-tricks in two weeks for Randburg CC, Johannesburg 2000-01,
including one spell of five wickets in six balls. Took three wickets in four balls in last
over of Norwich Union League match at Canterbury 2001, preventing Yorkshire from
scoring the 13 needed to win. Underwood Award (Kent leading wicket-taker) 2001,
2002. Took 5-18 for The Brits v Rest of the World XI in the indoor Power Cricket
tournament at the Millennium Stadium, Cardiff 2002. Took 5-42 v Somerset at
Canterbury 2002 to register his third five-wicket return in consecutive Championship
matches. *Kent Messenger* Group Readers Player of the Season 2002. Shepherd Neame
Award for Best Bowler 2002. Cowdrey Award (Kent Player of the Year) 2002. Joint
leading wicket-taker in English first-class cricket 2002 (with Kevin Dean) with 83
wickets (av. 21.51)
Opinions on cricket: 'It is great to have the two division system. However, there
should only be two teams being promoted and relegated. Three is one too many.'
Best batting: 61* Kent v Lancashire, Canterbury 2001
Best bowling: 7-79 Kent v Durham, Riverside 2000
Stop press: Included in provisional England squad of 30 for the 2002-03 World Cup

2002 Season

	M	Inns	NO	Runs	HS	Avge	100s	50s	Ct	St	O	M	Runs	Wkts	Avge	Best	5wI	10wM
Test																		
All First	16	19	6	73	16 *	5.61	-	-	6	-	571	111	1786	83	21.51	6-39	6	-
1-day Int																		
C & G	4	2	2	0	0 *	-	-	-	1	-	33	3	153	4	38.25	3-41	-	
B & H	5	4	2	16	10 *	8.00	-	-	3	-	39.2	2	170	3	56.66	2-19	-	
1-day Lge	13	5	2	6	4 *	2.00	-	-	5	-	104.1	8	467	20	23.35	4-37	-	

Career Performances

SALES, D. J. G.   Northamptonshire

Name: <u>David</u> John Grimwood Sales
Role: Right-hand bat
Born: 3 December 1977, Carshalton, Surrey
Height: 6ft **Weight:** 14st 7lbs
Nickname: Jumble, Grimmers,
Johnny Hartson, Peanut
County debut: 1994 (one-day),
1996 (first-class)
County cap: 1999
1000 runs in a season: 1
1st-Class 50s: 19
1st-Class 100s: 6
1st-Class 200s: 2
1st-Class 300s: 1
1st-Class catches: 66
Place in batting averages: 180th av. 25.04
Strike rate: (career 33.66)
Parents: John and Daphne
Wife and date of marriage: Abigail, 22 September 2001
Family links with cricket: 'Father played club cricket, and father-in-law bowls a
mean ball in the back garden'
Education: Cumnor House Prep School, Croydon; Caterham Boys' School
Qualifications: 7 GCSEs, cricket coach
Career outside cricket: 'Fishing, golf'
Off-season: 'Working on a building site for Friar Tuck'
Overseas tours: England U15 to South Africa 1993; England U19 to West Indies
1994-95, to Zimbabwe 1995-96, to Pakistan 1996-97; England A to Kenya and Sri Lanka
1997-98, to Bangladesh and New Zealand 1999-2000, to West Indies 2000-01; Northants
to Grenada 2000
Overseas teams played for: Wellington Firebirds, New Zealand 2001-02
Career highlights to date: '303 not out v Essex'

Cricket moments to forget: 'Watching White and Powell for five hours, then getting 0' (*Rob White and Mark Powell shared in a new record Northamptonshire opening partnership of 375 v Gloucestershire at Northampton 2002*)
Cricket superstitions: 'None'
Cricketers particularly admired: Graham Gooch, Darren Cousins
Young players to look out for: Mark Powell, Robert White ('Zorro')
Other sports followed: Football (Crystal Palace), golf
Relaxations: Golf and fishing
Extras: Sir John Hobbs Silver Jubilee Memorial Prize 1993. In 1994, became youngest batsman (16 years 289 days) to score a 50 in the Sunday League with his 56-ball 70* v Essex at Chelmsford. Scored 210* v Worcs 1996 to become first Englishman to score a double century on his Championship debut and the youngest ever to score a double century. Became the youngest Englishman to score a first-class 300 (303*) v Essex at Northampton 1999 aged 21 years 240 days (and became the first Englishman to 1000 runs for 1999 in the process). PCA/CGU Young Player of the Year 1999. Scored 276 off 375 balls v Nottinghamshire at Northampton 2000. Scored 62 for Wellington v Canterbury in the final of New Zealand's State Shield at Wellington 2001-02, winning the Man of the Match award
Best batting: 303* Northamptonshire v Essex, Northampton 1999
Best bowling: 4-25 Northamptonshire v Sri Lanka A, Northampton 1999

2002 Season

	M	Inns	NO	Runs	HS	Avge	100s	50s	Ct	St	O	M	Runs	Wkts	Avge	Best	5wI	10wM
Test																		
All First	14	22	0	551	179	25.04	1	3	11	-								
1-day Int																		
C & G	2	2	0	53	44	26.50	-	-	-	-								
B & H	5	5	1	138	76	34.50	-	1	4	-								
1-day Lge	15	14	0	459	93	32.78	-	5	7	-								

Career Performances

	M	Inns	NO	Runs	HS	Avge	100s	50s	Ct	St	Balls	Runs	Wkts	Avge	Best	5wI	10wM
Test																	
All First	90	141	10	4374	303 *	33.38	9	19	66	-	303	163	9	18.11	4-25	-	-
1-day Int																	
C & G	11	11	1	341	65	34.10	-	3	5	-	12	13	0	-	-	-	-
B & H	12	12	2	269	76	26.90	-	2	6	-							
1-day Lge	81	76	10	1861	93	28.19	-	12	28	-	24	17	0	-	-	-	-

SALISBURY, I. D. K.   Surrey

Name: <u>Ian</u> David Kenneth Salisbury
Role: Right-hand bat, leg-break bowler
Born: 21 January 1970, Moulton,
Northampton
Height: 5ft 11in   **Weight:** 12st 7lbs
Nickname: Solly, Dingle, Sals
County debut: 1989 (Sussex), 1997 (Surrey)
County cap: 1991 (Sussex), 1998 (Surrey)
Test debut: 1992
Tests: 15
One-Day Internationals: 4
50 wickets in a season: 6
1st-Class 50s: 18
1st-Class 100s: 1
1st-Class 5 w. in innings: 34
1st-Class 10 w. in match: 6
1st-Class catches: 171
One-Day 5 w. in innings: 1
Place in batting averages: 233rd av. 18.88 (2001 149th av. 25.88)
Place in bowling averages: 80th av. 32.10 (2001 122nd av. 42.62)
Strike rate: 55.21 (career 63.38)
Parents: Dave and Margaret
Wife and date of marriage: Emma Louise, 25 September 1993
Children: Anya-Rose, 10 August 2002
Family links with cricket: 'Dad is vice-president of my first club, Brixworth. He also re-lays cricket squares (e.g. Lord's, Northampton, Leicester)'
Education: Moulton Primary; Moulton Comprehensive (both Northampton)
Qualifications: 7 O-levels, NCA coaching certificate, 'life'
Off-season: 'More coaching qualifications. Coaching at Surrey Cricket Academy'
Overseas tours: England A to Pakistan 1990-91, to Bermuda and West Indies 1991-92, to India 1994-95, to Pakistan 1995-96; England to India and Sri Lanka 1992-93, to West Indies 1993-94, to Pakistan 2000-01; World Masters XI v Indian Masters XI November 1996 ('Masters aged 26?')
Overseas teams played for: University of New South Wales, Sydney 1997-2000
Cricketers particularly admired: 'Any that keep performing day in, day out, for both country and county (e.g. Saqlain, Martin Bicknell, Andrew Caddick, Steve Waugh)'
Young players to look out for: Jim Troughton, Kyle Hogg, Ricky Anderson, Scott Newman, Rikki Clarke, Akbar Ansari
Other sports played: 'Most sports'
Other sports followed: Football (Southampton FC, Northampton Town FC), rugby union (Northampton Saints), 'any England team'

Relaxations: 'Spending time with wife, Emma; meeting friends and relaxing with them and eating out with good wine. Also, Sydney has its moments!!'

Extras: Picked to play two Tests for England against Pakistan in 1992, 'proudest moments of my career'. Originally selected for England A tour to Australia 1992-93 but was asked to stay on in India and played in the first two Tests of the series. In 1992 was named Young Player of the Year by both the Wombwell Cricket Lovers and the Cricket Writers. One of *Wisden*'s Five Cricketers of the Year 1993. Left Sussex during the 1996-97 off-season to join Surrey. Won the Bill O'Reilly Medal for Sydney first-grade player of the year 1999-2000, taking 36 wickets at 10.31 and averaging 40 with the bat playing for University of New South Wales

Opinions on cricket: 'Two up/two down in the Championship.'

Best batting: 100* Surrey v Somerset, The Oval 1999

Best bowling: 8-60 Surrey v Somerset, The Oval 2000

2002 Season

	M	Inns	NO	Runs	HS	Avge	100s	50s	Ct	St	O	M	Runs	Wkts	Avge	Best	5wI	10wM
Test																		
All First	14	20	2	340	59	18.88	-	1	11	-	340.3	50	1188	37	32.10	4-59	-	-
1-day Int																		
C & G	1	0	0	0	0	-	-	-	-	-	2	0	14	0	-	-	-	-
B & H	3	3	1	38	18	19.00	-	-	1	-	16	1	79	2	39.50	2-48	-	
1-day Lge	9	7	2	80	21	16.00	-	-	5	-	49.1	0	236	7	33.71	3-44	-	

Career Performances

	M	Inns	NO	Runs	HS	Avge	100s	50s	Ct	St	Balls	Runs	Wkts	Avge	Best	5wI	10wM
Test	15	25	3	368	50	16.72	-	1	5	-	2492	1539	20	76.95	4-163	-	-
All First	261	336	68	5201	100 *	19.40	1	18	171	-	46079	23276	727	32.01	8-60	34	6
1-day Int	4	2	1	7	5	7.00	-	-	1	-	186	177	5	35.40	3-41	-	
C & G	29	17	5	164	34 *	13.66	-	-	5	-	1697	980	33	29.69	3-28	-	
B & H	42	26	10	213	19	13.31	-	-	16	-	2151	1530	48	31.87	4-53	-	
1-day Lge	140	94	24	885	48 *	12.64	-	-	51	-	5167	4281	124	34.52	5-30	1	

SAMPSON, P. J.   Surrey

Name: <u>Philip</u> James Sampson

Role: Right-hand bat, right-arm fast-medium bowler

Born: 6 September 1980, Manchester

Height: 6ft 1in **Weight:** 14st

Nickname: Sammo, Boss Hogg

County debut: 2000 (one-day), 2002 (first-class)

Strike rate: 37.71 (career 37.71)

Parents: Les and Kay

Marital status: Single

Family links with cricket: Father played league cricket and was chairman of the Harlequins club in Pretoria. Brother was captain of Northern Transvaal (Northerns) at Youth level

Education: Waterkloof House Preparatory School, Pretoria; Pretoria Boys High School

Qualifications: Matriculation (A-level equivalent)

Overseas teams played for: Harlequins, Pretoria 1999, 2000, 2001

Cricketers particularly admired: Allan Donald, Alec Stewart, Steve Waugh, Sachin Tendulkar

Young players to look out for: Carl Greenidge

Other sports played: Golf, social football

Other sports followed: Football (Manchester United), Formula One motor racing

Relaxations: Going to the theatre and movies, socialising with friends, listening to music

Extras: Captain of school 1st XI 1998. Trophy for best all-round cricketer at school. Represented Northerns at U15, U18, U19. Played for Buckinghamshire in the Minor Counties 1999. Played for Surrey Board XI in the NatWest 2000. Is not considered an overseas player

Best batting: 42 Surrey v CUCCE, Fenner's 2002

Best bowling: 3-52 Surrey v Leicestershire, The Oval 2002

2002 Season

	M	Inns	NO	Runs	HS	Avge	100s	50s	Ct	St	O	M	Runs	Wkts	Avge	Best	5wI	10wM
Test																		
All First	2	3	1	43	42	21.50	-	-	-	-	44	11	160	7	22.85	3-52	-	-
1-day Int																		
C & G																		
B & H	2	2	1	3	3 *	3.00	-	-	1	-	19	0	92	4	23.00	3-42	-	
1-day Lge	3	2	0	17	16	8.50	-	-	1	-	17	0	100	3	33.33	2-18	-	

Career Performances

	M	Inns	NO	Runs	HS	Avge	100s	50s	Ct	St	Balls	Runs	Wkts	Avge	Best	5wI	10wM
Test																	
All First	2	3	1	43	42	21.50	-	-	-	-	264	160	7	22.85	3-52	-	-
1-day Int																	
C & G	1	1	1	4	4 *	-	-	-	1	-	60	26	0	-	-	-	
B & H	2	2	1	3	3 *	3.00	-	-	1	-	114	92	4	23.00	3-42	-	
1-day Lge	6	3	0	21	16	7.00	-	-	1	-	228	192	4	48.00	2-18	-	

SAQLAIN MUSHTAQ   Surrey

Name: Saqlain Mushtaq
Role: Right-hand bat, off-spin bowler
Born: 29 December 1976, Lahore, Pakistan
Height: 5ft 9in **Weight:** 11st 4lbs
Nickname: Saqi, Baba
County debut: 1997
County cap: 1998
Test debut: 1995-96
Tests: 40
One-Day Internationals: 156
50 wickets in a season: 5
1st-Class 50s: 8
1st-Class 100s: 1
1st-Class 5 w. in innings: 50
1st-Class 10 w. in match: 13
1st-Class catches: 53
One-Day 5 w. in innings: 6
Place in batting averages: 176th av. 25.27

(2001 235th av. 13.66)
Place in bowling averages: 32nd av. 25.64 (2001 15th av. 20.74)
Strike rate: 55.32 (career 51.65)
Parents: Nasim Akhtar and Mushtaq Ahmed
Wife and date of marriage: Sana ('Sunny') Saqlain, 11 April 2000
Education: Lahore MAO College
Overseas tours: Pakistan to Australia 1995-96, 1996-97, 1999-2000, to England 1996,
2001, to Sri Lanka 1996-97, 1997-98, to India 1996-97, 1998-99, to South Africa
1997-98, 2002-03, to Zimbabwe 1997-98, 2002-03, to Bangladesh (Wills International
Cup) 1998-99, to UK, Ireland and Holland (World Cup) 1999, to West Indies 1999-
2000, to Kenya (ICC Knockout Trophy) 2000-01, to New Zealand 2000-01, to
Bangladesh 2001-02, to Sharjah (v West Indies) 2001-02, to Morocco (Morocco Cup)
2002, plus other one-day tournaments in Toronto, Sharjah, Kenya and Singapore
Overseas teams played for: PIA 1994-95 – ; Islamabad Cricket Association 1994-95
Cricketers particularly admired: Imran Khan, Wasim Akram, Waqar Younis
Young players to look out for: Younis Khan, Shoaib Malik
Other sports played: Squash
Other sports followed: Hockey (Pakistan), football (Manchester United and Arsenal)
Relaxations: 'I like listening to music when free or travelling'
Extras: Scored 79 v Zimbabwe in the first Test at Sheikhupura 1996-97, in the process
sharing with Wasim Akram (257*) in a world record eighth-wicket partnership in Tests
(313). Joined Surrey as overseas player in 1997. Won Man of the Series award in
1998-99 two-match Test series v India (20 wickets – 10-187/10-216; av. 20.15). Took
only the second hat-trick in World Cup cricket (Olonga, Huckle and Mbangwa), v

Zimbabwe at The Oval 1999; it was his second hat-trick in One-Day Internationals v Zimbabwe. Took the fifth hat-trick of his career, for Surrey v Sussex at Hove 1999. Topped the English first-class bowling averages in 1999, taking 58 wickets at an astonishing average of 11.37 in the seven games he played for Surrey. One of *Wisden*'s Five Cricketers of the Year 2000. Took 7-11 from 9.3 overs v Derbyshire at The Oval 2000. Returned his best One-Day International figures (5-20) in the third One-Day International v England at Rawalpindi 2000-01, winning the Man of the Match award. Took 8-164 (all eight wickets to fall) from 74 overs in England's first innings in the first Test at Lahore 2000-01, winning the Man of the Match award. Scored maiden first-class century (101*) in second Test v New Zealand at Christchurch 2000-01. Bowled unchanged for Surrey from 11 a.m. until 6 p.m. (47.2 overs) on the second day v Leicestershire at Leicester 2001, finishing with innings figures of 5-172 from a total of 52.2 overs. Holds record for taking fewest matches to reach 100 ODI wickets (53 matches) and 150 ODI wickets (78); also holds record for the most ODI wickets in a calendar year (69 in 1997)

Best batting: 101* Pakistan v New Zealand, Christchurch 2000-01
Best bowling: 8-65 Surrey v Derbyshire, The Oval 1998
Stop press: Took 7-66 (10-155 the match) in second Test v Zimbabwe at Bulawayo 2002-03; was man of the two-match series for his 15 wickets at 21.53. Selected for Pakistan squad for 2002-03 World Cup

2002 Season

	M	Inns	NO	Runs	HS	Avge	100s	50s	Ct	St	O	M	Runs	Wkts	Avge	Best	5wI	10wM
Test																		
All First	10	13	2	278	60	25.27	-	2	4	-	488.4	112	1359	53	25.64	6-121	3	1
1-day Int																		
C & G	4	1	0	5	5	5.00	-	-	-	-	30	0	180	2	90.00	1-14	-	
B & H																		
1-day Lge	9	5	1	51	28	12.75	-	-	2	-	68	4	242	6	40.33	1-17	-	

Career Performances

	M	Inns	NO	Runs	HS	Avge	100s	50s	Ct	St	Balls	Runs	Wkts	Avge	Best	5wI	10wM
Test	40	61	13	778	101 *	16.20	1	2	14	-	11604	4821	169	28.52	8-164	12	2
All First	137	191	50	2302	101 *	16.32	1	8	53	-	33111	13660	637	21.44	8-65	50	13
1-day Int	156	89	34	667	37 *	12.12	-	-	39	-	8131	5793	271	21.37	5-20	6	
C & G	17	5	2	44	24	14.66	-	-	1	-	931	610	28	21.78	4-17	-	
B & H	9	5	3	21	11	10.50	-	-	3	-	435	287	14	20.50	4-46	-	
1-day Lge	46	29	9	217	38 *	10.85	-	-	11	-	2002	1372	51	26.90	3-12	-	

SAVILL, T. E.　　　　　　　Nottinghamshire

Name: <u>Thomas</u> Edward Savill
Role: Right-hand bat, right-arm fast bowler
Born: 16 May 1983, Sheffield
Height: 6ft 6in **Weight:** 14st
Nickname: Lurch, Sav, ST
County debut: 2002
1st-Class catches: 2
Strike rate: 64.50 (career 64.50)
Parents: John and Barbara
Marital status: Single
Family links with cricket: 'Dad and brother both play. Mum is qualified umpire and coach'
Education: Fernwood Junior School; Fernwood Comprehensive; Bilborough Sixth Form; Homerton College, Cambridge University
Qualifications: 10 GCSEs, 3 A-levels
Career outside cricket: Student
Off-season: 'Attempting to survive university life'
Overseas tours: Nottinghamshire to Johannesburg 2002
Career highlights to date: 'Claiming the wicket of Andy Flower in both innings, playing for Cambridge UCCE v Essex [2002]'
Cricket moments to forget: 'Being sent out to open the batting for Notts 2nd XI on a pair, and being caught behind first ball. Annoying, bearing in mind I was a regular number eight'
Cricket superstitions: 'No superstitions, just routines'
Cricketers particularly admired: Dennis Lillee, Richard Stanley ('local hero')
Young players to look out for: Paul McMahon, Simon Marshall, Adrian Shankar
Other sports played: Football (county age groups, Forest Centre of Excellence), hockey
Other sports followed: Football (Brentford FC)
Injuries: Sent home early from 2002 pre-season tour with a broken toe
Relaxations: 'All the normal boring stuff'
Extras: Played for Nottinghamshire Board XI in the C&G 2001. Granted special permission to play three first-class games in 2002 for Cambridge University CCE despite not being a student at that point but having a firm offer of a place
Opinions on cricket: 'I believe two overseas players is a good idea and that the future is in being made to field a team with eight players available for England selection.'
Best batting: 18* CUCCE v Essex, Fenner's 2002
Best bowling: 2-42 Nottinghamshire v West Indies A, Trent Bridge 2002

2002 Season

	M	Inns	NO	Runs	HS	Avge	100s	50s	Ct	St	O	M	Runs	Wkts	Avge	Best	5wl	10wM
Test																		
All First	4	6	2	58	18 *	14.50	-	-	2	-	86	10	422	8	52.75	2-42	-	-
1-day Int																		
C & G																			
B & H																			
1-day Lge																			

Career Performances

	M	Inns	NO	Runs	HS	Avge	100s	50s	Ct	St	Balls	Runs	Wkts	Avge	Best	5wl	10wM
Test																	
All First	4	6	2	58	18 *	14.50	-	-	2	-	516	422	8	52.75	2-42	-	-
1-day Int																	
C & G	2	2	2	50	35 *	-	-	-	1	-	111	90	1	90.00	1-45	-	
B & H																	
1-day Lge																	

SAYERS, J. J. Yorkshire

Name: Joseph (Joe) John Sayers
Role: Left-hand bat, right-arm off-spin bowler
Born: 5 November 1983, Leeds
Height: 6ft **Weight:** 13st 2lbs
Nickname: Bradders, Machine, Joey
County debut: No first-team appearance
1st-Class 50s: 1
1st-Class catches: 1
Place in batting averages: 232nd av. 19.00
Parents: Geraldine and Roger
Marital status: Single
Family links with cricket: 'Father played at school, but otherwise none'
Education: St Joseph's Primary School, Otley; St Mary's RC Comprehensive School, Menston; Worcester College, Oxford University
Qualifications: 12 GCSEs, 4 A-levels
Career outside cricket: 'Undecided at present, but would like to work in the City, or design engineering'
Off-season: 'Captaining Oxford University Academy squad; studying physics at Worcester College'

Overseas tours: Leeds Schools to South Africa 1998; Yorkshire U17 to South Africa 2001; England U17 to Australia 2001

Career highlights to date: 'Being 12th man for the Test at Headingley [2002]'

Cricket superstitions: 'None'

Cricketers particularly admired: Mike Atherton, Mike Brearley, Sachin Tendulkar, Jonty Rhodes, Steve Waugh

Young players to look out for: Tim Bresnan, Jamie Dalrymple, Kadeer Ali

Other sports played: Football ('played as goalkeeper for Bradford City AFC for three years'), rowing (Worcester College)

Other sports followed: Football (Liverpool FC), baseball (New York Yankees)

Relaxations: 'Playing guitar; drawing/painting; reading autobiographies'

Extras: Captained England U17 against Australia U17 in Adelaide 2001. Played for Oxford University CCE in 2002. Oxford Blue 2002. Represented England U19 v India U19 in 'Test' series (1/3) 2002

Opinions on cricket: 'Recent introductions such as Power Cricket and the 20-over competition to come are and will continue to be beneficial. The sport should continue its efforts to appeal to the young, while maintaining the prominence of Test cricket.'

Best batting: 55 OUCCE v Gloucestershire, The Parks 2002

2002 Season (did not make any first-class or one-day appearances for his county)

Career Performances

	M	Inns	NO	Runs	HS	Avge	100s	50s	Ct	St	Balls	Runs	Wkts	Avge	Best	5wl	10wM
Test																	
All First	4	8	0	152	55	19.00	-	1	1	-	18	12	0	-	-	-	-
1-day Int																	
C & G																	
B & H																	
1-day Lge																	

SCHOFIELD, C. P.   Lancashire

Name: Christopher (Chris) Paul Schofield

Role: Left-hand bat, leg-break bowler

Born: 6 October 1978, Rochdale

Height: 6ft 1in **Weight:** 11st 5lbs

Nickname: Scoey, Junior, Scoffer

County debut: 1998

County cap: 2002

Test debut: 2000

Tests: 2

1st-Class 50s: 15

1st-Class 5 w. in innings: 4
1st-Class catches: 31
One-Day 5 w. in innings: 1
Place in batting averages: 121st av. 32.75
(2001 103rd av. 32.50)
Place in bowling averages: 2nd av. 18.38
(2001 141st av. 54.07)
Strike rate: 40.77 (career 60.21)
Parents: David and Judith
Marital status: Single
Family links with cricket: Father played
with local club team Whittles and brother
plays with local team Littleborough
Education: St John's; Wardle High School
Qualifications: 4 GCSEs, NVQ Levels 2 and
3 in Information Technology
Overseas tours: England U17 to Bermuda
1997; England U19 to South Africa (including

U19 World Cup) 1997-98; England A to Bangladesh and New Zealand 1999-2000, to
West Indies 2000-01; ECB National Academy to Australia 2001-02
Cricketers particularly admired: Shane Warne, Stuart Law
Young players to look out for: Graeme Swann, Robert Key
Other sports played: Football (Littleborough FC, Whittles FC), snooker (Wardle
Con Club – handicap of four)
Other sports followed: Football ('like watching Liverpool FC')
Relaxations: Listening to music, playing snooker, socialising
Extras: Was part of England U19 World Cup winning squad 1997-98. Won double
twice in two years with Littleborough CC (Wood Cup and Lancashire Cup 1997;
League and Wood Cup 1998). Awarded 2nd XI cap 1998. Won Sir Ron
Brierley/Crusaders Scholarship 1998. NBC Denis Compton Award for the most
promising young Lancashire player 1998, 1999, 2000. Was the only uncapped player
to be contracted to England in 2000. Made Test debut in first Test v Zimbabwe at
Lord's 2000 but did not get a bowl as Gough, Caddick and Giddins bowled the
opposition out twice. Leading first-class wicket-taker on England A tour to West Indies
2000-01 (22 wickets; av. 26.27). Awarded Lancashire cap 2002
Best batting: 91 Lancashire v Warwickshire, Old Trafford 2002
Best bowling: 6-120 England A v Bangladesh, Chittagong 1999-2000

	M	Inns	NO	Runs	HS	Avge	100s	50s	Ct	St	O	M	Runs	Wkts	Avge	Best	5wI	10wM
Test																		
All First	7	9	1	262	91	32.75	-	2	4	-	122.2	27	331	18	18.38	4-35	-	-
1-day Int																		
C & G	2	1	0	13	13	13.00	-	-	-	-	12	0	60	3	20.00	2-28	-	
B & H	7	4	1	52	21	17.33	-	-	2	-	27	0	126	5	25.20	2-27	-	
1-day Lge	10	9	2	188	52	26.85	-	1	2	-	53.1	1	286	6	47.66	2-38	-	

Career Performances

	M	Inns	NO	Runs	HS	Avge	100s	50s	Ct	St	Balls	Runs	Wkts	Avge	Best	5wI	10wM
Test	2	3	0	67	57	22.33	-	1	-	-	108	73	0	-	-	-	-
All First	56	77	12	1834	91	28.21	-	15	31	-	9334	4626	155	29.84	6-120	4	-
1-day Int																	
C & G	10	3	0	56	42	18.66	-	-	5	-	401	317	16	19.81	4-34	-	
B & H	11	8	1	99	23	14.14	-	-	2	-	366	259	13	19.92	4-34	-	
1-day Lge	38	31	8	442	52	19.21	-	1	7	-	1345	1119	42	26.64	5-31	1	

SCHOFIELD, J. E. K.   Hampshire

Name: James Edward Knowle Schofield
Role: Right-hand bat, right-arm
fast-medium bowler
Born: 1 November 1978, Blackpool
Height: 6ft **Weight:** 12st 7lbs
Nickname: Schoey, Doc, Doctor, Ebenezer
County debut: 2001
1st-Class catches: 1
Place in bowling averages: (2001 20th
av. 21.92)
Strike rate: 53.00 (career 44.89)
Parents: Victoria and David
Marital status: Single
Family links with cricket: Great-grandfather
played for Lancashire CCC
Education: Hagley Middle School;
RGS Worcester; University of Bradford
Qualifications: 9 GCSEs, 4 A-levels,
BSc (Hons) Business and Management
Off-season: 'Playing and training in Sydney'
Overseas teams played for: Melville, Perth 2000-02
Career highlights to date: 'Beating the Aussies at the Rose Bowl [2001] and getting

wicket with my first ball in first-class cricket. Playing against the champions, Surrey, and bowling at the likes of Ward and Thorpe'

Cricket moments to forget: 'Being sacked by Hampshire'

Cricket superstitions: 'None'

Cricketers particularly admired: Ian Botham, Jacques Kallis, Wasim Akram, Richard Hadlee, Shaun Pollock, Brett Lee, Glenn McGrath

Young players to look out for: John Francis, James Tomlinson, Kabir Ali

Other sports played: Football, rugby, tennis (played for Hereford and Worcester)

Other sports followed: Football (Liverpool FC), rugby league (Bradford Bulls), 'all rugby internationals, and tennis'

Injuries: Out for five months during winter 2001-02 and for first month of 2002 season with a stress reaction in the back

Relaxations: 'Lying on the beach; listening to music; watching live sporting events; spending time with friends'

Extras: Part of Hampshire's 2nd XI Championship winning side 2001. Took a wicket (Matthew Hayden) with his first ball in first-class cricket v Australians at the Rose Bowl 2001 (as Hampshire beat the Australians for the first time since 1912) and also a wicket (Anurag Singh) with his first ball in the Norwich Union League on one-day debut v Worcestershire at Worcester 2001 – 'apparently a world record'. Released by Hampshire at the end of the 2002 season

Opinions on cricket: 'EU players need to be monitored. Too many infiltrating into the game in England.'

Best batting: 21* Hampshire v Durham, Riverside 2001

Best bowling: 4-51 Hampshire v Worcestershire, Worcester 2001

2002 Season

	M	Inns	NO	Runs	HS	Avge	100s	50s	Ct	St	O	M	Runs	Wkts	Avge	Best	5wI	10wM
Test																		
All First	1	2	1	18	18 *	18.00	-	-	-	-	53	14	192	6	32.00	3-94	-	-
1-day Int																		
C & G																		
B & H																		
1-day Lge																		

Career Performances

	M	Inns	NO	Runs	HS	Avge	100s	50s	Ct	St	Balls	Runs	Wkts	Avge	Best	5wI	10wM
Test																	
All First	4	7	3	43	21 *	10.75	-	-	1	-	853	477	19	25.10	4-51	-	-
1-day Int																	
C & G																	
B & H																	
1-day Lge	1	0	0	0	0	-	-	-	-	-	36	22	1	22.00	1-22	-

SCOTT, B. J. M.   Surrey

Name: Benjamin (<u>Ben</u>) James Matthew Scott
Role: Right-hand bat, wicket-keeper
Born: 4 August 1981, Isleworth
Height: 5ft 8in **Weight:** 11st 5lbs
Nickname: Scotty, Head
County debut: 2002 (one-day)
Parents: Terry and Edna
Marital status: Single
Family links with cricket: Father and
brother played local club cricket
Education: Chatsworth School, Hounslow;
Whitton School, Richmond; Richmond
College
Qualifications: 9 GCSEs, 3 A-levels studied,
ECB Level 1 coach, YMCA Fitness
Instructor's Award
Career outside cricket: Fitness/gym
instructor
Overseas tours: MCC YC to South Africa 1999-2000
Overseas teams played for: Portland CC, Victoria, Australia 1999-2000
Career highlights to date: 'ECB U19 v Australia U19. Surrey 2nd XI Trophy 2001'
Cricketers particularly admired: Alec Stewart, Alan Knott, Steve Waugh,
Jack Russell
Young players to look out for: Alan Coleman, Chad Keegan, Nick Compton
Other sports played: Squash, football
Relaxations: Music, piano, guitar
Extras: Middlesex YC cap. Represented ESCA U14 and U15. Played for
Development of Excellence XI v Australia U19 1999. Played for Middlesex Board XI
in the NatWest 1999. Finchley CC Player of the Season 2000

2002 Season

	M	Inns	NO	Runs	HS	Avge	100s	50s	Ct	St	O	M	Runs	Wkts	Avge	Best	5wI	10wM
Test																		
All First																		
1-day Int																		
C & G																		
B & H																		
1-day Lge	1	1	0	4	4	4.00	-	-	-	-								

Career Performances

	M	Inns	NO	Runs	HS	Avge	100s	50s	Ct	St	Balls	Runs	Wkts	Avge	Best	5wI	10wM
Test																	
All First																		
1-day Int																		
C & G	1	1	0	11	11	11.00	-	-	-	-							
B & H																		
1-day Lge	1	1	0	4	4	4.00	-	-	-	-							

SCOTT, G. M. Durham

Name: <u>Gary</u> Michael Scott
Role: Right-hand bat, right-arm off-spin bowler
Born: 21 July 1984, Sunderland
Height: 6ft 1in **Weight:** 12st 9lbs
Nickname: Scotty
County debut: 2001
1st-Class catches: 1
One-Day 100s: 1
Parents: Mary and Michael
Marital status: Single
Education: Hetton Lyons Primary School; Hetton Comprehensive
Qualifications: 8 GCSEs
Overseas tours: England U17 to Australia 2000-01
Career highlights to date: 'Making first-class debut'

Cricket moments to forget: 'Can't remember; like to forget straightaway'
Cricketers particularly admired: Jacques Kallis, the Waugh brothers, Mike Atherton
Young players to look out for: Gordon Muchall, Bilal Shafayat
Other sports played: Football (represented Sunderland Schoolboys)
Other sports followed: Football (Newcastle Utd)
Relaxations: Football, music
Extras: Sir John Hobbs Silver Jubilee Memorial Prize 1999. Played for Durham Board XI in the C&G 2001 and 2002; scored maiden one-day century (100) for Durham Board XI v Herefordshire at Darlington in the second round of the C&G 2003, which was played in September 2002. Became youngest to play first-class cricket for Durham when he made his debut v Derbyshire at Riverside 2001 aged 17 years and 19 days. Is a Durham Academy player
Opinions on cricket: 'The standards that have been set by the England team should be set in the first-class game.'

Best batting: 25 Durham v Derbyshire, Riverside 2001

2002 Season (did not make any first-class or one-day appearances for his county)

Career Performances

	M	Inns	NO	Runs	HS	Avge	100s	50s	Ct	St	Balls	Runs	Wkts	Avge	Best	5wl	10wM
Test																	
All First	1	2	0	33	25	16.50	-	-	1	-	18	11	0	-	-	-	-
1-day Int																	
C & G	3	3	0	130	100	43.33	1	-	2	-	174	107	4	26.75	2-32	-	
B & H																	
1-day Lge																	

SEHWAG, V. Leicestershire

Name: Virender Sehwag
Role: Right-hand bat, right-arm
off-spin bowler
Born: 20 October 1978, Delhi, India
County debut: No first-team appearance
Test debut: 2001-02
Tests: 9
One-Day Internationals: 38
1st-Class 50s: 16
1st-Class 100s: 12
1st-Class 200s: 1
1st-Class catches: 51
One-Day 100s: 1
Strike rate: 98.50 (career 71.54)
Education: Jamia Millia Islamia University,
New Delhi
Career outside cricket: Works for Oil and
Natural Gas Commission

Overseas tours: India to Zimbabwe 2001 (one-day series), to Sri Lanka 2001
(one-day series), to South Africa 2001-02, to West Indies 2001-02 (one-day series),
to England 2002, to Sri Lanka (ICC Champions Trophy) 2002-03, to New Zealand
2002-03
Overseas teams played for: Delhi 1997-98 –
Extras: Scored 745 runs (av. 62.08) in eight Ranji Trophy appearances 1998-99 and
674 runs (av. 61.27) in eight appearances 1999-2000. Scored 54-ball 58 and took 3-59
in the first ODI v Australia at Bangalore 2000-01, winning Man of the Match award.
Scored 70-ball century (100) v New Zealand in the Coca-Cola Cup at Colombo 2001,
winning Man of the Match award. Made Test debut in first Test v South Africa at

Bloemfontein 2001-02, scoring century (105). Found himself at the centre of a selection controversy ahead of first Test v England at Mohali 2001-02 after having been fined and banned for one Test by referee Mike Denness during previous series in South Africa and omitted from team for unofficial 'Test' at Centurion; in the end omitted from Mohali line-up. Scored 62-ball 82 in the fourth ODI v England at Kanpur 2001-02, winning Man of the Match award. Has joined Leicestershire as an overseas player for 2003

Best batting: 274 North Zone v South Zone, Agartala 1999-2000
Best bowling: 4-32 North Zone v South Zone, Mumbai (Bombay) 1998-99
Stop press: Man of the Match awards at the ICC Champions Trophy at Colombo 2002-03 for his 104-ball 126 v England and 58-ball 59 plus 3-25 in semi-final v South Africa. Scored century (147) in first Test v West Indies at Mumbai (Bombay) 2002-03, in the process sharing with Sanjay Bangar (55) in a record first-wicket stand for India in Tests v West Indies (201) and winning Man of the Match award. Man of the Match award for his 82-ball 114* in third ODI v West Indies at Rajkot 2002-03. ODI Man of the Match awards v New Zealand 2002-03 for his 108 at Napier and 112 at Auckland. Selected for India squad for 2002-03 World Cup

2002 Season

	M	Inns	NO	Runs	HS	Avge	100s	50s	Ct	St	O	M	Runs	Wkts	Avge	Best	5wI	10wM
Test	4	6	0	237	106	39.50	1	1	6	-	19		63	1	63.00	1-32	-	-
All First	8	13	0	640	142	49.23	3	1	13	-	65.4	8	232	4	58.00	2-52	-	-
1-day Int	7	7	0	229	71	32.71	-	1	3	-	7	0	47	0	-	-	-	-
C & G																		
B & H																		
1-day Lge																		

Career Performances

	M	Inns	NO	Runs	HS	Avge	100s	50s	Ct	St	Balls	Runs	Wkts	Avge	Best	5wI	10wM
Test	9	12	0	546	106	45.50	2	3	11	-	180	101	1	101.00	1-32	-	-
All First	47	69	3	3690	274	55.90	13	16	51	-	3434	1761	48	36.68	4-32	-	-
1-day Int	38	36	3	981	100	29.72	1	6	14	-	797	719	15	47.93	3-59	-	
C & G																	
B & H																	
1-day Lge																	

SELWOOD, S. A. Derbyshire

Name: Steven (<u>Steve</u>) Andrew Selwood
Role: Left-hand bat, left-arm spin bowler
Born: 24 November 1979, Barnet, London
Height: 5ft 11in **Weight:** 12st
Nickname: Sellers, Hollywood
County debut: 2001
1st-Class 50s: 2
1st-Class catches: 2
Place in batting averages: 193rd av. 24.05
Strike rate: 39.00 (career 39.00)
Parents: Tim and Sarah
Marital status: 'Taken'
Family links with cricket: 'Father played for
Middlesex 1969-74, Central Districts 1972-73
and is now youth coach at Finchley CC'
Education: Belmont School, Mill Hill;
Mill Hill School; Loughborough University
Qualifications: 9 GCSEs, 2 A-levels,
BA (Hons) Politics, Level 1 coaching

Career outside cricket: 'Surfer'
Off-season: 'Playing and training in Perth, Western Australia'
Overseas tours: Middlesex Prep Schools to Australia 1990-91; British Universities to
South Africa 2002
Overseas teams played for: Manly-Warringah, Sydney 1996-97;
Claremont-Nedlands, Perth 1998-99
Career highlights to date: 'Every time we win'
Cricket moments to forget: 'Any time we lose and every time I fail'
Cricket superstitions: 'None'
Cricketers particularly admired: Darren Lehmann, Ian Botham
Young players to look out for: Rob White, Mark Powell, Jake Milton (Finchley),
Geoff Cullen (Western Australia)
Other sports played: Football, rugby
Other sports followed: Football (Tottenham Hotspur)
Injuries: Out for four weeks with a broken hand
Relaxations: 'Spending time with my girlfriend, Melissa; travel; going out with
friends'
Extras: Represented England U14 1994. Played for Finchley v Uxbridge in the
Evening Standard final 2000, winning Man of the Match award. Played for
Loughborough University CCE 2001 and 2002. Scored 93 v Gloucestershire at Bristol
in the NUL 2002, in the process sharing with Mathew Dowman (45) in a new record
sixth-wicket partnership for Derbyshire in the one-day league (123)

Opinions on cricket: 'There needs to be more aggressive marketing of the game worldwide. We must set our standards much higher in regard to wickets and practice facilities. There is too much four-day cricket. Club cricket must change to a two-day format.'

Best batting: 99 Derbyshire v Worcestershire, Derby 2002
Best bowling: 1-8 Derbyshire v Essex, Derby 2002

2002 Season

	M	Inns	NO	Runs	HS	Avge	100s	50s	Ct	St	O	M	Runs	Wkts	Avge	Best	5wI	10wM
Test																		
All First	10	19	0	457	99	24.05	-	2	1	-	13	3	67	2	33.50	1-8	-	-
1-day Int																		
C & G	1	1	0	1	1	1.00	-	-	-	-								
B & H	5	3	0	97	62	32.33	-	1	1	-	10	1	48	1	48.00	1-48	-	
1-day Lge	14	13	2	426	93	38.72	-	4	5	-								

Career Performances

	M	Inns	NO	Runs	HS	Avge	100s	50s	Ct	St	Balls	Runs	Wkts	Avge	Best	5wI	10wM
Test																	
All First	12	23	0	500	99	21.73	-	2	2	-	78	67	2	33.50	1-8	-	-
1-day Int																	
C & G	1	1	0	1	1	1.00	-	-	-	-							
B & H	5	3	0	97	62	32.33	-	1	1	-	60	48	1	48.00	1-48	-	
1-day Lge	17	16	2	501	93	35.78	-	4	5	-	2	8	0	-	-	-	-

74. Which Pakistan Test cricketer was out obstructing the field for Warwickshire v Hampshire at Coventry in 1963?

SHAFAYAT, B. M.   Nottinghamshire

Name: <u>Bilal</u> Mustafa Shafayat
Role: Right-hand bat, right-arm medium
bowler, occasional wicket-keeper
Born: 10 July 1984, Nottingham
Height: 5ft 8in **Weight:** 10st
Nickname: Billy, Mussy
County debut: 2001
1st-Class 50s: 4
1st-Class 100s: 1
1st-Class catches: 5
Place in batting averages: 92nd av. 37.50
(2001 76th av. 38.50)
Parents: Mohammad Shafayat and
Mahfooza Begum
Marital status: Single
Family links with cricket: Brother played
for Notts Youth and 2nd XI. Uncle Nadeem
Khan played for PCC

Education: Greenwood Juniors; Greenwood Dale; Nottingham Bluecoat School
Qualifications: 8 GCSEs
Off-season: England U19 tour to Australia
Overseas tours: ZRK to Pakistan 2000; England U17 to Australia 2000-01; England
U19 to Australia and (U19 World Cup) New Zealand 2001-02, to Australia 2002-03
(captain)
Career highlights to date: 'Notts debut at age 16 – scored 72 v Middlesex'
Cricketers particularly admired: Sachin Tendulkar, Nasser Hussain,
Andrew Jackman, Usman Afzaal
Young players to look out for: Ehsan Hussain, Akhil Patel
Other sports played: Football, squash
Other sports followed: Football (Liverpool), snooker (Ronnie O'Sullivan),
golf (Tiger Woods), boxing ('Naz')
Relaxations: 'Praying Namaz and spending time with loved ones'
Extras: Played for Nottinghamshire Board XI in the NatWest 2000 and for
Nottinghamshire Board XI and Nottinghamshire in the C&G 2001. Represented
England U19 v West Indies U19 in one-day series (3/3) and 'Test' series (2/3) 2001.
Scored 72 on Championship debut v Middlesex at Trent Bridge 2001; aged 16, he also
became the youngest player to represent Nottinghamshire in the competition. NBC
Denis Compton Award for the most promising young Nottinghamshire player 2001.
Represented England U19 v India U19 in 'Test' series (3/3) 2002; scored 118 and
201* in the third 'Test' at Northampton, in the process sharing with Kadeer Ali (97 and
111) in partnerships of 212 and 256; only Mark Ramprakash had previously scored
two centuries in a match for England U19, v Sri Lanka in 1987. Scored maiden first-

class century (104) v Worcestershire at Trent Bridge 2002, becoming the youngest Nottinghamshire centurion

Opinions on cricket: 'More day/night games should be introduced and better wickets in league cricket.'

Best batting: 104 Nottinghamshire v Worcestershire, Trent Bridge 2002

Stop press: Scored 108 and 66 and had second innings figures of 6-54 in England U19's victory over Australia U19 in the first 'Test' at Adelaide 2002-03

2002 Season

	M	Inns	NO	Runs	HS	Avge	100s	50s	Ct	St	O	M	Runs	Wkts	Avge	Best	5wI	10wM
Test																		
All First	7	13	1	450	104	37.50	1	2	5	-	14	0	52	0	-	-	-	-
1-day Int																		
C & G	1	1	1	28	28 *	-	-	-	-	-								
B & H	4	2	0	27	14	13.50	-	-	1	-	1	0	4	0	-	-	-	
1-day Lge	9	9	0	219	66	24.33	-	1	4	-	36.4	1	194	8	24.25	4-35	-	

Career Performances

	M	Inns	NO	Runs	HS	Avge	100s	50s	Ct	St	Balls		Runs	Wkts	Avge	Best	5wI	10wM
Test																		
All First	10	19	1	681	104	37.83	1	4	5	-	84		52	0	-	-	-	-
1-day Int																		
C & G	4	4	1	72	36	24.00	-	-	-	-								
B & H	4	2	0	27	14	13.50	-	-	1	-	6		4	0	-	-	-	
1-day Lge	14	14	0	295	66	21.07	-	1	7	-	220		194	8	24.25	4-35	-	

75. Which current international umpire made his debut
for Derbyshire in 1973?

SHAH, O. A. Middlesex

Name: <u>Owais</u> Alam Shah
Role: Right-hand bat, off-spin bowler, county vice-captain
Born: 22 October 1978, Karachi, Pakistan
Height: 6ft 1in **Weight:** 12st
Nickname: Ace
County debut: 1995 (one-day), 1996 (first-class)
County cap: 1999
One-Day Internationals: 9
1000 runs in a season: 2
1st-Class 50s: 24
1st-Class 100s: 11
1st-Class 200s: 1
1st-Class catches: 61
One-Day 100s: 4
Place in batting averages: 45th av. 47.13 (2001 61st av. 41.60)

Strike rate: (career 58.58)
Parents: Jamshed and Mehjabeen
Marital status: Single
Family links with cricket: Father played for his college side
Education: Berkley's Junior School; Isleworth and Syon School; Lampton School; Westminster University, Harrow
Qualifications: 7 GCSEs, 2 A-levels
Off-season: 'Back at university until January, then off to Perth to work on batting and fitness'
Overseas tours: England U19 to Zimbabwe 1995-96, to South Africa (including U19 World Cup) 1997-98; England A to Australia 1996-97, to Kenya and Sri Lanka 1997-98; ECB National Academy to Australia 2001-02; England to Zimbabwe (one-day series) 2001-02, to India and New Zealand 2001-02 (one-day series), to Sri Lanka (ICC Champions Trophy) 2002-03, to Australia 2002-03 (VB Series)
Overseas teams played for: University of Western Australia, Perth
Career highlights to date: 'Playing for England in one-day game v Australia [2001]'
Cricket moments to forget: 'Getting a pair in first-class cricket'
Cricketers particularly admired: Viv Richards, Sachin Tendulkar, Mark Waugh
Young players to look out for: Ed Joyce, Andrew Strauss, Rikki Clarke
Other sports played: Snooker
Other sports followed: Football ('enjoy watching Manchester United play')
Relaxations: 'Movies, eating out'
Extras: Scored record 232 for England U15 against England U16. Man of the Series in U17 'Test' series against India 1994. Awarded 2nd XI cap in 1996. Captained the

England U19 side to success in the 1997-98 U19 World Cup in South Africa, scoring 54 not out in the final. Captain of England U19 against Pakistan U19 (one-day and 'Test' matches) 1998. B&H Gold Award for his 109-ball 118* v Hampshire at Lord's 2001. Scored 62 v Pakistan at Lord's in the NatWest Series 2001, in the process sharing in a record fourth-wicket partnership for England in One-Day Internationals (170) with Marcus Trescothick. Cricket Writers' Young Player of the Year 2001. Called up to the England one-day squad for the ICC Champions Trophy in Sri Lanka 2002-03 as a replacement for the injured Michael Vaughan. Middlesex Player of the Year 2002. Vice-captain of Middlesex since 2002

Opinions on cricket: 'There is not enough time between games to work on faults that creep into your game.'

Best batting: 203 Middlesex v Derbyshire, Southgate 2001

Best bowling: 3-33 Middlesex v Gloucestershire, Bristol 1999

Stop press: Scored century (127) for England XI v Sir Donald Bradman XI in 50-over match at Bowral 2002-03

2002 Season

	M	Inns	NO	Runs	HS	Avge	100s	50s	Ct	St	O	M	Runs	Wkts	Avge	Best	5wI	10wM
Test																		
All First	17	26	3	1084	172 *	47.13	3	6	5	-	2	0	15	0	-	-	-	-
1-day Int																		
C & G	1	1	0	20	20	20.00	-	-	-	-								
B & H	4	4	1	100	50 *	33.33	-	1	2	-								
1-day Lge	13	12	1	439	110	39.90	1	2	5	-								

Career Performances

	M	Inns	NO	Runs	HS	Avge	100s	50s	Ct	St	Balls	Runs	Wkts	Avge	Best	5wI	10wM
Test																	
All First	95	156	11	5075	203	35.00	12	24	61	-	996	627	17	36.88	3-33	-	-
1-day Int	9	9	2	168	62	24.00	-	2	4	-							
C & G	11	11	1	247	49	24.70	-	-	3	-	30	36	1	36.00	1-36	-	
B & H	18	16	3	394	118 *	30.30	1	1	8	-	50	37	4	9.25	2-2	-	
1-day Lge	86	80	9	2098	134	29.54	3	10	23	-	151	176	3	58.66	1-4	-	

SHAHID AFRIDI   Derbyshire

Name: Sahibzaha Mohammad Shahid
Khan Afridi
Role: Right-hand bat, leg-break bowler
Born: 1 March 1980, Kohat, Pakistan
County debut: 2001 (Leicestershire)
Test debut: 1998-99
Tests: 14
One-Day Internationals: 157
1st-Class 50s: 16
1st-Class 100s: 7
1st-Class 5 w. in innings: 5
1st-Class catches: 46
One-Day 100s: 3
One-Day 5 w. in innings: 1
Place in batting averages: (2001 84th
av. 36.11)
Place in bowling averages: (2001 124th
av. 43.76)

Strike rate: (career 53.65)
Overseas tours: Pakistan U19 to West Indies 1996-97; Pakistan to Kenya (one-day series) 1996-97, to Australia (one-day series) 1996-97, to India (one-day series) 1996-97, to Zimbabwe and South Africa 1997-98 (one-day series), to Bangladesh (Wills International Cup) 1998-99, to India 1998-99, to UK, Ireland and Holland (World Cup) 1999, to Australia 1999-2000 (one-day series), to West Indies 1999-2000 (one-day series), to New Zealand 2000-01 (one-day series), to England 2001 (one-day series), to Sharjah (v West Indies) 2001-02, to Australia (Super Challenge II) 2002, to Morocco (Morocco Cup) 2002, to Kenya (Nairobi Triangular) 2002, to Sri Lanka (ICC Champions Trophy) 2002-03, to Zimbabwe 2002-03, to South Africa 2002-03 (one-day series), plus other one-day tournaments in Toronto and Sharjah
Overseas teams played for: Karachi Cricket Association; Habib Bank
Extras: Set record for fastest One-Day International century – 37 balls (out for 102) v Sri Lanka in Kenya 1996-97 in first ODI innings, aged 16 years 217 days; innings included a record-equalling 11 sixes and won him Man of the Match award. Recorded his maiden Test five-wicket innings return (5-52) on debut v Australia at Karachi 1998-99, going on to score his maiden Test century (141) v India at Chennai (Madras) in his second match. Joined Leicestershire during the 2001 season as overseas player, replacing the injured Dan Marsh. Struck 32-ball 70 on Norwich Union League debut v Kent at Leicester 2001. C&G Man of the Match awards for his 44-ball 67 in the quarter-final v Worcestershire at Worcester and for his 58-ball 95 in the semi-final v Lancashire at Leicester 2001. Struck 30-ball 68 v Somerset at Taunton and a 25-ball 58, including six sixes, v Somerset at Leicester, both in the Norwich Union League 2001. Scored 121-ball 164, including a 74-ball century, v Northamptonshire at

Northampton 2001. Released by Leicestershire at the end of the 2001 season. Has won numerous ODI awards, among them Man of the Finals in the Carlton & United Series in Australia 1996-97 and Man of the Match for his 5-40 and 61 v England at Lahore 2000-01, for his 43-ball 70 plus 2-49 v New Zealand at Sharjah 2000-01, and for his 44-ball 83 v Bangladesh at Dhaka 2001-02. His quicker ball was once timed at 86mph. Has joined Derbyshire as an overseas player for the start of 2003

Best batting: 164 Leicestershire v Northamptonshire, Northampton 2001
Best bowling: 6-101 Habib Bank v KRL, Rawalpindi 1997-98
Stop press: Struck 18-ball 55* v Holland at Colombo in the ICC Champions Trophy 2002-03, equalling his own record for the second-fastest fifty in ODIs (behind Sanath Jayasuriya's 17-ball fifty v Pakistan in Singapore 1995-96) set during his 37-ball century v Sri Lanka in Kenya 1996-97. Selected for Pakistan squad for 2002-03 World Cup

---

2002 Season (did not make any first-class or one-day appearances)

Career Performances

	M	Inns	NO	Runs	HS	Avge	100s	50s	Ct	St	Balls	Runs	Wkts	Avge	Best	5wI	10wM
Test	14	25	1	780	141	32.50	2	4	8	-	1331	661	21	31.47	5-52	1	-
All First	65	109	3	3279	164	30.93	7	16	46	-	7458	3829	139	27.54	6-101	5	-
1-day Int	157	153	6	3660	109	24.89	3	21	59	-	5821	4456	111	40.14	5-40	1	
C & G	4	4	0	205	95	51.25	-	2	1	-	216	158	7	22.57	3-47	-	
B & H																	
1-day Lge	8	8	0	276	70	34.50	-	3	-	-	336	266	11	24.18	3-45	-	

76. Who took 66 wickets in only seven Championship matches in 1999 and for which county?

SHAHID, N.   Surrey

Name: Nadeem Shahid
Role: Right-hand bat, 'leg-spin, googly, back-spinner …'
Born: 23 April 1969, Karachi, Pakistan
Height: 6ft **Weight:** 12st
Nickname: Nad, Gonad, 'too many to mention'
County debut: 1989 (Essex), 1995 (Surrey)
County cap: 1998 (Surrey)
1000 runs in a season: 1
1st-Class 50s: 33
1st-Class 100s: 9
1st-Class catches: 149
One-Day 100s: 2
Place in batting averages: 93rd av. 37.47 (2001 213th av. 17.33)
Strike rate: 132.00 (career 71.54)
Parents: Ahmed and Salma
Marital status: Single
Family links with cricket: 'Brother plays in the leagues in Suffolk'
Education: Stoke High; Northgate High; Ipswich School; Plymouth Polytechnic
Qualifications: 6 O-levels, 1 A-level, coaching certificate
Off-season: 'Playing and coaching in a black township – Langa, Cape Town'
Overseas tours: Ipswich School to Barbados (Sir Garfield Sobers Trophy) 1987; England (South) to Northern Ireland (Youth World Tournament) 1988
Overseas teams played for: Gosnells, Perth, Western Australia 1989-91; Fairfield, Sydney 1992-93
Career highlights to date: 'Every day is a highlight in this great Surrey dressing room'
Cricket moments to forget: 'Cannot remember … maybe a dropped catch against Gloucestershire that cost us the game some years back'
Cricket superstitions: 'Not eating duck the night before I'm due to bat'
Cricketers particularly admired: 'All players at Surrey plus Ed Giddins and Gavin Hamilton'
Young players to look out for: Rikki Clarke, Tim Murtagh
Other sports played: 'Golf, tennis, golf, football (centre forward), golf, snooker, golf … most sports'
Other sports followed: Football (Ipswich Town), 'follow most sports'
Relaxations: 'Playing as much golf as possible; eating out; watching movies'
Extras: Youngest Suffolk player, aged 17. Played for HMC, MCC Schools, ESCA U19, NCA Young Cricketers, England U25 and at every level for Suffolk. TSB Young Player of the Year 1987, *Daily Telegraph* Bowling Award 1987 and 1988 and Cricket

Society's Leading All-rounder in English Schools Cricket 1988. Laidlaw Young Player of the Year for Essex and Essex Society Player of the Year 1993. Released by Essex at end of 1994 season and signed for Surrey. Member of the Surrey Sunday League winning side of 1996. Member of Surrey County Championship winning squad of 1999, 2000 and 2002. Scored career best 150 v Sussex at The Oval 2002, in the process sharing with Alistair Brown (177) in a record fifth-wicket partnership for Surrey v Sussex (262). Surrey Team Man of the Year and Fielder of the Year 2002

Opinions on cricket: 'The two overseas players and the unlimited European passport holders playing county cricket cannot be good for the English game. You will have several counties fielding teams with half of the players not eligible to play for England. Cannot see how that can be good for English cricket. Cricket pitches have improved in general, which is good news as this will produce better quality cricketers. We shouldn't get too down over the Ashes loss as currently the Aussies are a world apart from any other nation. We have competed with all other nations and beaten some home and away.'

Best batting: 150 Surrey v Sussex, The Oval 2002
Best bowling: 3-91 Essex v Surrey, The Oval 1990

2002 Season

	M	Inns	NO	Runs	HS	Avge	100s	50s	Ct	St	O	M	Runs	Wkts	Avge	Best	5wI	10wM
Test																		
All First	13	20	1	712	150	37.47	2	3	24	-	22	1	72	1	72.00	1-55	-	-
1-day Int																		
C & G	2	2	1	86	65 *	86.00	-	1	-	-								
B & H	5	5	0	53	22	10.60	-	-	2	-								
1-day Lge	15	14	3	293	74 *	26.63	-	2	4	-								

Career Performances

	M	Inns	NO	Runs	HS	Avge	100s	50s	Ct	St	Balls	Runs	Wkts	Avge	Best	5wI	10wM
Test																	
All First	141	223	26	6268	150	31.81	9	33	149	-	3148	2071	44	47.06	3-91	-	-
1-day Int																	
C & G	12	9	2	249	85 *	35.57	-	2	6	-	72	30	4	7.50	3-30	-	
B & H	28	21	5	356	65 *	22.25	-	2	6	-	150	131	1	131.00	1-59	-	
1-day Lge	125	111	18	2232	109 *	24.00	2	7	38	-	66	72	0	-	-	-	

SHANTRY, A. J.   Northamptonshire

Name: <u>Adam</u> John Shantry
Role: Left-hand bat, left-arm
fast-medium bowler
Born: 13 November 1982, Bristol
Height: 6ft 2in **Weight:** 13st 8lbs
Nickname: Shants
County debut: No first-team appearance
Parents: Brian and Josephine
Marital status: Single
Family links with cricket: 'Father played for
Gloucestershire; younger brother plays for
Shropshire U15'
Education: Oxon C of E; The Priory School;
Shrewsbury Sixth Form College
Qualifications: 11 GCSEs, 4 A-levels,
Level 1 coaching
Career outside cricket: 'Hair stylist'
Off-season: 'Investigating methods of nut
dispersal (putting nuts on trifles)'
Overseas teams played for: Balwyn, Melbourne 2001-02
Career highlights to date: 'Representing ESCA v West Indies U19 2001'
Cricket moments to forget: 'Bowling a no-ball in a bowl-out. Or any time I get a lift
to a game with Chris Park'
Cricket superstitions: 'Never believe Chris Park'
Cricketers particularly admired: Wasim Akram
Young players to look out for: Chris Park, Jack Shantry
Other sports played: Football ('used to play for Shrewsbury Area team')
Other sports followed: Football (Bristol City – 'come on you Reds!')
Injuries: Out for two weeks with a strained ligament in the pelvis; for two weeks with
an injured arm after a car crash
Relaxations: 'Football, fishing, gym, listening to music – Feeder, Ash, Blake'
Extras: England U17 squad. Represented ESCA U18 v West Indies U19 2001. Radio
Shropshire Young Player of the Year 2001. Played for Northamptonshire Board XI in
the first round of the C&G 2003, which was played in August 2002. Leading wicket-
taker for Northamptonshire Colts 2002; took 7-18 v Warwickshire U19 2002
Opinions on cricket: 'Needs to attract more younger fans. More floodlit cricket. Far
too much cricket played – results in sub-standard performance.'

Career Performances

	M	Inns	NO	Runs	HS	Avge	100s	50s	Ct	St	Balls	Runs	Wkts	Avge	Best	5wI	10wM
Test																	
All First																	
1-day Int																	
C & G	1	1	0	15	15	15.00	-	-	-	-	42	21	2	10.50	2-21	-	
B & H																	
1-day Lge																	

SHARIF, Z. K. Essex

Name: <u>Zoheb</u> Khalid Sharif
Role: Left-hand bat, leg-spin bowler
Born: 22 February 1983, Leytonstone, London
Height: 5ft 10in **Weight:** 12st
Nickname: Omar, Bundles, Bomber
County debut: 2001
1st-Class catches: 1
Strike rate: 46.50 (career 49.50)
Parents: Khalid and Robina
Marital status: Single
Education: Henry Maynard Junior School; Warwick School; Chigwell School; Coopers Company and Coborn School
Qualifications: 10 GCSEs, 3 A-levels
Overseas tours: Essex U13 to Holland 1995
Overseas teams played for: PNT CC, Pakistan 1997; Rawalpindi District 2001-02

Career highlights to date: 'Making my first-team debut'
Cricket moments to forget: 'No day should be worth forgetting about; it is an opportunity for a person to learn and correct things for the future'
Cricketers particularly admired: Saeed Anwar, Sachin Tendulkar, Inzamam, Wasim Akram, Imran Khan
Young players to look out for: Gurdeep Kandola, Irfan Shah, Ravi Bopara, James Foster, Carl Greenidge, Bilal Shafayat, Tony Palladino
Other sports followed: Football (Manchester United)
Relaxations: 'Music; following Islam; chillin' with my mates'
Extras: MCC Lord's Taverners' Player of the Year at U13, U15 and U19 level. Was on MCC groundstaff. Was in England U17 squad v Scotland 2000. Took 4-98 v Northamptonshire at Northampton 2002 in his second first-class match

Opinions on cricket: 'Not many people enjoy it.'
Best batting: 42 Essex v Gloucestershire, Gloucester 2002
Best bowling: 4-98 Essex v Northamptonshire, Northampton 2002

2002 Season

	M	Inns	NO	Runs	HS	Avge	100s	50s	Ct	St	O	M	Runs	Wkts	Avge	Best	5wI	10wM
Test																		
All First	2	1	0	42	42	42.00	-	-	-	-	31	0	164	4	41.00	4-98	-	-
1-day Int																		
C & G																		
B & H																		
1-day Lge																		

Career Performances

	M	Inns	NO	Runs	HS	Avge	100s	50s	Ct	St	Balls	Runs	Wkts	Avge	Best	5wI	10wM
Test																	
All First	3	3	0	59	42	19.66	-	-	1	-	198	187	4	46.75	4-98	-	-
1-day Int																	
C & G																	
B & H																	
1-day Lge																	

SHAW, A. D. Glamorgan

Name: Adrian David Shaw
Role: Right-hand bat, wicket-keeper
Born: 17 February 1972, Neath
Height: 6ft **Weight:** 13st 6lbs
Nickname: Shawsy, AD, Hitler, Adolf,
ADS, Eddie
County debut: 1992 (one-day),
1994 (first-class)
County cap: 1999
50 dismissals in a season: 1
1st-Class 50s: 9
1st-Class 100s: 1
1st-Class catches: 180
1st-Class stumpings: 14
Parents: David Colin and Christina
Wife and date of marriage: Wendy,
December 2002
Children: Seren Georgia, 8 January 2002
Education: Catwg Primary; Llangatwg Comprehensive; Neath Tertiary College

Qualifications: 9 O-levels, 3 A-levels, various coaching badges
Career outside cricket: 'Currently open to offers. I feel I have a lot to offer, but that's what everyone says, isn't it?'
Off-season: 'Wiping bottoms, changing nappies, pacifying a teething child (that's my darling!); also trying to educate my daughter in the world of Neath RFC'
Overseas tours: Welsh Schools U17 to Barbados 1987; England YC to New Zealand 1990-91; Glamorgan pre-season tours, including to Cape Town 1999
Overseas teams played for: Welkom Police, Free State 1995-96
Career highlights to date: 'The older I get, the more I realise whatever I've achieved, while I am proud, is not that important in the grander scheme of things, since Seren popped her head out!'
Cricketers particularly admired: 'Anyone who can laugh at themselves and not take it all too seriously'
Young players to look out for: 'Those who can cope with the ups and downs. It's 90 per cent temperament'
Other sports played: Rugby (formerly centre with Neath RFC – Back of the Year 1993-94; Welsh U19 and U21 squad member)
Other sports followed: Rugby (Neath)
Relaxations: 'As anyone with a baby will tell you, no time'
Extras: One of youngest players (18 years 7 days) to play first-class rugby for Neath. Voted Glamorgan 2nd XI Player of the Year and Glamorgan Young Player of the Year in 1995. 2nd XI Player of the Month, June 1996. Claimed eight catches in the second innings and 12 for the match v Gloucestershire 2nd XI at Usk in 1998, setting two records for the 2nd XI Championship. Awarded county Young Player of the Month for August 1999 'at the geriatric age of 27'. Glamorgan 2nd XI player/coach since 2002
Opinions on cricket: 'Perspective – get that right and if you work hard and luck's on your side, you'll be OK. And if it's not, then so what? You tried. Over-inflated egos – we're only cricketers, and no one really notices a county player walking down the road, do they?'
Best batting: 140 Glamorgan v Oxford University, The Parks 1999

2002 Season (did not make any first-class or one-day appearances)

Career Performances

	M	Inns	NO	Runs	HS	Avge	100s	50s	Ct	St	Balls	Runs	Wkts	Avge	Best	5wl	10wM
Test																	
All First	76	102	16	1873	140	21.77	1	9	180	14	6	7	0	-	-	-	-
1-day Int																	
C & G	9	8	2	151	47	25.16	-	-	13	-							
B & H	19	17	3	166	39	11.85	-	-	16	7							
1-day Lge	56	38	9	436	48	15.03	-	-	29	10							

SHEIKH, M. A. Warwickshire

Name: <u>Mohammed</u> Avez Sheikh
Role: Left-hand bat, right-arm
medium bowler
Born: 2 July 1973, Birmingham
Height: 6ft
Nickname: Sheikhy
County debut: 1997
1st-Class 50s: 1
1st-Class catches: 1
Place in batting averages: 143rd av. 29.66
Strike rate: 130.50 (career 89.85)
Education: Broadway School
Overseas teams played for: Western
Province CC 1997-98
Extras: Played for Warwickshire U19 and
played for both Worcestershire and Essex 2nd
XIs in 1995. Played for the Warwickshire
Board side that won the last ECB 38-County
competition 2002, taking 4-37 in the final
Best batting: 58* Warwickshire v Northamptonshire, Northampton 2000
Best bowling: 4-36 Warwickshire v Hampshire, Edgbaston 2001

2002 Season

	M	Inns	NO	Runs	HS	Avge	100s	50s	Ct	St	O	M	Runs	Wkts	Avge	Best	5wI	10wM
Test																		
All First	5	8	2	178	43	29.66	-	-	1	-	130.3	25	396	6	66.00	4-78	-	-
1-day Int																		
C & G	2	2	0	27	14	13.50	-	-	-	-	20	1	94	1	94.00	1-32	-	
B & H	3	2	0	3	3	1.50	-	-	-	-	22	2	86	4	21.50	2-28	-	
1-day Lge	11	5	2	15	9	5.00	-	-	-	-	83	5	411	12	34.25	2-19	-	

Career Performances

	M	Inns	NO	Runs	HS	Avge	100s	50s	Ct	St	Balls	Runs	Wkts	Avge	Best	5wI	10wM
Test																	
All First	14	19	4	401	58 *	26.73	-	1	1	-	1887	838	21	39.90	4-36	-	-
1-day Int																	
C & G	8	4	1	44	14	14.66	-	-	2	-	456	309	9	34.33	2-18	-	
B & H	13	6	1	37	19 *	7.40	-	-	3	-	673	363	16	22.68	3-27	-	
1-day Lge	45	21	8	118	36	9.07	-	-	8	-	1995	1308	51	25.64	4-17	-	

SHERIYAR, A.   Kent

Name: Alamgir Sheriyar
Role: Right-hand bat, left-arm fast bowler
Born: 15 November 1973, Birmingham
Height: 6ft 1in **Weight:** 13st
Nickname: Sheri
County debut: 1993 (one-day, Leics),
1994 (first-class, Leics), 1996 (Worcs)
County cap: 1997 (Worcs; colours, 2002)
50 wickets in a season: 4
1st-Class 5 w. in innings: 21
1st-Class 10 w. in match: 3
1st-Class catches: 19
Place in batting averages: 294th av. 9.72
(2001 273rd av. 6.45)
Place in bowling averages: 58th av. 28.86
(2001 32nd av. 25.28)
Strike rate: 56.03 (career 49.97)
Parents: Mohammed Zaman (deceased) and
Safia Sultana
Marital status: Single
Family links with cricket: Brothers play a bit
Education: George Dixon Secondary School, Birmingham; Joseph Chamberlain Sixth
Form College, Birmingham; Oxford Brookes University
Qualifications: 6 O-levels
Overseas tours: Leicestershire to South Africa 1995; Worcestershire to Barbados
1996; England A to Bangladesh and New Zealand 1999-2000
Cricketers particularly admired: Wasim Akram
Other sports followed: Football, basketball
Relaxations: Time at home, music
Extras: Played for English Schools U17 and has also played in the Indoor National
League. Became only the second player to take a hat-trick on his Championship debut,
for Leics v Durham at Durham University 1994 (Vince Wells took a hat-trick for Leics
in the same match); the first player to achieve the feat was H. A. Sedgwick, for Yorks
v Worcs in 1906. Asked to be released by Leicestershire at the end of the 1995 season
and joined Worcestershire for 1996. First bowler to reach 50 first-class wickets in 1999
and ended season as leading wicket-taker with 92 wickets (av. 24.70). Took second
first-class hat-trick of his career v Kent at Worcester 1999. Left Worcestershire at the
end of the 2002 season and has joined Kent for 2003
Best batting: 21 Worcestershire v Nottinghamshire, Trent Bridge 1997
              21 Worcestershire v Pakistan A, Worcester 1997
Best bowling: 7-130 Worcestershire v Hampshire, Southampton 1999

2002 Season

	M	Inns	NO	Runs	HS	Avge	100s	50s	Ct	St	O	M	Runs	Wkts	Avge	Best	5wI	10wM
Test																		
All First	18	20	9	107	18	9.72	-	-	1	-	616.2	160	1905	66	28.86	6-71	5	-
1-day Int																		
C & G	1	0	0	0	0	-	-	-	-	-	6	3	8	1	8.00	1-8	-	
B & H	4	2	2	5	3*	-	-	-	-	-	32	3	189	4	47.25	2-70	-	
1-day Lge	7	1	1	0	0*	-	-	-	-	-	47.2	3	229	7	32.71	3-30	-	

Career Performances

	M	Inns	NO	Runs	HS	Avge	100s	50s	Ct	St	Balls	Runs	Wkts	Avge	Best	5wI	10wM
Test																	
All First	127	134	50	683	21	8.13	-	-	19	-	22091	12875	442	29.12	7-130	21	3
1-day Int																	
C & G	9	4	1	14	10	4.66	-	-	1	-	389	299	9	33.22	2-47	-	
B & H	19	8	5	34	15	11.33	-	-	1	-	874	639	24	26.62	4-19	-	
1-day Lge	76	21	12	63	19	7.00	-	-	5	-	2662	2265	86	26.33	4-18	-	

SHRECK, C. E.   Nottinghamshire

Name: Charles (<u>Charlie</u>) Edward Shreck
Role: Right-hand bat, right-arm
fast-medium bowler
Born: 6 January 1978, Truro
Height: 6ft 7in   **Weight:** 15st 7lbs
Nickname: Shrecker, Ogre, Stoat, Chough
County debut: 2002 (one-day)
One-Day 5 w. in innings: 2
Parents: Peter and Sheila
Marital status: Single
Family links with cricket: 'Grandfather
watched Southampton'
Education: Polwhele House School, Truro;
Truro School
Qualifications: Level 1 coaching
Career outside cricket: 'Sleeping'
Off-season: 'Playing cricket in the southern
hemisphere; chasing the sun'
Overseas tours: Cornwall U17 to South Africa 1997
Overseas teams played for: Merewether District CC, NSW 1997-98;
Hutt District CC, New Zealand 2000-03
Cricket moments to forget: 'Being run out off the last ball of the game against
Shropshire, walking off – we lost!'

Cricket superstitions: 'None'
Cricketers particularly admired: Viv Richards, Michael Holding, Ian Botham
Young players to look out for: Michael Munday, Carl Gazzard
Relaxations: 'Swimming, music'
Extras: Played for Cornwall in the NatWest 2000, in the C&G 2001 and 2002, and in the second round of the C&G 2003, which was played in September 2002; C&G Man of the Match award for his 5-19 (his maiden one-day five-wicket return) v Worcestershire at Truro in the third round 2002. Took wicket (Vikram Solanki) with his third ball in county cricket v Worcestershire at Trent Bridge in the NUL 2002, going on to record maiden one-day league five-wicket return (5-35)
Opinions on cricket: 'The batters are trying to have it too easy. Put the boundaries back out.'

2002 Season

	M	Inns	NO	Runs	HS	Avge	100s	50s	Ct	St	O	M	Runs	Wkts	Avge	Best	5wI	10wM
Test																		
All First																		
1-day Int																		
C & G	2	1	0	0	0	0.00	-	-	2	-	15	2	67	6	11.16	5-19	1	
B & H																		
1-day Lge	1	1	1	1	1 *	-	-	-	1	-	9	1	35	5	7.00	5-35	1	

Career Performances

	M	Inns	NO	Runs	HS	Avge	100s	50s	Ct	St	Balls	Runs	Wkts	Avge	Best	5wI	10wM
Test																	
All First																	
1-day Int																	
C & G	7	3	1	11	9	5.50	-	-	2	-	360	298	12	24.83	5-19	1	
B & H																	
1-day Lge	1	1	1	1	1 *	-	-	-	1	-	54	35	5	7.00	5-35	1	

77. Who scored 1300 Championship runs and took 50 Championship wickets for Nottinghamshire in 1977?

SIDEBOTTOM, R. J.   Yorkshire

Name: <u>Ryan</u> Jay Sidebottom
Role: Left-hand bat, left-arm fast bowler
Born: 15 January 1978, Huddersfield
Height: 6ft 4in **Weight:** 14st 7lbs
Nickname: Siddy, Sexual, Jazz
County debut: 1997
County cap: 2000
Test debut: 2001
Tests: 1
One-Day Internationals: 2
1st-Class 50s: 1
1st-Class 5 w. in innings: 6
1st-Class 10 w. in match: 1
1st-Class catches: 19
One-Day 5 w. in innings: 1
Place in batting averages: 296th av. 9.64
Place in bowling averages: 60th av. 29.02
(2001 41st av. 26.29)
Strike rate: 55.73 (career 54.77)
Parents: Arnie and Gillian
Marital status: Single

Family links with cricket: Father played cricket for Yorkshire and England and football for Manchester United and Huddersfield Town
Education: Almondbury Primary, Huddersfield; Lepton Middle; King James Grammar School, Almondbury
Qualifications: 5 GCSEs
Overseas tours: England U17 to Holland 1995; MCC to Bangladesh 1999-2000; England A to West Indies 2000-01; England to Zimbabwe (one-day series) 2001-02; ECB National Academy to Australia 2001-02
Overseas teams played for: Ringwood, Melbourne 1998
Cricketers particularly admired: Darren Gough, Chris Silverwood, Glenn McGrath
Young players to look out for: Joe Sayers, Scott Richardson
Other sports played: Football (once with Sheffield United), 'all sports'
Other sports followed: 'Love rugby league (any team)', football (Man Utd)
Relaxations: 'Music (R&B), films, clubbing, going out with my team-mates'
Extras: NBC Denis Compton Award for the most promising young Yorkshire player 1999, 2000. Recorded maiden first-class five-wicket return (5-27) v Kent at Headingley 2000, following up with 6-16 in second innings for maiden ten wickets in a match. Top English bowler in first-class averages in 2000 (second overall) with 24 wickets at 12.50. Took 5-31 (8-65 in the match) in the Busta Cup for England A v Jamaica at Kingston 2000-01, winning the Man of the Match award; topped tour first-class bowling averages (16 wickets; av.16.81). Made Test debut in first Test v Pakistan

at Lord's 2001 (England's 100th Test at the ground), becoming the tenth player to follow his father into the England Test team. Made One-Day International debut in third ODI v Zimbabwe at Harare 2001-02. Called into the ECB National Academy squad in Australia 2001-02 as cover in the pace-bowling department

Best batting: 54 Yorkshire v Glamorgan, Cardiff 1998
Best bowling: 6-16 Yorkshire v Kent, Headingley 2000

2002 Season

	M	Inns	NO	Runs	HS	Avge	100s	50s	Ct	St	O	M	Runs	Wkts	Avge	Best	5wI	10wM
Test																		
All First	13	21	7	135	28	9.64	-	-	4	-	380.5	85	1190	41	29.02	5-60	1	-
1-day Int																		
C & G	4	0	0	0	0	-	-	-	2	-	34	1	149	5	29.80	2-49	-	
B & H	3	1	0	1	1	1.00	-	-	3	-	12	2	52	1	52.00	1-7	-	
1-day Lge	12	6	4	36	30 *	18.00	-	-	2	-	75	7	344	8	43.00	2-32	-	

Career Performances

	M	Inns	NO	Runs	HS	Avge	100s	50s	Ct	St	Balls	Runs	Wkts	Avge	Best	5wI	10wM
Test	1	1	0	4	4	4.00	-	-	-	-	120	64	0	-	-	-	-
All First	51	68	22	502	54	10.91	-	1	19	-	7887	3719	144	25.82	6-16	6	1
1-day Int	2	1	1	2	2 *	-	-	-	-	-	84	84	2	42.00	1-42	-	
C & G	13	2	1	13	7 *	13.00	-	-	4	-	624	419	20	20.95	4-39	-	
B & H	20	7	2	20	8	4.00	-	-	8	-	928	622	12	51.83	2-26	-	
1-day Lge	57	29	16	153	30 *	11.76	-	-	8	-	2310	1683	57	29.52	6-40	1	

---

78. For which county did current first-class umpire Vanburn Holder play from 1968 to 1980?

SILLENCE, R. J.　　　　　Gloucestershire

Name: <u>Roger</u> John Sillence
Role: Right-hand bat, right-arm
fast-medium bowler
Born: 29 June 1977, Salisbury, Wiltshire
Height: 6ft 3in　**Weight:** 12st 10lbs
Nickname: Silly, Sillo
County debut: 2001
1st-Class 100s: 1
1st-Class 5 w. in innings: 2
1st-Class catches: 2
Place in batting averages: 196th av. 23.85
Place in bowling averages: 102nd av. 34.53
Strike rate: 46.15 (career 43.27)
Parents: Angela
Marital status: Single
Family links with cricket: 'Dad played local
cricket'

Education: Farley, Salisbury; Highbury,
Salisbury; Salisbury Art College
Qualifications: 7 GCSEs, ND and HND Graphic Design, ECB Level II coach
Career outside cricket: Graphic design
Off-season: 'Working on fitness, batting and bowling. Catching up with old friends.
Having a holiday in the sun'
Overseas teams played for: Napier Old Boys, New Zealand 1997-98;
St Augustine's, Cape Town 1998-99; East Keilor, Melbourne 2000-01;
Hamersley Carine, Perth 2001-02
Career highlights to date: 'First 100 v Derby on home debut'
Cricket moments to forget: 'Whenever I drop a catch'
Cricket superstitions: 'Always bowl in a short-sleeve shirt'
Cricketers particularly admired: Mike Smith ('good advice')
Young players to look out for: 'JP'
Other sports played: Football ('social')
Other sports followed: Football
Relaxations: 'Design, music, eating out, coffee'
Extras: Played for Wiltshire in the NatWest 1999 and 2000. Wiltshire Player of the
Year 2000. Recorded maiden first-class five-wicket return (5-97) on debut v Sussex at
Hove 2001. Took 4-35 v West Indies A in a 50-over match at Cheltenham 2002.
Scored maiden first-class century (101) v Derbyshire at Bristol 2002 in only his third
Championship match and batting at No. 9
Opinions on cricket: 'Need more people (spectators) interested in the game. Give the
young guys a go.'

Best batting: 101 Gloucestershire v Derbyshire, Bristol 2002
Best bowling: 5-63 Gloucestershire v Durham, Bristol 2002

2002 Season

	M	Inns	NO	Runs	HS	Avge	100s	50s	Ct	St	O	M	Runs	Wkts	Avge	Best	5wI	10wM
Test																		
All First	5	7	0	167	101	23.85	1	-	2	-	100	11	449	13	34.53	5-63	1	-
1-day Int																		
C & G																			
B & H																			
1-day Lge	1	1	0	11	11	11.00	-	-	-	-								

Career Performances

	M	Inns	NO	Runs	HS	Avge	100s	50s	Ct	St	Balls	Runs	Wkts	Avge	Best	5wI	10wM
Test																	
All First	6	9	0	173	101	19.22	1	-	2	-	779	549	18	30.50	5-63	2	-
1-day Int																	
C & G	4	3	0	89	82	29.66	-	1	-	-	96	75	4	18.75	3-47	-	
B & H																	
1-day Lge	1	1	0	11	11	11.00	-	-	-	-							

SILVERWOOD, C. E. W.   Yorkshire

Name: Christopher (<u>Chris</u>) Eric
Wilfred Silverwood
Role: Right-hand bat, right-arm
fast bowler
Born: 5 March 1975, Pontefract
Height: 6ft 1in **Weight:** 12st 9lbs
Nickname: Spoons, Silvers, Chubby
County debut: 1993
County cap: 1996
Test debut: 1996-97
Tests: 5
One-Day Internationals: 7
50 wickets in a season: 1
1st-Class 50s: 5
1st-Class 5 w. in innings: 18
1st-Class 10 w. in match: 1
1st-Class catches: 27
One-Day 5 w. in innings: 1

Place in batting averages: 250th av. 16.64 (2001 189th av. 20.87)
Place in bowling averages: 84th av. 32.83 (2001 10th av. 19.51)

Strike rate: 61.23 (career 51.39)
Parents: Brenda
Marital status: Single
Family links with cricket: 'Dad played a bit'
Education: Gibson Lane School, Kippax; Garforth Comprehensive
Qualifications: 8 GCSEs, City and Guilds in Leisure and Recreation
Overseas tours: England A to Kenya and Sri Lanka 1997-98, to Bangladesh and New Zealand 1999-2000, to West Indies 2000-01; England to Zimbabwe and New Zealand 1996-97, to West Indies 1997-98, to Bangladesh (Wills International Cup) 1998-99, to South Africa 1999-2000, to Zimbabwe (one-day series) 2001-02; England VI to Hong Kong 2002
Overseas teams played for: Wellington, Cape Town 1993-94, 1995-96
Career highlights to date: 'Making Test debut. Winning the Championship [2001]'
Cricketers particularly admired: Ian Botham, Allan Donald
Other sports played: Karate (black belt), rugby league (Kippax Welfare), athletics (represented Yorkshire)
Other sports followed: Rugby league (Castleford)
Relaxations: 'Listening to music, watching videos, riding my motorbike'
Extras: Attended the Yorkshire Cricket Academy. Played for England U19 in the home series against India U19 in 1994. Recorded his first five-wicket innings return in Tests (5-91) in the fourth Test v South Africa at Cape Town 1999-2000. Took 4-45 from 32 overs for England A in Trinidad and Tobago's first innings in the Busta Cup match at Port of Spain 2000-01. Called up for England one-day tour to Zimbabwe 2001-02 after the withdrawal of James Ormond through injury. Struck a 44-ball 56 in the B&H quarter-final v Essex at Chelmsford and a 32-ball 58 in the NUL v Durham at Riverside 2002. C&G Man of the Match award for his 61 and 2-35 v Northamptonshire at Northampton 2002
Best batting: 70 Yorkshire v Essex, Chelmsford 2001
Best bowling: 7-93 Yorkshire v Kent, Headingley 1997
Stop press: Called up to the England Test squad in Australia 2002-03 as a replacement for the injured Simon Jones; was himself injured (ankle) during the third Test at Perth and forced to return home

---

2002 Season

	M	Inns	NO	Runs	HS	Avge	100s	50s	Ct	St	O	M	Runs	Wkts	Avge	Best	5wl	10wM
Test																		
All First	12	19	2	283	44 *	16.64	-	-	3	-	306.1	68	985	30	32.83	4-28	-	-
1-day Int																		
C & G	5	4	0	117	61	29.25	-	1	1	-	39	6	143	3	47.66	2-35	-	
B & H	5	5	0	93	56	18.60	-	1	1	-	32	4	123	5	24.60	3-23	-	
1-day Lge	7	7	0	182	58	26.00	-	2	2	-	51	6	227	8	28.37	3-15	-	

Career Performances

	M	Inns	NO	Runs	HS	Avge	100s	50s	Ct	St	Balls	Runs	Wkts	Avge	Best	5wI	10wM
Test	5	6	3	19	7 *	6.33	-	-	3	-	804	415	11	37.72	5-91	1	-
All First	122	161	32	2013	70	15.60	-	5	27	-	20094	10493	391	26.83	7-93	18	1
1-day Int	7	4	0	17	12	4.25	-	-	-	-	306	244	6	40.66	3-43	-	
C & G	21	9	3	142	61	23.66	-	1	7	-	1091	672	20	33.60	3-24	-	
B & H	32	17	2	150	56	10.00	-	1	7	-	1564	1136	50	22.72	5-28	1	
1-day Lge	89	53	24	425	58	14.65	-	2	9	-	3685	2610	123	21.21	4-11	-	

SINGH, A. Worcestershire

Name: Anurag Singh
Role: Right-hand bat, right-arm 'all sorts'
Born: 9 September 1975, Kanpur, India
Height: 5ft 11½in **Weight:** 11st
Nickname: Ragi
County debut: 1995 (Warwickshire),
2001 (Worcestershire)
County colours: 2002 (Worcestershire)
1000 runs in a season: 2
1st-Class 50s: 17
1st-Class 100s: 8
1st-Class catches: 31
One-Day 100s: 1
Place in batting averages: 103rd av. 36.46
(2001 80th av. 36.34)
Parents: Vijay and Rajul
Marital status: Single
Education: Sacred Heart, Roehampton/
Bishop Gilpin, Wimbledon/Mayfield Prep, Walsall; King Edward's School,
Birmingham; Gonville and Caius College, Cambridge; College of Law, London
Qualifications: 12 GCSEs, 1 AO-level, 4 A-levels, passed Law School exams
Career outside cricket: Solicitor at Wragge & Co in Birmingham
Overseas tours: England U19 to West Indies 1994-95; Warwickshire U21 to
South Africa; Warwickshire CCC to South Africa; Quidnuncs to South Africa 2002
Overseas teams played for: Gordon CC, Sydney; Avendale CC, Cape Town
Career highlights to date: 'Scoring 62 v McGrath, Warne & Co at New Road 2001.
Reaching the 2000 NatWest final. Scoring 187 v Gloucestershire last year [2002]'
Cricket moments to forget: 'No regrets – I've enjoyed my career thus far'
Cricketers particularly admired: Steve Waugh, Sachin Tendulkar, Michael Atherton
Young players to look out for: Nick Warren, Kabir Ali
Other sports played: Hockey ('college and school'), football ('college and firm')
Other sports followed: Football (Aston Villa FC)

Relaxations: Reading, socialising with friends

Extras: Broke school record for number of runs in a season (1102). *Daily Telegraph* regional award for batting (twice) and bowling (once). Tiger Smith Memorial Award for Warwickshire's Most Promising Young Cricketer 1994, Coney Edmonds Trophy for Warwickshire's Best U19 Cricketer 1994, Lord's Taverners' Trophy for Best Young Cricketer 1994, Gray-Nicolls Len Newbery Award for ESCA U19 Best Player 1994. Scored two centuries for England U19 against India U19 in 1994. Scored one century against West Indies U20 and was Man of the Series 1994-95. Awarded 2nd XI cap in 1995. Cambridge Blue 1996-98; captain of Cambridge University 1997-98. Scored 85 in NatWest semi-final v Hampshire at Edgbaston 2000, in the process sharing with Nick Knight (100) in a Warwickshire record first-wicket stand (185) for the competition. Left Warwickshire at the end of the 2000 season and joined Worcestershire for 2001. Scored maiden Championship century (168) v Middlesex at Worcester 2001, in the process passing 1000 runs in a season for the first time and sharing with Philip Weston (71) in a record opening partnership for Worcestershire in matches against Middlesex (180)

Opinions on cricket: 'Given the influx of EU players, counties should only be allowed to sign one overseas player. Very few household names are available anyway, so the argument that having two overseas players will attract bigger crowds or more sponsors does not hold water, as they take more money out of the game than they bring in. In addition, the only way to learn is to play. It is one thing having an English player's place taken up by a Glenn McGrath or a Sachin Tendulkar; it is quite another to have a spot taken up by a run-of-the-mill state cricketer from another country who is admittedly maybe slightly better/more experienced than an English player but whose presence in the team serves only to prevent that English player improving. There is only so much you can learn from dominating second-team cricket.'

Best batting: 187 Worcestershire v Gloucestershire, Bristol 2002

2002 Season

	M	Inns	NO	Runs	HS	Avge	100s	50s	Ct	St	O	M	Runs Wkts	Avge	Best	5wl	10wM
Test																	
All First	18	32	0	1167	187	36.46	2	6	11	-							
1-day Int																	
C & G	2	2	0	13	9	6.50	-	-	1	-							
B & H	2	2	0	30	30	15.00	-	-	2	-							
1-day Lge	11	10	1	282	75 *	31.33	-	2	2	-							

Career Performances

	M	Inns	NO	Runs	HS	Avge	100s	50s	Ct	St	Balls	Runs	Wkts	Avge	Best	5wl	10wM
Test																	
All First	79	130	5	4050	187	32.40	8	17	31	-	95	111	0	-	-	-	-
1-day Int																	
C & G	9	9	0	282	85	31.33	-	2	3	-							
B & H	24	24	1	573	123	24.91	1	4	7	-							
1-day Lge	49	48	2	1105	86	24.02	-	9	13	-							

SMETHURST, M. P.   Lancashire

Name: Michael (<u>Mike</u>) Paul Smethurst
Role: Right-hand bat, right-arm fast bowler
Born: 11 October 1976, Oldham
Height: 6ft 5in **Weight:** 14st 6lbs
County debut: 1999
50 wickets in a season: 1
1st-Class 50s: 1
1st-Class 5 w. in innings: 3
1st-Class catches: 5
Place in batting averages: (2001 280th av. 4.14)
Strike rate: 73.33 (career 50.42)
Parents: Julie Martin ('Mum')
Marital status: Single
Education: Middleton Parish Primary School; Hulme Grammar School, Oldham; University of Salford
Qualifications: 9 GCSEs, 4 A-levels, BA (Hons) Leisure Management, Level 2 coaching award
Overseas tours: Lancashire to Cape Town 1999, 2000, 2001, 2002
Young players to look out for: James Anderson, Kyle Hogg, Mark Currie, Steven Crook, Sajid Mahmood
Other sports followed: Football (Manchester United)
Extras: Recorded maiden first-class five-wicket return (7-50) v Durham at Riverside 2000
Best batting: 66 Lancashire v Surrey, Old Trafford 2000
Best bowling: 7-37 Lancashire v New Zealand A, Liverpool 2000

2002 Season

	M	Inns	NO	Runs	HS	Avge	100s	50s	Ct	St	O	M	Runs	Wkts	Avge	Best	5wI	10wM
Test																		
All First	4	4	2	32	13	16.00	-	-	1	-	110	20	471	9	52.33	3-68	-	-
1-day Int																		
C & G																		
B & H	1	0	0	0	0	-	-	-	-	-								
1-day Lge	1	1	1	1	1*	-	-	-	-	-	6	0	45	0	-		-	-

Career Performances

	M	Inns	NO	Runs	HS	Avge	100s	50s	Ct	St	Balls	Runs	Wkts	Avge	Best	5wI	10wM
Test																	
All First	30	35	13	227	66	10.31	-	1	5	-	4286	2372	85	27.90	7-37	3	-
1-day Int																	
C & G	5	1	1	4	4 *	-	-	-	1	-	250	173	9	19.22	4-46	-	
B & H	3	1	1	10	10 *	-	-	-	-	-	96	77	3	25.66	2-34	-	
1-day Lge	18	9	4	12	3 *	2.40	-	-	3	-	590	500	9	55.55	2-13	-	

SMITH, A. M.   Gloucestershire

Name: Andrew <u>Michael</u> Smith
Role: Right-hand bat ('put bat to ball!'),
left-arm swing bowler
Born: 1 October 1967, Dewsbury
Height: 5ft 9in **Weight:** 12st 3lbs
Nickname: Smudge, Cyril
County debut: 1991
County cap: 1995
Benefit: 2001
Test debut: 1997
Tests: 1
50 wickets in a season: 5
1st-Class 50s: 4
1st-Class 5 w. in innings: 21
1st-Class 10 w. in match: 5
1st-Class catches: 29
One-Day 5 w. in innings: 2

Place in batting averages: 273rd av. 13.14
Place in bowling averages: 64th av. 29.54
Strike rate: 52.25 (career 49.61)
Parents: Hugh and Margaret
Wife and date of marriage: Sarah, 2 October 1993
Children: William James, 9 October 1994; Amelia Lucy, 14 June 1997
Family links with cricket: Father (Birstall club) and brother (East Ardsley club) local
league cricketers in Yorkshire
Education: Queen Elizabeth Grammar School, Wakefield; Exeter University;
University of the West of England, Bristol
Qualifications: 9 O-levels, 4 A-levels, BA (Hons) French and German, PGDip Law
Career outside cricket: Studying to be a lawyer
Off-season: 'Still studying law (nearly finished now); decorating, golf, going to the
races, ferrying the kids about, keeping fit'

Overseas tours: Queen Elizabeth Grammar School to Holland 1985; Bradford Junior Cricket League to Barbados 1986; Exeter University to Barbados 1987; Gloucestershire to Kenya 1990, to Sri Lanka 1992-93, to Zimbabwe 1996, to Cape Town 2000, to South Africa 2001; England A to Pakistan 1995-96; MCC to New Zealand 1999

Overseas teams played for: Waimea, New Zealand 1990; WTTU, New Zealand 1991

Career highlights to date: 'My one Test match and the 1999 NatWest final v Somerset'

Cricket moments to forget: 'My batting in my one Test match'

Cricket superstitions: 'I try not to rely on superstitions to bring me good luck'

Cricketers particularly admired: Wasim Akram, Malcolm Marshall, Richard Hadlee, Darren Gough, Jacques Kallis, Adam Gilchrist

Young players to look out for: 'My daughter (5) bowls quality left-arm seamers'

Other sports played: Football, golf

Other sports followed: Football (Leeds United), horse racing

Injuries: Out for the first month of the 2002 season with a sore groin

Relaxations: Looking after the kids ('hardly relaxing!'), crosswords, computers

Extras: Played for Yorkshire age groups. Played for English Schools U19, NAYC and represented Combined Universities in the B&H Cup in 1988 and 1990. Finished the 1997 English season as leading first-class wicket-taker with 83 wickets (av. 17.63). Gloucestershire Player of the Year 1997. Took 400th first-class wicket when Jack Russell caught Keith Parsons v Somerset at Bath 1999

Opinions on cricket: 'Good move to have two overseas players. The game needed more spark and more appeal, and two overseas players will help that. Not so sure about 20-over cricket, though, but I hope it works. Please make balls that stay harder for longer. It's not easy to bowl with a marshmallow. The decision as to whether a catch has carried to a fielder should only be made by umpire on the field, not third umpire.'

Best batting: 61 Gloucestershire v Yorkshire, Gloucester 1998

Best bowling: 8-73 Gloucestershire v Middlesex, Lord's 1996

2002 Season

	M	Inns	NO	Runs	HS	Avge	100s	50s	Ct	St	O	M	Runs	Wkts	Avge	Best	5wI	10wM
Test																		
All First	9	13	6	92	21	13.14	-	-	3	-	270	55	916	31	29.54	5-69	1	-
1-day Int																		
C & G	2	0	0	0	0	-	-	-	2	-	17	4	49	2	24.50	1-9	-	
B & H	1	0	0	0	0	-	-	-	1	-	10	2	29	1	29.00	1-29	-	
1-day Lge	13	6	4	22	12 *	11.00	-	-	3	-	100.1	14	353	24	14.70	5-30	1	

Career Performances

	M	Inns	NO	Runs	HS	Avge	100s	50s	Ct	St	Balls	Runs	Wkts	Avge	Best	5wI	10wM
Test	1	2	1	4	4 *	4.00	-	-	-	-	138	89	0	-	-	-	-
All First	143	190	54	1686	61	12.39	-	4	29	-	24164	12133	487	24.91	8-73	21	5
1-day Int																	
C & G	28	10	6	53	13	13.25	-	-	8	-	1603	849	40	21.22	4-46	-	
B & H	46	22	12	91	15 *	9.10	-	-	11	-	2532	1663	56	29.69	6-39	1	
1-day Lge	152	78	47	342	26 *	11.03	-	-	24	-	6349	4422	170	26.01	5-30	1	

SMITH, B. F.   Worcestershire

Name: Benjamin (<u>Ben</u>) Francis Smith
Role: Right-hand bat, right-arm
medium bowler, county captain
Born: 3 April 1972, Corby
Height: 5ft 9in **Weight:** 11st
Nickname: Turnip, Sven
County debut: 1990 (Leicestershire),
2002 (Worcestershire)
County cap: 1995 (Leicestershire),
2002 (Worcestershire colours)
1000 runs in a season: 4
1st-Class 50s: 50
1st-Class 100s: 26
1st-Class 200s: 2
1st-Class catches: 109
One-Day 100s: 1
Place in batting averages: 55th av. 44.51
(2001 56th av. 43.64)
Strike rate: 102.00 (career 179.66)
Parents: Keith and Janet
Wife and date of marriage: Lisa, 10 October 1998
Family links with cricket: Father, grandfather and uncles all played club and
representative cricket
Education: Tugby C of E; Kibworth High School; Robert Smyth, Market Harborough
Qualifications: 5 O-levels, 8 GCSEs, NCA coaching certificate
Off-season: 'A winter off and Christmas at home; maybe some time away pre-season.
Mainly keeping fit, along with some time on the golf course'
Overseas tours: England YC to New Zealand 1990-91; MCC to Bangladesh 1999-
2000; 'numerous pre-season tours to South Africa, Caribbean and Sri Lanka'
Overseas teams played for: Alexandria, Zimbabwe 1990; Bankstown-Canterbury,
Sydney 1993-96; Central Hawke's Bay CC, New Zealand 1997-98; Central Districts,
New Zealand 2000-01

Career highlights to date: 'Winning 1996 County Championship'
Cricket moments to forget: 'Lord's finals'
Cricketers particularly admired: Viv Richards, David Gower, Steve Waugh
Other sports played: Tennis (Leicestershire aged 12), golf, touch rugby, 'Vortex'
Other sports followed: Rugby union (Leicester Tigers)
Relaxations: 'Music, DIY, good wine'
Extras: Cricket Society Young Player of the Year 1991. Took part in Leicestershire record fifth-wicket partnership (322) with Phil Simmons v Notts at Worksop 1998. 'Two Championship medals so far!' Played in the Central Districts Shell Cup winning side in New Zealand 2000-01. Vice-captain of Leicestershire 2001. Scored 110 v Kent at Canterbury 2001, in the process sharing with Iain Sutcliffe in a Leicestershire record second-wicket partnership for matches against Kent (190). Left Leicestershire at the end of the 2001 season and joined Worcestershire for 2002. Scored 200* for Central Districts v Canterbury at New Plymouth in the New Zealand State Championship 2001-02, following up with 78 in the second innings. Scored century (137) on first-class debut for Worcestershire v Oxford University CCE at The Parks and another (129) on Championship debut for the county v Gloucestershire at Worcester 2002 to become the first player to achieve this 'double' for Worcestershire. Scored 2024 runs for Worcestershire in all cricket 2002. Worcestershire Supporters' Player of the Year 2002. Appointed captain of Worcestershire for 2003
Opinions on cricket: 'An even amount of teams in each division to play Championship games starting on the same day, to eliminate *some* weather and selection problems.'
Best batting: 204 Leicestershire v Surrey, The Oval 1998
Best bowling: 1-5 Leicestershire v Essex, Ilford 1991

2002 Season

	M	Inns	NO	Runs	HS	Avge	100s	50s	Ct	St	O	M	Runs	Wkts	Avge	Best	5wI	10wM
Test																		
All First	18	30	3	1202	137	44.51	4	6	6	-	17	2	77	1	77.00	1-45	-	-
1-day Int																		
C & G	3	3	2	115	85 *	115.00	-	1	-									
B & H	7	6	1	53	23 *	10.60	-	-	4	-								
1-day Lge	16	15	5	654	92 *	65.40	-	7	5	-	2	0	15	0	-	-	-	-

Career Performances

	M	Inns	NO	Runs	HS	Avge	100s	50s	Ct	St	Balls	Runs	Wkts	Avge	Best	5wI	10wM
Test																	
All First	214	330	40	11448	204	39.47	28	50	109	-	539	350	3	116.66	1-5	-	-
1-day Int																	
C & G	25	24	5	609	85 *	32.05	-	4	12	-	18	15	0	-	-	-
B & H	44	41	3	991	90	26.07	-	8	20	-							
1-day Lge	172	168	24	4492	115	31.19	1	27	43	-	30	30	0	-	-	-

SMITH, E. T.   Kent

Name: <u>Edward</u> Thomas Smith
Role: Right-hand bat, right-arm
medium bowler
Born: 19 July 1977, Pembury, Kent
Height: 6ft 2in **Weight:** 12st 8lbs
Nickname: Smudge
County debut: 1996
County cap: 2001
1000 runs in a season: 3
1st-Class 50s: 29
1st-Class 100s: 11
1st-Class catches: 27
Place in batting averages: 77th av. 41.30
(2001 74th av. 39.03)
Parents: Jonathan and Gillie
Marital status: Single
Family links with cricket: Father wrote
Good Enough? with Chris Cowdrey
Education: Tonbridge School; Peterhouse, Cambridge University
Qualifications: 11 GCSEs, 3 A-levels, degree in History
Career outside cricket: Writer
Off-season: 'Partly in America; partly in Australia'
Overseas teams played for: 'Several Australian club sides'
Career highlights to date: 'Scoring 175 at Chester-le-Street in 2000'
Cricket superstitions: 'Too many to mention'
Cricketers particularly admired: Steve Waugh, Rahul Dravid
Young players to look out for: James Tredwell
Other sports played: Squash, rugby
Other sports followed: Football (Arsenal FC), baseball (New York Mets)
Relaxations: 'Travel, music, reading, socialising'
Extras: Scored a century (101) on his first-class debut against Glamorgan in 1996 and in doing so became the youngest player to score a century on debut for Cambridge University. He was also the first person to score 50 or more in each of his first six first-class games. Cambridge Blue in 1996. Played for England U19 against New Zealand U19 in 1996. Published book *Playing Hard Ball* in 2001
Opinions on cricket: 'We should try to improve county cricket, but stop running it down. Is the standard really worse than other Test-playing nations? I doubt it.'
Best batting: 190 Cambridge University v Leicestershire, Fenner's 1997

2002 Season

	M	Inns	NO	Runs	HS	Avge	100s	50s	Ct	St	O	M	Runs	Wkts	Avge	Best	5wl	10wM
Test																		
All First	17	32	2	1239	154	41.30	2	8	4	-								
1-day Int																		
C & G																		
B & H	4	4	1	72	27	24.00	-	-	1	-								
1-day Lge	6	6	0	134	83	22.33	-	1	-	-								

Career Performances

	M	Inns	NO	Runs	HS	Avge	100s	50s	Ct	St	Balls	Runs	Wkts	Avge	Best	5wl	10wM
Test																	
All First	96	163	9	5800	190	37.66	11	29	27	-	54	45	0	-	-	-	-
1-day Int																	
C & G	3	3	0	33	19	11.00	-	-	-	-							
B & H	9	9	1	151	43	18.87	-	-	4	-							
1-day Lge	28	25	2	455	83	19.78	-	3	2	-							

SMITH, G. J.   Nottinghamshire

Name: Gregory (Greg) James Smith
Role: Right-hand bat, left-arm fast bowler
Born: 30 October 1971, Pretoria, South Africa
Height: 6ft 4in **Weight:** 15st
Nickname: Claw, Smudge, G
County debut: 2001
County cap: 2001
50 wickets in a season: 1
1st-Class 50s: 2
1st-Class 5 w. in innings: 10
1st-Class 10 w. in match: 2
1st-Class catches: 19
One-Day 5 w. in innings: 1
Place in batting averages: 236th av. 18.61 (2001 212th av. 17.72)
Place in bowling averages: 36th av. 26.56 (2001 31st av. 25.12)
Strike rate: 50.00 (career 57.27)
Parents: Fred and Nellie
Wife and date of marriage: Thea, 5 September 1999
Children: Rob, 1989; Keeghan, 1999

Education: Valhalla Primary; Pretoria BHS
Off-season: Playing for Northerns Titans in South Africa
Overseas tours: South Africa A to England 1996
Overseas teams played for: Northern Transvaal/Northerns Titans 1993-94 –
Career highlights to date: 'Playing for South Africa A. Being capped by Notts'
Cricket moments to forget: 'Losing to Surrey in semi-final of B&H Cup [2001]. Losing to Natal in final of Standard Bank Cup [2000-01]'
Cricketers particularly admired: Wasim Akram, Fanie de Villiers, Kepler Wessels
Young players to look out for: Bilal Shafayat, Krier van Wyk, Jacques Rudolph
Other sports played: Golf
Other sports followed: Football (Arsenal), South African rugby
Relaxations: 'Spending time with my family and friends'
Extras: Attended National Academy in South Africa. Made first-class debut for Northern Transvaal B v Transvaal B at Johannesburg 1993-94. Took hat-trick v Border in a semi-final. Took 4-18 from ten overs in the B&H quarter-final v Warwickshire at Trent Bridge 2001. Nottinghamshire Player of the Year 2001. B&H Gold Awards for his 5-39 (his maiden one-day five-wicket return for Notts) v Yorkshire and his 3-8 (in a 10-over match) v Derbyshire, both at Trent Bridge 2002. Scored 16* v Derbyshire at Derby 2002, in the process sharing with Jason Gallian (111*) in a Nottinghamshire record stand for the last wicket to win a Championship match (46*). Holds a British passport and is not considered an overseas player
Opinions on cricket: 'Too much cricket in the county season.'
Best batting: 68 Northerns v Western Province, Centurion 1995-96
Best bowling: 8-53 Nottinghamshire v Essex, Trent Bridge 2002

2002 Season

	M	Inns	NO	Runs	HS	Avge	100s	50s	Ct	St	O	M	Runs	Wkts	Avge	Best	5wI	10wM
Test																		
All First	15	20	7	242	38 *	18.61	-	-	4	-	400	85	1275	48	26.56	8-53	1	1
1-day Int																		
C & G	2	0	0	0	0	-	-	-	-	-	18	2	65	2	32.50	2-25	-	
B & H	5	2	1	18	11	18.00	-	-	-	-	34	2	155	9	17.22	5-39	1	
1-day Lge	7	6	1	33	16 *	6.60	-	-	-	-	58	8	283	9	31.44	3-41	-	

Career Performances

	M	Inns	NO	Runs	HS	Avge	100s	50s	Ct	St	Balls	Runs	Wkts	Avge	Best	5wI	10wM
Test																	
All First	99	124	47	1087	68	14.11	-	2	19	-	17413	8531	304	28.06	8-53	10	2
1-day Int																	
C & G	4	1	0	1	1	1.00	-	-	-	-	216	126	9	14.00	4-25	-	
B & H	12	3	1	20	11	10.00	-	-	2	-	617	409	21	19.47	5-39	1	
1-day Lge	22	11	2	52	16 *	5.77	-	-	1	-	1025	778	30	25.93	3-25	-	

SMITH, N. M. K.   Warwickshire

Name: <u>Neil</u> Michael Knight Smith
Role: Right-hand bat, off-spin bowler
Born: 27 July 1967, Solihull
Height: 6ft **Weight:** 14st 7lbs ('early
season'); 15st 7lbs ('end of season')
Nickname: Gert
County debut: 1987
County cap: 1993
Benefit: 2002
One-Day Internationals: 7
1000 runs in a season: 1
1st-Class 50s: 34
1st-Class 100s: 4
1st-Class 5 w. in innings: 18
1st-Class catches: 71
One-Day 100s: 2
One-Day 5 w. in innings: 3

Place in batting averages: 210th av. 22.46
(2001 186th av. 21.16)
Place in bowling averages: 101st av. 34.25 (2001 73rd av. 32.52)
Strike rate: 63.00 (career 74.47)
Parents: Mike (M.J.K.) and Diana
Wife and date of marriage: Rachel, 4 December 1993
Family links with cricket: Father (M.J.K.) captained Warwickshire and England
Education: Warwick School
Qualifications: 3 O-levels, cricket coach Grade 1
Career outside cricket: Sports coach
Off-season: Coaching Warwick School
Overseas tours: England to South Africa 1995-96, to India and Pakistan (World Cup)
1995-96; England XI to New Zealand (Cricket Max) 1997-98
Overseas teams played for: Phoenix, Perth, Western Australia 1989-90
Career highlights to date: 'Playing for England'
Cricket moments to forget: 'Being known for spoiling people's breakfasts in the UK
by throwing up in Pakistan during the World Cup'
Cricketers particularly admired: 'Anyone who has played for a long time'
Young players to look out for: Naqaash Tahir
Other sports played: Golf, squash, real tennis
Other sports followed: Rugby union (England, Leicester Tigers)
Relaxations: Sport, walking the dogs
Extras: Followed in his father's footsteps when he led the Warwickshire side out
against Northamptonshire at Edgbaston in the Sunday League 1997 – the first time
both father and son had captained Warwicks. His 147 v Somerset at Taunton 1998 is

the highest score by a Warwickshire No. 9. Warwickshire captain 1999-2000

Opinions on cricket: 'Cricket this year has been too predictable and boring. We must get our wickets better and try to bring spinners into the game. We will not attract spectators if all we have to offer is seam bowlers on pitches that are slow with unpredictable bounce. Typified by England trying to win the Trent Bridge Test with a batter who bowls – M. Vaughan.'

Best batting: 161 Warwickshire v Yorkshire, Headingley 1989
Best bowling: 7-42 Warwickshire v Lancashire, Edgbaston 1994

2002 Season

	M	Inns	NO	Runs	HS	Avge	100s	50s	Ct	St	O	M	Runs	Wkts	Avge	Best	5wI	10wM
Test																		
All First	8	15	0	337	96	22.46	-	2	7	-	126	27	411	12	34.25	5-42	1	-
1-day Int																		
C & G	2	2	1	37	28 *	37.00	-	-	-	-	18	3	80	3	26.66	2-25	-	
B & H	7	6	1	112	29	22.40	-	-	1	-	45	0	199	2	99.50	1-40	-	
1-day Lge	15	12	3	104	23 *	11.55	-	-	2	-	90.3	2	451	13	34.69	3-25	-	

Career Performances

	M	Inns	NO	Runs	HS	Avge	100s	50s	Ct	St	Balls	Runs	Wkts	Avge	Best	5wI	10wM
Test																	
All First	199	281	34	6645	161	26.90	4	34	71	-	27557	13560	370	36.64	7-42	18	
1-day Int	7	6	1	100	31	20.00	-	-	1	-	261	190	6	31.66	3-29	-	
C & G	45	40	9	671	72	21.64	-	4	14	-	1882	1201	50	24.02	5-17	1	
B & H	52	44	5	837	125	21.46	1	3	6	-	1829	1385	39	35.51	3-29	-	
1-day Lge	212	175	23	3286	111 *	21.61	1	18	74	-	6832	5267	199	26.46	6-33	2	

SMITH, R. A.   Hampshire

Name: Robin Arnold Smith
Role: Right-hand bat, slip fielder
Born: 13 September 1963, Durban, South Africa
Height: 6ft **Weight:** 15st
Nickname: Judge
County debut: 1982
County cap: 1985
Benefit: 1996
Test debut: 1988
Tests: 62
One-Day Internationals: 71
1000 runs in a season: 11
1st-Class 50s: 126
1st-Class 100s: 60

1st-Class 200s: 1
1st-Class catches: 224
One-Day 100s: 27
Place in batting averages: 112th av. 34.66
(2001 154th av. 24.91)
Strike rate: (career 78.50)
Parents: John and Joy
Wife and date of marriage: Katherine,
21 September 1988
Children: Harrison Arnold, 4 December
1991; Margaux Elizabeth, 28 July 1994
Family links with cricket: Grandfather
played for Natal in Currie Cup. Brother Chris
played for Natal, Hampshire and England
Education: Northwood High School, Durban
Qualifications: Matriculation, '62 England
caps'
Career outside cricket: 'Sports tours.
Developing my manufacturing business (Chase Sport, Masuri Helmets)'
Off-season: 'Hosting and organising Robin Smith Worldwide Tours to South Africa
for the World Cup. Selling and promoting Chase Sport (manufacturers of cricket
equipment)'
Overseas tours: England to India and West Indies 1989-90, to Australia 1990-91,
to Australia and New Zealand (World Cup) 1991-92, to India and Sri Lanka 1992-93,
to West Indies 1993-94, to South Africa 1995-96, to India and Pakistan (World Cup)
1995-96; England XI to New Zealand (Cricket Max) 1997-98
Overseas teams played for: Natal 1980-84; Perth, Australia 1984-85 (grade cricket)
Career highlights to date: '167* against Australia in an ODI at Edgbaston [1993] –
currently still an England record for highest ODI score'
Cricket moments to forget: 'Too many to mention!'
Cricket superstitions: 'Four-leaf clover on the back of my bat'
Cricketers particularly admired: Malcolm Marshall, Brian Lara, Graeme Hick,
Graham Gooch, Allan Lamb, Ian Botham
Young players to look out for: Steve Harmison, Rob Key, Ian Bell, Simon Jones
Other sports played: Golf
Other sports followed: Football (Southampton FC), golf
Relaxations: 'Reading (Leslie Thomas in particular), trout fishing, assembling a
good wine cellar, keeping fit; enjoying the company of my wife and children (most of
the time!); drinking in my local pub (the Lamb Inn) in the New Forest'
Extras: Played rugby for Natal Schools and for Romsey RFC as a full-back. Held 19
school athletics records and two South African schools records in shot putt and 100-
metre hurdles. One of *Wisden*'s Five Cricketers of the Year 1990. Cornhill England
Player of the Year 1991-92. Set record for the highest individual score for England in
One-Day Internationals (167*) against Australia at Edgbaston 1993. Passed 6000 runs
in one-day league v Gloucestershire at Southampton 1999. Awarded an honorary MA

by Southampton Institute, November 2001, for services to the institute. Scored a century (113) in Hampshire's victory over the Australians in the Vodafone Challenge match at West End 2001. Passed 25,000 first-class career runs during the match v Warwickshire at Edgbaston 2002. Hampshire captain 1998-2002. Granted a testimonial for 2003 (becoming only the second Hampshire player after Peter Sainsbury to be thus rewarded)

Opinions on cricket: 'I support the two-divisional system – it encourages more meaningful cricket throughout the season. Younger players should take the opportunity to speak more to experienced players in the bar after the game. This is where you learn your trade – I don't mean drinking five pints!'

Best batting: 209* Hampshire v Essex, Southend 1987
Best bowling: 2-11 Hampshire v Surrey, Southampton 1985

2002 Season

	M	Inns	NO	Runs	HS	Avge	100s	50s	Ct	St	O	M	Runs	Wkts	Avge	Best	5wI	10wM
Test																		
All First	15	25	1	832	104	34.66	2	3	6	-								
1-day Int																		
C & G	2	2	1	30	28	30.00	-	-	-	-								
B & H	4	4	0	116	64	29.00	-	1	1	-								
1-day Lge	2	2	0	11	8	5.50	-	-	2	-								

Career Performances

	M	Inns	NO	Runs	HS	Avge	100s	50s	Ct	St	Balls	Runs	Wkts	Avge	Best	5wI	10wM
Test	62	112	15	4236	175	43.67	9	28	39	-	24	6	0	-	-	-	-
All First	416	702	86	25633	209 *	41.61	61	126	224	-	1099	993	14	70.92	2-11	-	-
1-day Int	71	70	8	2419	167 *	39.01	4	15	26	-							
C & G	47	46	14	2364	158	73.87	8	10	22	-	19	14	2	7.00	2-13	-	-
B & H	70	67	10	2490	155 *	43.68	5	12	23	-	6	2	0	-	-	-	-
1-day Lge	215	206	25	6793	131	37.53	10	40	78	-	2	0	1	0.00	1-0	-	-

SMITH, W. R.   Nottinghamshire

Name: William (<u>Will</u>) Rew Smith
Role: Right-hand bat, right-arm off-spin bowler, occasional wicket-keeper
Born: 28 September 1982, Luton
Height: 5ft 9in **Weight:** 11st 4lbs
Nickname: Jiggy, Jigs, Posh Kid, Smudger
County debut: 2002
Parents: Jim and Barbara
Marital status: Single
Family links with cricket: 'Brother, Ben, plays club cricket'
Education: Polam School, Bedford; Bedford School; Durham University

Qualifications: 11 GCSEs, 3 A-levels
Career outside cricket: Student
Off-season: At Durham University
Overseas tours: Bedford School to Barbados (Sir Garfield Sobers International Tournament) 1998
Overseas teams played for: Gordon CC, Sydney 2001-02
Career highlights to date: 'Scoring 120 for Gordon CC in their Sydney grade final win [2001-02]. Scoring 38* on first-class debut v West Indies A. But hopefully better moments will come along!'
Cricket moments to forget: 'Bagging my first ever pair for Notts 2nd XI v Hampshire at the Rose Bowl'
Cricket superstitions: 'None'
Cricketers particularly admired:
Ian Botham, Brian Lara, Sachin Tendulkar, Paul Johnson
Young players to look out for: Bilal Shafayat, Samit Patel, Alistair Cook
Other sports played: Rugby (East Midlands age group), hockey (Eastern Counties age group)
Other sports followed: Football (Rushden & Diamonds)
Relaxations: 'Going out with friends; music'
Extras: Captained Harrold CC U13 to Ken Barrington Trophy (national club championship – 'a moment I'm very proud of!')
Opinions on cricket: 'Not played long enough to start telling everyone how to run the game.'
Best batting: 38* Nottinghamshire v West Indies A, Trent Bridge 2002

2002 Season

	M	Inns	NO	Runs	HS	Avge	100s	50s	Ct	St	O	M	Runs	Wkts	Avge	Best	5wI	10wM
Test																		
All First	1	1	1	38	38 *	-	-	-	-	-	-							
1-day Int																		
C & G																		
B & H																		
1-day Lge	3	2	0	25	16	12.50	-	-	1	-								

79. Which West Indies Test spinner took 92 first-class wickets (from 952.1 overs) for Lancashire in 1964?

	M	Inns	NO	Runs	HS	Avge	100s	50s	Ct	St	Balls	Runs	Wkts	Avge	Best	5wI	10wM
Test																	
All First	1	1	1	38	38 *	-	-	-	-	-							
1-day Int																	
C & G																	
B & H																	
1-day Lge	3	2	0	25	16	12.50	-	-	1	-							

SNAPE, J. N. Leicestershire

Name: <u>Jeremy</u> Nicholas Snape
Role: Right-hand bat, off-spin bowler;
all-rounder
Born: 27 April 1973, Stoke-on-Trent
Height: 5ft 8in **Weight:** 12st
Nickname: Snapey, Coot, Jez, Snapper
County debut: 1992 (Northamptonshire),
1999 (Gloucestershire)
County cap: 1999 (Gloucestershire)
One-Day Internationals: 9
1st-Class 50s: 19
1st-Class 100s: 3
1st-Class 5 w. in innings: 1
1st-Class catches: 62
One-Day 100s: 1
One-Day 5 w. in innings: 1
Place in batting averages: 266th av. 14.62
(2001 35th av. 48.22)

Strike rate: 150.00 (career 93.40)
Parents: Keith and Barbara
Marital status: Single
Family links with cricket: 'Brother Jonathan plays league cricket for Rode Park CC
in Cheshire. Dad loves cricket now, and Mum hates the sweep shot!'
Education: Denstone College, Staffordshire; Durham University
Qualifications: 8 GCSEs, 3 A-levels, BSc Natural Science
Career outside cricket: Director of Capetours – tailor-made holidays to Southern
Africa (www.capetours.co.uk)
Off-season: Touring with England
Overseas tours: England U18 to Canada (International Youth Tournament) 1991
(captain); England U19 to Pakistan 1991-92; Durham University to South Africa 1993,
to Vienna (European Indoor Championships) 1994; Northamptonshire to Cape Town

1993; Christians in Sport to Zimbabwe 1994-95; Troubadours to South Africa 1997; Gloucestershire to Kimberley, South Africa 1999; England to Zimbabwe (one-day series) 2001-02, to India and New Zealand 2001-02 (one-day series), to Sri Lanka (ICC Champions Trophy) 2002-03, to Australia 2002-03 (VB Series)

Overseas teams played for: Petone, Wellington, New Zealand 1994-95; Wainuiamata, Wellington, New Zealand 1995-96; Techs CC, Cape Town 1996-99

Cricketers particularly admired: Allan Lamb, Anil Kumble, Jack Russell

Relaxations: Travelling, music, cooking, good food and wine

Extras: Sir John Hobbs Silver Jubilee Memorial Prize 1988. B&H Gold Award for his 3-34 for Combined Universities v Worcestershire at The Parks 1992. Player of the Tournament at European Indoor 6-a-side Championships in 1994. Left Northants at end of 1998 season and joined Gloucestershire for 1999. Scored maiden one-day century (104*) in the Norwich Union League v Nottinghamshire at Trent Bridge 2001, in the process sharing with Mark Hardinges (65) in a record seventh-wicket partnership for domestic one-day competitions (164). Made One-Day International debut in first ODI v Zimbabwe at Harare 2001-02, winning Man of the Match award for his 2-39 (the Flower brothers both stumped in the same over) and brilliant catch to dismiss Guy Whittall. BBC West Country Sports Cricketer of the Year for 2001. Left Gloucestershire at the end of the 2002 season and has joined Leicestershire for 2003

Best batting: 131 Gloucestershire v Sussex, Cheltenham 2001

Best bowling: 5-65 Northamptonshire v Durham, Northampton 1995

Stop press: Suffered fractured right thumb after being struck by a ball from Brett Lee v New South Wales in a warm-up match at Sydney ahead of the VB Series 2002-03; Gareth Batty called up as cover

2002 Season

	M	Inns	NO	Runs	HS	Avge	100s	50s	Ct	St	O	M	Runs	Wkts	Avge	Best	5wI	10wM
Test																		
All First	5	8	0	117	28	14.62	-	-	2	-	50	6	179	2	89.50	2-54	-	-
1-day Int	1	1	1	15	15 *	-	-	-	1	-	10	2	34	1	34.00	1-34	-	
C & G	1	0	0	0	0	-	-	-	-	-								
B & H	6	4	1	42	35	14.00	-	-	2	-	14.4	1	77	5	15.40	3-7	-	
1-day Lge	9	8	2	137	38 *	22.83	-	-	2	-	35	3	140	5	28.00	2-36	-	

Career Performances

	M	Inns	NO	Runs	HS	Avge	100s	50s	Ct	St	Balls	Runs	Wkts	Avge	Best	5wI	10wM
Test																	
All First	90	134	23	3240	131	29.18	3	19	62	-	9060	4559	97	47.00	5-65	1	-
1-day Int	9	6	3	111	38	37.00	-	-	4	-	493	385	12	32.08	3-43	-	
C & G	21	17	4	259	54	19.92	-	1	8	-	535	381	10	38.10	2-19	-	
B & H	42	32	7	546	52	21.84	-	2	17	-	1468	1056	36	29.33	5-32	1	
1-day Lge	107	85	24	1365	104 *	22.37	1	3	35	-	2952	2313	91	25.41	4-27	-	

SOLANKI, V. S.   Worcestershire

Name: <u>Vikram</u> Singh Solanki
Role: Right-hand bat, right-arm
off-spin bowler
Born: 1 April 1976, Udaipur, India
Height: 6ft **Weight:** 12st
Nickname: Vik
County debut: 1993 (one-day),
1995 (first-class)
County cap: 1998; colours, 2002
One-Day Internationals: 8
1000 runs in a season: 2
1st-Class 50s: 42
1st-Class 100s: 14
1st-Class 5 w. in innings: 3
1st-Class 10 w. in match: 1
1st-Class catches: 175
One-Day 100s: 3
Place in batting averages: 65th av. 42.90

(2001 140th av. 27.65)
Strike rate: (career 78.01)
Parents: Mr Vijay Singh and Mrs Florabel Solanki
Marital status: Single
Family links with cricket: 'Father played in India. Brother Vishal is a
keen cricketer'
Education: Merridale, Wolverhampton; Regis School, Wolverhampton;
Open University
Qualifications: 9 GCSEs, 3 A-levels
Off-season: 'Playing in Australia'
Overseas tours: England U18 to South Africa 1992-93, to Denmark (ICC Youth
Tournament) 1994; England U19 to West Indies 1994-95; Worcestershire CCC
to Barbados 1996, to Zimbabwe 1997; England A to Zimbabwe and South Africa
1998-99, to Bangladesh and New Zealand 1999-2000, to West Indies 2000-01;
England to South Africa and Zimbabwe 1999-2000 (one-day series), to Kenya
(ICC Knockout Trophy) 2000-01, to Pakistan 2000-01 (one-day series)
Overseas teams played for: Midland-Guildford, Perth, Western Australia
Career highlights to date: 'Playing for England'
Cricket moments to forget: 'Losing to Scotland (NatWest 1998)'
Cricketers particularly admired: Sachin Tendulkar, Graeme Hick
Young players to look out for: Kabir Ali, Kadeer Ali, Gareth Batty
Other sports played: 'Enjoy most sports'
Injuries: Out for two weeks with a split finger

Relaxations: 'Reading; spending time with family and friends'
Extras: Scored more first-class runs (1339) in 1999 season than any other English player. Topped batting averages with 597 first-class runs (av. 59.70) on England A tour of Bangladesh and New Zealand 1999-2000. Took 22 catches at slip in seven first-class matches on England A tour of West Indies 2000-01. B&H Gold Award for his 90 v Glamorgan at Worcester 2002. C&G Man of the Match award for his 108 v Nottinghamshire at Trent Bridge 2002. Scored century (119*) v Warwickshire at Worcester in the NUL 2002, in the process passing 2000 runs in the one-day league
Best batting: 185 England A v Bangladesh, Chittagong 1999-2000
Best bowling: 5-69 Worcestershire v Middlesex, Lord's 1996

2002 Season

	M	Inns	NO	Runs	HS	Avge	100s	50s	Ct	St	O	M	Runs	Wkts	Avge	Best	5wI	10wM
Test																		
All First	16	26	4	944	153 *	42.90	2	5	18	-	39	6	128	0	-		-	-
1-day Int																		
C & G	3	3	0	165	108	55.00	1	1	-	-	5	0	25	1	25.00	1-25	-	
B & H	7	7	2	209	90	41.80	-	2	1	-								
1-day Lge	16	15	1	555	119 *	39.64	1	4	8	-	2	0	17	0	-		-	-

Career Performances

	M	Inns	NO	Runs	HS	Avge	100s	50s	Ct	St	Balls	Runs	Wkts	Avge	Best	5wI	10wM
Test																	
All First	142	235	18	7826	185	36.06	14	42	175	-	5623	3300	72	45.83	5-69	3	1
1-day Int	8	7	1	96	24	16.00	-	-	2	-							
C & G	15	14	0	364	108	26.00	1	2	3	-	225	174	3	58.00	1-25	-	
B & H	24	22	2	465	90	23.25	-	2	11	-	18	17	1	17.00	1-17	-	
1-day Lge	118	101	13	2530	120 *	28.75	2	15	38	-	210	223	4	55.75	1-9	-	

80. Which New Zealand Test bowler was Lancashire's overseas player in 1992?

SPEARMAN, C. M.   Gloucestershire

Name: <u>Craig</u> Murray Spearman
Role: Right-hand bat
Born: 4 July 1972, Auckland, New Zealand
Height: 6ft **Weight:** 13st 5lbs
Nickname: Spears
County debut: 2002
County cap: 2002
Test debut: 1995-96
Tests: 19
One-Day Internationals: 51
1000 runs in a season: 1
1st-Class 50s: 31
1st-Class 100s: 14
1st-Class catches: 99
One-Day 100s: 2
Place in batting averages: 39th av. 48.13
Strike rate: (career 78.00)
Parents: Murray and Sandra
Marital status: Single
Education: Henderson Primary, Auckland; Kelston Boys High School, Auckland;
Massey University, Palmerston North, New Zealand
Qualifications: Bachelor of Business Studies (BBS; Finance major)
Off-season: 'Overseas pro for my old team in New Zealand – Central Districts'
Overseas tours: New Zealand to India and Pakistan (World Cup) 1995-96, to West
Indies 1995-96, to Sri Lanka 1997-98, to India 1999-2000, to South Africa 2000-01
Overseas teams played for: Auckland 1993-96; Central Districts 1997-2001, 2002-03
Career highlights to date: 'Playing international cricket; Test century; winning ICC
Knockout Trophy in Kenya [2000-01]'
Cricket moments to forget: 'Misfielding on the boundary at the SCG in the fifth over
and hearing about it for the next 45 overs'
Cricketers particularly admired: Desmond Haynes and Gordon Greenidge
Young players to look out for: Alex Gidman
Other sports played: Golf
Other sports followed: 'Follow most sports except motor sport'
Relaxations: 'Travelling, seeing new places and cultures'
Extras: Scored maiden Test century (112) at Auckland 1995-96, in the process sharing
with Roger Twose in a record first-wicket partnership for New Zealand in Tests against
Zimbabwe (214). Played in the Central Districts Shell Cup winning side in New
Zealand 2000-01. Scored century (111) on Championship debut for Gloucestershire v
Worcestershire at Worcester 2002, reaching his hundred with a six. B&H Gold Award
for his 60-ball 73 v Glamorgan at Cardiff 2002. C&G Man of the Match award for his
77-ball 104* (his maiden one-day century for Gloucestershire) v Durham at Bristol

2002. Scored an 85-ball 107 (his maiden one-day league century) v Hampshire at Cheltenham in the NUL 2002. Carried his bat for 180* (out of 293) v Glamorgan at Cheltenham 2002. Gloucestershire Players' Player of the Year 2002. Awarded Gloucestershire cap 2002. 'Qualify to play for Gloucestershire because of my mother's Welsh background'

Opinions on cricket: 'Opponents seem to be getting younger – wonder why?!'
Best batting: 180* Gloucestershire v Glamorgan, Cheltenham 2002
Best bowling: 1-37 Central Districts v Wellington, New Plymouth 1999-2000

2002 Season

	M	Inns	NO	Runs	HS	Avge	100s	50s	Ct	St	O	M	Runs	Wkts	Avge	Best	5wI	10wM
Test																		
All First	17	34	4	1444	180 *	48.13	5	7	16	-								
1-day Int																		
C & G	3	3	1	114	104 *	57.00	1	-	-	-								
B & H	6	6	0	138	73	23.00	-	1	2	-								
1-day Lge	15	14	0	542	107	38.71	1	4	3	-								

Career Performances

	M	Inns	NO	Runs	HS	Avge	100s	50s	Ct	St	Balls	Runs	Wkts	Avge	Best	5wI	10wM
Test	19	36	2	920	112	27.05	1	3	21	-							
All First	102	184	13	6332	180 *	37.02	14	31	99	-	78	55	1	55.00	1-37	-	-
1-day Int	51	50	0	936	86	18.72	-	5	15	-	3	6	0	-	-	-	-
C & G	3	3	1	114	104 *	57.00	1	-	-	-							
B & H	6	6	0	138	73	23.00	-	1	2	-							
1-day Lge	15	14	0	542	107	38.71	1	4	3	-							

81. For which county did Eldine Baptiste play before joining Northamptonshire in 1991?

Name: James (<u>Jamie</u>) Ashley Spires
Role: Right-hand bat, slow left-arm bowler
Born: 12 November 1979, Solihull
Height: 6ft **Weight:** 12st 9lbs
Nickname: Spiro, Guff, Highlights, Younis, Woolly
County debut: 2001
1st-Class 5 w. in innings: 1
1st-Class catches: 3
Place in bowling averages: 97th av. 34.05
Strike rate: 57.22 (career 66.50)
Parents: Carol and Stuart
Marital status: Single
Family links with cricket: 'Dad is "chief exec" at Knowle and Dorridge!'
Education: Eversfield School; Solihull School; Leeds University ('for three months')
Qualifications: 11 GCSEs, 4 A-levels
Career outside cricket: 'Socialite'
Off-season: 'Catching up with mates!'
Overseas tours: Warwickshire U19 to Cape Town 1998; Warwickshire to Bloemfontein 2000, to Cape Town 2001, 2002
Overseas teams played for: SA Police, Bloemfontein 1999-2000; Tygerburg, Cape Town 2002
Career highlights to date: 'Debut at Lord's for Warwickshire 2001'
Cricket moments to forget: 'Colliding with team-mate while fielding for club side. His knee went straight into my cheekbone – sidelined for two weeks!'
Cricketers particularly admired: Gavin Franklin, Phil Tufnell
Young players to look out for: Tom Mees, Huw Jones, Ian Westwood
Other sports played: Football
Other sports followed: Football ('big Forest fan')
Injuries: Out for two weeks with a bruised cheekbone
Relaxations: 'Spending time with friends; PlayStation 2'
Extras: Warwickshire U19 Player of the Year 1999. Played for ECB U19 v Pakistan U19 1999. Played for Warwickshire Board XI in the first round of the C&G 2002, which was played in August 2001. Recorded maiden first-class five-wicket return (5-165; 9-264 the match) v Yorkshire at Edgbaston 2002
Opinions on cricket: 'Clubs should have more faith in their youth system, rather than looking elsewhere!'
Best batting: 37* Warwickshire v Sussex, Hove 2002
Best bowling: 5-165 Warwickshire v Yorkshire, Edgbaston 2002

2002 Season

	M	Inns	NO	Runs	HS	Avge	100s	50s	Ct	St	O	M	Runs	Wkts	Avge	Best	5wI	10wM
Test																		
All First	6	7	3	70	37 *	17.50	-	-	3	-	171.4	25	613	18	34.05	5-165	1	
1-day Int																		
C & G																		
B & H																		
1-day Lge																		

Career Performances

	M	Inns	NO	Runs	HS	Avge	100s	50s	Ct	St	Balls	Runs	Wkts	Avge	Best	5wI	10wM
Test																	
All First	7	7	3	70	37 *	17.50	-	-	3	-	1330	768	20	38.40	5-165	1	-
1-day Int																	
C & G	1	0	0	0	0	-	-	-	-	-	60	33	1	33.00	1-33	-	
B & H																	
1-day Lge																	

SRINATH, J.   Leicestershire

Name: Javagal Srinath
Role: Right-hand bat, right-arm
fast-medium bowler
Born: 31 August 1969, Mysore, India
Height: 6ft 3in
County debut: 1995 (Gloucestershire),
2002 (Leicestershire)
County cap: 1995 (Gloucestershire)
Test debut: 1991-92
Tests: 64
One-Day Internationals: 204
50 wickets in a season: 1
1st-Class 50s: 7
1st-Class 5 w. in innings: 23
1st-Class 10 w. in match: 3
1st-Class catches: 61
One-Day 5 w. in innings: 3
Place in batting averages: 270th av. 14.00
Place in bowling averages: 3rd av. 18.70
Strike rate: 35.86 (career 53.15)

Overseas tours: India to Australia and New Zealand (including World Cup) 1991-92,
to Zimbabwe and South Africa 1992-93, to Sri Lanka 1993-94, to New Zealand

1993-94, to New Zealand (NZ Centenary Tournament) 1994-95, to England 1996, to South Africa 1996-97, to Zimbabwe 1998-99, to Bangladesh (Wills International Cup) 1998-99, to New Zealand 1998-99, to UK, Ireland and Holland (World Cup) 1999, to Australia 1999-2000, to Bangladesh 2000-01, to Zimbabwe 2001, to South Africa 2001-02, to West Indies 2001-02, to New Zealand 2002-03 (one-day series)

Overseas teams played for: Karnataka 1989-90 –

Extras: Took hat-trick on first-class debut for Karnataka v Hyderabad at Secunderabad 1989-90. Was Gloucestershire's overseas player in 1995. Represented India in 1995-96 World Cup. Had match figures of 13-132 v Pakistan at Kolkata (Calcutta) 1998-99, a new best Test match analysis for the ground. Took 5-140 in the first Test v South Africa at Bloemfontein 2001-02, his return including his 200th Test wicket (Shaun Pollock). Retired from Test cricket after India's tour of West Indies 2001-02 but later reconsidered his decision. Has taken more Test wickets for India than any other pace bowler except Kapil Dev. Was Leicestershire's overseas player for the latter part of the 2002 season, replacing Michael Bevan, absent on international duty. Took Championship hat-trick (Ormond, Hollioake, Sampson) v Surrey at The Oval 2002 and ended up with 30 wickets (av. 18.70) from his five Championship appearances 2002

Best batting: 76 India v New Zealand, Hamilton 1998-99

Best bowling: 9-76 Gloucestershire v Glamorgan, Abergavenny 1995

Stop press: Selected for India squad for 2002-03 World Cup

2002 Season

	M	Inns	NO	Runs	HS	Avge	100s	50s	Ct	St	O	M	Runs	Wkts	Avge	Best	5wI	10wM
Test																		
All First	5	7	0	98	52	14.00	-	1	2	-	179.2	29	561	30	18.70	5-25	2	-
1-day Int																		
C & G																		
B & H																		
1-day Lge	2	1	1	2	2 *	-	-	-	3	-	18	2	48	3	16.00	3-18	-	

Career Performances

	M	Inns	NO	Runs	HS	Avge	100s	50s	Ct	St	Balls	Runs	Wkts	Avge	Best	5wI	10wM
Test	64	88	21	872	76	13.01	-	4	22	-	14786	7069	232	30.46	8-86	10	1
All First	141	182	31	2115	76	14.00	-	7	61	-	27796	13674	523	26.14	9-76	23	3
1-day Int	204	107	32	844	53	11.25	-	1	31	-	10637	7945	276	28.78	5-23	3	
C & G	3	2	1	11	11 *	11.00	-	-	1	-	152	63	7	9.00	4-38	-	
B & H	6	6	1	12	6	2.40	-	-	1	-	386	176	15	11.73	4-33	-	
1-day Lge	8	5	2	15	11	5.00	-	-	6	-	371	261	14	18.64	3-18	-	

STEMP, R. D. Leicestershire

Name: <u>Richard</u> David Stemp
Role: Right-hand bat, slow left-arm bowler
Born: 11 December 1967, Erdington, Birmingham
Height: 6ft **Weight:** 12st 4lbs
Nickname: Stempy, Sheriff, Badger
County debut: 1990 (Worcestershire), 1993 (Yorkshire), 1999 (Nottinghamshire), 2002 (Leicestershire)
County cap: 1996 (Yorkshire), 2000 (Nottinghamshire)
1st-Class 50s: 3
1st-Class 5 w. in innings: 14
1st-Class 10 w. in match: 1
1st-Class catches: 68
Place in batting averages: (2001 226th av. 15.00)
Place in bowling averages: (2001 126th av. 44.18)

Strike rate: 102.00 (career 81.72)
Parents: Arnold and Rita Homer
Marital status: Single
Family links with cricket: Father played Birmingham League cricket for Old Hill
Education: Britannia High School, Rowley Regis
Qualifications: NCA coaching award
Career outside cricket: Foreman with a civil engineering firm
Overseas tours: England A to India 1994-95, to Pakistan 1995-96
Overseas teams played for: Pretoria Technikon 1988-89
Cricketers particularly admired: Ian Botham, Phil Tufnell
Other sports followed: Indoor cricket, American football (New England Patriots)
Relaxations: Ornithology, music, driving
Extras: Played for England indoor cricket team v Australia in ManuLife 'Test' series 1990. Moved to Yorkshire at end of 1992 season (first English non-Yorkshireman to be signed for the county). Included in England Test squad against New Zealand in 1994. Left Yorkshire at the end of the 1998 season and joined Notts for 1999. Released by Notts at the end of the 2001 season. Signed by Leicestershire in September 2002 as emergency cover; released at the end of the 2002 season
Best batting: 66 Nottinghamshire v Hampshire, West End 2001
Best bowling: 6-37 Yorkshire v Durham, Durham University 1994

2002 Season

	M	Inns	NO	Runs	HS	Avge	100s	50s	Ct	St	O	M	Runs	Wkts	Avge	Best	5wl	10wM
Test																		
All First	1	2	1	8	8 *	8.00	-	-	-	-	17	2	59	1	59.00	1-18	-	-
1-day Int																		
C & G																		
B & H																		
1-day Lge	1	0	0	0	0	-	-	-	-	-	7	1	39	1	39.00	1-39	-	

Career Performances

	M	Inns	NO	Runs	HS	Avge	100s	50s	Ct	St	Balls	Runs	Wkts	Avge	Best	5wl	10wM
Test																	
All First	166	198	64	1657	66	12.36	-	3	68	-	31463	13554	385	35.20	6-37	14	1
1-day Int																	
C & G	16	6	3	13	12	4.33	-	-	1	-	874	550	19	28.94	4-45	-	
B & H	26	6	1	34	29	6.80	-	-	-	-	1371	913	23	39.69	3-22	-	
1-day Lge	105	32	13	177	29 *	9.31	-	-	27	-	4329	3403	112	30.38	4-25	-	

STEPHENSON, J. P.   Essex

Name: John Patrick Stephenson
Role: Right-hand bat, right-arm
medium bowler
Born: 14 March 1965, Stebbing, Essex
Height: 6ft 1in   **Weight:** 12st 7lbs
Nickname: Stan
County debut: 1985 (Essex), 1995 (Hants)
County cap: 1989 (Essex), 1995 (Hants)
Benefit: 2001 (Hants; £192,092)
Test debut: 1989
Tests: 1
1000 runs in a season: 5
1st-Class 50s: 74
1st-Class 100s: 24
1st-Class 200s: 1
1st-Class 5 w. in innings: 11
1st-Class 10 w. in match: 1
1st-Class catches: 181
One-Day 100s: 7
One-Day 5 w. in innings: 3
Place in batting averages: 108th av. 35.12
Place in bowling averages: 14th av. 22.54
Strike rate: 36.95 (career 58.35)

Parents: Pat and Eve
Wife and date of marriage: Fiona Maria, 24 September 1994
Children: Emma-Lydia, 19 May 1997; Camilla, 30 April 2000
Family links with cricket: 'Father was member of Rugby Meteors *Cricketer* Cup winning side in 1973. Three brothers played in Felsted 1st XI; Guy played for Essex 2nd XI and now plays for Teddington'
Education: Felsted Prep School; Felsted Senior School; Durham University
Qualifications: 7 O-levels, 3 A-levels, BA General Arts, Level 3 coaching award, SFA registered representative
Career outside cricket: Stockbroker at Durlachers
Overseas tours: English Schools U19 to Zimbabwe 1982-83; England A to Kenya and Zimbabwe 1989-90, to Bermuda and West Indies 1991-92; MCC to Kenya 1999
Overseas teams played for: Fitzroy, Melbourne 1982-83, 1987-88; Boland, South Africa 1988-89; Gold Coast Dolphins and Bond University, Australia 1990-91; St George's, Argentina 1994-95; Belgrano, Argentina 1994-95; Victoria CC, South Africa 1995-96
Career highlights to date: 'Playing for England. Winning Championship in 1992 with Essex. Captaining Hampshire'
Cricketers particularly admired: Brian Hardie
Young players to look out for: Matthew Wood
Relaxations: 'Watching cricket, reading (*Sunday Telegraph*, *Wisden*, *The Cricketer*), alternative music'
Extras: Awarded 2nd XI cap in 1984 when leading run-scorer with Essex 2nd XI. Essex Young Player of the Year 1985. Captained Durham University to victory in UAU Championship 1986 and was captain of Combined Universities team 1987 in the first year that it was drawn from all universities. Was leading wicket-taker on England A tour to Bermuda and West Indies 1991-92. Carried bat in first innings for 113* and scored 159* in the second v Somerset at Taunton in 1992 and was on the field for the whole game (the first Essex player to achieve this). First Essex player to achieve 500 runs and 20 wickets in a Sunday League season 1993. Joined Hampshire for 1995. Scored 107 v Norfolk in the NatWest at Southampton 1996, in the process sharing with Jason Laney (153) in a then competition record stand for the first wicket (269). Took over the captaincy of Hampshire in 1996, but relinquished it at the end of the 1997 season. Founded the One Test Wonder Club in 1996. Scored 83* v Durham 2000, becoming the first opening batsman to carry his bat five times in the Sunday/National League. Released by Hampshire at the end of the 2001 season; rejoined Essex for 2002 as 2nd XI captain/coach and ended up as the county's leading wicket-taker in the Championship with 48 wickets (av. 22.54) as well as scoring 562 runs (av. 35.12). Recorded maiden first-class ten-wicket match return (3-60 and a career-best 7-44) v Worcestershire at Worcester 2002, in his first Championship match since rejoining Essex
Best batting: 202* Essex v Somerset, Bath 1990
Best bowling: 7-44 Essex v Worcestershire, Worcester 2002

2002 Season

	M	Inns	NO	Runs	HS	Avge	100s	50s	Ct	St	O	M	Runs	Wkts	Avge	Best	5wI	10wM
Test																		
All First	13	24	8	562	100 *	35.12	1	2	7	-	295.4	59	1082	48	22.54	7-44	1	1
1-day Int																		
C & G	2	0	0	0	0	-	-	-	-	-	5	0	45	0	-		-	-
B & H	7	7	0	38	27	5.42	-	-	1	-	49	1	186	8	23.25	3-22	-	
1-day Lge	15	13	2	204	44	18.54	-	-	8	-	57.4	1	295	12	24.58	3-14	-	

Career Performances

	M	Inns	NO	Runs	HS	Avge	100s	50s	Ct	St	Balls	Runs	Wkts	Avge	Best	5wI	10wM
Test	1	2	0	36	25	18.00	-	-	-	-							
All First	294	498	53	14409	202 *	32.37	25	74	181	-	22175	12335	380	32.46	7-44	11	1
1-day Int																	
C & G	35	31	1	930	107	31.00	1	7	16	-	1225	965	29	33.27	5-34	1	
B & H	61	55	7	1611	142	33.56	2	11	15	-	1912	1358	51	26.62	3-22	-	
1-day Lge	199	179	25	4338	110 *	28.16	4	19	82	-	5733	4528	178	25.43	6-33	2	

STEVENS, D. I.   Leicestershire

Name: <u>Darren</u> Ian Stevens
Role: Right-hand bat, right-arm
medium bowler
Born: 30 April 1976, Leicester
Height: 5ft 11in **Weight:** 12st
Nickname: Stevo
County debut: 1997
County cap: 2002
1st-Class 50s: 12
1st-Class 100s: 2
1st-Class catches: 37
One-Day 100s: 2
Place in batting averages: 123rd av. 32.69
(2001 183rd av. 21.58)
Strike rate: 294.00 (career 195.50)
Parents: Maddy and Bob
Marital status: Single
Family links with cricket: Father and
grandfather played league cricket in Leicestershire
Education: Richmond Primary School; Mount Grace High School; John Cleveland
College, Hinckley; Hinckley Tech; Charles Klein College
Qualifications: 5 GCSEs, BTEC National in Sports Studies
Off-season: 'England National Academy in Adelaide!'

Overseas tours: Leicestershire U19 to South Africa 1994-95; Leicestershire to Barbados 1998, to Sri Lanka 1999, to Potchefstroom 2001; ECB National Academy to Australia and Sri Lanka 2002-03

Overseas teams played for: Wanderers CC, Johannesburg, South Africa 1996-97; Rhodes University, Grahamstown, South Africa 1997-98; Fairfield CC, Sydney 1998-99; Hawthorn-Waverley, Melbourne 1999-2000; Taita CC, Wellington, New Zealand 2000-01; Ringwood CC, Melbourne 2001-02

Career highlights to date: 'The build-up to my first final at Lord's'

Cricket moments to forget: 'Losing in my first final in the C&G against Somerset 2001'

Cricketers particularly admired: Steve Waugh, Viv Richards, Ian Botham

Young players to look out for: Steve Adshead, Ian Blackwell

Other sports played: Golf, squash

Other sports followed: Football (Leicester City), rugby union (Leicester Tigers)

Relaxations: 'Music, spending time with close friends'

Extras: Received painting from Sir Colin Cowdrey on day of maiden first-class 100 (130 in fourth Championship match), v Sussex at Arundel 1999. Won Sir Ron Brierley/Crusaders Scholarship 1999. Scored 83 v Sussex at Leicester in the C&G 2002, in the process sharing with Trevor Ward (112) in a competition record second-wicket partnership for Leicestershire (171). Scored a 114-ball 125 v Durham at Riverside in the NUL 2002; it was his maiden one-day league century and the highest individual one-day score recorded at Riverside. Awarded Leicestershire cap 2002

Opinions on cricket: 'A wonderful game. Not enough quality time to practise between games.'

Best batting: 130 Leicestershire v Sussex, Arundel 1999

Best bowling: 1-5 Leicestershire v Sussex, Eastbourne 1997

Stop press: Included in provisional England squad of 30 for the 2002-03 World Cup

2002 Season

	M	Inns	NO	Runs	HS	Avge	100s	50s	Ct	St	O	M	Runs	Wkts	Avge	Best	5wI	10wM
Test																		
All First	17	29	3	850	125	32.69	1	6	16	-	49	3	201	1	201.00	1-125	-	-
1-day Int																		
C & G	2	2	0	119	83	59.50	-	1	-	-								
B & H	6	5	1	83	44 *	20.75	-	-	2	-								
1-day Lge	16	15	0	651	125	43.40	1	5	5	-	22	1	114	2	57.00	2-43	-	

Career Performances

	M	Inns	NO	Runs	HS	Avge	100s	50s	Ct	St	Balls	Runs	Wkts	Avge	Best	5wI	10wM
Test																	
All First	54	89	5	2166	130	25.78	2	12	37	-	391	254	2	127.00	1-5	-	-
1-day Int																	
C & G	10	9	0	370	133	41.11	1	2	2	-	24	26	2	13.00	2-26	-	
B & H	12	11	1	200	54	20.00	-	1	3	-	4	2	0	-	-	-	-
1-day Lge	58	54	5	1431	125	29.20	1	10	18	-	135	115	2	57.50	2-43	-	

STEWART, A. J.   Surrey

Name: <u>Alec</u> James Stewart
Role: Right-hand bat, wicket-keeper,
honorary club captain
Born: 8 April 1963, Merton, London
Height: 5ft 11in **Weight:** 13st 2lbs
Nickname: Stewie, Ming
County debut: 1981
County cap: 1985
Benefit: 1994 (£202,187)
Test debut: 1989-90
Tests: 122
One-Day Internationals: 153
1000 runs in a season: 8
50 dismissals in a season: 1
1st-Class 50s: 138
1st-Class 100s: 46
1st-Class 200s: 2
1st-Class catches: 668
1st-Class stumpings: 31
One-Day 100s: 18

Place in batting averages: 24th av. 53.64 (2001 75th av. 38.73)
Strike rate: (career 162.33)
Parents: Michael and Sheila
Wife and date of marriage: Lynn, 28 September 1991
Children: Andrew James, 21 May 1993; Emily Elizabeth, 6 September 1996
Family links with cricket: Father (Micky) played for England (1962-64), Surrey
(1954-72) and Malden Wanderers and was team manager of England (1987-1992).
Brother Neil captained Malden Wanderers
Education: Tiffin Boys School
Qualifications: 'Streetwise'
Off-season: 'Ashes tour'
Overseas tours: England to India (Nehru Cup) 1989-90, to West Indies 1989-90,
1993-94, 1997-98, to Australia 1990-91, 1994-95, 1998-99 (captain), 2002-03, to
Australia and New Zealand (World Cup) 1991-92, to India and Sri Lanka 1992-93, to
South Africa 1995-96, 1999-2000, to Pakistan and India (World Cup) 1995-96, to
Zimbabwe and New Zealand 1996-97, to Sharjah (Champions Trophy) 1997-98, to
Sharjah (Coca-Cola Cup) 1998-99, to Kenya (ICC Knockout Trophy) 2000-01, to
Pakistan and Sri Lanka 2000-01, to Sri Lanka (ICC Champions Trophy) 2002-03
Overseas teams played for: Midland-Guildford, Perth, Western Australia 1981-89
Cricketers particularly admired: Graham Monkhouse, Graham Gooch, Alan Knott,
Geoff Arnold, K. Gartrell
Young players to look out for: Tim Murtagh

Other sports followed: Football (Chelsea)

Relaxations: 'Spending as much time with my family as possible'

Extras: Cornhill England Player of the Year (jointly with Chris Lewis) 1992-93. One of *Wisden*'s Five Cricketers of the Year 1993. Shared in a record fifth-wicket partnership for England in Tests v West Indies (150) with Graham Thorpe at Bridgetown 1993-94, becoming in that match the first Englishman to score a century in each innings (118/143) against West Indies. Cornhill England Player of the Year (for the second time) 1996-97. Captain of England 1998-99 (though had captained England in a Test match for the first time v India at Madras 1992-93). Awarded MBE in HM The Queen's birthday honours list 1998. Leading run-scorer in world Test cricket in the 1990s with 6407 runs (av. 40.81); leading scorer in Test cricket in the 1996 calendar year (with 793 runs). Made 126th One-Day International appearance v Zimbabwe at The Oval 2000, breaking Graham Gooch's England record of 125 ODIs. Became the second wicket-keeper (after Adam Gilchrist) to record six dismissals in a One-Day International, v Zimbabwe at Old Trafford 2000. Scored century (105) on his 100th Test appearance in the third Test v West Indies 2000, in the process taking part (with Marcus Trescothick) in a record England partnership for any wicket v West Indies at Old Trafford (179); his century, taking place as it did on The Queen Mother's 100th birthday, won him the Slazenger 'Sheer Instinct' award for 2000. Took 200th Test catch for England when he caught Rashid Latif off Darren Gough at Lord's 2001 in England's 100th Test match at the ground; it was Gough's 200th Test wicket. Shared in new record seventh-wicket partnership for Surrey in matches v Essex (206) with Alex Tudor at The Oval 2001. Scored 65 v Australia at Edgbaston 2001, in the process sharing with Andrew Caddick in the first century stand for the last wicket (103) since 1903-04 for England in Tests v Australia. Made ten dismissals in Championship match v Lancashire at The Oval 2002. Made 200th Test dismissal as a wicket-keeper (Kumar Sangakkara) in the second Test v Sri Lanka at Edgbaston 2002 and 200th Test catch as a wicket-keeper (Saurav Ganguly) v India at The Oval 2002. Scored 123 in England's first innings in third Test v Sri Lanka at Old Trafford 2002, in the process passing the late Lord Cowdrey's career total of 7624 Test runs to move into fifth place on the England list of Test run-scorers. Became first England player to win 150 ODI caps, v India at Riverside 2002. Won 119th Test cap, surpassing Graham Gooch's England record of 118, in first Test v India at Lord's 2002. ECB 12-month contract 2002-03. Granted a testimonial by Surrey for 2003

Opinions on cricket: 'Too many "overseas" players in our domestic game.'

Best batting: 271* Surrey v Yorkshire, The Oval 1997

Best bowling: 1-7 Surrey v Lancashire, Old Trafford 1989

Stop press: Scored 60-ball 64 v Sri Lanka at Brisbane in the VB Series 2002-03, winning Man of the Match award. Scored 71 in fifth Test v Australia at Sydney 2002-03, in the process passing Geoffrey Boycott's career total of 8114 Test runs to move into third place on the list of England's all-time Test run-scorers behind Graham Gooch (8900) and David Gower (8231). Selected for England squad for 2002-03 World Cup

2002 Season

	M	Inns	NO	Runs	HS	Avge	100s	50s	Ct	St	O	M	Runs	Wkts	Avge	Best	5wI	10wM
Test	7	10	2	450	123	56.25	1	2	16	2								
All First	11	16	2	751	123	53.64	1	5	34	4								
1-day Int	7	5	2	157	83	52.33	-	1	6	2								
C & G	3	2	1	5	3	5.00	-	-	3	-								
B & H	5	5	0	94	52	18.80	-	1	7	-								
1-day Lge	3	3	0	27	11	9.00	-	-	6	1								

Career Performances

	M	Inns	NO	Runs	HS	Avge	100s	50s	Ct	St	Balls	Runs	Wkts	Avge	Best	5wI	10wM
Test	122	217	19	7919	190	39.99	15	40	236	13	20	13	0	-		-	-
All First	428	705	77	25085	271 *	39.94	48	138	668	31	487	423	3	141.00	1-7	-	-
1-day Int	153	146	13	4257	116	32.00	4	24	142	13							
C & G	50	46	8	1842	125 *	48.47	3	13	57	5							
B & H	80	80	12	3134	167 *	46.08	4	24	64	11							
1-day Lge	186	170	17	4652	125	30.40	7	26	148	14	4	8	0	-		-	-

STRAUSS, A. J.   Middlesex

Name: <u>Andrew</u> John Strauss
Role: Left-hand bat, left-arm medium bowler, county captain
Born: 2 March 1977, Johannesburg, South Africa
Height: 5ft 11in **Weight:** 13st
Nickname: Straussy, Johann, Levi, Mareman, Muppet
County debut: 1997 (one-day), 1998 (first-class)
County cap: 2001
1000 runs in a season: 2
1st-Class 50s: 19
1st-Class 100s: 7
1st-Class catches: 35
Place in batting averages: 40th av. 48.08 (2001 50th av. 44.81)
Parents: David and Dawn
Marital status: Engaged to Ruth
Education: Caldicott Prep School; Radley College; Durham University
Qualifications: 4 A-levels, BA (Hons) Economics
Off-season: 'Working for the club'

Overseas tours: Durham University to Zimbabwe 1997-98; Middlesex to South Africa 2000; ECB National Academy to Australia 2001-02

Overseas teams played for: Sydney University 1998-99; Mosman, Sydney 1999-2001

Career highlights to date: 'My first first-class hundred, v Northants 2000'

Cricket moments to forget: 'Getting out second ball of the season 2001'

Cricket superstitions: 'Never call Yes to a David Nash call for a single!'

Cricketers particularly admired: Allan Donald, Brian Lara, Saqlain Mushtaq

Young players to look out for: Nick Compton

Other sports played: Golf (Durham University 1998), rugby (Durham University 1996-97)

Other sports followed: 'Anything with a ball'

Injuries: Out for the last two games of the season with a broken jaw

Relaxations: 'Any interesting set of cricket statistics will keep me happy for hours!'

Extras: Scored 112* v Hampshire at West End 2001, in the process becoming the first Middlesex batsman to carry his bat since Mark Ramprakash did so against Kent at Lord's in 1997. Middlesex Player of the Year 2001. Scored century (113) in ECB National Academy's innings victory over Commonwealth Bank [Australian] Cricket Academy in Adelaide 2001-02. Appointed Middlesex vice-captain for 2002, then took over as captain following the retirement of Angus Fraser early in the 2002 season

Opinions on cricket: 'The absence of England's contracted players has only fuelled the arguments of those who continue to belittle the standard of county cricket. The presence of two overseas players next year should help alleviate concerns, but at what cost to the game? Who will make way for them – young, promising players with little experience or the dead wood?'

Best batting: 176 Middlesex v Durham, Lord's 2001

2002 Season

	M	Inns	NO	Runs	HS	Avge	100s	50s	Ct	St	O	M	Runs	Wkts	Avge	Best	5wl	10wM
Test																		
All First	17	27	2	1202	141	48.08	3	5	16	-								
1-day Int																		
C & G	1	1	0	10	10	10.00	-	-	-	-								
B & H	4	4	0	56	24	14.00	-	-	1	-								
1-day Lge	12	11	0	356	74	32.36	-	4	1	-								

Career Performances

	M	Inns	NO	Runs	HS	Avge	100s	50s	Ct	St	Balls	Runs	Wkts	Avge	Best	5wl	10wM
Test																	
All First	63	106	6	3908	176	39.08	7	19	35	-	12	16	0	-	-	-	-
1-day Int																	
C & G	5	5	0	124	56	24.80	-	1	-	-							
B & H	12	11	1	216	61	21.60	-	1	3	-							
1-day Lge	48	45	2	1009	90	23.46	-	8	8	-							

STUBBINGS, S. D. Derbyshire

Name: <u>Stephen</u> David Stubbings
Role: Left-hand bat, occasional right-arm medium/spin bowler, 'very occasional wicket-keeper'
Born: 31 March 1978, Huddersfield
Height: 6ft 3in **Weight:** 15st
Nickname: Stubbo
County debut: 1997
County cap: 2001
1000 runs in a season: 2
1st-Class 50s: 11
1st-Class 100s: 5
1st-Class catches: 18
Place in batting averages: 208th av. 22.52 (2001 95th av. 33.77)
Parents: Marie and David
Marital status: Single
Family links with cricket: 'My father used to play in Cambridge, while my brother Jonathan (18) plays his cricket at my old club Delacombe Park in Melbourne, Australia'
Education: Belvedere Park Primary; Frankston High School; Swinburne University – all in Melbourne, Australia
Qualifications: Victorian Certificate of Education (VCE), ACB Level 1 coaching
Career outside cricket: 'Rocket surgery'
Off-season: 'Coaching and eventually playing cricket at Frankston Peninsula CC in Melbourne, Victoria'
Overseas tours: Derbyshire to Portugal 2000
Overseas teams played for: Delacombe Park CC, Melbourne 1990-94; Frankston Peninsula CC, Victoria 1994-2000, 2002-03; Kingborough CC, Tasmania 2000-02
Career highlights to date: 'Being presented with my Derbyshire county cap at the end of the 2001 season and receiving Player of the Year award'
Cricket moments to forget: 'Making a pair of noughts against Glamorgan at Derby during the 2002 season'
Cricket superstitions: 'No sex during a cricket season!'
Cricketers particularly admired: Mark Taylor, Michael Atherton, Steve Waugh, Ricky Ponting 'and a couple of Derbyshire players who shall remain anonymous!'
Young players to look out for: Sam Patel, Steve Selwood, Neil Gunter
Other sports followed: Australian Rules football (Essendon Bombers)
Relaxations: 'Chris Bassano fishing adventures; eating, drinking, sleeping'
Extras: Represented Victoria at all junior levels. Spent two years on the cricket programme at the Victorian Institute of Sport. Scored maiden first-class century (135*) v Kent at Canterbury 2000, taking part in an unbroken opening partnership of 293 with

Steve Titchard (141*); it was the first occasion on which Derbyshire had batted all day without losing a wicket. Derbyshire Player of the Year 2001. Took over as wicket-keeper in the B&H v Durham at Riverside 2002 after an injury to Karl Krikken
Opinions on cricket: 'Derbyshire's chef John Palmer is by far the best on the circuit!'
Best batting: 135* Derbyshire v Kent, Canterbury 2000

2002 Season

	M	Inns	NO	Runs	HS	Avge	100s	50s	Ct	St	O	M	Runs	Wkts	Avge	Best	5wl	10wM
Test																		
All First	11	20	1	428	128	22.52	1	1	5	-								
1-day Int																		
C & G																		
B & H	5	3	0	27	26	9.00	-	-	1	-								
1-day Lge	10	10	1	245	98 *	27.22	-	1	2	-								

Career Performances

	M	Inns	NO	Runs	HS	Avge	100s	50s	Ct	St	Balls	Runs	Wkts	Avge	Best	5wl	10wM
Test																	
All First	52	95	5	2604	135 *	28.93	5	11	18	-	54	77	0	-	-	-	-
1-day Int																	
C & G	3	2	0	63	47	31.50	-	-	-	-							
B & H	14	10	1	77	26	8.55	-	-	1	-							
1-day Lge	45	44	3	885	98 *	21.58	-	4	6	-							

82. Which South African bowler was Lancashire's
overseas player in 1996?

SUPPIAH, A. V. Somerset

Name: <u>Arul</u> Vivasvan Suppiah
Role: Right-hand bat, left-arm orthodox
spin bowler
Born: 30 August 1983, Kuala Lumpur,
Malaysia
Height: 6ft **Weight:** 12st 7lbs
Nickname: Ruley, Ja Rule
County debut: 2002
1st-Class catches: 1
Strike rate: 30.00 (career 30.00)
Parents: Suppiah and Baanumathi
Marital status: Single
Family links with cricket: 'Brother Rohan
Vishnu plays cricket for Malaysia. Dad plays
club cricket in Malaysia. Mum scores for
Malaysia'

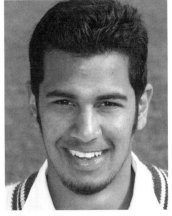

Education: Attended primary school in
Malaysia; Millfield School; Exeter University
Qualifications: 9 GCSEs, 4 A-levels, Level 1 coaching qualification
Career outside cricket: Studying for BA in Accounting and Finance at Exeter
University
Off-season: 'University'
Overseas tours: Millfield School to South Africa 1997, to Sri Lanka 1999; West of
England U15 to West Indies 1998; Malaysia to Sharjah (Asian Cricket Council
Trophy) 2000-01
Career highlights to date: 'Making my first-class debut v West Indies A for Somerset
2002; making my debut in the NUL for Somerset v Durham 2002; being the youngest
ever cricketer to play for Malaysia; playing for England through the age groups'
Cricket moments to forget: 'Being bowled out for a golden duck off the seventh ball
of the over'
Cricketers particularly admired: Sachin Tendulkar, Wasim Akram,
Marcus Trescothick
Young players to look out for: Richard Timms, Bilal Shafayat, Kadeer Ali,
Matthew Wood
Other sports played: Hockey (Somerset U16), badminton (Millfield School 1st team)
Other sports followed: Football (Manchester United)
Relaxations: 'Web surfing, listening to music'
Extras: Youngest ever cricketer to play for Malaysia (aged 15 years). Has represented
England at U14, U15, U17 and U18 levels. Somerset U15 Player of the Year 1998.
West of England U15 Player of the Year 1998. Most Promising Sportsman for
Malaysia 2000. Played for Somerset Board XI in the first round of the C&G 2003,
which was played in August 2002

Opinions on cricket: 'Fast-moving game. There is always action. The game is moving forward.'
Best batting: 21 Somerset v Lancashire, Taunton 2002
Best bowling: 3-46 Somerset v West Indies A, Taunton 2002

2002 Season

	M	Inns	NO	Runs	HS	Avge	100s	50s	Ct	St	O	M	Runs	Wkts	Avge	Best	5wI	10wM
Test																		
All First	2	4	0	27	21	6.75	-	-	1	-	15	4	55	3	18.33	3-46	-	-
1-day Int																		
C & G	1	1	0	70	70	70.00	-	1	2	-	10	0	36	0	-		-	-
B & H																		
1-day Lge	4	4	0	45	22	11.25	-	-	1	-	11	0	62	2	31.00	2-36	-	

Career Performances

	M	Inns	NO	Runs	HS	Avge	100s	50s	Ct	St	Balls	Runs	Wkts	Avge	Best	5wI	10wM
Test																	
All First	2	4	0	27	21	6.75	-	-	1	-	90	55	3	18.33	3-46	-	-
1-day Int																	
C & G	1	1	0	70	70	70.00	-	1	2	-	60	36	0	-		-	-
B & H																	
1-day Lge	4	4	0	45	22	11.25	-	-	1	-	66	62	2	31.00	2-36	-	

SUTCLIFFE, I. J.   Lancashire

Name: Iain John Sutcliffe
Role: Left-hand bat, leg-spin bowler
Born: 20 December 1974, Leeds
Height: 6ft 2in **Weight:** 13st
Nickname: Sutty
County debut: 1995 (Leicestershire)
County cap: 1997 (Leicestershire)
1000 runs in a season: 2
1st-Class 50s: 29
1st-Class 100s: 8
1st-Class 200s: 1
1st-Class catches: 58
One-Day 100s: 3
Place in batting averages: 70th av. 41.84 (2001 96th av. 33.46)
Strike rate: (career 52.12)
Parents: John and Valerie
Marital status: Single

Education: Leeds Grammar School; Oxford University
Qualifications: 10 GCSEs, 4 A-levels, 2.1 PPE degree
Overseas tours: Leeds GS to Kenya; Leicestershire to South Africa, to West Indies, to Sri Lanka
Career highlights to date: 'Championship winner's medal 1998'
Cricket moments to forget: 'Losing C&G final 2001 and B&H final 1998'
Cricketers particularly admired: Brian Lara, David Gower
Young players to look out for: S. Jones, T. Roberts
Other sports played: Boxing (Oxford Blue 1994, 1995; British Universities Light-middleweight Champion 1993)
Other sports followed: Football (Liverpool)
Relaxations: Socialising, cinema
Extras: Played NCA England U14 and NCA Development Team U18/U19. Scored 163* v Hampshire at The Parks 1995, in the process sharing with C. Gupte (119) in a record partnership for Oxford University against a first-class county (283). Scored 55 out of Leicestershire's first innings total of 96 v Pakistanis at Leicester 2001. Scored 64 v Kent at Canterbury 2001, in the process sharing with Ben Smith (110) in a Leicestershire record second-wicket partnership for matches against Kent (190). Leicestershire vice-captain 2002. Leicestershire Player of the Year 2002. Left Leicestershire at the end of the 2002 season and has joined Lancashire for 2003
Opinions on cricket: 'Need to play less cricket in order to improve preparation and recovery.'
Best batting: 203 Leicestershire v Glamorgan, Cardiff 2001
Best bowling: 2-21 Oxford University v Cambridge University, Lord's 1996

2002 Season

	M	Inns	NO	Runs	HS	Avge	100s	50s	Ct	St	O	M	Runs	Wkts	Avge	Best	5wI	10wM
Test																		
All First	16	29	3	1088	125 *	41.84	2	5	4	-	7	0	39	0	-		-	-
1-day Int																		
C & G	2	2	0	24	13	12.00	-	-	-	-								
B & H	6	6	1	222	65	44.40	-	3	-	-								
1-day Lge	16	16	3	512	104 *	39.38	1	4	3	-								

Career Performances

	M	Inns	NO	Runs	HS	Avge	100s	50s	Ct	St	Balls	Runs	Wkts	Avge	Best	5wI	10wM
Test																	
All First	121	192	16	5735	203	32.58	9	29	58	-	417	318	8	39.75	2-21	-	-
1-day Int																	
C & G	10	10	2	401	103 *	50.12	1	2	2	-							
B & H	21	21	2	647	105 *	34.05	1	6	2	-							
1-day Lge	45	44	4	1092	104 *	27.30	1	6	12	-							

SUTTON, L. D. Derbyshire

Name: <u>Luke</u> David Sutton
Role: Right-hand bat, wicket-keeper
Born: 4 October 1976, Keynsham
Height: 5ft 11in **Weight:** 12st 7lbs
Nickname: Sutts
County debut: 1997 (Somerset),
2000 (Derbyshire)
County cap: 2002 (Derbyshire)
1st-Class 50s: 6
1st-Class 100s: 2
1st-Class catches: 69
1st-Class stumpings: 2
Place in batting averages: 214th av. 22.22
(2001 133rd av. 28.66)
Parents: David and Molly
Marital status: Single
Education: Edgarley Hall, Glastonbury,
Somerset; Millfield School, Street, Somerset;
Durham University

Qualifications: 9 GCSEs, 4 A-levels, 2.1 degree in Economics
Off-season: Playing grade cricket in Sydney, Australia
Overseas tours: Various Somerset Schools tours to Holland; West of England U15
to West Indies 1991; Millfield School to Zimbabwe 1993, to Sri Lanka 1994; Durham
University to Zimbabwe 1997
Overseas teams played for: UNSW, Sydney 1998-99; Northville, Port Elizabeth,
South Africa 1999-2000; Subiaco Marist, Perth 2000-01
Career highlights to date: 'Scoring my maiden first-class 100 [110*] v Warwickshire
in 2001. Carrying my bat v Sussex in 2001, scoring 140 not out. Captaining
Derbyshire in final two games of 2002 season'
Cricket moments to forget: 'Scoring 0 on my Championship debut for Somerset
v Leicestershire in 1997'
Cricketers particularly admired: Ian Healy, Steve Waugh, Adrian Pierson,
Alec Stewart, Paul Nixon, Ian Salisbury, Anthony Wilcox, Marcus Trescothick
Young players to look out for: Steve Selwood, Tom Lungley, Lian Wharton
('although he is in fact very old but looks young!')
Other sports followed: Football (Newcastle United), rugby (Bath)
Injuries: Out for one NUL game with an 'annoying back problem'
Relaxations: 'Keeping fit; eating out; going to the cinema'
Extras: Captain of the England U15 side that played against South Africa and also
played for England U18 and U19. Won Sir John Hobbs Silver Jubilee Memorial Prize
for the U16 Cricketer of the Year in 1992 and the Gray-Nicolls Award for the English
Schools Cricketer of the Year in 1995. Left Somerset at the end of the 1999 season and

joined Derbyshire for 2000. Voted Derbyshire 2nd XI Player of the Year 2000. NBC Denis Compton Award for the most promising young Derbyshire player 2000, 2001. Scored 140* v Sussex at Derby 2001, in the process becoming the first Derbyshire batsman for five years to carry his bat. Awarded Derbyshire cap 2002

Opinions on cricket: 'The game's moving in the right direction. Still a bit concerned about the standard of wickets. Does two overseas players give big clubs more chance to flex their chequebooks?!'

Best batting: 140* Derbyshire v Sussex, Derby 2001

2002 Season

	M	Inns	NO	Runs	HS	Avge	100s	50s	Ct	St		O	M	Runs	Wkts	Avge	Best	5wI	10wM
Test																			
All First	10	19	1	400	80	22.22	-	3	30	1									
1-day Int																			
C & G	1	1	0	14	14	14.00	-	-	-	-									
B & H																			
1-day Lge	14	12	3	109	29	12.11	-	-	17	2									

Career Performances

	M	Inns	NO	Runs	HS	Avge	100s	50s	Ct	St	Balls	Runs	Wkts	Avge	Best	5wI	10wM
Test																	
All First	38	68	8	1536	140 *	25.60	2	6	69	2							
1-day Int																	
C & G	4	4	0	82	45	20.50	-	-	1	-							
B & H	10	10	1	147	60	16.33	-	1	3	-							
1-day Lge	34	31	6	381	53 *	15.24	-	1	30	5							

SWANEPOEL, P. J.   Yorkshire

Name: Pieter Johannes Swanepoel
Role: Right-hand bat, right-arm medium bowler
Born: 30 March 1977, Paarl, South Africa
Height: 6ft 4in **Weight:** 13st 9lbs
Nickname: Swanny
County debut: No first-team appearance
Parents: André and Johanita
Wife and date of marriage: Tara Jayne, 12 December 1999
Children: Jessica, 6 August 1992; Olivia, 24 December 2000
Education: Paarl Gymnasium Primary; Paarl Gymnasium High School
Qualifications: ECB Level 3 coach, UCBSA Level 3 coach
Career outside cricket: Cricket and football groundsman
Off-season: 'One to one coaching and holiday in South Africa'
Overseas teams played for: Boland Academy 1995-98; Boland 2nd XI 1994-96

Career highlights to date: 'Took hat-trick v Somerset in C&G Trophy 2002 for Yorkshire Cricket Board side'

Cricket superstitions: 'No – get on with it'

Cricketers particularly admired: Hansie Cronje, Justin Ontong

Young players to look out for: Justin Ontong 'and all young players at Yorkshire CCC'

Other sports played: Rugby union

Other sports followed: Rugby

Relaxations: '[Being] with family'

Extras: Played for South Africa Development XI 1998. Played for Yorkshire Board XI in the C&G 2001 and 2002, taking a hat-trick (K. Parsons, Dutch, Rose) v Somerset at Scarborough in the third round 2002; also played for Yorkshire Board XI in the second round of the C&G 2003, which was played in September 2002

Opinions on cricket: 'Too much travelling.'

2002 Season (did not make any first-class or one-day appearances for his county)

Career Performances

	M	Inns	NO	Runs	HS	Avge	100s	50s	Ct	St	Balls	Runs	Wkts	Avge	Best	5wI	10wM
Test																	
All First																	
1-day Int																	
C & G	4	4	2	59	28 *	29.50	-	-	1	-	216	139	8	17.37	3-9	-	
B & H																	
1-day Lge																	

---

83. Which future New Zealand captain made his debut for Surrey in 1971?

SWANN, A. J. Lancashire

Name: <u>Alec</u> James Swann
Role: Right-hand bat, off-spin bowler,
occasional wicket-keeper
Born: 26 October 1976, Northampton
Height: 6ft 2in **Weight:** 13st
Nickname: 'I get called EW nowadays'
County debut: 1996 (Northamptonshire),
2002 (Lancashire)
County cap: 2002 (Lancashire)
1000 runs in a season: 1
1st-Class 50s: 13
1st-Class 100s: 7
1st-Class catches: 40
Place in batting averages: 98th av. 37.00
(2001 178th av. 21.77)
Strike rate: (career 100.20)
Parents: Ray and Mavis
Marital status: Single

Family links with cricket: Father played for Northumberland, Bedfordshire,
Northants 2nd XI and England Amateurs. 'Brother Graeme [Northants] still refuses to
play defensive shots'
Education: Sponne School, Towcester
Qualifications: 9 GCSEs, 4 A-levels, coaching badge
Off-season: 'Playing seven-a-side football in Blackburn for the "Lancashire No Stars"
team'
Overseas tours: Northants to Zimbabwe 1998, to Grenada 2000, 2001; Lancashire to
Cape Town 2002
Overseas teams played for: Wallsend, NSW 1995-96, 1997-98; Montrose CC,
Cape Town 1998-99
Career highlights to date: 'Maiden first-class 100 and first Lancs 100 at Headingley'
Cricket moments to forget: 'A pair at Taunton and a missed run-out from a yard'
Cricket superstitions: 'Bar towel in my front pad'
Cricketers particularly admired: Steve and Mark Waugh, 'veteran paceman' Peter
Martin
Young players to look out for: Michael Lumb, Mark Powell
Other sports played: Golf, snooker, football
Other sports followed: Football (Newcastle United)
Relaxations: 'Reading, watching films, discussing property with property magnate
Chapple'
Extras: Played for England Schools U15 and U19. Opened batting for Bedfordshire
(with father in Minor Counties game). *Daily Telegraph* U15 Young Cricketer of the
Year 1992. Midlands Club Cricket Conference Young Cricketer of the Year 1992.

Played for England U19 against New Zealand U19 in 1996. Released by Northamptonshire at the end of the 2001 season and joined Lancashire for 2002. Carried his bat for 84* v Hampshire at Old Trafford 2002, becoming the first Lancashire batsman to achieve the feat since Gehan Mendis did so v Glamorgan at Swansea 1988. Scored 112 v Yorkshire at Old Trafford 2002 to become the first Lancashire batsman to score a century in each of his first two Roses matches, having scored 128 at Headingley earlier in the season. Scored 1000 first-class runs in a season for the first time in his first season at Lancashire 2002. Awarded Lancashire cap 2002

Opinions on cricket: 'I'm not sure 20-over cricket is the way forward. Why don't we just play each county at football?'

Best batting: 154 Northamptonshire v Nottinghamshire, Northampton 1999
Best bowling: 2-30 Northamptonshire v Gloucestershire, Northampton 2000

2002 Season

	M	Inns	NO	Runs	HS	Avge	100s	50s	Ct	St	O	M	Runs	Wkts	Avge	Best	5wI	10wM
Test																		
All First	18	31	2	1073	128	37.00	2	6	12	-	8	1	40	0	-		-	-
1-day Int																		
C & G	1	1	0	4	4	4.00	-	-	-	-								
B & H	1	1	0	1	1	1.00	-	-	1	-								
1-day Lge	7	6	0	109	61	18.16	-	1	-	-	1	0	16	0	-		-	-

Career Performances

	M	Inns	NO	Runs	HS	Avge	100s	50s	Ct	St	Balls	Runs	Wkts	Avge	Best	5wI	10wM
Test																	
All First	62	101	4	2838	154	29.25	7	13	40	-	501	286	5	57.20	2-30	-	-
1-day Int																	
C & G	5	4	0	153	74	38.25	-	1	1	-	18	16	0	-		-	-
B & H	5	3	2	138	83 *	138.00	-	2	1	-	18	20	0	-		-	-
1-day Lge	27	26	4	569	61	25.86	-	3	3	-	18	32	0	-		-	-

---

84. Which Australian Test pace bowler played for
Middlesex in 1969 and 1970?

SWANN, G. P.   Northamptonshire

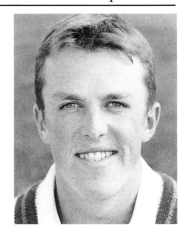

Name: <u>Graeme</u> Peter Swann
Role: Right-hand bat, right-arm off-spin bowler, 'benefit wicket-keeper'
Born: 24 March 1979, Northampton
Height: 6ft **Weight:** 12st
Nickname: G-spot, Swanny, Cygnet
County debut: 1997 (one-day), 1998 (first-class)
County cap: 1999
One-Day Internationals: 1
50 wickets in a season: 1
1st-Class 50s: 13
1st-Class 100s: 4
1st-Class 5 w. in innings: 9
1st-Class 10 w. in match: 2
1st-Class catches: 53
One-Day 5 w. in innings: 1
Place in batting averages: 117th av. 33.68 (2001 181st av. 21.72)
Place in bowling averages: 54th av. 28.51 (2001 131st av. 45.50)
Strike rate: 52.41 (career 62.97)
Parents: Ray and Mave
Marital status: Single
Family links with cricket: Dad has played Minor Counties cricket for Bedfordshire and Northumberland and also for England Amateurs. Brother was contracted to Northants, now at Lancs. 'Cat is named after Gus Logie'
Education: Abington Vale Lower School; Sponne School, Towcester
Qualifications: 10 GCSEs, 4 A-levels, Levels 1 and 2 coaching awards
Off-season: 'Christchurch'
Overseas tours: England U19 to South Africa (including U19 World Cup) 1997-98; England A to Zimbabwe and South Africa 1998-99, to West Indies 2000-01; England to South Africa 1999-2000; ECB National Academy to Australia 2001-02
Career highlights to date: 'Being selected to field at backward point ahead of Monty "Hands Like Knives" Panesar'
Cricket moments to forget: 'Being edged for four by Monty "Bats Like Sachin" Panesar'
Cricket superstitions: 'Never wash jockstrap on a Tuesday'
Cricketers particularly admired: Waugh twins, Neil Foster, Devon Malcolm
Young players to look out for: Monty 'Luton's No. 1' Panesar
Other sports played: Rugby (Northants U14, U15, U16), golf, football
Other sports followed: Football (Newcastle United), rugby (Northampton Saints)
Injuries: No bowling for two months with ligament damage in spinning hand

Relaxations: 'Music, films, Cluedo, feeding the ducks'
Extras: Played for England U14, U15, U17 and U19. *Daily Telegraph* Regional Bowling Award 1994. Gray-Nicolls Len Newbery Schools Cricketer of the Year in 1996. Took 8-118 for England U19 in second 'Test' v Pakistan U19 1998, the best ever figures in an U19 'Test'. Completed Championship double of 500 runs and 50 wickets 1999. Had match figures of 9-62 and scored 49 runs for England A v Windward Islands in St Lucia in the Busta Cup 2000-01, winning the Man of the Match award. Scored half-century (77) and had match figures of 3-91 in ECB National Academy's innings victory over Commonwealth Bank [Australian] Cricket Academy in Adelaide 2001-02. Struck 82-ball 109 as Northamptonshire successfully chased 353 to win Championship match v Durham at Northampton 2002. Scored 183 v Gloucestershire at Bristol 2002, in the process sharing with Mike Hussey (310*) in a stand of 318
Opinions on cricket: 'Free hits for no-balls should be in all cricket. Bowlers should have a three-ball blocking limit.'
Best batting: 183 Northamptonshire v Gloucestershire, Bristol 2002
Best bowling: 6-41 Northamptonshire v Leicestershire, Northampton 1999

2002 Season

	M	Inns	NO	Runs	HS	Avge	100s	50s	Ct	St	O	M	Runs	Wkts	Avge	Best	5wI	10wM
Test																		
All First	11	16	0	539	183	33.68	2	1	5	-	270.5	60	884	31	28.51	6-126	1	1
1-day Int																		
C & G	1	1	0	13	13	13.00	-	-	-	-	9	1	24	0	-	-	-	-
B & H	5	5	0	65	24	13.00	-	-	2	-	23	2	115	6	19.16	4-29	-	
1-day Lge	11	9	1	66	19	8.25	-	-	3	-	42.5	0	194	9	21.55	3-16	-	

Career Performances

	M	Inns	NO	Runs	HS	Avge	100s	50s	Ct	St	Balls	Runs	Wkts	Avge	Best	5wI	10wM
Test																	
All First	85	126	7	3238	183	27.21	4	13	53	-	13918	7032	221	31.81	6-41	9	2
1-day Int	1	0	0	0	0	-	-	-	-	-	30	24	0	-	-	-	
C & G	9	7	0	155	42	22.14	-	-	6	-	418	324	8	40.50	2-25	-	
B & H	12	10	1	181	51 *	20.11	-	1	3	-	360	281	11	25.54	4-29	-	
1-day Lge	64	51	4	926	83	19.70	-	6	14	-	1922	1575	56	28.12	5-35	1	

85. Which West Indian took a Lancashire competition best 6-10 v Scotland in the B&H at Old Trafford in 1982?

SYMINGTON, M. J.   Durham

Name: <u>Marc</u> Joseph Symington
Role: Right-hand bat, right-arm medium bowler
Born: 10 January 1980, Newcastle upon Tyne
Height: 5ft 8in **Weight:** 12st 7lbs
Nickname: Simo, Skids
County debut: 1998
1st-Class catches: 7
Place in batting averages: 258th av. 16.00
Place in bowling averages: 103rd av. 34.70
Strike rate: 51.88 (career 50.08)
Parents: Keith and Sheila
Marital status: Single
Family links with cricket: Grandfather (Ron Symington) played for 24 years in Northumberland League, then umpired in same league for 21 years. Father currently plays for Norton CC in North East Premier League. Brother (Craig) plays for Norton CC and played for Durham U19. Mother is club committee member
Education: St Joseph's, Norton, Stockton-on-Tees; St Michael's, Billingham, Stockton-on-Tees; Stockton Sixth Form College
Qualifications: 5 GCSEs, BTEC in Sports Science, Level I coach
Overseas tours: Durham U21 to Sri Lanka 1996; England U19 to New Zealand 1998-99
Overseas teams played for: Claremont-Nedlands, Perth 2000-01
Career highlights to date: 'Championship debut v Derbyshire. Promotion to division one of NUL [2001]. Watching Pengy bowl'
Cricket moments to forget: 'Being hit in box against own Academy'
Cricketers particularly admired: Graham Thorpe, Darren Gough, Adam Gilchrist
Young players to look out for: Nicky Peng, Ian Bell
Other sports played: Football ('played for Middlesbrough U16'), golf, hockey, snooker
Other sports followed: Football (Middlesbrough FC)
Relaxations: Playing golf and snooker and socialising with friends
Extras: Contracted player for Norton CC in 2000, scoring 466 runs (av. 42.36) and taking 25 wickets (av. 16.20). Released by Durham at the end of the 2002 season
Best batting: 42 Durham v Northamptonshire, Northampton 2002
Best bowling: 4-27 Durham v Sri Lankans, Riverside 2002

	M	Inns	NO	Runs	HS	Avge	100s	50s	Ct	St	O	M	Runs	Wkts	Avge	Best	5wI	10wM
Test																		
All First	10	16	2	224	42	16.00	-	-	6	-	147	29	590	17	34.70	4-27	-	-
1-day Int																		
C & G	2	2	1	34	34	34.00	-	-	-	-	4	0	37	0	-		-	-
B & H	3	3	0	55	32	18.33	-	-	-	-	18	1	111	0	-		-	-
1-day Lge	5	2	0	35	22	17.50	-	-	3	-	21	1	98	5	19.60	2-11	-	

Career Performances

	M	Inns	NO	Runs	HS	Avge	100s	50s	Ct	St	Balls	Runs	Wkts	Avge	Best	5wI	10wM
Test																	
All First	13	19	4	276	42	18.40	-	-	7	-	1202	805	24	33.54	4-27	-	-
1-day Int																	
C & G	2	2	1	34	34	34.00	-	-	-	-	24	37	0	-		-	-
B & H	3	3	0	55	32	18.33	-	-	-	-	108	111	0	-		-	-
1-day Lge	15	10	0	78	22	7.80	-	-	7	-	402	380	9	42.22	2-11	-	

SYMONDS, A.   Kent

Name: Andrew Symonds
Role: Right-hand bat, right-arm
medium or off-spin bowler
Born: 9 June 1975, Birmingham, England
Height: 6ft 1in **Weight:** 13st 5lbs
Nickname: Roy
County debut: 1995 (Gloucestershire),
1999 (Kent)
County cap: 1999 (Kent)
One-Day Internationals: 48
1000 runs in a season: 2
1st-Class 50s: 37
1st-Class 100s: 25
1st-Class 200s: 1
1st-Class 5 w. in innings: 1
1st-Class catches: 103
One-Day 5 w. in innings: 2
Place in batting averages: 84th av. 39.00
(2001 41st av. 46.91)
Place in bowling averages: 141st av. 46.30 (2001 82nd av. 33.30)
Strike rate: 86.46 (career 73.75)
Parents: Ken and Barbara

Marital status: Single
Family links with cricket: Father played Minor Counties cricket
Education: All Saints Anglican School, Gold Coast, Australia; Ballarat and Clarendon College, Australia
Qualifications: Level 2 coaching, professional fisherman
Off-season: Playing cricket for Queensland and Australia
Overseas tours: Australia U19 to India 1993-94; Australia A to Los Angeles 1999, to South Africa 2002-03; Australia to Pakistan 1998-99 (one-day series), to Sri Lanka and Zimbabwe 1999-2000 (one-day series), to New Zealand 1999-2000 (one-day series), to India 2000-01 (one-day series), to England 2001 (one-day series), to Kenya (Nairobi Triangular) 2002
Overseas teams played for: Queensland Academy of Sport 1992-93 – 1997-98; Australian Cricket Academy 1993-94; Queensland 1994-95 –
Cricketers particularly admired: Viv Richards, Shane Warne, Michael Holding
Other sports followed: Hockey, rugby, football
Relaxations: Fishing, camping and hunting
Extras: Nickname 'Roy' reportedly coined by his father after comic-book character 'Roy of the Rovers'. Born in England, he was brought up in Australia and has played for Queensland at various levels since 1991-92; attended the Commonwealth Bank [Australian] Cricket Academy 1994. In his first season of first-class cricket he scored a century (108*) for Queensland against England on their 1994-95 tour of Australia, sharing in an unbroken fifth-wicket partnership of 205 with Jimmy Maher (100*). Hit a world record number of sixes in a first-class innings (16) during his 254* for Gloucestershire v Glamorgan at Abergavenny 1995; struck four more sixes in the second innings to set a new world record for a first-class match. Professional Cricketers' Association Young Player of the Year 1995. Turned down the invitation to tour with England A in 1995 so that he could remain eligible to play for Australia, for whom he made One-Day International debut v Pakistan at Lahore 1998. Scored 113 off 116 balls and took 4-83 for Queensland v Western Australia in the 1998-99 Sheffield Shield final. Joined Kent for 1999 as overseas player; awarded Kent cap 1999; released by Kent at the end of the 1999 season. Rejoined Kent as overseas player part-way through the 2001 season as replacement for the injured Daryll Cullinan. C&G Man of the Match award for his 5-21 and 40-ball 39* v Northamptonshire at Canterbury 2001. Took 5-18 in title-clinching Norwich Union League victory v Warwickshire at Edgbaston 2001. Man of the Match in the Pura Cup final 2001-02 for his first innings 91 and match figures of 6-65 v Tasmania at Brisbane. Recorded maiden first-class five-wicket return (6-105) v Sussex at Tunbridge Wells 2002. ACB central contract 2002-03
Best batting: 254* Gloucestershire v Glamorgan, Abergavenny 1995
Best bowling: 6-105 Kent v Sussex, Tunbridge Wells 2002
Stop press: Selected for Australia squad for 2002-03 World Cup

2002 Season

	M	Inns	NO	Runs	HS	Avge	100s	50s	Ct	St	O	M	Runs	Wkts	Avge	Best	5wI	10wM
Test																		
All First	12	24	2	858	118	39.00	2	4	16	-	187.2	34	602	13	46.30	6-105	1	-
1-day Int																		
C & G	4	4	0	160	55	40.00	-	1	2	-	26	2	129	6	21.50	3-21	-	
B & H	5	5	0	31	21	6.20	-	-	1	-	36	0	172	10	17.20	3-28	-	
1-day Lge	11	11	0	195	46	17.72	-	-	6	-	39.2	1	192	8	24.00	2-23	-	

Career Performances

	M	Inns	NO	Runs	HS	Avge	100s	50s	Ct	St	Balls	Runs	Wkts	Avge	Best	5wI	10wM
Test																	
All First	145	245	21	9141	254 *	40.80	26	37	103	-	9293	4796	126	38.06	6-105	1	-
1-day Int	48	34	6	707	68 *	25.25	-	2	20	-	1580	1299	43	30.20	4-11	-	
C & G	15	14	1	486	87	37.38	-	3	4	-	437	308	16	19.25	5-21	1	
B & H	16	16	0	322	95	20.12	-	2	5	-	240	195	10	19.50	3-28	-	
1-day Lge	58	57	2	1420	95	25.81	-	7	29	-	1011	805	32	25.15	5-18	1	

TAHIR, N.   Warwickshire

Name: Naqaash Tahir
Role: Right-hand bat, right-arm fast bowler
Born: 14 November 1983, Birmingham
Height: 5ft 10in **Weight:** 10st
Nickname: Naq, Naqy
County debut: No first-team appearance
Parents: Mohammed Amin and
Ishrat Nasreen
Marital status: Single
Family links with cricket: Brother Sheraz
played for Worcestershire U16; father also
plays cricket
Education: Nelson Mandela Community
Primary School; Moseley School; Spring Hill
College
Qualifications: GCSEs, Level 1 coaching
Overseas tours: Warwickshire U15 to South
Africa 1999
Career highlights to date: 'Taking six wickets for just one run in four overs when I
was 15. Taking six wickets for West Bromwich Dartmouth 2001'
Cricket moments to forget: 'When I bowled two overs for 20 runs, bowling six wides
and eight no-balls'

Cricketers particularly admired: Darren Gough, Saeed Anwar, Ricky Ponting, Glenn McGrath, Waqar Younis, Wasim Akram
Young players to look out for: Moeen Munir Ali, Vishaal (Warwickshire U15)
Relaxations: Swimming, going to the gym, listening to music
Extras: Scored 103 in a 20-over match, setting a record for Moseley Ashfield U15. Has been Moseley Ashfield U15 Player of the Year, Warwickshire U15 Youth Player of the Year and top wicket-taker for Warwickshire U16
Opinions on cricket: 'I think that today's game is very competitive. There are lots of good players who are ready to play good cricket. You need to work really hard on your fitness and on the game.'

TAYLOR, B. V. Sussex

Name: <u>Billy</u> Victor Taylor
Role: Left-hand bat, right-arm medium-fast bowler
Born: 11 January 1977, Southampton
Height: 6ft 3in **Weight:** 13st 6lbs
Nickname: Crusty, BT, Howzat
County debut: 1999
1st-Class 5 w. in innings: 1
1st-Class catches: 2
One-Day 5 w. in innings: 1
Place in batting averages: 312th av. 5.83
Place in bowling averages: 81st av. 32.53
Strike rate: 59.78 (career 66.81)
Parents: Jackie and Victor
Marital status: Single
Family links with cricket: Brother James plays for Wiltshire CCC
Education: Townhill Park; Bitterne Park; Southampton Tech College; Sparsholt College, Hampshire
Qualifications: 5 GCSEs, NVQ Level 2 Carpentry and Joinery, NTPC Tree Surgery, Level 2 coaching
Career outside cricket: Arboriculturist (tree surgeon)
Off-season: 'Working as a tree surgeon and just enjoying my winter'
Overseas tours: Sussex/Hampshire to Cyprus 1999; Sussex to Grenada 2002
Overseas teams played for: Central Hawke's Bay, New Zealand 1996-97; Manawatu Foxton CC and Horowhenua rep team, New Zealand 1998-99, 2000-01; Te Puke 2002
Career highlights to date: 'Taking five wickets at Lord's last year in the B&H and taking a hat-trick against Surrey on Sky in the B&H last year'
Cricket moments to forget: 'When I had to keep running off every four to five overs at Lord's last year to use the toilet, thanks to a crispy duck from the night before'

Cricket superstitions: 'Don't eat crispy duck the night before a match. Always kiss whalebone carving around neck'

Cricketers particularly admired: Malcolm Marshall, Glenn McGrath, Michael Bevan

Other sports played: Golf – 'just to relax (sometimes!)'

Other sports followed: Football (Havant & Waterlooville), cricket (Wiltshire CCC) – 'brother James plays for both'

Relaxations: 'Golf, swimming, watching football'

Extras: Played for Wiltshire in Minor Counties cricket 1996-98 and in the NatWest 1999. Took 98 wickets in New Zealand club cricket in 1998-99. Sussex 2nd XI Player of the Year 1999, 2000. B&H Gold Award for his 5-28 (his maiden one-day five-wicket return) v Middlesex at Lord's 2002. Took hat-trick (Ormond, Sampson, Giddins) v Surrey at Hove in the B&H and another (G. Flower, Maddy, Malcolm) v Leicestershire at Leicester in the C&G 2002. Recorded maiden first-class five-wicket return (5-90) v Warwickshire at Hove 2002

Opinions on cricket: 'Matches should start at 10.30. Should have a new ball at 80 overs. We should play three or four less four-day matches, so then we would all have more time to recover and practise for the next game – which would mean a better standard in the matches as we would be more ready and less tired.'

Best batting: 24* Sussex v Gloucestershire, Cheltenham 2001

Best bowling: 5-90 Sussex v Warwickshire, Hove 2002

2002 Season

	M	Inns	NO	Runs	HS	Avge	100s	50s	Ct	St	O	M	Runs	Wkts	Avge	Best	5wI	10wM
Test																		
All First	10	14	2	70	18 *	5.83	-	-	1	-	318.5	73	1041	32	32.53	5-90	1	-
1-day Int																		
C & G	3	0	0	0	0	-	-	-	-	-	28	6	119	7	17.00	4-37	-	
B & H	6	0	0	0	0	-	-	-	-	-	54.5	4	192	13	14.76	5-28	1	
1-day Lge	16	9	2	22	16	3.14	-	-	2	-	107.2	12	416	22	18.90	4-22	-	

Career Performances

	M	Inns	NO	Runs	HS	Avge	100s	50s	Ct	St	Balls	Runs	Wkts	Avge	Best	5wI	10wM
Test																	
All First	20	25	7	128	24 *	7.11	-	-	2	-	3207	1812	48	37.75	5-90	1	-
1-day Int																	
C & G	7	1	0	1	1	1.00	-	-	1	-	378	245	13	18.84	4-26	-	
B & H	6	0	0	0	0	-	-	-	-	-	329	192	13	14.76	5-28	1	
1-day Lge	46	22	8	87	21 *	6.21	-	-	9	-	1898	1350	60	22.50	4-22	-	

TAYLOR, C. G. Gloucestershire

Name: Christopher (<u>Chris</u>) Glyn Taylor
Role: Right-hand bat, right-arm
off-spin bowler
Born: 27 September 1976, Bristol
Height: 5ft 8in **Weight:** 10st
Nickname: Tales, Tootsie
County debut: 2000
County cap: 2001
1st-Class 50s: 6
1st-Class 100s: 5
1st-Class catches: 29
Place in batting averages: 184th av. 24.59
(2001 43rd av. 46.50)
Strike rate: (career 75.00)
Parents: Chris and Maggie
Wife and date of marriage: Sarah,
8 December 2001
Family links with cricket: Father and
grandfather both played local club cricket
Education: Brentry Primary School; Colston's Collegiate School
Qualifications: GCSEs and A-levels
Career outside cricket: Teaching
Overseas teams played for: Harbord CC, Manly, Australia 2000
Cricket moments to forget: 'B&H loss to Surrey at Lord's [2001]'
Cricketers particularly admired: Jonty Rhodes, Mark Waugh
Other sports played: Rugby, hockey (both county level); squash, tennis
Other sports followed: Rugby
Relaxations: Fishing
Extras: Represented England Schools U18. In 1995 won the Cricket Society's
A. A. Thomson Fielding Prize and Wetherell Award for Leading All-rounder in English
Schools Cricket. Set school record of 278* v Hutton Grammar School. Made his
highest score of 300* for Gloucestershire 2nd XI v Somerset 2nd XI at Taunton 1999.
Scored maiden first-class century (104) in the Championship match v Middlesex 2000,
becoming the first player from any county to score a century at Lord's on
Championship debut; also the first player to score a century for Gloucestershire in
match that was both first-class and Championship debut. NBC Denis Compton Award
for the most promising young Gloucestershire player 2000. His 196 v Nottinghamshire
at Trent Bridge 2001 included 100 runs scored between lunch and tea on the first day.
B&H Gold Award for his 93 v Warwickshire at Bristol 2002
Opinions on cricket: 'We must try to make the game more appealing to children.'
Best batting: 196 Gloucestershire v Nottinghamshire, Trent Bridge 2001
Best bowling: 3-126 Gloucestershire v Northamptonshire, Cheltenham 2000

2002 Season

	M	Inns	NO	Runs	HS	Avge	100s	50s	Ct	St	O	M	Runs	Wkts	Avge	Best	5wl	10wM
Test																		
All First	15	29	2	664	126	24.59	1	2	15	-	10	1	36	0	-	-	-	-
1-day Int																		
C & G	2	2	1	40	29 *	40.00	-	-	1	-								
B & H	5	5	1	152	93	38.00	-	1	-	-								
1-day Lge	10	9	0	97	23	10.77	-	-	2	-								

Career Performances

	M	Inns	NO	Runs	HS	Avge	100s	50s	Ct	St	Balls	Runs	Wkts	Avge	Best	5wl	10wM
Test																	
All First	39	71	5	2086	196	31.60	5	6	29	-	225	172	3	57.33	3-126	-	-
1-day Int																	
C & G	11	10	3	154	41	22.00	-	-	7	-							
B & H	18	15	3	277	93	23.08	-	1	5	-							
1-day Lge	32	26	3	283	63 *	12.30	-	1	7	-							

TAYLOR, C. R.   *Yorkshire*

Name: Christopher (<u>Chris</u>) Robert Taylor
Role: Right-hand opening bat, right-arm fast-medium bowler
Born: 21 February 1981, Leeds
Height: 6ft 4in **Weight:** 14st 6lbs
Nickname: CT, Barthez
County debut: 2001
1st-Class 50s: 2
1st-Class catches: 5
Place in batting averages: 235th av. 18.75 (2001 261st av. 10.00)
Parents: Phil and Elaine
Marital status: Single
Family links with cricket: 'Brother Matthew plays in Bradford League for Drighlington. Dad slogged a few in Dales Council League. Mum gives good throw-downs in back garden!'
Education: Waterloo Infant and Junior School, Pudsey; Benton Park High School, Leeds
Qualifications: 9 GCSEs, 4 A-levels
Off-season: 'Playing first grade cricket in Sydney again'

Overseas tours: Yorkshire to Grenada 2002
Overseas teams played for: Western Suburbs Magpies, Sydney 1999-2003
Career highlights to date: 'To have played in County Championship winning team 2001. On a personal note, my maiden first-class half-century v Surrey at Headingley, April 2002' (*A 3¼-hour rearguard action of 52**)
Cricket moments to forget: 'To have bagged 'em in my first Roses match v Lancashire, which just also happened to be my first game live on Sky TV (I turned my phone off for a week after it!)'
Cricket superstitions: 'Always have two pieces of chewing gum and always wet my face before going out to bat'
Cricketers particularly admired: Geoffrey Boycott, Michael Vaughan, Matthew Elliott
Young players to look out for: Michael Clarke (NSW), Steve Phillips (NSW)
Other sports played: Rugby, football, tennis, basketball (all for Benton Park HS 1st teams); 'possibly the world's best goalkeeper for "the Young Ones" in pre-match football (much to the dismay of W. Clark, G. Hamilton and colleagues)'
Other sports followed: Football (Everton – 'since I was four years old'), 'enjoy watching all sports'
Relaxations: 'Watching cricket; going to the beaches of Sydney'
Extras: Represented Yorkshire U10-U17. Represented North of England at Bunbury Festival 1996 and was awarded Neil Lloyd Trophy for top run-scorer in festival. Selected for England U15 team for Lombard World Cup 1996. Has also represented England U17 and U19. Yorkshire CCC Supporters' Club Young Player of the Year 1999. Awarded Yorkshire 2nd XI cap 2001
Opinions on cricket: 'Two overseas players will be detrimental to our game. It will be beneficial for youngsters to watch and learn from the overseas, but when they are doing this sitting on the edge because the overseas has taken their place in the team, this is not allowing own young talent to develop. Australian state teams have no overseas at all, and they are the most successful country in the world game. Great game, though!'
Best batting: 52* Yorkshire v Surrey, Headingley 2002

2002 Season

	M	Inns	NO	Runs	HS	Avge	100s	50s	Ct	St	O	M	Runs	Wkts	Avge	Best	5wI	10wM
Test																		
All First	5	9	1	150	52*	18.75	-	1	2	-								
1-day Int																		
C & G																		
B & H																		
1-day Lge																		

Career Performances

	M	Inns	NO	Runs	HS	Avge	100s	50s	Ct	St		Balls	Runs	Wkts	Avge	Best	5wI	10wM
Test																		
All First	8	15	1	210	52 *	15.00	-	2	5	-								
1-day Int																		
C & G																		
B & H																		
1-day Lge																		

THOMAS, I. J.   Glamorgan

Name: <u>Ian</u> James Thomas
Role: Left-hand bat, right-arm off-spin bowler
Born: 9 May 1979, Newport, Gwent
Height: 5ft 11in   **Weight:** 14st
Nickname: Bolts, Homer
County debut: 1998
1st-Class 50s: 4
1st-Class catches: 9
Place in batting averages: 230th av. 19.50 (2001 198th av. 19.40)
Strike rate: 37.00 (career 55.00)
Parents: Amanda and Alun
Marital status: Single
Family links with cricket: 'Father and brother play local league cricket for Machen; local legends for the Buzzards. Mother loves washing the whites'
Education: Machen Primary School; Bassaleg Comprehensive; University of Wales Institute Cardiff (UWIC)
Qualifications: 9 GCSEs, 2 A-levels, BSc (Hons) Sports Development
Career outside cricket: Management/marketing
Off-season: 'Training hard; doing a few jobs, including coaching etc.; looking at all aspects of my game'
Overseas tours: Wales U16 to Jersey and Isle of Wight; British Universities to Port Elizabeth 1999; Glamorgan to Cape Town 2002
Overseas teams played for: Mt Lawley Hawks, Perth 2001-02
Career highlights to date: 'Winning the NUL Division One 2002'
Cricket moments to forget: 'First first-class pair, v Derbys 2002'
Cricketers particularly admired: Steve James, David Hemp, Matt Maynard, Mike Powell

Young players to look out for: David Harrison and brother; Jon Hughes
Other sports played: Rugby (Machen RFC), golf (24 handicap), fishing
Other sports followed: Rugby (Newport RFC)
Relaxations: 'Golf, fishing, training'
Extras: Captained Welsh Schools at all age groups. Glamorgan Young Player of the Month June, July, August and September 2000. Scored 82 on Championship debut v Essex at Southend 2000
Opinions on cricket: 'Still not enough experience to make comments.'
Best batting: 82 Glamorgan v Essex, Southend 2000
Best bowling: 1-26 Glamorgan v Nottinghamshire, Colwyn Bay 2002

2002 Season

	M	Inns	NO	Runs	HS	Avge	100s	50s	Ct	St	O	M	Runs	Wkts	Avge	Best	5wI	10wM
Test																		
All First	9	15	1	273	76	19.50	-	2	2	-	6.1	0	30	1	30.00	1-26	-	-
1-day Int																		
C & G	1	1	0	23	23	23.00	-	-	1	-								
B & H																		
1-day Lge	11	11	1	310	72	31.00	-	3	4	-								

Career Performances

	M	Inns	NO	Runs	HS	Avge	100s	50s	Ct	St	Balls	Runs	Wkts	Avge	Best	5wI	10wM
Test																	
All First	19	32	4	653	82	23.32	-	4	9	-	55	32	1	32.00	1-26	-	-
1-day Int																	
C & G	2	2	0	34	23	17.00	-	-	2	-							
B & H																	
1-day Lge	22	21	1	589	72	29.45	-	4	7	-							

THOMAS, S. D.   Glamorgan

Name: Stuart Darren Thomas
Role: Left-hand bat, right-arm fast-medium bowler
Born: 25 January 1975, Morriston
Height: 6ft **Weight:** 13st
Nickname: Teddy
County debut: 1992
County cap: 1997
50 wickets in a season: 5
1st-Class 50s: 13
1st-Class 100s: 1
1st-Class 5 w. in innings: 18
1st-Class 10 w. in match: 1

1st-Class catches: 47
One-Day 5 w. in innings: 3
Place in batting averages: 274th av. 13.04
(2001 128th av. 29.57)
Place in bowling averages: 74th av. 31.48
(2001 135th av. 50.54)
Strike rate: 53.90 (career 52.15)
Parents: Stu and Ann
Wife and date of marriage: Claire,
30 September 2000
Children: Ellie Sofia, 20 August 2002
Family links with cricket: 'Dad used to play
local club cricket for Llanelli'
Education: Old Road, Llanelli; Graig
Comprehensive, Llanelli; Neath
Tertiary College
Qualifications: 5 GCSEs, BTEC National
Diploma in Sports Studies, Level 2 coaching
award, 'and all the DIY knowledge in the world'
Career outside cricket: Sales rep
Off-season: 'Changing nappies and selling trucks'
Overseas tours: Glamorgan to Cape Town 1993, 1999, 2002, to Zimbabwe 1994,
to Pretoria 1995, to Portugal 1996, to Jersey 1998; England U18 to South Africa
1992-93; England U19 to Sri Lanka 1993-94; England A to Zimbabwe and South
Africa 1998-99, to Bangladesh and New Zealand 1999-2000
Overseas teams played for: Rovers CC, Welkom, Free State 1994
Career highlights to date: 'Winning the County Championship 1997 and NUL 2002.
Also my two England A tours'
Cricket moments to forget: 'Being left out of B&H final 2000'
Cricket superstitions: 'None'
Cricketers particularly admired: 'Anyone who plays or has played for Glamorgan'
Young players to look out for: 'Any young Glamorgan players'
Injuries: Out for one NUL match (v Yorkshire) with a back spasm
Relaxations: 'Enjoy seeing the globe, eating out'
Extras: Became youngest player (17 years 217 days) to take five wickets (5-80) on
debut, v Derbyshire in 1992, and finished eighth in national bowling averages. BBC
Welsh Young Sports Personality 1992. Played in third U19 'Test' against India U19 at
Edgbaston 1994. Bettered Alan Wilkins's Glamorgan best B&H bowling figures on his
debut in the competition with 6 for 20 v Combined Universities at Cardiff in 1995.
Took 7-16 v Surrey at Swansea in the Sunday League in 1998, the best analysis by a
Glamorgan bowler in the competition. Glamorgan Player of the Year 1998. Took 8-50
for England A v Zimbabwe A at Harare on 1998-99 tour – the first eight-wicket haul
by an England A tourist. Scored maiden first-class century v Essex at Chelmsford
2001, his 138 being a record Championship score by a Glamorgan No. 8. Recorded
maiden first-class ten-wicket match return (10-83, including first innings figures of

7-33) v Durham at Cardiff 2002. Scored a 41-ball 71* v Surrey at The Oval in the C&G 2002 as Glamorgan made 429 in reply to Surrey's 438-5

Opinions on cricket: 'Need a day's rest in between four-day cricket and one-day cricket. Body needs time to recover. Please!'

Best batting: 138 Glamorgan v Essex, Chelmsford 2001

Best bowling: 8-50 England A v Zimbabwe A, Harare 1998-99

2002 Season

	M	Inns	NO	Runs	HS	Avge	100s	50s	Ct	St	O	M	Runs	Wkts	Avge	Best	5wI	10wM
Test																		
All First	16	22	1	274	47	13.04	-	-	4	-	467.1	66	1637	52	31.48	7-33	3	1
1-day Int																		
C & G	2	1	1	71	71 *	-	-	1	1	-	16	0	132	4	33.00	3-108	-	
B & H	4	4	1	48	19	16.00	-	-	1	-	23	2	128	3	42.66	2-34	-	
1-day Lge	11	9	2	137	28 *	19.57	-	-	2	-	60.4	2	339	10	33.90	3-31	-	

Career Performances

	M	Inns	NO	Runs	HS	Avge	100s	50s	Ct	St	Balls	Runs	Wkts	Avge	Best	5wI	10wM
Test																	
All First	143	193	36	3058	138	19.47	1	13	47	-	23367	13867	448	30.95	8-50	18	1
1-day Int																	
C & G	16	13	3	238	71 *	23.80	-	1	3	-	909	770	29	26.55	5-74	1	
B & H	24	19	7	228	29	19.00	-	-	6	-	986	873	29	30.10	6-20	1	
1-day Lge	84	64	13	708	38 *	13.88	-	-	13	-	3006	2545	101	25.19	7-16	1	

THORNICROFT, N. D.   *Yorkshire*

Name: Nicholas (Nick) David Thornicroft
Role: Left-hand bat, right-arm fast bowler
Born: 23 January 1985, York
Height: 5ft 11in **Weight:** 12st 8lbs
Nickname: Thorny, Mad Dog, Harry Potter
County debut: 2002
Strike rate: 91.75 (career 91.75)
Parents: Lyn and David
Marital status: Single
Education: Sheriff Hutton CP; Easingwold
Qualifications: 'Common sense'
Career outside cricket: Groundworker
Off-season: 'A bit of work up to Christmas, then preparing to go to Australia with England U19'
Overseas tours: Yorkshire U16 to Cape Town, to Jersey; England U19 to Australia 2002-03

Career highlights to date: 'Getting Neil Fairbrother as my first first-class wicket'
Cricket moments to forget: 'Haven't got one yet'
Cricketers particularly admired: Darren Gough, Brett Lee, Ian Botham, Craig White, Andrew Flintoff
Young players to look out for: Charlie Thornicroft, Haroon Rashid, Andrew Gale, Liam Plunkett
Other sports played: Athletics, football, basketball, 'Physio Cup football ("the Young Ones")'
Other sports followed: Football (York City FC), horse racing
Relaxations: 'Spending time with family; music; fox hunting; shooting'
Extras: Played for Yorkshire Board XI in the second round of the C&G 2002, which was played in September 2001. Became youngest ever Roses match debutant, v Lancashire at Old Trafford 2002, aged 17. Represented England U19 v India U19 in one-day series (1/3) 2002. Shared new ball with fellow 17-year-old Tim Bresnan v Warwickshire at Edgbaston in the NUL 2002
Opinions on cricket: 'I think the game is becoming more entertaining, especially with the introduction of the new 20-over competition. This may also give more youngsters a chance, which is also very positive for the future.'
Best batting: 4* Yorkshire v Lancashire, Old Trafford 2002
Best bowling: 2-51 Yorkshire v Lancashire, Old Trafford 2002

2002 Season

	M	Inns	NO	Runs	HS	Avge	100s	50s	Ct	St	O	M	Runs	Wkts	Avge	Best	5wI	10wM
Test																		
All First	3	6	3	9	4 *	3.00	-	-	-	-	61.1	14	248	4	62.00	2-51	-	-
1-day Int																		
C & G																		
B & H																		
1-day Lge	3	1	1	0	0 *	-	-	-	-	1	-	15	2	89	3	29.66	2-35	-

Career Performances

	M	Inns	NO	Runs	HS	Avge	100s	50s	Ct	St	Balls	Runs	Wkts	Avge	Best	5wI	10wM
Test																	
All First	3	6	3	9	4 *	3.00	-	-	-	-	367	248	4	62.00	2-51	-	-
1-day Int																	
C & G	1	0	0	0	0	-	-	-	-	-	30	19	0	-	-	-	-
B & H																	
1-day Lge	3	1	1	0	0 *	-	-	-	-	1	-	90	89	3	29.66	2-35	-

THORPE, A. M.   Durham

Name: <u>Ashley</u> Michael Thorpe
Role: Left-hand bat, right-arm
medium bowler
Born: 2 April 1975, Kiama,
New South Wales, Australia
Height: 5ft 11in   **Weight:** 14st 6lbs
Nickname: Thorpedo
County debut: 2002
1st-Class 50s: 2
1st-Class catches: 5
Place in batting averages: 223rd av. 20.84
Parents: Michael and Helen
Wife and date of marriage: Kathleen,
18 April 1998
Children: Michael, 11 December 1998
Family links with cricket: 'Father played for
Albion Park and now plays for Scarborough
CC veterans in Western Australia'
Education: Albion Park Primary School, NSW; Kent St Senior High School, WA
Career outside cricket: Qualified trainer with London Electricity
Off-season: 'Working for LE Group. Training for 2003. One month in Perth (March)'
Overseas tours: Qantas to Malaysia 1995; Durham to Cape Town 2002
Overseas teams played for: Scarborough CC, Western Australia 1996-97
Career highlights to date: 'First-class debut [for Durham] v Sri Lanka'
Cricket superstitions: 'Right pad on first'
Cricketers particularly admired: Mark and Steve Waugh, Brad Hodge ('Cannon'),
N. Kent, Paul Collingwood
Young players to look out for: Gary Pratt, Gordon Muchall, Michael Gough
Other sports followed: Football (Newcastle United FC), rugby union (ACT
Brumbies), rugby league (Canberra Raiders)
Relaxations: 'Watching TV, sleeping; family time'
Extras: Played for Western Australia U17 and U19. Has played for Chester-le-Street
in the North East Premier League. Scored 138 and 85 on 2nd XI debut v Yorkshire 2nd
XI. Is not considered an overseas player
Opinions on cricket: 'Reduce to 90 overs per day. More day/night cricket. More
televised domestic four-day cricket.'
Best batting: 95 Durham v Essex, Riverside 2002

2002 Season

	M	Inns	NO	Runs	HS	Avge	100s	50s	Ct	St	O	M	Runs	Wkts	Avge	Best	5wl	10wM
Test																		
All First	7	13	0	271	95	20.84	-	2	5	-	8	0	32	0	-	-	-	-
1-day Int																		
C & G																		
B & H																		
1-day Lge	4	4	0	83	53	20.75	-	1	-	-	11	0	67	2	33.50	2-49	-	

Career Performances

	M	Inns	NO	Runs	HS	Avge	100s	50s	Ct	St	Balls	Runs	Wkts	Avge	Best	5wl	10wM
Test																	
All First	7	13	0	271	95	20.84	-	2	5	-	48	32	0	-	-	-	-
1-day Int																	
C & G																	
B & H																	
1-day Lge	4	4	0	83	53	20.75	-	1	-	-	66	67	2	33.50	2-49	-	

THORPE, G. P.   Surrey

Name: <u>Graham</u> Paul Thorpe
Role: Left-hand bat, occasional right-arm medium bowler
Born: 1 August 1969, Farnham
Height: 5ft 10in **Weight:** 12st 9lbs
Nickname: Chalky
County debut: 1988
County cap: 1991
Benefit: 2000
Test debut: 1993
Tests: 77
One-Day Internationals: 82
1000 runs in a season: 8
1st-Class 50s: 100
1st-Class 100s: 39
1st-Class 200s: 4
1st-Class catches: 256
One-Day 100s: 8
Place in batting averages: 91st av. 37.57 (2001 11th av. 61.42)
Strike rate: (career 92.84)
Parents: 'Mr and Mrs Thorpe'
Children: Henry and Amelia

Education: Weydon Comprehensive; Farnham College
Qualifications: 7 O-levels, PE Diploma
Overseas tours: England A to Zimbabwe and Kenya 1989-90, to Pakistan 1990-91, to Bermuda and West Indies 1991-92, to Australia 1992-93; England to West Indies 1993-94, to Australia 1994-95, to South Africa 1995-96, to India and Pakistan (World Cup) 1995-96, to Zimbabwe and New Zealand 1996-97, to Sharjah (Champions Trophy) 1997-98, to West Indies 1997-98, to Australia 1998-99, to Sharjah (Coca-Cola Cup) 1998-99, to Kenya (ICC Knockout Trophy) 2000-01, to Pakistan and Sri Lanka 2000-01, to India and New Zealand 2001-02
Cricketers particularly admired: Grahame Clinton, Waqar Younis, Ian Botham, Viv Richards
Other sports followed: Football (Chelsea FC), golf
Relaxations: Sleeping
Extras: Played for English Schools cricket U15 and U19 and England Schools football U18. Scored a century (114*) against Australia on his Test debut at Trent Bridge 1993. Scored 84 v West Indies at Bridgetown 1993-94, in the process sharing with Alec Stewart (143) in a record fifth-wicket partnership for England in Tests v West Indies (150). Scored 138 v Australia at Edgbaston 1997, in the process sharing with Nasser Hussain (207) in a record fourth-wicket partnership for England in Tests v Australia (288). England's Player of the Series and leading run-scorer in the 1997 Ashes campaign with 453 runs at an average of 50.33. Scored 103 v West Indies at Bridgetown 1997-98, in the process sharing with Mark Ramprakash (154) in a record sixth-wicket partnership for England in Tests v West Indies (205). Cornhill England Player of the Year 1997-98. One of *Wisden*'s Five Cricketers of the Year 1998. Represented England in the 1999 World Cup. With Craig White (93), shared in a new record sixth-wicket partnership for England in Tests v Pakistan (166) in the first Test at Lahore 2000-01; his century was the first in Test history to contain only one boundary (he added a second four before being out for 118). Scored match-winning 64* in third Test at Karachi 2000-01 to steer England to a series victory v Pakistan. Man of the Match in third Test v Sri Lanka at Colombo 2000-01 for his 113* followed by 32* out of 74-6 as England completed series win over Sri Lanka. Captained England in one-day series v Sri Lanka 2000-01. Scored 138 v Pakistan at Old Trafford 2001, in the process sharing with Michael Vaughan (120) in a record partnership for any wicket for England in Tests v Pakistan (267). England Man of the Series v Pakistan 2001. Scored maiden Test double century (200*) v New Zealand in the first Test at Christchurch 2001-02, in the process sharing with Andrew Flintoff in a stand of 281 that set several new records, including that for the highest sixth-wicket partnership for England in Tests; his 200 took 231 balls and was the second fastest for England in terms of balls received (after Ian Botham's 220-ball double hundred v India at The Oval in 1982) and, briefly, the third fastest in Tests overall until Nathan Astle struck his 153-ball double hundred later in the same Test. Scored century (123) in the second Test v Sri Lanka at Edgbaston 2002, in the process passing 5000 runs in Test cricket and sharing with Matthew Hoggard (17*) in a record tenth-wicket stand for England in Tests v Sri Lanka (91). Retired from One-Day International cricket after the NatWest Series 2002, then stood down from all cricket for some six weeks after the first Test v India at

Lord's in July. Scored century (114) v Gloucestershire at The Oval in the NUL 2002 to help Surrey clinch the runners-up spot in the second division. Originally selected for England tour of Australia 2002-03 but withdrew for personal reasons
Best batting: 223* England v South Australia, Adelaide 1998-99
Best bowling: 4-40 Surrey v Australians, The Oval 1993

2002 Season

	M	Inns	NO	Runs	HS	Avge	100s	50s	Ct	St	O	M	Runs	Wkts	Avge	Best	5wI	10wM
Test	4	6	0	252	123	42.00	1	1	5	-								
All First	8	14	0	526	143	37.57	2	1	6	-								
1-day Int	3	3	0	45	18	15.00	-	-	2	-								
C & G																		
B & H	1	1	0	61	61	61.00	-	1	-	-								
1-day Lge	1	1	0	114	114	114.00	1	-	-	-								

Career Performances

	M	Inns	NO	Runs	HS	Avge	100s	50s	Ct	St	Balls	Runs	Wkts	Avge	Best	5wI	10wM
Test	77	140	18	5109	200 *	41.87	11	30	86	-	138	37	0	-	-	-	-
All First	290	485	66	18625	223 *	44.45	43	100	256	-	2321	1305	25	52.20	4-40	-	-
1-day Int	82	77	13	2380	89	37.18	-	21	43	-	120	97	2	48.50	2-15	-	
C & G	30	29	8	1159	145 *	55.19	1	9	18	-	13	12	0	-	-	-	
B & H	54	52	5	1779	103	37.85	1	13	20	-	168	131	4	32.75	3-35	-	
1-day Lge	130	120	17	3945	126 *	38.30	6	26	51	-	318	307	8	38.37	3-21	-	

86. Who was the only batsman to top 2000
first-class runs in 2001?

TOMLINSON, J. A. Hampshire

Name: <u>James</u> Andrew Tomlinson
Role: Left-hand bat, left-arm
fast-medium bowler
Born: 12 June 1982, Appleshaw, Hants
Height: 6ft 2in **Weight:** 12st 7lbs
Nickname: Tommo, Dangerous Dave, Mr T
County debut: 2002
1st-Class catches: 2
Place in bowling averages: 156th av. 62.33
Strike rate: 84.25 (career 84.25)
Parents: Ian and Janet
Marital status: Single
Family links with cricket: Grandfathers
played cricket for Carlisle CC and in
Yorkshire leagues

Education: Appleshaw Primary School;
Harrow Way Secondary School, Andover;
Cricklade College, Andover; Cardiff
University
Qualifications: 9 GCSEs, 3 A-levels
Career outside cricket: Student (BA Education)
Off-season: 'Trying to get a degree'
Career highlights to date: 'My NUL debut. Playing against India and Sri Lanka.
Playing on Sky TV against Lancashire and Surrey. Playing with Robin Smith'
Cricket moments to forget: 'My Hampshire Southern League debut v Andover –
everything went wrong'
Cricket superstitions: 'Not applicable'
Cricketers particularly admired: Dimitri Mascarenhas, Shaun Udal, Peter Sadler,
Wasim Akram 'and the first-choice bowling attack of Australia'
Young players to look out for: James Anderson, Will Jefferson, Jamie Dalrymple,
Chris Tremlett, John Francis
Other sports played: Darts, football
Other sports followed: Football (West Ham United)
Relaxations: 'Walking the dog, Tinker; '80s nite at Cardiff University; R 'n' B music'
Extras: Played for Hampshire Board XI in the NatWest 2000 and for Wiltshire in the
C&G 2001. Played for Development of Excellence XI (South) v West Indies U19 at
Arundel 2001. Part of Hampshire's 2nd XI Championship winning side 2001. Played
for Cardiff University CCE 2002, taking 5-104 (7-134 the match) v Somerset at
Millfield School. Represented British Universities v Sri Lankans at Northampton 2002
Opinions on cricket: 'National league cricket has been great fun. The more floodlit
matches the better. Two-division cricket is excellent. Do not agree with having two
overseas players. Looking forward to next year.'

Best batting: 23 Hampshire v Indians, West End 2002
Best bowling: 2-55 Hampshire v Indians, West End 2002

2002 Season

	M	Inns	NO	Runs	HS	Avge	100s	50s	Ct	St	O	M	Runs	Wkts	Avge	Best	5wl	10wM
Test																		
All First	6	10	5	34	23	6.80	-	-	2	-	168.3	14	748	12	62.33	2-55	-	-
1-day Int																		
C & G																		
B & H																		
1-day Lge	9	4	2	7	6	3.50	-	-	1	-	65.2	3	319	10	31.90	2-15	-	

Career Performances

	M	Inns	NO	Runs	HS	Avge	100s	50s	Ct	St	Balls	Runs	Wkts	Avge	Best	5wl	10wM
Test																	
All First	6	10	5	34	23	6.80	-	-	2	-	1011	748	12	62.33	2-55	-	-
1-day Int																	
C & G	2	2	0	4	4	2.00	-	-	-	-	102	46	1	46.00	1-29	-	
B & H																	
1-day Lge	9	4	2	7	6	3.50	-	-	1	-	392	319	10	31.90	2-15	-	

TREDWELL, J. C.   Kent

Name: James Cullum Tredwell
Role: Left-hand bat, right-arm
off-spin bowler
Born: 27 February 1982, Ashford, Kent
Height: 5ft 11in   **Weight:** 14st 2lbs
Nickname: Tredders, Chad, Penguin
County debut: 2001
1st-Class 50s: 2
1st-Class catches: 8
Place in batting averages: 165th av. 26.83
Place in bowling averages: 107th av. 35.80
Strike rate: 74.60 (career 75.16)
Parents: John and Rosemary
Marital status: Single
Family links with cricket: 'Father played
league cricket for Ashford and Folkestone'
Education: Dymchurch County Primary
School; Southlands Community
Comprehensive
Qualifications: 10 GCSEs, 2 A-levels, ECB Level 1 coach

Off-season: 'Working, coaching, training'
Overseas tours: Kent U17 to Sri Lanka 1998-99; Kent to Port Elizabeth 2002
Overseas teams played for: Redlands Tigers, Brisbane 2000-02
Career highlights to date: 'Captaining England U19. Fifty against Somerset first time opening the innings in first-class cricket'
Cricket moments to forget: 'Being hit for six in a crucial B&H Cup match v Essex, which probably cost Kent's qualification to next stage'
Cricketers particularly admired: Mark Waugh, 'all the great spinners'
Young players to look out for: Gary Pratt, Rob Ferley
Extras: Played for Kent Board XI in the NatWest 2000 and in the C&G 2001. Called up from England U19 for first-class debut for Kent v Leicestershire 2001, entailing a dash from Hove to Leicester on the day of the game. Represented England U19 v West Indies U19 in 'Test' series (3/3) 2001 (captain in second 'Test'). Captained Kent to victory in the 2nd XI Trophy final at West End 2002, scoring 111
Best batting: 61 Kent v Yorkshire, Headingley 2002
Best bowling: 4-103 Kent v Warwickshire, Edgbaston 2002

2002 Season

	M	Inns	NO	Runs	HS	Avge	100s	50s	Ct	St	O	M	Runs	Wkts	Avge	Best	5wI	10wM
Test																		
All First	4	6	0	161	61	26.83	-	2	8	-	124.2	29	358	10	35.80	4-103	-	-
1-day Int																		
C & G	3	1	1	15	15 *	-	-	-	2	-	23	4	68	5	13.60	3-7	-	
B & H	3	2	0	9	5	4.50	-	-	2	-	18	0	110	4	27.50	2-44	-	
1-day Lge	11	9	4	10	3 *	2.00	-	-	4	-	53.5	1	265	11	24.09	3-28	-	

Career Performances

	M	Inns	NO	Runs	HS	Avge	100s	50s	Ct	St	Balls	Runs	Wkts	Avge	Best	5wI	10wM
Test																	
All First	5	7	0	171	61	24.42	-	2	8	-	902	481	12	40.08	4-103	-	-
1-day Int																	
C & G	9	6	1	181	71	36.20	-	2	3	-	372	237	8	29.62	3-7	-	
B & H	3	2	0	9	5	4.50	-	-	2	-	108	110	4	27.50	2-44	-	
1-day Lge	11	9	4	10	3 *	2.00	-	-	4	-	323	265	11	24.09	3-28	-	

87. Which Australian leg-spinning Test all-rounder
joined Nottinghamshire in 1953?

TREGO, P. D.   Kent

Name: <u>Peter</u> David Trego
Role: Right-hand bat, right-arm
'quickish' bowler
Born: 12 June 1981, Weston-super-Mare
Height: 6ft **Weight:** 12st 7lbs
Nickname: Tregs 'and many more'
County debut: 2000 (Somerset)
1st-Class 50s: 1
1st-Class 100s: 1
1st-Class catches: 5
Place in batting averages: 85th av. 38.57
Strike rate: 75.60 (career 63.59)
Parents: Carol and Paul
Marital status: Single
Family links with cricket: 'Brother Sam
played for Somerset; Dad plays for Uphill
Castle – both strong batsmen'
Education: St Martins, Weston-super-Mare;
Wyvern Comprehensive

Cricketers particularly admired: Ian Botham and Graham Rose – 'they have both
been huge inspirations to me'
Other sports played: Football
Other sports followed: Football (Man Utd), darts, golf
Relaxations: Golf, snooker, music, socialising with friends, shopping
Extras: Won Best Batsman award at U16 – averaged 137 in nine games. Attended
Lilleshall with England U17. Represented England U19 v Sri Lanka U19 in one-day
and 'Test' series 2000, scoring 53* and taking 3-41 in the second 'One-Day
International' at Cardiff. NBC Denis Compton Award for the most promising young
Somerset player 2000. Played for Somerset Board XI in the C&G 2001 and in the
second round of the C&G 2002, which was played in September 2001. Scored maiden
first-class century (140) at Taunton 2002 as Somerset, chasing 454 to win, tied with
West Indies A. Left Somerset at the end of the 2002 season and has joined Kent for
2003
Best batting: 140 Somerset v West Indies A, Taunton 2002
Best bowling: 4-84 Somerset v Yorkshire, Scarborough 2000

2002 Season

	M	Inns	NO	Runs	HS	Avge	100s	50s	Ct	St	O	M	Runs	Wkts	Avge	Best	5wI	10wM
Test																		
All First	4	8	1	270	140	38.57	1	-	2	-	63	6	357	5	71.40	3-65	-	-
1-day Int																		
C & G																		
B & H	3	3	1	23	15 *	11.50	-	-	1	-	16	1	110	2	55.00	1-32	-	
1-day Lge	6	5	1	36	24	9.00	-	-	1	-	26	3	140	6	23.33	3-14	-	

Career Performances

	M	Inns	NO	Runs	HS	Avge	100s	50s	Ct	St	Balls	Runs	Wkts	Avge	Best	5wI	10wM
Test																	
All First	14	21	3	521	140	28.94	1	1	5	-	1717	1203	27	44.55	4-84	-	-
1-day Int																	
C & G	3	2	0	11	11	5.50	-	-	-	-	132	93	6	15.50	2-21	-	
B & H	3	3	1	23	15 *	11.50	-	-	1	-	96	110	2	55.00	1-32	-	
1-day Lge	14	11	2	94	24	10.44	-	-	2	-	366	316	9	35.11	3-14	-	

TREMLETT, C. T. Hampshire

Name: <u>Christopher</u> Timothy Tremlett
Role: Right-hand bat, right-arm
fast-medium bowler
Born: 2 September 1981, Southampton
Height: 6ft 7in **Weight:** 16st 1lb
Nickname: Twiggy, Goober
County debut: 2000
1st-Class 5 w. in innings: 2
1st-Class catches: 6
Place in batting averages: 209th av. 22.50
Place in bowling averages: 62nd av. 29.47
(2001 12th av. 20.05)
Strike rate: 56.00 (career 48.80)
Parents: Timothy and Carolyn
Marital status: Single
Family links with cricket: Grandfather
[Maurice] played for Somerset and three
Tests for England. Father played county
cricket for Hampshire and is now director of cricket at the county
Education: Otterbourne Primary, Chandlers Ford; Thornden School, Chandlers Ford;
Taunton's College, Southampton
Qualifications: 5 GCSEs, BTEC National Diploma in Sports Science, Level 2 coach
Off-season: 'Going to Australia with National Academy'

Overseas tours: West of England U15 to West Indies 1997; Hampshire U16 to Jersey; England U17 to Northern Ireland (ECC Colts Festival) 1999; England U19 to India 2000-01; ECB National Academy to Australia 2001-02, to Australia and Sri Lanka 2002-03

Career highlights to date: 'Taking first five-wicket haul against Lancashire at the Rose Bowl'

Cricket moments to forget: 'Getting injured against Essex in an NUL game and being put out for the rest of the 2002 season'

Cricketers particularly admired: Glenn McGrath, Mark Waugh, Shane Warne

Young players to look out for: John Francis

Other sports played: Basketball, volleyball

Other sports followed: Football (Arsenal)

Injuries: Out for the remainder of the 2002 season after suffering a stress fracture of a toe in August

Relaxations: 'Socialising with friends; cinema'

Extras: Played for Hampshire Board XI in the NatWest 2000. Took wicket (Mark Richardson) with first ball in first-class cricket v New Zealand A at Portsmouth 2000; finished with debut match figures of 6-91. Hit 30 not out off 15 balls on National League debut. Represented England U19 v Sri Lanka U19 in 'Test' series 2000 and v West Indies U19 in one-day series (3/3) 2001. NBC Denis Compton Award for the most promising young Hampshire player 2000, 2001. Hampshire Young Player of the Year 2001. Recorded maiden first-class five-wicket return (5-68) v Lancashire at West End 2002

Opinions on cricket: 'The game is a lot more exciting with the introduction of two leagues. However, there is far too much cricket played in this country and it puts a strain on players, especially fast bowlers. The Australian system seems to be a better way of doing things. They play less games and the injury rate doesn't seem to be as high. The intensity of the game would rise as well.'

Best batting: 40* Hampshire v Kent, Canterbury 2002

Best bowling: 5-57 Hampshire v Lancashire, Old Trafford 2002

2002 Season

	M	Inns	NO	Runs	HS	Avge	100s	50s	Ct	St	O	M	Runs	Wkts	Avge	Best	5wI	10wM
Test																		
All First	11	14	6	180	40 *	22.50	-	-	4	-	336	83	1061	36	29.47	5-57	2	-
1-day Int																		
C & G	2	0	0	0	0	-	-	-	-	-	18.5	3	72	4	18.00	3-20	-	
B & H	4	4	1	10	7 *	3.33	-	-	-	-	29	0	151	3	50.33	2-42	-	
1-day Lge	9	7	2	44	18	8.80	-	-	3	-	62.1	6	240	13	18.46	4-25	-	

Career Performances

	M	Inns	NO	Runs	HS	Avge	100s	50s	Ct	St	Balls	Runs	Wkts	Avge	Best	5wI	10wM
Test																	
All First	19	25	10	296	40 *	19.73	-	-	6	-	3026	1553	62	25.04	5-57	2	-
1-day Int																	
C & G	4	1	0	10	10	10.00	-	-	-	-	185	142	6	23.66	3-20	-	
B & H	4	4	1	10	7 *	3.33	-	-	-	-	174	151	3	50.33	2-42	-	
1-day Lge	26	18	6	133	30 *	11.08	-	-	7	-	1192	789	39	20.23	4-25	-	

TRESCOTHICK, M. E.   Somerset

Name: Marcus Edward Trescothick
Role: Left-hand bat, right-arm swing bowler, reserve wicket-keeper
Born: 25 December 1975, Keynsham, Bristol
Height: 6ft 3in **Weight:** 14st 7lbs
Nickname: Banger
County debut: 1993
County cap: 1999
Test debut: 2000
Tests: 26
One-Day Internationals: 44
1st-Class 50s: 44
1st-Class 100s: 12
1st-Class catches: 140
One-Day 100s: 11
Place in batting averages: 7th av. 69.11
(2001 63rd av. 41.17)
Strike rate: (career 69.27)
Parents: Martyn and Lin
Marital status: Single
Family links with cricket: Father played for Somerset 2nd XI; uncle played club cricket; girlfriend plays for Taunton Ladies and Somerset Ladies CC
Education: Sir Bernard Lovell School
Qualifications: 7 GCSEs
Off-season: Touring with England
Overseas tours: England U18 to South Africa 1992-93; England U19 to Sri Lanka 1993-94, to West Indies 1994-95 (captain); England A to Bangladesh and New Zealand 1999-2000; England to Kenya (ICC Knockout Trophy) 2000-01, to Pakistan and Sri Lanka 2000-01, to Zimbabwe (one-day series) 2001-02, to India and New Zealand 2001-02, to Sri Lanka (ICC Champions Trophy) 2002-03, to Australia 2002-03
Overseas teams played for: Melville CC, Perth 1997-99

Career highlights to date: 'Scoring my first Test hundred in Galle, Sri Lanka [2001]'
Cricketers particularly admired: Adam Gilchrist, Andy Caddick
Young players to look out for: Pete Trego, Matthew Wood
Other sports followed: Golf, football (Bristol City FC)
Injuries: Out for about six weeks with a broken left thumb
Relaxations: 'Spending time at home (it's such a rare thing), playing golf'
Extras: England U19 squad v West Indies U19 1993; represented England U19 v India U19 1994 (Man of the Series) and v South Africa U19 1995 (captain); scored more than 1000 runs for England U19. Took a hat-trick for Somerset against Young Australia at Taunton 1995. Scored 322 v Warwickshire 2nd XI 1997, being the last man out with the score on 605 as Somerset 2nd XI chased 612. Made ODI debut v Zimbabwe in NatWest Series at The Oval 2000, scoring 79; scored 87 in same series v West Indies at Riverside, winning Man of the Match award. Made Test debut in third Test v West Indies 2000, scoring 66 and sharing with Alec Stewart (105) in record England partnership for any wicket in Tests v West Indies at Old Trafford (179). Scored 78 in fifth Test v West Indies 2000, sharing with Michael Atherton (83) in a new record first-wicket stand for England in Tests v West Indies at The Oval (159). PCA Player of the Year 2000. Scored 147 v Glamorgan at Cardiff 2001, in the process sharing with Piran Holloway (78) in a Somerset record opening stand for matches v Glamorgan (240). B&H Gold Awards for his 113 v Glamorgan at Cardiff, 109* v Northamptonshire at Northampton and 99-ball 112 v Gloucestershire at Taunton 2001 (three B&H centuries in eight days). Man of the Match for his 142-ball 137 (his maiden ODI century) v Pakistan at Lord's in the NatWest Series 2001, in the process of scoring which he shared in a record fourth-wicket partnership for England in One-Day Internationals (170) with Owais Shah (62). C&G Man of the Match award for his 83-ball 121 v Glamorgan at Taunton 2001. Sports.com Cricketer of the Year 2001. Captained England v Zimbabwe in fourth One-Day International at Bulawayo 2001-02, deputising for Nasser Hussain. BBC West Country Sports Sportsman of the Year for 2001. Man of the Match award v India at Kolkata (Calcutta) 2001-02 for his 109-ball 121, which included the fastest century for England in One-Day Internationals (80 balls). Man of the Match award for his 80-ball 95 in England's series-equalling One-Day International victory over India at Mumbai (Bombay) 2001-02. Scored 76 as England followed on in first Test v Sri Lanka at Lord's 2002, in the process sharing with Michael Vaughan (115) in a record first-wicket partnership for England in Tests v Sri Lanka (168). Took part in first-wicket stand of 50 in five overs with Michael Vaughan to bring England victory with an over to spare in the third Test v Sri Lanka at Old Trafford 2002. C&G Man of the Match award for his 133 v Hampshire at Taunton 2002. Scored 100-ball 109 v India in the final of the NatWest Series at Lord's 2002, and was named Man of the Series for his 362 runs (av. 51.71). ECB 12-month contract 2002-03. Vice-captain of Somerset 1999-2002; captained the county on his appearances in 2002
Opinions on cricket: 'Two divisions are working well. Central contracts are still causing problems for the counties. If we are serious about England getting better, it's something we have to live with.'
Best batting: 190 Somerset v Middlesex, Taunton 1999

Best bowling: 4-36 Somerset v Young Australia, Taunton 1995
Stop press: Scored 102-ball 119 v Zimbabwe at Colombo in the ICC Champions Trophy 2002-03, winning the Man of the Match award. Selected for England squad for 2002-03 World Cup

2002 Season

	M	Inns	NO	Runs	HS	Avge	100s	50s	Ct	St	O	M	Runs	Wkts	Avge	Best	5wI	10wM
Test	4	7	2	469	161	93.80	1	4	5	-								
All First	6	11	2	622	161	69.11	2	4	5	-								
1-day Int	7	7	0	362	109	51.71	1	2	2	-								
C & G	3	2	0	160	133	80.00	1	-	-	-								
B & H	2	2	0	67	47	33.50	-	-	1	-								
1-day Lge	2	2	0	41	41	20.50	-	-	1	-								

Career Performances

	M	Inns	NO	Runs	HS	Avge	100s	50s	Ct	St	Balls	Runs	Wkts	Avge	Best	5wI	10wM
Test	26	49	4	1952	161	43.37	3	14	21	-	120	52	1	52.00	1-34	-	-
All First	138	234	11	7589	190	34.03	12	44	140	-	2494	1438	36	39.94	4-36	-	-
1-day Int	44	44	1	1610	137	37.44	3	8	15	-	46	45	2	22.50	2-7	-	
C & G	18	16	0	715	133	44.68	3	1	4	-	174	141	4	35.25	2-23	-	
B & H	22	22	4	857	122	47.61	4	2	9	-	325	255	12	21.25	3-30	-	
1-day Lge	85	76	10	1821	110	27.59	1	9	28	-	978	823	31	26.54	4-50	-	

TROTT, B. J.   Kent

Name: Benjamin (<u>Ben</u>) James Trott
Role: Right-hand bat, right-arm fast-medium bowler
Born: 14 March 1975, Wellington, Somerset
Height: 6ft 5in **Weight:** 14st
Nickname: Tony Rott, Trotsky, Trotty
County debut: 1997 (Somerset), 2000 (Kent)
1st-Class 5 w. in innings: 4
1st-Class 10 w. in match: 1
1st-Class catches: 5
One-Day 5 w. in innings: 1
Place in batting averages: (2001 277th av. 5.70)
Place in bowling averages: (2001 40th av. 26.27)
Strike rate: 49.71 (career 47.70)
Parents: Alan Robert and Jane Elizabeth

Marital status: Single
Family links with cricket: 'Younger brother Thom plays for Somerset youth sides and also plays club cricket for Wellington along with my dad'
Education: Wellesley Park Primary School, Wellington; Court Fields Community School, Taunton; The Richard Huish College, Taunton; The College of St Mark and St John, Plymouth
Qualifications: 8 GCSEs, 3 A-levels, BEd (Hons) Physical Education and Information Technology; sports coaching – cricket, rugby, football, hockey
Career outside cricket: Teacher (primary)
Overseas teams played for: Claremont-Nedlands, Perth 1998-99
Career highlights to date: 'Winning the Norwich Union League 2001 with the last game of the season'
Cricketers particularly admired: Glenn McGrath, Darren Gough, Andrew Caddick
Young players to look out for: Alex Loudon, James Tredwell, Robert Ferley
Other sports played: Golf, football
Other sports followed: Football (Manchester United)
Relaxations: 'Spending time with my girlfriend, music, golf'
Extras: Wellington Young Player of the Year in 1993. Wellington Players' Player of the Year in 1996. Played for Somerset 1997-99; has also played for Devon. Joined Kent in 2000. Recorded maiden first-class five-wicket return (5-65) v Essex at Tunbridge Wells 2001, going on to take 6-13 in the second innings for a maiden first-class ten-wicket match return. Also recorded maiden one-day five-wicket return in 2001, 5-18 v Cumberland at Barrow on C&G debut, winning Man of the Match award. Scored 26 v Sussex at Tunbridge Wells 2002, in the process sharing with Mark Ealham (83*) in a ground record tenth-wicket partnership for Kent (77)
Opinions on cricket: 'There should be more one-day floodlit matches as they gain the increased interest of children; they are the future of English cricket.'
Best batting: 26 Kent v Sussex, Tunbridge Wells 2002
Best bowling: 6-13 Kent v Essex, Tunbridge Wells 2001

2002 Season

	M	Inns	NO	Runs	HS	Avge	100s	50s	Ct	St	O	M	Runs	Wkts	Avge	Best	5wI	10wM
Test																		
All First	3	3	0	27	26	9.00	-	-	-	-	58	8	260	7	37.14	3-83	-	-
1-day Int																		
C & G																		
B & H	1	1	1	0	0 *	-	-	-	-	-	10	0	43	3	14.33	3-43	-	
1-day Lge	4	3	1	1	1 *	0.50	-	-	-	-	32	1	183	3	61.00	2-39	-	

Career Performances

	M	Inns	NO	Runs	HS	Avge	100s	50s	Ct	St	Balls	Runs	Wkts	Avge	Best	5wI	10wM
Test																	
All First	22	20	6	85	26	6.07	-	-	5	-	3101	1812	65	27.87	6-13	4	1
1-day Int																	
C & G	3	1	0	0	0	0.00	-	-	1	-	175	117	8	14.62	5-18	1	
B & H	1	1	1	0	0 *	-	-	-	-	-	60	43	3	14.33	3-43	-	
1-day Lge	18	9	5	6	2 *	1.50	-	-	2	-	810	643	19	33.84	2-19	-	

TROTT, I. J. L. Warwickshire

Name: Ian Jonathan Leonard Trott
Role: Right-hand bat, right-arm
medium bowler
Born: 22 April 1981, Cape Town,
South Africa
Height: 6ft **Weight:** 13st 5lbs
Nickname: Booger
County debut: No first-team appearance
1st-Class 50s: 7
1st-Class catches: 13
Strike rate: (career 84.25)
Parents: Ian and Donna
Marital status: 'Long-term girlfriend
Lesli-Anne'
Family links with cricket: Father is a
professional cricket coach. Brother (Kenny
Jackson) plays for Boland and used to play for
Western Province
Education: Rondebosch Boys' Prep; Rondebosch Boys' High; Stellenbosch University
Qualifications: Level 2 coaching
Off-season: 'Playing club cricket in Cape Town'
Overseas tours: South Africa U15 to England (U15 World Cup) 1996; South Africa
U19 to Pakistan 1998-99, to Sri Lanka (U19 World Cup) 2000
Overseas teams played for: Western Province; Boland
Career highlights to date: 'Winning the Standard Bank Cup 2000'
Cricket moments to forget: 'Losing in the final of the Standard Bank Cup 2002'
Cricket superstitions: 'Personal'
Cricketers particularly admired: Sachin Tendulkar, Steve Waugh
Young players to look out for: Jacques Rudolph, John McInroy
Other sports played: Hockey (Western Province U16, U18, U21), golf ('socially')
Other sports followed: Football (Tottenham Hotspur)

Relaxations: 'Music, watching sport'
Extras: Represented South Africa A. Struck a record debut score of 245 for Warwickshire 2nd XI v Somerset 2nd XI at Knowle & Dorridge 2002, sharing in a third-wicket stand of 397 with Trevor Penney. Is related to the late-19th-century Test cricketers Albert (Australia and England) and Harry Trott (Australia). Is a British passport holder and is not considered an overseas player
Opinions on cricket: 'Need to get the crowds back to the domestic game.'
Best batting: 93 Boland v Western Province, Cape Town 2000-01
Best bowling: 1-10 Western Province v North West, Potchefstroom 2001-02

2002 Season (did not make any first-class or one-day appearances)

Career Performances

	M	Inns	NO	Runs	HS	Avge	100s	50s	Ct	St	Balls	Runs	Wkts	Avge	Best	5wI	10wM
Test																	
All First	17	32	3	800	93	27.58	-	7	13	-	337	220	4	55.00	1-10	-	-
1-day Int																	
C & G																	
B & H																	
1-day Lge																	

TROUGHTON, J. O. — Warwickshire

Name: Jamie (<u>Jim</u>) Oliver Troughton
Role: Left-hand bat, slow left-arm bowler
Born: 2 March 1979, London
Height: 5ft 11in **Weight:** 12st 12lbs
Nickname: Troughts, JT
County debut: 2001
County cap: 2002
1000 runs in a season: 1
1st-Class 50s: 6
1st-Class 100s: 3
1st-Class catches: 8
One-Day 100s: 1
Place in batting averages: 32nd av. 50.80
Parents: Ali and David
Wife and date of marriage: Naomi, 28 September 2002
Family links with cricket: Father was a Middlesex Colt. Great-grandfather Henry Crichton played for Warwickshire

Education: Bridgetown School, Stratford-upon-Avon; Trinity School, Leamington Spa; Birmingham University
Qualifications: 8 GCSEs, 3 A-levels, BSc Sport & Exercise Psychology
Career outside cricket: Coaching/acting
Off-season: 'National Academy, Australia'
Overseas tours: Warwickshire Development of Excellence squad to Cape Town 1998; MCC to Australia and Singapore 2001; ECB National Academy to Australia and Sri Lanka 2002-03
Overseas teams played for: Harvinia CC, Free State, South Africa 2000; Avendale CC, Cape Town 2001-02
Career highlights to date: 'Getting first-team cap after back-to-back centuries'
Cricket moments to forget: 'Having to bowl at Graeme Hick on 194'
Cricket superstitions: 'None'
Cricketers particularly admired: Graham Thorpe, Steve Waugh, Allan Donald, Ashley Giles
Young players to look out for: Jimmy Anderson, Graham Wagg
Other sports played: Football (Stoke City youth player)
Other sports followed: 'Hooked on Manchester United since going to their soccer school aged five'
Injuries: Out for the last three weeks of the season with shin splints
Relaxations: 'Music, films, playing my guitar, spending time with Naomi, going abroad'
Extras: Is grandson of *Dr Who* actor Patrick Troughton; father also an actor. County colours U12-U19. Has represented England U15, U16 and U17. Represented ECB Midlands U19 v Pakistan U19 1998. Has won the Alec Hastilow Trophy and the Coney Edmonds Trophy (Warwickshire awards). Played for Warwickshire Board XI in the NatWest 1999 and 2000 and in the first and second rounds of the C&G 2002, which were played in August and September 2001; scored maiden one-day century (115*) v Cumberland at Millom in first round of C&G 2002. Warwickshire 2nd XI Player of the Year 2001. Scored maiden first-class century (131*) v Hampshire at West End 2002, following up with another century (130) in his next innings, v Leicestershire at Edgbaston 2002. Scored 115 v Kent at Edgbaston 2002, in the process sharing with Ashley Giles (68) in a record sixth-wicket partnership for Warwickshire in matches against Kent (124). Scored 63 in Warwickshire's second innings v Surrey at Edgbaston 2002, in the process passing 1000 runs in his first full season. Awarded Warwickshire cap 2002
Opinions on cricket: 'Tight cricketing schedule sometimes overshadows the importance of improving techniques in the nets. Good to see a higher emphasis placed on fitness; you need to be an athlete in today's game. Hope summers don't get any wetter.'
Best batting: 131* Warwickshire v Hampshire, West End 2002

2002 Season

	M	Inns	NO	Runs	HS	Avge	100s	50s	Ct	St	O	M	Runs	Wkts	Avge	Best	5wI	10wM
Test																		
All First	14	24	3	1067	131 *	50.80	3	6	8	-	18	0	89	0	-	-	-	-
1-day Int																		
C & G	1	1	0	32	32	32.00	-	-	1	-								
B & H	5	5	0	145	42	29.00	-	-	1	-								
1-day Lge	10	10	3	215	66 *	30.71	-	1	1	-								

Career Performances

	M	Inns	NO	Runs	HS	Avge	100s	50s	Ct	St	Balls	Runs	Wkts	Avge	Best	5wI	10wM
Test																	
All First	15	26	4	1099	131 *	49.95	3	6	8	-	120	106	0	-	-	-	-
1-day Int																	
C & G	5	5	1	254	115 *	63.50	1	1	3	-	130	83	7	11.85	4-23	-	
B & H	5	5	0	145	42	29.00	-	-	1	-							
1-day Lge	10	10	3	215	66 *	30.71	-	1	1	-							

TUDOR, A. J. — Surrey

Name: Alexander (<u>Alex</u>) Jeremy Tudor
Role: Right-hand bat, right-arm fast bowler
Born: 23 October 1977, West Brompton, London
Height: 6ft 4in **Weight:** 13st 7lbs
Nickname: Big Al, Bambi, Tudes
County debut: 1995
County cap: 1999
Test debut: 1998-99
Tests: 9
One-Day Internationals: 3
1st-Class 50s: 5
1st-Class 100s: 1
1st-Class 5 w. in innings: 13
1st-Class catches: 22
Place in batting averages: 260th av. 15.85 (2001 108th av. 31.76)
Place in bowling averages: 38th av. 26.76 (2001 92nd av. 35.65)
Strike rate: 46.00 (career 45.55)
Parents: Daryll and Jennifer
Marital status: Single

Family links with cricket: Brother was on the staff at The Oval
Education: Wandle Primary, Earlsfield; St Mark's C of E, Fulham; City of Westminster College
Off-season: With ECB National Academy in Australia
Overseas tours: England U15 to South Africa 1992-93; England U19 to Zimbabwe 1995-96, to Pakistan 1996-97; England to Australia 1998-99, to South Africa 1999-2000, to Pakistan 2000-01; England A to West Indies 2000-01; ECB National Academy to Australia 2001-02, to Australia 2002-03
Cricketers particularly admired: Curtly Ambrose, Brian Lara
Other sports followed: Basketball, football (QPR)
Relaxations: Listening to music
Extras: Played for London Schools at all ages from U8. Played for England U17 against India in 1994. MCC Young Cricketer. Took 4-89 in Australia's first innings on Test debut at Perth 1998-99; his victims included both Waugh twins. Scored 99* in second innings of the first Test v New Zealand at Edgbaston 1999, bettering the highest score by a nightwatchman for England (Harold Larwood's 98 v Australia at Sydney 1932-33) and winning the Man of the Match award; in total he scored 131 unbeaten runs in the match. Scored maiden first-class century (116) at The Oval 2001, in the process sharing in a new record seventh-wicket partnership for Surrey in matches v Essex (206) with Alec Stewart (106). Recorded match figures of 7-109 in third Test v Sri Lanka at Old Trafford 2002, winning Man of the Match award
Best batting: 116 Surrey v Essex, The Oval 2001
Best bowling: 7-48 Surrey v Lancashire, The Oval 2000
Stop press: Called up from the ECB National Academy squad in Adelaide to the England Test squad in Australia 2002-03 as cover in the pace bowling department

2002 Season

	M	Inns	NO	Runs	HS	Avge	100s	50s	Ct	St	O	M	Runs	Wkts	Avge	Best	5wI	10wM
Test	4	5	0	46	21	9.20	-	-	1	-	119.5	30	385	11	35.00	4-65	-	-
All First	10	14	0	222	61	15.85	-	1	2	-	322	74	1124	42	26.76	5-66	1	-
1-day Int	3	2	1	9	6	9.00	-	-	1	-	21.1	1	136	4	34.00	2-30	-	
C & G	1	1	1	17	17 *	-	-	-	-	-	9	0	40	0	-			
B & H	4	4	1	51	28 *	17.00	-	-	2	-	35.5	2	179	7	25.57	3-28	-	
1-day Lge	5	3	1	11	6	5.50	-	-	-	-	33	1	169	2	84.50	2-32	-	

Career Performances

	M	Inns	NO	Runs	HS	Avge	100s	50s	Ct	St	Balls	Runs	Wkts	Avge	Best	5wI	10wM
Test	9	14	3	226	99 *	20.54	-	1	1	-	1338	819	26	31.50	5-44	1	-
All First	82	108	24	1831	116	21.79	1	5	22	-	11891	7004	259	27.04	7-48	13	-
1-day Int	3	2	1	9	6	9.00	-	-	1	-	127	136	4	34.00	2-30	-	
C & G	7	3	2	28	17 *	28.00	-	-	2	-	399	269	10	26.90	4-39	-	
B & H	16	11	1	110	28 *	11.00	-	-	4	-	802	591	29	20.37	3-28	-	
1-day Lge	33	23	5	173	29 *	9.61	-	-	7	-	1280	1017	40	25.42	4-26	-	

TUFNELL, P. C. R. Middlesex

Name: Philip (<u>Phil</u>) Clive Roderick Tufnell
Role: Right-hand bat, left-arm spinner
Born: 29 April 1966, Hadley Wood, Hertfordshire
Height: 6ft **Weight:** 12st 7lbs
Nickname: The Cat, Tuffers
County debut: 1986
County cap: 1990
Benefit: 1999
Test debut: 1990-91
Tests: 42
One-Day Internationals: 20
50 wickets in a season: 9
1st-Class 50s: 1
1st-Class 5 w. in innings: 53
1st-Class 10 w. in match: 6
1st-Class catches: 106
One-Day 5 w. in innings: 1
Place in batting averages: 276th av. 12.71 (2001 279th av. 4.33)
Place in bowling averages: 70th av. 30.88 (2001 55th av. 28.68)
Strike rate: 68.64 (career 72.83)
Parents: Alan
Education: Highgate School
Qualifications: O-level in Art
Career outside cricket: Media work
Off-season: 'Working for my company Paragon Sports Management'
Overseas tours: England YC to West Indies 1984-85; England to Australia 1990-91, to New Zealand and Australia (World Cup) 1991-92, to India and Sri Lanka 1992-93, to West Indies 1993-94, to Australia 1994-95, to Zimbabwe and New Zealand 1996-97, to West Indies 1997-98, to South Africa 1999-2000
Overseas teams played for: Queensland University, Australia
Career highlights to date: 'The Oval v Aussies 1997'
Cricket moments to forget: 'None'
Cricketers particularly admired: 'All'
Young players to look out for: Rikki Clarke, James Anderson
Other sports followed: Football (Arsenal)
Relaxations: 'Sleeping and partying'
Extras: MCC Young Cricketer of the Year 1984 and Middlesex Uncapped Bowler of the Year 1987. Had match figures of 11-93 in the final Test v Australia at The Oval in 1997, winning the Man of the Match award. Took his 900th first-class wicket (Guy Welton) v Nottinghamshire at Lord's 2000. Middlesex Player of the Season 2000. Took his 1000th first-class wicket (Martin Love) v Durham at Lord's 2001. Took 6-96

v Glamorgan at Cardiff 2002 to record his 50th first-class five-wicket return
Best batting: 67* Middlesex v Worcestershire, Lord's 1996
Best bowling: 8-29 Middlesex v Glamorgan, Cardiff 1993

2002 Season

	M	Inns	NO	Runs	HS	Avge	100s	50s	Ct	St	O	M	Runs	Wkts	Avge	Best	5wI	10wM
Test																		
All First	14	15	8	89	45	12.71	-	-	3	-	514.5	104	1390	45	30.88	8-66	4	-
1-day Int																		
C & G																		
B & H																		
1-day Lge																		

Career Performances

	M	Inns	NO	Runs	HS	Avge	100s	50s	Ct	St	Balls	Runs	Wkts	Avge	Best	5wI	10wM
Test	42	59	29	153	22 *	5.10	-	-	12	-	11288	4560	121	37.68	7-47	5	2
All First	316	349	136	2066	67 *	9.69	-	1	106	-	76987	31026	1057	29.35	8-29	53	6
1-day Int	20	10	9	15	5 *	15.00	-	-	4	-	1020	699	19	36.78	4-22	-	
C & G	9	1	0	8	8	8.00	-	-	4	-	630	338	11	30.72	3-29	-	
B & H	18	9	4	62	18	12.40	-	-	2	-	971	700	18	38.88	3-32	-	
1-day Lge	39	14	8	36	13 *	6.00	-	-	5	-	1652	1277	47	27.17	5-28	1	

TURK, N. R. K. Sussex

Name: <u>Neil</u> Richard Keith Turk
Role: Left-hand bat, right-arm
medium bowler
Born: 28 April 1983, Cuckfield
Height: 6ft **Weight:** 11st 8lbs
Nickname: Turkish, Neilo
County debut: 2002 (one-day)
Parents: Keith and Lorraine
Marital status: Single
Family links with cricket: 'Father PE
teacher and grade coach. Brother county
junior. Mother junior cricket coach/manager'
Education: Estcots CP School, East
Grinstead; Sackville Community College,
East Grinstead; Exeter University (Sports
Science degree)
Qualifications: 9 GCSEs, 3 A-levels,
1 AS-level, FIFA-approved referee
Career outside cricket: 'Student/barman at present'

Off-season: 'Studying for my degree at Exeter University; playing hockey and golf'
Career highlights to date: 'County debut 2002 v Essex Eagles. Maiden 2nd XI Championship century (123) v Hampshire'
Cricket moments to forget: 'Being dismissed by Hampshire's wicket-keeper in a match for Sussex 2nd XI, having scored a century in the first innings; his only wicket to date'
Cricket superstitions: 'I don't believe you need superstitions to help you'
Cricketers particularly admired: Brian Lara, Jacques Kallis
Young players to look out for: Arul Suppiah
Other sports played: Hockey (West of England U21, Exeter University, ISCA HC), golf, football
Other sports followed: Football (Liverpool FC), rugby league (Wigan Warriors), hockey (East Grinstead HC)
Relaxations: 'I enjoy most sports; I also like to spend time on the golf course when I'm not playing cricket'
Extras: Youngest player ever to score a Sussex League century. Sussex U17 Player of the Year. Played for Sussex Board XI in the second round of the C&G 2003, which was played in September 2002. Appeared in one NUL match for Sussex 2002; is a Sussex Academy player. 'I never missed an episode of Dream Team on Sky One'
Opinions on cricket: 'The quality of cricket at present hopefully will attract a greater audience and help to promote the game to those people who do not already enjoy it. It is also good to see a number of young players given a chance at the top level.'

2002 Season

	M	Inns	NO	Runs	HS	Avge	100s	50s	Ct	St	O	M	Runs	Wkts	Avge	Best	5wI	10wM
Test																		
All First																		
1-day Int																		
C & G	1	1	0	20	20	20.00	-	-	-	-	2	0	21	0	-		-	-
B & H																		
1-day Lge	1	1	0	36	36	36.00	-	-	-	-								

Career Performances

	M	Inns	NO	Runs	HS	Avge	100s	50s	Ct	St	Balls	Runs	Wkts	Avge	Best	5wI	10wM
Test																		
All First																		
1-day Int																		
C & G	1	1	0	20	20	20.00	-	-	-	-	12	21	0	-		-	-
B & H																		
1-day Lge	1	1	0	36	36	36.00	-	-	-	-								

TURNER, R. J.   Somerset

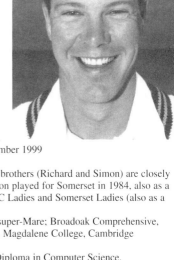

Name: Robert (<u>Rob</u>) Julian Turner
Role: Right-hand middle-order bat,
wicket-keeper
Born: 25 November 1967, Malvern
Height: 6ft 2in **Weight:** 14st
Nickname: Noddy, Turns
County debut: 1991
County cap: 1994
Benefit: 2002
1000 runs in a season: 2
50 dismissals in a season: 7
1st-Class 50s: 42
1st-Class 100s: 9
1st-Class catches: 555
1st-Class stumpings: 40
Place in batting averages: 140th av. 30.04
(2001 98th av. 33.08)
Parents: Derek and Doris
Wife and date of marriage: Lucy, 25 September 1999
Children: Jamie Jonathan Paul, 4 April 2001
Family links with cricket: 'Father and both brothers (Richard and Simon) are closely associated with Weston-super-Mare CC. Simon played for Somerset in 1984, also as a wicket-keeper. My wife, Lucy, plays for MCC Ladies and Somerset Ladies (also as a wicket-keeper!)'
Education: Uphill Primary School, Weston-super-Mare; Broadoak Comprehensive, Weston-super-Mare; Millfield School, Street; Magdalene College, Cambridge University
Qualifications: BEng (Hons) Engineering, Diploma in Computer Science, NCA coaching award, SFA securities representative of the London Stock Exchange
Career outside cricket: Rowan Dartington stockbrokers
Off-season: 'Completing benefit year, including an Ashes tour (Melbourne and Sydney), and then back working for club sponsors Rowan Dartington'
Overseas tours: Millfield School to Barbados 1985; Combined Universities to Barbados 1989; Qantas Airlines Tournament, Kuala Lumpur, Malaysia 1992-93; English Lions to New Zealand (Cricket Max) 1997; MCC to New Zealand 1999, to Canada 2000; England A to Bangladesh and New Zealand 1999-2000 (vice-captain)
Overseas teams played for: Claremont-Nedlands, Perth, Western Australia 1991-93
Career highlights to date: 'Winning the C&G Trophy 2001 at Lord's – especially catching a skyer to remove Afridi'
Cricket moments to forget: 'None – I enjoy it all!'
Cricket superstitions: 'Being last out onto the pitch (but that is just an excuse for being late, really!)'

Cricketers particularly admired: Jack Russell
Young players to look out for: Lachlan Cox, Adam Burns, Jamie Turner, Robert Bowler, Fraser Caddick, Felix Rose, Jack and Thomas Shine
Other sports played: Golf ('badly, but holed in one at the par three fourth at Oake Manor GC!')
Other sports followed: Football ('The Villa'), hockey (Taunton Vale Ladies)
Injuries: Out for one NUL game 'after twisted back getting up to speak at a benefit dinner!'
Relaxations: 'Being entertained by my son (18 months)'
Extras: Captain of Cambridge University (Blue 1988-91) and Combined Universities 1991. Equalled Somerset records of six catches in an innings and eight dismissals in a match v West Indians at Taunton 1995; also had eight dismissals in a match v Durham at Riverside in the same season. Wombwell Cricket Lovers' Society Wicket-keeper of the Year 1999. Highest-placed Englishman in the 1999 batting averages (6th with 1217 runs at 52.91). Sheffield Cricket Lovers' Society Allrounder of the Year 1999. Was on stand-by for England tours of West Indies 1997-98 and South Africa and Zimbabwe 1999-2000. Made nine dismissals (all caught) in the match v Surrey at Taunton 2001, breaking his own (shared) Somerset record. Took seven catches in an innings v Northamptonshire at Taunton 2001, breaking his own (shared) Somerset record
Opinions on cricket: 'If an overseas player has played in a cup competition for his county, then any overseas replacements should be cup-tied. If an English Test player is unable to play for his county, then he is not able to be replaced, so why should it be different?'
Best batting: 144 Somerset v Kent, Taunton 1997

2002 Season

	M	Inns	NO	Runs	HS	Avge	100s	50s	Ct	St	O	M	Runs	Wkts	Avge	Best	5wI	10wM
Test																		
All First	16	27	4	691	83 *	30.04	-	4	50	1								
1-day Int																		
C & G	5	4	1	88	47	29.33	-	-	4	1								
B & H	4	4	1	110	36	36.66	-	-	2	2								
1-day Lge	14	13	5	246	53 *	30.75	-	1	17	6								

Career Performances

	M	Inns	NO	Runs	HS	Avge	100s	50s	Ct	St	Balls	Runs	Wkts	Avge	Best	5wI	10wM
Test																	
All First	209	323	55	8255	144	30.80	9	42	555	40	79	58	0	-	-	-	-
1-day Int																	
C & G	27	22	8	491	52	35.07	-	2	39	3							
B & H	38	33	12	684	70	32.57	-	1	33	3							
1-day Lge	135	118	36	1904	67	23.21	-	6	128	23							

UDAL, S. D. Hampshire

Name: <u>Shaun</u> David Udal
Role: Right-hand bat, off-spin bowler
Born: 18 March 1969, Farnborough, Hants
Height: 6ft 3in **Weight:** 13st 10lbs
Nickname: Shaggy
County debut: 1989
County cap: 1992
Benefit: 2002
One-Day Internationals: 10
50 wickets in a season: 7
1st-Class 50s: 22
1st-Class 100s: 1
1st-Class 5 w. in innings: 29
1st-Class 10 w. in match: 4
1st-Class catches: 92
One-Day 5 w. in innings: 1
Place in batting averages: 174th av. 25.80
(2001 169th av. 23.00)

Place in bowling averages: 87th av. 33.17 (2001 60th av. 29.81)
Strike rate: 67.19 (career 69.80)
Parents: Robin Francis and Mary Elizabeth
Wife and date of marriage: Emma Jane, 5 October 1991
Children: Katherine Mary, 26 August 1992; Rebecca Jane, 17 November 1995
Family links with cricket: Grandfather (G. F. Udal) played for Leicestershire and Middlesex. Father played for Camberley CC and also for Surrey Colts; brother Gary is captain of Camberley 1st XI
Education: Tower Hill Infants and Junior; Cove Comprehensive
Qualifications: 8 CSEs, qualified print finisher, company director
Career outside cricket: Sales, PR and marketing for the Karran Group
Off-season: 'Holiday, work, golf tour to Spain, benefit, ankle operation, Christmas, recovery, two weeks in Barbados, then pre-season!'
Overseas tours: England to Australia 1994-95; England A to Pakistan 1995-96; England XI to New Zealand (Cricket Max) 1997; Hampshire to Anguilla 1998, to Cape Town 2001
Overseas teams played for: Hamilton Wickham, Newcastle, NSW 1989-90
Career highlights to date: 'Winning NatWest and B&H with Hants and playing for England'
Cricket moments to forget: 'Getting out hooking as nightwatchman – twice! Any time Robin Smith goes near the ball while fielding'
Cricket superstitions: 'Always put left pad, glove etc. on first'
Cricketers particularly admired: Ian Botham, Shane Warne, Robin Smith
Young players to look out for: Chris Tremlett, John Francis, Jimmy Anderson

Other sports played: Golf (14 handicap), 'football on a Sunday morning until two sendings-off in successive weeks!'
Other sports followed: Football (West Ham Utd, Aldershot Town, Basingstoke Town)
Injuries: Operation during winter 2002-03 for an ankle complaint ('screws rubbing against bone')
Relaxations: 'Going out in good company, and my two lovely daughters and wife'
Extras: Has taken two hat-tricks in club cricket. Has scored a double hundred (202) in a 40-over club game. Man of the Match on NatWest debut against Berkshire 1991. Took 8-50 v Sussex in the first game of the 1992 season, his seventh Championship match. Named Hampshire Cricket Association Player of the Year 1993. Vice-captain of Hampshire 1998-2000. Passed 550 first-class wickets and 5000 first-class runs during the 2002 season. Hampshire Players' Player of the Year 2001, 2002. B&H Gold Award for his 4-36 v Surrey at The Oval 2002
Opinions on cricket: 'Not convinced two overseas players is right for English cricket. Pitches have to improve. County cricket does have a future if people give it a chance. Please support the players and the game more – i.e. ex-players who continually criticise on TV commentaries.'
Best batting: 117* Hampshire v Warwickshire, Southampton 1997
Best bowling: 8-50 Hampshire v Sussex, Southampton 1992

2002 Season

	M	Inns	NO	Runs	HS	Avge	100s	50s	Ct	St	O	M	Runs	Wkts	Avge	Best	5wI	10wM
Test																		
All First	17	26	6	516	88	25.80	-	1	9	-	627.1	146	1858	56	33.17	5-56	4	-
1-day Int																		
C & G	2	0	0	0	0	-	-	-	-	-	20	1	90	2	45.00	2-33	-	
B & H	5	4	1	77	24	25.66	-	-	-	-	49	4	177	7	25.28	4-36	-	
1-day Lge	15	13	3	197	58	19.70	-	2	4	-	104.2	2	467	17	27.47	4-31	-	

Career Performances

	M	Inns	NO	Runs	HS	Avge	100s	50s	Ct	St	Balls	Runs	Wkts	Avge	Best	5wI	10wM
Test																	
All First	200	286	52	5293	117 *	22.61	1	22	92	-	39232	19105	562	33.99	8-50	29	4
1-day Int	10	6	4	35	11 *	17.50	-	-	1	-	570	371	8	46.37	2-37	-	
C & G	30	12	5	136	39 *	19.42	-	-	12	-	1695	1003	39	25.71	4-20	-	
B & H	48	30	7	341	34	14.82	-	-	13	-	2694	1738	54	32.18	4-36	-	
1-day Lge	189	129	36	1421	78	15.27	-	8	63	-	8031	6323	209	30.25	5-43	1	

VAN DER GUCHT, C. G.   Hampshire

Name: <u>Charlie</u> Graham Van der Gucht
Role: Left-hand bat, left-arm orthodox
spin bowler
Born: 14 January 1980, London
Height: 6ft 1in **Weight:** 11st 5lb
Nickname: Gucht
County debut: 2000
Strike rate: (career 51.00)
Parents: Nicky and Mike
Marital status: Single
Family links with cricket: Grandfather (P. I.
Van der Gucht) played for Gloucestershire
Education: Cothill House; Radley College;
Durham University
Qualifications: 9 GCSEs, 3 A-levels, 2.1
degree in History, Level 2 coaching award
Off-season: 'Six months' training in Sydney'
Overseas tours: West of England to West
Indies 1995; British Universities to Port Elizabeth 1999; Durham University to Cape
Town 2000
Overseas teams played for: Gordon CC, Sydney 1998-99
Career highlights to date: 'First-class debut v Zimbabweans'
Cricketers particularly admired: Phil Tufnell, Muttiah Muralitharan, Garry Sobers,
Henry Fitz
Young players to look out for: Chris Tremlett
Other sports played: Rackets
Other sports followed: Football (Southampton)
Relaxations: Reading
Extras: Leading wicket-taker at Gordon club in Sydney 1998-99. Played for
Hampshire Board XI in NatWest 1999, winning Man of the Match award (3-35) in
fourth round v Glamorgan at Southampton. Played for Durham University CCE in
2001. Took 4-36 for Durham University v Loughborough University in the BUSA final
at Fenner's 2001
Opinions on cricket: 'Good game.'
Best batting: 38 DUCCE v Lancashire, Durham 2001
Best bowling: 3-75 Hampshire v Zimbabweans, Southampton 2000

2002 Season (did not make any first-class or one-day appearances)

Career Performances

	M	Inns	NO	Runs	HS	Avge	100s	50s	Ct	St	Balls	Runs	Wkts	Avge	Best	5wI	10wM
Test																	
All First	2	2	1	38	38	38.00	-	-	-	-	204	138	4	34.50	3-75	-	-
1-day Int																	
C & G	3	2	0	4	3	2.00	-	-	-	-	144	95	5	19.00	3-35	-	
B & H																	
1-day Lge																	

VAUGHAN, M. P. — Yorkshire

Name: Michael Paul Vaughan
Role: Right-hand bat, off-spin bowler
Born: 29 October 1974, Eccles, Manchester
Height: 6ft 2in **Weight:** 11st 7lbs
Nickname: Frankie, Virgil
County debut: 1993
County cap: 1995
Test debut: 1999-2000
Tests: 23
One-Day Internationals: 17
1000 runs in a season: 4
1st-Class 50s: 47
1st-Class 100s: 26
1st-Class catches: 85
One-Day 100s: 1
Place in batting averages: 5th av. 75.07
(2001 25th av. 52.43)
Strike rate: 89.00 (career 78.64)
Parents: Graham John and Dee
Marital status: Single
Family links with cricket: Father played league cricket for Worsley CC. Brother plays for Sheffield Collegiate. Mother is related to the famous Tyldesley family (Lancashire and England)
Education: St Marks, Worsley, Manchester; Dore Juniors, Sheffield; Silverdale Comprehensive, Sheffield
Qualifications: 7 GCSEs
Off-season: Touring with England
Overseas tours: Yorkshire to West Indies 1994, to South Africa 1995, to Zimbabwe 1996; England U19 to India 1992-93, to Sri Lanka 1993-94 (captain); England A to India 1994-95, to Australia 1996-97, to Zimbabwe and South Africa 1998-99 (captain);

England to South Africa 1999-2000, to Pakistan and Sri Lanka 2000-01, to India and New Zealand 2001-02, to Australia 2002-03

Cricket moments to forget: 'My one-day series in 2001'

Cricketers particularly admired: Darren Lehmann, 'all the Yorkshire and England squads'

Young players to look out for: Richard Dawson, Matthew Wood

Other sports played: Football (Baslow FC), golf

Other sports followed: Football (Sheffield Wednesday), all golf

Injuries: Knee surgery

Relaxations: Most sports. 'Enjoy a good meal with friends'

Extras: *Daily Telegraph* U15 Batsman of the Year 1990. Maurice Leyland Batting Award 1990. The Cricket Society's Most Promising Young Cricketer 1993. A. A. Thompson Memorial Trophy – The Roses Cricketer of the Year 1993. Scored 1066 runs in first full season of first-class cricket in 1994. Captained England U19 in home series v India U19 1994. Scored two 100s (100 and 151) v Essex at Chelmsford 1999. Became the 600th player to represent England when he made his Test debut v South Africa at Johannesburg 1999-2000. Struck 69 in England's only innings of the rain-shortened fifth Test at Centurion, January 2000, a match-winning maiden Test fifty that earned him the Man of the Match award. Man of the Match for his 76 in England's only innings in the fourth Test v West Indies at his home ground of Headingley 2000. B&H Gold Award for his 128-ball 125* in the quarter-final v Somerset at Taunton 2001; it was his maiden one-day century. Scored maiden Test century (120) at Old Trafford 2001, in the process sharing in a record partnership for any wicket for England in Tests v Pakistan (267) with Graham Thorpe (138). Became the second England cricketer (after Graham Gooch) and the seventh cricketer overall in Tests to be given out handled the ball, when he was out for 64 v India in the third Test at Bangalore 2001-02. Scored 115 as England followed on in first Test v Sri Lanka at Lord's 2002, in the process completing 10,000 runs in first-class cricket and sharing with Marcus Trescothick (76) in a record first-wicket partnership for England in Tests v Sri Lanka (168). Took part in first-wicket stand of 50 in five overs with Marcus Trescothick to bring England victory with an over to spare in the third Test v Sri Lanka at Old Trafford 2002. Scored 197 in the second Test v India at Trent Bridge 2002, winning the Man of the Man award. Scored 195 in the fourth Test v India at The Oval 2002, in the process becoming only the sixth batsman to score four Test centuries in an English summer; ended rubber v India with 615 runs (av. 102.50) to become England's Man of the Series. Professional Cricketers' Association Player of the Year 2002. Selected for the England one-day squad for the ICC Champions Trophy in Sri Lanka 2002-03 but was ruled out after requiring knee surgery; replaced by Owais Shah. ECB 12-month contract 2002-03

Best batting: 197 England v India, Trent Bridge 2002

Best bowling: 4-39 Yorkshire v Oxford University, The Parks 1994

Stop press: Scored 177 in second Test v Australia at Adelaide 2002-03, equalling England's second highest Test score on the ground (by Wally Hammond in 1929) and falling just ten runs short of the highest (187 by Jack Hobbs in 1912). Scored 145 in England's second innings of fourth Test v Australia at Melbourne 2002-03, becoming the highest-scoring batsman in Test cricket for the calendar year 2002 with 1481 runs; it was the third highest total by any Test batsman in a calendar year after Viv Richards' 1710 in 1976 and Sunil Gavaskar's 1555 in 1979. Scored century (183) in fifth Test v Australia at Sydney 2002-03, becoming only the fifth England batsman to score three Test centuries (or more) in a series in Australia; he ended the rubber with 633 runs (av. 63.30), more than any other batsman on either side, was named Man of the Series and rose to second place behind Matthew Hayden in the PricewaterhouseCoopers Ratings for Test batsmen to become the highest ranked England batsman since Graham Gooch occupied the top spot in the early 1990s. Selected for England squad for 2002-03 World Cup

2002 Season

	M	Inns	NO	Runs	HS	Avge	100s	50s	Ct	St	O	M	Runs	Wkts	Avge	Best	5wI	10wM
Test	7	12	2	900	197	90.00	4	2	5	-	56	10	164	4	41.00	2-71	-	-
All First	9	15	2	976	197	75.07	4	3	5	-	59.2	10	185	4	46.25	2-71	-	-
1-day Int	4	3	0	47	30	15.66	-	-	-	-	6	1	22	4	5.50	4-22	-	
C & G	4	3	1	136	63 *	68.00	-	1	2	-	4	0	20	0	-		-	-
B & H	3	3	0	77	32	25.66	-	-	-	-								
1-day Lge	3	3	0	20	20	6.66	-	-	-	-								

Career Performances

	M	Inns	NO	Runs	HS	Avge	100s	50s	Ct	St	Balls	Runs	Wkts	Avge	Best	5wI	10wM
Test	23	39	3	1710	197	47.50	5	5	17	-	540	310	4	77.50	2-71	-	-
All First	176	308	17	10791	197	37.08	26	47	85	-	8808	4910	112	43.83	4-39	-	-
1-day Int	17	16	1	295	63	19.66	-	2	3	-	166	134	6	22.33	4-22	-	
C & G	23	22	2	619	85	30.95	-	5	6	-	294	176	5	35.20	1-4	-	
B & H	40	38	3	1190	125 *	34.00	1	7	12	-	765	515	19	27.10	4-46	-	
1-day Lge	92	90	6	1886	72	22.45	-	8	29	-	998	813	31	26.22	4-27	-	

---

88. Which West Indies bowler took 134 County Championship wickets in 1982?

WADE, J. — Northamptonshire

Name: James Wade
Role: Right-hand middle-order bat, slip fielder
Born: 7 May 1981, Bedford
Height: 6ft **Weight:** 12st
Nickname: Wadey, Woo
County debut: No first-team appearance
Parents: Nigel and Jo
Marital status: Single
Family links with cricket: 'Dad played club cricket locally'
Education: Bedford Modern School; Loughborough University
Qualifications: 9 GCSEs, 3 A-levels, Level I coaching
Career outside cricket: 'Investor, entrepreneur'
Off-season: 'Loughborough University'
Overseas tours: Bedford Modern School to Caribbean 1997, 1999; Northamptonshire U19 to South Africa 2000
Overseas teams played for: South Sydney 1999-2000
Career highlights to date: 'Being in the 12 for a first-class game v Durham 2002'
Cricketers particularly admired: Mark Waugh
Young players to look out for: Rob White, Andy Umpleby
Other sports played: Football (Watford School of Excellence 1994-95)
Other sports followed: 'England'
Relaxations: 'Investing, horses, football'
Extras: Played for Northamptonshire Board XI in the C&G 2001 and in the first round of the C&G 2002, which was played in August 2001
Opinions on cricket: 'Need for a higher turnover of players. Too many hangers-on with limited ambition in 2nd XIs.'

2002 Season (did not make any first-class or one-day appearances)

Career Performances

	M	Inns	NO	Runs	HS	Avge	100s	50s	Ct	St	Balls	Runs	Wkts	Avge	Best	5wI	10wM
Test																	
All First																	
1-day Int																	
C & G	2	2	0	50	38	25.00	-	-	1	-	12	37	0	-	-	-	-
B & H																	
1-day Lge																	

WAGG, G. G. Warwickshire

Name: <u>Graham</u> Grant Wagg
Role: Right-hand bat, left-arm
fast-medium bowler
Born: 28 April 1983, Rugby
Height: 6ft **Weight:** 12st 10lbs
Nickname: Stiggy, Waggy, Captain
Caveman, Wild Card, Ug
County debut: 2002
1st-Class 50s: 1
1st-Class catches: 1
Place in batting averages: 166th av. 26.83
Place in bowling averages: 55th av. 28.58
Strike rate: 41.41 (career 41.41)
Parents: John and Dawn
Marital status: Girlfriend Emma
Family links with cricket: Father is
qualified coach

Education: Boughton-Leigh Primary, Rugby;
Ashlawn School, Rugby
Qualifications: Level 1 cricket coach
Off-season: 'Doorman at Flores in Rugby'; ECB National Academy
Overseas tours: Warwickshire CCC Development tour to South Africa 1998,
to West Indies 2000
Overseas teams played for: Hams Tech, East London, South Africa 1999
Career highlights to date: 'Four wickets and 50 on first-class debut'
Cricket moments to forget: 'Being hit for 10 off the last two balls against India U19
when they needed eight to win'
Cricketers particularly admired: Stuart MacGill, John Wagg
Other sports played: Golf, carp fishing
Other sports followed: Football (Man United), cricket (Leamington CC)
Injuries: Out for the last three weeks of the season with a lower back injury
Relaxations: 'Fishing, music, clubbing'
Extras: Represented England U16, U17 and U18. Played for Warwickshire Board XI
in the NatWest 2000 and in the C&G 2002. Member of Warwickshire's ECB U19
County Championship winning squad 2001. Took 5-57 and scored 40* for
Development of Excellence (Midlands) XI v West Indies U19 at Oakham School 2001.
Represented England U19 v India U19 in 'Test' series (3/3) and one-day series (2/3)
2002. Scored 42* from 50 balls, 51 from 57 balls and took 4-43 on first-class debut v
Somerset at Edgbaston 2002. Took 4-50 on NUL debut, v Kent at Edgbaston 2002
Opinions on cricket: 'Should be allowed to play for county instead of having to play
for the [England] U19s.'

715

Best batting: 51 Warwickshire v Somerset, Edgbaston 2002
Best bowling: 4-43 Warwickshire v Somerset, Edgbaston 2002
Stop press: Selected for the ECB National Academy squad to Australia and Sri Lanka 2002-03 but was forced to withdraw with a back injury

2002 Season

	M	Inns	NO	Runs	HS	Avge	100s	50s	Ct	St	O	M	Runs	Wkts	Avge	Best	5wI	10wM
Test																		
All First	5	8	2	161	51	26.83	-	1	1	-	82.5	13	343	12	28.58	4-43	-	-
1-day Int																		
C & G	1	1	0	21	21	21.00	-	-	-	-	10	3	35	3	11.66	3-35	-	
B & H																		
1-day Lge	3	1	0	2	2	2.00	-	-	2	-	22	1	106	6	17.66	4-50	-	

Career Performances

	M	Inns	NO	Runs	HS	Avge	100s	50s	Ct	St	Balls	Runs	Wkts	Avge	Best	5wI	10wM
Test																	
All First	5	8	2	161	51	26.83	-	1	1	-	497	343	12	28.58	4-43	-	-
1-day Int																	
C & G	2	2	0	21	21	10.50	-	-	-	-	90	52	3	17.33	3-35	-	
B & H																	
1-day Lge	3	1	0	2	2	2.00	-	-	2	-	132	106	6	17.66	4-50	-	

WAGH, M. A. Warwickshire

Name: <u>Mark</u> Anant Wagh
Role: Right-hand bat, off-spin bowler
Born: 20 October 1976, Birmingham
Height: 6ft 2in **Weight:** 13st
Nickname: Waggy
County debut: 1997
County cap: 2000
1000 runs in a season: 1
1st-Class 50s: 20
1st-Class 100s: 11
1st-Class 200s: 1
1st-Class 300s: 1
1st-Class 5 w. in innings: 1
1st-Class catches: 38
Place in batting averages: 157th av. 27.94 (2001 16th av. 58.04)
Place in bowling averages: 124th av. 40.26 (2001 100th av. 36.38)

Strike rate: 81.20 (career 95.75)
Parents: Mohan and Rita
Marital status: Single
Education: Harborne Infants and Junior School; King Edward's School, Birmingham; Keble College, Oxford
Qualifications: BA degree, Level 2 coaching award
Overseas tours: Warwickshire U19 to South Africa 1992; ECB National Academy to Australia 2001-02
Career highlights to date: '315 at Lord's 2001'
Cricket moments to forget: 'Too many to mention'
Cricketers particularly admired: Andy Flower
Young players to look out for: Jim Troughton
Extras: Oxford Blue 1996-98; Oxford University captain 1997. Scored maiden first-class century (116) v Glamorgan at The Parks 1997, following up with another 100 (101) in the second innings to become the first batsman to score a century in each innings of a match for Oxford University since Imran Khan did so v Notts in 1974 and the fourth youngest batsman (at 20 years, 230 days) to score twin centuries in English first-class cricket. Attended Zimbabwe Cricket Academy 1999. With Michael Powell, shared in record first-wicket stand for Warwickshire in matches v Essex (230) at Chelmsford 2000. His 315 v Middlesex at Lord's 2001 is the second highest score by a batsman for Warwickshire (behind Brian Lara's 501* in 1994) and the equal second highest individual Championship score made at Lord's (behind Jack Hobbs's 316 in 1926). Recorded maiden first-class five-wicket return (5-137) v Yorkshire at Edgbaston 2002
Best batting: 315 Warwickshire v Middlesex, Lord's 2001
Best bowling: 5-137 Warwickshire v Yorkshire, Edgbaston 2002

2002 Season

	M	Inns	NO	Runs	HS	Avge	100s	50s	Ct	St	O	M	Runs	Wkts	Avge	Best	5wI	10wM
Test																		
All First	10	18	0	503	109	27.94	1	2	3	-	203	43	604	15	40.26	5-137	1	-
1-day Int																		
C & G																		
B & H																		
1-day Lge	6	6	0	181	84	30.16	-	1	-	-	15	0	71	0	-	-	-	-

Career Performances

	M	Inns	NO	Runs	HS	Avge	100s	50s	Ct	St	Balls	Runs	Wkts	Avge	Best	5wI	10wM
Test																	
All First	92	148	13	5074	315	37.58	13	20	38	-	5554	2803	58	48.32	5-137	1	-
1-day Int																	
C & G	3	3	0	68	46	22.66	-	-	-	-							
B & H	9	9	1	137	39	17.12	-	-	-	-	174	119	3	39.66	1-39	-	
1-day Lge	24	22	1	478	84	22.76	-	4	1	-	132	112	0	-	-	-	-

WALKER, G. W. Leicestershire

Name: <u>George</u> William Walker
Role: Left-hand bat, slow left-arm bowler
Born: 12 May 1984, Norwich
Height: 5ft 10in **Weight:** 10st 7lbs
Nickname: Walksy
County debut: 2002
1st-Class catches: 1
Parents: John and Sarah
Marital status: Single
Education: Town Close Prep School,
Norwich; Norwich School
Qualifications: 9 GCSEs, 4 AS-levels,
ECB Level 1 coach
Career highlights to date: 'First Minor
Counties wicket – Derek Randall in his last
game for Suffolk'

Cricketers particularly admired:
Ashley Giles, Brian Lara
Other sports played: Hockey, tennis, football, 'anything'
Other sports followed: Football (Norwich City); cricket, football, rugby (England
national teams)
Relaxations: 'Meeting up with friends; listening to a lot of music; films, videos, golf'
Extras: Played for Norfolk from U12 to 1st XI. Represented Midlands U13 and U14
and England U14, U15 and U17
Opinions on cricket: 'Introduce what they've done in New Zealand – Cricket Max –
faster, more exciting game for the crowd.'
Best batting: 37* Leicestershire v Kent, Canterbury 2002

2002 Season

	M	Inns	NO	Runs	HS	Avge	100s	50s	Ct	St	O	M	Runs	Wkts	Avge	Best	5wl	10wM
Test																		
All First	1	2	1	44	37 *	44.00	-	-	1	-	13	2	50	0	-	-	-	-
1-day Int																		
C & G																		
B & H																		
1-day Lge																		

Career Performances

	M	Inns	NO	Runs	HS	Avge	100s	50s	Ct	St	Balls	Runs	Wkts	Avge	Best	5wI	10wM
Test																	
All First	1	2	1	44	37 *	44.00	-	-	1	-	78	50	0	-	-	-	-
1-day Int																	
C & G																	
B & H																	
1-day Lge																	

WALKER, M. J.   Kent

Name: <u>Matthew</u> Jonathan Walker
Role: Left-hand bat, right-arm medium-fast bowler
Born: 2 January 1974, Gravesend
Height: 5ft 6in **Weight:** 12st 6lbs
Nickname: Walks, Walkdog, Pumba, Sweetie Pud, Cheeky Monkey, Dicky Neurerker, Merse
County debut: 1992-93
County cap: 2000
1st-Class 50s: 14
1st-Class 100s: 6
1st-Class 200s: 1
1st-Class catches: 59
One-Day 100s: 2
Place in batting averages: 231st av. 19.10 (2001 51st av. 44.77)
Strike rate: (career 113.00)
Parents: Richard and June
Wife and date of marriage: Claudia, 25 September 1999
Family links with cricket: Grandfather Jack played one game for Kent as a wicket-keeper. Father played for Kent and Middlesex 2nd XIs and was on Lord's groundstaff. Mother coached ex-England Ladies captain Megan Lear
Education: Shorne C of E Primary School; King's School, Rochester
Qualifications: 9 GCSEs, 2 A-levels, advanced coaching award
Career outside cricket: Teacher
Overseas tours: Kent U17 to New Zealand 1990-91; England U19 to Pakistan 1991-92, to India 1992-93 (captain); Kent to Zimbabwe 1992-93, to Port Elizabeth 2001
Career highlights to date: 'Captaining England U19. Winning Norwich Union League 2001'
Cricket moments to forget: 'Losing Lord's [B&H] final against Surrey 1997'

Cricketers particularly admired: Sachin Tendulkar, Darren Lehmann, Damien Martyn

Young players to look out for: Alex Loudon, James Tredwell

Other sports played: Hockey (England U14-U21 [captain U15-U17], Kent U14-U21, South East U16-U18), rugby (Kent U18), football (trials for Chelsea and Gillingham), athletics (Kent U15 javelin champion)

Other sports followed: Football (Charlton Athletic), rugby (Gravesend RFC), hockey (Canterbury HC)

Relaxations: Music and films ('avid collector of both')

Extras: Captained England U16 cricket team and England U16 hockey team in same year. Captained England U19 v West Indies U19 in 1993 home series. Sir John Hobbs Silver Jubilee Memorial Prize for outstanding U16 cricketer 1989; *Daily Telegraph* U15 batting award 1989. Woolwich Kent League's Young Cricketer of the Year 1994. Scored 275* against Somerset in 1996 – the highest ever individual score by a Kent batsman at Canterbury – and was on the pitch for the whole game. B&H Gold Award for his 106* v Essex at Chelmsford 2001. Scored 94 v Worcestershire at Canterbury in the NUL 2002, in the process sharing with Paul Nixon (60) in a record sixth-wicket partnership for Kent in the one-day league (116). Became an Eminent Roffensian in 1995

Best batting: 275* Kent v Somerset, Canterbury 1996

Best bowling: 1-3 First-Class Counties XI v New Zealand A, Milton Keynes 2000

2002 Season

	M	Inns	NO	Runs	HS	Avge	100s	50s	Ct	St	O	M	Runs	Wkts	Avge	Best	5wl	10wM
Test																		
All First	12	23	3	382	46	19.10	-	-	3	-	24.3	4	98	0	-	-	-	-
1-day Int																		
C & G	4	4	1	59	35	19.66	-	-	1	-	5	0	22	0	-	-	-	
B & H	5	4	1	167	64	55.66	-	1	-	-	3	0	22	0	-	-	-	
1-day Lge	13	13	2	444	94	40.36	-	3	2	-								

Career Performances

	M	Inns	NO	Runs	HS	Avge	100s	50s	Ct	St	Balls	Runs	Wkts	Avge	Best	5wl	10wM
Test																	
All First	99	165	18	4212	275 *	28.65	7	14	59	-	904	488	8	61.00	1-3	-	-
1-day Int																	
C & G	14	13	3	313	73	31.30	-	2	3	-	132	92	2	46.00	1-33	-	
B & H	34	31	5	1105	117	42.50	2	7	10	-	42	38	1	38.00	1-16	-	
1-day Lge	112	106	11	2070	94	21.78	-	10	26	-	351	281	15	18.73	4-24	-	

WALLACE, M. A.   Glamorgan

Name: <u>Mark</u> Alex Wallace
Role: Left-hand bat, wicket-keeper
Born: 19 November 1981, Abergavenny
Height: 5ft 10in **Weight:** 12st
Nickname: Wally, Gromit, Marcellus
County debut: 1999
50 dismissals in a season: 1
1st-Class 50s: 6
1st-Class 100s: 1
1st-Class catches: 107
1st-Class stumpings: 4
Place in batting averages: 171st av. 26.33
(2001 173rd av. 22.30)
Parents: Ryland and Alvine
Marital status: Single
Family links with cricket: 'Father plays for
Abergavenny Beavers and Wales Over 50s'
Education: Crickhowell Primary School;
Crickhowell High School
Qualifications: 10 GCSEs, 2 A-levels
Off-season: 'In Adelaide with ECB National Academy'
Overseas tours: Gwent U15 to South Africa 1996; Wales U16 to Jersey 1996, 1997;
England U19 to New Zealand 1998-99, to Malaysia and (U19 World Cup) Sri Lanka
1999-2000, to India 2000-01; ECB National Academy to Australia 2001-02, to
Australia and Sri Lanka 2002-03
Career highlights to date: 'Every team song I've ever been involved in. Winning
NUL 2002. Academy selection'
Cricket moments to forget: 'The relegation of the Beavers from the Thomas Carroll
East Wales Premier League'
Cricketers particularly admired: Ian Healy, Steve Rhodes, Keith Piper, Alec Stewart,
Adam Gilchrist
Young players to look out for: David Harrison, Jamie Pipe, Jon Hughes, Matthew
Wood ('both'), Kyle Hogg
Other sports played: Football, golf, touch rugby, pool ('Number 2 seed')
Other sports followed: Football ('the mighty Merthyr Tydfil FC')
Injuries: 'A few slipped discs facing Bolts in the nets'
Relaxations: 'Golf, sleep, a few racks with Long, PR work'
Extras: Represented England U17 at the ECC Colts Festival in Northern Ireland 1999.
Represented England U19 against Pakistan U19 1998, Australia U19 1999 and Sri
Lanka U19 (as captain for second 'Test') 2000. Made first-class debut v Somerset
1999 aged 17 years 287 days – youngest ever Glamorgan wicket-keeper. NBC Denis
Compton Award 1999. Took eight catches in match v Kent at Maidstone 2001, one

short of Colin Metson's Glamorgan record. Took seven catches in the match and scored 63* and 18* in win over Surrey at The Oval 2001. Captained ECB National Academy to innings victory over Commonwealth Bank [Australian] Cricket Academy in Adelaide 2001-02. Scored maiden first-class century (106*) v Derbyshire at Cardiff 2002. Recorded 50 first-class dismissals (61) in a season for the first time 2002
Opinions on cricket: 'Roger Skyrme is the finest room attendant on the circuit. EU passport situation needs to be sorted. Tea break too short.'
Best batting: 106* Glamorgan v Derbyshire, Cardiff 2002

2002 Season

	M	Inns	NO	Runs	HS	Avge	100s	50s	Ct	St	O	M	Runs	Wkts	Avge	Best	5wI	10wM
Test																		
All First	17	25	4	553	106 *	26.33	1	2	58	3								
1-day Int																		
C & G	2	1	0	5	5	5.00	-	-	2	-								
B & H	2	2	0	70	39	35.00	-	-	2	-								
1-day Lge	15	12	3	157	37 *	17.44	-	-	17	6								

Career Performances

	M	Inns	NO	Runs	HS	Avge	100s	50s	Ct	St	Balls	Runs	Wkts	Avge	Best	5wI	10wM
Test																	
All First	33	50	9	1057	106 *	25.78	1	6	107	4							
1-day Int																	
C & G	2	1	0	5	5	5.00	-	-	2	-							
B & H	2	2	0	70	39	35.00	-	-	2	-							
1-day Lge	22	17	4	175	37 *	13.46	-	-	24	9							

WARD, D. M.   Surrey

Name: <u>David</u> Mark Ward
Role: Right-hand bat, right-arm off-spin bowler, occasional wicket-keeper
Born: 10 February 1961, Croydon
Height: 6ft 1in
Nickname: Cocker, Wardy, Jaws, Gnasher, Fat Boy, Piano Man
County debut: 1985
County cap: 1990
Benefit: 1996
1000 runs in a season: 2
1st-Class 50s: 33
1st-Class 100s: 13
1st-Class 200s: 3
1st-Class catches: 122
1st-Class stumpings: 3

One-Day 100s: 5
Education: Haling Manor High School;
Croydon Technical College
Qualifications: 2 O-levels, Advanced
City & Guilds in Carpentry and Joinery
Overseas tours: Surrey to Barbados 1984,
1989, 1991; Lancashire to Mombasa 1990;
MCC to Bahrain 1994-95, to Canada 2000-
01; England VI to Hong Kong 1996
Overseas teams played for: Caulfield,
Melbourne 1984-87; Sunshine, Melbourne
1988-89; Perth, Western Australia 1990-91;
St Augustine, Cape Town 1992-93
Cricketers particularly admired:
Adam Hollioake, Graham Thorpe, Joey
Benjamin, Ian Austin, Andy Pick
Extras: Scored 2072 first-class runs in 1990,
becoming the first Surrey batsman since John

Edrich to score 2000 runs in a season. Scored 263 v Kent at Canterbury 1990, in the
process sharing with Darren Bicknell (186) in a record third-wicket partnership for
Surrey (413). Scored 55-ball century (out for 108) v Durham at Stockton-on-Tees in
the one-day league 1996; during his innings he struck eight sixes in the space of 14
deliveries and his second fifty took just 13 balls. Retired at the end of the 1996 season
and was recalled by Surrey for one NUL match in 2002, scoring a 52-ball 78 v
Northamptonshire at Whitgift School, where he is cricket coach. Has played for
Hertfordshire since 1997
Best batting: 294* Surrey v Derbyshire, The Oval 1994
Best bowling: 2-66 Surrey v Gloucestershire, Guildford 1991

2002 Season

	M	Inns	NO	Runs	HS	Avge	100s	50s	Ct	St	O	M	Runs	Wkts	Avge	Best	5wl	10wM
Test																		
All First																		
1-day Int																		
C & G	1	1	0	0	0	0.00	-	-	-	-								
B & H																			
1-day Lge	1	1	0	78	78	78.00	-	1	1	-								

---

89. Which Australian scored 1001 first-class runs and took
61 first-class wickets for Sussex in 1990?

Career Performances

	M	Inns	NO	Runs	HS	Avge	100s	50s	Ct	St	Balls	Runs	Wkts	Avge	Best	5wI	10wM
Test																	
All First	156	246	34	8139	294 *	38.39	16	33	122	3	107	113	2	56.50	2-66	-	-
1-day Int																	
C & G	30	26	3	808	101 *	35.13	1	6	10	-	48	37	2	18.50	2-31	-	
B & H	42	38	6	838	73	26.18	-	4	13	2							
1-day Lge	161	143	23	3645	112	30.37	4	22	77	1							

WARD, I. J. Surrey

Name: Ian James Ward
Role: Left-hand bat
Born: 30 September 1973, Plymouth
Height: 5ft 9in **Weight:** 13st
Nickname: Wardy, Cocker, Son of Baboon, Dwarf, Stumpy, Pig in a Passage
County debut: 1996
County cap: 2000
Test debut: 2001
Tests: 5
1000 runs in a season: 2
1st-Class 50s: 36
1st-Class 100s: 14
1st-Class catches: 55
Place in batting averages: 13th av. 62.82
(2001 144th av. 26.53)
Strike rate: 19.33 (career 71.33)
Parents: Tony and Mary

Wife and date of marriage: Joanne, 15 February 1998
Children: Robert, 21 September; Lennox, 10 April
Family links with cricket: Grandfather and father played for Devon
Education: Valley End; Millfield School
Qualifications: 8 GCSEs, 3 A-levels, NCA coaching award
Career outside cricket: Media
Off-season: 'Working for Sky TV. Holidaying in Perth. Practising and improving'
Overseas tours: Surrey U19 to Barbados 1990; Millfield to Jamaica 1991, to Australia; Malden Wanderers to Jersey 1994; England A to Bangladesh and New Zealand 1999-2000, to West Indies 2000-01
Overseas teams played for: North Perth CC, Western Australia 1996-97; Perth CC, Western Australia; Marist Newman Old Boys CC, Perth
Career highlights to date: 'Test debut'

Cricket moments to forget: 'Getting nailed on the neck at silly point by Chris Adams. Thanks'

Cricketers particularly admired: Ben Hollioake, Graham Thorpe, Adam Gilchrist, Mark Wasley (North Perth CC)

Young players to look out for: Scott Newman, Matthew Prior, Jim Troughton

Other sports played: Golf and 'Foxball'

Other sports followed: Football (Liverpool), beach volleyball, Formula One motor racing

Injuries: 'Sore neck'

Relaxations: 'Spending time with my wife, walking dog, running'

Extras: Released by Surrey at 18 and missed four years of cricket, returning to the county in 1996. Scored centuries in three successive Busta Cup matches for England A in West Indies 2000-01 and was leading first-class run-scorer on tour (769 av. 64.08); during his 135 v Barbados at Bridgetown, he shared in record opening stand for England A (224) with Michael Powell. Made Test debut v Pakistan at Lord's 2001 in England's 100th Test at the ground. Scored 95-ball 97 v Glamorgan at The Oval in the C&G 2002 as Surrey posted 438-5 from 50 overs. Scored 168* opening the innings as Surrey scored 410-8 to beat Kent in the Championship at Canterbury 2002 (at one point Surrey had been 208-7); scored another match-winning century (124*) in the next Championship match as Surrey successfully chased 237 to beat Yorkshire at Guildford. Scored four centuries in consecutive Championship innings 2002 – including two centuries in match (112/156) v Hampshire at West End – to equal a Surrey record last achieved by Jack Hobbs in 1925; in scoring the fourth (118), v Leicestershire at The Oval, he shared with Scott Newman (183) in a new record opening partnership for Surrey in matches v Leicestershire (227). Leading run-scorer in English first-class cricket 2002 with 1759 runs (av. 62.82). Surrey Player of the Year 2002

Opinions on cricket: 'Qualification laws are a farce – who is English and who's not? Only two up and down in Division One. Need to focus precious resources into Academy, A team and Team England and away from underperforming counties. An A team to tour and play four-day and one-day games in English summer against touring sides.'

Best batting: 168* Surrey v Kent, Canterbury 2002

Best bowling: 1-1 Surrey v Hampshire, West End 2002

2002 Season

	M	Inns	NO	Runs	HS	Avge	100s	50s	Ct	St	O	M	Runs	Wkts	Avge	Best	5wI	10wM
Test																		
All First	17	31	3	1759	168 *	62.82	7	7	10	-	9.4	3	19	3	6.33	1-1	-	-
1-day Int																		
C & G	4	4	0	169	97	42.25	-	2	1	-								
B & H	5	5	0	92	46	18.40	-	-	2	-	5	0	40	2	20.00	2-27	-	
1-day Lge	15	15	0	335	62	22.33	-	2	3	-	1	0	8	0	-	-	-	-

Career Performances

	M	Inns	NO	Runs	HS	Avge	100s	50s	Ct	St	Balls	Runs	Wkts	Avge	Best	5wI	10wM
Test	5	9	1	129	39	16.12	-	-	1	-							
All First	97	165	15	6067	168 *	40.44	14	36	55	-	214	121	3	40.33	1-1	-	-
1-day Int																	
C & G	17	15	2	497	97	38.23	-	4	1	-							
B & H	17	15	1	348	71 *	24.85	-	3	4	-	30	40	2	20.00	2-27	-	
1-day Lge	78	75	8	1683	91	25.11	-	10	16	-	59	92	0	-	-	-	-

WARD, T. R. Leicestershire

Name: <u>Trevor</u> Robert Ward
Role: Right-hand bat, occasional off-spin bowler
Born: 18 January 1968, Farningham, Kent
Height: 5ft 11in **Weight:** 13st
Nickname: Wardy, Chikka
County debut: 1986 (Kent), 2000 (Leicestershire)
County cap: 1989 (Kent), 2001 (Leicestershire)
Benefit: 1999 (Kent)
1000 runs in a season: 6
1st-Class 50s: 76
1st-Class 100s: 27
1st-Class 200s: 1
1st-Class catches: 219
One-Day 100s: 9
Place in batting averages: 202nd av. 23.08 (2001 45th av. 45.89)
Strike rate: 66.00 (career 127.66)
Parents: Robert Henry and Hazel Ann
Wife and date of marriage: Sarah Ann, 29 September 1990
Children: Holly Ann, 23 October 1995; Samuel Joseph, 25 April 1998
Family links with cricket: Father played club cricket
Education: Anthony Roper County Primary; Hextable Comprehensive
Qualifications: 7 O-levels, NCA coaching award
Overseas tours: NCA to Bermuda 1985; England YC to Sri Lanka 1986-87, to Australia (U19 World Cup) 1987-88
Overseas teams played for: Scarborough, Perth, Western Australia 1985; Gosnells, Perth 1993
Cricketers particularly admired: Ian Botham, Graham Gooch, Robin Smith

Other sports followed: 'Most sports'
Relaxations: Fishing, watching television, golf
Extras: Was awarded £1000 for becoming the first player to score 400 runs in the Benson and Hedges Cup in 1995. Released by Kent at the end of the 1999 season and joined Leicestershire for 2000. Awarded Leicestershire cap on the same day as he scored a century (110) against his old county Kent at Leicester 2001. B&H Gold Award for his 127 v Durham at Leicester 2002. Scored 112 v Sussex at Leicester in the C&G 2002, in the process sharing with Darren Stevens (83) in a competition record second-wicket partnership for Leicestershire (171)
Best batting: 235* Kent v Middlesex, Canterbury 1991
Best bowling: 2-10 Kent v Yorkshire, Canterbury 1996

2002 Season

	M	Inns	NO	Runs	HS	Avge	100s	50s	Ct	St	O	M	Runs	Wkts	Avge	Best	5wI	10wM
Test																		
All First	14	24	0	554	89	23.08	-	4	7	-	11	0	47	1	47.00	1-32	-	-
1-day Int																		
C & G	2	2	0	141	112	70.50	1	-	-	-								
B & H	6	6	0	200	127	33.33	1	-	1	-								
1-day Lge	16	16	1	285	91	19.00	-	2	10	-								

Career Performances

	M	Inns	NO	Runs	HS	Avge	100s	50s	Ct	St	Balls	Runs	Wkts	Avge	Best	5wI	10wM
Test																	
All First	239	410	22	13433	235 *	34.62	28	76	219	-	1149	694	9	77.11	2-10	-	-
1-day Int																	
C & G	29	29	1	1164	120	41.57	2	9	5	-	174	154	4	38.50	2-25	-	
B & H	62	62	3	1939	127	32.86	3	12	13	-	12	10	0	-	-	-	
1-day Lge	212	206	7	5522	131	27.74	4	35	55	-	228	187	6	31.16	3-20	-	

90. Who scored a Somerset individual record 322
v Warwickshire at Taunton in 1985?

WARN, C. J.   Derbyshire

Name: Christopher (<u>Chris</u>) James Warn
Role: Right-hand bat, wicket-keeper
Born: 22 April 1979, Little Waltham, Essex
Height: 5ft 11in **Weight:** 12st
Nickname: Warny
County debut: 2002
1st-Class catches: 3
Parents: David and Janet
Marital status: Single
Family links with cricket: Father has always played village cricket at Little Waltham
Education: Little Waltham Primary; Chelmer Valley High School
Career outside cricket: Family construction business
Off-season: In South Africa – coaching and playing
Overseas teams played for:
Southern Districts, Adelaide, 1999-2001; Claremont, Cape Town 2001-02
Career highlights to date: 'Getting the call to keep for Derbyshire when both Karl Krikken and Luke Sutton were unavailable'
Cricket moments to forget: 'Not playing as well as I would have liked on my first-class debut'
Cricketers particularly admired: Andy Brown, Ian Healy, Shane Dietz, Mark Waugh
Young players to look out for: Andy Fairburn
Other sports followed: Ipswich Town
Relaxations: 'I play a bit of golf; socialising'
Extras: Played for Essex U17 and 2nd XI. Regular member of the Suffolk team for the past three years; Suffolk Young Player of the Year 2000; played for Suffolk in the C&G 2001 and 2002. Appeared for Derbyshire in one first-class match v Indians 2002; is not contracted
Best batting: 1 Derbyshire v Indians, Derby 2002

2002 Season

	M	Inns	NO	Runs	HS	Avge	100s	50s	Ct	St	O	M	Runs	Wkts	Avge	Best	5wI	10wM
Test																		
All First	1	1	0	1	1	1.00	-	-	3	-								
1-day Int																		
C & G	1	1	0	7	7	7.00	-	-	2	-								
B & H																		
1-day Lge																		

Career Performances

	M	Inns	NO	Runs	HS	Avge	100s	50s	Ct	St	Balls	Runs	Wkts	Avge	Best	5wI	10wM
Test																	
All First	1	1	0	1	1	1.00	-	-	3	-							
1-day Int																	
C & G	5	5	3	89	52 *	44.50	-	1	9	2							
B & H																	
1-day Lge																	

WARREN, N. A. Warwickshire

Name: <u>Nick</u> Alexander Warren
Role: Right-hand bat, right-arm medium-fast bowler
Born: 26 June 1982, Moseley
Height: 5ft 11in **Weight:** 12st 7lbs
Nickname: Wazza
County debut: 2002
Strike rate: 60.00 (career 60.00)
Parents: Lesley
Marital status: Single
Education: St Martins; Wheelers Lane Boys School; Solihull Sixth Form College
Qualifications: 9 GCSEs, BTEC Sports Science
Overseas tours: Warwickshire U19 to Cape Town 1998-99; England U17 to Ireland 1999; England U19 to Malaysia and (U19 World Cup) Sri Lanka 1999-2000
Cricketers particularly admired: Allan Donald, Graeme Welch
Young players to look out for: Jim Troughton
Other sports played: Football
Other sports followed: Football (Birmingham City)
Relaxations: Watching films; planes, music
Extras: Played for Warwickshire Board XI in the second round of the C&G 2002, which was played in September 2001. Played for the Warwickshire Board XI side that won the final ECB 38-County competition 2002
Best batting: 11 Warwickshire v West Indies A, Edgbaston 2002
Best bowling: 2-48 Warwickshire v West Indies A, Edgbaston 2002

2002 Season

	M	Inns	NO	Runs	HS	Avge	100s	50s	Ct	St	O	M	Runs	Wkts	Avge	Best	5wI	10wM
Test																		
All First	1	2	1	13	11	13.00	-	-	-	-	20	3	90	2	45.00	2-48	-	-
1-day Int																		
C & G																		
B & H	1	0	0	0	0	-	-	-	-	-	6	0	45	0	-		-	-
1-day Lge	1	1	0	2	2	2.00	-	-	-	-	5	0	34	3	11.33	3-34	-	

Career Performances

	M	Inns	NO	Runs	HS	Avge	100s	50s	Ct	St	Balls	Runs	Wkts	Avge	Best	5wI	10wM
Test																	
All First	1	2	1	13	11	13.00	-	-	-	-	120	90	2	45.00	2-48	-	-
1-day Int																	
C & G	1	1	0	0	0	0.00	-	-	2	-	36	29	0	-		-	-
B & H	1	0	0	0	0	-	-	-	-	-	36	45	0	-		-	-
1-day Lge	1	1	0	2	2	2.00	-	-	-	-	30	34	3	11.33	3-34	-	

WARREN, R. J.   Nottinghamshire

Name: <u>Russell</u> John Warren
Role: Right-hand bat, wicket-keeper
Born: 10 September 1971, Northampton
Height: 6ft 2in **Weight:** 13st 4lbs
Nickname: Rab C, Rabbit
County debut: 1992 (Northamptonshire)
County cap: 1995 (Northamptonshire)
1000 runs in a season: 1
1st-Class 50s: 31
1st-Class 100s: 9
1st-Class 200s: 1
1st-Class catches: 106
1st-Class stumpings: 3
One-Day 100s: 1
Place in batting averages: 99th av. 36.90
(2001 22nd av. 54.29)
Parents: John and Sally
Marital status: Single
Family links with cricket: 'Dad likes a bet. Mum follows scores on Teletext'
Education: Whitehills Lower School; Kingsthorpe Middle and Upper Schools
Qualifications: 8 O-levels, 2 A-levels
Overseas tours: England YC to New Zealand 1990-91; Northamptonshire to Cape Town 1993, to Zimbabwe 1995, to Johannesburg 1996, to Grenada 2000

Overseas teams played for: Lancaster Park, Christchurch, and Canterbury B, New Zealand 1991-93; Riverside CC, Lower Hutt, New Zealand 1994-95; Petone CC, Wellington, New Zealand 1995-96; Alma Marist CC, Cape Town, South Africa 1997-98

Cricketers particularly admired: Allan Lamb, Wayne Larkins

Young players to look out for: Mark Powell

Other sports played: Golf, snooker

Other sports followed: Football (Manchester United and Northampton Town), rugby (Northampton Saints), golf, snooker and horse racing

Relaxations: 'Music, having a bet'

Extras: Scored 175 v Glamorgan at Northampton 2001, in the process sharing with Tony Penberthy (132*) in a record sixth-wicket partnership for Northants in matches against Glamorgan (250). Scored 144 v Somerset at Taunton 2001, in the process sharing with Mike Hussey (208) in a record third-wicket partnership for Northants in matches against Somerset (287). Released by Northamptonshire at the end of the 2002 season and has joined Nottinghamshire for 2003

Best batting: 201* Northamptonshire v Glamorgan, Northampton 1996

2002 Season

	M	Inns	NO	Runs	HS	Avge	100s	50s	Ct	St	O	M	Runs	Wkts	Avge	Best	5wI	10wM
Test																		
All First	6	11	1	369	150 *	36.90	1	1	1	-								
1-day Int																		
C & G	2	2	0	27	21	13.50	-	-	-	-								
B & H	5	4	1	123	78 *	41.00	-	1	-	-								
1-day Lge	3	3	1	26	17	13.00	-	-	1	-								

Career Performances

	M	Inns	NO	Runs	HS	Avge	100s	50s	Ct	St	Balls	Runs	Wkts	Avge	Best	5wI	10wM
Test																	
All First	110	179	20	5767	201 *	36.27	10	31	106	3	6	0	0	-	-	-	-
1-day Int																	
C & G	21	19	3	459	100 *	28.68	1	2	21	1							
B & H	24	22	4	282	78 *	15.66	-	1	18	-							
1-day Lge	96	85	13	1760	93	24.44	-	8	75	9							

91. Who was Derbyshire's overseas player in 1998 and 1999?

WATKINSON, M. Lancashire

Name: Michael Watkinson
Role: Right-hand bat, right-arm
medium or off-spin bowler
Born: 1 August 1961, Westhoughton
Height: 6ft 1½in **Weight:** 13st
Nickname: Winker
County debut: 1982
County cap: 1987
Benefit: 1996 (£209,000)
Test debut: 1995
Tests: 4
One-Day Internationals: 1
1000 runs in a season: 1
50 wickets in a season: 7
1st-Class 50s: 50
1st-Class 100s: 11
1st-Class 5 w. in innings: 27
1st-Class 10 w. in match: 3
1st-Class catches: 156
One-Day 100s: 2
One-Day 5 w. in innings: 3

Strike rate: (career 64.69)
Parents: Albert and Marian
Wife and date of marriage: Susan, 12 April 1986
Children: Charlotte, 24 February 1989; Liam, 27 July 1991
Education: Rivington and Blackrod High School, Horwich
Qualifications: 8 O-levels, HTC Civil Engineering
Career outside cricket: Draughtsman
Overseas tours: England to South Africa 1995-96
Cricketers particularly admired: Clive Lloyd, Imran Khan
Other sports followed: Football
Relaxations: Watching Bolton Wanderers
Extras: Played for Cheshire in Minor Counties Championship and in NatWest Trophy
(v Middlesex) 1982. Man of the Match in the first Refuge Assurance Cup final 1988
and for his 50 plus 2-37 in B&H Cup final 1990. Lancashire captain 1994-97, leading
the county to one NatWest and two B&H titles. Lancashire Player of the Year 1995.
2nd XI captain and coach 2000-01. Cricket manager since 2002; retired but
registration retained
Best batting: 161 Lancashire v Essex, Old Trafford 1995
Best bowling: 8-30 Lancashire v Hampshire, Old Trafford 1994

Career Performances

	M	Inns	NO	Runs	HS	Avge	100s	50s	Ct	St	Balls	Runs	Wkts	Avge	Best	5wI	10wM
Test	4	6	1	167	82 *	33.40	-	1	1	-	672	348	10	34.80	3-64	-	-
All First	308	459	49	10939	161	26.68	11	50	156	-	47806	24960	739	33.77	8-30	27	3
1-day Int	1	0	0	0	0	-	-	-	-	-	54	43	0	-	-		
C & G	46	40	7	1064	130	32.24	1	7	12	-	2681	1751	46	38.06	3-14	-	
B & H	73	53	12	837	76	20.41	-	4	22	-	3740	2636	88	29.95	5-44	2	
1-day Lge	236	189	38	3262	121	21.60	1	9	59	-	8730	7113	225	31.61	5-46	1	

WAUGH, M. E. Essex

Name: <u>Mark</u> Edward Waugh
Role: Right-hand bat, right-arm off-spin bowler
Born: 2 June 1965, Canterbury, Sydney, Australia
Height: 6ft 1in
Nickname: Junior, Tugga
County debut: 1988
County cap: 1989
Test debut: 1990-91
Tests: 125
One-Day Internationals: 244
1000 runs in a season: 4
1st-Class 50s: 126
1st-Class 100s: 76
1st-Class 200s: 5
1st-Class 5 w. in innings: 3
1st-Class catches: 417
One-Day 100s: 23
One-Day 5 w. in innings: 1
Strike rate: (career 73.60)
Parents: Rodger and Beverley
Family links with cricket: Younger twin brother of Steve Waugh. Brothers Dean (NSW and South Australia) and Danny have also played for the Bankstown club (formerly Bankstown-Canterbury); uncle Dion Bourne captained Bankstown. Father played A grade tennis; mother played A grade squash
Education: East Hills Boys' High School
Qualifications: Higher School Certificate, cricket coach
Off-season: Playing for Australia and New South Wales

Overseas tours: Young Australia to Zimbabwe 1985-86; New South Wales to Zimbabwe 1987-88; Australia to West Indies 1990-91, 1994-95, 1998-99, to Sri Lanka 1992-93, to New Zealand 1992-93, 1999-2000, to England 1993, 1997, 2001, to South Africa 1993-94, 1996-97, 2001-02, to Pakistan 1994-95, 1998-99, to India and Pakistan (World Cup) 1995-96, to India 1996-97, 1997-98, 2000-01, to Bangladesh (Wills International Cup) 1998-99, to UK, Ireland and Holland (World Cup) 1999, to Sri Lanka and Zimbabwe 1999-2000, to Kenya (ICC Knockout) 2000-01, to Sri Lanka and Sharjah (v Pakistan) 2002-03

Overseas teams played for: Bankstown, Sydney; NSW 1985-86 –

Extras: Sheffield Shield Player of the Year 1987-88 (jointly with D. Tazelaar of Queensland) and 1989-90. Was Essex overseas player 1988-90, 1992 and 1995. Scored 103 for Essex v Nottinghamshire at Colchester 1988, becoming the first player to score a century on Sunday League debut. Scored 3079 runs in the calendar year 1990. Scored 229* for NSW v Western Australia at Perth 1990-91, in the process sharing in a world record fifth-wicket partnership for first-class cricket (464*) with his brother Steve (216*). Scored 138 on Test debut v England at Adelaide 1990-91, having replaced Steve in the Australia side. In the third Test v West Indies in Trinidad 1990-91, he and Steve became the first twins to play in the same Test side. One of *Wisden*'s Five Cricketers of the Year 1991. Represented Australia in the 1991-92 World Cup. Scored 126 v West Indies in the fourth Test in Jamaica 1994-95, in the process sharing in a key fourth-wicket partnership of 231 with brother Steve (200). Scored three centuries as an opening batsman in the 1995-96 World Cup. Played in Australia's 1999 World Cup winning side. Set Australian record for the highest individual score in an ODI (173), v West Indies at Melbourne 2000-01. Scored 120 v England in the fifth Test at The Oval 2001, in the process sharing in a third-wicket partnership of 197 with brother Steve (157*), the second time that the brothers had scored centuries in the same Test innings. Holds world record for the number of catches in Test cricket (181 at time of retirement; *see Stop press*). Was Essex's overseas player towards the end of the 2002 season, replacing Andy Flower, absent on international duty; scored a century (117) in his first innings for the county in seven years, v Durham at Riverside. ACB central contract 2002-03

Best batting: 229* New South Wales v Western Australia, Perth 1990-91

Best bowling: 6-68 Australians v President's XI, Patiala 1996-97

Stop press: Reached 8000 runs in Test cricket during first Test v Pakistan at Colombo 2002-03. Retired from international cricket in October 2002. Scored match-winning century (108*) as captain of Sir Donald Bradman XI v England XI in 50-over match at Bowral 2002-03

---

92. Which British Guiana batsman and later first-class umpire in England scored 109* against the Australians on his Somerset debut in 1953?

2002 Season

	M	Inns	NO	Runs	HS	Avge	100s	50s	Ct	St	O	M	Runs	Wkts	Avge	Best	5wI	10wM
Test																		
All First	2	3	0	242	117	80.66	1	1	4	-	4	1	14	0	-	-	-	-
1-day Int																		
C & G																		
B & H																		
1-day Lge	2	2	0	28	26	14.00	-	-	-	-	3.3	0	14	3	4.66	3-14	-	

Career Performances

	M	Inns	NO	Runs	HS	Avge	100s	50s	Ct	St	Balls	Runs	Wkts	Avge	Best	5wI	10wM
Test	125	205	17	7949	153 *	42.28	20	46	173	-	4739	2358	59	39.96	5-40	1	-
All First	346	553	70	25715	229 *	53.24	81	126	417	-	15309	8208	208	39.46	6-68	3	-
1-day Int	244	236	20	8500	173	39.35	18	50	108	-	3687	2937	85	34.55	5-24	1	
C & G	8	7	0	145	47	20.71	-	-	1	-	252	222	2	111.00	1-45	-	
B & H	16	14	1	438	100	33.69	1	2	5	-	95	76	4	19.00	3-31	-	
1-day Lge	65	63	11	2374	112 *	45.65	4	15	24	-	1318	1248	43	29.02	3-14	-	

WAUGH, S. R.   Kent

Name: Stephen (<u>Steve</u>) Rodger Waugh
Role: Right-hand bat, right-arm
medium bowler
Born: 2 June 1965, Canterbury, Sydney,
Australia
Height: 5ft 11in
Nickname: Tugga
County debut: 1987 (Somerset), 2002 (Kent)
County cap: 1988 (Somerset), 2002 (Kent)
Test debut: 1985-86
Tests: 148
One-Day Internationals: 325
1000 runs in a season: 1
1st-Class 50s: 88
1st-Class 100s: 64
1st-Class 200s: 4
1st-Class 5 w. in innings: 5
1st-Class catches: 251
One-Day 100s: 5
Strike rate: (career 68.53)
Parents: Rodger and Beverley
Wife: Lynette

Family links with cricket: Elder twin brother of Mark Waugh. Brothers Dean (NSW and South Australia) and Danny have also played for the Bankstown club (formerly Bankstown-Canterbury); uncle Dion Bourne captained Bankstown. Father played A grade tennis; mother played A grade squash

Education: East Hills Boys' High School

Off-season: Playing for Australia

Overseas tours: Australia to New Zealand 1985-86, 1989-90, 1992-93, 1999-2000 (captain), to India 1986-87, 1996-97, 1997-98, 2000-01 (captain), to India and Pakistan (World Cup) 1987-88, to Pakistan 1988-89, 1994-95, 1998-99, to England 1989, 1993, 1997, 2001 (captain), to West Indies 1990-91, 1994-95, 1998-99 (captain), to South Africa 1993-94, 1996-97, 2001-02 (captain), to India and Pakistan (World Cup) 1995-96, to Bangladesh (Wills International Cup) 1998-99 (captain), to UK, Ireland and Holland (World Cup) 1999 (captain), to Sri Lanka and Zimbabwe 1999-2000 (captain), to Kenya (ICC Knockout) 2000-01 (captain), to Sri Lanka and Sharjah (v Pakistan) 2002-03 (captain)

Overseas teams played for: Bankstown, Sydney; NSW 1984-85 –

Extras: Played in Australia's World Cup winning side 1987 and represented Australia in the 1991-92 World Cup. Was Somerset's overseas player 1987-88. One of *Wisden*'s Five Cricketers of the Year 1989. Scored 506 runs at an average of 126.50 in the 1989 Ashes series. Scored 216* for NSW v Western Australia at Perth 1990-91, in the process sharing in a world record fifth-wicket partnership for first-class cricket (464*) with his brother Mark (229*). In the third Test v West Indies in Trinidad 1990-91, he and Mark became the first twins to play in the same Test side. Scored 200 v West Indies in the fourth Test in Jamaica 1994-95, in the process sharing in a key fourth-wicket partnership of 231 with brother Mark (126). Scored 160 at Johannesburg 1996-97, sharing in a record fifth-wicket partnership for Australia in Tests v South Africa, 385 with Greg Blewett (214). Scored a century in each innings (108 and 116) in the third Test v England at Old Trafford 1997. Was Australia's one-day captain from December 1997 to February 2002; skippered Australia's 1999 World Cup winning side. Was appointed Australia's Test captain in February 1999, leading his country to a world record 16 successive Test victories 1999-2000 – 2000-01. Scored 157* v England in the fifth Test at The Oval 2001, in the process sharing in a third-wicket partnership of 197 with brother Mark (120), the second time that the brothers had scored centuries in the same Test innings. *Wisden Australia* Cricketer of the Year 1999-2000. Winner of the Allan Border Medal 2001. Was Kent's overseas player for the latter part of the 2002 season, replacing Andrew Symonds, absent on international duty; awarded Kent cap 2002. ACB central contract 2002-03

Best batting: 216* New South Wales v Western Australia, Perth 1990-91

Best bowling: 6-51 New South Wales v Queensland, Sydney 1988-89

Stop press: Became second player to win 150 Test caps in second Test v Pakistan in Sharjah 2002-03. Scored century (103*) in third Test v Pakistan in Sharjah 2002-03, in the process passing Allan Border's total of 27 Test hundreds to take second place in the list of Australian Test century-makers behind Sir Donald Bradman (29). Overtook Allan Border's Australian record of 32 Test wins as captain when he led Australia to victory over England in the fourth Test at Melbourne 2002-03. Equalled Allan

Border's world record of 156 Test appearances in fifth Test v England at his home ground of Sydney 2002-03, scoring a century (102) to equal Sir Donald Bradman's Australian record of 29 Test hundreds and become (on 69*) the third batsman to reach 10,000 runs in Test cricket; he reached his century from the last ball of the second day

2002 Season

	M	Inns	NO	Runs	HS	Avge	100s	50s	Ct	St	O	M	Runs	Wkts	Avge	Best	5wI	10wM
Test																		
All First	4	6	1	224	146	44.80	1	-	3	-	3	0	15	0	-	-	-	-
1-day Int																		
C & G																			
B & H																			
1-day Lge	5	5	1	159	59 *	39.75	-	2	2	-	10	0	74	2	37.00	2-6	-	

Career Performances

	M	Inns	NO	Runs	HS	Avge	100s	50s	Ct	St	Balls	Runs	Wkts	Avge	Best	5wl	10wM
Test	148	233	41	9600	200	50.00	27	44	102	-	7193	3197	89	35.92	5-28	3	-
All First	319	492	81	21351	216 *	51.94	68	88	251	-	16654	7812	243	32.14	6-51	5	-
1-day Int	325	288	58	7569	120 *	32.90	3	45	111	-	8847	6730	195	34.51	4-33	-	
C & G	2	2	0	21	21	10.50	-	-	1	-	132	96	4	24.00	2-45	-	
B & H	3	3	1	161	79	80.50	-	2	1	-	84	63	2	31.50	2-16	-	
1-day Lge	16	15	3	693	140 *	57.75	2	3	6	-	180	188	4	47.00	2-6	-	

WEEKES, P. N. Middlesex

Name: <u>Paul</u> Nicholas Weekes
Role: Left-hand bat, right-arm
off-spin bowler
Born: 8 July 1969, Hackney, London
Height: 5ft 10in **Weight:** 12st 6lbs
Nickname: Weekesy, Twidds
County debut: 1990
County cap: 1993
Benefit: 2002
1000 runs in a season: 1
1st-Class 50s: 37
1st-Class 100s: 15
1st-Class 5 w. in innings: 4
1st-Class catches: 169
One-Day 100s: 3
Place in batting averages: 30th av. 52.10
(2001 102nd av. 32.68)
Place in bowling averages: 155th av. 57.04
(2001 61st av. 29.95)

Strike rate: 113.42 (career 85.59)
Parents: Robert and Carol
Marital status: Partner Christine
Children: Cherie, 4 September 1993; Shyann, 5 May 1998
Family links with cricket: Father played club cricket
Education: Manderville Primary; Homerton House, Hackney; Hackney Technical College
Qualifications: 2 O-levels, senior cricket coach
Career outside cricket: Cricket coach
Overseas tours: England A to India and Bangladesh 1994-95; BWIA to Trinidad (twice); Middlesex to Johannesburg
Overseas teams played for: Newcastle University, NSW 1988-89; Sunrise CC, Zimbabwe 1990-91
Career highlights to date: 'Scoring more than 150 (171* and 160) in each innings of a four-day match, v Somerset at Uxbridge 1996. Scoring 102* v South Africa' (*The latter innings was in a World Cup warm-up match 1999*)
Cricket moments to forget: 'Getting a pair against Essex in 1996'
Cricketers particularly admired: Viv Richards, Courtney Walsh
Young players to look out for: Owais Shah
Other sports followed: Boxing, football (Arsenal)
Relaxations: 'Music, laughing, talking rubbish'
Extras: Scored 50 in debut innings for both 2nd and 1st teams. Took two catches whilst appearing as 12th man for England in the second Test against West Indies at Lord's in 1995. Middlesex Player of the Year 1999. Only Englishman to have scored more than 150 in both innings of a first-class game. Has won six one-day Man of the Match awards (two NatWest; four B&H), including B&H Gold Award for his 4-17 v Kent at Lord's 2001. Captained Middlesex to their one-day victory over the Australians at Lord's 2001
Best batting: 171* Middlesex v Somerset, Uxbridge 1996
Best bowling: 8-39 Middlesex v Glamorgan, Lord's 1996

2002 Season

	M	Inns	NO	Runs	HS	Avge	100s	50s	Ct	St	O	M	Runs	Wkts	Avge	Best	5wI	10wM
Test																		
All First	18	25	6	990	127 *	52.10	4	3	23	-	397	61	1198	21	57.04	3-27	-	-
1-day Int																		
C & G	1	1	1	76	76 *	-		1	-	-	9	0	50	1	50.00	1-50	-	
B & H	4	3	1	34	24	17.00	-	-	3	-	22	0	100	2	50.00	2-22	-	
1-day Lge	15	13	4	159	53 *	17.66	-	1	8	-	95.5	7	441	19	23.21	3-17	-	

Career Performances

	M	Inns	NO	Runs	HS	Avge	100s	50s	Ct	St	Balls	Runs	Wkts	Avge	Best	5wI	10wM
Test																	
All First	178	276	36	8109	171 *	33.78	15	37	169	-	19173	9135	224	40.78	8-39	4	-
1-day Int																	
C & G	21	21	5	596	143 *	37.25	2	3	6	-	1041	752	20	37.60	3-35	-	
B & H	41	36	7	865	77	29.82	-	5	15	-	1790	1290	41	31.46	4-17	-	
1-day Lge	180	153	22	3138	119 *	23.95	1	13	80	-	6308	5226	192	27.21	4-26	-	

WELCH, G.   Derbyshire

Name: Graeme Welch
Role: Right-hand bat, right-arm medium-fast bowler
Born: 21 March 1972, Durham
Height: 6ft **Weight:** 13st
Nickname: Pop
County debut: 1992 (one-day, Warwickshire), 1994 (first-class, Warwickshire), 2001 (Derbyshire)
County cap: 1997 (Warwickshire), 2001 (Derbyshire)
50 wickets in a season: 2
1st-Class 50s: 12
1st-Class 5 w. in innings: 9
1st-Class 10 w. in match: 1
1st-Class catches: 41
One-Day 5 w. in innings: 3
Place in batting averages: 175th av. 25.55 (2001 201st av. 18.92)
Place in bowling averages: 31st av. 25.61 (2001 103rd av. 37.06)
Strike rate: 53.03 (career 60.32)
Parents: Jean and Robert
Wife and date of marriage: Emma, 4 October 1997
Children: Ethan, 4 April 2000
Family links with cricket: Brother and father play club cricket in Leeds and Durham respectively
Education: Hetton Primary; Hetton Comprehensive
Qualifications: 9 GCSEs, City and Guilds in Sports and Leisure, senior coaching award
Career outside cricket: Coaching
Overseas tours: Warwickshire to Cape Town 1992-97; England XI to New Zealand (Cricket Max) 1997

Overseas teams played for: Avendale, Cape Town 1992-94; Wellington Collegians and Wellington 1996
Career highlights to date: 'Winning the treble with Warwickshire in 1994'
Cricket moments to forget: 'Benson and Hedges game against Lancashire in 1995' (*Became first bowler to concede 100 runs in B&H match*)
Cricketers particularly admired: Brian Lara, Allan Donald, Sachin Tendulkar
Young players to look out for: Ian Bell, Nicky Peng
Other sports played: Football
Other sports followed: Football (Newcastle United)
Relaxations: 'A beer at "The Brook"; spending time with Emma and Ethan'
Extras: Played for England YC v Australian YC 1991. Took two hat-tricks in the 2nd XI, against Durham in 1992 and against Worcestershire. Warwickshire's Most Improved Player in 1994. Won seven trophies with Warwickshire 1994-97. Left Warwickshire at the end of the 2000 season and joined Derbyshire for 2001. Recorded five-wicket innings return (5-53) and scored a fifty (64) against his old county Warwickshire at Edgbaston 2001
Best batting: 84* Warwickshire v Nottinghamshire, Edgbaston 1994
Best bowling: 6-30 Derbyshire v Durham, Riverside 2001

2002 Season

	M	Inns	NO	Runs	HS	Avge	100s	50s	Ct	St	O	M	Runs	Wkts	Avge	Best	5wI	10wM
Test																		
All First	14	23	5	460	64	25.55	-	3	8	-	486.1	157	1409	55	25.61	6-60	2	-
1-day Int																		
C & G	1	1	1	31	31 *	-	-	-	-	-	5.5	0	37	0	-	-	-	-
B & H	5	2	0	12	11	6.00	-	-	-	-	25.2	3	118	1	118.00	1-51	-	
1-day Lge	14	13	4	95	23	10.55	-	-	-	-	117.3	14	517	23	22.47	6-31	2	

Career Performances

	M	Inns	NO	Runs	HS	Avge	100s	50s	Ct	St	Balls	Runs	Wkts	Avge	Best	5wI	10wM
Test																	
All First	108	161	25	2866	84 *	21.07	-	12	41	-	17072	9276	283	32.77	6-30	9	1
1-day Int																	
C & G	18	13	4	176	41	19.55	-	-	-	-	953	609	9	67.66	4-31	-	
B & H	27	18	4	253	55 *	18.07	-	1	1	-	1047	822	23	35.73	3-20	-	
1-day Lge	102	83	23	1038	71	17.30	-	3	16	-	4094	3030	90	33.66	6-31	3	

---

93. For which county did Imran Khan play before joining Sussex in 1977?

WELLS, V. J.   Durham

Name: Vincent (<u>Vince</u>) John Wells
Role: Right-hand bat, right-arm medium
bowler, occasional wicket-keeper
Born: 6 August 1965, Dartford
Height: 6ft **Weight:** 13st 4lbs
Nickname: Vinny, Wellsy, Both
County debut: 1987 (one-day, Kent),
1988 (first-class, Kent), 1992 (Leicestershire)
County cap: 1994 (Leicestershire)
Benefit: 2001 (Leicestershire)
One-Day Internationals: 9
1000 runs in a season: 2
1st-Class 50s: 44
1st-Class 100s: 14
1st-Class 200s: 3
1st-Class 5 w. in innings: 5
1st-Class catches: 123
One-Day 100s: 3
One-Day 200s: 1

One-Day 5 w. in innings: 2
Place in batting averages: 97th av. 37.20 (2001 123rd av. 29.90)
Place in bowling averages: 11th av. 22.15 (2001 50th av. 27.66)
Strike rate: 48.94 (career 54.16)
Parents: Pat and Jack
Wife and date of marriage: Deborah Louise, 14 October 1989
Children: Harrison John, 25 January 1995; Molly Louise, 2 June 1996
Family links with cricket: Brother plays club cricket for Chestfield
Education: Downs School, Dartford; Sir William Nottidge School, Whitstable
Qualifications: 1 O-level, 8 CSEs, junior and senior coaching certificates
Overseas tours: Leicestershire to Jamaica 1993, to Bloemfontein 1994, 1995,
to Western Transvaal 1996, to Durban 1997, to Barbados 1998, to Anguilla 2000;
England to Australia 1998-99 (CUB Series), to Sharjah (Coca-Cola Cup) 1998-99
Overseas teams played for: Parnell, Auckland 1986; Avendale, Cape Town 1986-89,
1990-91; Potchefstroom University, North West Transvaal 1996-97; Cornwall CC,
Auckland 1998-99
Career highlights to date: 'Winning trophies for Leicestershire. Playing for England'
Cricket moments to forget: 'Losing any game, especially Lord's finals'
Cricketers particularly admired: James Whitaker, Phil Simmons, Mike Kasprowicz,
Anil Kumble – 'all play hard, practise hard and all respect the game; top people'
Other sports followed: Football (Chelsea and Leicester)
Relaxations: 'Good food, pint of Guinness, spending time with my family and
walking Jasper the dog'

Extras: Was a schoolboy footballer with Leyton Orient. Scored 100* on NatWest debut v Oxfordshire at Oxford 1990. Left Kent at the end of 1991 season to join Leicestershire. Hat-trick for Leicestershire v Durham at Durham 1994; Alamgir Sheriyar also took hat-trick for Leicestershire in same match. Scored 201 v Berkshire at Leicester in the NatWest 1996. Member of England's 1999 World Cup squad and was reserve wicket-keeper. Captain of Leicestershire from retirement of James Whitaker during 1999 season to end of 2002 season. Scored century (138) and recorded five-wicket innings return (5-36) against his old county Kent at Canterbury 2001. C&G Man of the Match award for his 54* v Notts at Trent Bridge 2001. Left Leicestershire at the end of the 2002 season and has joined Durham for 2003

Opinions on cricket: 'Would like to see the toss given to away side in Championship cricket to hopefully make the pitches better and take away a luck element of the game. Two up/two down promotion and relegation.'

Best batting: 224 Leicestershire v Middlesex, Lord's 1997

Best bowling: 5-18 Leicestershire v Nottinghamshire, Worksop 1998

2002 Season

	M	Inns	NO	Runs	HS	Avge	100s	50s	Ct	St	O	M	Runs	Wkts	Avge	Best	5wI	10wM
Test																		
All First	11	17	2	558	150	37.20	1	3	9	-	155	41	421	19	22.15	5-39	1	-
1-day Int																		
C & G	2	2	1	53	49*	53.00	-	-	2	-	14	1	64	3	21.33	3-32	-	
B & H	6	5	1	23	13	5.75	-	-	1	-	33	1	146	6	24.33	4-32	-	
1-day Lge	10	10	0	256	68	25.60	-	2	3	-	66.2	4	291	9	32.33	2-17	-	

Career Performances

	M	Inns	NO	Runs	HS	Avge	100s	50s	Ct	St	Balls	Runs	Wkts	Avge	Best	5wI	10wM
Test																	
All First	184	285	21	8894	224	33.68	17	44	123	-	15165	7405	280	26.44	5-18	5	-
1-day Int	9	7	0	141	39	20.14	-	-	7	-	220	189	8	23.62	3-30	-	
C & G	28	27	7	885	201	44.25	2	5	5	-	1149	708	31	22.83	3-30	-	
B & H	50	43	4	952	90	24.41	-	5	14	-	1870	1388	51	27.21	6-25	1	
1-day Lge	162	155	13	3359	101	23.65	2	14	40	-	5329	4103	145	28.29	5-10	1	

WELTON, G. E.   Nottinghamshire

Name: <u>Guy</u> Edward Welton
Role: Right-hand opening bat
Born: 4 May 1978, Grimsby
Height: 6ft 1in **Weight:** 13st 7lbs
Nickname: Trigger, Giggs, Welts
County debut: 1997
1st-Class 50s: 14

1st-Class 100s: 1
1st-Class 200s: 1
1st-Class catches: 37
One-Day 100s: 1
Place in batting averages: 100th av. 36.69 (2001 225th av. 15.31)
Parents: Robert and Diana
Marital status: Single
Family links with cricket: Father is a qualified cricket coach and keen club cricketer
Education: Keelby Primary; Healing Comprehensive; Grimsby College of Technology; Nottingham Trent University
Qualifications: 9 GCSEs, BTEC in Business and Finance, senior level cricket coach
Overseas tours: England U17 to Holland (International Youth Tournament) 1995; Nottinghamshire to South Africa 1998
Overseas teams played for: Randfontein CC, Johannesburg, South Africa 1996-97; Willetton CC, Perth, Western Australia 1997-98; Coolbinia CC, Perth 1998-99
Cricketers particularly admired: David Gower, Viv Richards, Steve Waugh, Sachin Tendulkar, Mark Lavender
Other sports played: Football ('youth trainee at Grimsby Town Football Club 1994-96')
Relaxations: Music and going to the gym
Extras: Completed a two-year YTS with Grimsby Town Football Club where he made one first-team appearance as a substitute. Played cricket for England U14, U15 and U17. Won the Lord's Taverners' Young Player Award in 1993 and was MCC Young Cricketer 1994-95. Was 12th man for England at Lord's and The Oval against West Indies in 1995. Scored maiden first-class century v Warwickshire at Edgbaston 2000, going on to score 200* and become Nottinghamshire's youngest ever double centurion; in the process he shared in a first-wicket stand of 406* with Darren Bicknell (180*) that broke several records, including that for the highest Nottinghamshire partnership for any wicket, formerly 398 by Arthur Shrewsbury and William Gunn v Sussex at Trent Bridge 1890, and that for the highest unbeaten first-wicket partnership in Championship history. B&H Gold Awards for his 71 v Leicestershire at Trent Bridge and 75 v Durham at Riverside 2001
Best batting: 200* Nottinghamshire v Warwickshire, Edgbaston 2000

2002 Season

	M	Inns	NO	Runs	HS	Avge	100s	50s	Ct	St	O	M	Runs	Wkts	Avge	Best	5wI	10wM
Test																		
All First	16	28	2	954	115	36.69	1	6	16	-								
1-day Int																		
C & G	1	1	0	26	26	26.00	-	-	1	-								
B & H	1	0	0	0	0	-	-	-	-	-								
1-day Lge	7	7	0	68	18	9.71	-	-	4	-								

Career Performances

	M	Inns	NO	Runs	HS	Avge	100s	50s	Ct	St	Balls	Runs	Wkts	Avge	Best	5wI	10wM
Test																	
All First	61	110	5	2727	200 *	25.97	2	14	37	-	12	5	0	-	-	-	-
1-day Int																	
C & G	3	3	0	55	26	18.33	-	-	2	-							
B & H	7	6	0	182	75	30.33	-	2	2	-							
1-day Lge	38	37	2	636	104 *	18.17	1	1	12	-							

WESTON, R. M. S.   Middlesex

Name: <u>Robin</u> Michael Swann Weston
Role: Right-hand bat, leg-break bowler
Born: 7 June 1975, Durham
Height: 6ft **Weight:** 12st 6lbs
County debut: 1995 (Durham),
1998 (Derbyshire), 2000 (Middlesex)
County cap: 2001 (Middlesex)
1st-Class 50s: 9
1st-Class 100s: 6
1st-Class catches: 37
Place in batting averages: 169th av. 26.33
(2001 59th av. 42.00)
Strike rate: (career 93.50)
Parents: Kathleen Mary (deceased) and
Michael Philip
Marital status: Single
Family links with cricket: Father played for
Durham (and played rugby union for
England); brother Philip plays for Worcestershire

Education: Bow School; Durham School; Loughborough University
Qualifications: 10 GCSEs, 4 A-levels, degree in Economics with Accountancy, basic
cricket coaching certificate
Career outside cricket: Working in marketing

Off-season: 'Setting up an international schools cricket festival at Durham School'
Overseas tours: England U18 to South Africa 1992-93, to Denmark (International Youth Tournament) 1993; England U19 to Sri Lanka 1993-94
Overseas teams played for: Fremantle, Western Australia 1996-98; Parnell CC, Auckland 1999-2000
Cricketers particularly admired: 'Anyone at the highest level'
Young players to look out for: Ed Joyce
Other sports played: Golf, rugby union (Loughborough Students 1994-96, England U18 1993)
Other sports followed: Football (Sunderland AFC)
Relaxations: Most sports, listening to music and socialising with friends
Extras: Sir John Hobbs Silver Jubilee Memorial Prize 1990. Became youngest to play for Durham 1st XI, in Minor Counties competition, aged 15 in 1991. Released by Durham at the end of the 1997 season and joined Derbyshire. Scored maiden first-class century (129*) v Essex at Chelmsford 1999 and followed up with centuries in the next two Championship matches (124 v Middlesex at Lord's; 156 v Somerset at Derby) to become the fourth Derbyshire batsman to score centuries in three successive Championship games. NBC Denis Compton Award 1999. Left Derbyshire at the end of 1999 season and joined Middlesex for 2000. 2nd XI Championship Player of the Year 2000
Best batting: 156 Derbyshire v Somerset, Derby 1999
Best bowling: 1-15 Derbyshire v Hampshire, Derby 1999

2002 Season

	M	Inns	NO	Runs	HS	Avge	100s	50s	Ct	St	O	M	Runs	Wkts	Avge	Best	5wI	10wM
Test																		
All First	9	11	2	237	72	26.33	-	2	4	-								
1-day Int																		
C & G																		
B & H																		
1-day Lge	3	3	0	22	21	7.33	-	-	-	-								

Career Performances

	M	Inns	NO	Runs	HS	Avge	100s	50s	Ct	St	Balls	Runs	Wkts	Avge	Best	5wI	10wM
Test																	
All First	60	100	6	2635	156	28.03	6	9	37	-	187	104	2	52.00	1-15	-	-
1-day Int																	
C & G	7	7	1	150	56	25.00	-	1	1	-							
B & H	2	2	0	28	18	14.00	-	-	-	-							
1-day Lge	39	38	3	621	80 *	17.74	-	3	9	-							

WESTON, W. P. C.   Worcestershire

Name: William <u>Philip</u> Christopher Weston
Role: Left-hand opening bat, left-arm
medium bowler
Born: 16 June 1973, Durham
Height: 6ft 4in **Weight:** 13st 9lbs
Nickname: Sven, Reverend, Wesso
County debut: 1991
County cap: 1995; colours, 2002
1000 runs in a season: 4
1st-Class 50s: 47
1st-Class 100s: 16
1st-Class 200s: 1
1st-Class catches: 90
One-Day 100s: 2
Place in batting averages: 188th av. 24.23
(2001 60th av. 41.92)
Strike rate: (career 241.25)
Parents: Kate (deceased) and Michael

Wife and date of marriage: Sarah, 30 September 2000
Family links with cricket: Brother plays for Middlesex. Father played Minor
Counties cricket for Durham (and rugby union for England)
Education: Bow School, Durham; Durham School
Qualifications: 9 GCSEs, 4 A-levels, coaching certificates
Career outside cricket: Cricket development, coaching; 'hoping to enter business
world!'
Off-season: 'Undertaking a diploma in business management and hoping to gain some
work experience'
Overseas tours: England U18 to Canada (International Youth Tournament) 1991
(vice-captain); England YC to New Zealand 1990-91; England U19 to Pakistan 1991-
92 (captain); Worcestershire to Zimbabwe 1996
Overseas teams played for: Melville, Perth 1992-94, 1996-97; Swanbourne,
Perth 1995-96
Career highlights to date: 'Any game in which I have made an important contribution
to a victory'
Cricket moments to forget: 'A pair against Middlesex in 2000. Most of the 2002
season!'
Cricket superstitions: 'Like to walk on field second when opening batting'
Cricketers particularly admired: 'Everyone who makes the most of their talent'
Young players to look out for: Kadeer Ali
Other sports followed: Rugby union, football (Sunderland AFC)
Injuries: Out for two weeks with tennis elbow
Relaxations: 'Spending time with Sarah; travelling, cinema, property'

Extras: Scored century (146) for England YC v Australia YC 1991. Scored century (107) for England U19 v Sri Lanka U19 1992 and was Man of the Series. Cricket Society's Most Promising Young Cricketer 1992. Worcestershire Uncapped Player of the Year 1992. Member of Whittingdale Fringe Squad 1993. Scored 71 v Middlesex at Worcester 2001, in the process sharing with Anurag Singh in a record opening partnership for Worcestershire in matches against Middlesex

Opinions on cricket: 'Pitches are improving, but need to continue in encouraging fast bowlers, spinners, and batsmen to play long innings. EU players and two overseas players rule will harm the development of English players.'

Best batting: 205 Worcestershire v Northamptonshire, Northampton 1997
Best bowling: 2-39 Worcestershire v Pakistanis, Worcester 1992

2002 Season

	M	Inns	NO	Runs	HS	Avge	100s	50s	Ct	St	O	M	Runs	Wkts	Avge	Best	5wI	10wM
Test																		
All First	8	15	2	315	82	24.23	-	3	7	-								
1-day Int																		
C & G																		
B & H																		
1-day Lge																		

Career Performances

	M	Inns	NO	Runs	HS	Avge	100s	50s	Ct	St	Balls	Runs	Wkts	Avge	Best	5wI	10wM
Test																		
All First	170	299	31	9132	205	34.07	17	47	90	-	965	640	4	160.00	2-39	-	-
1-day Int																		
C & G	11	11	0	150	40	13.63	-	-	1	-							
B & H	26	25	3	325	65	14.77	-	2	11	-							
1-day Lge	90	76	8	1655	134	24.33	2	5	17	-	6	2	1	2.00	1-2	-	

94. Which South African batsman scored a Derbyshire season record eight first-class centuries in 1982?

WHARF, A. G. B. Glamorgan

Name: Alexander (<u>Alex</u>) George Busfield Wharf
Role: Right-hand bat, right-arm fast-medium bowler; all-rounder
Born: 4 June 1975, Bradford
Height: 6ft 4in **Weight:** 15st
Nickname: Gangster
County debut: 1994 (Yorks), 1998 (Notts), 2000 (Glamorgan)
County cap: 2000 (Glamorgan)
1st-Class 50s: 3
1st-Class 100s: 2
1st-Class 5 w. in innings: 2
1st-Class catches: 22
Place in bowling averages: (2001 70th av. 32.00)
Strike rate: 73.71 (career 55.84)
Parents: Jane and Derek

Wife and date of marriage: Shelley Jane, 1 December 2001
Children: Tristan Jack Busfield Wharf, 15 November 1997; Alf Alexander Busfield Wharf, 30 June 2001
Family links with cricket: Father played local cricket and brother Simon plays local cricket
Education: Marshfields First School; Preistman Middle School; Buttershaw Upper School; Thomas Danby College
Qualifications: 6 GCSEs, City and Guilds in Sports Management, NCA coaching award, junior football coaching award
Career outside cricket: 'House husband'
Off-season: 'Getting myself into shape, so I can give myself every opportunity to stay fit all season!'
Overseas tours: Various pre-season tours with Yorks, Notts and Glamorgan
Overseas teams played for: Somerset West, Cape Town 1993-95; Johnsonville CC, Wellington, New Zealand 1996-97; Universities, Wellington 1998-99
Career highlights to date: 'Playing alongside some great players!'
Cricket moments to forget: 'Too many to mention'
Cricket superstitions: 'None'
Cricketers particularly admired: Ian Botham
Young players to look out for: 'Plenty of youngsters out there, but only if they get the chance!'
Other sports played: Football ('goalkeeper – watch this space')
Other sports followed: 'Follow most sports but my passion is Manchester United; also very proud of Bradford City'

Injuries: Injury to left ankle
Relaxations: 'Spending time with family and friends, movies, PlayStation 2, eating (too much), TV, gym, football'
Extras: Attended Dennis Lillee coaching school, Chennai (Madras), during winter 1997-98. Scored 78 for Notts v Glamorgan at Colwyn Bay 1999, having arrived at the wicket with his side on 9 for 6. Left Nottinghamshire at end of the 1999 season and joined Glamorgan for 2000
Opinions on cricket: 'Maybe regional cricket should come into play to bridge the gap between first-class and Test cricket.'
Best batting: 101* Glamorgan v Northamptonshire, Northampton 2000
Best bowling: 5-63 Glamorgan v Yorkshire, Swansea 2001

2002 Season

	M	Inns	NO	Runs	HS	Avge	100s	50s	Ct	St	O	M	Runs	Wkts	Avge	Best	5wI	10wM
Test																		
All First	3	2	0	6	6	3.00	-	-	-	-	86	9	266	7	38.00	4-71	-	-
1-day Int																		
C & G	1	0	0	0	0	-	-	-	-	-	10	0	27	0	-		-	-
B & H																		
1-day Lge	4	3	2	34	18	34.00	-	-	1	-	27	0	164	5	32.80	3-39	-	

Career Performances

	M	Inns	NO	Runs	HS	Avge	100s	50s	Ct	St	Balls	Runs	Wkts	Avge	Best	5wI	10wM
Test																	
All First	46	62	8	914	101 *	16.92	2	3	22	-	6087	3657	109	33.55	5-63	2	-
1-day Int																	
C & G	6	4	1	42	24 *	14.00	-	-	-	-	336	172	7	24.57	3-18	-	
B & H	12	8	1	75	20	10.71	-	-	2	-	658	539	15	35.93	4-29	-	
1-day Lge	38	23	10	251	38 *	19.30	-	-	7	-	1504	1245	33	37.72	3-23	-	

95. Which West Indies Test fast bowler made his debut for Hampshire in 1973?

WHARTON, L. J. Derbyshire

Name: <u>Lian</u> James Wharton
Role: Left-hand bat, slow left-arm bowler
Born: 21 February 1977, Derby
Height: 5ft 9in **Weight:** 10st 4lbs
Nickname: Tetley, King, Two Thumbs,
Weasel
County debut: 2000
1st-Class 5 w. in innings: 3
1st-Class catches: 10
Place in batting averages: 303rd av. 7.54
(2001 283rd av. 3.22)
Place in bowling averages: 49th av. 27.80
Strike rate: 50.12 (career 78.71)
Parents: Pete and Di
Marital status: Single
Education: Ravensdale Primary School;
Ecclesbourne; Mackworth College
Qualifications: 9 GCSEs, BTEC National
Computer Studies, Level 2 coach
Career outside cricket: Sports manager
Off-season: 'Playing in Australia'

Overseas tours: MCC to Kenya 2002
Overseas teams played for: Merewether CC, Newcastle, NSW 2000-01
Career highlights to date: 'Taking nine wickets against the West Indians' (*Match figures of 9-179 at Derby 2000*)
Cricket moments to forget: 'Had complete nightmare fielding at Durham – running wrong way for balls, balls going through my legs etc.'
Cricket superstitions: 'None'
Cricketers particularly admired: Phil Tufnell, Ian Botham, Shane Warne, Stewart Edge, Ian Fraser, Daniel Vettori, Rory Williams, Andrew Williams, Ewan Craig, Alec Stubbs
Young players to look out for: James Dakin, George Moulds, Chris Windmill, Luke Sutton, Steve Stubbings, Tom Lungley, Sam Patel, Steve Selwood
Other sports played: Indoor cricket ('train with England squad'), golf, football, tennis, 'spoof'
Other sports followed: Football (Derby County), basketball (Derby Storm)
Relaxations: 'Reading, going to the cinema, socialising, sleeping'
Extras: Had match figures of 10-58 from 37 overs on debut for Derbyshire 2nd XI. Recorded maiden Championship five-wicket return (6-103) v Glamorgan at Cardiff 2002
Best batting: 16 Derbyshire v Worcestershire, Derby 2002
Best bowling: 6-62 Derbyshire v Middlesex, Lord's 2002

750

2002 Season

	M	Inns	NO	Runs	HS	Avge	100s	50s	Ct	St	O	M	Runs	Wkts	Avge	Best	5wI	10wM
Test																		
All First	14	23	12	83	16	7.54	-	-	7	-	208.5	45	695	25	27.80	6-62	2	-
1-day Int																		
C & G																		
B & H	1	1	1	2	2 *	-	-	-	1	-	5	0	24	1	24.00	1-24		-
1-day Lge	9	4	2	15	11 *	7.50	-	-	-	-	52.5	2	219	8	27.37	2-30		-

Career Performances

	M	Inns	NO	Runs	HS	Avge	100s	50s	Ct	St	Balls	Runs	Wkts	Avge	Best	5wI	10wM
Test																	
All First	32	50	25	127	16	5.08	-	-	10	-	3542	1803	45	40.06	6-62	3	-
1-day Int																	
C & G	1	1	1	0	0 *	-	-	-	-	-	60	41	1	41.00	1-41		-
B & H	1	1	1	2	2 *	-	-	-	1	-	30	24	1	24.00	1-24		-
1-day Lge	26	12	10	41	11 *	20.50	-	-	2	-	1103	772	24	32.16	3-23		-

WHILEY, M. J. A.   Leicestershire

Name: Matthew (Matt) Jeffrey Allen Whiley
Role: Right-hand bat, left-arm fast bowler
Born: 6 May 1980, Nottingham
Height: 6ft 3in **Weight:** 13st 8lbs
Nickname: Whibley, Stretch
County debut: 1998 (Nottinghamshire),
2001 (Leicestershire)
1st-Class catches: 2
Place in batting averages: 311th av. 5.85
Place in bowling averages: 146th av. 50.18
Strike rate: 65.87 (career 85.00)
Parents: Paul and Barbara
Marital status: Single
Family links with cricket: 'Dad played in
the local "bucket bangers" league; claims he
was quicker than Donald. Mum made the
business teas'
Education: Whitegate Primary School,
Clifton; Harry Carlton Comprehensive School, East Leake
Qualifications: 10 GCSEs, Level 1 coaching certificate
Overseas tours: England U19 to New Zealand 1998-99; Nottinghamshire to
Johannesburg 1999; Leicestershire to Potchefstroom 2001; MCC to Kenya 2002

Overseas teams played for: Manawatu-Foxton CC and Horowhenua District Cricket Association, both New Zealand 1997-98; Melville CC, Perth 2000-01

Career highlights to date: 'Although only at U19 level, representing my country. Making first-class debut'

Cricketers particularly admired: Devon Malcolm, Dennis Lillee, Graham Dilley, Bernard Allen 'for motivation'

Young players to look out for: Paul Franks, Stephen Randall, Richard Logan, Guy Welton

Other sports followed: Football (Man Utd)

Relaxations: 'Training, R&B music, clothes shopping'

Extras: Represented England U19. Visited the Dennis Lillee MRF Pace Foundation, February 2000. Awarded Nottinghamshire 2nd XI cap September 2000. Came second in the Freeserve Speedster Challenge; bowled the fastest delivery (86.6 mph) but was adjudged to have bowled a no-ball. Left Nottinghamshire in the 2000-01 off-season and joined Leicestershire for 2001. NBC Denis Compton Award for the most promising young Leicestershire player 2001

Opinions on cricket: 'Happy to be given an opportunity that others aren't.'

Best batting: 13* Leicestershire v Warwickshire, Edgbaston 2002

Best bowling: 3-60 Leicestershire v Kent, Leicester 2002

2002 Season

	M	Inns	NO	Runs	HS	Avge	100s	50s	Ct	St	O	M	Runs	Wkts	Avge	Best	5wI	10wM
Test																		
All First	7	9	2	41	13 *	5.85	-	-	1	-	175.4	28	803	16	50.18	3-60	-	-
1-day Int																		
C & G	1	1	1	0	0 *	-	-	-	-	-	4	0	27	0	-		-	-
B & H	6	1	1	3	3 *	-	-	-	1	-	43	3	182	9	20.22	2-20	-	
1-day Lge	12	5	4	25	14 *	25.00	-	-	4	-	60.2	3	321	6	53.50	2-37	-	

Career Performances

	M	Inns	NO	Runs	HS	Avge	100s	50s	Ct	St	Balls	Runs	Wkts	Avge	Best	5wI	10wM
Test																	
All First	13	18	4	43	13 *	3.07	-	-	2	-	1700	1235	20	61.75	3-60	-	-
1-day Int																	
C & G	1	1	1	0	0 *	-	-	-	-	-	24	27	0	-		-	-
B & H	6	1	1	3	3 *	-	-	-	1	-	258	182	9	20.22	2-20	-	
1-day Lge	12	5	4	25	14 *	25.00	-	-	4	-	362	321	6	53.50	2-37	-	

WHITE, C.

Yorkshire

Name: Craig White
Role: Right-hand bat, right-arm
fast-medium bowler, cover fielder
Born: 16 December 1969, Morley, Yorkshire
Height: 6ft 1in **Weight:** 11st 11lbs
Nickname: Chalky, Bassey
County debut: 1990
County cap: 1993
Benefit: 2002
Test debut: 1994
Tests: 26
One-Day Internationals: 42
1st-Class 50s: 44
1st-Class 100s: 14
1st-Class 5 w. in innings: 10
1st-Class catches: 140
One-Day 100s: 3
One-Day 5 w. in innings: 3
Place in batting averages: 64th av. 43.04 (2001 107th av. 31.84)
Place in bowling averages: 131st av. 42.26 (2001 91st av. 35.23)
Strike rate: 77.53 (career 53.42)
Parents: Fred Emsley and Cynthia Anne
Wife and date of marriage: Elizabeth Anne, 19 September 1992
Family links with cricket: Father played for Pudsey St Lawrence
Education: Kennington Primary; Flora Hill High School; Bendigo Senior High School
(all Victoria, Australia)
Off-season: Touring with England
Overseas tours: Australian YC to West Indies 1989-90; England A to Pakistan
1995-96, to Australia 1996-97; England to Australia 1994-95, to India and Pakistan
(World Cup) 1995-96, to Zimbabwe and New Zealand 1996-97, to South Africa and
Zimbabwe 1999-2000 (one-day series), to Kenya (ICC Knockout Trophy) 2000-01, to
Pakistan and Sri Lanka 2000-01, to India and New Zealand 2001-02, to Australia 2002-
03 (VB Series)
Overseas teams played for: Victoria, Australia 1990-91
Cricketers particularly admired: Graeme Hick, Mark Waugh, Brian Lara
Other sports followed: Leeds RFC, motocross, golf, tennis
Injuries: Torn abdominal muscle
Relaxations: Playing guitar, reading, gardening and socialising
Extras: Recommended to Yorkshire by Victorian Cricket Academy, being eligible to
play for Yorkshire as he was born in the county. Formerly bowled off-spin. Took 5-21
and scored 26 in the second One-Day International v Zimbabwe at Bulawayo in
February 2000, winning the Man of the Match award. Took National League hat-trick

(Fleming, Patel, Masters) v Kent at Headingley 2000. Recorded maiden Test five-wicket return (5-57) in fourth Test v West Indies on his home ground of Headingley 2000, following up with 5-32 in the fifth Test at The Oval. Scored 93 in England's first innings in the first Test at Lahore 2000-01, in the process sharing with Graham Thorpe (118) in a new record sixth-wicket partnership for England in Tests v Pakistan (166); also took 4-54 in Pakistan's only innings of the match. Selected for England one-day tour to Zimbabwe 2001-02 but was forced to withdraw with an injury to his right knee; replaced by Graham Thorpe. Scored maiden Test century (121) in second Test v India at Ahmedabad 2001-02, winning Man of the Match award and sharing with James Foster in a record seventh-wicket partnership for England in Tests in India (105). Ruled out of the one-day series v India 2001-02 with an injury to his left knee. B&H Gold Award for his 71 v Durham at Riverside 2002. C&G Man of the Match awards for his 87 v Devon at Exmouth and for his 4-35 and 78-ball 100* in the semi-final v Surrey at Headingley 2002. Scored 64 and then took a career one-day best 5-19 v Somerset at Scarborough in the NUL 2002. Selected for the England one-day squad for the ICC Champions Trophy in Sri Lanka 2002-03 but was forced to withdraw with a torn abdominal muscle; replaced by Dominic Cork

Best batting: 186 Yorkshire v Lancashire, Old Trafford 2001
Best bowling: 8-55 Yorkshire v Gloucestershire, Gloucester 1998
Stop press: Called up to the England Test squad in Australia 2002-03 as cover for Andrew Flintoff, recovering from surgery. Took 5-127 in Australia's only innings in third Test at Perth 2002-03. Scored 85* in England's first innings of fourth Test v Australia at Melbourne (once his home ground), in the process passing 1000 runs in Test cricket. Selected for England squad for 2002-03 World Cup

2002 Season

	M	Inns	NO	Runs	HS	Avge	100s	50s	Ct	St	O	M	Runs	Wkts	Avge	Best	5wI	10wM
Test	2	3	2	153	94 *	153.00	-	2	1	-	48.4	7	178	5	35.60	2-46	-	-
All First	13	24	2	947	161	43.04	2	7	6	-	193.5	33	634	15	42.26	4-49	-	-
1-day Int																		
C & G	5	5	1	237	100 *	59.25	1	1	2	-	33	1	126	7	18.00	4-35	-	
B & H	6	6	0	265	93	44.16	-	3	3	-	29	1	165	4	41.25	1-19	-	
1-day Lge	11	11	0	309	64	28.09	-	1	2	-	43.2	1	204	14	14.57	5-19	1	

Career Performances

	M	Inns	NO	Runs	HS	Avge	100s	50s	Ct	St	Balls	Runs	Wkts	Avge	Best	5wI	10wM
Test	26	42	6	898	121	24.94	1	4	14	-	3226	1688	45	37.51	5-32	2	-
All First	211	331	43	9129	186	31.69	14	44	140	-	19341	10067	362	27.80	8-55	10	-
1-day Int	42	33	3	368	38	12.26	-	-	10	-	1884	1385	53	26.13	5-21	1	
C & G	31	28	7	1043	113	49.66	2	7	11	-	1368	880	32	27.50	4-35	-	
B & H	46	42	7	924	93	26.40	-	5	15	-	1974	1479	47	31.46	5-25	1	
1-day Lge	143	128	15	2770	148	24.51	1	9	42	-	4456	3200	143	22.37	5-19	1	

WHITE, G. W.   Hampshire

Name: <u>Giles</u> William White
Role: Right-hand bat, leg-break bowler
Born: 23 March 1972, Barnstaple
Height: 6ft **Weight:** 12st
Nickname: Chalky
County debut: 1991 (Somerset),
1994 (Hampshire)
County cap: 1998 (Hampshire)
1000 runs in a season: 1
1st-Class 50s: 30
1st-Class 100s: 9
1st-Class catches: 107
1st-Class stumpings: 2
Place in batting averages: 229th av. 19.50
(2001 145th av. 26.39)
Strike rate: 73.00 (career 72.58)
Parents: John and Tina
Wife and date of marriage: Samantha,
25 September 1999

Children: Talia, 25 September 2002
Family links with cricket: Father played club cricket for Exeter CC
Education: Sandford Primary School, Devon; Exeter Cathedral School; Millfield School; Loughborough University
Qualifications: 10 O-levels, 3 A-levels, BA (Hons) Sports Management, Computing diploma, coaching certificates
Career outside cricket: Works for Exbury Developments (property development)
Overseas tours: Millfield School to Australia 1989; Hampshire to Anguilla, Cork and Guernsey
Overseas teams played for: Waverley, Sydney 1990-91; Tigers Parrow, Cape Town 1994-95; Techs Mutual CC, Cape Town 1995-96; Rygersdaal, Cape Town 1996-97; Wanneroo, Perth 1997-98
Cricketers particularly admired: Peter Hartley, Shane Warne, Darren Lehmann, Robin Smith, Peter Bowler
Young players to look out for: Chris Tremlett, Lawrence Prittipaul, Simon Francis
Other sports played: Golf, squash
Other sports followed: Football (Southampton FC)
Relaxations: Pubs, music, travel, friends, family
Extras: Hants Exiles Young Player of the Year 1997. Carried bat twice in 2000 – for 78* v Somerset at Southampton (the first time by a Hants player since Paul Terry at Headingley 1994); for 80* v Kent at Portsmouth. Retired at the end of the 2002 season
Best batting: 156 Hampshire v Sri Lankans, Southampton 1998
Best bowling: 3-23 Hampshire v Nottinghamshire, Trent Bridge 1999

2002 Season

	M	Inns	NO	Runs	HS	Avge	100s	50s	Ct	St	O	M	Runs	Wkts	Avge	Best	5wI	10wM
Test																		
All First	8	14	2	234	36	19.50	-	-	6	-	12.1	1	64	1	64.00	1-17	-	-
1-day Int																		
C & G	2	1	0	2	2	2.00	-	-	-	-	0.1	0	4	0	-		-	-
B & H	4	4	0	104	60	26.00	-	1	1	-								
1-day Lge	7	7	0	99	30	14.14	-	-	3	-								

Career Performances

	M	Inns	NO	Runs	HS	Avge	100s	50s	Ct	St	Balls	Runs	Wkts	Avge	Best	5wI	10wM
Test																	
All First	128	223	21	6195	156	30.66	9	30	107	2	871	629	12	52.41	3-23	-	-
1-day Int																	
C & G	13	12	0	161	69	13.41	-	1	6	-	73	49	1	49.00	1-45	-	
B & H	20	19	1	336	60	18.66	-	2	3	-							
1-day Lge	90	86	5	1809	76	22.33	-	11	29	-	22	23	0	-		-	-

WHITE, R. A. Northamptonshire

Name: Robert (<u>Rob</u>) Allan White
Role: Right-hand bat, leg-spin bowler
Born: 15 October 1979, Chelmsford
Height: 5ft 11in **Weight:** 11st 7lbs
Nickname: Chalky, Toff, Zorro,
Whitey, Lamb
County debut: 2000
1st-Class 50s: 3
1st-Class 200s: 1
1st-Class catches: 3
Place in batting averages: 3rd av. 92.66
Strike rate: 32.00 (career 35.60)
Parents: Dennis and Ann
Marital status: Single
Family links with cricket: 'Grandfather on
Essex committee for many years. Dad flailed
the willow and brother travels the local
leagues high and low'
Education: Spratton Hall; Stowe School; St John's College, Durham University;
Loughborough University
Qualifications: 9 GCSEs, 3 A-levels
Cricket moments to forget: 'Franklyn Rose telling me my mates had bet £10 that he
couldn't injure me, as I walked out to play Lashings'

Cricketers particularly admired: Ian Botham, Viv Richards, Steve Waugh
Young players to look out for: Monty Panesar, Mark Powell
Other sports played: Badminton, squash, golf, kabaddi
Other sports followed: Football (West Ham), rugby (Northampton Saints)
Extras: Northamptonshire League Young Player of the Year and Youth Cricketer of the Year 1999. Scored the first ever double century (206) in the history of the *Cricketer* Cup, for Stowe Templars v Old Whitgiftians at Stowe 2001. Northamptonshire Young Player of the Year (Frank Rudd Trophy) 2001. Played for Loughborough University CCE in 2001 and 2002; scored 99 v Nottinghamshire at Trent Bridge 2001 and received the Man of the Match award for his 58 in the first UCCE final at Lord's 2001. Recorded the highest maiden century in the history of English first-class cricket (277, including a hundred before lunch on the first day), v Gloucestershire at Northampton 2002 in his fifth first-class match; in the process he shared with Mark Powell (107; also a maiden first-class century) in a new record opening partnership for Northamptonshire (375)
Best batting: 277 Northamptonshire v Gloucestershire, Northampton 2002
Best bowling: 2-30 Northamptonshire v Gloucestershire, Northampton 2002

2002 Season

	M	Inns	NO	Runs	HS	Avge	100s	50s	Ct	St	O	M	Runs	Wkts	Avge	Best	5wI	10wM
Test																		
All First	4	7	1	556	277	92.66	1	3	1	-	26.4	3	91	5	18.20	2-30	-	-
1-day Int																		
C & G																		
B & H																		
1-day Lge	5	5	0	70	18	14.00	-	-	-	-	6	0	37	2	18.50	2-18	-	

Career Performances

	M	Inns	NO	Runs	HS	Avge	100s	50s	Ct	St	Balls	Runs	Wkts	Avge	Best	5wI	10wM
Test																	
All First	6	11	1	593	277	59.30	1	3	3	-	178	98	5	19.60	2-30	-	-
1-day Int																	
C & G																	
B & H																	
1-day Lge	5	5	0	70	18	14.00	-	-	-	-	36	37	2	18.50	2-18	-	

96. Name the overseas cricketers who played
for Worcestershire in 2002.

WIGLEY, D. H. Worcestershire

Name: <u>David</u> Harry Wigley
Role: Right-hand bat, right-arm
fast-medium bowler
Born: 26 October 1981, Bradford
Height: 6ft 4in **Weight:** 14st
Nickname: Wiggers, Reverend
County debut: 2002 (Yorkshire)
Strike rate: 124.00 (career 124.00)
Parents: Max and Judith
Marital status: Girlfriend Sarah
Family links with cricket: 'Dad played
league cricket in Liverpool Competition,
Bradford League and Durham Senior League'
Education: Pudsey Waterloo Infants and
Junior Schools; St Mary's Roman Catholic
Comprehensive, Menston; Loughborough
University

Qualifications: 9 GCSEs, 3 A-levels, ECB
Level I coaching
Off-season: 'Studying at Loughborough University while training with ECB Centre of
Excellence there'
Overseas teams played for: Gormandale CC, Victoria, Australia 2001
Career highlights to date: 'Making Yorkshire first-team debut v Surrey at Guildford.
Taking "five-for" at Lord's in University final'
Cricket moments to forget: 'Going for sevens in first innings of first-team debut
against Surrey!'
Cricket superstitions: 'Prefer to receive ball from right and must turn left to run in
when bowling'
Cricketers particularly admired: Darren Gough, Allan Donald, Jason Gillespie
Young players to look out for: Joe Sayers, Monty Panesar, Tim Bresnan
Other sports played: Rugby union ('played until 17 for district; had county trials')
Other sports followed: Football (Leeds United), rugby (Wales)
Injuries: 'Stop-start beginning of season at uni; fully fit for Yorkshire'
Relaxations: 'Watching films; listening to music'
Extras: Played for ECB Schools v Sri Lanka U19 2000. Yorkshire U19 Bowling
Award 2000. Played for Loughborough University CCE 2002, taking 5-71 v
Hampshire at West End and 5-52 v Oxford in the UCCE final at Lord's. Left Yorkshire
at the end of the 2002 season and has joined Worcestershire for 2003
Opinions on cricket: 'Too many teams playing too much cricket. Far cry from the
Australians, who play ten one-dayers a season and ten first-class games a season. This
would allow more rest and preparation time.'

Best batting: 15 Yorkshire v Surrey, Guildford 2002
Best bowling: 1-71 Yorkshire v Surrey, Guildford 2002

2002 Season

	M	Inns	NO	Runs	HS	Avge	100s	50s	Ct	St	O	M	Runs	Wkts	Avge	Best	5wI	10wM
Test																		
All First	1	2	1	19	15	19.00	-	-	-	-	20.4	2	116	1	116.00	1-71	-	-
1-day Int																		
C & G																			
B & H																			
1-day Lge																			

Career Performances

	M	Inns	NO	Runs	HS	Avge	100s	50s	Ct	St	Balls	Runs	Wkts	Avge	Best	5wI	10wM
Test																	
All First	1	2	1	19	15	19.00	-	-	-	-	124	116	1	116.00	1-71	-	-
1-day Int																	
C & G																		
B & H																		
1-day Lge																		

WINDOWS, M. G. N.   Gloucestershire

Name: <u>Matthew</u> Guy Newman Windows
Role: Right-hand bat, left-arm
medium bowler
Born: 5 April 1973, Bristol
Height: 5ft 7in **Weight:** 11st 7lbs
Nickname: Steamy, Bedos, Boat
County debut: 1992
County cap: 1998
1000 runs in a season: 3
1st-Class 50s: 39
1st-Class 100s: 15
1st-Class catches: 73
One-Day 100s: 3
Place in batting averages: 101st av. 36.62
(2001 89th av. 35.00)
Strike rate: (career 68.50)
Parents: Tony and Carolyn
Wife and date of marriage: Emma,
12 October 2002

Family links with cricket: 'Father (A.R.) played for Gloucestershire (1960-69) and
was Cambridge cricket Blue'

Education: Clifton College Prep; Clifton College; Durham University
Qualifications: 9 GCSEs, 3 A-levels, BA (Hons) Sociology (Dunelm), SFA securities representative of the London Stock Exchange
Career outside cricket: Working with Rowan Dartington stockbrokers
Overseas tours: Clifton College to Barbados 1991; England U19 to Pakistan 1991-92; Durham University to South Africa 1992-93; England A to Zimbabwe and South Africa 1998-99; Gloucestershire's annual pre-season tour to South Africa
Overseas teams played for: Gold Coast Dolphins, Queensland 1996-97
Career highlights to date: 'Winning all the Lord's finals, but [especially] being not out against Glamorgan in the 2000 [B&H] final'
Cricketers particularly admired: David Boon, Courtney Walsh
Young players to look out for: Monty Panesar, Alex Gidman
Other sports played: Rackets (British Open runner-up 1997)
Relaxations: 'Travelling and understanding financial jargon'
Extras: Played for Lincolnshire. Represented England U19 in home series v Sri Lanka U19 1992. Scored 71 on county debut v Essex at Bristol in 1992. Gloucestershire Young Player of the Year 1994. Set record for highest individual score for Durham University (218*), v Hull University in the BUSA Championships 1995. Gloucestershire Player of the Year 1998. B&H Gold Award for his 54 in the semi-final v Yorkshire at Headingley 2001. C&G Man of the Match award for his 82 v Sussex Board XI at Horsham 2001. At the close of the 2002 season, his last three one-day innings against Northants had been centuries – 108* in the B&H 2001, his maiden one-day hundred and for which he won the Gold Award; 117 off 94 balls in the NUL at Cheltenham 2001, his maiden one-day league century; 112* in the NUL 2002, in which innings he equalled the most sixes hit in an innings at Bristol
Best batting: 184 Gloucestershire v Warwickshire, Cheltenham 1996
Best bowling: 1-6 Combined Universities v West Indians, The Parks 1995

2002 Season

	M	Inns	NO	Runs	HS	Avge	100s	50s	Ct	St	O	M	Runs	Wkts	Avge	Best	5wI	10wM
Test																		
All First	17	31	2	1062	145	36.62	2	7	6	-	3.2	0	20	0	-	-	-	-
1-day Int																		
C & G	2	1	1	13	13 *	-	-	-	1	-								
B & H	6	5	1	109	86	27.25	-	1	2	-								
1-day Lge	12	12	1	333	112 *	30.27	1	1	2	-								

Career Performances

	M	Inns	NO	Runs	HS	Avge	100s	50s	Ct	St	Balls	Runs	Wkts	Avge	Best	5wI	10wM
Test																	
All First	129	229	17	7358	184	34.70	15	39	73	-	137	131	2	65.50	1-6	-	-
1-day Int																	
C & G	19	17	4	384	82	29.53	-	2	6	-							
B & H	28	27	7	703	108 *	35.15	1	3	8	-							
1-day Lge	108	101	7	2106	117	22.40	2	7	33	-	48	49	0	-	-	-	-

WOOD, J. Lancashire

Name: John Wood
Role: Right-hand bat, right-arm
fast-medium bowler
Born: 22 July 1970, Crofton, Wakefield
Height: 6ft 3in **Weight:** 16st 7lbs
Nickname: Woody
County debut: 1992 (Durham),
2001 (Lancashire)
County cap: 1998 (Durham)
50 wickets in a season: 1
1st-Class 50s: 3
1st-Class 5 w. in innings: 11
1st-Class catches: 25
One-Day 5 w. in innings: 1
Place in batting averages: 246th av. 16.81
(2001 231st av. 14.11)
Place in bowling averages: 106th av. 35.05
Strike rate: 60.27 (career 55.04)
Parents: Brian and Anne
Wife and date of marriage: Emma Louise, 30 October 1994
Children: Alexandra Mae, 7 April 1996; Joseph Samuel, 3 July 1998
Family links with cricket: 'Brother Ian plays for Spen Victoria in Bradford League;
Dad played local league cricket for Crofton'
Education: Crofton Junior School; Crofton High School; Wakefield District College;
Leeds Polytechnic
Qualifications: 6 O-levels, BTEC Diploma Electronic Engineering, HND Electrical
and Electronic Engineering, Level III cricket coach
Overseas tours: Durham CCC to South Africa 1994-95
Overseas teams played for: Griqualand West Cricket Union, South Africa 1990-91;
TAWA, Wellington and Wellington B, New Zealand 1993-95
Career highlights to date: 'Reaching C&G semi-final'
Cricket moments to forget: 'C&G semi-final' (*Lancashire lost to Leicestershire as
Shahid Afridi struck a 58-ball 95*)
Cricketers particularly admired: Wasim Akram, David Boon, Wayne Larkins
Young players to look out for: Andrew Pratt, Steve Harmison, Paul Collingwood,
Jimmy Anderson
Other sports played: Golf
Other sports followed: Football (Leeds United), rugby (England)
Relaxations: 'Spending time with my family; playing golf'
Extras: Played in the Bradford League. Made his debut for Durham (Minor Counties)
in 1991. Durham Players' Player of the Year 1998. Left Durham at the end of the 2000
season and joined Lancashire for 2001. Recorded maiden one-day five-wicket return

(5-49) v Gloucestershire at Old Trafford in the NUL 2002
Opinions on cricket: 'Umpires should treat batsmen 1-11 the same.'
Best batting: 64 Lancashire v Yorkshire, Headingley 2002
Best bowling: 7-58 Durham v Yorkshire, Headingley 1999

2002 Season

	M	Inns	NO	Runs	HS	Avge	100s	50s	Ct	St	O	M	Runs	Wkts	Avge	Best	5wl	10wM
Test																		
All First	8	11	0	185	64	16.81	-	1	2	-	180.5	34	631	18	35.05	4-17	-	-
1-day Int																		
C & G	2	1	0	1	1	1.00	-	-	-	-	10.3	1	46	0	-		-	-
B & H	7	3	1	13	6	6.50	-	-	-	-	51	4	211	16	13.18	4-31	-	
1-day Lge	13	7	3	46	13	11.50	-	-	3	-	103	5	418	22	19.00	5-49	1	

Career Performances

	M	Inns	NO	Runs	HS	Avge	100s	50s	Ct	St	Balls	Runs	Wkts	Avge	Best	5wl	10wM
Test																	
All First	104	153	21	1647	64	12.47	-	3	25	-	15804	9690	287	33.76	7-58	11	-
1-day Int																	
C & G	14	7	2	50	25	10.00	-	-	-	-	606	419	12	34.91	3-43	-	
B & H	27	16	5	116	28 *	10.54	-	-	1	-	1340	861	42	20.50	4-26	-	
1-day Lge	94	62	23	412	28 *	10.56	-	-	18	-	4095	3254	96	33.89	5-49	1	

WOOD, M. J. Somerset

Name: <u>Matthew</u> James Wood
Role: Right-hand bat, occasional right-arm
off-spin bowler
Born: 30 September 1980, Exeter
Height: 5ft 11in **Weight:** 12st 3lbs
Nickname: Woody, Grandma
County debut: 2001
1st-Class 50s: 9
1st-Class 100s: 4
1st-Class catches: 7
Place in batting averages: 111th av. 34.67
(2001 55th av. 44.08)
Parents: James and Trina
Marital status: Single
Family links with cricket: Father is
chairman of Exmouth CC
Education: St Joseph's Primary, Exmouth;
Exmouth Community College; Exeter
University (first year)

Qualifications: 8 GCSEs, 2 A-levels, ECB Level II coach
Off-season: 'Training and coaching'
Overseas tours: West of England U15 to West Indies 1995
Overseas teams played for: Doubleview CC, Perth 2000, 2001
Career highlights to date: 'Two hundreds in the match v Surrey 2002'
Cricketers particularly admired: Marcus Trescothick
Young players to look out for: Arul Suppiah
Other sports played: Football, golf
Other sports followed: Football (Liverpool FC)
Relaxations: 'Music, spending time with friends, golf'
Extras: Scored 71 on debut v Yorkshire at Bath 2001. NBC Denis Compton Award for the most promising young Somerset player 2001. Scored century in each innings (106/131) v Surrey at Taunton 2002, becoming (at 21 years, 279 days) the fourth youngest batsman to score twin centuries in the Championship. Somerset Player of the Year 2002. Has played for Devon
Best batting: 196 Somerset v Kent, Taunton 2002

2002 Season

	M	Inns	NO	Runs	HS	Avge	100s	50s	Ct	St	O	M	Runs	Wkts	Avge	Best	5wI	10wM
Test																		
All First	15	28	0	971	196	34.67	3	5	5	-								
1-day Int																		
C & G	3	2	0	25	19	12.50	-	-	1	-								
B & H	2	2	0	6	4	3.00	-	-	1	-								
1-day Lge	13	12	1	324	88 *	29.45	-	3	3	-								

Career Performances

	M	Inns	NO	Runs	HS	Avge	100s	50s	Ct	St	Balls	Runs	Wkts	Avge	Best	5wI	10wM
Test																		
All First	22	40	0	1500	196	37.50	4	9	7	-	42	30	0	-	-	-	-
1-day Int																		
C & G	3	2	0	25	19	12.50	-	-	1	-								
B & H	2	2	0	6	4	3.00	-	-	1	-								
1-day Lge	19	17	1	410	88 *	25.62	-	3	4	-								

97. Who was Hampshire's overseas player
in 1998 and 1999?

WOOD, M. J.   Yorkshire

Name: <u>Matthew</u> James Wood
Role: Right-hand bat, off-spin bowler
Born: 6 April 1977, Huddersfield
Height: 5ft 9in **Weight:** 12st
Nickname: Ronnie, Chuddy
County debut: 1997
County cap: 2001
1000 runs in a season: 2
1st-Class 50s: 13
1st-Class 100s: 8
1st-Class 200s: 1
1st-Class catches: 54
One-Day 100s: 2
Place in batting averages: 280th av. 11.82
(2001 36th av. 48.18)
Parents: Roger and Kathryn
Marital status: Single
Family links with cricket: 'Father played for
local team Emley. Mum made the teas and sister Caroline scored'
Education: Emley First School; Kirkburton Middle School; Shelley High School and
Sixth Form Centre
Qualifications: 9 GCSEs, 2 A-levels, NCA coaching award
Off-season: 'Club cricket in Australia'
Overseas tours: England U19 to Zimbabwe 1995-96; Yorkshire CCC to West Indies
1996-97, to Cape Town 1997, 1998; MCC to Kenya 1999, to Bangladesh 1999-2000;
ECB National Academy to Australia 2001-02
Overseas teams played for: Somerset West CC, Cape Town 1994-95; Upper Hutt
United CC, New Zealand 1997-98; Mosman Park, Western Australia 2000-01
Career highlights to date: 'Being on the pitch as fielding 12th man for England
series win v South Africa at Headingley [1998]. Winning the Championship in 2001
and winning the C&G 2002 at Lord's'
Cricket moments to forget: 'Last three months of 2002 season!'
Cricketers particularly admired: Darren Lehmann, Michael Slater, Martyn Moxon,
Matthew Maynard
Young players to look out for: Nick Thornicroft, Ben Heritage
Other sports played: Football (Kirkburton FC)
Other sports followed: Football (Liverpool FC)
Injuries: Out for ten days after being struck above the eye and requiring nine stitches
Relaxations: 'Music, dining out, socialising, watching sport'
Extras: Played for England U17 against India 1994. Attended Yorkshire Academy.
Has Yorkshire 2nd XI cap. Scored 81 on first-class debut v Lancs at Headingley 1997.
Scored 1000 runs in first full season 1998. Shared in the highest first-wicket stand for

Yorks in matches against Kent for 49 years (152) with Scott Richardson at Headingley 2001. Scored 85* v Surrey at Headingley 2001, in the process sharing with Darren Lehmann in a record third-wicket partnership for Yorkshire in matches against Surrey (190*). B&H Gold Award for his 115 (his maiden one-day century) v Derbyshire at Derby 2002

Opinions on cricket: 'One-day cricket is changing fast and must be more entertaining for the crowds.'

Best batting: 200* Yorkshire v Warwickshire, Headingley 1998

2002 Season

	M	Inns	NO	Runs	HS	Avge	100s	50s	Ct	St	O	M	Runs	Wkts	Avge	Best	5wI	10wM
Test																		
All First	9	17	0	201	43	11.82	-	-	12	-								
1-day Int																		
C & G	5	5	1	208	91	52.00	-	2	3	-								
B & H	5	5	1	159	115 *	39.75	1	-	2	-								
1-day Lge	15	13	1	258	105 *	21.50	1	-	8	-								

Career Performances

	M	Inns	NO	Runs	HS	Avge	100s	50s	Ct	St	Balls		Runs	Wkts	Avge	Best	5wI	10wM
Test																		
All First	72	123	10	3228	200 *	28.56	9	13	54	-	18		16	0	-	-	-	-
1-day Int																		
C & G	10	10	2	305	91	38.12	-	2	4	-								
B & H	12	10	2	248	115 *	31.00	1	1	4	-								
1-day Lge	50	41	3	821	105 *	21.60	1	3	20	-								

98. Which future West Indies Test batsman made
his debut for Middlesex in 1973?

WRIGHT, A. S.   Leicestershire

Name: <u>Ashley</u> Spencer Wright
Role: Right-hand bat, right-arm
medium bowler
Born: 21 October 1980, Grantham
Height: 5ft 11in **Weight:** 11st 7lbs
Nickname: Monkey
County debut: 2001
1st-Class catches: 1
One-Day 100s: 1
Place in batting averages: 272nd av. 13.42
Parents: Keith and Anna
Marital status: Single
Family links with cricket: 'Father very keen
cricketer and senior coach'; brother Luke also
on Leicestershire staff
Education: Redmile Primary School;
Belvoir High School; King Edward VII,
Melton Mowbray
Qualifications: 10 GCSEs, coaching award
Cricketers particularly admired: 'All the Leicestershire players'
Young players to look out for: Darren Stevens
Other sports played: Squash
Other sports followed: Football (Leicester City, Notts County, Notts Forest)
Relaxations: 'Music, cinema, going to gym, going out'
Extras: Hit a highest score of 158 against Staffordshire U15. Won the Livingstone
Cup for outstanding batting performance in the 2nd XI 1999. Played for Leicestershire
Board XI in the NatWest 1999 and 2000, scoring maiden one-day century (112) v
Durham Board XI at Gateshead Fell 2000. Also played for Leics Board XI in the
second round of the C&G 2002, which was played in September 2001; played for
Leicestershire in the third round. Released by Leicestershire at the end of the 2002
season
Best batting: 30 Leicestershire v Pakistanis, Leicester 2001

2002 Season

	M	Inns	NO	Runs	HS	Avge	100s	50s	Ct	St	O	M	Runs	Wkts	Avge	Best	5wI	10wM
Test																		
All First	5	8	1	94	28	13.42	-	-	1	-								
1-day Int																		
C & G	1	1	0	10	10	10.00	-	-	-	-								
B & H	1	0	0	0	0	-	-	-	-	-								
1-day Lge	4	2	1	38	20	38.00	-	-	-	-								

Career Performances

	M	Inns	NO	Runs	HS	Avge	100s	50s	Ct	St	Balls	Runs	Wkts	Avge	Best	5wI	10wM
Test																	
All First	6	10	1	124	30	13.77	-	-	1	-							
1-day Int																	
C & G	4	4	0	191	112	47.75	1	1	-	-	36	32	0	-		-	-
B & H	1	0	0	0	0	-	-	-	-	-							
1-day Lge	4	2	1	38	20	38.00	-	-	-	-							

WRIGHT, L. J.   Leicestershire

Name: <u>Luke</u> James Wright
Role: Right-hand bat, right-arm medium-fast bowler
Born: 7 March 1985, Grantham
Height: 5ft 11in **Weight:** 11st 6lbs
County debut: No first-team appearance
Parents: Keith and Anna
Marital status: Single
Family links with cricket: 'Father very keen cricketer (Level 2 coach).' Brother Ashley played for Leicestershire
Education: Redmile Primary School; Belvoir High School, Bottesford; Ratcliffe College
Qualifications: 8 GCSEs, 'currently studying sports science and sports massage'
Off-season: England U19 tour to Australia
Overseas tours: Leicestershire U13 to South Africa; Leicestershire U15 to South Africa; England U19 to Australia 2002-03
Career highlights to date: 'Getting a contract with Leicestershire'
Cricketers particularly admired: Jacques Kallis
Young players to look out for: Ashley Wright, Stephen Adshead, Damian Brandy, Tom New
Other sports played: Football, hockey, squash, tennis
Other sports followed: Football (Newcastle United)
Relaxations: Music, cinema, going out
Extras: Set record for best debut for Ratcliffe College with 130. Scored 86 v MCC, the highest score by a Ratcliffe player against the club. Played for Leicestershire Board XI in the second round of the C&G 2002, which was played in September 2001

2002 Season (did not make any first-class or one-day appearances)

Career Performances

	M	Inns	NO	Runs	HS	Avge	100s	50s	Ct	St	Balls	Runs	Wkts	Avge	Best	5wl	10wM
Test																	
All First																	
1-day Int																	
C & G	1	1	0	16	16	16.00	-	-	-	-							
B & H																	
1-day Lge																	

YARDY, M. H. Sussex

Name: <u>Michael</u> Howard Yardy
Role: Left-hand bat, left-arm fast-medium bowler
Born: 27 November 1980, Pembury, Kent
Height: 6ft **Weight:** 14st
Nickname: Yards, Savage
County debut: 1999 (one-day), 2000 (first-class)
1st-Class 50s: 7
1st-Class catches: 20
Place in batting averages: 149th av. 28.94 (2001 91st av. 34.60)
Strike rate: 174.00 (career 220.00)
Parents: Beverly D'Inverno and Howard Yardy
Marital status: Single
Family links with cricket: Brother plays
Education: St Pauls School, Hastings; William Parker School, Hastings

Qualifications: 5 GCSEs, 2 A-levels, Level 1 coach, Sports Psychology diploma
Overseas tours: Sussex Academy to Cape Town 1999; Sussex to Grenada 2001, 2002
Overseas teams played for: Cape Town CC 1999
Career highlights to date: 'Winning division two Championship with Sussex 2001'
Cricket moments to forget: 'Losing B&H quarter-final v Warwickshire 2002'
Cricket superstitions: 'Lots and lots'
Cricketers particularly admired: Chris Adams, James Kirtley, Matt Prior, 'anyone who has represented their country'
Young players to look out for: Russ Jones, Greg Hobbs, Jon McSweeney, Jon Gardener, Martin Smith, Fraser Key ('the Hastings Academy')

Other sports played: American football
Other sports followed: Football (West Ham)
Injuries: Out for two months with medial ligament damage
Relaxations: 'Anything really'
Extras: Played in the Sussex U15 side that won the U15 County Championship 1996, the U16 side that won the U16 County Championship in 1997 and the U19 side that were runners-up in the NAYC Two-Day Cup 1997. Represented England U17 1998. Attended Sussex Academy. Played for Sussex Board XI in the NatWest 1999 and 2000. Sussex Most Improved Player 2001
Opinions on cricket: 'Go to Matt Prior's!'
Best batting: 93 Sussex v Surrey, The Oval 2002
Best bowling: 1-13 Sussex v Derbyshire, Arundel 2001

2002 Season

	M	Inns	NO	Runs	HS	Avge	100s	50s	Ct	St	O	M	Runs	Wkts	Avge	Best	5wI	10wM
Test																		
All First	10	17	0	492	93	28.94	-	2	11	-	58	9	231	2	115.50	1-17	-	-
1-day Int																		
C & G	3	2	0	62	52	31.00	-	1	-	-	18	0	107	4	26.75	3-39	-	
B & H	6	4	4	43	22 *	-	-	-	5	-	46	0	204	7	29.14	3-30	-	
1-day Lge	6	6	1	82	31	16.40	-	-	2	-	23	1	107	4	26.75	3-36	-	

Career Performances

	M	Inns	NO	Runs	HS	Avge	100s	50s	Ct	St	Balls	Runs	Wkts	Avge	Best	5wI	10wM
Test																	
All First	31	54	7	1352	93	28.76	-	7	20	-	660	376	3	125.33	1-13	-	-
1-day Int																	
C & G	8	7	0	90	52	12.85	-	1	4	-	254	235	6	39.16	3-39	-	
B & H	9	7	4	110	59	36.66	-	1	5	-	306	221	8	27.62	3-30	-	
1-day Lge	12	11	1	138	31	13.80	-	-	2	-	270	200	6	33.33	3-36	-	

99. Who was Lancashire's overseas player in 2000?

YATES, G.   Lancashire

Name: Gary Yates
Role: Right-hand bat, right-arm
off-spin bowler
Born: 20 September 1967,
Ashton-under-Lyne
Height: 6ft 1in **Weight:** 13st 1lb
Nickname: Sweaty, Yugo, Pearly,
Backyard, Zippy
County debut: 1990
County cap: 1994
1st-Class 50s: 5
1st-Class 100s: 3
1st-Class 5 w. in innings: 5
1st-Class catches: 38
Strike rate: (career 74.73)
Parents: Alan and Patricia
Marital status: Single – 'girlfriend Christine
B. Haigh'
Children: Francis Leonard George, 1 May 1999
Family links with cricket: 'Father played for Denton St Lawrence and other teams in
the Lancashire League'
Education: Corrie County Primary School, Denton; Corrie County Junior School,
Denton; Manchester Grammar School
Qualifications: 6 O-levels, Level 2 coach, Australian Cricket Coaching Council coach
Career outside cricket: 'Sales rep with family business (Digical Ltd), selling diaries,
calendars and business gifts'
Off-season: 'Training with Lancashire; taking Level 3 coaching award'
Overseas tours: Lancashire to Tasmania and Western Australia 1990, to Western
Australia 1991, to Johannesburg 1992, to Barbados and St Lucia 1992, to Calcutta
1997, to Cape Town 1997-98; MCC to Bangladesh 1999-2000
Overseas teams played for: South Barwon, Geelong, Australia 1987-88; Johnsonville,
Wellington, New Zealand 1989-90; Western Suburbs, Brisbane 1991-92; Old
Selbornian, East London, South Africa 1992-93; Hermanus CC, South Africa 1995-96
Career highlights to date: 'All trophies won while playing with Lancashire'
Cricket moments to forget: 'Not being selected for a 2nd XI Bain Hogg final after
playing all ten round matches and semi-final'
Cricket superstitions: 'They vary – at the moment my car outside the house has to be
parked facing the same way'
Cricketers particularly admired: Michael Atherton, Ian Botham, John Emburey
Young players to look out for: Chris Schofield, James Anderson
Other sports played: Golf ('represented Lancashire CCC at National *Times* Corporate
Golf Challenge, La Manga, Spain, December 2001')

Other sports followed: 'All sports, especially football (Manchester City season-ticket holder), golf, motor rallying'

Relaxations: 'Playing golf, watching football and good films, eating; spending time with my son'

Extras: Scored century (106) on Championship debut v Nottinghamshire at Trent Bridge 1990. Rapid Cricketline Player of the Month April/May 1992. 2nd XI captain/coach since 2002. Won the double with Bowden CC (Cheshire County League) 2002

Opinions on cricket: 'I feel that over the next few years the game will enter a transitional period. There will be more emphasis on England and the number of English contracted players. There may well be less County Championship matches. I hope to see relegation and promotion restricted to two teams only.'

Best batting: 134* Lancashire v Northamptonshire, Old Trafford 1993
Best bowling: 6-64 Lancashire v Kent, Old Trafford 1999

2002 Season

	M	Inns	NO	Runs	HS	Avge	100s	50s	Ct	St	O	M	Runs	Wkts	Avge	Best	5wI	10wM
Test																		
All First	1	2	0	17	14	8.50	-	-	-	-	29	7	76	0	-	-	-	-
1-day Int																		
C & G																		
B & H																		
1-day Lge	5	5	1	61	32	15.25	-	-	1	-	34	2	149	2	74.50	1-27	-	

Career Performances

	M	Inns	NO	Runs	HS	Avge	100s	50s	Ct	St	Balls	Runs	Wkts	Avge	Best	5wI	10wM
Test																	
All First	82	107	36	1789	134 *	25.19	3	5	38	-	13751	7025	184	38.17	6-64	5	-
1-day Int																	
C & G	21	10	5	91	34 *	18.20	-	-	5	-	1206	692	18	38.44	2-15	-	
B & H	34	15	3	135	26	11.25	-	-	6	-	1566	1093	35	31.22	3-42	-	
1-day Lge	114	53	25	435	38	15.53	-	-	28	-	4068	3280	104	31.53	4-34	-	

100. Which West Indies pace bowler was Durham's overseas player in 1993 and 1994?

ZUIDERENT, B. Sussex

Name: Bastiaan (<u>Bas</u>) Zuiderent
Role: Right-hand top-order bat,
right-arm off-spin bowler
Born: 3 March 1977, Utrecht, Holland
Height: 6ft 3in **Weight:** 14st 2lbs
Nickname: Bazy, Bastil
County debut: 1999 (one-day),
2001 (first-class)
One-Day Internationals: 5
1st-Class 50s: 3
1st-Class 100s: 1
1st-Class catches: 18
One-Day 100s: 1
Place in batting averages: (2001 162nd
av. 23.80)
Parents: Eduard and Jacqueline
Marital status: Girlfriend Kelly
Family links with cricket: Cousins
J. J. Esmeijer and Ben Goedegebuur have represented Holland
Education: Van Oldebarnevelt School, Rotterdam; Erasmiaans Gymnasium,
Rotterdam; University of Amsterdam ('two years; Economics')
Qualifications: Level 2 coaching
Career outside cricket: 'Still studying part-time'
Overseas tours: Various Holland sides to Denmark, Kenya, South Africa and Scotland;
Holland to India and Pakistan (World Cup) 1995-96, to Malaysia (ICC Trophy) 1998, to
Sri Lanka (ICC Champions Trophy) 2002-03
Overseas teams played for: VOC Rotterdam 1989-97; Wits Technikon, Johannesburg
1997; VRA Amsterdam 1998
Career highlights to date: 'Winning [Championship] division two with Sussex 2001.
Participating in 1995-96 World Cup'
Cricket moments to forget: 'My first-class debut'
Cricketers particularly admired: Tim de Leede, Steven Lubbers, P. J. Bakker
Young players to look out for: Daan van Bunge
Other sports played: Football (VOC Rotterdam), golf (Broekpolder), skiing,
squash, tennis
Other sports followed: Football (PSV Eindhoven 'and Man United especially for
Wayne and Sam Tucknott')
Relaxations: 'Cooking, DIY'
Extras: Has represented Holland at various levels since the age of 12. Player of the
Tournament, International Youth Tournament, Denmark 1993. Scored 54 v England in
1995-96 World Cup, becoming the second youngest player (after Sachin Tendulkar) to
score 50 in a World Cup. Played for Holland in the NatWest 1996-98; scored 99 (run

out) v Worcestershire in the 1997 competition, winning the Man of the Match award. B&H Gold Award for his 102* v Hampshire at West End 2001 (his maiden one-day century); two days later scored maiden first-class century (122) v Nottinghamshire at Hove in only his second first-class match. Is not considered an overseas player
Opinions on cricket: 'Still too many games played! We need more exposure and promotion of the game in the country (also Holland) to get more kids interested.'
Best batting: 122 Sussex v Nottinghamshire, Hove 2001
Stop press: Selected for Holland squad for 2002-03 World Cup

2002 Season

	M	Inns	NO	Runs	HS	Avge	100s	50s	Ct	St	O	M	Runs	Wkts	Avge	Best	5wI	10wM
Test																		
All First	1	2	0	10	10	5.00	-	-	-	-								
1-day Int																		
C & G	1	1	0	50	50	50.00	-	1	-	-								
B & H	1	1	0	15	15	15.00	-	-	-	-								
1-day Lge	5	4	0	53	39	13.25	-	-	-	-								

Career Performances

	M	Inns	NO	Runs	HS	Avge	100s	50s	Ct	St	Balls	Runs	Wkts	Avge	Best	5wI	10wM
Test																	
All First	18	29	1	629	122	22.46	1	3	18	-							
1-day Int	5	5	1	91	54	22.75	-	1	4	-							
C & G	7	7	0	199	99	28.42	-	2	3	-	12	15	0	-	-	-	-
B & H	7	7	1	185	102 *	30.83	1	-	3	-							
1-day Lge	24	21	0	406	68	19.33	-	3	6	-							

THE UMPIRES

BENSON, M. R.

Name: <u>Mark</u> Richard Benson
Born: 6 July 1958, Shoreham, Sussex
Height: 5ft 10in
Nickname: Benny
Wife and date of marriage: Sarah Patricia,
20 September 1986
Children: Laurence, 16 October 1987;
Edward, 23 June 1990
Education: Sutton Valence School
Off-season: 'Coaching; trying to improve my
golf and bridge'
Other sports played: Bridge, golf,
swimming, cycling
Relaxations: 'Walking with my wife'
Appointed to 1st-Class list: 2000
One-Day Internationals umpired: 1 as
TV umpire
County as player: Kent
Role: Left-hand bat
County debut: 1980
County cap: 1981
Benefit: 1991 (£174,619)
Test debut: 1986
Tests: 1
One-Day Internationals: 1
1000 runs in a season: 11
1st-Class 50s: 99
1st-Class 100s: 47
1st-Class 200s: 1
1st-Class catches: 140
One-Day 100s: 5
Overseas tours: None

Highlights of playing career: '257 v Hampshire. Winning Sunday League as captain of Kent. Two 90s to win a game against Hampshire with Malcolm Marshall bowling'
Extras: Scored 1000 runs in first full season. Kent captain 1991-95. Captained England in two one-day matches against Holland in 1993. Retired from county cricket in 1995, finishing first-class career with a batting average in excess of 40
Opinions on cricket: 'Wish the game was played in an honest fashion (à la golf). Why fellow pros cheat fellow pros is beyond me. If it happened in golf, the guilty player would probably be ostracised for the rest of his career.'
Best batting: 257 Kent v Hampshire, Southampton 1991
Best bowling: 2-55 Kent v Surrey, Dartford 1986

First-Class Career Performances

	M	Inns	NO	Runs	HS	Avge	100s	Ct	St	Runs	Wkts	Avge	Best	5wI	10wM
Test	1	2	0	51	30	25.50	-	-	-						
All First	292	491	34	18387	257	40.23	48	140	-	493	5	98.60	2-55	-	-

BURGESS, G. I.

Name: <u>Graham</u> Iefvion Burgess
Born: 5 May 1943, Glastonbury, Somerset
Education: Millfield School
Appointed to 1st-Class list: 1991
One-Day Internationals umpired: 2 as
TV umpire
County as player: Somerset
Role: Right-hand bat, right-arm
medium bowler
County debut: 1966
County cap: 1968
Testimonial: 1977
1st-Class 100s: 2
1st-Class 5 w. in innings: 18
1st-Class 10 w. in match: 2
1st-Class catches: 120
One-Day 5 w. in innings: 2
Extras: Played Minor Counties cricket for
Wiltshire 1981-82 and for Cambridgeshire 1983-84
Best batting: 129 Somerset v Gloucestershire, Taunton 1973
Best bowling: 7-43 Somerset v Oxford University, The Parks 1975

First-Class Career Performances

	M	Inns	NO	Runs	HS	Avge	100s	Ct	St	Runs	Wkts	Avge	Best	5wI	10wM
Test															
All First	252	414	37	7129	129	18.90	2	120	-	13543	474	28.57	7-43	18	2

CLARKSON, A.

Name: Anthony (Tony) Clarkson
Born: 5 September 1939, Killinghall,
North Yorkshire
Height: 6ft
Wife's name: Cheryl
Children: André, 5 September 1964;
Chantal, 27 May 1967; Pierre, 1 May 1969
Family links with cricket: Father was a
league professional
Education: Killinghall C of E; Harrogate
Grammar School; Leeds College of Building;
Bradford Polytechnic; Brunel College, Bristol
Career outside cricket: Architectural, civil
engineering and surveying consultant
Other sports followed: Golf and rugby
Relaxations: Golf, DIY, and gardening
Appointed to 1st-Class list: 1996
Counties as player: Yorkshire, Somerset
Role: Right-hand bat, right-arm off-spin
bowler

County debut: 1963 (Yorkshire), 1965 (Somerset)
County cap: 1969 (Somerset)
1000 runs in a season: 2
1st-Class 50s: 23
1st-Class 100s: 2
1st-Class catches: 52
One-Day 100s: 1
Extras: First English player to score a century in the Sunday League. Was league
professional 1973-89
Best batting: 131 Somerset v Northamptonshire, Northampton 1969
Best bowling: 3-51 Somerset v Essex, Yeovil 1967

First-Class Career Performances

	M	Inns	NO	Runs	HS	Avge	100s	Ct	St	Runs	Wkts	Avge	Best	5wI	10wM
Test															
All First	110	189	12	4458	131	25.18	2	52	-	367	13	28.23	3-51	-	-

CONSTANT, D. J.

Name: <u>David</u> John Constant
Born: 9 November 1941,
Bradford-on-Avon, Wiltshire
Height: 5ft 7in
Nickname: Connie
Wife's name: Rosalyn
Children: Lisa, 6 July 1966;
Julie, 21 February 1969
Family links with cricket: Father-in-law,
G.E.E. Lambert, played for Gloucestershire
Education: Grove Park Secondary Modern
Off-season: Bowls
Other sports followed: Football (Millwall)
Interests/relaxations: 'Six grandchildren
and bowls'
Appointed to 1st-Class list: 1969
First appointed to Test panel: 1971
Tests umpired: 36 (plus 5 as TV umpire)
One-Day Internationals umpired: 33 (plus
5 as TV umpire)
Other umpiring honours: Stood in 1975, 1979 and 1983 World Cups
Counties as player: Kent, Leicestershire
Role: Left-hand bat, slow left-arm bowler
County debut: 1961 (Kent), 1965 (Leicestershire)
1st-Class 50s: 6
1st-Class catches: 33
Extras: County bowls player for Gloucestershire 1984-86 (outdoors). Also represented
Somerset at indoor version of the game in the Liberty Trophy
Best batting: 80 Leicestershire v Gloucestershire, Bristol 1966
Best bowling: 1-28 Leicestershire v Surrey, The Oval 1968

First-Class Career Performances

	M	Inns	NO	Runs	HS	Avge	100s	Ct	St	Runs	Wkts	Avge	Best	5wI	10wM
Test															
All First	61	93	14	1517	80	19.20	-	33	-	36	1	36.00	1-28	-	-

COWLEY, N. G.

Name: <u>Nigel</u> Geoffrey Cowley
Born: 1 March 1953, Shaftesbury, Dorset
Height: 5ft 6½in
Marital status: Divorced
Children: Mark Antony, 14 June 1973;
Darren James, 30 October 1976
Family links with cricket: Darren played
Hampshire Schools U11, U12, U13; Natal
Schools 1993, 1994, 1995; and toured India
with South Africa U19 1996
Education: Duchy Manor, Mere, Wilts
Other sports played: Golf (8 handicap)
Other sports followed: Football
(Liverpool FC)
Appointed to 1st-Class list: 2000
Counties as player: Hampshire, Glamorgan
Role: Right-hand bat, off-spin bowler
County debut: 1974 (Hampshire),
1990 (Glamorgan)

County cap: 1978 (Hampshire)
Benefit: 1988 (Hampshire; £88,274)
1000 runs in a season: 1
50 wickets in a season: 2
1st-Class 50s: 36
1st-Class 100s: 2
1st-Class 5 w. in innings: 5
1st-Class catches: 105
One-Day 5 w. in innings: 1
Overseas tours: Hampshire to Barbados 1985, 1986, 1987, to Dubai 1989
Overseas teams played for: Paarl CC, 1982-83; Amanzimtoti, 1984-96
(both South Africa)
Extras: Played for Dorset 1972. NatWest Man of the Match award
Best batting: 109* Hampshire v Somerset, Taunton 1977
Best bowling: 6-48 Hampshire v Leicestershire, Southampton 1982

First-Class Career Performances

	M	Inns	NO	Runs	HS	Avge	100s	Ct	St	Runs	Wkts	Avge	Best	5wI	10wM
Test															
All First	271	375	62	7309	109*	23.35	2	105	-	14879	437	34.04	6-48	5	-

DUDLESTON, B.

Name: Barry Dudleston
Born: 16 July 1945, Bebington, Cheshire
Height: 5ft 9in
Nickname: Danny
Wife and date of marriage: Louise Wendy, 19 October 1994
Children: Sharon Louise, 29 October 1968; Matthew Barry, 12 September 1988; Jack Nicholas, 29 April 1998
Family links with cricket: 'Dad was a league cricketer'
Education: Stockport School
Career outside cricket: Managing director of Sunsport Tours & Travel
Other sports played: Golf
Other sports followed: All sports
Relaxations: Bridge, red wine
Appointed to 1st-Class list: 1984

First appointed to Test panel: 1991
Tests umpired: 2 (plus 14 as TV umpire)
One-Day Internationals umpired: 4 (plus 10 as TV umpire)
Other umpiring honours: Stood in C&G final 2001 and B&H final 2002
Players to watch for the future: James Anderson
Counties as player: Leicestershire, Gloucestershire
Role: Right-hand opening bat, slow left-arm bowler, occasional wicket-keeper
County debut: 1966 (Leicestershire), 1981 (Gloucestershire)
County cap: 1969 (Leicestershire)
Benefit: 1980 (Leicestershire; £25,000)
1000 runs in a season: 8
1st-Class 50s: 64
1st-Class 100s: 31
1st-Class 200s: 1
1st-Class catches: 234
One-Day 100s: 4
Overseas tours: Kent (as guest player) to West Indies 1972; D.H. Robins' XI to West Indies 1973; Wisden XI to West Indies 1984; MCC to Kenya 1993
Overseas teams played for: Rhodesia 1976-80
Highlights of playing career: 'Winning County Championship [with Leicestershire]'
Extras: Played for England U25. Holder with John Steele of the highest first-wicket partnership for Leics, 390 v Derbys at Leicester in 1979. Fastest player in Rhodesian cricket history to 1000 first-class runs in Currie Cup; second fastest ever in Currie Cup
Opinions on cricket: 'My team-mate Duncan Fletcher is doing a great job.'

Best batting: 202 Leicestershire v Derbyshire, Leicester 1979
Best bowling: 4-6 Leicestershire v Surrey, Leicester 1972

First-Class Career Performances

	M	Inns	NO	Runs	HS	Avge	100s	Ct	St	Runs	Wkts	Avge	Best	5wl	10wM
Test															
All First	295	501	47	14747	202	32.48	32	234	7	1365	47	29.04	4-6	-	-

EVANS, J. H.

Name: Jeffrey (<u>Jeff</u>) Howard Evans
Born: 7 August 1954, Llanelli
Height: 5ft 8in
Wife and date of marriage: Christine,
29 December 1983
Children: Rhian, 9 February 1986;
Siân, 3 September 1987; Seren (golden
retriever)
Education: Llanelli Boys Grammar School;
Dudley College of Education
Career outside cricket: Supply teacher
Off-season: Teaching; coaching
Other sports followed: 'Most sports, rugby
in particular'
Relaxations: Keeping fit, walking,
cycling, skiing
Appointed to 1st-Class list: 2001
Highlights of umpiring career: 'First
Championship match – Yorkshire v Somerset
at Headingley 2001'

Cricket moments to forget: 'Any error of judgment!'
Players to watch for the future: James Anderson, Ian Bell
County as player: Did not play first-class cricket. Played league cricket in South
Wales as a right-hand bat
Extras: Coach to Welsh Schools Cricket Association team on tour to Australia 1993.
Taught in the Gwendraeth Grammar School – 'the old "outside half factory"'
Opinions on cricket: 'Would like to see more honesty throughout the game!'

Did not play first-class cricket

GOULD, I. J.

Name: Ian James Gould
Born: 19 August 1957, Taplow, Bucks
Height: 5ft 7in
Nickname: Gunner
Wife and date of marriage: Joanne,
27 September 1986
Children: Gemma; Michael; George
Education: Westgate Secondary Modern,
Slough
Career outside cricket: 'Learning to be a
groundsman'
Other sports played: Golf
Other sports followed: Football (Arsenal),
racing
Relaxations: 'Spending many hours
listening to Richard Edmondson (Racing
Correspondent of *The Independent*) telling
me what might win tomorrow'

Appointed to 1st-Class list: 2002
Players to watch for the future: John Maunders
Counties as player: Middlesex, Sussex
Role: Left-hand bat, wicket-keeper
County debut: 1975 (Middlesex), 1981 (Sussex)
County cap: 1977 (Middlesex), 1981 (Sussex)
Benefit: 1990 (Sussex; £87,097)
One-Day Internationals: 18
1st-Class 50s: 47
1st-Class 100s: 4
1st-Class catches: 536
1st-Class stumpings: 67
Overseas tours: England YC to West Indies 1976; D.H. Robins' XI to Canada
1978-79; International XI to Pakistan 1980-81; England to Australia and New Zealand
1982-83; MCC to Namibia
Overseas teams played for: Auckland 1979-80
Highlights of playing career: 'Playing in the World Cup'
Extras: Represented England in the 1983 World Cup. Retired from county cricket in
1991
Opinions on cricket: 'Too many long faces. Things that are funny should be
laughed at!'
Best batting: 128 Middlesex v Worcestershire, Worcester 1978
Best bowling: 3-10 Sussex v Surrey, The Oval 1989

First-Class Career Performances

	M	Inns	NO	Runs	HS	Avge	100s	Ct	St	Runs	Wkts	Avge	Best	5wI	10wM
Test															
All First	297	399	63	8756	128	26.06	4	536	67	365	7	52.14	3-10	-	-

HAMPSHIRE, J. H.

Name: <u>John</u> Harry Hampshire
Born: 10 February 1941, Thurnscoe, Yorks
Height: 6ft
Nickname: Hamps
Marital status: Widowed
Wife and date of marriage: Judith Ann,
5 September 1964 (deceased 20 April 2002)
Children: Ian Christopher, 6 January 1969;
Paul Wesley, 12 February 1972
Family links with cricket: Father (J.) and
brother (A.W.) both played for Yorkshire
Education: Oakwood Technical High School,
Rotherham
Other sports followed: Most sports
Relaxations: Gardening and cooking
Appointed to 1st-Class list: 1985
First appointed to Test panel: 1989
International panel: 1999-2002
Tests umpired: 21 (plus 4 as TV umpire)
One-Day Internationals umpired: 20 (plus 8 as TV umpire)
Other umpiring honours: Umpired four Tests in Pakistan 1989-90. Toured
Bangladesh 1999-2000 with MCC (as umpire). Stood in Coca-Cola Cup, Sharjah
2000. Umpired NatWest final 2000 and B&H final 2001, 2002
Counties as player: Yorkshire, Derbyshire
Role: Right-hand bat, leg-spin bowler
County debut: 1961 (Yorkshire), 1982 (Derbyshire)
County cap: 1963 (Yorkshire), 1982 (Derbyshire)
Benefit: 1976 (Yorkshire)
Test debut: 1969
Tests: 11
1000 runs in a season: 15
1st-Class 50s: 142
1st-Class 100s: 43
1st-Class 5 w. in innings: 2
1st-Class catches: 445
One-Day 100s: 7

Overseas tours: MCC (England) to Australia and New Zealand 1970-71
Overseas teams played for: Tasmania 1966-69, 1977-79
Extras: Captained Yorkshire 1979-80. Scored a century (107) at Lord's on Test debut (v West Indies 1969); the only England player to have done so. Manager/coach of the Zimbabwe squad for their first Test matches against India and New Zealand 1992-93
Best batting: 183* Yorkshire v Surrey, Hove 1971
Best bowling: 7-52 Yorkshire v Glamorgan, Cardiff 1963

First-Class Career Performances

	M	Inns	NO	Runs	HS	Avge	100s	Ct	St	Runs	Wkts	Avge	Best	5wI	10wM
Test	8	16	1	405	107	26.86	1	9	-						
All First	577	924	112	28059	183*	34.55	43	445	-	1637	30	54.56	7-52	2	-

HARRIS, M. J.

Name: <u>Michael</u> John Harris
Born: 25 May 1944, St Just-in-Roseland, Cornwall
Height: 6ft 1in
Nickname: Pasty
Wife and date of marriage: Danielle Ruth, 10 September 1969
Children: Jodie, Richard
Education: Gerrans Comprehensive
Career outside cricket: Sports teacher
Other sports followed: Squash, golf
Appointed to 1st-Class list: 1998
Counties as player: Middlesex, Notts
Role: Right-hand bat, leg-break bowler, wicket-keeper
County debut: 1964 (Middlesex), 1969 (Notts)
County cap: 1967 (Middlesex), 1970 (Notts)
1000 runs in a season: 11
1st-Class 50s: 98
1st-Class 100s: 40
1st-Class 200s: 1
1st-Class catches: 288
1st-Class stumpings: 14
One-Day 100s: 3
Overseas teams played for: Eastern Province 1971-72; Wellington 1975-76
Extras: Shared Middlesex then-record first-wicket partnership of 312 with Eric Russell v Pakistanis at Lord's 1967. Scored nine centuries in 1971 to equal

Nottinghamshire county record for a season, scoring two centuries in a match twice and totalling 2238 runs at an average of 50.86
Best batting: 201* Nottinghamshire v Glamorgan, Trent Bridge 1973
Best bowling: 4-16 Nottinghamshire v Warwickshire, Trent Bridge 1969

First-Class Career Performances

	M	Inns	NO	Runs	HS	Avge	100s	Ct	St	Runs	Wkts	Avge	Best	5wI	10wM
Test															
All First	344	581	58	19196	201*	36.70	41	288	14	3459	79	43.78	4-16	-	-

HARTLEY, P. J.

Name: Peter John Hartley
Born: 18 April 1960, Keighley
Height: 6ft
Nickname: Jack
Wife and date of marriage: Sharon, 12 March 1988
Children: Megan, 25 April 1992; Courtney, 25 July 1995
Family links with cricket: Father played local league cricket
Education: Greenhead Grammar School, Keighley; Bradford College
Career outside cricket: Sports footwear agent
Off-season: 'Developing and sales of footwear within cricket'
Other sports played: Golf
Other sports followed: Football (Chelsea)

Relaxations: 'Gardening, walking the hound'
Appointed to 1st-Class list: 2003
Counties as player: Warwickshire, Yorkshire, Hampshire
Role: Right-hand bat, right-arm fast-medium bowler
County debut: 1982 (Warwickshire), 1985 (Yorkshire), 1998 (Hampshire)
County cap: 1987 (Yorkshire), 1998 (Hampshire)
Benefit: 1996 (Yorkshire)
50 wickets in a season: 7
1st-Class 50s: 14
1st-Class 100s: 2
1st-Class 5 w. in innings: 23
1st-Class 10 w. in match: 3
1st-Class catches: 68

One-Day 5 w. in innings: 5
Overseas tours: Yorkshire pre-season tours to Barbados 1986-87, to South Africa 1991-92, 1992-93, to Zimbabwe
Overseas teams played for: Melville, New Zealand 1983-84; Adelaide, Australia 1985-86; Harmony and Orange Free State, South Africa 1988-89
Extras: Returned 8-65, his best figures for Hampshire, against Yorkshire, his former county, at Basingstoke 1999. Recorded his highest B&H score (32*) and best one-day analysis (5-20) v Sussex at Hove 2000. Retired at the end of the 2000 season
Best batting: 127* Yorkshire v Lancashire, Old Trafford 1988
Best bowling: 9-41 Yorkshire v Derbyshire, Chesterfield 1995

First-Class Career Performances

	M	Inns	NO	Runs	HS	Avge	100s	Ct	St	Runs	Wkts	Avge	Best	5wI	10wM
Test															
All First	232	283	66	4321	127*	19.91	2	68	-	20635	683	30.21	9-41	23	3

HOLDER, J. W.

Name: <u>John</u> Wakefield Holder
Born: 19 March 1945, St George, Barbados
Height: 6ft
Nickname: Benson, Hod
Wife's name: Glenda
Children: Christopher, 1968; Nigel, 1970
Education: St Giles Boys School; Combermere High School, Barbados; Rochdale College
Off-season: Keeping fit
Other sports followed: Football (Manchester United)
Relaxations: Keeping fit and watching wildlife documentaries
Appointed to 1st-Class list: 1983
First appointed to Test panel: 1988
Tests umpired: 11 (plus 5 as TV umpire)
One-Day Internationals umpired: 19 (plus 3 as TV umpire)
Other umpiring honours: Umpired in Nehru Cup in India and four Tests in Pakistan 1989-90. Has stood in Refuge Assurance Cup, B&H Cup and NatWest Trophy finals and umpired in C&G Trophy final 2002
Players to watch for the future: Jim Troughton
County as player: Hampshire
Role: Right-hand bat, right-arm fast bowler

County debut: 1968
50 wickets in a season: 1
1st-Class 5 w. in innings: 5
1st-Class 10 w. in match: 1
1st-Class catches: 12
Extras: Championship hat-trick v Kent at Southampton 1972
Opinions on cricket: 'I can see the day coming when umpires in international cricket as they are now will become redundant. TV technology is so advanced and commentators are so critical of mistakes that I think TV technology will be used more and more widely and eventually the TV umpire will make all the decisions. When that happens, for me the game will become far more impersonal.'
Best batting: 33 Hampshire v Sussex, Hove 1971
Best bowling: 7-79 Hampshire v Gloucestershire, Gloucester 1972

First-Class Career Performances

	M	Inns	NO	Runs	HS	Avge	100s	Ct	St	Runs	Wkts	Avge	Best	5wI	10wM
Test															
All First	47	49	14	374	33	10.68	-	12	-	3415	139	24.56	7-79	5	1

HOLDER, V. A.

Name: <u>Vanburn</u> Alonza Holder
Born: 8 October 1945, St Michael, Barbados
Height: 6ft 3in
Nickname: Van
Wife's name: Christine
Children: James Vanburn, 2 September 1981
Education: St Leonard's Secondary Modern; Community High
Off-season: 'Working'
Other sports followed: Football (Liverpool)
Relaxations: Music, doing crosswords
Appointed to 1st-Class list: 1992
One-Day Internationals umpired: 2 as TV umpire
County as player: Worcestershire
Role: Right-hand bat, right-arm fast-medium bowler
County debut: 1968
County cap: 1970
Benefit: 1979
Test debut: 1969
Tests: 40

One-Day Internationals: 12
1st-Class 50s: 4
1st-Class 100s: 1
1st-Class 5 w. in innings: 38
1st-Class 10 w. in match: 3
1st-Class catches: 98
One-Day 5 w. in innings: 3
Overseas tours: West Indies to England 1969, 1973, 1975 (World Cup), 1976, to India, Sri Lanka and Pakistan 1974-75, to Australia 1975-76, to India and Sri Lanka 1978-79 (vice-captain); Rest of the World to Pakistan 1973-74
Overseas teams played for: Barbados 1966-78
Extras: Made his debut for Barbados in the Shell Shield competition in 1966-67. Won John Player League 1973 and County Championship 1974 with Worcestershire. Played in West Indies 1975 World Cup winning side
Best batting: 122 Barbados v Trinidad, Bridgetown 1973-74
Best bowling: 7-40 Worcestershire v Glamorgan, Cardiff 1974

First-Class Career Performances

	M	Inns	NO	Runs	HS	Avge	100s	Ct	St	Runs	Wkts	Avge	Best	5wI	10wM
Test	40	59	11	682	42	14.20	-	16	-	3627	109	33.27	6-28	3	-
All First	311	354	81	3559	122	13.03	1	98	-	23183	948	24.45	7-40	38	3

JESTY, T. E.

Name: <u>Trevor</u> Edward Jesty
Born: 2 June 1948, Gosport, Hampshire
Height: 5ft 9in
Nickname: Jets
Wife and date of marriage: Jacqueline, 12 September 1970
Children: Graeme Barry, 27 September 1972; Lorna Samantha, 7 November 1976
Family links with cricket: Daughter played for England XI 2000
Education: Privett County Secondary Modern, Gosport
Off-season: Cricket coaching
Other sports followed: Football (Arsenal)
Relaxations: Gardening, reading
Appointed to 1st-Class list: 1994
One-Day Internationals umpired: 3 as TV umpire
Counties as player: Hampshire, Surrey, Lancashire

Role: Right-hand bat, right-arm medium bowler
County debut: 1966 (Hampshire), 1985 (Surrey), 1988 (Lancashire)
County cap: 1971 (Hampshire), 1985 (Surrey), 1990 (Lancashire)
Benefit: 1982 (Hampshire)
One-Day Internationals: 10
1000 runs in a season: 10
50 wickets in a season: 2
1st-Class 50s: 110
1st-Class 100s: 33
1st-Class 200s: 2
1st-Class 5 w. in innings: 19
1st-Class catches: 265
1st-Class stumpings: 1
One-Day 100s: 7
Overseas tours: International XI to West Indies 1982; joined England tour to Australia 1982-83; Lancashire to Zimbabwe 1989
Overseas teams played for: Border, South Africa 1973-74; Griqualand West 1974-76, 1980-81; Canterbury, New Zealand 1979-80
Highlights of playing career: 'Winning Championship with Hampshire in 1973. Playing against Australia for England in one-day match on 1982-83 tour'
Extras: One of *Wisden*'s Five Cricketers of the Year 1983
Best batting: 248 Hampshire v Cambridge University, Fenner's 1984
Best bowling: 7-75 Hampshire v Worcestershire, Southampton 1976

First-Class Career Performances

	M	Inns	NO	Runs	HS	Avge	100s	Ct	St	Runs	Wkts	Avge	Best	5wI	10wM
Test															
All First	490	777	107	21916	248	32.71	35	265	1	16075	585	27.47	7-75	19	-

JONES, A. A.

Name: <u>Allan</u> Arthur Jones
Born: 9 December 1947, Horley, Surrey
Height: 6ft 4in
Nickname: Jonah
Marital status: Single
Education: St John's College, Horsham
Career outside cricket: Sports tours
Off-season: 'Enjoying life'
Other sports played: Golf
Other sports followed: Football (Arsenal)
Relaxations: English history, reading, cooking
Appointed to 1st-Class list: 1985

First appointed to Test panel: 1996
Tests umpired: 3 as TV umpire
One-Day Internationals umpired: 1
(plus 4 as TV umpire)
Other umpiring honours: Has umpired at
Hong Kong Sixes. Chairman of the First-
Class Umpires' Association
Players to watch for the future: Ed Joyce
Counties as player: Sussex, Somerset,
Middlesex, Glamorgan
Role: Right-hand bat, right-arm fast bowler
County debut: 1964 (Sussex),
1970 (Somerset), 1976 (Middlesex),
1980 (Glamorgan)
County cap: 1972 (Somerset),
1976 (Middlesex)
50 wickets in a season: 4
1st-Class 5 w. in innings: 23
1st-Class 10 w. in match: 3
1st-Class catches: 50
One-Day 5 w. in innings: 5
Overseas teams played for: Northern Transvaal 1971-72; Orange Free State 1976-77;
Auckland (Birkenhead)
Highlights of playing career: '9-51 v Sussex 1972'
Extras: Won two Championship medals with Middlesex (1976 and 1977). Was on
stand-by for England tour of India 1976-77. Represented MCC v Australians 1977.
Was the first person to play for four counties
Opinions on cricket: 'Groundsmen should be appointed and retained by ECB and not
their counties, to achieve higher standard of pitches and more uniformity. Second XI
should be scrapped; integrate club sides into counties to bring on younger players and
revive more interest in amateur game, thus creating more money for schools of
excellence.'
Best batting: 33 Middlesex v Kent, Canterbury 1978
Best bowling: 9-51 Somerset v Sussex, Hove 1972

First-Class Career Performances

	M	Inns	NO	Runs	HS	Avge	100s	Ct	St	Runs	Wkts	Avge	Best	5wI	10wM
Test															
All First	214	216	68	799	33	5-39	-	50	-	15414	549	28.07	9-51	23	3

KITCHEN, M. J.

Name: Mervyn (<u>Merv</u>) John Kitchen
Born: 1 August 1940, Nailsea, Somerset
Height: 5ft 11in
Nickname: MJ
Wife and date of marriage: Anne,
March 1972
Children: Faye, 30 September 1975;
Jody, 5 March 1977
Family links with cricket: Father played
local cricket for the village of Nailsea
Education: Backwell Secondary Modern,
Backwell
Career outside cricket: 'Many varied winter
jobs – driver, labourer, decorator, printing;
worked on the racetracks, horses and
greyhounds, for a bookmaker for ten years'
Off-season: 'Relaxing at home; walking our
retriever; playing golf'

Other sports played: Golf, bowls, skittles
Other sports followed: 'Love TV football now the coverage is so good; no allegiance
to any teams'
Relaxations: 'Like crosswords but very rarely complete one; DIY'
Appointed to 1st-Class list: 1982
First appointed to Test panel: 1990
International panel: 1995-99
Tests umpired: 20 (plus 3 as TV umpire)
One-Day Internationals umpired: 28 (plus 8 as TV umpire)
Other umpiring honours: Stood in 1983 World Cup. Has umpired finals of each of
the domestic one-day competitions. Umpired in a one-day series in Kenya between the
hosts, Bangladesh and Zimbabwe, including the final, 1997-98
Highlights of umpiring career: 'My first Test match, England v New Zealand at
Lord's with D. Shepherd'
Players to watch for the future: James Troughton
County as player: Somerset
Role: Left-hand bat, occasional right-arm medium bowler
County debut: 1960
County cap: 1966
Testimonial: 1973
1000 runs in a season: 7
1st-Class 50s: 68
1st-Class 100s: 17
1st-Class catches: 157

One-Day 100s: 1
Overseas tours: Whitbread Wanderers to Rhodesia
Highlights of playing career: 'Many happy memories but perhaps playing with such talent as Viv Richards, Ian Botham and Joel Garner all in the same side ranks the top of my list'
Cricket moments to forget: 'I once scored three ducks in three days – one on Saturday in the Championship, one on the Sunday in the John Player League and another, second, Championship innings on the Monday'
Extras: Won two Gillette Cup Man of the Match awards and two B&H Gold Awards. Retired in September 1979 and played local cricket for Mendip Acorns
Opinions on cricket: 'Microscopic examination of umpires and players by TV replays. Tremendous coverage of cricket all over the world by TV, which I think has increased the knowledge of the armchair watcher.'
Best batting: 189 Somerset v Pakistanis, Taunton 1967
Best bowling: 1-4 Somerset v Sussex, Taunton 1969

First-Class Career Performances

	M	Inns	NO	Runs	HS	Avge	100s	Ct	St	Runs	Wkts	Avge	Best	5wI	10wM
Test															
All First	354	612	32	15230	189	26.25	17	157	-	109	2	54.50	1-4	-	-

LEADBEATER, B.

Name: Barrie Leadbeater
Born: 14 August 1943, Leeds
Height: 6ft
Nickname: Leady
Marital status: Widowed
Wife and date of marriage: Jacqueline, 18 September 1971 (deceased 1997)
Children: Richard Barrie, 23 November 1972; Michael Spencer, 21 March 1976; Daniel Mark Ronnie, 19 June 1981
Education: Harehills County Secondary, Leeds
Career outside cricket: LGV Class 1 driver – Renshaw Scotts
Off-season: As above
Other sports played: Golf, snooker, table tennis
Other sports followed: All sport – football (Leeds United), rugby league (Leeds Rhinos)
Relaxations: 'Reading, going to the pub, running'

Appointed to 1st-Class list: 1981
Tests umpired: 2 as TV umpire
One-Day Internationals umpired: 5 (plus 2 as TV umpire)
Other umpiring honours: Stood in 1983 World Cup. MCC tours to New Zealand 1999 and to Argentina and Chile 2001. Former chairman of the First-Class Umpires' Association
County as player: Yorkshire
Role: Right-hand opening bat, right-arm medium bowler, slip fielder
County debut: 1966
County cap: 1969
Benefit: 1980 (joint benefit with G.A. Cope)
1st-Class 50s: 27
1st-Class 100s: 1
1st-Class catches: 82
Overseas tours: Duke of Norfolk's XI to West Indies 1970
Overseas teams played for: Johannesburg Municipals 1978-79
Highlights of playing career: 'Man of the Match in Gillette Cup final 1969'
Cricket moments to forget: 'I've forgotten'
Extras: Took part in London Marathon 1997, 1998, 2000. Retired from county cricket in 1979 and played social cricket (still playing)
Best batting: 140* Yorkshire v Hampshire, Portsmouth 1976
Best bowling: 1-1 Yorkshire v Middlesex, Headingley 1971

First-Class Career Performances

	M	Inns	NO	Runs	HS	Avge	100s	Ct	St	Runs	Wkts	Avge	Best	5wI	10wM
Test															
All First	147	241	29	5373	140*	25.34	1	82	-	5	1	5.00	1-1	-	-

LLONG, N. J.

Name: Nigel James Llong
Born: 11 February 1969, Ashford, Kent
Height: 6ft
Nickname: Nidge
Wife and date of marriage: Melissa, 20 February 1999
Children: Andrew Stuart, 30 August 2002
Family links with cricket: Father and brother played local club cricket
Education: North School for Boys, Ashford
Off-season: Coaching – Kent Cricket Board; Duke of York School, Dover
Other sports followed: Football (Arsenal), 'generally most sports'
Relaxations: Fishing, clay-pigeon shooting
Appointed to 1st-Class list: 2002
Players to watch for the future: Ben Phillips

County as player: Kent
Role: Left-hand bat, right-arm off-spin bowler
County debut: 1991
County cap: 1993
1st-Class 50s: 16
1st-Class 100s: 6
1st-Class 5 w. in innings: 2
1st-Class catches: 59
One-Day 100s: 2
Overseas tours: Kent to Zimbabwe 1993
Overseas teams played for: Ashburton, Melbourne 1988-90, 1996-97; Greenpoint, Cape Town, 1990-95
Highlights of playing career: 'B&H final 1997. Sunday League winners 1995. First Championship hundred, Lord's 1993'
Cricket moments to forget: 'Sunday League [1993], last match against Glamorgan at Canterbury – lost the match and were runners-up. Plus not making the most of my ability'
Extras: Kent Young Player of the Year 1992. Man of the Match in 2nd XI Trophy semi-final and final 1999. Retired from county cricket in September 1999 and played for Norfolk in 2000
Opinions on cricket: 'Good pitches produce good players. With central contracts, we now need two overseas players per club (especially bowlers).'
Best batting: 130 Kent v Hampshire, Canterbury 1996
Best bowling: 5-21 Kent v Middlesex, Canterbury 1996

First-Class Career Performances

	M	Inns	NO	Runs	HS	Avge	100s	Ct	St	Runs	Wkts	Avge	Best	5wI	10wM
Test															
All First	68	108	11	3024	130	31.17	6	59	-	1259	35	35.97	5-21	2	-

LLOYDS, J. W.

Name: <u>Jeremy</u> William Lloyds
Born: 17 November 1954, Penang, Malaya
Height: 5ft 11in
Nickname: Jerry
Wife and date of marriage: Janine,
16 September 1997
Children: Kaeli, 16 November 1991
Family links with cricket: Father played
cricket in Malaya. Brother Chris played for
Somerset 2nd XI
Education: Curry Rivel Primary School;
St Dunstan's Prep School; Blundell's School,
Tiverton
Career outside cricket: Coaching and
setting up Western Province Youth
Programme 1992-95 in South Africa. Works
for National Car Rental

Other sports played: Golf (6 handicap)
Other sports followed: Golf, football (Tottenham Hotspur), American football
(San Francisco 49ers), Formula One and saloon car racing, rugby (Gloucester)
Relaxations: 'Reading, music and spending time at home with my family'
Appointed to 1st-Class list: 1998
International panel: 2002 – (as TV umpire)
Tests umpired: 4 as TV umpire
One-Day Internationals umpired: 2 (plus 6 as TV umpire)
Counties as player: Somerset, Gloucestershire
Role: Left-hand bat, off-spin bowler
County debut: 1979 (Somerset), 1985 (Gloucestershire)
County cap: 1982 (Somerset), 1985 (Gloucestershire)
1000 runs in a season: 3
1st-Class 50s: 62
1st-Class 100s: 10
1st-Class 5 w. in innings: 13
1st-Class 10 w. in match: 1
1st-Class catches: 229
Overseas tours: Somerset to Antigua 1982; Gloucestershire to Barbados 1985,
to Sri Lanka 1987
Overseas teams played for: St Stithian's Old Boys, Johannesburg 1978-79; Toombull
DCC, Brisbane 1980-82; North Sydney District 1982-83; Alberton, Johannesburg
1984; Preston CC, Melbourne 1986; Orange Free State 1987; Fish Hoek CC,
Cape Town 1988-92
Highlights of playing career: 'Winning 1983 NatWest final'

Extras: Highest score in Brisbane Premier League 1980-81 (165). Britannic Player of the Month July 1987. Gloucestershire Player of the Year 1987. Leading run-scorer in Western Province Cricket League 1988, 1989

Opinions on cricket: 'Too much overseas influence on how to play the game in England. We have more variations in wickets and weather conditions than in most other countries. Yes, take the best of what they have and work it into our game. Also, too much emphasis on all the various levels of coaching certificates. We have been dragged too far away from the *basics* – batting, bowling and fielding. The game hasn't really changed – people's perception of it has! We show people how to play but not the thinking side of it. At times, some players are too robotic. Whatever happened to natural flair?'

Best batting: 132* Somerset v Northamptonshire, Northampton 1982
Best bowling: 7-88 Somerset v Essex, Chelmsford 1982

First-Class Career Performances

	M	Inns	NO	Runs	HS	Avge	100s	Ct	St	Runs	Wkts	Avge	Best	5wI	10wM
Test															
All First	267	408	64	10679	132*	31.04	10	229	-	12943	333	38.86	7-88	13	1

MALLENDER, N. A.

Name: <u>Neil</u> Alan Mallender
Born: 13 August 1961, Kirk Sandall, Doncaster
Height: 6ft
Nickname: Ghostie
Marital status: Divorced
Children: Kirstie, 14; Dominic, 11; Jacob, 6
Education: Beverley Grammar School
Off-season: 'Umpired five ODIs in South Africa – South Africa v Pakistan. Due to umpire in 2003 World Cup'
Other sports played: Golf (3 handicap)
Other sports followed: 'Most sports'
Relaxations: 'Most sports; music'
Appointed to 1st-Class list: 1999
International panel: 2002 –
Tests umpired: 3 as TV umpire
One-Day Internationals umpired:
10 (plus 4 as TV umpire)

Other umpiring honours: Went with MCC to umpire in Namibia March/April 2001. PCA Umpire of the Year 2001
Highlights of umpiring career: 'First ODI at Lord's, England v Pakistan – and game went to the last ball'

Players to watch for the future: Michael Lumb, James Troughton, Ian Hunter
Counties as player: Northamptonshire, Somerset
Role: Right-hand bat, right-arm fast-medium bowler
County debut: 1980 (Northamptonshire), 1987 (Somerset)
County cap: 1984 (Northamptonshire), 1987 (Somerset)
Benefit: 1994 (Somerset)
Test debut: 1992
Tests: 2
50 wickets in a season: 6
1st-Class 50s: 10
1st-Class 100s: 1
1st-Class 5 w. in innings: 36
1st-Class 10 w. in match: 5
1st-Class catches: 111
One-Day 5 w. in innings: 3
Overseas tours: England YC to West Indies 1979-80
Overseas teams played for: Kaikorai, Dunedin, New Zealand; University, Wellington, New Zealand; Otago, New Zealand 1983-84 – 1992-93
Highlights of playing career: 'Test debut at Headingley'
Extras: Represented England YC 1980-81. Took 5-50 on Test debut v Pakistan at Headingley in 1992. Retired from county cricket in 1996
Best batting: 100* Otago v Central Districts, Palmerston North 1991-92
Best bowling: 7-27 Otago v Auckland, Auckland 1984-85

First-Class Career Performances

	M	Inns	NO	Runs	HS	Avge	100s	Ct	St	Runs	Wkts	Avge	Best	5wI	10wM
Test	2	3	0	8	4	2.66	-	-	-	215	10	21.50	5-50	1	-
All First	345	396	122	4709	100*	17.18	1	111	-	24654	937	26.31	7-27	36	5

PALMER, R.

Name: Roy Palmer
Born: 12 July 1942, Hampshire
Height: 6ft 3in
Nickname: Arp
Wife and date of marriage: Alyne, 5 November 1983
Children: Nick, 7 October 1968
Family links with cricket: Brother of Ken Palmer, former Test umpire and Somerset player; nephew Gary also played for Somerset
Education: Southbroom Secondary Modern, Devizes
Off-season: Golf, DIY
Relaxations: Golf
Appointed to 1st-Class list: 1980

First appointed to Test panel: 1992
Tests umpired: 2 (plus 1 as TV umpire)
One-Day Internationals umpired: 8 (plus 2 as TV umpire)
Other umpiring honours: Stood in 1983 World Cup
Players to watch for the future: Matthew Wood (Somerset)
County as player: Somerset
Role: Right-hand bat, right-arm fast-medium bowler
County debut: 1965
50 wickets in a season: 1
1st-Class 50s: 1
1st-Class 5 w. in innings: 4
1st-Class catches: 25
One-Day 5 w. in innings: 1
Extras: Won two Man of the Match Awards in the Gillette Cup
Best batting: 84 Somerset v Leicestershire, Taunton 1967
Best bowling: 6-45 Somerset v Middlesex, Lord's 1967

First-Class Career Performances

	M	Inns	NO	Runs	HS	Avge	100s	Ct	St	Runs	Wkts	Avge	Best	5wI	10wM
Test															
All First	74	110	32	1037	84	13.29	-	25	-	5439	172	31.62	6-45	4	-

SHARP, G.

Name: George Sharp
Born: 12 March 1950, West Hartlepool,
County Durham
Height: 5ft 11in
Nickname: Sharpy, Blunt, Razor, Toffee
Wife and date of marriage: Audrey,
14 September 1974
Children: Gareth James, 27 June 1984
Education: Elwick Road Secondary Modern,
Hartlepool
Career outside cricket: Watching all sports
Off-season: Working as joint director of GSB
Loams Ltd for soils and top dressing
Other sports played: Golf (8 handicap)
Other sports followed: Football (Newcastle
Utd and Middlesbrough), rugby
(Northampton Saints)
Relaxations: Golf; 'spend a lot of time in the
gym during the off-season'
Appointed to 1st-Class list: 1992
International panel: 1996-2002
Tests umpired: 15 (plus 1 as TV umpire)
One-Day Internationals umpired: 31 (plus 13 as TV umpire)
Other umpiring honours: Has umpired three B&H finals and one NatWest final and
stood in the inaugural C&G final 2001 and the 2002 final. Has stood in four overseas
tournaments, including the Singer Cup (India, Sri Lanka, Pakistan) in Singapore 1995-
96 and the Singer Champions Trophy (Pakistan, Sri Lanka, New Zealand) in Sharjah
1996-97
County as player: Northamptonshire
Role: Right-hand bat, wicket-keeper
County debut: 1967
County cap: 1973
Benefit: 1982
1st-Class 50s: 21
1st-Class catches: 565
1st-Class stumpings: 90
Overseas tours: England Counties XI to Barbados and Trinidad 1975
Best batting: 98 Northamptonshire v Yorkshire, Northampton 1983
Best bowling: 1-47 Northamptonshire v Yorkshire, Northampton 1980

First-Class Career Performances

	M	Inns	NO	Runs	HS	Avge	100s	Ct	St	Runs	Wkts	Avge	Best	5wI	10wM
Test															
All First	306	396	81	6254	98	19.85	-	565	90	70	1	70.00	1-47	-	-

SHEPHERD, D. R.

Name: <u>David</u> Robert Shepherd
Born: 27 December 1940, Bideford, Devon
Height: 5ft 10in
Nickname: Shep
Marital status: Single
Family links with cricket: Father: club cricketer and local umpire. Brother Bill: MCC Young Professional, Devon CCC and North Devon CC; local umpire
Education: Barnstaple Grammar School; St Luke's College, Exeter
Career outside cricket: Schoolteacher
Off-season: 'With international umpiring now, there is no close season'
Other sports played: 'Used to play rugby (school, Devon Public & Grammar Schools XV, South Molton RFC)'
Other sports followed: 'All sports'
Relaxations: Stamp collecting
Appointed to 1st-Class list: 1981
First appointed to Test panel: 1985
International panel: 1994-2002
Elite panel: 2002 –
Tests umpired: 69
One-Day Internationals umpired: 116 (plus 13 as TV umpire)
Other umpiring honours: Has stood in each World Cup since 1983, including the 1995-96 final between Australia and Sri Lanka in Lahore and the 1999 final between Australia and Pakistan at Lord's. Umpired the MCC Bicentenary Test, England v Rest of the World, at Lord's in 1987. Has umpired numerous domestic finals. Received National Grid/ICC 'bronze award' in March 1998 for long service as a Test umpire. Umpired 50th Test, India v South Africa, Mumbai (Bombay) February 2000, receiving ICC 'silver award' to acknowledge this achievement. Known for his superstition regarding 'Nelson' score 111, and multiples – 222, 333 etc.
Highlights of umpiring career: 'Standing in first Test match. Two World Cup finals.'
County as player: Gloucestershire

Role: Right-hand bat, right-arm ('occasional!') medium bowler
County debut: 1965
County cap: 1969
Benefit: 1978 (joint benefit with J. Davey)
1000 runs in a season: 2
1st-Class 50s: 55
1st-Class 100s: 12
1st-Class catches: 95
One-Day 100s: 2
Highlights of playing career: 'Winning two domestic finals with Gloucestershire at Lord's – the Gillette Cup in 1973 and the B&H Cup in 1977'
Extras: Played Minor Counties cricket for Devon 1959-64. First player to score a century for Gloucestershire on his first-class debut, v Oxford University 1965. Retired from county cricket in 1979 and played a little cricket for his original club, North Devon CC. Was awarded the MBE in 1997 for services to cricket. Wrote autobiography (*Shep*) 2001
Opinions on cricket: 'Players at the highest level must realise that they have a tremendous responsibility to the game as a whole. Their behaviour on the field is of the utmost importance, as they set an example to the rest of the sport. We must get some trust back in the game between players and officials and administrators, as well as between players themselves. How I hate the cheats!! Any batsman who stands at the crease knowing he is out is in my book a cheat! Any player who appeals knowing the batsman is not out is also a cheat!'
Best batting: 153 Gloucestershire v Middlesex, Bristol 1968
Best bowling: 1-1 Gloucestershire v Northamptonshire, Gloucester 1968

First-Class Career Performances

	M	Inns	NO	Runs	HS	Avge	100s	Ct	St	Runs	Wkts	Avge	Best	5wI	10wM
Test															
All First	282	476	40	10672	153	24.47	12	95	-	106	2	53.00	1-1	-	-

STEELE, J. F.

Name: <u>John</u> Frederick Steele
Born: 23 July 1946, Stafford
Height: 5ft 10in
Nickname: Steely
Wife and date of marriage: Susan, 17 April 1977
Children: Sarah Jane, 2 April 1982; Robert Alfred, 10 April 1985
Family links with cricket: Uncle Stan played for Staffordshire. Brother David played for Northamptonshire, Derbyshire and England. Cousin Brian Crump played for Northamptonshire and Staffordshire
Education: Endon School, Stoke-on-Trent; Stafford College

Other sports followed: Soccer (Stoke City, Port Vale), golf
Relaxations: Music and walking
Appointed to 1st-Class list: 1997
Counties as player: Leicestershire, Glamorgan
Role: Right-hand bat, slow left-arm bowler
County debut: 1970 (Leicestershire), 1984 (Glamorgan)
County cap: 1971 (Leicestershire), 1984 (Glamorgan)
Benefit: 1983 (Leicestershire)
1000 runs in a season: 6
1st-Class 50s: 69
1st-Class 100s: 21
1st-Class 5 w. in innings: 16
1st-Class catches: 414
One-Day 100s: 1
One-Day 5 w. in innings: 4

Overseas teams played for: Springs HSOB, Northern Transvaal 1971-73; Pine Town CC, Natal 1973-74, 1982-83; Natal 1975-76, 1978-79
Extras: Played for England U25. Was voted Natal's Best Bowler in 1975-76. First-wicket record partnership for Leicestershire of 390 with Barry Dudleston v Derbyshire at Leicester 1979. Won two Man of the Match Awards in the Gillette Cup and four in the Benson and Hedges Cup. Won the award for the most catches in a season in 1984
Best batting: 195 Leicestershire v Derbyshire, Leicester 1971
Best bowling: 7-29 Natal B v Griqualand West, Umzinto 1973-74
           7-29 Leicestershire v Gloucestershire, Leicester 1980

First-class career performances

	M	Inns	NO	Runs	HS	Avge	100s	Ct	St	Runs	Wkts	Avge	Best	5wI	10wM
Test															
All First	379	605	85	15053	195	28.94	21	414	-	15793	584	27.04	7-29	16	-

WHITEHEAD, A. G. T.

Name: <u>Alan</u> Geoffrey Thomas Whitehead
Born: 28 October 1940, Butleigh, Somerset
Appointed to 1st-Class list: 1970
First appointed to Test panel: 1982
Tests umpired: 5 (plus 5 as TV umpire)
One-Day Internationals umpired: 14
(plus 2 as TV umpire)
Other umpiring honours: Stood in the 1979
and 1983 World Cups
County as player: Somerset
Role: Left-hand bat, slow left-arm bowler
County debut: 1957
1st-Class 5 w. in innings: 3
1st-Class catches: 20
Best batting: 15 Somerset v Hampshire,
Southampton 1959
Best bowling: 6-74 Somerset v Sussex,
Eastbourne 1959

First-Class Career Performances

	M	Inns	NO	Runs	HS	Avge	100s	Ct	St	Runs	Wkts	Avge	Best	5wI	10wM
Test															
All First	38	49	25	137	15	5.70	-	20	-	2306	67	34.41	6-74	3	

WILLEY, P.

Name: Peter Willey
Born: 6 December 1949, Sedgefield, County Durham
Height: 6ft 1in
Nickname: Will, 'many unprintable'
Wife and date of marriage: Charmaine, 23 September 1971
Children: Heather Jane, 11 September 1985; David, 28 February 1990
Family links with cricket: Father played local club cricket in County Durham
Education: Seaham Secondary School, County Durham
Other sports followed: All sports
Relaxations: Gardening, dog-walking
Appointed to 1st-Class list: 1993
International panel: 1996 –
Tests umpired: 24 (plus 4 as TV umpire)
One-Day Internationals umpired: 26 (plus 10 as TV umpire)

Other umpiring honours: Stood in the 1999 World Cup and in the 1999 Benson and Hedges Super Cup final
Counties as player: Northamptonshire, Leicestershire
Role: Right-hand bat, off-break bowler
County debut: 1966 (Northamptonshire), 1984 (Leicestershire)
County cap: 1971 (Northamptonshire), 1984 (Leicestershire)
Benefit: 1981 (Northamptonshire; £31,400)
Test debut: 1976
Tests: 26
One-Day Internationals: 26
1000 runs in a season: 10
50 wickets in a season: 2
1st-Class 50s: 101
1st-Class 100s: 43
1st-Class 200s: 1
1st-Class 5 w. in innings: 26
1st-Class 10 w. in match: 3
1st-Class catches: 235
One-Day 100s: 9

Overseas tours: England to Australia and India 1979-80, to West Indies 1980-81, 1985-86; unofficial England XI to South Africa 1981-82
Overseas teams played for: Eastern Province, South Africa 1982-85
Extras: Became youngest player ever to play for Northamptonshire, at 16 years 180 days v Cambridge University in 1966. Leicestershire captain 1987. Played for Northumberland in 1992. Offered membership of the ICC Elite Panel of umpires in 2002 but declined because of the amount of time the appointment would require away from his family
Best batting: 227 Northamptonshire v Somerset, Northampton 1976
Best bowling: 7-37 Northamptonshire v Oxford University, The Parks 1975

First-Class Career Performances

	M	Inns	NO	Runs	HS	Avge	100s	Ct	St	Runs	Wkts	Avge	Best	5wI	10wM
Test	26	50	6	1184	102*	26.90	2	3	-	456	7	65.14	2-73	-	-
All First	559	918	121	24361	227	30.56	44	235	-	23400	756	30.95	7-37	26	3

THE 2002 SEASON
ROLL OF HONOUR

ROLL OF HONOUR 2002

FRIZZELL COUNTY CHAMPIONSHIP

Division One

		P	W	L	D	T	Bt	Bl	Pts
1	Surrey (I/4)	16	10	2	4	0	59	48	242.75
2	Warwickshire (II/3)	16	7	2	7	0	42	44	198
3	Kent (I/3)	16	7	4	5	0	48	44	195.50
4	Lancashire (I/6)	16	6	4	6	0	33	43	172
5	Leicestershire (I/5)	16	5	5	6	0	42	46	171
6	Sussex (II/1)	16	3	6	7	0	43	47	154
7	Hampshire (II/2)	16	2	5	9	0	35	44	131
8	Somerset (I/2)	16	1	7	8	0	39	44	126.75
9	Yorkshire (I/1)	16	2	8	6	0	35	45	124.75

The bottom three counties were relegated to Division Two for the 2003 season

Division Two

		P	W	L	D	T	Bt	Bl	Pts
1	Essex (I/9)	16	10	3	3	0	42	46	219
2	Middlesex (II/5)	16	7	3	6	0	61	43	211.75
3	Nottinghamshire (II/7)	16	8	5	3	0	47	48	201.75
4	Worcestershire (II/6)	16	7	4	5	0	53	43	200
5	Glamorgan (I/8)	16	5	5	6	0	41	44	169
6	Derbyshire (II/9)	16	7	7	2	0	37	48	167.75
7	Northamptonshire (I/7)	16	5	7	4	0	46	41	162.50
8	Gloucestershire (II/4)	16	2	7	7	0	42	44	136.50
9	Durham (II/8)	16	1	11	4	0	21	42	90.75

The top three counties were promoted to Division One for the 2003 season

Teams are docked 0.25 points for each over they fail to bowl of the target figure of 16 per hour

NORWICH UNION LEAGUE

Division One

		P	W	L	T	NR	Pts
1	Glamorgan (II/1)	16	12	3	1	0	50
2	Worcestershire (II/3)	16	11	3	0	2	48
3	Warwickshire (I/3)	16	9	6	0	1	38
4	Yorkshire (I/6)	16	8	7	0	1	34
5	Kent (I/1)	16	7	8	1	0	30
6	Leicestershire (I/2)	16	7	8	0	1	30
7	Somerset (I/4)	16	5	10	0	1	22
8	Durham (II/2)	16	5	11	0	0	20
9	Nottinghamshire (I/5)	16	3	11	0	2	16

The bottom three counties were relegated to Division Two for the 2003 season

Division Two

		P	W	L	T	NR	Pts
1	Gloucestershire (I/7)	16	10	4	0	2	44
2	Surrey (I/8)	16	10	5	0	1	42
3	Essex (II/7)	16	10	6	0	0	40
4	Derbyshire (II/9)	16	8	7	0	1	34
5	Lancashire (II/6)	16	7	7	0	2	32
6	Northamptonshire (I/9)	16	7	8	0	1	30
7	Hampshire (II/4)	16	6	9	0	1	26
8	Sussex (II/5)	16	4	10	0	2	20
9	Middlesex (II/8)	16	4	10	0	2	20

The top three counties were promoted to Division One for the 2003 season

CHELTENHAM & GLOUCESTER TROPHY

Winners: Yorkshire
Runners-up: Somerset

BENSON AND HEDGES CUP

Winners: Warwickshire
Runners-up: Essex

FIRST-CLASS
AVERAGES
2002

2002 AVERAGES (all first-class matches)

BATTING AVERAGES – including fielding
Qualifying requirements: 6 completed innings

Name	Matches	Inns	NO	Runs	HS	Avge	100s	50s	Ct	St
R.Dravid	7	9	1	773	217	96.62	3	3	14	-
N.V.Knight	10	19	3	1520	255*	95.00	5	5	10	-
R.A.White	4	7	1	556	277	92.66	1	3	1	-
M.L.Love	6	8	1	576	251	82.28	2	2	3	-
M.P.Vaughan	9	15	2	976	197	75.07	4	3	5	-
S.R.Tendulkar	6	8	0	573	193	71.62	2	2	2	-
M.E.Trescothick	6	11	2	622	161	69.11	2	4	5	-
M.E.K.Hussey	13	23	2	1442	310*	68.66	5	4	21	-
A.J.Hollioake	9	13	2	738	208	67.09	2	5	10	-
D.S.Lehmann	10	18	1	1136	216	66.82	3	7	5	-
M.G.Bevan	9	14	3	697	146	63.36	2	4	4	-
D.P.M.D.Jayawardene	6	11	2	567	125*	63.00	3	1	3	-
I.J.Ward	17	31	3	1759	168*	62.82	7	7	10	-
K.P.Pietersen	12	17	3	871	254*	62.21	4	-	12	-
M.J.DiVenuto	15	28	3	1538	230	61.52	4	7	29	-
R.C.Irani	12	19	3	977	207*	61.06	3	1	-	-
Abdul Razzaq	6	9	3	364	203*	60.66	1	-	1	-
M.R.Ramprakash	15	25	4	1194	218	56.85	4	6	6	-
G.A.Hick	18	30	4	1453	315*	55.88	4	6	30	-
M.P.Maynard	13	20	1	1058	151	55.68	3	6	14	-
D.Ganga	5	8	2	325	139*	54.16	2	-	3	-
M.T.G.Elliott	5	10	1	487	127	54.11	1	4	7	-
J.P.Crawley	15	25	4	1130	272	53.80	2	7	8	-
A.J.Stewart	11	16	2	751	123	53.64	1	5	34	4
K.J.Barnett	8	15	3	641	182*	53.41	3	1	1	-
P.D.Collingwood	7	12	0	636	190	53.00	1	4	5	-
S.P.James	14	22	1	1111	249	52.90	4	3	7	-
S.G.Law	15	26	3	1216	218	52.86	2	6	21	-
E.C.Joyce	18	27	3	1267	129	52.79	4	6	16	-
P.N.Weekes	18	25	6	990	127*	52.10	4	3	23	-
M.A.Gough	8	14	2	616	103	51.33	1	3	6	-
J.O.Troughton	14	24	3	1067	131*	50.80	3	6	8	-
R.Clarke	10	16	2	711	153*	50.78	2	4	9	-
A.D.Brown	16	26	2	1211	188	50.45	5	3	18	-
M.J.Powell	16	26	3	1152	135	50.08	3	7	7	-
A.Flower	16	29	6	1151	172*	50.04	2	6	35	1
P.A.de Silva	8	12	2	500	88	50.00	-	6	-	-

Name	Matches	Inns	NO	Runs	HS	Avge	100s	50s	Ct	St
V.Sehwag	8	13	0	640	142	49.23	3	1	13	-
C.M.Spearman	17	34	4	1444	180*	48.13	5	7	16	-
A.J.Strauss	17	27	2	1202	141	48.08	3	5	16	-
S.C.Ganguly	7	11	1	477	128	47.70	1	4	3	-
D.L.Maddy	16	29	4	1187	156	47.48	2	8	22	-
M.S.Atapattu	7	12	1	522	185	47.45	2	1	1	-
R.J.Blakey	16	29	7	1041	103	47.31	1	8	29	1
O.A.Shah	17	26	3	1084	172*	47.13	3	6	5	-
M.A.Butcher	13	21	1	936	123	46.80	3	5	8	-
D.S.Smith	6	10	0	465	181	46.50	1	2	4	-
S.G.Koenig	18	29	2	1251	141*	46.33	4	7	6	-
D.C.Nash	15	19	5	646	100	46.14	1	4	36	1
D.D.J.Robinson	18	34	2	1474	175	46.06	5	6	17	-
H.P.Tillekeratne	8	13	5	366	81	45.75	-	2	8	-
U.Afzaal	18	32	4	1275	134	45.53	5	6	12	-
R.C.Russell	17	28	6	991	119*	45.04	3	5	39	2
C.J.Adams	10	19	0	848	217	44.63	3	3	2	-
B.F.Smith	18	30	3	1202	137	44.51	4	6	6	-
A.Habib	15	25	3	964	123	43.81	2	8	12	-
D.P.Fulton	17	33	2	1358	177	43.80	4	4	33	-
D.J.Bravo	6	11	3	350	77*	43.75	-	3	4	-
N.M.Carter	9	12	5	305	103	43.57	1	1	4	-
I.J.Harvey	6	10	1	390	123	43.33	1	2	6	-
D.A.Leatherdale	14	23	4	823	154	43.31	2	4	4	-
D.P.Ostler	14	25	1	1039	225	43.29	2	5	24	-
R.P.Arnold	9	12	0	518	112	43.16	2	3	5	-
C.White	13	24	2	947	161	43.04	2	7	6	-
V.S.Solanki	16	26	4	944	153*	42.90	2	5	18	-
M.E.Cassar	7	9	1	343	101*	42.87	1	3	4	-
C.W.G.Bassano	14	26	1	1063	152	42.52	1	8	13	-
M.W.Goodwin	16	28	0	1179	162	42.10	5	3	13	-
R.S.C.Martin-Jenkins	16	28	4	1008	205*	42.00	1	5	1	-
I.J.Sutcliffe	16	29	3	1088	125*	41.84	2	5	4	-
R.W.T.Key	17	31	1	1255	160	41.83	3	6	12	-
V.V.S.Laxman	8	13	1	502	85	41.83	-	3	5	-
A.S.Rollins	6	12	1	460	107	41.81	1	2	6	-
J.E.R.Gallian	16	29	3	1087	171	41.80	4	6	16	-
S.D.Peters	10	16	0	667	146	41.68	2	3	6	-
A.L.Penberthy	16	25	3	909	130*	41.31	2	5	9	-
E.T.Smith	17	32	2	1239	154	41.30	2	8	4	-
R.O.Hinds	5	9	2	289	75	41.28	-	3	2	-
J.W.M.Dalrymple	8	14	1	535	148	41.15	2	1	2	-
J.W.R.Parker	4	7	0	284	86	40.57	-	2	1	-
N.Hussain	8	12	0	483	155	40.25	2	2	8	-

Name	Matches	Inns	NO	Runs	HS	Avge	100s	50s	Ct	St
M.M.Patel	16	20	6	561	82	40.07	-	5	9	-
S.J.Rhodes	15	22	6	636	124	39.75	1	2	37	4
A.Symonds	12	24	2	858	118	39.00	2	4	16	-
P.D.Trego	4	8	1	270	140	38.57	1	-	2	-
P.J.Martin	12	16	5	422	117*	38.36	1	1	4	-
I.D.Blackwell	14	23	0	879	114	38.21	3	3	4	-
R.R.Montgomerie	16	28	1	1026	196	38.00	2	4	16	-
T.R.Ambrose	13	22	1	798	149	38.00	2	2	9	-
P.A.Nixon	16	30	7	865	103	37.60	1	6	49	4
G.P.Thorpe	8	14	0	526	143	37.57	2	1	6	-
B.M.Shafayat	7	13	1	450	104	37.50	1	2	5	-
N.Shahid	13	20	1	712	150	37.47	2	3	24	-
G.D.Lloyd	7	13	1	449	80	37.41	-	5	4	-
M.Burns	16	30	2	1047	99	37.39	-	9	14	-
A.Dale	16	24	1	859	127*	37.34	2	3	7	-
V.J.Wells	11	17	2	558	150	37.20	1	3	9	-
A.J.Swann	18	31	2	1073	128	37.00	2	6	12	-
R.J.Warren	6	11	1	369	150*	36.90	1	1	1	-
G.E.Welton	16	28	2	954	115	36.69	1	6	16	-
M.G.N.Windows	17	31	2	1062	145	36.62	2	7	6	-
M.B.Loye	13	22	1	768	139	36.57	4	1	7	-
A.Singh	18	32	0	1167	187	36.46	2	6	11	-
R.D.B.Croft	17	24	3	747	101*	35.57	1	5	8	-
J.W.Cook	15	24	3	746	90	35.52	-	4	4	-
B.J.Hodge	4	8	0	284	73	35.50	-	2	3	-
J.N.Batty	13	23	2	742	151	35.33	2	3	41	5
J.P.Stephenson	13	24	8	562	100*	35.12	1	2	7	-
M.A.Ealham	14	24	7	594	83*	34.94	-	3	14	-
A.P.R.Gidman	10	17	1	558	117	34.87	1	4	5	-
M.J.Wood	15	28	0	971	196	34.67	3	5	5	-
R.A.Smith	15	25	1	832	104	34.66	2	3	6	-
C.M.W.Read	18	28	5	797	127	34.65	1	4	66	2
R.S.Clinton	5	8	1	242	107	34.57	1	1	2	-
A.P.Grayson	7	9	0	309	105	34.33	1	1	7	-
N.Millar	3	6	0	203	67	33.83	-	2	2	-
G.P.Swann	11	16	0	539	183	33.68	2	1	5	-
P.D.Bowler	14	25	2	766	94	33.30	-	7	22	-
A.W.Laraman	11	13	3	330	82*	33.00	-	1	3	-
P.C.L.Holloway	7	13	0	428	88	32.92	-	3	4	-
C.P.Schofield	7	9	1	262	91	32.75	-	2	4	-
N.D.Burns	16	24	2	720	101	32.72	1	5	61	2
D.I.Stevens	17	29	3	850	125	32.69	1	6	16	-
W.I.Jefferson	15	29	4	815	165*	32.60	2	2	17	-
A.McGrath	14	26	1	803	165	32.12	1	3	7	-

Name	Matches	Inns	NO	Runs	HS	Avge	100s	50s	Ct	St
D.J.Bicknell	13	23	0	734	112	31.91	2	2	5	-
K.J.Innes	13	22	7	478	60*	31.86	-	2	3	-
P.A.Cottey	13	22	0	699	137	31.77	3	1	5	-
N.C.Johnson	17	29	2	857	117	31.74	1	6	27	-
J.Cox	13	25	2	724	176	31.47	1	3	6	-
M.J.Prior	16	27	3	741	102*	30.87	1	5	39	2
T.Frost	7	11	1	308	103	30.80	1	1	6	2
A.I.Gait	17	33	1	983	175	30.71	1	8	14	-
A.B.Agarkar	7	9	1	244	109*	30.50	1	-	-	-
A.J.Bichel	9	11	2	274	78*	30.44	-	2	7	-
D.G.Cork	11	16	0	487	80	30.43	-	5	12	-
M.V.Fleming	5	8	1	211	102	30.14	1	-	-	-
P.Johnson	14	25	3	662	96	30.09	-	5	7	-
M.J.Powell	17	31	2	872	103	30.06	1	6	13	-
R.J.Turner	16	27	4	691	83*	30.04	-	4	50	1
J.I.D.Kerr	7	12	2	299	68	29.90	-	3	2	-
D.Byas	15	25	2	684	101	29.73	1	4	15	-
M.A.Sheikh	5	8	2	178	43	29.66	-	-	1	-
M.S.Kasprowicz	12	19	7	352	72*	29.33	-	1	7	-
N.Boje	9	16	2	409	84	29.21	-	2	10	-
S.B.Bangar	7	11	1	291	74	29.10	-	3	2	-
P.A.J.DeFreitas	16	23	2	609	114	29.00	1	3	10	-
T.H.C.Hancock	9	17	3	406	112	29.00	1	2	1	-
M.H.Yardy	10	17	0	492	93	28.94	-	2	11	-
B.L.Hutton	11	19	1	518	116	28.77	1	4	20	-
M.P.Bicknell	10	14	5	258	35*	28.66	-	-	6	-
A.Flintoff	7	10	0	284	137	28.40	1	1	8	-
D.R.Law	6	10	1	253	72*	28.11	-	2	2	-
T.J.Phillips	8	13	3	281	75	28.10	-	1	6	-
D.L.Hemp	12	20	2	505	108	28.05	1	2	6	-
D.R.Brown	16	28	4	671	79*	27.95	-	3	9	-
M.A.Wagh	10	18	0	503	109	27.94	1	2	3	-
G.J.Pratt	16	27	0	746	78	27.62	-	4	12	-
R.S.Bopara	4	7	1	165	48	27.50	-	-	6	-
G.M.Fellows	10	18	0	493	109	27.38	1	1	9	-
R.S.Morton	5	8	0	218	79	27.25	-	2	4	-
Harbhajan Singh	8	10	2	218	54	27.25	-	1	1	-
M.J.Chilton	17	29	1	761	107	27.17	1	4	15	-
S.T.Jayasuriya	8	12	0	322	57	26.83	-	3	4	-
J.C.Tredwell	4	6	0	161	61	26.83	-	2	8	-
G.G.Wagg	5	8	2	161	51	26.83	-	1	1	-
M.J.Lumb	16	30	1	777	124	26.79	1	4	8	-
K.C.Sangakkara	9	15	2	345	113	26.53	1	1	12	1
R.M.S.Weston	9	11	2	237	72	26.33	-	2	4	-

Name	Matches	Inns	NO	Runs	HS	Avge	100s	50s	Ct	St
M.J.G.Davis	15	22	4	474	111	26.33	1	2	7	-
M.A.Wallace	17	25	4	553	106*	26.33	1	2	58	3
M.L.Pettini	3	6	0	157	64	26.16	-	2	2	-
S.J.Marshall	4	7	0	182	99	26.00	-	1	1	-
S.D.Udal	17	26	6	516	88	25.80	-	1	9	-
G.Welch	14	23	5	460	64	25.55	-	3	8	-
Saqlain Mushtaq	10	13	2	278	60	25.27	-	2	4	-
M.W.Alleyne	14	25	3	555	142*	25.22	1	2	12	-
L.M.P.Simmons	5	8	1	176	81	25.14	-	1	7	2
P.J.Franks	10	14	2	301	67	25.08	-	3	2	-
D.J.G.Sales	14	22	0	551	179	25.04	1	3	11	-
S.M.Pollock	10	18	1	425	66	25.00	-	4	13	-
J.Hughes	7	10	1	225	74	25.00	-	1	2	-
I.D.Fisher	16	26	3	568	103*	24.69	1	4	8	-
C.G.Taylor	15	29	2	664	126	24.59	1	2	15	-
G.J.Muchall	15	25	0	613	127	24.52	1	3	14	-
I.R.Bell	16	28	1	658	77	24.37	-	3	6	-
W.S.Kendall	17	31	2	705	88	24.31	-	4	12	-
W.P.C.Weston	8	15	2	315	82	24.23	-	3	7	-
K.A.Parsons	15	26	2	581	68	24.20	-	4	16	-
N.Peng	12	21	0	508	108	24.19	1	2	8	-
M.J.Brown	4	6	0	145	57	24.16	-	1	6	-
W.Jaffer	7	13	1	290	53	24.16	-	2	9	-
S.A.Selwood	10	19	0	457	99	24.05	-	2	1	-
A.D.Mascarenhas	16	26	2	574	94	23.91	-	2	8	-
N.Pothas	16	26	1	597	99	23.88	-	5	30	4
R.J.Sillence	5	7	0	167	101	23.85	1	-	2	-
A.A.Shankar	4	7	0	167	143	23.85	1	-	4	-
J.J.B.Lewis	11	18	1	402	102	23.64	1	2	2	-
M.M.Betts	9	16	5	259	56	23.54	-	1	2	-
A.P.Cowan	10	15	2	305	60*	23.46	-	2	6	-
V.J.Craven	11	21	2	439	72	23.10	-	3	8	-
T.R.Ward	14	24	0	554	89	23.08	-	4	7	-
W.P.U.J.C.Vaas	5	7	1	138	50*	23.00	-	1	2	-
J.D.Francis	10	17	0	391	82	23.00	-	3	6	-
N.C.Phillips	10	16	6	226	58*	22.60	-	1	4	-
N.H.Fairbrother	12	19	1	406	101	22.55	1	-	10	-
A.A.Noffke	8	10	1	203	76	22.55	-	1	3	-
S.D.Stubbings	11	20	1	428	128	22.52	1	1	5	-
C.T.Tremlett	11	14	6	180	40*	22.50	-	-	4	-
N.M.K.Smith	8	15	0	337	96	22.46	-	2	7	-
G.Chapple	16	23	1	493	65	22.40	-	4	6	-
R.L.Johnson	9	17	4	290	61	22.30	-	1	2	-
J.S.Laney	7	13	0	289	89	22.23	-	1	7	-

Name	Matches	Inns	NO	Runs	HS	Avge	100s	50s	Ct	St
L.D.Sutton	10	19	1	400	80	22.22	-	3	30	1
R.K.J.Dawson	15	24	1	511	87	22.21	-	2	2	-
A.F.Giles	9	12	0	264	68	22.00	-	1	3	-
T.M.B.Bailey	17	25	4	457	68	21.76	-	4	43	6
H.R.Jones	3	6	0	130	97	21.66	-	1	3	-
G.J.Batty	18	27	4	491	74	21.34	-	3	9	-
M.P.Dowman	8	14	0	298	71	21.28	-	1	6	-
J.M.Dakin	14	20	3	359	57	21.11	-	1	3	-
G.R.Napier	9	13	2	230	54*	20.90	-	1	6	-
A.M.Thorpe	7	13	0	271	95	20.84	-	2	5	-
D.R.Hewson	11	20	1	393	102*	20.68	1	1	7	-
A.Pratt	17	30	3	556	93	20.59	-	3	42	3
K.J.Dean	17	26	9	347	54*	20.41	-	2	6	-
A.Ratra	7	11	2	183	101*	20.33	1	-	14	2
W.K.Hegg	16	23	2	416	62	19.80	-	1	44	2
G.W.White	8	14	2	234	36	19.50	-	-	6	-
I.J.Thomas	9	15	1	273	76	19.50	-	2	2	-
M.J.Walker	12	23	3	382	46	19.10	-	-	3	-
J.J.Sayers	4	8	0	152	55	19.00	-	1	1	-
I.D.K.Salisbury	14	20	2	340	59	18.88	-	1	11	-
R.C.Driver	5	8	2	113	56	18.83	-	1	5	-
C.R.Taylor	5	9	1	150	52*	18.75	-	2	4	-
G.J.Smith	15	20	7	242	38*	18.61	-	-	4	-
I.D.Hunter	8	12	1	204	65	18.54	-	1	2	-
D.A.Kenway	8	15	2	238	54	18.30	-	1	15	-
S.P.Jones	13	18	6	218	44	18.16	-	-	5	-
K.P.Dutch	16	27	3	432	74	18.00	-	2	20	-
J.R.C.Hamblin	5	9	0	162	50	18.00	-	1	4	-
M.P.L.Bulbeck	16	27	7	359	53*	17.95	-	1	3	-
M.S.Mason	7	8	2	107	50	17.83	-	1	1	-
J.D.Middlebrook	18	28	4	417	67	17.37	-	1	7	-
J.P.Pyemont	4	7	0	121	43	17.28	-	-	2	-
J.Wood	8	11	0	185	64	16.81	-	1	2	-
M.C.J.Ball	7	10	3	117	63	16.71	-	1	5	-
D.D.Masters	8	7	0	117	68	16.71	-	1	3	-
S.J.Cook	15	18	2	267	43*	16.68	-	-	4	-
C.E.W.Silverwood	12	19	2	283	44*	16.64	-	-	3	-
R.S.G.Anderson	5	10	0	166	51	16.60	-	1	-	-
A.Richardson	10	12	4	132	91	16.50	-	1	5	-
K.J.Piper	8	12	2	163	64*	16.30	-	1	14	1
V.H.Kumar	4	7	0	114	64	16.28	-	1	3	1
P.A.Patel	5	8	2	97	32	16.16	-	-	5	-
D.D.Cherry	5	8	0	129	47	16.12	-	-	4	-
J.Ormond	15	17	4	208	43*	16.00	-	-	6	-

Name	Matches	Inns	NO	Runs	HS	Avge	100s	50s	Ct	St
M.J.Symington	10	16	2	224	42	16.00	-	-	6	-
Kabir Ali	17	21	4	271	51*	15.94	-	1	3	-
A.J.Tudor	10	14	0	222	61	15.85	-	1	2	-
M.J.Hoggard	9	11	5	95	32	15.83	-	-	3	-
G.Keedy	16	22	8	219	57	15.64	-	1	4	-
A.Khan	16	19	5	213	58	15.21	-	1	5	-
Mohammad Ali	15	24	2	333	53	15.13	-	1	5	-
D.R.Heath	4	7	1	88	75	14.66	-	1	2	-
J.N.Snape	5	8	0	117	28	14.62	-	-	2	-
J.Lewis	16	25	6	273	57	14.36	-	1	6	-
C.D.Crowe	12	16	4	172	34	14.33	-	-	4	-
G.D.Bridge	10	15	2	184	49	14.15	-	-	4	-
J.Srinath	5	7	0	98	52	14.00	-	1	2	-
R.J.Cunliffe	5	10	1	121	30	13.44	-	-	1	-
A.S.Wright	5	8	1	94	28	13.42	-	-	1	-
A.M.Smith	9	13	6	92	21	13.14	-	-	3	-
S.D.Thomas	16	22	1	274	47	13.04	-	-	4	-
T.Lungley	7	13	0	168	44	12.92	-	-	4	-
P.C.R.Tufnell	14	15	8	89	45	12.71	-	-	3	-
R.J.Kirtley	11	15	3	146	36*	12.16	-	-	4	-
K.W.Hogg	7	9	0	109	50	12.11	-	1	5	-
A.D.Simcox	4	7	1	72	30	12.00	-	-	2	-
M.J.Wood	9	17	0	201	43	11.82	-	-	12	-
A.J.Harris	14	20	7	151	41*	11.61	-	-	6	-
D.M.Cousins	11	16	7	103	23*	11.44	-	-	4	-
K.M.Krikken	9	16	1	169	48	11.26	-	-	26	-
M.A.Davies	14	24	7	184	33	10.82	-	-	3	-
J.F.Brown	8	11	5	64	19	10.66	-	-	2	-
N.Killeen	15	22	5	178	27*	10.47	-	-	5	-
D.A.Cosker	10	13	2	115	37	10.45	-	-	8	-
J.M.M.Averis	5	8	0	83	43	10.37	-	-	3	-
J.B.Hockley	5	9	1	82	46	10.25	-	-	1	-
I.Pattison	3	6	0	61	27	10.16	-	-	2	-
S.P.Kirby	10	17	3	141	57	10.07	-	1	-	-
D.E.Malcolm	16	22	8	138	44	9.85	-	-	4	-
J.E.Bishop	6	9	2	69	23*	9.85	-	-	2	-
A.Sheriyar	18	20	9	107	18	9.72	-	-	1	-
A.P.Davies	5	6	0	58	30	9.66	-	-	-	-
R.J.Sidebottom	13	21	7	135	28	9.64	-	-	4	-
R.J.Logan	13	19	4	143	32	9.53	-	-	5	-
C.G.Greenidge	15	19	2	160	46	9.41	-	-	7	-
J.D.Lewry	10	15	5	91	21*	9.10	-	-	5	-
S.R.G.Francis	10	16	8	67	17	8.37	-	-	-	-
S.C.G.MacGill	6	7	1	48	22	8.00	-	-	5	-

Name	Matches	Inns	NO	Runs	HS	Avge	100s	50s	Ct	St
J.B.Grant	11	12	4	64	30	8.00	-	-	-	-
L.J.Wharton	14	23	12	83	16	7.54	-	-	7	-
L.R.Prittipaul	3	6	0	45	32	7.50	-	-	1	-
A.R.Caddick	10	14	2	89	16	7.41	-	-	2	-
J.M.Anderson	13	16	8	58	16	7.25	-	-	2	-
K.E.A.Upashantha	5	6	0	43	25	7.16	-	-	1	-
J.A.R.Blain	7	9	2	47	17*	6.71	-	-	2	-
D.J.Pagon	4	6	0	37	18	6.16	-	-	-	-
S.J.Harmison	11	18	3	88	19*	5.86	-	-	4	-
M.J.A.Whiley	7	9	2	41	13*	5.85	-	-	1	-
B.V.Taylor	10	14	2	70	18*	5.83	-	-	1	-
C.B.Keegan	9	10	0	58	24	5.80	-	-	3	-
M.J.Saggers	16	19	6	73	16*	5.61	-	-	6	-
M.N.Malik	7	7	1	33	19	5.50	-	-	1	-
A.D.Mullally	13	16	5	54	23	4.90	-	-	1	-
I.J.Clifford	4	6	0	20	7	3.33	-	-	15	1

BOWLING AVERAGES
Qualifying requirements: 10 wickets taken

Name	Overs	Mdns	Runs	Wkts	Avge	Best	5wI	10wM
Azhar Mahmood	109.2	27	345	20	17.25	8-61	1	-
C.P.Schofield	122.2	27	331	18	18.38	4-35	-	-
J.Srinath	179.2	29	561	30	18.70	5-25	2	-
D.G.Cork	403.4	101	1210	64	18.90	6-51	5	1
I.J.Harvey	152.2	29	533	28	19.03	6-68	3	1
R.C.Irani	227.5	72	591	29	20.37	6-71	1	-
P.J.Martin	452	143	1126	53	21.24	5-54	1	-
R.L.Johnson	307.1	66	914	43	21.25	7-43	2	1
M.J.Saggers	571	111	1786	83	21.51	6-39	6	-
A.J.Harris	413.4	93	1475	67	22.01	7-54	3	2
V.J.Wells	155	41	421	19	22.15	5-39	1	-
J.M.Anderson	326.4	61	1114	50	22.28	6-23	3	-
M.P.Dowman	72	24	223	10	22.30	4-28	-	-
J.P.Stephenson	295.4	59	1082	48	22.54	7-44	1	1
R.J.Kirtley	379	94	1199	53	22.62	6-107	4	1
S.C.G.MacGill	227.4	37	930	40	23.25	8-111	4	1
K.J.Dean	590	148	1951	83	23.50	7-42	3	2
D.L.Maddy	334.3	78	1025	43	23.83	5-37	2	-
T.Lungley	117.4	32	416	17	24.47	3-43	-	-
M.I.Black	113.1	32	344	14	24.57	4-32	-	-
N.Boje	238	58	671	27	24.85	6-128	2	-
T.J.Murtagh	122.1	23	424	17	24.94	5-39	1	-
A.Richardson	300.2	64	951	38	25.02	8-46	2	-
A.J.Bichel	297	77	902	36	25.05	9-93	1	1
A.A.Noffke	305.1	57	1128	45	25.06	8-24	3	1
Kabir Ali	547.1	129	1781	71	25.08	7-43	5	2

Name	Overs	Mdns	Runs	Wkts	Avge	Best	5wI	10wM
A.D.Mullally	463.2	145	1156	46	25.13	6-56	1	-
P.J.Franks	234.5	53	813	32	25.40	5-51	1	-
P.D.R.L.Perera	115	13	433	17	25.47	4-66	-	-
M.N.Malik	146.4	29	562	22	25.54	5-67	1	-
G.Welch	486.1	157	1409	55	25.61	6-60	2	-
Saqlain Mushtaq	488.4	112	1359	53	25.64	6-121	3	1
P.D.Collingwood	96.4	24	258	10	25.80	4-31	-	-
M.A.Davies	357.5	106	942	36	26.16	5-61	1	-
S.M.Pollock	301.3	101	733	28	26.17	4-37	-	-
G.J.Smith	400	85	1275	48	26.56	8-53	1	1
M.S.Kasprowicz	418.4	78	1413	53	26.66	6-47	4	1
A.J.Tudor	322	74	1124	42	26.76	5-66	1	-
J.J.C.Lawson	123.4	19	484	18	26.88	6-76	1	-
S.J.Cook	367.2	71	1305	48	27.18	8-63	2	-
A.P.Cowan	276.1	70	843	31	27.19	5-68	1	-
A.R.Caddick	423.3	89	1313	48	27.35	6-84	4	-
S.E.Bond	95.4	23	330	12	27.50	5-64	1	-
S.P.Jones	323.5	53	1101	40	27.52	6-45	2	-
R.C.Driver	105	28	331	12	27.58	5-70	1	-
A.Kumble	212	51	607	22	27.59	4-58	-	-
Harbhajan Singh	243.2	43	773	28	27.60	7-83	2	-
A.McGrath	174.3	38	498	18	27.66	4-49	-	-
L.J.Wharton	208.5	45	695	25	27.80	6-62	2	-
M.S.Mason	224.4	55	613	22	27.86	5-50	1	-
A.P.Davies	116.2	14	420	15	28.00	5-79	1	-
R.D.King	151	31	451	16	28.18	4-48	-	-
S.B.Bangar	132.5	25	395	14	28.21	4-40	-	-
G.P.Swann	270.5	60	884	31	28.51	6-126	1	1
G.G.Wagg	82.5	13	343	12	28.58	4-43	-	-
M.W.H.Inness	116.4	25	429	15	28.60	7-90	1	-
K.J.Innes	268.3	65	834	29	28.75	4-41	-	-
A.Sheriyar	616.2	160	1905	66	28.86	6-71	5	-
M.E.Cassar	113.3	18	464	16	29.00	6-34	1	1
R.J.Sidebottom	380.5	85	1190	41	29.02	5-60	1	-
Abdul Razzaq	206.3	25	757	26	29.11	7-133	2	-
C.T.Tremlett	336	83	1061	36	29.47	5-57	2	-
G.Chapple	539.3	128	1594	54	29.51	6-30	3	1
A.M.Smith	270	55	916	31	29.54	5-69	1	-
D.B.Powell	81	19	303	10	30.30	3-55	-	-
S.J.Harmison	324.2	75	1001	33	30.33	5-65	1	-
D.E.Malcolm	477.5	79	1826	60	30.43	7-76	4	1
J.M.Dakin	360.2	77	1233	40	30.82	4-17	-	-
A.D.Mascarenhas	420.5	144	1141	37	30.83	5-87	1	-
P.C.R.Tufnell	514.5	104	1390	45	30.88	8-66	4	-
G.J.Batty	613.1	162	1733	56	30.94	6-71	3	-
P.A.J.DeFreitas	566.4	150	1594	51	31.25	6-101	2	-
M.P.Bicknell	326	78	1067	34	31.38	6-42	2	-
S.D.Thomas	467.1	66	1637	52	31.48	7-33	3	1
N.Killeen	391.1	108	1165	37	31.48	4-26	-	-
C.G.Greenidge	431	67	1681	53	31.71	6-40	3	-

Name	Overs	Mdns	Runs	Wkts	Avge	Best	5wI	10wM
A.Khan	485	75	2004	63	31.80	6-52	4	-
G.R.Napier	172	33	639	20	31.95	3-47	-	-
N.C.Phillips	210	47	671	21	31.95	4-103	-	-
I.D.K.Salisbury	340.3	50	1188	37	32.10	4-59	-	-
B.V.Taylor	318.5	73	1041	32	32.53	5-90	1	-
M.S.Panesar	190.5	55	554	17	32.58	4-42	-	-
K.W.Hogg	175	41	621	19	32.68	5-48	1	-
C.E.W.Silverwood	306.1	68	985	30	32.83	4-28	-	-
J.B.Grant	267.5	50	1086	33	32.90	5-38	1	-
D.R.Brown	493.4	75	1716	52	33.00	7-110	2	-
S.D.Udal	627.1	146	1858	56	33.17	5-56	4	-
J.M.M.Averis	128	33	432	13	33.23	5-51	1	-
D.A.Leatherdale	140.3	22	535	16	33.43	4-23	-	-
M.P.L.Bulbeck	534	93	1940	58	33.44	6-93	1	-
E.S.H.Giddins	232.5	49	736	22	33.45	4-113	-	-
M.M.Patel	525.3	152	1206	36	33.50	5-56	1	-
R.O.Hinds	105.1	18	338	10	33.80	3-54	-	-
S.R.G.Francis	222.3	26	947	28	33.82	5-73	1	-
A.F.Giles	419.1	67	1222	36	33.94	7-142	3	1
R.J.Logan	319.3	71	1191	35	34.02	4-64	-	-
J.A.Spires	171.4	25	613	18	34.05	5-165	1	-
M.A.Ealham	351	107	954	28	34.07	3-22	-	-
A.W.Laraman	262.4	47	920	27	34.07	4-55	-	-
S.P.Kirby	331.1	68	1262	37	34.10	5-129	1	-
N.M.K.Smith	126	27	411	12	34.25	5-42	1	-
R.J.Sillence	100	11	449	13	34.53	5-63	1	-
M.J.Symington	147	29	590	17	34.70	4-27	-	-
M.J.Hoggard	364	71	1250	36	34.72	5-92	1	-
J.Ormond	485.1	87	1780	51	34.90	5-62	2	1
J.Wood	180.5	34	631	18	35.05	4-17	-	-
J.C.Tredwell	124.2	29	358	10	35.80	4-103	-	-
G.D.Bridge	247.5	61	753	21	35.85	4-50	-	-
R.S.C.Martin-Jenkins	470.2	100	1477	41	36.02	7-51	2	-
Mohammad Ali	405	63	1708	47	36.34	3-48	-	-
N.C.Johnson	242.2	52	814	22	37.00	3-22	-	-
C.D.Crowe	193.2	51	593	16	37.06	4-63	-	-
J.D.Lewry	304.3	45	1227	33	37.18	5-88	1	-
D.D.Masters	243.1	47	864	23	37.56	4-36	-	-
I.D.Blackwell	312.5	83	830	22	37.72	5-49	1	-
J.Lewis	536.1	137	1662	44	37.77	6-54	2	1
M.C.J.Ball	287	66	876	23	38.08	6-54	1	-
M.J.G.Davis	347.2	71	1081	28	38.60	6-97	1	-
I.D.Hunter	206	42	775	20	38.75	3-44	-	-
R.K.J.Dawson	488.5	104	1551	40	38.77	5-42	2	-
K.A.Parsons	216.3	30	830	21	39.52	3-44	-	-
G.Keedy	437.4	102	1313	33	39.78	5-122	1	-
M.C.Ilott	193.5	45	639	16	39.93	4-67	-	-
M.A.Wagh	203	43	604	15	40.26	5-137	1	-
M.Burns	101.4	15	444	11	40.36	3-54	-	-

Name	Overs	Mdns	Runs	Wkts	Avge	Best	5wI	10wM
J.F.Brown	352.5	76	1138	28	40.64	4-88	-	-
J.I.D.Kerr	147.2	29	652	16	40.75	4-32	-	-
R.Clarke	94.3	15	451	11	41.00	3-41	-	-
B.W.Gannon	162	36	626	15	41.73	3-41	-	-
D.N.T.Zoysa	110.2	15	421	10	42.10	3-93	-	-
C.White	193.5	33	634	15	42.26	4-49	-	-
R.D.B.Croft	619	138	1701	40	42.52	5-71	1	-
J.E.Bishop	120	17	470	11	42.72	3-59	-	-
A.Nehra	114	14	473	11	43.00	4-85	-	-
Z.Khan	147	32	483	11	43.90	3-90	-	-
A.P.R.Gidman	99	16	442	10	44.20	3-33	-	-
P.S.Jones	239.2	45	845	19	44.47	6-110	1	1
C.B.Keegan	211.5	32	855	19	45.00	4-47	-	-
J.D.Middlebrook	555.2	121	1736	38	45.68	4-38	-	-
A.B.Agarkar	162.3	32	640	14	45.71	4-55	-	-
A.Symonds	187.2	34	602	13	46.30	6-105	1	-
D.M.Cousins	311.2	67	1024	22	46.54	4-75	-	-
T.J.Phillips	209.5	32	844	18	46.88	4-102	-	-
N.M.Carter	228.1	35	957	20	47.85	4-46	-	-
A.L.Penberthy	292	76	833	17	49.00	3-21	-	-
M.J.A.Whiley	175.4	28	803	16	50.18	3-60	-	-
D.A.Cosker	317.5	60	1012	20	50.60	4-135	-	-
M.M.Betts	248.4	34	1023	20	51.15	3-75	-	-
M.W.Alleyne	266	59	876	17	51.52	3-76	-	-
T.C.B.Fernando	113.5	14	524	10	52.40	4-72	-	-
I.D.Fisher	514	103	1725	32	53.90	5-87	1	-
A.Flintoff	251	53	768	14	54.85	2-22	-	-
K.P.Dutch	268.3	59	852	15	56.80	3-104	-	-
J.A.R.Blain	192.4	21	909	16	56.81	4-144	-	-
P.N.Weekes	397	61	1198	21	57.04	3-27	-	-
J.A.Tomlinson	168.3	14	748	12	62.33	2-55	-	-
S.J.Marshall	215.2	42	657	10	65.70	6-128	1	-

INDEX OF PLAYERS
BY COUNTY

INDEX OF PLAYERS BY COUNTY

*denotes not registered for the 2003 season. Where a player is known to have moved in the off-season he is listed under his new county.

DERBYSHIRE

ALDRED, P.*
BASSANO, C.W.G.
CORK, D.G.
DEAN, K.J.
DIVENUTO, M.J.
DOWMAN, M.P.*
DUMELOW, N.R.C.
GAIT, A.I.
GUNTER, N.E.L.
HEWSON, D.R.
KERR, J.I.D.
KHAN, R.M.
KRIKKEN, K.M.
LUNGLEY, T.
MOHAMMAD ALI
PYEMONT, J.P.*
SELWOOD, S.A.
SHAHID AFRIDI
STUBBINGS, S.D.
SUTTON, L.D.
WARN, C.J.*
WELCH, G.
WHARTON, L.J.

DURHAM

BRIDGE, G.D.
BROWN, S.J.E.*
COLLINGWOOD, P.D.
DALEY, J.A.*
DAVIES, M.A.
GOUGH, M.A.
HARMISON, S.J.
HATCH, N.G.
HUNTER, I.D.

KILLEEN, N.
LAW, D.R.
LEWIS, J.J.B.
LOVE, M.L.
MANN, C.
MUCHALL, G.J.
MUSTARD, P.
PATTISON, I.
PENG, N.
PHILLIPS, N.C.
PRATT, A.
PRATT, G.J.
PRETORIUS, D.
SCOTT, G.M.
SYMINGTON, M.J.*
THORPE, A.M.
WELLS, V.J.

ESSEX

BISHOP, J.E.
BOPARA, R.S.
BRANT, S.A.
CLARKE, A.J.
CLINTON, R.S.*
COWAN, A.P.
DAKIN, J.M.
DENNING, N.A.
FLOWER, A.
FOSTER, J.S.
GRANT, J.B.
GRAYSON, A.P.
HABIB, A.
HUSSAIN, N.
HYAM, B.J.
ILOTT, M.C.*
IRANI, R.C.

JEFFERSON, W.I.
MCCOUBREY, A.G.A.M.
MCGARRY, A.C.
MIDDLEBROOK, J.D.
NAPIER, G.R.
PETTINI, M.L.
PHILLIPS, T.J.
ROBINSON, D.D.J.
SHARIF, Z.K.
STEPHENSON, J.P.
WAUGH, M.E.*

GLAMORGAN

CHERRY, D.D.
COSKER, D.A.
CROFT, R.D.B.
DALE, A.
DAVIES, A.P.
HARRISON, D.S.
HEMP, D.L.
HUGHES, J.
JAMES, S.P.
JONES, S.P.
KASPROWICZ, M.S.
MAYNARD, M.P.
NEWELL, K.*
PARKIN, O.T.
POWELL, M.J.
SHAW, A.D.
THOMAS, I.J.
THOMAS, S.D.
WALLACE, M.A.
WHARF, A.G.B.

INDEX OF PLAYERS BY COUNTY

GLOUCESTERSHIRE

ALLEYNE, M.W.
ANGEL, J.*
AVERIS, J.M.M.
BALL, M.C.J.
BARNETT, K.J.*
BRESSINGTON, A.N.
FISHER, I.D.
GANNON, B.W.*
GIDMAN, A.P.R.
HANCOCK, T.H.C.
HARDINGES, M.A.
HARVEY, I.J.
LEWIS, J.
PEARSON, J.A.
POPE, S.P.
RHODES, J.N.
RUSSELL, R.C.
SILLENCE, R.J.
SMITH, A.M.
SPEARMAN, C.M.
TAYLOR, C.G.
WINDOWS, M.G.N.

HAMPSHIRE

ADAMS, J.H.K.
AYMES, A.N.*
BENHAM, C.C.
BRUNNSCHWEILER, I.
CRAWLEY, J.P.
FRANCIS, J.D.
GIDDINS, E.S.H.
HAMBLIN, J.R.C.
JOHNSON, N.C.*
KATICH, S.M.
KENDALL, W.S.

KENWAY, D.A.
LANEY, J.S.*
MASCARENHAS, A.D.
MORRIS, A.C.
MULLALLY, A.D.
POTHAS, N.
PRITTIPAUL, L.R.
SCHOFIELD, J.E.K.*
SMITH, R.A.
TOMLINSON, J.A.
TREMLETT, C.T.
UDAL, S.D.
VAN DER GUCHT, C.G.
WHITE, G.W.*

KENT

BANES, M.J.
CARBERRY, M.A.
EALHAM, M.A.
FERLEY, R.S.
FLEMING, M.V.*
FULTON, D.P.
GOLDING, J.M.*
HEWITT, J.P.
HOCKLEY, J.B.*
JONES, G.O.
KEY, R.W.T.
KHAN, A.
LOUDON, A.G.R.
PATEL, M.M.
SAGGERS, M.J.
SHERIYAR, A.
SMITH, E.T.
SYMONDS, A.
TREDWELL, J.C.
TREGO, P.D.
TROTT, B.J.

WALKER, M.J.
WAUGH, S.R.*

LANCASHIRE

ANDERSON, J.M.
BYAS, D.*
CHAPPLE, G.
CHILTON, M.J.
CROOK, S.P.
CURRIE, M.R.
DRIVER, R.C.*
FAIRBROTHER, N.H.*
FLINTOFF, A.
HARBHAJAN SINGH
HAYNES, J.J.
HEGG, W.K.
HOGG, K.W.
KEEDY, G.
LAW, S.G.
LLOYD, G.D.*
LOYE, M.B.
MAHMOOD, S.I.
MARTIN, P.J.
REES, T.M.
ROBERTS, T.W.*
SCHOFIELD, C.P.
SMETHURST, M.P.
SUTCLIFFE, I.J.
SWANN, A.J.
WATKINSON, M.
WOOD, J.
YATES, G.

INDEX OF PLAYERS BY COUNTY

LEICESTERSHIRE

AMIN, R.M.
BEVAN, M.G.*
BRANDY, D.G.
BRIGNULL, D.S.
BURNS, N.D.*
CROWE, C.D.*
CUNLIFFE, R.J.
DAGNALL, C.E.
DEFREITAS, P.A.J.
FLOWER, G.W.*
GROVE, J.O.
HODGE, B.J.
KAIF, MOHAMMAD*
MADDY, D.L.
MALCOLM, D.E.
MASTERS, D.D.
MAUNDERS, J.
NEW, T.J.
NIXON, P.A.
SADLER, J.L.
SEHWAG, V.
SNAPE, J.N.
SRINATH, J.*
STEMP, R.D.*
STEVENS, D.I.
WALKER, G.W.
WARD, T.R.
WHILEY, M.J.A.
WRIGHT, A.S.*
WRIGHT, L.J.

MIDDLESEX

ABDUL RAZZAQ
ALLEYNE, D.
BLOOMFIELD, T.F.
BROWN, M.J.
COLEMAN, A.J.
COMPTON, N.R.D.
COOK, S.J.
DALRYMPLE, J.W.M.
FRASER, A.R.C.*
HUNT, T.A.
HUTTON, B.L.
JONES, I.*
JOYCE, E.C.
KEEGAN, C.B.
KOENIG, S.G.
NASH, D.C.
NOFFKE, A.A.
RICHARDS, M.A.
SHAH, O.A.
STRAUSS, A.J.
TUFNELL, P.C.R.
WEEKES, P.N.
WESTON, R.M.S.

NORTHAMPTONSHIRE

ANDERSON, R.S.G.
BAILEY, T.M.B.
BAKER, T.M.
BLAIN, J.A.R.
BROPHY, G.L.
BROWN, J.F.
CASSAR, M.E.*
CAWDRON, M.J.
COOK, J.W.
COUSINS, D.M.
COVERDALE, P.S.
GOODE, C.M.
GREENIDGE, C.G.
HUSSEY, M.E.
INNESS, M.W.H.*
KING, R.E.
NEL, A.
PANESAR, M.S.
PARK, C.L.
PAYNTER, D.E.
PENBERTHY, A.L.
PHILLIPS, B.J.
POWELL, M.J.
ROLLINS, A.S.*
SALES, D.J.G.
SHANTRY, A.J.
SWANN, G.P.
WADE, J.
WHITE, R.A.

NOTTINGHAMSHIRE

AFZAAL, U.
ATRI, V.
BICKNELL, D.J.
BOJE, N.*
CAIRNS, C.L.
CLOUGH, G.D.
FRANKS, P.J.
GALLIAN, J.E.R.
HARRIS, A.J.
JOHNSON, P.*
KLUSENER, L.*
LOGAN, R.J.
LUCAS, D.S.
MACGILL, S.C.G.
MCMAHON, P.J.
MALIK, M.N.
NOON, W.M.

INDEX OF PLAYERS BY COUNTY

INDEX OF PLAYERS BY COUNTY

POWELL, M.J.
RICHARDSON, A.
SHEIKH, M.A.
SMITH, N.M.K.
SPIRES, J.A.
TAHIR, N.
TROTT, I.J.L.
TROUGHTON, J.O.
WAGG, G.G.
WAGH, M.A.
WARREN, N.A.

WORCESTERSHIRE

BATTY, G.J.
BICHEL, A.J.*
CATTERALL, D.N.*
DONALD, A.A.*
FARROW, J.C.
GUEST, C.S.
HALL, A.
HARRITY, M.A.
HAYWARD, M.
HICK, G.A.
KABIR ALI
KADEER ALI
LAMPITT, S.R.*
LEATHERDALE, D.A.
LEE, S.*
LIPTROT, C.G.
MASON, M.S.
MOORE, S.C.
PETERS, S.D.
PIPE, D.J.
RAWNSLEY, M.J.*
RHODES, S.J.
SINGH, A.
SMITH, B.F.
SOLANKI, V.S.

WESTON, W.P.C.
WIGLEY, D.H.

YORKSHIRE

BLAKEY, R.J.
BRESNAN, T.T.
CRAVEN, V.J.
DAWSON, R.K.J.
ELLIOTT, M.T.G.
ELSTUB, C.J.*
FELLOWS, G.M.
GALE, A.W.
GOUGH, D.
GRAY, A.D.K.
GUY, S.M.
HAMILTON, G.M.
HOGGARD, M.J.
KIRBY, S.P.
LEHMANN, D.S.
LUMB, M.J.
MCGRATH, A.
PYRAH, R.M.
RICHARDSON, S.A.
SAYERS, J.J.
SIDEBOTTOM, R.J.
SILVERWOOD, C.E.W.
SWANEPOEL, P.J.
TAYLOR, C.R.
THORNICROFT, N.
VAUGHAN, M.P.
WHITE, C.
WOOD, M.J.

THE PRIMARY CLUB

PO Box 12121, London NW1 9▓
Telephone: 020 7267 3316
Fax: 020 7485 6808
e-mail: primaryclub @aol.com▓
website: www.primaryclub.org

Derek Underwood, the patron of the Primary Club, qualified fo▓ membership in some style in 1965. Playing for Kent against the South Africans he was out first ball twice in the same match.

However, members do not have to be playing Test or count▓ cricket when the ultimate disaster strikes in order to qualify for the club. As long as you are out first ball at ANY level of cricke▓ you are eligible to join The Primary Club.

Why join? The Primary Club is a charity (Registered Charity No. 285285) and all profits from subscriptions, donations and t▓ range of items for sale (ties, sweaters, shirts, mugs, umbrellas, etc.) go to pay for sporting and recreational facilities for the blind and partially sighted. All the club's workers are volunteers.

For many of us sport is an important part of our every day lives; for the blind and partially sighted, sport can mean so much more. The confidence and sense of achievement they g▓ from mastering a physical skill helps them a great deal in tackling the problems of their lives.

MEMBERSHIP APPLICATION

Name

Address

Joining subscription:	
To include City tie – £20	
To include Club tie – £20	
To include City & Club tie – £30	
To include 100% silk tie (City) – £30	
To include 100% silk tie (Country) – £30	
To include Bow tie – £20	
Lady, to include brooch – £15	
DONATION	
REMITTANCE TO 'THE PRIMARY CLUB' £	

Registered Charity No. 285285

The value of your remittance to The Prima▓ Club can be increased by 28p for every £▓ you give under Gift Aid tax reclaim arrangements, *at no extra cost to you.* To enable the Club to benefit from this scheme, please sign and date the declarat▓ below, provided that you pay income tax, capital gains tax, of an amount equal to t▓ tax to be reclaimed.

I wish The Primary Club to reclaim tax on a▓ donations I make on or after the date of this declaration.

Signed   **Date**

It would be of great benefit to the Club if yo▓ pay future donations by banker's standing order. Please tick the box and a form will be sent to you.

QUIZ ANSWERS

1. Brendon Julian
2. Justin Langer (Australia and Middlesex); Matthew Hayden (Australia and Northamptonshire)
3. Roy Marshall; also West Indies
4. Ravi Shastri
5. Intikhab Alam
6. David Gilbert (Australia)
7. Michael Bevan (A), Grant Flower (Z), Mohammad Kaif (I), Javagal Srinath (I)
8. Northamptonshire
9. Jimmy Cook (South Africa)
10. Darren Lehmann (Yorkshire)
11. Fanie de Villiers
12. Aamir Sohail and Shoaib Akhtar
13. Durham
14. Martin Crowe (New Zealand)
15. Lance Klusener (SA), Nicky Boje (SA), Stuart MacGill (A)
16. Dion Nash
17. David Boon (Durham); Jamie Cox (Somerset)
18. Daryll Cullinan
19. 1988; Steve played for Somerset, Mark for Essex
20. Kent
21. Martin Donnelly
22. Darren Lehmann (A), Simon Katich (A), Matthew Elliott (A)
23. Asif Iqbal
24. Aravinda de Silva
25. Shaun Pollock (South Africa and Warwickshire)
26. Brian Lara (West Indies and Warwickshire)
27. Middlesex
28. Vintcent van der Bijl
29. Gordon Greenidge (West Indies)
30. Dean Jones (Australia)
31. Tom Moody (Australia)
32. A.H. (Abdul Hafeez) Kardar
33. Hansie Cronje
34. Azhar Mahmood (P), Mushtaq Ahmed (P), Saqlain Mushtaq (P)
35. Garfield Sobers played for Nottinghamshire; the remainder for Warwickshire
36. Michael Bevan (Sussex)
37. Gloucestershire and Nottinghamshire
38. Waqar Younis (Surrey)
39. Chris Cairns
40. Vasbert Drakes (West Indies and Sussex, Nottinghamshire and Warwickshire)
41. Barry Richards (South Africa)
42. Eddie Barlow
43. Mushtaq played for Northamptonshire; Sadiq for Gloucestershire (he also played one match for Essex v Jamaica in 1970)
44. Paul Reiffel (Australia)
45. Michael Kasprowicz (Australia)
46. Essex
47. Curtly Ambrose (Northamptonshire)
48. George Tribe
49. Heath Streak
50. John Shepherd
51. Ian Harvey (Gloucestershire)
52. Phil Simmons
53. Shaun Young
54. Kepler Wessels
55. Bill Alley
56. a) Northamptonshire; b) Leicestershire
57. Glenn Turner's (New Zealand)
58. Paul Strang (Zimbabwe); Kent
59. Yorkshire
60. Andrew Symonds (then not an overseas player; now of Australia and Kent)
61. Ken McEwan
62. Majid Khan
63. Clive Inman
64. Mohammad Akram
65. Worcestershire
66. Zaheer Abbas (Pakistan)
67. Colin McCool
68. Stuart Law (Essex)
69. Anthony Gray and Sylvester Clarke
70. Nawab of Pataudi Jr.
71. Graham McKenzie (Australia)
72. Courtney Walsh (West Indies and Gloucestershire)
73. Shaun Pollock (SA), Shane Bond (NZ), Damien Fleming (A)
74. Billy Ibadulla
75. Srinivasaraghavan Venkataraghavan (India)
76. Muttiah Muralitharan (Sri Lanka); Lancashire
77. Clive Rice (South Africa)
78. Worcestershire
79. Sonny Ramadhin
80. Danny Morrison
81. Kent
82. Steve Elworthy
83. Geoff Howarth
84. Alan Connolly
85. Colin Croft
86. Mike Hussey (Northants and Western Australia)
87. Bruce Dooland
88. Malcolm Marshall (Hampshire)
89. Tony Dodemaide
90. Viv Richards (West Indies)
91. Michael Slater (Australia)
92. Peter Wight
93. Worcestershire
94. Peter Kirsten
95. Andy Roberts
96. Andy Bichel (A), Allan Donald (SA), Shane Lee (A)
97. Nixon McLean (West Indies)
98. Larry Gomes
99. Saurav Ganguly (India)
100. Anderson Cummins